PSYCHOLOGY

PSYCHOLOGY:
An Introduction
fourth edition

Josh R. Gerow
Indiana University –
Purdue University at Fort Wayne

HarperCollinsCollegePublishers

Acquisitions Editor: Catherine Woods
Developmental Editor: Phil Herbst
Project Editor: Shuli Traub
Design Supervisor / Text Designer: Jill Yutkowitz
Cover Photograph: David Madison / Tony Stone Images
Art Studio: Burmar
Photo Researcher: Kelly Mountain / Sandy Schneider
Electronic Production Manager: Mike Kemper
Electronic Desktop Manager: Heather A. Peres
Manufacturing Manager: Joe Campanella
Electronic Page Makeup: RR Donnelley Barbados
Printer and Binder: R. R. Donnelley & Sons Company
Cover Printer: Lehigh Press

Psychology: An Introduction, Fourth Edition

Library of Congress Cataloging-in-Publication Data

Gerow, Joshua R.
   Psychology :: an introduction / Josh R. Gerow.—4th ed.
      p. cm.
   Includes bibliographical references and index.
   ISBN 0-673-46869-0 (student edition)
   ISBN 0-673-46870-4 (teacher edition)
   1. Psychology.   I. Title.
BF121.G44 1995
150—dc20
                                             94-16489
                                               CIP

94 95 96 97 9 8 7 6 5 4 3 2 1

To Nancy

$\mathscr{B}$RIEF CONTENTS

Detailed Contents   *ix*
Preface   *xix*
About the Author   *xxvii*

Chapter 1   Psychology: What Psychologists Do   1
Topic 1A   Toward a Definition of Psychology   4
Topic 1B   The Research Methods of Psychology   21

Chapter 2   The Nervous Systems and Behavior   49
Topic 2A   Neurons: Building Blocks of the Nervous Systems   52
Topic 2B   The Human Nervous Systems and How They Are Studied   62
Topic 2C   The Central Nervous System   71

Chapter 3   Sensation and Perception   93
Topic 3A   Sensing and Perceiving: A Few Basic Concepts   96
Topic 3B   Vision   108
Topic 3C   Hearing and the Other Senses   140

Chapter 4   Types of Consciousness   163
Topic 4A   Levels of Consciousness   166
Topic 4B   Sleeping and Dreaming   173
Topic 4C   Voluntary Alterations of Consciousness   182

Chapter 5   Learning   201
Topic 5A   Classical Conditioning   204
Topic 5B   Operant Conditioning   222
Topic 5C   Cognitive Approaches to Learning   241

Chapter 6   Memory   253
Topic 6A   How Can We Describe Human Memory?   256
Topic 6B   Improving Memory: Factors Affecting Retrieval   277

Chapter 7   Higher Cognitive Processes   305
Topic 7A   Concepts and Language   308
Topic 7B   Problem Solving   328

Chapter 8   Developmental Psychology   351
Topic 8A   Prenatal Influences on Development   354
Topic 8B   Development in Childhood   365
Topic 8C   Development in Adolescence   390
Topic 8D   Development in Adulthood   402

Chapter 9   Personality and Intelligence   421
   Topic 9A   Issues and Theories of Personality   424
   Topic 9B   Intelligence as an Aspect of Personality   455

Chapter 10   Motivation and Emotion   491
   Topic 10A   Issues of Motivation   494
   Topic 10B   The Sex Drive and Human Sexual Behaviors   517
   Topic 10C   The Psychology of Emotion   529

Chapter 11   Psychology, Stress, and Physical Health   547
   Topic 11A   Stress, Stressors, and How to Cope   550
   Topic 11B   Health Psychology   569

Chapter 12   The Psychological Disorders   585
   Topic 12A   Defining and Classifying Psychological Disorders   588
   Topic 12B   A Sampling of Psychological Disorders   594

Chapter 13   Treatment and Therapy   633
   Topic 13A   History and Biomedical Treatments   636
   Topic 13B   The Psychotherapies   650

Chapter 14   Social Psychology   677
   Topic 14A   Social Cognitions: Attitudes, Attributions, and Attractions   680
   Topic 14B   Social Influence   700

Chapter 15   Industrial-Organizational, Environmental, and
             Sport Psychology   721
   Topic 15A   Industrial-Organizational Psychology   724
   Topic 15B   Environmental and Sport Psychology   743

         Statistical Appendix   763
         Glossary   G1
         References   R1
         Credits   C1
         Name Index   I1
         Subject Index   I11

$\mathcal{D}$ETAILED CONTENTS

Preface   xix
About the Author   xxvii

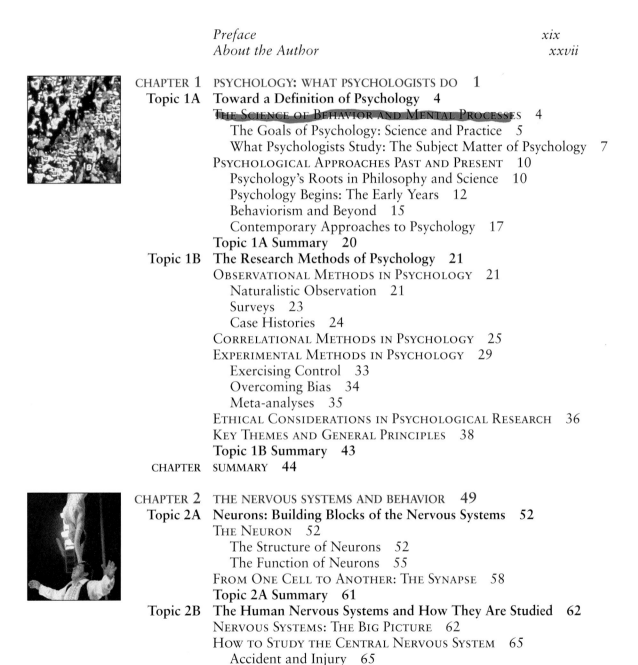

CHAPTER 1   PSYCHOLOGY: WHAT PSYCHOLOGISTS DO   1
Topic 1A   **Toward a Definition of Psychology   4**
THE SCIENCE OF BEHAVIOR AND MENTAL PROCESSES   4
    The Goals of Psychology: Science and Practice   5
    What Psychologists Study: The Subject Matter of Psychology   7
PSYCHOLOGICAL APPROACHES PAST AND PRESENT   10
    Psychology's Roots in Philosophy and Science   10
    Psychology Begins: The Early Years   12
    Behaviorism and Beyond   15
    Contemporary Approaches to Psychology   17
Topic 1A Summary   20
Topic 1B   **The Research Methods of Psychology   21**
OBSERVATIONAL METHODS IN PSYCHOLOGY   21
    Naturalistic Observation   21
    Surveys   23
    Case Histories   24
CORRELATIONAL METHODS IN PSYCHOLOGY   25
EXPERIMENTAL METHODS IN PSYCHOLOGY   29
    Exercising Control   33
    Overcoming Bias   34
    Meta-analyses   35
ETHICAL CONSIDERATIONS IN PSYCHOLOGICAL RESEARCH   36
KEY THEMES AND GENERAL PRINCIPLES   38
Topic 1B Summary   43
CHAPTER   SUMMARY   44

CHAPTER 2   THE NERVOUS SYSTEMS AND BEHAVIOR   49
Topic 2A   **Neurons: Building Blocks of the Nervous Systems   52**
THE NEURON   52
    The Structure of Neurons   52
    The Function of Neurons   55
FROM ONE CELL TO ANOTHER: THE SYNAPSE   58
Topic 2A Summary   61
Topic 2B   **The Human Nervous Systems and How They Are Studied   62**
NERVOUS SYSTEMS: THE BIG PICTURE   62
HOW TO STUDY THE CENTRAL NERVOUS SYSTEM   65
    Accident and Injury   65
    Surgical Interventions   67
    Electrical Stimulation   67
    Recording Electrical Activity   67

Observing the Brain Directly and Indirectly   69
Topic 2B Summary   71
Topic 2C   **The Central Nervous System   71**
THE SPINAL CORD   71
The Structure of the Spinal Cord   72
The Functions of the Spinal Cord   73
"LOWER" BRAIN CENTERS   75
The Brain Stem   75
The Cerebellum   76
The Reticular Activating System (RAS)   78
The Limbic System   78
The Hypothalamus   79
The Basal Ganglia   80
The Thalamus   81
THE CEREBRAL CORTEX   81
Lobes and Localization   82
The Two Cerebral Hemispheres—Splitting the Brain   85
The Two Sexes—Male and Female Brains   87
Topic 2C Summary   89
CHAPTER   SUMMARY   **89**

CHAPTER 3   SENSATION AND PERCEPTION   **93**
Topic 3A   **Sensing and Perceiving: A Few Basic Concepts   96**
SENSORY THRESHOLDS AND ADAPTATION   97
Absolute Thresholds   97
Difference Thresholds   100
Signal Detection   100
Sensory Adaptation   101
PAYING ATTENTION: A PROCESS OF SELECTION   102
Stimulus Factors in Selectivity   103
Personal Factors in Selectivity   105
Topic 3A Summary   107
Topic 3B   **Vision   108**
THE STIMULUS FOR VISION: LIGHT   108
THE RECEPTOR FOR VISION: THE EYE   112
Important Structures of the Human Eye   112
More on Rods and Cones and What They Do   116
The Visual Pathway After the Retina   119
COLOR VISION AND COLOR BLINDNESS   121
PERCEPTUAL ORGANIZATION   124
Stimulus Factors   125
Personal Factors   128
THE PERCEPTION OF DEPTH AND DISTANCE   128
Ocular Cues   129
Physical Cues   130
THE PERCEPTION OF MOTION   134
Perceiving Real Motion   134
The Perception of Apparent Motion   134
THE CONSTANCY OF VISUAL PERCEPTION   135
Perceptual Constancy   136
When Constancy Fails: Geometric Illusions and
Impossible Figures   137

Topic 3B Summary   140
Topic 3C **Hearing and the Other Senses   140**
         HEARING   141
            The Stimulus for Hearing: Sound   141
            The Receptor for Hearing: The Ear   145
         THE CHEMICAL SENSES   147
            Taste   148
            Smell   148
         THE SKIN, OR CUTANEOUS, SENSES   151
         THE POSITION SENSES   153
         PAIN: A SPECIAL SENSE   154
         Topic 3C Summary   157
   CHAPTER SUMMARY   157

CHAPTER 4 TYPES OF CONSCIOUSNESS   **163**
Topic 4A **Levels of Consciousness   166**
         NORMAL, WAKING CONSCIOUSNESS   166
         IS THERE AN UNCONSCIOUS AND WHAT MIGHT IT BE
         LIKE?   167
            The Freudian View of Levels of Consciousness   168
            Contemporary Investigations of the Unconscious   170
         Topic 4A Summary   172
Topic 4B **Sleeping and Dreaming   173**
         THE STAGES OF A "GOOD NIGHT'S SLEEP"   173
         REM AND NREM SLEEP   176
         SLEEP DEPRIVATION AND DISORDERS OF SLEEP   178
            Sleep Deprivation—In the Real World and in the
            Laboratory   179
            Disorders of Sleep   180
         Topic 4B Summary   181
Topic 4C **Voluntary Alterations of Consciousness   182**
         HYPNOSIS   182
         MEDITATION   185
         ALTERING CONSCIOUSNESS WITH DRUGS   188
            Stimulants   189
            Depressants   191
            Hallucinogens   193
            Marijuana—A Special Case   195
         Topic 4C Summary   196
   CHAPTER SUMMARY   197

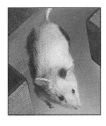

CHAPTER 5 LEARNING   **201**
Topic 5A **Classical Conditioning   204**
         WHAT IS LEARNING?   204
         PAVLOV AND A CLASSIC DEMONSTRATION   206
         CLASSICAL CONDITIONING PHENOMENA   209
            Acquisition   209
            Extinction and Spontaneous Recovery   209
            Generalization and Discrimination   211
         THE SIGNIFICANCE OF CLASSICAL CONDITIONING: WHAT ABOUT
         PEOPLE?   212

In the Laboratory   212
Conditioned Emotional Responses   212
An Example: The Case of "Little Albert"   214
An Application: Phobias and Their Treatment   216
RETHINKING WHAT REALLY HAPPENS IN CLASSICAL
CONDITIONING   218
Can *Any* Stimulus Serve as a CS?   219
Must the Time Interval Between the CS and UCS
Always Be Brief?   220
Topic 5A Summary   222
Topic 5B   **Operant Conditioning   222**
THE BASICS OF OPERANT CONDITIONING   222
Defining Operant Conditioning   223
The Procedures of Operant Conditioning   225
The Course of Conditioning   225
REINFORCEMENT   228
Positive and Negative Reinforcers   228
Primary and Secondary Reinforcers   230
Scheduling Reinforcers   232
PUNISHMENT   235
GENERALIZATION AND DISCRIMINATION   237
CAN ANY RESPONSE BE OPERANTLY CONDITIONED?   239
Topic 5B Summary   241
Topic 5C   **Cognitive Approaches to Learning   241**
LATENT LEARNING AND COGNITIVE MAPS   242
SOCIAL LEARNING AND MODELING   245
Topic 5C Summary   248
CHAPTER   SUMMARY   **249**

CHAPTER 6   MEMORY   **253**
Topic 6A   **How Can We Describe Human Memory?   256**
MEMORY AS INFORMATION PROCESSING   256
SENSORY MEMORY   258
SHORT-TERM MEMORY (STM)   259
The Duration of STM   260
The Capacity of STM   263
How Information Is Represented in STM   264
LONG-TERM MEMORY (LTM)   265
How Large Is Long-term Memory?   265
What Is the Duration of Long-term Memories?   266
How Accurate Are Long-term Memories?   267
How Do We Get Information into Long-term Memory?   271
Are There Different Types of Long-term Memories?   272
WHERE CAN WE FIND MEMORIES IN THE BRAIN?   275
Topic 6A Summary   276
Topic 6B   **Improving Memory: Factors Affecting Retrieval   277**
MEASURING RETRIEVAL   277
Direct, Explicit Measures of Memory   278
Indirect, Implicit Measures of Memory   280
ENCODING AND RETRIEVAL   281
The Effects of Context   282

Strategies That Guide Encoding and Aid Retrieval 285
The Amount and Distribution of Encoding Practice 292
INTERFERENCE AND RETRIEVAL 296
Retroactive Interference 297
Proactive Interference 298
Topic 6B Summary 299
CHAPTER SUMMARY **301**

CHAPTER 7 HIGHER COGNITIVE PROCESSES 305
Topic 7A **Concepts and Language 308**
THE CONCEPT OF CONCEPT 308
FORMING CONCEPTS 311
A Classic Demonstration 312
Developing Strategies and Testing Hypotheses 314
LANGUAGE 316
Let's Talk: What *Is* Language? 316
Describing the Structure in Language 318
Language Use as a Social Process 321
Language Acquisition 322
Topic 7A Summary 327
Topic 7B **Problem Solving 328**
WHAT *IS* A PROBLEM? 328
PROBLEM REPRESENTATION 330
PROBLEM-SOLVING STRATEGIES 332
Algorithms 333
Heuristics 334
BARRIERS TO EFFECTIVE PROBLEM SOLVING 336
Mental Set and Functional Fixedness 336
Biased Heuristics and Decision Making 338
Overcoming Barriers with Creative Problem Solving 340
CAN WE TEACH PROBLEM-SOLVING SKILLS? 343
Topic 7B Summary 345
CHAPTER SUMMARY **346**

CHAPTER 8 DEVELOPMENTAL PSYCHOLOGY 351
Topic 8A **Prenatal Influences on Development 354**
GENETICS AND PSYCHOLOGY 354
Inheritance of Physical Traits 355
The Interactionist Position 356
THE STAGES OF PRENATAL DEVELOPMENT 357
ENVIRONMENTAL INFLUENCES ON PRENATAL DEVELOPMENT 361
Nourishment 361
Smoking, Drinking, and Drugs 362
Maternal Stress 363
What About Dad? 363
Topic 8A Summary 364
Topic 8B **Development in Childhood 365**
MOTOR DEVELOPMENT: GETTING FROM HERE TO THERE 365
The Neonate 365
The Motor Development of Children 367
SENSORY AND PERCEPTUAL DEVELOPMENT 367

Cognitive and Social Development   370
   The Cognitive Abilities of the Neonate: What Does the
     Newborn Know?   370
   Piaget's Theory of Cognitive Development   372
   Reactions to Piaget   377
   Kohlberg's Theory of Moral Development   379
   Erikson's Theory of Psychosocial Development   382
   Developing Gender Identity   384
   Developing Social Attachments   387
Topic 8B Summary   390
Topic 8C   Development in Adolescence   390
What Are Adolescents Really Like?   391
   The Limits of Adolescence   391
   Are Adolescents Always in Turmoil, and "Stressed Out"?   391
Physical Changes During Adolescence   392
Some Challenges of Adolescence   396
   Identity Formation   396
   Drug Use by Adolescents   397
   Adolescent Sexuality   399
Topic 8C Summary   401
Topic 8D   Development in Adulthood   402
Early Adulthood   402
   Marriage and Family   403
   Career Choice   406
Middle Adulthood   408
Late Adulthood   410
What It Means to Be Old   410
   Death and Dying   412
Topic 8D Summary   414
Chapter Summary   **414**

Chapter 9   Personality and Intelligence   421
Topic 9A   Issues and Theories of Personality   424
The Psychoanalytic Approach   425
   Freud's Approach   425
   The Psychoanalytic Approach After Freud   431
The Behavioral/Learning Approach   433
The Humanistic-Phenomenological Approach   435
The Trait Approach   437
   Two Classic Examples   437
   A Contemporary Perspective: The Big Five   439
Pros and Cons of the Four Approaches to Personality   440
Issues Related to Personality   442
   Is There a Personality?: Interactionism   442
   Gender and Personality   444
   Personality Measurement, or Assessment   446
Topic 9A Summary   454
Topic 9B   Intelligence as an Aspect of Personality   455
Just What *Is* Intelligence?   456
   Defining Intelligence   456

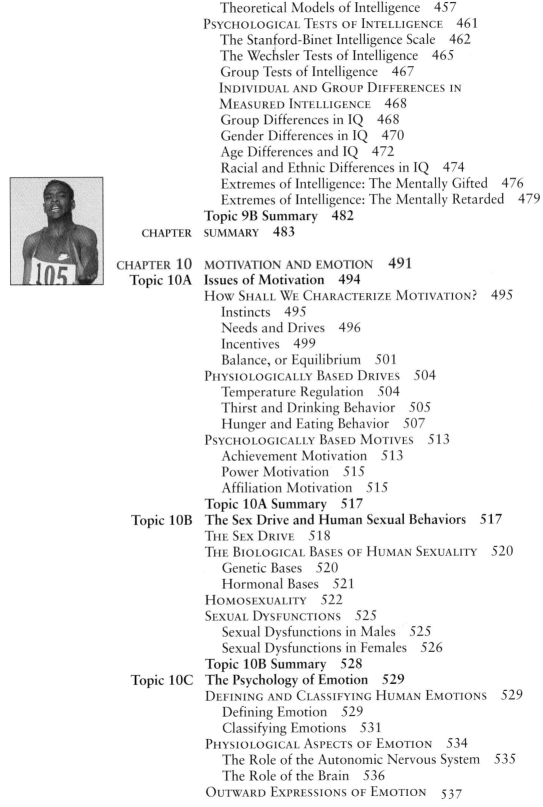

Theoretical Models of Intelligence   457
PSYCHOLOGICAL TESTS OF INTELLIGENCE   461
The Stanford-Binet Intelligence Scale   462
The Wechsler Tests of Intelligence   465
Group Tests of Intelligence   467
INDIVIDUAL AND GROUP DIFFERENCES IN
MEASURED INTELLIGENCE   468
Group Differences in IQ   468
Gender Differences in IQ   470
Age Differences and IQ   472
Racial and Ethnic Differences in IQ   474
Extremes of Intelligence: The Mentally Gifted   476
Extremes of Intelligence: The Mentally Retarded   479
Topic 9B Summary   482
CHAPTER   SUMMARY   **483**

CHAPTER 10   MOTIVATION AND EMOTION   **491**
Topic 10A   **Issues of Motivation   494**
HOW SHALL WE CHARACTERIZE MOTIVATION?   495
Instincts   495
Needs and Drives   496
Incentives   499
Balance, or Equilibrium   501
PHYSIOLOGICALLY BASED DRIVES   504
Temperature Regulation   504
Thirst and Drinking Behavior   505
Hunger and Eating Behavior   507
PSYCHOLOGICALLY BASED MOTIVES   513
Achievement Motivation   513
Power Motivation   515
Affiliation Motivation   515
Topic 10A Summary   517
Topic 10B   **The Sex Drive and Human Sexual Behaviors   517**
THE SEX DRIVE   518
THE BIOLOGICAL BASES OF HUMAN SEXUALITY   520
Genetic Bases   520
Hormonal Bases   521
HOMOSEXUALITY   522
SEXUAL DYSFUNCTIONS   525
Sexual Dysfunctions in Males   525
Sexual Dysfunctions in Females   526
Topic 10B Summary   528
Topic 10C   **The Psychology of Emotion   529**
DEFINING AND CLASSIFYING HUMAN EMOTIONS   529
Defining Emotion   529
Classifying Emotions   531
PHYSIOLOGICAL ASPECTS OF EMOTION   534
The Role of the Autonomic Nervous System   535
The Role of the Brain   536
OUTWARD EXPRESSIONS OF EMOTION   537

Topic 10C Summary 541
CHAPTER SUMMARY 541

CHAPTER 11 PSYCHOLOGY, STRESS, AND PHYSICAL HEALTH 547
Topic 11A Stress, Stressors, and How to Cope 550
STRESSORS: THE CAUSES OF STRESS 550
Frustration-induced Stress 551
Conflict-induced Stress 552
Life-change-induced Stress 555
REACTING TO THE STRESSORS IN OUR LIVES 558
Individual Differences 558
Stress as a Physiological Reaction: Selye's GAS 559
Effective Strategies for Coping with Stressors 562
Ineffective Strategies for Coping with Stressors 566
Topic 11A Summary 568
Topic 11B Health Psychology 569
PSYCHOLOGICAL FACTORS THAT INFLUENCE PHYSICAL HEALTH 570
PROMOTING HEALTHY BEHAVIORS 572
Why Do People Die? 572
Helping People to Stop Smoking 574
Sexually Transmitted Diseases 575
Helping Patients "Follow Doctors' Orders" 579
Topic 11B Summary 580
CHAPTER SUMMARY 581

CHAPTER 12 THE PSYCHOLOGICAL DISORDERS 585
Topic 12A Defining and Classifying Psychological Disorders 588
JUST WHAT *Is* "ABNORMAL"? 589
THE CLASSIFICATION OF ABNORMAL REACTIONS 590
The DSM Series 591
Problems with Classification and Labeling 591
On "Insanity" 593
Topic 12A Summary 594
Topic 12B A Sampling of Psychological Disorders 594
ANXIETY DISORDERS 595
Generalized Anxiety Disorder 596
Panic Disorder 596
Phobic Disorder 597
Obsessive-compulsive Disorder (OCD) 599
Posttraumatic Stress Disorder (PTSD) 601
SOMATOFORM DISORDERS 603
Hypochondriasis 603
Conversion Disorder 604
DISSOCIATIVE DISORDERS 605
Dissociative Amnesia 605
Dissociative Fugue 605
Dissociative Identity Disorder 606
PERSONALITY DISORDERS 607
DISORDERS USUALLY FIRST DIAGNOSED IN INFANCY,
CHILDHOOD, OR ADOLESCENCE 610
The Example of Autism 610

DELIRIUM, DEMENTIA, AMNESTIC, AND OTHER
COGNITIVE DISORDERS   611
   The Example of Alzheimer's   612
MOOD DISORDERS   614
   Types of Mood Disorder   615
   Observations on the Causes of Depression   616
SCHIZOPHRENIA   618
   Incidence and Types of Schizophrenia   620
   Observations on the Causes of Schizophrenia   623
Topic 12B Summary   627
CHAPTER   SUMMARY   **627**

CHAPTER 13   TREATMENT AND THERAPY   633
Topic 13A   **History and Biomedical Treatments   636**
A HISTORICAL PERSPECTIVE   636
BIOMEDICAL TREATMENTS OF PSYCHOLOGICAL DISORDERS   639
   Psychosurgery   639
   Electroconvulsive Therapy   641
   Drug Therapy   643
DEINSTITUTIONALIZATION: BLESSING OR CURSE?   647
Topic 13A Summary   650
Topic 13B   **The Psychotherapies   650**
WHO PROVIDES PSYCHOTHERAPY?   650
PSYCHOANALYTIC TECHNIQUES   653
   Freudian Psychoanalysis   654
   Post-Freudian Psychoanalysis   656
HUMANISTIC TECHNIQUES   657
BEHAVIORAL TECHNIQUES   659
COGNITIVE TECHNIQUES   662
   Rational-Emotive Therapy   663
   Cognitive Restructuring Therapy   664
GROUP APPROACHES   665
EVALUATING PSYCHOTHERAPY   667
Topic 13B Summary   670
CHAPTER   SUMMARY   **670**

CHAPTER 14   SOCIAL PSYCHOLOGY   677
Topic 14A   **Social Cognitions: Attitudes, Attributions, and Attractions   680**
ATTITUDES   681
   The Components of Attitudes   682
   Attitude Formation   683
   Attitude Change and Persuasion   686
ATTRIBUTION THEORY   691
INTERPERSONAL ATTRACTION   694
   Theories of Interpersonal Attraction   694
   Factors Affecting Interpersonal Attraction   696
Topic 14A Summary   700
Topic 14B   **Social Influence   700**
CONFORMITY   701
OBEDIENCE TO AUTHORITY   703
   Attribution Errors and a Word of Caution   705

A Reminder About Ethics in Research   706
BYSTANDER INTERVENTION   706
   A Cognitive Model of Bystander Intervention   707
   The Bystander Effect: A Conclusion   710
SOCIAL LOAFING   711
SOCIAL FACILITATION   712
DECISION MAKING IN GROUPS   713
Topic 14B Summary   715
CHAPTER   SUMMARY   **716**

CHAPTER 15   INDUSTRIAL-ORGANIZATIONAL, ENVIRONMENTAL, AND
                SPORT PSYCHOLOGY   **721**
Topic 15A   **Industrial-Organizational Psychology   724**
FITTING THE PERSON TO THE JOB   724
   Defining "Good Work": The Job Analysis   725
   Selecting People Who Can Do Good Work   727
   Training People to Do Good Work   730
   Motivating People to Do Good Work   734
FITTING THE JOB TO THE PERSON   737
   Job Satisfaction   737
   Job Satisfaction and Work Behaviors   739
   Worker Safety   741
Topic 15A Summary   743
Topic 15B   **Environmental and Sport Psychology   743**
PSYCHOLOGY AND THE ENVIRONMENT   744
   Space and Territory   744
   Life in the City: An Example   749
   Noise, Temperature, and Environmental Toxins   750
   Changing Behaviors That Impact on the Environment   753
PSYCHOLOGY AND SPORT   755
   The Psychological Characteristics of Athletes   756
   Maximizing Athletic Performance   756
Topic 15B Summary   758
CHAPTER   SUMMARY   **759**

STATISTICAL APPENDIX   **763**
AN EXAMPLE TO WORK WITH   764
ORGANIZING DATA   765
   Frequency Distributions   765
   Graphic Representations   766
DESCRIPTIVE STATISTICS   767
   Measures of Central Tendency   768
   Variability   770
INFERENTIAL STATISTICS   772
SOME NORMAL CURVE STATISTICS   776
APPENDIX SUMMARY   778

Glossary   G1
References   R1
Credits   C1
Name Index   I1
Subject Index   I11

PREFACE

THE ORIGINAL VERSION

I had been reviewing other people's books for years, so when I was first approached to write an introductory psychology textbook, I had a reasonably clear vision of what I wanted that text to be like. What I find most encouraging about seeing *Psychology: An Introduction* evolve to a fourth edition is that so many psychology instructors seem to share that vision. Two general principles have remained constant throughout:

1. The text is written for the student who is unlikely to take more than one or two additional psychology classes. I have come to call these our "terminal introductory" students. By far, they comprise the majority of the students in my classes over the past twenty-five years. This may be our only opportunity to have an impact on these students.

2. The text puts into practice what we teach about making learning an effective, interesting, meaningful experience.

From these general principles, several guidelines flow naturally:

■ Help beginning students understand the basic methods, concepts, and principles of psychology. Do not try to impress readers with how much you know. Cover the basics fully, but don't overwhelm them with details.

■ Provide examples and applications. Then provide more examples. Show how psychology in all its aspects is relevant to daily life experience.

■ Help the student space or distribute his or her practice. Provide guidance within the text to help the student understand which points are central and which are less so.

■ Avoid distracting features, such as built-in quizzes or "boxes" of tangentially related material. If it's interesting and relevant, put it in the text.

■ As often as possible, show that today's psychology has emerged from a historical context. All of the "good stuff" of psychology has not been discovered within the last five years.

■ Be as intellectually honest as possible. Avoid taking any one point of view when many are possible. Acknowledge that we have many important questions in psychology for which we do not have adequate answers.

- Without disrupting the flow of the text, include as many pedagogical aids as is reasonable. (See "Features of This Text" below.)

- Include illustrations, graphs, tables, and photos that are relevant and instructive as well as attractive.

- Assemble a package of ancillary materials that will allow the student to learn and the instructor to teach as easily and effectively as possible.

To remain true to these principles and guidelines and to put them into practice has been a challenge, but with each edition we get closer to that original vision.

FEATURES OF THIS TEXT

There are several things I have done to make the task of learning about psychology as easy and painless as I know how. For one thing, I've provided each instructor with a large assortment of supplementary materials and media to help in teaching the class. These are described below in the section of this preface called "Supplements to Accompany the Text." What I will do here is describe briefly those features that are built into the text.

Topics. Each of the fifteen chapters is divided into Topics. Each Topic is designed to be freestanding and comprehensible on its own. I see two advantages of this system: (1) It allows the instructor an added degree of flexibility, and (2) it provides material to the student in smaller, manageable pieces that are coherent and meaningful.

Chapter Outline. Each of the fifteen chapters (and the Statistical Appendix) opens with a complete outline. This should be the first thing a student reads when beginning an assignment. The outline provides a general overview and shows how the material in the chapter is interrelated.

Chapter Introduction. Following the chapter outline is a prefatory section made up of two parts: (1) a short vignette that attempts to engage the student/reader and ease him or her into the flow of the chapter and (2) a short introductory section that describes precisely what sorts of issues will be covered in the chapter.

Marginal, Boldface Glossary. In large measure, learning about psychology is a matter of developing the appropriate vocabulary. Key words and concepts are printed in the text in **boldface** type. Each term is defined in the text and the definition is repeated in the margin for ready reference. All definitions are collected in a complete, page-referenced glossary at the end of the text.

***Before You Go On* Questions.** A series of questions labeled *Before You Go On* appear throughout each chapter. They typically occur after major content sections. This remains one of the most popular features of the text *from the students' point of view.* The questions help prompt active learning by the reader and should serve the purpose implied in their name. Before you go on, stop and answer this question. If you cannot, perhaps you'd better reread the previous section. *Before You Go On* questions provide a quick and simple intermediate review.

Chapter Summary. As its name suggests, this section provides a review of the important material presented in each chapter. Each *Chapter Summary* repeats all of the of *Before You Go On* questions in that chapter, and provides brief answers. You realize, of course, that the answers provided in the *Chapter Summaries* are to be taken as suggestions only. Each item in the summary is page referenced.

Practice Test Items. These tests for *Psychology: An Introduction,* Fourth Edition, come shrink-wrapped free with each new copy of the text. For each chapter in the text, the student will find twenty-five multiple-choice and 10 true-false items—525 items in all. Two things make this feature unique. First, every item was written by the textbook's author. Second, answers are provided in annotated form. A student cannot simply glance at a list of letters to see if he or she correctly answered an item. Reasons—or justifications—are provided to let the student know which alternatives are correct, which are incorrect, and *why.*

In order to prepare for a classroom exam, it should not be necessary to reread all of the assigned material. Students should only have to reexamine the *Chapter Outline,* review the *Marginal Glossary* terms and the *Chapter Summaries* for answers to the *Before You Go On* questions, and then test themselves by attempting the questions in the *Practice Test Items* booklet.

WHAT IS NEW IN THIS EDITION

New Topic Organization

Those of you who have used any of the first three editions of *Psychology: An Introduction* will see that the basic structure of the text has not changed. I still have 15 chapters in which each chapter is divided into short, manageable Topics. You will notice, however, that I have given up my compulsive adherence to having two Topics in every chapter. Most chapters still do have two Topics, a few now have three, and the chapter on developmental psychology has four. I've simply let content—and not design—drive the decision of how many Topics to include. In previous editions, each Topic had its own Outline, Introduction, and Summary. Although we have retained the Topic summary, to underscore the integration and coherence of the material within each chapter, we now have a Chapter Outline, a Chapter Introduction, and a Chapter Summary. Each chapter also begins with a short, "soft," introductory "vignette." Within chapters, all of the previously used pedagogical aids have been retained and are described in the section "Features of This Text."

Reordered Chapters

Another change is immediately noticeable: I have recast and reordered some of the chapters. Perception is now paired with sensation (Chapter 3), leaving Chapter 4 to deal with matters of consciousness. Developmental psychology has been moved forward to Chapter 8. Chapter 9 now pairs issues of personality with issues of intelligence (surely part of what we mean by "personality"), and includes the discussion of psychological tests and measurement. Chapter 10, on motivation and emotion, has a new free-standing Topic on the sex drive and human sexuality. Finally, Chapter 11 is a new combination of Topics dealing with issues of physical health and stress—just before Chapter 12 on the psychological disorders. All other changes have been made within the Topics of the text.

Increased Attention to Gender and Cross-Cultural Issues

Two areas have received special attention for this edition. I have worked with two very special consultant-reviewers: Richard Brislin, Director of Intercultural Programs, East-West Center, Honolulu, for help on cross-cultural and ethnic issues, and Carol Lawton, of Indiana–Purdue at Fort Wayne, for help with gender-related issues. Our intent has been to place new material on gender and cultural matters within the flow of the text. That is, there is no new, separate Topic on cross-cultural psychology; the new content has been woven into extant coverage. A few examples of this coverage include:

> A discussion of the contributions of three key women, Margaret Floy Washburn, Mary Calkins, and Christine Ladd-Franklin, in psychology's history (Chapter 1)
>
> A new section on brain differences as a function of male-female differences, particularly in the areas of lateralization and "split-brain" research (Chapter 2)
>
> A discussion of the perception of depth and distance as a function of cultural experience (Chapter 3)
>
> A look at the extent to which reinforcers for individual achievements make sense in cultures where the group or the tribe is valued above the individual (Chapter 5)
>
> "What About Dad?" a new section on the role of fathers in prenatal development (Chapter 8)
>
> A new section devoted to a discussion of developing gender identity (Chapter 8)
>
> A look at how valued traits for mates differ across cultures (Chapter 8)
>
> A new section on gender and personality traits (Chapter 9)

A look at social loafing and social facilitation in different cultures (Chapter 14)

A dicussion of motivating workers in different cultures (Chapter 15)

Key Content Changes

A brief sampling of what is new in this edition includes the following:

Chapter 1—shortened the section on history and added the role of women.

Chapter 2—restructured into three Topics; added section on sex differences in brain structure and function.

Chapter 3—totally reorganized, adding perception to discussion of the senses.

Chapter 4—nearly a new chapter, extending coverage of sleep and dreaming, and adding a section on levels of consciousness; updated coverage of psychoactive drugs.

Chapter 5—reorganized into three Topics, extending coverage of cognitive maps.

Chapter 6—added sections on the accuracy of long-term memories; added to measures of implicit memory.

Chapter 7—restructured to put student-oriented problems at beginning of chapter; added section on gender and language use.

Chapter 8—essentially a new chapter, in four Topics; added section on role of the father in prenatal development; expanded neonatal cognitions section; added cross-cultural concerns in moral development; added section on the development of gender identity; expanded discussion of social attachments; added section on adolescent "turmoil"; updated section on adolescent drug use; expanded treatment of the elderly.

Chapter 9—a new combination of personality with intelligence; added section on psychosexual stages of development; extended coverage of the "Big Five"; added "gender and personality"; expanded treatment of gender and racial differences in intelligence.

Chapter 10—reorganized, with a new Topic on sexuality; expanded coverage of homosexuality; expanded section on expression of emotion.

Chapter 11—a new combination of Topics; 82 new references; more on "hassles" and stress; STDs moved to here, greatly expanded and updated.

Chapter 12—restructured for consistency with the *DSM-IV*; expanded coverage of OCD; added section on childhood autism; restructured section on mood disorders.

Chapter 13—expanded section on deinstitutionalization; added Gestalt therapy.

Chapter 14—nearly new section on attitudes; updated attribution and attraction, with cross-cultural references.

Chapter 15—52 new references; new section on being "in the zone" or "having a hot hand" in sports psychology section.

I should also note that **541** new reference citations were added for this edition, about half of them (271) published in the 1990s.

SUPPLEMENTS TO ACCOMPANY THE TEXT

Two Test Banks (Test Bank I ISBN: 0-673-55253-5; Test Bank II ISBN: 0-673-55255-1). The first test bank includes over 2500 professionally reviewed multiple-choice and essay questions. Each of these items was written, revised, or reviewed by the author. The second test bank, includes over 2000 new items.

TestMaster Computerized Test Bank. A powerful test-generation system. TestMaster allows the instructor to construct test files using multiple-choice and essay questions from the Gerow test banks. Questions can be exchanged between the TestMaster program and the instructor's word processing software allowing instructors to modify questions and create entirely new questions. It is available for both IBM and Macintosh computers.

Instructor's Resource Kit (ISBN: 0-673-55253-5). Revised by Maria Lasaga of the University of Wyoming, this comprehensive supplement contains an extensive collection of demonstration ideas, teaching strategies, and supplementary lecture notes. The Resource Kit provides a rich source of ideas for experienced teachers, as well as for new instructors of introductory psychology. This kit is available in a tabbed three-ring binder for adopters.

Study Guide (ISBN: 0-673-99423-6). Written by Glenda Smith of North Harris College, this manual is designed to help students get the most from the Gerow introductory text by including a lot of practice test questions. Each chapter concludes with study tips especially developed for college students.

SuperShell: Computerized Tutorial. This interactive software, also written by Glenda Smith, features diagnostic and feedback capabilities. SuperShell provides immediate correct answers and the text page reference on which the topic is presented. When students miss a question, the question begins to appear more frequently. A "flash cards" feature provides a drill to help students learn important terms and concepts. Available for IBM computers.

For further information on how to obtain any of the package components, please contact your local representative or HarperCollins, College Marketing Group, 10 East 53rd Street, New York, NY 10022-5299.

ACKNOWLEDGMENTS

I must first mention my wife, Nancy. She has provided encouragement and sound advice throughout this project.

Once again, my colleagues at IPFW have proven to be a source of support and information. I have "borrowed" their expertise freely and I appreciate their generosity: Bruce Abbott, Ken Bordens, Lenore DeFonso, Dennis Cannon, Nancy Kelley, Carol Lawton, and W. Jeffrey Wilson.

Four others deserve "special" recognition: Carol Lawton and Richard Brislin, again, for educating me on matters of gender and culture. Much of what is new in this edition reflects their good work. Phil Herbst, Developmental Editor, working for HarperCollins out of their Glenview office, has his good work reflected on every page of this text. And Catherine Woods has proven to be an exceptional psychology editor. She has provided continuous support for all the vagaries it takes to get a book from concept stage through production. Working with Carol, Richard, Phil, and Catherine has been a most pleasant, rewarding experience.

Many of the people with whom I worked at HarperCollins were unknown to me before this revision began. Those who deserve special mention for their role in putting this text together are: Shuli Traub, Project Editor; Michael Kemper, Electronic Production Manager; Jill Yutkowitz, Design Supervisor; Kelly Mountain, Photo Researcher; Evelyn Owens, Supplements Editor; Mark Paluch, Marketing Manager; Lesly Atlas, Assistant Editor; and Margaret Loftus, Assistant Editor. Finally, a special thanks to Marcus Boggs, Art Pomponio, and Susan Driscoll for their continued support and creativity throughout this project.

Right from the start it was obvious to me that—these days—no one person can write a complete survey of general psychology, even at the introductory level. Previous editions have benefited from the advice and suggestions of scores of fine reviewers. The friends and colleagues who took so much time from their busy schedules to contribute to this revision as supplement authors, test bank reviewers, and manuscript reviewers were enormously helpful. Simply listing names here seems a woefully inadequate acknowledgment of their contribution: Lynn Augsbach, Morehead State University; William M. Beneke, Lincoln University; Joyce Bishop, Golden West College; Shirley Cole-Harding, Minot State University; Marla J. Colvin, Cuyahoga Community College; James Dooley, Mercy College; John Flannagan, Eastern Kentucky University; Sue Gordon, Hudson Valley Community College; Martha B. Haslam, Laredo Community College; Barbara Honhart, Baker College; Robert Johnson, Arkansas State University; Neil J. Lavender, Ocean County College; Kit Lowder, Illinois Central College; William McVough, Weber State University; John Nichols, Tulsa Junior College; David Pick, Purdue University Calumet; Gerald Rubin, Central Virginia Community College; Michael Shaughnessy, Eastern New Mexico University; Donald M. Stanley, North Harris College; Janice C. Stapley, Monmouth College; and Patrick S. Williams, University of Houston.

I would also like to acknowledge the reviewers of the Third Edition: Michael Aamodt, Radford University; Sharon Akimoto, University of

Utah; Mark Alcorn, University of Northern Colorado; Gary Bothe, Pensacola Junior College; Thomas Brothen, University of Minnesota; Robert Brown, Georgia State University; Bill Buskist, Auburn University; Roy Cain, Pan American University; James Calhoun, University of Georgia; Charlotte Callens, Prince George Community College; Karen Christoff, University of Mississippi; Philip Compton, Ohio Northern University; Richard T. Comstock, Monroe Community College; Alfrieda Daly, Rutgers University; Marc DesLauriers, Kansas City Community College; George Diekhoff, Midwestern State University; David Donovan, Northwestern University; Sherry Ellis, Virginia Commonwealth University; Warren Fass, University of Pittsburg/Bradford; William Filbert, Dodge City Community College; John Flanagan, Eastern Kentucky University; Donald Foshee, Valdosta State University; Margaret Fulton, Edison Community College; David Geary, University of Missouri; Judy Gentry, Columbus State Community College; Robert Gentry, College of Charleston; Fredrich Gibbons, Iowa State University; Bryan Gibson, University of Utah; William Gibson, Northern Arizona State; John Goodwyn, School of the Ozarks; Susan Goodwyn, University of California/Davis; Paula Goolkasian, University of North Carolina; William Gray, University of Toledo; Larry Gregory, New Mexico State University; Bruce Hill, Triton College; Wendy James-Alderidge, Pan American University; Philip Langer, University of Colorado; Robert MacAleese, Spring Hill College; Marian Miller, Fort Wayne, Indiana; Daniel D. Moriarty, University of San Diego; Arthur Mueller, Community College of Baltimore; Dennis Nagi, Hudson Valley Community College; James Pate, Georgia State University; Carrol S. Perrino, Morgan State University; Virginia Philo, State University of New York/Albany; John Pinto, Morningside College; Lillian Range, University of Southern Mississippi; Robert Riesenberg, Raymond Walters College; Ernst E. Roberts, El Paso Community College; Aaron Roy, Ashland College; Robert Seibel, Pennsylvania State University; Paul Sheldon, Villanova University; Frank Sjursen, Shoreline Community College; Randall Smith, Ouachita Baptist University; Roy Smith, Mary Washington College; Leo Spindel, Centennial College; Dalmus A. Taylor, Wayne State University; Laura Thompson, New Mexico State; Roscoe Thornthwaite, Pembroke State University; Ann Weber, University of North Carolina; Lisa Whitten, State University of New York/Old Westbury; Clair Wiederholt, Madison Area Technical College; Robert Wiley, Montgomery College; Cynthia Willis, Kansas State University; Richard Willis, University of Pittsburg; Randall Wright, Ouachita Baptist University; and Cecilia K. Yoder, Oklahoma City Community College.

Josh R. Gerow

Josh Gerow began his college training at Rensselaer Polytechnic Institute, where he majored in chemistry, and earned his B.S. in psychology at the University of Buffalo. At the University of Tennessee, Knoxville, he was awarded a doctorate in experimental psychology. His graduate area of specialization was developmental psycholinguistics. Having taught for two years at the University of Colorado at Denver, he joined the faculty at Indiana University–Purdue University at Fort Wayne (IPFW), an undergraduate institution, where he still teaches. Dr. Gerow has conducted research and published articles in the field of instructional psychology, focusing on factors that affect performance in introductory psychology. His teaching background is extensive: During his more than twenty-seven years as a college professor, he has taught courses on the psychology of learning, memory, the history of psychology, and his favorite course, introduction to psychology; he has brought college-level introductory psychology to high school students; and he has made frequent presentations at regional and national conferences on the teaching of psychology.

A Visual Guide To:

PSYCHOLOGY
AN INTRODUCTION
Fourth Edition

Josh R. Gerow
Indiana University—Purdue University at Fort Wayne

ISBN 0-673-46869-0

One of the most accessible and effective texts for students at all levels, the fourth edition of *Psychology: An Introduction* continues to provide a straightforward, sensible introduction to psychology. As always, Gerow's best-selling presentation is based on his learning system, predicated on the basic psychological principles of learning and memory. Each chapter breaks down into two, three, or four "Topics" in order to help students digest manageable chunks of information one section at a time, while providing instructors with greater flexibility. Numerous examples and applications reinforce topics by demonstrating how psychology is relevant to students' daily experiences. To prompt students' active learning, "Before You Go On" questions appear after each major discussion and provide a quick review of material just covered. In addition, Gerow's own Practice Test Items provide numerous questions with in-depth answers that not only explain whether an answer is correct or incorrect, but also why. Both the Practice Tests and SuperShell Interactive Electronic Study Guide are shrink-wrapped free with every copy of the text, providing students with valuable learning tools and rounding out the Gerow Learning Package. This new edition of the text features a thorough integration of material on cross-cultural and gender issues.

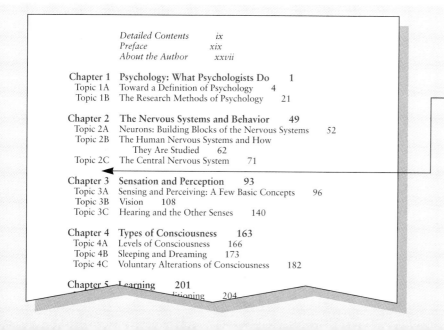

Detailed Contents ix
Preface xix
About the Author xxvii

Chapter 1   **Psychology: What Psychologists Do**   1
Topic 1A   Toward a Definition of Psychology   4
Topic 1B   The Research Methods of Psychology   21

Chapter 2   **The Nervous Systems and Behavior**   49
Topic 2A   Neurons: Building Blocks of the Nervous Systems   52
Topic 2B   The Human Nervous Systems and How
They Are Studied   62
Topic 2C   The Central Nervous System   71

Chapter 3   **Sensation and Perception**   93
Topic 3A   Sensing and Perceiving: A Few Basic Concepts   96
Topic 3B   Vision   108
Topic 3C   Hearing and the Other Senses   140

Chapter 4   **Types of Consciousness**   163
Topic 4A   Levels of Consciousness   166
Topic 4B   Sleeping and Dreaming   173
Topic 4C   Voluntary Alterations of Consciousness   182

Chapter 5   **Learning**   201
Topic ... ditioning   204

TOPIC ORGANIZATION

Gerow has always practiced the principles that psychologists teach, and now his effective learning system has evolved one step further. Chapters contain two, three, or four topics: manageable "chunks" of material that provide instructors with greater flexibility and students with easy access to material.

CHAPTER-OPENING OUTLINE

Each chapter begins with a complete outline designed to introduce the assignment, provide students with a general overview, and show how the material in the chapter is interconnected.

CHAPTER OUTLINE

TOPIC 7A CONCEPTS AND LANGUAGE
The Concept of Concept
Forming Concepts
  A Classic Demonstration
  Developing Strategies and Testing Hypotheses
Language
  Let's Talk: What *Is* Language?
  Describing the Structure in Language
  Language Use as a Social Process
  Language Acquisition
TOPIC 7A SUMMARY

TOPIC 7B PROBLEM SOLVING
What *Is* a Problem?
Problem Representation
Problem-Solving Strategies
  Algorithms
  Heuristics
Barriers to Effective Problem Solving
  Mental Set and Functional Fixedness
  Biased Heuristics and Decision Making
  Overcoming Barriers with Creative Problem Solving
Can We Teach Problem-Solving Skills?
TOPIC 7B SUMMARY

CHAPTER SUMMARY

I've never had the nerve to try this classroom demonstration. I've always thought it a bit too dangerous, and probably unethical. However, when I was a graduate student, I had a chance to see it done about as well as it has ever been done. The demonstration is something of a classic now, and it has been replicated in many forms.

I took a seat at the rear of the introductory psychology class, unnoticed by the more than six hundred students filling the large, old lecture hall. The professor entered the room through a side door and began his lecture on the basic principles of sensation and perception. After a few minutes, the class settled down to taking notes and listening to the lecture.

Suddenly, a student burst through the large doors at the rear of the lecture hall. I recognized him as the professor's graduate-student assistant, but no one else in the class knew who he was. I felt he overacted a bit as he stomped down the center aisle of the lecture hall, screaming the foulest of obscenities at the professor. "Dr. X, you failed me for the last time, you *&%@#$ so-and-so. You're going to pay for this!" Needless to say, the class was stunned. Everyone gasped as the student leaped over the lectern to grab the professor.

The student and the professor struggled briefly, and then—in clear view of everyone—there was a chrome-plated revolver! Down behind the lectern they fell. bang! The sound of a gunshot filled the room. The students sat frozen in their seats. The graduate assistant raced out of the same side door the professor had entered just a few minutes earlier. The professor lay sprawled out on the floor, moaning loudly.

Six hundred students sat stunned in their seats. At just the right dramatic moment, the professor slowly drew himself up to the lectern and in a calm, soft voice said, "Now, I want everyone to take out a pen and some paper and write down exactly what you saw."

I'm sure I need not describe all the results of this demonstration. You can guess what happened. I never did read all 600 descriptions of the events that took place in class that day, but I did help summarize the responses. I was very impressed. The "enraged" graduate student was described as being from 5'4" to 6'3" tall, weighing between 155 and 225 pounds, and wearing either a gray sweatshirt or a blue blazer. Although there was some agreement, one would have a difficult time coming up with a good physical description of the suspect in this mock shooting.

The most remarkable misperception that took place had to do with the gun. As I watched the professor take his place at the front of the class, I was sure he had ruined the demonstration. I clearly saw him remove the pistol from his suit coat pocket and place it on top of his notes. When the "crazed student" crashed into the room, the first thing the professor did was to reach down, grab the gun, and point it at the student as he came charging down the center aisle. In fact, the student never had the gun in his hands. The professor had it all along. The first move the student made was to grab the professor's wrist.

CHAPTER INTRODUCTION

Following the chapter outline is a two-part introductory section: a short vignette, which eases students into the flow of the chapter, and a brief section that introduces the issues to be discussed in the chapter.

we most clearly share with other animals. In no way should you think of these lower centers as being less important. As you will soon see, our very survival depends on them. You can use figure 2.10 as a guide to lacate the various structures as we discuss them.

Before You Go On

Why does spinal cord injury sometimes cause paralysis?

Describe the major features of a spinal reflex.

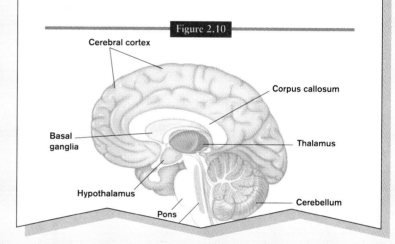

Figure 2.10

Cerebral cortex

Corpus callosum

Basal ganglia

Thalamus

Hypothalamus

Cerebellum

Pons

"BEFORE YOU GO ON" QUESTIONS

Appearing after each major discussion, these popular questions provide a quick review and prompt students' active learning. As the name implies, students are encouraged to stop and answer a question before going on to the next section. If students have difficulty with the question, they are encouraged to go back and re-read the previous section.

MOOD DISORDERS

The **mood disorders** (called *affective disorders* until the publication of the *DSM-III-R*) clearly demonstrate a disturbance in one's emotional reactions or feelings. We have to be a little careful here. Almost all psychological disorders have an impact on one's mood or affect. With mood disorders, however, the intensity or extremeness of mood is the major, primary symptom.

Types of Mood Disorder

Mood disorders are defined in terms of extremes of mood, depression being the more common of the two extremes. Under the label *mood disorder* are several specific disorders differentiated in terms of such criteria as length of episode and severity.

Major depression is the diagnosis for a constellation of symptoms that includes feeling sad, low, and hopeless, coupled with a loss of pleasure or interest in almost all usual activities. Associated with major depression are such factors as poor appetite, insomnia, decrease in sexual activity, loss of energy, and feelings of worthlessness. At the same time, there is no event or situation that could reasonably account for the observed depression.

This form of mood disorder is diagnosed about two times more often in women than in men; during any 6-month period, approximately 6.6 percent of women and 3.5 percent of men will have an episode of major depression (NIMH, 1991). The ratio of about two women to every man developing major depression holds across nationalities and across ethnic groups (Cross-National Collaborative Group, 1992; McGrath et al., 1990). Worldwide, major depression is on the increase, with current rates at more than 100 million persons (Gotlib, 1992; Weissman & Klerman, 1992). Unfortunately, research also tells us that relapse and reoccurrence are common for those who

dysthymia   a mood disorder that is basically a mild case of depression; it is chronic, with recurrent pessimism, low energy level, and low self-esteem

major depression   a mood disorder characterized by inexplicable moods of sadness and hopelessness, accompanied by a loss of pleasure or interest in usual activities

MARGINAL, BOLDFACE GLOSSARY

To help students develop their psychology vocabulary, key words and concepts are printed in the text in boldfaced type. Each term is defined in the text and the definition is repeated in the margin for easy reference. All definitions are collected in a complete, page-referenced glossary at the end of the text.

TOPIC SUMMARIES

As part of the Gerow Learning System, Topic Summaries provide reviews of the information in each section, helping to improve students' retention of material.

Adolescence is an exciting period of development. It is a period of transition—from the dependence of childhood to the independence of adulthood. It is difficult, however, to specify exactly when adolescence begins and when it ends. We'll begin defining adolescence and seeing how psychologists have attempted to characterize this stage. We'll review some of the physical changes that occur during adolescence, and we'll sample three of the issues that concern developmental psychologists who study adolescents: identity formation, drug use, and adolescent sexuality.

TOPIC 8B SUMMARY

With birth, the neonatal period begins. Although several useful reflexes and sensory capacities are available to the newborn, interaction with the environment shapes and modifies the developmental process. Throughout childhood we find that motor development varies from child to child, but usually progresses in the same, orderly sequence.

Theories concerning the pattern of cognitive, social, and moral development have stimulated much research in child psychology. In this Topic, we first reviewed Piaget's theory of cognitive development. Piaget argued that children go through a distinct sequence of stages in their efforts to find out about the world in which they live, thus developing new schemas along the way. Few theories have generated the sort of research activity as has Piaget's. We saw that there are problems with some of the particular points of Piaget's theory, but we also saw that his theory has found support in cross-cultural research efforts. We then looked at Kohlberg's theory of the development of moral reasoning, essentially a six-stage theory. There is support for

TOPIC 4A

What is normal, waking consciousness, and, according to William James, what are its four basic characteristics?

We define normal, waking consciousness as the perception or awareness of our environment and our own mental processes. According to William James, consciousness can be characterized as (1) always changing, (2) personal, (3) continuous, and (4) selective.

What are the three levels of consciousness proposed by Freud?

Sigmund Freud proposed that consciousness could be classified into one of three levels. (1) That which is in your *conscious* mind is that of which you are aware at the moment, that is, information that is readily available. (2) Below the conscious level of awareness is the *preconscious*, memories, feelings, desires, and the like that are not immediately known to you, but that can be brought to your attention, to consciousness, with relatively little effort. (3) Most of the contents of our minds, Freud said, are at an *unconscious* level of awareness. Information, feelings, and desires are stored at the unconscious level because becoming aware of these issues might lead to feelings of anxiety and distress. Although information stored at the unconscious level could influence our behaviors and could show itself in slips of the tongue and in our dreams, it can be retrieved only with considerable effort.

How may we characterize unconscious processing?

Cite an example of experimental evidence for unconscious processing.

The notion of the unconscious processing of information has returned to mainstream psychology. Unconscious processing occurs when information is processed without one's conscious awareness of it. For example, when subjects are shown words presented so quickly or dimly that they do not report seeing them, those words will still influence the subjects' choice of a word that is related to the word they claimed they did not see.

What are REM and NREM sleep?

What occurs during REM sleep?

REM sleep is "rapid eye movement sleep," which constitutes about one-fourth of each night's sleep. Several events occur during REM, most noticeably vivid, storylike dreams. During REM sleep we find loss of muscle tone (atonia), excitement of the sexual organs, rapid breathing, and increased heart rate and blood pressure. NREM is "non-REM" sleep, and predictably, the eyes are still and there is little dream activity.

CHAPTER SUMMARY

CHAPTER SUMMARIES

Chapter Summaries review key points presented in each chapter. Each summary repeats all of the "Before You Go On" questions in that chapter, lists brief answers, and includes page references for each item.

At least three factors influence the choice of a marriage partner (Newman & Newman, 1984). The first deals with availability. Before we can develop an intimate relationship with someone, we need the opportunity to develop the relationship in the first place. Availability is one thing, eligibility is a second. Here, matters of age, race, religion, politics, and background come into play. Available and eligible, a third factor enters the picture: attractiveness. To a degree, attractiveness in this context means physical attractiveness, but as we all know, judgments of physical beauty depend on who's doing the judging. "Attractiveness" also involves psychological characteristics such as understanding, emotional supportiveness, and similarity in values and goals.

Let's pause here momentarily and remind ourselves of two points that have come up before.

(1) The conclusion of the studies previously cited are true only in general, on the average. There may be happy couples that have few of the traits listed in Figure 8.5 in common.

(2) These general conclusions only hold in Western, largely Anglo, North American cultures. Buss and many colleagues are studying preferences in selecting mates around the world. In one report of their efforts (Buss et al., 1990), people from 33 countries on six continents and five islands were studied. There were some similarities among all of the cultures studied, but cultures tended to show significantly different rankings of preferences for mates. The trait that varied most across cultures was *chastity*.

You'll note that chastity is nowhere to be found on the list of preferred characteristics presented in Figure 8.5. Choosing a marriage partner is not always a matter of making sound, rational decisions, regardless of one's culture. Many factors, including romantic love and the realities of economic hardship, sometimes affect such choices. As sound and sensible as choices at marriage may seem, approximately 50 percent of all first marriages end in divorce (75 percent of second marriages suffer the same fate). In the United States, 9.4 years is the average span of a first marriage (U.S. Bureau of the Census, 1991).

We turned next to gender identity, and learned that although adults may treat boys and girls differently, their behavior as infants and young children provides no basis for doing so. Most children become aware of gender differences by the age of 4 years. Differences are noticeable in matters from peer group interactions to the choice of toys. Finally, we examined the lasting importance of the early development of social attachments. These bidirectional, largely emotional bonds are established between young children and their primary caregivers. We continue our story of human development now by considering that span that falls between childhood and adulthood: adolescence.

CROSS-CULTURAL COVERAGE

With the help of Richard Brislin, Director of Intercultural Programs, East-West Center, Honolulu, *Psychology* features solid coverage of cross-cultural and ethnic issues. This provides students with a more inclusive overview of material discussed.

Let's say that Ken agrees to a friendly racquetball game, just for the exercise. At first all goes well, and Ken, a superior player, really takes it easy on his opponent. After all, they're just playing for the exercise. In their second game, Ken's opponent makes a few good shots and moves ahead in the score. Ken now notices that a small group of spectators is watching them play. As the situation changes, so does Ken's perception of it. "This is no longer fun and games," he thinks to himself, as he starts smashing low line drives off the front wall. Within just a few minutes, Ken's behavior shows a considerable change. The situation has changed, and now his behavior is aggressive and forceful. As the situation changed, it brought about a change in Ken's behavior: a perceived challenge to his ability brought out competitive reactions. Ken's personality also brought about a change in the situation: to some degree, his trait of competitiveness changed a friendly game into an athletic contest. With interactionism we have an approach that acknowledges the impact of the environment, but also allows for the influence of stable, internal personality traits.

Gender and Personality

Personality traits give us reasonable ways to describe people and to express differences among them. We observe differences among them. We can note Kathy's assertiveness and Juan's sociability. We can say that Chick is friendlier than Steve or that Melissa is more impulsive than Jesse. An issue that intrigues personality psychologists is the extent to which personality traits can be used to characterize *groups* of people, and if there are consistent personality differences, in general, among groups. The two groups that have been studied most closely in this regard are men and women.

What do you think about these differences? Boys have higher self-esteem than girls. Girls are more social than boys. Men are more analytical than women. Men are better at rote learning, whereas women are more creative. Women are more open to suggestion and influence than are men. These assertions might sound sensible to some people, but there is no research evidence to support any of them. There are no gender differences in self-esteem, sociability, analytic skills, rote learning, creativity, or suggestibility.

What do you think about these differences? Boys have higher self-esteem than girls. Girls are more social than boys. Men are more analytical than women. Men are better at rote learning, whereas women are more creative. Women are more open to suggestion and influence than are men. These assertions might sound sensible to some people, but there is no research evidence to support any of them. There are no gender differences in self-esteem, sociability, analytic skills, rote learning, creativity, or suggestibility.

These were the findings of the first large-scale exploration of gender differences, reported by Eleanor Maccoby and Carol Jacklin in 1974. Maccoby and Jacklin's work was not the first to ask whether there are consistent differences between males and females (their's was a reanalysis of data that existed at the time). It did, however, stimulate

GENDER COVERAGE

Consultant Carol Lawton, of Indiana—Purdue at Fort Wayne, has contributed her expertise to give gender issues prominence throughout this edition.

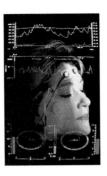

Effective Strategies for Coping with Stressors

In the long run, the most effective way to deal with stress is to make relatively permanent changes in our behaviors as a result of the experience of stress. You will recall that we defined learning as a relatively permanent change in behavior that occurs as the result of practice or experience. To respond to a stressor with learning makes particularly good sense for frustration-induced stress. Here, our pathway to a goal is being blocked or thwarted. An adaptive way to handle such a stressor is to find some new way to reach our goal or to learn to modify our goal.

A variety of operant conditioning called **biofeedback** can provide relief from the tension associated with stress (Kamiya et al., 1977; Shirley, Matt, & Burish, 1992; Yates, 1980). Biofeedback is "the process of providing information to an individual about his [or her] bodily processes in some form which he [or she] might be able to use to modify those processes" (Hill, 1985, p. 201). One's heart rate, let us say, is constantly monitored, and the rate is fed back to the person, perhaps in the form of an audible tone. As heart rate increases, the pitch of the tone becomes higher. As heart rate decreases, the tone gets lower. Once the learner knows (through the feedback) what his or her heart rate (or blood pressure, or muscle tension, and so on) is doing, a certain degree of control over that response is possible. The reinforcement involved here is simply the newly gained knowledge that a desired change is being made. As a result of being reinforced, the stress-fighting responses increase in their frequency (Kaplan, 1991; Kimmel, 1974; Miller, 1978; Thackwray-Emerson, 1989).

Learn techniques of relaxation. Learning effective ways to relax may not be as easy as it sounds, and may take some time and effort. The logic is simple: feeling stressed and being relaxed are incompatible responses. If you can become relaxed, the experience (feelings) of stress will be diminished (e.g., Lehrer & Woolfolk, 1984). Hypnosis may help. Meditation may help. So may relaxation training.

In fact, much of our everyday learning is motivated by frustration-induced stress. We've had to learn many new responses as a means of coping with frustration. Let's look at a few imaginary examples. Having been frustrated once (or twice) by locking yourself out of your house or car, you have learned to hide another set of keys somewhere where you can easily find them. Having been denied promotion because you didn't have a college degree, you are learning about general psychology on the way toward earning such a degree. Having been caught at home in a blizzard with no cookies in the house, you have learned to bake them yourself. Having discovered you're too short to make the basketball team, you have learned to play tennis. You may have learned as a child to get what you wanted from your parents by smiling sweetly and asking politely. In each of these cases, what prompted, or motivated, the learning of new responses or the establishment of new goals was the stress resulting from frustration.

EXAMPLES AND APPLICATIONS

Using numerous examples and applications to reinforce topics, Gerow demonstrates how all aspects of psychology are relevant to students' daily lives.

The Limbic System

The **limbic system** is actually a collection of structures rather than a single, unified one. It is of utmost importance in controlling the behaviors of nonhuman animals, which do not have as large or well-developed a cerebral cortex as humans do. The limbic system controls many of the complex behavioral patterns we usually think of as instinctive. The location of the limbic system and its constituent parts is presented in Figure 2.11.

Figure 2.11

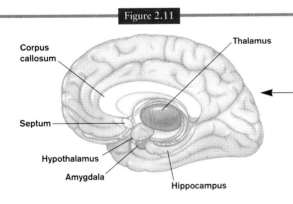

Within the human brain, parts of the limbic system are intimately involved in the display of emotional reactions. One center in the system, the *amygdala,* produces reactions of rage or aggression when stimulated, while another area, the *septum,* seems to have the oppo-

---

ART PROGRAM

Striking and engaging photography and line art clearly illustrate important points.

story? In most cases, the accuracy of our recollection of experiences from the distant past is of little or no consequence. In some situations, the accuracy of the report of one's long-term memory for events can be of critical importance.

Repressed Memories

One example of the importance of the accuracy of information retrieved from long-term storage involves what are called "repressed memories." We discussed the Freudian concept of repression in Chapter 4 (p.160). Repression is said to have occurred when extremely unpleasant or traumatic events of one's life are pushed deep into the unconscious corners of one's memory, from which retrieval is very difficult at best. That repression—or in more modern, non-Freudian terminology, "motivated forgetting"—can help us forget unpleasant events of the past is a notion that has gained wide acceptance in psychology (Baddeley, 1990; Erdelyi, 1985; Erdelyi & Goldberg, 1979; Loftus, 1993a.)

In recent years, a disturbing number of cases have become public in which an adult (often in psychotherapy for any one of a number of disorders, mild to severe) comes to remember being abused when a child. Most cases of the recall of repressed memories of child abuse involve women, and the "recall" of the abusive events is often impressively detailed. The trauma of child abuse (sexual or not) seems a likely event to be repressed—put out of one's conscious awareness. Without questioning the enormity of the problem of child abuse or challenging reports of it prevalence, Loftus (1993a, 1993b) has recently challenged the authenticity of the "repressed memories" of some adults who "remember" as adults events that may never have happened in the first place. It may be, Loftus argues, that some people genuinely come to believe that they were abused as children in order to help make some sense of the difficulties they are encountering as adults. In some cases, the notion that a person has been set

CUTTING-EDGE REFERENCES

Providing a perfect balance of traditional and contemporary material, this edition features 541 new reference citations, with over half of them (271) from the 1990s.

PRACTICE TEST ITEMS   CHAPTER 14: SOCIAL PSYCHOLOGY
TOPIC 14B: *SOCIAL INFLUENCE*

1. Muzafer Sherif performed some of the first experiments on conformity using the auto-kinetic effect, which is:
   __ a. an illusion of motion of a point of light in a dark room.
   __ b. tasks in which subjects judge the length of lines.
   __ c. an ambiguous picture of an old hag or a young woman.
   __ d. a device for presenting visual information for very brief periods of time.

2. When Solomon Asch studied conformity, he found each of the following EXCEPT that:
   __ a. even subjects' perceptual judgments could be influenced by perceived group pressure.
   __ b. most of his subjects (more than 75%) conformed at least once.
   __ c. the least amount of social support was sufficient to help a subject resist group pressure.
   __ d. most of the subjects continued to conform even after they knew the group members were confederates of the experimenter.

3. The major difference between conformity and obedience is:
   __ a. peer pressure.
   __ b. the presence of an authority figure.
   __ c. the nature of the task involved.
   __ d. the subject's perception of social influence.

4. Which result does NOT follow from Milgram's studies of obedience?
   __ a. Personality characteristics of the subjects allowed Milgram to predict who would obey and who would not.
   __ b. When told about the experiment, virtually no one believes that he or she would have delivered shocks.
   __ c. No subject in his experiment stopped delivering shocks before the 300-volt level when the "learner" protested.
   __ d. More than half the subjects "delivered" the highest level of shock to the "learner."

5. Which conclusion from Milgram's research on obedience is justified?
   __ a. Persons of some nationalities are more likely to obey than are others.
   __ b. When told to harm another, few subjects felt guilty about it.
   __ c. The perception of authority is a strong force in conformity.
   __ d. Women are more likely to obey than are men.

6. What is the major reason why some have criticized Milgram's study of obedience as being unethical?
   __ a. He made a fundamental attribution error.
   __ b. He shocked subjects without their consent.
   __ c. He allowed subjects to believe they were hurting someone.
   __ d. He failed to adequately debrief his subjects.

7. Which of the following is NOT taken to be a necessary step in considering whether or not to intervene in an emergency?
   __ a. One must notice or perceive the emergency.
   __ b. One must interpret the situation as an emergency.
   __ c. One must know or care about the victim.
   __ d. One must decide to take responsibility to do something.

PRACTICE TEST/ SUPERSHELL

Practice Tests (written by Gerow) include 525 questions, as well as all answers in annotated form. Students learn which answers are correct, which are incorrect, and why.

SuperShell Interactive Electronic Study Guide (by Glenda Smith) is an interactive software (featuring diagnostic and feedback capabilities) that provides students with quick answers and page references. When a student misses a question, the question begins to appear more frequently. A "flash cards" feature provides a drill to help students learn important terms and concepts.

Both Practice Tests and SuperShell are shrink-wrapped free with each text (*Psychology* is the first introductory psychology text to offer students complimentary software).

chapter one

PSYCHOLOGY: WHAT PSYCHOLOGISTS DO

CHAPTER OUTLINE

TOPIC 1A TOWARD A DEFINITION OF PSYCHOLOGY
The Science of Behavior and Mental Processes
    The Goals of Psychology: Science and Practice
    What Psychologists Study: The Subject Matter of Psychology
Psychological Approaches Past and Present
    Psychology's Roots in Philosophy and Science
    Psychology Begins: The Early Years
    Behaviorism and Beyond
    Contemporary Approaches to Psychology
TOPIC 1A SUMMARY

TOPIC 1B THE RESEARCH METHODS OF PSYCHOLOGY
Observational Methods in Psychology
    Naturalistic Observation
    Surveys
    Case Histories
Correlational Methods in Psychology
Experimental Methods in Psychology
    Exercising Control
    Overcoming Bias
    Meta-analyses
Ethical Considerations in Psychological Research
Key Themes and General Principles
TOPIC 1B SUMMARY

CHAPTER SUMMARY

*J*ust what *is* psychology? Let's begin with a definition implied in the chapter's title: Psychology is what psychologists do.

Your first inclination might be to dismiss this definition as circular and silly. Although I can't claim that this definition is totally satisfactory, there may be something to say for it. You will come to appreciate as you read through this book that psychology is a very diverse discipline that uses many techniques to study a wide range of reactions of many types of organisms.

To give you some idea of the diversity of interests and activities of psychologists, let me take you on a quick tour of a few of the laboratories and offices in the psychology department on my campus. If you were to ask me, "What is psychology?" I might say, "Well,

> it's Ken Bordens, interested in those factors other than guilt and innocence that influence a jury in a criminal trial;
>
> it's David Young, interested in the psychological adjustment of adolescents whose parents are undergoing a divorce;
>
> it's Leni DeFonso and Nancy Kelley, interested in how skilled musicians and rank amateurs process music;
>
> it's Carol Lawton, interested in how people acquire a 'sense of direction';
>
> it's Bruce Abbott, interested in the question, 'If a rat is going to get shocked, would the rat rather know the shock is coming, or be surprised?';
>
> it's Dennis Cannon, interested in attitudes about sexuality and the actual sexual behaviors of college students;
>
> it's Elaine Blakemore, interested in how a child's understanding of gender impacts on his or her behaviors;

. . . and it's so much more." The colleagues I've listed constitute only about half our psychology department. Their interests and activities go well beyond the one research area I've mentioned here. How do we get this variety, this range of subject matter, condensed into one, simple definition?

*I*n this introductory chapter, the intent is to define psychology and to describe its major goals and methods. In Topic 1A, I will offer a working definition, and explain the basic goals of psychology. We'll then examine some of the approaches that have characterized psychology since it first emerged as an independent science late in the nineteenth century. Among other things, we'll note how the definition of psychology has changed over the past hundred years.

In Topic 1B, I will describe the methods that psychologists use to reach their goals. As you will see, most of the questions of today's psychology are ancient questions. What sets psychology apart are the methods that psychologists use to answer these questions. To consider the methods of psychology is to get to the heart of what makes psychology psychology.

This chapter ends with a brief discussion of some of the abiding themes, or general principles, that have been central to psychology throughout the years. These themes are overarching areas of concern within psychology. We will find them interwoven throughout the rest of our discussion.

When studying behavior and mental processes, psychologists often find it convenient, if not necessary, to use nonhuman animals in research.

psychology *the science of behavior and mental processes.*

Topic 1A

TOWARD A DEFINITION OF PSYCHOLOGY

In the following chapters we'll explore in detail questions about our emotions, motivations, sexuality, and psychological development. We'll examine the nature and causes of psychological disorders and see how they can be treated. We'll see psychology applied in business settings, in athletics, in classrooms, and in other social situations. We'll examine the relationships between our brains and our behaviors. We'll look at how we process information about the world in which we live through sensation, perception, learning, and memory. But we should start at the beginning and generate a working definition of psychology. Doing so will enable us to focus on psychology's subject matter and its general approach to that subject matter (Henley et al., 1989).

THE SCIENCE OF BEHAVIOR AND MENTAL PROCESSES

Psychology is the science of behavior and mental processes. This is a fairly standard definition—one that millions of students before you have committed to memory. If there is a problem with this definition, it's that it is a bit sterile; it doesn't tell us very much about what psychologists actually study or how they go about it. It will take the rest of this book to fill in the details and make this definition truly meaningful. First let's see what it means to say that psychology is a science; then we'll consider the subject matter of psychology.

The Goals of Psychology: Science and Practice

There are many ways to find out about ourselves and the world in which we live. Some of our beliefs we have taken as a matter of faith (There is a God—or there isn't). Some of our understanding has come through tradition, passed on from one generation to the next, accepted simply because "they said it is so." Some of what we believe is credited to common sense ("You beat a dog often enough and sooner or later it will get mean"). Some of the insights we have about ourselves and the human condition are taken from works of art, literature, poetry, and drama. Psychologists, however, claim that there is a better way to come to an understanding of its subject matter: by applying the values and methods of science.

One of the goals of psychology is to use scientific methods to discover and understand the relationships that exist among the behaviors and mental processes of organisms. Put another way, one goal of psychology is to understand the *scientific laws* that govern our subject matter. In this context, a scientific law is a statement about one's subject matter that one believes to be true—not on the basis of faith, or tradition, or common sense, but on the basis of evidence.

If psychology is a science, we should have an appreciation of what it is that qualifies a discipline to be a science. Most simply put, a **science** is an organized body of knowledge gained through application of scientific methods. So to qualify as a science, a discipline has to demonstrate two things: (1) an organized body of knowledge and (2) the use of scientific methods.

science an organized body of knowledge gained through application of scientific methods

Over the years, psychologists have accumulated a great deal of information about their subject matter. They have learned much about the behaviors and mental processes of organisms, both human and nonhuman. They are coming to understand how feelings, behaviors, and thoughts affect our nervous systems, and vice versa. They have developed a reasonably clear vision of how we learn about the world in which we live and how we remember what we have learned. They can now identify many of the determinants of individual growth and development. Psychologists have isolated many of the factors that influence the adjustments organisms make to their environments and to one another, and they have a sense of how such adjustments can become maladaptive.

Many interesting and important questions can still be asked for which there are no good answers. Not having all of the answers can be frustrating at times, but that is part of the excitement of psychology—there are still so many questions left to be answered. The truth is, nonetheless, that psychologists *have* learned much about their subject matter. What is known is reasonably well organized. You have in your hands one version of the organized collection of knowledge that is psychology. In terms of our first requirement, then, psychology is a science.

What we know in psychology we have learned through the application of **scientific methods**—a series of procedures that involve observation, description, control, and replication. To explain something scientifically is a matter of ruling out, or eliminating, alternative

scientific methods a series of procedures that involve observation, description, control, and replication used to explain phenomena

explanations. The scientific method is an attitude or approach to problem solving. Science is "a process of inquiry, a particular way of thinking," not a carefully delineated set of procedures that must be followed rigorously (Graziano & Raulin, 1993, p. 2). There is no one way to do science.

There are, however, some guidelines. The basic process goes something like this: The scientist (psychologist) makes observations about his or her subject matter (behavior and/or mental processes). Based on these observations, a **hypothesis** is developed. A hypothesis is a tentative explanation of some phenomenon that can be tested and then either supported or rejected. In a way, a hypothesis is an educated guess about one's subject matter.

hypothesis a tentative explanation that can be tested and confirmed or rejected

After formulating a hypothesis, the scientist again observes and describes relevant events, while controlling or eliminating irrelevant ones. These observations are then analyzed to see if the hypothesis was well founded. Alternative hypotheses or explanations may be examined also. The results of one's investigation are shared with others, who may test them further to see if these results can be replicated.

In science, one's hypothesis may be rejected or it may be supported, but it cannot be "proven" as true. This is because no matter how much support one finds for a hypothesis, there still may be other hypotheses, as yet unthought of, that will do a better job of explaining the observed phenomenon. "Scientists may have confidence in their explanations, but are nevertheless willing to entertain the possibility that their explanations are faulty" (Bordens & Abbott, 1991, p. 4).

And so it is with all sciences. Specific techniques and procedures vary from one science to another. The scientific status of psychology does not depend on the extent to which it resembles chemistry, physics, or biology, but on how well it explains behavior and mental processes (Simon, 1990). For that matter, the specific procedures that psychologists use vary considerably. We'll review some of the more commonly used methods of psychologists in Topic 1B, where we'll consider a number of examples. What is important is the realization that through its reliance on scientific methods, psychology fulfills our second requirement for qualifying as a science.

Although psychologists are scientists, most of my colleagues in psychology are what we call *scientist-practitioners*. This means that they are not so much involved in discovering new scientific laws about behavior and mental processes as they are in *applying* what we already know. Thus, we say that psychology has two interrelated goals: (1) the discovery and understanding of relationships that exist among the behaviors and mental processes of organisms, and (2) the application of this understanding in the real world.

Of those psychologists who are practitioners, most are clinical or counseling psychologists. Their goal is to apply what we know to help people deal with problems that are affecting their ability to cope or to adjust to the demands of their environments, including other people. Some scientist-practitioners in psychology have as their goal the application of psychological principles to issues that arise in the workplace; these are industrial/organizational (or I/O) psychologists.

Psychological practitioners can be found in many settings, dealing with a variety of issues. Some apply psychology to improve the performance of athletes; some advise attorneys on how best to present arguments in the courtroom; some intervene to reduce ethnic prejudice; some establish programs to increase the use of automobile safety belts; some help people train their pets; and the list goes on.

I hope you recognize that the science of psychology and the practice of psychology are *not* mutually exclusive endeavors. For one thing, many psychologists who are practicing clinical, counseling, or industrial psychologists *are* active scientific researchers. And much of the scientific research in psychology gets its initial spark or impetus from problems that arise in real-world applications of psychology (Hoshmand & Polkinghorne, 1992).

Before You Go On

Why may we claim that psychology is a science?

What are the two major goals of psychology?

What Psychologists Study: The Subject Matter of Psychology

Skimming through the pages of this book should quickly convince you that trying to list everything that psychologists study would not be very instructive. Our list would be much too long to be useful. However, it is fair to say, as our definition does, that the subject matter of psychology is behavior and mental processes. I've already noted that psychologists study both human and nonhuman organisms. Let's now explore more fully what it is about organisms that psychologists seek to understand.

Psychologists Study Behavior. By **behavior** I mean what organisms *do:* their actions, reactions, and responses. The behaviors of organisms are observable and—at least potentially—measurable. If I am concerned with whether a rat will press a lever under some circumstance, I can observe its behavior directly. If I wonder about Susan's ability to draw a circle, I can ask her to do so and observe her efforts. Observable, measurable behaviors such as lever pressing and circle drawing offer an advantage as subject matters of a science because they are **publicly verifiable**. In other words, several observers (public) can agree on (verify) the behavior or the event being studied. We can all agree that the rat did or did not press the lever or that Susan drew a circle, not a triangle. Events, including behaviors, that can be publicly verified have greater credibility in science. Susan may believe that she can draw a circle (and that belief may be of some interest), but if she cannot or will not actually do so, why should we believe her?

Psychologists Study Mental Processes. When psychology first emerged as a separate discipline late in the nineteenth century, it was

behavior what an organism does; an action of an organism that can be observed and measured

publicly verifiable the agreement (verifiability) of observers (public) that a behavior or an event did or did not take place

mental processes *internal activities of consciousness, including cognitions and affect*

defined as the science of **mental processes,** or the science of consciousness. Eventually, it became clear that mental processes were not easy to study, particularly for a discipline struggling to demonstrate that it was a science. The problem was (and still is) that mental processes are private and personal, and thus are difficult to verify publicly. After all, your mental activities go on *in your mind,* and I can't get into your mind to share those activities with you. For nearly fifty years in this century (from the 1920s to the 1970s), mental processes were virtually ignored by psychology, which focused instead on the study of observable behaviors. No one ever denied that mental processes existed, or claimed that they were unimportant or uninteresting. The issue was that psychology simply was not prepared to study mental processes in a scientific manner.

Mental processes can be divided into two major types: cognitions and affects. **Cognitions** include perceptions, beliefs, thoughts, ideas, memories, and the like. *Cognitive processes* include perceiving, thinking, knowing, understanding, problem solving, and remembering. On the other hand, **affect** refers to one's feelings, mood, or emotional state.

cognitions *one's perceptions, beliefs, thoughts, ideas, memories, and the like*

affect *one's feelings or mood, or emotional state*

Here we have a scheme we will encounter repeatedly: the *ABCs* that make up the subject matter of psychology. The subject matter of psychology may be taken to be *a*ffect, *b*ehavior, and *c*ognition. To understand a person at any given time, or to predict what one will do next, we have to understand what he or she is feeling (*A*), doing (*B*), and thinking (*C*).

The study of mental processes is now clearly entrenched in mainstream psychology. We'll see throughout this book many examples of how psychologists have managed to learn about internal, private, and personal mental events and at the same time maintain scientific respectability. After all, a psychology silent on such matters as thinking, planning, problem solving, and feeling would be barren indeed (Bourne, 1992; Kimble, 1989).

operational definition *a definition of a concept given in terms of the methods (or operations) used to measure or create that concept*

Psychologists Use Operational Definitions. Psychologists study how organisms feel, what they do, and what they think. Psychologists find it useful, and occasionally imperative, to define their subject matter in terms of the operations they use to measure it. When they do so, they are using **operational definitions.** Operational definitions define concepts in terms of the procedures used to measure or create them. Let's look at a few examples.

Let's say we are interested in the conditions under which a rat turns left, rather than right, in a maze (see Figure 1.1). It seems like a relatively simple matter to determine the direction a rat turns in a maze. But just what will constitute *a turn?* How will you *measure* the turn of a rat in a maze? Will sticking its nose around the corner be taken as a turn? What if it gets most of its body around the corner and then scoots back? Does the rat's tail have to make it all the way around? As silly as it may sound, you may have to operationally define *a turn in the maze* by specifying just how you intend to measure it.

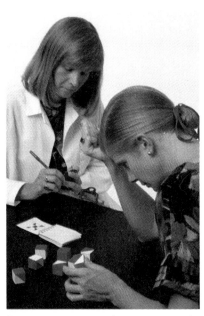

Because we cannot observe a person's intelligence directly, we may choose to define intelligence operationally as "that which an IQ test measures."

What if we wanted to compare the behaviors of hungry and non-hungry rats in a maze? How do we know when a rat is hungry? How will we define *hungry rat*? What we can do is offer an operational definition, specifying that—at least for our study—a hungry rat is one that has been deprived of food for 24 hours. Alternatively, we may operationally define a hungry rat as one that has lost 15 or 20 percent of its normal body weight. Here, we're defining a concept in terms of the procedures used to create it.

Operational definitions become particularly useful when we consider mental processes. How shall we define *anxiety* in a study comparing the performance of students who experience either high or low anxiety during test taking? How shall we define *intelligence* if we want to compare the intelligence of students who have had access to a preschool program with students who have not? Terms such as *anxiety* and *intelligence* are difficult to define precisely or in ways with which all psychologists would agree. Sometimes our only recourse is to use operational definitions and specify how we intend to measure these concepts during the course of our study. We might operationally define *anxiety* in terms of measurable changes in physiological processes such as blood pressure, heart rate, and sweat gland activity. We might operationally define *intelligence* as the score on a certain psychological test.

There are some limitations of operational definitions. They may *over*simplify truly complex concepts (surely there is more to intelligence than a few numbers from a test). On the other hand, they *do* allow us to specify exactly how to measure the behavior or mental process we are studying, so they help us communicate accurately with others. Operational definitions can be used to sidestep lengthy philosophical discussions. Rather than agonizing over the "true" nature of intelligence, we can operationally define intelligence as "that which an IQ test measures." Rather than considering all factors that affect the aging process, we can operationally define old age as "living 65 years or more." Notice that someone else may choose to define old age as "living 75 years or more." Such a definition would be no more right or wrong than ours. It is simply different. Have you noticed that medical science has had to resort to an operational definition of what it means to be dead? With increases in organ transplant surgery, one must be quite certain what one means when declaring a patient "dead." We will see many examples of operational definitions throughout this text.

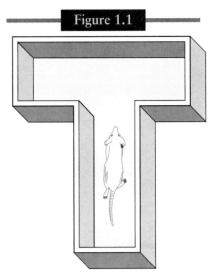

Figure 1.1

A rat moves down a simple T-maze. Determining whether this rat turns left or right in the maze may necessitate operationally defining what we mean by "turn."

Before You Go On

What is the subject matter of psychology?

What are operational definitions, why do we use them, and what are their limitations?

PSYCHOLOGICAL APPROACHES PAST AND PRESENT

No two psychologists approach their subject matter exactly the same way. As individuals, psychologists bring their own experiences, expertise, values, and prejudices to the study of behavior and mental processes. This is true today, and it always has been the case. In this section, we add to our definition of psychology by considering some of the major perspectives, or approaches, developed throughout psychology's history. Let's begin by considering the origins of the independent discipline of psychology.

Psychology's Roots in Philosophy and Science

Psychology did not suddenly appear as the full-blown, productive scientific enterprise we know today. The roots of psychology are to be found in philosophy and science.

We credit the philosophers for first suggesting that it is both reasonable and potentially profitable to seek explanations of human behaviors at a human level. Most of the earliest explanations of the human experience tended to be at the level of God—or the gods. If someone was smarter than you it was because God willed it that way. If someone suffered from fits of terrible depression it was because that someone had offended the gods. What philosophers did was to convince us that we might be able to explain why people do what they do and feel and think as they do without constant reference to God's intentions in the matter.

The French philosopher René Descartes (1596–1650) provides a good example. Descartes liked to think about the nature of thinking. As he "lay abed of a morning thinking" (something his schoolmaster allowed, given that Descartes was so good at it), he pondered how the human body and mind produced the very process he was then engaged in—thinking. Descartes envisioned the human body as a piece of machinery, intricate and complicated to be sure, but machinery nonetheless. If the body consisted essentially of tubes, gears, valves, and fluids, its operation must be subject to natural, physical laws, and those laws could be, and should be, discovered. Then, Descartes went further. Humans possess more than just a body. They have minds. It is likely that the mind also functions through the actions of knowable laws, but getting at these laws is surely to be more difficult. Here's where Descartes had a truly important insight. We *can* learn about the mind, and the laws under which it operates, because the mind and the body *interact* with each other. That interaction takes place in the brain. We call Descartes's position in these matters **interactive dualism**. *Dualism* because the mind and the body are separate entities, said Descartes, and *interactive* because they influence each other. Thus we have with Descartes the real possibility of understanding the mind and how it works.

Nearly a hundred years later, across the English Channel, a group of British thinkers moved that part of philosophy concerned with the human mind and how it worked very close to what was soon to become psychology. This group got their start from the writings of John Locke (1632–1704). Locke was sitting with some friends after

interactive dualism Descartes's position that a separate body and mind influence each other and are thus knowable

dinner one evening discussing philosophical issues when it became clear that no one in the group really understood how the human mind comes to understand anything, much less complex philosophical issues. Locke thought that within a week he could provide the group with a short explanation of the nature of human understanding. What was to have been a simple exercise took Locke many years to finish and gave philosophers a new set of ideas to deal with.

The major concern of Locke was how we come to represent—in the internal world of the mind—the world "out there." Others (including Descartes) had asked this question before, and many had assumed that we are born with certain basic ideas—notions about ourselves, the world, and, of course, God. Locke thought otherwise. He believed we are born into this world with our minds empty, essentially like blank slates. [The notion of the mind as a blank slate, or *tabula rasa,* was not new with Locke; it had been introduced as far back as Aristotle (384–322 B.C.)]. So how does the mind come to be filled with ideas, thoughts, and memories? To this question Locke answered, "In one word, from *experience.*" Locke, and those who followed his initiative, are known as **British empiricists**, where empiricists credit experience and observation as the source of mental life.

British empiricists philosophers (including Locke) who claimed, among other things, that the contents of the mind come from experience and observation

Philosophy had gone nearly to the brink. Attention had been focused on the mind, how it worked, where its contents (ideas) came from, how those ideas could be manipulated, and how mind and body could influence each other. But philosophers are not scientists. Could the methods of science provide answers to some of the questions posed by philosophers?

During the nineteenth century, natural science was making progress on every frontier. By the middle of the century, Charles Darwin (1809–1882) had returned from his lengthy sea voyage on the *Beagle,* and in 1859 published his revolutionary *The Origin of Species,* which reported his observations from his trip and spelled out the details of evolution. Few nonpsychologists were ever to have as much influence on psychology. What Darwin did for psychology was to confirm that the human species was part of the natural world of animals. The methods of science could and should be turned to try to understand this creature of nature called human. Darwin also made it clear that all species of this planet are, in a nearly infinite number of ways, related to one another. The impact of this, of course, is that something we discover about the sloth or the ground squirrel or the rhesus monkey may enlighten us about ourselves. Another major point that Darwin emphasized was *adaptation.* Species will survive and thrive only to the extent that they can, over the years, adapt to their environments.

In 1860, a year after publication of *The Origin of Species,* a German physicist, Gustav Fechner (1801–1887), published a volume that was unique as a physics text. Fechner applied his training in the methods of physics to the psychological process of sensation. What, Fechner wondered, was the relationship between the physical characteristics of a stimulus and the psychological experience of sensing that stimulus? For example, if the intensity of a light source is doubled, will an observer see that light as being twice as bright? Fechner found that the answer was no. Using the precise scientific procedures of a physicist, Fechner went on to determine the mathematical relationship that exists between certain physical aspects of stimuli and a person's psychological experience of those stimuli. What Fechner did was to apply the methods of science to a fundamentally psychological question about the mind and experience.

The mid-1800s also found physiologists coming to a better understanding of how the human body functions. By then it was known that nerves carried electrical messages to and from various parts of the body, that the nerves serving vision are different from those that serve hearing and the other senses, and are different, too, from those that activate muscles and glands. Of all the biologists and physiologists of the nineteenth century, the one whose work is most relevant to psychology is Hermann von Helmholtz (1821–1894). Although a physician by trade, von Helmholtz's true love was pure science, the laboratory, and research. In the physiology laboratory, von Helmholtz developed an interest in matters that were clearly psychological. He did experiments and wrote theories on how long it takes the nervous system to react to stimuli, on how we process information through our senses, on how we experience color, and other, similar psychological issues. But in the mid-1800s there was no formal, recognized science of psychology as we know it today.

By the late nineteenth century, psychology's time had come. Philosophy had become intrigued with mental processes, the origin and nature of ideas, and the contents of the mind. Physiology and physics had begun to look at the nervous system, at sensation and perception, and were doing so using scientific methods. Biologists were raising questions about relations between humans and other species. What was needed was someone with a clear vision to unite these interests and methods and to establish a separate discipline. That person was Wilhelm Wundt.

Before You Go On

In what ways did the philosophies of Descartes and Locke prepare the way for psychology?

In what ways did the science of Darwin, Fechner, and von Helmholtz influence the emergence of psychology?

Psychology Begins: The Early Years

It is generally claimed that psychology began in 1879 when Wilhelm Wundt (1832–1920) officially opened his laboratory at the University of Leipzig. Wundt had been educated to practice medicine, and had studied physiology. At the University of Heidelberg he served as a laboratory assistant to the great von Helmholtz. He also held an academic position in philosophy. Wundt was a scientist-philosopher with an

Late in the nineteenth century, Wilhelm Wundt (center) and his students at the University of Leipzig used scientific methods in their attempts to understand human consciousness.

interest in such psychological processes as sensation, perception, attention, word associations, and emotions.

For Wundt, psychology was the scientific study of the mind, of consciousness. He was a scientist who left nothing to chance. All of his hypotheses were to be tested and retested in his laboratory under carefully controlled conditions. Wundt wanted to systematically describe the contents of the human mind. The focus of most of the work in Wundt's laboratory was to discover the basic elements of thought and how they were related to one another. Because the psychologists in Wundt's laboratory were interested in describing the structure of the mind and its operations, we refer to Wundt's approach to psychology as **structuralism.**

About the same time that Wundt's laboratory was flourishing, an American philosopher at Harvard University, William James (1842–1910), began to take issue with the sort of psychology that was practiced there. James never thought of himself as a psychologist, although he taught classes in the subject and published a two-volume textbook in 1890, *Principles of Psychology.* William James did agree that psychology should study consciousness. He defined psychology as "the science of mental life," a definition very similar to Wundt's. However, he thought the German-trained psychologists were off base trying to discover the contents and structure of the human mind. James argued that consciousness could not be broken down and analyzed into elements or particles. Consciousness is dynamic, a stream of events—personal, changing, and continuous. Psychology should be concerned not with the structure of the mind but with its function. The focus of psychology should be on the practical *uses* of the mind and mental life. In this regard, James was responding to the lead of Darwin. To survive requires that a species adapt to its environment.

structuralism the approach to psychology associated with Wundt that concerned itself with the structure and operations of the human mind and consciousness

functionalism an approach to
psychology emphasizing the study
of the mind and consciousness as
they help an organism adapt to its
environment

How does the mind function to help organisms adapt and survive in the world?

James's practical approach to psychology found favor in North America, and a new type of psychology emerged—largely at the University of Chicago. Psychologists there continued to focus on the mind, but emphasized its utilitarian, adaptive functions. As a result, we refer to this approach to psychology as **functionalism**. Functionalist psychologists relied heavily on experimental methods, and introduced the study of animals to psychology. Accepting the study of animals in the psychology laboratory reflects another influence of Darwin. One of the most popular textbooks of this era was *The Animal Mind* by Margaret Floy Washburn (1871–1939), the first American woman to be awarded a Ph.D. in psychology. Published in 1908, the book focused on animal consciousness. In fact, one of the characteristics of functionalism was its willingness to be open to a wide range of topics—as long as they were in some way related to mental life, adaptation, and practical application. As a result, we can trace the origin of child psychology, educational psychology, and social, industrial, and organizational psychology to this approach.

In those early days of psychology, societal pressures were such that getting a graduate-level education or any academic appointment was exceedingly difficult for women, no matter how bright and able they were (Furumoto & Scarborough, 1986; Scarborough & Furumoto, 1987). Nonetheless, one woman, Mary Calkins (1863–1930) so impressed William James that he allowed her into his classes even though Harvard would not allow her to enroll formally (nor would Harvard award her a Ph.D. for which she met all academic requirements). Mary Calkins went on to do significant experimental work on human learning and memory and, in 1905, was the first woman to be elected president of the American Psychological Association (Madigan & O'Hara, 1992). Christine Ladd-Franklin (1847–1930) did finally receive her Ph.D., but not until 40 years after it was earned and Johns Hopkins University had lifted its ban on awarding advanced degrees to women. In the interim she authored an influential theory on how humans perceive color.

As more and more bright young students were drawn to the science of psychology, academic departments and laboratories began to prosper throughout the United States and Canada. Scientific psychology was well under way. Regardless of one's particular interest, psychology was the scientific study of the mind—its structures and/or its functions. Such was the case until, early in the twentieth century, John Watson turned psychology's attention to the study of behavior.

Before You Go On

When and where did psychology begin?

How did the functionalists change psychology's approach to its subject matter?

Behaviorism and Beyond

John B. Watson (1878–1958) was born on a small farm in South Carolina. In his last year at nearby Furman University, Watson's mother died, thus relieving one of the pressures he felt to enter the ministry. Instead, he enrolled as a graduate student in psychology at the University of Chicago. He had read about the new science of psychology as an undergraduate and thought Chicago would be the best place to study. He was soon disappointed. It turned out he had little sympathy for attempts to study mental processes and consciousness with scientific methods. Even so, he stayed on at the university as a psychology major, studying the behavior of animals—white rats in particular.

With his Ph.D. in hand, at the age of 29, Watson moved to Johns Hopkins University in Baltimore, where, almost single-handedly, he changed the focus and the definition of psychology. Watson argued that if psychology were to become a mature, productive scientific enterprise, it had to give up its preoccupation with consciousness and mental activity. Psychology should concentrate on events that can be observed and measured. It should give up the study of the mind and focus on *behavior;* hence the name of a new approach to psychology: **behaviorism**.

behaviorism an approach to psychology emphasizing the overt, observable, measurable behavior of organisms

Neither Watson nor the behaviorists who followed him claimed that people do not think, have ideas, or form mental images. What Watson did say was that such processes were not the proper subjects of scientific investigation. Science must focus on those events that observers can measure and agree on, and behaviors fit the bill. No one else, after all, can share your thoughts, your ideas, or your images. We have no way of seeing what you see in your mind's eye. Watson argued that we ought to leave private, mental events to the philosophers and theologians and make psychology as rigorously scientific as possible. Watson once referred to behaviorism as "common sense grown articulate. Behaviorism is a study of what people *do*" (Watson, 1926, p. 724).

No one has epitomized the behaviorist approach to psychology more than B. F. Skinner (1904–1990). Skinner took Watson at his word and spent a long and productive career in psychology trying to demonstrate that we can predict and control the behaviors of organisms by studying relationships between their overt, observable responses and the circumstances under which those responses occur (Lattal, 1992).

Skinner simply avoided any reference to the internal states of his subjects, be they rats, pigeons, or people. What mattered for Skinner is how behaviors are modified by events in the environment. Behaviorists would not address the question of why a rat turns left in a maze by talking about what the rat wanted or what the rat was thinking at the time. Rather, they would try to specify the environmental conditions (the presence of food, perhaps) under which a rat is likely to make left turns. We should focus on observable events and leave the internal affairs of the organism out of our explanations. For more than fifty years, Skinner consistently held to the argument that

John B. Watson introduced behaviorism to psychology, but it was B. F. Skinner, shown here, who made behaviorism a dominant force in American psychology for nearly fifty years.

psychology should be defined as "the science of behavior" (Skinner, 1987, 1990).

Since the introduction of behaviorism in the 1920s, psychology has flourished and grown in many different directions. Here, I'll briefly describe just three.

Psychoanalytic Psychology. Sigmund Freud (1856–1939) was a practicing physician in Vienna who became interested in mental disorders. Freud was not a laboratory scientist. Most of his insights about the mind came from his careful observations of his patients and himself. Freud's works were particularly perplexing to the behaviorists. Just as they were arguing against a psychology that concerned itself with consciousness, here was Freud declaring that we are often subject to forces of which we are not aware. Our feelings, actions, and thoughts (A, B, and C) are often under the influence of the *unconscious* mind, wrote Freud. Many of our behaviors are expressions of instinctive strivings, he claimed. Freud's views were clearly at odds with Watson's. We call the approach to psychology that traces its origins to Sigmund Freud **psychoanalytic psychology**.

Humanistic Psychology. The approach we call **humanistic psychology** arose in many respects as a reaction against behaviorism *and* psychoanalysis. The leaders of this approach were Carl Rogers (1902–1987) and Abraham Maslow (1908–1970). Humanistic psychologists take the position that the individual, or the self, should be the central concern of psychology. It is their argument that we need to focus on the *person* in psychology. If we attend only to stimuli in the environment and overt responses to those stimuli, we are leaving the person out of the middle—and that's dehumanizing. Such matters as caring, intention, concern, will, love, and hate are real phenomena and worthy of scientific investigation whether they can be directly observed or not. Attempts to understand people without considering

psychoanalytic psychology the approach to psychology associated with Freud that emphasizes instincts and unconscious mental processes

humanistic psychology an approach to psychology emphasizing the person, or self, as a central matter of concern

Sigmund Freud brought the psychoanalytic approach to psychology. Among other things, this approach focused interest on human instincts and the unconscious.

such processes will be doomed. To humanists, the Freudian reliance on instincts was too controlling. Our biology notwithstanding, we are—or can be—in control of our destinies. Rogers and Maslow, and their intellectual heirs, emphasize the possibility of personal growth and achievement. This approach led Maslow to develop a theory of human motivation (see Topic 10A), and Rogers to develop a system of psychotherapy (see Topic 13B).

Gestalt Psychology. In the first quarter of the twentieth century, a group of German scientists was taking an approach to psychology decidedly different from that of Wundt, James, Watson, or Maslow. Under the leadership of Max Wertheimer (1880–1943), this approach became known as Gestalt psychology. **Gestalt psychology** focuses on the process of perception, concerned in particular with how we select and organize information from the outside world. *Gestalt* is a word difficult to translate literally into English. It means "configuration," or "whole," or "totality." In general terms, if you can see the big picture, if you can focus on the forest and not the trees, you have formed a gestalt. Indeed, it was the big picture of perception and consciousness that intrigued the Gestalt psychologists, who argued against trying to analyze perception, or awareness, or consciousness into discrete, separate entities. To do so would be to destroy the essence of what was being studied. "The whole is more than the sum of its parts," they said. When we look at a drawing of a cube, we do not see individual lines, angles, and surfaces, but naturally combine these elements to form a whole, a gestalt, which we recognize as a cube.

Gestalt psychology the approach to psychology that emphasized perception, in particular how we select and organize information

Before You Go On

What is the basic thrust of behavioristic, psychoanalytic, humanistic, and Gestalt approaches to psychology?

Contemporary Approaches to Psychology

Psychology has come a long way from those few students gathered around Wilhelm Wundt in his laboratory at Leipzig, but many of the insights provided by the early pioneers are still with us. Today, there are well over 500,000 psychologists in the world, with about half of these working in the United States (Rosenzweig, 1992). The largest professional organization of psychologists, the American Psychological Association, or APA, claims nearly 120,000 members, and lists over forty divisions or specialty areas to which its members belong (Fowler, 1992). A list of "Psychological Specialty Areas" from the APA—to use in responding to items on a 1993 survey of its members—lists 236 areas in which psychologists may be employed.

For now, we need only briefly sketch a few of the areas of current concern in psychology, just to give you an idea of the variety of interests that fall under the one label, "psychologist." This short list combines many of the APA divisions into broader categories. A danger

Abraham Maslow, shown here, and Carl Rogers are two psychologists associated with humanistic psychology.

inherent in such lists is that someone may infer that it provides a ranking in some order of importance. Be assured, none is intended.

Physiological/biological psychology is concerned with the interactions between bodily activity, behavior, and mental processes. This is the subfield in psychology most concerned with the structures and functions of the nervous system and the brain, and the role they play in guiding behavior. When we ask, "Why did I do (or feel, or think) that?," psychologists who take this approach will look to physiological, genetic, or biochemical explanations.

Developmental psychology is concerned with the psychological development of the individual from conception through death. Most developmental psychologists focus on the childhood years; some attend primarily to adolescence, adulthood, or old age; and others take a broader, life span approach. Developmental psychologists share interests with those in many other areas because they deal with numerous psychological functions: cognitive, emotional, perceptual, social, and moral development, to name a few.

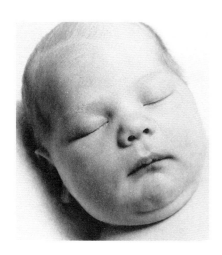 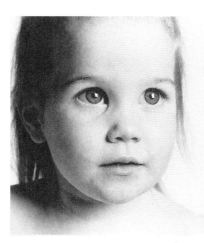 

Some developmental psychologists study the growth and development of the individual throughout the life span. Each of these images is of the same person.

Educational/instructional psychology is devoted to the processes of learning and memory and to the application of what we know about these processes to real-life situations. In both academic and business settings, educational and instructional psychologists often serve as consultants to improve training and educational programs.

Clinical psychology includes those psychologists concerned with the psychological well-being of the individual. The training of clinical psychologists provides them with the means to diagnose and treat persons with psychological disorders. Clinical psychologists usually have Ph.D.s in psychology (or the more recent Psy.D.). This distinguishes them from psychiatrists, who have earned a medical degree (M.D.) and, as a result, can prescribe medication and use other forms of medical treatment. Clinical psychology is by far the largest subfield in psychology. When combined with counseling psychology (see the following section), this subfield accounts for nearly 60 percent of all psychologists.

Counseling psychology is another applied area of psychology, which is very much like clinical psychology. Counseling psychologists, however, tend to serve persons with less severe and less chronic (long-lasting) disorders. They are more likely to be involved in such processes as grief counseling for disaster victims, divorce counseling, or short-term counseling with college students who are having adjustment problems.

Health psychology is one of the newer—and fastest growing—subfields in psychology. In general, health psychologists are commited to the notion that one's physical health is (or can be) affected by psychological variables, and vice versa. Finding ways to change or reduce behaviors that are known to have an adverse effect on one's health is typical of the activities of the health psychologist.

Cognitive psychology includes psychologists who investigate the basic processes of the mind: perception, learning, memory, and thinking. There are many specialty areas within cognitive psychology. Psycholinguists, for example, focus on language—how it is acquired, how it is produced, how it is perceived and interpreted. Some cognitive psychologists are interested in artificial intelligence—using computers to increase our understanding of the human mind.

Psychometrics involves the development and use of psychological tests and the statistical interpretation of data. Psychological testing is a big business in our society, particularly in educational and business settings.

Personality psychology is the subfield that most directly seeks to identify those traits or characteristics that unite us as a species and at the same time can be used to differentiate among us. The questions asked by personality psychologists are among the most basic and difficult: What *is* human nature? To what extent are our affects, behaviors, and cognitions a reflection of internal aspects of our personality, and to what extent do they reflect the environment or situation in which we find ourselves?

Social psychology reflects the observation that most organisms do not and cannot live without the company of others. How the behaviors of an individual affect others, and vice versa, is the general concern of social psychology. Predictably, this area, too, has many subfields, with interests in sex roles, attitudes, prejudice, intergroup conflict, conformity, and the like.

Cultural psychology goes further, recognizing that people live in a variety of cultures and ethnic environments. The aim of cultural psychology is to examine ethnic (e.g., Caucasian-American, African-American, Native American, Hispanic-American, and so forth) and cultural sources of psychological diversity (Shweder & Sullivan, 1993).

Industrial/organizational (I/O) psychology is defined largely by the work setting of the psychologist. What he or she may do there covers a wide range of possibilities. Some I/O psychologists are concerned with marketing and advertising; some with group productivity or with consumer satisfaction; some with the design of machines; others with personnel decisions of hiring, firing, or training; and still others with helping those who suffer from the stress of the workplace.

Of course, this list is incomplete and provides only an overview. No doubt there are psychologists who could claim that they do not fit any of these categories. Others might claim that they fit two or more. Still, as you read through the rest of this text, you'll be introduced to many psychologists who follow the approaches we have outlined in Topic 1A. The diversity of psychology is one of the things that makes it such an exciting field to study.

Before You Go On

What are some of the specialty areas of modern psychology, and what might we expect from a psychologist working in a particular area?

TOPIC 1A SUMMARY

In Topic 1A we have defined psychology as the scientific study of behavior and mental processes. That is, psychologists use scientific methods to study *a*ffect, *b*ehavior, and *c*ognition. The goals of psychology are to discover and understand scientific laws concerning affect, behavior, and cognition, and to apply these laws in the real world. We have also taken a brief look at psychology's history, noting that although it emerged as a separate, scientific discipline only a hundred years ago, its roots in philosophy and science date much further back. We have seen that the discipline of psychology includes many areas and approaches, and many perspectives from which psychologists view their subject matter. This is true today, and always has been. Now we need to consider in more detail just how psychologists go about doing what they do. These are the issues covered in Topic 1B.

Topic 1B
THE RESEARCH METHODS OF PSYCHOLOGY

In Topic 1A we saw that psychology is a science because it has an organized body of knowledge and because it uses scientific methods to discover and understand the laws of its subject matter: affect, behavior, and cognition. Scientific methods were defined as systematic procedures of observation, description, control, and replication. Now it is time to see what this general definition means as it applies to the methods psychologists use. To understand psychology, it is imperative that we understand its research methods.

OBSERVATIONAL METHODS IN PSYCHOLOGY

Our discussion of research in psychology begins with comments about observational methods. Before we can explain what people do, we must first make valid observations of just what it is that people do. As it happens, many of our casual, commonsense observations about behaviors are simply not true. "You can spot a gay guy a mile away, they're so effeminate." (No, not necessarily.) "Most people older than 65 are unhappy complainers." (No, they're not.) "Mothers pay more attention to good babies than they do to bad babies." (No, they don't.) If many of our casual, everyday observations lead to conclusions that are incorrect, how, then, can psychologists go about making valid observations? In the next few sections, we'll review some of the steps psychologists take to do just that.

Naturalistic Observation

As its name implies, the approach called **naturalistic observation** involves carefully watching behaviors as they occur, without any involvement from the observer. There is a logical appeal to the argument that if you are trying to understand what organisms do in real life, you should simply watch them while they are doing it, noting their behaviors and the conditions under which those behaviors occur.

As straightforward and logically appealing as naturalistic observation may sound, it does present a few difficulties. For one thing, if

naturalistic observation the method of observing and noting behaviors as they occur, without the involvement of the observer

Naturalistic observation requires skill and great patience. The observer here is using a night-vision lens to look for frogs as tape recorders play the frogs' mating call.

observer bias when one's own motives, expectations, and past experiences interfere with the objectivity of one's observations

we truly do want to observe people (or any other organism) *the way they naturally act*, we must make sure they do not realize we are watching them. As you know from your own experience, people may act very differently if they think they are being watched. You may do all sorts of things in the privacy of your own home that you would never do if you thought someone was watching you.

A second problem of which we must be aware is **observer bias**. Observers should not let their own motives, expectations, and previous experiences interfere with the objectivity of their observations. It might be difficult for a researcher to be objective in her observations of a group of children in a preschool setting if she is aware of the hypothesis under consideration, say, that boys are more verbally aggressive than girls. Observer bias may also result from gender and cultural bias. For example, men often have different visions of what constitutes "sexual harassment" than do women (see Fitzgerald, 1993). One person shoving another might be seen as an aggressive act by a person from a culture in which the crime rate is very low (e.g., Japan), but as not aggressive at all by a person from a culture in which the crime rate is very high. One solution for observer bias is to have observers note behaviors as they occur without knowledge of the particular hypotheses that are under investigation in the research. Another protection against observer bias is to check the reliability (dependability) of observations by using several observers, and relying only on those observations that can be verified by a number of observers.

A third potential problem with naturalistic observation is a bit more difficult to deal with. The behaviors you want to observe may not be there when you are. For example, if you are interested in conformity and want to observe people conforming naturally, in the real world, just where would you go? Where are you likely to observe conformity happening naturally? There are some environments in which conformity behaviors are more likely to occur than others. But there is no guarantee that during any particular day, or week, the people you are watching will provide any evidence of conformity. If you start manipulating a situation so that people are more likely to conform, you are no longer doing *naturalistic* observation. To use this method you often have to be lucky, and you almost certainly will have to be patient.

Although it has its problems, there are times when naturalistic observation *is* the most suitable method psychologists have available. For example, studying chimpanzees in zoos and laboratories (even when we use observational methods to do so) will tell us little about the behaviors of chimpanzees in the wild. Many other examples come from psychologists who have been frustrated in their attempts to study the language development of young children. By the time they are 3 or 4 years old, children demonstrate all sorts of interesting language behaviors. However, these same children may be too young to understand and properly follow the instructions that many experiments require. Almost certainly, they are unable to respond sensibly to questions about their own language usage. Perhaps all we *can* do is watch and listen carefully to young children as they use their language and try to determine what is going on by observing them as they interact naturally with their environments. A psychologist who studies language development with her husband reports that they often spend their summers "looking quite foolish" following behind toddlers, "recording their every utterance in dime-store notebooks" (Gelman et al., 1987).

Before You Go On

What is naturalistic observation?

List some of the potential problems that can arise with this method.

Surveys

When we want to make systematic observations about a large number of people, we may use a **survey** method. Doing a survey amounts to asking many people the same question or set of questions. The questions may be asked in person, in a telephone interview, or in a written

survey a means of collecting observations from a large number of subjects, usually by interview or questionnaire

The data from surveys can tell us what a large sample of persons thinks about a limited number of issues.

questionnaire. Survey studies yield data that would be difficult to gather otherwise.

If we wanted to know, for example, whether there was a relationship between income level and the type of automobile one drives or television programs one watches regularly, we could ask about these issues in a survey of a large number of persons. Surveys can tell us what segments of the population think or feel and can provide insights about preferences for products or services (or political candidates). If the staff of the cafeteria on your campus really wanted to know what students preferred to eat, they could survey a sample of the student population. Publishers often survey psychology and other instructors to see what they would like to have included in the books they use.

Perhaps the most critical aspect of observations made from survey data is the size and representativeness of the **sample** surveyed. A sample is a subset, or portion, of a larger population chosen to be studied. We would like to be able to generalize, or extend, observations beyond those persons we survey in our sample. Textbook publishers who survey instructors only at small liberal arts colleges, or cafeteria managers who survey students attending only morning classes, may very easily collect information (make observations) that do not generalize to the intended population, that is, the larger, complete set of persons from which the sample is drawn.

sample the subset or portion of a larger population chosen for study

Case Histories

case history an intensive, retrospective, and detailed study of some aspects of one (or a few) individual(s)

The **case history** method provides another sort of observational information. In the case history method, one person—or a small sample of persons—is studied in depth, often over a long period. Use of this method usually involves an intense and detailed examination of a wide range of variables. The method is retrospective, which means that we start with some given state of affairs (a situation that exists today) and go back in time to see if there is any relationship between this state of affairs and previous experiences and events. We may use interviews or psychological tests as a means of collecting our data.

As an example, let's say that we are interested in Mr. X, a known child abuser. Our suspicion (hypothesis) is that Mr. X's own childhood experiences might be related to his present behavior as a child abuser. We talk to Mr. X at length and interview his family and friends—those who knew him as a child—trying to form a retrospective picture of Mr. X's childhood. If we find some clues—for example, Mr. X was punished with severe spankings, or he missed class at school significantly more often than other children—we may then explore the early childhood experiences of other known child abusers, looking to find common experiences that might be related to their abuse of children now that they are adults.

I have always been intrigued by the choices college students make when they decide on a major course of study. Why do some students major in psychology, whereas others choose mathematics or fine arts as a major? Perhaps the case history method could provide some insights about the factors related to one's choice of a college major. How would we proceed? We would choose a sample of students, perhaps seniors, from each major, and ask them a number of penetrating (it is hoped) questions about their experiences, looking for something that all students of one major had in common but that was different from the experiences of those who opted for other majors.

As we shall see, Freud based most of his theory of personality on his intensive examination of the case histories of his patients (and himself). The advantage of the case history method is that it can provide a wealth of detailed information about a few individual cases. The disadvantage is that we have to be particularly careful when we try to generalize our findings beyond those individuals we have chosen to study.

Now that we have briefly reviewed some of the ways in which psychologists make careful, reliable observations, we need to see how these observations can be used to make predictions about behaviors not yet observed. This is our focus in the following section.

Before You Go On

**How can surveys and case history studies
be used to help us understand behavior
and mental processes?**

CORRELATIONAL METHODS IN PSYCHOLOGY

As you know from your own experience, observations are often very useful in their own right. Observations about people's behaviors, thoughts, or feelings can provide us with interesting insights. How many people in the United States and Canada *do* smoke cigarettes? What do the majority of Americans really think about abortions performed during the first trimester of pregnancy? How do most people feel about making yet another *Home Alone* movie? They may be interesting, informative, and insightful, but observations take the form of scientific laws only when they can be related consistently to other observations. **Correlation** is a statistical procedure used to assess the nature and degree to which sets of observations are lawfully related. In fact, to say that observations are correlated is to say that they are related to each other (co-related) in some way.

Let's work through an example to see how this method works. Imagine that we are interested in whether there is a relationship—a correlation—between reading ability and performance in introductory psychology. The only difficult part of this study is devising acceptable operational definitions for the responses in which we are interested. That is, we need to decide on how we will actually measure *reading ability* and *performance in introductory psychology.* Once we've done that, we can make our measurements, which will provide us with two sets of numbers. Then we can determine if a relationship exists between our two observed responses. We'll look at this procedure step by step.

First, we need to come up with operational definitions for the responses we care about. *Performance in introductory psychology* isn't difficult to deal with. We'll take that to mean the total number of points earned by a student on classroom exams over the course of a semester. *Reading ability* is a little tougher. What do we mean by *reading ability?* We could design a test of our own to measure behaviors we think reflect reading ability, but it turns out we're in luck. There are several tests of reading ability already available, and after reviewing them, we decide to use the Nelson Denny Reading Test, the NDRT (Brown, 1973).

Now we're ready to collect some data (make our observations). We give a large group of students our reading test (the NDRT). Once the tests are scored, we have one large set of numbers. At the end of the semester, we add up the points earned by each of our students, and we have a second set of numbers. For each student in our study we now have a pair of numbers—one indicating reading ability and one indicating performance in the introductory psychology course. We want to know if these observations are correlated. From here on out, our method is more statistical than psychological.

We enter our pairs of numbers into a calculator, or a computer if we have a very large set of numbers. A series of arithmetic procedures is applied (there are prescribed formulas for these calculations). The result is called the **correlation coefficient**—a number between −1.00 and +1.00 that tells us about the nature and the extent of the relationship between the responses we have measured. What does this number mean? How can it be the basis for a scientific law? It takes experience to be truly comfortable with the interpretation of correlation coefficients, but we can make some general observations.

---

correlation a largely statistical technique used to determine the nature and extent of the relationship between two measured responses

correlation coefficient a number that indicates the nature (+ or −) and the strength (0.00 to +1.00 or −1.00) of the relationship between measured responses

First, let's deal with the sign of the correlation coefficient, which will be positive (+) or negative (−). A positive coefficient tells us that our two measured responses are related to each other and that high scores on one of our responses are associated with high scores on the other. It also tells us that low scores on one measure are associated with low scores on the other. Most of the correlations with which we are familiar are of this positive type—the correlation between SAT scores and college grade point averages, for example. In our example, a student who does well on the reading test probably does well in an introductory psychology course. Those students who do poorly on the reading test are likely to earn lower grades in the psychology course. We can make these predictions only if our two measured responses are positively correlated. As it happens, there is ample evidence that such is the case (Gerow & Murphy, 1980). Figure 1.2(A) shows what a graph of the scores measured in our example might look like, showing a positive correlation. This example shows us a major use of correlations: if we determine that two responses are correlated, we can use our observation of one response to make predictions about the other.

What if our calculations result in a correlation coefficient that is a negative number? Here, too, we have a useful psychological law. We can still use scores on one response to predict scores on the other. But,

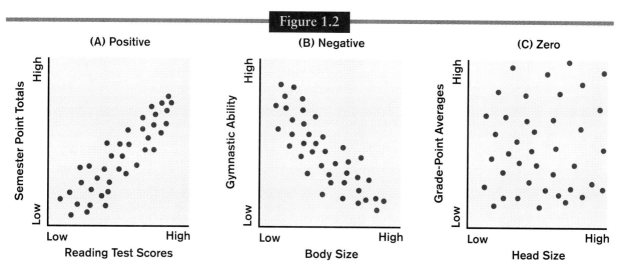

Figure 1.2

Positive, negative, and zero correlations. (A) A graph depicting the reading test scores and semester point totals earned by 40 students. These data indicate a positive (+) correlation between the two measured responses. As reading test scores increase, so do semester point totals. (B) A graph depicting the body size and gymnastic ability of 40 students. These data indicate a negative (−) correlation between the two measured responses. As body size increases, gymnastic ability decreases. (C) A graph depicting the head sizes and grade-point averages of 40 students. These data indicate a zero (0) correlation between the two measured responses. There is no relationship between head size and grade-point average.

U.S. gymnast Christy Phillips with her coach Bela Karolyi at the 1992 Olympic Games. Is it reasonable to hypothesize a negative correlation between gymnastic ability and body size?

when our correlation coefficient is negative, we know that the relationship between our two measured responses is inverse, or upside down. With negative correlation coefficients, high scores on one response predict low scores on the other.

If we measured body size and looked to see if it was related to gymnastic ability, we might find a negative correlation: large body sizes are associated with poor gymnastic ability (low scores), whereas small body sizes are associated with good gymnastic ability (high scores). Notice that if these two sets of observations are negatively correlated, we can still use body size to predict gymnastic ability. Figure 1.2(B) shows a set of data depicting the possible relationship between gymnastic ability and body size, a negative correlation.

What if our correlation coefficient turns out to be zero, or nearly so (say, .003)? In this case, we would have to conclude that the two sets of observations are simply not related to each other in any consistent, lawful way. Let's say that I worked from the faulty notion that intelligence is a function of brain size, and that one's head size tells us how big a person's brain is. No doubt if I were to measure the head size of a large number of students and also measure grade point average, I would find that the calculations for the correlation coefficient would result in a number very close to zero. As correlations approach zero, predictability decreases. Figure 1.2(C) completes our set of examples by showing what a graph of data from two sets of unrelated measures would look like.

So much for the sign of the correlation coefficient. What about its numerical value? Again, it takes a little practice to get used to working with numbers such as −.46, +.55, and +.002. There are statistical tests we can use to determine the usefulness (or significance) of a correlation coefficient. Among other things, these tests can tell us the likelihood that our coefficient is or is not significantly different from zero. For now, let us just say that the closer we get to the extreme of +1.00 or −1.00, the stronger the relationship between the responses we have measured. This means that as our correlation coefficient approaches +1.00 or −1.00 (say, +.84 or −.93), we will have increased confidence in our ability to predict one response knowing the other. The closer our coefficient gets to zero (say, −.12 or +.004), the weaker the relationship and the less useful it is for making predictions. I should mention that the confidence we have in the usefulness of correlations for making predictions is largely determined by the number of observations used in our calculations. In general, the larger the sample (the more observations we have made) the greater the confidence we can put in our correlation coefficient, whatever its value.

As you read this text, you'll encounter many studies that use a correlational analysis of measured observations. As you do so, you'll need to keep in mind two important points. (1) *Cause-and-effect conclusions are inappropriate for correlational studies*. Even if two responses are very well correlated with each other, we cannot claim that one causes the other. For some reason, this seems difficult to remember. Sometimes logic overwhelms us. It does make sense that an inability to read will actually cause some students to do poorly in an introductory psychology class where reading is so important. Yes, it does make sense, but if all we have to guide us is knowing that reading ability and grades are correlated, we can make no statement at all about cause and effect; all we can say is that the two responses are related to each other. (2) *Even when two responses are well correlated, we cannot make predictions for individual cases.* As I said, reading ability and introductory psychology grades are positively correlated. By and large, students who read well do well in the course, and, by and large, students who do not read well tend to do poorly. So, *in general,* we can use reading test scores to predict grades, but we have to allow for exceptions. A few poor readers may do very well indeed, and a few excellent readers may still fail the course. Exceptions are to be expected. In fact, the further from +1.00 or −1.00 our correlation coefficient is, the more exceptions we can expect. Like most scientific laws in psychology, statements of correlation hold true only "by and large," "generally," "in the long run," or "more often than not."

Before You Go On

**What data are needed to calculate
a correlation coefficient?**

**What does a correlation coefficient tell us
about the relationship between
two measured responses?**

EXPERIMENTAL METHODS IN PSYCHOLOGY

Most of what is known today in psychology has been learned by doing **experiments**. Experiments involve a series of operations used to investigate relationships between manipulated events and measured events, while other extraneous events are controlled or eliminated. In the abstract, that's quite a mouthful, but the actual procedures are not that difficult.

In fact, before we go on, we should pause momentarily to reiterate some of the general comments made earlier about scientific research. All research begins with observations; psychologists deal with observations about an organism's behaviors or mental processes. On the basis of initial observations we formulate a hypothesis, which, you will recall, is a tentative explanation of our subject matter that can be tested to determine whether it can be supported or must be rejected. Sometimes all we need to do to find support for our hypothesis is to make additional observations. If we think students would like the cafeteria to make pizza available every day, we need only survey students to find out. Sometimes we need to see if two or more responses are related to each other in some lawful way. If we hypothesize that performance in a course is related to students' reading ability, we need to measure reading ability and performance and calculate a correlation coefficient. In other words, we need to put our hypothesis to the test.

experiments operations used to investigate relationships between manipulated events (independent variables) and measured events (dependent variables) while other events (extraneous variables) are controlled or eliminated

One of the important things about experiments is that they are intended to discover cause-and-effect relationships. With experiments we're no longer content to discover that two measured observations are simply related; now we want to be able to claim that, at least to some degree, one is caused by the other. To see if such a claim can be made, an experimenter manipulates one variable to see if that manipulation causes any measurable changes in another variable. A variable is simply something that can vary—a measurable event (e.g., a score on a reading test or classroom performance) that can take on various values. Experimental methods are described in terms of variables.

The events or conditions an experimenter manipulates are called **independent variables**. Those the experimenter measures are **dependent variables**: their value should *depend* on the experimenter's manipulation of independent variables. The hope is that the manipulation of the independent variable will cause predictable changes in the dependent variable—changes predicted by one's hypothesis. If there *are* changes in the measured dependent variable, the experimenter would like to claim that these changes are due *solely* to the influence of the manipulated independent variable. In order to make such a claim, it must be shown that all other variables that could have influenced what is being measured have been controlled or eliminated. Those factors that need to be eliminated from consideration are called **extraneous variables** (extraneous means "not essential" or "irrelevant"). So, to do an experiment, a researcher manipulates independent variables, measures dependent variables, and eliminates, or controls, the effects of extraneous variables. If you haven't encountered this before, don't be discouraged. It's not as confusing as it may sound. Going over a couple of examples will help.

After a few quizzes in your biology class you notice that the student sitting in front of you is consistently scoring higher than you are—not by much, but by enough to be annoying. You ask this student how she does it, and she tells you she has a system she learned in high school. To help remember a series of unrelated concepts, she weaves the terms together to form a story. Recalling the story is fairly easy and can be used to help recall terms for quizzes. This system sounds sensible to you, and you decide to do an experiment to test if there is a cause-and-effect relation here—a decision that was also made in 1969 by Gordon Bower and M. C. Clark.

You get some volunteers from your introductory psychology class and divide them into two groups. One group (A) is asked to memorize a list of ten unrelated nouns. They are left to their own resources to learn the list however they would like. The other group (B) is asked to memorize the very same list of nouns, but they are told about the scheme of tying the words together to form a meaningful story, and they are told to try to use this strategy in learning the list.

Now for some terminology. Your hypothesis is that how one goes about memorizing has an effect on how much one remembers. You have manipulated this process, so using or not using a strategy in memorizing is your *independent variable*. You believe this variable will have an effect on memory. How will you measure this to see if it is so; that is, what will be your *dependent variable?* You ask all of the

independent variables those events in an experiment that are manipulated by the experimenter; they are hypothesized to produce changes in responses

dependent variables those responses measured in an experiment whose values are hypothesized to depend on manipulations of the independent variable

extraneous variables those factors in an experiment that need to be minimized or eliminated so as not to affect the dependent variable

students to return three weeks later. At that time you ask them all to "write down as many of the words as you can recall from the list you learned three weeks ago." Thus, you operationally define your dependent variable to be the average number of words from the list recalled three weeks later. When you look at your data, you discover that, on the average, group A recalls 3.5 words of the original 10, and group B (those who made up a story) recalls 8.2 words correctly. It seems that a story-generating strategy is useful in memorizing words. That strategy seems to cause significantly better recall.

Before we get too carried away, we had better consider the possible *extraneous variables* that might have been operating in this experiment. These are factors that might have affected the average recall of our two groups of students over and above what was manipulated (memorization strategy). Such factors should have been considered before you actually did the experiment. What extraneous variables might be involved in this experiment? For one thing, we need to be certain that the students in each of our groups are of essentially the same ability to begin with. It would not do if the students in group A were poor, struggling students and those in group B were honor students. It is also the case that both groups of learners need to be presented with identical materials to be learned, and the words need to be presented in the same way to both groups.

The essence of it is—and this is a very important point—that when we are done with our experiment and find differences in our dependent variable, we want to be able to claim that these differences are due to our manipulation of the independent variable, and to nothing else. It is the extent to which extraneous variables are anticipated and eliminated that determines the quality of an experiment. Figure 1.3 reviews the steps in our example experiment.

Let's take a quick look at another potential experimental question. Suppose you believe (hypothesize) that a stimulating environment in early childhood improves intellectual functioning at adolescence. How could you do an experiment to support your observation? Somehow, you would have to manipulate the nature or quality of the environment in which young children were reared. One group of children would have to be reared in relative isolation, in quiet, empty rooms. We'll consider ethical issues in psychological research shortly, but doesn't it seem likely that such a manipulation would be judged to be unethical? You wouldn't isolate or deprive a group of children this way—particularly if your own hypothesis is that doing so would have negative consequences.

Although there are alternatives, this problem provides a good example of an experiment that could be done with rats. Rats could be raised in cages that provide differing amounts of stimulation. When the rats approach maturity, you could test their ability to negotiate mazes or learn a variety of responses. Early exposure to stimulation would be your independent variable, and scores on your tests of learning ability would be your dependent variable.

One advantage of using rats in experiments is that extraneous variables are usually easy to deal with. You seldom have to worry about previous experience, inherited differences, parental influences,

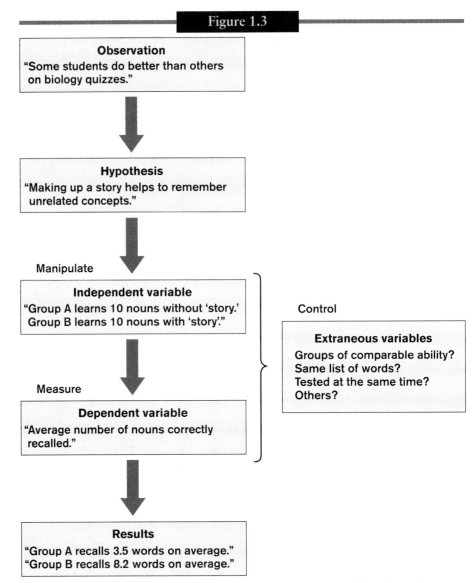

Figure 1.3

The steps, or stages, involved in doing an experiment. Note the relationship among the types of variables.

and the like (all of your rats have a known and very similar genetic history, and all have been reared in very similar conditions). The problem with using rats is also obvious. Even if you do demonstrate your point with rats, you may then have to argue that the data you have collected for rats are, in some way, applicable to humans. As we shall see, in many cases this argument is relatively easy to make, and with the advantage of ease of control, we can see why the use of non-human organisms in psychology is commonplace. Now that we have covered the essential procedures involved in doing experiments, we can examine some of the considerations that often determine the quality of an experiment.

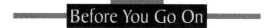

Before You Go On

What is the essence of doing an experiment?

Define independent, dependent, and extraneous variables in the context of doing an experiment.

Exercising Control

As I have said, the value of an experimental finding is often related to the researcher's ability to eliminate or control the influence of extraneous variables. The most difficult extraneous variables to control are often those that involve individual differences that exist among the participants in the experiment. Such was the case in our example involving a memory strategy. In a typical experiment, the independent variable is manipulated by presenting one group of participants with some treatment (such as a hint about how to memorize a list of words) while withholding that treatment from another group. Participants in both groups are then measured to see if the treatment produced any effect in the chosen dependent variable. By definition, those participants who receive a treatment or manipulation constitute the **experimental group**. An experiment may have a number of experimental groups. Our example of memorizing lists used just one. If an additional group had been available, we might have given them a different type of hint to aid their recall. Participants who do not receive the experimental treatment are the **control group**. Experiments usually have just one control group: In our example, this was group A, which received no hint about how to memorize the words.

    To make sure your control and experimental groups begin the experiment on an equal footing, you could do one of a number of things. You could try to match the groups on the characteristic of interest. In our example, you might have given all participants a recall test before the experiment began and then assigned them to either group A or B so that the average scores on this test were equal, or nearly so.

    A more common technique is to assign participants to groups by **random assignment**, which means that each participant in the research has an equal chance of being assigned to any one of the groups used in your experiment. If assignment is truly random, the honor students would be equally likely to be in either of your two groups—the one that does or the one that doesn't get a hint about weaving the words into a story. And remember, this sort of consideration—matching or randomly assigning subjects—is something that must be made before the experiment is actually begun.

experimental group those participants in an experiment who receive some treatment or manipulation; there may be more than one in an experiment

control group those participants in an experiment who do not receive any experimental treatment or manipulation

random assignment the selection of members of a population in such a way that each has an equal chance of being assigned to any one group

baseline design a method in which subjects' performance with an experimental treatment is compared with performance without that treatment (the baseline)

Another method for dealing with the control of variables that arises from the differing past experiences of subjects is called a **baseline design**. Although there are several such designs, each amounts to arranging things so that each participant serves in both experimental and control group conditions. Imagine, for example, that you wished to see if a certain drug caused an increase in the running speed of white rats. Using a baseline design, you would first measure the running speed of rats without giving them the drug (a control, or baseline measure). Then you would check the running speed of the same rats after they were given the drug. Changes in their behavior (your dependent variable) could then be attributed to the drug (your independent variable). You could then check the running speed of the rats again, after the effects of the drug wore off, to see if their behavior returned to its baseline rate.

Overcoming Bias

Human participants in psychology experiments are usually helpful and well motivated to do whatever is asked of them. In their efforts to please, they may act in an experimental situation in ways they would never act otherwise. That is, experimental subjects sometimes do what they think the experimenter wants them to do. When participants in an experiment are reacting to their perception of the experimenter's wishes, they are not responding to the independent variables of the experiment. In order to overcome this difficulty, subjects are generally not told anything about how the experimenter expects them—or wants them—to act. This is called the **single-blind technique** because the subjects are not aware of (are blind to) the purpose or the hypothesis of the experiment.

single-blind technique a protection against bias in which participants are kept from knowing the purpose, or hypothesis, of an experiment

For similar reasons, it is often helpful to keep the person who is to measure the dependent variable unaware of the goals or hypotheses of the experiment. At times, one can easily misread a clock, misperceive a rat's reaction in a maze, misinterpret a subject's verbal response, or give unintentional cues to a subject. This is particularly true when one *wants* a clock to give a certain time or *expects* a rat to make a given response. Note that I'm not talking about downright dishonesty here; I'm talking about honest errors that can be made in analyzing data when one has a stake in the outcome of the analysis. To offset this possible source of bias, we can use the **double-blind technique**, in which neither the participants nor the person collecting the data knows what the hypothesis of the experiment is. Obviously, *somebody* has to know what is going on, and that somebody is the person who will analyze the data—but not collect it.

double-blind technique a protection against bias in which both participants and data collector are kept from knowing the hypothesis of an experiment

For example, in our experiment that involved memorizing a list of words with and without a hint to aid the process, we would not tell the students or the participants in the experiment about our hypothesis, nor would we tell the people counting the number of words correctly recalled which group any participant belonged to. In our example of raising rats under differing levels of stimulation, we would see to it that the experimenters rating the learning ability of the rats (our dependent variable) did not know the conditions under which the rats were raised (our independent variable). (We don't have to worry about keeping hypotheses from the rats, which is another good reason to consider using nonhuman subjects.)

Meta-analyses

Before we leave our discussion of research methods in psychology, there is one technique that has become popular of late that deserves at least a brief note here. Some experiments may be impossible or difficult (or too expensive) to do on a large scale with many subjects. For example, ethics may prevent us from rearing children in isolation, deprived of environmental stimulation, but we might be able to identify a few adolescents who had relatively isolated, deprived childhoods. We might now compare their learning abilities with adolescents whose childhood experiences were apparently normal and with adolescents who seem to have had particularly stimulating childhood experiences. Our findings, based on only a few adolescents, with many variables not under careful control, would be tentative at best, no matter what those findings happened to be.

But, what if, over the years, many similar studies were conducted by several different researchers in many different places? Although each such study, in and of itself, would not be convincing, what if there were some way to combine the results of these studies? Such is precisely the intent of a procedure called **meta-analysis**, a statistical procedure of combining the results of many studies to see more clearly the relationship, if any, between independent and dependent variables. What a meta-analysis does is minimize the errors (confounding) that can plague single, smaller studies (Schmidt, 1992).

Meta-analysis research sometimes uncovers relationships that are not clear in individual studies, and sometimes produces results that even contradict some of the studies being analyzed. A recently reported meta-analysis (Hyde et al., 1990) examined an issue we'll look at in detail in Topic 9B: gender differences in mathematics performance. The researchers analyzed 100 studies, which involved the testing of a combined total of 3,175,188 subjects. (It's difficult to imagine any one research project that could involve over 3 million subjects.) What these researchers found was that there aren't many differences between males and females in mathematical performance. Girls show a slight advantage in computational skills in elementary and middle school. Males do slightly better than females in mathematical problem solving in high school and college, particularly in tests of advanced mathematics. But, what differences that do exist were found to be very small, and in most comparisons there were no real differences at all. This is the sort of finding that any one study, no matter how well conceived, is unlikely to give us.

There are many issues that researchers in psychology must attend to, whether they are doing correlational studies, collecting survey

meta-analysis a statistical procedure of combining the results of many studies to see more clearly any relationships among observations that may be present

data, recording case histories, making naturalistic observations, or doing experiments. The major intent is to see to it that one's observations and descriptions of relationships are as free from bias, error, and extraneous variables as possible. Another factor that researchers must consider is ethics. Ethical considerations are relevant to all methods psychologists use in their efforts to understand behavior and mental processes. In our next section, we'll take a brief look at ethics in psychological research.

Before You Go On

How do random assignment, baseline designs,
single- and double-blind techniques, and
meta-analyses help to minimize error
in psychological experiments?

ETHICAL CONSIDERATIONS IN PSYCHOLOGICAL RESEARCH

Ethical and moral concerns can be found in all of the sciences. In most of the sciences, ethical issues usually center on the application of knowledge. We know how to split the atom; should we build a bomb? We can manufacture effective insecticides; should we use them? We have the means to render people infertile; should we? We can use machines to keep people alive indefinitely; should we? We can bury toxic or radioactive waste; where should we?

Psychology has something of a unique problem with regard to ethics. To be sure, ethical matters are important in the application of psychological knowledge, be it in diagnosis, therapy, counseling, training, or whatever. (These we'll deal with in later chapters.) A unique aspect of psychology is that ethical considerations are often central in the *gathering*, accumulation, or discovery of information. After all, the focus of our studies is living organisms. Their physical and psychological welfare need to be protected as we investigate their behaviors and mental processes. Psychologists have long been concerned with the ethical implications of their work. Since 1953, the American Psychological Association has regularly revised and published *Ethical Principles of Psychologists* for practitioners and researchers. The most recent version was published in 1992 (American Psychological Association). We'll deal briefly with a few of the issues these guidelines address with regard to research.

As one plans his or her research, the degree to which subjects will be put at risk should be assessed. What are the potential dangers, physical or psychological, that might accompany participation? Even if potential risks are deemed slight, they need to be considered and balanced in the light of what potential good might come from the experiment. Researcher Gregory Kimble put it this way: "Is it worth it? Do the potential benefits to science and eventually to animal and human lives justify the costs to be extracted here and now?" (Kimble, 1989, p. 499). Seldom will any one psychologist have to make the ultimate decisions about the potential benefits or risks of research. Advisory committees of researchers, familiar with the techniques and the problems of the proposed research, will have to approve it before the project begins.

What are some other ethical issues related to research in psychology?

1. The participant's confidentiality must be guaranteed. Often, the person's name is not even used; it is replaced instead with an identification number. No matter what you are asked to do or say, you should be confident that no one will have access to your responses but the researchers.

2. Participation in research should be voluntary. There are no circumstances under which you should feel coerced or compelled to participate in psychological research. Volunteers should be allowed the option of dropping out of any research project, even after it has begun. For example, college students *cannot* be offered extra credit to participate in psychological research unless other options are available for earning the same amount of extra credit.

3. Subjects should participate in experiments only after they have given their advised consent. Participants must know the potential dangers of participation, why a project is being done, and what is going to be expected of them. For example, no one can have access to your college records (your GPA, your entrance exam scores, and so on) without your specific knowledge and approval. Obviously, some deception may be required when doing experiments. Even so, the amount of deception needs to be balanced with the promise of the outcome of the research.

4. Particularly if subjects have been deceived about the true nature of an experiment, and even if they haven't been, all subjects should be **debriefed** after the experiment has been completed. That means, if nothing else, that the true nature of the project and its basic intent should be fully explained to all those who participated in it. This becomes particularly relevant for studies using a single- or double-blind procedure. Subjects should also be provided with a copy of the results of the project when they are available.

debrief to fully inform a subject about the intent and/or hypotheses of one's research once data have been collected

Published ethical guidelines for the use of animals in research are also quite stringent. Only experts trained and experienced in the proper and humane care and housing of animals should have responsibility for laboratory animals. Those experts must then provide training to all others working with the animals. Every effort must be made to minimize discomfort, illness, and pain of animals. Putting animals in a situation in which they might experience injury, pain, or stress is acceptable *only* if no other procedure is available and the goal is justified by its prospective scientific, applied, or educational value. As

Even though the welfare of animals is carefully monitored in most laboratories, many animal-rights activists would prefer that animals not be used in research under any circumstances. Such is the point of this demonstration.

with human subjects, there are usually review committees that approve the design of any research using nonhuman animals, where the major concern is the ethical, humane protection of the animals.

Before You Go On

Cite four ethical issues that must be considered when doing psychological research.

KEY THEMES AND GENERAL PRINCIPLES

Psychologists have learned a lot about the behaviors and mental processes of organisms. Some of the conclusions we can now draw about psychology and its subject matter seem so important, so basic, that they deserve special mention. The principles listed here are so well established that they are almost part of our definition of psychology. In every chapter that follows you will recognize a reflection of these important ideas.

1. *Our biological nature and our psychological nurture interact to make us who we are.* How much of who we are—our affect, behavior, and cognition—is the result of our inheritance, our biological *nature*? How much of who we are reflects the influences of our environment, our experiences, or our *nurture*? Is intelligence inherited (nature) or due to experience (nurture)? Is aggressiveness inborn (nature), or is it learned (nurture)? Does alcoholism reflect one's innate nature, or is it a learned reaction to events in the environment?

In fact, nearly all behaviors and mental processes result from the *interaction* of inherited, genetic influences and environmental influences. In this context, interaction is a difficult concept. We'll extend our understanding as we go along. But for now, the logic is that any psychological characteristic is not going to be the result of *either* heredity *or* experience, but will reflect the extent to which these two forces have influenced each other. "For all psychological characteristics, inheritance sets limits on, or creates a range of potentials for, development. Environment determines how near the individual comes to developing these potentials" (Kimble, 1989).

Taking intelligence as an example, what this means is that person A may be born with the inherited, genetic potential, or predisposition, to be extremely bright. But what if person A is born into a poor neighborhood in a large city and receives less than adequate childhood care, nourishment, educational opportunities, and the like? That person may not turn out to be very intelligent—at least in an academic sense. If person B is born with genes that severely limit his or her intelligence, all of the training, education, and experience the environment can provide may not raise that person's intelligence very far above those limits set by nature. On the other hand, person B will probably be better off as a result of training than he or she would be without it. Many psychologists are now ready to argue that several complex, psychological traits, such as extroversion, leadership, parenting styles, and artistic abilities, at least have a basis in genetic, inherited predispositions (Lykken et al., 1992). Although there are obviously many factors involved, even the likelihood that one's marriage will end in divorce may be affected by genetic influences (McGue & Lykken, 1992).

2. *No two persons are exactly alike.* This observation may be psychology's most common and well documented. Given the diversity of genetic constitutions and the diversity of environments, including societal and cultural pressures, when we pause to contemplate the number of ways in which people can be (and often are) different from each other, it is sometimes a wonder that we can get along with each other at all. Not only is each organism unique and different from all others, but no one organism is the same from one point in time to another. Depending on your experiences, your mental processes and behaviors are different today from what they were yesterday. Most likely, you have not changed in any major, significant way, but some observations that may have been true of you yesterday may not be true of you today.

Imagine that a psychologist wants to study your behavior and mental activity and draw some conclusions she can apply to people in general. Do you see the problem she is going to have? Because there is variability in you and because you are not exactly like everyone else, the best this psychologist will be able to do is make statements in general terms, in terms of probability. For example, we know that high school grades are reasonable predictors of success in college. But because of the fact that people differ, the best we can do is say that students who do well in high school will *probably* do well in college. In fact, it is because no two people are exactly alike that virtually all psychological laws are statements made "in general, in the long run, by and large."

phenomenology the study of events
as they are experienced by the
individual, not as they actually
occur

3. *Our experience of the world may reflect something other than what is actually "out there."* The deceptively simple and classic notion has a name: **phenomenology**. Phenomenology has to do with the study of events *as they are experienced by the individual,* not as they actually occur. As you might imagine, we can easily get involved in some fairly deep philosophical discussions here, but we need not. What we need to appreciate, and what we need to keep an eye out for as we go along, is the notion that as active agents in the world, we each select, attend to, interpret, and remember (i.e., experience) different aspects of the very same world.

Here's a very simple example of what I am talking about. (It is also a classic example, attributed to the philosopher John Locke.) Imagine that you have before you three pails of water. The water in the pail on your left is quite hot, the water in the pail on your right is nearly ice cold, and the water in the center pail is at about body temperature. You put your left hand into the hot water and your right hand into the cold. Then, after a minute, you place both hands in the center pail. What is its temperature? How does the water feel? To your left hand, the water seems quite cool, whereas to your right hand the very same water feels quite warm. Well, what *is* the temperature of the water in the center pail? Is it cool or is it warm? A physicist may come along and measure the temperature of the water in that center pail with astonishing accuracy. But we're not interested in the physics of the water. We're interested in the psychology of your *experience* of the water, and we may—with a smug smile—report that the water in the center pail is both warm *and* cool. What matters is not the actual, physical temperature of the water but your experience of that water.

This principle has practical relevance in many areas of psychology. It will show up most clearly in our discussion of sensation and perception, where we note that what we perceive often depends more on what we want to perceive or expect to perceive than what is really there. A quick study of Figure 1.4 will give you an idea of what I mean.

4. *For many questions in psychology, there are no simple answers.* There are many good questions in psychology for which there are, as yet, no good answers. For some questions we do have answers with which almost all psychologists agree. On the other hand, for some questions we don't even have reasonably acceptable hypotheses. What you will encounter in your study of psychology is that complex phenomena often have complex explanations.

As an example, let's briefly anticipate a discussion we'll have later when we cover psychological disorders. What causes schizophrenia? For the moment, let us simply acknowledge that schizophrenia is one of the most devastating and debilitating of all psychological disorders, afflicting approximately 2.5 million people in the United

Figure 1.4

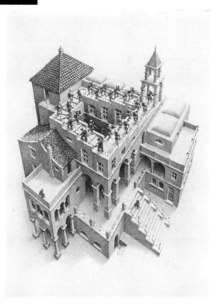

Things are not always as they may first appear. (A) The highlighted letter is neither A nor H. It is interpreted to be one or the other, however, based on our experience with the English language. (B) This ambiguous drawing may be of an old hag with her chin tucked down into her coat collar or a young woman in Victorian clothing, depending on the context in which it is viewed. (C) Are the soldiers marching up or down the stairs?

States today. What causes the distortions in the way a person feels, thinks, and acts that define schizophrenia? The truth is that we do not know. As it happens, we have several hypotheses, and each holds some promise, but the issue is complex. Part of the answer is genetic; schizophrenia tends to run in families. Part of the answer is biochemical; the brains of persons with schizophrenia do not function the same way as the brains of those who do not have schizophrenia. Part of the answer is environmental, or situational; stress and experience can bring on symptoms, or at least make symptoms worse than they would be otherwise. What causes schizophrenia? Answer: a number of interacting factors; some genetic, some physiological, some environmental, perhaps all operating at the same time. And so it goes for virtually all of our behaviors and mental processes.

The main point of this principle is that if you are looking for simple answers to explain your behavior or the behavior of others, you are bound to be disappointed. Disappointed you may be, but please don't be discouraged. Behaviors and mental processes are complex, and explaining them is going to take a degree of complexity. Complexity in and of itself should not be worrisome. Behaviors and mental processes generally have multiple causes. Our challenge is to discover them.

5. *Psychology is relevant to our daily lives.* We might get an argument from biologists, chemists, physicists, geologists, and even some astronomers, but I'm willing to make the claim that no other science has more practical, useful application in the real world than does the science of psychology. In everyday life, people *can* get by without thinking about physics or geology or biology, but they cannot get by without thinking *psychologically.* They must take into consideration a multitude of sensations, perceptions, memories, feelings, and consequences of their actions if they are going to survive, and certainly if they are going to prosper. As you read about psychology on the following pages, you should be on the lookout for how the material you're reading can be put to use in your own life.

Here's an example you can put to use right now. When we get to the chapters on learning and memory, I'll make the point that material is easier to learn and remember if it is meaningful. One of your jobs as a learner—as a student in a beginning psychology class—is to make the material you are learning as meaningful as possible. What that means, among other things, is that part of your job is to find ways in which you can personally relate to the issues you are reading about. In psychology, finding such relevance is fairly easy. After all, the subject matter of psychology is the behavior and mental processes of organisms—and that includes you and me.

Let's here consider just one area in which psychological principles can be usefully applied. Getting old and dying are natural processes,

Health psychologists are applying psychological principles to help people stop smoking, lose weight, exercise, and generally change their behaviors to live healthier lives.

but the truth is that many people never get old, they just die—unnaturally, and in many cases the cause of their death was preventable. It is possible to prevent some deadly diseases, such as polio, smallpox, or measles, by being vaccinated against them. What we have come to appreciate in the last decade or so is the extent to which illness and even death can be attributed to dangerous lifestyles (Matarazzo, 1980; Miller, 1983). In fact, "7 of the 10 leading causes of death in the United States are in large part behaviorally determined. We believe these unhealthy behaviors can be significantly reduced with help from psychologists" (Heffernan & Albee, 1985, p. 202). We understand that it is not necessarily easy, but principles of psychology *can* be used to help people stop smoking, cut down on alcohol use, increase exercise, wear safety belts, cope with life's stresses, decrease overeating, engage in safe(er) sexual practices, and otherwise control many behaviors for which the application of psychology can help ensure or even improve the physical health of the individual.

Before You Go On

Describe five general principles that will appear repeatedly throughout our study of psychology.

TOPIC 1B SUMMARY

The major aim of this Topic was to describe the research methods used in psychology in general terms, leaving the specifics and details to subsequent chapters. We have learned that psychologists use scientific methods that can be classified as methods of observation, correlation, and experimentation. Most research begins with careful, reliable observation. In psychology, this process may use naturalistic observation, surveys, or case history studies. Once observations have been made, we can discover the extent to which they are related to each other by using the statistical procedure of correlation. If two responses are correlated, we can use one to predict the other.

It is only from doing experiments that cause-and-effect relationships can be inferred. Doing experiments involves manipulating independent variables, measuring dependent variables while controlling or eliminating the influence of extraneous variables. We've learned that psychologists have concerns about the ethics of their work, be it with humans or nonhumans. And, finally, we've learned that a few general themes or principles concerning behavior and mental processes have evolved that are applicable to many areas of psychological inquiry.

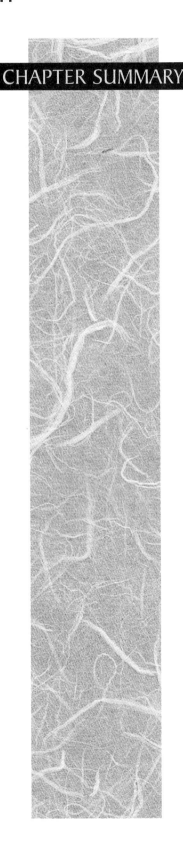

CHAPTER SUMMARY

TOPIC 1A

Why may we claim that psychology is a science?

What are the two major goals of psychology?

We may claim scientific status for psychology because it meets two criteria: it has an organized body of knowledge and it uses scientific methods. Psychology has two interrelated goals: (1) to use scientific methods to discover and understand the laws that govern its subject matter, and (2) to apply what is already known about behavior and mental processes in the real world. /*p. 7*

What is the subject matter of psychology?

What are operational definitions, why do we use them, and what are their limitations?

The subject matter of psychology includes the *a*ffects, *b*ehaviors, and *c*ognitions of organisms. Operational definitions define concepts in terms of the procedures, or operations, used to measure or create those concepts. Although they foster precise communication, they often give the appearance of oversimplifying complex issues. /*p. 9*

In what ways did the philosophies of Descartes and Locke prepare the way for psychology?

In what ways did the science of Darwin, Fechner, and von Helmholtz influence the emergence of psychology?

Both René Descartes and John Locke directed the attention of philosophers to the study of the mind—how it interacts with the body and how it acquires understanding—and did so with the belief that the human mind was part of the natural world and could be studied without reference to divine intervention. Charles Darwin (from biology), Gustav Fechner (from physics), and Hermann von Helmholtz (from physiology) brought scientific methodology to bear on questions that were basically psychological. /*p. 12*

When and where did psychology begin?

How did the functionalists change psychology's approach to its subject matter?

We credit Wilhelm Wundt for having founded psychology when he officially opened his laboratory at the University of Leipzig in 1879. Wundt wanted to use scientific methods to discover the contents and structure of the mind, and how the mind operates. We call his approach *structuralism*. Following the lead of Charles Darwin and William James, the functionalists were concerned with the mind and mental activity, but focused on the adaptive value or function of consciousness. The functionalists, including Washburn, added the study of animals to mainstream psychology. /*p. 14*

What is the basic thrust of behavioristic, psychoanalytic, humanistic, and Gestalt approaches to psychology?

Behaviorism (associated with Watson and Skinner) holds that the subject matter of the science of psychology should be measurable and observable—thus, behavior. Psychoanalytic psychology (associated with Freud) investigated the importance of instincts and the unconscious mind as influences on our behaviors. Humanistic psychology (associated with Rogers and Maslow) focuses on the person, or the self, emphasizing internal processes and the potential for growth and development. Gestalt psychologists were particularly interested in how people select and organize their perceptions of the world, emphasizing the whole as more than the sum of its parts. /p. 17

What are some of the specialty areas of modern psychology, and what might we expect from a psychologist working in a particular area?

Physiological psychologists study the nervous system and how it affects behaviors and mental processes. Developmental psychologists study the growth and development of the individual throughout the life span. Educational psychologists study and try to improve the processes of learning and memory. Clinical psychologists have many subspecialties, but generally are involved in the diagnosis and treatment of mental and behavioral disorders. Counseling psychologists tend to focus on the treatment of persons with less severe psychological problems. Health psychologists are involved with how psychological factors affect one's physical health and well-being. Cognitive psychologists study mental processes such as memory, perception, language, and problem solving. Psychometric psychologists are involved in the construction and evaluation of psychological tests. Personality psychologists seek to understand the extent to which one's behaviors are determined by internal dispositions as opposed to external influences. Social psychologists study how the behaviors of an individual influence and are influenced by others. Cultural psychologists focus on the impact of the diverse cultures and ethnic contexts in which individuals live. Industrial/organizational (I/O) psychologists work in business and industry to use psychological principles to solve the many problems that arise in those settings. /p. 20

TOPIC 1B

What is naturalistic observation?

List some of the potential problems that can arise with this method.

Naturalistic observation involves the careful, reliable observation of behaviors as they occur naturally. This method requires that (1) those being observed are not aware that they are being studied, (2) the

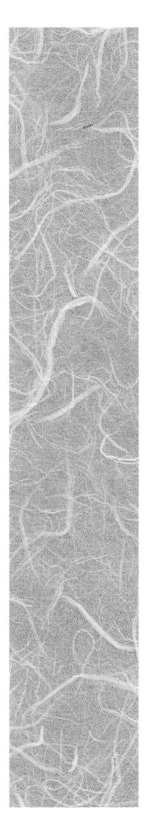

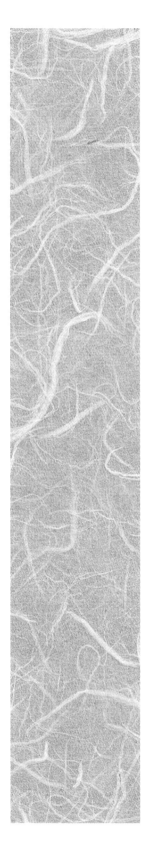

observers' biases not influence observations, and (3) patience be exercised for those behaviors that occur infrequently. /p. 23

How can surveys and case history studies be used to help us understand behavior and mental processes?

Surveys provide a few responses (observations) from large samples of respondents, whereas case histories tend to provide detailed and specific information about just a few persons. In either case, one may discover relationships among the observations made. /p. 25

What data are needed to calculate a correlation coefficient?

What does a correlation coefficient tell us about the relationship between two measured responses?

In order to calculate a correlation coefficient, one needs to measure two responses made by the same group of subjects, yielding a set of paired observations. Positive correlation coefficients tell us that high scores on one response are associated with (predict) high scores on the other, and that low scores on one response are associated with low scores on the other. Negative correlations tell us that the two responses are inversely related, with high scores on one predicting low scores on the other, and vice versa. Correlation coefficients of zero (or nearly zero) tell us that our measured responses are not related to each other in any lawful way. The closer the coefficient is to its possible extreme of +1.00 or −1.00, the stronger the relationship between the responses, but in no case can one infer a cause-and-effect relationship from correlational data. /p. 29

What is the essence of doing an experiment?

Define independent, dependent, and extraneous variables in the context of doing an experiment.

An experiment involves manipulating independent variables and measuring dependent variables, while minimizing the influence of extraneous variables. Independent variables are those hypothesized to have a measurable effect on some behavior or mental process. To see if such is the case, one looks for changes in some measured dependent variable that are consistent with changes in the manipulated independent variable. In order to claim a cause-and-effect relationship between the independent and dependent variables, all other (extraneous) events that could have influenced the dependent variable must have been controlled or eliminated. /p. 33

How do random assignment, baseline designs, single- and double-blind techniques, and meta-analyses help to minimize error in psychological experiments?

The random assignment of participants to experimental (those who receive one's treatment) or control (those who do not receive one's treatment) conditions of an experiment ensures that each participant has an equal opportunity to be in any of the treatment groups of the experiment. Any existing differences among the participants should thus balance out over groups. With baseline designs, the same subjects serve in both control and experimental conditions, thus acting as their own control. Single- and double-blind techniques protect against bias by not informing the participant (single-blind) or the participant and the data collector (double-blind) about the hypothesis under consideration. A meta-analysis is a statistical procedure of control that essentially combines the results of numerous smaller studies in one large analysis. /p. 36

Cite four ethical issues that must be considered when doing psychological research.

Participants in psychological research must have their confidentiality maintained. They should provide their advised consent before voluntarily participating in the research and should be debriefed about the project when it is over. Above all else, one should always consider whether any potential risks in the research are offset by the present or future value of the results that come from the research. Similar considerations are given to the use of animals in research. /p. 38

Describe five general principles that will appear repeatedly throughout our study of psychology.

(1) Who we are—all of our psychological functioning—is a result of the interaction of our biological nature and our psychological nurture. (2) In virtually any way imaginable, no two persons are alike. (3) Our experience of the world is often influenced by psychological processes, such as expectation and motivation, as well as what is "really" there in the world to be experienced. (4) Most psychological phenomena are complex, and few questions in psychology have simple answers. (5) Psychology is a relevant science, with many applications to our daily lives. /p. 43

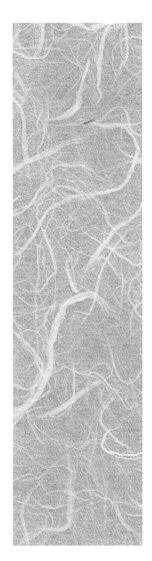

chapter two

THE NERVOUS SYSTEMS AND BEHAVIOR

CHAPTER OUTLINE

TOPIC 2A NEURONS: BUILDING BLOCKS OF THE NERVOUS SYSTEMS

The Neuron
    The Structure of Neurons
    The Function of Neurons
From One Cell to Another: The Synapse
TOPIC 2A SUMMARY

TOPIC 2B THE HUMAN NERVOUS SYSTEMS AND HOW THEY ARE STUDIED

Nervous Systems: The Big Picture
How to Study the Central Nervous System
    Accident and Injury
    Surgical Interventions
    Electrical Stimulation
    Recording Electrical Activity
    Observing the Brain Directly and Indirectly
TOPIC 2B SUMMARY

TOPIC 2C THE CENTRAL NERVOUS SYSTEM

The Spinal Cord
    The Structure of the Spinal Cord
    The Functions of the Spinal Cord
"Lower" Brain Centers
    The Brain Stem
    The Cerebellum
    The Reticular Activating System (RAS)
    The Limbic System
    The Hypothalamus
    The Basal Ganglia
    The Thalamus
The Cerebral Cortex
    Lobes and Localization
    The Two Cerebral Hemispheres—Splitting the Brain
    The Two Sexes—Male and Female Brains
TOPIC 2C SUMMARY

CHAPTER SUMMARY

$\mathcal{Y}$ou are walking down the hall late at night in your bare feet when—ouch! You've stepped on a tack. Soon, you are hopping around on one foot, trying to grab the other, and rapidly becoming furious at whomever it was who left a tack on the hallway floor. What was involved in producing this series of experiences? One answer is: a series of incredibly complex biological processes—processes that you, no doubt, did not care about at the time. Roughly, here's what happened, with some intriguing questions you might ask yourself following in parentheses. We'll get back to these questions throughout the chapter.

As your injured foot jerks up off the floor, your arms flail out so that you can maintain your balance. (What stimulated the muscles in my leg to pull up my foot?)

You realize your foot hurts. (Where does that realization take place? In my brain?)

To be more specific, the point of the tack punctures the sole of your foot and stimulates a nerve cell. (What does it mean to say that a nerve cell is stimulated? For that matter, what *is* a nerve cell?)

The cell stimulated by the tack sends a message to other nerve cells. (Wait a minute! What do you mean, "message?" How do messages get from one nerve cell to another?)

Messages now race up your leg to the base of the spinal cord. (Why to the spinal cord? What does the spinal cord look like? What does it do?)

Once in the spinal cord, messages now go in two directions: up to the brain and back down to the muscles in your leg. (How do the messages get to my brain? For that matter, how do they get back down to my leg? Do they go to my brain first?)

Messages from the spinal cord to your leg stimulate muscles to quickly lift your leg off the floor. At the same time, those messages sent to your brain are being interpreted. (Do you mean to say that my leg lifts up off the floor without my brain even thinking about it? Doesn't my brain have to control that movement?)

You identify the source of your pain as a tack. Still hopping on one foot, you wonder who left the tack there, and start to get angry. (To recognize a tack implies that I'm using my memory. Where are memories stored? Are there separate areas of the brain involved in emotions like anger?)

Even in a stimulus-response chain of events as simple as stepping on a tack, a remarkable series of physiological and biochemical reactions takes place. Ultimately, all of our behaviors and mental processes—from the simple blink of an eye to profound, abstract thought—are no more, and no less than the integrated reactions of our nervous systems.

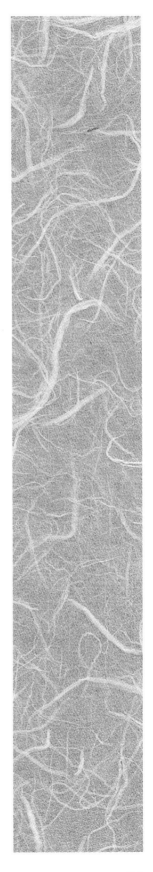

e'll take a building-block approach in this chapter. First, in Topic 2A, we'll deal with the single, individual nerve cell and how it works. Then we'll see how these cells interact with each other and with other cells. In Topic 2B, we'll discuss how the billions of nerve cells in our bodies work together to form the major nerve systems of the human body, and we'll review the methods that scientists use to discover the intricate workings of the human nervous systems.

Our goal for Topic 2C is to examine some of the more important structures and functions of the central nervous system. Starting with the spinal cord, we'll work our way up to the base of the brain, through its midsection, and on to the outer layers of the brain, the cerebral cortex. As we go, I'll describe anatomical features and point out how they are involved in our everyday lives.

Discussions of nervous systems, spinal cords, and brains may sound rather impersonal, as if we were talking about some strange mass of gooey tissue in a glass jar. However, remind yourself from time to time that we're talking about your brain, your nervous system—and mine, too. As you read these words, it is your spinal cord that carries the impulses in your arm to turn the page, your brain that directs your eyes to move across the page, your brain that processes the impulses from your eyes, your brain that seeks understanding and forms memories, and your brain that monitors your heart rate and keeps you breathing as you read.

Topic 2A

NEURONS: BUILDING BLOCKS OF THE NERVOUS SYSTEMS

THE NEURON

neuron a nerve cell that transmits neural impulses; the basic building block of the nervous system

Our exploration of the nervous system begins at the level of the nerve cell, or **neuron**, the microscopically small cell that transmits information, in the form of neural impulses, from one part of the body to another. Neurons were not recognized as separate structures until about the turn of the century. They are so tiny and complex that estimating their number is difficult. To give you an idea of the sizes and numbers we're talking about, there are approximately *125 million* specialized neurons that line the back, inside surface of each human eye, and it has been estimated that there are about *100 billion* neurons in the human brain (Hubel, 1979; Kolb, 1989).

The Structure of Neurons

We may not be sure about snowflakes, but it is a sure bet that no two neurons are identical. There really is no such thing as a typical neu-

Figure 2.1

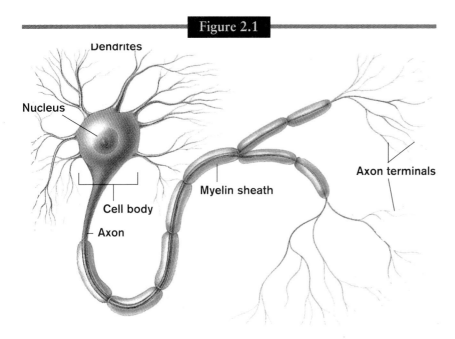

A typical neuron with its major structures.

ron, but most do have a few structures in common. Figure 2.1 illustrates these common features, and Figure 2.2 is a photograph that shows what neurons actually look like.

One structure that all neurons are certain to have is a **cell body**. The cell body is the largest concentration of mass of the neuron. It contains the nucleus of the cell, which contains the genetic information that keeps the cell functioning. Extending away from the cell body are several tentaclelike structures called **dendrites**, and one particularly long structure called the **axon**. Our drawing in Figure 2.1 is simplified, showing only a few dendrites; in a mature neuron there may be thousands. Typically, dendrites reach out to receive messages, neural impulses, from nearby neurons. These impulses are sent along to the cell body and then on down the axon to other neurons, or to muscles or glands. In the cerebral cortex of the human brain there are as many as 1 million billion interconnections among neurons (Edelman, 1992). Some axons are quite long—as much as 2 to 3 feet long in the spinal cord. Within a neuron, then, impulses travel from dendrite to cell body to axon, and most of the trip will be made along the axon.

The neuron illustrated in Figure 2.1 has a feature not found on all neurons. You can see that the axon of this neuron has a cover, or sheath, of **myelin**. Myelin is a white substance consisting of fat and protein that is found on about half the axons in an adult's nervous system. The presence or absence of myelin allows us to tell the difference between the gray matter (dendrites, cell bodies, and unmyelinated axons) and the white matter (myelinated axons) we see when we look at sections of nervous system tissue.

cell body the largest mass of a neuron, containing the cell's nucleus

dendrites extensions from a neuron's cell body where most neural impulses are received

axon the long, tail-like extension of a neuron that carries an impulse away from the cell body toward a synapse

myelin a white, fatty covering found on some axons that serves to insulate and protect them, while increasing the speed of impulses

Figure 2.2

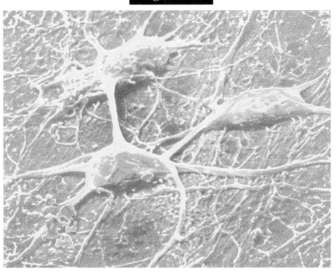

A photograph of a neuron taken through a powerful electron microscope.

We tend to find myelin sheaths on axons that carry impulses relatively long distances. Fibers that carry messages up and down the spinal cord, for instance, are myelinated, whereas those that carry impulses back and forth across the spinal cord are not. Myelin serves several useful functions. It protects the long, delicate axon. It acts as an insulator, keeping the activity of one neuron separate from those that happen to be nearby. Myelin speeds impulses along the length of the axon. Myelinated fibers carry impulses nearly 10 times faster than unmyelinated ones (up to 120 meters per second). Myelin sheaths are not fully developed at birth; myelin develops and adheres to axons as the nervous system matures (a process usually not complete until the age of 11 or 12 years). There are some diseases (multiple sclerosis is the most common) that attack the myelin on axons, which slows and ultimately stops the neural impulses that activate muscle fibers.

Whether they are myelinated or not, axons end in a branching series of bare end points called **axon terminals**. It is at the axon terminal that each neuron communicates with other neurons. To quickly review: within a neuron, impulses travel from the dendrites, to cell body, to axon (which may be myelinated), and then to axon terminals.

Here's a far-reaching observation about neurons, particularly those in our brains: virtually no neurons are generated after we are born. We are born with more neurons than we will ever have again. In fact, we are born with about twice as many neurons as we'll ever use. What happens to the rest? They just die off. Bryan Kolb (1989) of the University of Lethbridge in Canada gives us this analogy: In normal development, the brain is "constructed" in a manner rather like that in which a statue is chipped away from a block of granite.

axon terminals the series of branching end points of an axon where one neuron communicates with the next in a series

Rather than building up the finished product one small piece at a time, more material than one needs is available. Then, what is needed or used is retained, and the rest dies away. Here is a related observation: In order to have billions of neurons in our brains at the time of birth, brain cells must be generated at a rate of about 250,000 per minute while the brain is being formed (Cowan, 1979). There are implications here about prenatal care, which we'll explore in Chapter 8.

The fact that when neurons die they are not replaced with new ones makes neurons unique among cells. We constantly make new blood cells to replace lost ones. If we didn't, we could never donate a pint of blood. Lost skin cells are rapidly replaced by new ones. You rinse away skin cells by the hundreds each time you wash your hands. Neurons are different; once they're gone, they're gone forever. We are often in luck, however, because the *functions* of lost neurons can be taken over by other, surviving neurons. Also, recent evidence from research on tissue removed from the brains of adult mice suggests that under just the right circumstances (when exposed to a substance called epidemal growth factor), *new* neurons and supporting cells *can be* regenerated (Reynolds & Weiss, 1992). Whether this research can be generalized to other organisms, or has any practical, real-life application, remains to be seen.

Have you noticed that in this section I have tried to focus on the structure of the neuron and have found it nearly impossible to do so without reference to the function of the neuron: the transmission of neural impulses? We have seen that impulses are typically received by dendrites, passed on to cell bodies, and then to axons. We know that myelin insulates some axons and speeds neural impulses along, but we haven't yet considered exactly what a neural impulse is. Let's do so now.

Before You Go On

What are the major structures of a neuron?

What is myelin, and what is its function?

The Function of Neurons

The function of a neuron is to transmit neural impulses from one place in the nervous system to another. The actual detailed story of how impulses are generated and transmitted is a complex one, dealing with electrical and chemical changes that are extremely delicate and subtle. Let's start with a definition: A **neural impulse** is a sudden and reversible change in the electrical charges within and outside a neuron that travels from the dendrites to the axon terminal when the neuron fires. Now let's see what all that means.

neural impulse a sudden and reversible change in the electrical charges within and outside a neuron, which travels from the dendrite to the axon terminal of a neuron

*ion an electrically charged (either +
or –) chemical particle*

Neurons exist in a complex biological environment. As living cells, they are filled with and surrounded by fluids. Only a very thin membrane (rather like skin) separates the fluids inside a neuron from fluids outside. These fluids contain microscopic, dissolved chemical particles called **ions**. Chemical ions carry a small, measurable electrical charge that is either positive (+) or negative (–). These electrically charged ions float around in all the fluids of the body, but are heavily concentrated in and around the nervous system. They come from the foods and liquids we eat and drink that are dissolved by our digestive system.

Neurons that are just lying around not doing anything are said to be neurons at rest, although "at rest" may not be a very accurate description. A tension develops between the electrical charge of ions that have moved and become trapped *inside* the neuron and the electrical charge of ions that have moved and are trapped *outside* the neuron. A balanced state would exist if the positive and negative charges on both sides of the neuron's membrane were equal. But this is not the case. When it is at rest, the inside of the neuron has a negative charge compared to the positive charge on the outside. Hence the tension (and why "at rest" is not very descriptive).

The positive and negative ions are drawn toward each other, but they cannot become balanced because of the neuron's membrane, which separates them. This imbalance of electrically charged chemical particles makes a neuron at rest like a tiny battery, holding a small electrical charge called a **resting potential**. The resting potential of a neuron is about –70 mV. The value is negative because we measure the inside relative to the outside, and the inside of the neuron is where we have the concentration of negative ions.

If this sounds at all mysterious, just think about a common D-cell battery of the sort you use in a flashlight. It, too, has two aspects (called poles), one positive and the other negative. The electrical charge possible with one of these batteries—its resting potential—is about 1500 mV, much greater than that of a tiny neuron.

When a neuron is stimulated to fire, or to produce an impulse of its own, the electrical tension of the resting potential is released. Very quickly, the polarity of the nerve cell changes. For a brief instant (about one-thousandth of a second) at one point along the length of the neuron, the electrical charge within the cell becomes more *positive* than the area outside the cell. The entire "charge" of the cell changes instantaneously. This new charge is called the **action potential**. The measurable electric potential is now about +40 mV, the positive sign indicating that the inside of the neuron is now more positive than the outside. There are more positive ions inside than outside. Now, for just a few thousandths of a second, there is a period (called the *refractory period*) during which the neuron cannot fire because there is no tension there to release as an action potential. In another fraction of a second, the neuron returns to its original state, with the tension redeveloped. It is ready to fire again.

To repeat, what happens is something like this. When a neuron is at rest, there is a difference between the electrical charge inside and

resting potential the difference in electrical charge between the inside of a neuron and the outside when it is at rest

action potential the short-lived burst caused by a change in the difference in electrical charge between the inside and outside of a neuron when it fires

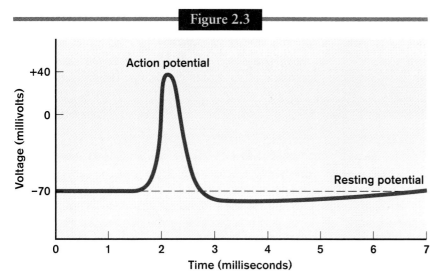

Figure 2.3

Changes in electrical potential that occur during the firing of a neuron. Note that the voltage is negative (– 70 millivolts) when the neuron is "at rest," and positive (+ 40 millivolts) during the firing of the impulse. Note, too, that the entire process lasts but a few milliseconds.

outside the neuron (the inside being slightly negative). When the neuron is stimulated, the difference suddenly reverses, so that the inside is slightly positive. Then the tension of the resting potential returns again. Figure 2.3 shows this process in the form of a graph.

When a neuron is stimulated, the impulse travels from the dendrite to the cell body, down the axon to the axon terminal. Notice that when an impulse "travels down a neuron," *nothing physically moves from one end of the neuron to the other.* The only movement of physical particles that occurs is the movement of the electrically charged ions *into and out of the neuron* through its membrane. What travels "down the neuron" is where this action potential takes place. What moves along the neuron is the location where the release of tension of the resting potential occurs.

When a neuron is stimulated, it either transmits an impulse or it doesn't. It either fires or it doesn't. This fact is called the **all-or-none principle**, which raises a psychological question: How does the nervous system react to differences in stimulus intensity? How do neurons react to the differences between a bright light and a dim one, a soft sound and a loud one, a tap on the shoulder and a slap on the back? Here's where the all-or-none principle comes in. The electrical charge of the resting potential is either released or it isn't. There is no in-between or degree of firing. We cannot say that for a dim light a neuron fires softly, slightly, or gently, releasing only some of the tension of the resting potential, while for brighter lights, more ions are exchanged.

It is also true that neurons do not *necessarily* generate impulses every time they are stimulated. Each neuron has a level of stimulation

all-or-none principle the fact that a neuron will either fire and generate a full impulse (an action potential) or not fire at all

that must be surpassed in order to get it to transmit an impulse. The minimum level of stimulation required to get a neuron to fire is called the **neural threshold**. When this concept is coupled with the all-or-none principle, we have some insight about how we process differences in stimulus intensity. High-intensity stimuli (bright lights, loud sounds, and so on) do not get neurons to fire more vigorously, but stimulate more neurons to fire and/or to fire more frequently. High-intensity stimuli are above the threshold of a greater number of neurons than are low-intensity stimuli. The difference in your experience of a flashbulb going off in your face and a candle viewed at a distance is a matter of the number of neurons involved and the rate at which they fire, not the intensity with which they fire.

neural threshold the minimum stimulation required to produce an impulse within a neuron

Now that we've examined the individual nerve cell in some detail, we had better see how neurons communicate with each other—how impulses are transmitted from one cell to another. The story of how impulses travel *between* neurons is just as remarkable, but quite different from, the story of how impulses travel *within* neurons.

Before You Go On

What is the basic process involved when
a neuron fires?

What is the all-or-none principle?

What is meant by the concept of
neural threshold?

FROM ONE CELL TO ANOTHER: THE SYNAPSE

The location at which an impulse is relayed from one neuron to another is called the **synapse**. Here's what happens there.

synapse the location where an impulse is relayed from one neuron to another by means of neurotransmitters

As we've noted, at the very end of an axon there are many branches called axon terminals (see Fig. 2.1). Throughout the neuron, but concentrated in the axon terminals, are incredibly small containers called **vesicles**. The vesicles hold complex chemicals called **neurotransmitters**. When a neural impulse reaches the axon terminal, the vesicles there at the very end, near the membrane, burst open and release the neurotransmitter they have been holding. Released from the vesicles, the neurotransmitter floods out into the **synaptic cleft**, the tiny space between two neurons. Note that the two neurons involved do not actually touch; they are separated by the synaptic cleft. Once in the synaptic cleft, some neurotransmitter molecules move to the membrane of the next neuron, where they may fit into "receptor sites" and enter the membrane. (See Figure 2.4.)

vesicles the small containers, concentrated in axon terminals, that hold neurotransmitter molecules

neurotransmitters chemical molecules released at a synapse that will, in general, either excite or inhibit neural impulse transmission

Then what happens? Actually, any number of things. Let's look at a few. The most reasonable scenario for synaptic activity is that in which neurotransmitters float across the synaptic cleft, enter into receptor sites in the next neuron in a chain of nerve cells, and by so

synaptic cleft the space between the membrane of an axon terminal and the membrane of the next neuron in a sequence

Figure 2.4

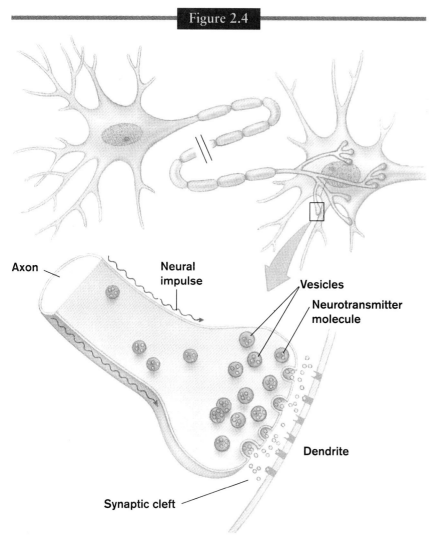

A synapse, in which transmission is from upper left to lower right. As an impulse enters the axon terminal, vesicles release neurotransmitter chemicals into the synaptic space or cleft. The neurotransmitter then either excites or inhibits an impulse in the next neuron.

doing excite that neuron to release the tension of its resting potential and fire a new impulse down to its axon terminals. There, neurotransmitter chemicals are released from vesicles, cross the synaptic cleft, and stimulate the next neuron in the sequence. This is the case when the neurotransmitter excites and stimulates the next neuron in a sequence to fire.

There are many neurons throughout our nervous systems that contain neurotransmitters that have the opposite effect. When they are released, they flood across the synaptic cleft and actually work to prevent the next neuron from firing. We refer to these synapses as *inhibitory.* If you think back to our last section, where we talked about neural thresholds, you can now see how that concept works. Imagine a neuron's dendrite, sitting there "at rest," with many axon terminals (of many neurons) just across the synaptic cleft. For this neuron to begin a new impulse, it may require more excitatory chemical than just one axon terminal can provide, particularly if nearby terminals are releasing inhibitory neurotransmitters about the same time.

The same sort of process also occurs at the synapse of neurons and nonneural cells. When a neuron forms a synapse with a muscle cell, for instance, the release of neurotransmitter from the neuron's axon terminals may excite that muscle to contract momentarily. In the same fashion, neurons that form synapses with a gland may cause that gland to secrete a hormone when stimulated by the appropriate neurotransmitter.

Not long ago, it was believed that neurons produced and released one of just two neurotransmitters. There were neurotransmitters that elicited further action, and those that inhibited neural impulse transmission. Now we realize that this view is much too simplistic. Today we know of nearly 60 neurotransmitters, and it is virtually certain that there are many others to be discovered.

We'll run into neurotransmitters again, when we discuss the actions of many drugs, when we consider what happens when memories are formed, and when we explore theories of what causes some psychological disorders, for example. But for now, we ought to at least briefly note some of the better-known neurotransmitters.

Acetylcholine (pronounced "uh-see'-til-kōh'-leen"), or ACh, can be found throughout the nervous system, where it acts as either an excitatory or an inhibitory transmitter, depending on where it is found. It is the most common neurotransmitter, and the first to have been discovered (in the 1920s). Not only is ACh found in the brain, but it commonly works in synapses between neurons and muscle tissue cells. Acetylcholine is also implicated in normal memory function and is thus a prime candidate for research on memory problems, such as those found in Alzheimer's disease. Nicotine is a chemical that in small amounts tends to increase the normal functioning of ACh, but in large doses acts to override the normal action of acetylcholine—a reaction that can lead to muscle paralysis and even death. Smoking or chewing tobacco will not (usually) cause such a dramatic effect because large amounts of nicotine first stimulate a brain center that causes vomiting before too much nicotine has been absorbed into one's system (Palfai & Jankiewicz, 1991, p. 141).

Norepinephrine is a relatively common and important neurotransmitter that seems to be involved in mood regulation. When there is an abundance of norepinephrine in a person's brain or spinal cord, the result is often a feeling of arousal, anxiety, or agitation. Normally, norepinephrine is involved in the physiological reactions associated with high levels of emotional arousal—such as increased heart rate, increased perspiration, and heightened blood pressure (Groves & Rebec, 1992). (One of the things that cocaine does is to increase the release of norepinephrine, leading to a state of agitation and a "high" mood state.) Too little norepinephrine in the brain and spinal cord has been linked to feelings of depression.

Dopamine, a common neurotransmitter also involved in mood regulation, is one that most intrigues psychologists. It is involved in a wide range of reactions. Either too much or too little dopamine within the nervous system seems to produce a number of effects, depending on which system of nerve fibers in the brain is involved. Dopamine has been associated with the thought and mood disturbances of some psychological disorders and with the impairment of movement responses. When there is not enough dopamine, we find difficulty in voluntary movement; too much and we find involuntary tremors. (See p. 80)

Endorphins (plural, because there are many of them) are our natural pain suppressors. By and large, what we call our pain threshold—our ability to tolerate levels of pain—is a function of the production of endorphins (Watkins & Mayer, 1982). With excess endorphins, we feel little pain; a deficit in endorphins results in more pain being experienced.

As you can imagine, we could continue this list, but for now it is the basic idea of what neurotransmitters do that matters: they are the agents that excite or inhibit the transmission of neural impulses throughout the nervous system, and that excitation or inhibition can have a considerable effect on our thoughts, feelings, and behavior.

Finally, so that our simplified description does not leave a false impression, let me make one point clear: neural impulse transmission is seldom a matter of just one neuron stimulating one other neuron that in turn stimulates yet one more. Remember that any neuron can have hundreds or thousands of axon terminals and synapses. Any one neuron, then, has the potential for exciting or inhibiting (or being excited by or inhibited by) many other neurons.

Before You Go On

Summarize neural impulse transmission at the synapse.

Name four neurotransmitters and indicate a psychological reaction with which they are involved.

TOPIC 2A SUMMARY

We simply cannot divorce who we are in this world from the biological bases of our behaviors and mental processes. Whatever else we may be, we are biological organisms, and it behooves us as students of psychology to appreciate the structures and functions of the nervous system. That living cells as tiny as neurons can provide the basis for all of our actions, mental or behavioral, is a notion that takes some time to get used to. But neurons do not act alone. The complexity of the individual nerve cell multiplies geometrically with the activity of neurotransmitters at synapses.

Neurons are individual, microscopic, living cells, consisting of a cell body, dendrites, and axons. The axons of some neurons are covered with a myelin sheath that insulates these axons and speeds impulses along them. Neurons communicate with one another at synapses, where neurotransmitter chemicals are released from the vesicles stored in the axons' terminals. These neurotransmitters, of which there are many, work either to excite an impulse in a subsequent neuron or to inhibit the generation of a new impulse. Neural impulses involve the release of electrical tension caused by the imbalance of chemical ions concentrated inside and outside the walls, or membranes, of the neuron.

Topic 2B

THE HUMAN NERVOUS SYSTEMS AND HOW THEY ARE STUDIED

Now that we have a sense of what neurons look like, and how they work, both individually and in combination, let's step back for a moment to consider the broader context in which they do what they do. Little of any consequence is accomplished by the actions of only a few individual neurons. In this Topic we will see what integrated systems of neurons do, and how we have come to discover how the various nervous systems work.

NERVOUS SYSTEMS: THE BIG PICTURE

Behavior and mental activity generally require large numbers of integrated neurons working together in complex, organized systems. Figure 2.5 depicts how these systems are related to one another.

The first major division of the nervous system is determined wholly on the basis of anatomy. The **central nervous system (CNS)** includes all neurons and nerve fibers found in the spinal cord and brain. In many ways, this system of nerves is the most complex and intimately involved in the control of our behavior and mental processes. The **peripheral nervous system (PNS)** consists of all neurons in our body *not* in the CNS; that is, the nerve fibers in our arms, face, fingers, intestines, and so forth. In general, neurons in the peripheral nervous system carry impulses either from the central nervous system

central nervous system (CNS) neurons and nerve fibers in the brain and spinal cord

peripheral nervous system (PNS) neurons not found in the brain or spinal cord, but in the periphery of the body

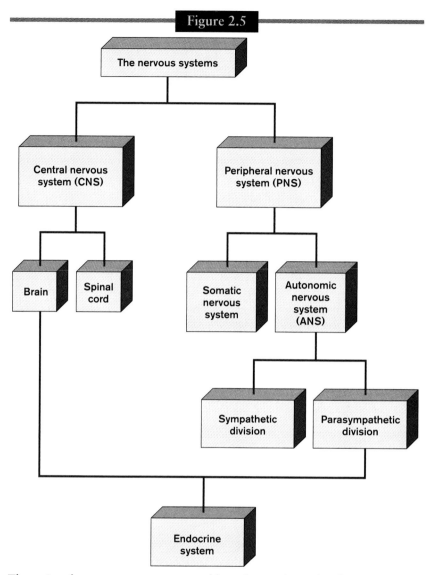

The various human nervous systems and how they are interrelated.

to the muscles and glands (on *motor neurons,* or *motor fibers*) or to the CNS from receptor cells (on *sensory neurons,* or *sensory fibers*).

The peripheral nervous system is itself divided into two parts, based largely on the part of the body being served. The **somatic nervous system** includes those neurons outside the CNS that serve the skeletal muscles and that pick up impulses from our sense receptors—the eyes and ears, for example. The other component of the PNS is the **autonomic nervous system** (**ANS**), where "autonomic" means essentially the same thing as "automatic." This implies that the activity of the ANS is in large measure (but not totally) independent of CNS control. The nerve fibers of the ANS are involved in activating

somatic nervous system sensory and motor neurons outside the CNS that serve sense receptors and skeletal muscles

autonomic nervous system (ANS) neurons of the PNS that activate smooth muscles and glands

the smooth muscles, such as those of the stomach and intestines, and the glands. The ANS does provide feedback to the CNS on the activity of these internal processes.

Because the autonomic nervous system is so intimately involved in emotional responding, we'll return to it again in that context. For now, we note only that the ANS also consists of two parts, the **sympathetic division** and the **parasympathetic division**. These two divisions commonly work in opposition to each other, the former being active when we are in states of emotional excitement or under stress, and the latter becoming active when we are relaxed and quiet. The sympathetic and the parasympathetic divisions of the ANS each act on the same organs, but they do so in opposite ways.

As you can see, there is one other system depicted in the overview of Figure 2.5: the **endocrine system**. The endocrine system is influenced by the central nervous system and, in turn, influences nervous system activity, but *it is not a system of nerves.* It is an interconnected network of glands that has its effect on behavior through the secretion of chemicals, called **hormones**, into the bloodstream. Curiously, many of the hormones produced by the endocrine system are chemically similar to neurotransmitters and have many of the same overall effects. The endocrine system's glands and hormones are controlled both by the brain of the central nervous system and by the autonomic nervous system, as is depicted in Figure 2.5. I have included the endocrine system here because its basic function is similar to that of the nervous systems: to transmit information from one part of the body to another. The nervous systems do so through the transmission of neural impulses; the endocrine system uses hormones sent through the bloodstream. As it happens, the endocrine system is slow to react, but many of its effects are long lasting. Most of the endocrine system's involvement in our behavior occurs in states of emotion and motivation. We'll return to a discussion of this system in the context of these topics.

There is good reason to categorize the various organizations of neurons. It is not just an academic exercise. It helps make a very complex system easier to deal with, and it reminds us that not all neurons in our body are doing the same thing, for the same purpose, at the same time. But we have to keep in mind that the outline of Figure 2.5 is very simplified to this extent: the nerve fibers in each of the systems have profound influences on one another. They are not at all as independent as our diagram might imply.

For example, let's return to our opening example of stepping on a tack. Receptor cells in your foot respond to the tack and send impulses up your leg (on sensory neurons of the somatic division of the PNS) to your spinal cord (CNS). There, some impulses are sent back down your leg (on motor neurons of the somatic division of the PNS) to get it to jerk up off the floor. At the same time, other impulses are sent up the spinal cord to your brain, where you become aware of what is happening (all in the CNS). Also at the same time, you are angry that someone left a tack on the floor (anger involving the sympathetic division of your ANS). Perhaps in your excitement of hopping about the

sympathetic division neurons (of the ANS) involved in states of emotionality

parasympathetic division neurons (of the ANS) involved in the maintenance of states of calm and relaxation

endocrine system a network of glands that secrete hormones directly into the bloodstream

hormones a variety of chemical compounds, secreted by the glands of the endocrine system, many of which have effects on behavior or mental states

kitchen and planning revenge for whoever left the tack on the floor, your endocrine system becomes active, flooding extra doses of hormones into your bloodstream. Eventually, you settle down, the parasympathetic division of your autonomic nervous system taking over again.

Even when we can classify a response as being determined by some part of the nervous system, we need to recognize that no division of the nervous system operates independently from the others.

We're almost ready to begin our discussion of the structures and functions of the human central nervous system. Before we do, however, we'll address the issue of how scientists have learned what they have about the intricate and complex structures of the spinal cord and brain.

Before You Go On

Name the human nervous systems, and indicate
how they are related to one another.

HOW TO STUDY THE CENTRAL NERVOUS SYSTEM

The complexity of the billions of neurons that make up the spinal cord and the brain is truly awesome. That we know as much as we do about their tiny and delicate structures is a credit to those scientists who have taken up the challenge of trying to understand this most important system of nerve fibers. In this section, we'll review five of the approaches that have helped us learn about the central nervous system.

Accident and Injury

One way to find out how the central nervous system (CNS) functions is to work backward. In this case, we ask what happens to an organism's behaviors or mental processes if a part of the spinal cord or brain is damaged by injury or disease. If, for example, a person is found to be blind after suffering a wound to the back of the head, we might hypothesize that vision is normally coded there, in the back of the brain. This was the method used by the neurologist Pierre-Paul Broca (1824–1880), who discovered that speech production is processed in a small area toward the front, and usually on the left side, of the brain. Broca's conclusions were based on observations he made of human brains during autopsies. People with similar speech disorders commonly had noticeable damage in the very same area of the brain. Logic led Broca to suspect that normal speech functions are controlled by this portion of the brain, which we now call Broca's area.

Figure 2.6

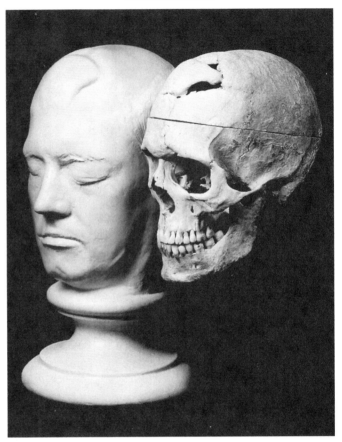

A cast of the head, and actual skull, of Phineas Gage. Note where the iron bar pierced Gage's skull.

One of the strangest cases of injury that expanded our understanding of brain function is the story of Phineas Gage. In 1848, Gage, a 25-year-old railroad construction foreman, had the misfortune of being too close to an explosion. That explosion, which he accidentally caused himself, drove an iron bar into his head through his left jaw and out through the top of his skull (Figure 2.6). To everyone's surprise, Gage survived this massive injury to his brain. He was declared recovered in just a few weeks. Although he survived until 1861, his behavior—in fact, his entire personality—changed completely. He became loud, profane, and irresponsible, and he seemed unable to plan and think ahead—an almost total reversal from the Phineas Gage his friends had known before the accident. The changes in his behavior were directly related to the damage to Gage's brain. Important pathways in the front, upper part of his brain, which normally exert voluntary control over the emotional behaviors originating in his lower brain centers, had been severed. After the accident, his emotions were expressed directly, without the supervision and restrictions of the higher brain areas.

Surgical Interventions

By definition, we cannot control the location or the extent of damage to the nervous system when it occurs by accident or disease. What we can do is surgically cut or remove some particular portion of the spinal cord or brain to see what effects might result. Obviously, no one cuts into human brains motivated solely by the curiosity of what might happen as a result. The procedure is used sparingly and almost always with animal subjects.

The logic of this method is the same as for naturally occurring CNS damage. A very small **lesion**, or cut, is made in a particular place in, say, a rat's brain. That rat then refuses to eat, even if food is readily available. The procedure is repeated with other rats, and the results are the same. We then can reasonably conclude that the lesioned part of the brain plays some role in the feeding behaviors of rats.

lesion a cut or incision that destroys specific areas of tissue

Electrical Stimulation

One of the most significant advances in technology that has aided the study of the central nervous system was the development of the **electrode** for stimulating or recording the activity of small areas of nervous system tissue. An electrode is a fine wire (often made of platinum) that can be eased into a specific area of the brain. Once in position, the electrode delivers a mild electric current, stimulating that region of the brain. The technique was first used in the early 1870s (Sheer, 1961).

electrode a fine wire used either to stimulate or record the electrical activity of neural tissue

By using a stimulating electrode, one can map out many of the functions of parts of the spinal cord and brain (e.g., Penfield, 1975; Penfield & Rasmussen, 1950). Most of the time, when an electrode stimulates an area of human brain, there is simply no discernible reaction. Sometimes, however, the artificial stimulation produces a noticeable reaction. For example, you might deliver a mild stimulus current to the tissues near the surface of the very back of the brain. When you do so, your subject reports a visual experience, a flash of lights not unlike fireworks—thus reinforcing your hypothesis that vision is processed in the back of the brain. A stimulus from an electrode in a particular location in the left side of the brain produces a muscle twitch in the patient's right arm, even though the patient claims not to have voluntarily moved. Here is evidence that perhaps this area of the brain controls muscles in the right arm.

Recording Electrical Activity

Electrodes can be used to stimulate nervous system tissue, and also to measure and record electrical activity there. Remember that nerve impulses are largely changes in electrical charges that sweep down nerve fibers. Some recording electrodes are so small and sensitive that they can be used to detect electrical changes in individual neurons. Most recordings of single nerve cell activity are made using nonhuman subjects, particularly those animals that have large neurons, such as the squid. These tiny recording electrodes have helped us learn about the true nature of the neural impulse and impulse transmission. Single-cell recordings allowed David Hubel and Thornton Wiesel (1979) to discover individual cells in the brains of cats and monkeys that respond only to very specific types of visual stimulation. The work of these researchers (which earned them a Nobel Prize) prompted them to propose that the entire visual field (what we see) is completely represented in the brain, although in somewhat distorted form. Their work confirmed the insight that neural impulses from the eyes are processed at the back of the brain.

In 1929, Hans Berger, a German psychiatrist who had been using the method for nearly twenty years, reported that electrodes attached to a person's scalp could pick up and record the general electrical activity of the brain. Recordings of brain activity are called **electroencephalograms**, or **EEGs**. Electroencephalograms do not provide much in the way of detailed information about the specific activity of small areas of the brain, but they do provide a wealth of information about overall brain activity (Figure 2.7). Electroencephalograms can be used to tell us about a person's level of arousal or what stage of sleep he or she is in (see Topic 4B). The technique is sensitive enough to help confirm impressions we may have gotten from other sources. For example, when a person looks at a bright, colorful, detailed picture, EEG activity at the back of the brain increases.

electroencephalogram (EEG)
recordings of the general electrical activity of the brain

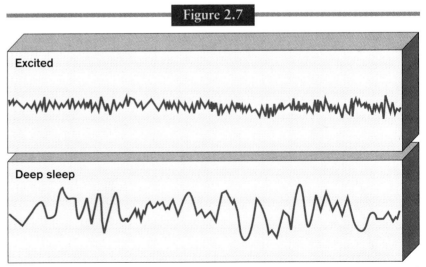

Figure 2.7

Slightly idealized EEG recordings of the electrical activity of the brain in states of excitement and deep sleep.

A relatively new technology (called a *magnetoencephalogram*, or MEG) can provide us with a more detailed description of the electrical activity of the brain. This procedure can record very slight and short-lived changes in electrical activity, but for now its usefulness as a research tool remains to be demonstrated (Adler, 1990a).

Observing the Brain Directly and Indirectly

One way to study regions of the central nervous system is to simply look at them. The development of the microscope helped a great deal in this regard, making small anatomical details of structure visible. The more powerful electron microscope allows us to look even closer and to take pictures of the sort presented in Figure 2.2. But normal microscopic examination restricts us to looking at dead tissue—cells removed from their usual surroundings. What a great advantage there would be in having a detailed look at the brain of a living, behaving organism. To some degree, X-ray technology allows us to do just that. We can get a fairly good view of the major structures of the brain, but the picture is not a clear one. Some important structures, such as tumors, may remain hidden behind less important ones.

Computer technology has joined with X-ray technology to create a **CAT scan** of the brain. *CAT* is an acronym for *computerized axial tomography*. This device takes a series of thousands of X-ray pictures of the brain from many angles. The images are fed into a computer that enhances their quality and combines them into a set of pictures of "slices" of the brain. The CAT scan can take a series of computer-enhanced pictures of the brain that together make what amounts to a three-dimensional view of the brain. Significantly, the CAT scan is noninvasive, which means that the pictures can be taken of a living subject without physically having to "invade" the brain with any sort of instrument.

CAT scan (computerized axial tomography) a method of imaging brain structures through the computer enhancement and combining of X-ray pictures

Since the CAT scan became generally available in the early 1980s, more powerful devices for imaging the brain have come into use. A clear picture of the structures of the living, intact, human brain are possible using **magnetic resonance imaging (MRI)**. This technique allows for precise, high-resolution pictures of the brain in cross section. MRI is not a form of X-ray technology. Magnetic resonance images are constructed (by computers, again) from the detection of very small waves of energy produced by cells when the brain is placed in a strong magnetic field. This, too, is a noninvasive method of studying brain structure.

magnetic resonance imaging (MRI) a process that provides clear, detailed pictures of the brain by recording energy from cells when the brain has been placed in a magnetic field

Whereas CAT scans and MRIs can tell us about the structure of the brain, the **PET scan** (PET stands for *positron emission tomography*), and its recent derivatives, go beyond structure: they not only give us a picture of the inside of the living brain, but provide us with insights about brain function. PET scans involve injecting a radioactive substance that makes its way to the brain. This substance tends to concentrate in areas of the brain that are most active—areas at which oxygen or glucose are being metabolized most rapidly. (In some forms

PET scan (positron emission tomography) a picture of brain functioning provided by an image of radioactive chemicals in a living, intact brain

 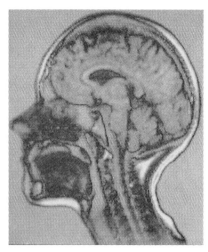

The MRI procedure, shown on the left, produces images such as the one on the right of a normal brain.

of PET scans a different chemical is used, which gravitates to areas of greatest blood flow.) The PET scan then provides a picture of those areas of the brain that are most active. PET scans of subjects who are looking at a complex visual stimulus show increased activity in the back regions of the brain. When the same subject is listening to a story, for example, the PET scan shows increased brain activity on the right side, near the temple. An even more recent development, with great potential, is the single-photon-emission computed tomography (SPECT) brain scan. This procedure can provide a picture of brain areas in action, and has the advantage of being able to examine smaller areas and areas deeper in the brain than can the standard PET scan (Holman & Tumeh, 1990).

Before You Go On

Briefly summarize five techniques used to study the central nervous system.

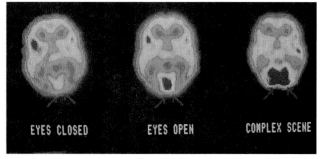

PET scan images can be used to confirm the hypothesis that visual information is processed at the back of the brain.

TOPIC 2B SUMMARY

In this Topic we have seen how the billions of nerve cells of the human body are organized in large, complex systems. For us, the most relevant of these systems is the central nervous system, consisting of the brain and the spinal cord. We have also seen some of the ways in which scientists studying the brain have discovered how the central nervous system functions. Some of what has been learned has come from chance actions such as accident or injury, some from surgical intervention, and some from the direct observation of the brain in action. Now that we have seen how scientists go about studying the brain and the spinal cord, it is time to explore some of what they have learned.

Topic 2C

THE CENTRAL NERVOUS SYSTEM

When we consider the central nervous system, the spinal cord and the brain, we can see most clearly how physiological structures and functions impact regularly on our behaviors and our mental processes. When we examine the spinal cord and its function, we can see the interaction of stimuli from the environment, cells within the nervous system, and responses of the organism—the spinal reflex.

Then there's the brain. The human brain. What is it like? A vast computer? The seat of understanding? The processor of information? A warehouse of memories of experiences past? A reservoir of emotion? The source of motivation? Yes, it is all of these, and more. It is in the brain that our conscious, voluntary actions begin. It is in the brain that our emotions are experienced, and that our cognitions are manipulated and stored.

Breaking the central nervous system down into small, manageable areas and discussing them one at a time is about the only choice we have. However, when we fragment our discussion of the spinal cord and brain this way, we can easily lose sight of the reality that they make up a unified system in which all parts work together and interact with other complex systems. Some functions can be localized in specific areas or structures of the CNS, but the adaptability and integration of its many different functions force us to consider the CNS as a whole, as more than the sum of its parts.

THE SPINAL CORD

As we have noted, the central nervous system consists of the brain and the spinal cord. In this section, we'll consider the structure and the function of the spinal cord, reserving our discussion of the brain for later. As we examine the spinal cord we can see clearly the role of the nervous system in behavior.

The Structure of the Spinal Cord

spinal cord a mass of interconnected neurons within the spine that conveys impulses to and from the brain and is involved in some reflex behaviors

The **spinal cord** is a mass of interconnected neurons, within the spinal column, that looks rather like a section of rope or thick twine. It is surrounded and protected by the hard bone and cartilage of the vertebrae.

A cross-sectional view of the spinal column and the spinal cord is illustrated in Figure 2.8. There are only a few structural details that need mention. Note that the spinal cord itself is located in the middle of the spinal column, which reaches from your lower back to high in your neck, just below your brain. Then note that the nerve fibers that enter and leave the spinal cord do so from the side. Neurons, and the impulses they transmit, enter the spinal cord on *dorsal roots* (dorsal means "toward the back"). Impulses that leave the spinal cord do so on *ventral roots* (ventral means "toward the front").

Also notice that the center area of the spinal cord itself consists of gray matter, rather in the shape of a butterfly, while the outside area is light, white matter. Remember, this means that the center portion is filled with cell bodies, dendrites, and unmyelinated axons, while the

Figure 2.8

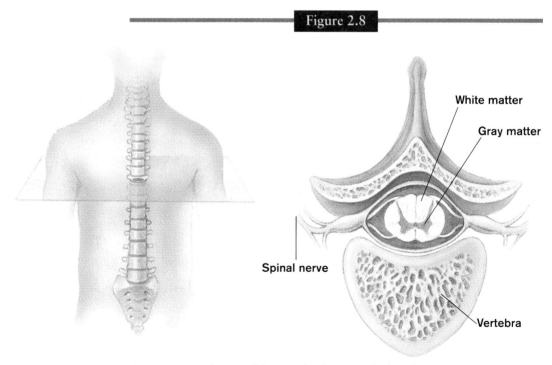

A cross-sectional view of the spinal column. Only the white matter and gray matter in the center represent actual spinal cord tissue.

outer section is filled with myelinated axons. Both of these observations about the structure of the spinal cord are keys to understanding its functions.

The Functions of the Spinal Cord

The spinal cord has two major functions, one of which is to transmit impulses rapidly to and from the brain. When sensory impulses originate in sense receptors below the neck and make their way to the brain, they do so through the spinal cord. When the brain transmits motor impulses to move or activate parts of the body below the neck, those impulses first travel down the spinal cord.

Impulses to and from various parts of the body leave and enter the spinal cord at different levels (impulses to and from the legs, for example, enter and leave at the very base of the spinal cord). If the spinal cord is damaged, the consequences can be disastrous, resulting in a loss of feeling from the part of the body served and a loss of voluntary movement (paralysis) of the muscles in the region. The higher in the spinal cord that damage takes place, the greater will be the resulting losses.

Once impulses get into the spinal cord, they race up and down the ascending and descending pathways found in the white matter areas (see Figure 2.8). Remember that this area looks white because of the myelin covering on the axons found there. Remember, too, that one of the functions of myelin is to speed impulses along their way—as in the relatively long distances up and down the spinal cord.

The second major function of the spinal cord is found in its role in **spinal reflexes**—simple automatic behaviors that occur without conscious, voluntary action of the brain. To understand how these reflexes work, follow along with the drawing in Figure 2.9. Here we have yet another drawing of the spinal cord, but we have added receptor cells in the skin and motor neurons to muscles in the hand, and have labeled the neurons within the spinal cord as interneurons (located, as they are, between sensory and motor neurons).

spinal reflex an automatic, involuntary response to a stimulus that involves sensory neurons, interneurons, and motor neurons

Let's trace your reaction to having your fingertip placed over the flame of a candle (assuming you're blindfolded at the time). Receptor cells in your fingertip respond to the flame, sending neural impulses racing along sensory neurons, through a dorsal root, and into the spinal cord. Then, two things happen at almost the same time. Impulses rush up the ascending pathways of the spinal cord's white matter to your brain. But impulses also travel through interneurons and go right back out of the spinal cord through a ventral root on motor neurons to your arm and hand, where muscles are stimulated to contract, and your hand jerks back from the flame.

Here we have a simple spinal reflex. Impulses travel *in* on sensory neurons, *within* on interneurons, and *out* on motor neurons. We are now clearly involved with behavior. We have an environmental stimulus (a flame), activity in the central nervous system (neurons in the spinal cord), and an observable response (withdrawal). Can you describe our example of stepping on a tack using this terminology?

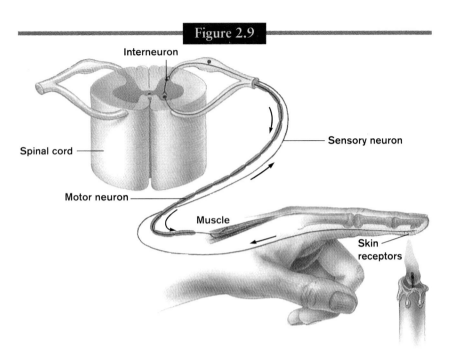

A spinal reflex. Stimulation of receptor cells in the skin, in turn, stimulates sensory neurons, interneurons, and motor neurons. Although a response is made without involvement of the brain, impulses also travel up fibers in the spinal cord's white matter to the brain.

There are a couple of observations I must make about the reflex of the type depicted in Figure 2.9 before we go on. First, the fact that impulses enter the spinal cord and immediately race to the brain is not indicated in the drawing. As you know, in a situation such as the candle flame example, you may jerk your hand back "without thinking about it," but very soon thereafter you are aware of what has happened. Awareness occurs in the brain, not in the spinal cord. The awareness that what happened was painful is a reaction of the brain, not the spinal cord. It is also true that some reflexes are even more simple than the one in Figure 2.9 in that no interneurons are involved. That is, it is possible for sensory neurons to form synapses directly with motor neurons inside the spinal cord, which is what happens in the familiar knee-jerk reflex. On the other hand, the complex pattern of behaviors involved in having one's finger burned in a flame actually involves many more than just three or four neurons.

Before You Go On

Why does spinal cord injury sometimes cause paralysis?

Describe the major features of a spinal reflex.

"LOWER" BRAIN CENTERS

There are several ways in which we could organize our discussion of the brain. We'll use a simple scheme and divide the brain into two parts: the cerebral cortex, and everything else—which we'll refer to as lower brain centers. Because the cerebral cortex plays so many important roles, this division is a reasonable one.

The lower brain centers are "lower" in two ways. First, they are physically located below, or under, the cerebral cortex. Second, they are the brain structures to develop first, both in an evolutionary sense and within the developing human brain. They are the brain structures we most clearly share with other animals. In no way should you think of these lower centers as being less important. As you will soon see, our very survival depends on them. You can use Figure 2.10 as a guide to locate the various structures as we discuss them.

The Brain Stem

As you look at the spinal cord and brain, you really cannot tell where one ends and the other begins. There is no abrupt dividing line separating these two aspects of the central nervous system. Just above the spinal cord there is a slight widening of the cord that suggests we are into brain tissue. Here, two important structures together form what we call the **brain stem**: the medulla and the pons.

brain stem the lowest part of the brain, just above the spinal cord, consisting of the medulla and the pons

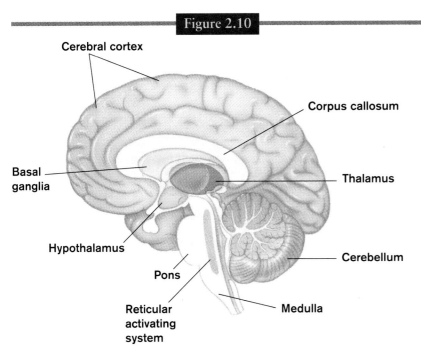

Figure 2.10

Cerebral cortex

Corpus callosum

Basal ganglia

Thalamus

Hypothalamus

Cerebellum

Pons

Reticular activating system

Medulla

Some of the major structures of the human brain, of which the cerebral cortex is clearly the largest.

medulla an area of the brain stem
that monitors breathing and heart
rate, and where most cross laterality
occurs

nuclei small collections or bundles
of neural cell bodies

The lowest structure in the brain is the **medulla**. In a sense, the medulla acts like the spinal cord in that its major functions involve involuntary reflexes. There are several small structures called **nuclei** (collections of neural cell bodies) in the medulla. These nuclei control such functions as coughing, sneezing, tongue movements, and reflexive eye movements. You don't, for example, have to think about blinking your eye as something rushes toward it; your medulla will produce that eye blink reflexively.

The medulla also contains nuclei that control breathing reflexes and that monitor the muscles of the heart to see that it keeps beating rhythmically. We *can* exercise some voluntary control over the nuclei of the medulla, of course, but only within limits. The medulla controls our respiration (breathing), but we can override the medulla and hold our breath. We cannot, however, hold our breath until we die. We can hold our breath until we lose consciousness, which is to say until we give up voluntary control, but the medulla then picks up where it left off, and breathing continues.

At the level of the medulla, nerve fibers to and from the brain cross over from left to right, and vice versa. Centers in the left side of the brain receive impulses from and send impulses to, the right side of the body. Similarly, the left side of the body sends impulses to, and receives messages from, the right side of the brain (explaining why electrically stimulating the correct area in the *left* side of the brain will produce a movement in the *right* arm). The process of fibers crossing from one side of the body to the opposite side of the brain is called **cross laterality**, and it takes place here in the brain stem.

cross laterality the process of nerve
fibers crossing over at the brain
stem so that the left side of the body
sends impulses to, and receives
impulses from, the right side of the
brain, and vice versa

pons a brain stem structure,
forming a bridge between the brain
and the spinal cord, that monitors
the sleep-wake cycle

Just above the medulla is a structure called the **pons**. (The pons is one structure; there is no such thing as a "pon.") The pons serves as a relay station, a bridge (which is what *pons* means), sorting out and relaying sensory messages from the spinal cord and the face up to higher brain centers and reversing the relay for motor impulses coming down from higher centers. The cross laterality that begins in the medulla continues in the pons. Nuclei in the pons are also responsible, at least in part, for the rapid movement of our eyes that occurs when we sleep and are dreaming (e.g., Sakai, 1985).

Before You Go On

**Name the two brain stem structures,
indicate where they are located, and describe what they do.**

The Cerebellum

cerebellum a spherical structure at
the lower rear of the brain involved
in the coordination of bodily
movements

Your **cerebellum** is just about the size of your closed fist. It is more or less spherical and sits right behind your pons, tucked up under the base of your skull. The cerebellum itself looks like a small brain. Its

The ability of an athlete, such as this gymnast, to perform a complex, coordinated movement over and over may involve training the cerebellum.

outer region (its cortex) is convoluted, meaning that the tissue there is folded in upon itself, creating many deep crevices and lumps.

The major role of the cerebellum is in smoothing and coordinating rapid body movements. Most intentional, voluntary movements originate in higher brain centers (usually the motor area of the cerebral cortex) and are only coordinated by the cerebellum. Because of the close relationship between body movement and vision, many eye movements originate in the cerebellum.

Our ability to casually stoop, pick a dime off the floor, and slip it into our pocket involves a complex series of movements made smooth and regular by our cerebellum. When athletes train a movement, such as a golf swing or a gymnastic routine, we may say that they are trying to "get into a groove," so that their movements can be made simply and smoothly. In a way, such athletes are training their cerebellum.

Few of our behaviors are as well coordinated or rapid as the movements we need to make speech sounds. The next time you're talking to someone, consider just how quickly and effortlessly your lips, mouth, and tongue are moving—all thanks to the cerebellum. Damage to the cerebellum disrupts coordinated movements. Speech can become slurred. One may shake and stagger when walking. Someone with cerebellum damage may appear to be drunk. (On what region of the brain do you suppose alcohol has a direct and noticeable effect? The cerebellum.)

Damage to the cerebellum can disrupt motor activity in other ways. If the outer region of the cerebellum is damaged, persons suffer **tremors**, or involuntary trembling movements, when they try to move

tremors *involuntary, trembling, jerky movements*

(called intention tremors). Damage to inner, deeper areas of the cerebellum leads to "tremors at rest," where the limbs or head may shake or twitch rhythmically even when the person tries to remain still.

Before You Go On

Where is the cerebellum located, and
what is its major function?

The Reticular Activating System (RAS)

reticular activating system (RAS) a network of nerve fibers, extending from the brain stem to the cerebrum, involved in maintaining levels of arousal

The **reticular activating system**, or **RAS**, is a different sort of brain structure. In fact, it is hardly a brain structure at all. It is a complex network of nerve fibers that begins in the brain stem and works its way up through and around other structures all the way to the top portions of the brain (Carlson, 1991).

Just exactly what the reticular activating system does, and how it does so, remains something of a mystery. As its name implies, however, the RAS is involved in determining our level of activation or arousal. It influences whether we are awake and attentive, drowsy, asleep, or at some level in between. Electrical stimulation of the RAS can produce EEG patterns of brain activity associated with being awake and alert. Lesions of the RAS cause a condition of constant sleep in laboratory animals (Lindsley et al., 1949; Moruzzi & Magoun, 1949). In a way, the reticular activating system acts like a valve that either allows sensory messages to pass from lower centers up to the cerebral cortex or shuts them off, partially or totally. What we don't know yet is just how the RAS does what it does, and what stimulates it to produce its effects.

The Limbic System

limbic system a collection of structures, including the amygdala and septum, involved in emotionality; and the hippocampus, involved in forming long-term memories

The **limbic system** is actually a collection of structures rather than a single, unified one. It is of utmost importance in controlling the behaviors of nonhuman animals, which do not have as large or well-developed a cerebral cortex as humans do. The limbic system controls many of the complex behavioral patterns we usually think of as instinctive. The location of the limbic system and its constituent parts is presented in Figure 2.11.

Within the human brain, parts of the limbic system are intimately involved in the display of emotional reactions. One center in the system, the *amygdala*, produces reactions of rage or aggression when stimulated, while another area, the *septum*, seems to have the opposite effect, reducing the intensity of emotional responses when stimu-

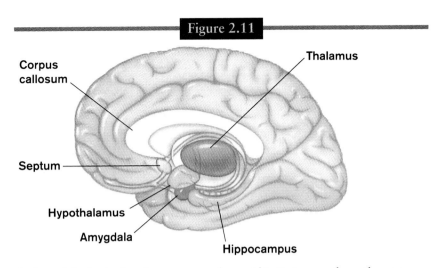

Figure 2.11

A view of the brain showing structures deep within it. Among these, the septum, amygdala, hippocampus, and hypothalamus constitute the limbic system.

lated. The influence of the amygdala and the septum on emotional responding is immediate and direct in nonhumans. In humans, it is more subtle, reflecting the influence of other brain centers in addition to the limbic system.

Another center in the limbic system, called the *hippocampus,* is less involved in emotion and more involved with the forming of memories. People with a damaged hippocampus are often unable to "transfer" experiences into permanent memory storage. They may remember events for short periods, and may be able to remember events from the distant past, but only if these events occurred before the hippocampus was damaged.

The Hypothalamus

Perhaps the first thing to say about the **hypothalamus** is that it is often considered a part of the limbic system. It is located near the limbic system, and it, too, is involved in motivational and emotional reactions. Among other things, it influences many of the functions of the endocrine system, which, as we have seen, is involved in emotional responding.

The major responsibility of the hypothalmus seems to be to monitor critical internal bodily functions. It has centers (nuclei again) that control feeding behaviors. It is sensitive to the amount of fluid in our bodies and indirectly gives rise to the feeling of being thirsty. The hypothalamus also acts something like a thermostat, triggering a number of automatic reactions should we become too warm or too cold. This small structure is also involved in aggressive and sexual behaviors. It acts as a regulator for many hormones. To be sure, we'll

hypothalamus a small structure near the limbic system in the center of the brain, associated with feeding, drinking, sex, and aggression

discuss the hypothalamus again when we study needs, motives, and emotions in later topics.

The Basal Ganglia

basal ganglia a collection of structures in front of the limbic system that produces and depends on dopamine to control large, slow body movements

A curious set of tissues is the **basal ganglia**. The basal ganglia are a collection of small, loosely connected structures located just in front of the limbic system. Like the cerebellum, the basal ganglia work primarily to control motor responding. Unlike the cerebellum, the role of the basal ganglia is more tied to large, slow movements—their initiation and their coordination. Although the basal ganglia are clearly related to the movements of some of our body's larger muscles, there are no pathways that lead directly from the ganglia, down the spinal cord, and off to those muscles.

Parkinson's disease a disorder of movement caused by damage to tissues in the basal ganglia

Some of the functions of the basal ganglia have become clearer as we have come to understand **Parkinson's disease**—a disorder, involving the basal ganglia, in which the most noticeable symptoms are impairment of movement and involuntary tremors. At first there may be a tightness or stiffness in the fingers or limbs. As the disease progresses, it becomes difficult, if not impossible, to initiate bodily movements. Walking, once begun, involves a set of stiff, shuffling movements. In advanced cases, voluntary movement of the arms is nearly impossible. Parkinson's disease is more common with increasing age, afflicting approximately 1 percent of the population.

The neurotransmitter *dopamine* is usually found in great quantity in the basal ganglia. The basal ganglia provide the source of much of the brain's dopamine. In Parkinson's disease, the cells that produce dopamine die off, and as a result, levels of the neurotransmitter in the basal ganglia (and elsewhere) decline. As dopamine levels in the basal ganglia become insufficient, behavioral consequences are noted as symptoms of the disease. Treatment, you might think, would be to inject a lot of dopamine back into the basal ganglia. As it happens, that isn't possible: simply put, there's no way to get the chemical in there so that it will stay. But another drug, *L-dopa,* can be used (in pill form) to the same effect: L-dopa increases dopamine availability in the basal ganglia, and as a result, the course of the disease can be slowed (reversing the course of Parkinson's disease is as yet not possible).

One treatment for Parkinson's disease has gotten considerable attention in the 1990s: the transplantation of brain cells from fetuses directly into the brain of someone suffering from the disease. After many studies with rats demonstrated that cells from the fetuses of rats could grow in the brains of adult rats—and increase the amount of dopamine there (e.g., Bjorklund et al., 1980)—the procedure was tried with humans. The results so far have been promising. Some studies have shown that transplanting brain cells from aborted human fetuses into the brains of persons with Parkinson's disease can actually reverse the course of the disease (e.g., Fahn, 1992; Freed et al., 1992; Spencer et al., 1992; Widner et al., 1992). As you can imagine, using brain cells from aborted fetuses—even if it is to treat a devastating disease—is a procedure with profound ethical, legal, and political ramifications.

The Thalamus

The last structure to discuss as a lower brain center is the **thalamus**. It sits right below the cerbral cortex and is involved with its functioning. Like the pons, it is a relay station for impulses traveling to and from the cerebral cortex. Many impulses traveling from the cerebral cortex to lower brain structures, the spinal cord, and out to the peripheral nervous system pass through the thalamus. Overcoming the normal function of the medulla (e.g., by voluntarily holding our breath) involves messages that pass through the thalamus. The major role of the thalamus, however, involves the processing of information from the senses.

In handling incoming sensory impulses, the thalamus "integrates" or collects, organizes, and then directs sensory messages to the appropriate area of the cerebral cortex. Sensory messages from the lower body, eyes, ears, and other sensory organs pass through the thalamus. For example, it is at the thalamus that nerve fibers from an eye are spread out and projected onto the back of the cerebral cortex.

Because of its role in monitoring impulses to and from the cerebral cortex, the thalamus has long been suspected to be involved in the control of our sleep-wake cycle (Moruzzi, 1975). Although this issue is not yet settled, some evidence (Lugaresi et al., 1986) suggests that nuclei in the thalamus (as well as some in the pons) do have a role in establishing a person's normal pattern of sleep and wakefulness.

thalamus the last sensory relay station; it sends impulses to the appropriate area of the cerebral cortex

Before You Go On

Indicate the location and briefly describe the major function of the RAS, limbic system, hypothalamus, basal ganglia, and thalamus.

THE CEREBRAL CORTEX

The human brain is a homely organ. There's just nothing very pretty about it. When we look at a human brain, the first thing we are likely to notice is the large, soft, lumpy, creviced outer covering of the **cerebral cortex** (in fact, *cortex* means "outer bark," or covering). The cerebral cortex (also called the cerebrum, or just cortex) of the human brain is significantly larger than any other brain structure. It is the complex and delicate development of the cerebral cortex that makes us uniquely human. It is our center for the processing and storage of information about the world in which we live. It is the starting place for virtually all of our voluntary action.

cerebral cortex (or cerebrum) the large, convoluted outer covering of the brain that is the seat of cognitive functioning and voluntary action

Lobes and Localization

Figure 2.12 presents two views of the cerebral cortex, one a top view, the other a side view. You can see from these illustrations that the deep folds of tissue of the human cerebral cortex provide us with markers for dividing the cerebrum into major areas. The most noticeable division of the cortex can be seen in the top view. Here, we can clearly see the deep crevice that runs down the middle of the cerebral cortex from front to back, dividing it into the left and right **cerebral hemispheres**.

A side view of a hemisphere (Figure 2.12 shows us the left one) allows us to see the four major divisions of the cerebral cortex found in each hemisphere. These divisions are referred to as *lobes* of the brain. The **frontal lobes** are the largest and are defined by two large crevices called the central fissure and the lateral fissure. The **temporal lobes** are located at the temples, below the lateral fissure, with one on each side of the brain. The **occipital lobes**, at the back of the brain, are defined somewhat arbitrarily, with no large fissures setting them off, and the **parietal lobes** are wedged in behind the frontal lobes and above the occipital and temporal lobes.

Using the methods we discussed in Topic 2B (see pages 65–75), researchers have learned much about what normally happens in the various regions of the cerebral cortex. Scientists have mapped out what goes on in most of the cortex, but many of the details of cerebral function are yet to be understood. Three major areas have been

cerebral hemispheres the two halves of the cerebral cortex, separated by a deep fissure running from front to back

frontal lobes the largest of the cerebral lobes, located in front of the central fissure and above the lateral fissure

temporal lobes the lobes of the cerebrum, located at the temples

occipital lobes the cerebral lobes at the very back of the brain

parietal lobes the lobes of the cerebrum found behind the frontal lobes, in front of the occipital lobes, and above the temporal lobes

Figure 2.12

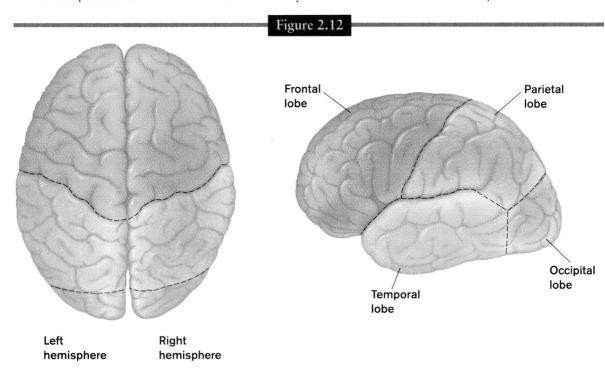

Left hemisphere   Right hemisphere

The human cerebral cortex is divided into left and right hemispheres, which in turn are divided into frontal, temporal, occipital, and parietal lobes.

mapped: *sensory areas,* where impulses from sense receptors are sent; *motor areas,* where most voluntary movements originate; and *association areas,* where sensory and motor functions are integrated, and where higher mental processes are thought to occur. We'll now review each of these areas in turn.

Sensory Areas. Let's review for just a minute. Receptor cells (specialized neurons) in our sense organs respond to stimulus energy from the environment. These cells then pass neural impulses along sensory nerve fibers, eventually to the cerebral cortex. Senses in our body below our neck first send impulses to the spinal cord. Then, it's up the spinal cord, through the brain stem and thalamus, and beyond. After they leave the thalamus, these impulses go to a **sensory area**—an area of the cerebral cortex that receives impulses from our senses. Which sensory area is involved depends on which sense is activated.

sensory areas those areas of the cerebral cortex that receive impulses from sense receptors

Reflecting their relative importance to us, large areas of the cerebral cortex are involved with vision and hearing. Virtually the entire occipital lobe handles visual information (labeled "visual area" in Figure 2.13). Auditory (hearing) impulses end up in large centers ("auditory areas") in the temporal lobes.

Our bodily senses (to touch, pressure, pain, and so on) send impulses to a strip at the very front of the parietal lobe (labeled "body sense area" in Figure 2.13). In this area of the parietal lobe we can map out specific regions that correspond to various parts of the body. When we do so, we find that some body parts—the face, lips, and fingertips, for example—are overrepresented in the body sense area of the cerebral cortex, reflecting their high sensitivity. (In other words, some parts of the body, even some very small ones, are processed in larger areas of the cortex than are other parts.)

Figure 2.13

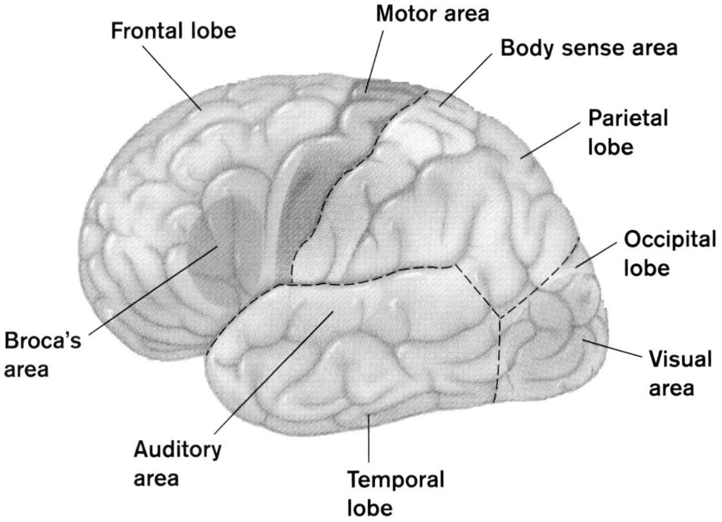

A side view of the left cerebral hemisphere, showing the four lobes of the cerebral cortex and areas of localization of function.

This is a good place to remind ourselves of *cross laterality* (page 76), the crossing over of information from senses on the left side of the body to the right side of the brain, and vice versa, with this crossing occurring in the brain stem. When someone touches your right arm, that information ends up in your left parietal lobe. A tickle to your left foot is processed by the right side of your cerebral cortex.

Motor Areas. We have already seen that some of our actions, at least very simple and reflexive ones, originate in our central nervous system below the cerebral cortex. Although lower brain centers, such as the basal ganglia, may be involved, most voluntary activity originates in the cerebral cortex—in strips at the very back of our frontal lobes. These **motor areas** (remember, there are two of them, left and right) are directly across the central fissure from the body sense areas in the parietal lobe (see Figure 2.13). I need to make the disclaimer that the actual, thoughtful decision-making process of whether one *should* move probably occurs elsewhere, almost certainly farther forward in the frontal lobes.

Electrical stimulation techniques have allowed us to map locations in the motor areas that correspond to, or control, specific muscles or muscle groups. As is the case for sensory processing, we find that some muscle groups (such as those that control movements of the hands and mouth) are represented by disproportionally larger areas of cerebral cortex.

As you know, we also find cross laterality at work with the motor area. It is your right hemisphere's motor area that controls movements of the left side of your body, and the left hemisphere's motor area that controls the right side. Someone who has suffered a cerebral stroke (a disruption of blood flow in the brain that results in the loss of neural tissue) in the left side of the brain will have impaired movement in the right side of the body.

Association Areas. Once we have located the areas of the cerebral cortex that process sensory information and originate motor responses, we find that we still have a lot of cortex left over. The remaining areas of the cerebral cortex are called **association areas**—areas of the cerebrum in which sensory input is "associated" with motor responses; where cognitive functions such as problem solving, memory, and thinking occur. There are three association areas in each hemisphere: frontal, parietal, and temporal. The occipital lobe is so "filled" with visual processing, there is no room left over for an occipital association area.

There is considerable support for the idea that it is in our association areas that so-called higher mental processes occur. Frontal association areas are involved in many such processes. As Broca discovered more than a century ago, some speech and language behaviors are localized in the frontal association area. Damage to the frontal lobes often interrupts or destroys the ability to plan ahead, to think quickly, or to think things through.

We should remind ourselves not to get carried away with cerebral localization of function. Let's not fall into the trap of coming to believe that separate parts of the cerebral cortex operate independently and have the sole responsibility for any one function. This is a

motor areas the strips at the back of the frontal lobes that control voluntary movement

association areas the areas of the frontal, parietal, and temporal lobes in which higher mental processing occurs

point that neurologist Marcel Kinsbourne makes: "There are no discontinuities in the brain. No independent channels traverse it; nor is its territory divisible into areas that house autonomous processors" (1982, p. 412). This will be particularly important to keep in mind as we now look at the division of the cerebral cortex into right and left hemispheres.

Before You Go On

Given a side view of the brain, locate the four lobes of the cerebral cortex.

Locate the primary sensory, motor, and association areas of the cerebrum, and describe what happens at each.

The Two Cerebral Hemispheres—Splitting the Brain

Even the ancient Greeks knew that the cerebral cortex was divided into two major sections, or hemispheres. That there should be a division of the cerebral cortex into halves seems quite natural. After all, we have two eyes, arms, legs, lungs, and so forth. Why not two divisions of the brain? In the last 30 years, interest in this division into hemispheres has heightened as scientists have accumulated evidence that suggests that each half of the cerebral cortex may have primary responsibility for a particular set of functions—particularly mental functions.

In most humans, the left hemisphere is the larger of the two halves, contains a higher proportion of gray matter, and is thought to be the dominant hemisphere (active to a greater degree in more tasks). We have already noted that the language center is housed in the left cerebral hemisphere. This is surely true for virtually all right-handed people. For most, but not all, left-handers, language may be processed primarily by the right hemisphere. Because humans are so language oriented, not much attention was given to the "lowly" right hemisphere until a remarkable surgical procedure, first performed in the 1960s, gave us new insights about the cerebral hemispheres (Sperry, 1968, 1982; Springer & Deutsch, 1981).

Normally, the two hemispheres of the cerebral cortex are interconnected by hundreds of thousands of fibers, collectively called the **corpus callosum** (which can be seen in Figure 2.11). Through the corpus callosum, one side of our cortex remains in constant and immediate contact with the other. Separating the functions of the two hemispheres is possible, however, through a surgical technique called a **split-brain procedure**, which is neither as complicated nor as dangerous as it may sound. The procedure amounts to destroying the corpus callosum's connections between the two hemispheres. The procedure was first tried on humans in 1961 by Joseph Brogan in an attempt to lessen the severity of the symptoms of epilepsy. As an irreversible

corpus callosum a network of nerve fibers that connects the two hemispheres of the cerebrum

split-brain procedure a surgical technique of severing the corpus callosum, allowing the two hemispheres to operate independently

treatment of last resort, the split-brain procedure was found to be very successful.

Most of what we know about the activities of the cerebral hemispheres has been learned from split-brain subjects, both human and animal. One of the things that makes this procedure remarkable is that under normal circumstances split-brain patients behave normally. Only in the laboratory, with specially designed tasks, can we see the results of having made the hemispheres of the cerebral cortex function independently (e.g., Gazzaniga & LeDoux, 1978; Hellige, 1983).

Experiments with split-brain patients confirm that speech production is a left-hemisphere function in a great majority of people. Suppose you have your hands behind your back. I place a house key in your left hand, and ask you to tell me what it is. Your left hand feels the key. Impulses travel up your left arm, up your spinal cord, and then cross over to your *right* cerebral hemisphere (remember cross laterality down in your brain stem). You can tell me that the object in your hand is a key because your brain is intact. Your right hemisphere passes information about the key to your left hemisphere, and your left hemisphere directs you to say, "It's a key." But suppose your corpus callosum is severed (that you are a split-brain subject). Now you cannot answer my question, even though you understand it perfectly. Why not? Your right brain knows that the object in your left hand is a key, but without the corpus callosum, it has no way to inform the left hemisphere where speech production is located. You *would*, however, be able to point out the key from among other objects placed before you, under the direction of the right cerebral hemisphere. Once your eyes saw you do so, they would communicate that information to your left hemisphere, and now it, too, would know, and tell us, what your right hemisphere knew all along.

A major task of the left hemisphere, then, is the production of speech and the use of language. But before we go any further, we need to pause and caution against overinterpretation. When results from early split-brain studies were first made known, many people—nonpsychologists and psychologists alike—rushed to some premature conclusions. What we now appreciate is that virtually no behavior, virtually no mental process, is the simple and single product of just one hemisphere (e.g., Hellige, 1990). What is more reasonable to assert is that one hemisphere dominates the other in regard to, or may be the primary processing area for, certain actions and reactions. The left hemisphere *is* dominant in the perception and interpretation of speech. But, some language processing seems to occur in the right hemisphere. The right side of the cerebral cortex is more involved in processing common phrases and clichés, such as "How do you do?" or "Have a nice day!" (e.g., Kempler & Van Lanker, 1987).

Granted that we shouldn't overinterpret, what are some of the activities that are processed *primarily* in one hemisphere or the other? We have seen that the left hemisphere can be given credit for processing most of our language skills, and given our heavy reliance on language, that's no small matter. Simple arithmetic tasks of calculation also seem to be primarily a left-brain function. Indeed, the left hemisphere has often been credited with the processing of information in

Although we must be careful not to overgeneralize, we may say that a major task of the left cerebral hemisphere is the use of language (as working a crossword puzzle). A major task of the right cerebral hemisphere is the appreciation of spatial relations (as in working on a jigsaw puzzle).

an analytical, one-piece-at-a-time sort of way, although the data here are a bit tenuous (Hellige, 1990, p. 59).

What, then, of the right hemisphere? The clearest evidence is that the right hemisphere dominates in the processing of visually presented information (Bradshaw & Nettleton, 1983; Kosslyn, 1987). Putting together a jigsaw puzzle, for instance, uses the right hemisphere more than the left. Skill in the visual arts (painting, drawing, and sculpting) is associated with the right hemisphere more than the left. Also, the right hemisphere is credited with being more involved in monitoring levels of emotionality, both in interpreting emotional stimuli and in expressing emotions. Consistent with the hypothesis that the left hemisphere tends to be analytic and sequential, the right hemisphere is thought to be better able to grasp the big picture—to see the overall view of things—and tends to be somewhat more creative.

These few possibilities are intriguing. It seems that there are differences in the way the two sides of the cerebral cortex normally process information. But these differences are slight, and many remain controversial. In fact, we are finding that the more we study hemispheric differences, the more we find similarities. Any special programs or courses that claim to be designed to train or educate one side of our brains to the exclusion of the other are misguided, no matter how well intentioned they may be.

The Two Sexes—Male and Female Brains

That there are anatomical and physical differences between women and men is obvious. Here we are talking about the function of the brain, however, and we may fairly ask if there are any differences between the brains of men (in general) and the brains of women (in general). Remember, we're asking about general differences; the brains of no two human beings are precisely the same. If there are differences in the anatomy of male and female brains, we must then ask if these differences are in any way significant. Do they have any impact on psychological functioning?

It turns out that what appears to be a loaded issue can be resolved fairly easily. Except for those differences in the brains of males and females that are directly related to reproductive function (which are not inconsequential), we know of no differences between the brains of women and the brains of men that are of any real consequence (e.g., Unger & Crawford, 1992).

Here's an example of how research in this area has gone. One possibility that seemed intriguing was that the hemispheres of the cerebral cortex are more separate and distinct (more "lateralized") in males than they are in females. At least one part of the corpus callosum in the brains of females seems to be larger than it is in the brains of males. There is also evidence that women are more likely to recover from strokes than are men, presumably because functions lost as a result of stroke damage in one hemisphere can be taken over more easily by the other, undamaged hemisphere (McGlone, 1977, 1978, 1980). An implication of this finding—usually left unspoken—is that intellectual functioning in women is more "balanced" than in men, whereas men are more likely to excel in the functioning of one hemisphere or the other. But as it happens, further research failed to find any differences at all in lateralization (Bleier et al., 1987). Nor is there evidence that differences in lateralization are associated with any differences in cognitive abilities between men and women (e.g., Unger & Crawford, 1992). There *is* a difference in the lateralization of the brains of left-handed persons compared to right-handed persons (brains of left-handed persons are less lateralized, or less separate), but there are *no* significant differences in the cognitive abilities of left- and right-handed persons (Kocel, 1977).

As we shall see repeatedly throughout this text, there are very few differences in the psychological functioning of women and men—in cognitive abilities or any others—so it should not be surprising that there are few, if any, differences in underlying brain structure. I would be remiss to leave this discussion without also mentioning that there are no known differences in the brain structures or brain functions of *any* identifiable groups of persons, whether those groups differ in culture, race, or ethnic background.

Before You Go On

What is a split-brain procedure, why is it done on humans, and what have we learned from it?

Briefly summarize the respective functions of the left and right cerebral hemispheres of the human brain.

Are there any significant differences between the brains of females and the brains of males?

TOPIC 2C SUMMARY

Although we have learned a great deal about the human nervous system, its structures, and how it affects our thoughts, feelings, and behaviors, many mysteries remain to be solved. If nothing else, we have learned not to look for simple answers, a point made in Chapter 1. We have learned that areas of the brain and spinal cord do not function independently. We have also learned that a true understanding of behavior and mental processes requires a working knowledge of the underlying anatomy and physiology. This observation will be reinforced in virtually every Topic that follows.

TOPIC 2A

What are the major structures of a neuron?

What is myelin, and what is its function?

Neurons are microscopic, living cells consisting of a cell body, which contains the cell's nucleus; dendrites that protrude from the cell body and that usually receive impulses; and an axon that carries an impulse away from the cell. The axons of some neurons are covered with a white, fatty myelin sheath that serves to protect and insulate the axon while speeding impulses along it. All axons, including myelinated ones, end with a set of bare, branching axon terminals. /p. 55

What is the basic process involved when a neuron fires?

What is the all-or-none principle?

What is meant by the concept of neural threshold?

When a neuron fires, a tension created by an imbalance of electrically charged chemical ions is quickly reversed. When a neuron is not firing, or is "at rest," the inside of the neuron is more negatively charged than the outside (the resting potential). Where the impulse occurs, this polarity changes, and the inside of the neuron becomes momentarily positive compared to the outside (the action potential). The all-or-none principle is the name for the observation that a neuron's firing either takes place totally or not at all; that is, there is no such thing as the partial firing of a neuron. The concept of neural threshold claims that there is a minimum amount of stimulation required to get a neuron to fire in the first place. /p. 58

Summarize neural impulse transmission at the synapse.

Name four neurotransmitters and indicate a psychological reaction with which they are involved.

At the synapse, an impulse triggers the release of neurotransmitter chemicals from small vesicles in the axon terminal. These chemicals flood into the synaptic cleft, embed themselves in receptor sites in the

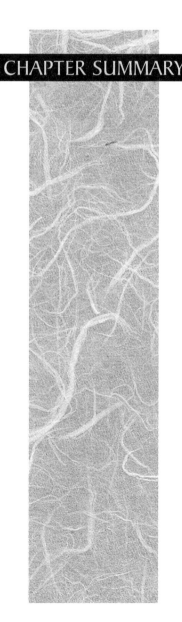

CHAPTER SUMMARY

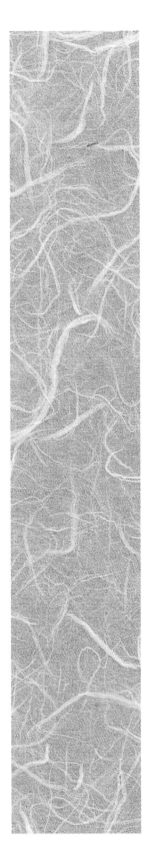

membrane of adjacent neurons, and, when sufficient amounts of the neurotransmitter are present, either excite or inhibit impulse transmission. Acetylcholine (ACh) is the most common excitatory neurotransmitter found in the central nervous system and at synapses between neurons and muscle cells. Norepinephrine and dopamine are inhibitory neurotransmitters, the former implicated in reactions of agitation, arousal, and depression; the latter implicated in cognitive and affective reactions and in movement responses. Endorphins are a class of neurotransmitter involved in the suppression of, or reaction to, pain. /p. 61

TOPIC 2B

Name the human nervous systems, and indicate how they are related to one another.

See Figure 2.5. The major division is into CNS and PNS, where the CNS consists of the spinal cord and brain, and the PNS is divided into the somatic and autonomic nervous systems. The ANS is further divided into sympathetic and parasympathetic divisions. The endocrine system is a network of glands that, under the influence of the brain and the ANS, secretes hormones into the bloodstream, which, in turn, influences behaviors and mental processes. /p. 65

Briefly summarize five techniques used to study the central nervous system.

We can study the central nervous system by (1) observing the effects of accident or injury; (2) lesioning parts of the CNS and noting the results; (3) electrically stimulating specific regions of the CNS; (4) recording the electrical activity of individual nerve cells, or, with the EEG, larger areas of the brain; and (5) looking at the brain with X rays, CAT scans, MRI procedures, and PET scans. /p. 70

TOPIC 2C

Why does spinal cord injury sometimes cause paralysis?

Describe the major features of a spinal reflex.

If the spinal cord is damaged, impulses originating in the brain to move parts of the body may not get past the damaged area to activate the appropriate muscles, resulting in paralysis. In a spinal reflex, impulses enter the spinal cord on sensory fibers, may or may not form a synapse with interneurons, and then exit the spinal cord on motor fibers to activate a muscle response. At the same time, impulses are sent to the brain on fibers in the spinal cord's white matter. /p. 74

Name the two brain stem structures, indicate where they are located, and describe what they do.

The brain stem consists of the *medulla,* at the very base of the brain, which controls important reflexes, monitors heart rate and breathing, and is where most cross laterality occurs, and the *pons,* just above the medulla, which acts like a bridge, passing impulses between the spinal cord and the brain. */p. 76*

Where is the cerebellum located, and what is its major function?

The cerebellum is located at the rear and base of the brain and is most involved in the smoothing and coordinating of rapid muscular responses. */p. 78*

Indicate the location and briefly describe the major function of the RAS, limbic system, hypothalamus, basal ganglia, and thalamus.

The RAS (or reticular activating system) extends from the brain stem through the middle of the brain to the cerebral cortex and is involved in maintaining levels of arousal. The limbic system, just above the brain stem, is involved in emotional expression (the amygdala and septum in particular) and the transfer of information into long-term memory (the hippocampus). The hypothalamus, which is near the limbic system, is involved in such motivated behaviors as feeding, drinking, sex, aggression, and temperature regulation. The basal ganglia, just in front of and above the limbic system, are a set of structures that control slow body movement and that produce much of the brain's dopamine. The thalamus, located just below the cerebral cortex, is a final relay station for sensory impulses it projects up to the appropriate area of the cerebrum. */p. 81*

Given a side view of the brain, locate the four lobes of the cerebral cortex.

Locate the primary sensory, motor, and association areas of the cerebrum, and describe what happens at each.

See Figures 2.12 and 2.13 to review the locations of the frontal, temporal, occipital, and parietal lobes, and the primary sensory, motor, and association areas. The sensory areas of the cerebral cortex (visual, auditory, and body sense) receive impulses (through the thalamus) from our senses. Voluntary motor activity is initiated in the motor area of the cortex, and cognitive processing, such as memory, thinking, and problem solving, are thought to take place in the so-called association areas. */p. 85*

What is a split-brain procedure, why is it done on humans, and what have we learned from it?

Briefly summarize the respective functions of the left and right cerebral hemispheres of the human brain.

Are there any significant differences between the brains of females and the brains of males?

The split-brain procedure severs the fibers of the corpus callosum, the structure that sends impulses back and forth between the two cerebral hemispheres, thus allowing them to operate independently. It is used

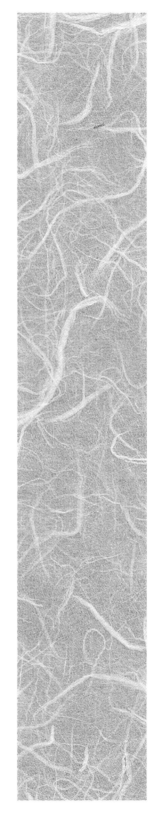

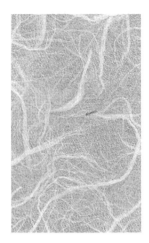

as a treatment of last resort for extreme cases of epilepsy. The procedure has allowed us to study the functions of the hemisphere separately and to localize the functions of each. Although one hemisphere may dominate the other in some cases, seldom does one have complete control of any important brain function. However, it is safe to say that language and speech are usually processed in the left hemisphere, while visual, spatial information is usually processed in the right. Also possible, but less certain, is the left hemisphere's dominance in simple calculations and the sequential, analytical processing of information, while the right hemisphere is thought to be more involved with the "big picture," with the visual arts, and with emotionality. Other than those brain structures that are involved in reproductive functioning, there seem to be no differences of consequence between the brains of females and the brains of males. */p. 88*

chapter three

SENSATION AND PERCEPTION

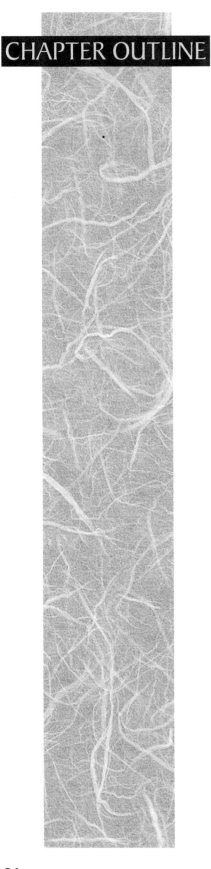

CHAPTER OUTLINE

TOPIC 3A SENSING AND PERCEIVING:
A FEW BASIC CONCEPTS
Sensory Thresholds and Adaptation
     Absolute Thresholds
     Difference Thresholds
     Signal Detection
     Sensory Adaptation
Paying Attention: A Process of Selection
     Stimulus Factors in Selectivity
     Personal Factors in Selectivity
TOPIC 3A SUMMARY

TOPIC 3B VISION
The Stimulus for Vision: Light
The Receptor for Vision: The Eye
     Important Structures of the Human Eye
     More on Rods and Cones and What They Do
     The Visual Pathway After the Retina
Color Vision and Color Blindness
Perceptual Organization
     Stimulus Factors
     Personal Factors
The Perception of Depth and Distance
     Ocular Cues
     Physical Cues
The Perception of Motion
     Perceiving Real Motion
     The Perception of Apparent Motion
The Constancy of Visual Perception
     Perceptual Constancy
     When Constancy Fails: Geometric Illusions
       and Impossible Figures
TOPIC 3B SUMMARY

TOPIC 3C HEARING AND THE OTHER SENSES
Hearing
     The Stimulus for Hearing: Sound
     The Receptor for Hearing: The Ear
The Chemical Senses
     Taste
     Smell
The Skin, or Cutaneous, Senses
The Position Senses
Pain: A Special Sense
TOPIC 3C SUMMARY

CHAPTER SUMMARY

I've never had the nerve to try this classroom demonstration. However, when I was a graduate student, I had a chance to see it done. The demonstration is a classic.

I took a seat at the rear of the introductory psychology class, unnoticed by the more than six hundred students filling the large, old lecture hall. The professor entered the room through a side door and began his lecture. After a few minutes, the class settled down to taking notes and listening.

Suddenly, a student burst through the large doors at the rear of the lecture hall. I recognized him as the professor's assistant, but no one else in the class knew who he was. I felt he overacted a bit as he stomped down the center aisle of the lecture hall, screaming the foulest of obscenities. "Dr. X, you failed me for the last time, you *&%@#$ so-and-so. You're going to pay for this!" The class was stunned. Everyone gasped as the student leaped over the lectern to grab the professor.

The student and the professor struggled briefly, and then—in clear view of everyone—there was a chrome-plated revolver! Down behind the lectern they fell. BANG! The sound of a gunshot filled the room. The students sat frozen in their seats. The graduate assistant raced out of the same side door the professor had entered just a few minutes earlier. The professor lay sprawled out on the floor, moaning loudly.

Six hundred students sat stunned in their seats. At just the right dramatic moment, the professor drew himself up to the lectern and in a calm voice said, "Now, I want everyone to take out some paper and write down exactly what you saw."

I need not describe all the results of this demonstration. I never did read all 600 descriptions but I did help summarize the responses. I was very impressed. The "enraged" graduate student was described as being from 5'4" to 6'3" tall, weighing between 155 and 225 pounds, and wearing either a gray sweatshirt or a blue blazer. Although there was some agreement, one would have a difficult time coming up with a good physical description of the suspect in this mock shooting.

The most remarkable misperception that took place had to do with the gun. As the professor took his place at the front of the class, he removed the pistol from his coat pocket and placed it on top of his notes. When the "crazed student" crashed into the room, the first thing the professor did was grab the gun, and point it at the student as he came charging down the center aisle. In fact, the student *never* had the gun in his hands. The professor had it all along. It was the professor who fired the shot that startled us all. *Fewer than 20 students of the 600 in class that day reported seeing these events the way they actually occurred.* The overwhelming majority of "witnesses" claimed it was the crazy student with the gun. As we will see in this chapter, our experience of the world is often flavored by factors over and above what happens.

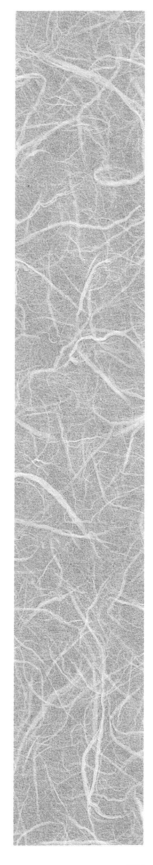

*T*his chapter is organized in three Topics. Topic 3A deals with basic concepts: thresholds, adaptation, and paying attention. These concepts are relevant to all of our senses. Sensory thresholds, adaptation levels, and the extent to which one pays attention all work together to determine whether events in the environment are recorded in one's experience. Topic 3B focuses on vision. First, we'll consider how visual information is processed by the eyes and the brain (matters of sensation), and then we'll look at some of the ways in which visual information is organized and interpreted (matters of perception). I've devoted an entire Topic to vision for two reasons: (1) it is a very important sense, and (2) psychologists understand how visual processes work to a greater degree than they understand the other senses. Topic 3C briefly covers the other human senses. As we did for vision, we'll first examine the nature of the relevant stimulus, and then consider the sense organ and sense receptor.

Topic 3A

SENSING AND PERCEIVING: A FEW BASIC CONCEPTS

In this chapter, we begin our discussion of *information processing*— how we find out about the world, make judgments about it, learn from it, and remember what we have learned. By the time we become adults, our memories are filled with all sorts of information, some of it critically important (e.g., knowing the difference between things that are edible and things that are not), some of it comparatively trivial (e.g., knowing the difference between hard rock and punk rock music). An important question for many psychologists is how information gets processed into our memories.

We really do not experience any breaks in the way we process information. The experience seems continuous. We hear someone say something in class and discover some time later that we remember what was said. If there were subprocesses involved along the way, we were not aware of them. What we are going to do in this chapter, then, is somewhat artificial, at least in terms of our everyday experience. We are going to divide information processing into two subprocesses—sensation and perception.

We begin with a discussion of sensory processes, or what we often call sensation. **Sensation** is the process that yields our immediate experience of stimuli in our environment. It is the process of receiving information from the environment and changing that input into nervous system activity. The psychology of sensation deals with how our various senses manage to do what they do. *Sense receptors* are the specialized neural cells in *sense organs* that change physical energy into neural impulses. In other words, each of our sense receptors is a

sensation the process of receiving information from the environment and changing that input into nervous system activity

transducer—a mechanism that converts energy from one form to another. A light bulb is a transducer. It converts electrical energy into light energy (and a little heat energy). Your eye is a sense organ that contains sense receptors that transduce light energy into neural energy. Your ear is a sense organ that contains sense receptors that transduce the mechanical energy of sound waves into neural energy.

transducer a mechanism that converts energy from one form to another—a basic process common to all of our senses

Compared to sensation, perception is a more active, complex, even creative, process. It acts on stimulation received and recorded by the senses. **Perception** is a process that involves the selection, organization, and interpretation of stimuli. We can think of perception as a more cognitive and central process than sensation. One way in which you can think about the role of perception in our daily lives is to say that our senses present us with information about the world in which we live, whereas perception represents (re-presents) that information, often flavored by our motivational states, our expectations, and our past experiences. Levine and Shefner (1991, p. 1) put it this way: "...we sense the presence of a stimulus, but we perceive what it is."

perception the cognitive process of selecting, organizing, and interpreting stimuli

Now, before we get into the story of how each of our sense organs goes about transducing physical energy from the environment, we'll consider a few concepts that apply to all of our senses.

SENSORY THRESHOLDS AND ADAPTATION

Psychophysics is the study of the relationships between the physical attributes of stimuli and the psychological experiences they produce. It is one of the oldest subfields in psychology. Many methods of psychophysics were developed before Wundt opened his psychology laboratory in Leipzig in 1879. There are two ways to think about what psychophysics is all about.

psychophysics the study of the relationship between the physical attributes of stimuli and the psychological experiences they produce

At a simple, applied level we can say that the techniques of psychophysics have been designed to assess the sensitivity of our senses, providing answers to such questions as "Just how good *is* your hearing after all these years of playing bass in a rock band?" At a more theoretical level, we can think of psychophysics as providing a means of systematically relating the outside, *physical* world to the inner, *psychological* world. Now the question we just asked gets recast to: "How much of a change in the physical intensity of this sound will it take for you to experience a difference in loudness?" Most psychophysical methods are designed to measure *sensory thresholds*, indicators of the sensitivity of our sense receptors. There are two types of sensory thresholds: absolute thresholds and difference thresholds.

Absolute Thresholds

Imagine the following experiment. You are seated in a dimly lighted room, staring at a small box. The side of the box facing you is covered by a sheet of plastic. Behind the plastic is a light bulb. I can decrease the physical intensity of the light bulb to the point where you cannot see it at all. I can also increase the light's intensity so that you can see it very clearly. I have many intensity settings available between these extremes. At what point of physical intensity will the light first become visible to you?

Common sense tells us that there should be some value of physical intensity below which you cannot see the light and above which you can. That point, for you, would be your absolute threshold. The term *threshold* here means the same thing it does in other contexts—a point of crossing over. Sensory thresholds are related to sensitivity, but inversely. That is, as threshold values decrease, sensitivity increases. The lower the threshold of a sense receptor, the more sensitive it is.

Let's return to our imaginary experiment. I repeatedly vary the light's intensity and ask you to respond "Yes, I see the light," or "No, I don't see the light," depending on your experience. (In this experiment, I won't allow you the luxury of saying you don't know or aren't sure.)

When this experiment is actually done, we discover something that at first seems strange. I can reduce the intensity of the light so low that you never report seeing it. And I can present light intensities so high that you always say you see them. However, there are intensities of the light to which you sometimes respond "yes" and sometimes respond "no," even though the actual, physical intensity of the light is unchanged.

In reality, there just isn't very much that's absolute about absolute thresholds. They keep changing from moment to moment, reflecting small, subtle changes in the sensitivity of our senses. (They also reflect such factors as momentary shifts in our ability to pay attention to the task at hand—an issue we'll get back to soon.) Figure 3.1 shows (A) what we might like to happen in an experiment such as the one we

Figure 3.1

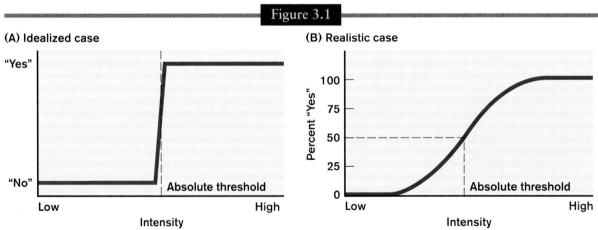

Results of a project to determine absolute threshold values. (A) The idealized case, for which there is a single point of intensity below which a stimulus is never detected and above which it is always detected, and (B) the realistic case, for which absolute threshold becomes the intensity of a stimulus below which it is detected less than 50 percent of the time and above which it is detected more than 50 percent of the time.

Figure 3.2		
Examples of Absolute Threshold Values for Five Senses **(i.e., These Stimuli Will Be Detected 50 Percent of the Time)**		
Vision	A candle flame seen from a distance of 30 miles on a clear, dark night	
Hearing	The ticking of a watch under quiet conditions from a distance of 20 feet	
Taste	1 teaspoon of sugar dissolved in 2 gallons of water	
Smell	One drop of perfume in a three-room apartment	
Touch	The wing of a bee dropped on your cheek from a height of one centimeter	

From Galanter, 1962.

have just considered, and (B) what actually does happen in such an experiment.

Because there are no absolute measures of sensory sensitivity, psychologists resort to the following operational definition of **absolute threshold**: the physical intensity of a stimulus a subject reports detecting 50 percent of the time. In other words, intensities below threshold are those detected less than 50 percent of the time, and intensities above threshold are those detected more than 50 percent of the time. This complication occurs for all of our senses, not just vision. I would have had the same general result if I had tested your ability to detect sounds, smells, touches, or tastes.

So what good is the notion of absolute threshold? Determining absolute thresholds is not just an academic exercise. For one thing, as a measure of sensitivity, absolute threshold levels can be used to determine if one's senses are operating properly and are detecting low levels of stimulation (which is what happens when you have your hearing tested, for example). Engineers who design sound systems need to know about absolute thresholds; stereo speakers that do not reproduce sounds above threshold levels aren't of much use. Warning lights must be designed to be well above absolute threshold if they are to be of any use to us. How much perfume do you need to use for it to be noticed? How low must you whisper so as not to be overheard in a classroom? Do I really smell natural gas in the house, or is it my imagination? Can one basil leaf in the tomato sauce be detected, or will two be required? These are psychophysical questions about absolute thresholds as they pertain to everyday experiences outside the laboratory. As it happens, our sense receptors are remarkably sensitive, as the examples in Figure 3.2 attest.

absolute threshold the physical intensity of a stimulus that one can detect 50 percent of the time

Before You Go On

How are the processes of sensation and perception defined?

What is psychophysics?

What is an absolute threshold, and how is it related to the sensitivity of our senses?

difference threshold *the minimal difference in a stimulus attribute that can be detected 50 percent of the time*

To be a professional wine taster requires that one's ability to detect just noticeable differences among various wines be extremely sensitive.

just noticeable difference (j.n.d.) *the minimal change in a stimulus attribute, such as intensity, that can be detected*

Difference Thresholds

The truth is, we don't often encounter situations that test our abilities to detect very-low-intensity stimuli. We *are* often called upon to detect differences between or among stimuli that are above our absolute thresholds. The issue here is not whether the stimuli can be detected, but whether they are in some way *different* from each other. So, a **difference threshold** is defined as the smallest difference between stimulus attributes that can be detected. As you may have anticipated, we do have the same complication here as we do when we try to measure absolute thresholds. To a slight degree, one's difference threshold for any stimulus attribute varies from moment to moment. So, again we say that to be above one's difference threshold, differences between stimuli need to be detected more than 50 percent of the time.

For example, imagine I have two cans of paint, both containing the exact same shade of red. You can easily see that they are the same color. I slowly add some white paint to one of the cans. At what point do the two cans of red paint no longer look the same to you? The point at which the difference between the paints is first barely detectable would be your difference threshold—for colors of paint, anyway.

Now let's go through an example dealing with hearing. I present you with two tones. You claim to be able to hear them both (both are above absolute threshold), and you say that they are equally loud. If I gradually increase the intensity of one of the tones, I will eventually reach a point at which you can just detect a difference in the loudness of the two tones. **Just noticeable difference**, or **j.n.d.**, is defined as the amount of change in a stimulus that makes it just noticeably different from what it was.

The concept of just noticeable difference is relevant in many contexts. A parent tells a teenager to "turn down that stereo!" The teenager reduces the volume, but not by a j.n.d. from the parent's perspective, and trouble may be brewing. Does the color of the belt match the color of the dress closely enough? Can anyone tell the difference between the expensive ingredients and the cheaper ones? Is this car so much cheaper than that one that the difference in price really makes a difference?

Signal Detection

Sensory thresholds are not stable, fixed values. They vary from moment to moment and are defined in terms of probability—as a 50-percent point, above which attributes of stimuli, or their differences, can be detected.

To say that sensory thresholds change is the same thing as saying the sensitivity of our senses changes. It changes because of momentary shifts in attention and because of the random electrical activity of the nerve cells in our sensory systems. Occasionally, nerve cells fire without any direct stimulation from the environment. Even if you were standing in a deep cave (or a closet, for that matter) where there was no light, with your eyes closed, you would still have some sort of visual experience—you would sense small flashes of light. The firing of sensory nerve cells creates a background noise that varies randomly from moment to moment.

When we are asked to determine if a stimulus has been presented, what we are really being asked to do is to judge if we can detect a signal against a background of other stimuli and randomly changing neural activity. When we think of threshold determination in this way, we are using the basics of what is called **signal detection theory**. Signal detection theory claims that stimulus detection is a decision-making process of determining if a signal exists against a background of noise (Green & Swets, 1966).

According to this theory, one's absolute threshold can be influenced by many factors in addition to the actual sensitivity of one's senses. We've already seen that we need to account for random nervous system activity. We also need to account for the individual's attention, expectations, and biases. For example, in an experiment to determine one's absolute threshold, subjects are simply more likely to say that yes, they can detect a stimulus, than they are to say that they don't. Everything else being equal, there is a general tendency to say "yes" more often than "no" (Block, 1965). On the other hand, some subjects may be overly cautious, saying "yes" only when they are absolutely sure that the stimulus in question has been presented.

Remember the basics of the absolute threshold study with which we began our discussion of psychophysics? I had a light in a box. I changed the intensity of the light and asked whether you could see it. Your absolute threshold was taken to be the intensity of the light to which you responded "yes" 50 percent of the time. Signal detection theory asks us to consider *all* of the factors that might have prompted you to say "yes" at any exposure to the light. What might some of these factors be? One might be the overall amount of light available in the room. Wouldn't you be more likely to detect the signal of my light in a room that was totally dark as opposed to a room in which all of the standard lights were on? What if I had offered you a reward, say $5, each time you detected the light? Wouldn't you tend to say "yes" often, whether you were really sure of yourself or not? By the same token, if I were to fine you $1 for each time you said "yes" when the light was not really on, might you not become more conservative, saying "yes" only when you were very sure of yourself? Might we expect a difference in your pattern of saying "yes" or "no" depending on whether we tested you in mid-morning, or late in the day when you were tired?

Signal detection procedures take into account such factors as background noise (e.g., the amount of other light in the room), levels of attention, and subject bias in the determination of sensory thresholds. The result is a better, clearer picture of sensory sensitivity.

Sensory Adaptation

Sensory adaptation is a process in which sensory experience decreases with continued exposure to a stimulus. There are many common examples of sensory adaptation. When we first jump into a pool or

signal detection theory *the view that signal detection is a matter of decision making, of separating a signal from ground (background) noise*

sensory adaptation *the process in which our sensory experience tends to decrease or diminish with continued exposure to a stimulus*

lake, the water feels very cold. But after only a few minutes we adapt and are reassuring our friends to "Come on in; the water's fine." When we first walk into a house in which cabbage is cooking, the odor is nearly overwhelming, but soon we adapt and do not notice it. When the compressor motor of the refrigerator first turns on, it seems to make a terribly loud noise—one we soon do not notice, until the compressor *stops* and silence returns to the kitchen. These are examples of sensory adaptation.

There is an important psychological point hidden in these examples. It is that one's ability to detect the presence of a stimulus (one's threshold) depends in large measure on the extent to which our sense receptors are being newly stimulated or have adapted to some degree. Another way to say the same thing is to note that our sense receptors respond to *changes* in stimulation. The constant stimulation of a receptor leads to adaptation and less of a chance that that stimulation will be detected.

There is an exception to this usage of the term *adaptation*. What happens when you move from a brightly lighted area to a dimly lighted area? At first you can barely see anything, but in a few minutes, you are seeing reasonably well. We say that you have "adapted to the dark." Here we are using the term adaptation in a different way. **Dark adaptation** refers to the process in which the visual receptors actually become *more* sensitive with time spent in the dark.

dark adaptation the process by which our eyes become more sensitive to light as we spend time in the dark

Before You Go On

What is a difference threshold, or a j.n.d.?

Briefly summarize the basic ideas of signal detection theory.

What is sensory adaptation?

PAYING ATTENTION: A PROCESS OF SELECTION

Imagine that you are at a party, engaged in a dreadfully boring conversation with someone you've just met. From time to time, it occurs to you that wearing your new shoes was not a good idea—your feet hurt. You are munching on an assortment of tasty appetizers. Music blares from a stereo at the other end of the room. Aromas of foods, smoke, and perfumes fill the air. There must be at least fifty people at this party, and you don't know any of them. Your senses are being bombarded simultaneously by all sorts of information: sights, sounds, tastes, smells, even pain. Suddenly, you hear someone mention your name. You redirect your attention, for the moment totally disregarding the person talking right in front of you.

What determines which of many competing stimuli attract our attention? In fact, there are many variables that influence our selection of stimuli. These variables are related to the basic concept of threshold, and this discussion expands on what I have been saying all along: whether we detect *any* stimulus depends on several factors, all acting at the same time. In this section, we'll discuss some of the more important variables that influence whether we attend to what is going on around us. These variables are of two general types: stimulus factors and personal factors. By stimulus factors, I mean those characteristics that make some stimuli more compelling (attention-grabbing) than others, no matter who the perceiver is. By personal factors, I mean those characteristics of the person, the perceiver, that influence which stimuli get attended to or perceived.

Stimulus Factors in Selectivity

Some stimuli are simply more compelling than others; they are more likely to get our attention, to be selected in for processing and interpretation. This is true regardless of who the perceiver is, and because individual differences seem to matter little here, they're called *stimulus factors.*

The most important stimulus factor in perceptual selection is **contrast,** the extent to which a given stimulus is physically different from the other stimuli around it. One stimulus can contrast with other stimuli in a variety of ways. For example, we are more likely to attend to a stimulus if its *intensity* is different from the intensities of other stimuli. Generally, the more intense a stimulus, the more likely we are to select it for further processing. Simply put, a shout is more compelling than a whisper; a bright light is more attention-grabbing than a dim one; an extreme temperature is more likely to be noticed than a moderate one.

Notice that this isn't always the case, however. The context in which stimuli occur can make a difference. A shout may be more compelling than a whisper, unless everyone is shouting; then it may very well be the soft, quiet, reasoned tone that gets our attention. If we are faced with a barrage of bright lights, a dim one, by contrast, may be the one we process more fully.

contrast the extent to which a stimulus is in some physical way different from surrounding stimuli

Because of the stimulus factor of contrast, it is easy to spot the green pine trees across the pond.

The same argument holds for the stimulus characteristic of physical *size*. In most cases, the bigger the stimulus, the more likely we are to attend to it. There is little point in building a small billboard to advertise your motel or restaurant. You'll want to construct the biggest billboard you can afford in hopes of attracting attention. Contrast effects are such that when we are faced with many large stimuli, one that is smaller may be the one to which we attend. The easiest player to spot on a football field is usually the placekicker, who tends to be much smaller than the other players and tends not to wear as much protective padding.

A third physical dimension that may determine perceptual selectivity, and for which contrast is relevant, is *motion*. Motion is a powerful factor in determining visual attention. A bird in flight is much easier to see than a bird sitting in a bush. In the fall, walking through the woods, you may come close to stepping on a chipmunk before you notice it, as long as it stays still—an adaptive response of camouflage that chipmunks do well. But if that chipmunk makes a dash to escape, it is easily noticed scurrying across the leaves. Again, the *contrast* created by movement is important. As you enter a nightclub, your attention is immediately drawn to the dance floor by the bright lights and the moving throng dancing to the loud music. How easy it is to spot the one person, in the middle of the dance floor, who, for whatever reason, is motionless, frozen against the background of moving bodies.

Although intensity, size, and motion are three physical characteristics of stimuli that readily come to mind, there are others. Indeed, any way in which two stimuli may be different (contrast) may provide a dimension that determines which stimulus we attend to. (Even a small grease spot can easily grab one's attention if it's located in the middle of a solid yellow tie.) This is precisely why we have printed important terms in boldface type throughout this book—so that you will notice them, attend to them, and then recognize them as important stimuli.

Here's yet another dimension that sometimes influences the stimuli we attend to: *novelty-familiarity*. The basic issue is still contrast. When we are in an old, familiar setting or environment, what is likely to catch our attention? Something new, different, and unusual. On the other hand, when we are in a new and different environment—out of town, perhaps—we are likely to notice something familiar. We may, for example, hardly notice our neighbors around the neighborhood. But if we're off on vacation, surrounded by hundreds or thousands of strange, unfamiliar people at an amusement park, we notice those neighbors almost immediately as familiar stimuli in a novel situation. (Note that which stimuli are novel and which are familiar depends, to some extent, on the experience of the individual. Thus, we could refer to this as a "personal factor" in perceptual selectivity. However, because the main issue here is contrast, I list novelty-familiarity as a stimulus factor in attention.)

There *is* another stimulus characteristic that can determine attention, but for which contrast really is not relevant, and that is *repetition*. Simply put, the more often a stimulus is presented, the more likely it is that it will be attended to—everything else being equal. Note that we have to say "everything else being equal" or we start to develop contradictions. We just agreed that novel stimuli attract attention. But if stimuli are repeated enough, they're no longer going to be very novel. In some situations novelty may determine attention, whereas in others, one's attention may be determined by repetition.

Instructors who want to get across an important point will seldom mention it just once, but will repeat it. This is why I repeat the definitions of important terms in the text, in the margin, *and again* in the glossary. If the leaky faucet only dripped once or twice in the night, you might not notice it. What gets your attention is that it drips and drips and drips. The people who write and schedule television commercials want you to attend to their messages, and obviously, repetition is one of their main techniques.

To summarize, there are many ways in which stimuli may differ—brightness, size, motion, color, pitch, and loudness, for example. The greater the contrast between any one stimulus and the others around it, the greater the likelihood that that stimulus will capture our attention. And, everything else being equal, the more often a stimulus is presented (at least up to a point), the greater the likelihood that it will be perceived and selected for further consideration and processing.

Before You Go On

**What stimulus factors determine the
selection of perceptions?**

Personal Factors in Selectivity

Sometimes, attention is determined not so much by the physical characteristics of the stimuli present but by personal characteristics of the perceiver. For example, imagine that two students are watching a football game on television. Both are being presented with identical stimulation from the same TV screen. One asks, "Wow, did you see that tackle?" The other responds, "No, I was watching the cheerleaders." The difference in perception here is hardly attributable to the nature of the stimuli, in that both students received exactly the same sensory information from the same TV. The difference is due to characteristics of the perceivers, or *personal factors,* which we can categorize as motivation, expectation, or past experience.

Imagine that two students watching a football game on TV are avid supporters of the two teams involved. One is a fan of the Chicago Bears; the other roots for the Dallas Cowboys. These viewers may have a wager on this important game. Suppose the Bears win the hard-fought contest with a last-second field goal. Both students have watched exactly the same game on the same TV, but which of the two is more likely to have perceived the officiating of the game as fair and honest? Which student is more likely to have seen the game as "one of the poorest refereed games ever"? The perception of the officiating may depend on who won or lost, and the *motivation* of the perceiver. The viewers tended to see what they wanted to see. You might not be surprised to learn that research confirms this very scenario (Hastorf & Cantril, 1954).

It is true that we often perceive what we want to perceive, and it is equally true that we often perceive what we *expect* to perceive, whether it's really there or not. We often do not notice stimuli when they *are* present simply because we did not "know" they were coming—we didn't expect them. When we are psychologically predisposed to perceive something, we say that we have formed a **mental set.**

Take just a second and quickly glance at the message in Figure 3.3. What did the message say? (If you've seen this before, you'll have to try it with someone who hasn't.) Many people say the message is PARIS IN THE SPRING. In fact, there are two THEs in the triangle: PARIS IN THE THE SPRING. Most people familiar with the English language (and with this phrase) do not expect there to be two *the*s right next to each other. Following their mental set, they report seeing only one. Others may develop a different mental set. Their line of reasoning goes something like this: "This is a psychology text, so there's probably a trick here, and I'm going to find it." In this instance, such skeptics get rewarded. There *is* a trick, and if their mental set was to find one, they did so. Sometimes our expectations not only affect what we perceive, but what we don't perceive. If you don't expect something to happen, if you're not "looking for it," you may miss it.

We will see later (Chapter 7) that our inability to change a mentally set way of perceiving a problem may interfere with our finding a solution to that problem. What we call "creative" problem solving is often a matter of perceiving aspects of a problem in new, unique, or unexpected ways. Thus, even as complex a cognitive process as problem solving often hinges on basic perceptual processes.

Have you noticed that when we say that paying attention is due to motivation and expectation we are claiming that what we perceive is often influenced by our *past experiences*? Much of our motivation comes from our past experiences. For example, the two television viewers of the football game between Chicago and Dallas were not born fans of those two teams. Their allegiances reflect their past experiences. By the same token, expectations develop from past experiences. We are likely to perceive, or be set to perceive, what we have perceived in the past in similar circumstances. Perhaps a personal example will make clear what I mean.

I once took a course in comparative psychology that examined the behaviors of nonhuman organisms. One of the co-teachers of the course was an ornithologist (a scientist who studies birds). A requirement of the course was to participate in an early-morning outing to go bird-watching. The memory is still vivid: Cold, tired, clutching my thermos of coffee, I slopped through the marshland looking for birds, as the sun was just rising. After 20 minutes of this unpleasantness, our instructor had identified ten or eleven different birds. I wasn't cer-

mental set a predisposed (set) way to perceive something; an expectation

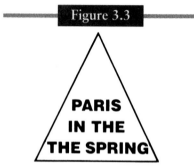

Figure 3.3

How we perceive the world is determined at least in part by our mental set or our expectations about the world. How many THEs did you see when you first glanced at this simple figure? Why?

tain, but I thought I'd seen a duck. I didn't know what sort of duck it was, but I did think that I'd seen a duck. The differences in perception between my instructor and me that cold, wet morning could be explained in terms of motivation (he *did* care more than I); but I suspect his ability to spot birds so quickly and surely reflected his experience. He knew where to look and what to look for.

Our perception of stimuli is usually accomplished without conscious effort, and the process is influenced by several factors. Some depend on the stimuli themselves. The implication is that what we perceive is determined to some extent by the bits and pieces of information we receive directly from our senses. This sort of processing is called *bottom-up processing*. We may attend to a particular stimulus because it is significantly larger, smaller, more colorful, louder, or slower than the other stimuli around it. Whether, or how, stimuli are perceived can also be influenced by the perceiver. In this case, selection is a matter of applying concepts and information already processed. To a degree, what one perceives depends on what the perceiver already knows, called *top-down processing*. Examples include the use of motivation, mental set, and past experience to influence perceptual selectivity.

Before You Go On

What personal factors are involved in perceptual
selectivity?

TOPIC 3A SUMMARY

Sensation and perception are processes that inform us about what is going on in the world. Sensation is the simpler of the two, involving the transduction of physical energy from the environment into the neural energy of the nervous system. Perception is a less physiological, more cognitive process that involves selection, organization, and the interpretation of sensory inputs.

Sensation begins when the intensity of environmental stimulation is sufficient to be above one's absolute threshold. Differences can be detected among stimuli only if they vary by at least a j.n.d., or a just noticeable difference. Whether stimuli are detected and how they are interpreted depend on several factors, including the physical nature of the stimulus (Is it loud, soft, hot, dim, large? To what extent does it contrast with other stimuli? Has it been presented repeatedly?), the nature of the receptor (What is its threshold value? Has it undergone adaptation?), and the nature of the perceiver (Has this stimulus been experienced before? Is it expected? Is it of value to the perceiver, something the perceiver wants?).

VISION

Discussing which of our senses is the most important is a pretty silly exercise. Each sense is of value in helping us process information about the environment. (I enjoy eating and think highly of the sense of taste.) It remains the case, nonetheless, that vision *is* a very important sense for humans. Occasionally we even equate our visual experience with truth, or reality, as in, "Seeing is believing." We have noted that the entire occipital lobe of the brain is devoted to the processing of visual information. In this Topic, we'll first consider both the stimulus for vision (light) and the receptor for vision (the eye). Then we'll explore a few perceptual phenomena that involve the visual sense: such matters as the perception of color, space, depth, and motion.

THE STIMULUS FOR VISION: LIGHT

Light is the stimulus for vision. It will be helpful to have an appreciation of the nature of light so that we can understand how it is related to our visual experiences. **Light** is thought of as a *wave form of radiant energy.* What that means is that light *radiates* from its source in the form of *waves* (which we call light waves). Light waves have three important physical characteristics that are related to psychological experience: wave amplitude, wavelength, and wave purity.

light a radiant energy that can be represented in wave form with wavelengths between 380 and 760 nanometers

---

Figure 3.4

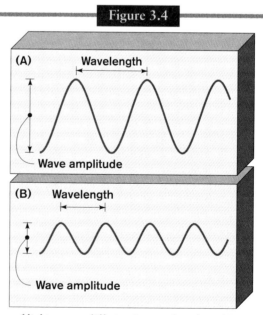

Representations of light waves differing in wavelength and in wave amplitude. Wavelength gives rise to our experience of the hue of a light, whereas wave amplitude determines our experience of brightness.

One of the ways in which light energy may vary is in its intensity. Differences in intensity correspond to differences in the **wave amplitude** of light. The amplitude of a wave is represented by its height. Refer to Figure 3.4 and assume that the two waves represent two different light waves. One of the physical differences between light A and light B is their wave amplitude. Our psychological experience of wave amplitude, or intensity, is **brightness**. The difference between a bright light and a dim light is due to the difference in wave amplitude. In Figure 3.4, A has the higher amplitude and thus would be experienced as brighter. Dimmer-switches that control the brightness of light fixtures are in essence controlling the amplitude of light waves.

Wavelength is the distance between any point in a wave and the corresponding point on the next cycle—from peak to peak, for example. In Figure 3.4, one difference between waves A and B is their wavelength, where A has the longer wavelength. Although it's difficult to imagine distances so small, we *can* measure the length of a light wave. The unit of measurement is the **nanometer (nm)**, which is equal to one-billionth of a meter, or one-millionth of a millimeter.

The human eye responds only to radiant energy in wave form that has a wavelength between roughly 380 and 760 nm. This is the range of energy waves that constitute the visible spectrum. Wave forms of energy with wavelengths shorter than 380 nm (e.g., X rays and ultraviolet rays) are too short to stimulate the receptors in our eyes, and they go unnoticed. Wave forms of energy with wavelengths in excess of 760 nm (e.g., microwaves and radar) do not stimulate the receptor cells in our eyes either.

Wavelength is the attribute of light energy that determines the **hue**, or color, we perceive. As light waves increase from the short 380-nm wavelengths to the long 760-nm lengths, our experience changes—from violet to blue to green to yellow-green to yellow to orange to red along the color spectrum (Figure 3.5). A source of radiant energy with a 700-nm wavelength will be seen as a red light. In fact, that's what a red light *is*. (A bright red light has a high amplitude, and a dim red light a low amplitude, but both have 700-nm wavelengths.) As we can see in Figure 3.5, if a light generated waves 550 nm long, it would be seen as a yellow-green light, and so on. Note that yellow-green is a single hue produced by wavelengths of light 550 nm long. It is *not* some sort of combination of yellow and green. We simply have no other name for this hue, so we call it yellow-green.

Here's an apparently easy problem: I have two lights, one red (700 nm) and the other yellow-green (550 nm). I adjust the *amplitudes* of these lights so that they are equal. They have different hues because their wavelengths are different. What about their brightness? With both amplitudes equal, will the lights appear equally bright?

Actually, they won't. The yellow-green light will appear much brighter than the red one. It will also appear brighter than a blue light of the same amplitude. We say that wavelength and wave amplitude *interact* to produce apparent brightness. Wavelengths in the middle of the spectrum (such as yellow-green) appear brighter than do wavelengths of light from either extreme, *if* their amplitudes are equal. To

wave amplitude *a characteristic of a wave form (the height of a wave) that determines the brightness of light*

brightness *the psychological experience associated with a light's intensity, or wave amplitude*

wavelength *the distance between any point on a wave and the corresponding point on the next cycle of the wave*

nanometer (nm) *one millionth of a millimeter; the unit of measurement for the wavelength of light*

hue *the psychological experience of color associated with a light's wavelength*

Figure 3.5

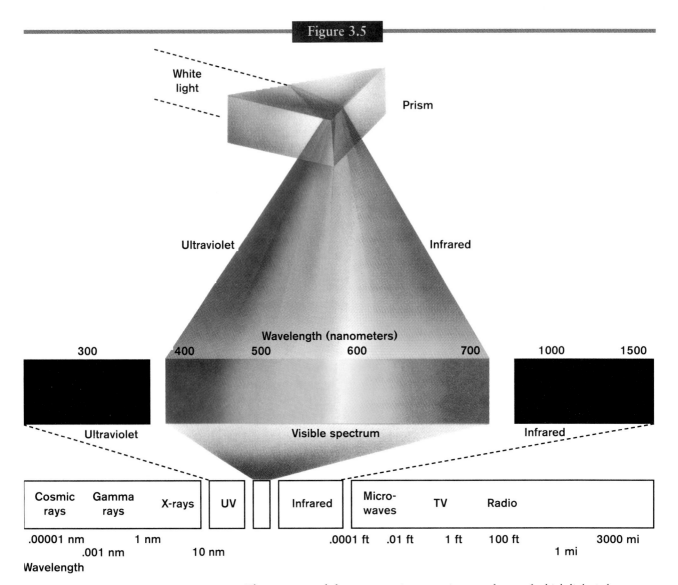

The spectrum of electromagnetic energy in wave form, of which light is but a small segment. Here we see that light is electromagnetic energy with a wavelength between 380 nm and 760 nm. As wavelength increases, our experience of light changes to produce a "rainbow."

be sure, I can get a red light to appear as bright as a yellow-green one, but to do so I'll have to increase its amplitude. Doing so can be expensive, however. Here is a fairly good argument that the lights on emergency vehicles should be yellow-green, not red. With *everything else being equal,* yellow-green lights appear brighter than red ones.

The relationship between wavelength and relative brightness is shown in Figure 3.6. Note: amplitude *does* determine brightness. If you have two red lights, one dim, one bright, the difference between them is a difference in amplitude. *But,* across the visible spectrum, apparent brightness—brightness as judged by a person, not a light

Figure 3.6

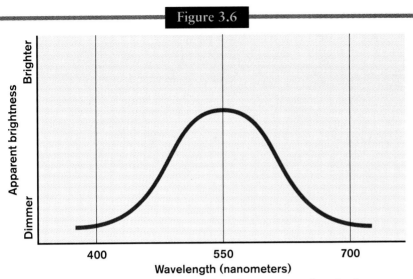

The perceived (apparent) brightness of lights of varying wavelength when wave amplitudes are held equal.

meter—is determined by amplitude *and* wavelength. Now we need to consider a third characteristic of light waves: their degree of purity.

Imagine a light of medium amplitude with all of its wavelengths exactly 700 nm long. The light would appear to be of medium brightness. Because the wavelengths are all 700 nm, it would appear red. More than that, it would appear as a pure, rich red. We call such a light **monochromatic** because it consists of light waves all of one (*mono*) length or hue (*chroma*). In truth, we seldom see such lights outside the laboratory because producing a pure, monochromatic light is expensive. The reddest of lights we see in our everyday experience have other wavelengths of light mixed in with the predominant 700-nm red. (If the 700-nm wave did not predominate, the light wouldn't look red at all.) Even the red light on top of a police car has some violet, green, and yellow wavelengths of light in it.

The physical purity of a light source determines the psychological experience called **saturation**. Pure, monochromatic lights are the most highly saturated; their hue is rich and obvious. As different wavelengths get mixed into a light, it becomes lower and lower in saturation, and starts to look pale and washed out.

What do we call a light that is of the lowest possible saturation, a light consisting of a random mixture of wavelengths of light? By definition, it is **white light**. It is something of a curiosity that white light is in fact as *impure* a light as possible. A pure light has but one wavelength; a white light contains many wavelengths. True white light is as difficult to produce as is a pure monochromatic light. Fluorescent bulbs produce reasonable approximations, but their light contains too many wavelengths from the short, or blue-violet, end of the spectrum. Light from regular incandescent bulbs contains too many light waves from the orange and red end of the spectrum, even if we paint the

monochromatic *literally* one-colored; *a pure light consisting of light waves all of the same wavelength*

saturation the psychological experience *associated with the purity of a light wave; the most saturated lights are monochromatic and the least saturated are white light*

white light *a light of the lowest possible saturation, containing a mixture of all visible wavelengths*

Figure 3.7	
The Relationships Between the Physical Characteristics of Light and Our Psychological Experience of That Light	
Physical characteristic	**Psychological experience**
Wave amplitude (intensity)	Brightness
Wavelength	Hue
Wave purity	Saturation

These two interact.

inside of the bulb with white paint. A prism can take a beam of white light (sunlight is a reasonable approximation) and break it down into its various parts, giving us the experience of a rainbow of hues. Where did all those hues come from? They were there all along, mixed together to form the white light.

We have seen that three physical characteristics of light influence our visual experience. These relationships are summarized in Figure 3.7.

Before You Go On

In what ways do the major physical characteristics of light waves of energy (amplitude, length, and purity) affect our psychological experience of light?

THE RECEPTOR FOR VISION: THE EYE

Vision involves changing light wave energy into the neural energy of the nervous system. This transduction of energy takes place in the eye, yet most of the structures of the eye have little to do with the actual process of transducing light energy into neural energy. Instead, they are there to ensure that light waves that enter the eye are well focused by the time they get back to the layer of cells that responds to them.

Important Structures of the Human Eye

Using Figure 3.8 as a guide, let's trace the path of light as it passes through the eye, ultimately to produce a visual experience. Light enters the eye through the **cornea**. The cornea is the tough, round, virtually transparent outer shell of the eye. Those of you who wear contact lenses float them on your corneas. The cornea has two major functions. One is to protect the delicate structures behind it. The other is to start bending the entering light waves in order to focus an image on the back surface of the eye.

cornea the outermost structure of the eye that protects the eye and begins to focus light waves

Figure 3.8

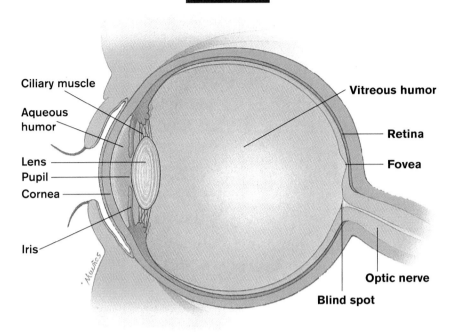

The major structures of the human eye.

Having passed through the cornea, light then travels through the **pupil**, which is an opening in the **iris**. The iris is the part of your eye that is pigmented, or colored. When we say that someone has blue, brown, or green eyes, we are referring to the color of the iris. The iris expands or contracts, changing the size of the pupil. This is a reflexive reaction. Contractions of the iris that change pupil size are usually made in response to the level of light present, opening the pupil wide when small amounts of light are present and reducing its size (protectively) in response to high-intensity lights. Increasing pupil size is also one of the automatic responses that occurs with heightened levels of emotionality—an adaptive reaction to let in as much light as possible.

After the pupil, the next structure light encounters is the **lens**. As in a camera, the main function of the lens of the eye is to *focus* a visual image. Unlike a camera, the lens of the eye changes shape to bring an image into focus, becoming flatter when we try to focus on an object at a distance and becoming fatter, or rounder, when we try to view something up close. This, too, is a reflex. Obviously, lenses are not normally as hard as glass or they wouldn't be able to change their shape. With age, lenses tend to harden, making it difficult to focus and requiring that we use glasses to help out.

Small, powerful muscles, called **ciliary muscles**, push on the lens or relax in order to change the shape of the lens—a process called **accommodation**. Often an image does not focus as it should, either

pupil the opening of the iris, which changes size in relation to the amount of light available and to emotional factors

iris the colored structure of the eye that reflexively opens or closes the pupil

lens the structure behind the iris that changes shape to focus visual images in the eye

ciliary muscles small muscles attached to the lens that control its shape and focusing capability

accommodation in vision, the process in which the shape of the lens is changed by the ciliary muscles to focus an image on the retina

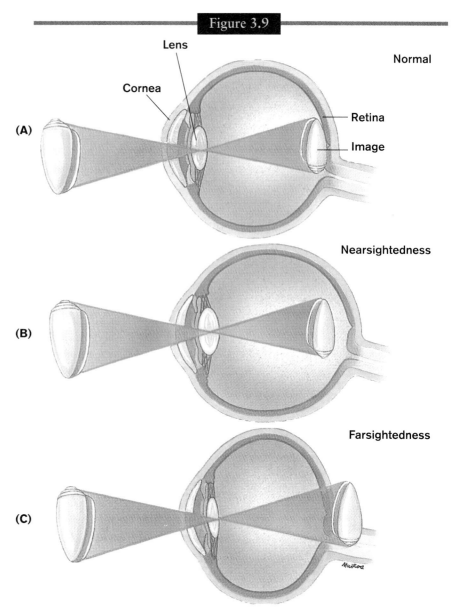

Figure 3.9

Normal

(A)

Cornea

Lens

Retina

Image

Nearsightedness

(B)

Farsightedness

(C)

Sightedness. (A) Normal vision, where the inverted image is focused by the cornea and the lens to fall directly on the retina. (B) Nearsightedness, where the focused image falls short of the receptors in the retina. (C) Farsightedness, where a focused image falls beyond, or behind, the retina.

because of the shape of the lens or a failure of accommodation. Sometimes, even a healthy lens and functioning ciliary muscles still can't get an image to focus because of the shape of the eyeball itself. The result is either nearsightedness or farsightedness. Figure 3.9 shows examples of what happens in these cases.

There is a space between the cornea and the lens filled with a clear fluid called **aqueous humor**. This humor (which means "fluid")

aqueous humor *watery fluid found in the space between the cornea and the lens that nourishes the front of the eye* provides nourishment to the cornea and the other structures at the front of the eye. The aqueous humor is constantly being produced and supplied to the space behind the cornea, filtering out blood to keep the fluid clear. If the fluid cannot easily pass out of this space, pressure builds within the eye, causing distortions in vision or, in extreme cases, blindness. This disorder is known as *glaucoma.*

There is another, larger space *behind* the lens that is also filled with a fluid, or humor. This fluid is called **vitreous humor.** It is not nearly as watery as aqueous humor. It is thick and filled with tiny structures that give it substance. Its major function is to keep the eyeball spherical.

It is at the **retina** of the eye that vision begins to take place. Here, light energy is transduced into neural energy. The retina is really a series of layers of specialized cells at the back surface of the eye. These cells are nerve cells and can be thought of as part of the brain. The location of the retina and its major landmarks are shown in Figure 3.8. Figure 3.10 shows the retina in more detail.

To describe the retina, let's move from the back of the retina toward the front. The layer of cells at the very back of the retina are the receptor cells for vision, the transducers, or **photoreceptors,** of the eye. It is here that light wave energy is changed into neural energy.

There are two types of photoreceptor cells: **rods** and **cones.** They are aptly named because that's just what they look like: small rods and cones. Their tips respond to light wave energy and begin a neural

vitreous humor the thick fluid behind the lens of the eye that helps keep the eyeball spherical

retina layers of cells at the back of the eye that contain the photosensitive rod and cone cells

photoreceptors light-sensitive cells (cones and rods) of the retina that convert light energy into neural energy

rods photosensitive cells of the retina that are most active in low levels of illumination and do not respond differentially to various wavelengths of light

cones photosensitive cells of the retina that operate best at high levels of illumination and that are responsible for color vision

Figure 3.10

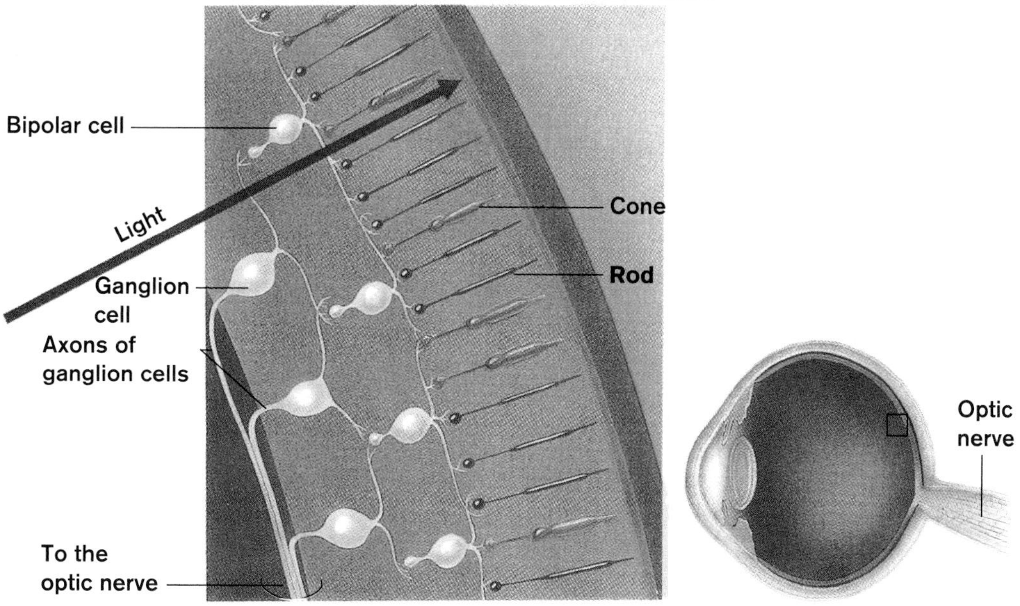

Bipolar cell

Light

Cone

Rod

Ganglion cell

Axons of ganglion cells

To the optic nerve

Optic nerve

The major features of the human retina.

impulse. The impulses travel down the rods and cones and pass on to (form a synapse with) other cells, also arranged in layers. Within these layers there is considerable combination and integration of neural impulses. No rod or cone has a single, direct pathway to the cerebral cortex of the brain. Impulses from many rods and cones are combined within the eye (by *bipolar cells* and *ganglion cells*, among others). Fibers from ganglion cells gather together to form the **optic nerve**, the collection of neurons that leaves the eye and starts back toward other parts of the brain.

The two main features of the retina depicted in Figure 3.8 are the **fovea** and the **blind spot**. The fovea is a small area of the retina where there are very few layers of cells between the entering light and the cone cells that fill the area. There are no rods in the fovea, only cones, which are tightly packed together. Here at the fovea our vision is best, our *acuity*, or ability to discern detail, is best—at least in daylight or in reasonably high levels of illumination. If you were to try to thread a needle, you would want to focus the image of the needle and thread on the fovea.

The blind spot of the retina is where the nerve impulses from the rods and cones, having passed through all of those other layers of cells, exit the eye. At the blind spot, there are no rods or cones—there's nothing there but the optic nerve threading its way back deeper into the brain. Because there are no rods or cones, there is no vision here, which is why this area is called the blind spot. Figure 3.11 shows you how to locate your own blind spot.

More on Rods and Cones and What They Do

Let's now deal with the fact that there are two types of receptor cells in our retinas, rods and cones. Although they are both nerve cells,

optic nerve *the fiber, consisting of many neurons, that leaves the eye and carries impulses to the occipital lobe of the brain*

fovea *the region at the center of the retina, consisting solely of cones, where acuity is best in daylight*

blind spot *the small region of the retina, containing no photoreceptors, where the optic nerve leaves the eye*

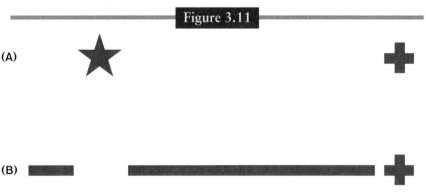

Figure 3.11

(A)

(B)

Two ways to find your blind spot. (A) Close your right eye and stare at the cross (+). Hold the page about a foot from your left eye and slowly move the page around until the star falls on your blind spot and disappears. (B) Close your right eye and stare at the cross. Hold the page about a foot from your left eye and slowly move the page around until the break in the line falls on your blind spot. The line will appear to be unbroken.

These two photos of lifeguard chairs approximate cone vision (daylight, clear, colorful) and rod vision (twilight, hazy, colorless).

rods and cones do not look alike. There are other differences, too. In each eye, there are about 120 million rods, but only 6 million cones. They are not distributed evenly throughout the retina. Cones are concentrated in the center of the retina, in the fovea. Rods are concentrated in a band or ring around the fovea, out toward the periphery. These observations have led psychologists to wonder if rods and cones have different functions.

In fact, cones function best in medium to high levels of illumination (such as in daylight) and are primarily responsible for our experience of color. On the other hand, rods operate best under conditions of reduced illumination. They are more sensitive to low-intensity light. Our rods do not discriminate among wavelengths of light, which means that rods do not contribute to our appreciation of color.

Some of the evidence supporting these claims can be verified by our own experiences. Don't you find it difficult to distinguish among different colors at night or in the dark? The next time you are at the movies eating some pieces of candy that are of different colors, see if you can tell them apart without holding them up to the light of the projector. You probably won't be able to tell a green piece from a red one because they all appear black. You can't discriminate colors very well in a dark movie theater because you are seeing them primarily with your rods, which are very good at seeing in the reduced illumination of the theater but don't differentiate among wavelengths of light.

If you are looking for something small outside at night, you'll probably not see it if you look directly at it. Imagine you're changing a tire along the road at night. You're replacing the wheel and can't

Nocturnal animals, such as this timber wolf, have a high concentration of rods in their retinas.

find one of the lug nuts you know is there someplace in the gravel. If you were to look directly at it, the image of the nut would fall on your fovea. Remember, your fovea consists almost entirely of cones. Cones do not operate well in relative darkness, and you'll not see the nut. To have the best chance of finding it, you have to get the image of the nut to fall on the periphery of your eye, where your rods are concentrated.

One of the reasons nocturnal animals (such as many varieties of owls) function so well at night is that they can see well in the dark. They see so well because their retinas are packed with rods. Such animals usually have no fovea, or at least have fewer cones and are demonstrably color blind. (How you might test the color vision of an owl is discussed in Topic 5B, page 238.)

Let's consider just one other piece of evidence that supports the idea that our rods and cones provide us with two distinct types of visual experience. Let's take a closer look at what happens during dark adaptation. Dark adaptation is the process of our eyes becoming more sensitive (our thresholds lowering) as we spend time in the dark.

Figure 3.12 is a graphic representation of the dark-adaptation process. It shows us that with time spent in the dark, our sensitivity increases, or our threshold decreases. At first, we can see only very bright lights (say, the light reflected from a movie screen), then we can see dimmer lights (reflected from people in the theater), and then still dimmer ones (reflected from pieces of candy perhaps) are detected as our threshold drops. The entire process takes about 30 minutes.

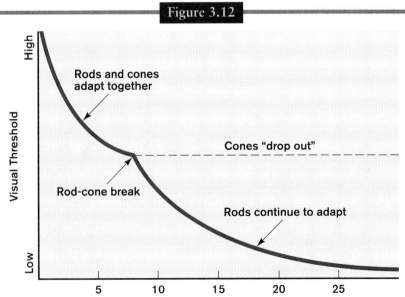

Figure 3.12

The dark-adaptation curve. At first, both rods and cones lower thresholds (increase their sensitivity). After 6 to 8 minutes, the cones have become as sensitive as possible, and drop out, leaving the rods alone to increase visual sensitivity.

But there is something strange going on. The dark-adaptation curve is not a smooth, regular one. At about the 7-minute mark, there is a change in the shape of the curve. This break in the smoothness of the curve is called the *rod-cone break*. At first, for 6 or 7 minutes, both rods *and* cones increase their sensitivity (represented by the first part of the curve). But our cones are basically daylight receptors. They're not cut out for seeing in the dark, and after a few minutes, they have become as sensitive as they are going to get. Rods, on the other hand, keep on lowering their threshold, becoming more and more sensitive (represented by the part of the curve after the "break").

Now that we've reviewed the nature of light and the basic structures of the eye, we'll finish this section by examining how the neural impulses that leave our retinas make their way back to the occipital lobes of the cerebral cortex.

Before You Go On

List the major structures of the eye, and describe the function of each.

How and why can we claim that rods and cones provide us with two distinct types of visual experience?

The Visual Pathway After the Retina

To keep track of what happens to impulses once they have left the eyes at their respective blind spots, follow along with Figure 3.13. Recall that considerable visual processing takes place within the layers of the retina; there are, after all, many more rods and cones in the retina than there are ganglion cell fibers leaving it. Visual information continues to be altered as it races back to the visual area of the occipital lobe of the cerebral cortex.

One challenge in tracing the pathway of nerve fibers between the eyes and the cortex is simply a matter of sorting out left and right. To do so, I need to introduce the concept of left and right *visual field*. All this means is that when you look out at the world, everything off to your left is said to be in your left visual field, whereas everything you see off to your right is said to be in your right visual field. Figure 3.13 is drawn so that the left visual field is red and the right visual field is purple. What happens is that stimuli located in our left visual field end up in our right occipital lobe, and stimuli from our right visual field end up in our left occipital lobe.

The sorting out of which fibers in the optic nerve get directed where occurs largely in the **optic chiasma**. Look at Figure 3.13 again and notice that, in fact, each of our eyes receives light energy from *both* visual fields. So what happens is this: light that enters our left

optic chiasma the location in the brain where impulses from light in the left visual field cross to the right side of the brain, and impulses from light in the right visual field cross to the left side of the brain

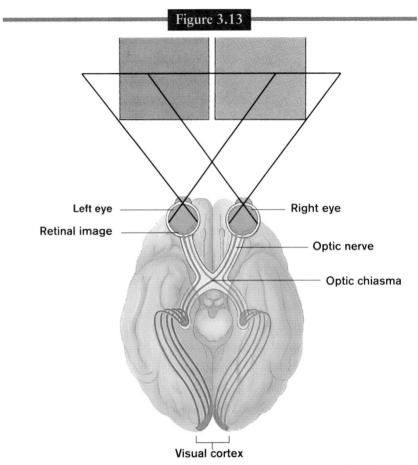

Figure 3.13

Left eye
Retinal image
Right eye
Optic nerve
Optic chiasma
Visual cortex

In keeping with the principle of cross-laterality, stimuli from the left visual field are sent to the right occipital lobe for processing, whereas stimuli from the right visual field are sent to the left occipital lobe.

eye from the left initiates neural impulses that cross at the chiasma and go over to the right side of the brain, whereas light that enters our left eye from the right visual field initiates neural impulses that go straight back to the left hemisphere. Now see if you can describe in words what happens to light that enters the right eye.

From the optic chiasma, nerve fibers pass through other centers in the brain. For example, there is, for each side of the brain, a cluster of cells, a superior colliculus, that controls the movement of our eyes over a patterned stimulus, perhaps fixing our gaze on some aspect of the pattern. Beyond the superior colliculus, nerve cells form synapses with neurons in the thalamus, which, as we saw in Chapter 2, project neural impulses to the layers of cells in the visual cortex of the occipital lobe.

Perhaps the most critical thing to realize about this brief description is that vision doesn't really happen in our eyes. Yes, the eye is the structure that contains the transducers that convert light energy into neural impulses, but the actual experience of "seeing" a stimulus is something that happens in our brains. Our brains reassemble in our awareness one complete visual field that we experience as continuous, not divided into right and left. To be sure, the detection, recognition, and interpretation of patterns of light, shade, color, and motion are functions of the cerebral cortex.

Before You Go On

Briefly trace the path of impulses from each eye to the cerebral cortex.

COLOR VISION AND COLOR BLINDNESS

Explaining how the eye codes or responds to various intensities of light is not difficult. Coding is handled largely by the frequency of the firing of the receptor cells in the retina. High-intensity lights cause more rapid firings of neural impulses than do low-intensity lights. It is also sensible that high-intensity lights stimulate more cells to fire than do lights of low intensity. How the eye codes differing wavelengths of light to produce differing experiences of color, however, is another story. Here things are not simple at all. Two theories of color vision have received research support, even though both were proposed many years ago. As is often the case with competing theories that try to explain the same phenomenon, both are probably partially correct.

The older of the two theories of color vision is the *trichromatic theory*. It was first proposed by Thomas Young very early in the nineteenth century and was revised by Hermann von Helmholtz, the noted physiologist, about fifty years later. As its name suggests, the *trichromatic* theory proposes that the eye contains *three* distinct receptors for color.

Although there is considerable overlap, each receptor responds best to one of three **primary hues** of light: red, green, and blue. These hues are primary because by the careful combination of the three, all other colors can be produced. You see this in action every day on your TV screen. The picture on your TV screen consists of a pattern of very small dots, each one being either red, green, or blue. From these three wavelengths alone, all other colors are constructed, or integrated. (Don't get confused here with the primary colors of *pigment*, which are red, blue, and yellow. These are the three colors of paint, dye, pastel, and so on that can be mixed together to form all other pigment colors. Our eyes respond to light, not to pigment, and the three primary hues of light are red, green and blue.)

Because the sensitivity of the three types of receptors overlaps, when our eyes are stimulated by a nonprimary color—say, orange—the orange-hued light will stimulate each receptor to varying degrees

primary hues red, green, and blue; those colors of light from which all others can be produced

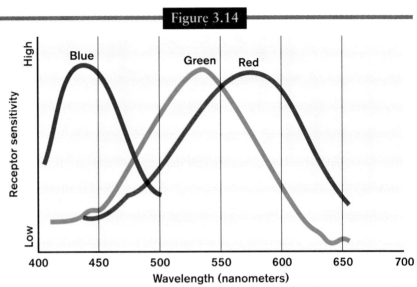

The relative sensitivities of three types of cones to lights of differing wavelengths. Although there is considerable overlap, each type is maximally sensitive to wavelengths corresponding to the primary hues of light: blue, green, and red.

to produce the experience of orange. What gives this theory credibility is that *there really are* such receptor cells in the human retina. Obviously, they are cones (which are responsible for color vision). The relative sensitivity of these three cone systems is shown in Figure 3.14.

Ewald Hering thought the Young-Helmholtz theory left a bit to be desired, and in 1870 he proposed a theory of his own, the *opponent-process theory*. Hering's position is that there are three *pairs* of visual mechanisms that respond to different wavelengths of light. One mechanism is a blue-yellow processor, one a red-green processor, and the third deals with black-white differences.

Each mechanism is capable of responding to *either* of the two hues that give it its name, but not both. That is, the blue-yellow processor can respond to blue *or* to yellow, but can't handle both at the same time. The second mechanism responds to red *or* green, but not both. The third codes brightness. Thus, the members of each pair work to oppose each other, giving the theory its name. If blue is excited, yellow is inhibited. If red is excited, green is inhibited. A light may appear to be a mixture of red and yellow perhaps, but cannot be seen as a mixture of red *and* green because both red and green cannot be excited at the same time. (It is difficult to imagine what a "reddish green" or a "bluish yellow" would look like, isn't it? Can you picture a light that is bright and dim at the same time?)

Although the opponent-process theory may at first appear overly complicated, there are some strong signs that Hering was on the right track. In the first place, excitatory-inhibitory mechanisms such as he proposed for red-green, blue-yellow, and black-white have been found. They are not at the level of rods and cones in the retina (as Hering had thought), but at the layer of the ganglion cells (see Figure 3.10) and in a small portion of the thalamus.

Some support for Hering's theory comes from our experiences with *negative afterimages.* If you stare at a bright green figure for a few minutes and then shift your gaze to a white surface, you will notice an image of a red figure. Where did that come from? The explanation for the appearance of this image is as follows: while you were staring at the green figure, the green component of the red-green process fatigued because of all the stimulation it was getting. When you stared at the white surface, both the red and green components of the process were equally stimulated, but because the green component was fatigued, the red predominated, producing the experience of seeing a red figure. Figure 3.15 gives an example for you to try.

Evidence supporting both theories of normal vision has come from studies of persons with color vision defects. Defective color vision of some sort occurs in about 8 percent of males and slightly less than 0.5 percent of females. Most cases are genetic in origin. It makes sense that if cones are our receptor cells for the discrimination of color, people with some deficiency in color perception should have a problem with their cones. Such logic is certainly consistent with the Young-Helmholtz theory.

In fact, for the most common of the color vision deficiencies (*dichromatism*) there is a noticeable lack of one particular type of cone; which type depends on the color that is "lost." Those people who are red-green color blind, for instance, have trouble telling the difference between red and green. People with this type of color blindness also have trouble distinguishing yellow from either red or green. The deficiency is not in actually seeing reds or greens. It is in distinguishing reds and greens from other colors. Put another way, someone who is red-green color blind can clearly see a bright red apple; it just looks no different from a bright green apple.

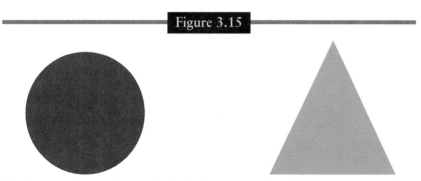

Figure 3.15

To illustrate the experience of color fatigue, or negative afterimages, stare at the blue circle for about 30 seconds; then quickly shift your gaze to a plain white surface. You should see the same figure, but it will appear yellow because the corresponding blue receptors are fatigued. Now try the same thing with the green triangle. What color did you see when you shifted your gaze?

Because cone cells have been found in the retina that respond differentially to red, blue, and green light, we cannot dismiss the trichromatic theory. Because there are cells that do operate the way the opponent-process theory predicts, we cannot dismiss this theory either. Well, which one is right? Probably both. Our experience of color likely depends on the interaction of cone cells *and* opponent-process cells within our visual pathway—a marvelous system indeed.

Before You Go On

Briefly summarize the trichromatic and
the opponent-process theories of color vision.

PERCEPTUAL ORGANIZATION

One of our basic perceptual reactions to the environment is to select certain stimuli from among all those that strike our receptors so that they may be processed further. A related perceptual process involves organizing and interpreting the bits and pieces of experience presented by our senses into meaningful, organized wholes. We do not really hear the individual sounds of speech; we organize them and perceive them as words, phrases, and sentences. Our visual experience is not one of bits of color and light and dark, as recorded at the retina, but of identifiable objects and events. We don't perceive a warm pat on the back as responses from hundreds of individual receptors in our skin.

As implied by these examples, organizing stimulus inputs is a perceptual process that applies to all of our senses, not just to vision. But, because so much of the information we get about the world *is* visual, it is reasonable to take up this issue here, in Topic 3B. In this section, most of our examples will involve the organization of visual information, but when appropriate, I'll include examples that involve our other senses.

Perceptual organization, or grouping, was a process of considerable interest to the Gestalt psychologists. Perhaps you recall from Chapter 1 that **gestalt** is a German word that, roughly translated, means something like "configuration," or "whole," or "totality." One forms a gestalt when one sees the overall scheme of things. If you have a general idea of how something works, or can appreciate the general nature of something without overly attending to details, you have formed a gestalt.

One of the most basic principles of Gestalt psychology is that of the **figure-ground relationship**. Of all the stimuli in your environment at any one time, those you attend to and group together are said to be *figures*, whereas all the rest become the *ground*. As you focus your attention on the words on this page, they form figures against the ground (or background, if you prefer) provided by the rest of the

gestalt *whole, totality, configuration; where the whole (gestalt) is seen as more than the sum of its parts*

figure-ground relationship *the Gestalt psychology principle that stimuli are selected and perceived as figures against a ground (background)*

Figure 3.16

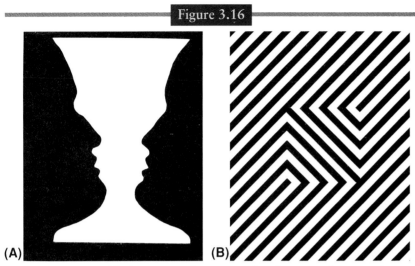

(A) **(B)**

(A) A classic, reversible figure-ground pattern. What do you see here? A white vase or two black profiles facing each other? Can you clearly see both figures at the same time? (B) After a few moments' inspection, a small square should emerge as a figure against a ground of diagonal lines.

page. When you hear your instructor's voice during a lecture, that voice is the figure against the ground of all other sounds in the room. Figure 3.16 provides a couple of visual examples of the figure-ground relationship.

Gestalt psychologists were interested in factors that influence our attention to stimuli in the environment. They were also intrigued by how perception enables us to group and organize stimuli together to form meaningful gestalts. As was the case for perceptual selection, many factors influence how we organize our perceptual worlds. Again, it will be useful to consider both stimulus factors (bottom-up processing) and personal factors (top-down processing).

Stimulus Factors

By stimulus factors, I am referring to those characteristics of stimuli that help us perceive them as being organized together in one figure or gestalt. We'll consider five of the most influential: proximity, similarity, continuity, common fate, and closure.

Glance quickly at Figure 3.17(A). Without giving it much thought, what did you see there? A bunch of Xs yes, but more than that, there were two identifiable groups of Xs, weren't there? The group of Xs on the left seems somehow separate from the group on the right, whereas the Xs within each group seem to go together, illustrating what the Gestalt psychologists called **proximity**, or *contiguity*. What this means is that events occurring close together in space or time are perceived as belonging together as part of the same figure. In

proximity the Gestalt principle of organization claiming that stimuli will be perceived as belonging together if they occur together in space or time

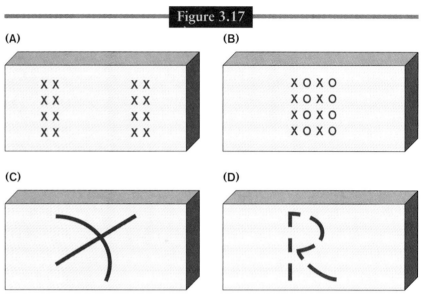

(A) These Xs are organized as two groups, not as four rows or four columns because of proximity. (B) Here we see two columns of Os and two columns of Xs because of similarity. (C) We tend to see this figure as two intersecting lines—one straight, the other curved—because of continuity. (D) This figure is perceived as an R, not because it is a well-drawn representation, but because of closure.

Figure 3.17(A), it's difficult to see the Xs as falling into four rows or four columns. They are best organized as two groups of eight Xs each.

Proximity operates on more than just visual stimuli. For example, sounds that occur together (are contiguous) in speech are perceived as going together to form words or phrases. In written language there are physical spaces between words on the printed page; with spoken language there are (usually) very brief pauses between words. Thunder and lightning usually occur together, the sound of thunder following shortly after our experience of the lightning. As a result of our experience, it's rather difficult to think about lightning without also thinking about thunder.

Now glance at Figure 3.17(B) and describe what you see there. Here we have a collection of Xs and Os that are clearly organized into a simple pattern—as two columns of Xs and two of Os. Perceiving rows of alternating Xs and Os is difficult. This demonstrates the Gestalt principle of **similarity**. Stimulus events that are in some way alike, or have properties in common, tend to be grouped together in our perception—a "birds of a feather are perceived together" sort of thing.

The Gestalt principle of **continuity** (or good continuation) is operating when we tend to see things as ending up consistent with the way they started off. Figure 3.17(C) illustrates this point with a simple line drawing. The clearest, easiest way to organize this drawing is as two

similarity *the Gestalt principle of organization claiming that stimuli will be perceived together if they share some common characteristics*

continuity *the Gestalt principle of organization claiming that a stimulus or a movement will be perceived as continuing in the same smooth direction as first established*

separate but intersecting lines—one straight, the other curved. It's difficult to imagine seeing this figure any other way.

The Gestalt principle of continuity may also account for some of the ways in which we organize our perceptions of people. Aren't we particularly surprised when a young man who was a hardworking, award-winning honor student throughout high school suddenly does poorly at college and flunks out? That's not the way we like to view the world working. We would not be as surprised to find that another student, who barely made it through high school, failed to pass at college. This is a lot like continuity, or good continuation: we want to see things continue as they started off; largely a matter of "as the twig is bent, so grows the tree."

Common fate describes our tendency to group together in the same figure those elements of a scene that appear to move together in the same direction and at the same speed. Common fate is not unlike continuity, but it applies to moving stimuli. The next time you get to look down on traffic from a tall building, notice how clear it is to see the lines of traffic moving—as if all vehicles were tied together—in opposite directions, up and down the street. Remember our example of a chipmunk sitting motionless on the leaves in the woods? As long as both the chipmunk and the leaves remain still, the chipmunk won't be noticed. When it moves, all of the parts of the chipmunk move together—sharing a common fate—and we see it scurrying away.

One of the most commonly encountered Gestalt principles of organization is called **closure**. This is our tendency to fill in gaps in our perceptual world. Closure provides an excellent example of what I mean when I say that perception is an *active* process. It underscores the notion that we constantly seek to make sense out of our environment, whether that environment presents us with sensible stimuli or not. This concept is illustrated by Figure 3.17(D). At a glance, anyone would tell you that this figure is the letter *R*, but of course it is not. That's not the way you make an *R*. However, it may be the way we *perceive* an *R* due to closure.

As an example of closure in hearing, tape-record a casual conversation with a friend. Then write down exactly what was said during the conversation. A truly faithful transcription will reveal that many words and sounds were left out. Even though they were not actually there as stimuli, they were not missed by the listener because he or she filled in the gaps (closure) and understood what was being said.

A phenomenon that many psychologists believe is a special case of closure is our perception of **subjective contours**, in which arrangements of lines and patterns enable us to see figures that are not actually there. If that sounds a bit spooky, look at Figure 3.18, in which we have an example of subjective contour. In Figure 3.18 you can "see" a triangle that is so clearly there it nearly jumps off the page. There is no one accepted explanation for subjective contours (Bradley & Dumais, 1975; Coren, 1972; Kanizsa, 1976; Rock, 1986), but it seems that the phenomenon is a good example of our perceptual processes filling in gaps in our perceptual world in order to provide us with sensible information.

common fate the Gestalt principle of organization claiming that we group together, within the same figure, elements of a scene that move together in the same direction and at the same speed

closure the Gestalt principle of organization claiming that we tend to perceive incomplete figures as whole, as complete

subjective contours the perception of a contour (a line or plane) that is not there, but is suggested by other aspects of a scene

Figure 3.18

An example of subjective contours.

Personal Factors

We can cover the personal factors that influence perceptual organization rather quickly because they are the same as those that influence perceptual selection: motivation, expectation, and past experience. We perceive stimuli as going together, as part of the same gestalt or figure, because we want to, because we expect to, or because we have perceived them together in the past.

I can think of no better example of the influence of personal factors on perceptual organization than the story at the opening of this chapter. Remember the classroom demonstration with the loud, attacking graduate student and the professor? It was the professor who had the gun all along, but virtually every one of the nearly six hundred witnesses organized the gun into the hands of the enraged student. No one was *mentally set* for, or expected, the professor to bring a gun to class. No one *wanted* to see their professor with a gun. And no one had ever *experienced* a professor bringing a gun to class. (Seeing crazed students with guns is not a common experience either, but with television and movies, it's certainly a more probable one.) Paying attention, or stimulus *selection*, was not at issue here. Everyone saw the gun. The students' reports of their perceptions differed from reality in terms of how they *organized* the gun in that classroom scene.

How we organize our experience of the world depends on several factors. Our perception that some stimuli go together with other stimuli to form coherent figures is a process influenced in part by characteristics of the stimuli themselves (such as their proximity or similarity), and by our own personal motives, expectations, and past experiences.

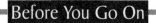

Before You Go On

**List stimulus and personal factors that determine
how we organize stimuli in perception.**

THE PERCEPTION OF DEPTH AND DISTANCE

Perception is a more complex and active process than is the simple reception of information we call sensation. Perception requires that we select and organize stimulus information. Perception involves recognizing, identifying, and assigning meaning to stimulus events. One of the ways in which we interpret a visual stimulus is to note not only *what* it is we are seeing, but *where* it happens to be. We perceive the world for what it is—three-dimensional. As long as we are paying attention (surely a required perceptual process), we don't fall off cliffs or run into buildings. We know with considerable accuracy just how far we are from objects in our environment. What is remarkable about this ability is that the light reflected from objects and events in our environment falls on *two*-dimensional retinas. The depth and distance in our world is not something we directly *sense;* it is something we *perceive.*

The ability to judge depth and distance accurately is an adaptive skill that plays an important role in determining many of our actions. Our ability to make such judgments reflects the fact that we are simultaneously responding to a large number of clues or cues to depth and distance. Some cues are built into our visual systems and are referred to as *ocular cues,* whereas others, called *physical cues,* have more to do with our appreciation of the physical environment.

Ocular Cues

Some of the cues we get about distance and depth reflect the way our eyes work. Cues that involve both eyes are called *binocular cues* (*bi* means "two"); those cues that only require one eye are called *monocular cues* (*mono* means "one").

Binocular cues for depth result from the fact that our eyes are separated. When we look at a nearby three-dimensional object, each eye gets a somewhat different view of it. Hold a pen with a clip on it a few feet in front of your eyes. Rotate the pen until the clip can be viewed by the left eye, but not the right. (You check that by closing first one eye, then the other, as you rotate the pen.) Now each eye (retina) is getting a different (disparate) view of the same object. This phenomenon is called **retinal disparity**. It is a cue that what we are looking at must be solid or three-dimensional. Otherwise, each eye would see the same image, not two disparate ones (Fig. 3.19).

Another binocular cue to depth and distance is **convergence**—the action of our eyes turning inward, toward each other, when we view something up close. Convergence reflects the fact that we know how our eyes are aligned in our heads, even if we seldom pay much attention to it. As we gaze off into the distance, our two eyes aim outward in almost parallel fashion. As we focus our view on objects close to us, our two eyes come together, or converge, and we simply interpret that convergence as an indication that what we are looking at is close to us. Convergence is also illustrated in Figure 3.19.

The rest of the cues we'll consider are monocular. (Even the physical cues that follow are often referred to as monocular cues because they can be appreciated by persons who can see with but one eye.) A unique monocular cue, at least for relatively short distances, is **accommodation**. This process, you'll remember, is the changing of the shape of the lens, by the ciliary muscles, to focus images on the retina. When we focus on distant objects, accommodation flattens our lens, and when we focus on nearby objects, our lens gets rounder or fatter, thanks to the action of the ciliary muscles. Although the process is reflexive and occurs automatically, our brain can react to the activity of our ciliary muscles in terms of the distance of an object from our eyes. That is, our brain knows what our ciliary muscles are doing to focus an image and interprets these actions in terms of distance.

retinal disparity the phenomenon in which each retina receives a different (disparate) view of the same three-dimensional object

Figure 3.19

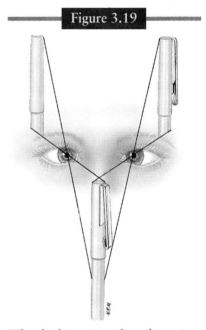

When looking at one three-dimensional object, the right eye sees a slightly different image than does the left eye—a phenomenon called retinal disparity. *This disparity gives us a cue that the object we are viewing is three-dimensional. Here we also note* convergence—*the fact that our eyes turn toward each other when we view an object close to us.*

convergence the tendency of the eyes to move toward each other as we focus on objects close up

accommodation in vision, the process in which the shape of the lens is changed by the ciliary muscles to focus an image on the retina

Figure 3.20

Although we know that the sides of the road are parallel, they appear to come together in the distance—an example of linear perspective.

Accommodation does not function as an effective cue for distances beyond arm's length because the changes in the activity of the ciliary muscles in such cases are too slight to be noticed. But it is within arm's length that accurate decisions about distance are most critical.

Physical Cues

The physical cues to distance and depth are those we get from the structure of our environment. These cues are sometimes called *pictorial cues* because they are used by artists to create the impression of three-dimensionality on a two-dimensional canvas or paper. Here are some of the most important.

1. *Linear perspective* (see Figure 3.20): As you stand in the middle of a road, looking off into the distance, the sides of the road—which you know to be parallel—seem to come together in the distance. Using this pictorial cue in drawing obviously takes some time and experience to develop.

2. *Interposition* (see Figure 3.21): This cue to distance reflects our appreciation that objects in the foreground tend to cover, or partially hide from view, objects in the background, and not vice versa. It seems a strange thing to contemplate, but one of the reasons I know that people sitting in the back of a classroom are farther away from me than people sitting in the front row is the information that I get from interposition. People (and other objects) in the front partially block my view of the people sitting behind them.

Figure 3.21

Interposition *occurs when objects in the foreground partially cover or obscure objects farther away.*

Figure 3.22

Although all of these hot air balloons are about the same size, those in the distance project much smaller images on our retinas, demonstrating the importance of relative size *as a cue to distance.*

3. *Relative size* (see Figure 3.22): This is a commonly used clue to our judgment of distance. As it happens, very few stimuli in this world change their size, but a lot of things get nearer to or farther away from us. So, everything else being equal, we tend to judge the object that produces the larger retinal image as being closer to us.

4. *Texture gradient* (see Figure 3.23): Standing on a gravel road, looking down at your feet, you can clearly make out the details of the texture of the roadway. You can see individual pieces of gravel. But as you look on down the road, the texture gradually changes, details giving way to a smooth blending of a textureless surface. We interpret this gradual change (which is what *gradient* means) in texture as indicating a gradual change in distance.

5. *Patterns of shading* (see Figure 3.24): Drawings that do not use shading look flat and two-dimensional. Children eventually learn that if they want their pictures to look lifelike, they should shade in tree trunks and apples and show them as casting shadows. Two-dimensional objects do not cast shadows, and how objects create

Gradients of texture *provide cues to distance because we can more clearly see the details of objects close to us.*

patterns of light and shade can tell us a great deal about their shape and solidity.

6. *Motion parallax:* This rather technical-sounding label names something with which we are all familiar. The clearest example may occur when we are in a car, looking out a side window. Even if the car is going at a modest speed, the nearby utility poles and fence

We see depth and distance in this image of sand dunes largely because patterns of light and shadow *provide us with information about the three-dimensionality of objects in our environment.*

posts seem to race by. Objects farther away from the car seem to be moving more slowly, and mountains or trees way off in the distance seem not to be moving at all. This difference in apparent motion is known as motion parallax.

In Chapter 8, we will discuss the development of depth perception and the extent to which it is a learned or an innate process. But now, in this context, I need to note that even so "natural" a reaction as perceiving depth and distance is susceptible to cultural constraints. I'll mention just two classic examples. Turnbull (1961) reported that the Bambuti people of the African Congo live so much of their lives in the dense Ituri Forest that they seldom can see much farther than 100 feet. When Turnbull first took his Bambuti guide out of the forest onto the open plains, the guide, Kenge, was disoriented with regard to cues for distance. Kenge thought that buffalo grazing a few miles away were, in fact, tiny insects, responding more to retinal size than relative size as a cue to distance.

As a second example, take a look at Figure 3.25. If the man with the spear was trying to kill an animal, which animal would it be? Because you are responding to well-known pictorial depth cues such as relative size and interposition, the answer is obvious: the antelope. When pictures such as this one were shown to persons from remote areas of Africa, a surprising number failed to react to these "standard" depth cues and responded that the hunter was trying to kill the elephant (Deregowski, 1972, 1973; Hudson, 1960). In this example, the problem was not with judging depth and distance in the real world, but in the interpretation of physical cues as represented in a picture or a drawing (Serpell & Deregowski, 1980). With just a little bit of training in how the real, physical world can be represented in

Figure 3.25

Which animal—the antelope or the elephant—is the hunter about to spear? One's response to this question depends on the interpretation of physical or pictorial cues to depth and distance. (Adapted from "Pictorial Perception and Culture," by Jan Deregowski. Copyright © 1972 by Scientific American, Inc. All rights reserved.)

pictures or drawings, most cultural differences in the perception of depth disappear (Mshelia & Lapidus, 1990).

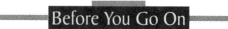

Name and describe some of the cues that inform
us about depth and distance.

THE PERCEPTION OF MOTION

As an object moves across our field of view—say, from right to left—how do we *know* that the object is moving? At first you may feel like ignoring what appears to be such a simple question. If you think about it for a while, you'll come to realize that our perception of motion is a complex process.

Perceiving Real Motion

As long as our heads, bodies, and eyes are still, the answer to our question of how we know a stimulus is moving *is* fairly simple. Light reflected from a moving object produces an image on the retina that successively stimulates adjoining rods and cones—stimulation we interpret (perceive) as motion.

Of course, our eyes, heads, and bodies are seldom perfectly still. As we scan a room, for example, images of the objects in the room stimulate successive rods and cones on the retina, but we don't see everything in the room as moving. Our brain is able to compensate for the movements of our eyes, head, and body (Wallach, 1987).

Our judgments of motion are influenced by details we seldom think about. All else being equal, we will tend to see small objects as moving faster than larger ones, even if their actual speeds are the same. Objects seen moving against a plain, empty background are perceived as moving more slowly than when they move against a patterned background (Gregory, 1977).

We have already discussed how factors such as motivation and expectations affect the organization of our perceptions. They also affect our perception of motion. First we see a sleek, bright red sports car, driven by a teenager, traveling down the street. It is followed soon after by an old clunker, driven by an elderly woman. If both cars were, in fact, traveling at the same rate of speed, we'd be more likely to perceive the first car as going faster. Notice how these judgments are yet another example of top-down processing. That is, our judgment is not based solely on the information provided us by our senses. Our perception of speed is also influenced by our experiences with teenagers, the elderly, sports cars, and clunkers.

The Perception of Apparent Motion

As interesting as our perception of real motion is, even more intriguing is our perception of motion when in fact there isn't any. When our perceptions (experiences) are at odds with what we know as reality, we are experiencing an **illusion**. Two classic illusions of motion are the phi phenomenon and the autokinetic effect.

The **phi phenomenon** is the illusion created when stationary lights flash on and off in sequence. This illusion can be illustrated with just two lights. If two equally bright lights of the same color flash on and off alternately, it is very easy to see them as one light moving back and forth. The phi phenomenon accounts for our perception of the movement of lights in theater marquees or on large signs. Consider Figure 3.26. The arrow may look as if it is moving through space, even though we know it is securely fastened to the wall. Perhaps you recognize this as a subset of the Gestalt principle of closure: we fill in the gaps between the flashing stimuli and see them as moving.

The **autokinetic effect** is the apparent movement of a stationary pinpoint of light in an otherwise dark environment. You might want to construct the apparatus for demonstrating this illusion yourself. To do so, first locate a reasonably large room you can completely darken. Get a good flashlight and cover the lens with black paper or tape so that no light escapes. Poke a very small hole in the paper or tape covering so that only a small pinpoint of light can be seen. Secure the light at one end of the room, with the hole pointed out toward the center of the room. Turn off all lights except for your flashlight. Within seconds a strange thing happens as you stare at that stationary point of light: it starts to move and float around. Even though you know very well that the light is stationary, it will appear to move.

Psychologists do not yet have a complete explanation for this phenomenon. The most commonly accepted view is that the apparent movement is caused by very small head and body movements (e.g., Pola & Martin, 1977; Post & Leibowitz, 1985). As you try to focus on the light, your eyes, head, and body move—drifting slowly—which causes the pinpoint of light to cast an image that moves across your retina. Because the image moves across the retina, and you do not feel your body moving, your brain perceives the light as moving.

illusion a perception that is at odds with (different from) what we know as physical reality

phi phenomenon the visual illusion of the apparent motion of stationary lights flashing on and off alternately

autokinetic effect the visual illusion of apparent motion of a stationary pinpoint of light in an otherwise dark environment

Figure 3.26

Although the individual lights in the "arrow" are stationary, the rapid consecutive flashing of them creates the illusion of motion. This is an example of the phi phenomenon.

Before You Go On

What are two illusions of motion and how are they produced?

THE CONSTANCY OF VISUAL PERCEPTION

Perceptual constancies help us organize and interpret the stimulus input we get from our senses. Because of the *constancy* of perception, we recognize a familiar object as being the same regardless of how far away it is, the angle from which we view it, or the color or intensity of the light reflected from it. You can recognize your textbook whether you view it from a distance or close up, straight on or from an angle, in a dimly or brightly lighted room, or in blue, red, or white light; it is still your textbook, and you will perceive it as such regardless of how your senses detect it. If it were not for perceptual constancy, every individual sensation might be perceived as a new experience and little would appear familiar to you.

Perceptual Constancy

size constancy the tendency to see objects as being of constant size regardless of the size of the retinal image

I have already mentioned **size constancy**—the tendency to see objects of constant size regardless of the size of the retinal image. A friend standing close to you may fill your visual field. At a distance, the image of the same person may take up only a fraction of your visual field. The size of the image on your retina may be significantly different, but you know very well that your friend has not shrunk but has simply moved farther away. Our tendency to view objects as remaining the same size depends on several factors, most importantly the quality of the depth perception cues available to us and our familiarity with the stimulus object.

shape constancy the tendency to see objects as being of constant shape regardless of the shape of the retinal image

Shape constancy refers to our perception of objects as maintaining their shape even though the retinal image they cast may change. Shape constancy may be simply demonstrated with any familiar object—say, the nearest door in your field of view. As you look at that door from various angles, the shape of the image of the door on your retina changes radically. Straight on it appears to be a rectangle; partially open, the image is that of a trapezoid; from the edge, fully open, the retinal image is of a straight line. Regardless of the retinal image, because of shape constancy, you still see that object as a door. (See Figure 3.27.)

brightness constancy the tendency to see objects as being of constant brightness regardless of the amount or type of light available

Because of **brightness constancy**, the apparent brightness of familiar objects is perceived as being the same regardless of the actual amount or type of light under which it is viewed. The white shirt you put on this morning may be *sensed* as gray when you pass through a

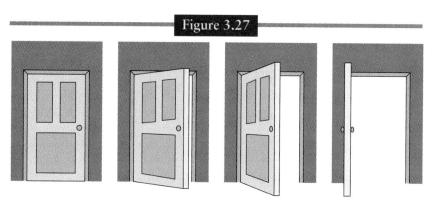

Figure 3.27

Although we see (at the retina) four different images, we know that we are looking at the same door because of shape constancy.

shadow, or as black when night falls, but it is still *perceived* as a white shirt—in no way darker than it was in the morning.

The same is true for color perception. If you know you put on a white shirt this morning, you would still perceive it as white even if I were to illuminate it with a red light. Most of the light waves reflected by the shirt will be associated with the experience of red (about 700 nm), but you will still know the shirt is white. Someone else, who didn't know any better, might perceive the shirt as red, but you'd perceive it as white because of color constancy.

When Constancy Fails:
Geometric Illusions and Impossible Figures

By now, you should appreciate that the relationship between the "real world" and our perception of that world is tenuous at best. What we come to perceive is often flavored by many factors above and beyond any physical reality that impinges on our sense receptors. We've seen a number of applications of this theme. The interaction between physical reality and our psychological experience can be appreciated clearly when we consider illusions and impossible figures. Illusions are experiences in which our perceptions are at odds with what we know as physical reality. In most cases, illusions occur when our usual reliance on perceptual constancies is challenged.

Several very simple and very compelling geometrical illusions are presented in Figure 3.28. Consider Figure 3.28(A). This drawing depicts the *vertical-horizontal illusion*. Figure 3.28(B) is the same illusion, of course, but in slightly more meaningful terms. Are the lines in Figure 3.28(A) the same length? Yes, you know they are—we're talking about illusions here. But, do they *appear* to be the same length? No, they do not. The vertical line seems significantly longer than the horizontal one. The hat in Figure 3.28(B) seems to be considerably taller than it is wide. Notice that the vertical-horizontal illusion works even after you have measured the two lines to confirm that they are the same length. They *still* don't look equal. This is one of three fundamental facts about illusions: they do not depend on our ignorance of the situation.

A second fact about illusions is that they do not occur at the retina. Figure 3.28(C) is the well-known *Müller-Lyer illusion*, named after the man who first drew it. The top line would continue to appear longer than the bottom one even if the two (equal) lines were presented to one eye, and the arrowlike vanes were presented to the other. A third fact about illusions is that their effects do not depend on movements of the eye. Illusions appear vividly even when they are flashed before the eyes so quickly that there is no opportunity to scan the presented image (Gillam, 1980).

Illusions of the sort presented in Figure 3.28 are not new. Psychologists have been searching for reasonable explanations for illusions for well over a hundred years. How do geometrical illusions give rise to perceptions, to visual experiences that are at odds with the

Figure 3.28

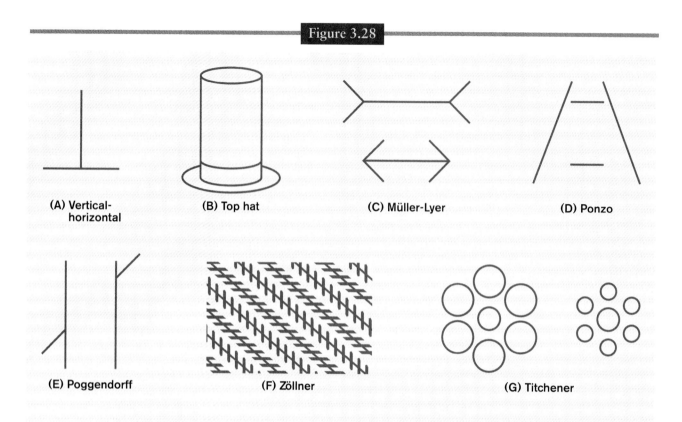

(A) Vertical-horizontal

(B) Top hat

(C) Müller-Lyer

(D) Ponzo

(E) Poggendorff

(F) Zöllner

(G) Titchener

A few classic geometrical illusions. In each case you know the answer, but the relevant quations are: (A) Are the vertical and horizontal lines the same length? (B) Is the brim as wide as the hat is tall? (C) Are the two horizontal lines the same length? (D) Are the two horizontal lines the same length? (E) Are the two diagonals part of the same line? (F) Are the long diagonal lines parallel? (G) Are the two center circles the same size?

physical reality detected by the eyes? Frankly, we just can't say. A number of factors seem to be working together to create illusions. In general, perhaps the most reasonable observation we can make about illusions is that they provide evidence of our perceptual constancies being overapplied. The effects of illusions largely depend on how we perceive and interpret clues to the size of objects in a three-dimensional world, and on inferences we make about the world based on our experience with it (Coren & Girgus, 1978; Gillam, 1980; Gregory, 1977; Hoffman, 1983).

Here's just one example. A reasonable-sounding explanation of the Müller-Lyer illusion is that the vanes of the arrows are taken to represent corners, as in a room. To see what I mean, refer to Figure 3.29(A). When corners are near to us or far away, we are presented with perspective cues to their distance. Hence, we "see" the "arrows" of the illusion as representing corners and edges. This point of view is known as the "carpentered world hypothesis" (e.g., Davidoff, 1975;

Gregory, 1977). In fact, in those cultures, such as the Zulu in Africa, who through most of their history have lived in circular houses with round doors and domed roofs—without all of our familiar corners and edges—the effects of the Müller-Lyer illusion are difficult to find (Segall et al., 1966). The carpentered world hypothesis sounds pretty good, doesn't it? Why, then in Figure 3.29(B) do we see the distance between circles *A* and *B* as greater than the distance between circles *B* and *C* when they are, in fact, equal?

The main instructional point of illusions is that they remind us that perception is a higher-level process than simple sensation; perception involves the organization and interpretation of the information we get from our senses, and things are not always as they seem. This point is made even more dramatically with what are called impossible figures (see Figure 3.30).

Before You Go On

**Name and give an example of four types of
perceptual constancy.**

Figure 3.29

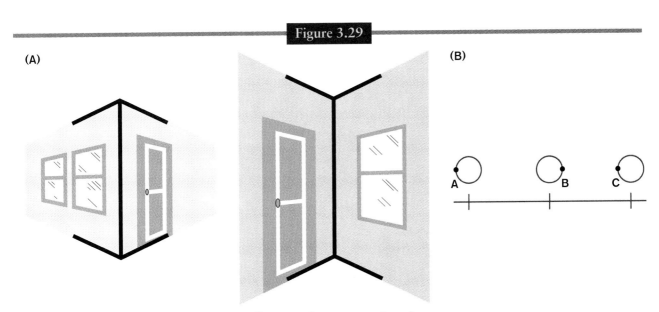

(A)   (B)

(A) One attempt to "explain" the Müller-Lyer illusion as the representation of edges and corners. (B) A variant of the Müller-Lyer illusion. The distance between circles A and B is equal to the distance between circles B and C. An explanation in terms of edges and corners no longer seems reasonable.

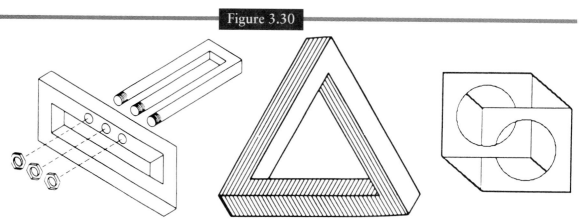

Impossible figures—examples of conflicting visual information.

TOPIC 3B SUMMARY

We have covered a lot of ground in this Topic, dealing with both sensation and perception. We have noted that the stimulus for vision is light—radiant energy in wave form where wave amplitude determines brightness, wavelength determines our experience of hue, and wave mixture determines our experience of saturation. We've seen that the receptor for vision is the eye, where only the rods and cones in the retina are actual photoreceptors, or transducers, for vision. Cones are responsible for our normal, daylight vision and for our experience of color, while rods function best in low levels of illumination. We've seen that objects in the right visual field are represented in the left side of our brains and that the left visual field is represented in the right side of our cerebral cortex. Our experience of color is due to the interaction of cones at the retina and opponent-process structures beyond the retina itself.

Our perception of the visual world is flavored by several factors, all of which operate together to give us the experience of a three-dimensional world, organized into meaningful gestalts on the basis of such factors as similarity, proximity, good continuation, closure, motivation, expectation, and past experience. Without a degree of perceptual constancy, each new or different view of a stimulus would have to be interpreted as a new and different perceptual experience.

Topic 3C

HEARING AND THE OTHER SENSES

There's no doubt that vision is an important sense. Try a little experiment on your own. Try to bypass your heavy reliance on vision and spend the better part of a day doing without it. Try to go about your normal everyday activities blindfolded.

One thing you will realize almost immediately is just how heavily you normally rely on vision. But consider for a moment the quantity and quality of information you *do* receive from your other senses. You soon may come to a new appreciation of your other senses as they inform you of the wonder of your environment: the aroma and taste of a well-prepared barbecue, the sounds of birds and music, the touch and feel of textures and surfaces, the sense of where your body is and what it's doing, the feedback from your muscles as you move.

In this Topic, we'll briefly discuss several senses, noting, as we did for vision, the relevant stimulus for each and indicating in general how each sense receptor works. We'll start with hearing and then move to the chemical senses of taste and smell. We'll consider the skin senses of touch, pressure, and temperature. We'll cover those senses that help us maintain our balance and tell us where various parts of our bodies are positioned. Finally, we'll take a look at pain—a sense as mysterious as it is important.

HEARING

Hearing (or more formally, *audition*) provides us with nearly as much useful information about our environment as vision. One of its main roles is its involvement in the development of language and speech. Without hearing, these uniquely human skills are difficult to acquire.

The Stimulus for Hearing: Sound

The stimulus for vision is light; for hearing, the stimulus is sound. Sound consists of a series of pressures of air (or some other medium, such as water) beating against our ear. We can represent these pressures as sound waves. As a source of sound vibrates, it pushes air against our ears. Figure 3.31 shows how we may depict sound as a wave form of energy.

As was the case for light waves, there are three major physical characteristics of sound waves: amplitude, frequency (the inverse of wavelength), and purity. Each is related to a different psychological experience. We'll briefly consider each in turn.

The *amplitude* of a sound wave depicts its intensity—the force with which the air strikes our ear. The intensity of a sound determines the psychological experience we call **loudness**. That is, the higher its amplitude, the louder we perceive the sound. Soft, quiet sounds have low amplitudes (see Figure 3.32).

Measurements of the physical intensity of sound are given in units of force per unit area (pressure). Loudness is a psychological characteristic. It is measured by people, not by instruments. The **decibel scale** of sound intensity has been constructed to reflect *perceived loudness*. Its zero point is the lowest intensity of sound that can be detected, or the absolute threshold. Our ears are very sensitive receptors and respond to very low levels of sound intensity. (In fact, if our ears were much more sensitive, we could hear molecules of air bouncing

loudness the psychological experience correlated with the intensity, or amplitude, of a sound wave

decibel scale a scale of our experience of loudness in which 0 represents the absolute threshold and 120 is sensed as pain

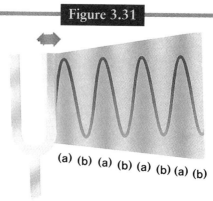

Figure 3.31

Sound waves are produced as air pressure is changed by the tine of the tuning fork vibrating to the right (A) and to the left (B). The point of greatest pressure is the high point or peak of the wave; least pressure is indicated by the low point of the wave.

against our eardrums.) Sounds that are louder than those produced by jet aircraft engines or fast-moving subway trains (about 120 decibels) are experienced more as pain than as sound. Figure 3.33 shows decibel levels for sounds we might find in our environment.

The second physical characteristic of sound to consider is *wave frequency*, the number of times a wave repeats itself within a given period. For sound, frequency is measured in terms of how many waves of pressure are exerted every second. The unit of sound frequency is the **hertz**, abbreviated **Hz**. If a sound wave repeats itself 50 times in one second, it is a 50-Hz sound; 500 repetitions is a 500-Hz sound, and so on. Waves of different frequency (A and C) are shown in Figure 3.32, where you can see the relationship between wavelength and frequency.

hertz (Hz) the standard measure of sound wave frequency that is the number of wave cycles per second

The psychological experience produced by sound wave frequency is **pitch**. Pitch is our experience of how high or low a tone is. The musical scale represents differences in pitch. Low frequencies correspond to bass tones, such as those made by foghorns or tubas. High-frequency vibrations give rise to the experience of high-pitched sounds, such as the musical tones produced by flutes or the squeals of smoke detectors.

pitch the psychological experience that corresponds to sound wave frequency and gives rise to high (treble) or low (bass) sounds

Just as the human eye cannot respond to all possible wavelengths of radiant energy, so the human ear cannot respond to all possible sound wave frequencies. A healthy human ear responds to sound wave frequencies between 20 Hz and 20,000 Hz. If air strikes our ears at a rate less than 20 times per second, we will not hear a sound. Sound vibrations faster than 20,000 cycles per second cannot be heard, at least not by the human ear. Many animals *can* hear sounds

Figure 3.32

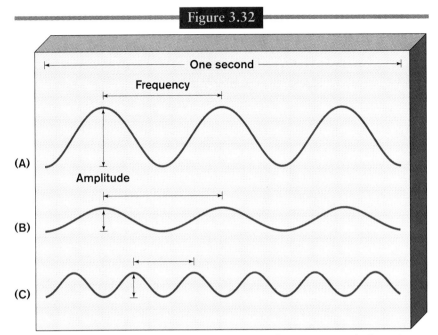

How the physical characteristics of sound waves influence our psychological experience of a sound. Although waves A and B have the same frequency, wave A has a higher amplitude and would be experienced as a louder sound. Although waves B and C have the same amplitude, wave C would be experienced as having a higher pitch because of its greater frequency.

with frequencies above 20,000 Hz, such as those produced by dog whistles.

A third characteristic of sound waves is *wave purity,* or complexity. You may recall that we seldom experience pure, monochromatic lights. Pure sounds are also uncommon in our everyday experience. A pure sound would be one in which *all* waves from the sound source were vibrating at exactly the same frequency. Such sounds can be produced electronically, and tuning forks produce approximations, but most of the sounds we hear every day are complex sounds, consisting of many sound wave frequencies.

A tone of middle C on the piano is a tone of 256 Hz. (Again, this means that the source of the sound, here a piano wire, is vibrating 256 times per second.) A *pure* 256-Hz tone consists of sound waves (vibrations) of only that frequency. As it happens, the middle C of the piano has many other wave frequencies mixed in with the predominant 256-Hz wave frequency. (If the 256-Hz wave did not predominate, the tone wouldn't sound like middle C.)

The quality or character of a sound, reflecting its degree of purity, is called **timbre.** For example, each musical instrument produces a

timbre *the psychological experience of wave purity by which we differentiate the qualities of tones*

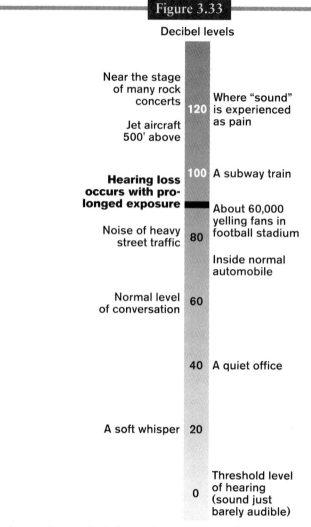

Figure 3.33

Decibel levels

Near the stage of many rock concerts

Jet aircraft 500' above

120 Where "sound" is experienced as pain

Hearing loss occurs with prolonged exposure

100 A subway train

About 60,000 yelling fans in football stadium

Noise of heavy street traffic **80**

Inside normal automobile

Normal level of conversation **60**

40 A quiet office

A soft whisper **20**

0 Threshold level of hearing (sound just barely audible)

Loudness values in decibel units for various sounds.

unique variety or mixture of overtones, so each type of musical instrument tends to sound a little different from all others. If a trumpet, a violin, and a piano were to play the same note, we could still tell the instruments apart because of our experience of timbre. In fact, any instrument can display different timbres, depending on how it is constructed and played.

With light, we found that the opposite of a pure light was white light—a light consisting of all wavelengths of the visible spectrum. Again, the parallel between vision and hearing holds up. Suppose I have a sound source that can produce all of the possible sound wave frequencies. What would that sound like? Actually, it would sound rather like a buzzing noise. The best example would be what one

Sound is a series of pressures of air that produce vibrations of the eardrum.

hears when a radio is tuned to a position between stations (as it happens, FM works better than AM). This soft, whispering, buzzing sound, containing a range of many audible sound frequencies, is useful in masking or covering other unwanted sounds. We call a random mixture of sound frequencies **white noise**, just as we called a random mixture of wavelengths of light white light.

 The analogy between light and sound, between vision and hearing, is striking. Both types of stimulus energy can be represented as waves. In both cases, each of the *physical* characteristics of the waves (amplitude, length or frequency, and purity or complexity) is correlated with a *psychological* experience. All of these relationships are summarized in Figure 3.34.

white noise a sound consisting of a random assortment of all wave frequencies from the audible spectrum

Before You Go On

**What are the three major physical characteristics
of sound, and which psychological experiences
do they produce?**

The Receptor for Hearing: The Ear

The energy of sound wave pressures is transduced into neural impulses deep inside the ear. As with the eye, most of the structures of the ear simply transfer energy from without to within. Figure 3.35 is a drawing of the major structures of the ear. We'll use it to follow the path of sound waves from the environment to the receptor cells.

Figure 3.34

A Summary of the Ways in Which the Physical Characteristics of Light and Sound Waves Affect Our Psychological Experiences of Vision and Hearing

Physical characteristic	Psychological experience for vision	Psychological experience for hearing
Wave amplitude	Brightness	Loudness
Wavelength or frequency	Hue	Pitch
Wave purity or mixture	Saturation	Timbre

pinna *the outer ear, which collects and funnels sound waves into the auditory canal toward the eardrum*

eardrum *the outermost membrane of the ear; set in motion by the vibrations of a sound; transmits vibrations to the ossicles*

malleus, incus, and stapes *(collectively, ossicles) three small bones that intensify sound vibrations and transmit them from the eardrum to the oval window*

cochlea *part of the inner ear where sound waves become neural impulses*

basilar membrane *a structure within the cochlea that vibrates and thus stimulates the hair cells of the inner ear*

hair cells *the receptor cells for hearing, located in the cochlea, stimulated by the vibrating basilar membrane; they send neural impulses to the temporal lobe of the brain*

The outer ear is called the **pinna**. Its function is to collect sound waves from the air around it and funnel them through the auditory canal toward the **eardrum**. Air waves push against the eardrum (technically, called the tympanic membrane), setting it in motion so that it vibrates at the same rate as the sound source.

The eardrum then transmits vibrations to three very small bones (collectively called *ossicles*) in the middle ear. In order, they are the **malleus, incus,** and **stapes** (pronounced *stape-eez*). These bones pass vibrations on to the *oval window,* another membrane, like the eardrum, only smaller. As the ossicles pass sound vibrations to the oval window, they amplify them, increasing their force.

When sound waves pass beyond the oval window, the vibrations are in the inner ear. The major structure of the inner ear is the snail-like **cochlea**, which contains the actual receptor cells—the transducers—for hearing. As the stapes vibrates against the oval window, fluid inside the cochlea is set in motion at the same rate.

When the fluid within the cochlea moves, the **basilar membrane** is bent up and down. The basilar membrane is a small structure that runs about the full length of the cochlea. Hearing takes place when very tiny **hair cells** are stimulated by the vibrations of the basilar membrane. Through a process not yet fully understood, the mechanical pressure of the basilar membrane on the hair cells starts neural impulses that leave the ear, traveling on the auditory nerve toward the temporal lobe. Thus, most of the structures of the ear are responsible for amplifying and directing waves of pressure to the hair cells in the cochlea, where the neural impulse begins.

Before You Go On

Summarize how sound wave pressures pass through the various structures of the ear.

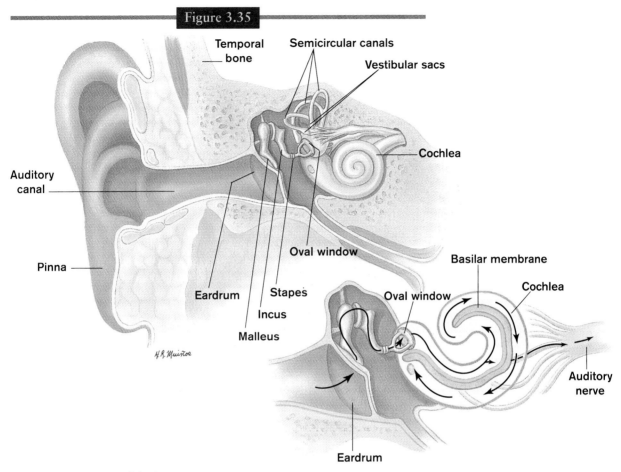

Figure 3.35

The major structures of the human ear.

THE CHEMICAL SENSES

Taste and smell are referred to as chemical senses because the stimuli for both of them are molecules of chemical compounds. For taste, the chemicals are dissolved in liquid (usually the saliva in our mouths). For smell, they are dissolved in the air that reaches the smell receptors high inside our noses. The technical term for taste is *gustation;* for smell, it is *olfaction.*

If you have ever eaten while suffering from a head cold that has blocked your nasal passages, you appreciate the extent to which our experiences of taste and smell are interrelated. Most foods seem to lose their taste when we cannot smell them. This is why we differentiate between the *flavor* of foods (which includes such qualities as odor and texture) and the *taste* of foods. A simple test demonstrates this point very nicely. While blindfolded, eat a small piece of peeled apple and a small piece of peeled potato, and see if you can tell the difference between the two. You shouldn't have any trouble making this discrimination. Now hold your nose very tightly and try again. Without your sense of smell to help you, such discrimination—on the basis of taste alone—is very difficult.

Taste

Our experience of the flavors of foods depends so heavily on our sense of smell, texture, and temperature that we sometimes have to wonder if there is any sense of taste alone. Well, there is. Even with odor and texture held constant, tastes can vary. Taste (gustation) has four basic psychological qualities (and many combinations of these four): sweet, salt, sour, and bitter. You should be able to generate a list of foods that produce each of these basic sensations. Most foods derive their special taste from a unique combination of the four basic taste sensations. Have you noticed that it is more difficult to think of examples of sour- and bitter-tasting foods than of sweet and salty ones? This reflects the fact that we usually don't like bitter and sour tastes and have learned to avoid them.

The tip of the tongue is the area most sensitive to sweet tastes.

taste buds *the receptors for taste located on the tongue*

The receptor cells for taste are located in the tongue and are called **taste buds**. We all have about ten thousand taste buds, and each one consists of a number of parts (see Figure 3.36). When parts of taste buds die (or are killed by foods that are too hot, for example), new segments are regenerated. Fortunately, we are always growing new taste receptor cells. That observation in itself makes taste a unique sense: as receptor cells, taste buds are essentially nerve cells, and we've already noted that nerve cells are usually not replaced when they die.

Different taste buds respond primarily to chemicals that produce one of the four basic taste qualities. Some receptor cells respond best to salts, whereas others respond primarily to sweet-producing chemicals, such as sugars. These cells are not evenly distributed on the surface of the tongue (Figure 3.37). Receptors for sweet are at the very tip of the tongue, receptors for salty tastes are toward the front, sour receptors are on the sides, and bitter receptors are at the back of the tongue. A sour vinegar solution dropped on the tip of the tongue might very well go unnoticed until some of it gets washed over to the side of the tongue. To best savor a lollipop, children learned ages ago to lick it with the tip of the tongue.

Smell

Smell (olfaction) is a poorly understood sense. It is a sense that often gives us great pleasure; think of the aroma of bacon frying over a

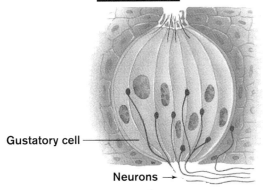

Figure 3.36

Gustatory cell

Neurons →

Enlarged view of a taste bud, the receptor for gustation.

wood fire or of freshly picked flowers. It can also produce consider-able displeasure; consider the smell of a skunk, old garbage, or rotten eggs.

The sense of smell originates in hair cells located high in the nasal cavity, very close to the brain itself. We know that the pathway from these receptors to the brain is the most direct and shortest of all the senses (see Figure 3.38). What we don't understand well is how mole-cules suspended in air, gases, actually stimulate the small hair cells of the olfactory receptor to fire neural impulses.

The sense of smell is very important for many nonhumans. The

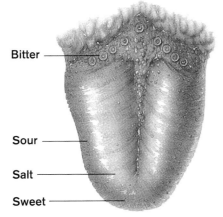

Figure 3.37

Bitter

Sour

Salt

Sweet

The four primary qualities of taste are experienced on distinct areas of the tongue.

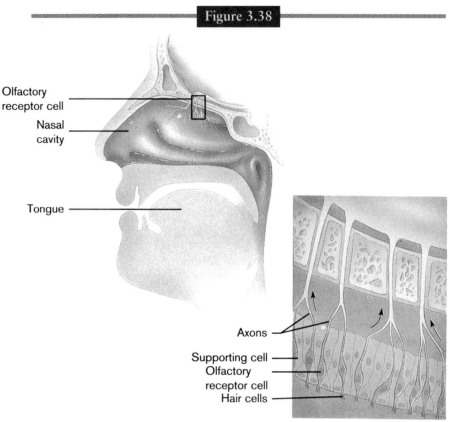

Figure 3.38

Olfactory receptor cell

Nasal cavity

Tongue

Axons

Supporting cell
Olfactory receptor cell
Hair cells

The olfactory system, showing its proximity to the brain and the transducers for smell—the hair cells.

pheromones chemicals that produce an odor used as a method of communication between organisms

dog's sense of smell is legendary. Many animals emit chemicals, called **pheromones**, that produce distinctive odors. Sometimes pheromones are released by cells in the skin, sometimes in the urine, and occasionally from special glands (in some deer, this gland is located near the rear hoof). One purpose of pheromones is to mark or delineate one's territory. If you take a dog for a walk around the block and discover that the pooch wants to stop and deposit small amounts of urine on just about every front lawn, that dog is leaving behind a pheromone message that essentially says, "*I* have been here; this is my odor; this is my turf."

Most commonly, pheromones carry sexually related messages to members of the opposite sex of the same species. Most often that message is roughly translated into, "I am available for sexual activities." Of course, the result is that the odor of these pheromones tends to attract members of the opposite sex. This knowledge can be useful. Japanese beetles are a common pest and are very difficult to kill safely with standard poisons. Traps are available that contain a small amount of a pheromone attractive to Japanese beetles. Beetles smell the odor the trap gives off, come rushing to investigate, and slide off a slippery plastic platform to their doom in a disposable bag.

It is likely that pheromone production is related to the sex hormones, even in humans. There is evidence that women who live in close quarters (say, in a college dormitory) for very long soon synchronize their menstrual cycles. The same thing happens in rats when the only contact between them is that they share the same air supply and thus the same odors (McClintock, 1971, 1979). It is possible that humans use pheromones to attract members of the opposite sex (Cutler et al., 1986; Wallace, 1977). If we do, the real effect is no doubt very small, although people who advertise perfumes and colognes would like to have us think otherwise (e.g., Doty, 1986).

For years, psychologists have been trying to determine if there are primary odors, perhaps not unlike the primary tastes. Several schemes have been proposed, and each seemed reasonable in its day. One scheme suggests that there are four basic odors from which all others may be constructed: fragrant, acid, burnt, and, of all things, goaty. Another scheme cites six primary odors. Yet another plan, called the stereochemical theory (Amoore, 1970), names seven primary qualities of smell, and further suggests that each primary quality is stimulated by a unique type or shape of chemical molecule. For the moment, it is just impossible to be any more definite, in that there seems to be evidence both for and against Amoore's theory—and each of the others that has been proposed.

Before You Go On

Discuss the chemical senses of taste and smell, noting the stimulus and sense receptor for each.

Do taste and smell each have primary qualities? If so, what are they?

THE SKIN, OR CUTANEOUS, SENSES

Most of us take our skin for granted—at least we seldom think about it very much. We frequently abuse our skin by overexposing it to the sun's rays in summer and to excess cold in winter. We scratch it, cut it, scrape it, and wash away millions of its cells every time we shower or bathe.

Figure 3.39 is a diagram of just some of the structures found in an area of skin from a hairy part of the human body. Each square inch of the layers that make up our skin contains nearly 20 million cells, including many special sense receptors. Some of the skin receptors have *free nerve endings*, whereas others have some sort of covering over them. We call these latter cells *encapsulated nerve endings*, of which are many types. Our skin somehow gives rise to our psychological experience of touch or pressure, and of warmth and cold. It

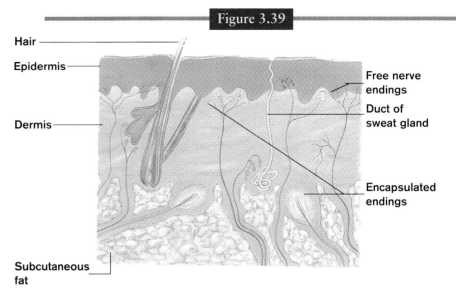

Figure 3.39

Hair
Epidermis
Dermis
Free nerve endings
Duct of sweat gland
Encapsulated endings
Subcutaneous fat

A patch of hairy skin, showing the layers of skin and various nerve cells.

The tips of the fingers contain many receptors for touch and pressure.

would be convenient if each of the various receptor cells within the layers of our skin gave rise to a different type of psychological sensation, but such seems not to be the case.

One of the problems in studying the cutaneous senses is trying to determine which cells in the skin give rise to different sensations of pressure and temperature. We can discriminate clearly between a light touch and a strong jab in the arm and between vibrations, tickles, and itches. A simple proposal is that there are different receptors in the skin responsible for each sensation, but this proposal is not supported by the facts. Although *some* types of receptor cells are more sensitive to *some* types of stimuli, current thinking is that our ability to discriminate among types of cutaneous sensation is due to the unique combination of responses the many receptor cells have to various types of stimulation.

By carefully stimulating very small areas of the skin, we can locate areas that are sensitive to temperature. We are convinced that warm and cold temperatures each stimulate specific, different locations on the skin. Even so, there is no consistent pattern of receptor cells found at these locations—or temperature spots, as they are called. That is, we have not yet located specific receptor cells for cold or hot. Actually, our experience of hot seems to come from the simultaneous stimulation of both warm and cold spots. A rather ingenious demonstration shows how this works. Cold water is run through one metal tube and warm water is run through another tube. The two tubes are coiled together (Figure 3.40). If you were to grasp the coiled tubes, your experience would be one of *heat;* the tubes would feel hot even if you knew they weren't.

Before You Go On

What are the cutaneous senses, and what are the transducers for each?

THE POSITION SENSES

Another sensory capacity we often take for granted is our ability to know how and where our bodies are positioned in space. Although we seldom worry about it, we can quickly become aware of how our bodies are positioned in regard to the pull of gravity. We also get sensory information about where various parts of our body are in relation to one another. We can tell if we are moving or standing still. And unless we are on a roller coaster, or racing across a field, we usually adapt to these sensory messages quickly and pay them little attention.

Most of the information about where we are in space comes to us through our sense of vision. If we want to know just how we are oriented in space, all we have to do is look around. But notice that we *can* do the same sort of thing even with our eyes closed. We have two systems of position sense over and above what vision can provide. One, the **vestibular sense**, tells us about balance, where we are in relation to gravity, and acceleration or deceleration. The other, the **kinesthetic sense**, tells us about the movement or position of our muscles and joints.

The receptors for the vestibular sense are located on either side of the head, near the inner ears. Five chambers are located there: three semicircular canals and two vestibular sacs. Their orientation is shown in Figure 3.35. Each of these chambers is filled with fluid. When our head moves in any direction, the fluid in the semicircular canals moves, drawn by gravity or the force of our head accelerating in space. The vestibular sacs contain very small, solid particles that float around in the fluid within the sacs. When these particles are forced against one side of a sac, as happens when we move, they stimulate hair cells that start neural impulses. Overstimulation of the receptor cells in the vestibular sacs or semicircular canals can lead to feelings of dizziness or nausea, reasonably enough called *motion sickness.*

Receptors for our kinesthetic sense are located primarily in our joints, but some information also comes from muscles and tendons. These receptors sense the position and movements of parts of the body—again, information to which we seldom attend. Impulses from

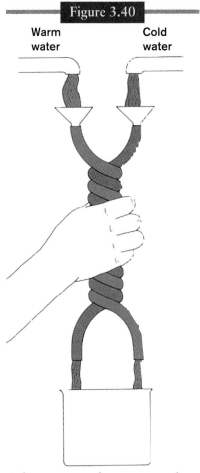

Figure 3.40

Warm water   Cold water

A demonstration that our sense of what is hot may be constructed from sensations of what is warm and cold. Even if you know that the coiled tubes contain only warm and cold water, when you grasp the tubes, they will feel hot.

vestibular sense *the position sense that tells us about balance, where we are in relation to gravity, and acceleration or deceleration*

kinesthetic sense *the position sense that tells us the position of various parts of our bodies and what our muscles and joints are doing*

A keen vestibular sense is a prime requirement for a tightrope walker.

these receptors travel to our brain through pathways in our spinal cord. They provide excellent examples of reflex actions. As muscles in the front of your upper arm (your biceps) contract, the corresponding muscles in the back of your arm (triceps) must relax if you are to bend your arm at the elbow successfully. How fortunate it is that our kinesthetic receptors, operating reflexively through the spinal cord, take care of these details without our having to consciously manipulate all of the appropriate muscular activity. In fact, about the only time we even realize that our kinesthetic system is functioning is when it stops working well, such as when our leg "falls asleep" and we have trouble walking.

Before You Go On

What are our position senses, and how do they operate?

PAIN: A SPECIAL SENSE

The sense of pain is a curious and troublesome one for psychologists who are interested in sensory processes. Pain, or the fear of it, can be a strong motivator; we'll do all sorts of things to avoid it. Pain is surely unpleasant, but at the same time, it is very useful. Pain alerts us to problems occurring somewhere in our bodies, warning us that steps might need to be taken to remove the source of pain. Without a sense of pain, a person might very well die of a burst appendix. Feelings of pain are private sensations—difficult to share or describe (Verillo, 1975).

What *is* pain? What causes the experience of pain? What are its receptors? At present, we have only partial answers. Many stimuli can cause pain. Very intense stimulation of virtually any sense receptor can produce pain. Too much light, strong pressures on the skin, excessive temperatures, very loud sounds, and even very "hot" spices can all result in our experiencing pain. But as we all know, the stimulus for pain need not be intense. In the right circumstances, even a light pinprick can be painful.

Our skin seems to have many receptors for pain, but pain receptors can also be found deep inside our bodies; consider stomachaches, lower back pain, and headaches. Pain is experienced in our brains, but pain is the only "sense" for which we can find no one specific center in the cerebral cortex.

A theory of pain still attracting attention from researchers (most of it supportive, some not) is Melzack and Wall's **gate-control theory** (1965; Melzack, 1973). It suggests that our experience of pain happens not at the level of the receptor (say, the skin), but within the central nervous system. The theory proposes that a gatelike structure in the spinal cord responds to stimulation from a particular type of

gate-control theory *the theory of pain sensation that argues that there are brain centers that regulate the passage of pain messages from various parts of the body to the brain*

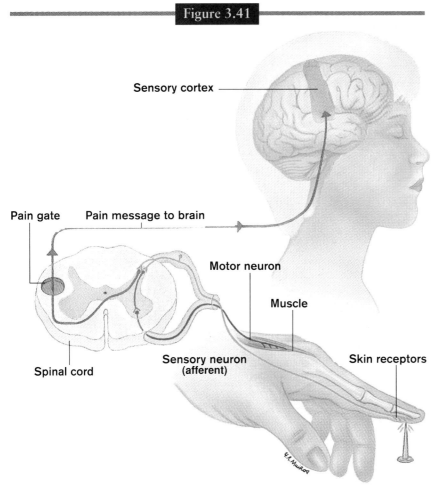

Figure 3.41

The gate-control theory of pain. A stimulus on the skin initiates neural impulses that enter the spinal cord and rush through a "pain gate" to the brain. Several mechanisms (including the release of endorphins) can act to "close the gate," at least to some degree, thus reducing the experience of pain by the cerebral cortex of the brain.

nerve fiber—one that "opens the gate" and allows for the sensation of pain by letting impulses travel to the brain. Other nerve fibers can off-set the activity of the pain-carrying fibers and "close the gate" so that pain messages are cut off and never make it to the brain. Figure 3.41 presents the basic idea of the gate-control theory.

There are several situations in which this idea of an opening and closing gate to pain seems reasonable. One of the things that happens when we are exposed to persistent pain is that certain neurotransmitters—*endorphins*—are released in the brain (Hughes et al., 1975; Terenius, 1982). We've already noted that endorphins naturally reduce our sense of pain and make us feel good. When the effects of endorphins are blocked, pain feels unusually severe. Endorphins stimulate nerve fibers that go to the spinal cord and effectively close the gate that monitors impulses from pain receptors.

Another situation that seems to fit the gate-control theory is that of abnormally persistent pain. Some patients who have received a trauma to some part of their body (through accident or surgery, for example) continue to experience extreme pain even after the initial wound is completely healed. Abnormal pain is also found in so-called "phantom-limb" pain, experienced by about 10 percent of amputees. Some patients continue to feel pain in an arm or leg even after that limb is no longer there. How can this be? Recent thinking is that the severe trauma of amputation overloads and destroys the function of important cells in the spinal cord that normally act to close the gate to pain messages, leaving pain circuits uninhibited and "open" (Gracely et al., 1991; Laird & Bennett, 1991).

Hypnosis and cognitive self-control (trying very hard to convince yourself that the pain you're experiencing is not really that bad and will go away) *are* effective in controlling the feeling of pain (Litt, 1988; Melzack, 1973). That pain can be controlled to some extent by cognitive training is clear from the success of many classes aimed at reducing the pain of childbirth. The idea is that psychological processes influence the gate-control center in the spinal cord. We also know that **placebos** can be effective in treating pain. A placebo is a substance (perhaps in pill form) a person *believes* will be effective in treating some symptom—such as pain—when, in fact, there is no pain-relieving ingredient in the substance. When subjects are given a placebo they genuinely believe will alleviate pain, endorphins are released in the brain that can close the gate to pain-carrying impulses (Levine et al., 1979).

Another process that works to ease the feeling of pain, particularly pain from or near the surface of the skin, is called counterirritation. The idea here is to stimulate forcefully (but not painfully, of course) an area of the body *near* the location of the pain. Dentists have discovered that rubbing on the gum near the spot a novacaine needle is to be inserted significantly reduces the patient's experience of the pain of the needle. Again, as you might have guessed, the logic is that the stimulation from the nearby rubbing action serves to close the pain gate, so the needle has less effect.

The ancient oriental practice of acupuncture can also be tied in to the gate-control theory of pain. What we don't know yet is exactly why acupuncture works as well as it does when it is effective. There are cases for which it doesn't work well at all, but these usually involve patients who are skeptics and "don't believe in" acupuncture. This observation suggests that at least some of acupuncture's benefits derive from its function as a placebo. But an important aspect may be its function as a counterirritant. There is also evidence that acupuncture releases endorphins in the brain. Perhaps each or all of these functions serve the major purpose of controlling pain by closing off impulses to the brain.

placebo   *an inactive substance that has its effect because a person has come to believe it will be effective*

Before You Go On

What produces the sensation of pain, and how might that sensation be controlled or reduced?

What is the gate-control theory of pain?

TOPIC 3C SUMMARY

In this Topic, we have reviewed the structures and functions of several human senses. We have seen that hearing, like vision, is stimulated by physical wave forms of energy and that the measurable characteristics of these waves (amplitude, frequency, and complexity) give rise to distinct psychological experiences of sounds (loudness, pitch, and timbre). We've noted the interrelationship between taste and smell. We've reviewed a number of our skin senses, as well as those senses (vestibular and kinesthetic) that inform us about our body's position in space. Finally, we have introduced some of the current thinking about the sense of pain. It is clear that at any one time our brains are receiving a remarkable amount of information from our sensory receptors.

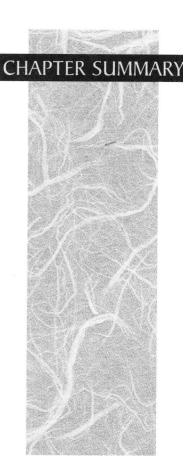

CHAPTER SUMMARY

TOPIC 3A

How are the processes of sensation and perception defined?

What is psychophysics?

What is an absolute threshold, and how is it related to the sensitivity of our senses?

Sensation is the first step in the processing of information. It involves the transduction of physical energy from the environment into the energy of the nervous system at our senses. Perception, on the other hand, is a more cognitive process, involving the selection, organization, and interpretation of the information provided by the senses. Psychophysics is a subfield of psychology that studies relationships between physical stimuli and our psychological experiences of them. This effort includes the determination of sensory thresholds. An absolute threshold is the intensity of a stimulus that can be detected 50 percent of the time. The lower one's threshold for any sense, the more sensitive it is; thus, sensitivity and threshold are inversely related. /p. 99

What is a difference threshold, or a j.n.d.?

Briefly summarize the basic ideas of signal detection theory.

What is sensory adaptation?

A difference threshold is the difference between two stimuli (on any dimension) that can be detected 50 percent of the time. It is that point

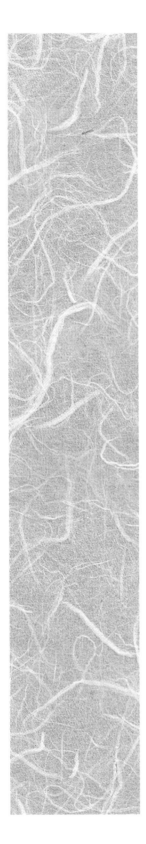

at which two stimuli are detected to be just noticeably different (j.n.d.). Signal detection theory considers threshold determination as a matter of detecting a signal against a ground (background) of shifting "noise," where the subjects' biases, motivation, and attention are also considered. Sensory adaptation is the process by which our sensory experience tends to decrease with continued exposure to a stimulus. /p. 102

What stimulus factors determine the selection of perceptions?

Of all information that stimulates our receptors, only a small portion is attended to, or selected for further processing. Characteristics of the stimuli themselves may determine which stimuli will be attended to. We are more likely to attend to a stimulus if it *contrasts* with others around it in terms of intensity, size, motion, novelty, or any other physical characteristic. The *repetition* of a stimulus also increases the likelihood that we will attend to it. /p. 105

What personal factors are involved in perceptual selectivity?

The selection of stimuli is partly based on such characteristics of the perceiver as motivation, expectation (or mental set), and past experience. In this case we say that information is processed from the top down, rather than from the bottom up. /p. 107

TOPIC 3B

In what ways do the major physical characteristics of light waves of energy (amplitude, length, and purity) affect our psychological experience of light?

We can think of light as a wave form of radiant energy having three major characteristics: wave amplitude, which determines our experience of the light's brightness; wavelength, which determines our experience of hue; and wave purity, which determines a light's degree of saturation, from the extremes of a monochromatic light to the lowest saturation, white light. /p. 112

List the major structures of the eye, and describe the function of each.

How and why can we claim that rods and cones provide us with two distinct types of visual experience?

Before light reaches the retina, it passes through several structures whose major function is to focus an image on the retina. In order, light passes through the cornea, the aqueous humors, the pupil (an opening in the iris), the lens (whose shape is controlled by ciliary muscles), and the vitreous humors. At the retina, after passing through layers of neural fibers that combine and integrate visual information, light reaches the photoreceptors (rods and cones), the transducers for vision. Neural impulses that originate at the rods and cones are collected and leave the eye at the blind spot. Cones, which are concentrated in the fovea, respond best to medium to high levels of illumination (e.g., daylight) and respond differentially to light of varying wavelength (or hue). Although rods, concentrated in the periphery of the retina, do not discriminate among hues, they do react to relatively low levels of illumination. Evidence for this point of view comes from common experience, the examination of the retinas of nocturnal animals, and data on adaptation to darkness. */p. 119*

Briefly trace the path of impulses from each eye to the cerebral cortex.

Once nerve fibers leave the eye at the blind spot, they travel to the optic chiasma, where some are sent straight back and others cross to the opposite side of the brain. The process works so that images from the left visual field are processed in the right side of the brain, whereas images from the right visual field are processed in the left side of the brain. From the optic chiasma, impulses travel through the superior colliculi, the thalamus, and finally to the occipital lobes of the cerebral cortex, where visual experiences are processed. */p. 121*

Briefly summarize the trichromatic and the opponent-process theories of color vision.

These theories attempt to explain how the visual system codes various wavelengths of light, giving us the experience of color. Young and Helmholtz's trichromatic theory claims that there are three types of cones, each maximally sensitive to one of the three primary hues—red, green, and blue. Hering's opponent-process theory claims that there are three pairs of mechanisms involved in our experience of color: a blue-yellow processor, a red-green processor, and a black-white processor. Each of these can respond to either of the characteristics that give it its name, but not to both at the same time. There is evidence that supports both of these theories, some of which comes from our understanding of why some people have defects in color vision. */p. 124*

List stimulus and personal factors that determine how we organize stimuli in perception.

The organization of stimuli depends in part on the characteristics of the available stimuli, such as proximity, similarity, continuity, common fate, and closure. The personal factors that affect perceptual organization are the same as those that influence attention: motivation, mental set, and past experience. */p. 128*

Name and describe some of the cues that inform us about depth and distance.

We are able to perceive three-dimensionality and distance even though we sense the environment on two-dimensional retinas because of the many cues with which we are provided. Some have to do with the visual system and are called ocular cues, such as retinal disparity

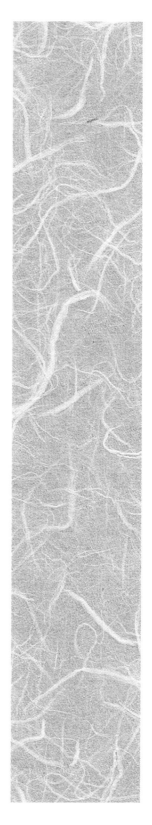

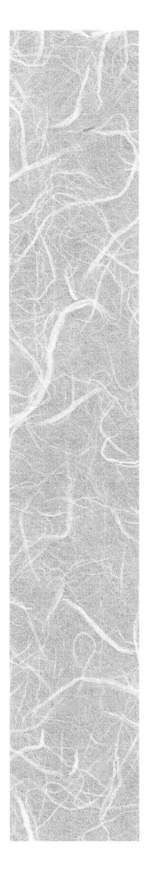

(each eye gets a different view of the same three-dimensional object), convergence (when we look at something up close our eyes move inward, toward each other), and accommodation (our lenses change shape to focus images as objects move toward or away from us). Cues also come from the environment, including the physical cues of linear perspective (parallel lines seem to come together in the distance), interposition (near objects partially obscure our view of more distant objects), relative size (everything else being equal, the smaller the stimulus, the farther away we judge it to be), texture gradients (details of texture that we can see clearly up close are difficult to determine at a distance), patterns of shading, and motion parallax (as we move toward stationary objects, those close to us seem to move past us more rapidly than do objects in the distance). The accurate reliance on some of these cues may be sensitive to the culture in which one lives. /*p. 134*

What are two illusions of motion and how are they produced?

The perception of motion when there is none is an example of an illusion. The *phi phenomenon* is such an illusion and can be demonstrated by flashing lights on and off in a sequence, giving the appearance of a light in motion. The *autokinetic effect* occurs when a stationary point of light is perceived as moving in an otherwise darkened environment. /*p. 135*

Name and give an example of four types of perceptual constancy.

Constancies bring stability to our perceptual world. With size constancy, we perceive objects as being of the same size regardless of how the size of their retinal images may change. Similarly, shape constancy refers to the stability of our perception of an object's shape regardless of the shape of its retinal image. With brightness and color constancy, we are able to perceive an object's true color and brightness regardless of the intensity or the wavelength of light reflected from it. The geometric illusions can be thought of as a distortion of normal perceptual constancy. They also demonstrate the impact of one's culture on perception. /*p. 139*

TOPIC 3C

What are the three major physical characteristics of sound, and which psychological experiences do they produce?

Like light, sound may be represented as a wave form of energy with three major physical characteristics: wave amplitude, frequency, and purity (or mixture). These in turn give rise to our experiences of loudness, pitch, and timbre. /*p. 145*

Summarize how sound wave pressures pass through the various structures of the ear.

Most of the structures of the ear (the pinna, auditory canal, eardrum, malleus, incus, stapes, and oval window) intensify and transmit sound wave pressures to the fluid in the cochlea, which then vibrates the basilar membrane, which in turn stimulates tiny hair cells to transmit neural impulses along the auditory nerve to the temporal lobes of the cerebral cortex. /*p. 146*

Discuss the chemical senses of taste and smell, noting the stimulus and sense receptor for each.

Do taste and smell each have primary qualities? If so, what are they?

The senses of taste (gustation) and smell (olfaction) are interrelated. They are referred to as chemical senses because both respond to chemical molecules. The receptors for smell are hair cells that line the upper regions of the nasal cavity; for taste, the receptors are cells in the taste buds located on the tongue. Taste appears to have four primary qualities: sweet, salt, sour, and bitter. For smell, the issue of primary qualities and how many there may be is far less certain. /*p. 151*

What are the cutaneous senses, and what are the transducers for each?

The cutaneous senses are our skin senses: touch, pressure, warmth, and cold. Specific receptor cells for each identifiable skin sense have not yet been localized, although they no doubt include free nerve endings and encapsulated nerve endings, which most likely work in combination. /*p. 153*

What are our position senses, and how do they operate?

One of our position senses is the vestibular sense, which, by responding to the movement of small particles suspended in a fluid within our vestibular sacs and semicircular canals, can inform us about orientation with regard to gravity or accelerated motion. The other position sense is kinesthesis, which, through receptors in our tendons, muscles, and joints, informs us about the orientation of various parts of our bodies. /*p. 154*

What produces the sensation of pain, and how might that sensation be controlled or reduced?

What is the gate-control theory of pain?

A wide variety of environmental stimuli can give rise to our experience of pain, from high levels of stimulus intensity, to light pinpricks, to internal stimuli of the sort that produce headaches. There is no one receptor for the pain sense. The central nervous system is involved in our experience of pain, as a gate-control mechanism in the spinal cord that either blocks or sends impulses carrying information about pain to the brain. Given the gate-control theory of pain, anything that can block the passage of pain impulses—close the gate—can control our experience of pain. This is directly accomplished by the action of endorphins and counterirritation. Closing of the gate can be controlled by hypnosis, placebo effects, self-persuasion, and acupuncture. /*p. 157*

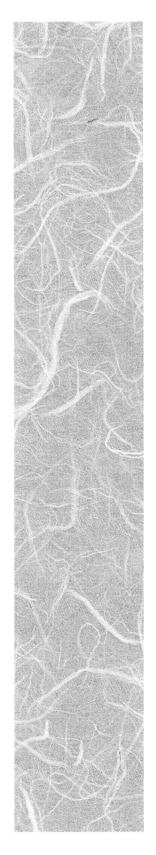

chapter four

TYPES OF
CONSCIOUSNESS

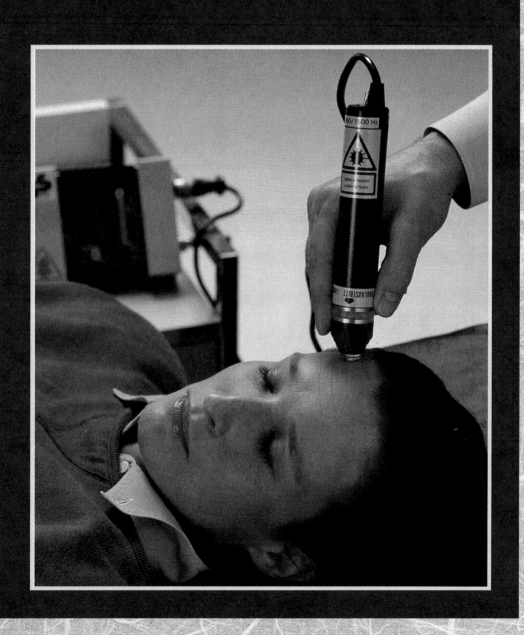

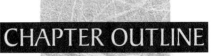
CHAPTER OUTLINE

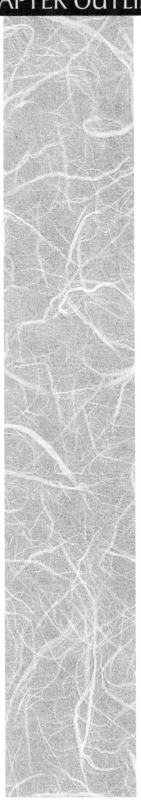

TOPIC 4A LEVELS OF CONSCIOUSNESS
Normal, Waking Consciousness
Is There an Unconscious, and What Might It Be Like?
    The Freudian View of Levels of Consciousness
    Contemporary Investigations of the Unconscious
TOPIC 4A SUMMARY

TOPIC 4B SLEEPING AND DREAMING
The Stages of a "Good Night's Sleep"
REM and NREM Sleep
Sleep Deprivation and Disorders of Sleep
    Sleep Deprivation—In the Real World and in the Laboratory
    Disorders of Sleep
TOPIC 4B SUMMARY

TOPIC 4C VOLUNTARY ALTERATIONS OF
CONSCIOUSNESS
Hypnosis
Meditation
Altering Consciousness with Drugs
    Stimulants
    Depressants
    Hallucinogens
    Marijuana—A Special Case
TOPIC 4C SUMMARY

CHAPTER SUMMARY

The National Commission on Sleep Disorder Research (NCSDR) released Volume One of its report *Wake Up America: A National Sleep Alert* in January of 1993. The commission found that approximately 40 million Americans suffer from chronic disorders of sleep and that another 20 to 30 million persons experience intermittent sleep-related problems. We will review some of the findings and recommendations of the NCSDR later in this chapter. For now, consider a few samples of the testimony presented at the commission's open hearings.

I was experiencing constant daytime drowsiness. I would fall asleep for short periods during meetings, conversations, and public functions. At times, I could awaken and make a very inappropriate comment only to realize that I was commenting on a dream I had just experienced. My associates began to question my mental stability. . . . It was my practice in those days to carry a large pin or pocket knife with which I would stab myself in the leg, arm or hand to stay awake during meetings and while driving. (p. 15)

The Exxon Valdez, grounded in Prince William Sound, Alaska, in March, 1989, cost our nation billions of dollars: $25 million in damage to the vessel itself; $3.4 million in lost cargo; and $1.85 billion in cleanup costs. We continue to assess the impact of the long-term devastation upon an extremely productive and unique ecosystem, for generations an important resource for local fishermen and the state's tourist industry. The National Transportation Safety Board (NTSB) determined that "the probable cause of the grounding . . . was the failure of the third mate to properly maneuver the vessel because of fatigue and excessive workload." The third mate was asleep on his feet and failed to respond to the warning light signaling Bligh Reef. (p. 16)

To help you understand narcolepsy, set your alarm for every 90 minutes, and stay awake for ten minutes every time it goes off. Alternate that with periods of 48 hours without sleep . . . Collapse on the floor each time you are angry, scared, surprised, laughing, or upset. Sleep for $1/2$ hour before you drive anywhere; sleep again for $1/2$ hour when you arrive . . . Be late for everything. Fall asleep at every traffic light . . . I figured out the difference between my life as a narcoleptic and dead people. The dead don't have to get up and go to work every day. (p. 35)

*C*onsciousness is such a central, integral part of our lives, we might argue that to be alive is to be conscious. You may remember that the earliest psychologists (e.g., Wilhelm Wundt and William James) actually defined psychology as the science of consciousness, or mental activity. Dealing with consciousness scientifically proved to be a very tricky business. After years of struggling with a science of consciousness, psychologists were more than happy to abandon consciousness altogether and turn their attention to observable behavior, as John B. Watson (and behaviorism) argued they should. But consciousness would not go away, and within the past 25 years, the scientific study of consciousness has reemerged, resuming its place in mainstream psychology.

In this chapter, we will first consider some matters of definition to gain a better appreciation of just what consciousness is. We'll then look at a number of "altered" states of consciousness. Perhaps we can better appreciate "normal" consciousness if we examine those conditions in which our consciousness, or awareness, is changed (distorted). We'll consider the changes that take place in our consciousness when it is affected by sleep, hypnosis, meditation, and drugs.

Topic 4A

LEVELS OF CONSCIOUSNESS

NORMAL, WAKING CONSCIOUSNESS

consciousness the awareness or perception of the environment and of one's own mental processes

Consciousness is the awareness, or perception, of the environment and of one's own mental processes. Consciousness, then, is a state of awareness. Normal, waking consciousness is the awareness of those thoughts, ideas, feelings, and perceptions that are active in our minds. With this as a working definition, we might ask how to best characterize consciousness. What are its aspects or dimensions?

When he addressed a group of psychologists at a national conference, Wilse Webb, a respected researcher in the field of sleep and dreaming, was faced with the task of describing consciousness. Webb (1981) claimed that we could do no better than to read what William James had to say about consciousness over a hundred years ago.

For James (1890, 1892, 1904), there were four basic aspects of what we are calling our normal, waking consciousness. We should try to keep these four factors in mind—in our own consciousness—as we read through this Topic.

1. Consciousness is always *changing*. Consciousness doesn't hold still. It cannot be held before the mind for study. "No state once gone can recur and be identical with what was before," James wrote (1892, p. 152).

2. Consciousness is a *personal* experience. Consciousness does not exist without an individual to have it. My consciousness and yours are separate and different. The only consciousness I can experience with certainty is mine. You may try to tell me about yours, but I will never be able to fully appreciate your consciousness.

3. Consciousness is *continuous*. Our awareness of our environment and of ourselves cannot be broken into pieces. There are no gaps in our awareness. We really can't tell where one thought begins and another leaves off. James wrote, "Consciousness, then, does not appear to itself chopped up in bits. Such words as 'chain' or 'train' do not describe it fitly as it presents itself in the first instance. It is nothing jointed; it flows. A 'river' or 'stream' is most naturally described. In talking of it hereafter, let us call it the stream of thought, of consciousness . . . " (1890, p. 243).

4. Consciousness is *selective*. Awareness is often a matter of making choices, of selectively attending to some aspect of experience while ignoring others. "We find it [consciousness] always doing one thing, choosing one out of several of the materials so presented to its notice, emphasizing and accentuating that and suppressing as far as possible all the rest" (James, 1890, p. 139). We had a good bit to say about the factors that influence the selective nature of consciousness in our last chapter.

I trust that you can appreciate that studying human consciousness scientifically, or experimentally, has been a challenge to psychologists over the years. An even more slippery notion is that consciousness is not an either-or proposition; that it functions to different degrees, or levels, of awareness. Let's now consider levels of consciousness and the possibility of subconscious mental processes.

Before You Go On

What is normal, waking consciousness, and, according to William James, what are its basic characteristics?

IS THERE AN UNCONSCIOUS, AND WHAT MIGHT IT BE LIKE?

The observation that levels or degrees of consciousness vary throughout the day seems intuitively obvious. There are times when we are wide awake, paying full attention to nearly everything around us, alert and aware, processing considerable information from the environment. On the other hand, there are those times when our "minds wander," when we seem "unfocused," don't seem to be paying attention to or processing much information of any sort from anywhere. And, of course, when we are asleep there are long periods when we are virtually unconscious, seemingly unaware of what is happening either in the environment or in our own minds.

It also seems intuitively obvious that the higher the degree, or level, of our consciousness, the better able we are to process (i.e., interpret, understand, recall, or react to) the information of which we are conscious. For example, is it not more likely that you will remember something said in class if your consciousness is focused; you are attentive, wide awake, and straining your attention to hear and understand what is being said? Are you not more likely to trip over something on the sidewalk if you are daydreaming about this weekend's plans rather than remaining fully conscious of the environment around you?

Now we come to the interesting question: Is it possible to process information about the environment without being aware of that information or that processing? Is it possible to process information *unconsciously*? The idea of an unconscious aspect of mind has a long history in philosophy and psychology (Greenwald, 1992; Hilgard, 1992; Kihlstrom, 1987; Whyte, 1960). In this section, we'll focus first on a classic view of the unconscious as proposed by Sigmund Freud, and then briefly consider some contemporary research.

The Freudian View of Levels of Consciousness

psychiatry the subfield of medicine that studies, diagnoses, and treats mental disorders

Sigmund Freud was trained in medicine, and can rightfully be called the Father of Psychiatry—where **psychiatry** refers to that subfield of medicine that studies, diagnoses, and treats mental disorders. Early in his career, Freud became intrigued by what were then called "nervous disorders." He was struck by how little was known about disorders wherein one's psychological experiences and mental life seemed to produce pain and suffering for which there was no known medical explanation. Using his observations of his patients and of himself, Freud developed theories that revolutionized the way we think about human nature. Freud proposed an elaborate theory of personality and how it develops (see Topic 9A). He put his ideas about human nature into practice by developing a new technique for treating mental disorders (the technique is called psychoanalysis, which will be covered in Topic 13B). So, you see, we shall be referring to Sigmund Freud again. For now, we are focusing on Freud's view of consciousness, a central aspect of his theory of human personality.

Freud's vision of consciousness is often depicted as an iceberg nearly totally submerged in the sea (Figure 4.1). This iceberg analogy is one that Freud used himself. What does it imply?

Freud wrote that only a small portion of one's mental life was readily available to one's awareness at any given time. Ideas, memories, feelings, or motives of which we are actively aware are said to be *conscious*. It is hoped you are right now conscious of the words you are reading, what they mean, and how you can relate them to your own experience.

Figure 4.1

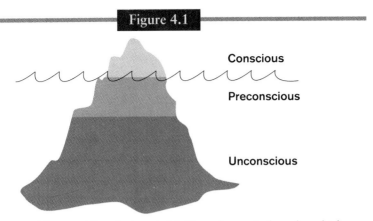

In the theories of Sigmund Freud, the mind is likened to an iceberg for which only a small part of one's mental life is available in normal waking consciousness; more is available, with some effort of retrieval, at a preconscious level; and most is stored away at an unconscious level from which retrieval occurs only with great difficulty.

Aspects of our experience that are not conscious at any one moment, but that can easily be brought to awareness, are, according to Freud, stored at a *preconscious* level. For example, right now you may not be thinking about what you had for dinner last night or what you might have for dinner tonight, but with just a little effort these matters can be brought into your conscious awareness.

Cognitions, feelings, or motives that are not available at the conscious or the preconscious level are said to be in the *unconscious*. At this level are ideas, desires, and memories of which we are not aware and cannot easily become aware. This is a strange notion: that there are thoughts and feelings stored away in our minds of which we are completely unaware. However, Freud theorized that the unconscious level of mind can and does influence us. Much of the content of our unconscious mind is put there because if we were to think about or dwell on these issues we would experience anxiety and distress. A husband, for instance, who constantly forgets his wedding anniversary and occasionally cannot even remember his wife's name when he tries to introduce her may be experiencing some unconscious conflict or doubts about being married in the first place. (There are, of course, other explanations.) Unconscious mental content—passing through the preconscious—can show itself in dreams, humor, and slips of the tongue. It might be significant that following a lively discussion of some issue, Nathan says to Heather, "Let's rape about this some more some time," when he "meant" to say, "Let's rap about this some more some time." As we shall see, many Freudian techniques of psychotherapy are aimed at helping the patient learn about the contents of his or her unconscious mind.

As you might imagine, demonstrating the reality of levels of consciousness as Freud proposed them has proven difficult in controlled, laboratory research. Nonetheless, Freud's basic ideas about levels of consciousness have gained wide acceptance in psychology, particularly among practicing clinical psychologists (Erdelyi, 1985; Greenwald, 1992; Lockhard & Paulus, 1988).

Before You Go On

**What are the three levels of consciousness
proposed by Freud?**

Contemporary Investigations of the Unconscious

In Chapter 1, I said that cognitive psychologists investigate the basic processes of the mind: perception, learning, memory, and thinking. The study of unconscious mental activity has had a long and honorable history in psychology, but lately there has been a resurgence of interest among cognitive psychologists in the unconscious processing of information. Contemporary research is trying to bring the unconscious mind to the laboratory and to describe how (or if) information from the environment can be processed, and how it can influence our behaviors without our awareness. At the moment, virtually all conclusions on these matters are tentative, awaiting further research, but here we can summarize some of the research being done. The major stumbling block is the "lack of consensus on where the division between conscious and unconscious processes lies" (Loftus & Klinger, 1992, p. 763).

There are two ways in which psychologists assess unconscious processing. In one sense, you have processed information unconsciously if you were not actively attending to that information when it was presented (a matter of perception without awareness). In another sense, you processed information unconsciously if you could not then verbally report that such information was presented (a matter of memory) (Erdelyi, 1992; Greenwald, 1992). In either sense, current research indicates that we sometimes do process things without awareness (Holyoak & Spellman, 1993; Loftus & Klinger, 1992). Let's look at an example of each type of "unconscious processing."

Picture this. You are sitting in a theater watching a movie. Bruce Willis is about to jump from a building just before it explodes. Suddenly, there on the screen, in big letters, is a message: BUY SODA, followed shortly by, HOW ABOUT SOME POPCORN? If this sort of interruption actually occurred, you would probably be upset, leave the theater, and demand your money back. You paid to see a movie, not a series of commercial messages. But what if the messages embedded in the movie were *so* brief, or *so* dim that you were not consciously aware of their presence? If you did not realize they were there, could they still influence you? Could they influence you to the point of actually going to the refreshment stand and placing an order for popcorn and a drink?

When we ask the question this way, the answer is clearly no. The issue here is known as **subliminal perception**, the process of perceiving and responding to stimuli presented below our absolute threshold—below our level of conscious processing. Although the implications for misuses are clear, it is almost a shame that subliminal perception in this sense does not work. Wouldn't it be useful *if we could* reduce shoplifting by embedding antishoplifting messages into the background music in retail stores? Wouldn't it be wonderful *if we could* increase our earning potential, or improve our study habits, or build our self-confidence simply by listening to audiotapes or watching videotapes into which subliminal messages have been inserted? But these tapes do not work—at least they do not work through anything like subliminal, unconscious processing. Many people claim to have been helped by such tapes, and perhaps they have been. A better explanation is that when people genuinely believe the tapes will help, and have invested time and money in them, they can easily convince themselves that the tapes are of value (Balay & Shevrin, 1988; Dixon, 1971; Duncan, 1985; Vokey & Read, 1985).

An experiment reported in 1991 by Anthony Greenwald and his colleagues looked at the changes that occurred when 237 motivated students listened to audiotapes supposed to either improve memory or enhance self-esteem through subliminal suggestion. What the students did not know was that the labels on some of the tapes were switched so that some of the students who believed they were using the memory enhancement tapes were actually using the self-esteem tapes, and vice versa. Although there was general improvement for both memory and self-esteem for everyone, "neither the memory nor the self-esteem tapes produced their claimed effects" (p. 119). Even so, more than a third of the participants in this experiment had the illusion of improvement that the tape's label promised.

Is it true then, that stimuli outside one's awareness or consciousness never have any effect? No, that's too strong a statement. Although messages directed only at your unconscious mind are not going to influence you to get up from your TV set and march down to the store to buy some new snack food, there is evidence that to some degree we may be sensitive to stimuli presented below our levels of immediate awareness. Here's one example of that sort of evidence.

A subject sits in front of a small screen. A word is flashed on the screen so dimly and so quickly that the subject does not report seeing the word. Let's say the word is EASTER. Now two words are flashed on the screen that the subject *can* see clearly. The task is to choose the word related in some way to the word that was not seen. Let's say the words used in this example are BUNNY and PENCIL. Even when subjects claim they are just guessing, they choose BUNNY significantly more frequently than chance would predict. If the "unconscious prompt" were PEN, not EASTER, they would tend to choose PENCIL. It is as if the initially presented word has influenced their choice (e.g., Cheesman &

subliminal perception the process of perceiving and responding to stimuli presented at levels below one's absolute threshold

Merikle, 1984; Dixon, 1971, 1981; Fowler et al., 1981; Tulving & Schacter, 1990). For that matter, simply reading a list of words at one point in time increases the ability of subjects to read those words later when they are flashed very briefly on a computer screen, even if the subjects did not recognize that the words had been read previously (Jacoby & Dallas, 1981). We'll be returning to this issue again when we discuss memory in Chapter 6.

So, is there an unconscious mind, and if so, what is it like? There is no doubt that consciousness occurs in degrees. There is little doubt that we can process some information without our full awareness or consciousness—unconsciously, if you will. At the present, the data suggest that the unconscious is simple, unsophisticated, and primitive in terms of the amount or type of information it can handle.

> A large body of research now suggests that the reality of unconscious processes is no longer questionable. Although there is not uniform agreement about how sophisticated these processes are, there seems to be a general consensus that the unconscious may not be as smart as previously believed. More important, there is absolute agreement that exciting times, both in research and theory, are ahead for the unconscious. (Loftus & Klinger, 1992, p. 764)

Before You Go On

How may we characterize
unconscious processing?

Cite an example of experimental evidence
for unconscious processing.

TOPIC 4A SUMMARY

Consciousness is the perception or awareness of the environment and of one's own mental processes. Normal, waking consciousness is always changing, personal, continuous, and selective. Human consciousness occurs to differing degrees or differing levels of awareness. In fact, the processing of some information may occur without our awareness and is said to be unconscious. Freud argued that the information in our unconscious minds is (typically, at least) the sort of information that would cause us anxiety or distress if it were to be dealt with on a conscious level. Contemporary research suggests that there may be something to unconscious processing, but, so far, that processing seems very limited and simple.

Our appreciation of levels of normal, waking consciousness may be enhanced if we examine consciousness when its nature is altered.

By definition, if we are in an altered state of consciousness, our perception of ourselves and the environment will be changed or altered. The nature of these changes and how they are produced is the focus of the rest of this chapter.

Topic 4B

SLEEPING AND DREAMING

Sleep alters our consciousness by reducing our alertness, awareness, and perception of events occurring around us. Sleep is a normal process, yet it is one we do not understand well. We are seldom aware or conscious of our own sleeping, even though we may spend more than 200,000 hours of our lifetime asleep. Sleep can be considered a temporary loss of consciousness. We can know that we have been asleep. We can be certain that we will sleep again. We can suspect that we are dreaming, but we find it difficult to be sure.

Just as the level or degree of our awareness varies during the day, so does our sleep vary in its level or quality from night to night and throughout the night. The study of sleep and dreams, as variants of consciousness, has intrigued psychologists for many years. In this Topic, we'll examine some of what we know about the altered state of consciousness we call sleep.

THE STAGES OF A "GOOD NIGHT'S SLEEP"

How do we know when someone is asleep? Self-reports of sleeping are notoriously unreliable. A person who claims that he or she "didn't sleep a wink last night" may have slept soundly for many hours (Dement, 1974).

Our best, most reliable indicators of sleep are measurements of brain activity and muscle tone. The **electroencephalogram** (**EEG**) is an instrument that measures and records the electrical activity of the brain. It does so by means of small electrodes pasted onto the scalp. The process is slightly messy, but it is in no way painful. The **electromyogram** (**EMG**) similarly produces a record of a muscle's activity, tone, or state of relaxation.

When you are in a calm, relaxed state, with your eyes closed, but not yet asleep, your EEG pattern shows a rhythmic cycle of brain wave activity called **alpha activity**. In this presleep stage, we find relatively smooth EEG waves cycling 8 to 12 times per second. If, as you sit or lie there, you start worrying about an event of the day or trying to solve a problem, the smooth alpha waves become disrupted and

electroencephalogram (EEG) an instrument used to measure and record the electrical activity of the brain

electromyogram (EMG) an instrument used to measure and record muscle tension/relaxation

alpha activity an EEG pattern associated with quiet relaxation and characterized by slow wave cycles of 8 to 12 per second

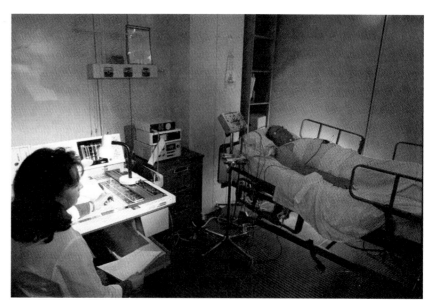

Subjects in sleep laboratories provide scientists with information about humans during sleep. Electrodes attached to the scalp provide an indication of brain activity with EEG records.

are replaced by an apparently random pattern of heightened electrical activity typical of what we usually find in wakefulness.

As you drift from rest and relaxation into sleep, your brain waves change, as alpha waves give way to the stages of sleep. The EEG tracings of sleeping subjects reveal that sleep can be divided into four stages (Borbely, 1986). As I review these four stages, you can refer to Figure 4.2, which shows the EEGs of a person in each of the stages of sleep. These tracings were chosen because they are good illustrations of the four stages. Actual EEG tracings are not always this clear.

Stage 1: This is a very light sleep from which you can be easily aroused. The smooth, cyclical alpha pattern disappears, replaced by the slower *theta waves* (3–7 cycles per second). The amplitude, or magnitude, of the electrical activity also lessens considerably. At the same time, your breathing is becoming more regular, and your heart rate is slowing and blood pressure is decreasing. This stage does not last long—generally less than 10 minutes. Then, you start to slide into stage 2 sleep.

Stage 2: In this stage, the EEG pattern is similar to stage 1—low amplitude, with no noticeable wavelike pattern. The difference is that we now see *sleep spindles* in the EEG record. These are brief, high-amplitude bursts of electrical activity that occur with regularity (about every 15 seconds). You're really getting off to sleep now, but still can be easily awakened.

Stage 3: You're getting into deep sleep. There is a reduction in the brain's electrical activity. Now we can clearly make out *delta wave* activity in your EEG. Delta waves are high, slow waves

Figure 4.2

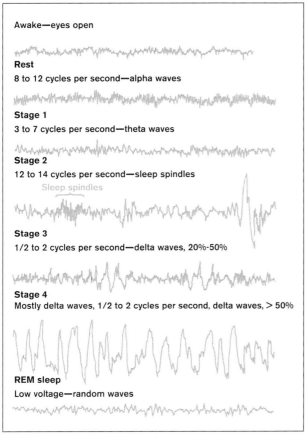

EEG records showing the general electrical activity of the brain for a person at various levels of wakefulness and sleep.

(from 0.5 to 3 cycles per second). In stage 3 of sleep, delta waves constitute between 20 and 50 percent of your EEG pattern. Your internal functions (temperature, heart rate, breathing) are lowering and slowing. It's going to be difficult to wake you now.

Stage 4: Now you're in deep sleep. Your EEG record is virtually filled with slow, recurring delta waves (as opposed to stage 3 sleep, where delta waves constituted only a portion of your brain wave activity). Readings from an electromyogram indicate that your muscles have become totally relaxed. About 15 percent of your night's sleep will be spent in this stage of sleep.

It usually takes about an hour to go from stage 1 to stage 4, depending on such things as how tired you are and the physical conditions that surround you. We'll assume a quiet, dark room, with a comfortable and familiar bed. After an hour's passage through these four stages, the sequence begins to reverse itself. You go back through stage 3, to stage 2, but before going through the stages in order again, something remarkable happens. Your eyes move rapidly under closed eyelids.

Before You Go On

What are the EEG and the EMG?

Briefly describe the four stages of sleep.

REM AND NREM SLEEP

REM sleep rapid-eye-movement sleep, during which vivid dreaming occurs, as do heightened levels of physiological functioning

In the early 1950s, Nathaniel Kleitman and Eugene Aserinsky made quite a discovery. They noticed that as sleeping subjects began their second series of stages into deeper levels of sleep, their eyes darted back and forth under their closed eyelids (Aserinsky & Kleitman, 1953; Kleitman, 1963b). This period of *rapid eye movement* is called **REM sleep**. A noteworthy aspect of this discovery is that when people are awakened during REM sleep, they usually (about 85 percent of the time) report that they are having a vivid, storylike dream. When awakened during sleep periods not accompanied by rapid eye movements—*NREM sleep*—people report fewer and much more fragmented dreams (Kleitman, 1963a; NCSDR, 1993). At first it was believed that eye movements during REM sleep were being made as the dreamer literally viewed, or scanned, images produced by the dream. It turns out that a dreamer's eye movements are unrelated to the content of his or her dream. Eye movements are produced instead by a cluster of cells in the brain stem near other clusters of cells that have been implicated in moving us in and out of REM and NREM sleep (Hobson, 1977; Kiester, 1980).

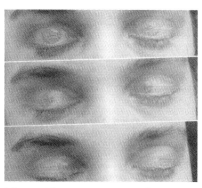

The rapid eye movements of REM sleep are captured in these double-exposure photographs.

Periods of REM sleep occur throughout the night, normally lasting from a few minutes to half an hour, occupying about 20 to 25 percent of the sleep of adult humans. About 90 to 120 minutes each night is spent "REMing." During these REM periods, we are probably dreaming. As one goes through a night's sleep, REM episodes tend to become longer and dreams more vivid (NCSDR, 1993). The normal pattern of REM occurrences is presented in Figure 4.3. Note that during the course of a night's sleep, one does not necessarily pass through all stages of sleep in an orderly fashion. Occasionally stage 3 may be passed over completely; later in the evening, stage 4 may be absent. Indeed, toward the end of our sleeping, we tend not to return to the deep sleep of stage 4 between REM episodes. If you refer to Figure 4.2, you will find an EEG tracing typical of the sort found during REM sleep. Note that it looks much like the tracing indicating wakefulness.

Everyone REMs. Everyone dreams. Some of us have difficulty remembering what we have dreamed when we awake in the morning, but we can be sure that in the course of a normal night's sleep, we

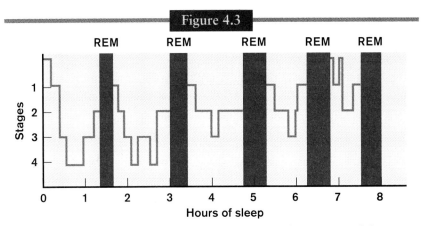

Figure 4.3

A typical sequence of sleep stages during a night's sleep for a young adult. Notice the recurring REM sleep throughout the night, and note that one does not need to enter each stage of sleep in the same order each night.

have dreamed several times. (There's no great mystery why we don't remember our dreams any better than we do. Most dreams are ordinary, boring, and forgettable. Unless we make some conscious effort to do so, we seldom try to store dream content in our memories so that it can be recalled later. That is, we are seldom motivated to remember our dreams.)

Although we're sure that everyone does dream, we're less sure *why* everyone dreams. Some theories have their basis in the writings of Freud (1900), who believed that dreaming allows us the opportunity to engage in fantasy and wish fulfillment of a sort that would probably cause us discomfort or embarrassment if we entertained such thoughts while we were awake. Freud saw dreams as a pathway (he called the "royal road") to the discovery of the contents of our unconscious mind.

More modern theories about the function of REM sleep and dreaming tend to emphasize the physiological activity that occurs during this phase of sleep. One hypothesis is that REM sleep helps the brain form, or consolidate, memories of events that occurred during the day. In one study, for example, students were less able to recall stories they read before they went to bed if their REM sleep was interrupted during the night (Tilley & Empson, 1978).

Another intriguing hypothesis is that dreams (and our recall of them) represent convenient cognitive "explanations" for what may be the random activity of our brains. For example, if the area of the brain associated with the movement of our legs is active while we are asleep, our brain will "manufacture" a reasonable story—a dream— that involves running, or kicking, or using our leg muscles (Hobson, 1988; Hobson & McCarley, 1977). These theories are consistent with those contemporary theories about why we sleep in the first place. One such theory argues that there are several networks, or groups, of

atonia muscular immobility, associated with REM sleep, caused by the total relaxation of the muscles

neurons involved in falling asleep, not just one brain center that controls whether we are awake or asleep. Some of these groups of neurons are involved in critical, but infrequent, activities (such as informing us that our body temperature is too high). We sleep, then, to activate these seldom-used neuron groups in order to maintain their function (Krueger & Obal, 1993; Saunders & Sullivan, 1994).

Dreaming isn't all that happens during REM sleep. From the outside, someone in REM sleep seems quiet and calm, except for those barely noticeable eye movements. On the inside, however, there is quite a different story. One noticeable change is a type of muscular immobility, called **atonia**, caused by the total relaxation of the muscles (Chase & Morales, 1990). It does seem adaptive to have the body lie still so that the dreamer does not react to the action of his or her dreams. This state of immobilization is occasionally interrupted by slight muscle "twitches" (which you may have seen if you've watched a sleeping dog that seems to be dreaming about chasing an imaginary rabbit). Some people do not demonstrate normal atonia but thrash about wildly during REM sleep, a condition reasonably called REM sleep disorder (Mahowald & Schenck, 1989).

In many ways, the REM sleeper is very active, even though he or she may be oblivious to, or not conscious of, most external stimulation. During REM sleep there is often an excitement of the sex organs, males having a penile erection, females having a discharge of vaginal fluids (although this latter finding is not as common). Breathing usually becomes shallow and rapid. Blood pressure levels may skyrocket and heart rates increase, all while the person lies "peacefully" asleep. There does not appear to be much that is quiet or peaceful about REM sleep. These changes occur regardless of what the sleeper is dreaming about. It matters little whether one is dreaming about lying on the beach getting a tan, enjoying a sexual encounter, or engaging in hand-to-hand combat; physiologically, the reactions are the same. This marked increase in physiological activity has long been suspected to be related to heart attacks, strokes, and other cardiovascular problems that can develop "even though the patient was asleep" (King et al., 1973; Kirby & Verrier, 1989; Somers et al., 1993).

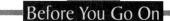

Before You Go On

What are REM and NREM sleep?

What occurs during REM sleep?

SLEEP DEPRIVATION AND DISORDERS OF SLEEP

"Each year, the lives of millions of American men, women, and children are disturbed, disrupted, or destroyed by sleep deprivation, sleep disorders, or sleep disturbances." So begins the report of the National

Commission on Sleep Disorders Research (NCSDR, 1993, p. 15). In this section, we'll consider some of the issues that have concerned this commission.

Sleep Deprivation—In the Real World and in the Laboratory

We are a nation in need of a good night's sleep. On the average, most people get about 1.5 hours less sleep each night than they need. This reflects a reduction in average nightly sleep time of nearly 20 percent over the last century—due to a myriad of factors, including demands of the workplace, school, home, and family. Interstate truck drivers, for instance, regularly get less than five hours of sleep a night (NCSDR, 1993). Each of us requires a specific amount of sleep in every 24-hour period to maintain optimal waking activity. "A good night's sleep" is the amount of sleep that will allow a person to awaken without the use of some device or environmental influence, such as an alarm clock. If a person does not get an adequate amount of sleep (there *are* individual differences in terms of how much sleep is adequate), he or she will be less alert and less able to function well the next day. What is particularly troubling is that sleep loss accumulates from one night to the next as a "sleep debt." The more sleep lost each day, the greater the debt, and the more severe the consequences.

Most sleep deprivation studies—in which humans or animals are awakened so as to disrupt their sleep—show remarkably few long-term adverse side-effects of that deprivation (Horne, 1988; Martin, 1986; Webb & Cartwright, 1978). Even when sleep is disrupted over several nights, there are few lasting changes in a person's reactions, particularly if the person is in good physical and psychological health to begin with. If the task at hand is interesting enough and if it is not lengthy or time-consuming, there is little impairment of intellectual functioning after sleep deprivation (Dement, 1974; Webb, 1975). At least up to a point, we can adapt to deprivation, perhaps by taking little catnaps while we're awake. Very short episodes of sleep, called **microsleeps**, can be found in the EEG records of waking subjects, both animal and human. These microsleep episodes increase in number when normal sleep is disrupted.

That's not to say that there aren't *any* effects of being deprived of sleep. Some people show signs of depression and irritability when their sleep is interrupted (e.g., Moorecroft, 1987, 1989). People deprived of REM sleep for a few nights and then left alone will spend long periods REMing, as if to catch up on lost REMs. This *REM rebound effect* is generally found only for the first night after deprivation, then patterns return to normal. There is some evidence that NREM sleep (particularly stage 4 deep sleep) also rebounds (Agnew et al., 1964). When, in 1965, 17-year-old Randy Gardner set the Guinness world record by going without sleep for nearly 266 hours, he slept for 14 hours the first night after deprivation, but by the second night he returned to his normal 8 hours of sleep. The current record holder for sleeplessness, Maureen Weston, went for nearly 19 days without sleep and similarly experienced no lasting effects once given the opportunity to reduce her sleep debt.

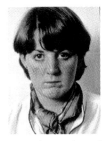

A study conducted at Loughborough University of Technology in England tested the effects of 72 hours of sleep deprivation on volunteers. Despite the weary looks of the "after" picture, volunteers suffered no ill effects of their deprivation.

microsleep a very brief episode of sleep discernible only by examination of an EEG record

Disorders of Sleep

A good night's sleep is a wonderful and apparently necessary thing. Some people have no difficulty sleeping, and seem to be able to sleep through anything. Others experience problems, either in getting to sleep in the first place, or during sleep itself. As is the case for so many psychological processes, we often take sleep for granted until we experience problems with it.

Insomnia. At some time or another, each of us has suffered from a bout of **insomnia**—the inability to fall asleep or stay asleep when we want to. We may be excited or worried about something that is going to happen the next day. We may have overstimulated our autonomic nervous systems with drugs, such as the caffeine in coffee, tea, or soft drinks. However, most people who chronically (regularly) suffer from insomnia haven't the slightest idea why they are unable to get a good night's sleep. Chronic, debilitating insomnia afflicts nearly 30 million Americans, women more commonly than men, and the elderly about 1.5 times as often as younger adults (Fredrickson, 1987; NCSDR, 1993).

insomnia the inability to fall asleep and/or stay asleep

An interesting finding from the sleep laboratory is that many people who *believe* they are not getting enough sleep are, in fact, sleeping much more than they think. The phenomenon is called *pseudoinsomnia,* and one hypothesis is that such people spend several dream episodes each night dreaming that they are awake and trying to get to sleep. Then, in the morning, they remember their dreams and come to believe that they haven't slept at all (e.g., Dement, 1974). Pseudoinsomnia can usually be cured simply by demonstrating to patients that they really are getting a good night's sleep, as indicated by their EEG records.

Prescribing sleeping pills (common in nursing home settings) and using over-the-counter medications to treat insomnia may cause more problems than it solves. The medication (usually sedatives or depressants) may have a positive effect for a while, but eventually dosages have to be increased as tolerance builds. When the drugs are discontinued, a rebound effect occurs that makes it even more difficult to get to sleep than it was before (Kales et al., 1979; Kripke & Gillin, 1985; Palfai & Jankiewicz, 1991).

Narcolepsy. **Narcolepsy** involves going to sleep, even during the day, without any intention to do so. Symptoms also include excessive sleepiness, brief episodes of muscle weakness or paralysis precipitated by strong emotion, paralysis upon falling asleep, and dreamlike images that occur as soon as one goes to sleep (in a narcoleptic episode, one immediately goes into REM sleep). No one knows exactly what causes narcolepsy, and the disorder seems resistant to treatment. Although only 50,000 cases of the disorder have been diagnosed, estimates are that nearly 350,000 Americans suffer from narcolepsy (NCSDR, 1993). The big problem with narcolepsy (in addition to the embarrassment it may cause) is the total relaxation of muscle tone that is associated with REM sleep (Dement, 1974; Lucas et al.,

narcolepsy a disorder that involves unintentional sleeping, muscle paralysis, and immediate REM sleep; is resistant to treatment

1979). The danger involved in suddenly going to sleep and losing muscle control during one's daily activities is obvious.

Sleep Apnea. Apnea means a sudden stoppage in breathing, literally "without breath." If we were to stop breathing when awake and conscious, we could do something about it. We can exercise conscious, voluntary control over our breathing. We cannot do so, however, when we are asleep. **Sleep apnea** involves patterns of sleep during which breathing stops entirely. Usually, episodes are short, and long-term dangers are few. When apnea episodes are longer—say, a minute or two—carbon dioxide in the lungs builds to such a level that the sleeper is awakened, draws a few gasps of air, and returns to sleep, probably oblivious to what just happened. Potential consequences of sleep apnea include hypertension, coronary heart disease, stroke, psychiatric problems, impotence, and memory loss. The Commission on Sleep Disorders Research estimates that 38,000 cardiovascular deaths due to sleep apnea occur each year (NCSDR, 1993, p. 33).

For reasons not clearly understood, sleep apnea appears most commonly in obese, middle-aged males. Sleep apnea is also a prime suspect in the search for a cause of Sudden Infant Death Syndrome, or SIDS. In this syndrome, young infants, apparently without any major illness, but sometimes with a slight cold or infection, suddenly die in their sleep. Such sudden death occurs at a rate of about two infants per thousand.

sleep apnea involves patterns of sleep during which breathing stops entirely

Before You Go On

What are the effects of sleep deprivation?

Name and describe three common disorders of sleep.

TOPIC 4B SUMMARY

We spend nearly one-third of our lives in that altered state of consciousness we call sleep. EEG tracings—the most reliable indicators of sleep—show us that sleep flows through four discernible stages, although not necessarily in predictable patterns. The distinction between REM and NREM sleep is made on the basis of involuntary rapid eye movements. Neither REM nor NREM sleep is considered one of the four "stages of sleep." REM sleep is associated with clear, vivid dreaming episodes and occupies about one-quarter of our sleeping time. During rapid eye movement (REM) sleep, we experience atonia (muscular immobility) and an activation of the sympathetic division of the ANS (including rapid, shallow breathing, increased heart rate, and

elevated blood pressure). Millions of persons are afflicted by disturbances of sleep, many simply not getting enough sleep. Short-term
consequences of sleep deprivation are not severe and can be rectified
with just one or two nights of normal sleep. Long-term effects can be
serious. Common disorders of sleep include insomnia (an inability to
fall asleep and stay asleep when one wants to), narcolepsy (rapidly
falling asleep, even in the daytime, without intention), and sleep apnea
(patterns of sleep in which one stops breathing).

Topic 4 C
VOLUNTARY ALTERATIONS OF CONSCIOUSNESS

Now that we have reviewed some of the evidence and theories of the
altered state of consciousness called sleep, we can turn to those states
that normally require some effort to attain. In this Topic, we'll consider three processes that result in "altered states of consciousness":
hypnosis, meditation, and the use of psychoactive drugs.

HYPNOSIS

hypnosis an altered state of consciousness characterized by an increase in suggestibility, attention, and imagination

Hypnosis is an altered state of consciousness that typically requires
the voluntary cooperation of the person being hypnotized. Hypnosis
is characterized by (1) a marked increase in suggestibility, (2) a focusing of attention, (3) an exaggerated use of imagination, (4) an unwillingness or inability to act on one's own, and (5) an unquestioning
acceptance of distortions of reality (Hilgard & Hilgard, 1975). There
is little truth to the belief that being hypnotized is like going to sleep.
In fact, few of the characteristics of sleep are to be found in the hypnotized subject. EEG patterns, for example, are significantly different.

Hypnosis has been used, with varying degrees of success, for a
number of purposes. As you know, it is used as entertainment, as a
show business routine where members of an audience are hypnotized—usually to do silly things in public. Hypnosis has long been
viewed as a method for gaining access to memories of events not in
immediate awareness. Hypnosis has also been touted as a process of
treatment for a wide range of psychological and physical disorders. In
this section, we'll consider some common questions about hypnosis.

1. *Can everyone be hypnotized?* No, probably not. The susceptibility to hypnosis varies widely from person to person. Some people
resist and cannot be hypnotized. Contrary to popular belief, you
cannot be hypnotized against your will, which is one reason why I
say that one enters a hypnotic state voluntarily (although I acknowledge that some hypnotists claim that they can hypnotize anyone under the right conditions, which is why I hedged and said
"probably" not) (e.g., Lynn et al., 1990).

Hypnosis is an altered state of consciousness that one enters voluntarily. It has been used for a variety of purposes, including treatment of some psychological and physical disorders.

2. *What best predicts who can be easily hypnotized?* Although not everyone can be easily hypnotized, some people are excellent subjects, can readily be put into deep hypnotic states, and can easily learn to hypnotize themselves (Hilgard, 1975, 1978). A number of traits are correlated with one's hypnotizability. The most important factor seems to be the ability to engage easily in daydreaming and fantasy, to be able to "set ordinary reality aside for awhile" (Lynn & Rhue, 1986; Wilkes, 1986, p. 25). Other factors include suggestibility and a degree of passivity or willingness to cooperate, at least during the hypnotic session. Another intriguing notion is that persons who were often punished in childhood, or are avid readers, runners, or actors, are good subjects for hypnosis. The logic is that these people have a history of self-induced trancelike states (to escape punishment, to focus and become absorbed in a task at hand, and so on), which makes them more likely to be hypnotized (Hilgard, 1970).

3. *Can I be made to do things under the influence of hypnosis that I would be embarrassed to do otherwise?* Next to being unknowingly hypnotized, this seems to be the greatest fear associated with hypnosis. Again, the answer is *probably* no. Under the influence of a skilled hypnotist, you may do some pretty silly things and do them publicly. Under the right circumstances, you might do those same things without being hypnotized. It is unlikely you would do under hypnosis anything you would not do otherwise. However, under certain (unusual) circumstances, people can do outrageous—and dangerous—things, which is why hypnosis should be used with caution.

4. *Are hypnotized subjects simply more open to the suggestions of the hypnotist, or is their consciousness really changed?* This issue is in dispute. Some believe that hypnosis is really no more than a heightened level of suggestibility (Barber, 1972; Spanos & Barber, 1974), whereas others believe it to be a special state, separate from the compliance of a willing subject. When hypnotized subjects are left alone, they usually maintain the condition induced by their hypnosis. Subjects not hypnotized, but simply complying as best they can with an experimenter, revert quickly to normal behaviors when left alone (Hilgard, 1975; Orne, 1969).

5. *Can hypnosis be used to alleviate pain—real, physical pain?* Yes. It won't (can't) cure the underlying cause, but it can be used to control the feeling of pain. Hypnosis can be used to create **hallucinations** in the hypnotized subject. Hallucinations are perceptual experiences that occur without sensory input; that is, false experiences. Some hallucinations are termed positive because the subject is led to perceive something that is not there. Pain reduction uses negative hallucinations: the failure to perceive something (e.g., pain) that *is* there. If a subject is a good candidate for hypnosis, there is a good chance that at least a portion of perceived pain can be blocked from conscious awareness (Hilgard & Hilgard, 1975; Long, 1986).

6. *Is a person in a hypnotic state in any sense aware of what he or she is doing?* Yes, but in a strange way. Within the hypnotized subject is what Hilgard calls a "hidden observer" who may be aware of what is going on. In one study (Hilgard & Hilgard, 1975), a subject was hypnotized and told that he would feel no pain as his hand was held in a container of ice water (usually very painful). When asked, the subject reported feeling little pain, just as expected. The hypnotic suggestion was working. The Hilgards then asked the subject if "some part of him" was feeling any pain and to indicate the presence of such pain by using his free hand to press a lever (or to write out a description of what he was feeling). Even though the subject continued to *verbally report* no feeling of pain, the free hand (on behalf of the "hidden observer") indicated that it "knew" there was pain in the immersed hand.

7. *Can I remember things under hypnosis I couldn't remember otherwise?* No, *probably* not, although there is no more hotly contested issue in regard to hypnosis than this. In the everyday sense of "Can you hypnotize me to remember psychology material better for the test next Friday?" the answer is an apologetic "Almost certainly not." I might be able to convince you under hypnosis that you had better remember your psychology and lead you to *want* to remember your psychology, but there is no evidence that hypnotic suggestion can *directly* improve your ability to learn and remember new material. In the more restrictive sense of "I don't remember all the details of the accident and the trauma that followed. Can hypnosis

hallucinations perceptual experiences without sensory input; that is, perceiving that which is not there or not perceiving that which is there

help me recall those events more clearly?" the answer is less sure. When we get to our discussion of memory (Chapter 6), we'll see that distortions of memory in recollection can easily occur in normal states.

In hypnotic states, the subject is suggestible and susceptible to distortions in recall furnished by the hypnotist (even assuming that the hypnotist has no reason to cause distortions). To the extent that hypnosis can reduce feelings of anxiety and tension, it may help in the recollection of anxiety-producing memories. The evidence is neither clear nor convincing on this issue in either direction (Dywan & Bowers, 1983; Kihlstrom, 1985). What of the related questions, "Can hypnosis make me go back in time (regress) and remember what it was like when I was only 3 or 4 years old?" or, "Can hypnosis help me recall past life experiences?" Here, we *do* have a clear-cut answer, and the answer is no. So-called age-regression hypnotic sessions have simply not proven valid (e.g., Nash, 1987; Spanos et al., 1991).

Hypnosis does alter one's consciousness, does open one to suggestions of the hypnotist, can be used to treat symptoms (if not their underlying causes), and can distort one's view of reality. However, we are learning that it is neither mystical nor magical; there are limits to what hypnosis can do.

Before You Go On

What is hypnosis, and who can be hypnotized?

What changes in consciousness does hypnosis produce?

MEDITATION

Meditation is a self-induced state of altered consciousness characterized by a focusing of attention and relaxation. Meditation is usually associated with ancient, particularly Eastern, cultures and has been practiced for many centuries. We tend to think of meditation in a religious context. Meditation became popular in North America in the 1960s. It was then that psychologists began to study the process seriously. In this section, we'll first review the process of meditation, and then look at some of the claims that have been made about its potential benefits.

There are several types of meditation, but the most popular are those that require mental focusing, or concentration. *Transcendental meditation (TM)* is a form of this variety (Maharishi, 1963). In TM, one begins meditating by assuming a comfortable position and becoming calm and relaxed. The meditator then directs his or her

meditation a self-induced state of altered consciousness characterized by a focusing of attention and relaxation

These University of Wisconsin football players are being trained to relax—reducing their somatic arousal, if you will.

attention to one particular stimulus. This could be some simple bodily function, such as one's own breathing. Attention could be focused on some softly spoken or chanted word or phrase, or *mantra,* such as "ōm," "one," or "calm." As attention is focused, other stimuli, either external (events in the environment) or internal (thoughts, feelings, or bodily processes), can be blocked from consciousness. The challenge is to stay relaxed, to remain peaceful and calm. By definition, a state of meditation cannot be forced; it just happens. Its practitioners claim that to reach an altered state of awareness through meditation is not difficult (Benson, 1975).

Once a person is in a meditative state, there *are* measurable physiological changes that take place that allow us to claim meditation to be an altered state of consciousness. The most noticeable is a predominance of alpha waves in the EEG record (remember, such waves characterize a relaxed state of the sort experienced just *before* one enters into sleep). Breathing slows and becomes deeper. Oxygen intake is reduced, and heart rate may decrease (Wallace & Benson, 1972).

There is no doubt that people can enter meditative states of consciousness. Doubts that have arisen concerning meditation center on the claims of its benefits. One of the major claims for meditation is that it is a reasonably simple, very effective, even superior way to enter into a state of relaxation. The reduction of somatic (bodily) arousal is taken to be one of the main advantages of meditation. The claim is that by meditating, one can slow bodily processes and enter into a state of physical as well as psychological calm.

Researcher David Holmes (1984, 1985, 1987) has reviewed the evidence for somatic relaxation through meditation. On several different measures of arousal and relaxation, including heart rate, respiration rate, muscle tension, and oxygen use, Holmes concluded that there were *no differences* between meditating persons and people who were "simply" resting or relaxing. After reviewing the data of dozens of experiments, he concluded:

> There is not a measure of arousal on which the meditating subjects were consistently found to have reliably lower arousal than resting subjects. Indeed, the most consistent finding was that there were not reliable differences between meditating and resting subjects. Furthermore, there appear to be about as many instances in which the meditating subjects showed reliably higher arousal as there are instances in which they showed reliably lower arousal than their resting counterparts. (1984, p. 5)

Another claim made for meditation is that those who practice it are better able to cope with stress, pressure, or threatening situations than are those who do not practice meditation. Once again, Holmes (1984, 1985) reports that he could find no evidence to support this claim. In fact, in four of the studies he reviewed, Holmes found that under mild threat, meditating subjects showed *greater* arousal than did nonmeditating subjects.

I must add two important notes here: (1) A number of psychologists have taken issue with Holmes's methods and conclusions, and argue that meditation *does* offer advantages over simply resting, suggesting also that "resting" is a difficult concept to define (e.g., Shapiro, 1985; Suler, 1985; West, 1985). (2) In no way does Holmes argue that meditation isn't of value. He simply says that with regard to somatic arousal there is no evidence that it is any better than resting.

Some of the claims made for meditation techniques go beyond relaxation and somatic arousal reduction. Claims that meditation can raise one's consciousness to transcendental heights of new awareness and thus make one a better person are viewed with considerable skepticism in psychology. Some people claim that they have an enormous "openness" to ideas and feelings, that they have hallucinatory experiences, and that they can divorce themselves from their bodies and minds when they meditate. Such experiences might, in some instances, be true. The idea that a meditating person can exist apart from present experience and view life "as if from without" is not far removed from Hilgard's concept of a "hidden observer" in hypnosis. Nonetheless, the majority of psychologists who have investigated meditation continue to question any claims for a heightened state of well-being that is achieved through such little effort and that relies more on testimonials of personal experience than on hard scientific evidence (Webb, 1981).

Before You Go On

What is meditation?
Is meditation an effective way to relax?

ALTERING CONSCIOUSNESS WITH DRUGS

In this section, we will discuss some of the chemicals that alter consciousness by inducing changes in perception, mood, or behavior. Because of their ability to alter psychological processes, these chemicals are referred to as **psychoactive drugs**.

Drugs have been used for centuries to alter consciousness. Psychoactive drugs are taken—at least initially—to achieve a state of consciousness the user considers to be good, positive, pleasant, even euphoric. No reasonable person would take a drug because he or she expected to have a bad, negative, or unpleasant experience. However, the use of drugs that alter our mood, perception, and behaviors often has seriously negative outcomes. In this regard, there are a few terms that will be relevant for our discussion. Although there is not total agreement on how these terms are used, for our purposes, we'll use the following definitions:

psychoactive drug a chemical that affects psychological processes and consciousness

1. *Dependence:* a state in which (a) the use of a drug is required to maintain bodily functioning (called physical dependence), or (b) continued use of a drug is believed to be necessary to maintain psychological functioning at some level (called psychological dependence). *"I just can't face the day without my three cups of coffee in the morning."*

dependence a state in which drug use is either necessary or believed to be necessary to maintain functioning at some desired level

2. *Tolerance:* a condition in which the use of a drug leads to a state in which more and more of it is needed to produce the same effect. *"I used to get high with just one of these; now I need three."*

tolerance in using a drug, a state in which more and more of the drug is required to produce the same desired effect

3. *Withdrawal:* a strongly negative response, either physical or psychological (including reactions such as headaches, vomiting, and cramps), that results when one stops taking a drug. *"When I take these, I don't feel real good, but it sure does hurt when I stop."*

withdrawal a negative reaction that may occur when one stops taking a drug

4. *Addiction:* an extreme dependency, physical or psychological, in which signs of tolerance and painful withdrawal are usually found (Schuckit, 1989). Addiction also implies seeking a short-term gain (say, a pleasurable feeling) at the expense of long-term negative consequences (Miller, 1992). *"No way I'm gonna give it up; no matter what. It feels too good; and the pain is too great without it."*

addiction an extreme dependency, usually accompanied by symptoms of tolerance and painful withdrawal

drug abuse a lack of control, a disruption of interpersonal relationships or difficulties at work, and a history of maladaptive use for at least one month

Another distinction we should make is between drug use and **drug abuse.** We are dealing with abuse when we find (1) a lack of control, as evidenced by daily intoxication and continued use, even knowing that one's condition will deteriorate; (2) a disruption of interpersonal relationships or difficulties at work that can be traced to drug usage; and (3) indications that maladaptive drug use has continued for at least one month (American Psychiatric Association, 1987). Hidden in this distinction is the reality that drug use may not have negative consequences; drug abuse will. There is no clear dividing line between drug use and drug abuse. For that matter, there are no clear dividing lines between drug use, dependency on drugs, and drug addiction. There is, instead, a continuum from total abstinence through heavy social use to clear-cut addiction (Doweiko, 1993; Peele et al., 1991). There are many psychoactive drugs. We'll focus on four types: stimulants, depressants, hallucinogens, and (as a separate category) marijuana.

Stimulants

Chemical **stimulants** do just that—they chemically stimulate, or activate, the nervous system. They produce a heightened sense of arousal, creating not only an increase in general activity but also an elevation of mood.

stimulants drugs (such as caffeine, cocaine, and amphetamines) that increase nervous system activities

Caffeine is one of the most widely used stimulants. It is found in many foods and drinks (coffee, tea, and chocolate), as well as in many varieties of painkillers. It is an ingredient in many soft drinks, notably colas. In moderate amounts, it seems to have no life-threatening effects on the user. At some point, a mild dependence may develop. Although it is not yet known precisely *how* caffeine does so, it temporarily increases cellular metabolism (the general process of converting food into energy), which then results in a burst of new-found energy. It also seems to block the effects of some inhibitory neurotransmitters in the brain (Julien, 1985). Caffeine disrupts sleep, making it more difficult to get to sleep in the first place and more difficult to stay asleep.

There is usually a rebound effect when caffeine intake is stopped. After long or excessive use, giving up sources of caffeine may result in the pain of withdrawal. If you tend to drink a lot of coffee and cola during the week, but take a break from them during the weekend, you may experience the headaches of caffeine withdrawal. You may drink coffee to help stay awake to withstand an all-night study session, but within a few hours after you stop drinking the caffeine, you may rebound and experience a streak of mental and physical fatigue—perhaps right at exam time!

Nicotine is another popular stimulant, usually taken by smoking. Nicotine is carried from the lungs to the brain very quickly—in a matter of seconds. Nicotine *is* a stimulant of central nervous system activity, but it does relax muscle tone slightly, which may explain in part the rationalization of smokers who claim that they can relax by having a cup of coffee and a cigarette. Nicotine seems to produce its effects by activating excitatory synapses in both the central and peripheral nervous systems (McKim, 1986).

Many individuals (but not all) develop a tolerance to nicotine, requiring more and more to reach a desired state of stimulation (Hughes et al., 1987). Indeed, beginning smokers generally cannot smoke more than one or two cigarettes without becoming ill. The drug often leads to dependency. In 1989, then Surgeon General C. Everett Koop declared cigarette smoking an addiction, calling it the single most preventable cause of death in our society, accounting for more than one-sixth of all deaths reported in 1985 (DeAngelis, 1989; Shiffman, 1992; Shiffman et al., 1990). More recent reports blame

Cocaine is a psychoactive stimulant that many individuals can become both psychologically and physically dependent on after just one or two episodes of use.

tobacco use for nearly half of all deaths in the United States. How addictive nicotine (or perhaps any other drug) becomes may depend primarily on how quickly it enters the brain. This means that people who take many quick deep puffs when smoking may become addicted more easily to nicotine than will people who take slow, shallow puffs (Bennett, 1980). We'll return to issues of smoking and nicotine addiction in our discussion of health psychology in Chapter 11.

Cocaine is a stimulant derived from leaves of the coca shrub (native to the Andes mountains in South America). The allure of cocaine and its derivative "crack" is the rush of pleasure and energy it produces when it first enters the bloodstream, either through the mucous membranes when inhaled as smoke ("free basing"), inhaled through the nose as a powder ("snorting"), or injected directly as a liquid. A cocaine "high" doesn't last very long; 15 to 20 minutes is typical.

There are many physiological reactions that can result from cocaine use. It elevates blood pressure and heart rate. Another reaction is that the drug blocks the reuptake of two important neurotransmitters (Julien, 1988). This means that once these neurotransmitters have entered a synapse, cocaine will prohibit their being taken back up into the neuron from which they have been released. The result is that, for some time at least, excessive amounts of these neurotransmitters are available in the nervous system. The two neurotransmitters in question are *norepinephrine*, which acts in both the central and peripheral nervous systems to provide arousal and the sense of extra energy, and *dopamine*, which acts in the brain to produce feelings of pleasure and euphoria.

Some of the physiological effects of cocaine use are long-lasting, if not permanent, even though the psychological effects last but a few minutes. Not only is the rush of the psychological reaction to cocaine or "crack" short-lived, but is followed by a period of letdown approaching depression. As users know, one way to combat letdown and depression is to take more of the drug—a vicious cycle that invariably leads to dependency and addiction. Cocaine is such a powerfully addictive drug that many individuals can become both psychologically and physically dependent on its use after just one or two episodes. Determining the number of cocaine users or addicts is difficult (after all, the drug *is* illegal), but estimates range from slightly less than 2 million to over 6 million users of cocaine or crack in the United States alone (Doweiko, 1993, pp. 82–83). Cocaine addiction tends to run in families to such an extent that current research is exploring the hypothesis that there is a genetic basis for cocaine addiction. Cocaine is a drug that no one can handle safely.

Amphetamines are synthetically manufactured stimulants that usually come in the form of capsules or pills, and are known by many "street names," such as bennies, uppers, wake-ups, cartwheels, dexies, or jellie babies. In addition to blocking reuptake, amphetamines cause the release of excess dopamine and norepinephrine. However, their action is considerably slower and somewhat less widespread than is that of cocaine. Once an amphetamine takes effect, users feel alert, awake, aroused, filled with energy, and ready to go. These results are short-lived and illusory. Whereas a reaction to cocaine fades after a few minutes, the impact of amphetamines may last for a few hours (Schuckit, 1989). The drug does not create alertness so much as it masks fatigue, which will ultimately overcome the user when the drug wears off. These are not the only effects of amphetamine use; it has a direct effect on the heart and circulatory system, causing, for example, irregular heartbeat and increased blood pressure (McKim, 1986). It may sound trite, but speed (another name for amphetamines) does kill. With amphetamine use, tolerance and dependency build quickly, and withdrawal can be a long, painful process.

Before You Go On

What are stimulant drugs, and what are their effects?

Depressants

In terms of their effects on consciousness, **depressants** are the opposite of stimulants. They reduce one's awareness of external stimuli, slow bodily functioning, and decrease levels of overt behavior. Predictably, one's reaction to depressant drugs depends largely on how much is taken. In small doses, they may produce relaxation, a sense of freedom from anxiety, and a loss of stifling inhibitions. In greater amounts, they may produce sedation, sleep, coma, or death.

Alcohol is the most commonly used of all depressants. It has been in use for thousands of years—perhaps since as long ago as 8000 B.C. (Ray & Ksir, 1987). Alcohol is a dangerous drug because of its popularity and widespread use, if for no other reason. It can be a deadly drug. Over 100,000 deaths a year in the United States can be attributed directly to alcohol consumption. The devastating effects of alcohol consumption by pregnant women are also well documented. Alcohol use has been associated with a myriad of problems of the newborn (see Topic 8A, page 362).

depressants drugs (such as alcohol, opiates, heroin, and barbiturates) that slow or reduce nervous system activity

The behavioral consequences of drug use often depend on dosage. With too much alcohol, for example, a pleasant altered state of consciousness can become a total loss of consciousness.

Perhaps the first thing to remember about alcohol is that it *is* a depressant. Some folks may feel that they are entertaining and stimulating when drinking alcohol, but their nervous system activity is actually being slowed. Alcohol increases urination, leading to an overall loss of fluids. It raises visual thresholds, making it more difficult to detect dim lights. Alcohol affects mood, leading to friendly elation as levels rise, and of anger, depression, and fatigue as alcohol levels drop (Babor et al., 1983).

The specific effects of alcohol on the drinker usually reflect several interacting factors. Primary among them (again) is *amount*. What matters most is the amount of alcohol that gets into a person's bloodstream. Blood alcohol level (BAL) is affected by how much one drinks and by how fast the alcohol can get into the bloodstream, which in turn is affected by what else is in the stomach. Drinking on an empty stomach is more dangerous than drinking while or soon after eating, because the alcohol will be more quickly absorbed. One-tenth of 1 percent alcohol in the bloodstream is enough to declare someone legally drunk in most states. Brain activity is so depressed at this level that decision making becomes distorted and motor coordination is impaired (and both are skills required to drive safely). Drinking more than one mixed drink or one can of beer or glass of wine *per hour* will raise blood alcohol levels (Maguire, 1990).

Drug use and abuse are susceptible to *sociocultural factors,* including race, religion, and socioeconomic level. This observation seems especially relevant in the context of alcohol. Consider the impact of the social pressures derived from religious beliefs and attitudes toward alcohol. The use of alcohol is virtually nonexistent among Muslims and Mormons, and used sparingly—usually in religious settings—by Chinese and Orthodox Jews. Alcoholism rates are also minimal among these groups. Such is the case even in the United States, where Irish Americans are six times more likely to suffer alcoholism than are Greek Americans—*in general.* Remember, there are Irish Americans who do not use alcohol at all (Valliant, 1983). Adolescent American Indians, especially those living on reservations, have much higher rates of alcohol use and abuse compared to any other American ethnic-racial population (Moncher et al., 1990; Swaim et al., 1993). Curiously, peer pressure, a major determining factor in drug and alcohol use for Anglo youths, is significantly less important in the culture of adolescent American Indians (Oetting & Beauvais, 1987). We also have to remember that economics are relevant. Research clearly demonstrates a relationship between alcohol use and economic indicators such as poverty, unemployment, and lack of opportunity (Beauvais et al., 1989; Ley, 1985).

Opiates, such as morphine and codeine, are called analgesics because they can be used to reduce or eliminate sensations of pain. It was for this purpose that they were first commonly used. In small doses, they create feelings of well-being and ease, relaxation, and a trancelike state. Unlike alcohol, they seem to have little effect on motor behavior. The catch, again, is that they produce dependence and addiction. Their removal results in extreme pain and depression.

Heroin is an opiate, originally (in the 1890s) derived from morphine, but thought not to be as addictive—a thought soon proven wrong. A strong dependency and addiction grow rapidly. Estimates generally suggest that more than 500,000 persons in the United States are addicted to heroin—and nearly half of them live in New York City. As with other drugs, we find that the addictive nature of heroin may be related to its rapid entry into the brain. Methadone, used in some treatment programs for long-term heroin users, is a drug with many of the chemical properties of heroin and many of the same psychological effects. A difference is that methadone is slow to reach the brain and, thus, tends not to produce heroin's predictable "rush," which makes methadone somewhat less addictive.

The effects of heroin (above whatever painkilling use it may have) seem to be most related to one's emotional state and mood. Unlike alcohol, or the opiates, there seldom are hallucinations or thought disturbances associated with heroin use. But as increased amounts of heroin become needed to produce the desired emotional states of pleasant euphoria, tolerance builds—and increased dosages of heroin can cause breathing to stop, often for long enough periods that death results.

Barbiturates are synthetically produced sedatives. Like the opiates, there are many varieties (well over 2,500 barbiturate chemicals have been isolated in laboratories [Doweiko, 1993]). They slow nervous system activity; in small amounts producing a sense of calm and tranquility, and in higher doses producing sleep or coma. They have this effect either by blocking receptor sites of excitatory synapses or by enhancing the effects of inhibitory neurotransmitters. Barbiturates also depress the cells and organs outside the central nervous system, slowing muscular reponses and reducing heart rate and respiration rates. Some barbiturates are addictive, producing strong withdrawal symptoms when discontinued. All produce dependency if used with regularity. As is generally the case, once addiction develops, getting off these drugs is very difficult.

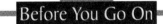

Before You Go On

What are depressant drugs, and what are their effects?

Hallucinogens

The chemicals called **hallucinogens** have the most unpredictable effects on consciousness. One of the reactions to these drugs is the formation of hallucinations, usually visual. That is, users often report seeing things when there is nothing there to see, or they see things in ways that others do not. Hallucinations of hearing, smell, taste, and touch are possible, but much less common.

There are nearly a hundred different types of hallucinogenic substances around the world, and many have been in use for centuries. In many cultures, the drugs are used in religious practices to induce

hallucinogens drugs (such as LSD) whose major effect is the alteration of perceptual experience and mood

trancelike states that may help the user communicate with the supernatural. In such settings, the hallucinogenic drug is often used as part of a religious ceremony, and may be given to young people by their elders. In such cases, "unauthorized" use of the drug, or abuse of the drug, is nearly unheard of (e.g., Grob & Dobkin de Rois, 1992).

A drug called ebene, for example, is used by the Yanomamö Indians, who live near the border of Brazil and Venezuela. They make a green pasty mixture from a powder derived from a tree that grows sparsely throughout the region. Wads of the mixture are placed in 3-foot-long hollow tubes and forcefully blown into the nostrils of a recipient. The initial experience is painful, but eventually becomes pleasurable, and may bring the person face to face with the spirit world.

> Dry heaves are also very common, as is out-and-out vomiting. Within a few minutes, one has difficulty focusing and begins to see spots and blips of light. Knees get rubbery.... Soon spirits can be seen dancing out of the sky and from the mountain tops, rhythmically prancing down their trails to enter the chest of their human beckoner, who by now is singing to lure them into his body where he can control them—send them to harm enemies or help cure sick kinsmen. (Chagnon, 1983, pp. 50–51)

LSD (lysergic acid diethylamide), a potent and popular hallucinogen in most Western cultures, was introduced in the United States in the 1940s. LSD raises levels of emotionality that can produce profound changes in perception, usually vivid visual hallucinations. One of the first steps in discovering how LSD works was finding that levels of the neurotransmitter serotonin increased when LSD was given to animals (Jacobs, 1987; Jacobs & Trulson, 1979). In itself, this was not too surprising, because LSD and similar hallucinogens (such as mescaline) have a chemical composition much like that of serotonin. Serotonin has its effects, both excitatory and inhibitory, on many areas of the brain (Jacobs, 1987). Now we know that serotonin levels

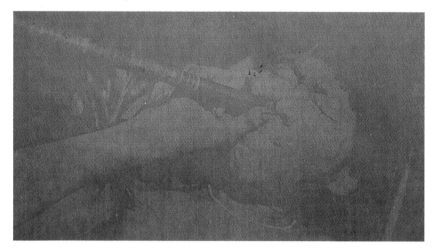

In some cultures, the use of hallucinogens is a sanctioned part of rites or ceremonies. Here, a Yanomamö Indian is receiving a wad of ebene—a powerful hallucinogen—blown up his nose.

increase because LSD acts on serotonin receptor sites, acting like a neurotransmitter. Small doses (measured in millionths of a gram) can produce major behavioral effects.

The changes in mood that take place with LSD are usually exaggerations of one's present mood. From the start, this has been viewed as one of the dangers of the drug. Some people may be drawn to drugs such as LSD because things are not going well for them. Perhaps they are depressed and are becoming hopeless. They think that LSD might help cheer them up. In fact, it may worsen their mood, resulting in a "bad trip," by exaggerating the feelings they had when they took the drug.

The hallucinations that occur under the influence of LSD usually involve an exaggeration of some actual perception. Colors seem more vivid, dimly lit stimuli take on a glow, stationary objects move, and otherwise unnoticed details become very apparent. On some occasions, LSD gives rise to an experience of *synesthesia*, in which a stimulus of one modality is perceived in a different modality. For example, the individual may "hear" colored lights, "see" sounds, "feel" odors, and so forth.

Before You Go On

**What are hallucinogenic drugs, and
what are their effects?**

Marijuana—A Special Case

Marijuana is a consciousness-altering drug that I'll consider a special case because it doesn't fit neatly into any of the three previous categories. In some ways, marijuana acts as a depressant. In small doses its effects are similar to those of alcohol: decreased nervous system activity and depression of thought and action. In greater doses, marijuana acts as if it were a hallucinogen, producing hallucinations and alterations in mood.

Marijuana is produced from the cannabis plant. This plant was the source of most of the rope manufactured for sailing ships in the eighteenth century and was an important crop in the American colonies, grown by George Washington, among other notables. As a source of raw materials for twine and rope, the plants were farmed in great numbers throughout the Midwest during World War II. The cannabis plant is hardy, and many of the remnants of those farms of the early 1940s can still be found in Illinois and Indiana, where every summer, adventurers come in search of a profitable—albeit illegal—harvest. More marijuana is grown in the United States than anywhere else in the world. Use of the drug is not uncommon, with estimates of Americans who have tried marijuana ranging from 40 to 60 million; as many as 3 to 6 million use the drug daily (Mirin et al., 1991).

The active ingredient in marijuana is the chemical compound tetrahydrocannabinol, commonly known as THC. THC is also the active ingredient in hashish, a similar but more potent drug also made from the cannabis plant. Although marijuana, in large doses, has been found to increase overall levels of some neurotransmitters, it is not known just how it produces this effect.

Marijuana is a difficult drug for society to deal with. In the United States, it is illegal to sell, possess, or use the drug, yet in some circumstances it can be prescribed to reduce the nausea associated with chemotherapy treatments for cancer. There is evidence that marijuana tolerance may develop rapidly, but little evidence that it is addictive. Is marijuana dangerous? Certainly, if for no other reason than it is usually smoked, and smoking is a danger to one's health. But smoking marijuana is more dangerous than cigarette smoking in terms of causing cancers, lung disease, and respiratory problems. It is also dangerous in the sense that alcohol is dangerous. Excessive use leads to impaired judgment, impaired reflexes, unrealistic moods, poor physical coordination, and hallucinations (Bennett, 1982; Weil et al., 1968).

The most debatable aspect of marijuana use involves the results of moderate to heavy long-term use. We are all tired of hearing this, but the truth is that enough evidence just isn't in yet. What data we have are more suggestive than definitive. The long-term use of marijuana may have genetic implications (producing chromosomal abnormalities in nonhumans). It can adversely affect the body's immune system and white blood cells. It is partially responsible for lowering the sperm count of male users. It can impair memory function, affecting memories of recent events in particular. It has predictably negative effects when taken during pregnancy, resulting in smaller babies, increased numbers of miscarriages, and so on (Bloodworth, 1987; Doweiko, 1993; Grinspoon, 1977; Julien, 1985; McKim, 1986). One issue of genuine concern is the considerable variability in the potency and quality, or purity, of marijuana available on the street today.

Before You Go On

**What is the active ingredient in marijuana,
and what effects does it produce?**

TOPIC 4C SUMMARY

To be conscious is to be aware of one's own mental processes and one's environment. We can voluntarily, consciously, alter our consciousness. In this Topic we examined three means of doing so: hypnosis, meditation, and using psychoactive drugs. What have we learned?

You cannot be hypnotized without your consent, nor is it likely that you can be made to do anything while hypnotized that you wouldn't do otherwise. Some people are easier to hypnotize than others, and although hypnosis can be used to alleviate pain, you cannot be hypnotized to improve your memory.

Meditation alters consciousness through relaxation and the focusing of one's attention. Although meditation may not be significantly different from several other techniques of relaxation, there are benefits to be gained from meditation, and there are measurable physiological changes that occur while one is in a meditative state.

Chemicals that alter consciousness are called psychoactive drugs, and they fall into three major categories, the names of which indicate the ultimate effect on one's nervous system activity. There are stimulants, including caffeine, nicotine, cocaine, and the amphetamines; depressants, including alcohol, the opiates (such as heroin), and the barbiturates; and hallucinogens, such as LSD. Marijuana is a special sort of psychoactive drug because it can produce the effects of stimulants and depressants, and can produce many of the effects of hallucinogens.

TOPIC 4A

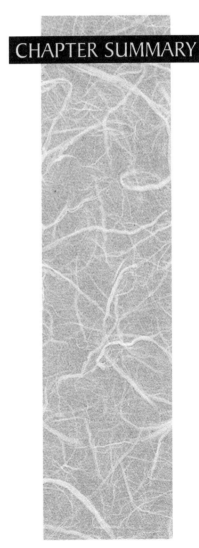

CHAPTER SUMMARY

What is normal, waking consciousness, and, according to William James, what are its four basic characteristics?

We define normal, waking consciousness as the perception or awareness of our environment and our own mental processes. According to William James, consciousness can be characterized as (1) always changing, (2) personal, (3) continuous, and (4) selective. /*p. 167*

What are the three levels of consciousness proposed by Freud?

Sigmund Freud proposed that consciousness could be classified into one of three levels. (1) That which is in your *conscious* mind is that of which you are aware at the moment, that is, information that is readily available. (2) Below the conscious level of awareness is the *preconscious*, memories, feelings, desires, and the like that are not immediately known to you, but that can be brought to your attention, to consciousness, with relatively little effort. (3) Most of the contents of our minds, Freud said, are at an *unconscious* level of awareness. Information, feelings, and desires are stored at the unconscious level because becoming aware of these issues might lead to feelings of anxiety and distress. Although information stored at the unconscious level could influence our behaviors and could show itself in slips of the tongue and in our dreams, it can be retrieved only with considerable effort. /*p. 170*

How may we characterize unconscious processing?

Cite an example of experimental evidence for unconscious processing.

The notion of the unconscious processing of information has returned to mainstream psychology. Unconscious processing occurs when information is processed without one's conscious awareness of it. For example, when subjects are shown words presented so quickly or

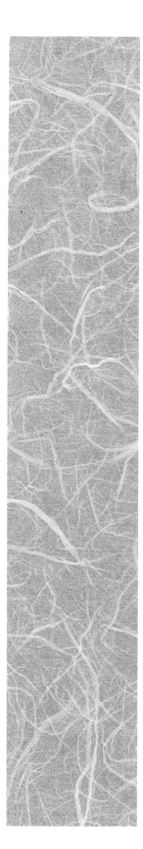

dimly that they do not report seeing them, those words will still influence the subjects' choice of a word that is related to the word they claimed they did not see. /*p. 172*

TOPIC 4B

What are the EEG and the EMG?

Briefly describe the four stages of sleep.

The EEG (electroencephalogram) is an instrument that measures the general pattern of electrical activity of the brain. This electrical activity is taken to be the most common indicator of the stages of sleep. The EMG (electromyogram) measures muscle tone, another indicator of sleep. In addition to a state of relaxed wakefulness characterized by EEG alpha waves, we say that there are four levels, or stages, of sleep: (1) light sleep with low-amplitude, slow theta waves, (2) sleep showing low-amplitude EEG waves with sleep spindles present, (3) a level where delta waves enter the EEG record, and (4) deep sleep, with more than 50 percent delta wave activity. /*p. 176*

What are REM and NREM sleep?

What occurs during REM sleep?

REM sleep is "rapid eye movement sleep," which constitutes about one-fourth of each night's sleep. Several events occur during REM, most noticeably vivid, storylike dreams. During REM sleep we find loss of muscle tone (atonia), excitement of the sexual organs, rapid breathing, and increased heart rate and blood pressure. NREM is "non-REM" sleep, and predictably, the eyes are still and there is little dream activity. /*p. 178*

What are the effects of sleep deprivation?

Name and describe three common disorders of sleep.

People who have been deprived of sleep show a rebound effect, making up for lost sleep, usually in just one night. There is more certainly going to be a rebound effect for REM sleep than for NREM sleep. Evidence suggests that millions of persons chronically get less sleep than they need. The effects of short-term deprivation are minimal and reversible; however, the effects of long-term deprivation are more negative. Insomnia is the perception of being unable to fall asleep and/or stay asleep when one wants to. Nearly thirty million Americans suffer from chronic insomnia. Narcolepsy involves going to sleep, even in the daytime, without any intention to do so. It is an underdiagnosed sleep disorder. Sleep apnea involves patterns of sleep during which one suddenly stops breathing, often long enough to awaken the sleeping person. /*p. 181*

TOPIC 4C

What is hypnosis, and who can be hypnotized?

What changes in consciousness does hypnosis produce?

Hypnosis is an altered state of consciousness into which one enters voluntarily. Those who most readily can be hypnotized easily engage in fantasy and daydreaming, show signs of suggestibility, and demonstrate a willingness to cooperate with the hypnotist. Hypnosis is characterized by an increase in suggestibility, a focusing of attention, an exaggeration of imagination, a reduction of spontaneous activity, and an unquestioning acceptance of distortions in reality. Not everyone can be hypnotized. /p. 185

What is meditation?

Is meditation an effective way to relax?

Meditation is a self-induced state of consciousness characterized by an extreme focusing of attention and relaxation. There are many claims for the benefits of meditation. It *is* an effective means of relaxing and reducing overall levels of somatic activity, but there is evidence that it is not significantly better in these regards than other relaxation techniques. /p. 187

What are stimulant drugs, and what are their effects?

Stimulants are psychoactive drugs such as caffeine, nicotine, cocaine, and amphetamines. Their basic effect is to increase the level of nervous system activity and to elevate mood, in the case of cocaine by affecting the neural synapse, increasing effective levels of the neurotransmitters norepinephrine and dopamine. With heavy or continued use, tolerance may develop, as may dependence and addiction. /p. 191

What are depressant drugs, and what are their effects?

The depressants include such drugs as alcohol, the opiates (including morphine, codeine, and heroin), and a variety of synthetically produced barbiturates. All depressants slow nervous system activity, reduce one's awareness of outside stimulation, and, in small doses, may alleviate feelings of nervousness and anxiety. In large doses, however, they produce sedation, sleep, coma, or death. Tolerance, dependence, and addiction may result from the use of these drugs. The use of these drugs (and virtually all others) is influenced to some degree by sociocultural factors. /p. 193

What are the hallucinogenic drugs, and what are their effects?

Hallucinogens are drugs that alter mood and/or perceptions. LSD is an example. Hallucinogens get their name from their ability to induce hallucinations, where a user may have an experience unrelated to what is going on in the user's environment. Synesthesia, a hallucinatory

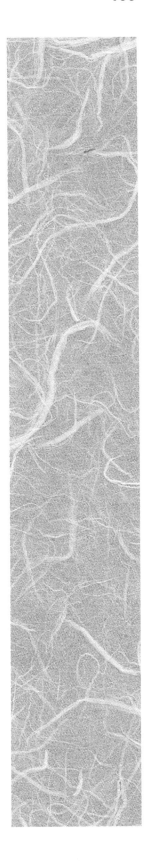

experience that crosses sense modalities ("hearing" lights, for example), may occur under the influence of LSD. /p. 195

What is the active ingredient in marijuana, and what effects does it produce?

The active ingredient in marijuana is the chemical compound THC. Listing its short- and long-term effects is difficult because of contradictory evidence. The use of marijuana through smoking is more dangerous to lungs and the respiratory system than is the smoking of regular cigarettes. Negative effects have been associated with long-term use: impaired judgment, unrealistic mood, impaired coordination, and hallucination. In addition, marijuana may have an adverse effect on the body's immune system and has been implicated in producing a range of negative consequences when taken during pregnancy. /p. 196

chapter five

LEARNING

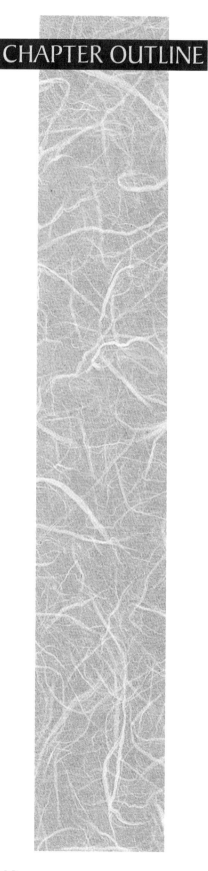

CHAPTER OUTLINE

TOPIC 5A CLASSICAL CONDITIONING
What Is Learning?
Pavlov and a Classic Demonstration
Classical Conditioning Phenomena
    Acquisition
    Extinction and Spontaneous Recovery
    Generalization and Discrimination
The Significance of Classical Conditioning: What About People?
    In the Laboratory
    Conditioned Emotional Responses
    An Example: The Case of "Little Albert"
    An Application: Phobias and Their Treatment
Rethinking What Really Happens in Classical Conditioning
    Can *Any* Stimulus Serve as a CS?
    Must the Time Interval Between the CS and the UCS Always
      Be Brief?
TOPIC 5A SUMMARY

TOPIC 5B OPERANT CONDITIONING
The Basics of Operant Conditioning
    Defining Operant Conditioning
    The Procedures of Operant Conditioning
    The Course of Conditioning
Reinforcement
    Positive and Negative Reinforcers
    Primary and Secondary Reinforcers
    Scheduling Reinforcers
Punishment
Generalization and Discrimination
Can Any Response Be Operantly Conditioned?
TOPIC 5B SUMMARY

TOPIC 5C COGNITIVE APPROACHES TO LEARNING
Latent Learning and Cognitive Maps
Social Learning and Modeling
TOPIC 5C SUMMARY

CHAPTER SUMMARY

The topic for the Psychology of Learning class was a process called operant conditioning. After stressing the importance of operant conditioning in their everyday lives, the instructor suggested that the 25 students use operant conditioning to change the behaviors of someone they knew.

The choice was an easy one. Following their learning class, most of the students moved across the hall for a class in child psychology. It was a larger class, with 75 to 80 students in attendance on a typical day. The professor in the child psychology class had a boring lecture style: he simply read his notes to the class. Every day he'd go through the same ritual. He would find his place in his notes, check the time on his pocket watch, and then read to the class for 50 minutes. While what he was reading was no doubt high-quality psychology, the students thought that this classroom style left much to be desired.

The students from the learning class decided to reward the professor for doing what they wanted him to do by smiling, looking attentive, and appearing to take many notes. Whenever the professor did what the students did not want him to do, they'd look away, appear bored, and stop taking notes.

The project began on a Wednesday. When the students met after class that day, they realized they weren't very well organized. They hadn't specifically defined just what it was they were to reward. They only knew that they wanted the professor to stop reading to them. They thought that by the end of the class the professor was looking up from his notes a little bit more than usual, but they weren't sure.

The students did get some results the following Friday. By the end of that class, the professor *was* looking up more than usual, and he was moving around in his chair. Monday's class brought a real breakthrough: the professor rose from his chair! From time to time he would sit down again (only to be ignored), and he would not give up physical contact with his notes. He was still reading, but occasionally he would stand to do so.

On the following Friday, about halfway through the class, the professor was standing in the corner of the room; notes still on the desk, he was just talking to the class about child psychology.

Think about that. In five days these students had lifted their professor from his chair and placed him in the corner! The students had no doubt that in 10 minutes they could have moved the professor from one corner to the other. And all this was done simply by rewarding some behaviors with attention and by ignoring other behaviors. The class was impressed.

This is a true story. I was one of those 25 students in both classes, and I was impressed indeed. The sight of our instructor leaning back in the corner of the classroom just talking about child psychology remains a vivid memory, even though the ethical implications of what we had done concern me more now than they did then.

ow we learn and adapt to our environments is a major issue in psychology. Directly or indirectly, learning has an impact on every aspect of our being. Learning affects how we find out about the world and ourselves as we grow and develop, how we form social relationships, and how we change during the course of psychotherapy. The human organism is poorly suited to survive without learning. If we are to survive, much less prosper, we must profit from our experiences.

In this chapter, we'll begin Topic 5A by defining learning. Then we'll focus on a simple form of learning: classical conditioning. At first, most of our descriptions of classical conditioning will be based on Ivan Pavlov's work with dogs. Then, once we have the basic principles in hand, we'll consider why classical conditioning is important to all of us and how the procedures of classical conditioning can be found regularly in our daily lives.

In Topic 5B we'll concentrate on operant conditioning—the type of learning employed in our opening story. The basic premise of operant conditioning is that our behaviors are shaped by the consequences they have produced in the past. This Topic will get us involved in the matters of reward, reinforcement, and punishment.

We'll close this chapter with a short Topic that focuses on the role of the learner in learning. Whereas both classical and operant conditioning tend to focus on observable stimuli and responses, what we call "cognitive approaches" to learning tend to emphasize the mental processes (cognitions) involved in a learning task. A good deal of your learning as a college student can be thought of in this way. You have altered many of your cognitions on the basis of your experiences. Let's start at the beginning and formulate a definition for this important psychological process we call learning.

Topic 5A
CLASSICAL CONDITIONING

WHAT IS LEARNING?

learning *demonstration of a relatively permanent change in behavior that occurs as the result of practice or experience*

We'll say that **learning** is demonstrated by a relatively permanent change in behavior that occurs as the result of practice or experience. This is a rather standard definition, and it raises some important points we should explore.

For one thing, when we say that learning is *demonstrated* by a change in behavior we're saying that learning (like many other psychological processes) cannot be observed directly. In a literal sense, there is no way that I can directly observe, or measure, what you have learned. All I can measure directly is your performance, or your behavior. To determine if you have learned something, I must ask you to perform and then make inferences about your learning on the basis of your performance. And sometimes I may be wrong.

For example, you may learn everything there is to know about the psychology of learning for your next exam. But just days before that exam, someone you care about becomes seriously ill. As a result, you don't get much sleep. Then, with your resistance weakened, you develop a sinus headache and catch the flu. When you come to class to take your exam, you have a high fever, feel miserable, and can't concentrate. You fail the exam. Your instructor may infer (incorrectly in this case) that you haven't learned very much about learning. On the other hand, there may be a student in class who hasn't studied at all and has actually learned very little. But the exam is of the multiple-choice type, and she correctly guesses the answers to 90 percent of the questions. Your instructor might infer (incorrectly again) that this student has learned a great deal.

One way to make this point is to say that what is learned is some *potential*, or predisposition, to respond. Because what is learned is simply potential, we will not recognize that learning has taken place until that potential is realized in behavior. (This issue will reemerge in our discussion of memory. What gets graded on most exams, after all, is not so much what you have learned as what you appear to have remembered at exam time.)

A second aspect of our definition that takes a bit of explaining is that learned changes in behavior are said to be *relatively permanent*. This means that they are not fleeting, short-lived, or cyclical changes, such as those due to fatigue or brief shifts in motivation. Consider, for example, the change in typing behavior that occurs—even for a skilled typist—between 8 and 10 AM on any given morning. There is likely to be a significant improvement in typing behavior that we really ought not attribute to learning but to what is called *warm-up*. That same skilled typist might not function as well at the end of the day—a change in behavior better attributed to *fatigue* than to forgetting. These are important changes in behavior, but they are not due to learning. Learned changes are relatively permanent.

We have another term in this definition to remind us that there are yet other, occasionally important, changes in our behavior that do not result from learning. We say, by definition, that learned changes in behavior result from *practice*, or *experience*. For one thing, some changes may be due to maturation. The fact that birds fly, that salamanders swim, or that humans walk probably has more to do with genes and physical development than with learning and experience. For another thing, some changes in our behaviors are due to automatic physiological reactions, such as sensory adaptation, and are not learned. When we enter a darkened theater, for example, we don't really "learn" to see in the dark. Our vision improves and our behaviors change as our eyes adapt to the lighting. Consider your own behavior when you sit in a tub of hot water. Your behaviors are likely to change as you settle down and relax, as you adapt to the hot water—more of a physiological change (adaptation again) than a learned one.

One final point about learning: as students, parents, and teachers, we often fall into the habit of thinking that learning is necessarily a good thing. Clearly, it isn't always so. We can learn bad, ineffective habits as readily as we learn good, adaptive ones. For example, no one I know honestly claims to have enjoyed the first cigarette that he or she smoked. Yet many people have learned the habit, which is hardly an adaptive one. Learning is simply reflected in a change in behavior, be it for better or worse.

When we put these ideas together, we come up with our definition: Learning is demonstrated by (or inferred from) a relatively permanent change in behavior that occurs as the result of practice or experience. We begin our discussion of learning by considering a variety of learning referred to as *classical conditioning*. Although conditioning and learning are not technically synonymous terms, they can be used interchangeably. For the sake of simplicity, we will follow common usage here and agree to call the most basic and fundamental types of learning "conditioning."

Before You Go On

How do we define learning?

PAVLOV AND A CLASSIC DEMONSTRATION

When we think about learning, we typically think about such activities as memorizing the Bill of Rights, studying for an exam, or learning to *do* things, such as ice-skate. But our study of learning begins nearly a hundred years ago in the laboratory of a Russian physiologist who taught dogs to salivate in response to tones. How salivating dogs could be relevant to college students may be difficult to imagine at first, but the relevance will soon become apparent.

Psychology was just beginning to emerge as a science late in the nineteenth century. At this time, Ivan Pavlov, a physiologist, was studying the basic processes of digestion—work for which he was awarded the Nobel Prize in 1904. Focusing on the salivation reflex in dogs, Pavlov knew he could produce salivation in his dogs by forcing food powder into their mouths. A **reflex**, is an unlearned, automatic response that occurs in the presence of a specific stimulus. Every time Pavlov presented the food powder, his dogs salivated.

Pavlov's reputation in psychology stems from the fact that he observed and pursued something not as simple as reflexive responses. He noticed that sometimes his dogs would salivate *before* the food was put in their mouths. They would salivate at the very sight of the food or even at the sight of the laboratory assistant who usually delivered the food. With this observation, Pavlov went off on a tangent he pursued for the rest of his life (Pavlov, 1927, 1928). We now call the phenomenon he studied **classical conditioning**—a type of learning in which an originally neutral stimulus comes to elicit a new response after having been paired with another stimulus that reflexively elicits that same response. In his honor, we sometimes call this type of learning Pavlovian conditioning.

reflex an unlearned, automatic response that occurs in the presence of a specific stimulus

classical conditioning learning in which an originally neutral stimulus comes to elicit a new response after having been paired with a stimulus that reflexively elicits that same response

To demonstrate classical conditioning, we first need a stimulus that reliably, or consistently, produces a predictable response. The relationship between this stimulus and the response it elicits is usually a natural, unlearned, reflexive one. Given this stimulus, the same response always follows. Here is where the food powder comes in. If we present the food powder to a dog, the salivation response reliably follows. There is no learning involved in this reflexive association, so we call the stimulus an **unconditioned stimulus (UCS)** and the response an **unconditioned response (UCR)**. We have a UCS (food powder) producing a UCR (salivation).

To get classical conditioning under way, we need a second, *neutral stimulus* that, when presented, produces a minimal response, or a response of no particular interest. For this neutral stimulus, Pavlov chose a tone.

At first, when a tone is sounded, a dog *will* respond. It will, among other things, perk up its ears and try to orient toward the source of the sound. We call this response an **orienting reflex**—a simple, unlearned response of attending to a new or unusual stimulus. After awhile, the dog will get used to the tone and will ignore it. This process is called **habituation**, a form of learning in which an organism comes to ignore a stimulus of no consequence. Essentially, the dog learns *not* to orient toward the tone.

Now we are ready to go. We have two stimuli: a tone that produces a minimal response, and food powder (UCS) that reliably produces salivation (UCR).

Neutral stimulus ⟶ No response
     (a tone)   (no salivation)

UCS ⟶ UCR
(food powder)   (salivation)

Once we get our stimuli and responses straight, the rest is easy. The two stimuli are paired. That is, they are presented at about the same time—the tone first, then the food powder. The salivation then occurs automatically in response to the food powder. We have a neutral stimulus, then a UCS, followed by the UCR (or tone-food-salivation).

Neutral stimulus + UCS ⟶ UCR
   (a tone)   (food powder)   (salivation)

Each pairing of the two stimuli may be considered a conditioning *trial*. If we repeat this procedure several times—for several trials—conditioning, or learning, takes place. We find a relatively permanent change in behavior as a result of this experience. After a number of trials, when we present the tone by itself, the dog salivates, something it did not do before. Now the dog salivates not just in response to the food powder, but to the tone. Clearly, the tone is no longer "neutral." Now it produces a response, so we call the tone a **conditioned stimulus (CS)**. To keep the salivation response that it elicits separate from the salivation in response to the food powder, we call it a **conditioned response (CR)**, indicating that it has been conditioned, or learned.

unconditioned stimulus (UCS) in classical conditioning, a stimulus (for example, food powder) that reflexively and reliably evokes a response

unconditioned response (UCR) in classical conditioning, a response (for example, salivation) reliably and reflexively evoked by a stimulus

orienting reflex the simple, unlearned response of orienting toward, or attending to, a new or unusual stimulus

habituation in classical conditioning, a simple form of learning in which an organism comes to ignore a stimulus of little or no consequence

conditioned stimulus (CS) in classical conditioning, an originally neutral stimulus (for example, a tone) that when paired with a UCS comes to evoke a new response (a CR)

conditioned response (CR) in classical conditioning, the learned response (for example, salivation) evoked by the CS after conditioning

$$\text{CS} \longrightarrow \text{CR}$$
(a tone) (salivation)

Let's review this one more time: (1) We start with two stimuli: the neutral stimulus, which elicits no response, and the UCS, which elicits the UCR. (2) We repeatedly present the two stimuli together. (3) We find that when we present the CS alone, it now elicits a CR.

The same type of stimulus—a tone, for example—can be either a neutral stimulus (before learning occurs), or a conditioned stimulus (when it elicits a learned response). Similarly, the same type of response—say, salivation—can be either an unconditioned response (if it is elicited without learning) or a conditioned response (if it is elicited as the result of learning).

If you have a pet at home, you've no doubt seen this process in action. If you keep your pet's food in the same cabinet all the time, you may note a range of excited, anticipatory behaviors by your pet every time you open that cabinet door. The open door (CS) has been paired with the food within it (UCS), now producing the same sort of reaction (CR) that was originally reserved for the food (UCR).

Shortly we'll look at how classical conditioning influences human behaviors, but before we go on, let's make it clear that classical conditioning is not something that occurs only in dogs and cats. You demonstrate a classically conditioned salivation response (particularly if you're hungry) when you see pictures or smell the aromas of your favorite foods. If you respond with anxiety at the sight of your instructor entering the classroom with a stack of exam papers, you're displaying a classically conditioned response.

We also need to consider two technical points. First, the CR seldom reaches the strength of the UCR no matter how many times the

Ivan Pavlov (seated) watches a dog in one of his laboratory's testing chambers.

CS and the UCS are paired. For example, in salivation conditioning, we never get as much saliva in response to the tone (as a CR) as we originally got in response to the food powder alone (as a UCR).

Second, *how* the conditioned stimulus and the unconditioned stimulus are paired does matter. If you think about it, you'll realize that there are many ways in which two stimuli can be presented at about the same time (e.g., simultaneously, or UCS then CS, or CS then UCS, with varying time intervals in between). Of all the alternatives, one method consistently works best: The CS comes first, followed shortly (within a second or so) by the UCS, or, again, tone-food-salivation. (I tell my classes that Pavlovian conditioning is basically a matter of "ding-food-slobber.")

Before You Go On

**Summarize the essential procedures involved
in classical conditioning.**

CLASSICAL CONDITIONING PHENOMENA

Now that we have the basics of classical conditioning in mind, we can turn to some of the details that go along with it—some of the procedures developed in Pavlov's laboratory. We'll first see how a classical conditioning experiment actually proceeds. Just to keep our terminology firmly in mind, I'll continue to use the original Pavlovian example of salivating dogs.

Acquisition

The stage of classical conditioning during which the strength of the CR increases—the stage in which a dog acquires the response of salivating to a tone—is called **acquisition**. When conditioning begins, the conditioned stimulus (CS) does not produce a conditioned response (CR), which is why we refer to it as a neutral stimulus at this point. After a few pairings of the CS and UCS (conditioning trials), we can demonstrate the presence of a CR. To do that, of course, we'll have to present the conditioned stimulus (CS) by itself. Now we discover that there is some saliva produced in response to the tone presented alone. The more trials of the CS and UCS together, the more the dog will salivate in response to the tone when it is presented alone. Over repeated trials, the increase in CR strength (here, the amount of saliva in response to the tone) is rather rapid at first, but soon slows, and eventually levels off. The first part of Figure 5.1 illustrates the acquisition phase of classical conditioning.

acquisition the process in classical conditioning in which the strength of the CR increases with repeated pairings of the CS and UCS

Extinction and Spontaneous Recovery

Assume we now have a well-conditioned dog producing a good deal of saliva at the sound of a tone. Continuing to present the CS-UCS

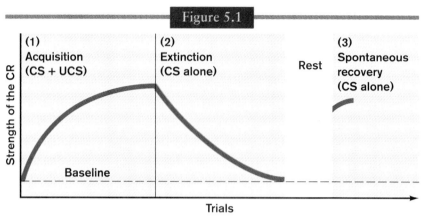

The stages of conditioning. (1) Acquisition is produced by the repeated pairing of a CS and a UCS. The strength of the CR increases rapidly at first, then slows, eventually leveling off. (2) Extinction is produced by presenting the CS without pairing it with the UCS. The strength of the CR then decreases. (3) After a rest interval (and following extinction), spontaneous recovery is demonstrated by a partial return of the CR.

pair adds little to the amount of saliva we get when we present the tone alone. Now suppose we go through a series of trials during which the CS (the tone) is presented but is *not* paired with the UCS (no more food powder). The result of this procedure is that the CR will weaken. As we continue to present the tone alone, the dog provides less and less saliva. If we keep it up, the dog eventually will stop salivating to the tone. This is called **extinction**—the process in which the strength of a CR decreases with repeated presentations of the CS alone (without the UCS).

It would appear that we're right back where we started. Because the CR has extinguished, when we present the tone, our dog does nothing—at least it no longer salivates. Let's return our dog to the kennel and give it a rest. When the dog returns to the laboratory and the tone is sounded, the dog salivates again! Not a lot, perhaps, but the salivation does return, or recover. It recovers automatically, or spontaneously, so we call this phenomenon **spontaneous recovery**. Extinction and spontaneous recovery are also illustrated in Figure 5.1.

Spontaneous recovery occurs after extinction and following a rest interval, which indicates two things. First, one series of extinction trials may not be sufficient to eliminate a conditioned response. Because of the possibility of spontaneous recovery, to get our dog to stop salivating altogether, we may have to run more than one series of extinction trials. Second, what is happening during extinction is not literally "forgetting"—at least not in the usual sense. The response is not forgotten so much as it is *suppressed*. That is, the learned salivation response is still there, but it is not showing up in performance during extinction, which is why it can (and does) return later, in spontaneous recovery.

extinction the process in classical conditioning in which the strength of the CR decreases with repeated presentations of the CS alone (without the UCS)

spontaneous recovery the phenomenon in classical conditioning in which a previously extinguished CR returns after a rest interval

Generalization and Discrimination

During the course of conditioning, assume we consistently use a tone of a given pitch as the conditioned stimulus. After repeated pairings of this tone with food powder, a dog salivates when the tone is presented alone.

What will happen if we now present a different tone, one the dog has not heard before? Typically, the dog will salivate in response to it also. This response may not be as strong as the original CR (there may not be as much saliva). How strong it is depends on how similar the new tone is to the original CS. The more similar it is to the original, the more saliva will be produced. This is **generalization**—the process by which a classically conditioned response is elicited by stimuli different from, but similar to, the CS.

This is a powerful process. It means that an unconditioned stimulus need not be paired with all possible conditioned stimuli. If you choose a mid-range CS, the conditioned response automatically generalizes to other, similar stimuli. Conditioning trials do not have to be applied over and over for separate stimuli. A graph of this process is presented in Figure 5.2. Imagine a young boy is bitten by a large, black Labrador retriever. Originally, this dog was a neutral stimulus, but having been paired (associated) with the trauma and pain of a bite, the dog is now feared by the boy (a conditioned response). Is it not predictable that the boy's conditioned fear will generalize to other large, black dogs—and, to a lesser extent, to small gray ones?

If a dog is conditioned to salivate to a tone of middle pitch, it also will salivate to higher and lower tones through generalization. What if we do not want it to? What if we want our dog to salivate to the CS alone and *not* to other tones? We would use **discrimination** training, a process in which an organism learns to make a CR in response to only one CS but not to other stimuli. In a way, discrimination is the opposite of generalization. To demonstrate discrimination training, we would present a dog with many tones, but would pair the UCS food powder with only one of them—the CS we want the dog to salivate to. We might, for example, pair the food powder with a tone of middle C. A lower tone would also be presented to the dog, but *would not* be followed by food powder. At first, there would be some saliva in response to the lower tone (generalization), but eventually our subject would learn to discriminate and would no longer salivate to the lower tone.

generalization *the phenomenon in classical conditioning in which a CR is elicited by stimuli different from, but similar to, the CS*

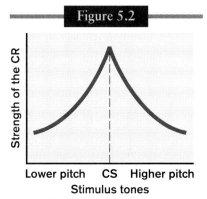

Figure 5.2

Generalization. Presenting stimuli other than the CS may produce a CR. How much CR is produced depends on the similarity between the new stimulus and the original CS.

discrimination *the phenomenon in classical conditioning in which an organism learns to make a CR in response to only one CS but not to other stimuli*

Before You Go On

In classical conditioning, what are acquisition, extinction, and spontaneous recovery?

In classical conditioning, what are generalization and discrimination?

THE SIGNIFICANCE OF CLASSICAL CONDITIONING: WHAT ABOUT PEOPLE?

It is time to leave our discussion of dogs, tones, salivation, and Pavlov's lab. We need to turn our attention to the practical application of all of this. First, let's see how classical conditioning can be demonstrated in the human learning laboratory. Then we'll deal with conditioned emotional responses, where I'll provide two examples, one an experimental demonstration, the other a real-world application.

In the Laboratory

Of one thing we can be sure: we can easily bring the procedures of classical conditioning into the human learning laboratory. Here's a procedure that has been used to demonstrate classical conditioning in undergraduate psychology laboratory classes; it's called finger-withdrawal conditioning. A student is presented with a small block of wood on which a metal plate is positioned. The student is instructed to place his or her fingertip on that metal plate. The metal plate is wired to a battery in such a way that when a button is pushed a slight electric current passes through the metal and presents the student with a very mild electric shock. The student is instructed to touch the metal plate and then relax. The experimenter taps on the table top. Nothing happens. The experimenter taps again, and again. Then the experimenter taps the table and pushes the button, delivering the shock. The response is immediate and predictable: the finger is jerked up off the metal plate. (In my experience, this "finger withdrawal conditioning" usually involves the entire body jumping up out of the seat, not just the withdrawal of a finger.)

The process can then be repeated, but after this one trial it is often difficult to get a student to return his or her finger to the metal plate; that is, one trial is usually all that is needed. To demonstrate conditioning, the experimenter then taps on the desk and the finger comes flying off the metal plate. What we have here may be trivial classical conditioning, but classical conditioning it is. There will be a relatively permanent change in the subject's behavior as a result of the experience of pairing together a tap and a mild electric shock. We start with a neutral stimulus (the tap); pair it with an unconditioned stimulus (the "shock"), which produces an unconditioned response (the finger withdrawal); and then pair it with the tap (now a conditioned stimulus), which elicits a learned or conditioned response (finger withdrawal again).

Conditioned Emotional Responses

One of the most significant aspects of classical conditioning is its role in affecting our emotional responses to stimuli in our environment. There are very few stimuli that naturally, or instinctively, produce an emotional response. Yet think of all those things that *do* directly influence how we feel.

For example, very young children seldom seem afraid of spiders, plane rides, or snakes. (Some children actually seem to enjoy them.) Now consider how many people you know who *are* afraid of these things. There are many stimuli in our environments that cause us to be afraid. There are stimuli that produce within us feelings of pleasure, calm, and ease.

What scares you? What makes you feel relaxed and at ease? Why? Might you feel particularly upset or distressed in a certain store because you once had an unpleasant experience there? Might you fondly anticipate a vacation at the beach because of a very enjoyable vacation you had there as a child? Do you shudder at the sight of a police car? Do you smile at the thought of a payroll envelope? In each of these cases, we are talking about classical conditioning. (To be fair, I must say that not all of our learned emotional reactions are acquired through classical conditioning alone. As we shall see, there are other possibilities.)

When I was a senior in high school, I agreed to have surgery on my nose. (A rather clumsy child, I had broken it a number of times.) The surgery was done under local anesthetic, was painful, messy, and altogether unpleasant. That surgery was done many years ago, but to this day, when I visit a hospital, I get a slight ache in my nose. Now, I know better. I know that the pain is just "in my head," but my nose still hurts! What is happening is that I am being reminded of some relatively permanent classical conditioning. The CS of hospital sights, sounds, and odors was paired with the UCS of an operative procedure that caused a UCR of pain and discomfort. This pairing, which lasted several days, produced a CR of discomfort associated with the CS of the hospital. My conditioned response *generalized* to many other hospitals, not just the one in which the surgery was performed. And the conditioned response has lasted a long time.

Here's another example: assume that I have before me two small boys, each 3 years old. I ask them to say quickly, out loud, everything they think of when I say a word. I say "dog." Boy 1 smiles broadly and responds, "Oh, doggie; my doggie; Spot; my friend; good dog; go fetch; friend; my dog; Spot." Boy 2 frowns and then responds, "Oooo dog; bite; teeth; blood; bad dog; hurts me; bad dog." Both of these boys know what a dog *is*. How they feel about dogs is another matter and is obviously a function of their experience with dogs—a classically conditioned emotional reaction.

Advertising provides us with many examples of attempts to use classical conditioning to change the way we feel about products or services. How many times have you seen TV ads showing healthy, good-looking young people having a great time—at the beach playing volleyball, riding bicycles down mountain trails, swinging on ropes over cool streams, and so on—while drinking large amounts of brand X. These attractive, "fun" stimuli are designed to make us "feel good." The intent of pairing "fun stimuli" (here the UCS) with brand X (the CS) is to have us acquire a "feel-good" response (CR) to the

Young children who have pleasant experiences with dogs probably will, when older, have pleasant thoughts and feelings about dogs.

beverage being advertised. We can analyze TV commercials in other ways as well, but claiming that the procedures of conditioning are at work here is quite reasonable.

Before You Go On

What sorts of responses are most readily influenced by classical conditioning?

For a long time, advertisers have understood the value of pairing their product with images of people having a good time. This ad appeared in 1948.

An Example: The Case of "Little Albert"

Let's take a somewhat detailed look at a famous example of the conditioning of an emotional response. In 1920, John B. Watson (the founder of behaviorism) and his student assistant, Rosalie Rayner, published a summary article on a series of experiments they performed with "Little Albert." Albert's experiences have become well known, and although Watson and Rayner's summary of their own work tended to oversimplify matters (Samuelson, 1980), the story of Little Albert still provides a good model for the classical conditioning of emotional responses.

Eleven-month-old Albert was given many toys to play with. Among other things, he was allowed to play with a live white rat. Albert seemed to enjoy the rat; he certainly showed no signs of fearing it. Then conditioning began. One day, just as Albert reached for the rat, one of the experimenters (Rayner) made a sudden loud noise by striking a metal bar with a hammer. The loud noise was frightening to Albert, a fact that Watson and Rayner had established two months earlier, during initial observations of Albert. At least, Albert made responses that Watson and Rayner felt indicated fear.

After repeated pairings of the rat and the noise, Albert's reaction to the rat underwent a relatively permanent change. Now when presented with the rat, Albert would at first start to reach out toward it, and then would recoil and cry, often trying to bury his head in his blanket. He was clearly making emotional responses to a stimulus that did not elicit those responses before it was paired with sudden loud noises. This sounds like classical conditioning: the rat is the CS and the sudden loud noise is the UCS that elicits the UCR of an emotional fear response. After repeated pairings of the rat and the noise (the CS and UCS), the rat elicits the same sort of fear response (or CR). Figure 5.3 presents a diagram of the procedures used to condition Little Albert to be afraid of a white rat.

Watson and Rayner went on to demonstrate that Albert's fear of the white rat *generalized* to all sorts of other stimuli: a dog, a ball of cotton, and even a Santa Claus mask with a white beard and mustache. In some cases, however, Watson and Rayner did not test for generalization as they should have. They occasionally paired the loud noise (UCS) with new stimuli before testing to see what the reaction might be (Harris, 1979).

Several issues have been raised concerning the Watson and Rayner demonstration of learned fear—not the least of which is the unethical treatment of poor little Albert. It is unlikely that anyone would even attempt such a project today. Watson had previously argued (1919) that emotional experiences of early childhood could

---

Figure 5.3

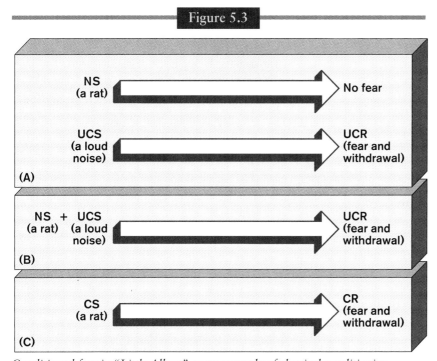

Conditioned fear in "Little Albert" as an example of classical conditioning.

affect an individual for a lifetime, yet here he was purposely frightening a young child (and without the advised consent of his mother). In fact, Albert's mother removed him from the hospital before Watson and Rayner had a chance to undo the conditioning. They were convinced that they could remove Little Albert's fear, but as fate would have it, they never got the chance. A number of researchers who tried to replicate Watson and Rayner's experiment, despite ethical considerations, were not totally successful (Harris, 1979).

Even with all of these technical disclaimers, it is easy to see how the Little Albert demonstration can be used as a model for describing how fear and other emotional responses can develop. When the project began, Albert didn't respond fearfully to a rat, cotton, or a furry mask. After a few trials of pairing a neutral stimulus (the rat) with an emotion-producing stimulus (the loud noise), Albert appeared to be afraid of a number of white, furry, fuzzy objects.

Before You Go On

Briefly summarize the "Little Albert"
experimental demonstration.

An Application: Phobias and Their Treatment

There are many things in this world that are life-threatening and downright frightening. Being afraid of certain stimuli is often a wise, rational, and appropriate reaction. Occasionally, however, we find people who experience distressing fears of stimuli that are *not* threatening in a real or rational sense.

Some people are intensely afraid of flying, of elevators, of heights, of small closed-in areas, of spiders, or of the dark. Psychologists say that these people are suffering from a **phobic disorder**—an intense, irrational fear of an object or event that leads a person to avoid contact with it. There are many explanations for how phobic disorders, or phobias, occur, but one clear possibility is classical conditioning.

This explanation goes as follows: a person experiences an intense, natural emotional response to a powerful, emotion-producing stimulus—perhaps a traumatic event, such as a severe injury or an accident. When an emotion-producing stimulus occurs in the presence of another, neutral stimulus, the pairing may result in the formation of a conditioned fear response to the originally neutral stimulus. A child at a local carnival becomes separated from his parents and gets swept away by a large crowd into a tent where clowns are performing. The youngster is (sensibly) frightened by the separation from his parents, and after they are reunited, requires considerable reassurance before he settles down. Should we be terribly surprised if this child—even much later, as an adolescent or an adult—appears to be irrationally afraid of carnivals, circuses, or clowns? Not if one believes that classical conditioning can account for the formation of phobias.

Sadly enough, phobic disorders are far from uncommon. Estimates place prevalence rates at between 7 and 20 percent of the

phobic disorder *an intense, irrational fear that leads a person to avoid the feared object, activity, or situation*

population; that's tens of millions of people (Marks, 1986; Robins et al., 1984). Phobias seldom extinguish on their own. Why don't they? There are many reasons, but one is that someone with a phobia is usually successful at avoiding the conditioned stimulus that elicits the fear. Someone with a fear of flying may get by driving or taking a bus or train.

Although there are various techniques used to treat phobic disorders (see Chapter 13), one of the most common is based on Pavlovian conditioning. The procedure, **systematic desensitization**, was introduced by therapist Joseph Wolpe (1958, 1969, 1981). As an example, we'll consider a college student with an extreme fear of public speaking, now enrolled in a speech class.

In its standard form, there are three stages of systematic desensitization. First, the therapist instructs or trains the subject to relax. There are many ways to go about such training. Some use hypnosis, but most simply have the subject relax one foot, then both feet, then one leg, then both, and so on, until the entire body is relaxed. Whatever method is used, this stage generally doesn't take very long, and after a few hours of training at most, the subject knows how to enter a relaxed state quickly.

systematic desensitization the application of classical conditioning procedures to alleviate anxiety; each item in a hierarchy of anxiety-producing stimuli is paired with a state of relaxation

A phobic fear of heights, probably not a problem for this daring skier, may be a conditioned emotional response. It can be lessened with systematic desensitization.

The second stage is to construct an "anxiety hierarchy"—a list of stimuli that gradually decrease in their ability to elicit anxiety. The most feared stimulus is placed at the top of the list (in our example, perhaps, "Giving a formal speech to a large group," followed by "Being called on in class," "Talking to a small group of strangers," "Being introduced to two or more people," "Talking with friends," and so on). Each item that follows elicits less and less fear until, at the bottom of the list, we place stimuli that elicit no fear.

Now treatment is ready to begin. The student relaxes completely and thinks about the stimulus lowest on the anxiety hierarchy. The student is then instructed to think about the next highest stimulus, and the next, and so on, all the while remaining as relaxed as possible. As progress is made up the list toward the anxiety-producing stimuli at the top, the therapist constantly monitors the subject's tension/relaxation level. When anxiety seems to be overcoming relaxation, the student is told to stop thinking about that item on the hierarchy and to think about an item lower on the list.

Systematic desensitization is more than the simple extinction of a previously conditioned fear response. A new response (relaxation) is being acquired to "replace" an old one (fear). The process is called *counterconditioning*. The logic is that a person cannot be relaxed and be anxious at the same time. These are incompatible responses. So, if I pair a stimulus (the CS) with the feeling associated with being relaxed (the UCS), through classical conditioning it will come to produce a reaction of calm (a new CR), not the incompatible response of tension and anxiety (the old CR). For many people, this technique can be effective (e.g., Wilson, 1982). It works best for those fears that are associated with easily identifiable, specific environmental stimuli; it works least well for a diffuse, generalized fear, for which hierarchies are difficult to generate.

Before You Go On

What is a phobic disorder?

How is systematic desensitization used to treat phobic disorders?

RETHINKING WHAT REALLY HAPPENS IN CLASSICAL CONDITIONING

Although much of our discussion of classical conditioning so far has dealt with procedures and phenomena associated with Pavlov's laboratory soon after the turn of the century, Pavlovian conditioning continues to be an active area of research (Adler & Cohen, 1993; Domjan, 1987; Lavond et al., 1993; Rescorla, 1987, 1988; Spear et al., 1990). Psychologists today are interested in understanding precisely what happens during classical conditioning. They want to understand the factors that influence the effectiveness or efficiency of the procedure.

Pavlov believed, as did generations of psychologists who followed him, that *any* stimulus paired with an unconditioned stimulus could effectively serve as a conditioned stimulus. It's easy to see how psychologists came to this conclusion. A wide variety of stimuli *can* be paired with food powder and as a result come to elicit a salivation response. It seemed reasonable to characterize Pavlovian conditioning as a matter of "stimulus substitution" in which one stimulus (the CS) comes to substitute for another (the UCS). The long-standing belief was that any neutral stimulus paired with a UCS could become a CS, *and* it was further understood that the time interval between the CS and the UCS had to be brief.

We now see conditioning in a much broader light. Classical conditioning is viewed as learning about relationships among events in the world. Conditioning is seen as an active search for sensible ways to represent the environment, a search for information that one stimulus gives about another (Rescorla, 1988; Spear et al., 1990).

> Pavlovian conditioning is not a stupid process by which the organism willy-nilly forms associations between any two stimuli that happen to co-occur. Rather, the organism is better seen as an information seeker using logical and perceptual relations among events, along with its own preconceptions, to form a sophisticated representation of its world. (Rescorla, 1988, p. 154)

Can *Any* Stimulus Serve as a CS?

At least two lines of research suggest that one cannot pair just *any* stimulus with an unconditioned stimulus and expect conditioning to result. One research program is associated with Robert Rescorla, the other with Leon Kamin.

A rat can be conditioned to fear the sound of a tone by presenting that tone and consistently following it with a mild electric shock. It doesn't take many pairings of the tone and shock for the conditioned response (fear of tone) to develop. This is a straightforward example of classical conditioning. Assume we present a second rat with a tone, occasionally following it with a mild shock. For this rat, we also present the shock from time to time, but *without the preceding tone*. This rat might end up with quite a few shocks without a preceding tone, but it will have as many tone-shock pairings as our first rat. Will this second rat demonstrate any conditional response to the tone when it is presented alone? No, it won't. Although this rat experienced the same number of tone-shock pairings, there will be no conditioning (Rescorla, 1968, 1987). Before I explain this failure of conditioning, let's consider Kamin's research.

In a demonstration of a phenomenon called *blocking*, rats are shocked (UCS) at the same time a noise (CS) is presented. Classically conditioned fear of the noise is readily established. The rats are then presented with several trials in which the noise *and* a light (a new "compound" CS) are paired with the UCS of a shock. Even though the light (now presented with the noise) is paired with the shock several times, no conditioned fear of the light can be found. That is, when the light is now presented to these rats *by itself,* no fear reaction can be detected. The light continues to act as a neutral stimulus. The rats had already learned that the noise was a good predictor of the shock; the light was redundant (Kamin, 1968, 1969).

In both cases (and in others; e.g., Miller & Spear, 1985; Pearce & Hall, 1980; Rescorla & Wagner, 1972), what matters most in determining whether a stimulus will act as a CS is the extent to which that stimulus *provides useful information,* or predicts (signals) the occurrence of another stimulus. In the original Pavlovian demonstration, the tone was highly informative. Every time the tone was presented, food powder followed, so in this case the tone was an effective CS. In Rescorla's experiments, we see that if the tone does not reliably predict the presence of a shock (as when some shocks occur without the previous tone), that tone will not be an effective CS no matter how many times it is paired with the UCS. And in Kamin's experiments we see that because rats had already learned that the noise predicted the shocks, adding a light as a potential CS provided no additional information and hence was ineffective.

Let's recast this issue in human terms. If we can talk about rats representing their environments by learning which stimuli predict other stimuli, isn't it reasonable to think about classical conditioning in humans in a similar vein? We may experience a warm, pleasant feeling when we see a picture of a beach because it is the beach that is best associated with one of our best vacations—not the fact that we happened to have left for that vacation on a Wednesday. Beaches predict fun and good times; Wednesdays don't. We have not learned to associate the fireplace with the pain of being burned, even though we may have first been burned when we placed our hand into a fire there. Little Albert's fear generalized to many stimuli, but Albert developed no particular fear of blankets, even though he was sitting on a blanket every time Raynor created the loud noise Albert did come to associate with the rat.

Now, let's consider two additional complications that have arisen in the search to understand the basic process of classical conditioning: the fact that the CS and the UCS do not have to be paired close together in time, and the fact that some responses are easier to condition than others.

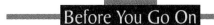

Before You Go On

Under what circumstances are stimuli likely
to serve effectively as CSs?

Must the Time Interval Between the CS and UCS Always Be Brief?

Pavlov recognized that the time interval between the CS and the UCS was a critical variable in classical conditioning. For nearly fifty years it was assumed that the most appropriate interval between the CS and UCS was a brief one—a few seconds, at most (Beecroft, 1966; Gormezano, 1972). The claim found in most textbooks on learning was that the shorter the interval between the CS and UCS, the faster conditioning would be. It now appears that there is at least one excellent example of classical conditioning in which the CS-UCS interval may be much longer than a few seconds—even hours long. This example also reinforces the point that some stimuli make more effective conditioned stimuli than others. The example is found in the research on the formation of aversions (very strong dislikes) to certain tastes.

Many experiments have confirmed that both rats and people (and many other organisms) can be classically conditioned to avoid particular foods (Garcia et al., 1966; Gemberling & Domjan, 1982; Revulsky & Garcia, 1970). In experiments using rats, subjects eat or drink a food that has been given a distinctive taste. Then they are given a poison, or treated with X rays, so that they will develop nausea. However, the feelings of nausea do not occur until hours after the food has been eaten. (In a few days, the rats are perfectly normal and healthy again.) Even though there has been a long delay between the flavored food (CS) and the feelings of nausea (UCS), the rats learn to avoid the food, often in just one trial. Patients being treated for cancer may experience nausea as an unpleasant side effect of chemotherapy. Such patients will often show a strong taste aversion for whatever they ate hours before their treatment—even if what they ate was something pleasant, such as ice cream (Bernstein, 1978).

The time delay between the CS and the UCS here is obviously at odds with the standard belief that to be effective the CS and the UCS need to be presented together in time. Another difficulty centers on why the *taste* of previously eaten food should so commonly serve as the CS for nausea that occurs hours later. That is, why is the nausea associated with the taste of food instead of some other stimulus event that could be paired with the nausea? Think of this experience happening to you. At a restaurant, you order a piece of pumpkin pie. Hours later, you suffer severe stomach cramps and nausea. Why should you associate these with the pie and not the type of chair you sat on, or the car you drove to the restaurant, or the person you were with? Actually, we may have a predisposition, or bias, rooted in our biology for associating some things with others, particularly if they have a functional basis (Mackintosh, 1975, 1983; Revulsky, 1985). Food followed by nausea is an excellent example of just such a predisposed association.

Taste aversion involves the classically conditioned association of nausea with foods eaten earlier. Seldom is the nausea associated with stimuli such as the restaurant at which the food was eaten or people you may have eaten with.

<hr>

Before You Go On

What do taste aversion studies tell us about the relationship between the CS and UCS in classical conditioning?

TOPIC 5A SUMMARY

Learning is a process inferred from our observation of relatively permanent changes in behavior that occur as the result of practice or experience. In this Topic, we have reviewed the procedures of classical, or Pavlovian, conditioning. In this sort of conditioning, when one stimulus precedes another, and is seen as predicting the occurrence of a second stimulus, that first stimulus comes to produce the response usually produced by the second one. We have seen that one of the major applications of Pavlovian conditioning is its role in eliciting emotional behaviors. Many of the stimuli to which we respond emotionally do not elicit these responses naturally or reflexively; they do so through classical conditioning. In other words, many of the stimuli in our environments that give rise to pleasant or unpleasant feelings do so because they have previously been paired with more inherently pleasant or unpleasant experiences or situations. We have looked at other ways in which classical conditioning can have an impact on our daily lives. In our next Topic, we consider another fundamental form of learning: operant conditioning.

Topic 5B
OPERANT CONDITIONING

The basic premise of operant conditioning is that behaviors are influenced by the consequences they produce. Learning is a matter of increasing the rate of those responses that produce positive consequences and decreasing the rate of responses that produce negative consequences. You'll see in this Topic that many behaviors can be understood in terms of operant conditioning. We will begin by defining some of the terminology of operant conditioning. Because the concept of reinforcement is so important in operant conditioning, we'll spend a good deal of time examining some of the varieties and principles of reinforcement. Then we'll discuss punishment.

THE BASICS OF OPERANT CONDITIONING

Most of the early research on operant conditioning was done by B. F. Skinner. Although we correctly associate operant conditioning with Skinner, he did not discover it or invent it in any literal sense. The techniques of operant conditioning had been in use for hundreds of years before Skinner was born. What Skinner did was bring that earlier work—most of it casual, some of it scientific—into the psychology laboratory. There, he studied the process of operant conditioning with a unique vigor that helped the rest of us realize the significance of the process.

Defining Operant Conditioning

Skinner used the term **operant** to refer to a behavior or group of behaviors an organism uses to *operate* on its environment. Operants are said to be controlled by their consequences: they will maintain or increase their rate (or probability) if they are reinforced; they will decrease their rate if they are not reinforced or if they are punished. Thus, **operant conditioning** changes the probability, or rate, of responses on the basis of the consequences that result from those responses. Responses that are followed by reinforcers tend to increase in rate; those not followed by reinforcers tend to decrease in rate. We are not claiming that the future governs what happens in the present, but we are claiming that past experiences influence present ones. As Skinner put it, ". . . behavior is shaped by its consequences, but only by consequences that lie in the past. We do what we do because of what *has* happened, not what *will* happen" (Skinner, 1989, p. 14).

The first clear statement of the essence of operant conditioning came not from Skinner, but from E. L. Thorndike, a psychologist at Columbia University early in the twentieth century, who tried to discover the "laws of learning." In one experiment, Thorndike placed a cat inside a wooden box. The door of the box was latched with a wooden peg. If manipulated correctly, the peg could be moved and the latch opened, and the cat could go outside the box to eat a small piece of fish that Thorndike had placed there (see Figure 5.4). When it was first placed in the box, the cat engaged in a wide range of behaviors: clawing, licking, biting, scratching, hissing, stretching, and so on. But eventually—and at first, by chance—the door was unlatched and the cat got to the food. The next time the cat was in Thorndike's "puzzle box," it exhibited many of the same behaviors, but it did unlatch the door and escape a bit sooner. Over a series of subsequent trials, Thorndike noted that his cat reduced its irrelevant behaviors and directly moved to open the door more and more quickly. After some experience, a cat placed in the box would go immediately to the latch, move the peg, open the door, and eat the fish provided by its trainer. Thorndike had discovered a law of learning—the *law of effect*.

The **law of effect** embodies the basics of operant conditioning, claiming that responses are learned ("stamped in," Thorndike said) when followed by a "satisfying state of affairs" (Thorndike, 1911, p. 245). When an organism makes a response and experiences a satisfying state of affairs (reinforcement), the organism will tend to make that response again. On the other hand, if a response is not followed by a satisfying state of affairs, or if a response leads to "discomfort," the organism will tend not to make that response again. Thorndike seemed to be saying, "We tend to do, and continue to do, whatever makes us feel good." This simple observation is also a profound one because it is true. Behaviors *are* shaped by their consequences.

operant behavior(s) used by an organism to operate on its environment

operant conditioning a procedure that changes the rate of a response on the basis of the consequences that result from that response

law of effect (Thorndike's) the observation that responses that lead to a "satisfying state of affairs" tend to be repeated; responses that do not lead to a satisfying state of affairs tend not to be repeated

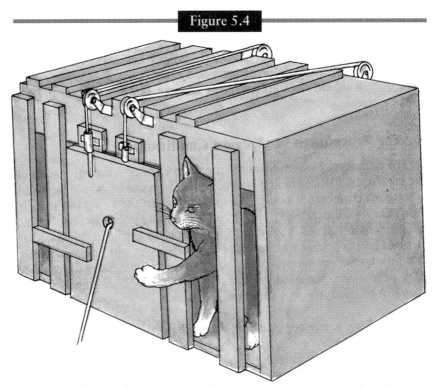

After noting that cats became more and more proficient at escaping from his "puzzle box," Thorndike believed that they were demonstrating lawful behaviors. Those behaviors could be explained, he thought, in terms of his law of effect.

Examples of operant conditioning are all around us. One hardly needs any apparatus or a laboratory to observe the principle at work. Imagine a father rushing through a supermarket with his toddler seated in a shopping cart. The youngster is screaming at the top of his lungs for a candy bar—over and over, echoing throughout the store, "I wanna candy bar! I wanna candy bar!" Father is doing a good (and an appropriate) job of ignoring this monstrous behavior until he spies a neighbor coming down the next aisle. The neighbor has her three children with her, and all three are acting like quiet, perfect angels. What's a parent to do? He races by the checkout lanes, grabs a chocolate bar, and gives it to his child. Does one have to be an expert in child psychology (or operant conditioning) to predict what will happen on the next visit to the store? Screaming "worked" this time, so it will be tried again. Reinforced behaviors tend to recur. Do you recognize that the story about my child psychology professor at the beginning of this chapter is an example of operant conditioning?

As we did with classical conditioning, we'll use examples from the laboratory to describe the procedures and phenomena of operant conditioning. You should have little difficulty finding similar examples in your own experience.

The Procedures of Operant Conditioning

To demonstrate operant conditioning in the controlled environment of the laboratory, Skinner built a special apparatus, which he called an operant chamber. Although Skinner never used the term, and said he didn't like it (Skinner, 1984), some psychologists call this device a *Skinner box*. Figure 5.5 shows a standard operant chamber. The chamber pictured here is designed for rats. The box is empty except for a small lever that protrudes from one wall and a small cup to hold a piece of rat food. Food pellets are automatically dispensed through a tube into the food cup. They are released one at a time when the lever is pressed all the way down.

Figure 5.5

Now that we have our chamber, we need a subject. If we put a hungry rat into the chamber and do nothing else, the rat will occasionally press the lever. There's little else for it to do in there. Rats naturally explore their environments and tend to manipulate objects in it. The rate at which the rat presses the lever is called its *base rate* of responding. Typically, a rat will press the lever 8 to 10 times an hour.

After a period of observation, we activate the food dispenser so that a food pellet is delivered every time the lever is pressed. As predicted by Thorndike's law of effect, the rate of the lever-pressing response increases. The rat may reach the point of pressing the lever at a rate of as many as 500 to 600 times an hour. Learning has taken place. There has been a relatively permanent change in behavior as a result of experience.

A typical operant chamber for rats.

Here is a little subtlety: has the rat learned to press the lever? In any sense can we say that we have taught the rat a lever-pressing response? No. The rat knew how to press the lever and did so long before we introduced the food pellets as a reward for its behavior. What it did learn—the change in behavior that took place—was a change in the *rate* of the response, not in the nature of the response.

Before You Go On

What is the essence of operant conditioning?

The Course of Conditioning

Now that we have the basic principles of operant conditioning in mind, let's briefly review just how one goes about using the procedure.

Shaping. One reality of operant conditioning is that before you can reinforce a response, you have to get that response to occur in the first place. If your rat never presses the lever, it will never get a pellet. What if you place your rat in an operant chamber and discover that after grooming itself, it stops, stares off into space, and settles down, facing away from the lever and the food cup? Your operant chamber is prepared to deliver a food pellet as soon as your rat presses the lever, but it appears that you may have a long wait. You want to get going now.

In such circumstances, you could use a procedure called **shaping**, reinforcing *successive approximations* of the response that you ultimately want to condition. You have a button that delivers a pellet to the food cup of the operant chamber even though the lever is not pressed. When your rat turns to face the lever, you deliver a pellet, reinforcing that behavior. This is not exactly the response you want, but at least the rat is facing in the correct direction. You don't give your rat another pellet until it moves toward the lever. It gets another pellet for moving even closer to the lever. The next pellet doesn't come until the rat touches the lever.

A reinforcer is delivered each time your rat successively approximates the lever-press response. Eventually the rat will press the lever to deliver a pellet by itself. Shaping is over, and the rat is on its own. In practice, this procedure is not as easy as it may sound. You have to be quick with your reinforcement, and you must be sure that each reinforced response is really closer to the one you ultimately want. Remember that your rat will continue to do whatever it was doing just before its behavior was reinforced. If you're not careful, your rat may be rewarded for just running to the lever, or bobbing its head up and down, or turning in circles, instead of pressing the lever. Or think back to the example of conditioning the professor to stand in the corner. If we had waited until he just wandered into the corner on his own, we would have had a very long wait indeed. We used shaping and reinforced successive approximations of the professor's corner-standing behaviors.

Acquisition. Once an organism begins to emit the responses you wish to reinforce, the procedures of operant conditioning are simple. Immediately following the desired response, reinforcement is provided. As responses produce reinforcers, those responses become more and more likely to occur. The increase in response rate that follows reinforcement will generally be slow at first, then become more rapid, and eventually will level off. This stage in which response rates increase is **acquisition**. Figure 5.6 is a curve showing the stages of operant conditioning. Note that the vertical axis (y-axis) in this curve is a measure of *rate* of response, not response strength. That is, what increases in acquisition for operant conditioning is the rate of a response.

Extinction and Spontaneous Recovery. Once an organism is responding at a high rate of response, what happens if reinforcers are withheld? Let's say that because we have reinforced its lever pressing, a rat is pressing a lever at a rate of 550 presses an hour. From now on, however, it will receive no more pellets of food for its efforts—no more reinforcers. What happens is predictable: the rate of lever-pressing response decreases gradually until it returns to the low base rate at which it began. That is, eventually the lever pressing returns to base rate (not to zero, because it didn't start at zero), and we say that extinction has taken place. In operant conditioning, **extinction** is the decrease in the rate of a response as reinforcers are withheld.

shaping a procedure of reinforcing successive approximations of a desired response until that desired response is made

acquisition the process in operant conditioning in which the rate of a reinforced response increases

extinction the process in operant conditioning in which the rate of a response decreases as reinforcers are withheld

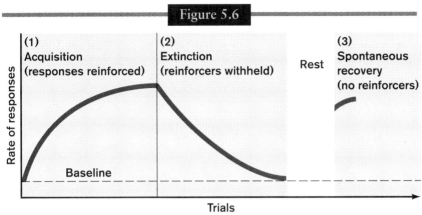

Figure 5.6

The stages of operant conditioning. (1) During acquisition, response rates increase as responses are reinforced. (2) In extinction, reinforcers are withheld and response rates return to their original baseline levels. (3) In spontaneous recovery, an increase in response rate is noted following a rest interval after extinction. Note that the vertical axis indicates a measure of the rate of a response, not its strength.

Now assume that extinction has occurred, and that the rat has been removed from the operant chamber and returned to its cage for a few days. When we again deprive it of food and return it to the chamber, what will it do? It will go to the lever and begin to press it again. Athough the lever pressing has undergone extinction (the last time this rat was in the operant chamber, it was not pressing the lever), it will resume once the rat is given a rest interval. A return of an extinguished response following a rest interval is called **spontaneous recovery**. As was the case in classical conditioning, the significance of spontaneous recovery is that once acquired, an operant

spontaneous recovery the phenomenon in operant conditioning in which a previously extinguished response returns after a rest interval

Operant conditioning techniques were used to train this whale to give his human friend a ride.

response can seldom be eliminated in just one series of extinction trials. Figure 5.6 also shows extinction and spontaneous recovery for operant conditioning.

REINFORCEMENT

reinforcement a process that increases the rate, or probability, of the response it follows

reinforcers stimuli that increase the rate, or probability, of the responses they follow

Reinforcement is a crucial concept in operant conditioning. **Reinforcement** is a process that increases the rate, or probability, of the response it follows. It is the operation of administering a reinforcer. In this section we'll define *reinforcer*, and discuss a number of types of reinforcers. We'll also examine the effects of scheduling reinforcers. We will then move on to consider punishment.

Positive and Negative Reinforcers

What qualifies as a good, effective reinforcer? What creates that satisfying state of affairs Thorndike claimed is necessary to increase response rate? For hungry rats in operant chambers, the answer seems deceptively simple. Here we can ensure that a rat is hungry, and can confidently predict that receiving food will be reinforcing. For people, or for rats who are no longer hungry, the answer may not be as obvious.

Skinner and his students have argued that we should define reinforcers only in terms of their effect on behavior. Reinforcers are stimuli. Stimuli that increase the rate, or probability, of the response they follow are **reinforcers**.

At first reading, this logic may sound a bit backward—or at least circular. A reinforcer is something that increases the rate of those responses it follows. This reasoning suggests that nothing is *necessarily* going to be reinforcing. Reinforcers are defined only after we have noted their effect on behavior. Thus, we do not know ahead of time what will or what will not produce an increased rate of response—or a satisfying state of affairs. We may have some strong suspicions, based on what has worked in the past, but we will not know for sure until we try.

For many people, money is a powerful reinforcer. What would happen if your instructor offered $10 for every test item answered correctly? Such a scheme might drastically increase the rate of students' studying behaviors. But, as difficult as it may be to believe,

For some students, a degree at graduation is a powerful reinforcer.

some students might not be interested in such a scheme. For them, the monetary reward would not be at all reinforcing. In such a case, it would not lead to an increase in the studying behaviors of those students.

In many cultures (mostly Eastern and African) the group (e.g., family, or tribe) is valued above the life of the individual. In such cultures, reinforcing an individual's achievements will have less effect than in those cultures (mostly Western) in which individual effort and achievement are valued (e.g., Brislin, 1993; Triandis, 1990). For example, in traditional Hawaiian culture, the sense of family is strong, and personal independence is not a sought-after goal. Thus, "the Hawaiian child may not be motivated by individual rewards (gold stars, grades) to the extent that his or her Caucasian counterpart may be" (Cushner, 1990, p. 107). The point is that we cannot tell whether a stimulus will be reinforcing until we try it. It is reinforcing *only* if it increases the rate or the likelihood of the response it follows (Kimble, 1981).

Now that we have a general idea of what a reinforcer is, we can get a bit more specific. A **positive reinforcer** is a stimulus *presented to* an organism that increases (or maintains) the rate of a response it follows. This sounds familiar, and perhaps redundant: if something is positive, it ought to be reinforcing. Examples include such stimuli as food for hungry organisms, water for thirsty ones, high letter grades for well-motivated students, and money, praise, and attention for most of us. Remember: the intention of the person doing the reinforcing does not matter at all. Reinforcers are defined solely on the basis of their effect on behavior.

A **negative reinforcer** is a stimulus that increases (or maintains) the rate of a response that precedes *its removal*. That is, to increase the rate of a response, one removes or terminates a negative reinforcer. *Negative reinforcer* is a strange term. There is something contradictory about the sound of it. If something is negative, how can it be a reinforcer? Part of the secret is to remember that the key word here is *reinforcer,* and that reinforcers increase the rate of responses. In terms of the law of effect, negative reinforcement must produce some sort of satisfying state of affairs. It does. The reinforcement comes not from the delivery or presentation of negative reinforcers, but from their removal. (Another secret is to remember that reinforce*ment* is a process. You may think of negative reinforcers as generally being unpleasant stimuli, whereas negative reinforcement is a pleasant outcome.)

So, negative reinforcers are stimuli that increase the probability of a response *when they are removed*. They may include such stimuli as shocks, enforced isolation, and ridicule. They are exactly the sorts of things an organism would work to avoid or escape. They are the very stimuli that could be used to punish an organism if they were presented following an undesired response. Although it may not sound like it, negative reinforcement is desirable. If offered "negative reinforcement, one should accept the offer. It is always good to have bad things terminated or removed" (Michael, 1985, p. 107).

positive reinforcer a stimulus that increases the rate of a response it follows

negative reinforcer a stimulus that increases the rate of a response when that stimulus is removed after the response is made

Let's consider a few examples, keeping in mind that the outcome of negative reinforcement is the increase in an organism's rate of response. A rat in an operant chamber is shocked (through the metal floor of the chamber). As soon as the rat presses a lever, the shock is turned off. The lever press has been reinforced. Because an unpleasant, painful stimulus was terminated, this was negative reinforcement—the negative reinforcer was the shock.

You take an aspirin when you have a headache and are reinforced: the pain stops. You will be likely to try aspirin again the next time you have a headache. When Wayne says "uncle" to get Ken to stop twisting his arm, Ken does stop, thereby reinforcing Wayne's saying "uncle." If this negative reinforcement is effective, Wayne will be more likely to say "uncle" in the future when Ken asks him to. (Notice that Ken could have used a positive reinforcer to get Wayne to say "uncle," perhaps by offering him 50 cents to do so.) When a prisoner is released from prison early, "for good behavior," the good behavior is being reinforced. The process is negative reinforcement.

Before we go on, here's one more hint for you, suggested by a few of my colleagues. Don't think of positive and negative reinforcement in terms of good and bad, but in terms of plus (+) and minus (−). In using positive reinforcement, one adds (+) a stimulus, whereas in negative reinforcement one takes away, or subtracts (−), a stimulus. Now that we have some of the basics laid down, let's make another distinction between reinforcers, this time between primary and secondary reinforcers.

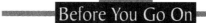

Before You Go On

Give an operational definition of reinforcement.

Distinguish between a positive and a negative reinforcer.

Primary and Secondary Reinforcers

Reinforcers are defined in terms of their effects on behavior. We have seen that both positive and negative reinforcers increase response rate. Now we need to make a distinction between primary and secondary reinforcers. What is at issue here is the extent to which reinforcers are unlearned and natural, or acquire their reinforcing capability through learning or experience.

Primary reinforcers do not require previous experience to be effective. They are, in some way, related to the organism's survival. They are usually biological or physiological in nature. Food for a hungry organism or water for a thirsty one are common examples. Providing a warm place by the fire to a cold, wet, stray dog involves primary reinforcement.

primary reinforcers stimuli (usually biologically or physiologically based) that increase the rate of a response with no previous experience required

Secondary reinforcers are often referred to as conditioned, learned, or acquired reinforcers. There is nothing about them that implies they are inherently reinforcing in any biological sense, yet they operate to strengthen responses.

Most of the reinforcers you and I work for are of this sort. Money, praise, high letter grades, and promotions are good examples. Money, in itself, is not worth much (the metal variety wears holes in your pockets, and the paper kind is dirty and carries germs). But previous learning experiences have convinced most of us of the reinforcing nature of money, and it can serve to increase the rate of a variety of responses. Among other things, we have learned that money can give us access to many other reinforcers, such as food and clothing.

The use of secondary reinforcers—and operant conditioning—can be illustrated by a type of psychotherapy called *contingency contracting* (see page 661 in Topic 13B). Contingency contracting amounts to setting up a system that provides secondary reinforcers for appropriate behaviors. The system established is referred to as a token economy.

Here's an example of a token economy I think is particularly clever. A colleague and his wife were having a difficult time with their preschool son, Mikey, whenever a baby-sitter was needed. Mikey had become a terror, to the point that getting baby-sitters had become difficult. So, his dad designed small stamps—tokens—each imprinted with a pink bunny. He also assembled stamp savings booklets. Each booklet could hold 40 stamps. A contract was (literally) written out on the back of the booklet: "When this book is filled with stamps, Daddy will take Mikey to the store to buy him _____." The deal was that each time Mom and Dad went out, Mikey could "earn" as many as five stamps. How many depended on the report of the previous night's baby-sitter. (When Mikey's dad first tried this, Mikey spent the entire evening sitting quietly in one chair because he "didn't want to mess up.") Contingency contracting techniques, and secondary reinforcers, are often remarkably effective.

Token economies need not be so elaborate. A child earns a check mark on the calendar for each day he or she makes the bed (or takes out the trash, walks the dog, clears the table, or whatever). The economy here hinges on the extent to which the check marks serve as tokens, as secondary reinforcers. In other words, the child must first learn that a certain number of check marks can be exchanged for something that already reinforces his or her behaviors (for example, an extra dessert, an hour of playing a video game, or a new toy).

Perhaps because of their effectiveness, examples such as these often disturb students and parents. "Why, this isn't psychology," they claim. "You're just bribing the child to behave." There are two reasons why we need not be concerned. First, bribery involves contracting to reward someone to do something that *both parties view as inappropriate*. People are bribed to steal, cheat, lie, change votes, or otherwise engage in behaviors they know they should not. Token economies are designed to reinforce behaviors judged in the first place to be appropriate. Second, as Skinner argued for many years, the long-term hope is that Mikey will come to appreciate that behaving

secondary reinforcers stimuli that increase the rate of a response because of their having been associated with other reinforcers; also called conditioned, *or* learned, reinforcers

oneself in the presence of baby-sitters can be its own reward. The hope is that the use of extrinsic reinforcers will be no longer needed as appropriate behaviors become reinforced by more subtle, intrinsic factors.

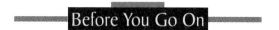

Before You Go On

Compare and contrast primary and secondary reinforcers, and give an example of each.

Scheduling Reinforcers

In all of our discussions and examples so far, I have implied that operant conditioning requires that a reinforcer be provided after every desired response. In fact, particularly at the start, it may be best to reinforce each response as it occurs. But once response rate begins to increase, there may be good reason for doing otherwise—for reinforcing responses intermittently.

The procedure of reinforcing every response after it occurs is called a **continuous reinforcement (CRF) schedule**. One problem with CRF schedules is that earning a reinforcer after each response may soon reduce the effectiveness of that reinforcer. For example, once a rat has eaten its fill, food pellets will no longer serve to reinforce its behavior, and the rat will have to be removed from the operant chamber until it becomes hungry again (Skinner, 1956). Another problem is that responses acquired under a CRF schedule tend to extinguish very quickly. Once reinforcement is withheld, response rates decrease drastically.

Alternatives to reinforcing every response are called **intermittent** (or partial) **reinforcement schedules**. Simply put, these are strategies for reinforcing a desired behavior less frequently than every time it occurs. There are any number of ways in which one might go about reinforcing responses according to an intermittent schedule. We'll review four such strategies: fixed-ratio, fixed-interval, variable-ratio, and variable-interval schedules. These schedules were devised in the laboratory. In the world outside the laboratory, there are not many good examples of the precise, literal application of intermittent schedules. There are some real-life examples that are fairly close, however, and they are instructive. For each type of schedule, we will look at how acquisition (see Figure 5.7) and—perhaps more important—extinction (see Figure 5.8) are affected.

With a *fixed-ratio (FR) schedule*, one establishes (fixes) a ratio of reinforcers to responses. In an FR 1:5 schedule, for example, one reinforcer would be delivered after every five responses. A 1:10 fixed-ratio schedule for a rat in an operant chamber means that the rat would receive a pellet only after it pressed the lever ten times. An example of a fixed-ratio schedule can be found in piecework: "I'll pay

continuous reinforcement (CRF) schedule a reinforcement schedule in which every response is followed by a reinforcer

intermittent reinforcement schedules reinforcement schedules in which responses are not reinforced every time they occur

Figure 5.7

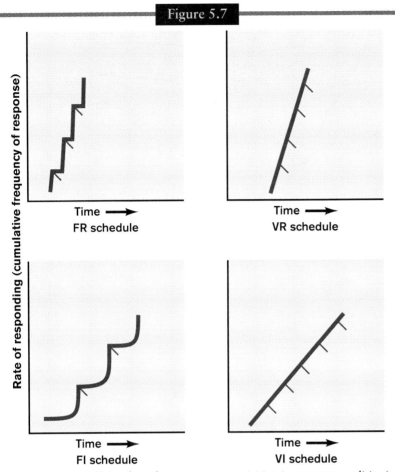

The effects of a schedule of reinforcement on acquisition in operant conditioning. Rates are high for the FR schedule, and there is a pause after each reinforcer. VR schedules produce even higher rates of response with no pause after each reinforcer. An FI schedule produces somewhat lower rates, with delays just after each reinforcement. Responses are at a more steady rate with a VI schedule.

you 25 cents for every 12 gizmos you assemble," or "You'll earn 10 points of extra credit for every three book reports you hand in." As you might imagine, there is a high and steady rate of responding under an effective fixed-ratio schedule. After all, the more one responds, the more reinforcement there will be. For most organisms, there is a brief pause just after a reinforcement occurs. Responses acquired under an FR schedule are more resistant to extinction than those acquired under a CRF schedule.

With a *fixed-interval (FI) schedule*, time is divided into set (fixed) intervals. After each fixed interval, a reinforcer is delivered when the next response occurs. An FI 30-second schedule, for example, calls for the delivery of a food pellet for the first lever press a rat makes after each 30-second interval passes. With such a schedule, you know from the start that you won't be dispensing more than two pellets every

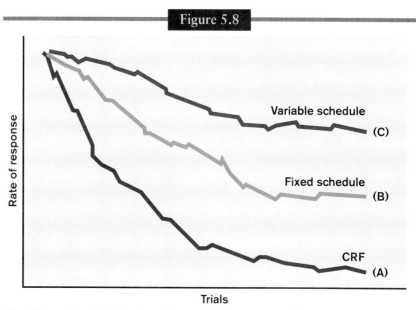

Figure 5.8

*The effects of a schedule of reinforcement on extinction. These are three hypo-
thetical extinction curves following operant conditioning on (A) continuous reinforcement (CRF), (B) a fixed schedule (FR or FI), and (C) a variable schedule (VR
or VI).*

minute. Note that the rat doesn't get a pellet just because 30 seconds
has elasped; it gets a pellet for the first response it makes after the
fixed interval. A common example is employees being paid on a regular interval of, say, every Friday, or once a month. Under an FI schedule, response rates decrease just after a reinforcer, then increase significantly as the time for the next reinforcer approaches. Fixed-interval
schedules also produce responses that are resistant to extinction.

There are two variable schedules of reinforcement: the *variable-
ratio (VR) schedule* and the *variable-interval (VI) schedule.* From the
learner's point of view, these schedules are very much alike. They differ mostly from the perspective of the experimenter, or the dispenser
of reinforcers. With a VR schedule, one varies the ratio of reinforcers
to responses. With a VR 1:5 schedule, for example, the experimenter
administers one reinforcer for every five responses *on the average,* but
always in a different ratio. That is, the first reinforcer may come after
five responses, the next after six, the next after nine, the next after
one, and so on. On the average, the ratio of reinforcers to responses is
1:5, but the patterning of actual ratios is variable. From the learner's
point of view, this is a random schedule. The most commonly cited
examples of VR reinforcement schedules are gambling devices, such
as slot machines. They are programmed to pay off (reinforce) on a
variable-ratio schedule where the ratios are usually quite large. Not
surprisingly, VR schedules produce high rates of responding, and produce responses that are very resistant to extinction.

Variable-interval schedules follow the same sort of logic as variable-ratio schedules. Here, time intervals are established randomly.

For a rat on a VI schedule in an operant chamber, a food pellet comes following the first lever press response after a 30-second interval; the next follows the first response after a 50-second interval; then after a 10-second interval, and so on. A VI 30-second schedule is one in which the varied intervals *average* 30 seconds in length. Again, though, keep in mind that it is a response that gets reinforced, not a time interval. An instructor who wants to keep a class on its toes, studying regularly and attending class consistently, may schedule pop quizzes on a variable-interval schedule. The students will learn that the quizzes are coming, but they never know when. What we find when VI schedules are used is a somewhat slower but very steady pattern of performance. If you know when your exams are coming, you may hold off studying until just before they occur. If they are scheduled to occur randomly throughout the semester, you'll keep your studying rate up just in case there's a test the next class period.

The terminology we have used here is standard, but it is somewhat technical. The main point to remember is that operant conditioning does not require that each response be reinforced. The scheduling of reinforcers will influence the pattern of the learned responses, and will affect their resistance to extinction.

Another point should be made regarding the scheduling of reinforcers that is true regardless of whether one is using a continuous or an intermittent reinforcement schedule. Reinforcers should come immediately after the desired response. Delayed reinforcement is likely to be ineffective. I'm not saying that delaying reinforcement destroys the possibility of learning; I'm simply suggesting that in most cases the more immediate the reinforcer, the better the learning. In one study, for example, rats were reinforced for entering a black box instead of a white one. The task was learned readily when reinforcers were delivered immediately. If the delivery of reinforcers was delayed only a second or two, very little learning took place; with a 10-second delay, there was no learning at all (Grice, 1948). Several experiments have demonstrated the same phenomenon with human subjects (Hall, 1976). The point here is sensible. What if parents buy tickets to the circus to reinforce their son's behavior with the baby-sitter? But the circus is not until Saturday. When the family does go off to the circus Saturday afternoon, what is being reinforced may not be the child's "good behaviors" of last Tuesday night but inappropriate behaviors of Wednesday, Thursday, Friday, and Saturday morning.

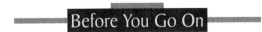

Before You Go On

**Define FR, FI, VR, and VI intermittent schedules
of reinforcement.**

PUNISHMENT

We've talked at length about reinforcers—positive and negative, primary and secondary—and how they can be scheduled. Let's now consider punishment. **Punishment** occurs when a stimulus delivered to an

punishment the administration of a punisher, which is a stimulus that decreases the rate, or probability, of a response that precedes it

organism *decreases* the rate, or probability, of occurrence of the response that preceded it. In common usage, punishment is usually in some way hurtful or painful, either physically (a spanking) or psychologically (ridicule). It is a painful, unpleasant stimulus presented to an organism after some response is made. If the rate, or probability, of the organism's response decreases, the response has been punished. It may have occurred to you that if punishers *are removed*, the result will be reinforcing; in fact, we would have an example of negative reinforcement.

Determining ahead of time what stimulus will be punishing is as difficult to do as determining what stimulus will serve as a reinforcer. Once again, one's intentions are irrelevant. We know for sure that something is a punisher only in terms of its effect on behavior. For example, we may *think* we are punishing Jon by sending him to his room because he has begun to throw a temper tantrum. It may be that "in his room" is exactly where Jon would like to be. We may have reinforced Jon's temper tantrum behaviors simply by attending to them. Once again, the only way to know for certain is to note the effect on behavior. If stimuli decrease the rate of the behaviors they follow, those stimuli may be called punishers. If Jon's tantrum-throwing behaviors become less frequent as a consequence of our actions, sending him to his room may indeed be a punishing thing to do.

We can think of punishers as being positive and negative in the same way that we explained positive and negative reinforcers. Positive punishment means giving or delivering (adding, +) a painful, unpleasant stimulus (a slap on the hand) following an inappropriate response, whereas negative punishment means removing (subtracting, −) a pleasant, valued stimulus ("No more TV for a week!") following an inappropriate response.

Is punishment an effective way of controlling behavior? Does punishment work? Yes, it does—sometimes. Punishment can be a rather impressive modifier of behavior. A rat has learned to press a lever to get a food reinforcer. Now you decide that you no longer want the rat to press the lever. You pass an electric current through the lever so that each time the rat touches the lever it receives a strong shock. What will happen? As a matter of fact, a number of things may happen, but—if your shock is strong enough—there's one thing of which we can be sure: the rat will stop pressing the lever. If punishment is all that effective, why do psychologists argue against its use, particularly the punishment of children for their misbehavior?

There are many potential problems, or side effects, of the use of punishment, even when it is used correctly. And often it is used incorrectly. Let's review some of what we know about the use of punishment (e.g., Axelrod & Apsche, 1983; Azrin & Holz, 1966; Walters & Grusec, 1977).

1. To be effective, punishment should be delivered immediately after the response. The logic here is the same as for the immediacy of reinforcement. Priscilla is caught in mid-afternoon throwing flour all over the kitchen. Father counts to ten (good), then says, "Just wait 'til your mother gets home" (not good). For the next three hours,

Priscilla's behavior is angelic. When mother does get home, what is punished, Priscilla's flour tossing or her appropriate behaviors that followed?

2. For punishment to be effective, it needs to be administered consistently. If one chooses to punish a certain behavior, it should be punished on every occasion—and often that is difficult to do.

3. Punishment may decrease (suppress) overall behavior levels. Although an effectively punished response may end, so may other responses. Not only will that rat who has been shocked for pressing the bar stop pressing the bar, but cower in the corner, doing very little of anything.

4. When responses are punished, alternatives should be introduced. Think about your rat for a minute. The poor thing knows what to do when it is hungry: press the lever. Now it gets shocked for doing that very thing. When the rat is given no alternative response to make in order to get food, it is in a conflict that has no solution. There is no way out. The result may be fear, anxiety, and even aggressiveness. One way to make this point is to say that punishment does not convey any information about what to do; it only communicates what *not* to do. Rubbing your puppy's nose in a "mess" it just made on the living room carpet doesn't give the dog much of a sense of what it is supposed to do when it feels a need to relieve itself.

5. Among other things, spanking or hitting provides a model for aggressive behavior. It conveys the message that when one is frustrated, to hit and to strike out is acceptable behavior—and particularly it conveys the message that it's okay for "big" people to hit smaller people. As we will soon see, such a message, provided by important models, can easily be taken as a model for the behavior of youngsters.

Punishment does not convey information about what to do; it communicates only what not to do.

Before You Go On

What is a punisher?

How can punishers be used effectively?

GENERALIZATION AND DISCRIMINATION

In classical conditioning, we saw that in the right circumstances a response conditioned to one particular stimulus could be elicited by other, similar stimuli. We have a similar phenomenon occurring in operant conditioning, and again we call it **generalization**—responses that have been conditioned in the presence of a specific stimulus may appear in the presence of other, similar stimuli.

generalization the phenomenon in operant conditioning in which a response that was reinforced in the presence of one stimulus appears in response to other, similar stimuli

For example, little Leslie may receive a reinforcer for saying "doggie" as a neighbor's poodle wanders across the front yard. "Yes, Leslie, good girl. That's a doggie." Having learned that calling the neighbor's poodle a "doggie" earns parental approval, the response is tried again, this time with a German shepherd from down the street. Leslie's operantly conditioned response of saying "doggie" in the presence of a poodle has generalized to the German shepherd. When it does, it will no doubt be reinforced again. The problem is, of course, that Leslie may overgeneralize "doggie" to virtually any small, furry, four-legged animal and start calling cats and raccoons "doggie" also. When a child turns to a total stranger and utters "Dada," generalization can (usually) be blamed for the embarrassing mislabeling.

The process of generalization can be countered with **discrimination** conditioning. Discrimination learning is basically a matter of *differential reinforcement*. What that means is that responses made to appropriate stimuli will be reinforced, while responses made to inappropriate stimuli will be ignored or extinguished (note: by withholding reinforcers, *not* by punishing the response).

To demonstrate how discrimination training works, let's consider a strange question. Are pigeons color blind? Disregarding for now why anyone would care, how might you go about testing the color vision of a pigeon? The standard tests we use for people certainly wouldn't work.

Pigeons *can* be trained to press levers in operant chambers, but they're much better at pecking at things, so we usually use a pecking response when we study the behavior of pigeons. A pigeon can be readily trained to peck at a single lighted disk in order to earn a food reward. A pigeon in an operant chamber pecks at a lighted disk, and a few grains of food are delivered. Soon the pigeon pecks the disk at a high rate.

Now let's present the pigeon with *two* lighted disks. One disk is red and one is green. Otherwise, they are identical: the same shape, brightness, size, and so on. The question is whether the pigeon can tell the difference between red and green. We decide that we will make the green disk the discriminative (positive) stimulus, and that responses to the red disk will be extinguished. This means that every peck at the green disk will be followed by grain, and pecks at the red disk will not be reinforced. The position of the colored disks is randomly altered, of course. We don't want simply to demonstrate that the pigeon can tell left from right.

The results of this sort of manipulation are depicted in Figure 5.9. At first, the red and green lighted disks are responded to at an approximately equal rate. But in short order, the pigeon is ignoring the red disk and pecking only at the green one, for which it receives its reinforcer.

In order to maintain such behavior, the pigeon must be able to discriminate between the two colored disks. We still do not know what red and green look like to a pigeon, but we may conclude that pigeons can tell the difference between the two. This is sensible because in many ways the eyes of pigeons are like those of humans. They contain cones in their retinas, and as you'll recall, cones are the

discrimination the process of differential reinforcement wherein one stimulus is reinforced while another stimulus is not

A pigeon in an operant chamber with a red disk and a green disk is able to distinguish one from the other.

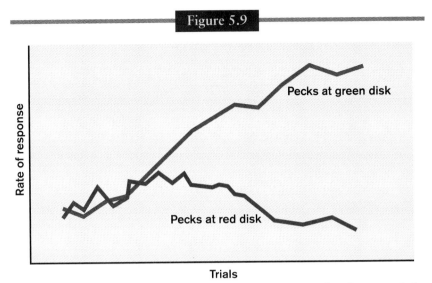

Figure 5.9

Discrimination training. Response rates for a pigeon presented with a green disk and a red disk. Pecks at the green disk are reinforced; those at the red disk are not.

receptors for color vision. Some varieties of owls are virtually without cone receptor cells in their retinas and thus are color blind. They cannot discriminate between red and green and appear very frustrated in a discrimination learning task based on color.

Please don't think that generalization and discrimination learning in operant conditioning are processes relevant only to young children, rats, and pigeons. A great deal of our own learning has involved learning to discriminate when behaviors are appropriate and are likely to be reinforced, and when they are inappropriate and likely to be ignored (at best) or punished. You have, I hope, learned that many of the behaviors that may be reinforced at a party are inappropriate responses to make in the classroom. You may have learned that it's okay to put your feet up on the coffee table at home, but not when you're at your boss's house or at Grandma's.

Before You Go On

In the context of operant conditioning, what are generalization and discrimination?

CAN ANY RESPONSE BE OPERANTLY CONDITIONED?

Animals can be trained to make many unusual responses. Rats *can* be trained through operant conditioning to press lighted disks in an operant chamber. Pigeons *can* be shaped to press levers. Yet, typically, we demonstrate conditioning with these organisms by having rats

In their studies of operant conditioning, Keller and Marion Breland found that even though they could get a racoon and other animals to perform certain tasks, they were unable to get them to do others, such as dropping coins into a bank. The Brelands concluded that there is a tendency for animals to return to their more instinctive, natural behaviors, even in the face of conditioning.

press bars and pigeons peck at disks. Somehow these responses seem more natural for the animals we're using. Even so, it was believed for a long time that if we could find the right reinforcer, we could train almost any animal to do almost anything.

Keller and Marion Breland, psychologists who had worked with B. F. Skinner, were convinced of the power of operant conditioning as a means of modifying behavior. They applied their expertise to the practical matter of animal training, and many of their trained animals became quite famous. Along with their many successes at training animals to do very involved things, the Brelands experienced noteworthy failures. Some of their animals just seemed totally contrary and unable to learn apparently simple routines. They described their frustrations in a 1961 article titled "The Misbehavior of Organisms," a takeoff on Skinner's book about operant conditioning, *The Behavior of Organisms* (1938).

As an example of the sort of difficulty the Brelands encountered, consider their efforts to teach a raccoon and a pig to deposit large coins in a bank. Both animals had demonstrated that they were capable of learning through operant conditioning. They were not in any way unintelligent animals. But the raccoon never did learn to drop coins into the bank. He'd grab the coins, rub them together, begin to enter them into the bank's slot, and then withdraw them at the last moment, rubbing them together again. The pig never got that close.

The pig would drop the coins from its mouth and then push them around the floor with its nose. Even when the coins were put into the pig's mouth, they were promptly dropped again and pushed around the ground.

What was happening here, the Brelands concluded, was that their animals were simply acting naturally. They were acting toward the coins the way they would instinctively act toward food—the raccoon manipulating the coin (food) with its hands, the pig rooting it around the ground. No training or reinforcement seemed sufficient to overcome this instinctive predisposition. Yes, reinforcement might get an animal to perform some task a few times, but even then it would eventually drift back to more natural, or instinctive, patterns of behavior. The Brelands labeled this phenomenon **instinctive drift**. It suggests that indeed there *are* limits on the types of responses an organism can learn, and many of these limits are established by the organism's genetic history.

instinctive drift the tendency of behaviors that have been conditioned to revert eventually to more natural, instinctive behaviors

Before You Go On

What is instinctive drift, and what does it tell us about the limits of operant conditioning?

TOPIC 5B SUMMARY

In this Topic we have explored the power of operant conditioning—a procedure in which an organism's rate of responding is altered by the consequences that follow that responding. Responses followed by reinforcers—be they positive or negative, primary or secondary, and regardless of how they are scheduled—will increase in their rate, or probability, of occurrence. Responses that are not reinforced, or that are punished, will decrease in their rate, or probability, of occurrence. Additionally, we have seen that to be effective, reinforcers or punishers should be administered as soon after a response of interest as possible. Now it is time to move on to consider a few varieties of basic learning procedures where the "relatively permanent change" in one's behaviors may not be readily observable—varieties of learning that produce relatively permanent changes in one's cognitions.

Topic 5C
COGNITIVE APPROACHES TO LEARNING

Cognitions, as you'll recall, are mental representations. They include ideas, beliefs, understanding, and knowledge. Cognitive approaches to learning emphasize changes that occur in an organism's system of cognitions—its mental representation of itself and its world. Cognitive learning, then, involves the acquisition of knowledge or understanding and need not be directly reflected in behavior. Remember my alerting you to this issue when we discussed the definition of learning. We said that learning is demonstrated by, or inferred from, changes in behavior. The implication is that there may be something less than a pefect correspondence between what one has learned and what one does. We anticipated this approach to learning with our coverage of the work of Rescorla and Kamin in Topic 5A, noting that a stimulus acted as an effective conditional stimulus only when it informed the organism about something happening in its world; as in, "When this tone sounds, food will follow it." Extracting useful information from one's experience in the world is largely a cognitive experience (see also Bolles, 1970, 1972, 1975). In this section, we'll briefly review the work of a few of the theorists who from the outset have stressed cognitive approaches to learning: Edward Tolman, David Olton, and Albert Bandura.

LATENT LEARNING AND COGNITIVE MAPS

Do rats have brains? Of course they do. Their brains aren't very large, and the cerebral cortex of a rat's brain is small indeed, but they do have brains. A more intriguing question about rats is whether they form and manipulate cognitions. Can they figure things out? Can they understand? Surely they can form simple associations. They can associate a light with a shock and a lever-press response with a reinforcer, and they can modify their behaviors on the basis of these associations. Can they do more?

Consider a now-classic experiment performed over 60 years ago by Tolman and Honzik (1930). Even at that time, it was well established that a rat could learn to run through a complicated maze of alleyways and dead ends to get to a goal box, where it would receive a food reward. Tolman and Honzik wanted to understand just *what* the rats were learning when they learned to negotiate such a maze. They used three groups of rats with the same maze.

One group of hungry rats was given a series of exposures (trials) to the maze. Each time they ran from the starting point to the goal box, they were given a food reward for their efforts. Over the course of 16 days, the rats in this group showed a steady and predictable improvement in their maze running. Their rate of errors dropped from approximately nine per trial to just two. Getting quickly and errorlessly from the start box to the goal box was just what had earned them their reinforcers.

A second group of rats was also given an opportunity to explore the maze for 16 days of test trials. However, they were not given a food reward for making it to the end of the maze. When they got to the goal box, they were simply removed from the maze. The average number of errors made by the rats in this group also dropped over the course of the experiment (from about nine errors per trial to about six). That the rats in this group *did* improve their maze-running skills suggests that simply being removed from the maze provided some measure of reinforcement. Even so, after 16 days, this group was having much more difficulty in their maze running than was the group being given a food reinforcer.

Now for the critical group of rats. A third group of rats was allowed to explore the maze on their own for ten days. They were *not* given a food reward upon reaching the goal box. But, beginning on day 11, a food reinforcer was introduced when they reached the end of the maze. The food was provided as a reinforcer on days 11 through 16. The introduction of the food reward had a very significant effect on the rats' behaviors. Throughout the first ten days in the maze—without the food—their performance showed only a slight improvement. Soon after the food was introduced, however, their maze running improved markedly. In fact, on days 13 through 16, they made fewer errors than did the rats who received the food all along. Figure 5.10 shows the performance of these three groups.

What do you make of this experiment? Why did that third group of rats do so much better after the food reward was introduced? Could they have learned something about the pattern of that maze *before* they received reinforcement for getting to the goal box? Could

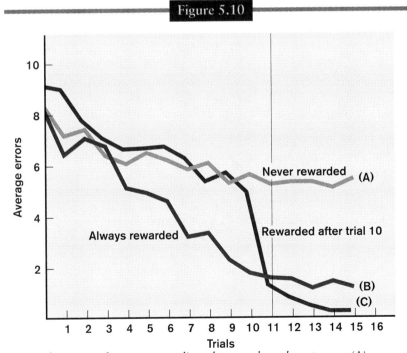

Figure 5.10

The performance of rats in a complicated maze where the rats were (A) never rewarded for reaching the maze's end, (B) rewarded every time they reached the maze's end, and (C) rewarded for reaching the end of the maze only on trials 11-16. (After Tolman & Honzik, 1930.)

they have figured out the maze early on, but failed to rush to the goal box until there was some good reason to do so?

Tolman thought they had. He argued that the food rewarded a change in the rats' performance, but that the actual learning had taken place earlier. This sort of learning is called **latent learning** because it is, in a sense, hidden and not shown in behavior until it is reinforced.

During those first ten days in the maze, the rats developed what Tolman called a **cognitive map** of the maze; that is, they formed a mental picture, or representation, of what the maze was like. The rats knew about the maze, but until food was provided at the goal box, there was no reason, or purpose, for getting there in any hurry. This logic led Tolman to refer to his approach as "purposive behaviorism" (Tolman, 1932). Introducing the notion of purpose, and drawing a distinction between performance and what was actually learned, tended to focus attention on what was happening to the learner during learning, which was one of Tolman's goals.

Here was Tolman, when behaviorism was dominating American psychology, arguing that rats form mental representations, or cognitive maps, of their environment. Interest in cognitive maps died out for awhile, but made a comeback thanks to a series of well-controlled experiments by David Olton (1976, 1978, 1979). Let's briefly review just one.

Olton used a maze such as the one pictured in Figure 5.11. A piece of food is placed at the end of each of the eight arms, or runways, that extend from the center of the maze. In order to "solve" this maze, a rat placed at the center has to learn to run to the end of each arm, eat the food there, and move on to other runways where food can still be found. Going back to a runway arm already visited constitutes an error (there is no food there).

Rats perform beautifully in this maze. Within 20 trials, they race from arm to arm without ever retracing their path down an "old" runway. What's more, on each trial the rats tend to run around the maze *in a different pattern*. Their behavior doesn't seem rigidly compulsive. They don't start with one arm and then move around the maze in any one direction. Their pattern of visits seems random. But still, they don't go down the same arm twice on any one trip around the maze.

The rats' performance is not disrupted even if odor cues are removed. (That is, the rats don't smell, or see, where the food is and isn't, and they don't smell where they have and have not been before.) On the other hand, if the maze is rotated after a trial has begun, the rats *do* make errors and go down runways they've traveled before, even though food is not present there. They may be "old" runways, but after the maze is rotated, they are in new positions. Olton and his colleagues argue that their rats have learned a mental representation of the maze (a cognitive map) and have learned where they have and have not been to get food.

If you stop and think for a minute about what Olton's rats did, you'll have to be impressed. But the cognitive maps learned by small

latent learning *hidden learning that is not demonstrated in performance until that performance is reinforced*

cognitive map *a mental representation of the learning situation or physical environment*

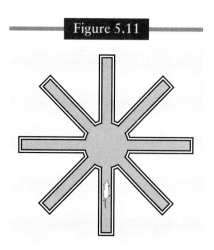

Figure 5.11

An eight-arm maze of the sort used by Olton to demonstrate the formation of cognitive maps in rats. (After Olton, 1978.)

birds that live in the Alps are even more impressive. These small birds spend most of the summer and early fall hiding away seeds in the ground (about four or five at a time). During the winter, they find their hidden seeds with remarkable accuracy. Have they formed cognitive maps of their seed placements? Apparently they have. Making their judgments on the basis of nearby landmarks, these small birds, called Clark's nutcrackers, can remember the location of at least 2,500 hiding places (Vander Wall, 1982)!

This may make some sense for rats and even for nutcrackers, but what about people? For one thing, there is the argument that if we can demonstrate that cognitive restructuring takes place when *rats* and *birds* learn, it seems clear that such processes also can occur in humans.

You should be able to find examples from your own experiences that closely approximate latent learning and cognitive maps. You may take the same route home from campus every day. If one day an accident blocks your path, won't you be able to use your knowledge of other routes (a cognitive map) to get where you are going? When you park your car in a new, large parking lot, what do you do as you walk away from your car? Don't you look around, trying to develop a mental image, a cognitive map or representation, of the parking lot and some of its major features? Imagine that you are to meet a friend in a new classroom building on campus. You arrive early, so you stroll around the building for a few minutes. Isn't it likely that this unreinforced, apparently aimless behavior will be useful if you have to locate a room in that building for class the next semester?

Another setting in which we may find Tolman's purposive behaviorism at work is athletics. Before the big game, the coaching staff may devise a perfect game plan—a set of ideas or cognitions dealing with what the team should do. The team members may learn the coaches' defensive strategy and may understand a number of offensive formations and plays. In theory, they know (latent learning) what they are supposed to do to win, but what will ultimately decide the contest is not their understanding but their performance. In sports, this is called execution. Knowing what to do and doing it are often different things

Before You Go On

What is learned when one forms a cognitive map?

What is latent learning?

SOCIAL LEARNING AND MODELING

Albert Bandura's approach to learning also is cognitive, but it adds a decidedly social flavor to the process and for that reason is often

Figure 5.12

In Albert Bandura's classic study, children who watched others (either in person, on film, or in a cartoon version) behave aggressively toward a "Bobo" doll displayed the same sort of behaviors themselves. Social learning theory claims that the children learned their aggressive behaviors through observation.

social learning theory *the theory that learning takes place through observation and imitation of models*

referred to as **social learning theory** (Bandura, 1974, 1977, 1982). The central idea of this theory is that learning often takes place through the observation and imitation of models. What makes social learning theory *social* is the notion that we often learn from others. What makes it *cognitive* is that what is learned through observation or modeling are changes in one's cognitions that may never be expressed as behavior nor be directly reinforced.

The classic demonstration of observational learning was reported in 1963 by Bandura, Ross, and Ross. For this demonstration, 96 preschoolers were randomly assigned to one of four experimental conditions. One group of children observed an adult model act aggressively toward an inflated plastic "Bobo" doll toy (Figure 5.12). The adult model vigorously attacked the doll. Children in the second group watched the same aggressive behaviors directed toward the "Bobo" doll, but in a movie. The third group watched a cartoon version of the same aggressive behaviors, this time performed by a cartoon cat. Children in the fourth group constituted the control group and did not watch anyone interact with "Bobo" dolls, either live or on film.

Then the test began. Each child (tested individually) was given new and interesting toys to play with, but only for a brief time. The child was then led to another room that contained fewer, older, and less interesting toys, including a small version of the inflated "Bobo" doll. Each child was left alone in the room while researchers watched the child's behavior. The children did not know they were being observed.

The children who had seen the aggressive behaviors of the model—whether live, on film, *or* in cartoon form—were more aggressive in their play than were the children who did not have the observational experience. Children from each of the first three experimental conditions attacked the "Bobo" doll (Figure 5.12). What's more, they attacked it the same way the model had.

According to social learning theory, children in the first three groups learned simply by observing. But as with latent learning, the learning was separated from performance. The children had no opportunity to imitate (to perform) what they had learned until they had a "Bobo" doll of their own. The learning that took place during observation was cognitive. As Bandura puts it, "Observational learning is primarily concerned with processes whereby observers organize response elements into new patterns of behavior at a symbolic level on the basis of information conveyed by modeling stimuli" (Bandura, 1976, p. 395).

Later studies have shown that reinforcement and punishment can play a significant part in observational learning. For example, a new twist was added to an experiment that basically replicated the one just described. The difference was that after attacking the "Bobo" doll, adult models were either rewarded or punished for their behavior. Children who saw the model being punished for attacking the doll engaged in very little aggressive behavior toward their own "Bobo" dolls. Those who saw the model receive reinforcement for attacking the doll acted aggressively, imitating the model's behaviors in considerable detail (Bandura, 1965).

The application of this sort of data is very straightforward. For example, most of Bandura's research suggests that children can and do learn all sorts of potential behaviors by watching TV. Our real concern, however, should be reserved for those occasions for which inappropriate behaviors are left unpunished. As long as children are exposed to the consequences of inappropriate behaviors, they will be less likely to imitate them. This logic suggests that it would be most unfortunate for one of a child's TV heroes to get away with murder, much less be rewarded for doing so. It is also the case that reinforced behaviors of valued models are more likely to be imitated than punished behaviors of less valued models (e.g., Bandura, 1965).

Learning about the consequences of one's behaviors by observing the results, or consequences, of someone else's behavior is called **vicarious reinforcement** or **vicarious punishment**. Our own experiences speak to the usefulness of these concepts. Aren't you much more likely to imitate (as best you can) the behaviors of a person who is rewarded for his or her efforts than you are to imitate the behaviors of someone who gets punished? Doesn't it make more sense to model your behaviors after a top-notch student than after someone failing the course? A child does not have to burn her fingers in a fire to learn to avoid the fireplace. Just watching someone else getting burned (or pretending to get burned) will usually suffice (Domjan, 1987).

In fact, learning through observation and imitation is a common form of human learning. Your television on any Saturday provides many examples, particularly if you watch a PBS station. All day long there are people (role models) trying to teach us how to paint landscapes, build solar energy devices, do aerobic exercises, improve our golf game, remodel the basement, replace a carburetor, or prepare a

There is little doubt that the behaviors and mannerisms of children are in large measure a reflection of their attempts to imitate adult models.

vicarious reinforcement (or punishment) increasing the rate (with reinforcement) or decreasing the rate (with punishment) of responses due to observing the consequences of someone else's behaviors

low-calorie meal. The basic message is, "Watch me; see how I do it. Then, try it yourself." Here, too, there are cultural variables that may come into play. For example, when a model performed a task correctly and received reinforcement for doing so, Japanese students learned more than did American students. One possible explanation is that Japanese observers are more attentive to high-status others and are more likely to learn more from their actions (Haruki et al., 1984).

Before You Go On

Summarize the basic concepts of social learning theory.

TOPIC 5C SUMMARY

In this Topic we have looked at a few types of learning in which what is learned are new cognitions—or changes in existing cognitions. Tolman's and Olton's research show us that rats can gain considerable knowledge of the structure of a complicated maze even though they do not act on that knowledge (perform) until their performance is reinforced—a process called latent learning. In the process of latent learning, rats (and certainly people) can and do form cognitive maps that provide them with an internalized, mental representation of their surroundings. Bandura's research shows us that learning can take place through the observation of others, particularly when those others are either reinforced or punished for their behaviors. These approaches remind us why we defined learning as being *demonstrated by* or *inferred from* relatively permanent changes in behavior that occur as the result of practice or experience.

But wait a minute! Here we are at the end of the chapter on learning, and we haven't yet said anything about memorizing all of those definitions one needs to know when talking about classical conditioning. We haven't yet said anything about how we go about learning concepts, theories, and "academic" sorts of things. Whatever happened to "human learning" as students generally think about human learning? Be assured I haven't forgotten about these concerns regarding human learning. Here are two points to keep in mind: (1) You should be convinced by now that to some degree classical conditioning, operant conditioning, and the cognitive approaches we have summarized so far *do* impact on everyday human learning. (2) Psychologists have moved much of their discussion of human learning to their treatment of human memory—and to the higher cognitive processes such as problem solving and concept formation. You will find most of the discussion of human learning you are looking for in the next two chapters.

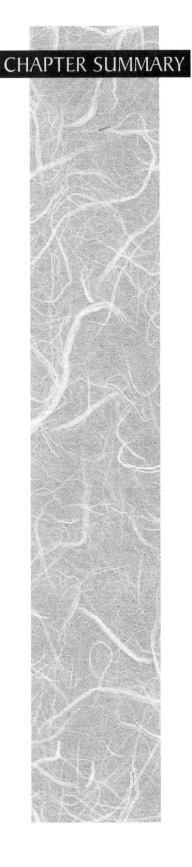

TOPIC 5A

How do we define learning?

Learning is demonstrated by a relatively permanent change in behavior that occurs as the result of practice or experience. We can use the same definition for "conditioning," in that it is a simple, basic form of learning. /*p. 206*

Summarize the essential procedures involved in classical conditioning.

In classical, or Pavlovian, conditioning, a neutral stimulus that originally does not elicit a response of interest is paired with an unconditioned stimulus (UCS), one that reliably and reflexively does produce a response—an unconditioned response (UCR). As a result, the once-neutral stimulus becomes a conditioned stimulus (CS) and elicits a conditioned response (CR) that is the same type of response as the original UCR. /*p. 209*

In classical conditioning, what are acquisition, extinction, and spontaneous recovery?

In classical conditioning, what are generalization and discrimination?

In classical conditioning, acquisition is an increase in the strength of the CR as the CS and the UCS continue to be presented together. Extinction is a decrease in the strength of the CR that occurs when the CS is repeatedly presented alone (without being paired with the UCS). Spontaneous recovery is demonstrated by the return of a CR after extinction and a rest interval. In generalization we find that a response (CR) conditioned to a specific stimulus (the CS) will also be elicited by other, similar stimuli. The more similar the new stimuli are to the original CS, the greater the resultant CR. In many ways, discrimination is the opposite of generalization. It is a matter of learning to make a CR in response to a specific CS (paired with the UCS), while learning not to make the CR in response to other stimuli, which are not paired with the UCS. /*p. 211*

What sorts of responses are most readily influenced by classical conditioning?

Classical conditioning has its most noticeable effect on emotion or mood. Most of the stimuli to which we respond emotionally have probably been classically conditioned to elicit those responses, called conditioned emotional responses. /*p. 214*

Briefly summarize the "Little Albert" experimental demonstration.

In the Watson and Rayner 1920 "Little Albert" demonstration, a sudden loud noise (the UCS) was paired with the presentation of the neutral stimulus, a white rat. As a result of several such pairings, Albert came to display a learned fear response (a CR) to the originally neutral rat (now the CS). The conditioned fear also generalized to other,

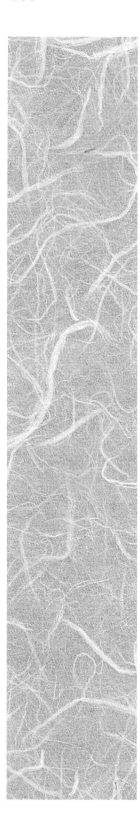

similar stimuli. This demonstration has been used to explain learned emotional reactions to events in our environments. /p. 216

What is a phobic disorder?

How is systematic desensitization used to treat phobic disorders?

A person with a phobic disorder suffers from an intense, irrational fear, which is assumed to have been learned, probably through classical conditioning. Systematic desensitization involves counterconditioning—training a person to relax and stay relaxed while thinking about a hierarchy of stimuli that are more and more likely to elicit anxiety or fear. If relaxation can be conditioned to thoughts of anxiety-producing stimuli, the sense of calm and relaxation will come to replace the competing response of anxiety. /p. 218

Under what circumstances are stimuli likely to serve effectively as CSs?

Pavlov, and others, believed that any stimulus could serve effectively as a conditioned stimulus if it were repeatedly paired with an unconditioned stimulus. We now believe that this is an oversimplification. Stimuli most effective as CSs are those that best or most reliably predict or signal the occurrence of the UCS. Stimuli are effective conditioned stimuli only if they provide useful information to the learner; for example, a shock *is* going to follow this tone. /p. 220

What do taste aversion studies tell us about the relationship between the CS and the UCS in classical conditioning?

Taste aversion studies, in which subjects develop strong dislikes and avoidance of particular foods or tastes, tell us that the time interval between the CS and the UCS may be very long, even hours. This result is in conflict with early conclusions that classical conditioning progressed most effectively with very short CS-UCS intervals (seconds or fractions of a second). These studies also provide evidence for the observation that some behaviors are more easily, or more naturally, conditioned than others. Associating nausea with the taste of food is more "natural," for example, than associating with other stimuli that may have been present when the nausea-inducing foods were eaten. /p. 221

TOPIC 5B

What is the essence of operant conditioning?

Operant conditioning is that type of learning in which the probability, or rate, of a response is changed as a result of the consequences that follow that response. Reinforced responses increase in rate, while nonreinforced responses decrease in rate. /p. 225

What is shaping and how does it work?

Describe acquisition, extinction, and spontaneous recovery as they occur in operant conditioning.

Shaping is a procedure used to establish a response that can then be reinforced; that is, shaping is used to get the organism to make a desired response in the first place. We shape a response by reinforcing successive approximations to the desired response. In operant conditioning, acquisition is produced by reinforcing a desired response so that its rate increases. Extinction decreases the rate of a response (to return to its original, baseline rate) by withholding reinforcement. After a rest interval, a previously extinguished response will return at a rate above baseline; that is, in the same situation, it will spontaneously recover. /p. 228

Give an operational definition of reinforcement.

Distinguish between a positive and a negative reinforcer.

In general, reinforcement is a process that increases the rate, or probability, of the response it follows. A positive reinforcer increases the rate of the response that precedes its presentation. Negative reinforcers increase the rate of the response that precedes their removal or termination. /p. 230

Compare and contrast primary and secondary reinforcers, and give an example of each.

Primary reinforcers are stimuli in some way biologically important or related to the organism's survival, such as food for a hungry organism or a warm shelter for a cold one. Secondary reinforcers increase response rates because of the organism's previous learning history. That is, secondary reinforcers, such as praise, money, letter grades, and the like, are acquired reinforcers. /p. 232

Define FR, FI, VR, and VI intermittent schedules of reinforcement.

Intermittent schedules of reinforcement provide a reinforcer for less than every response. The FR (fixed-ratio) schedule calls for delivering one reinforcer after a set number of responses (e.g., one reinforcer after every five responses). The FI (fixed-interval) schedule calls for a reinforcer at the first response following a specified, or fixed, interval. A VR (variable-ratio) schedule randomly changes the ratio of reinforcers to responses, but maintains some given ratio as an average. A VI (variable-interval) schedule calls for the delivery of a reinforcer for the first response after a time interval whose length is randomly varied. In general, responses reinforced with fixed schedules are more resistant to extinction than are responses that have been reinforced each time they occur (which is a CRF, or continuous reinforcement schedule). Responses acquired under variable schedules of reinforce-

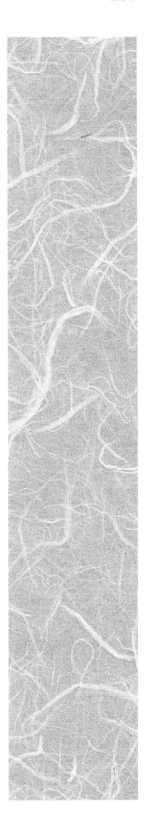

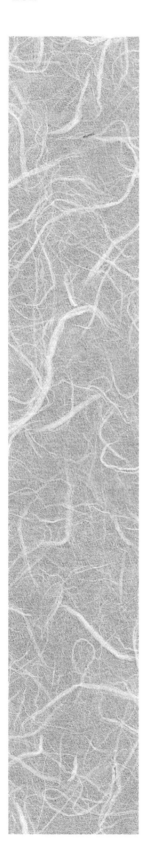

ment are even more resistant to extinction than are those acquired by fixed schedules. /*p. 235*

What is a punisher?

How can punishers be used effectively?

A punisher is a stimulus that decreases the rate of the response it follows. Punishers can be effective in suppressing a response when they are strong enough and are delivered immediately after the response to be punished. Fear, anxiety, aggression, and an overall suppression of behavior may accompany punishment, which, in itself, provides no information about what an organism should do in a given situation. Punishing one response should thus be paired with the reinforcement of another, more appropriate response. /*p. 237*

In the context of operant conditioning, what are generalization and discrimination?

In operant conditioning, generalization occurs when a response reinforced in the presence of one stimulus also occurs in the presence of other, similar stimuli. Discrimination, on the other hand, is a matter of differential reinforcement; reinforcing responses to some stimuli while extinguishing responses to other (inappropriate) stimuli. /*p. 239*

What is instinctive drift, and what does it tell us about the limits of operant conditioning?

Instinctive drift is the term used by the Brelands to note that some behaviors are more difficult to operantly condition than others. That is, in spite of conditioning efforts, an organism will "drift" toward "doing what comes naturally." /*p. 241*

TOPIC 5C

What is learned when one forms a cognitive map?

What is latent learning?

According to Tolman, when one acquires a cognitive map, one develops a cognitive representation (or picture) of one's surroundings—an appreciation of general location and where key objects are located. The formation of a cognitive map can be viewed as a type of latent learning. This is because latent learning is the acquisition of information (an internal, mental, cognitive process) that may not be demonstrated in performance until later, if at all. /*p. 245*

Summarize the basic concepts of social learning theory.

Bandura's social learning theory emphasizes the role of the observation of others (models) and imitation in the acquisition of cognitions and behaviors. We often learn by imitating models through vicarious reinforcement and vicarious punishment. /*p. 248*

chapter six

MEMORY

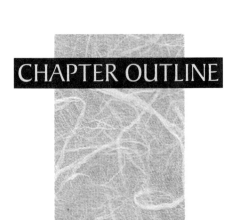

CHAPTER OUTLINE

TOPIC 6A HOW CAN WE DESCRIBE HUMAN MEMORY?
Memory as Information Processing
Sensory Memory
Short-term Memory (STM)
    The Duration of STM
    The Capacity of STM
    How Information Is Represented in STM
Long-term Memory (LTM)
    How Large Is Long-term Memory?
    What Is the Duration of Long-term Memories?
    How Accurate Are Long-term Memories?
    How Do We Get Information into Long-term Memory?
    Are There Different Types of Long-term Memories?
Where Can We Find Memories in the Brain?
TOPIC 6A SUMMARY

TOPIC 6B IMPROVING MEMORY: FACTORS AFFECTING RETRIEVAL
Measuring Retrieval
    Direct, Explicit Measures of Memory
    Indirect, Implicit Measures of Memory
Encoding and Retrieval
    The Effects of Context
    Strategies That Guide Encoding and Aid Retrieval
    The Amount and Distribution of Encoding Practice
Interference and Retrieval
    Retroactive Interference
    Proactive Interference
TOPIC 6B SUMMARY

CHAPTER SUMMARY

Human memory is involved in nearly everything we do. Perhaps we can gain some appreciation of the importance of memory in our daily lives by briefly considering two real cases in which one aspect of memory was stolen away by illness and disease (from Baddeley, 1990; Corkin, 1984; Milner, 1959, 1965; Milner et al., 1968).

A patient known to us only as "H. M." suffered from epilepsy. For nearly eleven years he experienced an average of one large convulsive attack and several partial seizures every day. Finally, it was decided that drastic treatment was called for. Parts of the temporal lobe would be severed, and the hippocampus would be removed from both sides of H. M.'s brain. The surgery was successful. Epileptic seizures became rare, and most intellectual functioning was left intact.

But there were disastrous effects on H. M.'s memory. He could not form new long-term memories. H. M. could remember all that had happened *before* the surgery, but he could not form new memories of events that happened after the surgery. If asked what year it was, he would say, "1953"—the year in which his surgery was performed. If you were to meet H. M. and then leave for a few minutes, he would have no idea who you were when you returned.

Or consider the fate of Clive Wearing, a bright musician who contracted encephalitis, which ultimately damaged his brain. He, too, was left after treatment with the inability to form new, lasting memories. "If his wife left the room for a few minutes, when she returned he would greet her with great joy, declaring that he had not seen her for months and asking how long he had been unconscious. Experienced once, such an event could be intriguing and touching, but when it happens repeatedly day in, day out, it rapidly loses its charm" (Baddeley, 1990, p. 5). Unlike H. M.'s experience, Mr. Wearing's memory for events that preceded his illness was poor. His recollections were spotty, and seldom included detail, *except* that throughout all of his memory failures, his memory for making beautiful music remained. Clive Wearing "has only the haziest access to his own past, and no apparent capacity to learn anything new. In his own words, life is 'Hell on earth—It's like being dead—all the bloody time'" (Baddeley, 1990).

I *t is nearly impossible to imagine what life would be like without memory. For one thing, this sentence in your textbook would make no sense. Without your memory, you'd have no idea what a textbook is or why you had it open in front of you. The black patterns of print you now recognize as words would appear to be no more than random marks. We care about memory in an academic, study-learn-test sense, but the importance of memory goes well beyond classroom exams. All of those things that define us as individuals—our feelings, beliefs, experiences, moods, behaviors, and attitudes—are stored away in our memories.*

Topic 6A will focus on what is involved in getting information into *memory and storing it there. First, we'll formulate a working definition of memory. Then, we'll explore the possibility that there are several types of memory, what these types of memory might be, and how they function. Topic 6B will deal with the practical matter of retrieval, or getting that information out of our memories when we want it.*

Topic 6A

HOW CAN WE DESCRIBE HUMAN MEMORY?

MEMORY AS INFORMATION PROCESSING

One common way to think about memory is to consider it as a final step in a series of psychological activities that process information. An *information-processing* view of memory takes the position that complex cognitive processes, such as those involved in remembering and forgetting, can be understood as a series of simpler, associated processes. In this view, we come into this world knowing very little about it. By the time we are adults, we have stored away a considerable amount of information. Much of that information may be trivial and irrelevant, but much of it is essential for survival. How do our minds come to be filled with so much information? As noted in Chapter 3, the processing of information begins when our sensory receptors are stimulated. Through perception, information from our senses is selected and organized. With memory, we form a record of the information we have processed.

Thus, we may think of **memory** as a capacity—the capacity to encode, store, and retrieve information. Using one's memory is a cognitive activity that involves three interrelated processes. The first is **encoding**, a process of putting information *into* memory. It is a matter of forming cognitive representations of information. Once those representations are in memory, we must keep them there—a process called **storage**. And, of course, to use stored information, we need to

memory *the cognitive capacity to encode, store, and retrieve information*

encoding *the active process of representing, or putting information into memory*

storage *the process of holding encoded information in memory*

get it out again. This process is **retrieval** (after Murdock, 1974). Memory, then, involves the cognitive processes of encoding, storing, and retrieving information.

Modern theories view memory as being complex and multidimensional. That is, not all of the information that gets into memory necessarily gets encoded or stored in the same way or even in the same place. As it happens, there is considerable disagreement over just how we should conceptualize human memory. Theories are plentiful, and often at odds with each other (Baddeley, 1992; Loftus, 1991; Roediger, 1990; Schacter, 1992; Squire et al., 1993; Watkins, 1990). Some psychologists argue that there actually are various memory storehouses and that each has its own unique characteristics and its own mechanisms for processing information. Psychologists who talk about separate, distinct memories, or stores of information, support what are called **multistore models of memory** (e.g., Atkinson & Shiffrin, 1968; Tulving, 1985; Waugh & Norman, 1965).

Other theorists claim that there is only one type of human memory, or storehouse of information, but that within that memory are various levels or depths to which information can be processed (e.g., Cermak & Craik, 1979; Craik, 1970; Craik & Lockhart, 1972). Their argument is that information can get more (deep) or less (shallow) processing within the same memory—that depth of processing is a function of work and effort and is related to the likelihood of retrieval. This position gives rise to what is called a **levels-of-processing model of memory**. Although it has wide support, it is but one theory that views memory as a single, unitary process.

So, which model shall we use? We can construct "our own" conceptualization of memory by combining the major aspects of both of these dominant positions. Our model will include three stores, or levels, of memory: sensory memory, short-term memory (STM), and long-term memory (LTM). Sometimes I'll refer to sensory, short-term, and long-term memories as if they were *stores* or *structures* (or something you put information in). Sometimes I will refer to memory in terms of *levels of processing*, as if the levels referred to activities (what you do with information in order to remember it). This mixing of viewpoints is intentional, because at the moment no one can claim with any certainty which model of memory provides the "best" way to think about human memory.

In any event, we will have questions about each memory structure or level. What is its capacity: how much information can it deal with? What is its duration: how long will information be held there without further processing? How does information get into this memory: how does it get processed to this depth? In what form is it stored?

retrieval *the process of locating, removing, and using information stored in memory*

multistore models of memory *descriptions of memory that propose a number of distinct types (or stores) of memory, each with its own manner of processing information*

levels-of-processing model of memory *the view that there is only one memory, but that information can be processed within that memory at distinct levels, or depths*

Before You Go On

How do we define memory?

Compare multistore and levels-of-processing models of memory.

SENSORY MEMORY

sensory memory *a type of memory that stores large amounts of information for very brief periods (a few seconds or less)*

Sensory memory involves the storage of large amounts of information for very short periods (a few seconds or less). The concept of such a brief memory is a strange one (we usually don't think about remembering something for only a few seconds), but it has a place in information-processing models. All of the information that gets stored in our memories must first have entered through our senses. Simply put, to be able to recall what a lecturer says, you must first be in class to hear the lecture. To remember a drawing from this book, the image of the drawing must first stimulate your visual system. You can't remember the aroma of fried onions if you've never smelled them in the first place.

The basic idea of a sensory memory is that information does not pass directly through our sensory systems; instead, it is held in sensory memory for a brief time. Even after a stimulus has left our environment and is no longer physically present, it has left its imprint, having formed a sensory memory.

The *capacity* of sensory memory seems, at least in theory, to be very large indeed. At one time it was believed that we are able to keep as much in our sensory memory as our sense receptors can respond to at any one time. Everything above our sensory thresholds—everything to which our senses react—gets stored in our sensory memory. Such claims may give sensory memory more credit than it is due. Sensory memory can hold much more information than we can attend to, but there are limits on its capacity.

The practical problem with sensory memory lies in its *duration*. We may be able to get a lot of information into our sensory memory, but we aren't able to keep it there (storage) very long. What *is* the duration of sensory memory? It's difficult to say exactly, but memories remain in sensory storage only very briefly—about 0.5 seconds for visually presented materials (Sperling, 1960, 1963), and perhaps as long as 3 to 10 seconds for orally presented information (Cowan, 1984; Darwin et al., 1972; Massaro, 1975). It certainly won't be of much help for your next psychology exam if you process information only to this memory and no further.

Sensory memory is typically viewed as being a rather mechanical or physical type of storage. The information stored there cannot be acted on. You can't *do* much of anything with it. Information is *not encoded* in sensory memory; you have to take the information in your sensory memory pretty much as your receptors deliver it to you. It is as if stimuli from the environment make an impression on our sensory systems and then rapidly fade or are replaced by new stimuli.

Here are two demonstrations of sensory memory. In a reasonably dark area, stand about 20 feet from a friend who is pointing a flashlight at you. Have your friend swing the flashlight around in a small circle, making about one revolution per second. What do you see? Your experience is that of a circle of light. At any one instant, you're seeing where the light *is*, and you are experiencing—from your sensory memory—where the light *has just been*. If your friend moves the light slowly, you may see a "tail" of light following it, but you won't see a circle anymore because the image of the light's position will have decayed from sensory memory.

Have you ever had this experience? Someone asks you a simple question, to which your reply is something like "Huh? What did you say?" Then, before the person even gets a chance to repeat her question, you answer it (which may in turn provoke a response such as, "Why didn't you answer me in the first place?"). Perhaps you did not clearly hear all of the question you were asked, but while it was still reverberating, or echoing, in your sensory memory, you listened to it again and formed your answer.

As I said, this notion of a sensory memory as the very brief storage of large amounts of minimally processed information is a strange one. There is evidence that sensory memory is a real phenomenon, at least for vision and audition. Perhaps that extra fraction of a second or two of storage in sensory memory gives us the time we need to attend to information so that we can then move it further along in our memory.

Before You Go On

What is sensory memory?

What is its capacity and duration?

SHORT-TERM MEMORY (STM)

We have seen that a good deal of information can get into sensory memory with relative ease. Once information gets to sensory memory, where does it go next? Most of it rapidly fades or is quickly replaced with new stimuli. But with a little effort, we can process material from our sensory memories more fully by moving it to short-term memory. **Short-term memory (STM)** is a level, or store, in human memory with a limited capacity and, without the benefit of rehearsal, a brief duration.

What we are here calling short-term memory is often referred to as *working memory* (Baddeley, 1982, 1990, 1992). It is viewed as something like a workbench or desk top on which we pull together, use, and manipulate the information to which we pay attention. To encode information into STM requires that we pay attention to it. This information can get into STM directly from our sensory memory or can be retrieved from our long-term memory for use at the mo-

short-term memory (STM) a type of memory with limited capacity and limited duration; also called working memory

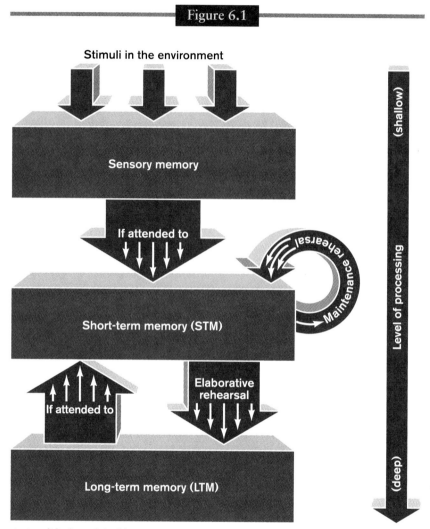

Figure 6.1

A simplified model of human memory.

ment. The capacity of short-term memory is limited by our span of attention. There are severe limits on the amount of information to which we can attend in a short period.

Figure 6.1 presents a schematic diagram of the model of memory we are constructing. At the top are stimuli from the environment impacting our senses, and moving directly into sensory memory. We see that information from sensory memory *or* from long-term memory can be moved into STM. It will be helpful to refer to this diagram as we continue to expand various aspects of our model.

The Duration of STM

Interest in short-term memory processing can be traced to two experiments reported independently in the late 1950s (Brown, 1958;

Peterson & Peterson, 1959). We'll review the Petersons' experiment.

On a typical trial, a subject is shown three letters, such as KRW, for 3 seconds. Presenting the letters for 3 seconds ensures that they are attended to and, hence, encoded into STM. The subject is then asked to recall the three letters after retention intervals ranging from 0 to 18 seconds. This doesn't sound like a very difficult task, and it isn't. Anyone can remember three letters for as long as 18 seconds. However, in this experiment, subjects are prohibited from rehearsing the letters during the retention interval. They are given a "distractor" task to perform right after they see the letters. They are asked to count backward, by threes, from a three-digit number.

For example, if you were a subject, you would be shown a letter sequence—say, KRW—and then asked to immediately start counting backward from, say, 397, by threes, or "397, 394, 391, 388," and so forth. You would be instructed to do your counting out loud and as rapidly as possible. The idea is that the counting task prohibits you from rehearsing the three letters you were just shown.

Under these conditions, your correct recall of the letters depends on the length of the retention interval. If you are asked to recall the letters after just a few seconds of counting, you won't do too badly. If you have to count as long as 15 to 20 seconds, your recall of the letters drops to almost zero (see Figure 6.2). Distracted by the counting task, you cannot rehearse the letters, and they are soon unavailable to you.

This laboratory example is not as abstract as it may first appear. Consider this scenario. Having studied psychology for three hours, you decide to reward yourself and have a pizza. You decide to splurge and have the pizza delivered. Never having called Pizza City before, you turn to the yellow pages to find the number: 555-5897. You repeat the number to yourself: 555-5897. You close the phone book, then dial the number without error. Buzzz-buzzz-buzzz-buzzz. Darn, the line's busy! Well, you'll call back in a minute.

Just as you hang up the phone, the doorbell rings. It's the paper boy. You owe him $11.60 for the past two weeks' deliveries. Discovering that you don't have enough cash on hand to pay for the paper *and* a pizza, you write a personal check. "Let's see, what is today's date? 10-15-95. How much did you say I owed you? Oh yes, $11.60, plus a dollar tip, comes to $12.60. This is check number 1079; I'd better write that down. There you go. Thanks a lot."

The paper boy leaves, and you return to your studying. Then you recall that you were going to order a pizza. Only five or six minutes have passed since you got a busy signal from Pizza City. As you go to dial the phone, however, you cannot for the life of you remember the phone number. Back to the yellow pages. A number once attended to became active in your STM. When you were kept from rehearsing it, and when other numbers entered STM as interfering information, that original telephone number was soon inaccessible.

One way in which we can increase the duration of short-term memory is to rehearse the information stored there. The type of

If we are not interrupted or distracted, we easily can hold a telephone number in STM long enough to dial it.

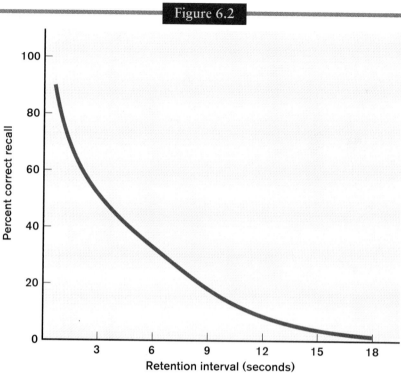

Figure 6.2

The recall of a stimulus of three letters as a function of retention interval when maintenance rehearsal is minimized. (After Peterson & Peterson, 1959.)

maintenance rehearsal a process of rote repetition (reattending) to keep information in short-term memory

rehearsal we use simply to keep material active in our short-term memory is called **maintenance rehearsal**, or rote rehearsal, and amounts to little more than simple repetition of the information already in our STM. To get material into STM (encoding), we have to attend to it. By repeating that material (as we might if we wanted to remember a telephone number until we could dial it), we are essentially reattending to it with each repetition.

The duration of STM is long enough to allow us to use it in several common activities. Again, the telephone number example is relevant. Usually all we want to do with a telephone number is remember it long enough to dial it. Few people feel the need to make a permanent record of every telephone number they dial.

Using STM in mathematical computations is a good example, particularly when we do computations "in our head." Multiply 28 by 6 without paper and pencil: "Let's see. Six times 8 is 48. Now I have to keep the 8 and carry the 4." Stop right there. Where do you "keep the 8" and where do you store the 4 until they are needed? Right, in your STM. For that matter, where did the notion that $6 \times 8 = 48$ come from in the first place? Where did the idea of what "multiply" means come from? How did *this* information get into STM? Right, again.

Many mathematical operations require the use of STM to hold information until we need it in our calculations.

This is an example of information entering STM, not "from the outside," through our senses and sensory memory, but from long-term storage (see Figure 6.1).

Yet another example of STM in action is in the processing of language. As you read one of my longer sentences, such as this one, it is useful to have a short-term storage place to keep the beginning of the sentence you are reading in mind until you finally get to the end of the sentence, so that you can figure out the basic idea of the sentence before deciding whether anything in the sentence is worth remembering.

Having discussed the duration of short-term memory, let's now deal with its capacity. Just how much information can we hold in STM for that 15 to 20 seconds?

Before You Go On

How long is information stored in STM?

What is required to get information into STM and then keep it there?

The Capacity of STM

In 1956, George Miller wrote a charming paper about "the magical number seven, plus or minus two." In it, he argued that the capacity of our short-term memories is very small—limited to just 5 to 9 (or 7 ± 2) bits, or "chunks," of information.

In the context of short-term memory, the concept of chunk is a rather technical, and at the same time imprecise, term (Anderson,

chunk a somewhat imprecise concept referring to a meaningful unit of information as represented in short-term memory

1980). A **chunk** may be defined as the representation in memory of a meaningful unit of information. Thus, the claim is that we can store 7 ± 2 meaningful pieces of information in STM.

We can easily attend to, encode, and store five or six letters in STM. Holding the letters YRDWIAADEFDNSYE in short-term memory would be a challenge. Fifteen randomly presented letters exceed the capacity of STM for most of us. What if I asked you to remember the words *Friday* and *Wednesday*? Keeping just these two simple *words* in STM is easy—even though they contain (the same) 15 letters. Here, you are storing just two chunks of meaningful information, not 15. In fact, you could easily store *50* letters in short-term memory if you recoded them into the one meaningful chunk: "days of the week."

As we all know, we can readily store a telephone number in our short-term memory. Adding an area code makes the task somewhat more difficult because the ten digits now come fairly close to the upper limit of our STM capacity. Notice, though, how we tend to cluster the digits of a telephone number into a pattern. The digit series 2194935661 is more difficult to deal with as a simple string than when it is seen and encoded as a telephone number: (219) 493-5661 (Bower & Springston, 1970). Grouping the digits this way lets us see them in a new, more meaningful, way.

So, by chunking bits and pieces of information, we can extend the apparent capacity of short-term memory. Here's one last example. Can you hold this number in your STM: 49162536496481? The 14 digits here are beyond the capacity of most people's short-term memory. But if you recognize this as a series of numbers, each being the *square* of the digits 2 through 9 (4/9/16/25/36/49/64/81), the task is an easy one because you have chunked (and recoded) the material in a meaningful way. Using a similar system of chunking digits into meaningful clusters, one student demonstrated an ability to recall more than 80 randomly presented digits (Ericsson & Chase, 1982).

Short-term memory works something like a leaky bucket. From the vast store-house of information available in our sensory memory, we scoop up some (not much, at that) by paying attention to it, and hold it for a while until we either use it, maintain it with rehearsal, move it along to long-term storage, or lose it. Before we go on to our discussion of long-term memory, we need to consider how information is encoded and stored in STM.

Before You Go On

How much information can be held in STM?

How can chunking affect the capacity of STM?

How Information Is Represented in STM

The material stored in our sensory memory is kept there in virtually the same form in which it was presented. Visually presented stimuli are held as visual images, auditory stimuli form auditory memories, and so on. Getting information into STM is not such an automatic process. We have to attend to the material to encode it into STM. How is that material stored, or represented, there?

R. Conrad (1963, 1964) was one of the first to argue that information is stored in STM with an acoustic code. This means that material is processed in terms of how it *sounds*. Conrad's conclusion was based on his interpretation of the errors people make in short-term memory experiments.

For example, in one experiment, Conrad presented a series of letters to his subjects. The letters were presented *visually*, one at a time, and subjects were asked to recall the letters they had just seen. Many errors were made over the course of the experiment. What was surprising was that when subjects responded with an incorrect letter, it was often a letter that *sounded* like the correct one. For example, if subjects were to recall the letter E and failed to do so, they commonly would recall V, G, or T, a letter that sounded like the E they were supposed to recall. They rarely responded with F, which certainly *looks* more like the E they had just seen than does V, G, or T. (This was true whether subjects gave their recall orally or in writing.)

Using STM is largely a matter of talking to ourselves. No matter how it is presented, we tend to encode information acoustically, the way it sounds. At least that's what the early evidence suggested. Subsequent research hasn't changed the view that acoustic coding is the most important means of representing information in STM. However, some material may be encoded in STM in other ways—visually or spatially (Cooper & Shepard, 1973; Martindale, 1981; Shulman, 1971, 1972; Squire et al., 1993; Wickens, 1973). Perhaps the most we can say is that there is a tendency to rely heavily on the acoustic coding of information in STM, but that other codes may also be used.

Before You Go On

How is information encoded (represented) in STM?

LONG-TERM MEMORY (LTM)

Long-term memory (LTM) is memory as you and I usually think of it: memory for large amounts of information held for long periods. As we did for sensory and short-term memory, we'll begin by considering two basic issues: capacity and duration.

long-term memory (LTM) a type of memory with virtually unlimited capacity and very long, if not limitless, duration

How Large Is Long-term Memory?

Our own experiences tell us that the capacity of our long-term memories is huge—virtually limitless. At times we may even impress ourselves with the amount of material we have stashed away in LTM (for

The capacity of our long-term memories is so large that sometimes we surprise ourselves with how much information we have stored there.

instance, when we play Trivial Pursuit or TV game shows). Just how much can be stored in human memory may never be measured, but we can rest assured there is no way we will ever learn so much that there won't be room for more.

As an example of long-term memory's huge capacity, consider an experiment by Standing, Conezio, and Haber (1970). Over five days, they presented 2,500 different pictures to subjects and asked them to remember them all. Even a day or so later, subjects correctly identified, from a new collection of pictures, 90 percent of the ones they had seen before. Standing (1973) increased the number of pictures that subjects viewed to 10,000. (As you can imagine, it took a long time simply to view 10,000 pictures.) Again, subjects later recognized more than 90 percent of them.

There seems to be no practical limit to the amount of information we can process, or encode, into long-term memory. (Getting that information out again when we want it is another matter, which we'll get to in Topic 6B.)

What Is the Duration of Long-term Memories?

How long will information stay in LTM once it is there? Assuming you remain free from disease or injury, you are likely never to forget some information, such as your own name, your parents' names, or the words to "Happy Birthday to You."

At the moment, it is impossible even to imagine an experiment that could tell us with any certainty how long information or experiences remain stored in LTM. One thing we know for a fact is that we often cannot remember things we know we once knew. We do tend to forget things. The issue is *why*. Do we forget because the information is no longer *available* to us in our long-term memories, just not there any more? Or do we forget because we are unable to get the information out of LTM, which implies that the information is still available but now somehow not *accessible*? "How can we ever be sure that a memory failure is due to the relevant information being unavailable and hence inaccessible under all conceivable conditions rather than just merely being inaccessible under the prevailing conditions?" (Watkins, 1990, p. 330).

Most psychologists believe that once information is in LTM, it stays there until we die. In fact, 84 percent of the psychologists who were asked agreed with the assertion that "everything we learn is permanently stored in the mind, although sometimes particular details are not accessible" (Loftus & Loftus, 1980, p. 410). In this view, forgetting is a failure of *retrieval* of stored information.

Have you ever handed in an exam paper, walked out of the classroom, and suddenly realized the answer to a question you could not think of minutes before? This sort of experience reinforces the notion that memories may be available but not always accessible. How pleasant it is to think that everything we ever knew, everything that ever happened to us, is still there someplace, ultimately retrievable if we only knew how to get it out. (On the other hand, we have all had unpleasant experiences we might never want to remember.)

As intriguing as it may be to think of the storage of information in long-term memory as permanent, there is reason to believe that this view is not totally accurate. A review article by Elizabeth and Geoffry Loftus (1980) focused on the issue of the duration of long-term memories. The Loftuses concluded that "the evidence in no way confirms the view that all memories are permanent and thus potentially recoverable" (p. 409). They claim that the bulk of such evidence is neither scientific nor reliable, and further claim that when we think we are recalling specific events of the long-distant past, we may be reconstructing a reasonable facsimile of that information from bits and pieces of our past. That is, when we do remember something that happened to us a long time ago, we don't recall the events as they actually happened. Instead, we recall a specific detail or two and then *actively reconstruct* a reasonable story. Even if we do reconstruct recollections of past experiences, that would not necessarily mean that our original memory was no longer available. It might only suggest that we can maintain several versions of the same event in long-term memory (e.g., McCloskey & Zaragoza, 1985). This discussion gives rise to our next question.

How Accurate Are Long-term Memories?

When we try to remember a fact we learned in school many years ago, it is often easy to determine the accuracy of our recall. As on many classroom tests, we are either right or wrong. Note that if we learned something many years ago that was wrong and recalled that incorrect information now, it might still be wrong, even though our memory would be accurate.

Determining the accuracy of our memories for our past experiences is difficult at best, and sometimes simply impossible. Do we *really* remember all those details of that vacation we took with our family when we were 6 years old, or are we recalling bits and pieces of what actually happened, bits and pieces of what we have been told happened, and adding in other details so as to reconstruct a likely story? In most cases, the accuracy of our recollection of experiences from the distant past is of little or no consequence. In some situations, the accuracy of the report of one's long-term memory for events can be of critical importance.

Repressed Memories. One example of the importance of the accuracy of information retrieved from long-term storage involves what are called "repressed memories." We discussed the Freudian concept of repression in Chapter 4 (page 169). Repression is said to have occurred when extremely unpleasant or traumatic events of one's life are pushed deep into the unconscious corners of one's memory, from which retrieval is very difficult at best. That repression—or in more modern, non-Freudian terminology, "motivated forgetting"—can help us forget unpleasant events of the past is a notion that has gained wide acceptance in psychology (Baddeley, 1990; Erdelyi, 1985; Erdelyi & Goldberg, 1979; Loftus, 1993a.)

In recent years, a disturbing number of cases have become public in which an adult (often in psychotherapy for any one of a number of disorders, mild to severe) comes to remember being abused when a child. Most cases of the recall of repressed memories of child abuse involve women, and the "recall" of the abusive events is often impressively detailed. The trauma of child abuse (sexual or not) seems a likely event to be repressed—put out of one's conscious awareness. Without questioning the enormity of the problem of child abuse or challenging reports of its prevalence, Loftus (1993a, 1993b) has recently challenged the authenticity of the "repressed memories" of some adults who "remember" as adults events that *may* never have happened in the first place. It may be, Loftus argues, that some people (genuinely) come to believe that they were abused as children in order to help make sense of the difficulties they are encountering as adults. In some cases, the notion that a person has been abused may come from a therapist who says something like, "You know, I've seen many cases like yours and often find that the person was abused or molested as a child. Do you suppose anything like that ever happened to you?" Simply questioning whether memories of child abuse are real, as Loftus has done, has elicited and will continue to elicit considerable debate—and research—for some time to come.

Eyewitness Testimony. Another area in which the accuracy of long-term memory is of critical importance is eyewitness testimony. We have touched on this topic earlier (in Chapter 4). Perhaps you recall my example of the crazed student who was perceived as bringing a gun to a lecture to threaten the professor, even though it was the professor who had the gun all along. The major issue, once again, is the accuracy or the distortion of one's long-term memory. If it is true that long-term memories may not be permanent and that they can be distorted or replaced by events processed later, we may have to reconsider the weight given to eyewitness testimony—eyewitness identification in particular (e.g., Buckhout, 1975; Clifford & Lloyd-Bostock,

When President John Kennedy was shot and killed in Dallas in 1963, the assassination was witnessed by many people. Memories of that day more than thirty years ago now appear to be considerably different and varied.

1983; Loftus, 1984; MacLeod & Ellis, 1986; McCloskey & Egeth, 1983).

Let's begin by reviewing two classic studies. In one (Loftus et al., 1978), subjects view a series of slides that show a red Datsun (a common, imported car at the time of this study) approach an intersection, turn right, and knock down a pedestrian who is crossing at the intersection. Some subjects see a yield sign at the corner, whereas others are shown a stop sign there. In all other respects, the slides are identical. After viewing the slides, subjects are asked a series of questions about what they have just seen. Some are asked, "Did another car pass the red Datsun while it was stopped at the *stop sign?*" Others are asked the same question, but with "*yield sign*" substituted for "*stop sign.*"

After the questioning, all subjects are shown a pair of slides and are asked to identify the one from the pair that was in the series they had seen earlier. As you now might guess, 80 percent of the subjects chose the picture that contained the sign that was consistent with the question they had been asked, not with the sign they had actually seen. That is, if you were a subject who had seen the red car at the *stop sign* and then were asked about a red car at a *yield sign*, chances are that you would "remember" the sign as being a yield sign, not a stop sign.

In a similar vein (Loftus & Zanni, 1975), subjects view a short film showing the collision of two cars. Later, the viewers were asked about what they had seen, and were asked to estimate the speed of the cars when they collided. Actually, some were asked about the cars "colliding," some were asked about the cars "hitting" each other, and others were asked about cars "contacting," "bumping," or "smashing" each other. Estimates varied in accord with the verb used in the question. The cars were reported to be going nearly 41 mph when they "smashed" together, but only about 31 mph when they "contacted" each other. Although these are laboratory studies—and there is danger in trying to generalize too much from the laboratory to the real world (Bekerian, 1993; Yuille, 1993)—the relevance for eyewitness testimony is fairly obvious.

What do the "experts" say about eyewitness testimony? On what issues would psychologists be willing to go to court and claim that valid, scientific evidence exists? Just this question was put to 113 researchers who had published data on eyewitness testimony (Kassin et al., 1989). Statements about eyewitness testimony that these experts claim are reliable and accurate are presented in Figure 6.3.

A more recent review article by Gary Wells of Iowa State University, who has researched eyewitness identification for many years, claims that there *are* steps that can be taken (asking the right questions, structuring lineups, properly instructing witnesses, and so on) that can improve the accuracy of eyewitness identification (Wells,

---

Figure 6.3

Statements About Eyewitness Testimony with Which the "Experts" Agree

1. An eyewitness's testimony about an event can be affected by how the questions put to the witness are worded.

2. Police instructions can affect an eyewitness's willingness to make an identification and/or the likelihood that he or she will identify a particular person.

3. Eyewitnesses' testimony about an event often reflects not only what they actually saw but information they obtained later on.

4. An eyewitness's confidence is not a good predictor of his or her identification accuracy.

5. An eyewitness's perception and memory for an event may be affected by his or her attitudes and expectations.

6. The less time an eyewitness has to observe an event, the less well he or she will remember it.

7. Eyewitnesses sometimes identify as a culprit someone they have seen in another situation or context.

8. The use of a one-person showup instead of a full lineup increases the risk of misidentification.

9. The rate of memory loss for an event is greatest right after the event, and then levels off with time.

10. White eyewitnesses are better at identifying other white people than they are at identifying black people.

From Kassin 1989, pp. 1089–1098.

1993). Other researchers remain more pessimistic, arguing that we still know too little about the real-world process of eyewitness testimony, or about the nature of witnesses (particularly those who are also crime victims), to be able to predict when the recollections of eyewitnesses are or are not accurate (Bekerian, 1993; Egeth, 1993; Yuille, 1993).

Before You Go On

What can we say about the capacity, duration, and accuracy of long-term memory?

How Do We Get Information into Long-term Memory?

We have seen how simple repetition (maintenance rehearsal) can be used to keep material active in short-term memory. This sort of rehearsal is also one way to move information from STM to LTM. Within limits, the more one repeats a bit of information, the more likely it will be remembered—beyond the limits of short-term memory. Although there *are* circumstances in which this is true, in most cases the simple repetition of information is not sufficient to process it into long-term storage. Simply attending to information—the essence of repetition—is an inefficient means of encoding information in long-term memory.

Getting information into long-term memory usually requires more than just repeating that information over and over. To get information into LTM we need to process it more thoroughly, or "elaborate" on it, to use the term proposed by Craik and Lockhart (1972). That is, we need to use **elaborative rehearsal**, which means we need to think about it, organize it, form images of it, and make it meaningful (relate it to something already in our long-term memories).

elaborative rehearsal a mechanism for processing information into LTM that involves thinking about information, organizing it, and making it meaningful

Do you see how the distinction between maintenance rehearsal and elaborative rehearsal fits the levels-of-processing model of memory we discussed earlier? When we do no more than attend to an item, as in maintenance rehearsal, our processing is fairly minimal, or shallow, and that item is likely to remain in memory for a relatively short time. The more we are able to rehearse an item elaboratively, the deeper into memory it is processed. And, as the model claims, the more we elaborate on it, the easier it will be to remember.

Consider a hypothetical experiment in which subjects are asked to respond to a list of words in different ways. In one case, they are asked to count the number of letters in each word on the list. In another, subjects are to generate a word that rhymes with the one they are reading. In a third, they are asked to use each word in a sentence. The logic is that in each case, the words were processed at an increasingly "deeper" level as subjects focused on (1) the simple, physical structure of the words, (2) the sounds of the words as they are said aloud, and (3) the meaning of the words and their role in sentence structure. In such an experiment, as processing increases, so does recall of the words being processed (Cermak & Craik, 1979; Craik & Tulving, 1975).

Before You Go On

Contrast elaborative rehearsal with maintenance
rehearsal as a means of encoding information
into long-term memory.

Are There Different Types of Long-term Memories?

Our own experiences tell us that what we have stored in LTM can be retrieved in various forms. We can remember the definitions of words. We can visualize or picture people and events from the past. We can remember the melodies of songs. We can recall how our bodies moved when we first tried to roller-skate or ski. Could it be that distinct types of information in our long-term memories are held in different subsystems, or types, of LTM? This amounts to asking if information can be encoded or represented in LTM in various ways. The notion of multiple long-term memory systems is a relatively new one in psychology, and as you might expect, there is little agreement on just what all of the systems within LTM might be, or how to label them (Johnson & Hasher, 1987). Here, we'll briefly review three LTM subsystems.

Procedural Memory. Endel Tulving has suggested that information in LTM is stored in one of three subsystems (1972, 1983, 1985, 1986). Although the three interact, he sees them as basically different. One type of long-term memory is called **procedural memory**. In this memory, we have stored recollections of learned responses, or chains of responses. Stored here are the patterned responses we have learned well, such as how to balance and ride a bicycle, how to type, how to shave, or how to apply makeup. Simply, what is stored in procedural memory are the basic procedures of our lives. What we have stored here is put into use with little or no effort. For example, at one time in your life, handwriting was difficult, as you strained to form letters and words correctly. But by now, your writing skills, or "procedures," are so ingrained in procedural memory that you can retrieve the processes involved almost without thinking. John Anderson (1986, 1987) calls the information in this subsystem of LTM *procedural information*, or "knowing how." The other types of LTM hold what Anderson calls *declarative knowledge*, or "knowing that."

Semantic Memory. In **semantic memory** we store all of our vocabulary, simple concepts, and rules (including the rules that govern our use of language). Here we have stored our concepts and

procedural memory a subsystem of LTM, in which stimulus-response associations and skilled patterns of responses are stored

semantic memory a subsystem of LTM, in which vocabulary, facts, simple concepts, and rules are stored

knowledge of the world in which we live. In a way, our semantic memories are crammed with facts, both important and trivial, such as the following:

Who opened the first psychology laboratory in Leipzig in 1879?
How many stripes are there on the American flag?
Is "Colorless green ideas sleep furiously" a well-formed, grammatically correct sentence?
What do dogs eat?

If we can answer these questions, we have found the answers in our long-term semantic memories.

The information we have stored in semantic memory seems to be stored there in an organized fashion. We're not yet sure how to characterize the (no doubt) complex structure of semantic memory, but there have been several ideas put forward. At the very least, concepts seem to be related in terms of their ability to evoke each other as associates. If I ask you to say the first thing that comes to mind when I say a word, and then say "hot," are you not likely to say "cold" in response? When people are asked to recall a list of randomly presented words from various categories (e.g., pieces of furniture, men's names, fruits, sports, and colors), they tend to categorize their recall by category, recalling first furniture pieces, then names, then fruits, and so on (Bousfield, 1953). In fact, when people are asked to recall lists of words that do not come from distinct categories, they still produce recall lists that reflect their own, associative organization (Tulving, 1962). Over the past twenty years, several *network models* have been proposed to describe the structure of semantic LTM. Although each theory is somewhat different, they all propose that the concepts (e.g., "animal," "bird," "canary," "yellow") or propositions ("birds are animals," "birds can fly," "canaries are birds," "canaries are yellow") stored in semantic memory are interrelated in highly structured, predictable ways (Anderson, 1976, 1983a, 1983b; Collins & Loftus, 1975; Collins & Quillian, 1969).

Semantic long-term memory is also abstract. By that I mean that although we may know how many stripes there are on the American flag, and although we have a general idea of the sorts of things that dogs eat, we have difficulty remembering how, why, or when we ever acquired that tidbit of information. Another way of saying the same thing is that the information in semantic memory is not tied in any real way to our memories of our own life experiences—which sets it apart from the third variety of LTM.

Episodic Memory. The third type or subsystem of memory proposed by Tulving is called **episodic memory**. Here we store the memories of our life events and experiences. It is a time-related memory, and the experiences stored there seem to be laid down in chronological order. Episodic memory seems to operate something like a video camera that simply registers all of our life's events on one continuous videotape. Essentially, episodic memory catalogues the episodes or

episodic memory a subsystem of LTM, in which personal experiences are stored

Basic procedures, or movements, such as those acquired when one learns how to swim, are stored in procedural memory. The rules that govern the structure, or grammar, of one's language are stored in semantic memory. Life experiences, mundane and dramatic, are stored in episodic memory.

events of our lives. In other words, episodic memories are memories of specific events, not abstract events. For example:

> What did you have for lunch yesterday?
> Did you have a good night's sleep?
> How did you spend last summer's vacation?
> What did your dog eat yesterday?

The answers to these sorts of questions are stored in our episodic memories.

Some memory researchers claim that there is a separate category of episodic memory that they call *autobiographical memory* (e.g., Baddeley, 1990). Although episodic memory contains those things that have happened to us, the events in autobiographical memory are particularly significant. What I had for lunch last Monday may be in my episodic memory, but the experience of teaching my first class in introductory psychology as a graduate student at the University of

Tennessee is probably in autobiographical memory as well. One's autobiographical memory does not seem to develop until about the age of $3–3^1/_2$ years, or until we are old enough to be able to talk to ourselves and to others about the events of our lives (Nelson, 1993; Pillemer & White, 1989).

Before You Go On

Name and briefly describe three possible subsystems, or types, of long-term memory.

WHERE CAN WE FIND MEMORIES IN THE BRAIN?

We may safely assume that memories of our experiences are stored in our brains. A very compelling logic suggests that as information is encoded, stored, and retrieved, there must be reliable changes in the structures or functions of the nervous system. The search for where and how memories are formed within the nervous system is not a new line of research, but within the last decade it has become one of the most exciting and most promising.

When information is encoded as a memory, changes take place in the central nervous system. In humans, most of these changes take place in the brain, and many such changes occur in the cerebral cortex. *That* sounds simple enough, but what sorts of changes take place as memories are stored? Exactly what is changed, and in what ways? Answers to these questions are not yet available, and what hints we do have tell us that the processes involved are incredibly complex. If the nervous system is in some way altered as memories are formed, that alteration must be at the level of the neuron or the synapse. Given the recency of most of the research in this area, the story changes regularly, but here is some of what psychologists suspect.

First, let's make sure we understand what *does not* happen. We do not grow or develop new neurons as a function of experience. Recall from our discussion in Chapter 2 that we are born with as many neurons as we'll ever have. Learning and memory must take advantage of existing neurons. There is evidence, however, that experience does increase the number of axon endings, dendrites, and synapses in the brain (Greenough, 1984; Rosenzweig et al., 1972).

By the 1970s, the best guess was that evidence for memory formation could be found by examining changes that take place at the synapse (Bartus et al., 1982; Deutsch, 1973; Kandel & Schwartz, 1982; Lavond et al., 1993; Matthies, 1989; McNaughton & Morris, 1987). The research—most of it done with simple, nonhuman animals—shows that with repetition or experience, the flow of impulses across synapses becomes easier and easier. It is as if synapses become more efficient with practice.

If memories are formed because repetition, experience, or practice allows some neurotransmitters to work more effectively at the synaptic level, what would happen if something disrupted or blocked the action of those neurotransmitters? You would predict that memories formed at synapses that used those neurotransmitters would be disrupted as well. This is essentially what happens. The neurotransmitters most often involved in studies such as these are acetylcholine (ACh) and serotonin.

A slightly different line of research claims that experience does not increase, or alter in any way, the neurotransmitter released at synapses. What matters most, these scientists argue, are changes in the postsynaptic membrane. The most common changes are thought to be increases in the number of effective or useful receptor sites (e.g., Lynch & Baudry, 1984). The point is that as synapses are used and used again, the number of receptor sites increases, and this is what makes for more efficient use of the synapse.

In brief, the formation of memories involves making some synaptic transmissions easier than they once were. What remains to be seen is whether changes at the synapse involve increases or decreases in the amount of neurotransmitter present, or physical changes in the neuronal membranes involved (or both), to allow existing neurotransmitters to function more effectively.

Before You Go On

What changes take place at a neural level when memories are formed?

TOPIC 6A SUMMARY

We have covered a lot of ground in this Topic, much of it quite theoretical or technical. I have tried to show that human memory is not a simple receptacle for information that passively enters through our senses and gets dumped someplace where we can get it out whenever we wish. Multistore models of memory claim that to encode and store information requires a series of steps needed to move that information through distinct memory stores. Levels-of-processing models claim that there is but one memory store where information is processed at various levels. What I've tried to do in this Topic is present a model of memory that borrows heavily from a multistore viewpoint, but that also acknowledges the usefulness of a levels-of-processing approach. Our model included sensory memory, short-term memory, and long-term memory components.

There may be various types of long-term memory, and information in long-term memory may be stored in an organized fashion, although we do not yet fully appreciate all of the complex patterns of organization that can best characterize our memory systems. It is still true, however, that on a practical level, what matters most to us, day in and day out, is whether we can get information out of our memory systems when we want to. We consider this process of retrieval in Topic 6B.

Topic 6B
IMPROVING MEMORY: FACTORS AFFECTING RETRIEVAL

As we have defined it, memory involves three related processes: encoding, storage, and retrieval. The first two processes were discussed in Topic 6A, where we saw how information is processed into memory (encoded) and kept there (storage). In this Topic, our focus shifts to the practical matter of retrieval—the process of getting that information out of memory.

Retrieval is an important memory process regardless of the type of information we have stored or where we have stored it. Whether we are talking about a simple, well-learned habit stored in procedural memory, a precise definition stored in semantic memory, a personal experience stored in episodic memory, or a telephone number temporarily stored in short-term memory, if retrieval fails at the critical time, that information will be of no use to us.

Consistent with the terminology we have been developing, we can say that *remembering* demonstrates successful retrieval and that *forgetting* demonstrates retrieval failure. You should recognize that this usage of retrieval and retrieval failure is both circular and trivial. To say that we forget something because we are unable to retrieve it *explains nothing*. The real issue, of course, is, *why* did retrieval fail? Was the information we were seeking simply not there—not available to us? Or was the information there, in memory, but inaccessible at the time? What factors influence the extent to which information can be retrieved on demand? What can be done to increase the likelihood that retrieval will succeed? These are the issues we explore in this Topic.

MEASURING RETRIEVAL

One factor affecting the retrieval of information from long-term memory is how one is asked to go about retrieving it. This is a factor over which you and I seldom have much control. For instance, unless you have an unusually democratic instructor, you will not be allowed to vote on what type of exams will be given in class. Students are generally asked to retrieve information in one of a number of standard exam formats chosen by their instructor. In this section, we'll see how retrieval is influenced by our choice of measuring technique.

Direct, Explicit Measures of Memory

Measures of retrieval are called direct, or explicit, when someone is asked to consciously, or purposively, retrieve specified information from his or her memory (as on a classroom exam). Both recall and recognition qualify as direct measures.

Let's design an experimental example to work with for a while. Imagine that we have students come to the laboratory on a given Tuesday to learn a list of 15 randomly chosen words. Some students take longer than others, but all eventually demonstrate that they have learned the list. The students report back to the laboratory two weeks later, when our basic question is: "How many of the words that you learned two weeks ago do you still remember?" How could we find out?

One thing we might do is ask for simple recall of the list of words. **Recall** asks someone to produce information to which he or she has been previously exposed. To use recall in our experiment, we need only give the students a blank sheet of paper and ask them to write, in any order, as many of the words from the previously learned list as they can. (Technically, this is "free recall." If, for example, we asked the students to recall the list in the order in which it was presented, we would be asking for "serial recall.") This is a difficult retrieval task. For recall, we provide the fewest possible cues to aid the retrieval. We merely specify the information we want and essentially say, "There, now go into your long-term memory, locate that information, get it out, and write it down." Let's assume that one student correctly recalls six words.

Now suppose that we furnish our student with a list of 50 words, including those on the previously learned list. We instruct her to "circle the words on this list that you *recognize* from the list you learned two weeks ago." In this case, we're not asking for recall, but for **recognition**, a retrieval task requiring a subject to identify material learned previously. Isn't it likely that our student will do better on this task? She was able to recall 6 words of the original 15, so let's say she recognizes 11 words. In a way, we now have a small dilemma. Should we say that our student remembered 6 words or 11 words? The answer is, both or either. Whether our student remembered 6 words or 11 words depends on how we asked her to go about remembering.

In virtually every case, retrieval by recognition is superior to retrieval by recall (e.g., Bahrick, 1984; Brown, 1976; Schacter, 1987). Figure 6.4 provides some clear-cut data in support of this point. It shows that over a two-day period, tests of retrieval by recognition are superior to tests of retrieval by recall. Most students I know would rather take a multiple-choice exam, in which they only have to recognize the correct response from among a few alternatives, than a fill-in-the-blank test (or an essay test), which requires recall.

recall a measure of retrieval in which an individual is given the fewest possible cues to aid retrieval and must produce information to which he or she has been previously exposed

recognition a measure of retrieval in which an individual is required to identify material previously learned

Figure 6.4

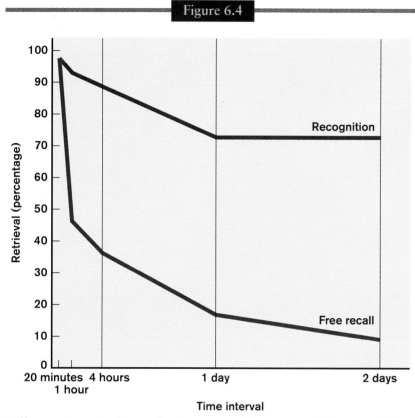

Differences in retrieval scores for the memory of nonsense syllables over a 2-day period. In one case, retrieval is measured with a test for recall, whereas in the other case, retrieval is measured by a recognition test. (From Luh, 1922.)

Recall and recognition *are* similar in that they both involve the retrieval of information that is usually stored in semantic memory (possibly episodic memory) (Hayman & Tulving, 1989; Tulving, 1983), and seem to involve the same physiological underpinnings in the brain (Haist et al., 1992; Squire et al., 1993). The major difference is that with recall, we provide minimal retrieval cues; with recognition, we provide maximum cues and ask the subject to identify a stimulus as being one that he or she has seen before (Mandler, 1980). Or, as Benton Underwood, a psychologist who studied memory processes for many years, described the difference: In recall we ask, "What is the item?" In a recognition task we ask, "Is this the item?" (cited in Houston, 1986, p. 280).

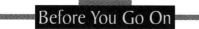

**How do recall and recognition measures affect
our assessment of retrieval?**

Indirect, Implicit Measures of Memory

Measures classified as indirect, or implicit, are more subtle than either recall or recognition. With indirect measures, someone demonstrates that information is stored in memory when he or she can take advantage of previous experiences without consciously trying to do so.

What if one of the students in our hypothetical example came back to the laboratory two weeks after memorizing a list of words and could neither recall nor recognize any of the items? I suspect that we'd be a bit surprised, but we might be wrong if we assumed that our subject retained nothing from the learning experience two weeks earlier. What if we ask this subject to relearn the list of 15 words? Two weeks ago it took the subject ten trials, or presentations of the list, before he or she learned the words. Now, when relearning the same list, we find it takes only seven trials. This is a common finding in memory research.

relearning a technique of noting the improvement in performance when learning material a second time

Relearning—the technique of noting the change in performance that occurs when one is required to learn material for a second time— almost always takes fewer trials, or less time, than did original learning. The difference is attributed to the benefit provided by one's memory of the original learning. The importance of relearning as a sensitive measure of memory dates back to 1885 and the research of Hermann Ebbinghaus. In order to minimize the impact of previous experience, Ebbinghaus designed "nonsense syllables"—such as *dax, wuj, lep, pib, loz*—to use in his research. [As it happens, not all syllables are equally nonsensical; some *are* more meaningful (e.g., *tix, luv, bot*) than others (e.g., *wuj, xyg, keq*).] Ebbinghaus served as his own subject, memorizing list after list of nonsense syllables under various conditions of practice. Later, he would assess his memory for what he had learned. He noted that even when recall was poor, he could relearn a list of syllables in just a few trials.

Because relearning does not require the direct, or conscious, retrieval of information from memory, it qualifies as an indirect, or implicit, test of memory retention (Graf & Schacter, 1985; Schacter, 1987, 1992). Implicit tests of memory have become an active area of research in cognitive psychology (Richardson-Klavehn & Bjork, 1988; Roediger, 1990; Schacter, 1987). Among other things, this research supports the hypothesis that information is stored in various types of long-term memory.

Although we may think of the relearning of verbal materials, such as words or nonsense syllables, as an indirect measure of memory, many implicit tests of retention focus on *procedural memories*, or what Anderson calls *procedural knowledge*. You'll recall from our last Topic that procedural memories include the storage of "knowing how to go about doing things," such as tying a shoelace, typing, speaking, or riding a bicycle. Remembering how to do these things is virtually automatic, or unconscious. When we specifically try to recall how to do them, our performance may deteriorate. "In some sense, these performances reflect prior learning, but seem to resist conscious remembering" (Roediger, 1990, p. 1043).

Let's look at an example of how implicit memory tests provide some intriguing data about amnesia. As we have noted (in Topic 6A), some people with amnesia (such as H. M.) are unable to transfer information from STM to LTM. What is learned today is forgotten by tomorrow.

Warrington and Weiskrantz (1968, 1970) had amnesic and control subjects learn a list of words. Retention of the list was tested. In two direct, explicit measures, recall and recognition, the control subjects were superior to the amnesic subjects, who predictably scored poorly. Then the subjects were given two implicit tests. Neither test was presented as a test of memory, but as a guessing game. In one, subjects were shown a few letters (such as *tab . . .*) and were asked to identify a word that began with those letters. In the other test, subjects were to identify words that had been mutilated so that they were very difficult to read. The question was, how many words from the previously learned list would be identified in either task? It turned out that words from the list learned previously were easier to identify than "new" words. In addition, there were no differences between the amnesic and nonamnesic subjects on these implicit tests of memory. These findings have been replicated many times (see also Bowers & Schacter, 1990; Graf & Mandler, 1984; Shimamura, 1986).

Even in the case of extreme amnesia, all of memory processing may not be lost. Some long-term memories—those in procedural memory in particular—may be resistant to destruction. Remember the last time you heard about a victim of amnesia? Typically, we hear about some adult found wandering about, totally unaware of who he is, where he came from, or how he got there. There seems to be no *direct* recollection of any long-term memories. But have you noticed that such amnesia patients usually *do* demonstrate all sorts of long-term memories? They remember how to talk, how to eat, and how to get dressed. They remember, in short, all those procedures stored in their procedural memories.

Before You Go On

What are implicit tests of retention, and what do they tell us about long-term memory?

ENCODING AND RETRIEVAL

I have made the point repeatedly that encoding, storage, and retrieval are interrelated memory processes. In this section, we'll explore the important relations that exist between retrieval and encoding. At one level, the issue is simple: If you do not encode information appropriately, you will have difficulty retrieving it. You cannot recall my mother's maiden name simply because you never knew it in the first place. You have never heard my mother's maiden name before, but

Figure 6.5

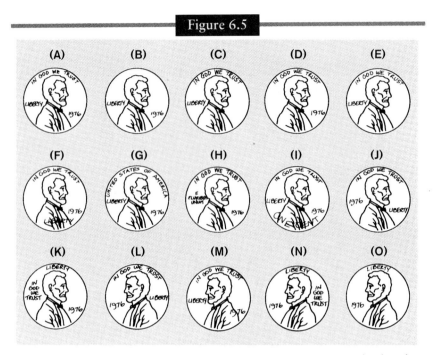

Fifteen drawings of the head of a penny. The fact that we cannot easily identify the correct rendition emphasizes that simple repetition of a stimulus does not guarantee that it will be stored usefully in long-term memory. (After Nickerson & Adams, 1979.)

you *have* had countless encounters with pennies. Can you draw a picture of a penny, locating each of its features? Can you recognize from a series of drawings which one most accurately depicts a penny (see Figure 6.5)? In fact, very few of us can correctly recognize a drawing of a penny, and even fewer can recall all of its essential features, nearly 90 percent forgetting that the word *Liberty* appears right behind Lincoln's shoulder (Nickerson & Adams, 1979; Rubin & Kontis, 1983). These retrieval failures do not result from a lack of experience but from a lack of proper encoding. There are three general encoding issues we'll discuss here: context effects, encoding strategies, and the amount and spacing of encoding practice.

The Effects of Context

encoding specificity principle the hypothesis that we can retrieve only what we have stored and that retrieval is enhanced to the extent that retrieval cues match encoding cues

Retrieval is best when the situation, or context, in which retrieval takes place matches the context that was present at encoding. When cues present at encoding are also present at retrieval, retrieval is enhanced. This observation is called the **encoding specificity principle**. Essentially, this principle asserts that how we retrieve information depends on how it was encoded in the first place (Flexser & Tulving, 1982; Newby, 1987; Tulving & Thompson, 1973). The principle suggests that not only do we encode and store particular items of information, but note and store the context in which those items occur. The encoding specificity principle is as valid for animals as it is for humans. "Ease of retrieval . . . is quite strongly influenced by the context in which the animal is asked to retrieve it. The closer the test context is to training conditions and the more unique the context is for specific memories, the better the retrieval" (Spear et al., 1990, pp. 190–191).

Here's a hypothetical experiment (based on Tulving & Thompson, 1973) that demonstrates encoding specificity. Subjects are asked to learn a list of 24 common words. Half the subjects are also given cue words to help them remember each item on the list. For the stimulus word *wood*, the cue word is *tree;* for *cheese*, the cue word is *green*, and so on for each of the 24 words. The other half of the subjects receive no such cue during their memorization (i.e., while encoding). Later, subjects are asked to recall as many words from the list as they can. What we discover at recall is that the cue helps those subjects who had seen it during learning, but *decreases* the recall for those subjects who had not seen it during learning. If learning takes place without a cue, recall will be better without it.

How-to-study-in-college books often recommend that you choose one special place for studying and that your kitchen table, for example, wouldn't be a good choice because that setting is already associated with eating experiences (and many others). In other words, the context of a kitchen is not a good one for encoding information unless you expect to be tested for retrieval in that same context— which seems highly unlikely. This advice was reaffirmed by a series of experiments by Steven Smith (1979). For example, he had subjects learn some material in one room, and then tested their recall for that material in either the same room or a different one. When a new

Research on the relationship between encoding and retrieval suggests that the best place to study for an exam is in the classroom where the exam will be taken. The greater the difference between the context available during studying and the context during retrieval, the poorer retrieval will be.

room—a different context, with different cues—was used, retrieval performance dropped substantially. Simply instructing students to try to remember and think about the room in which learning took place helped recall considerably. As an extreme example, consider a study by Godden and Baddeley (1975) in which deep-sea divers learned lists of words either on dry land or under 15 feet of water. If they were tested in the same environment in which learning took place, subjects recalled significantly more than if recall took place in a different context.

These context effects are related to what has been called **state-dependent memory**. The idea here is that, to a degree, retrieval depends on the extent to which a person's *state of mind* at retrieval matches the person's state of mind at encoding (Leahy & Harris, 1989, p. 146). If learning takes place while a person is under the influence of a drug, for example, being under the influence of that drug at retrieval has beneficial effects (e.g., Eich et al., 1975; Goodwin et al., 1969; Parker et al., 1976). Intriguing research by Gordon Bower (Bower et al., 1978; Bower, 1981) and others suggests that one's mood may also predict retrieval. Using moods (sad or happy) induced by posthypnotic suggestion, Bower found that retrieval was best when mood at retrieval *matched* mood at learning, regardless of whether that mood was happy or sad. There also is considerable evidence that a given mood or frame of mind tends to evoke memories that are consistent with that mood (e.g., Blaney, 1986). Simply: when you are in a good mood, you tend to remember pleasant things, and when you are in a bad or depressed mood, you tend to remember unpleasant, depressing things.

Furthermore, our memories for emotionally arousing experiences are likely to be easier to recall than memories of emotionally neutral events (Thompson, 1982). This may be because emotional arousal increases the levels of certain hormones that, in turn, help form vivid memories associated with the emotional arousal (Gold, 1987; McGaugh, 1983). That emotional arousal may help to form particularly vivid memories may help us understand what Brown and Kulik (1977) call **flashbulb memories**—memories of events that are unusually clear and vivid. You probably have flashbulb memories of several events: your high school graduation; the funeral of a close friend; or what you were doing on January 28, 1986, when the space shuttle *Challenger* exploded, killing all on board. Which flashbulb memories *you* have depends on how old you are, of course. I also should mention that although flashbulb memories *are* particularly clear and vivid, there is little reason to believe that they are necessarily any more complete or accurate than any other memories. Although we seem to recall these events in vivid detail, much of that detail may be totally wrong or may never have really happened (McCloskey et al., 1988; Neisser, 1982, 1991).

We have seen that the retrieval of information from memory depends in large measure on the context and cues provided by events that occur at the time of encoding. Retrieval is enhanced to the extent that the situation, or one's state of mind, is the same at retrieval as it

state-dependent memory the hypothesis that retrieval can be enhanced by the extent to which one's state of mind at retrieval matches one's state of mind at encoding

flashbulb memories particularly clear, vivid memories that are easily retrieved but not necessarily accurate in all detail

Flashbulb memories are particularly clear and vivid, though not necessarily accurate, recollections of events that had some emotional impact at the time they occurred. Different people have different flashbulb memories, reflecting one's age, if nothing else. Some remember clearly what they were doing when they first heard that Elvis Presley had died or that John Lennon had been shot.

was at encoding. Emotional arousal at encoding seems to strengthen the encoded information.

Before You Go On

How does the situation, or context, in which
one encodes information affect retrieval
of that information?

Strategies That Guide Encoding and Aid Retrieval

To once again use the term of Craik and Tulving (1975), to practice material in a way that maximizes the chance of retrieving it when we want it, we need to use *elaborative rehearsal*. We need to develop strategies that will encode information in long-term memory in such a way that we can easily get it out again. In this section, we'll examine a few elaboration strategies. We'll begin by considering meaningfulness in general; then we'll briefly review some specific mnemonic devices (after the Greek goddess of memory, Mnemosyne). These techniques use existing memories to make new information more meaningful. We'll end this section with a discussion of how memory schemas—complex cognitive representations of general knowledge—affect our elaboration of information at encoding and retrieval.

Meaningfulness. I have a hypothesis. I believe I can determine the learning ability of students by noting where they sit in a classroom. The good, bright students tend to choose seats farthest from the door. The poor, dull students sit by the door, apparently interested in getting easily into and out of the room. (Although there may be some truth to this, I'm not serious.) To make my point, I do an experiment. Students seated away from the door are asked to learn a list of words I read aloud only once. I need a second list of words for the students seated by the door because they've already heard my first list.

The list my "smart students" hear contains words such as *cat, dog, mother, father, black, white,* and so forth. As I predicted, they have no problem recalling this list after just one presentation. The students huddled by the door get my second list: *insidious, tachistoscope, sophistry, flotsam, episcotister,* and so forth. Needless to say, my hypothesis will be confirmed.

This obviously is not a very fair experiment. Those students sitting by the door will yell foul. My second list of words is clearly more difficult to learn and recall than the first. The words on the first list are shorter, more familiar, and easier to pronounce. However, the major difference between these two lists is the **meaningfulness** of the items—the extent to which they elicit existing associations in one's memory. The *cat, dog, mother* list is easy to remember because each word in it is meaningful. Each word makes us think of many other things, or produces many associations. That is, these items are easy to elaborate. Words such as *episcotister* are more difficult because they evoke few, if any, associations.

Meaningfulness is not a characteristic or feature built into materials to be learned. *Meaningfulness resides in the learner. Episcotister* may be a meaningless collection of letters for many people, but for others it is a word rich in meaning, a word with which they can readily form many associations. What is meaningful is a function of our individual experiences. (An episcotister, by the way, is a type of apparatus used in psychology. To make this word meaningful for you, you might want to do some research on episcotisters.)

It follows that one of your tasks as a learner is to do whatever you can to make the material you are learning meaningful. You need to seek out and form associations between what you are learning and what you already know. You need to elaboratively rehearse what you are encoding so that you can retrieve it later. You need to ask about what you are studying. What does this mean? What does it make me

meaningfulness the extent to which new information evokes associations with information already in memory

think of? Does this remind me of something I already know? Can I make this more meaningful? If you cannot, there is little point in going on to more confusing material. Perhaps you now see a reason for including Before You Go On questions within each chapter.

Before You Go On

What is meaningfulness, and how is it related to retrieval?

Mnemonic Devices. Retrieval is enhanced to the extent that we elaborate on the material we are learning. Often this is simply a matter of reflecting on what we are learning and actively forming associations with previously stored memories. Now let's examine some specific encoding techniques, **mnemonic devices**, that can aid our retrieval by helping us to organize and add meaningfulness to new material.

An experiment by Bower and Clark (1969) shows us that we can improve the retrieval of otherwise unorganized material if we weave that material into a meaningful story. This technique is called **narrative chaining**. A group of college students was asked to learn a list of 10 simple nouns in order. This isn't a difficult task, and subjects had little trouble with it. Then they were given another list of 10 nouns to learn, and then another—12 lists in all. These students were given no instructions other than to remember each list of words in order.

A second group of students was given the same 12 lists of 10 nouns each to learn. They were asked to make up little stories that used each of the words on the list in turn. Immediately after each list was presented, both groups were asked to recall the list of words they had just heard. There was virtually no difference in the recall scores for the two groups. Then came a surprise. *After all 12 lists had been recalled,* the students were tested again on their recall for each of the lists. The students were given a word from one of the 12 lists, and then were asked to recall the other nine words from that list. The difference in recall between the two groups of students in this instance was striking (see Figure 6.6). Those who used a narrative-chaining technique recalled 93 percent of the words (on average), whereas those who did not so organize the random words recalled only 13 percent of them.

The message seems clear and consistent with what we've learned so far. A technique that adds organization and meaningfulness to otherwise meaningless or unorganized material is a means of elaborative rehearsal that will improve retrieval. Stringing together unrelated words into sensible stories helps us remember them.

Forming *mental images*, or pictures in our minds, also can improve memory. Using imagery at encoding to improve retrieval has proven to be very helpful in many different circumstances (Begg &

mnemonic devices strategies for improving retrieval that take advantage of existing memories in order to make new material more meaningful

narrative chaining the mnemonic device of relating words in a story, thus organizing them in a meaningful way

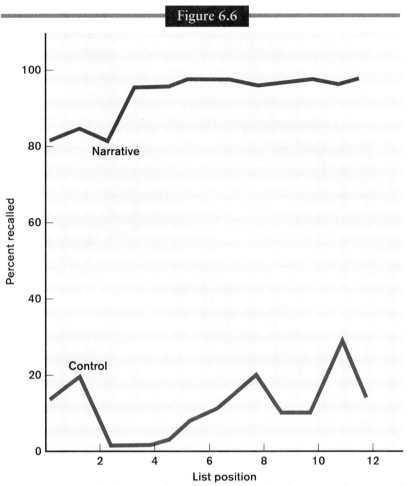

Figure 6.6

Percent correct recall for words from 12 lists learned under two study, or encoding, conditions. In the narrative condition, subjects made up short stories to relate words meaningfully, whereas in the control condition, simple memorization without any specified mnemonic device was used. (After Bower & Clark, 1969.)

Paivio, 1969; Marschark et al., 1987; Paivio, 1971, 1986). It is Paivio's contention that visual images provide a unique way of encoding meaningful information; that is, we are at an advantage when we can encode not only what a word means, but also what it looks like. It is because imagery helps retrieval that words such as *horse, rainbow,* and *typewriter* can be recalled more readily than words such as *treason, session,* and *effort*—even when factors such as frequency of occurrence and meaningfulness are equated.

Assume, for example, that you have to learn the meanings of a large number of Spanish words. You could use simple rote repetition, but this technique is tedious and not very efficient. Atkinson (1975) suggested that to improve memory for foreign language vocabulary, it is useful to imagine some connection visually tying the two words together. He calls this the *key word* method of study. For example, the Spanish word for "horse" is *caballo,* pronounced *cab-eye-yo.* To remember this association, you might choose *eye* as the key word and picture a horse actually kicking someone in the eye. Or, if you are not prepared to be that gruesome, you might imagine a horse with a very large eye. The Spanish word for "duck" is *pato.* Here your key word might be *pot,* and you could picture a duck wearing a pot on its head (Figure 6.7) or sitting in a large pot on the stove. This may sound strange, but research suggests that it works very well (Pressley et al., 1982).

The same basic technique works whenever you need to remember any paired sort of information. Gordon Bower (1972), for example, asked students to learn lists of pairs of English words. Some students were instructed to form a mental image that showed some interaction between the two words. One pair, for instance, was *piano-cigar.* There are many ways to form an image of a piano and a cigar: The cigar could be balanced on the edge of the piano, for one. Recall for word pairs was much better for those students who formed mental images than it was for those who did not. It is also the case that more commonplace and interactive images are *more useful* than strange and bizarre ones (Bower, 1970; Wollen et al., 1972). That is, to remember the *piano-cigar* pair, it would be better to picture a cigar balanced on a piano than it would be to picture a piano actually smoking a cigar (Figure 6.8). If you wanted to remember that it was Bower and Clark who did the experiment on narrative chaining, try to picture two *storytellers chained* together, each holding a *Clark Bar* in their hands as they take a *bow* on a theater stage. Again, it sounds silly, but it works.

The last formal mnemonic device I'll mention may be the oldest in recorded history. It is attributed to the Greek poet Simonides and is called the **method of loci** (Yates, 1966). The idea here is to get in your mind a well-known location (*loci* are locations); say, the floor plan of your house or apartment. Visually place the material you are trying to recall in various places throughout your house in a sensible order. When the time comes for you to retrieve the material, mentally walk through your chosen locations, recalling the information you have stored at each place.

Some time ago, I was asked to present a short talk. There were several points I wanted to make, and I didn't want to use written notes as a memory aid. I also didn't want to appear as nervous as I knew I was going to be, so I decided to try the method of loci. I divided my talk into five or six major ideas, imagined my house, and walked through it in my mind. I stored my introduction at the front door, point 1 got me to the living room, point 2 to the dining room, and so on through the house until I got to my conclusion at the back door. Even though I have been telling others about the method of loci for many years, this was the first time I had chosen to use it. I was impressed with how easy it was to remember my little speech.

Figure 6.7

An illustration of how the key word method can be used to help foreign language retrieval. (After Atkinson, 1975.)

method of loci the mnemonic device that mentally places information to be retrieved at a series of familiar locations (loci)

Figure 6.8

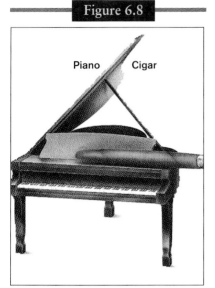

Piano   Cigar

The key word method can also be used to help us remember pairs of English words. (After Wollen et al., 1972.)

schema *a system of organized, general knowledge, stored in long-term memory, that guides the encoding and retrieval of information*

Mnemonic devices don't have to be formal techniques with special names. You used a mnemonic trick to learn which months of the year had 30 days and which had 31 when you learned the ditty "Thirty days has September, April, June, and November. All the rest have . . . ". Some students originally learned the colors of the rainbow (we called it the visible spectrum) in order by remembering the name "ROY G. BIV," which I grant you isn't terribly meaningful, but it does help us remember "red, orange, yellow, green, blue, indigo, and violet." My guess is that you can think of several mnemonic devices you have used to organize material to be learned and make it meaningful. In each case, the message is that when we can organize otherwise unrelated material in a meaningful way, retrieval will be enhanced.

Before You Go On

What are mnemonic devices and, in general, how do they work? Cite examples.

Schemas. The encoding specificity hypothesis tells us that how we retrieve information will be affected by how we encode that information. One of the processes that influences how we encode and retrieve information is our use of schemas (sometimes referred to as scripts). A **schema** is an organized, general knowledge structure stored in long-term memory (R. E. Mayer, 1983). Sir Frederic Bartlett, who first used the term in the context of memory, saw schemas as an organized

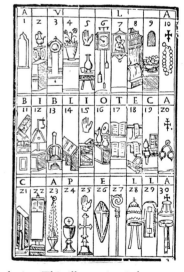

The method of loci is an ancient mnemonic device. This illustration is by a Dominican monk in the sixteenth century. On the left are the abbey and the surrounding buildings through which the speaker will mentally walk, placing the ideas (illustrated on the right) that he or she needs to recall.

part of our memories that held what we knew about some aspect of the world and guided our expectations about it (Bartlett, 1932). Schemas give us a general framework we use to understand new information and to remember or retrieve that information later (Alba & Hasher, 1983; Lord, 1980).

Let's take a look at a few examples of research that involve using schemas as encoding strategies. Before you go any further, stop and read the short passage in Figure 6.9. As it stands, the paragraph doesn't make much sense, does it? All of the words are sensible. Even individual sentences seem reasonable. But as a story, it seems virtually meaningless because without additional information you have no way, no schema, available to comprehend the meaning of the passage (Bransford & Johnson, 1972). Now look at the drawing in Figure 6.14 at the very end of this Topic. This drawing provides a schema that gives meaning to the paragraph. Subjects who were shown this picture *before* they read the passage recalled more than twice as much about it than did subjects who did not see the picture at all or who were shown the picture *after* they read the paragraph. Schemas seem to help retrieval only if the same schemas are available at or before encoding.

I've never learned to play chess. I know what a chessboard looks like and I can probably name most of the pieces. I realize that there are rules, or restrictions, on how pieces can be moved in a chess game, but I don't know what those restrictions are. In other words, I have a very sketchy schema for chess. If you were to show me a chessboard with the pieces positioned as if in the midst of a game and then later ask me to reconstruct what I had seen, I'm afraid I would do very poorly. When chess experts are shown the board and are later asked to reconstruct the positions of the pieces from memory, they do very well (DeGroot, 1965, 1966). Part of the explanation for their success is that they have complete, detailed schemas for chess games,

---

Figure 6.9

The Balloons Passage

If the balloons popped, the sound would not be able to carry since everything would be too far away from the correct floor. A closed window would also prevent the sound from carrying since most buildings tend to be well insulated. Since the whole operation depends on a steady flow of electricity, a break in the middle of the wire would also cause problems. Of course the fellow could shout, but the human voice is not loud enough to carry that far. An additional problem is that a string could break on the instrument. Then there could be no accompaniment to the message. It is clear that the best situation would involve less distance. Then there would be fewer potential problems. With face-to-face contact, the least number of things could go wrong.

From Bransford & Johnson, 1972.

which helps them encode and later retrieve the positions of the pieces on the board. In fact, when chess pieces are positioned randomly on a chessboard (not consistent with the rules of the game), the memory of chess experts for the location of the pieces is no better than mine or that of other novices (Chase & Simon, 1973). This is because the randomly positioned pieces don't fit the experts' schemas for chess, taking away their advantage. A detailed schema is not necessarily going to help one's retrieval, unless the retrieval task takes advantage of the information stored in that schema (Brewer & Nakamura, 1984). This result has been found for expertise in a number of areas, including computer programming (Adelson, 1984) and medicine (Norman et al., 1989).

The role of prior knowledge at encoding was also nicely demonstrated by an experiment by Anderson and Pichert (1978). All subjects read the same story about a couple of boys playing alone in a house. The story contained several details about the house and its contents. One group of subjects was asked to read the story from the perspective of a potential buyer of the home, while a second group of subjects was asked to read the story from the point of view of a burglar who is planning to rob the house. When recalling the story from the buyer's perspective, subjects remembered details such as a leaky roof and a large living room. Subjects who took the burglar's point of view remembered where jewelry was kept and that the house contained a large television set. Think in terms of your own memory. If I ask you to tell me all of the details of your last trip to the dentist, won't you rely heavily on your knowledge of what it is like to go to the dentist in general? Then you'll supplement your recall of your last specific visit by adding whatever details you can recall.

So, what's the bottom line? When to-be-remembered information is consistent with prior, existing information (such as schemas), retrieval is enhanced. When to-be-remembered material is at odds with existing schemas, those schemas may actually inhibit retrieval.

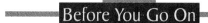

Before You Go On

What are schemas, and how do they affect retrieval?

The Amount and Distribution of Encoding Practice

One point I have made over and over is that retrieval, no matter how it is measured, depends largely on how one goes about encoding, rehearsing, or practicing information in the first place. We'll end this section on encoding with the related observation that retrieval is a function of the amount of practice and how that practice is spaced or distributed.

One of the reasons some students do not do as well on classroom exams as they would like is that they simply do not have (or make) enough time to study or practice the material covered on the exams. A related reason is that some students do not schedule wisely what time they do have.

A schema is an organized, general knowledge system stored in LTM. We have formed many schemas, including the general idea of what is involved in waiting for an appointment at the doctor's office. Note: a schema is not the recollection of any one particular visit to the doctor, but an abstract composite formed after many such visits.

Overlearning. What you and I often do once we decide to learn something is to read, practice, and study the material until we know it. We practice until we are satisfied that we have encoded and stored the required information in our memories, and then we quit. Another way of expressing this is to say that we often fail to engage in **overlearning**, the process of practicing or rehearsing material over and above what is needed to learn it. Consider this fictitious example, and see if you can extend this evidence to your own study habits.

A student comes to the laboratory to learn a list of nonsense syllables such as *dax, wuj, pib,* and *zuw*. There are 15 items on the list, and the material has to be presented repeatedly before our student can recall all of the items correctly. Having correctly recalled the items once, our student is dismissed with instructions to return two weeks later for a test of his recall of the syllables. Not surprisingly, he does not fare very well on the retrieval task.

What do you think would have happened to our student's recall if we had continued to present him with the list of syllables at the time of learning, well beyond the point at which he first learned them? Let's say the list was learned in 12 trials. We have the subject practice the list for 6 more presentations (50-percent overlearning—practice that is 50 percent over and above that required for learning). What if we required an additional 12 trials of practice (100-percent overlearning), or an additional 48 trials of practice (400-percent overlearning)?

The effects of overlearning are well documented and very predictable. The recall data for this imaginary experiment might look like those in Figure 6.10. Notice three things about these data: (1) If we measure retrieval at various times after learning, forgetting is

overlearning the practice, or rehearsal, of material over and above what is needed to learn it

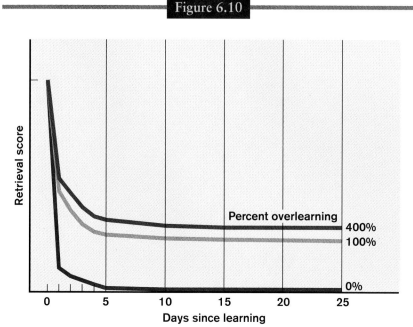

Figure 6.10

Idealized data showing the short- and long-term advantage of overlearning. Note the "diminished returns" with additional overlearning. From Krueger, 1929.

rather impressive and quite sudden. (This is one of the results of his research on memory that Ebbinghaus reported in 1885.) (2) Overlearning improves retrieval, having its greatest effects with longer retention intervals. (3) There is a "diminishing returns" phenomenon present; that is, 50-percent overlearning is much more useful than no overlearning; 100-percent overlearning is somewhat better than 50 percent; and 400 percent is better than 100 percent, but not by very much. For any learning task, or individual, there is probably an optimum amount of overlearning.

In summary, with everything else being equal, the more we practice what we are learning, the easier it will be to retrieve it. How one *schedules* one's practice or learning time is also an important factor in determining the likelihood of retrieval, and it is to this issue we turn next.

Scheduling Practice. Some of the oldest data in psychology support the notion that retrieval can be improved if practice (encoding) is spread out over time, with rest intervals spaced in between. The data shown in Figure 6.11 are fairly standard. In fact, this 1946 experiment provides such reliable results that it is commonly used as a student project in psychology laboratory classes. The task is to write the letters of the alphabet, upside down and from right to left. (If you think that sounds easy, give it a try.)

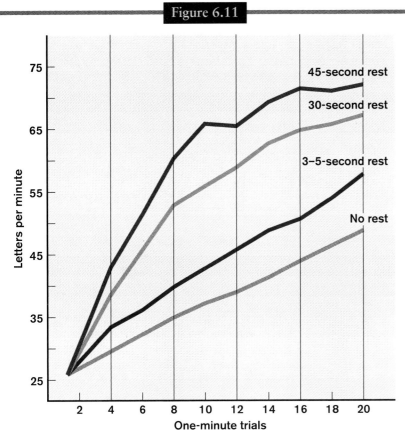

Figure 6.11

Improvement in performance as a function of distribution of practice time. The task involved was printing the letters of the alphabet upside-down and backward with twenty 1-minute trials separated by rest intervals of various lengths. (After Kientzle, 1946.)

Subjects are given the opportunity to practice the task under four conditions. The *massed-practice* group works without a break between trials. The three *distributed-practice* groups receive the same amount of actual practice, but get rest intervals interspersed between each 1-minute practice trial. One group gets a 3- to 5-second break between trials, a second group receives a 30-second rest, and a third group gets a 45-second break between practice trials.

As we can see in Figure 6.11, subjects in all four groups begin at about the same (poor) level of performance. After 20 minutes of practice, the performance of all groups shows improvement. By far, however, the massed-practice (no rest) group does the poorest, and the 45-second-rest group does the best.

The conclusion to be drawn from years of research is that almost without exception distributed practice is superior to massed practice. There are exceptions, however. Some tasks might suffer from having rest intervals inserted in practice time. In general, whenever you must keep track of many things at the same time, you should mass your practice until you have finished what you are working on. If, for example, you are working on a complex math problem, you should work it through until you find a solution, whether it's time for a break or not. And, of course, you should not break up your practice in such a way as to disrupt the meaningfulness of the material you are studying.

What we're talking about here is the scheduling of study time. Discussions of study schedules constitute the major part of all how-to-study books. The message is always the same: many short (and meaningful) study periods with rest periods interspersed are more efficient than a few study periods massed together. There may be occasions when cramming is better than not studying at all, but as a general strategy, cramming is inefficient.

Now let's assume you're going to follow this advice to prepare for a test scheduled for next week. The test will cover two chapters of material in your text, and material covered in class. What this means, of course, is that you'll schedule several short (45-minute or so) study periods throughout the week. You'll not even try to study an entire chapter, but will break it into shorter, meaningful topics (as we've done with this text). And when you're studying any one topic, you'll break it up into even shorter, meaningful chunks (separated, perhaps, by Before You Go On questions). Such a strategy of spreading out study sessions will be much more efficient than trying to get all of your studying done in one or two sessions, say, over one weekend.

Before You Go On

What is overlearning, and how does
it affect retrieval?

Compare and contrast massed and distributed
practice, noting their effects on retrieval.

INTERFERENCE AND RETRIEVAL

Think back to when you were in third grade. Can you remember the name of the student who sat behind you at school? I know I can't. I can guess who it might have been, but there seems to be no way I can directly access and retrieve that information from my long-term memory with any certainty. One possibility is that that information is no longer there. It may, in some literal sense, be lost forever. Perhaps I never encoded that information in a way that would allow me to retrieve it effectively. Another possibility is that the name of that student is in fact available in memory, but inaccessible at the moment simply because I have been in so many classes since third grade. So much has happened and entered my memory since third grade that the material I am looking for is covered up and being *interfered with* by information that entered later.

How about your most recent class? Can you recall who sat behind you in your last class? That may be a little easier, but remembering with confidence is still not easy. Again, our basic retrieval problem may be one of interference. Assuming that what we are searching for is still there (and that *is* an assumption), we may not be able to retrieve it because so many *previous* experiences (classes attended earlier) are getting in the way, interfering with retrieval.

Retroactive Interference

The basic idea that interference can account for retrieval failure is an old one in psychology. Some early experiments, for example, demonstrated that subjects who were active for a period after learning remembered what they had learned less well than did subjects who used the intervening period for sleep (Jenkins & Dallenbach, 1924). The graphs in Figure 6.12 show apparently comparable data from two studies, one with college students who had learned a list of nonsense syllables, and the other with cockroaches that had learned to avoid an area of their cage. In both cases, subjects who engaged in normal waking activity did more poorly on tests of retrieval over several retention intervals.

When interfering activities come *after* the learning of material to be retrieved or remembered, we are dealing with **retroactive interference**. Let's go back into the laboratory. We'll need two groups of subjects randomly assigned to either a control or an experimental group. The subjects in both groups are required to learn something (almost anything will do; we'll assume it's a list of nonsense syllables). Having learned their lists, the groups are then treated differently. Subjects in the experimental group are now required to learn something else, perhaps a new list of nonsense syllables. At the same time, control group subjects are asked to do nothing (which is impossible, of course, in a literal sense). These subjects might be asked to rest quietly or to play some simple game.

Now for the test. Both groups of subjects are asked to retrieve the material presented in the *first* learning task. Control group subjects will show a higher retrieval score than experimental group subjects. For the experimental group, the second set of learned material interferes with the retrieval of the material learned first. Figure 6.13(A) summarizes this research design.

Most of us are familiar with retroactive interference from our own experiences. A student who studied French in high school takes a few Spanish courses in college and now can't remember very much French. The Spanish keeps getting in the way. I have two students who are scheduled to take a psychology exam tomorrow morning at 9:00. Both are equally able and equally well motivated. One is taking only one class—mine. She studies psychology for two hours, watches TV for two hours, and goes to bed. She comes in the next morning to take the exam. The second student also studies psychology for two hours, but then must read a chapter and a half from her sociology text, just in case she is called on in class. After reading sociology, she goes to bed, comes to class, and takes the exam. Everything else being equal, this second student will be at a disadvantage. The sociology she

retroactive interference the inhibition of retrieval of previously learned material caused by material learned later

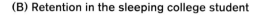

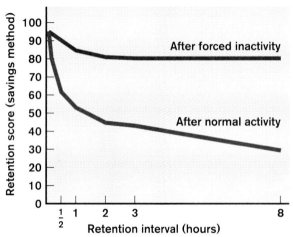

(A) Retention in the immobilized cockroach

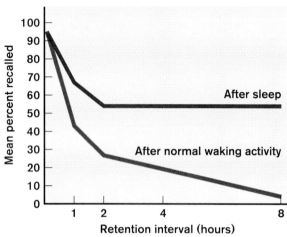

(B) Retention in the sleeping college student

These graphs illustrate how activity following learning can interfere with the retrieval of the learned material. In both cases, normal waking activity caused more interference than did forced inactivity (for cockroaches) or sleeping (for college students). (After Minami & Dallenbach, 1946.)

studied will retroactively interfere with her retrieval of the psychology she learned previously. What is this student to do? She has to study psychology, and she knows that she had better read her sociology, too. About all she can do is to set herself up for proactive interference.

Proactive Interference

proactive interference the inhibition of retrieval of recently learned material caused by material learned earlier

Proactive interference occurs when *previously* learned material interferes with the retrieval of material learned later. First follow along in

---

Figure 6.13		
Designs of Experiments to Demonstrate Retroactive Interference and Proactive Interference		

(A) Retroactive interference

	Learn	**Learn**	**Test**
Experimental group	Task A	Task B	Retrieval of Task A
Control group	Task A	Nothing	Retrieval of Task A

(B) Proactive interference

	Learn	**Learn**	**Test**
Experimental group	Task A	Task B	Retrieval of Task B
Control group	Nothing	Task B	Retrieval of Task B

Note: If interference is operating, the control group will demonstrate better retrieval than will the experimental group.

Figure 6.13(B), then we'll get back to our student and her studying problem. Again, we have two groups of subjects, experimental and control. The experimental group again starts by learning something—that same list of syllables, perhaps. This time the control group subjects begin by resting quietly while the experimental group goes through the learning task. Both groups then learn a different list of syllables. We test for retrieval, but this time we test for the retrieval of the more recently learned material. Again, the control group subjects will have an advantage. They have none of that first list in their memories to interfere with the retrieval task. But the advantage is not as great as it was in the case of retroactive interference. Proactive interference is not as detrimental as retroactive interference, which is why I would advise my student to study what she thinks is her most important assignment last.

Although both retroactive and proactive interference are well documented, there are many factors that influence the *extent* of such interference (Underwood, 1957). For example, meaningful, well-organized material is less susceptible to interference than is less meaningful material, such as nonsense syllables.

The nature of the interfering task matters a great deal. As a rule, the more similar the interfering material is to the material being retrieved, the greater will be the interference (e.g., McGeoch & McDonald, 1931). My student who had to study for a psychology exam *and* read a sociology text will experience more interference (retroactive *or* proactive) than will a student who has to study for the psychology exam and work on calculus problems. In this context, I might suggest that working on calculus is rather like doing "nothing." I would make such a suggestion only in the sense that there is little about calculus to get in the way, or interfere, with the psychology lesson. So, my advice is that if you're going to take more than one course at a time, those courses should be as different from each other as possible, to minimize interference effects.

Before You Go On

Briefly describe retroactive and proactive interference.

Which of these two generally has the greater impact on retrieval?

TOPIC 6B SUMMARY

A few pages back, I claimed that this Topic would cover practical advice about improving human long-term memory. Have you noted any useful or practical ideas? In very general terms, here's what we've

Figure 6.14

A picture providing a possible schema for the story about balloons presented in Figure 6.9. (From Bransford & Johnson, 1972.)

learned. The most practical aspect of human memory is our ability to retrieve information stored there. Retrieval generally depends on how it is measured, as well as the number and quality of retrieval cues available to us. The quality of learning (how well we have elaborated new information by making it meaningful or organizing it, perhaps with the help of mnemonic devices or existing schema) and the quantity of learning (the extent to which one has overlearned and distributed one's practice) have a definite influence on memory. To improve our chances of retrieving information from memory, we need to spend time with the material we are learning, encoding that information in a meaningful and well-organized way, whenever possible matching cues available at retrieval with those present at encoding. We also need to do what we can to avoid the effects of interference.

One final point: we can improve our retrieval of information from memory by *practicing retrieval* itself. Perhaps you'll recall from our discussion of the definition of learning that we cannot assess or measure learning directly. We can only measure performance and, on that basis, make inferences about what may have been learned. We say that classroom exams are designed to measure what you have learned. But they do so indirectly by measuring what you can remember or retrieve at the time of the test. Why don't we spend more time, then, practicing what is really going to matter—getting learned material out of our memories? Retrieval is a skill that can be practiced. Try to anticipate test questions. Work example problems at the end of textbook chapters or in accompanying study guides, if they are available. Ask yourself questions about the material you are studying. The time you spend doing so will pay off.

TOPIC 6A

How do we define memory?

Compare multistore and levels-of-processing models of memory.

Memory refers to the interrelated cognitive processes of actively representing information in memory (encoding), keeping it there (storage), and bringing it out again later (retrieval). There are many theories about the nature of human memory. One view, the multistore model, suggests that there are a number (usually three) of distinct memories, or storehouses of information, each with its own mechanisms for processing information. A levels-of-processing model contends that there is but one sort of human memory store but various depths, levels, or degrees to which new information is processed into that memory. /p. 257

What is sensory memory?

What is its capacity and duration?

Sensory memory provides storage for large amounts of information for very brief periods. In sensory memory we cannot manipulate or encode information, but have to deal with it as it is presented to us by our senses. The duration of storage in this store, or level, is measured in fractions of a second to a maximum of just a few seconds. /p. 259

How long is information stored in STM?

What is required to get information into STM and then keep it there?

Once entered into short-term memory, information will be held there approximately 15 to 20 seconds (occasionally up to 1 minute) before it fades or is replaced with new information. Some of the contents of STM become inaccessible very soon after encoding. Processing information into this memory requires that we attend to it. Information may be passed on from sensory memory or retrieved from long-term memory. We keep material in STM by reattending to it, a process called maintenance rehearsal. /p. 263

How much information can be held in STM?

How can chunking affect the capacity of STM?

The capacity of short-term memory is limited to approximately 7 ± 2 "chunks of information." This assumes that the information is unrelated and nearly meaningless. By "chunking" information into mean-

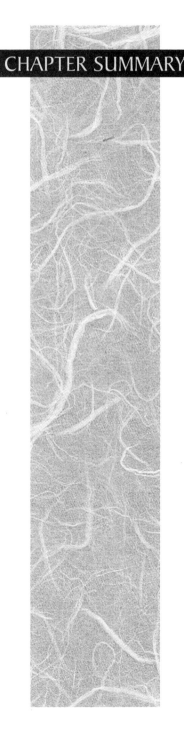

CHAPTER SUMMARY

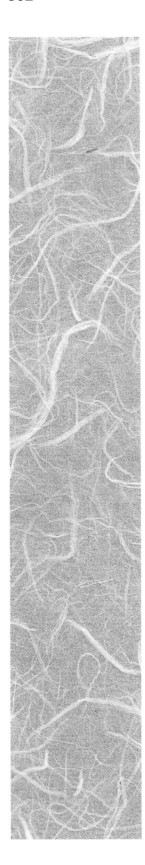

ingful clusters or units, more information can be processed into STM, but the limit remains 7 ± 2 chunks. /p. 264

How is information encoded (represented) in STM?

Information in our short-term memories may be encoded in several forms, but acoustic coding seems to be the most common. *p. 265*

What can we say about the capacity, duration, and accuracy of long-term memory?

There seem to be no limits on the amount of information that can be held in human long-term memory. As is clear from our own experiences, some of the information in LTM has been there, and can remain for very long periods. Whether memories are permanent is, for the moment at least, a question that does not have a good, scientific answer. We are often unable to tell if memories are unavailable or inaccessible when retrieval fails. There is also little doubt that our recollections of memories are often in error or, at best, inaccurate. There *is* evidence that events that have occurred *after* a to-be-recalled event can influence our memory of that event. /p. 271

Contrast elaborative rehearsal with maintenance rehearsal as a means of encoding information into long-term memory.

Although maintenance rehearsal may sometimes be sufficient to encode or move material from STM to LTM, there is little doubt that the best way to place information in LTM is elaborative rehearsal; that is, to think about the material, organize the material, and form associations with or images of the material to relate it to something already stored in LTM. The more one can elaborate, or the "deeper" the elaboration, the better retrieval will be. /p. 272

Name and briefly describe three possible subsystems, or types, of long-term memory.

Information can be stored in any one of at least three types of LTM systems. One of the most basic is procedural memory, in which we retain learned connections between stimuli and responses—how we perform simple, well-learned behaviors. Episodic memories are those that record one's life experiences and events. They are autobiographical and tied to a specific time and place. Semantic long-term memory holds one's knowledge and concepts—the facts, vocabulary, and rules one has accumulated. /p. 275

What changes take place at a neural level when memories are formed?

There is considerable uncertainty about the details of the changes that take place at the neural level when memories are formed, stored, and/or retrieved. Promising research suggests that synaptic pathways that are used repeatedly become more and more efficient in their ability to transmit neural impulses. This may be because more neurotransmitter chemical is available as memories are formed, or because new receptor sites are formed on the postsynaptic membrane as memories are formed. /*p. 276*

TOPIC 6B

How do recall and recognition measures affect our assessment of retrieval?

One's ability to retrieve information from LTM is often a function of how we ask for that retrieval. When we ask for retrieval by recall, we provide the fewest possible retrieval cues, identifying only the information to be retrieved. With recognition, we actually provide the information to be retrieved and ask that it be identified as familiar. Retrieval measured by recognition is generally superior to retrieval measured by recall. /*p. 279*

What are implicit tests of retention, and what do they tell us about long-term memory?

As opposed to explicit tests of retrieval, implicit tests assess the extent to which previously experienced material is helpful in subsequent tasks. For example, relearning shows us that even when information can be neither recalled nor recognized, that information will be easier to relearn than it was to learn in the first place. Even though people do not recall being shown a word, it will be easier to identify when subsequently mutilated or masked. These tests show us that even material that appears inaccessible through conscious effort may be available and useful in LTM. /*p. 281*

How does the situation, or the context, in which one encodes information affect retrieval of that information?

The greater the extent to which the cues or context available at retrieval match the cues or context available at encoding, the better retrieval will be. Even matching a person's state of mind at encoding and retrieval may improve retrieval. Heightened emotionality at encoding may also produce memories that seem more vivid than others, even if they are not more accurate. /*p. 285*

What is meaningfulness, and how is it related to retrieval?

Meaningfulness is the extent to which material is associated with, or related to, information already stored in memory. In general, meaningful material (or material that is made meaningful) is easier to retrieve than meaningless material. Meaningfulness resides in the individual and not in the material to be learned. /*p. 287*

What are mnemonic devices and, in general, how do they work? Cite examples.

In general, mnemonic devices are strategies used at encoding to organize and add meaningfulness to material to be retrieved. *Narrative*

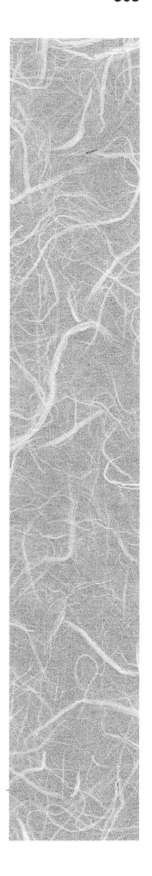

chaining involves making up a story that meaningfully weaves together a set of otherwise unorganized words or information. Several mnemonic devices (such as the "key word method" and the "method of loci") use *visual imagery* to add organization and meaningfulness. /p. 290

What are schemas, and how do they affect retrieval?

Schemas are organized, general knowledge systems we have stored in LTM. Based on one's past experiences, schemas summarize the essential features of common events or situations. They are used as a means of guiding the organization of and giving meaning to new information. The more complete and relevant one's available schemas for to-be-remembered information, the better will be encoding and retrieval. /p. 292

What is overlearning, and how does it affect retrieval?

Compare and contrast massed and distributed practice, noting their effects on retrieval.

Overlearning involves the rehearsal or practice of information above and beyond that necessary for immediate recall. Within limits, the more one overlearns, the greater the likelihood of accurate retrieval. In massed practice, study, or rehearsal, continues without intervening rest intervals. Distributed practice uses shorter segments of rehearsal interspersed with rest intervals. In almost all cases, distributed practice is superior to massed practice. /p. 296

Briefly describe retroactive and proactive interference.

Which of these two generally has the greater impact on retrieval?

Retroactive interference occurs when previously learned material cannot be retrieved because it is inhibited or blocked by material or information learned *later*. Proactive interference occurs when information cannot be retrieved because it is inhibited or blocked by material or information learned *earlier*. Retroactive interference is typically more detrimental to retrieval than is proactive interference. /p. 299

chapter seven

HIGHER COGNITIVE
PROCESSES

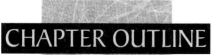

CHAPTER OUTLINE

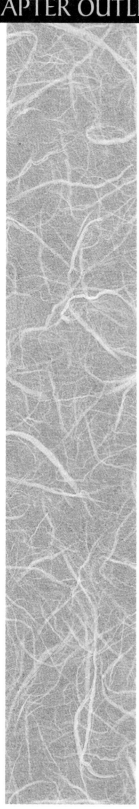

TOPIC 7A CONCEPTS AND LANGUAGE
The Concept of Concept
Forming Concepts
    A Classic Demonstration
    Developing Strategies and Testing Hypotheses
Language
    Let's Talk: What *Is* Language?
    Describing the Structure in Language
    Language Use as a Social Process
    Language Acquisition
TOPIC 7A SUMMARY

TOPIC 7B PROBLEM SOLVING
What *Is* a Problem?
Problem Representation
Problem-Solving Strategies
    Algorithms
    Heuristics
Barriers to Effective Problem Solving
    Mental Set and Functional Fixedness
    Biased Heuristics and Decision Making
    Overcoming Barriers with Creative Problem Solving
Can We Teach Problem-Solving Skills?
TOPIC 7B SUMMARY

CHAPTER SUMMARY

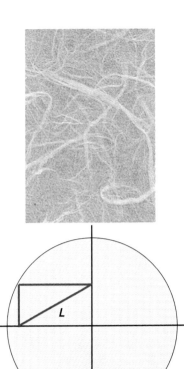

This chapter is about complex cognitive processes—the sorts of things you and I often call "thinking." We'll discuss forming and manipulating concepts, using language, and solving problems. Your study of this chapter will be enhanced—and more fun—if you give the following problems or activities a try on your own before you go on. Answers to the questions and problems will be scattered throughout the chapter—in order.

1. If I tell you that a *rogaritz* is usually white, is hard and dry, can be used to write on a blackboard, can fit comfortably in one hand, shouldn't be put in your mouth, and often creates a messy dust when used, can you tell me what a *rogaritz* is?

2. Which of the following is the best example of a piece of furniture: bed, lamp, chair, picture, stereo, telephone? Can you put these items in order in terms of the extent to which they represent examples of furniture?

3. Is "Colorless green ideas sleep furiously" a sentence in English? What about, "The dog looks terrifying"? Or, "The dog looks barking"?

4. In the figure to the right, the diameter of the circle is exactly 10 inches long. What is the length of line *L*? (From Köhler, 1969.)

5. One morning, exactly at sunrise, a Buddhist monk began to climb a tall mountain. A narrow path, only a foot or two wide, spiraled around the mountain to a glittering temple at the summit. The monk ascended at varying rates of speed, stopping many times along the way to rest and eat dried fruit he carried with him. He reached the temple shortly before sunset. After several days of fasting and meditation, he began his journey back down along the same path, starting at sunrise again and walking at variable speeds, with many pauses along the way. His average speed going down was, of course, greater than his average climbing speed. Show that there is a spot along the path the monk occupied on both trips at precisely the same time of day. (From Duncker, 1945.)

6. Imagine that you have a very large sheet of paper, 1/100 of an inch thick. Imagine folding it over on itself so that now you have two layers of paper. Fold it again so that there are four layers. It is impossible to actually fold a sheet of paper 50 times, but imagine that you could. About how thick would the paper be if it were folded 50 times? (From Adams, 1974.)

7. Without moving the book and without removing your standard pen or pencil from the page, connect the nine dots to the right with four (4) straight lines. (From Scheerer, 1963.)

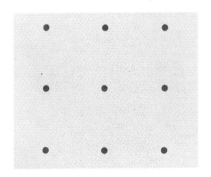

*C*ognitions include ideas, beliefs, thoughts, and images. When we know, understand, or remember something, we use cognitions to do so. Thus, cognitive processes involve the formation, manipulation, and use of cognitions. In this chapter, we will consider three complex cognitive tasks: concept formation, language use, and problem solving. Topic 7A deals with concepts—how they are formed and how they are used to communicate through language. In Topic 7B, we discuss problem solving. Because these cognitive tasks rely on perception, learning, and memory, I refer to them as "higher" cognitive processes.

Although the activities described in this chapter can qualify as higher cognitive processes, it should be clear that they are in no way rare or unusual. Particularly as a student, you encounter concept formation, effective communication with language, and problem solving as important, day-to-day activities. In your study of psychology, you have already formed many new concepts, some of them simple, some of them complex. Forming concepts, using language, and solving problems may be higher cognitive processes, but they are processes upon which we rely every day.

At first, the question "What is a chair?" may sound silly, but actually defining the concept in terms of attributes and rules that combine them is not easily done—even though we all "know" what a chair is.

Topic 7A

CONCEPTS AND LANGUAGE

THE CONCEPT OF CONCEPT

Think about chairs. Really. Take a minute or two to think about chairs. As you do this, try to notice what is happening.

Images come to mind. You can "see" a large variety of chairs. You may have thought about high chairs, armchairs, dining room chairs, rocking chairs, chairs in a classroom, easy chairs, chairs with smooth leather seats, broken chairs, overstuffed chairs upholstered with flowery fabric, kitchen chairs, and so on. We all know what a chair is. We have all formed a concept or a category that we've agreed to label *chair*.

As you thought about chairs, did any one particular chair—any one standard, definitional chair—come to mind? Were there any features or attributes that all chairs you thought of had in common? What are the defining characteristics of chairs? Most have four legs, but beanbag chairs have no legs at all. Most chairs are used for sitting, although we do stand on chairs to reach high places. Many chairs are used with tables, and some with desks. Most chairs have a back. However, if the back gets too low, you have a stool, not a chair. Chairs have limited widths: they usually hold only one person at a time. If they are wider, they are love seats or sofas. Chairs are usually considered to be pieces of furniture.

Now consider problem 1 (page 307). Did you figure out what a rogaritz is? Would you recognize a rogaritz if you saw one? If you know what a rogaritz is, you have acquired a new concept: the concept of rogaritz (after Werner & Kaplan, 1950). You recognize it as a piece of chalk. Because we already have a perfectly good word with which to label this concept, I suppose there's no reason to try to remember the new concept label "rogaritz."

I've asked you to go through these mental gymnastics so that you can better appreciate the definition of concept. A **concept** is the mental representation of a category, or class, of events or objects. Concepts represent categories, classes, or groups of things, not just individual cases.

A world without concepts would be unimaginable. If there were no way to mentally organize or classify our experiences, our impressions of our environments and of ourselves would be chaotic. *Because* we have a concept of chair, we do not have to treat every encounter with a chair as a new experience. We do not have to make up a new and different label, or word, for every chair we see, nor do we have to decide what a chair is every time we see one. We only have to recognize an object as having the characteristics appropriate for this category and refer to it as a chair. We may think of concepts as "building blocks for human thought and behavior" (Medin, 1989, p. 1469).

One way we can describe a concept is in terms of attributes or features that are related to each other according to some rule or rules. This *attribute-rule* approach is a classic view of concepts, and works fairly well for a concept such as chair. We have considered some of the *attributes* associated with the category of objects called "chair." Perhaps you've thought of others. The *rule* that relates these attributes is that chairs share many, if not all, of these attributes at the same time. Accordingly, learning a new concept is a matter of learning the attributes that characterize it and the rule that relates those attributes (Bourne et al., 1983).

Talking about attributes and the rules that unite them is useful and reasonable for some concepts, but what about concepts as they are encountered in real life? Is it always possible to define concepts in terms of attributes and rules? Real, or *natural concepts,* are often not easily defined. Much of our experience involves "fuzzy" concepts (Barsalou, 1989; Labov, 1973; Medin, 1989; Oden, 1987; Zadeh, 1965).

How would you describe the difference between a cup and a bowl? We know what a cup is, and we know what a bowl is, but sometimes there is no clear distinction between the two. Each is a fuzzy concept. If you think this distinction *is* clear, consider the drawings of cups in Figure 7.1. Do any of these "cups" look at least a little like a bowl? Consider the concept of "family" these days. What constitutes membership in the concept or category of "family"? A mom, a dad, and two children. Sure. What about single-parent families? (Remember the Murphy Brown–Dan Quayle brouhaha during the 1992 presidential campaign?) What about children being raised by gay or lesbian couples? Are these families? How does the definition of what constitutes a family change depending on one's culture? To what extent are grandparents taken to be "members of the family"—common in Asian cultures, but less so in Western cultures?

concept a mental representation of a category or class of events or objects

Membership in some categories or concepts is difficult to determine for all cases. These days, the concept of soldier *must be broad enough to include females, although women are seldom thought of as prototypical soldiers.*

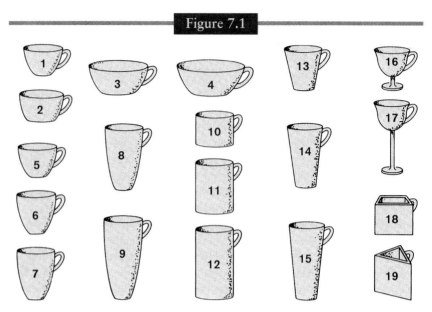

Just what is a cup? To some degree, each of these objects may be classified as members of the concept "cup," but some seem to be much better examples, suggesting that "cup" is a "fuzzy concept."

prototype *the member of a category that best typifies or represents that category*

One way to deal with the complication of fuzzy concepts is to follow the lead of Eleanor Rosch and her colleagues (1973, 1975, 1978). Rosch has proposed that we consider naturally occurring concepts in terms of **prototypes**. A prototype is a member of a category that best typifies or represents the category to which it belongs; it is the ideal or best member of the concept.

Rosch suggests that within our concept of chair, for example, there are some instances that are more typical and better examples—more "chairish" than others. A robin may be a prototypic bird. Crows are less prototypic. Vultures are even less so, and the fact that a penguin even *is* a bird can be difficult to remember. (For that matter, just who does decide on category membership? "Penguins, of course, really are birds biologically speaking, although it is not clear why we should be willing to give biologists the last word on the matter" [Oden, 1987, p. 215].)

Figure 7.2 lists members of a "furniture" category (Rosch, 1978). You can see which are the *best* examples of the concept of furniture. In this list you find the ranking of the terms presented in problem 2 on page 307. Within this category, *lamp* turns out be a poor example, and of the 60 items rated, *fan, ashtray,* and *telephone* ranked at the bottom of the list, barely qualifying as furniture.

In Rosch's view, some categories are poorly delineated and may spill over into others. Some instances of a concept provide good examples; others provide poor examples. Excellent examples (prototypes) share the largest number of attributes common to members of the category *and* have few attributes that cause them to be confused with others (Lasky & Kallio, 1978).

Using prototypes is one way to define natural concepts. In this way, a penguin is less prototypic than a robin for the concept of "bird."

As it happens, the prototype approach to defining concepts is not without a few problems of its own. For one thing, what we've said so far about this view fails to take context or situational variables into account. What does this mean? Essentially, the problem is that what is most typical, or prototypical, of a given category depends on the situation (e.g., Roth & Shoben, 1983). "Robin" may be a prototypic bird in some general, diffuse way, but not in the minds of hunters, out in the field with their "bird dogs." Is there really such a thing as a most typical "chair"? Don't we have to ask, "In what context?" What is the best example of a beverage? Water? Coffee? Tea? Beer? Soda? For whom and in what context?

Before You Go On

How can we use attributes and rules to define concepts?

How does the concept of prototype help our understanding of what a concept is?

FORMING CONCEPTS

By the time we get to be college students, our minds are crammed with a huge variety of mental representations. How were those concepts acquired? Where did they come from? Back in the seventeenth century, philosopher John Locke (1690) asked, "How comes it [the mind] to be furnished?" To his own question, Locke replied, "I answer in one word, from experience." Few psychologists today would argue with Locke's conclusion that concepts are learned—are acquired through experience.

Figure 7.2

Goodness of Example Rankings for the Concept "Furniture"

Member	Goodness of example rank	Member	Goodness of example rank	Member	Goodness of example rank
Chair	1.5	Vanity	21	Mirror	41
Sofa	1.5	Bookcase	22	Television	42
Couch	3.5	Lounge	23	Bar	43
Table	3.5	Chaise lounge	24	Shelf	44
Easy chair	5	Ottoman	25	Rug	45
Dresser	6.5	Footstool	26	Pillow	46
Rocking chair	6.5	Cabinet	27	Wastebasket	47
Coffee table	8	China closet	28	Radio	48
Rocker	9	Bench	29	Sewing machine	49
Love seat	10	Buffet	30	Stove	50
Chest of drawers	11	Lamp	31	Counter	51
Desk	12	Stool	32	Clock	52
Bed	13	Hassock	33	Drapes	53
Bureau	14	Drawers	34	Refrigerator	54
Davenport	15.5	Piano	35	Picture	55
End table	15.5	Cushion	36	Closet	56
Divan	17	Magazine rack	37	Vase	57
Night table	18	Hi-fi	38	Ashtray	58
Chest	19	Cupboard	39	Fan	59
Cedar chest	20	Stereo	40	Telephone	60

From Rosch, 1975.

A Classic Demonstration

Figure 7.3 shows some of the stimulus materials that Edna Heidbreder used in her 1946 study of concept formation. Stimuli in a set (there are five sets here) were presented to a subject in the study *one item at a time.* As each picture was presented, Heidbreder named it orally, using the nonsense label included in Figure 7.3 for the first three sets. The participants in the experiment *did not* see these names.

Subjects were told to learn the name associated with each picture. Each set of pictures was presented over and over until the correct name was paired with each picture. This wasn't too difficult to do, and soon subjects could provide a label for all items in set 1. Then the items in set 2 were presented one at a time. Subjects were asked to learn the label for each of *these* pictures. As you can see, the names for the items of set 2 are the same as those used for set 1.

This procedure was repeated for 16 different sets of pictures. Each time, the subjects had to learn the label or name associated with a picture. The pattern behind what Heidbreder was doing is obvious to us as we look at all of the pictures and their labels in Figure 7.3. It is clear that all drawings of people are labeled *relk.* Collections of six small things are named *mank.* Circular items are *fards,* and so on. *Ling* is the label for a concept—roughly, things appearing in pairs.

Figure 7.3

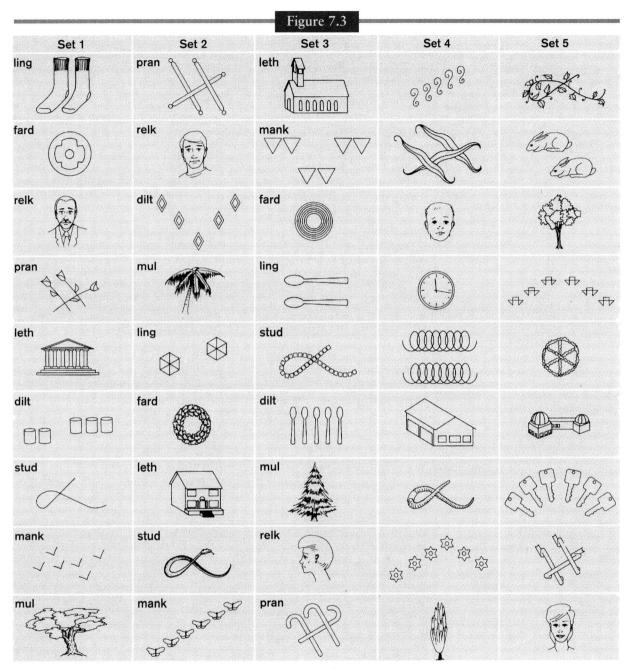

Sets of images Heidbreder used in her experiments on concept formation. As each image was presented, it was given a nonsense label (labels are shown for the first three sets). The subjects were presented the images and labels until they could provide the labels themselves. Thus, they came to label drawings of trees, for example, as "mul"—and a new concept had been formed.

Heidbreder's subjects eventually formed the same concepts you and I can see so clearly in Figure 7.3. Remember, though, that they were seeing these items one at a time, could not see the label, and didn't even realize they were in a concept formation experiment. They thought they were simply learning verbal labels for pictures.

As subjects progressed through the sets of picture-label pairs, they required fewer and fewer presentations to form the picture-label association. Toward the end, some subjects provided the correct response name for a pictured item even before Heidbreder had a chance to say it. Significantly, subjects often could not state what rule *or* attributes were underlying a particular concept, but they could identify new members of that concept. Among other things, this finding implies that we may form concepts we can use but cannot easily describe, or talk about, to others. Heidbreder's study not only suggested how we form (at least some) concepts, but convinced psychologists that concept formation tasks could be brought into the laboratory and studied systematically.

Developing Strategies and Testing Hypotheses

People in concept formation experiments often go about forming concepts in systematic ways. To be sure, some folks just guess at random whether a presented stimulus belongs in a given category, particularly at first. Most, however, develop some strategy to guide their responses (Bruner et al., 1956; Johnson, 1978). In this context, we may define a strategy as a systematic plan or procedure for identifying members of a category or concept.

One way to think about concept formation is to say that people go through a process of *hypothesis testing*. That is, they develop a

Sometimes we develop new concepts and new concept labels. When surfing and sailing combined to form a new sport, we had a new concept, commonly called "windsurfing."

hypothesis, or reasonable guess, about what is going on and test that hypothesis when presented with new stimuli. For example, saying to yourself "I think that all members of this concept are green" is a hypothesis. You test it by finding another green stimulus and seeing if it also fits within the category.

Notice that this approach to concept formation works whether we are dealing with concepts defined in terms of rules and attributes or natural categories defined in terms of prototypes. In the former, classical case, hypotheses about specific attributes and rules are formed and tested. In the latter, probabilistic case, new stimuli are tested in terms of their similarity to a prototype (Posner & Keele, 1968, 1970).

In a sense, concepts are formed in accord with theories we have about the world. For example, "I think a spider looks a lot like my idea of what an insect is. It may not be the best example of an insect, but it sure looks like one to me." When you test this hypothesis (perhaps in a biology class), you discover you're wrong, because as much as a spider may appear similar to your prototypic insect, it happens to belong in a different category (that of *arachnid*).

This hypothesis-testing view of concept formation helps explain the presence of some concepts that are otherwise difficult to account for (Medin, 1989). Consider this list: *children, money, photo albums,* and *pets*. Are they in any way members of the same category, or concept? Once I tell you that I am thinking about "items to remove quickly if one's house is on fire," the list makes perfectly good sense, because it fits our view, our theory, of the way the world works, or should work (Barsalou, 1983).

Notice also that forming concepts requires the active involvement of one's memory. When presented with a new stimulus, we retrieve from memory, other similar stimuli and make judgments concerning whether we can match the new stimulus with any already-existing category or concept. If the newly presented stimulus matches the prototypic example of a concept (stored in memory), we will have little difficulty adding it to our preexisting concept. If the new stimulus does *not* match a prototype, we have to decide if we're faced with a poor example of a known concept or if we should devise a new category to include the new stimulus (Stern, 1985).

What many experiments since Heidbreder's in 1946 have demonstrated is that we form concepts in a very systematic way, based on what we know at the time, developing strategies and testing hypotheses. But even as Heidbreder's study suggests, people cannot always tell us what strategies they are using. For example, young children (ages 6 to 8) have a very reasonable notion of the concept of *family*, but even much older children (ages 12 and 13) can seldom tell you the rule, attributes, or prototype that defines *family* for them (Watson & Amgott-Kwan, 1984).

We have defined the concept of concept and have seen some of the ways in which concepts are formed. Now we will see how the cognitive process of language use allows us to communicate to others our concepts, or mental representations, of the world.

Before You Go On

What does Edna Heidbreder's classic study of
concept formation tell us about the process?

What does it mean to say that people use
hypothesis testing in forming concepts?

LANGUAGE

Because we form concepts, we bring order and economy to our
understanding of objects and events in the world. Because we use language, we are able to communicate that understanding to others. In
this sense, using language is a social process, which reflects a mar-
velously complex cognitive activity. The philosopher Suzanne Langer
put it this way:

> Language is, without a doubt, the most momentous and at the same
> time the most mysterious product of the human mind. Between the
> clearest animal call of love or warning or anger, and a man's least, triv-
> ial *word*, there lies a whole day of Creation—or in modern phrase, a
> whole chapter of evolution. (1951, p. 94)

psycholinguistics the science that studies the cognitive processes involved in the use and acquisition of language

In this section, we'll review some of the issues involved in the subfield of psychology called psycholinguistics. **Psycholinguistics** is a
hybrid discipline, consisting of scientists trained in psychology *and*
linguistics. Psycholinguists "are interested in the underlying knowledge and abilities which people must have in order to use language
and to learn language in childhood" (Slobin, 1979, p. 2). First, let's
define the concept of language.

Let's Talk: What *Is* Language?

language a large collection of arbitrary symbols that have significance for a language-using community and that follow certain rules of combination

How shall we characterize this mysterious product of the human
mind called language? **Language** is a large collection of arbitrary symbols that have significance for a language-using community, and that
follow certain rules of combination (after Morris, 1946). Now let's
pull apart this definition and examine the points it raises.

First, language consists of a large number of *symbols*. The symbols that constitute language are commonly referred to as words—
labels we have assigned to concepts, or our mental representations.
When we use the word *chair* as a symbol, we don't use it to label one
specific instance of a chair. We use the word as a symbol to represent
our concept of chairs. Notice that as symbols, words do not have to
stand for real things in the real world. We have words to describe
objects or events that cannot be perceived directly, such as *ghost* or,
for that matter, *mind*. With language, we can communicate about
owls and pussycats in teacups; four-dimensional, time-warped hyper-
space; and a beagle that flies his doghouse into battle against the Red
Baron. Words stand for our cognitions, our concepts, and we have a
great number of them. They allow us to communicate what we know.

It is important that we define the symbols of language as being *arbitrary*. By doing so we imply that there is no requirement or reason for representing anything with the particular symbol we do. You call what you are reading a book (or a textbook, to use a more specific symbol). We have all agreed (in English) that *book* is the appropriate symbol for what you are reading. But we don't have to. We could agree to call it a *relm*. Or a *poge*. The symbols of a language are arbitrary; they are not genetically determined. They can be whatever we like, but once established by common use or tradition, they become part of one's language and must be learned and applied consistently by each new language user.

To be part of a language, at least in a practical sense, language symbols need to have *significance for a language-using community.* That is, people have to agree on the symbols used in a language and have to agree on what those symbols mean. This is another way of saying that language use is a social enterprise. For example, there is a language-using community for which *"Kedinin üstünde halt var"* makes sense, or has significance. I'm not part of that community, but many people are. To them—to people who know Turkish—the statement reads, roughly, "The cat is on the mat" (Slobin, 1979, p. 4). You and I might decide to call what you are now reading a *relm*, but then you and I would be in a terribly small language-using community. We're better off going along with the majority and using the word *book*.

The final part of our definition tells us that the symbols of a language must *follow certain rules of combination.* What this means is that language is structured. Language is rule-governed. Language is used to communicate ideas, to share our thoughts and feelings with others. Of course, there are ways of communicating that do not involve language. What makes language use a special form of communication is the fact that it is governed by rules of combination. For one thing, there are rules about how we can and cannot string symbols together in language. In English, we say, "The small boy slept late." We do not say, "Slept boy late small the." Well, we could say it, but no one will know for sure exactly what we mean by it, and everyone will recognize that the utterance violates the combinatorial rules of English. When the rules of language are violated, utterances lose their meaning, and the value of language as a means of communication is lost. I'll have much more to say about the structure of language in the next section.

Even with this complex definition of language, there are a few points left out. For one, using language is a remarkably *creative, generative* process; very few of the utterances we make are utterances we've ever made before or even encountered before. It's unlikely, for example, that you have ever before read a sentence just like this one. Almost every time we use our language, we use it in a new and creative way, which emphasizes the importance of the underlying rules, or structure, of language. Another point: language allows for *displacement*—the ability to communicate about the "*not* here and the *not* now." We can use language to talk about yesterday's lunch and

Although the symbols of a language are arbitrary, many people have to agree on what the symbols are, what they mean, and how they will be used.

Language is a vehicle for communicating our understanding of events to others.

tomorrow's class schedule. We can talk about things that aren't here, never were, and never will be. Language is the only form of communication that allows us to do so.

Finally: Language and speech are not synonymous terms. Speech is but one way in which language is expressed as behavior. There are others, including writing, coding (as in Morse code), or signing (as in American Sign Language).

Before You Go On

What are some of the defining characteristics of language?

Describing the Structure in Language

When psycholinguists analyze a language, they usually do so at three levels. The first level involves the sounds that are used when we express the language as speech. The second level deals with the meaning of words and sentences, and the third concerns the rules used for combining words and phrases to generate sentences. At all three levels, we can see structure and rules at work.

Speech Sounds and Structure. Individual speech sounds of a language are called **phonemes**. These are the sounds we make when we talk to each other. Phonemes themselves have no meaning, but when they are put together in the proper order, the result is a meaningful utterance. The word *cat*, for example, consists of three phonemes: the initial consonant sound (a "k" sound here), the vowel sound of "a," and a final consonant sound, "t." How phonemes are combined to

phoneme the smallest unit of sound in the spoken form of a language produce words and phrases is rule-governed. If we were to inter-change the two consonant sounds in *cat,* we would have an altogether different utterance, *tack,* with an altogether different meaning. There are approximately 45 phonemes in English. (Because those 45 sounds are represented by only 26 letters in our alphabet, it is no wonder many of us have problems spelling.)

To use a language requires that one knows which speech sounds are part of that language and how they may be combined to form larger language units. For example, the difference between *time, climb, rhyme,* and *grime* is the initial phoneme, or phonemes, of each utterance. We recognize each of these as acceptable words in English. We also recognize that *blime* and *frime* are not English words, although we also know that they could be. The "bl" and "fr" sound combinations of *blime* and *frime* are acceptable in English: they fol-low the rules. You recognize that *gzlime* or *wbime* are not words. They violate the English rules for combining sounds into words.

Before You Go On

What are phonemes, and in what way are they rule-governed?

Meaning and Structure. Describing a language's phonemes, not-ing which sounds are relevant and which combinations are possible, is only a small part of a complete description of a language. Another level of analysis involves *meaning* in the language. The study of mean-ing in language is called **semantics.**

Researchers interested in semantics take the morpheme as their unit of analysis. A **morpheme** is the smallest unit of meaning in a spo-ken language. A morpheme is a collection of phonemes that means something. In most cases, *morpheme* and *word* are synonymous. In addition to words, morphemes include all of the prefixes and suffixes of a language. For example, *write* is a morpheme and a word; it has meaning, and it is not possible to subdivide it into smaller, meaningful units. *Rewrite* is also a word and has meaning, but it consists of two morphemes, *write* and *re,* which in this context has meaning—rough-ly, "write it again." *Tablecloth* is a word composed of two mor-phemes, *table* and *cloth.* When we change a noun from singular to plural—*boy* to *boys* or *ox* to *oxen,* for example—we are adding a morpheme to the noun (a morpheme that indicates plurality and that changes our meaning).

Notice that how we generate morphemes is governed by rules. For example, we cannot go around making nouns plural in any old way. The plural of ox is oxen, not oxes. The plural of mouse is mice, not mouses, mousen, or meese. If I want you to write something over again, I have to ask you to *rewrite* it, not *write-re* it. Note too, how morphemes are verbal labels for concepts (mental representations).

semantics the study of the meaning of words and sentences

morpheme the smallest unit of meaning in a language

Asking you to rewrite something would make no sense if we did not share a concept of "writing" and a concept of "doing things over again."

Before You Go On

What is semantics?

What are morphemes?

Sentences and Structure. The aspect of our language that most obviously uses rules is the generation of sentences—stringing words (or morphemes) together to create meaningful utterances (Hörmann, 1986). The rules that govern how sentences are formed (or structured) in a language are referred to as the **syntax** of a language.

To know the syntax, or syntactic rules, of one's language involves a peculiar sort of knowledge or cognitive ability. We all know the rules of English in the sense that we can and do use them, but few of us know what those rules are in the sense that we can tell anyone else what they are. We say that people have a *competence,* a cognitive ability that governs their language use. That ability allows us to judge the extent to which an utterance is a meaningful, well-formed sentence. Competence with the syntactic rules of English can be demonstrated with a few examples of what are called linguistic intuitions (Howard, 1983; Slobin, 1979). **Linguistic intuitions** are judgments about the extent to which utterances are acceptable in a language. What makes them intuitive is that we make these judgments without being able to specify exactly how they are being made.

For example, we know that "The dog looks terrifying" fits the rules of English and that "The dog looks barking" does not. Somehow, we recognize that "The dog looks watermelon" is downright absurd. The first utterance means something. The second and third do not. At the same time, we recognize that the utterance "Colorless green ideas sleep furiously" does fit the rules of English, even though it doesn't make any sense (Chomsky, 1957). It may be a silly thing to say, but we realize intuitively that it is an acceptable thing to say.

We also know that these two utterances communicate the same message, even though they look (and sound) quite different:

The student read the textbook.
The textbook was read by the student.

In either case, we know who is doing what. Putting this basic idea into either of two forms can change the psychological focus of what is being said. In the first case, we find out what the student did, and in the second, we focus on the notion that it was the textbook that was read. The way elements are structured in language affects the meaning

syntax the rules that govern how the morphemes of a language may be combined to form meaningful utterances

linguistic intuitions judgments or decisions about the syntactic acceptability of utterances without the ability to specify why

of what is being communicated. Semantics and syntax cannot be separated.

Another linguistic intuition that demonstrates our competence with the rules of our language is in our ability to detect ambiguity. Consider these two sentences:

They are cooking apples.
They are cooking apples.

There is no doubt that they appear to be identical, but upon reflection we can see that they may be communicating very different (ambiguous) ideas. In one case, we may be talking about what some people are cooking (apples as opposed to spaghetti). In another, we may be identifying a variety of apple (those best suited for cooking as opposed to those best suited for eating). In yet another case, we may be describing what is being done to the apples (cooking them as opposed to eating them). You may be able to think of yet other ways in which this simple sentence can be interpreted.

In part, this sentence is ambiguous only if we are not aware of the context in which it was used. Is the sentence in response to a question about what some people are doing or in response to a question about different types of apples? This is not an isolated example of ambiguity in language. There are many, such as, "The shooting of the policemen was terrible," or "Flying airplanes can be dangerous." When we start referring to context, we again are reminded of the *social* nature of language use.

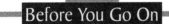

Before You Go On

What is syntax?

What are linguistic intuitions?

Language Use as a Social Process

The main reason for language is communication. Language helps us share our thoughts, feelings, intentions, and experiences with others. Language is social behavior. **Pragmatics** is the study of how linguistic events are related to the social context in which they occur. Our understanding of sarcasm (as in "Well, it certainly is a beautiful day!" when in fact it is rainy, cold, and miserable), or simile (as in "Life is like a sewer . . . "), or metaphor (as in "His slam dunk to start the second half delivered the knockout blow"), or cliché (as in "It rained cats and dogs") depends on many things, including our appreciation of the context of the utterance and the intention of the speaker.

Pragmatics involves decisions made by language users that are based on the perception of the social situation at the moment. Think how you modify your language use when you talk to your best friend, a preschool child, a professor in her office, or a poor driver who cut

pragmatics the study of how social context affects the meaning of linguistic events

you off at an intersection. Contemporary concerns about "political correctness" seem relevant here, don't they? In some contexts, words such as *pig, Uncle Tom, boy,* and *girl* can be reasonable and proper, while in other contexts they may evoke angry responses. In many American Indian cultures, periods of silence—even lengthy periods of silence—during conversation are acceptable and common. Someone not familiar with this pragmatic reality could become anxious and upset about long pauses in the midst of a conversation (e.g., Basso, 1970; Brislin, 1993, pp. 217–221). Once again, how you use language to communicate depends on certain general rules you have acquired about matching one's style of speech—in terms of formality, content, complexity, intonation, intensity, and so on—to the social situation.

One part of the social context of language communication psychologists have researched is the gender of the language user. Are there differences in the ways men and women use language? What few differences in "language style" do exist depend mostly on pragmatics—the context and purpose of the conversation. Even so, differences are slight (Pearson et al., 1991; Simkins-Bullock & Wildman, 1991). For example, men are more talkative than are women and are more likely to interrupt the speech of others (Key, 1975). *In some situations,* the speech of women is less assertive than that of men, and includes more hedges, qualifiers, and indirect statements such as, "It seems to me that ... " or "In my opinion ... " or "The test wasn't really quite so bad" (Lakoff, 1975; Quina et al., 1987). *In some situations,* women are more likely than men to make "self-disclosing" statements, which means that they are more likely to share ideas and feelings about themselves (Cozby, 1973).

To understand the cognitive competence people must have to use language requires understanding how we use the sounds (phonemes) of spoken language, how we assign meaning to morphemes, how we combine words and morphemes to form sentences, and how we alter our language to match the social situation. Next, we look at developmental psycholinguistics—the study of language acquisition.

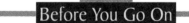

Before You Go On

What is pragmatics, and what can it tell us about language use?

Language Acquisition

One of the most significant achievements of childhood is the acquisition of language. There are few, if any, cognitive skills that can compare to language use in complexity and utility. How children acquire language skills has been a concern of many psycholinguists. The process seems nearly magical: gooing, cooing, babbling one day, then

When violin teacher Shinichi Suzuki realized how easily and quickly children acquire language at an early age, Suzuki reasoned that children could acquire violin-playing skills in much the same way, and the so-called Suzuki Method of instruction was born.

a word or two, then "Why is the sky blue, Daddy, why is the sky blue?"—and all in the span of just a few months' time.

Steven Pinker, director of the Center for Cognitive Science at MIT, calls language acquisition "the jewel in the crown of cognition—it is what everyone wants to explain" (deCuevas, 1990, p. 63). At best, we have tentative theories and hypotheses. We are only now getting reasonably close to adequately describing *what* happens. Describing *how* it happens will take longer.

What Happens in Language Acquisition. We've seen that language can be described at three levels: sounds (phonemes), meanings (morphemes), and structure (syntax). Let's consider the development of each of these facets of language use in turn.

Infants create speech sounds spontaneously. They come into the world with a cry, and make noise with regularity forever after. At about the age of 6 months, random cries and noises are replaced by the more regular sounds of **babbling**. Babbling is the production of speech phonemes, often in repetitive, rhythmic patterns. A curiosity is that when children babble, they do so by producing all of the known phonemes of all known languages. Phonemes that are not part of one's language eventually drop out of the child's repertoire. All babies babble in the same general way (Nakazima, 1962; Oller, 1981). An adult cannot distinguish the babbling of a Chinese infant from that of a Greek infant or an American infant. Even deaf infants produce babbling sounds that are indistinguishable from those of hearing children (Lenneberg et al., 1965).

The acquisition of vocabulary follows soon after babbling begins. In all cases, comprehension, or understanding, comes before production. Children understand and respond appropriately to the meaning of utterances long before they are able to produce those utterances themselves. A child's first word or two usually appears at about the

babbling speech phonemes produced in rhythmic, repetitive patterns

age of 1 year (parents often argue that the onset of meaningful speech is earlier, but independent observers often fail to confirm what may be parental wishful thinking). Once it begins, word or morpheme acquisition is remarkable. A 1-year-old may produce only two or three words (remember, he or she may very well understand dozens of words, but can produce only a few). By the age of 2 years, word production is up to about 50. In terms of comprehension, by age 2, a child understands 200 to 300 words; by age 3, over 1,000; and by age 6, somewhere between 8,000 and 14,000 (Benedict, 1979; Brown, 1973; Carey, 1978).

Describing the development of syntactic rules in children has proven difficult. For one thing, as linguists began to understand the rules that govern adult language, it seemed reasonable to look for these same rules in the language of children. What soon became apparent was that the syntax of adult forms of language do not emerge until long after children have begun stringing words and morphemes together in utterances. Even though we do not find adult structure or rules in the language use of very young children, they still use language in a rule-governed way. In other words, young children do not speak adult language badly; instead, their language follows its own rules (e.g., Radford, 1990).

The first use of vocalization as language is called **holophrastic speech**. Holophrastic speech is the use of just one word to communicate a range of intentions and meanings dependent on gestures, intonation, and so on. Before this stage is apparent, a child may produce a number of words, but will do so only as a naming exercise. Words are used as labels for concepts and nothing else. With holophrastic speech, individual words are used to communicate a range of possibilities. Imagine it yourself. Picture a young child sitting in a high chair. Can't you just see how the one-word utterance *milk* could be used to communicate such things as *"I want my milk!"* or "Uh-oh, I dropped my milk," or "Oh yea! here's my milk," or "Yuck, not milk again."

At about the age of 2 years, we can note the appearance of two-word utterances. When carefully analyzed, these two-word utterances are very regular, as if they were being put together according to strict rules. Given an understanding of the words *big* and *little* and many nouns, a child may say, "big ball," "big plane," "big doggie," "little stick," "little cup," and so on. What is curious is that this child will never reverse this word order. He or she will not say "ball big" or "cup little" (Braine, 1976).

From the point of the two-word utterance on, language development—syntax development—is so rapid that it is difficult to even note the stages through which the process passes. From the two-word utterance stage there is a period typified by **telegraphic speech**—spoken language consisting of nouns, verbs, and adjectives, but hardly any "function words" such as articles or prepositions. We hear children say such things as "Daddy go store" or "Billy draw pictures." Then, at roughly age 2 years, language use expands at an explosive rate. There really is no noticeable three-word or four-word stage of development. Phrases are lengthened, noun phrases first, so that "Billy's ball" becomes "Billy's red ball," which soon becomes "Billy's

holophrastic speech the use of one word to communicate a number of meanings

telegraphic speech utterances characterized by the use of nouns, verbs, and adjectives, and generally few "function words"

red ball that Mommy got at the store." By the time children are ready to begin grade school, at about age 5, they demonstrate both the understanding and the production of virtually every acceptable type of sentence structure in their language. Now that we have a basic idea of what happens when children acquire language, we'll briefly consider how psycholinguists try to account for the process.

Before You Go On

What are some of the landmark events that occur during language acquisition?

Theories of Language Acquisition. How does language acquisition happen? If you took a foreign language in high school or are taking one now, did it ever occur to you that there were children somewhere in the world who were acquiring the same language you were struggling with but were not having any problems with it at all. Acquiring one's language is a cognitive feat at which all (normal) humans succeed.

Have you noticed that I have referred to language *acquisition* or language *development*, but have avoided any reference to language *learning*? This was intentional because I do not want to suggest that acquiring language is simply a matter of learning. On the other hand, language is certainly not innate or instinctive in the usual sense, or everyone would speak the very same language. What we have here is a reminder of an observation made in Topic 1B: Our biological nature and our psychological nurture interact to make us who we are. Some of language acquisition can be accounted for by learning (in ways discussed in Chapter 5), but some aspects of language acquisition defy explanation in terms of learning and suggest an inherited basis for language acquisition.

Theories of language development in terms of learning (e.g., Skinner, 1957; Whitehurst, 1982) certainly have their place. No one will claim that language emerges free of the influence of learning, experience, conditioning, reinforcement, and the like. We can be most comfortable with learning approaches when we try to account for the acquisition of phonemes and morphemes. Indeed, acquiring the phonemes of one's language seems to be a straightforward process, albeit slightly backward. The infant spontaneously produces phonemes from all languages, but learns, through imitation and reinforcement, which sounds need to be "saved" for use in his or her language. Speech sounds not appropriate for the child's language are simply not used and disappear from the child's repertoire (deVillers & deVillers, 1978).

Learning theories are not terribly strained when it comes to the acquisition of words and morphemes. What we're dealing with here is largely the development of labels for concepts—concepts that are, clearly, learned, as we noted earlier in this Topic. There are, no doubt, many varieties of learning involved in word acquisition. Some of the meaning of words comes from classical conditioning. The use of some words or morphemes is reinforced and the use of others is not, as operant conditioning predicts. Some vocabulary growth results from observational learning—using words that others use. Some words develop through direct instruction. In general, learning seems to handle morpheme acquisition rather nicely, but there are a few problems.

For one thing, as children acquire morphemes that change the meaning of a word (called bound morphemes), they do so with a disturbing regularity. For no good reason that learning theory can account for, children learn to add *-ing* to words before they learn to form possessives (by adding *-'s*), which they learn before learning to form the past tense of verbs (by adding *-ed*). That is, when asked what he is doing, a child may be expected first to respond, "I draw." Later will come "I drawing." Only after the *-ing* morpheme is in use may we expect "That Billy's picture." Only later will we hear something like "I drawed it yesterday." In other words, there is a predictable sequence in which many morphemes are acquired. This may reflect limits set by the child's genetic constitution, or it may reflect limits set by the child's cognitive growth (i.e., he or she may not understand the basic concept of past tense until the concept of possessive is acquired), but in either case, simple learning theory is strained.

Another example that provides a problem for learning theory is called **overregularization**. By definition, overregularization is the continued application of an acquired language rule (e.g., for forming plurals or past tense) in a situation for which it is not appropriate. A child might say, "I have two foots," or "four mans," or "I goed to the store," even after using the words *feet, men,* and *went* appropriately in similar contexts. What accounts for overregularization? Biologically oriented theories (e.g., Chomsky, 1965, 1975, 1986; Lenneberg, 1967; McNeil, 1970) suggest that there must be some innate, "prewired" biological mechanism that compels the child to seek out and apply rules during acquisition. This mechanism (called a *language acquisition device,* or LAD), becomes active and useful when we are about 1 year old, and usually turns off by the time we are 5 or 6 years old. The child is so predisposed to find and use rules that she or he will do so with consistency, even when a particular application of the rule is wrong. In many ways, "two foots" is a more reasonable construction than "two feet," even though "two foots" is not likely to have been heard in adult speech (Anisfeld, 1984).

Reliance on some sort of innate LAD becomes even more sensible when we consider the acquisition of rules reflected in the generation of sentences. (I should add that nobody has the slightest idea of what an LAD would look like, where it would be found, or exactly how it would work.) The argument for an innate predisposition for the acquisition of language rules comes once again from the orderliness of language development. The ages of the children are not always the same, but with uncanny regularity, children everywhere go about acquiring their different languages in virtually the same pattern. The phenomenon of holophrastic speech, the stability of the two-word utterance, the expansion of noun phrases, and the ordered acquisition

overregularization the excessive application of an acquired language rule (e.g., for plurals or past tense) in a situation for which it is not appropriate

of bound morphemes has been noted over and over as a consistent pattern—a pattern much more consistent than we could ever expect of the learning histories of the children being observed (Slobin, 1979).

Another point often raised against the learning approach is that when it comes to the rules of syntax, most adults cannot begin to tell us what the rules of their language *are*. How, then, can you teach something to someone else if you haven't got any idea yourself of what it is you're teaching? The argument is sensible. Yet, there is the logic that as adults we *do* have certain linguistic intuitions. We can tell when an utterance is correctly formed, even if we can't specify why. We can use this intuition to reinforce proper use and to correct improper use. When we carefully watch adults interacting with young children, however, we find that they are much more likely to correct the *content* of what the child says than the *form* in which it is said. If a child says, "Me no like cereal," a parent is likely to respond with a statement such as, "Sure you do; you eat it all the time" (Brown, 1973; Brown et al., 1969).

Here's the way Mabel Rice summarized some of these issues:

> There is a remarkable similarity in the general acquisition sequence for language skills across languages and cultures, although there is considerable individual variability in learning strategies and rate of acquisition. . . . Explicit language teaching from adults is not necessary. In fact, if adults try to structure and direct a child's language learning, the outcome may be interference . . . . (1989, p. 153)

So, when it comes to explaining language acquisition, where are we? We're far from final answers, but we seem to be where we commonly are when faced with two opposing theoretical positions—particularly when one position favors learning (or nurture) and the other favors innate factors (or nature). Some aspects of language are learned. For most language acquisition processes, learning, reinforcement, and imitation provide unsatisfactory explanations. A reasonably conservative position, for now, is an interactionist position: humans are born with a predisposition to acquire certain aspects of language. Which language they acquire, and which aspects, will reflect their experiences in their language-using community.

Before You Go On

Briefly summarize the learning-oriented and biologically oriented theories of language acquisition.

TOPIC 7A SUMMARY

In this Topic, we have examined two related and complex cognitive processes: concept formation and language use. Concepts are mental representations of the world, both real and imagined. Concepts represent classes, or categories, of objects and events, and in so doing, help us bring order and meaningfulness to our everyday experiences. In a formal sense, concepts may be defined in terms of attributes of objects or events and the rules that unite those attributes. Concepts may also be defined in terms of the extent to which objects or events are similar to prototypic, best examples of category membership.

Most of our concepts can be symbolized by words—the meaningful, arbitrary units of language. Language use provides an excellent example of structured, rule-governed behavior at three levels of analysis: sound (phonemes), meaning (morphemes), and morpheme order (syntax). All language users demonstrate a knowledge—a competence—of the rules of their language, whether or not they can state explicitly what those rules are. It is this competence, this implicit knowledge of the structure of one's language, that is most difficult to account for when one considers how language is acquired.

Some problems are ill defined, such as the problem of where to go to college and which classes to take.

Topic 7B
PROBLEM SOLVING

Our daily lives are filled with problems of various sorts. Some are simple, straightforward, or trivial; others are complex and very important to us. In this Topic, we'll focus our attention on cognitive, or intellectual, problems: those that require the manipulation of cognitions for their solution. The first thing to do is define what a problem is, and then to consider how we can go about solving one. Solving problems requires several interrelated processes. First, we need to recognize that a problem exists. Then we have to decide how to represent the problem in such a way as to maximize our chances of solving it. Then we have to devise some strategy to help us reach the goal of solving the problem. Finally, we have to assess whether or not our proposed solution actually does solve the problem at hand.

As was the case for concept formation and language use, problem solving is a "higher" cognitive process. It requires that we *perceive* the nature of the problem and *learn* the most efficient path toward a solution, using our *memories* as we go along.

WHAT *IS* A PROBLEM?

Sometimes our goals are obvious, our present situation is clear, and the way to get from where we are to where we want to be is also obvious. In such cases, we really don't have a problem, do we? Say you want to have a nice breakfast. You have eggs, bacon, and bread available. You also have the implements needed to prepare these foods, and you know how to use them. You know that, for you, a nice breakfast would be two eggs over easy, three strips of fried bacon, and a piece of buttered toast. With little hesitation, you engage in the appropriate behaviors and reach your goal.

On the other hand, a **problem** exists when there is a discrepancy between one's present state and one's perceived goal state *and* there is

problem *a situation in which there is a discrepancy between one's current state and one's desired, or goal, state, with no clear way of getting from one to the other*

no readily apparent way to get from one to the other. In situations in which the path to goal attainment is not clear, a problem exists, and you need to engage in problem-solving behaviors—as might be the case if halfway through the preparation of breakfast, you discover you have no butter or margarine.

A problem-solving situation has three major components: (1) an *initial state*, which is the situation as it exists, or is perceived to exist, at the moment; (2) a *goal state*, the situation as the problem solver would like it to be, or the end product; and (3) *possible routes or strategies* for getting from the initial state to the goal state.

Psychologists also make a distinction between well-defined and ill-defined problems. Well-defined problems are those in which both the initial state and the goal state are clearly defined. We know what the current situation is, know what the goal is, and may even know some of the possible ways to go about getting from one to the other. "What English word can be made from the letters *teralbay*?" We recognize this question as presenting a problem. We understand what the question is asking, have some ideas about how we might go about answering it, and will surely know when we have succeeded. "How do you get home from campus if you discover that your car, which is in the campus parking lot, won't start?" Again, we know our initial state (on campus with a car that won't start), and we'll know when we have reached our goal (when we're at home), but we have to find a different way to get there.

Most of the problems you and I face every day are of the ill-defined variety. In such cases, we do not have a clear idea of what we are starting with, nor are we able to clearly identify or define any one ideal solution. "What should my college major be?" Many high school seniors (and some college seniors) don't even know what their options are. They have few ideas about how to find out about college majors. And, once they have selected a major, they're not at all sure that their choice was the best one—which may explain why so many college students change their majors so often.

"Write the script for a movie that will be a smashing success." The screenwriter certainly knows what a script is and probably knows what the producers mean by "smashing success." Beyond that, however, this problem is certainly ill defined. This is the same sort of ill-defined problem you may face when assigned to write a term paper. All you may know is that the paper must be on some topic in psychology, at least 15 pages long, well-written, and original! Because ill-defined problems usually involve many variables that are difficult to define (much less, control), psychologists usually study problems that are at least reasonably well defined.

Before You Go On

What are the three components of a problem?

Contrast well-defined and ill-defined problems.
Give an example of each.

PROBLEM REPRESENTATION

Once we realize we're facing a problem, the first thing we should do is put it in some form that allows us to think about it in familiar terms. We need to come up with a way to *represent* the problem in our own minds, interpreting the problem so that the initial state and the goal state are clear to us. We also need to note if there are any restrictions on how we can go about seeking solutions. (For a crude example, if you were charged with determining whether male or female cats swim better, you could hardly just throw one of each into a pool to see which survived the longest.) In short, we need to understand the nature of the problem. We should try to make the problem meaningful, relating it to information we have available in our memories.

By examining a few of the problems of the sort that have been used in the psychology laboratory, we can see that how we choose to represent a problem can be critical. Consider problem 4 at the beginning of this chapter. The problem was to calculate the length of line L. On first inspection, you might decide that this problem is just too difficult to attempt, requiring an in-depth knowledge of trigonometry or geometry. But if you work with the representation of the problem for a moment, you may recognize that if you know the diameter of the circle is 10 inches, any radius of the circle must be 5 inches long. That in itself doesn't help much until you see that line L is a diagonal of the rectangle, and that the other diagonal is a radius of the circle. It then becomes obvious that line L must be 5 inches long (see Figure 7.4). If the problem's initial state is not restated, or represented, in this way, the problem is very difficult to solve.

Now refer to problem 5, about a monk climbing up a mountain to a temple and then back again. Thinking about this problem as it is presented—in words—can be maddening. You may picture yourself walking up and down a mountain, mentally visualizing a narrow path, trying to find a point on the path at which you might be at precisely the same time on two different days.

As is often the case with real-life problems, this statement of the problem contains a good deal of irrelevant information. Useful problem representation often involves sorting out what matters and what doesn't. The fact that we're dealing with a monk is not relevant, and neither are the temple, the dried fruit, the fact that the path is a narrow one, or that the trip was made on two different days.

You might think about, or represent, this problem in terms of just one climber making the trip in one day. Or, better still, imagine that there are two climbers: one starting from the top of the mountain, the other starting from the bottom. Because both take the same path, surely they will meet somewhere on that mountain trail sometime during the day (see Figure 7.5). When you represent the problem this way, the solution becomes readily apparent. So, it might help to represent the mountain-climbing problem visually, drawing out the ascending and descending pathways on a sheet of paper.

As it happens, visually representing the problem presented in Figure 7.6 would not be wise. One can readily imagine a subject

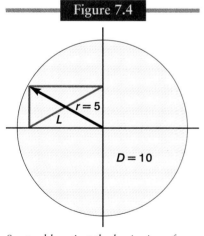

Figure 7.4

See problem 4 at the beginning of Chapter 7. Here we have an example of a problem in which representation is critical. The diagonal of this circle is exactly 10 inches long. What, then, is the length of line L? (From Köhler, 1969.)

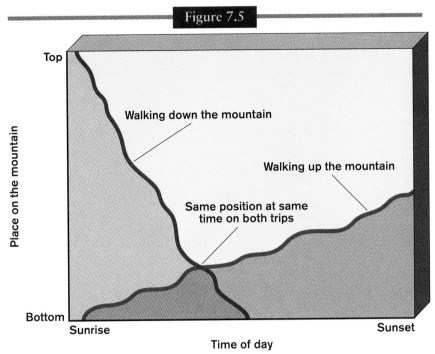

Figure 7.5

Top

Place on the mountain

Walking down the mountain

Walking up the mountain

**Same position at same
time on both trips**

Bottom

Sunrise

Sunset

Time of day

*See problem 5 at the beginning of Chapter 7. A way to represent graphically the
problem of a hill-climbing monk to make its solution more accessible.*

working on this problem by drawing little train stations with trains
moving toward each other, tracing the path of a bird racing back and
forth between the trains. If you tried this, you discovered it didn't
help much.

Instead of visualizing this problem, think about the logic
involved. The stations are 50 miles apart, and the trains travel at 25
mph. At this rate, how long will it take for the trains to meet? Exactly
one hour. You also know that the bird flies at a rate of 100 mph. If
the bird flies for one hour (back and forth—or any place else for that

Figure 7.6

Another Problem Whose Solution May Depend on
How It Is Represented by the Problem Solver

Two train stations are fifty miles apart. At 2:00 P.M. one Saturday afternoon two
trains start toward each other, one from each station. Just as the trains pull out
of the stations, a bird springs into the air in front of the first train and flies ahead
to the front of the second train. When the bird reaches the second train it turns
back and flies toward the first train. The bird continues to do this, flying back
and forth between the two trains until the trains meet.

If both trains travel at the rate of twenty-five miles per hour and the bird flies at
one hundred miles per hour, how many miles will the bird have flown before the
two trains meet?

From Posner, 1973.

matter), how far will it fly? Right. Exactly 100 miles. As with most problems, solutions become more accessible when they are represented as simply as possible.

As a final example of the importance of problem representation, consider problem 6 at the beginning of this chapter again. On the one hand, it sounds so simple: imagine what it would be like to fold a piece of paper over and over. Unfortunately, picturing just what a piece of paper folded 50 times really would look like is very difficult. Some people guess a few inches, whereas some imagine that the folded paper would be a few feet thick. Many have no idea at all. So, representing this problem in visual terms will be of little help. If one recognizes this as a problem of mathematics, involving exponents, a correct solution is more likely. Actually, 50 folds will increase the paper's thickness by a factor of 2^{50}. That comes to 1,100,000,000,000,000 inches, and the resulting paper would be so thick it would nearly reach from the earth to the sun!

Choosing the best way to represent a problem is not a simple task. Very often problem representation provides *the* stumbling block to problem solution (Bourne et al., 1983). Once you realize you're faced with a problem, your first step in solving it should be to represent it in a variety of ways. To the extent you can, eliminate unessential information. Relate the problem to other problems of a similar type you have solved before. Having done so, if the solution is still not obvious, you may choose to develop some strategy to move from your representation of the problem to the goal of its solution. We now turn to how one might go about generating possible problem solutions.

Before You Go On

In the context of problem solving, what is meant by problem representation?

PROBLEM-SOLVING STRATEGIES

Once you have represented the initial state of a problem and have a clear idea of what an acceptable goal state might be, you still have to figure out how to get to your goal. Even after you have adequately represented a problem, how to solve it may not be readily apparent. You might spend a few minutes guessing wildly at a solution, but soon you'll have to settle on some strategy. In this context, a **strategy** is a systematic plan for generating possible solutions that can be tested to see if they are correct. The main advantage of cognitive strategies is that they permit the problem solver to exercise some degree of control over the task at hand. They allow solvers to choose the skills and knowledge they will bring to bear on any particular problem at any time (Gagné, 1984). There are several strategies one might choose

strategy in problem solving, a systematic plan for generating possible solutions that can be tested to see if they are correct

to try. We'll consider two types of strategies: algorithms and heuristics.

Algorithms

An **algorithm** is a problem-solving strategy that *guarantees* that eventually you will arrive at a solution if the strategy is correctly applied. Algorithms involve systematically exploring and evaluating all possible solutions until the correct one is found. It is sometimes referred to as a *generate-test* strategy, in which one generates hypotheses about potential solutions and then tests each one in turn. Given their speed of computation, most computer programs designed to solve problems use algorithmic strategies.

Simple anagram problems (letters of a word in a scrambled fashion) *can* be solved using an algorithmic strategy. "What English word has been scrambled to make *uleb?*" With sufficient patience, you can systematically rearrange these four letters until you hit on a correct solution: *leub, lueb, elub, uleb, buel, beul, blue.* There it is, *blue.* With only four letters to deal with, finding a solution generally doesn't take very long; there are only 24 possible arrangements of four letters ($4 \times 3 \times 2 \times 1 = 24$).

On the other hand, consider the eight-letter anagram I mentioned earlier: *teralbay.* In fact, there are 40,320 possible combinations of these eight letters: $8 \times 7 \times 6 \times 5 \times 4 \times 3 \times 2 \times 1 = 40,320$ (Reynolds & Flagg, 1983). Unless your system for moving letters around just happens to start in a good place, you could spend a lot of time trying to come up with a combination that produces an English word. If we were dealing with a ten-letter word, there would be 3,628,800 possible combinations to check!

Imagine that you go the supermarket to buy just one item: a jar of horseradish. You're quite sure the store has horseradish, but you have

algorithm a problem-solving strategy in which all possible solutions are generated and tested and an acceptable solution is guaranteed

The problem of searching a large supermarket to find a specific item would not be solved quickly if one used an algorithmic strategy. Although finding a solution is not guaranteed, heuristic strategies are typically less time consuming.

no idea where to find it. One plan would be to go up and down every aisle of the store, checking first the top shelf, then the second, then the third, until you spied the horseradish. This strategy would work *if* the store carried horseradish *and if* you searched carefully enough. There must be a better way to solve such problems. Here's where heuristic strategies come in.

Heuristics

heuristic an informal and economical method of testing problem solutions without guarantee of success

A **heuristic** strategy is an informal, rule-of-thumb method of generating and testing problem solutions. Heuristics are more economical techniques for solving problems than are algorithms, but when one uses a heuristic, there is no guarantee of success. On the other hand, such strategies are usually much less time consuming than algorithm strategies and do lead searches for goals in a logical, sensible way.

A heuristic strategy for finding horseradish in a supermarket might take you to various sections in the store in the order you believed to be most reasonable. You might start with spices, but you would be disappointed. Next, you might look among the fresh vegetables. Then, upon recalling that horseradish needs to be refrigerated, you go next to the dairy case, and there you'll find the horseradish. You would not have wasted time searching the cereal aisle or the frozen food section—real possibilities if you tried an algorithmic strategy. Another, more reasonable, heuristic strategy would be to ask an employee where the horseradish is kept. Let's look at three heuristic strategies: *means-ends analysis, working backward,* and *hill climbing.*

If you tried the *teralbay* anagram problem, it is likely you used a heuristic strategy. To do so, you rely on your experience with the English language (remember that basic cognitive processes such as the use of memory are required for problem solving). You seriously consider only those letter combinations you know occur frequently. You generate and test the most common combinations first. You just don't worry much about the possibility that the solution may contain a combination such as *brty*. Nor do you search for a word with an *aae* string in it. You explore words that end in *able* because you know these to be fairly common. But that doesn't work. What about *br* words? No, that doesn't work either. How about words with the combination *tray* in them? *Traybeal*? No. *Baletray*? No. "Oh! Now I see it: *betrayal*."

This heuristic strategy is a *means-ends analysis* (Newell & Simon, 1972). In this strategy, one always keeps the final goal in mind, but first works toward reaching subgoals. In the *teralbay* anagram example, subgoals are defined in terms of letter combinations that make sense or are commonly found. Once subgoals are reached, they are manipulated in an attempt to reach the final goal. The example of the search for horseradish also involved a means-ends analysis: first find the right section of the store, then search for the specific product.

Here's another example. If José has decided that it is his goal to be a family-practice physician, he cannot simply rent an office and practice medicine. Getting to the ultimate goal of being a physician (or almost anything else) involves establishing a series of subgoals and procedures for reaching subgoals before moving on to others. The final goal state (getting into medical school) may always be in José's mind, but right now he has to get a good grade in introductory psychology (a subgoal along the way) or he's going to have difficulty graduating (another subgoal).

A related heuristic strategy you have probably used involves *working backward*. In this strategy, the goal state of a problem may be better defined than either the initial state *or* the means to get to the goal. It may be easier to trace a path from the goal of a maze to its starting point than it is to trace the same path in the other direction.

Suppose you know what you want to have for supper tonight: a Chinese dinner of egg rolls, shrimp in lobster sauce, and fried rice. There's your goal state, now how do you get there? "What would I have to do to get that dinner on my table tonight? I'd have to fry rice. In order to fry rice, I'll need something to fry it in. No problem; I'll use my new wok. But I need the rice to fry. How *do* you fry rice, anyway?" When you check your Chinese cookbook, you discover that to fry rice, you need to first cook the rice and then let it cool, or chill it, before frying. "I haven't got the time to buy rice, then boil it, then cool it, then fry it. How else could I get fried rice to the table?" It may be at this point you decide your problem has no reasonable solution, and decide to stop at a neighborhood Chinese restaurant for a carry-out on the way home.

Note how this "fried rice" example is different from a problem in which you want to try out a new wok and don't know what to do with it until you work through a series of decisions, finally settling on the goal of fried rice. The *working backward* example starts with the goal.

A problem-solving strategy called *hill climbing* requires that every action (real or imagined) moves us somehow closer to our ultimate goal state (Atwood & Polson, 1976). Problem solving is often a matter of, "Let's just forge ahead; we'll get there sooner or later, as long as we keep moving forward" (or upward to maintain the hill-climbing analogy). For example, as one stands on the tee of a golf course, the goal is to get the ball into the hole on the green while hitting it as few times as possible. Logic says that no matter how far we hit the ball, if it moves toward the green, we're at least going in the right direction. But in real life, as in golf, successful problem solving may require that we make a move *away from* our ultimate goal. If your ball lands behind a tree, your only course of action may be to hit it to the side or backward out onto the fairway so that your *next* shot can be successful. Sometimes it may be wiser to hit the ball around a sand trap rather than over it, even if the latter shot is more directly aimed at the hole.

By now you realize that these heuristic strategies are *not* mutually exclusive. Mostly, they differ in emphasis. When faced with complex problems in real life, we may use all of these strategies. You want to do as well in this course as possible. How do you go about it? First, you make sure you understand the ultimate goal—exactly what will it take (how many points) to get the grade of your choice? By what *means* can these *ends* be attained? Then *work backward*. How many points will you need at the end of the semester? How many points will you need just before the final? How many will you need after the next test to keep on track toward your goal? Then engage in a bit of *hill climbing*. Every point you earn on your next test, paper, or project is one more point that moves you closer to your ultimate goal.

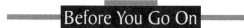

Before You Go On

How are algorithmic and heuristic strategies used
to solve problems?

BARRIERS TO EFFECTIVE PROBLEM SOLVING

By and large, it is difficult to solve problems without relying heavily on one's memory. If you failed to remember that the radius of a circle is equal to one-half its diameter, you couldn't solve problem 4 at the beginning of the chapter. If you forgot how fast the bird was flying, you couldn't deal with the problem in Figure 7.6. If you couldn't remember the recipe for something you wanted to have for supper, you would have a hard time buying the correct ingredients when you went to the store. Regardless of the type of problem or the type of strategy employed to solve it, solving problems effectively requires that we use our memories.

There are times, however, when previous experiences (and memories of them) create difficulties in problem solving. We'll look at three such cases.

Mental Set and Functional Fixedness

In Topic 3A, we saw that our perceptions can be influenced by expectations, or mental set. We said that we often perceive what we are set to perceive. The concept of mental set is also very relevant in problem solving. A **mental set** is a tendency to perceive or respond to something in a given, or set, way. It is, in essence, a cognitive predisposition. We may have or develop expectations that interfere with effective problem solving.

mental set a predisposed (set) way to perceive or respond to something; an expectation

One clever (but quite nasty) demonstration of the negative consequences of mental set involves giving a class a lengthy surprise test, perhaps 50 true-false items. The instructions at the top of the first page state clearly: "Place all of your answers on the attached answer sheet. Do not write on this exam. *Read all of the items on this test before making any marks on the answer sheet.*" Having taken so many true-false tests before, many students do not read any of the instructions. They just start into the test, working away. Some students read the instructions and choose to ignore the warning about first reading all the items. Only those students who do so get to read item 50 before they begin to answer the questions. Item 50 is, "This is not a test. I just wanted to see if you would follow directions. Please sit quietly until I collect the exams."

Problem 7 at the beginning of the chapter provides another example of how an inappropriate mental set can interfere with problem solving. This is the problem of connecting nine symmetrically arranged dots with just four straight lines. Most people, when first presented with this problem, make an assumption (form a mental set). They assume the nine dots form a square and that their lines somehow must stay within that square. Only when this mental set is "broken" can the problem be solved. Figure 7.7 provides one solution to the nine-dot problem.

Mental sets do not necessarily interfere with problem solving. A proper, or appropriate, mental set can be facilitating. For example, if I were to have told you to look beyond the confines of any imagined square when attempting the nine-dot problem, *that* mental set—which seems strange out of context—could have made the problem easier to solve.

The phenomenon of **functional fixedness** may be thought of as a type of mental set. The process was defined by Duncker (1945) as the inability to discover an appropriate new use for an object because of experience using the object in some other function. That is, the problem solver fails to see a solution to a problem because he or she has "fixed" some "function" to an object that makes it difficult to see how it could help with the problem at hand.

A standard example is one used by Maier (1931). Two strings dangle from the ceiling. The problem is that they are so far apart a subject cannot reach both of them at the same time. The goal is to do just that: to hold on to both strings at once. If there were nothing else in the room, this problem might never get solved. However, there are other objects in the room that the subject can use, including a pair of pliers (see Figure 7.8). One solution to this problem is to tie the pliers to one string and start the pliers swinging like a pendulum. As the subject holds the other string, the string with the pliers attached can be grasped as it swings over to the subject. Because many subjects fail to see pliers as useful (functioning) for anything but turning nuts and bolts, they fail to see the pliers as a potential pendulum weight and thus may fail to solve the problem. They have "fixed" the "function" of the pliers in their mind.

Another famous example that demonstrates functional fixedness is one reported by Duncker (1945). Here, subjects are provided with a box of tacks, a candle, and some matches. The task is to use these materials to mount the candle on the wall and light it. Obviously, one cannot just tack a candle to the wall. The solution to this problem requires breaking the mental set of functional fixedness for the box in which the tacks are presented, seeing it as a potential candleholder, tacking *it* to the wall, and mounting the candle on it (see Figure 7.9 on page 339).

A number of experiments (e.g., Glucksberg & Danks, 1968) have shown that some subtle changes in the way in which the materials are

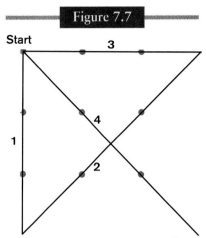

Figure 7.7

See problem 7 at the beginning of Chapter 7. Here is one solution to the classic nine-dot problem. (From Scheerer, 1963.)

functional fixedness a type of mental set that interferes with the discovery of a new use for an object because of the experience of using the object in some other function

Figure 7.8

Maier's two-string problem. The subject is to manage to get both strings in his grasp. They are separated so that when one string is held, the other cannot be reached. See text for solution. (After Maier, 1931.)

presented have an effect on solving this problem. For example, when the box of tacks is labeled TACKS, the problem is much more difficult to solve. Using an empty box and having the tacks scattered about increases the likelihood that subjects will overcome the functional fixedness of seeing the box as something that holds things.

Before You Go On

What is a mental set, and how might a mental set hinder problem solving?

What is functional fixedness, and how might it hinder problem solving?

Biased Heuristics and Decision Making

For some of the problems we encounter in real life, we are provided with a set of possibilities from which we must choose a correct or "best" alternative. Looked at this way, we see that some decision-making tasks are very much like the problems we have been considering in this Topic. We've seen that problem solving requires us to use our past experience—knowledge of common letter strings in English,

Figure 7.9

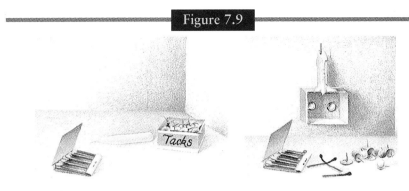

The materials provided in the candle problem—and one possible solution. (After Duncker, 1945.)

for example—to devise strategies for reaching goal states. Occasionally, our heuristic strategies—those rules of thumb used to guide problem solving—based on perceptions of past experience are biased. Such biases create a barrier to effective problem solving.

Some of the strategies we use to make decisions require that we estimate the probability of events. As it happens, many of them are notoriously poor (Hastie & Park, 1986; Payne et al., 1992). Most of the research on judging probabilities and frequencies has been reported by Daniel Kahneman and Amos Tversky (1973, 1979, 1984) (Tversky and Kahneman, 1974).

The **availability heuristic** is the assumption that things that come readily to mind are more common, or more frequently occurring, than things difficult to recall or think of. For example, I show you a list that includes the names of 19 famous women and 20 less famous men. Later, you will almost certainly overestimate the number of women on the list, because those famous names were more available to you. The media (newspapers, TV, radio, and so on) often draw our attention to events (make them available) in such a way that we tend to overestimate their frequency of occurrence. For example, when reports of terrorist bombings at foreign airports make the televison news, many Americans cancel their plans for European vacations, overestimating the risk of flying to Europe. Even without terrorists, most people will *over*estimate the number of airplane crashes that occur each year, compared to the number of automobile crashes that occur, simply because we tend to hear more about the airplane accidents; they are more available in our memories.

The **representativeness heuristic** is the assumption that judgments made about the most prototypic member of a category will hold for all members of the category. You are told that a group of men consists of 70 percent lawyers and 30 percent engineers. You are told that one of the men, chosen at random from the group, has hobbies that include carpentry, sailing, and mathematical puzzles. You are to decide if this man is an engineer or a lawyer. Because you believe

availability heuristic the assumption that whatever is more available in our memory is also more common or probable

representativeness heuristic the assumption that judgments made about a prototypic member of a category will hold for all members of the category

these hobbies to be representative of engineers, not lawyers, you may say that the man is an engineer, even though (by chance) the likelihood that he is a lawyer is more than twice (7 to 3) the chance that he is an engineer.

Which group includes more tobacco chewers, professional baseball players or college students? The answer is college students (mostly because there are so many of them, even though a smaller *percentage* actually uses chewing tobacco). Let me ask you this: if I flip a coin (you may assume that it's a fair coin) and it turns up heads five times in a row, what is the chance of getting tails on the next flip? Actually, the probability is no better than it's been all along, 50-50 (the fact that heads have appeared the previous five times is of absolutely no consequence to the coin).

There are other heuristic strategies that may bias our decision making and interfere with problem solving. You recognize a multiple-choice test item as the sort of problem that requires you to decide which of a number of alternatives best answers a question. A problem-solving heuristic that may cause trouble is called the **positive test strategy**. This is the strategy that claims that if something works, don't drop it to try something else (e.g., Klayman & Ha, 1987). In many ways, this is the heuristic that suggests: "If it isn't broken, don't fix it." In many cases this approach is a sensible one, but there certainly are instances when even *better* solutions—more useful decisions—could be found if only one continued to look. Have you ever fallen into the "trap" of saying that alternative A was the correct answer to a multiple-choice item simply because it was correct, only to discover later that alternatives B and C were also correct, thus making alternative D, "all of the above," the *best* answer to the question?

Successful problem solving often requires that we break out of the restraints imposed by improper mental sets, functional fixedness, and some heuristic strategies. To be able to overcome these barriers is to be able to solve problems creatively, and it is to this subject we turn next.

positive test strategy the heuristic of sticking with an acceptable decision or solution, even if a better one might exist

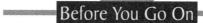

Before You Go On

What are the availability and representativeness heuristics, and how might they hinder problem solving?

Overcoming Barriers with Creative Problem Solving

Creative solutions to problems are new, innovative, and useful. It is important to note that in the context of problem solving, *creative* means more than unusual, rare, or different. Someone may generate a very original plan to solve a given problem, but unless that plan

Flattop haircut for balancing fruit

Bow tie with folding trays

Drop-shelf patch pockets

Extension trays from pants pockets

Shirt studs with folding cups for salt and pepper

Special long-distance fork

Creative problem solutions must be more than unusual or different—they must provide a workable solution to the problem at hand.

works, we shouldn't view it as creative (Newell et al., 1962; Vinacke, 1974). If you were to think about how to keep warm on a cold winter's night, you might come up with the idea of popping bushels of warm popcorn for everyone to sit in. This solution may border on the unique, unusual, and creative, but it certainly doesn't seem very workable, no matter how creative it may be. Creative solutions should be put to the same test as more ordinary solutions: do they solve the problem at hand?

Creative solutions generally involve a different organization of elements of the problem. As mentioned earlier, it is often at the stage of problem representation that creativity is most noticeable. Seeing a problem in a new light, or combining elements of a problem in a new and different way, can lead to creative solutions.

One observation has been made many times: there is virtually no correlation between creative problem solving and intelligence (Barron & Harrington, 1981; Horn, 1976; Kershner & Ledger, 1985). At least

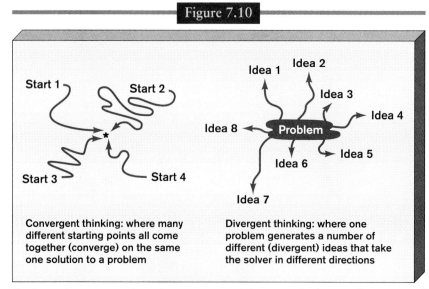

Figure 7.10

A schematic representation of convergent and divergent thinking in the context of problem solving.

divergent thinking the creation of many ideas or potential problem solutions from one idea

convergent thinking the reduction or focusing of many ideas into one possible problem solution

there are virtually no significant correlations between tests for creativity and tests for intelligence.

We say that creative problem solving often involves **divergent thinking**; that is, starting with one idea and generating from it a number of alternative possibilities and new ideas (Dirkes, 1978; Guilford, 1959b). When we engage in **convergent thinking**, we take many ideas, or bits of information, and try to focus and reduce them to just one possible solution (See Figure 7.10). Obviously, convergent thinking has its place in problem solving. But for creative problem solving, divergent thinking is generally more useful because many possibilities are explored. We must remember, however, that all of these new possibilities for a problem's solution need to be judged ultimately in terms of whether or not they really solve the problem.

Creative problem solving can be divided into four interrelated stages. This view of the problem-solving process is attributed to Wallas (1926). It is an old one in psychology, but it has held up rather nicely over the years.

1. *Preparation:* This is not unlike problem representation. The basic elements of the problem are considered. Past experience is relevant, but should not become restrictive. At this stage of problem solving, it is important to overcome the negative effects of mental set and functional fixedness. Various ways of expressing the problem are considered, but a solution is not found.

2. *Incubation:* In this stage, the problem is "put away" and not thought about. Perhaps fatigue that has developed during

failed efforts can then dissipate. Perhaps inappropriate strategies can be forgotten. Perhaps unconscious processes can be brought to bear on the problem. Why setting aside a problem may lead to its creative solution we cannot say for sure. We do know, however, that it is often very useful (cf. Koestler, 1964; Yaniv & Meyer, 1987).

3. *Illumination:* This is the most mysterious stage of the process. Like insight, a potential solution to a problem seems to materialize as if from nowhere. Some critical analogy becomes apparent, as does a new path to the problem's solution (Glass et al., 1979; Metcalfe & Wiebe, 1987).

4. *Verification:* Now the proposed solution must be tested, or verified, to see if it does in fact provide an answer to the question posed by the problem.

You have probably noted that there is really nothing that extraordinary about Wallas's description of the creative problem-solving process. It sounds very much like the sort of thing anyone should do when faced with a problem to solve. The truth is, however, that we often fail to go through these stages in any systematic fashion. To do so consciously often helps problem solving. It has long been recognized that good problem solvers show more conscious awareness of what they are doing during the course of problem solving than do poor problem solvers (Glaser, 1984).

Before You Go On

What is the difference between divergent and convergent thinking?

What are the four stages of creative problem solving, according to Wallas?

CAN WE TEACH PROBLEM-SOLVING SKILLS?

Have you ever heard someone say something like, "We don't want schools to teach our children just the facts, but to teach them how to think as well"? Many psychologists and educators believe that thinking and problem-solving skills are somehow "teachable" and that these cognitive abilities *ought* to be part of the school curriculum. In the 1930s and 1940s, education in America tended to focus on drill, repetition, and rote practice, with little regard for higher cognitive functions. In the 1950s and 1960s, Skinner's behaviorism and reinforcement theory flooded into the classroom with teaching machines and programmed instruction. With the rebirth of interest in cognitive psychology, there has been an increased call for educators to teach

An unresolved issue in psychology today is the extent to which problem-solving skills can be taught independently from content knowledge.

cognitive skills such as concept formation, problem solving, decision making, and critical thinking in the classroom (Glaser, 1984; Greeno, 1989; Resnick, 1987).

As it happens, this increased interest in teaching cognitive skills has not been reflected in the performance of schoolchildren. According to one major study of the impact of education in this country, there is evidence that the basic skills of students are improving, but that higher cognitive skills are declining. For example, in math, "There appears to be an increase in the performance associated with basic skill and computation, but little improvement and even a reported decline in mathematical understanding and problem solving" (cited in Glaser, 1984).

What can be done to improve the problem-solving skills of students? This question is one of the most actively researched issues in cognitive psychology today. It has a number of tentative answers. For one thing, it *is* helpful for students simply to know about the basic nature of problem solving. Teaching students about problem representation, algorithms, heuristics, mental sets, and functional fixedness is in itself a helpful thing to do (e.g., Adams, 1974; Greeno, 1978; Hayes, 1987; Newell & Simon, 1972). Most programs of this sort are "knowledge free" in the sense that they do not require any particular expertise on the part of the student. "In large part, abstract tasks, puzzlelike problems, and informal life situations are used as content"

(Glaser, 1984, p. 96). In other words, most of the material used to teach students about thinking and problem solving has been similar to what we have used in this Topic: anagrams, puzzles, and mountain-climbing monks.

It is the position of cognitive psychologist Robert Glaser (1984) that instruction in problem-solving strategies and techniques needs to rely on a sound knowledge base. The ability to solve problems requires, Glaser says, an interaction between general cognitive abilities to manipulate information (higher cognitive processes) *and* a base of adequate information to manipulate (knowledge). The essence of this argument is this: if you don't *know* much about the particular elements of a given problem, you are going to have difficulty solving it regardless of how much you know about heuristics, strategies, and problem solving in general.

Consider an experiment reported by Chi in 1978. Chi found that on a test of memory for digits, 10-year-old children did significantly less well than adults. The children in Chi's study were expert chess players, however, and the adults were not. When children and adults were tested on their memory of chess pieces arranged on a chessboard, the children's memories were far superior to those of the adults. The adults may have had better, more efficient strategies for performing the memory task at hand, but the children simply knew more about chess, and that gave them the edge.

One of Glaser's arguments, then, is that problem-solving skills can be taught, but need to be taught in the context of a specific "domain" of knowledge and understanding (Chi & Glaser, 1985). On the one hand, it makes little sense to try to teach students the higher cognitive skills of concept formation and problem solving if they do not have an adequate base of knowledge or information with which to work. On the other hand, it makes little sense to do no more than drill students over and over again on basic facts without exploring theories, concepts, relationships, and how such facts can be used to solve problems. Or, as Glaser puts it, "As individuals acquire knowledge, they also should be empowered to think and reason" (1984, p. 103).

Before You Go On

Briefly summarize Glaser's position on teaching
problem-solving skills.

TOPIC 7B SUMMARY

Problem solving is obviously a higher cognitive process. To solve problems requires that we rely on our perceptions, learning, and memories. To solve a problem requires that we understand a situation as it exists, understand the situation as we would like it to be, and then discover some way to reach this desired goal state. To do so effectively and efficiently often requires that we represent the nature of the problem correctly, generate an appropriate problem-solving strategy, and overcome inhibiting influences of mental set, functional fixedness, or the choice of a misleading heuristic strategy. It is clear that an important goal of education is to teach effective and efficient problem-solving strategies. What is less clear is the extent to which problem-solving strategies—or thinking skills in general—can be taught outside the context of a knowledge base.

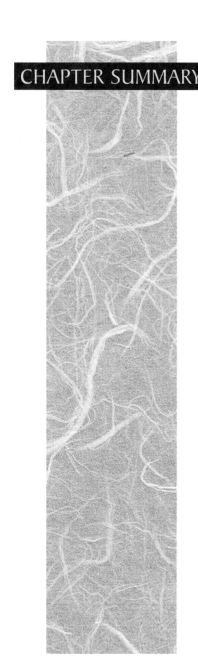

CHAPTER SUMMARY

TOPIC 7A

How can we use attributes and rules to define concepts?

How does the concept of prototype help our understanding of what a concept is?

Concepts are mental representations of categories or classes of objects and events. They are often defined in terms of critical attributes or features related to each other by some rule. A prototype is the best example, or most typical member, of a category or concept. It is the member of a concept class that has most of the attributes that define that concept and few attributes that cause it to be confused with other concepts. The notions of prototype and best fit allow us to deal with the fuzzy concepts we often encounter in real life. The standard notion of prototype, however, often fails to take context into account. /p. 311

What does Edna Heidbreder's classic study of concept formation tell us about the process?

What does it mean to say that people use hypothesis testing in forming concepts?

Heidbreder's 1946 study demonstrated that concept labels are learned, that concept formation can be meaningfully studied in the laboratory, and that concepts may be acquired by strategies of which even the learner is unaware. Concepts are usually learned by developing a systematic plan, or strategy, for discovering the essential attributes of a concept and the rule that unites those attributes. Concept formation strategies involve generating and then testing hypotheses about potential membership in a class or concept. Forming and testing hypotheses about concept membership applies to natural as well as formal concepts. /p. 316

What are some of the defining characteristics of language?

Language is a complex and creative cognitive skill used for communication. A language consists of a large number of arbitrary symbols, usually words, that stand for, or label, our conceptualization of objects and events, that have meaning for users of that language, and that are combined in accordance with certain rules. The use of language is a generative process that, among other things, allows us to communicate about the "*not* here and the *not* now." /*p. 318*

What are phonemes, and in what way are they rule-governed?

A phoneme is the smallest unit of sound in the spoken form of a language; that is, a speech sound. Phonemes are rule-governed in the sense that each language comprises only a portion of all possible phonemes. How phonemes may be combined within a given language follows strict rules. /*p. 319*

What is semantics?

What are morphemes?

Semantics is the name we give to the study of meaning; in the context of this chapter, the meaning of words and sentences. Morphemes are the smallest units, or elements, of meaning in a language. Morphemes include words, prefixes, and suffixes. They provide labels that allow us to communicate about concepts. The way in which morphemes are ordered, or structured, in language generally affects their meaning. /*p. 320*

What is syntax?

What are linguistic intuitions?

Syntax refers to the rules that govern the way morphemes in a language are ordered, or structured, to produce sentences. Language users demonstrate a competence with these rules even though they may not be able to state them explicitly. Our knowledge of syntax, or sentence structure, is reflected in linguistic intuitions—judgments that language users make about the structure of utterances. For example, we can determine intuitively (without being able to explain why) when utterances are syntactically correct and when they are not. We can tell when two sentences that take different forms are communicating the same idea or message. We can identify ambiguous sentences and can often remove that ambiguity, but only when we are aware of a larger context in which the utterance occurred. /*p. 321*

What is pragmatics, and what can it tell us about language use?

Pragmatics is the study of how the social situation, or context, in which language is used influences the meaning of what is being said. An appreciation of that context allows us to recognize the use of sarcasm, simile, metaphors, and the like. Research evidence suggests that any differences in language use as a function of gender are very small. In some contexts, however, the language of women may tend to be less assertive, more self-disclosing, and contains more qualifiers than does the language of men, who, in most situations, tend to be more talkative and interrupt others more than women do. /*p. 322*

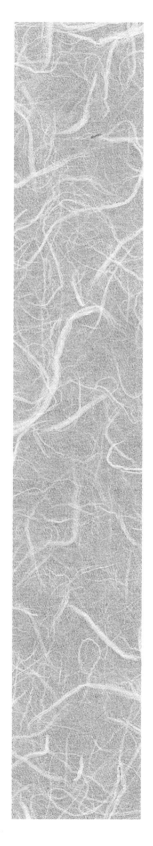

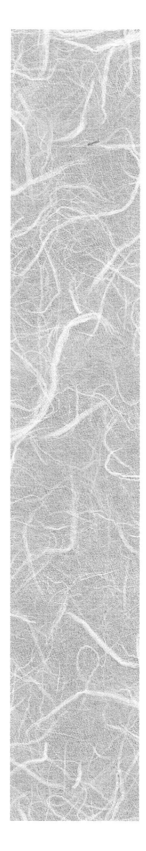

What are some of the landmark events that occur during language acquisition?

Although infants cry and babble, the first truly linguistic utterances are called holophrastic speech. This occurs when one word is used to communicate a range of feelings, intentions, and meanings. A two-word stage of development shows the presence of structure in word ordering—a syntax that is not merely a copy of adult language structure. From the two-word utterance on, language development is extremely rapid. By the time a child is 5 years old, he or she will know thousands of words (will understand more than she or he will produce) and combine those words in virtually every acceptable sentence structure in the language. /p. 325

Briefly summarize the learning-oriented and biologically oriented theories of language acquisition.

Neither learning nor biological theories can totally account for language acquisition. Clearly, one's learning history has an impact on language development, particularly in the formation of words and morphemes (we do not all speak the same language in the same way). At the same time, learning theory is challenged by the cross-cultural regularities that seem to occur in language acquisition—by the fact that all children of all languages seem to develop their languages in the same general, patterned way. The complex process just seems too rapid and too regular not to have a strong biological basis. /p. 327

TOPIC 7B

What are the three components of a problem?

Contrast well-defined and ill-defined problems. Give an example of each.

We say that a problem has three components: (1) an initial state—the situation as it exists at the moment), (2) a goal state (the situation as the problem solver would like it to be), and (3) routes or strategies for getting from the initial state to the goal state. Whether a problem is well defined or ill defined is a matter of the extent to which the elements of the initial state and goal state are well delineated and clearly understood by the problem solver. An example of a well-defined problem might be that which you face when a familiar route home from campus is blocked. An example of an ill-defined problem might be that which you face when you have to write a term paper on a topic of your choice. /p. 329

In the context of problem solving, what is meant by problem representation?

Problem representation involves the mental activity of thinking about a problem so as to put it into a form with which we can deal effectively. In essence, representation involves putting a problem into familiar terms. /*p. 332*

How are algorithmic and heuristic strategies used to solve problems?

Algorithms and heuristics are types of strategies, or systematic plans, we use to solve problems. Algorithms involve a systematic search of all possible solutions until the goal is reached; with algorithms, a solution is guaranteed. A heuristic strategy—of which there are many—is a more informal, rule-of-thumb approach that involves generating and testing hypotheses that *may* lead to a problem solution in a sensible, organized way. /*p. 336*

What is a mental set, and how might a mental set hinder problem solving?

What is functional fixedness, and how might it hinder problem solving?

A mental set is a tendency, or predisposition, to perceive or respond in a particular way. Mental sets generally develop from past experience and involve the continued use of strategies that have been successful in the past. Because those ways of perceiving or solving a problem that have worked in the past may no longer be appropriate for the problem at hand, mental sets often hinder effective problem solving. Functional fixedness is a type of mental set in which an object is seen as serving only a few fixed functions. Because we may not see a familiar object as being able to serve different functions, fixedness often interferes with effective problem solving. /*p. 338*

What are the availability and representativeness heuristics, and how might they hinder problem solving?

These two heuristic strategies, based on our past experience, often mislead us in problem solving. For example, we tend to judge as more likely or more probable those events more readily available to us in memory—the availability heuristic. We also tend to overgeneralize about events that are prototypic representatives of a category or concept—the representativeness heuristic. /*p. 340*

What is the difference between divergent and convergent thinking? According to Wallas, what are the four stages of creative problem solving?

Divergent thinking is seen as a useful technique in problem solving, in which a large number of alternative possibilities are generated to be tested later for usefulness. Convergent thinking involves taking a large number of ideas or possibilities and reducing them to one or a few. Problem solving in general, and creative problem solving in particular, have four interrelated stages: (1) preparation (in which the problem is represented mentally), (2) incubation (in which the problem is put aside for a while), (3) illumination (in which a potential solution

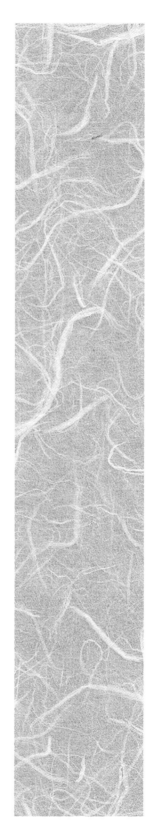

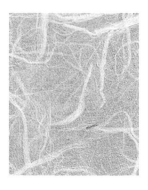

becomes known), and (4) verification (in which the potential solution is tested to see if it does solve the problem at hand). /p. 343

Briefly summarize Glaser's position on teaching problem-solving skills.

Although there is evidence that students can profit from instruction in problem-solving strategies in general, it is Robert Glaser's view that problem solving first requires an extensive knowledge base or understanding of the content area that needs to be manipulated in the problem-solving process. /p. 345

chapter eight

DEVELOPMENTAL PSYCHOLOGY

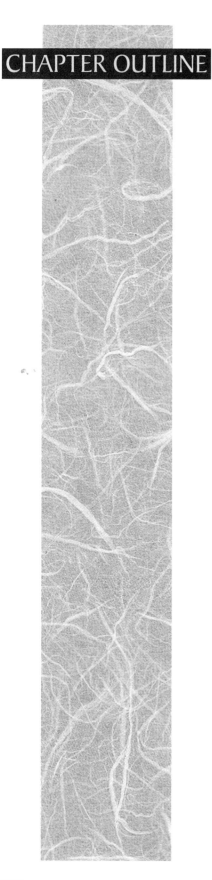

CHAPTER OUTLINE

TOPIC 8A PRENATAL INFLUENCES ON DEVELOPMENT
Genetics and Psychology
    Inheritance of Physical Traits
    The Interactionist Position
The Stages of Prenatal Development
Environmental Influences on Prenatal Development
    Nourishment
    Smoking, Drinking, and Drugs
    Maternal Stress
    What About Dad?
TOPIC 8A SUMMARY

TOPIC 8B DEVELOPMENT IN CHILDHOOD
Motor Development: Getting from Here to There
    The Neonate
    The Motor Development of Children
Sensory and Perceptual Development
Cognitive and Social Development
    Cognitive Abilities of the Neonate: What Does the Newborn
        Know?
    Piaget's Theory of Cognitive Development
    Reactions to Piaget
    Kohlberg's Theory of Moral Development
    Erikson's Theory of Psychosocial Development
    Developing Gender Identity
    Developing Social Attachments
TOPIC 8B SUMMARY

TOPIC 8C DEVELOPMENT IN ADOLESCENCE
What Are Adolescents Really Like?
    The Limits of Adolescence
    Are Adolescents Always in Turmoil, and "Stressed Out"?
Physical Changes During Adolescence
Some Challenges of Adolescence
    Identity Formation
    Drug Use by Adolescents
    Adolescent Sexuality
TOPIC 8C SUMMARY

TOPIC 8D DEVELOPMENT IN ADULTHOOD
Early Adulthood
    Marriage and Family
    Career Choice
Middle Adulthood
Late Adulthood
    What It Means to be Old
    Death and Dying
TOPIC 8D SUMMARY

CHAPTER SUMMARY

I have attempted only one experiment that involved young children: a study of word associations. The procedure was simple: present a stimulus word and have a child respond with the first thing that came to mind.

Two undergraduate research assistants went off to a local nursery school to collect data. I couldn't go with them that first day because I had a class to teach. When I met the assistants upon their return, they were upset. One said, "It was just awful! The kids won't do it. It was a mess!" I became very paternalistic and reassured the assistants, "Now, now, don't worry, I'll go with you tomorrow and everything will be alright." It wasn't. My assistants were right. The kids wouldn't do it.

I approached a 4-year-old with a proposition. "Hi. How are you? Let's play a game, okay? Would you like to play a game with words?" My first discovery was that 8 percent of the children simply did not want to play. They just walked away, back to the sandbox or some other activity. When children did agree to "play," they did some peculiar things. I gave my simple instructions: "I'm going to say a word, and then you tell me the first word you think of when you hear my word. Okay? My first word is *black*." After a moment's pause, a child looked up and responded, "My Mommy has a black dress and she wears it to church sometimes."

"Okay, that's fine," I'd say, "but next time tell me just one word. Do not tell me a story. If *black* makes you think of your Mommy's dress, just say, 'dress,' okay?" I gave the next word on the list. "The word is *happy*." "Dress," the child quickly responded. "No. No. You have to tell me what *happy* makes you think of." "Oh. I'm happy when we have ice cream."

Some children demonstrated that they were learning the alphabet and how to spell. "What's the first thing you think of when I say *black*?" The response: "Bee." To *man*, the response was "Em," and so on. Some children came up with sounds I didn't even know how to record. In response to *black*, one child responded with a series of "buh-buh-buh" noises. To *happy*, the response was "hap-hap-puh-puh-puh."

I eventually included more than 300 children in this study, just to see how they would respond to my "word game." Most of the responses produced by young children were nonword responses.

The word association procedure is one of the most straightforward techniques in all of psychology. But "playing the game" is a task that some children may do with their own set of rules, and some may not be ready to play the game at all. I had failed to take into account the cognitive level of my "research participants." Even doing simple experiments with children is often not as simple as it may sound. To study the behavior of children scientifically requires that we be particularly clever—and patient. Some experiments may not work at all, and other methods, such as naturalistic observation, may be needed. To varying degrees, similar problems arise throughout our study of human development.

rom conception to death, human beings share certain developmental events that unite us as one species. As we have already noted a number of times, it is also true that each of us is unique. Developmental psychologists are interested in the common patterns of our growth and development, and in the ways in which we differ as we grow and develop throughout our lives.

There are several ways in which a discussion of human development could be organized. I've chosen to take a chronological approach and have divided this chapter into four Topics.

We tend to think that a person's development begins at birth. In fact, growth and development begin earlier—at conception, and with the first division of one cell into two. Topic 8A focuses on the factors that influence the development of the human organism from conception to birth—the prenatal period *of development. We'll turn our attention to the development of children in Topic 8B, considering some of the major landmarks in three areas of development: physical-motor, sensory-perceptual, and cognitive-social. In each case, we will focus first on the capabilities of the newborn child.*

Topics 8C and 8D are relatively short topics that acknowledge the fact that one's growth and development do not come to a halt when one is no longer a child. We continue to develop throughout adolescence and adulthood. Most of the changes that reflect our development during these periods are more gradual and subtle than those that occur in childhood. They may be more difficult to observe, but they are no less significant.

Topic 8A

PRENATAL INFLUENCES ON DEVELOPMENT

GENETICS AND PSYCHOLOGY

genetics the science that studies the transmission of traits or characteristics from one generation to the next

The science of **genetics** studies how traits and characteristics are passed from one generation to the next. As often has been the case in psychology, the actual application of genetics often came well before scientists understood the underlying principles involved. For example, humans have engaged in the selective breeding of plants and animals for thousands of years. Without fully appreciating why it was the case, farmers discovered that when meaty bulls mated with meaty cows, the resulting calves tended to be meaty also. Rose growers have been creating new varieties of flowers for centuries through selective breeding (they call it hybridization). To some degree, it has always been understood that children tend to be more like their parents than anyone else; that many traits seem to "run in families."

Inheritance of Physical Traits

The formal discipline of genetics began about the time of the U.S. Civil War, after an Austrian monk, Gregor Mendel, discovered one of the mechanisms of heredity as he studied the selective breeding of the lowly pea. What Mendel discovered in his studies of peas was the **gene**, the basic mechanism of hereditary transmission. The genes Mendel assumed to exist (at the time there was no way he could actually *see* a gene) can be found on microscopically tiny structures called **chromosomes**, which means "colored" (*chroma*) "bodies" (*somes*). Chromosomes, in turn, live in the nucleus of every cell in a living organism (even bacteria have them). They live there in pairs.

gene the basic mechanism of hereditary transmission

chromosome literally, "colored body," found in 23 pairs in human cells; chromosomes carry genes

So, exactly how does the process of genetic transmission work in humans? You probably recognize that the process is very complex, even though the basics are straightforward. The nuclei of all human cells normally contain 23 pairs of chromosomes, *except* for the sex cells (the sperm in males, the ovum in females), which hold only half of each of the 23 possible pairs. At **conception**, the male and female sex cells unite to form a new cell, producing a new mixture of 23 chromosome pairs (and genes), half from the father and half from the mother.

conception the moment when the father's sperm cell unites with the mother's ovum to produce a new cell

If both parents contribute a gene that is ultimately responsible for a physical characteristic, such as blue eyes, their child will have blue eyes. If both parents contribute a gene that results in brown eyes, their child will be brown-eyed. The story starts to get interesting when one parent contributes a gene that develops blue eyes and the other parent contributes a gene that develops brown eyes. Here's where the notion of dominant and recessive genes becomes relevant. A **dominant gene** is one whose characteristics will be expressed no matter what gene is paired with it. With eye coloration, the gene for brown is dominant, so a child who inherits a "brown-eye" gene from either parent also will have brown eyes. A **recessive gene** expresses its characteristic only when it is paired with another, similar recessive gene. With eye color, the gene for blue eyes is recessive; so, a child who inherits a "blue-eye" gene from either parent (who may be either brown-eyed or blue-eyed) will have blue eyes only if another "blue-eye" gene is inherited from the other parent. It's really not all that complicated; perhaps Figure 8.1 will help.

dominant gene a gene that carries a trait that will be expressed regardless of the gene it is paired with

recessive gene a gene that carries a trait that will be expressed only if it is paired with another, similar recessive gene

When we talk about the genetic transmission of physical traits, we often use eye color as an example. This is because the color of the human eye is one of the few characteristics that actually can be accounted for by just a couple of known genes. Even eye color is often a complicated matter of gene interaction. Many genes will express their characteristic, or have an impact, only if other genes are present as well.

There are a few other complications that deserve mention. One is that genes do not directly create any physical characteristics. For example, a gene for brown eyes does not "make brown eyes," but causes a certain chemical to be manufactured during the early stages of development which, in turn, *has the effect of* producing brown

Figure 8.1

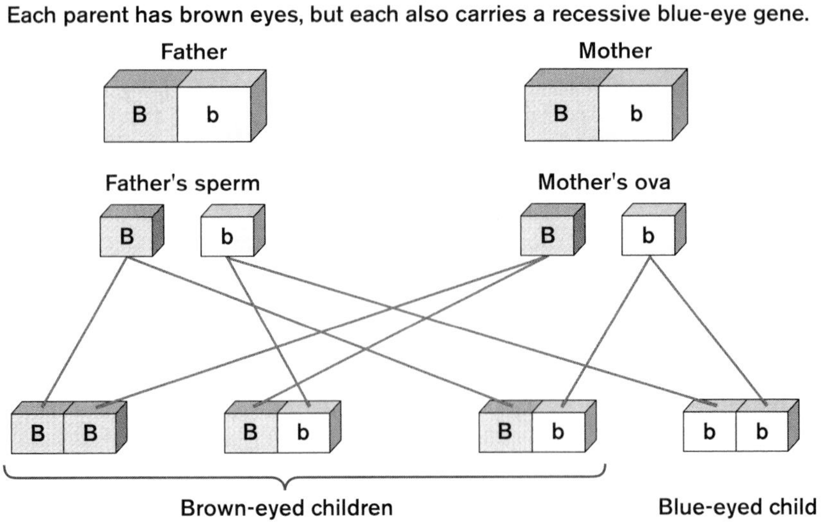

Each parent has brown eyes, but each also carries a recessive blue-eye gene.

This figure depicts what is likely to happen when two brown-eyed (B) parents who each carry a recessive blue-eye gene (b) have children. Only a child who receives the recessive gene (b) from both parents will, in fact, have blue eyes. Note that—in the long run, and on the average—three of four of their children will be able to transmit a blue-eye gene to their children.

eyes. Another complication is that the noticeable effects of some genes require time before they are expressed. For example, there is a type of baldness called "male pattern baldness" that is inherited in quite a straightforward fashion. Obviously, the consequences of this "gift" of heredity take time to be expressed. A third complication is that even physical characteristics determined primarily by genetic factors require at least some environmental interaction for those traits to be evidenced. Now we are at the point where we can ask about the inheritance of behaviors, not just physical characteristics.

The Interactionist Position

At any point in the developmental process, we encounter the same question: what determines a particular behavior, our nature or our nurture? How much of any given behavior can be attributed to heredity (one's nature), and how much can be attributed to the environment (one's nurture)? Which is more important, our genes or our experiences? Developmental psychologists now recognize that these are often the wrong questions to be asking. *Both* heredity and the environment shape the course of development; *neither* is sufficient alone.

Today, most psychologists ascribe to what is called the **epigenetic model** of development (Gottlieb, 1970; Lerner, 1978; Plomin et al., 1988; Rowe, 1981). This is an *interactionist* position, claiming that development *emerges* based on one's genetic history *and* one's experiences in the environment. Development is influenced by the forces of

epigenetic model an interactionist view of development claiming that development emerges based on one's genetic programming and one's experiences nature and nurture, "experienced in an inseparable tangle" (McGraw, 1987, p. 103). "The complex interplay between environment and genes is most apparent in the case of development" (Plomin, 1989, p. 110).

Our genes provide the foundation, or framework, for development, but we have to recognize the extent to which the environment often produces variation within that framework. As a simple example, consider why I happen to be 6′ 4″ tall. A lot of it has to do with the fact that both my parents were taller than average, and that on both sides of their families there were many relatives who were also tall. There happened to be a good number of genes around that promote tallness, and I got some of them. But that I am 6′ 4″ tall also reflects the fact that I was well fed and cared for. My environment, in other words, allowed those genes to be expressed.

Developing organisms demonstrate a capacity to be molded and shaped by their experiences with the environment. This capacity is called **plasticity**, and we now recognize that developing organisms are enormously plastic in the sense of being able to express genetic predispositions in a variety of ways (Hall & Oppenheim, 1987). The extent of plasticity may vary throughout one's development (Kolb, 1989), and varies from species to species, with humans showing the greatest plasticity (Gallagher & Ramey, 1987).

plasticity a capacity to be molded and shaped by experiences with the environment

As we cover the processes of development in this chapter, you should be ever mindful of the interaction of heredity and the environment, of nature and nurture. This will be particularly true in this Topic on prenatal development.

Before You Go On

What are some of the basic concepts involved in any discussion of the genetic transmission of physical characteristics?

What is the epigenetic model of development, and what does it say about the impact of heredity and the environment?

THE STAGES OF PRENATAL DEVELOPMENT

Human development begins at conception, when the father's sperm cell unites with the mother's ovum. At that time, 23 chromosomes from each parent pair off within a single cell, called the **zygote**. We have in that one action the complete transmission of all inherited characteristics. Within the next 30 hours or so, that one-celled zygote will divide and become two. In three days, there may be about 10 to 15 cells; after five days, there will be slightly more than 100 (Moore, 1982; Torrey & Feduccia, 1979). No one knows how many cells the human organism has at birth, and few are willing to even hazard a guess; "more than a trillion" is a conservative estimate (Moore,

zygote the one-cell product of the union of sperm and ovum at conception

prenatal period the period of
development from conception to
birth

stage of the zygote developmental
period from conception to the age
of 2 weeks

1982). As we review the physical stages of prenatal development, I
hope you will keep in mind that our knowledge of these *physical
processes* helps us understand the ultimate development of *psychological processes*. At the simplest level: if there are problems at any stage
of physical development, the likelihood is that there will be problems
in terms of psychological development.

The time from conception to birth is the **prenatal period**. Until
recently, this period received only minor attention from psychologists.
We now recognize that many events that can have lifelong consequences occur during this very sensitive period.

Throughout this discussion I will use *growth* and *development* to
mean slightly different things. Growth refers to rather simple enlargement—getting bigger. A child demonstrates growth just by becoming
taller and heavier. Development, on the other hand, implies a differentiation of structure or function. Something develops when it appears
for the first time and remains. Thus, we say that the nervous system
"develops" between week 2 and week 8 after conception.

Prenatal development is divided into three different stages: the
stage of the zygote, the embryo, and the fetus. These stages are not all
of the same duration, and each is characterized by its own landmarks
of development.

The **stage of the zygote** is the shortest of the prenatal stages, lasting from conception until approximately two weeks later. The ovum
is usually fertilized as it moves along the fallopian tubes from the
ovaries, where ova (the plural of ovum) are stored and released at
approximately 28-day intervals. It typically takes the zygote about
seven days to travel down the fallopian tube to the uterus, and another seven days to become firmly implanted there (see Figure 8.2). At

Figure 8.2

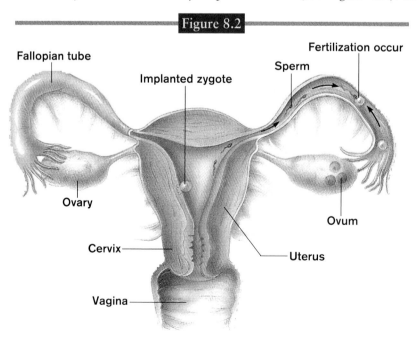

*The female reproductive organs, indicating where fertilization and implantation
normally take place.*

this point, the zygote has grown to include hundreds of cells, and for the first time it is clear that not all of the cells are exact replicas of each other. That is, there is now some *differentiation* among the cells in the zygote. Some cells develop to form the protective placenta, whereas others form the umbilical cord that will supply nourishment to the developing organism.

The **stage of the embryo** lasts about six weeks. During this period, the embryo develops at a rapid rate. At the beginning of this stage, we can differentiate only three types of cells: those that will become the nervous system, the sense organs, and the skin; those that will form the internal organs; and those that will become the muscles, skeleton, and blood vessels. By the end of this stage, we can identify the face, eyes, ears, fingers, and toes. At this point, not only does the number of cells increase, but the types of cells also increase.

stage of the embryo developmental period from 2 to 8 weeks

During this stage—conservatively, within the first three months— the unborn is most sensitive to external or environmental influences. If there are to be problems (e.g., birth defects), they are most likely to develop during this stage. If the heart, eyes, and hands do not become differentiated and develop during this period, for example, there will be no way to compensate later. Figure 8.3 shows the periods during which defects are most likely to occur. Note, for example, that there is little risk of damage to the zygote. Note, too, that the central nervous system is at risk throughout prenatal development—particularly in weeks 3 through 6.

Two months after conception, the stage of the embryo draws to a close. The 1-inch-long embryo now has enough of a primitive nervous system to respond to a light touch, exhibiting a simple reflex movement.

The final stage of prenatal development is also the longest, the **stage of the fetus**. This period includes months 3 through 9. Not only do the organs of the body continue to increase in complexity and size, but they begin to function. The arms and legs move spontaneously by

stage of the fetus developmental period from week 8 until birth

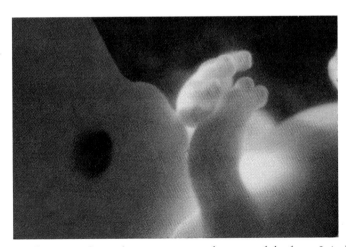

A human embryo at eight weeks, soon to enter the stage of the fetus. It is during the embryonic stage that environmental toxins are most likely to have an impact on the developing prenatal organism.

Figure 8.3

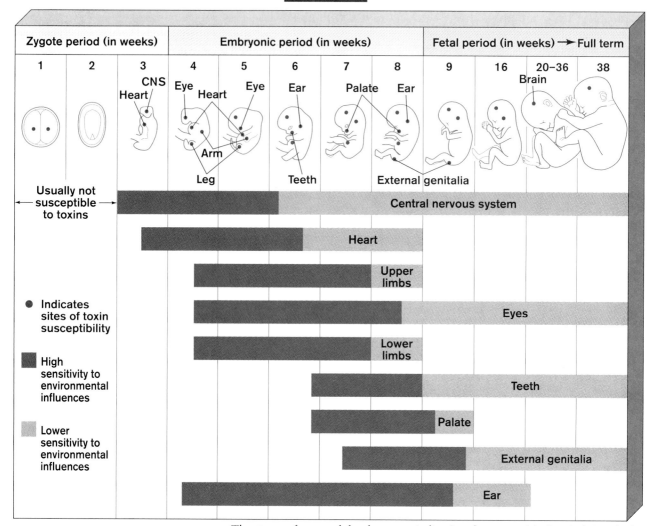

The stages of prenatal development, indicating the most critical periods in which defects are likely to occur and which aspect of the developing organism is likely to be affected. (After Moore, 1982.)

the end of the third month. In two more months, these movements will be substantial enough for the mother to feel them. At the end of the fifth month, the fetus is 10 inches long. Internal organs have developed, but not to the point of sustaining life outside the uterus. The brain has developed, but the neurons within it have not formed many synapses.

Development and growth continue through the last few months of pregnancy. The most noticeable change—certainly most noticeable to the mother—is the significant increase in weight and overall movement of the fetus. Sometime during the seventh month, most fetuses have reached the point of **viability**. This means that if they were forced to do so, they could survive, without interference or medical

viability the ability to survive without interference or intervention

intervention, if they were born prematurely. During its last few weeks in the uterus, the fetus grows more slowly. Its movements may be more powerful, but overall activity is also slowed because of the cramped quarters in which the fetus finds itself. After nearly 270 days, the fetus is ready to enter the world as a newborn.

Before You Go On

Briefly summarize the stages of prenatal development.

ENVIRONMENTAL INFLUENCES ON PRENATAL DEVELOPMENT

In most cases, the growth and development of the human organism from zygote to embryo to fetus progress according to the blueprint laid down in the genes. Even in the prenatal stage, however, the human organism is not immune to influences from the environment.

"Until the early 1940s, it was generally accepted that human embryos were protected from environmental agents by their fetal membranes and their mother's abdominal walls and uterus" (Moore, 1982, p. 140). It was then discovered that birth defects often resulted when a pregnant woman contracted rubella (German measles). Twenty years later, it was discovered that many drugs taken by a pregnant woman have measurable effects on the development of the embryo and fetus. It is now common knowledge that during the very rapid period of prenatal development, even small environmental disturbances can have serious and lasting consequences. Most of the external influences on prenatal development we know about are those that tend to have negative consequences (as is noted in Figure 8.3).

Nourishment

Never meant to be taken literally, the old expression "You are what you eat" does have some truth to it. By the same token, before we are born, we are what our mothers eat. When pregnant women eat poorly, their unborn children may share in the results. Maternal malnutrition often leads to increases in miscarriages, stillbirths, and premature births. At best, we can expect the newborn child of a malnourished mother to be similarly malnourished (e.g., Lozoff, 1989). Nutrition during the last three months of pregnancy is more critical than in the previous six months because it is in this latter stage that growth of the fetus is most rapid and significant.

It is also the case that deficiencies in specific vitamins and minerals affect the prenatal organism (Bratic, 1982). For example, a mother's calcium deficiencies affect the development of bones and teeth in the fetus. As is the case for many nutrients, it may very well be the mother who suffers more. If there are inadequate supplies of calcium in the mother's system, "the fetal need for calcium will be met at the expense of the mother" (Hughes & Noppe, 1985, p. 140). It should go without saying, but I need also mention that taking certain vitamins can be overdone. What works best is a balanced, sensible diet. Overdosing many vitamins (vitamins A and D, in particular) can be toxic, with negative effects for both mother and unborn child.

Smoking, Drinking, and Drugs

There is ample evidence that smoking has harmful effects on the smoker. Research also clearly shows that smoking by pregnant women has harmful effects on their unborn children (Frazier et al., 1961; Fribourg, 1982; Jacobson, 1984; Vorhees & Mollnow, 1987). Exactly *how* smoking affects the fetus is not known for certain. It may simply be a matter of reducing the oxygen and/or blood supply to the fetus. It may be that the tar and nicotine of the smoke act directly as poisons. What we do know is that cigarette smoking is well established as a cause of retarded prenatal growth (Golbus, 1980). Mothers who smoke during pregnancy give birth to children who are more likely to have hearing defects, and the more the mother smokes, the more serious the defects are likely to be (Fried, 1993). Mothers who smoke a pack a day or more double the chances of having a low-weight baby. Smoking mothers have many more miscarriages, stillbirths, and babies who die soon after birth than do mothers who do not smoke (Frazier et al., 1961; Golbus, 1980).

Alcohol is a commonly abused drug that can be injurious to unborn children. Alcohol is quickly and directly passed through the umbilical cord from the mother to the fetus. Heavy drinking (3 drinks or more per day) significantly increases the probability of having smaller babies and babies with retarded physical growth, poor coordination, poor muscle tone, intellectual retardation, and other problems, collectively referred to as **fetal alcohol syndrome** (**FAS**) (Jones et al., 1973; Mattson et al., 1988). In the United States, fetal alcohol syndrome is *the* leading preventable cause of birth defects that produce mental retardation (e.g., Streissguth et al., 1991). The Center for Disease Control estimates that 8,000 babies with fetal alcohol syndrome are born in the U.S. every year. In the 1970s, it was believed that an occasional drink or two had no particular lasting effect on prenatal development. Now experts agree that there is no safe dose of alcohol, nor is there a safe time to drink during pregnancy. The best advice is total abstinence (Abel, 1981, 1984; Barr et al., 1990).

Mothers who use or abuse psychoactive drugs such as heroin or cocaine, or "crack," during pregnancy cause considerable complications for their unborn children. At best, such children enter the world with low birth weights, difficulty regulating their sleep-wake cycles, and many symptoms of fetal alcohol syndrome, perhaps because their mothers *also* used or abused alcohol (Finnegan, 1982; Zuckerman & Bresnahan, 1991). At worst, they are born addicted themselves and must, within days of birth, suffer the pains of withdrawal, requiring a hospital stay averaging 42 days instead of the usual 3 days (Adler, 1989; Chasnoff et al., 1989; Finnegan, 1982).

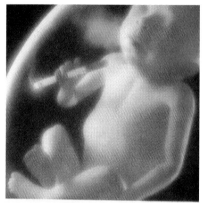

WOULD YOU GIVE A CIGARETTE TO YOUR UNBORN CHILD?

YOU DO EVERY TIME YOU SMOKE!

AMERICAN CANCER SOCIETY

Studies reveal that women who smoke during pregnancy significantly increase their chances of having miscarriages, stillbirths, low-weight babies, and babies who die shortly after birth.

fetal alcohol syndrome (FAS) a cluster of symptoms (e.g., low birth weight, poor muscle tone, and intellectual retardation) associated with a child born to a mother who was a heavy drinker of alcohol during pregnancy

Some drugs taken by the mother during her pregnancy seem to have few if any effects on the developing child; penicillin, for example (Golbus, 1980). Some have predictable effects that are not life-threatening; the antibiotic tetracycline, for instance, which directly passes to the developing fetus, is deposited in the teeth and bones, coloring them yellow. Even common aspirin has become suspect as a potential cause of several complications of pregnancy and labor (Briggs et al., 1986; Govoni & Hayes, 1988; Sibai et al., 1993).

Other prescription drugs may have devastating effects. One example is the drug thalidomide, routinely prescribed in Europe in the early 1960s as a tranquilizer and treatment for nausea associated with pregnancy. "Thalidomide children," as they are called, developed shortened, malformed limbs, or no limbs at all, and very often were mentally retarded. (Ironically, in 1993 researchers discovered that—at least in the laboratory—thalidomide can effectively retard the reproduction of the virus that causes AIDS. Although the drug is certainly worth pursuing for this reason, the long-term effects of its use are not known.)

Also in the 1950s and 1960s, many women who had problems during earlier pregnancies were given the drug DES (diethylstilbestrol) to reduce the likelihood of miscarriage. This synthetic hormone is now believed to be related to cervical cancer in the *daughters* of women who took the drug years earlier. Even the *sons* of women who received DES are found to have higher than normal rates of infertility (Stenchever et al., 1981), and subtle differences in brain functioning (Reinisch & Sanders, 1992). The bottom-line advice again seems very clear: pregnant women should use drugs of any sort only with great care, if at all, and only after consultation with their physicians.

Maternal Stress

There is a certain logic that tells us that a mother's emotional health can affect her unborn baby. There is even some logic to the physiology of the argument. As we shall see, emotionality is accompanied by many hormonal changes that may have some influence on the development of the embryo or fetus. It is also true that when a pregnant mother is under stress, the blood flow in her body is, for a short while at least, diverted from the uterus to other organs in the body, reducing the amount of oxygen available to the prenatal organism (Stechler & Halton, 1982). As logical and time-honored as the argument may be, the research evidence is difficult to find (Istvan, 1986). Imagine trying to find data that could relate stress during pregnancy to some measurable outcome at and after birth, while controlling for all other influences, and perhaps you can see why there is no clear-cut conclusion for us on this issue.

What About Dad?

As you read through this last section on nourishment, drugs, and stress, did it occur to you that the discussion seemed somewhat sexist? All of what we've covered here puts the focus on the mother— what the mother should and should not do. Eat a balanced diet.

Don't drink. Don't smoke. Don't get upset. Nowhere has there been any concern about the father's role in the process. To some degree it makes sense. After all, how is a father's diet going to directly impact on the development of a fetus residing in someone else's body? Psychologists Vicky Phares and Bruce Compas recently reviewed the literature on factors that influence the pathological development of children and adolescents and found that only *1 percent* of the 577 studies they looked at focused exclusively on the role of fathers. Their ultimate conclusion was that "the most global statement that can be made about the role of fathers in child and adolescent psychopathology is that fathers count" (Phares & Compas, 1993, p. 164).

But times *are* changing, and researchers are looking at the role of the father in determining the quality of life even of the prenatal child. The main issue, of course, revolves around the quality of the father's sperm at the moment of conception and the factors that affect sperm quality. Just as one example, consider the known causes of Down's syndrome, a collection of birth defects associated with mental retardation (See also page 481). Down's syndrome was first described in the mid-1800s, and is the result of a child being born with 47 chromosomes per cell instead of the standard 23 pairs. From the beginning, it was assumed that some problem with the mother's ovum ultimately caused this syndrome. Among other things, this was because the likelihood of having a child with Down's syndrome increases as the mother's age increases (much beyond the age of 35 to 40). What we now recognize is that the age of the father matters just as much as the age of the mother; that as many as one-third of all Down's cases are due to difficulties with the father's sperm; that the syndrome is more likely in children whose fathers have jobs that subject them to toxic chemicals. Alcohol use by fathers has been implicated as a probable cause of prenatal and birth abnormalities, but nearly all of this research has been on rats and mice (Hood, 1990). It may be that many difficulties of pregnancy, birth, and development are due to the condition of the father—who may be undernourished, an alcohol abuser, a drug user, or under stress—at or near the time of conception (Brown, 1985; Soyka & Joffee, 1980).

Before You Go On

Briefly review the impact of diet, drugs, and stress on prenatal development.

TOPIC 8A SUMMARY

Human development begins at conception when genes from the father's sperm cell unite with the genes from the mother's ovum to form a zygote. For the next nine months, the human organism grows and develops in the mother's uterus. This prenatal period of development has three discernible stages: zygote, embryo, and fetus. During the prenatal stages, development is governed largely by genetics, but in this stage, the developing organism is not beyond the influence of the environment. Most noteworthy environmental influences on prenatal development result in negative consequences, which leads us to advise pregnant women to eat well, to avoid smoking and drinking alcohol, and to use any drug with extreme care and a physician's awareness. Recent interest has also reinforced the notion that the father's physical condition at the time of conception may be a matter of concern.

Topic 8B
DEVELOPMENT IN CHILDHOOD

Now we turn our attention to development in *childhood*, the period between birth and adolescence. In the first section, we focus on the physical growth of children and note the orderly sequence of the development of their motor responses—their ability to do things with their bodies. We'll begin by considering some of the abilities of the newborn infant, or neonate.

neonate the newborn, from birth through the first 2 weeks

MOTOR DEVELOPMENT: GETTING FROM HERE TO THERE

The Neonate

As recently as 20 years ago, textbooks on child psychology seldom devoted more than a few paragraphs to the behaviors of the **neonate**—the newborn through the first two weeks of life. It seemed as if the neonate did not do much worth writing about. Today, most child psychology texts devote considerable space to a discussion of the abilities of newborns. It is unlikely that over the past 20 years neonates have gotten any smarter or more able. Psychologists have, though: They have devised new and better ways of assessing the abilities of neonates.

When a baby is first born, it looks like it can't do much of anything. It can cry, and dirty a diaper, but mostly it just sleeps. In fact, newborns *do* sleep a lot, about 15 to 17 hours each day. But as parents are quick to discover, that sleep tends to occur in a series of short naps, seldom lasting more than a few hours at a time.

A careful examination of babies reveals that they are capable of a wide range of behaviors. Nearly all of these behaviors are *reflexive*—simple, unlearned, involuntary reactions to specific stimuli. Many of the neonate's reflexes serve a useful purpose; mainly they help the child in responding to the demands of its environment. Some do not seem to have any particular survival value, but even these are important to know about because they can be used as diagnostic indicators

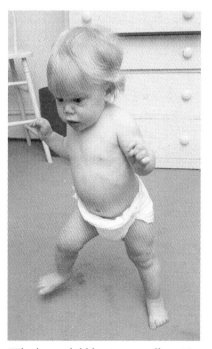

Whether a child begins to walk at 10 months or 13 months, he or she will still follow the same sequence of sitting, crawling, then walking. Here, an 11-month-old works on mastering that first step.

Figure 8.4

Reflexes of the Neonate

Name	Stimulus	Response	Age when disappears
Moro	Loud sound, or sudden loss of support	Arms and legs thrown outward; fingers spread; then, with fists clenched, arms and legs pulled back	4–6 months
Rooting	Light stroke on cheek	Head turns toward stimulus; mouth opens; sucking begins	3–4 months
Sucking	Object (e.g., nipple) inserted in mouth 3–4 cm.	Rhythmic sucking and mouth movements	Variable
Grasping	Rod pressed in palm	Close fist and grasp firmly	3–5 months
Walking/ stepping	With feet just touching surface, baby moved forward	Coordinated rhythmic stepping movements	2–4 months
Babinski	Stroke sole of foot from heel to toes	Small toes spread; big toe raised	9–12 months
Tonic neck	With baby on its back, turn head to one side	Arm and leg thrust outward, while other arm and leg drawn in to body	3–4 months
Swimming	Place infant in water	Rhythmic swimming movements	4–6 months

of the quality of the neonate's development, particularly the development of the nervous system. More than a dozen reflexes can be observed and measured (for strength and duration, for example) in the newborn child. Figure 8.4 summarizes some of the major neonatal reflexes. Remember that *psychologically* the major importance of these reflexes and the standard ages at which they occur is that they give us some behavioral landmarks by which we can assess the progress of development.

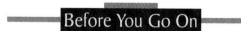

Before You Go On

What are some of the reflexes that can be observed in neonates?

Why do we care about neonatal reflexes?

The Motor Development of Children

Parents trying to keep their young children in properly fitting clothes know how quickly children grow. In their first three years, children's height and weight normally increase at a rate never again equaled. Although changes in size and motor skills are rapid, they do tend to be orderly and well sequenced, following a prescribed pattern. It is with this pattern that we are concerned here.

No two children are alike. No two children can be expected to grow at exactly the same rate or to develop control over their bodies at the same time. Joan may walk unaided at the age of 10 months. Bill may not venture forth on his own until he's 13 months old. Children who happen to develop more slowly might benefit from having others appreciate the notion of individual differences in developmental rates. (They might also benefit from the realization that the rate of physical development in infancy and early childhood is largely unrelated to adult characteristics, such as intelligence or even physical coordination.)

Regardless of the *rate* of one's motor development, there are regularities in the *sequence* of motor development. No matter when Joan does walk, she will first sit, then crawl.

Figure 8.5 summarizes the development of common motor skills. There are two important things for you to notice about this figure: first, the sequence of events is very regular, and second, *when* each stage develops includes a wide range of ages that should be considered normal. It is also true that the sequence and timing of the events listed in this figure hold equally for boys and girls. That is, in these basic motor skills there are no significant sex differences.

The regularity of physical growth and development seems to be guided by two "principles": (1) *Cephalocaudal sequencing* refers to the fact that a child's growth and bodily control proceed from top to bottom, or from head to upper torso to lower body. For example, children's heads and upper torsos develop before their trunks and lower bodies; hands and arms can be manipulated before feet and legs can. (2) *Proximodistal sequencing* refers to the observation that a child's growth and bodily control proceed from the center core to the extremities; from the internal organs to the arms and legs, to the hands and feet, to the fingers.

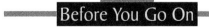

Before You Go On

What general observations can we make about physical growth and motor control in childhood?

SENSORY AND PERCEPTUAL DEVELOPMENT

Psychologists used to think that newborn children couldn't do much, in part because of the belief that newborns could not sense or perceive

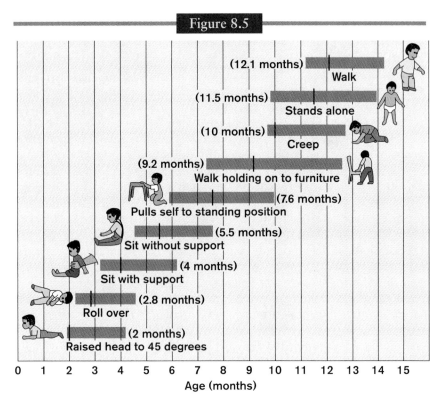

Figure 8.5

The sequence of human motor development. Each bar represents the ages at which between 25 percent of children (left end) and 90 percent of children (right end) engage in a given behavior. The short vertical line indicates the age at which 50 percent of children exhibit that behavior. (After Frankenburg & Dodds, 1967.)

very much. We now understand that neonates can and do respond to a wide range of stimuli. To some degree, all human senses are functioning at birth, having developed in order: touch, body position, balance, taste, smell, hearing, and finally, vision (Gibson, 1987, 1988; Hall & Oppenheim, 1987).

The neonate's ability to sense even subtle changes is remarkable. However, there *are* limitations. The ability of the eyes to focus on an object, for example, does not develop fully until the child is about 4 months old. The neonate can focus well on objects held 1 to 2 feet away, but everything nearer or farther appears out of focus. This means, however, that even newborns can focus on the facial features of the persons cradling or feeding them. Visual acuity—the ability to discern detail—shows at least a threefold to fourfold improvement during the first year (Aslin & Smith, 1988).

For their first few weeks, babies have difficulty coordinating the movements of their eyes, although within hours after birth they can follow (track) a stimulus object swung slowly back and forth in front of them. Newborns can detect differences in brightness, and soon develop the ability to detect surfaces, edges, and borders and to differentiate among colors (Cohen et al., 1978; Termine et al., 1987).

An issue that has been of interest to psychologists is just when the perception of depth and distance develops. Even newborns show some simple reactions to distance. They will close their eyes and squirm away if you rush an object toward their face (Bower et al., 1971).

In the late 1950s, two Cornell University psychologists, Eleanor Gibson and Richard Walk (1960), built an apparatus to test the depth perception of young children. The *visual cliff* is a deep box covered by a sheet of thick, clear Plexiglas. It is divided into two sides, one shallow, one deep. The deep and shallow sides are separated by a center board (Figure 8.6). Gibson and Walk found that 6-month-old children would not leave the center board to venture out over the deep side of the box, even to get to their mothers. By crawling age, therefore, the child seems able to perceive depth *and* to make an appropriate response to it.

It seems likely that the perception of depth develops even before the age of 6 months. When neonates (who obviously can't crawl) are placed on the Plexiglas over the deep side of the visual cliff, their heart rates *decrease,* indicating that at least they notice the change in visual stimulation (Campos et al., 1978). When 7-month-old infants are placed over the deep side of the visual cliff, their heart rates *increase.* The increase in heart rate is taken as indicating fear—a response that develops after the ability to discriminate depth (Bertenthal & Campos, 1989; Campos, 1976). There is also ample evidence that retinal disparity (the discrepancy in images received by the retinas of the two eyes) does not develop until the fourth month after birth (Birch et al., 1983; Fox et al., 1980). So, in some rudimentary form, even neonates sense depth, but reacting appropriately to depth requires experiences and learning that come later.

What about the other senses? Newborn infants can hear very well. They can direct their attention to the source of a sound, even a faint one. Wertheimer (1961) reports a study demonstrating sound localization in a newborn between 3 and 10 *minutes* after birth. (The child moved her eyes to the left or right in response to a loud clicking sound.) Sounds probably don't *mean* much to neonates, but they can respond differently to sounds of varied pitch and loudness. Even 3-day-old newborns are able to discriminate the sound of their mother's voice from other sounds (DeCasper & Fifer, 1980; Kolata, 1987; Martin & Clark, 1982).

Newborns also respond to differences in taste and smell. They discriminate among the four basic taste qualities of salt, sweet, bitter, and sour. They display a distinct preference for sweet-tasting liquids. Although they are unable to use it then, the sense of smell is established before birth. Immediately after birth, neonates respond predictably—drawing away and wrinkling their noses—to a variety of strong odors.

In summary, a wide range of sensory and perceptual capabilities appears to be available to the newborn child. The neonate may require some time to learn what to do with the sensory information it acquires from its environment, but many of its senses are operational.

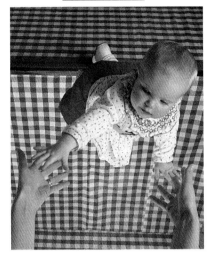

Figure 8.6

The visual cliff was designed to determine if depth perception is innate or learned. By the time an infant can move about, most will avoid the "deep" side of the apparatus.

What the newborn makes of the sensations it receives will depend on the development of its mental, or cognitive, abilities. This is the subject we turn to now.

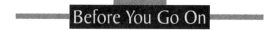

Before You Go On

Summarize the basic sensory capacities of the neonate.

COGNITIVE AND SOCIAL DEVELOPMENT

In preceding Topics, I have referred to cognitive skills many times. Cognitive processes are those that enable us to know and understand ourselves and the world around us. In this section, we'll look at how these skills develop throughout childhood, beginning with a summary of the cognitive capacities of the newborn infant. Our major focus will be on the theories of Jean Piaget. We'll consider Lawrence Kohlberg's theory of moral development, followed by the psychosocial theory of Erik Erikson. We will take a moment to consider gender and cultural issues in our discussion, and we'll end this Topic with a brief section on the development of social attachments. (We discussed the development of another cognitive skill—language—in Topic 7A.)

Cognitive Abilities of the Neonate: What Does the Newborn Know?

As we have seen, reflex reactions can help neonates survive. For long-term survival, however, neonates must learn to adapt to their environments and profit from their experiences. Neonates have to form memories of their experiences and learn to make discriminations among the many stimuli with which they are presented. Are these cognitive processes possible in a baby just a couple of days or weeks old? In several specific ways, the answer seems to be yes.

The first thing we can note is that even newborns demonstrate the ability to engage in simple learning tasks. A neonate (only two hours old!) is stroked on the forehead and seems not to respond. This stimulus is then paired with a sugar solution delivered to the infant's lips. The (unconditioned) sugar solution stimulus elicits the (unconditioned) response of turning the head and making sucking movements. After several trials of pairing the stroking of the forehead and the sugar solution, the baby makes sucking and head movements simply when its forehead is touched (Blass et al., 1984). This is an excellent example of classical conditioning (for a review, see Topic 5A, pages 204–209).

Head turning and sucking movements of neonates can also be brought under the control of operant conditioning (see Topic 5B). The rates of these responses increase when they are followed (reinforced) by sugar solutions, the sound of mother's voice, or the recorded sound of mother's heartbeat (DeCasper & Sigafoos, 1983; Moon & Fifer, 1990; Sameroff & Cavanaugh, 1979).

Friedman (1972) reported a demonstration of what we might call memory in neonates only 1 to 4 *days* old. Babies were shown a picture of a simple figure—say, a checkerboard pattern—for 60 seconds. Experimenters recorded how long the baby looked at the stimulus pattern. After the same pattern was shown over and over again, the baby appeared to be bored and gave it less attention. (You should recognize *this* as "habituation," which, in Topic 5A, we characterized as a simple form of learning.) When a different stimulus pattern was introduced, the baby stared at it for the full 60 seconds of its exposure. So, what does this have to do with memory? The argument is that for the neonate to stare at the new stimulus, it must have formed some memory of the old one. Otherwise, how would it recognize the new pattern as being new or different? In fact, if the new stimulus pattern was very similar to the old one, the baby would not give it as much attention as it would if it were totally different. It is as if a judgment is being made about the distinctiveness of the new stimulus and the old (remembered) ones.

In talking about recognizing visual patterns, I should mention the research of Robert Fantz (1961, 1963). Fantz presented newborn children with pairs of visual stimuli. In most pairs, one stimulus was more complex than the other. As the babies lay on their backs, looking up at the stimuli, the experimenters could note which of the two stimuli received more attention from the child. In nearly every case, the babies showed a preference for the more complex stimulus pattern.

This in itself is interesting, but difficult to explain. The major finding is that the newborns could at least discriminate between the two stimuli. That attention equals "preference" is more of an assumption than a research finding. Fantz also discovered something curious when he found that even newborn infants show a preference for (choose to attend to) drawings of a human face. They chose the face pattern as the focus of their attention no matter what it was paired with. It is also clear that human newborns just a few hours old can recognize a picture of their own mother's face, and prefer to look at it over any other face paired with it (Bushnell et al., 1989; Walton et al., 1992; Walton & Bower, 1993). Researchers have also demonstrated that young infants can even discriminate among facial expressions displaying various emotional states, looking more at facial expressions of joy than of anger, for instance (Malatesta & Isard, 1984).

One more step takes us to the research of Meltzoff and Moore (1977, 1989), who discovered something in the controlled setting of a laboratory that many parents have discovered by accident. Not only do newborns look at a human face, but often try to imitate facial expressions. When experimenters stick out their tongues at babies, the babies stick out their tongues, too. Infants open their mouths to imitate the same facial expression of the experimenter. These attempts at imitation—a cognitive skill indicating an appreciation of the environment—are clearly present by the age of 2 weeks, and are often found in neonates only 1 hour old. These attempts at imitation serve a useful social skill, encouraging additional interaction with delighted parents. It hardly needs mentioning that many parents—and unrelated adults—seem to take great joy in imitating the facial expressions of infants.

Jean Piaget's observations on the cognitive development of children remain the most comprehensive and influential. Nonetheless, some of Piaget's ideas have been challenged.

Before You Go On

Cite an example of research evidence demonstrating a cognitive reaction in neonates.

Piaget's Theory of Cognitive Development

The physical growth and development of a child is remarkable. Even more impressive are the increases in cognitive and intellectual abilities that occur during childhood. By the time the human reaches adolescence, he or she has acquired an enormous stockpile of information. More than just learning facts, the child comes to appreciate *how* to learn. Strategies for survival or success begin to develop in childhood (Siegler, 1983).

Accounting for *how* children's intellectual capacities and abilities change is a difficult business. It is important to be able to describe the changes that occur, but it is even more important to be able to specify the principles that underlie cognitive development (Siegler, 1989; Wellman & Gelman, 1992). The theory that has attracted the most attention in this regard is that of the Swiss psychologist Jean Piaget (1896–1980). Although there *are* others, Piaget's theory of cognitive development has been so influential that it will be the focus of our discussion (Piaget, 1932/1948, 1954, 1967).

In Piaget's theory, cognitive development relies on the formation of **schemas**, or organized mental representations of the world. For example, children develop a schema for "daddy," for "mommy," for "eating breakfast," and for "bedtime." Schemas aid the child in adapting to the demands and pressures of the environment. Schemas are formed by experience. (Indeed, you are correct if it seems to you that *schema* in this context sounds like our earlier use of terms such as *concepts* and *categories* [pages 308–311]). Organizing the world into schemas is, for Piaget, a process found in all children.

Forming mental representations of the environment involves two fundamental processes, assimilation and accommodation. **Assimilation** involves taking on new information and fitting it into an existing schema. Children develop a rather complex schema for mealtime, for instance. When, for the first time, they are taken to a fast-food restaurant, new information will have to be added to the mealtime schema, such as the understanding that meals must be paid for and that others (strangers, in fact) will be eating in the same room.

Accommodation involves changing or revising existing schemas—not just adding to them—in the face of new experiences. As children are shifted away from the bottle to strained foods, to chunkier foods,

schemas organized mental representations of the world that are adaptive and formed by experience

assimilation the process of adding new material or information to an existing schema

accommodation in Piaget's theory, the process of changing or revising an existing schema as a result of new experiences

to regular food, they must accommodate their schemas for efficient feeding; what used to work in the past doesn't work any longer. Once the child gets to go out to the fast-food restaurant, not only will new information have to be assimilated, but old ideas about how and where one eats will have to be accommodated. Learning that mommy or daddy won't *necessarily* come running when one cries may require accommodation.

Piaget proposed that as children assimilate new ideas into existing schemas and modify or make accommodations to old ones, they progress through four stages of development: the sensorimotor stage, the preoperational stage, the concrete operations stage, and the formal operations stage. Determining precisely when each stage begins or ends is not always possible, in that adjacent stages may overlap and blend for a while. Even so, each stage is characterized by its own schemas, cognitive methods, insights, and abilities.

Sensorimotor Stage. (Ages birth to 2 years.) For children younger than age 2, language is not an effective means of finding out about the world. Children of this age are unable to discover much about their world by asking questions about it or by trying to understand long-winded explanations. Trying to explain to a 10-month-old baby *why* it shouldn't chew on an electrical extension cord is likely to be an unrewarding piece of parental behavior. In the **sensorimotor stage**, children discover by *sensing* (sensori) and by *doing* (motor). A child may come to appreciate, for example, that a quick pull on a dog's tail (a motor activity) reliably produces a loud yelp (a sensory experience), perhaps followed in turn by parental attention.

sensorimotor stage in Piaget's theory, from ages birth to 2 years, when a child learns by sensing and doing

One of the most useful schemas to develop in the sensorimotor stage is that of *causality*. Infants gradually come to realize that events may have knowable causes and that some behaviors cause predictable reactions. Pushing a bowl of oatmeal off the high chair causes a mess and gets mommy's attention: if *A*, then *B*—a practical insight. Another important discovery that occurs during this developmental stage is that objects may exist even when they are not immediately in view. Early in this stage, an object that is out of sight is more than out of mind. The object ceases to exist for the child. By the end of the sensorimotor period, children have learned that objects can and do still exist even if they are not physically present, and that their reappearance can be anticipated. This awareness is called **object permanence** (see Figure 8.7).

object permanence the appreciation that an object no longer in view can still exist and reappear later

A useful skill that characterizes the sensorimotor period is imitation. As long as it is within its range of abilities, a baby will imitate almost any behavior it sees. A cognitive strategy has developed, one that will be used for a lifetime: trying to imitate the behaviors of a model.

Before You Go On

How are schemas formed during the sensorimotor stage?

What characterizes this stage of development?

Figure 8.7

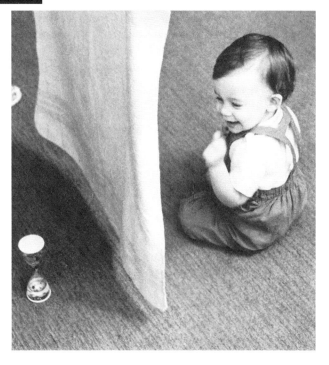

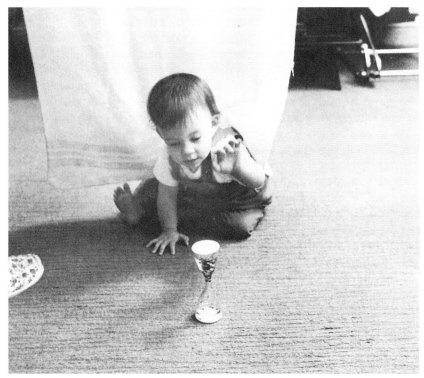

By the end of the sensorimotor stage of development, a child comes to appreciate that simply because an object is no longer in view does not mean that object ceases to exist. Here, the infant sees a toy, and even when it is blocked from view, realizes that it is still there and crawls under the blanket to get at it.

Preoperational Stage. (Ages 2 to 6 years.) By the end of the senso-rimotor stage, a child recognizes that he or she is a separate, independent person. Through most of the **preoperational stage**, a child's thinking is self-centered, or *egocentric.* According to Piaget, the child has difficulty understanding life from someone else's perspective. In this stage, the world is very much *me-, mine-,* and *I*-oriented.

preoperational stage in Piaget's theory, from ages 2 to 6 years, characterized by egocentrism and the beginning of symbol development

Perhaps you have seen two preschool children at play. They are right next to each other, one playing with a truck, the other coloring in a coloring book. They are jabbering at each other, taking turns, but each seems to be oblivious to what the other is saying:

Jill: "This sure is a neat truck!"
Leslie: "I think I'll paint the sky a kinda purple."
Jill: "I'm gonna be a truck driver some day."
Leslie: "But if I make the sky a kinda purple, what'll I make the trees?"
Jill: "Maybe I'll drive a milk truck. Broooom!"
Leslie: "I know, blue."

Such exchanges, called *collective monologues,* reflect the egocentrism of children's thinking in this stage.

In the preoperational stage, children begin to develop symbols, usually in the form of words to represent concepts. At this stage, children do not appreciate how to manipulate symbols in a consistent, rule-governed way (remember my difficulties with preschoolers and a simple word association task). It's not until the end of this period that they can play word games or understand why riddles about rabbits throwing clocks out of windows in order to "see time fly" are funny. It is similarly true that children at this stage have great difficulty with many "abstract" concepts, such as those involved with religious beliefs.

Before You Go On

In Piaget's theory, what characterizes the
preoperational stage of development?

Concrete Operations Stage. (Ages 7 to 12 years.) In the **concrete operations stage**, children begin to develop many concepts *and* show that they can manipulate those concepts. For example, they can organize objects into categories of things: balls over here, blocks over there, plastic soldiers in a pile by the door, and so on. Each of these items is recognized as a toy, ultimately to be put away in the toy box and not in the closet, which is where clothes are supposed to go. Thus, it is in this period that rule-governed behavior begins. The concrete, observable objects of the child's world can be classified, ranked, ordered, or separated into more than one category, according to systematic rules.

concrete operations stage in Piaget's theory, from ages 7 to 12 years, when concepts can be manipulated, but not in an abstract fashion

In a demonstration of the concept of "conservation of volume," a child in Piaget's preoperational stage of development will claim that there is more water in the tall beaker than in the shorter, wider one, even though the amounts of liquid are, in fact, equal.

conservation *in Piaget's theory, an appreciation that changing the physical properties of an object does not necessarily change its essence*

A sign of the beginning of the concrete operations stage is an ability to solve conservation problems. **Conservation** involves the awareness that changing the form or the appearance of something does not necessarily change what it really is. Many experiments convinced Piaget that the ability to demonstrate conservation marked the end of the preoperational stage of development. Figure 8.8 shows a test for conservation of *volume*. We can show *size* conservation by giving two equal-size balls of clay to a 4-year-old. One is then rolled into a long cigar shape, and the child will now assert that it has more clay in it than the ball does. A 7-year-old will seldom hesitate to tell you that each form contains the same amount of clay. The 7-year-old has moved on to the next stage of cognitive development.

During the concrete operations stage, youngsters enjoy games if the rules are simple. Moving pieces around a board to squares that match the color indicated by a spinner is easy. Problems arise when choices need to be made that force decisions beyond the concrete here and now: "Should I buy this property now or build a house on Boardwalk?" "If I move my piece there, I'll get jumped, but then I can jump two of his pieces." "Should I save sevens, or should I save clubs?"

As its name suggests, in the concrete operations stage, children begin to use and manipulate (operate on) concepts and ideas. These manipulations are still very concrete, however—very much tied to real objects in the here and now. An 8-year-old can be expected to find her way to and from school, even if she throws in a side trip along the way. What she will have a difficult time doing is *telling* you with any precision just how she gets from one place to another. Drawing a sensible map is very difficult for her. If she actually stands on the corner of Maple Street and Oak Avenue, she knows where to go next to get home. Dealing with the concrete reality, here and now, is fairly easy. Dealing with such knowledge, in abstract terms, is what is difficult.

Before You Go On

What cognitive skills might we expect from a child in the concrete operations stage of development?

Formal Operations Stage. (Ages over 12 years.) The logical manipulation of abstract, symbolic concepts appears in the last of Piaget's stages of development: **formal operations.** The key to this stage, usually begun at adolescence, is abstract, symbolic reasoning. By the age of 12 years, most children can develop and mentally test hypotheses—can work through problems in their mind. Many problem-solving strategies of the sort that we discussed in Topic 7B develop at this stage.

formal operations stage in Piaget's theory, ages older than 12 years, when one can generate and test abstract hypotheses and manipulate symbolic concepts

It is only at the stage of formal operations that youngsters are able to reason through hypothetical problems: "What if you were the only person in the world who liked rock music?" "If nobody had to go to school, what would happen?" Similarly, children are now able to deal with questions that are literally contrary to fact: "What if John F. Kennedy or Ronald Reagan were still president of the United States?" The stages of Piaget's theory and the cognitive milestones associated with each are summarized in Figure 8.9.

Before You Go On

What cognitive ability characterizes the stage of formal operations?

Reactions to Piaget

There can be no doubt of the significance of Piaget's influence. His insights and observations about intellectual development spanned decades. Considerable research has supported many of these insights. Finding evidence of Piagetian stages and the experiences people need to have to demonstrate that they've reached a given stage is one of cross-cultural research's success stories. The bulk of that evidence tells

---

Figure 8.9

Piaget's Stages of Cognitive Development

1. **Sensorimotor stage (ages birth to 2 years)**
   "Knows" through active interaction with environment
   Becomes aware of cause-effect relationships
   Learns that objects exist even when not in view
   Imitates crudely the actions of others
2. **Preoperational stage (ages 2 to 6 years)**
   Begins by being very egocentric
   Language and mental representations develop
   Objects are classified on just one characteristic at a time
3. **Concrete operations stage (ages 7 to 12 years)**
   Develops conservation of volume, length, mass, etc.
   Organizes objects into ordered categories
   Understands relational terms (e.g., bigger than, above)
   Begins using simple logic
4. **Formal operations stage (ages over 12)**
   Thinking becomes abstract and symbolic
   Reasoning skills develop
   A sense of hypothetical concepts develops

---

us that the stages we have just reviewed can be identified in children around the world (e.g., Brislin, 1993; Dasen & Heron, 1981; Dasen & de Ribaupierre, 1987; Segall et al., 1990). There will be individual differences, of course. Remember my example of *conservation* that involved estimating the amount of clay one has when it is rolled into varied shapes? Sons and daughters of potters understand the conservation of sizes of clay with great ease (Price-Williams et al., 1969). In other words, experience does matter.

On the other hand, some research has brought into question some of Piaget's basic ideas. The two major criticisms of Piaget's theory are that (1) the borderlines between his proposed stages are much less clear-cut than his theory suggests, and (2) Piaget underestimated the cognitive talents of preschool children (Flavell, 1982, 1985; Gelman, 1978; Wellman & Gelman, 1992).

For example, the egocentrism said to characterize the preoperational child may not be as flagrant as Piaget would have us believe. In one study (Lempers et al., 1977), children were shown a picture pasted inside a box. They were asked to show the picture to someone else. In showing the picture, they turned it so that it would be right side up to the viewer. Every child over 2 years of age indicated such an appreciation of someone else's point of view. Similarly, object permanence may be neither universal nor consistently found in any one child; it depends on how you test for it (Harris, 1983).

Even Piaget's notion of conservation may not be such an obvious indicator of cognitive development as was once thought. When experimenters pour liquid from a short beaker into a tall one, a 5-year-old will probably say that the taller beaker now holds more liquid—evidence of a failure to conserve in the preoperational stage. If the *child* does the pouring from one beaker to the other, as opposed to just watching, even 5-year-olds show conservation and recognize that the amount of liquid is the same in both containers (Rose & Blank, 1974).

A further criticism is that Piaget's theory, focusing on a stage approach, gives little attention to the impact of language development. Nor did Piaget have much to say about the smooth and gradual increase in the capacity of a child's memory.

So, it seems that some of Piaget's observations and assumptions have come under attack. This is to be expected in science. In fact, one of the most important contributions of Jean Piaget is that he developed a theory of cognitive development in children that was so rich, so detailed, so thought-provoking, that it will continue to challenge researchers for years to come.

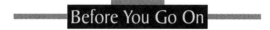

Cite two criticisms of Piaget's theory of cognitive development.

Kohlberg's Theory of Moral Development

How children learn to reason about and make judgments about what is right and wrong is an aspect of cognitive development that has received considerable attention. This is true even though psychologists do not have a generally acceptable model of moral reasoning in adults (Darley & Schultz, 1990; Vitz, 1990). Piaget included the study of moral development in his theory, arguing that morality is closely related to cognitive awareness, and that children are unable to make moral judgments until they are at least 3 or 4 years old (Piaget, 1932/1948). Lawrence Kohlberg (1963, 1969, 1981, 1985) has offered a theory of moral development that, like Piaget's theory of cognitive development, is a theory of stages, in which one progresses from one stage to another in an orderly fashion. Kohlberg's original data include responses made by young boys who were asked a number of questions about stories that involve some moral dilemma. The most commonly cited example of such a story concerns whether or not a man should steal a drug in order to save his wife's life after the pharmacist who invented the drug refuses to sell it to him. Should the man steal the drug; why or why not?

On the basis of responses to such dilemmas, Kohlberg proposed three levels of moral development, with two stages (or "orientations") at each level. The result is the six stages of moral development briefly summarized in Figure 8.10. A child who says, for example, that the man should not steal the drug because "he'll get caught and be put in jail" would be at the first, *preconventional*, level of reasoning because the prime interest of the child is simply with the punishment that comes from breaking a rule. A child who says the man should

Figure 8.10

Kohlberg's Stages of Moral Development

Level 1	**Preconventional morality**
1. Obedience and punishment orientation	Rules are obeyed simply to avoid punishment; If I take the cookies, I'll get spanked."
2. Naive egotism and instrumental orientation	Rules are obeyed simply to earn rewards; "If I wash my hands, will you let me have two desserts?"
Level 2	**Conventional (conforming) morality**
3. Good boy/girl orientation	Rules are conformed to in order to avoid disapproval and gain approval; "I'm a good boy 'cause I cleaned my room, aren't I?"
4. Authority-maintaining orientation	Social conventions blindly accepted to avoid criticism from those in authority; "You shouldn't steal because it's against the law, and you'll go to jail if the police catch you."
Level 3	**Postconventional morality**
5. Contractual-legalistic orientation	Morality is based on agreement with others to serve the common good and protect the rights of individuals; "I don't like stopping at stop signs, but if we didn't all obey traffic signals, it would be difficult to get anywhere."
6. Universal ethical principle orientation	Morality is a reflection of internalized standards; "I don't care what anybody says, what's right is right."

steal the drug because "it will make his wife happy, and probably most people would do it anyway" is reflecting a type of reasoning at the second, *conventional,* level because the judgment is based on a blindly accepted social convention, and social approval matters as much as or more than anything else. The argument that, "no, he shouldn't steal the drug for a basically selfish reason, which in the long run would just promote more stealing in the society in general" is an example of moral reasoning at Kohlberg's third, *postconventional,* level because it reflects complex, internalized standards. Notice that what matters is not the choice the child makes, but the reasoning behind that choice.

Research tells us that Kohlberg's theory has merit (Rest, 1983). It also has cross-cultural application. To varying degrees, Kohlberg's descriptions are valid for several cultures, including Israel, Turkey, India, and Nigeria (Edwards, 1977, 1981; Magsud, 1979; Nisan & Kohlberg, 1982; Snarey, 1987; Snarey et al., 1985).

Problems with the theory also exist. For one thing, very few people (including adults) operate at the higher stages of moral reasoning described by the theory (Colby & Kohlberg, 1984). This is particularly true in cultures that emphasize communal or group membership—such as the Israeli kibbutz or tribal groups in New Guinea—more than individuality (Snarey, 1987).

This brings us to a key concept in cross-cultural psychology: the dimension of individualism-collectivism (Bhawuk & Brislin, 1992; Erez & Early, 1993; Triandis, 1990, 1993; Triandis et al., 1988). People in some cultures are raised and socialized to take others (members of the family, the tribe, the neighborhood, the society) into account when setting goals and making decisions. Such a tendency toward **collectivism** is found more commonly in Asia and South America. People in other cultures are raised and socialized to think mostly about themselves and their own individual behaviors, a sort of "pull yourself up by your own boot straps; make it on your own; you'll get what you deserve" sort of mentality. A tendency toward **individualism** is more common in North America and Western Europe. Remember, we are talking about a dimension of comparison here; even within the same culture, individualism and collectivism exist to varying degrees.

collectivism in cross-cultural psychology, the tendency to set goals and make decisions based on a concern for the group or the common good

individualism in cross-cultural psychology, the tendency to set goals and make decisions based on a concern for one's self or the individual

This discussion relates to Kohlberg's theory and the subsequent research it generated because most ratings or measures of moral reasoning put a high value on the sort of thinking found in individualistic (largely Western) cultures, and devalue the sorts of thinking typical of collective cultures. This does not mean that Kohlberg was wrong, of course. It just means that much of what is true for one culture may not be for another, and neither is necessarily any "better" or more moral.

A similar argument has been raised about Kohlberg's theory as it applies to women (Ford & Lowery, 1986; Gilligan, 1982). All of Kohlberg's original data came from the responses of young boys, remember. Later, when young girls were tested, some studies seemed to suggest that girls showed slower moral development when compared to boys. Carol Gilligan's argument is that the moral reasoning of females is neither slower nor faster but is simply *different* from the reasoning of males. Males (at least males in Western cultures) are concerned with rules, justice, and an individual's rights. As a result, they approach moral dilemma problems differently than do females, who are characteristically more concerned with caring, personal responsibility, and interpersonal relationships (Gilligan, 1982). Gilligan's book brought a new approach to research on morality and value development. The issue is not a judgmental one in the sense of trying to determine if men are more or less moral in their thinking than women. The question is whether women and men develop different styles of moral reasoning or different types of moral behaviors, a question for which final answers are not yet available. In fact, most studies show that differences between men and women in resolving moral conflicts are really quite insignificant (Darley & Schultz, 1990; Donneberg & Hoffman, 1988; Mednick, 1989; Walker, 1989).

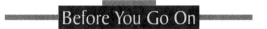

Before You Go On

Briefly summarize the stages of Kohlberg's theory of moral development.

Erikson's Theory of Psychosocial Development

Erik Erikson (1902–1994) was a psychologist who, like Piaget, proposed a stage theory of human development (Erikson, 1963, 1965, 1968). Unlike Piaget, his theory focuses on more than cognitive development, although this aspect is included. Erikson's theory is based on his observations of a wide range of types of people of various ages. As we'll see, his theory extends from childhood through adolescence into adulthood. Many of his observations had more of a cross-cultural basis than did Piaget's. Erikson was born in Germany, studied with Anna Freud (Sigmund Freud's daughter) in Vienna, and came to the United States to do his research. Erikson's views were influenced more by Freud than by Piaget. Unlike Freud, Erikson chose to focus on the *social* environment, which is why his theory is called *psychosocial.*

Erikson's theory lists eight stages of development through which an individual passes. These stages are not so much periods of time as they are a series of conflicts, or crises, that need to be resolved. Each of the eight stages is referenced by a pair of terms that indicates the nature of the conflict that needs to be resolved in this period of development.

As a stage theory, Erikson's implies that we naturally go through the resolution of each conflict, or crisis, in order and that facing any one type of crisis usually occurs at about the same age for all of us. Figure 8.11 is a summary of each of Erikson's eight stages of development.

As you can see, only the first four stages, or crises, are relevant for children. In fact, one of the major strengths of Erikson's view of development is that it covers the entire life span. Whereas Piaget focused only on the stages of development of children, Erikson extended his views to late adulthood. For now, we'll describe Erikson's first four crises, but we will return to his theory in Topics 8C and 8D.

During one's first year of life, according to Erikson, one's greatest struggle centers around the establishment of a sense of *trust or mistrust*. There's just not very much a newborn can accomplish on its own. If its needs are met in a reasonable fashion, the child will develop a basic sense of safety and security, optimistic that the world is a predictable place. If a child's needs aren't adequately met, what develops is a sense of mistrust—feelings of frustration and insecurity.

Figure 8.11

Erikson's Eight Stages of Development

Approximate age	Crisis	Adequate resolution	Inadequate resolution
0–1½	Trust vs. mistrust	Basic sense of safety	Insecurity, anxiety
1½–3	Autonomy vs. self-doubt	Perception of self as agent capable of controlling own body and making things happen	Feelings of inadequacy to control events
3–6	Initiative vs. guilt	Confidence in oneself as initiator, creator	Feeling of lack of self-worth
6–puberty	Competence vs. inferiority	Adequacy in basic social and intellectual skills	Lack of self-confidence, feelings of failure
Adolescent	Identity vs. role confusion	Comfortable sense of self as a person	Sense of self as fragmented; shifting, unclear sense of self
Early adult	Intimacy vs. isolation	Capacity for closeness and commitment to another	Feeling of aloneness, separation; denial of need for closeness
Middle adult	Generativity vs. stagnation	Focus on concern beyond oneself to family, society, future generations	Self-indulgent concerns; lack of future orientation
Later adult	Ego-integrity vs. despair	Sense of wholeness, basic satisfaction with life	Feelings of futility, disappointment

During the period of *autonomy versus self-doubt,* what emerges most plainly is a sense of self-esteem. The child begins to act independently; to dress and feed himself or herself, for example. Physically more able, the child can strike off on its own, exploring ways of assuming personal responsibility. Frustration at this level of development leads to feelings of inadequacy and doubts of one's self-worth.

From ages 3 years to 6 years is Erikson's period of *initiative versus guilt.* Now the challenge is to develop as a functioning, contributing member of social groups, particularly the family. If the child is encouraged to do so, he or she should develop a strong sense of initiative, a certain joy of trying new things. How reinforcing it is to a 5-year-old to be asked for an opinion on what the family should do this evening. Without such encouragement, the child is likely to feel guilty and resentful.

The final childhood period, *competence versus inferiority*, lasts from about age 6 years to puberty. During this period of choices, the child is challenged to move beyond the safety and comfort of the family unit. The main focus of development is "out there" in the neighborhood and the school. Children have to begin to acquire those skills that will enable them to become fully functioning adults in society. If the child's efforts of industry are constantly belittled, criticized, or ignored, the child may develop a sense of inadequacy and inferiority, and remain dependent on others even into adulthood.

Before You Go On

Briefly describe the first four stages, or crises, of development according to Erikson.

Developing Gender Identity

gender one's maleness or femaleness; the state of being male or female

The theories of Piaget, Kohlberg, Gilligan, and Erikson deal with how (and when) children develop concepts or cognitions about themselves and the world in which they live. In this section we'll focus on the concept of **gender**—one's maleness or femaleness, as opposed to one's sex, which is a biological term. Janet Hyde defines gender as "the state of being male or female" (1986, p. 3).

One of the first proclamations made upon the birth of a baby is, "It's a girl!" or "It's a boy!" Parents then may wrap up little girls in pink things, boys in blue things. Many parents dress an infant or small child in clothes that clearly label the child as a boy or a girl, and are concerned that their baby's gender be correctly identified.

One question we might ask is what differences do we find between boys and girls? Let me give you the general answer first, then we'll fill in some of the details. Sex differences between male and female infants and children are few and subtle. They are more likely to be in the eye of the beholder than in the behaviors of children.

As infants, boys do develop a bit more slowly than girls, have a little more muscle tissue than girls do, and are slightly more active, but even these differences are slight (e.g., Eaton & Enns, 1986). During the first year of life there are virtually no differences in temperament or "difficulty" between boys and girls (Thomas & Chess, 1977).

Adults often believe that there are, or ought to be, differences between the sexes (Paludi & Gullo, 1986) and often do choose toys, clothing, and playmates on the basis of their understanding of what is acceptable for them as boys or girls (Schau et al., 1980). Surprisingly, however, when averaged over many research studies, there are few areas in which parents consistently treat their sons and daughters differently (Lytton & Romney, 1991). The only area in which North

Adults react to gender differences in children at a very young age, often dressing girls in pink and boys in blue. This phenomenon is not a new one. These two works of art are often hung together. "Pinkie," by Sir Thomas Lawrence, was painted about 1795, and "The Blue Boy," by Thomas Gainsborough, was painted in 1770.

American parents show significant differentiation is in the encouragement of different sex-typed activities for girls and boys. For example, in one study (Snow et al., 1983), fathers were more likely to give dolls to 1-year-old girls than to boys. However, even at this age, children themselves already have their own toy preferences; when offered dolls, boys were less likely to play with them than girls were. During the first few years of elementary school, girls have a different view of areas of their own competence and activities of value than boys do. Girls tend to value (and see themselves as competent in) reading and instrumental music, for example, whereas boys value math and sports activities (Eccles et al., 1993.)

Children's peer groups provide significant experiences for both girls and boys (Maccoby, 1988, 1990; Maccoby & Jacklin, 1987). By the age of 3 or 4, girls and boys gravitate toward playmates of the same sex. This pattern is shown cross-culturally, and increases in strength from the preschool to school-age years. Girls tend to be dominated in mixed-sex interactions, even in children as young as 33 months (Jacklin & Maccoby, 1978). Boys develop the tendency to use direct commands to influence others, whereas girls tend to use polite suggestions, which are effective with other girls but not with boys (Serbin et al., 1984). Girls develop more intensive friendships than boys and are more distressed when those friendships end. Maccoby (1990) has suggested that the interactive styles that develop in same-sex groups in childhood lay the foundation for differences in social relationships of adult men and women, with more supportive, intimate relationships among women and more direct, hierarchical relationships among men.

Here's a different, but related, question: At what point do boys and girls begin to see each other as "different"? More technically, when do children develop **gender identity**, the basic sense or self-awareness of one's maleness or femaleness? It has been found that even 5-month-old infants are capable of distinguishing gender in faces shown in pictures (Fagan & Singer, 1979). Most of us develop a sense of our own gender identity by the time we are 2 or 3 years old (Money, 1972; Paludi & Gullo, 1986). By the age of 4, most children demonstrate common gender stereotypes, showing that they believe that certain occupations, activities, or toys go better with males and some with females. By the time they are ready to start school, most children have a notion of associating various personality traits with men and women. This pattern has been found in several cultures (Williams & Best, 1990). Once gender identity is established, it remains quite invulnerable to change (Bem, 1981; Spence, 1985).

Cognitive psychologists believe that once children are able to discriminate between the sexes, they develop schemas for gender-related

gender identity *a basic sense or self-awareness of one's maleness or femaleness*

It's recess time at school. Notice that every boy is wearing pants; every girl is wearing a dress.

information (e.g., Martin, 1991). You'll recall that a schema is an organized system of general information, stored in one's memory, that guides the processing of new information. For example, children show more interest in and a better memory for new toys when those toys are labeled as appropriate for their own sex than appropriate for the other sex (Bradbard & Endsley, 1983). If information is inconsistent with the gender schema the child has developed, that information is likely to be distorted in memory. Children shown a picture of a female doctor tend to remember her as a nurse (Cordua et al., 1979). Children shown a girl sawing wood may remember a boy sawing wood. As Martin (1991) has pointed out, such distortions in memory may serve to perpetuate gender stereotypes, because information that does not fit the child's existing schema regarding gender is simply changed so that it conforms to the stereotype.

Before You Go On

What conclusions may we draw about the development of gender identity in children?

attachment a strong two-way emotional bond, usually between a child and parent, or primary caregiver

Developing Social Attachments

To a large degree, we adapt and thrive in this world to the extent that we can profit from interpersonal relationships (Hartup, 1989). The roots of social development can be found in early infancy—in the formation of attachment. **Attachment** is defined as a strong, two-way, emotional bond, usually referring to the relationship between a child and his or her mother or primary caregiver (Bowlby, 1982). Thus, attachment is a product of our evolutionary history—a means for keeping the individual near significant others. It has survival value by "increasing the chances of an infant being protected by those to whom he or she keeps proximity" (Ainsworth, 1989). Well-formed attachment provides a child with freedom to explore the environment, curiosity, adaptive problem solving, and competence when interacting with peers (Collins & Gunnar, 1990).

Harlow's Studies with Monkeys. The best place to begin our discussion of human attachment is with Harry Harlow and his research with rhesus monkeys (Harlow, 1959; Harlow et al., 1971). Harlow raised some baby monkeys with their biological mothers and raised others in cages with "artificial mothers." Some artificial mothers were made from wire mesh and fitted with wooden heads. Small, doll-size baby bottles within the models provided nourishment to the baby monkeys. One style of artificial mother was covered with a soft, terry-cloth wrap, whereas the other was left as bare wire (see Figure 8.12).

There was no doubt which model the young monkeys preferred. Whether or not it provided food, baby monkeys clung tightly to the soft, terry-cloth model. Harlow realized that mother rhesus monkeys

Figure 8.12

One of Harlow's monkeys and its artificial, terry cloth "mother." Harlow found that the contact comfort mothers usually provide is essential for normal social development.

provide more to their young than just food. The opportunity to cling to something soft, warm, and cuddly, called *contact comfort,* is also important.

What were the long-term implications of raising baby rhesus monkeys under these varied conditions? Those raised in isolation, or with bare-wire model mothers, or, to a lesser degree, even with the cloth mothers, showed signs of abnormal development. As adults, they tended to show inappropriate social behaviors, either withdrawing or acting aggressively. Normal sexual behavior patterns were disrupted. Many never successfully mated. When mating was possible, females turned out to be very poor mothers. For rhesus monkeys, then, forming an early attachment bond is an important step in social development.

As is usually the case, we need to exercise caution when translating data from the animal laboratory to humans, but it seems that a bond of attachment is often (not always) formed between a human child and its primary caregiver(s). Forming an attachment between infant and mother (as an example) involves regular interaction and active give-and-take between the two. Strong attachments are most likely to be formed if the mother is sensitive to the needs of the child, picking up the baby when he or she cries, changing the diaper as soon as it is soiled, feeding on a regular basis, and so on. Simply spending time with an infant is seldom enough to produce successful attachment. Attachment is promoted by spontaneous hugging, smiling, eye contact, and vocalizing (Lamb et al., 1982; Stern, 1977). It is fostered by qualities such as warmth and gentleness (Londerville & Main, 1981). When the process is successful, we talk of children who are "securely attached." But forming an attachment is a two-way street. Attachment will be most secure when the baby reciprocates by smiling, cooing, and clinging to mother when attended to (Ainsworth, 1979; Pederson et al., 1990). About 65 percent of American children become securely attached by the age of 1 year—a percentage close to that found in seven other countries (van Ijzendorn & Koonenberg, 1988).

Are there long-term benefits of becoming securely attached in infancy? Yes. Secure attachment in infancy tends to lead to (1) *sociability* (less fear with strangers, better relationships with peers, more popularity, and more friends), (2) higher *self-esteem,* (3) better *relationships with siblings,* (4) fewer *tantruming* or *aggressive behaviors,* (5) less concern by teachers over controlling behaviors *in the classroom,* (6) more *empathy* and concern for the feelings of others, (7) fewer *behavioral problems* at later ages, and (8) better *attention spans* and more *confidence in solving problems* (from a summary by Bee, 1992, p. 433).

Before we go on, I need to mention that infants can and do form attachments with persons other than their mothers. Although fathers do typically spend less time with young children than do mothers (fathers' time increases as children get older), father-child attachments are common and are beneficial for the long-term development of the child (Lamb, 1977, 1979; Lynn, 1974). One researcher found that she could predict the extent to which a child showed signs of attachment to its father simply by knowing how often Dad changed the baby's diaper (Ross et al., 1975). And there is no evidence that fathers are any less sensitive to the needs of their children than are mothers (Parke, 1981), although they may be a little more physical and a little less verbal in their interactions (Parke & Tinsley, 1987).

Consequences of Day Care for Forming Attachments. Finally, we need to consider attachment formation for those children who spend time—occasionally a lot of time—in day care facilities, cared for by people other than their mother or father. What are the consequences of the reality that in the United States in the 1990s more than half the mothers of children younger than three are employed, and that the care of those children is at least in part taken over by others? I'll bet you've anticipated my answer to this (often controversial) question: it depends. It depends mostly on the quality of the care the children receive—no matter where they receive it. Children who are given warm, supportive, attentive care, adequate stimulation, and opportunities for exploration demonstrate secure attachment (Howes, 1990; Phillips et al., 1987). The impact of day care also depends on the likelihood that the child would have received good, warm, supportive, loving care at home (Scarr & Eisenberg, 1993). The answer to questions about the impact of nonparental child care may also depend on the age of the child. "There is little dispute about the conclusion that children who enter day care at 18 months, 2 years, or later show *no* consistent loss of security of attachment to their parents" (Bee, 1992, p. 510). The main debate centers on children less than one year old, and there is some evidence that secure attachment is less likely among those children who are not cared for at home during their first year (Belsky, 1990; Belsky & Rovine, 1988; Hennessy & Melhuish, 1991; Lamb & Sternberg, 1990).

It may tentatively be concluded that forming secure attachments is important for the later development of the human infant, just as contact comfort is important for the development of the rhesus monkey. Because we have not been able to do the sort of controlled experiments with human infants that Harlow did with monkeys, the data are not as impressive. They do suggest, however, that there are long-term benefits (ranging from improved emotional stability to improved problem-solving skills) to be derived from strong attachments formed early in childhood (Ainsworth, 1989; Bowlby, 1982; Etaugh, 1980; Schwartz, 1983). Further, attachments formed with father or other caregivers seem as useful for long-term development as do attachments to mother.

Attachment between parents and children is a two-way street, where signs of mutual affection and interest are exchanged. Studies tell us that early father-child attachments are beneficial later in life.

Before You Go On

In child development, what is meant by attachment, and what are the consequences of developing attachments?

TOPIC 8B SUMMARY

With birth, the neonatal period begins. Although several useful re-flexes and sensory capacities are available to the newborn, interaction with the environment shapes and modifies the developmental process. Throughout childhood we find that motor development varies from child to child, but usually progresses in the same, orderly sequence.

Theories concerning the pattern of cognitive, social, and moral development have stimulated much research in child psychology. In this Topic, we first reviewed Piaget's theory of cognitive development. Piaget argued that children go through a distinct sequence of stages in their efforts to find out about the world in which they live, thus devel-oping new schemas along the way. Few theories have generated the sort of research activity as has Piaget's. We saw that there are prob-lems with some of the particular points of Piaget's theory, but we also saw that his theory has found support in cross-cultural research efforts. We then looked at Kohlberg's theory of the development of moral reasoning, essentially a six-stage theory. There is support for this theory, too, but it seems that support is mostly to be found in Western, individualistic cultures particularly among men. We may need different means of assessing moral development in women or in people from collective societies. Erikson's theory of psychosocial development is also a stage theory, but unlike Piaget's it considers developmental stages throughout adolescence and adulthood as well as childhood. Erikson's stages are defined in terms of conflicts that need to be resolved at various times in one's life.

We turned next to gender identity, and learned that although adults may treat boys and girls differently, their behavior as infants and young children provides no basis for doing so. Most children become aware of gender differences by the age of 4 years. Differences are noticeable in matters from peer group interactions to the choice of toys. Finally, we examined the lasting importance of the early devel-opment of social attachments. These bidirectional, largely emotional bonds are established between young children and their primary care-givers. We continue our story of human development now by consid-ering that span that falls between childhood and adulthood: adoles-cence.

Topic 8C
DEVELOPMENT IN ADOLESCENCE

Adolescence is an exciting period of development. It is a period of transition—from the dependence of childhood to the independence of adulthood. It is difficult, however, to specify exactly when adolescence begins and when it ends. We'll begin defining adolescence and seeing how psychologists have attempted to characterize this stage. We'll re-view some of the physical changes that occur during adolescence, and we'll sample three of the issues that concern developmental psychologists who study adolescents: identity formation, drug use, and adolescent sexuality.

WHAT ARE ADOLESCENTS REALLY LIKE?

When does adolescence begin and when is this period of development over? Are there any general principles that characterize adolescence? These are the two questions we deal with in this section.

The Limits of Adolescence

We may define adolescence in biological terms. In that case, adolescence begins with the onset of puberty (with sexual maturity and a readiness to reproduce) and ends with the end of physical growth, which is usually late in the teen years. An individual's developing sexuality and physical growth certainly do have psychological implications we could address, but there are other ways of defining adolescence.

A more psychological perspective would emphasize the development of the cognitions, feelings, and behaviors that characterize adolescence. Psychological approaches emphasize the development of problem-solving skills and an increased reliance on the use of symbols, logic, and abstract thinking. Such perspectives stress the importance of identity formation and the appreciation of self and self-worth.

We may also consider adolescence from a social perspective by looking at the role of adolescents in society (Kett, 1977). These approaches define adolescence in terms of being in between: not yet an adult, but no longer a child (Peterson & Ebata, 1987). In this context, adolescence usually lasts from the early teen years through one's highest educational level, when the person is thought to enter the adult world. Here, the limits of adolescence may be changing as more and more youngsters opt to go on to college immediately after high school, still maintaining contact with and dependence on family and other support groups developed during the teen years.

Actually, whether we accept a biological, psychological, or social perspective, we are usually talking about people who, in our culture, are between the ages of 12 and 20. For the sake of our discussion, **adolescence** will be defined as the period of development begun at puberty and lasting through the teen years. This is fairly close to the definition chosen by Anne Peterson for her review of adolescent development. She decided to focus on the second decade of life (Peterson, 1988).

adolescence the developmental period between childhood and adulthood, often begun at puberty and ending with full physical growth; generally between the ages of 12 and 20

Are Adolescents Always in Turmoil, and "Stressed Out"?

One of the intriguing issues in the psychology of adolescence today is how to characterize this stage of development. Is adolescence a time of personal growth, independence, and positive change? Or is it a period of rebellion, stress, turmoil, and negativism?

The view that adolescence should be characterized in terms of turmoil, storm, and stress is actually the older of the two, attributed to

G. Stanley Hall (who wrote the first textbook on adolescence in 1904) and to Anna Freud (who applied Freudian psychoanalytic theory to adolescents). This position claims that normal adolescence involves all sorts of difficulties of adjustment. Anna Freud wrote, "To be normal during the adolescent period is by itself abnormal" (1958, p. 275). In this view, "Adolescents may be expected to be extremely moody and depressed one day and excitedly 'high' the next. Explosive conflict with family, friends, and authorities is thought of as commonplace" (Powers et al., 1989, p. 200).

Over the past 25 years, psychologists have come to appreciate that such a characterization is probably inappropriate. Adolescence is not just a period of great emotional distress that, with time, one outgrows (e.g., Larson & Lampman-Petraitis, 1989). As we'll see shortly, the teen years often present conflicts and pressures that require difficult choices, and some teenagers *do* react to the pressures of their adolescence in maladaptive ways (Larson & Ham, 1993; Quadrel et al., 1993; Takanishi, 1993). However, the adjustments required of adolescents are *usually made in psychologically healthy ways* (Garbarino, 1985; Jessor, 1993; Manning, 1983; Offer & Offer, 1975; Peterson & Ebata, 1987; Rutter et al., 1976). Psychologist John Conger puts it this way: "While many adolescents face occasional periods of uncertainty and self-doubt, loneliness and sadness, and anxiety and concern for the future, they are also likely to experience joy, excitement, curiosity, a sense of adventure, and a feeling of competence as they master new challenges" (Conger, 1991, p. 24). The picture of the seriously troubled, rebellious adolescent may be based on real experience, but is more often a reflection of a social stereotype.

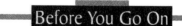
Before You Go On

How might adolescence be defined, and how can the period best be characterized?

PHYSICAL CHANGES DURING ADOLESCENCE

The onset of adolescence is marked by two biological or physical changes. First, there is a marked increase in height and weight, known as a growth spurt, and second, there is sexual maturation.

The growth spurt of early adolescence usually occurs in girls at an earlier age than it does in boys. Girls begin their growth spurt as early as age 9 or 10, and then slow down at about age 15. Boys generally show increased rates of growth between the ages of 12 and 17 years. Indeed, males usually don't reach their adult height until their early twenties, whereas girls generally attain their maximum height by their late teens (Roche & Davila, 1972; Tanner, 1981). Figure 8.13 shows one way to represent the adolescent growth spurt in graphic form.

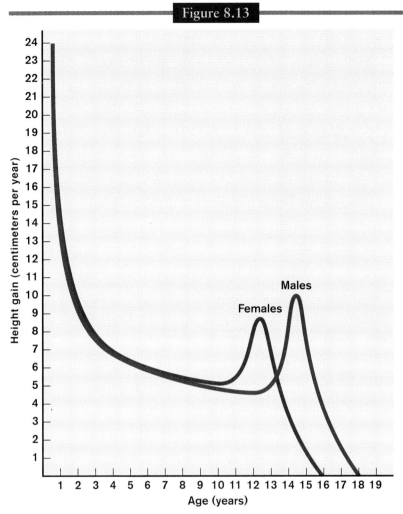

Figure 8.13

Females begin their growth spurt at about age 10, whereas the growth spurt in males does not begin until about age 12. In general, males will grow faster and for a longer period than females. (After Tanner et al., 1966.)

At least some of the challenge of early adolescence is a direct result of the growth spurt. It is not uncommon to find increases in weight and height occurring so rapidly that they are accompanied by real, physical growing pains, particularly in the arms and legs. Unfortunately, the spurt of adolescent growth seldom affects all parts of the body uniformly, especially in boys. Thirteen- and 14-year-old boys often appear incredibly clumsy and awkward as they try to coordinate their large hands and feet with the rest of their body. One of the most noticeable areas of growth in boys is that of the larynx and vocal cords. As the vocal cords lengthen, the pitch of the voice lowers. Much to the embarrassment of many a teenage boy, this transition is seldom a smooth one, and he may suffer through weeks of a squeaking, crackling change of pitch in the middle of a serious conversation (Adams, 1977; Adams & Gullotta, 1983).

Adolescence brings physical changes and psychological challenges, some major, some minor, including learning how to shave.

puberty *the stage of physical development at which one becomes capable of sexual reproduction*

By definition, **puberty** occurs when one becomes physically capable of sexual reproduction. With the onset of puberty, there is a marked increase in the production of the sex hormones, primarily androgens in males and estrogens in females. (All of us have androgens *and* estrogens in our bodies. Males have more androgens; females have more estrogens.) Boys seldom know when their own puberty begins. For some time they have experienced penile erections and nocturnal emissions of seminal fluid. Puberty in males begins with the appearance of live sperm, and most males have no idea when *that* happens; such determinations require a laboratory test.

menarche *a female's first menstrual period, a sure sign of the beginning of adolescence*

In females, puberty is noticeable. It is indicated by the first menstrual period, called **menarche**. With puberty, both boys and girls are ready, in a biological sense, to reproduce. Coming to deal with that readiness and making the adjustments we associate with psychological maturity do not come automatically with sexual maturity.

By now you recognize that the ages I indicate for the start and end of major developmental periods vary considerably from person to person, and such is the case for puberty. Many boys and girls reach puberty before or after most of their age mates, and are referred to as early or late bloomers. Reaching puberty well before or after others of the same age may have some psychological effects, although few are long-lasting. Let's first get an idea of what early and late puberty means. Figure 8.14 shows the age ranges during which the major developments associated with puberty may be expected to occur. In some cases, the age range is quite large. Many of the ages in this figure are subject to change. For example, in the United States 150 years ago, the average age of menarche was 16; now it's close to 12 (Hamburg & Takanishi, 1989). The age of puberty also varies around the world. African girls, for example, experience menarche at a significantly younger age than do European girls (Eveleth & Tanner, 1978).

What are the advantages and disadvantages of early maturation? As you might suspect, there are differences for girls and boys. A girl who enters puberty early will probably be taller, stronger, faster, and

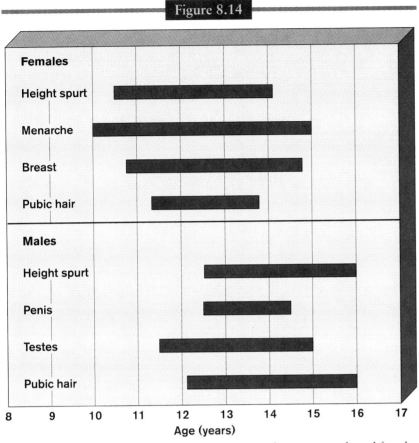

The ages at which certain physical changes occur in the average male and female during puberty. (Adapted from "Growing Up" by J. M. Tanner, *Scientific American, September 1973, Volume 229, Number 3. Copyright © 1973 by Scientific American. All rights reserved. Reprinted by permission.)*

more athletic than other girls (and many of the boys) in her class at school. She is more likely to be approached for dates, have more early sexual encounters, and marry at a younger age than her peers. There is a small but consistent advantage on objective tests of intelligence (Newcomb & Dubas, 1987). She may have self-image problems, seeing herself as unattractive, particularly if she puts on extra weight and shows marked breast development (Conger & Peterson, 1984; Crockett & Peterson, 1987).

Because of the premium put on physical activity in boys, the early-maturing boy is at a greater advantage than the early-maturing girl. He will have more dating and sexual experiences than his age mates, which will raise his status among his peers. He will have a *better* body image and higher self-esteem (Peterson, 1988).

For teens of both sexes, being a late bloomer is more negative in its impact (*at the time*) than is being an early bloomer (Gross & Duke, 1980). Late-maturing boys *may* carry a sense of inadequacy and poor self-esteem into adulthood (Jones, 1957). Late maturity for girls has little long-term negative consequence. Some feel, at least in retrospect, that being a late bloomer was an advantage because it allowed them to develop other, broadening interests, rather than becoming "boy-crazy" like so many of their peers in early adolescence (Tobin-Richards et al., 1984).

Summary generalizations can be dangerous, but I may suggest that (1) early maturity is more advantageous than late maturity, at least at the time of adolescence, and (2) boys profit from early maturity more than do girls, but may also suffer more from late maturity.

Before You Go On

Briefly describe the physical changes that accompany the beginnings of adolescence.

SOME CHALLENGES OF ADOLESCENCE

Adolescence is a developmental period marked by the stage of formal operations in Piaget's theory of cognitive development and by identity formation in Erikson's psychosocial theory. According to Piaget, in adolescence one is now able to think abstractly and to imagine, to think about what *is*, and to ponder what *might be*. This new, higher level of cognition often gets turned toward self-analysis, toward a contemplation of one's self in a social context (Keating, 1980). In this section, we'll examine a few issues that present specific challenges to the adolescent: identity formation, drug use, and sexuality.

Identity Formation

Adolescents typically give the impression of being great experimenters. They experiment with hairstyles, music, religions, drugs, sexual outlets, fad diets, part-time jobs, part-time relationships, and part-time philosophies of life. In fact, it often appears that most of a teenager's commitments are made on a part-time basis. Teens are busy trying things out, doing things their own way, off on a grand search for Truth.

This perception of adolescents as experimenters is not without foundation. It is consistent with the view that one of the major tasks of adolescence is the resolution of an **identity crisis**—the effort to define and integrate the sense of who one is, what one is to do in life, and what one's attitudes, beliefs, and values should be. As we saw in Topic 8B, the concept of identity formation is associated with Erik Erikson (1963), where the search for identity is the fifth of eight stages of psychosocial development and occurs during the adolescent years (Figure 8.11). During adolescence, we come to grips with questions such as: "Who am I?" "What am I going to do with my life?"

identity crisis the effort to define and integrate one's sense of self and what one's attitudes, beliefs, and values should be

One of the challenges of adolescence is identity formation. Who am I? What kind of a person am I to be? What shall be my values? What will I do with my life as I give up dependence on my parents?

"What is the point of it all?" Needless to say, these are not trivial questions.

For many young people, resolving one's identity crisis is a relatively simple and straightforward process. In such cases, adolescence brings very little confusion or conflict in terms of attitudes, beliefs, or values. Many teenagers are able and willing to accept the values and sense of self they began to develop in childhood.

For many teenagers, however, the conflict of identity formation is quite real. They have a sense of giving up the values of parents and teachers in favor of new ones—their own. Physical growth, physiological changes, increased sexuality, and the perception of societal pressures to decide what they want to be when they "grow up" may lead to what Erikson calls *role confusion*, in which wanting to be independent, to be one's own self, does not fit in with the values of the past, of childhood. Hence, the teenager experiments with various possibilities in an attempt to see what works out best, occasionally to the dissatisfaction of bewildered parents.

Before You Go On

**Summarize the adolescent's search for identity
as described by Erikson.**

Drug Use by Adolescents

There simply is no doubt that many adolescents experiment with using drugs, many use drugs on a regular basis, and many abuse

Resisting the temptations of alcohol and drug use is a struggle for many adolescents.

drugs. Smoking (79 percent) and drinking alcohol (65 percent) lead the list of drug-related activities teenagers have tried at least once by the ninth grade (Gans & Blyth, 1990). About 5 percent of high school seniors are daily drinkers, and 37.5 percent report at least one occasion of heavy drinking (five or more drinks in a row) per month (Newcomb & Bentler, 1989). Nearly 30 percent have tried illegal drugs (usually marijuana) at least once (Millstein, 1989; National Institute on Drug Abuse, 1987). Surveys tell us that among high school students, there are no racial differences in drug use or drug abuse (Oetting & Beauvais, 1990). *There is also no difference in rate of drug use between adolescents and adults.*

The use of most drugs by high school seniors increased between the mid-1970s and the 1981–1982 school year, but for the next decade there was a gradual but steady decline (Oetting & Beauvais, 1990). In that same time period, attitudes about the use of drugs became more negative among teenagers (Newcomb & Bentler, 1989). Then in January of 1994, a team of researchers at the University of Michigan reported a modest but noteworthy reversal: cigarette and drug use among 8th-, 10th-, and 12th-grade students was again on the increase. Only 53 percent of the eighth graders saw a significant risk in smoking a pack of cigarettes a day. Lloyd Johnson, principal investigator of the project, believes one cause may be that less attention is being paid to the issue of drugs, cigarette smoking, and alcohol use among teenagers. "The whole issue fell off the screen in the country, figuratively and literally," he said.

Jonathan Shedler and Jack Block, researchers at the University of California, Berkeley, reported on a study of adolescent drug use and psychological health that is bound to affect the way we view drug use among teenagers (1990). The participants in this investigation were 18-year-olds who had been under study since they were 3 years old. Based on reports of their drug use, they were divided into three groups: (1) *abstainers* (N = 29), who had never tried any drug; (2) *experimenters* (N = 36), who had used marijuana "once or twice, or a few times," and who tried no more than one other drug; and (3) *frequent users* (N = 20), who reported using marijuana frequently and tried at least one other drug. There were no socioeconomic or IQ differences among the groups.

The major findings of this study had to do with personality characteristics of the 18-year-olds in each group. *Frequent users* were generally maladjusted, alienated, deficient in impulse control, and "manifestly" distressed. The *abstainers* were overly anxious, "emotionally constricted," and lacking in social skills. These same results were apparent when the researchers examined records from when the same subjects were 7 and 11 years old. By and large, the *experimenters* were better adjusted and psychologically "healthier" than either of the other two groups.

The authors of this study believe their data may be misinterpreted. Their concern is that these data might be taken to indicate "that drug use might somehow improve an adolescent's psychological health" (p. 628). Clearly, this interpretation would be in error. You recognize these as correlational data from which no conclusion regarding cause and effect is justified (Topic 1B, p. 28). Make no mistake, drug use among adolescents is, and should be, a matter of great concern. A drug-free society is a noble goal. On the other hand, there are data that suggest we need not get hysterical about infrequent, occasional drug use among teenagers. In a review of substance use among teenagers, Newcomb and Bentler (1989) put it this way:

> Not all drug use is bad and will fry one's brain (as the commercials imply). Such claims as reflected in the national hysteria and depicted in media advertisements for treatment programs repeat the failed scare tactics of the past. All drug abuse is destructive and can have devastating consequences for individuals, their families, and society. The difference or distinction lies in the use versus abuse of drugs. (p. 247)

What may we conclude? Adolescents do use and do abuse drugs. We can say that drug use is no greater among teenagers than for any other segment of the population, but there are signs that drug use among teens is again on the rise.

Before You Go On

Briefly summarize the data on drug use and abuse in adolescence.

Adolescent Sexuality

For the adolescent, going through puberty is an intensely personal, private, and potentially confusing process. Under the direction of the hypothalamus and the pituitary gland, large doses of sex hormones enter the bloodstream, stimulating the development of secondary sex characteristics. In males, the neck and shoulders expand, hips narrow, facial and body hair begins to sprout, and the voice crackles and then lowers in pitch. In females, the breasts begin to develop, the hips broaden and become more rounded, and the shoulders narrow. All of this takes time, of course, but then, puberty is more of a process than a single event. It is during this process that sex hormones give rise to sex drives, which are expressed in sexual behaviors. With puberty, sexual behaviors can lead to pregnancy.

As you might imagine, collecting data on the sexual behaviors of adolescents isn't easy. Many surveys are biased because samples are small or not representative of the general population. Truthfulness is a potential problem with any survey data, even if anonymity is ensured. This is particularly the case when we are asking young people about an issue as sensitive as their own sexual behaviors. Some respondents stretch reality with tales of numerous sexual exploits, whereas others, perhaps somewhat anxious or guilt-ridden, tend to minimize reports of their sexual activities. Quality data can be found, however, and they tell us that adolescents are a sexually active group.

A report from the Centers for Disease Control (CDC) released in 1991 tells us that the incidence of premarital sex has risen in the last two decades, with a sharp increase since 1985. The CDC survey reports that nearly twice as many female teenagers (51.5 percent) had engaged in premarital sex by their late teens in 1988, compared to 1970 (28.6 percent). The largest relative increase occurred among girls 15 years old. When the report was released, Sevgi Aral, of the CDC, was quoted as saying, "This is really important because it happened during a time when we thought we were doing so much in terms of health education and AIDS prevention."

How do adolescents feel about sex? Most teens do not "plan" to be sexually active; it "just happens" (Chilman, 1983). The implication, of course, is that there is little consideration of short- and long-term consequences when behaviors "just happen." There are gender differences in how sexual activity is evaluated. One study (Coles & Stokes, 1985) tells us that about 60 percent of the males, but only 23 percent of the females, "felt glad" about their first intercourse (34 percent of the males and 61 percent of the females reported feeling "ambivalent"). These data mirror those of Darling and Davidson (1986), who reported that 67.4 percent of the males in their survey were "psychologically satisfied after their first sexual experience," whereas only 28.3 percent of the females in the study shared that satisfaction.

With all of this sexual activity among adolescents, it is not surprising that teenage pregnancy has become a significant social problem. What is a bit surprising is that the problem did not gain national recognition until the 1970s, by which time childbearing among teenagers had begun a decline that still continues. Again, there are statistics to review. Each year more than half a million babies are born to adolescent mothers, of whom nearly two-thirds of the white mothers and virtually all of the black mothers (97 percent) are single (Furstenberg et al., 1989). Girls in the United States younger than 15

When adolescents become parents, both those parents and their child face a myriad of problems and challenges.

are *five times more likely* to give birth than are young girls from any other developed country for which comparable data are available (Landers, 1987b). Between 1973 and 1987, pregnancy among teenagers between the ages of 10 and 14 increased 23 percent (Moore, 1992). Hayes (1987) estimates that approximately 400,000 teenage pregnancies end in abortion each year. It is difficult to assess exactly, but estimating teenage pregnancies (which includes births, abortions, and miscarriages) at over a million a year is probably not far off (Auletta, 1984; Millstein, 1989; Zelnick & Kantner, 1980).

The physical, psychological, and financial costs of teenage pregnancy—to individuals, families, and society—are very high. The child of a teenage mother is certainly a baby at risk. Teenage mothers face innumerable hurdles: they are much more likely to drop out of school, are more likely to be on welfare, are more likely to have poorer access to health care, and are more likely to suffer economic hardships (Hayes, 1987; Hofferth & Hayes, 1987). But remember, most adolescents do not plan to become pregnant. Teenage pregnancy may reflect a poor understanding of human sexuality. For example, a significant number of adolescents do not believe they can become pregnant the first time they have intercourse, and teenagers generally hold negative attitudes about the use of contraceptives (Morrison, 1985).

What can we conclude about adolescents on the basis of the statistics we've reviewed here? Millions of adolescents are sexually active. Many adolescents are ignorant of the consequences of their own sexual behaviors. Those for whom sexual activity results in pregnancy may exceed a million each year. But, let's not lose sight of the fact that most teenagers are not involved with unwanted pregnancies. Many adolescents know a great deal about sex. Dealing with one's sexuality effectively may not be easy, but it is just one of the challenges that must be addressed as one passes through adolescence.

Before You Go On

What evidence supports the notion that adolescents are a sexually active group?

Briefly summarize the data on teenage pregnancy.

TOPIC 8C SUMMARY

Adolescence is a developmental stage of challenge, and for some it is a stage of risk and danger. On the other hand, adolescence is a stage of growth, newfound freedom, responsibility, and independence.

Adolescence begins with a growth spurt and puberty—that series of processes that brings a person to full sexual maturity. Reaching puberty before or after most of one's peers can have implications for both boys and girls, although the consequences of early or late blooming are seldom long-lasting, especially for girls.

In this Topic we briefly explored three challenges of the teen years: (1) identity formation, in which one struggles to define one's self and to integrate just how he or she will fit into the world; (2) drug use, which is not uncommon among adolescents, but is no more common in adolescence than in adulthood (smoking and alcohol use seem to continue on the rise, whereas use of illegal drugs shows signs of decreasing); and (3) sexuality, where we noted that regardless of concerns for AIDs or other parental pressures, adolescents are sexually active. A particularly unfortunate consequence of adolescent sexual behaviors is a still-rising rate of teenage pregnancies and teenage parenthood, especially among very young teens—children having children.

Topic 8D

DEVELOPMENT IN ADULTHOOD

The changes that occur during our adult years may not seem as striking or dramatic as those that typify our childhood and adolescence, but they are no less real. Many of the adjustments we make as adults go unnoticed as we accommodate physical changes and psychological pressures. As an adult, one's health may become a concern for the first time. Psychological and social adjustments need to be made to marriage, parenthood, career, the death of friends and family, retirement, and ultimately, one's own death.

Following the lead of Erikson (1968) and Levinson (1978, 1986), we will consider adulthood to consist of three overlapping periods, eras, or seasons: early adulthood (roughly ages 18 to 45), middle adulthood (approximately ages 45 to 65), and late adulthood (over age 65). Presenting adult development in this way may be misleading, so we must be careful. Although there is support for developmental stages in adulthood, these stages may be better defined by the individual adult than by the developmental psychologist (Datan et al., 1987). In fact, some psychologists find little evidence for orderly transitions in the life of adults at all (Costa & McCrae, 1980; McCrae & Costa, 1984), while others find that there are sex differences in what determines the stage or status of one's adult life (Reinke et al., 1985).

EARLY ADULTHOOD

If anything marks the transition from adolescence to adulthood it is choice and commitments independently made. The sense of identity one began to fashion during adolescence now needs to be put into action. In fact, the achievement of a sense of self by early adulthood is a good predictor of the success of intimate relationships later in adulthood (Kahn et al., 1985). With adult status, there are new and often difficult choices to be made. Advice may be sought from elders, parents, teachers, or friends, but as adults, individuals make their own choices. Should I get married? Should I get a job? Which one? Do I need more education? What sort of education? Where? Should we have children? How many? Many of these issues are first addressed in adolescence, during identity formation. For the adult, these questions are no longer abstract. They are very real questions that demand some sort of response.

Levinson calls early adulthood the "era of greatest energy and abundance and of greatest contradiction and stress" (1986, p. 5). In terms of our physical development, we are at something of a peak during our twenties and thirties, and we are apparently willing to work hard to maintain that physical condition (McCann & Holmes, 1984; Shaffer, 1982). On the one hand, young adulthood is a season for finding our niche, for working through the aspirations of our youth, for raising a family. On the other hand, it is a period of stress, taking on parenthood, finding and keeping the "right" job, and maintaining a balance among self, family, job, and society at large. Let's take a look at two important decision-making processes of young adulthood, the choice of mate and family, and the choice of job or career.

Marriage and Family

It is Erikson's claim (1963) that early adulthood revolves around the choice of *intimacy versus isolation*. A failure to establish close, loving, or intimate relationships may result in loneliness and long periods of social isolation. Marriage is certainly not the only source of interpersonal intimacy, but it is the first choice of most Americans. More young adults than ever before are postponing marriage plans, but fully 95 percent of us do marry (at least once). In 1950, the average (median) age at the time of their first marriage was 20.3 years for women and 22.8 years for men. By 1989, the age of women at their first marriage was 23.8 and the age of men was 26.2 years (U.S. Bureau of the Census, 1991). Americans claim that happiness in adulthood depends more on a successful marriage than any other factor, including friendship, career, community activities, and hobbies (Glenn & Weaver, 1981).

Individuals reach the point of being ready to marry at diverse ages. Some people decide to marry simply because they perceive that it is "the thing to do." Others choose marriage as an expression of an intimacy that has already developed (Stinnett et al., 1984). In addition to the choices of *when* to marry, of no small consequence is the choice of *whom* to marry. We've learned over the past 30 years that mate selection is a complex process.

At least three factors influence the choice of a marriage partner (Newman & Newman, 1984). The first deals with availability. Before we can develop an intimate relationship with someone, we need the opportunity to develop the relationship in the first place. Availability is one thing, eligibility is a second. Here, matters of age, race, religion, politics, and background come into play. Available and eligible, a third factor enters the picture: attractiveness. To a degree, attractiveness in this context means physical attractiveness, but as we all know, judgments of physical beauty depend on who's doing the judging. "Attractiveness" also involves psychological characteristics such as understanding, emotional supportiveness, and similarity in values and goals.

Psychologist David Buss has reviewed the evidence on mate selection with a focus on the question of whether opposites attract (Buss, 1985). He concluded that, in marriage, they do not. He found that "we are likely to marry someone who is similar to us in almost every variable" (Buss, 1985, p. 47). Most important (in order) are age, education, race, religion, and ethnic background, followed by attitudes and opinions, mental abilities, socioeconomic status, height, weight, and even eye color. In addition, he found that men and women are in nearly total agreement on the characteristics they commonly seek in a mate (Buss, 1985; Buss & Barnes, 1986). Figure 8.15 presents 13 such characteristics ranked by men and women. There is a significant *difference* in ranking for only two: good earning potential and physical attractiveness.

Let's pause here momentarily and remind ourselves of two points that have come up before. (1) The conclusions of the studies previously cited are true only in general, on the average. There may be happy couples that have few of the traits listed in Figure 8.5 in common. (2) These general conclusions only hold in Western, largely Anglo, North American cultures. Buss and many colleagues are studying preferences in selecting mates around the world. In one report of their efforts

Figure 8.15
Characteristics Sought in Mates

Rank (most important)	Male choices	Female choices
1	Kindness and understanding	Kindness and understanding
2	Intelligence	Intelligence
3	Physical attractiveness	Exciting personality
4	Exciting personality	Good health
5	Good health	Adaptability
6	Adaptability	Physical attractiveness
7	Creativity	Creativity
8	Desire for children	Good earning capacity
9	College graduate	College graduate
10	Good heredity	Desire for children
11	Good earning capacity	Good heredity
12	Good housekeeper	Good housekeeper

From Buss & Barnes, 1986.

(Buss et al., 1990), people from 33 countries on six continents and five islands were studied. There were some similarities among all of the cultures studied, but cultures tended to show significantly different rankings of preferences for mates. The trait that varied most across cultures was *chastity.*

> . . . desiring a mate with no previous experience in sexual intercourse. Samples from China, India, Indonesia, Iran, Taiwan, and Arab Palestine placed great importance on chastity in a potential mate. Samples from Ireland and Japan placed moderate importance on chastity. In contrast, samples from Sweden, Finland, Norway, the Netherlands, and West Germany generally judged chastity to be irrelevant or unimportant. (Buss et al., 1990, p. 16)

You'll note that chastity is nowhere to be found on the list of preferred characteristics presented in Figure 8.15. Choosing a marriage partner is not always a matter of making sound, rational decisions, regardless of one's culture. Many factors, including romantic love and the realities of economic hardship, sometimes affect such choices. As sound and sensible as choices at marriage may seem, approximately 50 percent of all first marriages end in divorce (75 percent of second marriages suffer the same fate). In the United States, 9.4 years is the average span of a first marriage (U.S. Bureau of the Census, 1991).

Just as men and women tend to agree on what matters in choosing a mate, so do they agree on what matters in maintaining a marriage, listing first such things as liking one's spouse as a friend, agreeing on goals, and a mutual concern for making the marriage work (Lauer & Lauer, 1985). It is also true that, typically, men tend to be more satisfied with their marriage than are women (Rhyne, 1981). One of the best predictors of a successful marriage is the extent to which marriage partners were able to maintain close relationships (such as with parents) *before* marriage (Wamboldt & Reiss, 1989). We'll return to this discussion, and expand on it in Chapter 14 when we consider interpersonal relationships in general (pages 694–700).

Beyond establishing an intimate relationship, becoming a parent is often taken as a sure sign of adulthood. For many couples, parenthood has become more a matter of choice than ever before because of more available means of contraception and new treatments for infertility. Having a family fosters the process of *generativity,* which Erikson associates with middle adulthood. Generativity reflects a concern for family and for one's impact on future generations (Chilman, 1980). Although such concerns may not become central until one is over age 40, parenthood usually begins much sooner.

There is no doubt that having a baby around the house significantly changes established routines. Few couples have a truly realistic vision of what having children will do to their lives. The freedom for spontaneous trips, intimate outings, and privacy is in large measure given up in trade for the joys of parenthood. As parents, men and women take on the responsibilities of new social roles—of father and mother. These new roles in adulthood add to the already established roles of being male or female, son or daughter, husband or wife, and so on. It seems that choosing to have children (or at least choosing to have a large number of children) is becoming less and less popular

Having a child around the house requires new adjustments in the daily lives of parents.

(Schaie & Willis, 1986). Although many people see the decision not to have children as selfish, irresponsible, and immoral (Skolnick, 1978), there is little evidence that such a decision leads to a decline in well-being or life satisfaction later in life (Beckman & Houser, 1982; Keith, 1983).

Career Choice

By the time a person has become a young adult, it is generally assumed that he or she has chosen a vocation or life's work. One's choice of occupation, and one's satisfaction with that choice, go a long way toward determining self-esteem, even one's identity. For women in early and middle adulthood, being employed outside the home is a major determinant of one's self-worth and satisfaction with one's self (Stein et al., 1990). Selection of a career is driven by many factors; family influence and the potential for earning money are just two. In truth, most young adults are dissatisfied with their initial choice(s) (Rhodes, 1983; Shertzer, 1985).

Jeffrey Turner and Donald Helms (1987) claim that choosing a career path involves seven identifiable stages. Let's review their list.

1. *Exploration:* Here, there is a general concern that something needs to be done; a choice needs to be made, but alternatives are poorly defined, and plans for making a choice are not yet developed. This period is what Daniel Levinson (1978) calls "formulating a dream."

2. *Crystallization:* Now some real alternatives are being weighed, pluses and minuses are associated with each possibility, and although some are eliminated, a choice is not made.

3. *Choice:* For better or worse, a decision is made. Now there is a sense of relief that at least one knows what one wants, and an optimistic feeling develops that everything will work out.

4. *Career clarification:* Now the individual's self-image and career choice are meshed together. Adjustments and accommodations are made. This is largely a matter of fine-tuning one's initial choice: "I know I want to be a teacher; now what do I want to teach, and to whom?"

5. *Induction:* The career decision is implemented. This presents a series of potentially frightening challenges to one's own values and goals. "Is this really what I want to do?"

6. *Reformation:* Here one finds that changes need to be made if one is to fit in with fellow workers and do the job as one is expected to do it. "This isn't going to be as simple as I thought it would be. I'd better take a few more classes."

7. *Integration:* The job and one's work become part of one's self, and one gives up part of one's self to the job. This is a period of considerable satisfaction.

Occasionally, a person makes the wrong career decision. This is most likely to happen, of course, in the third stage of choosing a career path, but probably won't be recognized until the fourth or fifth stage. In such cases, there is little to do but begin again and work through the process, seeking the self-satisfaction that comes at the final stage.

▬▬ Before You Go On ▬▬

What developments may be said to
characterize early adulthood?

MIDDLE ADULTHOOD

As the middle years of adulthood approach, many aspects of one's life
have become settled. By the time most people reach the age of 40,
their place in the framework of society is fairly well set. They have
chosen their life-style and have grown accustomed to it. They have a
family (or have decided not to). They have chosen what is to be their
major life work or career. "Most of us during our 40s and 50s
become 'senior members' in our own particular worlds, however
grand or modest they may be" (Levinson, 1986, p. 6).

The movement to middle adulthood involves a transition of reexamination, at least for men (Levinson et al., 1974). During the middle
years, one is forced to contemplate one's own mortality. "Middle-age
spread," loss of muscle tone, facial wrinkles, and graying hair are evi-
dent each day in the mirror. At about the age of 40, sensory capacities
begin to slowly diminish. Most people in this stage now notice obitu-
aries in the newspaper, where more and more people of the same age
(or even younger) are listed every day.

For some people, perhaps for men more than women, the realization that time is running out produces something of a crisis, even
approaching panic. But, by and large, the notion of a mid-life crisis is
mostly myth (Costa & McCrae, 1980; Farrell & Rosenberg, 1981;
Hunter & Sundel, 1989). For most, middle age is a time of great satisfaction and true opportunity (Rossi, 1980). In most cases, children
are grown and gone. Careers are in full bloom. Time is available as
never before for leisure and commitment to community, perhaps in
the form of volunteer work.

There are several major tasks that one must face in the middle
years (from Havighurst, 1972). For one thing, we must accept and
adjust to the physiological changes of middle age. Although there certainly are many physical activities that middle-aged persons can
engage in, they sometimes must be selective or must modify the vigor
with which they attack such activities. Heading out to the backyard
for pickup basketball with the neighborhood teenagers is something a
45-year-old may have to think twice about.

Career choices may have been made earlier, but in middle age one
comes to expect satisfaction with one's job, and the experience necessary to demonstrate an adequate performance of that job. If career
satisfaction is not attained, one may attempt a mid-career job change.
Of course, there are also situations in which changing jobs in middle
age is more a matter of necessity than choice. In either case, the
potential for further growth and development or for crisis and conflict exists.

By middle adulthood, most people have chosen career paths and have developed life-styles that allow for more leisure time.

A major set of challenges that middle-aged persons face is dealing with other members of the family. At this stage in one's life, parents are often in the throes of helping their teenagers adjust to adolescence and prepare to "leave the nest," at the same time caring for their own parents. Adults in this situation have been referred to as being in "the sandwich generation" (Brody, 1981; Neugarten & Neugarten, 1989). In spite of widespread opinions to the contrary, individual responsibility and concern for the care of the elderly has not deteriorated in recent years (Brody, 1985). In fact, 80 percent of all day-to-day health care for the elderly is provided by the family.

One task of middle adulthood is similar to what Erikson calls the crisis of *generativity versus stagnation*. People shift from thinking about all they have done with their life to considering what they will do with what time is left for them and how they can leave a mark on future generations (Erikson, 1963; Harris, 1983).

Although all of these "tasks," as Havighurst calls them, are clearly related and interdependent, this is particularly true of these last two: relating to one's spouse as a person and developing leisure-time activities. As children leave home and financial concerns diminish, there may be more time for one's spouse and for leisure. In the eyes of adults, these tasks may seem like "enjoying each other, enjoying one's status, enjoying one's retirement, vacations, and travel." In truth, taking advantage of these changes in meaningful ways provides a challenge for some adults whose lives have previously been devoted to children and career.

Before You Go On

What are some of the issues typically faced
during the middle years of adulthood?

LATE ADULTHOOD

The transition to late adulthood generally occurs in our early to mid-
sixties. Perhaps the first thing we need to acknowledge is that persons
over the age of 65 constitute a sizable and growing proportion of the
population in the United States. More than 30.4 million Americans
were in this age bracket in 1988, and the numbers are increasing by
an average of 1,400 per day (Fowles, 1990; Kermis, 1984; Storandt,
1983). By the year 2020, Americans over 65 will constitute nearly 20
percent of the population, compared to the current 12 percent
(Cavenaugh & Park, 1993). Because of the coming of age of the
"baby boom" generation, by the year 2030, there will be about 66
million older persons in the United States (Fowles, 1990). According
to a Census Bureau report, by the year 2050, the number of persons
of age 65-plus years will be *78.9 million*—with an average life span of
82.1 years (AARP, 1993). The data also tell us that "aging is disproportionally a women's issue"; the vast majority of the oldest old—
over age 80—are women, and that the number of older ethnic minority adults is increasing more rapidly than for the population in general
(Cavenaugh & Park, 1993).

WHAT IT MEANS TO BE OLD

agism discrimination or prejudice against someone formed solely on the basis of age

Agism is the name given to discrimination and prejudice against a
group on the basis of age. Agism is particularly acute in our attitudes
about the elderly (Kimmel, 1988). One misconception about the aged
is that they live in misery. We cannot turn away from the realities of
some losses with age, but matters may not be as bad as many people
believe. For example, sensory capacities are not what they used to be.
But as Skinner (1983) suggested, "If you cannot read, listen to book
recordings. If you do not hear well, turn up the volume of your
phonograph (and wear headphones to protect your neighbors)."
Some cognitive abilities decline with age, but others often develop to
compensate for most losses (Salthouse, 1989). Some apparent memory loss may reflect more of a choice of what one wants to remember
than an actual loss. There is no doubt that mental speed is reduced,
but the accumulated experience of years of living can, and often does,
outweigh any advantages of speed.(Meer, 1986). It's almost a matter
of there being some good news to accompany the bad news of growing old.

Death does become a reality. As many as 50 percent of the
women over the age of 65 in this country are widows, and about one-
fifth as many are widowers. *But,* many elderly people choose this time

Many people find late adulthood both enjoyable and productive. They look forward to good times with friends and also have time to do volunteer community service work.

of their lives to marry for the first time (Kalish, 1982). Children have long since left the nest, *but* they're still in touch, and now there are grandchildren with whom to interact. The children of the elderly have now reached adulthood themselves, and are more able and likely to provide support for aging parents. Most older adults live in a family setting. In fact, only about 5 percent of Americans over the age of 65 live in nursing homes (Fowles, 1990; Harris, 1975, 1981, 1983). Even among those elderly in the United States classified as "poor" or "near poor," almost two-thirds own and live in their own homes—a percentage higher than that for their children (USGAO, 1992).

Some individuals dread retirement, but most welcome it as a chance to do things they have planned on for years (Haynes et al., 1978). Many people over the age of 65 become *more* physically active after retiring, perhaps from a job in which they sat at a desk all day long.

Although we often assume that old age necessarily brings with it the curse of poor health, in 1987 only 31 percent of respondents to a survey over age 65 claimed poor health to be a serious problem (Fowles, 1990). That may sound like a high percentage, but it compares to 7 percent in the 18-to-54 age range and 18 percent in the 55-to-65 age range. So, although health problems *are* more common in the elderly, they are not as widespread or as devastating as we might think.

One scheme developmental psychologists are finding useful is to divide those over age 65 into two groups: the *young-old* and the *old-old*. This distinction is not made on the basis of one's actual age, but on the basis of psychological, social, and health characteristics (Committee on an Aging Society, 1986; Neugarten & Neugarten, 1986). This distinction reinforces the notion that aging is not some sort of disease. The young-old group constitutes the large majority of those over 65 years of age (80 to 85 percent). They are "vigorous and competent men and women who have reduced their time investments in work or homemaking, are relatively comfortable financially and relatively well educated, and are well-integrated members of their families and communities" (Neugarten & Neugarten, 1989).

The concept of "successful aging" is a similar one and has been with us for some time. It is, however, a concept that seldom gets much attention. John Rowe and Robert Kahn (1987) would have us change the entire focus of the study of aging. Most research has focused on *average* age-related losses and deficits. Rowe and Kahn argue "that the role of aging per se in these losses has often been over-stated and that a major component of many age-associated declines can be explained in terms of life-style, habits, diet, and an array of psychosocial factors extrinsic to the aging process" (p. 143). The argument is that the declines, deficits, and losses of the elderly are not the result of advanced age but of factors over which we all can exercise some degree of control (Schaie, 1993). The major contributors to decline in old age include such things as poor nutrition, smoking, alcohol use, inadequate calcium intake, failure to maintain a sense of autonomy or control over one's life circumstances, and lack of social support (as long as the support does not erode self-control). Attention to these factors may not significantly lengthen the life span, but should extend what the authors call the "health span, the maintenance of full function as nearly as possible to the end of life" (Rowe & Kahn, 1987, p.149). Research suggests, for example, that maintaining close family relationships and involvement in effective exercise programs predict successful aging (Clarkson-Smith & Hartley, 1989; Valliant & Valliant, 1990).

Death and Dying

Of the two sure things in life, death and taxes, the former is the surer. There are no loopholes. Dealing with the reality of our own death is the last major conflict or crisis we face in life. As it happens, many people never have to deal with their own death in psychological terms. These are the people who die young or suddenly, from natural or accidental causes. Many individuals *do* have the time to contemplate their own death, and this usually takes place in late adulthood.

Much attention was focused on the confrontation with death in the popular book *On Death and Dying*, by Elisabeth Kübler-Ross (1969). Her description of the stages one goes through when facing death was based on hundreds of interviews with terminally ill patients who were aware that they were dying. Kübler-Ross suggests that the process takes place in five stages: (1) *denial* (a firm, simple avoidance of the evidence; a sort of "No, this can't be happening to me" reaction), (2) *anger* (often accompanied by resentment and envy of others, along with a realization of what is truly happening; a sort of "Why me? Why not someone else?" reaction), (3) *bargaining* (a matter of dealing, or barter, usually with God; a search for more time; a sort of "If you'll just grant me a few more weeks, or months, I'll go to church every week; no, every day" reaction), (4) *depression* (a sense of hopelessness that bargaining won't work, that a great loss is imminent; a period of grief and sorrow over both past mistakes and what will be missed in the future), and (5) *acceptance* (a rather quiet facing of the reality of death, with no great joy or sadness; simply a realization that the time has come).

It turns out that the Kübler-Ross description may be an idealized one (Kastenbaum & Costa, 1977). Many dying patients do not fit this pattern at all (Butler & Lewis, 1981). Some may show behaviors consistent with one or two of the stages, but seldom all five (Schultz & Alderman, 1974). There is some concern that this pattern of approaching death may be viewed as the "best" or the "right'" way to go about it. The concern here is that caretakers may try to force dying people into and through these stages, instead of letting each face the inevitability of death in his or her own way (Kalish, 1976, 1985).

Although elderly people have to deal with dying and death, they are generally less morbid about it than are adolescents (Lanetto, 1980). In one study (Kalish, 1976), adults over age 60 did more frequently think about and talk about death than did the younger adults surveyed. However, of all of the adults in the study, the oldest group expressed the least fear of death, some even saying they were eager for it.

The one sure thing about life is death. In old age, people think and talk about death more than when they were younger, but they are no more morbid about or afraid of death than younger adults.

Before You Go On

Briefly summarize some of what we
know about the elderly.

TOPIC 8D SUMMARY

I find it a curiosity that of the major periods of human development, childhood, adolescence, and adulthood, it has been only recently that psychologists have begun to focus on that period in which we will spend most of our lives: adulthood. Adulthood begins, for most of us, in our late teen or early twenties and is characterized by both independence (largely from parents) and interdependence (on new family ties). The process of development throughout adulthood may be slower than in other stages, but still, choices need to be made and crises resolved. Often, these choices or transitions (if not crises) involve marriage, family, and career.

If you have read all four of the Topics in this chapter, you might now be quite impressed with the orderliness and predictability of human development. Ova and sperm cells unite to form zygotes. Zygotes become embryos, fetuses, and, through birth, neonates. Neonates are born with a range of adaptive reflexes and sensory capabilities. Motor development progresses through identifiable stages. Depending on the theory, cognitive development appears to progress through four stages, psychosocial development passes through eight stages, and moral development through six. Many of the conflicts of adolescence are predictable. Adulthood moves from choice to commitment to preparation for death.

As easy as it is to be impressed with the orderliness of human development, we must remember not to take this too literally. Orderly sequences of development emerge from examining averages and progressions *in general*. Developmental trends and stages are like so many other things: if one looks hard enough, they can be found. But the individual differences we see around us constantly remind us that for any one individual—child, adolescent, or adult—many of our observations may not hold true. The orderliness of development may exist only in the eyes of the observer. The picture we have drawn in this chapter is one of general conclusions to which there will always be exceptions.

CHAPTER SUMMARY

TOPIC 8A

What are some of the basic concepts involved in any discussion of the genetic transmission of physical characteristics?

What is the epigenetic model of development, and what does it say about the impact of heredity and the environment?

Physical characteristics are inherited to the extent that genes, carried on chromosomes, are passed from the sex cells of both parents to the child. Genes may be dominant (the trait they represent will be expressed no matter what other gene is paired with it) or recessive, in which case they must be paired with a similarly recessive gene for that characteristic to be expressed. Even for characteristics that are inherited, the impact of the environment is relevant. The epigenetic model is an interactionist one, claiming that psychological characteristics are the result of neither heredity nor the environment alone. Rather, organisms develop through the interaction of one's genetic programming *and* one's experiences in the environment. Nature may set limits on what nurture may provide through development. The extent to which the environment can impact on genetic predispositions is referred to as plasticity. /*p. 357*

Briefly summarize the stages of prenatal development.

Prenatal development begins at conception and ends at birth. The period is divided into three stages: the stage of the zygote (conception to 2 weeks), at which time the zygote becomes implanted in the uterus; the stage of the embryo (week 2 to week 8), during which there is rapid growth and differentiation of developing cells; and the stage of the fetus (month 3 until birth), during which the organs begin to function. /*p. 361*

Briefly review the impact of diet, drugs, and stress on prenatal development.

A mother's diet and use of drugs can have profound effects on prenatal development. Malnutrition in the mother, or deficiencies of specific vitamins or minerals, are usually shared by the embryo or the fetus. Smoking and alcohol use during pregnancy have well-documented negative effects. Research on the effects of stress on prenatal development has not produced clear-cut results. Severe or chronic stress may produce negative consequences, for the mother and for her child. Although most attention is focused on the health and behaviors of the pregnant mother, the health and behaviors of the father at or about the time of conception are not irrelevant in predicting the birth of a healthy child. /*p. 364*

TOPIC 8B

What are some of the reflexes that can be observed in neonates?

Why do we care about neonatal reflexes?

Some reflexes have survival value for the neonate; for example, the rooting reflex, in which the newborn turns toward pressure on its

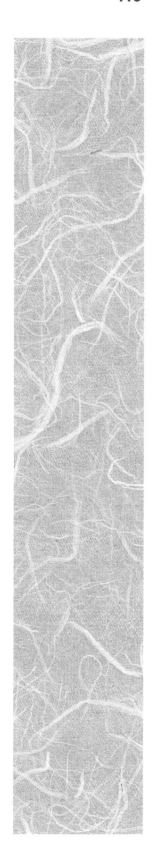

cheek, the sucking reflex, or the grasping reflex. Other reflexes, such as the Moro reflex (thrusting arms to the sides and then bringing them back to the chest in reaction to a sudden noise or loss of support) or the walking reflex seem to serve no particular function for the neonate but can be used to diagnose developmental delays or confirm normal physical development. /*p. 366*

What general observations can we make about physical growth and motor control in childhood?

The age at which motor abilities develop varies considerably from child to child, but the sequence is quite regular and predictable. Review Figure 8.5. Growth and development follow two patterns: (1) cephalocaudal, or from head to torso to feet, and (2) proximodistal, or from center to extremities. /*p. 367*

Summarize the basic sensory capacities of the neonate.

The neonate's senses function reasonably well from birth. The eyes can focus well at arm's length, although they will require a few months to focus over a range of object distances. Rudimentary depth perception seems to be present even in the neonate, but improves considerably within the first year. Hearing and auditory discrimination are quite good, as are the senses of taste, smell, and touch. /*p. 370*

Cite an example of research evidence demonstrating a cognitive reaction in neonates.

Newborns just a few hours old give evidence of learning through both classical and operant conditioning. Neonates (in one case only 1 to 4 days old) can demonstrate memory. They will attend to a new visual pattern after coming to ignore a familiar one, showing an appreciation of the difference between familiar and new. They show definite preferences for complex visual patterns over simple ones, and seem to prefer (attend to) visual representations of the human face, their mother's face in particular. Babies only 1 hour old make attempts to imitate facial expressions of someone within their field of view. /*p. 372*

How are schemas formed during the sensorimotor stage? What characterizes this stage of development?

During Piaget's sensorimotor stage of cognitive development, the child develops schemas (assimilating new information and accommodating old concepts) through an active interaction with the environment—by sensing and doing. The baby begins to appreciate cause-and-effect relationships, imitates the actions of others, and by the end of the period, develops a sense of object permanence; that is, he or she understands that just because something is no longer in view does not mean it is gone. /*p. 373*

In Piaget's theory, what characterizes the preoperational stage of development?

Egocentrism is a cognitive reaction that occurs during the preoperational stage of development. The child becomes *me-* and *I*-oriented, unable to appreciate the world from anyone else's perspective or point of view. In addition, children begin to develop and use symbols, in the form of words to represent concepts. */p. 375*

What cognitive skills might we expect from a child in the concrete operations stage of development?

In the concrete operations stage, a child organizes concepts into categories, and begins to use simple logic and to understand relational terms. The skills of conservation are not acquired until the end of the preoperational stage, and mark the beginning of the concrete operations stage. Conservation involves understanding that changing something's form (rolling out a ball of clay or pouring liquid from one type of container to another) does not change its nature or quantity. */p. 377*

What cognitive ability characterizes the stage of formal operations?

The essence of the formal operations stage is the ability to think, reason, and solve problems symbolically, or in abstract rather than concrete, tangible form. */p. 377*

Cite two criticisms of Piaget's theory of cognitive development.

Piaget's theory of cognitive development has been very influential, and has received support from cross-cultural studies, but it has not escaped criticism. Two criticisms of the theory are that (1) there is little evidence that cognitive abilities develop in a series of well-defined stages (that is, the borders between stages are poorly defined), and (2) preschool children in particular seem to have more cognitive abilities than Piaget suggested. */p. 379*

Briefly summarize the stages of Kohlberg's theory of moral development.

Kohlberg claims that moral reasoning develops through three levels and six stages. First, one decides right from wrong on the basis of avoiding punishment and gaining rewards (preconventional morality), then on the basis of conforming to authority or accepting social convention (conventional morality), and finally on the basis of one's understanding of the common good, individual rights, and internalized standards (postconventional morality). Although much of the theory has been supported, there is little evidence that many individuals reach the higher levels of moral reasoning. Also, there may be serious deficiencies in applying the theory equally to both sexes or to all cultures, wherein what is "moral, or right," may vary. */p. 382*

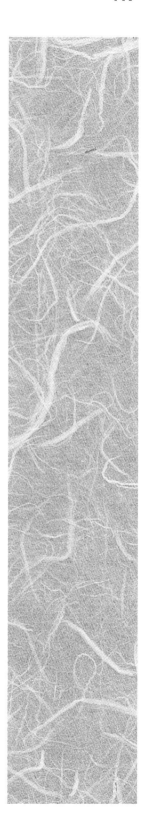

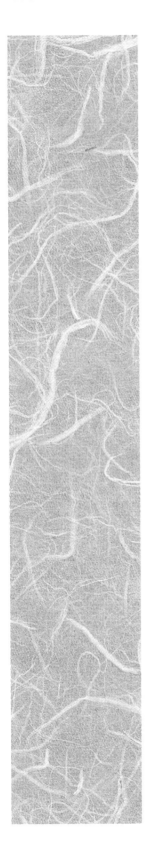

Briefly describe the first four stages, or crises, of development according to Erikson.

Of Erikson's eight stages of development, four occur during childhood. These stages are described in terms of crises that need resolution, and include (1) trust versus mistrust (whether the child develops a sense of security or anxiety), (2) autonomy versus shame and doubt (whether the child develops a sense of competence or doubt), (3) initiative versus guilt (whether the child gains confidence in his or her own ability or develops a sense of inadequacy), and (4) industry versus inferiority (whether the child develops a sense of confidence in intellectual and social skills or develops a sense of failure and lack of confidence.) /p. 384

What conclusions may we draw about the development of gender identity in children?

Gender identity is the sense or self-awareness of one's maleness or femaleness. There is a notion that males and females, even as children are different and should be treated differently, although there is no evidence to support this notion. Most children have a firm sense of their own gender by the age of 2 to 3 years, with gender identity most strongly reinforced by peer groups and play activities. A child's cognitive sense of gender stereotypes may flavor how new information is accommodated. /p. 387

In child development, what is meant by attachment, and what are the consequences of developing attachments?

Attachment is a strong, two-way, emotional bond, formed early in childhood between the child and primary caregiver(s). It has survival value in an evolutionary sense, keeping the child in proximity to those who can best care for him or her. Secure attachment in childhood has been associated with improved self-esteem later in life. Harlow first demonstrated a need for *contact comfort* in rhesus monkeys. Fathers, as well as mothers, demonstrate appropriate attachment-related behaviors, and to date, most evidence is that day care for young children need not have negative consequences (depending mostly on the quality of that day care). /p. 389

TOPIC 8C

How might adolescence be defined, and how can the period be best characterized?

Adolescence may be defined in several ways. Physically, it begins with puberty (attainment of sexual maturity) and lasts until the end of one's physical growth. Psychologically, it is defined in terms of the cognitions and feelings that characterize the period, searching for identity and abstract thinking. Socially, it is a marginal period of transition, coming between childhood and adulthood and reflecting how the adolescent is viewed by others. Historically, the period has been seen as one of stress, distress, and abnormality. More contemporary views see adolescence as a period of challenges, but a period that most survive with no lasting negative consequences. /p. 392

Briefly describe the physical changes that accompany the beginnings of adolescence.

Two significant physical developments mark adolescence: a spurt of growth, seen at an earlier age in girls (9 to 15) than in boys (12 to 20), and the beginning of sexual maturity, a period called *puberty*. That is, as adolescents, individuals are for the first time physically prepared for sexual reproduction and begin to develop secondary sex characteristics. The consequences of reaching puberty early are a bit more positive for males than females, although the long-term consequences are few and slight. /p. 396

Summarize the adolescent's search for identity as described by Erikson.

The search for one's identity—a sense of who one is and what one is to do with one's life—is, for Erikson, the major crisis of adolescence. Most do develop such a sense of identity, but some do enter adulthood in a state of what Erikson calls role confusion. /p. 397

Briefly summarize the data on drug use and abuse in adolescence.

Most teenagers have experimented with drugs (mostly alcohol, tried by 92 percent of high school seniors), and a disturbing number use drugs quite frequently. One study demonstrated that among frequent users, experimenters, and abstainers, the experimenters evidenced the fewest psychological problems as 18-year-olds. Drug use and abuse among teenagers is no worse (but no better) than among the adult population. /p. 399

What evidence supports the notion that adolescents are a sexually active group?

Briefly summarize the data on teenage pregnancy.

By the time they are 19 years old, more than half of all females and nearly three-quarters of all males report having had sexual intercourse. Sexual activity is on the increase for both males and females. One's first sexual encounter most often just "happens," without forethought. This may help explain the fact that over 1 million teenagers become pregnant each year. Slightly more than half of those pregnancies will result in live births. About two-thirds of white teenage mothers are unmarried, and virtually all black teenage mothers are single. /p. 401

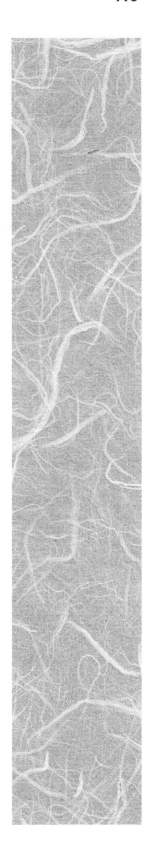

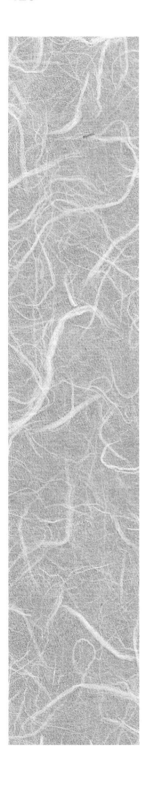

TOPIC 8D

What developments may be said to characterize early adulthood?

Early adulthood (ages 18 to 45) is characterized by choices and commitments independently made. One assumes new responsibilities and is faced with difficult decisions concerning career, marriage, and family. For Erikson, the period is marked by the conflict between intimacy and social relationships on the one hand and social isolation on the other. Although many marriages fail, most young adults list a good marriage as a major source of happiness in their lives. Psychologists have found that many factors determine one's selection of a mate. There is little support for the notion that opposites attract. Characteristics of desired mates vary considerably from culture to culture. Choosing one's career or occupation is a decision of early adulthood. It is a process that goes through several stages, and often fails at first. /p. 408

What are some of the issues typically faced during the middle years of adulthood?

Middle adulthood (ages 45 to 65) is often a period first of reexamination and then of settling down to one's life goals. Entering into the period may be troublesome for some, but most find middle age a period of great satisfaction and opportunity. The person comes to accept his or her own mortality in several ways. The tasks of middle age involve one's changing physiology, one's occupation, aging parents and growing children, social and civic responsibilities, and the use of leisure time. /p. 410

Briefly summarize some of what we know about the elderly.

There are more than 30 million Americans over age 65, and the number of elderly is growing rapidly. Although there may be sensory, physical, and cognitive limits forced by old age, only 21 percent of elderly people rate health problems as a major concern. Although some elderly are isolated and lonely, fewer than 5 percent live in nursing homes and only 8 percent consider themselves lonely. Older people are concerned about death, but they are neither consumed by it nor morbid about it. With good nutrition and diet, the development of a healthy life-style, proper social support, and the maintenance of some degree of autonomy and control over one's life, "successful aging" can become even more common than it is today. This is another way of saying that we can increase the already large percentage (now 80 to 85 percent) of those over the age of 65 who have been characterized as young-old, as opposed to old-old. /p. 414

chapter nine

PERSONALITY AND INTELLIGENCE

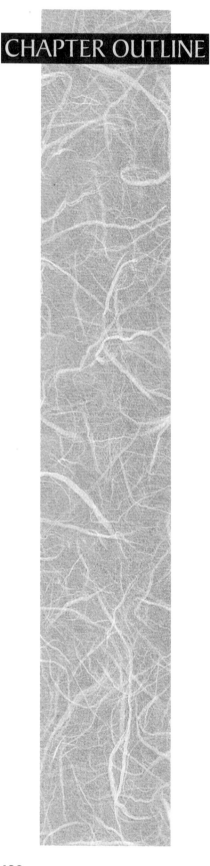

CHAPTER OUTLINE

TOPIC 9A ISSUES AND THEORIES OF PERSONALITY
The Psychoanalytic Approach
    Freud's Approach
    The Psychoanalytic Approach After Freud
The Behavioral/Learning Approach
The Humanistic-Phenomenological Approach
The Trait Approach
    Two Classic Examples
    A Contemporary Perspective: The Big Five
Pros and Cons of the Four Approaches to Personality
Issues Related to Personality
    Is There a Personality?: Interactionism
    Gender and Personality
    Personality Measurement, or Assessment
TOPIC 9A SUMMARY

TOPIC 9B INTELLIGENCE AS AN ASPECT OF PERSONALITY
Just What *Is* Intelligence?
    Defining Intelligence
    Theoretical Models of Intelligence
Psychological Tests of Intelligence
    The Stanford-Binet Intelligence Scale
    The Wechsler Tests of Intelligence
    Group Tests of Intelligence
Individual and Group Differences in Measured Intelligence
    Group Differences in IQ
    Gender Differences in IQ
    Age Differences and IQ
    Racial and Ethnic Differences in IQ
    Extremes of Intelligence: The Mentally Gifted
    Extremes of Intelligence: The Mentally Retarded
TOPIC 9B SUMMARY

CHAPTER SUMMARY

I have been teaching introductory psychology for over 25 years. By now, I feel I understand the basic personalities of most introductory psychology students quite well. Some of my observations are listed below. To test their accuracy, go through the list and indicate the extent to which each statement applies to you. If you think the statement is a true, accurate appraisal, mark it with a 1. If you think it is only partially accurate, or true only some of the time, give it a 2. If you think the statement does not apply to you at all, give it a 3.

_____You have a rather strong need for other people to like you and for them to admire you.

_____You have a tendency to be critical of yourself.

_____You feel somewhat uncomfortable when called on in class, even if you know the answer to the question.

_____While you have some personality weaknesses, you generally are able to compensate for them.

_____Disciplined and controlled on the outside, you tend to be a bit insecure and worrisome on the inside.

_____You prefer a certain amount of change and variety, and become dissatisfied when hemmed in by restrictions.

_____You have found it unwise to be too frank in revealing yourself to others.

_____At times you are extroverted, easy-going, and sociable, while at other times you are introverted, wary, and reserved.

_____Some of your aspirations tend to be pretty unrealistic.

_____You occasionally have difficulty relating what you are reading in your psychology class to your experiences.

_____Your sexual adjustments have presented some problems for you.

_____At times you have serious doubts as to whether you have made the right decision or done the right thing.

Add up the scores so that we can see how well I've done. A low score means I did fairly well; a score of 12 indicates that I was accurate with every observation.

When I do this exercise in class, nearly 90 percent of my students have a score of 18 or less. That's pretty good, isn't it? But wait a minute! How could I possibly have any insight about the personalities of the students in my class, most of whom I hardly know at all? How could I describe *your* personality accurately, when we've never met?

This little "test" is a version of a demonstration that dates back at least to 1956 (Munn, 1956). Ten of these twelve items come from the Generalized Personality Test (or GPT) described in an article by Ulrich, Stachnick, and Stainton in 1963. The truth is that these statements are so general that they are virtually meaningless, and could be applied to nearly everyone. Also notice that these "items" are very similar to the statements one commonly finds in daily horoscopes.

*M*ost of us think we understand ourselves fairly well. We believe we have a good sense of who we are, how we tend to think and feel, and what we are likely to do in most situations. To a somewhat lesser extent, we also feel we understand a few other people, perhaps a few close friends and family members. We have come to believe that knowing someone's personality is required if we are to truly understand that person. We have also come to appreciate that it is not easy to know someone's personality, because a personality consists of internal, private experiences, often difficult to determine from the outside.

Psychology has valued the concept of personality throughout its history. Over the years, many theories have emerged that have sought to describe the nature of personality. In this chapter, we'll begin by examining some of those theories. Each of these theories, in its own way, has added to our contemporary understanding of personality.

Once we've reviewed a few theories of personality in Topic 9A, we'll consider how psychologists go about measuring those traits or characteristics that can be taken to constitute the aggregate we call personality. This will get us into a brief side trip for a discussion of psychological testing and measurement in general.

Topic 9B focuses on a major component of personality: intelligence. We will find that defining the concept of intelligence is nearly as difficult as defining the more general concept of personality. We'll look at how intelligence is measured, and we'll end the chapter with a brief discussion of group and individual differences in measured intelligence.

Topic 9A

ISSUES AND THEORIES OF PERSONALITY

As I said, the major task of this Topic is to briefly describe some of the major theories of personality. We'll organize this discussion of specific personality theories into four basic approaches. But, before we do, let's see what we mean by *theory* and what we mean by *personality* in this context.

A theory is a series of assumptions; in our particular case, these assumptions are about people and their personalities. The ideas or assumptions that constitute a theory are based on the theorist's observations, and are reasonably and logically related to each other. Further, the ideas of a theory should lead, through reason, to specific, testable hypotheses. In short, a good **theory** is an organized collection of testable ideas used to explain a particular subject matter.

Okay, so what, then, is personality? Few terms have been as difficult to define. In many ways, each of the theoretical approaches we will study in this topic generates its own definition of personality. **Personality** includes the *affects*, *behaviors*, and *cognitions* of people

theory *an organized collection of ultimately testable ideas used to explain a particular subject matter*

personality *those affects, behaviors, and cognitions that characterize a person in a variety of situations*

that characterize them in a number of situations over time. (Here again is our *ABC* mnemonic from Topic 1A.) We assume that these affects, behaviors, and cognitions help individuals adapt to their environments. Personality also includes those dimensions we can use to judge people to be different from one another. So, we are looking for ways to describe how individuals remain the same over time and circumstances, and allow us to describe differences we know exist among people (R. F. Baumeister, 1987). Personality somehow resides *inside* the person; it is something a person brings to his or her interactions with the environment. David Buss (1984) put it this way: "The field of personality psychology is centrally concerned with the traits that characterize our species as well as the major ways in which individuals characteristically differ" (p. 1143).

THE PSYCHOANALYTIC APPROACH

We begin our discussion of personality theories by considering the psychoanalytic approach. This approach is associated with Sigmund Freud and his students. We begin with Freud because he was the first to present a unified theory of personality.

Freud's theory of personality has been one of the most influential and, at the same time, most controversial in all of science. Although there are many facets to Freud's theory (and those of his students), two basic premises characterize the **psychoanalytic** approach: (1) reliance on innate drives as explanatory concepts for human behavior, and (2) acceptance of the power of unconscious forces to mold and shape behavior.

psychoanalytic the approach to personality associated with Freud and his followers that relies on instincts and the unconscious as explanatory concepts

Freud's Approach

Freud's ideas about personality arose largely from his reading of the works of many philosophers, observations of his patients, and intense self-examination. His private practice provided Freud with experiences from which he proposed a general theory of personality and developed a technique of therapy called *psychoanalysis*. Freud's approach to psychotherapy is discussed in Topic 13B. For now, let's review some of Freud's basic ideas about the structure and dynamics of human personality.

Levels of Consciousness. Central to Freudian personality theory is the notion that information, feelings, wants, drives, desires, and the like can be found at various levels of awareness, or consciousness. You'll recall that Topic 4A centered on a discussion of levels of human consciousness—and Freud's views about such levels. Let's quickly review that discussion. (You might want to check Figure 4.1 on page 169 again.)

Mental events of which we are actively aware at the moment are *conscious*, or "in consciousness." Aspects of our mental life of which we are not conscious at any one moment, but that can be easily brought to awareness, are stored or housed at a *preconscious* level.

When you shift your awareness to think about something you may do this evening, those plans probably were already there, in your preconscious mind.

Cognitions, feelings, and motives not available to us at the conscious or preconscious level are said to be in the *unconscious*. At this level we keep ideas, memories, and desires of which we are not aware and cannot easily become aware. Remember the significance of the unconscious level of the mind: even though ideas, thoughts, and feelings are stored there so that we are completely unaware of them, the contents of the unconscious mind still influence us. Unconscious content passing through the preconscious may show itself in slips of the tongue, humor, neurotic symptoms, and, of course, dreams. Freud believed that unconscious forces could be used to explain behaviors that otherwise seemed irrational and beyond description.

Before You Go On

What are the three levels of consciousness
proposed by Freud?

Basic Instincts. According to Freudian theory, our behaviors, thoughts, and feelings are largely governed by innate biological drives, referred to as *instincts* in this context. These are inborn impulses or forces that rule our personalities. There may be many separate drives or instincts, but they can be grouped into two categories.

On the one hand are **life instincts** (**eros**), or impulses for survival, including those that motivate sex, hunger, and thirst. Each instinct has its own energy that compels us into action (drives us). Freud called the energy through which the sexual instincts operate **libido**. Opposed to life instincts are **death instincts** (**thanatos**). These are largely impulses of destruction. Directed inward, they give rise to feelings of depression or suicide; directed outward, they result in aggression toward other people or their property. In large measure, life (according to Freud) is an attempt to resolve conflicts between these two natural but diametrically opposed instincts.

The Structure of Personality. As we have seen, Freud believed the mind operates on three interacting levels of awareness: conscious, preconscious, and unconscious. Freud also proposed that the human personality consists of three separate, though interacting, structures or subsystems: the id, ego, and superego. Each of these subsystems has its own job to do and its own principles to follow.

The **id** is the totally inborn or inherited portion of personality. The id resides in the unconscious level of the mind, and it is through the id that basic instincts develop. The driving force of the id is libido, or sexual energy, although it may be more fair to say "sensual" rather than "sexual" so as not to leave the impression that Freud was always talking about adult, sexual intercourse.

life instincts (eros) inborn impulses, proposed by Freud, that compel one toward survival; they include hunger, thirst, and sex

libido the energy that activates the sexual instincts

death instincts (thanatos) the inborn impulses, proposed by Freud, that compel one toward destruction; they include feelings of depression and aggression

id the instinctive aspect of personality that seeks immediate gratification of impulses; it operates on the pleasure principle

The id operates on what Freud labeled the **pleasure principle**, indicating that the major function of the id is to find satisfaction for basic pleasurable impulses. Although the two other divisions of personality develop later, our id remains with us always and is the basic energy source in our lives.

The **ego** is the part of the personality that develops through one's experience with reality. In many ways, it is our self, the rational, reasoning part of our personality. The ego operates on the **reality principle**. One of the ego's main jobs is to try to find satisfaction for the id, but in ways that are reasonable and rational. The ego may have to delay gratification of some libidinal impulse or may need to find an acceptable outlet for some need.

The last of the three structures to develop is the **superego**, which we can liken to one's sense of morality, or conscience. It reflects our internalization of society's rules. The superego operates on the **idealistic principle**. One problem we have with our superegos is that they, like our ids, have no contact with reality and therefore often place unrealistic demands on the individual. The superego demands that we do what *it* deems to be right and proper, no matter what the circumstances. Failure to do so may lead to guilt and shame. Again, it falls to the ego to try to maintain a realistic balance between the conscience of the superego and the libido of the id.

This isn't as complicated as it may sound. Let's suppose a bank teller discovers an extra $20 in her cash drawer at the end of the day. She certainly could use an extra $20. "Go ahead. Nobody will miss it. The bank can afford a few dollars here and there. Think of the fun you can have with an extra $20," is the basic message from her id. "The odds are that you'll get caught if you take this money. If you *are* caught, you may lose your job; then you'll have to find another one," reasons her ego. "But you shouldn't even think about taking that money. Shame on you! It's not yours. It belongs to someone else and should be returned," the superego protests. Clearly, the interaction of the three components of one's personality is not always this simple and straightforward, but this example illustrates the general idea.

pleasure principle the impulse of the id to seek immediate gratification to reduce tensions

ego the aspect of personality that encompasses the sense of "self"; it is in contact with the real world, and operates on the reality principle

reality principle the force that governs the ego, arbitrating between the demands of the id, the superego, and the real world

superego the aspect of personality that refers to ethical or moral considerations; it operates on the idealistic principle

idealistic principle the force that governs the superego; opposed to the id, it seeks adherence to standards of ethics and morality

Before You Go On

According to Freud, what are the three
structures of personality, and by what principle
does each operate?

The Defense Mechanisms. When the ego cannot find acceptable ways to satisfy the drives of the id, or when it cannot deal with the demands of the superego, conflict and anxiety result. Then, ways must be found to combat the resulting anxiety. It was for this purpose that Freud proposed the existence of **defense mechanisms**—*unconsciously* applied techniques that protect the self (ego) against strong

defense mechanisms unconsciously applied techniques that protect the self (ego) from feelings of anxiety

feelings of anxiety. What follows is a list of some of the more common ego defense mechanisms, with an example of each.

repression a defense mechanism referring to motivated forgetting of an anxiety-producing event or desire

Repression is the most basic of the defense mechanisms. It is sometimes referred to as *motivated forgetting*, which gives you a good idea of what is involved. Repression is a matter of (conveniently) forgetting about some anxiety-producing event or desire. Paul had a teacher with whom he did not get along. After spending an entire semester trying to do his best, Paul failed the course. The following summer, while Paul was out walking with his girlfriend, the teacher approached Paul, and Paul could not remember the instructor's name. He had repressed it. Surely, forgetting about everything and everyone who ever caused you anxiety is not a very adaptive response, but pushing some anxiety-producing memories into the depths of the unconscious mind can protect us from dwelling on unpleasantness.

denial a defense mechanism wherein one refuses to believe the realities of an anxiety-producing situation

Denial is a mechanism of defense in which a person simply refuses to acknowledge the realities of an anxiety-producing situation. When a physician first tells a patient that he or she has a terminal illness, a common reaction is denial; the patient refuses to believe or accept that the diagnosis is accurate.

rationalization a defense mechanism that excuses one's behaviors rather than facing the anxiety-producing reasons for them

Rationalization amounts to making up excuses for one's behaviors rather than facing the (anxiety-producing) real reasons for them. The real reason Kevin failed his psychology midterm is that he didn't study for it and had missed several classes. Kevin hates to admit, even to himself, that he could have been so stupid as to flunk this big exam because of his own actions or inactions. So, he rationalizes: "It really wasn't my fault. I had a terrible instructor. The test was grossly unfair. We used a lousy textbook. And I've been fighting the flu all semester."

fantasy a defense mechanism that involves the imagination or daydreaming as a reaction to stress and anxiety

Fantasy provides an escape from anxiety through imagination or daydreaming. It is one of the more common of the defense mechanisms used by college students. Particularly after a week of exams and term paper deadlines, isn't it sort of pleasant to sit back in a comfortable chair and fantasize about finally graduating from college with honors? To engage in fantasy occasionally is a normal and acceptable reaction to stress and anxiety. On the other hand, there are potential dangers here. One needs to be able to keep separate those activities that are real and those that occur in fantasies. Surely you recognize that fantasy in itself will not solve the problems or resolve the conflicts that caused the anxiety in the first place. Daydreaming about academic success may help one feel better for a while, but it is not likely to make anyone a better student.

projection a defense mechanism that involves seeing in others traits or motives that would make one anxious if seen in oneself

Projection is a matter of seeing in others those motives or traits that would make one anxious if seen in oneself. Under enormous pressure to do well on an exam, Kirsten decides to cheat. But at exam time, her conscience (superego) won't let her. Because of projection, Kirsten may think that she sees cheating going on all around her. Projection is a defense mechanism that often is used in conjunction with aggression or hostility. When people feel uncomfortable with their own levels of hostility, they often project their aggressiveness onto others, coming to believe that others are "out to do me harm," and "I'm only protecting myself."

To employ the defense of **regression** is to return to earlier, more primitive, even childish levels of behavior that were once effective. Oddly enough, we often see regression occurring in children. Imagine a 4-year-old who until very recently was an only child. Now Mommy has returned from the hospital with a new baby sister. The 4-year-old is no longer the "center of attention." He reverts to earlier behaviors and starts wetting the bed, screaming for a bottle of his own, and crawling on all fours. He is regressing.

regression a defense mechanism that involves returning to earlier, more primitive levels of behavior that were once effective

The defense mechanism of **displacement** is usually discussed in the context of aggression. It is a matter of directing one's motives or behaviors at some substitute person or object rather than expressing them directly—which would be anxiety-producing. Dorothy expects to get promoted at work, but someone else gets the new job she wanted. She's upset and angry at her boss, but feels, perhaps correctly, that blowing her top at her boss will do more harm than good, so she displaces her hostility toward her husband, the children, or the family cat.

displacement a defense mechanism in which one's behaviors or motives (usually aggressive) are directed at a substitute rather than the real object of those behaviors or motives

This list of defense mechanisms is not an exhaustive one. These are among the more common, however, and should give you an idea of what Freud had in mind. There are two points about defense mechanisms that deserve special mention. (1) Using defense mechanisms is a normal reaction. You shouldn't be alarmed if you find that some of these mechanisms sound like reactions you have used. In moderation they help us to cope with the anxieties and conflicts of everyday life. (2) Although they are normal, even common, defense mechanisms can become maladaptive. As long as these mechanisms are successful in alleviating the unpleasant feelings of anxiety, we may no longer feel the need to search for the true sources of anxiety and thus will be less likely to resolve the conflicts that produced the anxiety in the first place. We'll have more to say about this point when we discuss effective and ineffective strategies for dealing with stress and anxiety in Chapter 11.

Before You Go On

**What are Freudian defense mechanisms and
what is their purpose?**

The Psychosexual Stages of Personality Development. Freud obviously put a lot of stock in the biological bases of personality, relying as he did on concepts such as drive and instinct. This same orientation flavored his view of personality development. According to Freud, personality develops naturally, in a biologically based series of overlapping stages. The events that occur in early stages have the potential to produce profound effects on later development.

One of Freud's most controversial assumptions about human behavior was that even infants and young children were under the influence of the sexual strivings of the id and its libidinal energy. The outlet for the sexual impulses (again, "*sensual*" may be a better word in today's usage) of young children is not the reproductive sex act. But Freud thought that much of the pleasure derived by children is essentially sexual; hence. we refer to Freud's stages of development as *psychosexual*. Freud claimed that there are five such stages.

1. *Oral Stage* (Birth to 1 year.) Pleasure and satisfaction come from oral activities: feeding, sucking, and making noises. The mouth continues to be a source of pleasure for many people long into adulthood, as demonstrated by overeating, fingernail biting, smoking, or talkativeness.

2. *Anal Stage* (Age 1 to 3 years.) Sometime in their second year, children develop the ability to control their bladder and bowel habits. At this time, the anus becomes the focus of pleasure. Satisfaction is gained through bowel control. Aggressiveness (the id again) can be displayed (particularly against parents) by either having bowel movements at inappropriate times or by refusing "to go" when placed on the potty chair. Here we clearly can see the thoughtful, reasoning ego emerging and exercising some control. After all, the parents can't *make* the child do what they want it to. The child is in control, and that control can lead to great satisfaction.

3. *Phallic Stage* (Age 3 to 5 years.) Here there is an awareness of one's sexuality. The genitals replace the mouth and the anus as the source of pleasure, and masturbation or fondling of the genitals may become a common practice. It is during this stage of development that children tend to form close (sexually based) attachments to the parent of the opposite sex, and feelings of jealousy and/or fear of the same-sex parent may arise. This pattern of reaction is called the *Oedipus complex* in boys and the *Electra complex* in girls. It is in the phallic stage that the superego begins to develop.

4. *Latency Stage* (Age 6 years until puberty.) At this stage in life, sexual development gets put on hold. Now the ego is developing very rapidly. There is much to be learned about the world and how it operates. Sexual development can wait. Sexuality is suppressed. Friends tend to be of the same sex. You have no doubt heard the protestations of a 9-year-old boy, "Oh, yuck; kiss a girl? No way! Yuck!" And you counsel, "Just wait; soon girls won't seem so 'yucky.'"

5. *Genital Stage* (After puberty.) With puberty, there is a renewal of sexual impulses, a reawakening of desire, and an interest in matters sexual and sensual.

Before You Go On

Briefly summarize Freud's psychosexual stages
of development.

According to Freud, from the age of 6 until puberty, children are in a "latency period," and tend to associate only with others of the same sex.

The Psychoanalytic Approach After Freud

Sigmund Freud was a persuasive communicator. He was a powerful speaker. In his writings, he was without peer. His ideas were challenging, and they attracted many students. Freud founded a psychoanalytic society in Vienna. There was an "inner circle" of colleagues and friends who shared his ideas, but some did not entirely agree with all aspects of his theory. Among other things, they were bothered by the very strong emphasis on biological instincts and libido, and what they perceived as a lack of concern for social influences. Some of these analysts left Freud and proposed theories of their own; they became known as **neo-Freudians**. Because they had their own ideas, they had to part from Freud; he would not tolerate disagreement with his theory. One had to accept all of Freudian theory, or one had to leave Freud's inner circle.

 We really cannot do justice to someone's theory of personality in a short paragraph or two. What we can do, perhaps, is sketch the basic idea(s) behind the theories of a few neo-Freudians.

 Alfred Adler (1870–1937). As the psychoanalytic movement was beginning to take shape, Adler was one of Freud's closest friends and associates. However, Adler left Freud and, in 1911, founded his own version of a psychoanalytic approach to personality. Two things seemed most to offend Adler: the negativity of Freud's views (the death instinct, for one) and the idea of sexual libido as the prime impulse in life.

 Adler argued that we are a product of the social influences on our personality. We are motivated not so much by drives and instincts as by goals and incentives. The future and one's hope for what it holds for us are often more important than one's past. For Adler, our major

neo-Freudians theorists (including Adler, Jung, and Horney) who supported the basics of psychoanalytic theory, but differed from Freud

inferiority complex *the feeling that we are less able than others to solve life's problems and get along in the world*

goal is the achievement of success or superiority. This goal is fashioned in childhood when, because we are then weak and vulnerable, we develop an **inferiority complex**—the feeling that we are less able than others to solve life's problems and get along in the world. Although we may seem inferior as children, with the help of social influences and our own creativity, we can overcome and succeed.

Carl Jung (1875–1961). Another student and colleague of Freud, Carl Jung left the inner circle in 1913. Jung was chosen by Freud to be his successor, but several disagreements developed, mostly about the role of sexuality and the nature of the unconscious—two central themes in psychoanalysis. Jung was more mystical in his approach to personality and, like Adler, certainly was more positive about one's ability to control one's own destiny. He believed our major goal in life was to unify all of the aspects of our personality, conscious and unconscious, introverted (inwardly directed) and extroverted (outwardly directed). Libido was energy for Jung, but not sexual energy; it was energy for personal growth and development.

Jung accepted the idea of an unconscious mind, and expanded on it, claiming that there are *two* types of unconscious: the *personal unconscious*, which is very much like Freud's view of the unconscious, and the *collective unconscious*, which contains very basic ideas that go beyond an individual's own personal experiences. The ideas of the collective unconscious are common to all of humanity and are inherited from all past generations. The contents of our collective unconscious include what Jung called *archetypes*—universal forms and patterns of thought. These are basic "ideas" that transcend generations and transcend history. They include certain themes that repeatedly show up in myths: motherhood, opposites, good, evil, masculinity, femininity, and the circle as a symbol representing travel from a beginning back to where one started, or the complete, whole self.

Karen Horney (1885–1952). Trained as a psychoanalyst in Germany, Horney came to the United States in 1934. She kept some Freudian concepts, but changed most of them significantly. Horney believed that the idea of levels of consciousness made sense, as did anxiety and repression, but she theorized that the prime impulses that motivate behavior are not biological and inborn or sexual and aggressive. A major concept for Horney was *basic anxiety*, which grows out of childhood when the child feels alone and isolated in a hostile environment. If proper parental nurturance is forthcoming, basic anxiety can be overcome. If parents are overly punishing, inconsistent, or indifferent, however, children may develop *basic hostility* and may feel very hostile and aggressive toward their parents. However, young children cannot express hostility toward their parents openly; so, the hostility gets repressed (into the unconscious), building even more anxiety.

Horney did place great emphasis on early childhood experiences, but from a perspective of social interaction and personal growth. Horney claimed that there are three distinct ways in which people interact with each other. In some cases, people *move away from* others, seeking self-sufficiency and independence. The idea here is something like, "If I am on my own and uninvolved, you won't be able to hurt me." On the other hand, some may *move toward* others, and are compliant and dependent. This style of interaction protects against anxiety in the sense of, "If I always do what you want me to do, you won't be upset with me." Horney's third interpersonal style involves *moving against* others, where the effort is to be in control, to gain power and dominate: "If I am in control, you'll have to do what I want you to." Now the ideal, of course, is to maintain a balance among these three styles, but Horney argued that many people tend to have just one style predominant in their dealings with others.

Before You Go On

Briefly summarize the contributions of Adler, Jung, and Horney to the psychoanalytic approach to personality.

THE BEHAVIORAL/LEARNING APPROACH

Many American psychologists in the early twentieth century did not think much of the psychoanalytic approach, regardless of its form or who happened to propose it. From its very beginnings, American psychology was oriented toward the laboratory and theories of learning. Explaining personality in terms of learning and focusing on observable behaviors seemed a reasonable course of action. In this section, we'll briefly review some of the behavioral approaches to personality.

John B. Watson (1878–1958). Watson and his followers in behaviorism argued that psychology should turn away from the study of consciousness and the mind because the contents of mental life were unverifiable and ultimately unscientific. Behaviorists argued that psychologists should study observable behavior. Yet here were the psychoanalysts arguing that *un*conscious and *pre*conscious forces are determiners of behavior. "Nonsense," the behaviorist would say. "We don't even know what we mean by consciousness, and you want to talk about levels of unconscious influence!"

Watson and his followers emphasized the role of the environment in shaping one's behaviors. Behaviorists could not accept the Freudian notion of inborn traits or impulses, whether called id or libido or anything else. What mattered was *learning*. A personality theory was not needed. A theory of learning would include all of the details about so-called personality that one would ever need.

Who we are has been determined by our learning experiences, and early experiences count heavily; on this point Watson and Freud might have agreed. Even our fears are conditioned (remember Watson's "Little Albert" study?). So convinced was Watson that instincts and innate impulses had little to do with the development of behavior that he could write, albeit somewhat tongue in cheek: "Give me a dozen healthy infants, well-formed, and my own specified world to bring them up in and I'll guarantee to take any one at random and train him to become any type of specialist I might select—doctor,

Learning theorists see no need for a separate theory of personality. Who we are is determined by our learning experiences, and early childhood experiences count heavily.

lawyer, artist, merchant, chief, and yes, even beggarman and thief, regardless of his talents, penchants, tendencies, abilities, vocations, and race of his ancestors" (Watson, 1925).

B. F. Skinner (1904–1990). Although he claimed to have proposed no particular theory of learning, much less of personality, Skinner should be mentioned in this context. Skinner's behaviorism refuses to refer to any internal variables to explain behavior—which is, essentially, what personality is taken to mean. Look at observable stimuli and observable responses, and for relationships among these; do not go meddling about in the mind of the organism, Skinnerians argue. Behavior is shaped by its consequences. Some behaviors result in reinforcement and are repeated. Some behaviors are not reinforced and thus tend not to be repeated. Consistency in one's behavior simply reflects the consistency of one's reinforcement history. The question is, how shall external conditions be manipulated to produce the consequences we want?

John Dollard (1900–1980) and Neal Miller (b. 1909). Dollard and Miller tried to see if they could use the principles of learning theory to explain personality and how it developed. What matters for one's personality, they argued, was the system of habits one developed in response to various cues in the environment. Behavior was motivated by primary drives (upon whose satisfaction survival depended,) and learned drives, which developed through experience. Motivated by drives, habits that get reinforced are those that tend to be repeated and, thus, become part of the stable collection of habits that constitute one's personality. For example, repression into the unconscious is simply a matter of learned forgetfulness: forgetting about some anxiety-producing experience is reinforcing and, consequently, tends to be repeated. It was Miller (1944) who proposed that conflict is explainable in terms of tendencies (habits) to approach or avoid goals and has little to do with the id, ego, and superego or with unconscious impulses of any sort.

Albert Bandura (b. 1925). Bandura is one learning theorist more than willing to consider the internal, cognitive processes of the learner. He claims that many aspects of behavior, of personality, *are* learned, but they are often learned through observation and social influence. For Bandura, learning involves more than forming connections between stimuli and responses or between responses and resulting reinforcers; it involves a cognitive rearrangement and representation. In simpler terms, this approach argues that you may learn to behave honestly, for example, through the observation of others. If you view your parents as being honest and see their behaviors being reinforced, you may acquire similar responses.

Before You Go On

Specify a contribution to the concept of personality made by Watson, Skinner, Dollard and Miller, and Bandura.

THE HUMANISTIC-PHENOMENOLOGICAL APPROACH

To some degree, the humanistic-phenomenological approach to personality contrasts with both the psychoanalytic and behavioral approaches. For one thing, it claims that people have the ability to shape their own destiny, to chart and follow their own course of action, and that biological, instinctive, or environmental influences can be overcome or minimized. The humanistic view may be thought of as more optimistic than either the Freudian approach (with its death instincts and innate impulses) or the learning approach (with its emphasis on control exerted by forces of the environment). It tends to focus more on the "here and now" than on early childhood experiences as important molders of personality. The humanistic-phenomenological point of view emphasizes the wholeness or completeness of personality, rather than focusing on its structural parts. Above all else, what matters most is *how people view themselves and others,* which is essentially what phenomenological means.

Carl Rogers (1902–1986). Rogers' approach to personality is referred to as a person-centered or self theory. Like Freud, Rogers developed his views of human nature through the observation of clients in a clinical setting. (Rogers preferred the term *client* to *patient* and even preferred the term *person-centered* to *client-centered* to describe his approach.) Rogers believed that the most powerful of human drives is the one to become fully functioning.

To be *fully functioning* implies that the person has become all that he or she can be. When we are children, some of what we do brings reward, but some of what we do does not. How we are regarded by those we care about is often conditional on how we behave. We tend to receive only conditional positive regard. *If* we do what is expected or desired, *then* we get rewarded. As a result, we try to act in ways that bring rewards and avoid punishments. Feelings of self and self-worth are thus dependent on the actions of others who either reward us, don't reward us, or punish us.

As long as we act only to please others, we are not fully functioning. To be fully functioning involves an openness to one's self and one's feelings and desires, an accurate awareness of one's inner self, and a positive self-regard. Helping children become fully functioning requires that we offer them what Rogers calls unconditional positive regard and that we separate the child's behaviors from the child's self. What this means is that we may punish a child for doing a bad thing, but never for being a bad child (e.g., "I love you very much, but what you have done is wrong and, therefore, will be punished"; or more simply, "You're a wonderful girl, but you've done a bad thing"). Helping people achieve positive self-regard is one of the major goals of person-centered therapy.

Notice that what matters here is often not so much what *is,* but what is *felt* or *perceived.* One's true self (whatever it may be) is less important than one's *image* of oneself. How the world is experienced is what matters—a clearly phenomenological point of view. You may be an excellent piano player (better, perhaps, than 98 percent of all of us), but if you feel you are a poor piano player, that perception or self-regard is what most matters.

Abraham Maslow (1908–1970). Maslow's basic criticism of the psychology he had studied was that it was altogether too pessimistic and negative. The individual was seen as being battered about by either a hostile environment or by depraved instincts, many of which propelled the person on a course of self-destruction.

There must be more to living than this, thought Maslow. He preferred to attend to the positive side of human nature. Maslow felt that people's needs are not low and base, but are positive, or at worst, neutral (Maslow, 1954). Our major goal in life is to actualize (realize and put into practice) those needs, or to *self-actualize.*

Let's look, Maslow argued, at the very best among us. Let's focus attention on the characteristics of those who have realized their fullest positive potential and have become self-actualized (see Figure 9.1). In his search for such individuals, however, Maslow couldn't find many. Most were historical figures, such as Thomas Jefferson and Eleanor Roosevelt. We'll look at Maslow's self-actualization again in our discussion of motivation in Topic 10A.

Figure 9.1

Some of the Characteristics or Attributes of Self-Actualizers

1. They tend to be realistic in their orientation.
2. They accept themselves, others, and the world for what they are, not for what they should be.
3. They have a great deal of spontaneity.
4. They tend to be problem-centered rather than self-centered.
5. They have a need for privacy and a sense of detachment.
6. They are autonomous, independent, and self-sufficient.
7. Their appreciation of others (and of things of the world) is fresh, free, and not stereotyped.
8. Many have spiritual or mystical (although not necessarily religious) experiences.
9. They can identify with humankind as a whole and share a concern for humanity.
10. They have a number of interpersonal relationships, some of them very deep and profound.
11. They tend to have democratic views in the sense that all are created equal and should be treated equally.
12. They have a sense of humor that tends more to the philosophical than the hostile.
13. They tend to be creative in their approach.
14. They are hard working.
15. They resist pressures to conform to society.

After Maslow, 1954.

═══ Before You Go On ═══

Briefly summarize the humanistic-phenomenological approach to personality as epitomized by Rogers and Maslow.

THE TRAIT APPROACH

Trait theories of personality have a markedly different flavor from any of the approaches we have looked at so far. Trait theories are more concerned with the adequate *description* of personality than with the *explanation* of personality. Arnold Buss puts the agenda of trait theorists this way: "Trait psychologists typically seek to reveal the psychological dimensions along which people differ and ways in which traits cluster within individuals" (1989, p. 1379). Thus, the argument is that a person's personality can be adequately described on the basis of certain traits. We may define a **trait** as "any distinguishable, relatively enduring way in which one individual differs from others" (Guilford, 1959a, p. 5).

Notice that traits are descriptive *dimensions*. In other words, any trait (e.g., friendliness) is not a simple either-or proposition. Friendliness falls on a continuum, ranging from extremely unfriendly to extremely friendly, with many possibilities in between. To be useful, personality traits need to be measurable so we can assess the extent to which people may differ on those traits (Hogan & Nicholson, 1988; Kagan, 1988).

The main issue or focus for psychologists who have taken this approach has been to try to determine which traits are the important ones. Which dimensions best characterize a person and how she or he is different from everyone else? How can personality traits be organized? The various answers to these and related questions have given rise to several trait theories. We'll briefly summarize two classic trait theories (Allport's and Cattell's) and then look at a contemporary trait theory.

trait a distinguishable, relatively enduring way in which individuals may be described and in which they may differ

Two Classic Examples

Gordon Allport (1897–1967). For Allport, personality traits exist within a person and can help to explain the consistency in that person's behavior. In various situations, a personality trait of friendliness might produce a range of specific responses, but those responses would be, in their essence, very much alike.

Allport's theory proposes that personality traits are of two types: *common traits* and *personal traits* (or personal dispositions) (e.g., Allport, 1961). By common traits, Allport means those dimensions of personality shared by almost everyone (to greater or lesser degrees perhaps, but shared in common with nearly everyone else). Aggressiveness is an example of a common trait, as is intelligence. These are traits we can use to make comparisons among people.

Personal dispositions, on the other hand, are traits unique to just some persons. How one displays a sense of humor (sharp wit, cutting sarcasm, dirty jokes, philosophical puns, and so on) is usually thought of as being a unique disposition.

Allport went on to claim that personal traits are of three subtypes. Allport wrote of cardinal, central, and secondary personal traits. A *cardinal trait* is one that is so overwhelming it influences virtually everything a person does. The personalities of few of us are ruled by cardinal traits. Even Allport could imagine only a few examples, even in history, literature, or mythology (Don Quixote, the Marquis de Sade, Mohandas Gandhi, and Don Juan among them). No, what influences your behaviors and mine are not likely to be cardinal traits, but *central traits,* or dispositions. These traits can usually be described in just one word, and they are the 5 to 10 traits that best characterize someone (e.g., honest, friendly, neat, outgoing, fair, and kind). Finally, each of us is occasionally influenced by *secondary traits.* These are traits (dispositions) that seldom govern many of our reactions, but may be found in specific circumstances. For example, people who are basically very calm and easygoing, even when threatened (reflecting their central traits), may be very aggressive and excited when threatened in their own home (by intruders, let's say).

Raymond Cattell (b. 1905). Cattell's approach to personality is an empirical one, relying on psychological tests, questionnaires, and surveys. Talking about personality traits without talking about how they are measured makes little sense to Cattell. He used a statistical technique called *factor analysis.* Factor analysis is a correlational procedure that identifies groups of highly related variables that may be assumed to measure the same underlying factor (here, a personality trait). The logic is that if you know that certain people are outgoing, you really don't need to test them to see if they are sociable or extroverted; such information would be redundant.

On the basis of his research, Cattell argues that there are two major types of personality traits (Cattell, 1973, 1979). *Surface traits* are the clusters of behaviors that go together, like those that make up curiosity, trustworthiness, or kindliness. These traits are easily observed and can be found in many settings. More important than surface traits are the fewer number of underlying traits from which surface traits develop. These are called *source traits.* It is one's pattern of source traits that determines which surface traits will get expressed in behavior. Source traits are not as easily measured as surface traits because they are not directly observable. Cattell's source traits are listed in Figure 9.2.

Before You Go On

What is a personality trait?

What are the major traits that influence personality according to Allport and Cattell?

Figure 9.2

Sixteen Source Traits as Identified by Cattell
(Remember that each trait is a dimension.)

Reserved ↔ Outgoing		Trusting ↔ Suspicious	
(detached, aloof)	(participating)	(accepting)	(circumspect)
Less intelligent ↔ More intelligent		**Practical ↔ Imaginative**	
(dull)	(bright)	(down-to-earth)	(absentminded)
Affected by feelings ↔ Emotionally stable		**Forthright ↔ Shrewd**	
(easily upset)	(calm)	(unpretentious)	(astute, wordly)
Submissive ↔ Dominant		**Self-assured ↔ Apprehensive**	
(obedient, easily led)	(assertive)	(secure, complacent)	(insecure, troubled)
Serious ↔ Happy-go-lucky		**Conservative ↔ Experimenting**	
(sober, taciturn)	(enthusiastic)	(disinclined to change)	(experimenting)
Expedient ↔ Conscientious		**Group-dependent ↔ Self-sufficient**	
(disregards rules)	(moralistic, staid)	(a joiner)	(resourceful)
Timid ↔ Venturesome		**Uncontrolled ↔ Controlled**	
(shy, restrained)	(socially bold)	(follows own urges)	(shows will power)
Tough-minded ↔ Sensitive		**Relaxed ↔ Tense**	
(rejects illusions)	(tender-minded)	(tranquil, composed)	(frustrated, driven)

From Cattell, 1973, 1979.

A Contemporary Perspective: The Big Five

We've taken a look at two theories that have tried to identify distinguishable, relatively enduring personality traits, and we've generated quite a list. Allport named common traits and personal dispositions, and Cattell found many surface traits and a smaller number of source traits. Which set is most reasonable? It may surprise you to learn that personality theorists have come to something of a consensus concerning which traits have the most research support to qualify as descriptors of personality. This model is referred to as the *Five-Factor Model* (Carson, 1989; Digman, 1990; McCrae & Costa, 1986, 1987; McCrae & John, 1992; Peabody & Goldberg, 1989; Wiggins & Pincus, 1992). What are these dimensions of personality that are being referred to now as the "Big Five?"

Although there may be some consensus that five major dimensions will suffice to characterize human pesonality, there is disagreement on exactly how to describe these five. The following dimensions are from Digman (1990) and Goldberg (1993). *Dimension I* is usually called "Extroversion/Introversion" and embodies such things as assurance, talkativeness, openness, self-confidence, and assertiveness on the one hand, and silence and passivity on the other. *Dimension II* is "Agreeableness" or "Friendliness," with altruism, caring, and emotional support at one end and hostility, indifference, selfishness, and distrust on the other. *Dimension III* is "Conscientiousness," and amounts to a "will to achieve" (or simply "Will"). It includes such things as self-control, dependability, planning, thoroughness, and persistence paired with carelessness, negligence, and unreliability. It is well correlated with educational achievement. *Dimension IV* is an "Emotionality" dimension. In many ways, this is a dimension of the extent to which one is emotionally stable or in some way disordered. It includes such things as nervousness and moodiness. *Dimension V* is "Intellect," "Intelligence," or "Openness to Experience and Culture." This factor includes such characteristics as curiosity, imagination, and creativity. The recurrent finding that all personality traits can be reduced to just five, with these names (or names like these), is remarkable.

These five traits have emerged from nearly fifty years of research. We find these five traits emerging from research in many cultures (e.g., Paunonen et al., 1992; Wiggins & Pincus, 1992). They have emerged repeatedly, regardless of the individuals being assessed, and "the Big Five have appeared now in at least five languages, leading one to suspect that something quite fundamental is involved here" (Digman, 1990, p. 433). On the other hand, Revelle (1987) notes that "the agreement among these descriptive dimensions is impressive, [but] there is a lack of theoretical explanation for the *how* and the *why* of these dimensions" (p. 437).

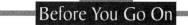

Before You Go On

What are the "Big Five" personality dimensions?

PROS AND CONS OF THE FOUR APPROACHES TO PERSONALITY

Given that we have reviewed only a few of the major personality theories, can we make any judgments about which approach is the best? Are any of these theories better than the others? These appear to be reasonable, natural questions to ask, but I suspect you can anticipate our answers. There are supporters and critics of each of the four approaches we've summarized in this Topic. As long as we recognize that our evaluations are going to be somewhat superficial, it still might be useful to take a moment to reflect on the strengths and weaknesses of each approach.

There is little doubt that the psychoanalytic approach, particularly as modified by the neo-Freudians, is the most comprehensive and complex of the theories we've reviewed. Psychologists have been debating the merits of Freud's contributions for decades. On the plus side, Freud and the other psychoanalytically oriented theorists must be credited for focusing our attention on the importance of the childhood years and for suggesting that some (even biologically determined) impulses may affect our behaviors even though they are beyond our immediate awareness. Although Freud may have overstated the matter, drawing our attention to the impact of sexual impulses as influences on one's personality was also a major contribution.

On the other hand, many psychologists have been critical of psychoanalytic theory. We have seen how several neo-Freudians tended to minimize innate biological drives and take a more social approach to personality development than did Freud. One major criticism of the psychoanalytic approach is that so many of its insights are untestable. Freud thought of himself as a scientist, but he tested none of his ideas about human nature experimentally. Some concepts seem to be beyond testing. Just what *is* libidinal energy? How can it be measured? How would we recognize it if we saw it? Concepts such as id, ego, and superego may make some sense, but how can we prove or disprove that they even exist? It also seems that such a heavy reliance on instincts, especially instincts with aggressive and sexual overtones, as explanatory concepts goes beyond where most psychologists are willing to venture.

With regard to the behavioral-learning approach, many psychologists argue that Watson, Dollard, Miller, and Skinner "dehumanize" personality, and that even the social learning theory of Bandura tends to be too deterministic. Virtually everything a person does, thinks, or feels is in some way determined by his or her environment through learning or conditioning. This leaves nothing for the person, for personality, to contribute. Behavioral-learning approaches to personality are often not theories at all—at least they are not comprehensive theories. To their credit, they demand that terms be carefully defined and that conclusions be verified experimentally.

Like the others, the humanistic-phenomenological approach has a number of strengths. For one, it reminds us of the wholeness of personality and of the danger in analyzing something so complex into artificial segments. That the approach, stressing as it does personal growth and development, is positive and upbeat in its flavor serves to inform us that at least such views are possible. As we shall see in our discussion of psychotherapy (Topic 13B), the humanistic-phenomenological approach has had a major impact on many therapists and counselors. A major problem with this approach is not unlike the basic problem with Freud's theory. It may make sense, but how does one go about testing any of the observations and statements made by proponents of the approach? Many of the key terms are defined in general, fuzzy ways. What really is self-image? How do we really know when someone is "growing"? How can one test the effects of unconditional positive regard? In many ways, what we have here is a blueprint, a vision for the nature of personality, not a scientific theory.

As I've already mentioned, trait approaches to personality are different from the others, even in their intent. Trait theories have a few obvious advantages. They provide us not only with descriptive terms, but with means of measuring the important dimensions of personality. They also give us an idea of how measured traits are related to one another. On the other hand, as theories, they offer little more than description. To say that someone acted in a certain way "because he is *introverted*" does not go far to *explain* that action. It functions merely as a label. And even with the so-called Big Five traits, there continues to be disagreement about how to define or characterize the most basic traits that describe personality. Another reality is that as we begin to look at people's behaviors in various cultures, we find that the basic idea of personality traits, as characteristics of individuals, may be important only in some cultures. Perhaps you recall the distinction between individualistic and collectivist cultures we made in Chapter 8 (page 381). The notion of individual personality traits seems to be relevant and sensible to people in individualistic societies, such as ours, and most Western cultures. Personality traits are less important and less frequently used when people describe others in collectivistic cultures, such as are found largely in Asia and South America (Miller, 1984; Shwedler & Sullivan, 1993).

So, as we might have predicted, when we try to evaluate various theories or approaches to personality *overall*, there are no real winners or losers. Each approach has its shortcomings, but each adds something to our appreciation of the complex concept of human personality.

Before You Go On

**What are some of the strengths and weaknesses
of each of the four approaches to personality
we have discussed?**

ISSUES RELATED TO PERSONALITY

All psychologists who claim "personality" as one of their areas of interest are not actively involved in trying to devise some grand theory of how to best describe and explain human nature. Many are involved in research and theory that focuses on just one or a few aspects of the complex concept we call personality. In this section we'll look at three areas: the extent to which reference to personality is useful when trying to explain behavior, male/female differences in personality, and personality assessment or measurement.

Is There a Personality?: Interactionism

Each approach we have reviewed in this Topic brings its own perspective to the study of personality. There is one theme, however, they have in common: they all address the *consistency* of personality.

Someone with an "overdeveloped superego" should be consistently conscientious and feel guilty whenever established standards are not met. Someone who has learned to "behave aggressively" should demonstrate aggressive responses in a range of settings. Someone trying to "grow personally and to self-actualize" should be consistently open to a wide variety of new opinions and ideas.

About 25 years ago, this very basic assumption about personality was severely challenged by Walter Mischel (1968). One problem with arguing for the consistency of personality is that personality just may not be consistent at all (Council, 1993; Epstein, 1979; Mischel, 1968, 1979; Mischel & Peake, 1982). Think carefully about your own behavior and your own personality. Assume for the moment you think of yourself as easygoing. Are you *always* easygoing, easy to get along with? Are there some situations in which you would be easygoing, but other situations in which you might fight to have your way? Are there some situations in which you tend to be social and outgoing, yet different situations in which your preference is to be alone and not mix in? Such was the thrust of Mischel's challenge: personality characteristics appear to be consistent only when they are viewed in similar or consistent situations.

We may observe consistency in the personality of others for two reasons: (1) It is convenient. We like to think that we can quickly and accurately categorize people. We see someone do something dishonest—pick up change left as a tip for a waiter, for example—and find it convenient to label that person as basically dishonest. It's easy to assume that the mean, aggressive football player will probably be mean and aggressive off the field as well. Such assumptions may not be true, but they make it easy to form judgments about others. (2) We tend to see others only in a restricted range of situations, where their behaviors and attitudes may very well *be* consistent. The real test would be to see those people in varied situations on several occasions (Epstein, 1979).

As you might suspect, arguments challenging the very definition of personality created quite a stir. Over the past 25 years, since Mischel brought it up, there has been an exciting barrage of research and debate on this issue. We now see that things may not be as unstable and situation-bound as Mischel suggested. One analysis, using methodology borrowed from the field of behavior genetics, argues strongly that most of the variability we see in behaviors *does* reflect individual differences even more than the pressures of the situation (Rowe, 1987; see also Digman, 1990; Wiggins & Pincus, 1993).

In fact, most personality theorists today are ready and willing to declare the debate of "personality traits versus the situation as determinants of behavior" resolved (Carson, 1989; Digman, 1990; Kendrick & Funder, 1988). Depending on how you look at it, neither side or both sides won. By and large, research supports the position that, indeed, there are some person-related characteristics that show remarkable stability over a wide range of situations. The research also supports the notion that it is folly *not* to take into account the situation in which behaviors occur.

Personality is a complex concept. We often are in error when we infer how someone will act in a situation simply on the basis of physical appearance.

One outcome of the debate stimulated by Mischel is a view of personality and situational variables known as *interactionism*. This approach is complex, but we can summarize the basic idea (Bandura, 1978; Magnusson & Edler, 1977; Mischel, 1981). Interactionism claims that how anyone behaves is a function of an interaction of stable personality characteristics *and* the individual's perception of the situation. Neither personality characteristics (inside the person) nor the situation (external environment) can be fully relied on to explain an individual's reaction.

Let's say that Ken agrees to a friendly racquetball game, just for the exercise. At first all goes well, and Ken, a superior player, really takes it easy on his opponent. After all, they're just playing for the exercise. In their second game, Ken's opponent makes a few good shots and moves ahead in the score. Ken now notices that a small group of spectators is watching them play. As the situation changes, so does Ken's perception of it. "This is no longer fun and games," he thinks to himself, as he starts smashing low line drives off the front wall. Within just a few minutes, Ken's behavior shows a considerable change. The situation has changed, and now his behavior is aggressive and forceful. As the situation changed, it brought about a change in Ken's behavior: a perceived challenge to his ability brought out competitive reactions. Ken's personality also brought about a change in the situation: to some degree, his trait of competitiveness changed a friendly game into an athletic contest. With interactionism we have an approach that acknowledges the impact of the environment, but also allows for the influence of stable, internal personality traits.

Before You Go On

Briefly summarize the debate concerning personality versus situational influences on behavior.

Gender and Personality

Personality traits give us reasonable ways to describe people and to express differences we observe among them. We can note Kathy's assertiveness and Juan's sociability. We can say that Chick is friendlier than Steve or that Melissa is more impulsive than Jesse. An issue that intrigues personality psychologists is the extent to which personality traits can be used to characterize *groups* of people, and if there are consistent personality differences, in general, among groups. The two groups that have been studied most closely in this regard are men and women.

What do you think about these differences? Boys have higher self-esteem than girls. Girls are more social than boys. Men are more analytical than women. Men are better at rote learning, whereas women are more creative. Women are more open to suggestion and influence than are men. These assertions might sound sensible to some people, but there is no research evidence to support any of them. There are no gender differences in self-esteem, sociability, analytic skills, rote learning, creativity, or suggestibility.

These were the findings of the first large-scale exploration of gender differences, reported by Eleanor Maccoby and Carol Jacklin in 1974. Maccoby and Jacklin's work was not the first to ask whether there are consistent differences between males and females (theirs was a reanalysis of data that existed at the time). It did, however, stimulate others to join in the search for ways in which gender could be used to predict how one would behave in a variety of situations. That search has turned up little. The research shows us that either there are no gender differences on personality variables, or that gender differences are insignificant and appear inconsistently (Huston, 1985; Hyde, 1984, 1986; Maccoby, 1990). There is one glaring exception, and that is overt, direct, physical aggression, which *is* consistently found to be more common in males than in females (e.g., Eagly & Steffen, 1986; Hyde, 1986; Maccoby, 1990).

The difference in aggression found between males and females seems to be there (to varying degrees) at all ages and in all cultural settings (e.g., Maccoby & Jacklin, 1980; Rushton et al., 1986; Whiting & Edwards, 1973). Although we may claim that males are more aggressive in their personalities than are females, there are two necessary cautions: (1) This is a generality made "on the average" for groups of persons. Any one female might be significantly more aggressive in all regards than any one male. (2) We do not have evidence that this difference is necessarily genetic or biologically based.

On the assumption that you will not overinterpret them, we can list instances, other than aggression, in which gender differences have been found.

1. *Communication style.* Men seem to be more talkative in a variety of settings and are more likely to interrupt others (Key, 1975), but in some situations, females are more likely to "self-disclose" and share their inner ideas and feelings (Cozby, 1973).

2. *Body language.* Women may be better at decoding or interpreting the body language of others (Hall, 1978), but there are no differences in the display of postures or gestures associated with dominance in nonverbal social situations (Halberstadt & Saitta, 1987).

3. *Altruism.* Women report that they more willing to engage in self-sacrifice for the good of others, but whether their behaviors are actually more altruistic than that of men is not clear (Rushton et al., 1986; Sennecker & Hendrick, 1983).

4. *Empathy.* As with altruism, when we rely on self-reports, women appear to be more empathic than men, more able to

appreciate and understand another's feelings. But when we look at laboratory or real-life evidence, differences disappear (Eisenberg & Lennon, 1983).

5. *Self-confidence.* Particularly when they are asked to do something usually associated with a male role (e.g., take a test on sports figures), women tend to be less self-confident in their performance than men (even when performances are equivalent [Beyer, 1990; Lenney, 1977]). This difference occurs only in social situations, in which females may be acting in accord with their perception of what is expected (Daubman et al., 1992).

Well, then, where are we on the issue of personality differences as a function of one's gender? We can say that there are gender differences in aggression. There may be insignificant gender differences on a few other traits, but even these differences are not found with consistency. On most identified personality traits, there simply are no differences between females and males.

Before You Go On

Briefly summarize what we know about gender differences in personality traits.

Personality Measurement, or Assessment

In this section, we'll summarize four ways to measure, or assess, personality: behavioral observations, interviews, paper-and-pencil tests, and projective methods. Before we do so, we'll consider a few basic ideas about psychological measurement in general. These ideas will also be relevant in our next Topic, in which we discuss the measurement of intelligence.

Characteristics of Good Psychological Tests and Measures. A **psychological test** is an objective, standardized measure of a sample of behavior (Anastasi, 1988; Dahlstrom, 1993). A psychological test measures behavior because that is all we *can* measure. We cannot directly assess those internal, mental processes we call feelings, abilities, or personality dispositions. On the basis of what we learn from our measurement of behavior, we may be willing to make assumptions or inferences about underlying mental processes.

All we can measure is a *sample* of one's behaviors. Let's say I want to know about your tendency to be aggressive. I cannot ask you everything that relates to aggression in your life ("List all of the situations in which you have ever acted aggressively," for instance). What I have to do instead is sample (systematically identify a portion of) the behaviors in which I am interested. Even a classroom exam asks you about only a sample of all the material you have learned in preparation for that exam. The quality of our psychological measurement is

psychological test an objective, standardized measure of a sample of behavior clearly dependent on the extent to which our sample is a fair and representative one.

There are other definitional points to consider. If a measurement technique is to have any value, its administration must be *standardized*. If a test is standardized, it will be given to everyone in the same way, and will be scored following the same procedures. Imagine taking a college placement test used to determine which courses in English composition you will be required to take. You are given 45 minutes to answer 50 multiple-choice questions and write a short essay on some prescribed topic. Later you discover that some students were given the same exam but with the instructions to "take as long as you'd like to finish the test." This testing system would lack standardization.

A psychological test should be *objective*. Objectivity in this context refers to the evaluation of the behaviors being measured. For example, several examiners (at least those of the same level of expertise) should be expected to give the same interpretation and evaluation of observed responses. If the same responses to a psychological test lead one psychologist to declare a person perfectly normal, a second to consider that person a mass of inner conflict and anxiety, and a third to wonder why that person is not now in a psychiatric institution, we have a problem, and it *may* be with the objectivity of our test. The quality of a psychological test or assessment technique depends on the extent to which it has three additional characteristics: reliability, validity, and adequate norms.

In the context of psychological measurement, **reliability** means the same as it does in other contexts: consistency or dependability. Suppose someone gives you a psychological test and on the basis of its interpretation tells you that you have an IQ just slightly below average—94, let's say. Three weeks later, you take the same test and are told that your IQ is now 127—nearly in the top 3 percent of the population! Something is wrong. We haven't yet discussed IQ scores, but surely we recognize that one's IQ—as a measure of intelligence—does not change 33 points in three weeks.

reliability consistency or dependability; in testing, the consistency of test scores

When people worry about the usefulness of a test or assessment procedure, their concern is usually with **validity**. Measures of validity tell us the extent to which a test or technique actually measures what it claims to be measuring. It is the extent to which there is agreement between a test score and the quality the test is believed to measure (Kaplan & Saccuzzo, 1989). "This test measures extroversion." Does it? "This observer rating scale will indicate degrees of cooperative play among children." Will it? "This technique predicts the extent to which someone will succeed at this job." Does it? These are questions of validity.

validity in testing, the extent to which a test measures what it claims to measure

Let's add just one more—but important—issue: adequacy of norms. Let's say you have completed a long paper-and-pencil questionnaire designed to measure the extent to which you are extroverted. You know the test is a reliable and valid instrument. You are told you scored a 50 on the test. What does that mean? It doesn't mean you answered 50 percent of the items correctly, because there are no right or wrong answers. You need to compare your score with the scores of other people like you. Results of a test taken by a large group of people whose scores are used to make comparisons are called **norms**. You may discover by checking the norms that a score of 50 is average and that you are neither extremely extroverted nor introverted. On the other hand, a score of 50 may be a very high or a very low score. You just can't tell without adequate norms. The fact is that constructing a good, useful technique or test to measure personality characteristics is not easily done. There are many factors to be considered. With these factors in mind, we can now turn to the techniques that have been used to measure or assess personality. (You also might think back to that little "test" at the beginning of this chapter and evaluate it in terms of the concepts introduced here.)

norms in testing, results of a test taken by a large sample of persons whose scores can be used to make comparisons, or give meaning to new scores

Before You Go On

What is a psychological test?

By what criteria do we evaluate psychological tests or assessment techniques?

Behavioral Observations. As you and I develop our own impressions of the personalities of our friends and acquaintances, we do so largely by relying on **behavioral observation**. As its name suggests, this approach involves drawing conclusions about an individual's personality on the basis of observations of his or her behaviors. We judge Dan to be bright because he was the only one who knew the answer to a question in class. We feel that Maria is submissive because she always seems to do whatever her husband demands.

behavioral observation the assessment technique of drawing conclusions about one's personality based on observations of that person's behaviors

As helpful as our observations may be to us, there may be problems with the casual, unstructured observations you and I normally make. Because we have observed only a small range of behaviors in a limited range of settings, we may be overgeneralizing when we assume that those same behaviors will show up in new, different situations. Dan may never again know the answer to a question in class. Maria may give in to her husband only because we are there.

Behavioral observation can be an excellent source of information, particularly when observations being made are purposeful, careful, and structured, as opposed to the casual observations you and I usually make, or when steps are taken to make the observations reliable and valid and to ensure our sample is representative.

Let's consider an example. A child is reportedly having trouble at school, behaving aggressively and generally being disruptive. One thing a psychologist may do is visit the school and observe the child's behaviors in the natural setting of the classroom. It may be that the child does behave aggressively and engage in fighting behavior, but

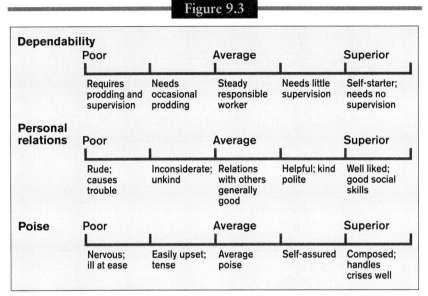

Dependability					
Poor		**Average**		**Superior**	
Requires prodding and supervision	Needs occasional prodding	Steady responsible worker	Needs little supervision	Self-starter; needs no supervision	

Personal relations					
Poor		**Average**		**Superior**	
Rude; causes trouble	Inconsiderate; unkind	Relations with others generally good	Helpful; kind polite	Well liked; good social skills	

Poise					
Poor		**Average**		**Superior**	
Nervous; ill at ease	Easily upset; tense	Average poise	Self-assured	Composed; handles crises well	

A graphic rating scale such as this might be used by an employer in evaluating employees or potential employees.

only when the teacher is in the room. Otherwise, the child is pleasant and passive. It may be that the child's aggressive behaviors reflect a ploy to get the teacher's attention.

In an attempt to add to her original observations, a psychologist may use *role-playing* as a means to collect more information. Role-playing is a matter of acting out a given life situation. "Let's say that I'm a student, and that you're the teacher, and that it's recess time," the psychologist says to a child. "Let's pretend that somebody takes a toy away from me, and I hit him on the arm. What will you do?"

Observational techniques can be supplemented with some sort of *rating scale* (see Figure 9.3). Rating scales provide many advantages over casual observation. For one thing, they focus the attention of the observer on a set of specified behaviors to be observed. Rating scales also yield a more objective measure of behavior. With rating scales, one can have behaviors observed by several raters. If several raters are involved in the observation of the same behaviors (say, children at play in a nursery school), you can check on the reliability of the observations. That is, if all five of your observers agree that Timothy engaged in "hitting behavior" on the average of five times per hour, the consistency of that assessment adds to its usefulness.

Behavioral observation involves drawing conclusions about an individual's personality on the basis of his or her behaviors. Role playing is one technique that psychologists use to gain insights about a child's behaviors. This child may make disclosures while "talking on the telephone" that she would not make otherwise.

Before You Go On

How are behavioral observations used to assess personality?

Although the data derived from casual, unstructured interviews are seldom reliable or valid, psychologists can gain useful insights about personality using formal, structured interviews.

interview the assessment technique involving a conversational interchange between an interviewer and another in order to gain information about the latter's personality

Interviews. We can learn some things about people by watching them. We can also gain insight about some aspects of their personality by simply asking them about themselves. In fact, the **interview** is "one of the oldest and most widely used, although not always the most accurate, of the methods of personality assessment" (Aiken, 1984, p. 296). Its popularity is largely due to its basic simplicity and flexibility.

The basic data of the interview are what people say about themselves, rather than what they do. The results of interviews are usually impressionistic and not easily quantifiable (although some interview techniques are clearly more structured and objective than others). The interview is more a technique of discovering generalities than specifics.

A major advantage of the interview is its flexibility. The interviewer may decide to drop a certain line of questioning if it is producing no useful information, to pursue some other area of interest. Unfortunately, there is little evidence that unstructured interviews have very much reliability or validity (Tenopyr, 1981).

As is the case for observational techniques, there is considerable variety in the degree to which interviews may be unstructured or structured. In the latter type of interview, there is a specific set of questions to be asked in a prescribed order. The structured interview, then, becomes more like a psychological test to the extent that it is objective and standardized, and asks about a particular sample of behavior.

■■■■■■ Before You Go On ■■■■■■

Cite an advantage and a disadvantage
of the interview as a technique
of personality assessment.

Paper-and-Pencil Tests. Observational and interview techniques barely qualify as psychological tests. They are seldom as standardized or as objective as we would like them to be. In this section, we'll focus on one of the most often used paper-and-pencil personality tests, the **Minnesota Multiphasic Personality Inventory**, or **MMPI** for short. The test is referred to as multiphasic because it measures several personality dimensions with the same set of items.

The MMPI was designed to aid the diagnosis of persons with mental disorders and, hence, is not a personality test in the sense of identifying personality traits. The test is the most researched test in psychology and remains one of the most commonly used (Lubin et al., 1984). In August of 1989, a revision of the MMPI (called the MMPI-2) was made available. The revision made two major changes and several lesser ones. Antiquated and offensive items (having to do with religion or sexual practices) were replaced. The norm group for the MMPI-2 was much larger (2,600 subjects) than for the MMPI (about 700 subjects) and is supposed to reflect a more representative sample of the population in regard to cultural background, ethnicity, and the like (Ben-Porath & Butcher, 1989). The intent of the authors of the MMPI-2 was to update and improve, but *not change*, the basic design or meaning of test scores. The extent to which the revision has succeeded remains to be seen (Adler, 1990a; Edwards & Edwards, 1991).

The MMPI-2 consists of 567 true-false questions that ask about feelings, attitudes, physical symptoms, and past experiences. Because of the way in which it was constructed, the MMPI is called a *criterion-referenced* test, which means that items on the test are referenced to one of the criterion groups—either normals or patients with a diagnosis of a particular mental disorder. Some of the items appear quite sensible. "I feel like people are plotting against me" seems like the sort of item someone with paranoia would call "true," whereas normals would tend to respond "false." Many items, however, are not as obvious. "I like to visit zoos," is not an MMPI-2 item, but it might have been if subjects of one diagnostic group responded to the item differently from other subjects. What the item *appears* to be measuring is irrelevant. The only thing that matters is whether subjects of different groups respond differently to the item. (No one will make even a tentative diagnosis of a psychological disorder on the basis of a person's response to just a few items. What matters is one's *pattern* of responding to a large number of items.)

The MMPI-2's "validity scales" consist of items from among the 567 that assess the extent to which the subject is attending to the task at hand, or is trying to present herself or himself in a favorable light

MMPI a paper-and-pencil personality test designed to indicate the presence of a psychological disorder

instead of responding truthfully to the items. For example, responding "true" to several statements such as "I always smile at everyone I meet" would lead an examiner to doubt the validity of the subject's responses.

Although the MMPI is commonly used, it certainly is not the only paper-and-pencil personality test. The *California Personality Inventory,* or *CPI,* for example, was written using only normal subjects, not people who were diagnosed as having a psychological problem or disorder. The CPI assesses 18 personality traits, including self-acceptance, dominance, responsibility, and sociability. Because it is designed to measure several traits, it can also be referred to as a multiphasic test.

Some multiphasic tests have been designed in conjunction with a particular personality theory. For example, Cattell's trait theory approach investigated a number of potential personality traits. These traits are what are measured with Cattell's *16 PF Questionnaire* (in which PF stands for personality factors). Analyses of responses on this test (of statements to which the subject responds yes or no) results in a personality profile. That profile can then be compared to one gathered from a large norm group.

Finally, some personality questionnaires or inventories are designed to measure just one trait and thus are not multiphasic. One example is the *Taylor Manifest Anxiety Scale.* Taylor began with a large pool of items, many of them from the MMPI, and then asked psychologists to choose those items they thought would best measure anxiety. The 50 items most commonly chosen as indicators of anxiety constitute this test, which has gained wide acceptance.

Before You Go On

What does multiphasic mean?

How was the MMPI constructed?

projective technique an assessment technique requiring a person to respond to ambiguous stimuli in hopes that the person will reveal aspects of his or her personality

Projective Techniques. A **projective technique** involves asking a person to respond to ambiguous stimuli. The stimuli can be any number of things, and clearly there are no right or wrong answers. The procedure is unstructured and open-ended. The idea is that because there is, in fact, so little content in the stimulus being presented, the subject will *project* some of his or her own self into the response. In many ways, projective techniques are more like aids to interviewing than they are psychological tests (Korchin & Scheldberg, 1981).

Some projective techniques are very simple. The word association technique, introduced by Galton in 1879 and used in psychoanalysis, is a projective technique. "I will say a word, and I want you to say the first thing that pops into your head. Do not think about your response; just say the first thing that comes to mind." There certainly are no right answers in this procedure. The hope is that the psychologist can gain some insight, perhaps into the problems of a patient, by using this technique.

A similar technique is the *unfinished sentences,* or *sentence completion,* test. For example, a sentence is begun, "My greatest fear is . . ." The subject is asked to complete the sentence. Although there are several published tests available (e.g., the *Rotter Incomplete Sentences Blank*), many clinical psychologists prefer to make up their own forms. There are no right or wrong responses, and interpreting responses is quite subjective, but a skilled examiner can use these procedures to gain new insights about a subject's personality.

Of all the projective techniques, none is as well known as the **Rorschach inkblot test.** This technique was introduced in 1921 by Hermann Rorschach, who believed that people with different personalities respond differently to inkblot patterns (Figure 9.4). There are 10 cards in the test: 5 are black on white, 2 are red and gray, and 3 are multicolored. Subjects are asked to tell what they see in the cards or what the inkblot represents.

Scoring Rorschach test responses has become quite controversial. Standard scoring procedures require attending to many factors: what the subject says (content), where the subject focuses attention (location), mention of detail versus global features, reacting to color or

Rorschach inkblot test a projective technique in which a person is asked to say what he or she sees in a series of inkblots

---

Figure 9.4

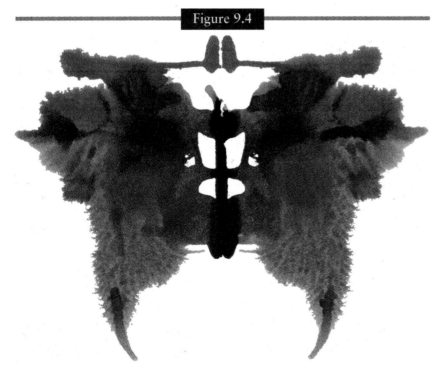

A sample Rorschach-like inkblot. The subject is asked what the inkblot represents and what she or he sees in it.

open spaces, and how many distinct responses there are per card. Many psychologists have questioned the efficiency of the Rorschach as a diagnostic instrument. Much of what it can tell an examiner may be gained directly. For example, Rorschach responses that include many references to death, sadness, and dying are probably indicative of a depressed person. One wonders if inkblots are really needed to discover such depression. As a psychological test, the Rorschach seems neither very reliable nor valid, yet it remains very popular. It is used primarily as an aid to assessment and the development of subjective impressions.

Thematic Apperception Test (TAT)
a projective technique in which a person is asked to tell a series of short stories about a set of ambiguous pictures

A projective test we'll see again in Chapter 10 (in the context of achievement motivation), is the **Thematic Apperception Test**, or **TAT**, devised by Henry Murray in 1938. This test consists of a series of ambiguous pictures about which a person is asked to tell a story. The person is asked to describe what is going on, what led up to this situation, and what the outcome is likely to be.

The test is designed to provide a mechanism to discover the subjects' hidden needs, desires, and emotions, which will be projected into their stories. The test is called a *thematic* test because scoring depends largely on the interpretation of the themes of the stories told. Although scoring schemes are available, scoring and interpretation are usually subjective and impressionistic. It is likely the TAT remains popular for the same reason as the Rorschach: psychologists are used to it, comfortable with the insights it provides, and willing to accept any source of additional information they can use to make a reasonable assessment or diagnosis.

Before You Go On

What is the essence of a projective technique,
the Rorschach and TAT in particular?

TOPIC 9A SUMMARY

We've covered a lot of ground in this Topic. We began with the realization that although we regularly talk about "personality," describing its nature is not easily done. What we did was briefly outline a few approaches to personality, examining a sample of specific theories.

We looked at psychoanalytic approaches, which, following the lead of Freud, tend to emphasize unconscious influences, early childhood experiences, and sexual and aggressive instincts, although the neo-Freudians placed more concern on social issues and less on biologically based strivings. We saw that many psychologists prefer to talk about personality in terms that derive from learning theories. In these cases, there is much less emphasis on what may be inside a person, and much more on how the environment molds the apparent consistency we sometimes see in behavior. The humanistic-phenomenological approach was characterized as being "optimistic," stressing such factors as personal growth and development and self-actualization. Trait approaches to personality have been more inclined to care about generating adequate descriptions of personality traits than with explaining where these traits may come from. Something of a consensus seems to be building among trait theorists that human personality can be described adequately by five clusters, or factors, of personality traits.

When we asked which of these various approaches or theories is the best, we found that this is an unanswerable question. Each approach is qualitatively different from the others and emphasizes different aspects of personality. In its own way, each has a contribution to make.

We have also explored a few issues in which personality psychologists are interested. We found emerging again an interactionist's position that claims that in any one case, both internal (personality) traits (or dispositions) and the environment (or one's perception of the environment) interact to produce a person's behaviors. We saw that with the only exception of aggression, there are no real, or significant, measurable differences between males and females on personality traits. Finally, we looked at some of the techniques psychologists use to assess personality: behavioral observations, interviews, paper-and-pencil tests, and projective techniques. Although none of these, in itself, can provide a full picture of one's personality, each can contribute to our understanding of the complex fabric we call human personality.

One aspect of our "self"—our being, our personality—that is part of nearly every personality theory is intelligence. Intelligence, its nature and its measurement, is the focus of our next Topic.

Topic 9B

INTELLIGENCE AS AN ASPECT OF PERSONALITY

This Topic focuses on the personality trait called intelligence. We've defined personality as a constellation of affects, behaviors, and cognitions that characterize an individual in many distinct situations over a period of time. Similarly, we have taken personality traits to be dimensions we can use to describe some stable, enduring way in which we can characterize an individual and that we can use to describe individual differences. It is clear that a defining trait of anyone's personality is his or her intelligence. Indeed, intelligence was listed as the fifth of the Big Five traits that best describe human personality.

JUST WHAT *IS* INTELLIGENCE?

Intelligence is another one of those troublesome concepts in psychology. We all know what we mean when we use the word, but we have a terrible time trying to define intelligence concisely. We wonder if John's failure in school is due to his lack of intelligence or to some other factor. You may argue that locking my keys in my car was not very intelligent. I may argue that a student with any intelligence can see the difference between reinforcement and punishment. In this section, we'll do two things. First, we'll develop a working definition of intelligence. Then, we'll review some of the ways in which psychologists have conceptualized the nature of intelligence.

Defining Intelligence

Intelligence has been variously defined as the total of everything you know, as the ability to learn and profit from experience, or as one's ability to solve problems and to cope with the environment. Of course, there is nothing wrong with any of these definitions. The problem is that none seems to say it all. We have gotten into the habit of using intelligence as a general label for so many cognitive abilities that it virtually defies specific definition.

Nonetheless, we should settle on some definition to guide our study through this Topic. I propose that we accept two definitions, one academic and theoretical, the other operational and practical. For our theoretical definition of **intelligence**, we will use the one offered by David Wechsler, who calls it "the capacity of an individual to understand the world about him [her] and his [her] resourcefulness to cope with its challenges" (1975, p. 139).

This definition, and others like it, presents some ambiguities. Just what does one mean by "capacity"? What is meant by "understand the world"? What if the world never really challenges one's "resourcefulness"? Would such people be less intelligent? What at first reading may seem like a very sensible, inclusive definition of intelligence may, upon reflection, pose even more definitional problems.

Perhaps we ought to follow our advice from Chapter 1, in which I suggested that defining concepts operationally often helps overcome such difficulties. We have to be careful here, but, as many psychologists do, we may operationally define intelligence as "that which intelligence tests measure." Note that using this definition sidesteps the thorny problem of coming to grips with the "true" nature of intelligence. It does what most operational definitions do—it gives us a definition we can work with for a while. To use this definition, however, we need to understand how intelligence tests measure intelligence. Before we get to a discussion of intelligence tests, it might be helpful if we spend a bit of time reviewing some of the ways in which psychologists have described intelligence.

intelligence the capacity to understand the world and the resourcefulness to cope with its challenges; that which an intelligence test measures

Before You Go On

Provide a theoretical and an operational
definition of intelligence.

Theoretical Models of Intelligence

Theoretical models of intelligence are attempts to categorize and
organize the various aspects of intellectual (cognitive) abilities into
sensible groupings. In a way, they are sophisticated attempts to provide a definition for what we mean when we talk about the personality trait we call intelligence.

Spearman's "g." One of the first theories of intelligence was proposed by a British psychologist, Charles Spearman. Spearman was
one of the pioneers of mental testing and the inventor of many statistical procedures that could be used to analyze test scores.

Spearman's image of intelligence came from his inspection of
scores earned by people on a wide range of psychological tests
designed to measure many cognitive skills. What impressed Spearman
was that no matter what cognitive ability a specific test was designed
to measure, some people always seemed to do better than others.
People who scored high on some tests tended to score high on all of

*Some people are born with a predisposition to become extremely intelligent, and
others may be born with a predisposition to develop musical talent. This inherited potential must be encouraged and nurtured in a stimulating environment to be
fully realized.*

"g" (g-factor) general intelligence; a global measure of intellectual ability

s-factors specific cognitive, intellectual skills or abilities; for Spearman, what makes up intelligence, when combined with a g-factor

the tests (to varying degrees, of course). It seemed as if there were some intellectual power that facilitated performance in general, whereas variations in performance reflected strengths and weaknesses in specific tasks. Spearman (1904) concluded that intelligence consists of two things: a general intelligence, called a **g-factor**, and a collection of specific intellectual skills, or **s-factors**. Spearman believed that "g" was independent of knowledge, of content—it went beyond knowing facts. It involved the ability to see, understand, and apply relationships in all content areas. In this view, everyone has a degree of "g," or general intelligence (which Spearman thought was inherited), *and* everyone has specific skills that are useful in some tasks but not in others.

Looking at intelligence in terms of what a variety of tests measure, and how such measures are interrelated, became a popular way to think about intelligence. Psychologists gave many types of tests to all sorts of people. They applied statistical techniques (many of them devised by Spearman) to their test scores and looked for areas of overlap and independence. This is still a very popular way to think about intelligence. In fact, there still is controversy about the extent to which "g" is an all-important, sometimes-important, or never-important component of the concept we think of as intelligence (Barrett & Depinet, 1991; Helms, 1992; Ree & Earles, 1992; Sternberg & Wagner, 1993; McClelland, 1973, 1993).

Thurstone's Primary Mental Abilities. When L. L. Thurstone examined the correlations among the various tests of cognitive abilities he administered, he found something different from what Spearman found. Thurstone (1938) saw little or no evidence to support the notion of a general g-factor of intellectual ability. Instead, he claimed that abilities fall into seven categories, which he called the seven **primary mental abilities** (Figure 9.5). Each of the factors in this

primary mental abilities in Thurstone's model, the seven distinct abilities that constitute intelligence

Figure 9.5	
Thurstone's Seven Primary Mental Abilities	
Verbal comprehension (V)	The ability to understand ideas, concepts, and words, as in a vocabulary test.
Number (N)	The ability to use numbers to solve problems quickly and accurately.
Spatial relations (S)	The ability to visualize and manipulate patterns and forms in space, as in the ability to recognize an object viewed from a different perspective.
Perceptual speed (P)	The ability to determine quickly and accurately whether or not two complex stimuli are identical or in some way different.
Word fluency (W)	The ability to use words quickly and fluently, as in the ability to solve anagrams and produce rhymes.
Memory (M)	The ability to remember lists of materials, such as digits, letters, or words presented previously.
Inductive reasoning (I)	The ability to discover a general rule from presented information, to discover relationships, as in, "what number comes next? 2, 4, 6, 8, —."

After Thurstone, 1938.

model is taken to be separate and independently measurable. To know one's intelligence requires that you know how one fares on all seven factors.

Guilford's Structure of Intellect. With the model of J. P. Guilford (1967), matters get much more complicated than either Spearman's or Thurstone's theories. Guilford claimed that intelligence can be analyzed as three intersecting dimensions. He said that any intellectual task can be described in terms of the mental *operations* used in the task, the *content* of material involved, and the *product* or outcome of the task. Each of these three main dimensions has a number of possible values. That is, there are five operations, four contents, and six possible products. The three dimensions of this model, and their values, are found in Figure 9.6.

If you study Figure 9.6, you'll see that there are 120 possible combinations of content, operations, and products in Guilford's model. (In 1988, Guilford increased the possible number of combinations to

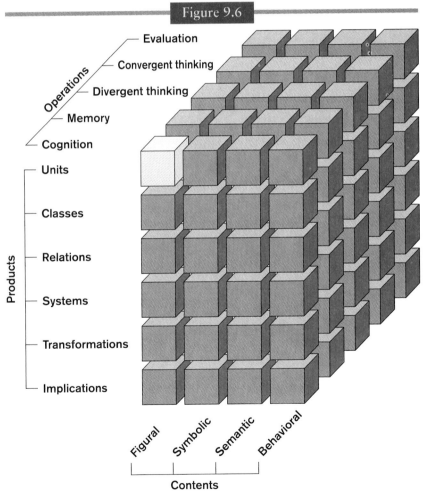

Figure 9.6

Guilford's model of intelligence. In this model, there are three major divisions (contents, products, and operations), each with its own subdivisions. Each subdivision may interact with all others, yielding 120 specific intellectual skills or abilities. (After Guilford, 1967.)

150 by coming up with two memory operations. His basic logic remained the same.) Given that Guilford's model is theoretical, we can still ask, "What does this mean in real life?" Just to give you an idea of how this system works, let's choose one of the 120 "cells," or intersections, depicted in Figure 9.6—the one at which *cognition*, *figural*, and *units* intersect (i.e., the little "block" in the uppermost left corner). What would this intellectual skill be like? Guilford says it's a matter of recognizing (cognitive) diagrams or pictures (figural) of simple, well-defined elements (units). To test this ability, one might be shown an incomplete drawing of a simple object and asked to identify it as quickly as possible.

Vernon's Hierarchical Model. Philip Vernon (1960, 1979) suggests we think of intelligence as a collection of skills and abilities arranged in a hierarchy (Figure 9.7). At the top is a general cognitive ability similar to Spearman's "g." Under it are two major factors; one is a *verbal*, *academic* sort of intelligence, whereas the other is a *mechanical*, *practical* sort. Either of these in turn is thought of as consisting of yet more specific intellectual skills. The verbal-academic skill, for example, consists of *numerical* and *verbal* abilities, among others. Each of these can be broken down still further (verbal skills include such things as *word usage* and *vocabulary*); and further still because vocabulary includes knowing *synonyms* and *antonyms*. Seeing intelligence as including a general factor and a structured set of specific factors gives us a model that combines some of the thinking of Spearman, Thurstone, and Guilford.

Sternberg's Triarchic Model. Robert Sternberg is a cognitive psychologist whose concern about intelligence reflects a more modern vision than the theories we've reviewed so far. His focus is on *how one uses intellectual abilities* rather than on describing one's intellectual abilities. Sternberg's approach is called triarchic because he sees intelligent behavior as a reflection of the input of three distinct processes, or components (1979, 1981, 1985, 1988). One set of components of intelligent behavior involves what Sternberg calls *metacomponents*. These are the skills we bring to bear when we set about to solve a problem. "Just what is the problem here?" "How shall I get started?" "What will I need to see this through?" "How will I know when I've succeeded?" The second set of abilities are *performance components*. These are the actual skills we use in our attempt to solve problems, and involve what we know about ourselves and the world. For example, when working on a math problem, once we realize that two numbers must be multiplied, it is the performance component of our cognitive abilities that gets that job done. Finally, Sternberg proposes that intelligence includes a set of abilities he calls *knowledge-acquisition* components. These are the techniques or strategies for collecting and assimilating new information. Part of "being intelligent" is to demonstrate that one can profit from experience.

What we have reviewed here so briefly is only a small sampling of the theoretical approaches to intelligence that have been proposed

Figure 9.7

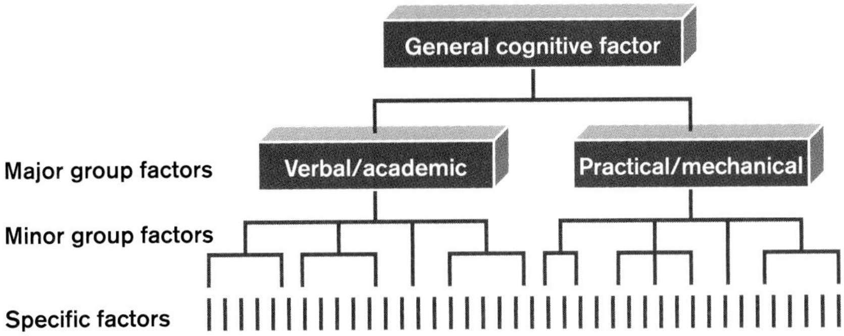

According to Philip Vernon, intellectual abilities may be represented in a hierarchy from very general intellectual skills at the top to very specific abilities at the bottom. (After Vernon, 1960.)

over the years. Given the diversity of opinion about what intelligence *really means*, it is not surprising that psychologists have often resorted to the operational approach of defining intelligence in terms of the tests they have devised to measure it. Now that we have a general idea of the sorts of theoretical issues psychologists have struggled with, we can turn our attention to our discussion of tests of intelligence.

Before You Go On

Briefly summarize the approaches to intelligence
taken by Spearman, Thurstone, Guilford,
Vernon, and Sternberg.

PSYCHOLOGICAL TESTS OF INTELLIGENCE

In this section, we'll move from theory to practical matters as we briefly review a few of the psychological tests designed to measure intelligence. As we do so, there are two things you'll need to keep in mind. You'll need to remember the definition of a test (an objective, standardized measure of a sample of behavior) and the criteria for evaluating psychological tests (reliability, validity, and norms). You'll also have to remember that test scores provide only one measure of intelligence, and, as we've seen, no one measure is going to provide a universally satisfactory indicator of intelligence.

The Stanford-Binet Intelligence Scale

Historians of psychology would refer to the contributions of Alfred Binet (1857–1911) even if he hadn't written the first practical test of general intelligence. He was the leading psychologist in France at the turn of the century. Of great concern in 1900 were those children in the Paris school system who seemed unable to profit from the educational experiences they were being given. What was the problem? Were they not interested? Did they have some emotional sickness? Or were they intellectually unable to grasp the material they were being presented? Binet set out to construct a test to measure the intellectual abilities of children. Binet and his main collaborator, Théodore Simon, wanted to identify students who should be placed in special (remedial) classes, where their education could proceed more efficiently than it had in the standard classroom.

Binet's first test appeared in 1905 and was an immediate success. It caught the attention of Lewis M. Terman at Stanford University, who supervised a translation and revision of the test in 1916. (This revision included changing some clearly French questions into items more suitable for American children.) Since then, the test has been referred to as the Stanford-Binet and has undergone a number of subsequent revisions. The most recent version of the Stanford-Binet was published in 1986. This edition—the fourth—made several significant changes in the test and in its scoring. So, what is this test like?

The test now follows what its authors call a three-level, hierarchical model of cognitive ability (Thorndike et al., 1986). As did Binet's original test, the current edition yields an overall test score that reflects **g**, or general intellectual ability (rather like Spearman's "g"). The test's authors describe this g-factor as "what an individual uses when faced with a problem that he or she has not been taught to solve" (Thorndike et al., 1986, p. 3). Underlying g are three second-level factors (see Figure 9.8). *Crystallized abilities* represent those skills needed for acquiring and using information about verbal and quantitative concepts to solve problems. They are influenced by schooling and could be called an academic ability factor. *Fluid-analytic abilities* are those needed to solve problems that involve figural or nonverbal types of information. The bases of these skills are less tied to formal schooling. They involve the ability to see things in new and different ways. The third factor at this level of the model is *short-term memory*. Items that test one's ability to hold information in memory for relatively short periods can be found on Binet's original test.

The next level of abilities tested on the new Stanford-Binet provides more specific, content-oriented definitions of the factors from level two. As you can see from Figure 9.8, at this level, crystallized abilities are divided into verbal and quantitative reasoning, fluid ana-

The intellectual factors tested by the Stanford-Binet Intelligence Scale, Fourth Edition, arranged in three levels below "g," or general intellectual ability. Each subtest is noted at the lowest level. (After Thorndike et al., 1986.)

lytic abilities are seen as abstract/visual reasoning, and there is no ability at this level that corresponds to short-term memory. At the very base of the hierarchy are the 15 subtests that constitute the actual Stanford-Binet test.

What all of this means is that the authors of the 1986 revision of the Stanford-Binet acknowledge that a person's measured intelligence should be reflected in more than just one test score. Now, not only can we determine an overall g score, but calculate scores for each factor at each of three levels. In addition, we can calculate scores for the 15 subtests by themselves, although it is difficult to say that individual subtest scores are very meaningful. It is unlikely an examiner would administer all 15 of the subtests to any one person. Figure 9.9 shows the way g-scores on the Stanford-Binet are distributed for the general population.

Before we go on, let's take a minute to discuss what has happened to the concept of IQ. **IQ** is an abbreviation for the term *intelligence quotient*. As you know, a quotient is the result you get when you divide one number by another. If one divides 8 by 6, the quotient is 1.33. For the early versions of the Stanford-Binet, the examiner's job was to determine a person's *mental age* (or *MA*), the age level at which the person was functioning in terms of intellectual abilities. A person with the intellectual abilities of an average 8-year-old would have an MA of 8. IQ was then determined by dividing the person's earned mental age by his or her actual age (called *chronological age*, or *CA*). This

IQ (intelligence quotient) a measure of intelligence found by dividing one's mental age by one's chronological age, and multiplying the result by 100

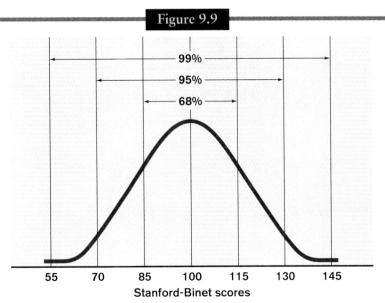

Figure 9.9

An idealized curve that shows the distribution of scores on the Stanford-Binet Intelligence Scale if the test were taken by a large sample of the general population. The numbers at the top of the curve indicate the percentage of the population expected to score within the indicated range of scores; that is, 68% earn scores between 85 and 115, 95% score between 70 and 130, and 99% earn scores between 55 and 145.

quotient was then multiplied by 100 to determine IQ, or IQ = (MA/CA) × 100. If an 8-year-old girl had a mental age of 8, she would be average, and her IQ would equal 100 (or $(^8/_8)$ × 100 = 1 × 100). If the 8-year-old were above average, with the intellectual abilities of an average 10-year-old, her IQ would be 125 $(^{10}/_8$ × 100, or 1.25 × 100). If she were below average, say with the mental abilities of an average 6-year-old, her computed IQ would be 75. Many people are used to the term *IQ* as a measure of general intellectual abilities. Because it is a term ingrained in our vocabulary, *we will continue to use "IQ" as a measure of general intelligence*, even though we now use standard scores, and no longer calculate MAs or quotients.

The Stanford-Binet test has been in use a long time, and there is much to be said for it. It is a well-recognized measure of those behaviors we commonly label intelligent—at least in an educational or academic sense—and is in that way a valid instrument. It is also reliable, or consistent, in the scores it yields (Matarazzo, 1990). Even so, we can expect a change in IQ scores of as much as eight points on repeated administrations (that is, a test score of 100 ought to be thought of as representing a "true'" score somewhere between 96 and 104). The Stanford-Binet also has some drawbacks. It is an individual test (one subject and one examiner) and should be administered, scored, and interpreted only by well-trained professionals. The test can take longer than an hour to administer and, hence, is quite expensive.

Before You Go On

Briefly describe the Stanford-Binet
Intelligence Scale.

The Wechsler Tests of Intelligence

David Wechsler published his first general intelligence test in 1939. Unlike the version of the Stanford-Binet that existed at the time, it was designed for use with adult populations and to reduce the heavy reliance on verbal skills that characterized Binet's tests. With a major revision in 1955, the test became known as the *Wechsler Adult Intelligence Scale (WAIS)*. The latest revision (the WAIS-R) was published in 1981. The WAIS-R is appropriate for persons between 16 and 74 years of age and is reported to be the most commonly used of all psychological tests (Lubin et al., 1984).

A natural extension of the WAIS was the *Wechsler Intelligence Scale for Children (WISC)*, originally published 11 years after the WAIS. After a major revision in 1974, it became known as the WISC-R. With updated norms and several new items (among other things, designed to minimize bias against any ethnic group or gender), the WISC-III appeared in 1991. The WISC-III is appropriate for testing children ages 6 to 16 (there is some overlap with the WAIS-R). A third test in the series is designed for younger children, between the ages of 4 and 6. It is called the *Wechsler Preschool and Primary Scale of Intelligence*, or *WPPSI*. It was published in 1967, was revised in 1989, and is now the WPPSI-R. There are some subtle differences among the three Wechsler tests, but each is based on the same general logic. Therefore, we will consider only one, the WAIS-R, in detail.

The WAIS-R consists of 11 subtests organized in two categories. Six subtests define the *verbal scale,* and five subtests constitute a *performance scale.* Figure 9.10 lists the subtests of the WAIS-R and describes some of the types of items found on each. With the Wechsler tests, we can compute three scores: a verbal score, a performance score, and a total (or full-scale) score. As with the Stanford-Binet, the total score can be taken as a measure of general intelligence.

Each item on each subtest is scored. (Some of the performance items have strict time limits that affect scoring.) You now have 11 scores earned by your subject. As is now the case with the fourth edition of the Stanford-Binet, each subtest score is compared to the score provided by the test's norms. How your subject's earned score compares to the score earned by subjects in the norm group determines

Figure 9.10

The Subtests of the Wechsler Adult Intelligence Scale, Revised (WAIS-R)

Verbal scales

Information	(29 items) Questions designed to tap one's general knowledge about a variety of topics dealing with one's culture; for example, "Who wrote *Huckleberry Finn*?" or "How many nickels in a quarter?"
Digit span	(7 series) Subject is read a series of three to nine digits and is asked to repeat them; then a different series is to be repeated in reverse order.
Comprehension	(16 items) A test of judgment, common sense, and practical knowledge; for example, "Why is it good to have prisons?"
Similarities	(14 pairs) Subject must indicate the way(s) in which two things are alike; for example, "In what way are an apple and a potato alike?"
Vocabulary	(35 words) Subject must provide an acceptable definition for a series of words.
Arithmetic	(14 problems) Math problems must be solved without the use of paper and pencil; for example, "How far will a bird travel in 90 minutes if it flies at the rate of 10 miles per hour?"

Performance scales

Picture completion	(20 pictures) Subject must identify or name the missing part or object in a drawing; for example, a truck with only three wheels.
Picture arrangement	(10 series) A series of cartoonlike pictures must be arranged in an order that tells a story.
Block design	(9 items) Using blocks whose sides are either all red, all white, or diagonally red and white, subject must copy a designed picture or pattern shown on a card.
Object assembly	(4 objects) Free-form jigsaw puzzles must be put together to form familiar objects.
Digit symbol	In a key, each of nine digits is paired with a simple symbol. Given a random series of digits, the subject must provide the paired symbol within a time limit.

the subject's *standard score* for each of the Wechsler subtests. In addition to one overall score, the Wechsler tests provide verbal and performance scores, which can tell us something about a person's particular strengths and weaknesses.

For many years, there has been controversy about the quality and use of individually administered intelligence tests such as the Wechsler tests and the Stanford-Binet. The extent to which the tests may be culturally biased, thus favoring one group of subjects over another, whether they truly measure intelligence and not just academic success, and whether test results can be used for political purposes, perhaps as a basis for racial discrimination, are just some of the questions that keep coming up. A survey of over 600 experts in psychological testing (from a number of disciplines, including education and psychology) indicates considerable agreement about the basic value of intelligence (or IQ) tests (Snyderman & Rothman, 1987). Although the experts are willing to allow that the tests may be somewhat biased on racial and socioeconomic grounds, they "believe that such tests adequately measure more important elements of intelligence" (p.143).

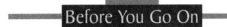

What are the major features of the Wechsler intelligence scales?

Group Tests of Intelligence

There are advantages of individually administered tests such as the Wechsler tests and the Stanford-Binet. Perhaps most important is that the examiner has the opportunity to interact with the person taking the test. The examiner develops opinions about the examinee and can observe how the subject goes about responding to test items. A disadvantage of the individually administered tests is that they are time consuming and expensive. There are alternatives. Group IQ tests are generally paper-and-pencil tests that can be administered to many individuals at one time.

By the beginning of World War I, Binet's test had already gained wide approval, and the notion of using psychological methods to measure intellectual abilities had been generally accepted. There was good reason to know the intellectual capabilities of the recruits who were entering the armed services, but obviously all could not be tested individually. A committee of psychologists was charged with the task of creating a group intelligence test. The result, published in 1917, was the *Army Alpha Test,* a paper-and-pencil test that made rough discriminations among examinees on the basis of intelligence. In the same year, the committee published the *Army Beta Test.* It was designed for illiterates who could not read the Army Alpha. Basically, it was a performance test, the instructions of which were given orally or were acted out.

The military continues to be a major publisher and consumer of group intelligence tests. The U.S. Army now uses the *Armed Forces Qualification Test (AFQT),* and anyone who goes through the process of military induction will have firsthand experience with this test.

When psychological tests of cognitive ability are used to predict future behaviors, we call them *aptitude tests.* Many of the aptitude tests used in the context of education are essentially tests of general intellectual ability. The difference is in the use to which the score is put: predicting future academic success. The two most commonly used college entrance tests are the *SAT (Scholastic Aptitude Test)*, which yields verbal and mathematics subscores as well as an overall score, and the *ACT (American College Testing Program)*. In 1990, the College Entrance Examination Board, which publishes the SAT, announced a major revision of the test (to be called the SAT-I). The SAT-I will include math items that are not in the usual multiple-choice format, and the verbal section will place more emphasis on reading comprehension. At the same time, a new, optional SAT-II will be made available. The SAT-II will include a written essay section, language proficiency tests for native speakers of Japanese and Chinese, and tests for nonnative English speakers.

Before You Go On

What are the advantages of group intelligence tests?

How are paper-and-pencil IQ tests and educational aptitude tests alike?

INDIVIDUAL AND GROUP DIFFERENCES IN MEASURED INTELLIGENCE

Throughout this text, I have made the point that no two people are exactly alike. Characteristic and distinctive ways in which people can differ are often referred to as personality traits. One of the most important ways in which people differ is in their intellectual abilities and capabilities. In this section, we'll review some of the psychological literature on group and individual differences in measured intelligence.

We'll briefly review the data on differences in intelligence as a function of sex and age. We will also look at the research on measured intelligence and academic achievement as a function of race. Finally, we'll consider the individual extremes of intelligence: the mentally gifted and the mentally retarded.

Throughout this section, I'll be referring to the concept of IQ. Please keep in mind that IQ is simply a convenient abbreviation for "intelligence as it is measured by psychological tests." *We should not take IQ to equal one's intelligence.* IQ scores reflect only a particular measure of intelligence.

Group Differences in IQ

Recognizing that there are individual differences in intelligence, can we make any statements about differences in IQ in general? Who are smarter, women or men? Do we become more or less intelligent with age? Are there differences in intelligence among ethnic groups? As you are aware, simple answers to such questions are often misleading and, if interpreted incorrectly, can be dangerous.

One thing we have to ask is why we care. What motivates an interest in group differences in IQ? Even the best scientific data can be put to questionable use. Issues of group differences are sometimes raised in order to justify what amounts to social or political ends. Some sexists (male and female), some racists (of whatever ethnicity), and some agists (young and old) like to point to any observed differences in IQ for groups of individuals to make claims of superiority or inferiority. It is in such cases that clear-cut answers can be dangerous.

More commonly, however, reported average differences in intelligence test scores are simply misleading. Let's imagine for a moment that I have tested two large groups of people: 1,000 Umaloos and 1,000 Takatees. On the average, the IQ score (measured general intelligence, remember) for Umaloos is 95; for Takatees, it is 110. Appropriate statistical analyses tell me that this observed difference of 15 points is too large to have been expected by chance. Are Takatees smarter than Umaloos? Yes, *on the average* they are—that's what I just discovered.

Now look at Figure 9.11. Here we find two curves that represent the IQ scores from my fictitious study. We can clearly see the difference in the averages (means) of the two groups. However, there *are* Takatees whose IQs are below the average IQ of Umaloos. And there

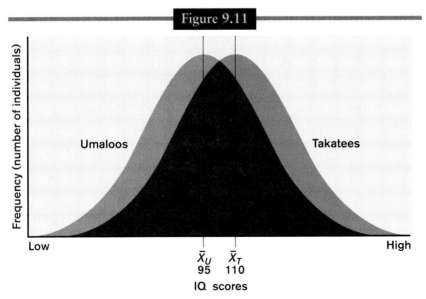

Figure 9.11

Hypothetical distributions of IQ scores for two imaginary groups (Umaloos and Takatees). The average IQs for Takatees is higher than that for Umaloos, but there is considerable overlap between the two distributions. That is, some Umaloos have IQs higher than the average for Takatees (110), and some Takatees have IQs lower than the average for Umaloos (95).

are Umaloos whose IQs are above the average IQ of Takatees. We may be able to draw some conclusions about average IQs, but making definitive statements about individual Takatees and Umaloos is not possible.

Perhaps the most sensible reason for caring about group differences in intelligence (beyond simple curiosity) is the hope that understanding such differences will help us understand the true nature of intelligence and the factors that influence its development (Mackintosh, 1986). Being able to demonstrate a significant difference between the average IQs of two groups of individuals in itself tells us nothing about *why* those differences exist. Are Takatees genetically superior to Umaloos? Maybe, maybe not. Have Umaloos had equal access to the sorts of things that IQ tests ask about? Maybe, maybe not. Are the tests themselves slanted to provide Takatees with an advantage? Maybe, maybe not. And so on. Learning that two groups of persons have different average IQ scores usually raises more questions than it answers. But if we can pursue those questions rigorously, we may learn more about that personality trait we call intelligence.

Before You Go On

If group A and group B have different IQ scores on the average, what may be true about two individuals, one from group A and the other from group B, with regard to intelligence?

Gender Differences in IQ

Here's a question to which we do have a reasonably definitive answer: Is there a difference between the measured IQs of males and females? Answer: no. At least there are very few studies that report any differences between men and women on any test of general intelligence of the sort represented by an IQ score; and further, what small differences have been found seem to be getting even smaller over the past two decades (Aiken, 1984; Halpern, 1986; Hyde et al., 1990; Maccoby & Jacklin, 1974). We must keep in mind that there may be no measurable differences between the IQs of men and women because our tests are constructed to minimize or eliminate any such differences. Usually, if an item on an intelligence test discriminates between women and men, it is dropped from consideration.

When we look beyond global measures of IQ, there are some indications of gender differences on specific intellectual skills (which balance each other out on general IQ tests). For example, females score (on the average) higher than males on tests of clerical speed and accuracy, verbal fluency, reading ability, and fine dexterity (ability to manipulate small objects). Males, on the other hand, outscore females on some tests of mathematical reasoning and spatial relations.

Some psychologists argue that males generally outscore females on tests of mathematics and spatial relations because of the courses they are encouraged to take in school. As more females are drawn to classes in math and science, such differences in test scores will continue to decrease.

Tests of spatial relations ask a subject to visualize and mentally manipulate figures and forms. What is curious about this rather specialized ability is that males seem to perform better than females on such tasks from an early age, widening the gap through the school years, even though this particular ability seems to be only slightly related to any academic course work (Linn & Peterson, 1985; McGee, 1979). This suggests that these sex differences cannot be easily attributed to differences in educational opportunity. Another possibility, however, is that the different recreational activities of boys and girls contribute to differences in spatial abilities.

On the other hand, educational experiences are related to differences in mathematical ability. Scores on tests of mathematics and arithmetic skills are well correlated with the number and type of math classes taken while a student is in high school (Kimball, 1989; Welch et al., 1982). For many reasons, males tend to enroll in advanced math courses at a higher rate than females. It is not surprising, then, that by the time they leave high school, there are differences between men and women on some tests of mathematical ability (those that assess mathematical reasoning and problem solving). We also now have evidence that the differences between males and females on tests of general mathematical abilities have been declining steadily over the past 25 years (Hyde et al., 1990; Jacklin, 1989). Still, some researchers, noting the higher scores males have earned on the math portion of the SAT over the past 17 years (among other things), suspect the possibility of genetic factors at work (Benbow, 1987, 1990).

Before You Go On

Are there gender differences in IQ?

Age Differences and IQ

We spent a lot of time in Chapter 8 discussing many of the cognitive changes that accompany one's lifelong development. Here we'll simply review a few important observations concerning the relationship between age and IQ.

You know a great deal more now than you did when you were 12 years old. You knew more when you were 12 than you did when you were 10. You learned a lot in the fifth and sixth grades. In fact, many 12-year-olds seem to think they know more than their parents do. Certainly, *what* we know changes with age, even *how much* we know changes with age, but neither what nor how much we know is a direct measure of intelligence. IQ scores are computed in such a way that, by definition, they remain consistent with age. The IQ score of the average 12-year-old is 100, the same as the IQ of the average 30-year-old and the average 60-year-old. This is true regardless of which test is used to measure general intellectual abilities. But what about the IQ of any one individual? If Kim's IQ is 112 at age 4, will it still be 112 at age 14, or age 40, or age 80? The measured IQs of individuals much younger than 7 don't correlate well with later IQ scores. We cannot put too much stock in IQs earned by 4-year-olds as predictors of adult intelligence (Baumeister, 1987). The data in Figure 9.12 are typical in this regard. They show the correlations between IQ

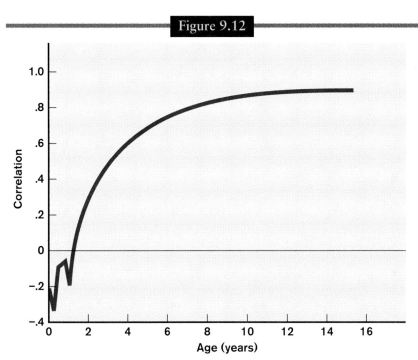

Figure 9.12

Correlations between IQ test scores earned by males between the ages of 16 and 18 with IQ test scores at a younger age (for the same subjects). There is virtually no correlation between IQ scores at 16 or 18 and IQs determined at ages younger than 3 years. That is, infant and preschool IQ test scores are poor predictors of IQ at older ages. (From Bayley & Schaefer, 1964.)

scores earned at ages 16 to 18 with IQ scores at younger ages. Notice that when previous testing was done before the age of 7 or 8 years, the correlations are quite low.

This does not mean that testing young children is without purpose. Knowing the intellectual abilities of young children is often useful, particularly if there is some concern about retardation or some thought that the child may be exceptional. The resulting scores may not predict adult intelligence well, but they may help in assessing the development of the child compared to other children. Even when scores are taken only as a guide, knowing as early as possible that there may be some intellectual problem with a youngster is useful information.

What about intellectual changes throughout the life span? Does intelligence decrease with old age? You may have guessed the answer: yes, no, and it depends. Most of the data we have on age differences in IQ scores have been gathered using a *cross-sectional method*. That is, IQ tests are given, at about the same time, to a large number of people of varied ages. When this is done, the results indicate that overall, global IQ peaks in the early twenties, stays stable for about 20 years, and then declines sharply (e.g., Schaie, 1983; Wechsler, 1958, 1981). A different approach would be to test the same individuals repeatedly, over a period of time. This is the *longitudinal method*. When this method is used, things don't look quite the same, usually showing IQ scores rising until the mid-fifties and then very gradually declining (Schaie, 1974; Schaie & Strother, 1968).

So far we have a qualified "yes" and "no" as answers to our question about age and IQ. Probably the best answer is "it depends." Studies of cognitive abilities demonstrate that we should ask about specific intellectual skills because they do not all decline at the same rate, and some do not decline at all. For example, tests of vocabulary often show no drop in scores with increasing age (Blum et al., 1970), whereas tests of verbal fluency often show steep declines beginning at age 30 (Schaie & Strother, 1968). A longitudinal study of more than 300 bright, well-educated adults showed a slight increase in general intellectual performance through adulthood (ages 18 to 54) on the Wechsler Adult Intelligence Scale (Sands et al., 1989). A closer look at scores on the Wechsler subtests for subjects between the ages of 40 and 61 showed improvement on the Information, Comprehension, and Vocabulary subtests, but a decline in scores on Digit Symbol and Block Design (see Figure 9.10).

Another "it depends" answer comes to the surface when we consider what are called **fluid intelligence** and **crystallized intelligence** (Horn & Cattell, 1966). It appears that fluid intelligence—abilities that relate to speed, adaptation, flexibility, and abstract reasoning—includes the skills that show the greatest decline with age. On the other hand, crystallized intelligence—abilities that depend on acquired knowledge, accumulated experiences, and general information—includes the skills that remain constant or even increase throughout one's lifetime (Horn, 1976; Vernon, 1979). If the concepts of fluid and crystallized intelligence sound familiar, you may be reminded of two of the dimensions the Stanford-Binet Intelligence

fluid intelligence *those cognitive skills dependent on speed, adaptation, flexibility, and abstract reasoning*

crystallized intelligence *those cognitive skills dependent on knowledge, accumulated experience, and general information*

Scale measures (see page 462). Put a bit differently, "increased age is assumed to be associated with declines in raw intellectual power or current ability to process information, but little or no declines are expected in measures of the accumulated products of past cognitive activity" (Salthouse, 1989, pp. 19–20). With age, one's abilities to acquire new information and to solve new and different types of problems may decline, but there is no reason to expect a decline in the intellectual abilities one has already acquired.

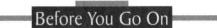

Before You Go On

Does intelligence decline with age, increase with age, or stay the same?

Racial and Ethnic Differences in IQ

That there are significant differences between the IQ test scores of black and white Americans is not a new discovery. It was one of the conclusions drawn from the testing program for army recruits during World War I. Since then, many studies have reconfirmed the fact that whites score as many as 15 points higher on tests of general intelligence (IQ) than do blacks. Blacks even earn lower scores on performance tests and on intelligence tests that supposedly minimize the influence of one's culture (so-called culture-fair tests) (Helms, 1992; Jensen, 1980; Rushton, 1988). There are also data that tell us that Japanese children between the ages of 6 and 16 score higher on IQ tests—about 11 points *on the average*—than do American children of the same age (e.g., Lynn, 1982, 1987). The superiority of Japanese children on mathematics tests is even greater (Stevenson, et al., 1986). Recently, Asian-American students have been scoring considerably higher on the SAT than have other students; again, particularly in mathematics (for example, average math scores on the SAT of 525 compared to 476) (College Board, 1989; Hsia, 1988; Lynn, 1991; Sue & Okasaki, 1990). The nagging question, of course, is *why*? Why do these differences appear?

The proposed answers have been controversial and point to several possibilities: (1) The *tests themselves are biased* and unfair. Current IQ tests may simply reflect mainstream life and the experiences of white Americans to a greater extent than they reflect the lives and experiences of most blacks or Hispanics. Whether such biases occur by intention is not relevant. (2) Differences in IQ scores can be attributed to *environmental factors*, such as available economic or educational opportunities, or the extent to which one is exposed to a wide range of stimuli. (3) There are *genetic factors* involved that place some groups at a disadvantage. (4) There are *cultural differences* in motivation and attitudes about performance on standardized tests. In most Western cultures, poor performance on an academic test is typically attributed to factors other than one's effort: "The test was bad;

my teachers were lousy, and I had the flu." In some cultures, including most Asian cultures, failure is more likely to be attributed to lack of effort: "I didn't work hard enough to prepare and should try harder next time."

Test bias may account for some of the observed differences in IQ scores, but assume for the moment that our available methods for assessing general intelligence are as valid as possible. What then? Let's first concentrate on black-white differences in IQ.

In the 1950s and 1960s, social scientists were confident that most if not all of the difference between the IQ scores of whites and blacks could be explained in terms of environmental conditions. There wasn't much research to support the position, but the logic was compelling and was consistent with prevailing attitudes. Blacks were at a disadvantage on standard tests of general intelligence, the argument went, because they were often denied access to enriching educational opportunities. Their generally lower socioeconomic status deprived blacks of many of the sorts of experiences that could positively affect IQ scores. The generally poor nutrition and health of blacks were also used to explain why their scores tended to be, on the average, lower.

In 1969, Arthur Jensen shocked the scientific community with an article published in the *Harvard Educational Review*. Simply put, Jensen argued that there was insufficient evidence to justify the conclusion that the environment could produce such a large racial difference in IQ scores. The alternative was obvious to Jensen: the differences were attributable to genetic factors. Many readers took Jensen's claim to mean that blacks are genetically inferior to whites. However, Jensen claims that his argument was meant only as a reasonable hypothesis, intended to provoke scientific efforts to explore such a possibility (Jensen, 1981).

Perhaps you can imagine the furor created by Jensen's article. Researchers took up the challenge and tried to find convincing evidence to demonstrate that the environment *is* the cause of lower black IQ scores. Along the way, it was learned that there *were* things about Jensen's argument, and about the data upon which he was basing his argument, that were problematic. Among other things, he based much of his conclusion on data about the IQs of twins that were simply fabricated and without basis. Nonetheless, one reviewer has asserted that "what is finally clear from such research is that environmental factors have not been identified that are sufficient to account for all or even most of the 15-point mean difference in IQ between blacks and whites in the United States. Jensen's conclusion that one-half to two-thirds of the gap remains unaccounted for by any proposed combination of environmental influences is still unrefuted" (Mackenzie, 1984, p. 1217).

Now what does *that* mean? Does it mean that racial differences in IQ *are* caused by genetic factors? *Are* blacks genetically less able than whites? Of course not; at the very least, there is not sufficient evidence to support such a conclusion (Mackintosh, 1986). To understand why we have not yet resolved this issue requires that we understand three points: (1) Just because there is evidence to suggest that genetic factors affect differences in intelligence *within* races, that evidence cannot be used as evidence of genetic factors affecting differences in intelligence *between* races. (2) It is improper to assume that the failure to identify any specific environmental causes of racial differences in IQ is sufficient reason to drop the environmental-factors argument. (3) Just because we have not identified the specific environmental factors that can cause racial differences in IQ does not mean we must accept genetic explanations. Again, when we consider the impact of heredity and environment, the issue is not a matter of either-or.

Similar arguments have been proposed by those trying to understand and account for the apparent superiority of Asian American students on standard tests of academic achievement. Some have argued for at least a degree of innate superiority (e.g., Lynn, 1977, 1991), whereas others have pointed to socioeconomic, cultural, and motivational factors (e.g., Caplan, 1989; Stevenson et al., 1986; Sue & Okasaki, 1990).

So where do we stand on the issue of racial-ethnic differences in IQ? We stand in a position of considerable uncertainty. As we have seen, there is a body of research data that underscores the contributions of both genetic and environmental influences on what we call intelligence. Whether any of these data can be used to settle the issue of racial differences in IQ scores is debatable.

Before You Go On

Briefly summarize the data on racial differences in IQ scores and arguments about the causes of such differences.

Extremes of Intelligence: The Mentally Gifted

When we look at the IQ scores earned by large random samples of people, we find that those scores are distributed in a predictable pattern. The most frequently occurring score is the average score, 100. Most other earned scores are close to this average. In fact, about 95 percent of all IQ scores fall between scores of 70 and 130 (see Figure 9.9, page 464). We'll end this chapter by considering those people who score at the extremes. We'll start with the upper extreme, and then consider the lower.

There are many ways in which a person can be gifted. A report of the United States Office of Education (1972) defines giftedness as *a demonstrated achievement or aptitude for excellence* in any one of six areas.

1. *Psychomotor ability:* One of the most overlooked areas in which some people clearly can excel. We are dealing with people of outstanding abilities in behaviors or skills that require agility, strength, speed, quickness, coordination, and the like.

Giftedness can be demonstrated in several behaviors, even in childhood. Some children show extraordinary talent in leadership, in psychomotor ability, or in performing arts.

2. *Visual and performing arts:* Some people, even as children, demonstrate an unusual talent for art, music, drama, and writing.

3. *Leadership ability:* Leadership skills are valued in most societies, and there seem to be individuals who are particularly gifted in this area. This is often true even with very young children. Youngsters with good leadership skills tend to be bright, but they are not necessarily the smartest of the group.

4. *Creative or productive thinking:* This aspect of giftedness has received much attention over the past 25 years. Here we are

talking about individuals who *may* be intellectually or academically above average, but not necessarily so. Indeed, scores on measures of creativity typically are *un*related to measures of general intelligence (e.g., Horn, 1976; Kershner & Ledger, 1985). Among other things, people with this type of giftedness are able to generate unique and different, but still useful, solutions to problems. (You might want to review our discussion of creative problem solving in Topic 7B.) Persons who demonstrate exceptional creative talents in one area (art, math, or language, for instance) usually show no particular creativity in other areas (e.g., Amabile, 1985; Weisberg, 1986).

5. *Specific academic aptitude:* In this case, we are talking about people who have a special ability in a particular subject or two. Someone who is a whiz in math, history, or laboratory science, without necessarily being outstanding in other academic areas, would fit this category.

6. *Intellectually gifted:* Inclusion in this group is based on scores earned on a general intelligence test, usually a Wechsler test or the Stanford-Binet Intelligence Scale. It is most likely that when people use the term *mentally gifted,* they are referring to individuals who would fit this category—people of exceptionally high IQ. (IQ scores of 130 or above usually qualify for inclusion in this category. Some prefer to reserve the label for those with IQs above 135. In either case, we are dealing with a very small portion of the population: fewer than 3 percent qualify.)

How can we describe intellectually gifted individuals? The truth is, there have been few large-scale attempts to understand mental giftedness or the cognitive processing of people at the upper end of the IQ distribution (Horowitz & O'Brien, 1985; Reis, 1989). A good deal of what we know about the mentally gifted comes directly, or indirectly, from a classic study begun by L. M. Terman in the early 1920s (the same Lewis Terman who revised Binet's IQ test in 1916). Terman supervised the testing of more than 250,000 children throughout California. His research group at Stanford University focused on those children who earned the highest scores—about 1,500 in all, each with an IQ above 135.

Lewis Terman died in 1956, but the study of those mentally gifted individuals, who were between the ages of 8 and 12 in 1922, continues. Ever since their inclusion in the study, and at regular intervals, they have been retested, surveyed, interviewed, and polled by psychologists from Stanford (Goleman, 1980; Oden, 1968; Sears & Barbee, 1977).

The Terman study has its drawbacks. Choosing a narrow definition of *gifted* in terms of IQ alone is an obvious one. Failing to control factors such as socioeconomic level or parents' educational level is another. There also is evidence that researchers may have excluded from the sample any children who showed signs of psychological disorders or problems, whether their IQ scores were high enough or not. Nonetheless, the study is an impressive one for having continued for more than 60 years, if nothing else. What can this longitudinal analysis tell us about people with very high IQs?

Most of Terman's results fly in the face of the common stereotype of the bright child as being skinny, anxious, clumsy, sickly, and wearing thick glasses (Sears & Barbee, 1977). In fact, if there is any overall conclusion to be drawn from the Terman-Stanford study, it is that, in general, gifted children experience advantages in virtually everything. They are taller, faster, better coordinated, have better eyesight, fewer emotional problems, and tend to stay married longer than average. These findings have been confirmed by others with different samples of subjects (Holden, 1980). All sorts of obvious things are also true of this sample of bright children, now oldsters. They received more education; found better, higher-paying jobs; and had brighter children than did people of average intelligence. By now, we know better than to overgeneralize. All of Terman's children (sometimes referred to as "Termites") did not grow up to be rich and famous and live happily ever after. Many did, but not all. These conclusions, like so many others, are valid only "in general, on the average."

Before You Go On

List six ways in which individuals can be considered gifted.

Summarize the basic findings of the Terman-Stanford study of intellectually gifted youngsters.

Extremes of Intelligence: The Mentally Retarded

Our understanding of mental retardation has changed considerably over the past 25 years. We have seen changes in treatment and care, and great strides in prevention. Part of the change in prevention and care is due to significant changes in how psychology *defines* mental retardation (Baumeister, 1987; Landesman & Ramey, 1989).

Issues of Definition. Intelligence as measured by IQ tests is often used to confirm suspected cases of **mental retardation**. As is true for the mentally gifted, however, there is more to retardation than IQ alone. The definition provided by the American Association of Mental Deficiency (AAMD) cites three factors: "subaverage general intellectual functioning which originated during the developmental period and is associated with impairment in adaptive behavior" (Grossman, 1973). Let's look at each of these three points.

The IQ cutoff for mental retardation is usually taken to be 70. The AAMD further categorizes mental retardation as follows:

IQ 70–85: *borderline or slow*
IQ 50–69: *mildly mentally retarded*
IQ 35–49: *moderately mentally retarded*
IQ 20–34: *severely mentally retarded*
IQ less than 19: *profoundly mentally retarded*

mental retardation a condition, indicated by an IQ below 70, that begins during the developmental period and is associated with impairment in adaptive functioning

As you review this list, you need to keep two things in mind. First, these IQ test scores are suggested limits. Given what we know about IQ tests and their reliability, it is ridiculous to claim after one administration of a test that a person with an IQ of 69 is mentally retarded, while someone else with an IQ of 71 is not. Second, diagnosis of mental retardation is not (should not be) made on the basis of IQ score alone.

To fit the AAMD definition of mental retardation, the cause or the symptoms of the below-average intellectual functioning must show up during the usual period of intellectual development (up to age 18). In many circles, the term *developmentally delayed* is coming to replace the narrower term *mentally retarded*. Diagnosis may come after the administration of an IQ test, but initial suspicions generally come from perceived delays in a person's developmental or adjustive patterns of behavior.

By making "impairment in adaptive behavior" a part of their definition of mental retardation, the AAMD is acknowledging that there is more to getting along in this world than the intellectual and academic sorts of skills that IQ tests emphasize. Being mentally retarded does not necessarily mean being helpless, particularly for those in the categories of borderline or mild levels of retardation. Of major consideration is, or ought to be, the individual's ability to adapt to his or her environment. In this regard, such skills as the ability to dress oneself, to follow directions, to make change, or to find one's way home from a distance become relevant (Coulter & Morrow, 1978).

Even without the simple, one-dimensional definition of retardation based on IQ, the population of mentally retarded or developmentally delayed citizens is large. It is difficult to obtain exact figures because many individuals who might fit the criteria and be classified as mildly retarded have never been diagnosed. Even so, estimates indicate that approximately 3 percent of the population at any one time falls within the IQ range for retardation. Two other relevant estimates are that approximately 900,000 children and young adults with mental retardation between the ages of 3 and 21 years are being served in the public schools (Schroeder et al., 1987) and that nearly 200,000 mentally retarded persons are found in community residential facilities: state and county mental hospitals, and nursing homes (Landesman & Butterfield, 1987). Let's now turn to a brief discussion of the causes, treatment, and prevention of mental retardation.

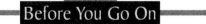

Before You Go On

How might we best define mental retardation?

Causes, Treatment, and Prevention. We don't really know what causes *average* intelligence. We have little to indicate what causes someone to be mentally gifted. We cannot begin to explain the causes of all types of mental retardation, but at least we have some good ideas. Psychologists suspect that there are hundreds of causes; at the moment, the list of known or highly suspected causes exceeds 100. The more we learn about the sources of mental retardation, the better able we will be to treat it or to prevent it altogether.

Approximately one-quarter of all cases of mental retardation reflect a problem that developed before, during, or just after birth. Between 15 and 20 percent of those persons referred to as mentally retarded were born prematurely, where prematurity is defined as being born at least three weeks before the due date *or* at a weight below 5 pounds, 8 ounces.

We appreciate that the health of the mother during pregnancy—and the health of the father at conception—can affect the health of the child. Several prenatal conditions can cause developmental delays, including hypertension, exposure to X rays, lowered oxygen intake, rubella, maternal syphilis, and the mother's use of drugs, from powerful narcotics to the frequent use of aspirin, alcohol, or nicotine. To greater and lesser degrees, all of these can be linked to mental retardation. In addition, there are those cases that stem from difficulties or injuries during the birth process itself.

As we've seen, the extent to which normal levels of intelligence are inherited is open to debate. Some types of mental retardation, however, are clearly genetic in origin. One of the clearest examples of such a case is the intellectual retardation accompanying **Down's syndrome**, first described in 1866. We don't know exactly why it happens, but occasionally a fetus develops with 47 chromosomes instead of the usual 46, or 23 pairs. We do know that Down's syndrome is more likely as the age of either parent increases. The physical signs are well known: small, round skull; flattened face; large tongue; short, broad nose; broad hands; and short, stubby fingers. During childhood, behavioral development is delayed. Down's syndrome children may fall into any of the levels of retardation previously listed. Many are educable and lead lives of considerable independence, although it remains true that even as adults many will require supervision at least some of the time.

Fragile X Syndrome is a variety of mental retardation with a genetic basis discovered more recently—in the late 1960s (Bregman et al., 1987). Although it does occur in females, it is found primarily in males. (The problem here is with the X chromosome, giving the disorder its name.) Males with Fragile X Syndrome usually have long faces, big ears, and—as adults—large testes (Zigler & Hodapp, 1991). Individuals with this form of retardation have difficulty processing sequences of events, or events in a series, which means that they have problems with language skills. One curiosity is that whereas males with Down's syndrome show a gradual but steady decrease in IQ scores with age, males with Fragile X Syndrome show their most noticeable declines during puberty.

Most cases of mental retardation do not have obvious causes. They are more subtle in their origin. About one-half to three-quarters of cases of mental retardation do not have known biological or genetic causes (Zigler & Hodapp, 1991).

Down's syndrome a condition of several symptoms, including mental retardation, caused by an extra (47th) chromosome

Many Down's syndrome children can benefit greatly from special education programs, as well as individualized instruction.

To some degree, our ability to treat mental retardation depends on our ability to specify its causes. Special-education programs have helped, but not all have been equally successful (Zigler & Hodapp, 1991). Preparing teachers and mental health professionals to be sensitive to the wide range of behaviors and feelings of which mentally retarded persons are capable has helped. Impressive changes can be made in raising the IQs of some mildly retarded and a few moderately retarded children (Landesman & Ramey, 1989). For severely and profoundly retarded persons, the outlook is not bright—certainly not in terms of raising IQ points (Spitz, 1986). But we always need to remind ourselves that quality of life is not necessarily a function of IQ. The emphasis in recent years has been to focus less on overall intellectual growth and more on those specific skills and abilities that *can* be improved.

There is greater hope in the area of prevention. As we continue to appreciate the influences of the prenatal environment on the development of cognitive abilities, we can educate mothers and fathers about how their behaviors can affect their child even before it is born. An excellent example of how mental retardation can be prevented concerns a disorder called **phenylketonuria**, or **PKU**. This disorder is genetic in origin, and over fifty years ago it was discovered to be a cause of mental retardation. PKU results when a child inherits genes that fail to produce an enzyme that normally breaks down chemicals found in many foods. Although a newborn with PKU usually appears normal, a simple blood test has been developed that can detect the disorder soon after birth. Once PKU has been detected, a prescribed diet (which must be maintained for about four years) can reduce or eliminate any of the retardation effects of the disorder. Unfortunately, most cases (about 70 percent) of mental retardation cannot be detected at birth, which means that preventive or therapeutic intervention also has to wait until the child is older (Scott & Carran, 1987).

phenylketonuria (PKU) a genetically caused disorder that produces mental retardation and that is now detectable and, thus, preventable

Before You Go On

List some of the possible causes of mental retardation.

TOPIC 9B SUMMARY

In this chapter we have been dealing with issues related to one's personality. We've defined personality traits as distinguishable, relatively enduring ways in which people may differ. One of the ways in which people differ is in their level or degree of intelligence. Having said that, we soon found that generating a complete, adequate definition of intelligence is not easily done. We looked at a few theoretical approaches and moved on to consider intelligence in operational terms—in terms of how it is typically measured—reviewing the two individual tests of intelligence (the Stanford-Binet and the Wechsler tests) in some detail.

Our ability to measure general intellectual abilities (which we continue to call IQ) is not without limitation. Nonetheless, IQ tests have raised several controversial and intriguing questions psychologists have attempted to answer. We have seen that some questions about IQ may be more important politically than scientifically. We briefly examined differences in measured intelligence as a function of sex, age, and race. IQ scores seem quite stable as a function of age, and differences in IQ scores between males and females are slight at best. There are some significant differences in measured intelligence when we look at various ethnic groups, but accounting for these differences remains an elusive goal. We have considered those individuals with extreme IQ scores. In every instance, we're confronted with the issue of the extent to which one's intelligence—at least as it is measured by our tests—is a function of one's nature or one's nurture. Beyond saying that both of these influences interact in some way, we must focus on the issue of how one's intelligence can be changed, regardless of the extent to which it reflects either genes or environment.

TOPIC 9A

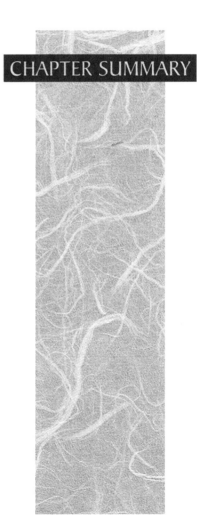

CHAPTER SUMMARY

What are the three levels of consciousness proposed by Freud?

Freud proposed that at any given time we are only aware, or *conscious*, of a few things. With a little effort, some ideas or memories can be accessed from our *preconscious*, whereas others—those in our *unconscious* mind—may be accessed only with great difficulty. */p. 426*

According to Freud, what are the three structures of personality, and by what principle does each operate?

The three structures of personality according to Freud are the inborn, instinctive *id*, operating on the *pleasure principle* and seeking immediate gratification; the *ego*, or sense of self, which operates on the *reality principle*, mediating needs in the context of the real world; and the *superego*, or sense of morality or conscience, which operates on the *idealistic principle*, attempting to direct one to do what is right and proper. */p. 427*

What are Freudian defense mechanisms and what is their purpose?

Defense mechanisms are unconscious devices employed to defend the ego against feelings of anxiety that may originate in conflicts with the id or the superego. They include *repression*, or motivated forgetting in which anxiety-producing ideas, wishes, or experiences are forced into the unconscious; *denial*, in which a person refuses to acknowledge the reality of anxiety-producing situations; *rationalization*, in which one generates excuses for anxiety-producing behaviors rather than facing the reasons for those behaviors; *fantasy*, in which a person uses daydreaming or imagination to escape the anxieties of daily living; *projection*, in which one sees in others those very traits or desires that

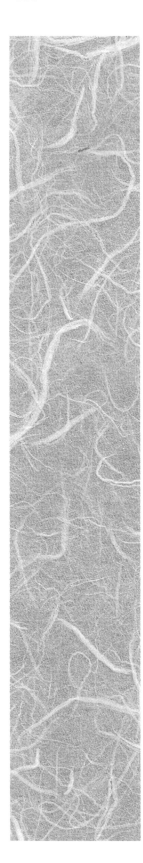

would make one anxious if seen in oneself; *regression*, in which one retreats to earlier, primitive levels of behavior that were once effective as a means of dealing with anxiety; and *displacement*, in which one's anxiety-producing motives or behaviors are directed at some "safe" object or person rather than at the person for whom they are intended. /*p. 429*

Briefly summarize Freud's psychosexual stages of development.

Freud believed that personality developed in a sequence of stages, each related to some expression of sexuality or sensuality, beginning with an *oral stage*, in which pleasure and satisfaction derive from oral activities such as sucking, feeding, and noise making; to an *anal stage*, in which the control of bladder and bowel movements become a source of satisfaction and pleasure; to a *phallic stage*, in which one becomes aware of one's sexuality and forms a close attachment with the opposite sex parent; to a *latency stage*, in which sexuality is "put on hold" during a period of rapid ego development; to a *genital stage*, which follows puberty and wherein there is a reawakening of sexual, sensual desires. /*p. 430*

Briefly summarize the contributions of Adler, Jung, and Horney to the psychoanalytic approach to personality.

Adler, Jung, and Horney each parted with Freud on theoretical grounds, whereas remaining basically psychoanalytic in their approaches to personality. For Adler, social influences and inferiority complexes mattered much more than did innate drives. Jung was less biological, more positive, and expanded on Freud's view of the unconscious mind, adding the notion of the collective unconscious. Horney also rejected the notion of instinctual impulses and discussed instead the notion of basic anxiety and how one reacts to it as the sculptor of one's personality. /*p. 433*

Specify a contribution to the concept of personality made by Watson, Dollard and Miller, Skinner, and Bandura.

Many psychologists have argued that personality can be approached using basic learning principles and observable behavior. Watson emphasized focusing on behavior and abandoning mental concepts. Dollard and Miller attempted to explain personality development in terms of learning theory and habits. Skinner emphasized the notion of the consequences of one's behavior. Bandura stressed the role of observation and social learning in the formation of personality. /*p. 434*

Briefly summarize the humanistic-phenomenological approach to personality as epitomized by Rogers and Maslow.

The theories of Rogers and Maslow are alike in many ways, emphasizing the integrity of the self and the power of personal growth and development. Both theorists deny the negativity and biological bias of psychoanalytic theory and the environmental determinism of behaviorism. /*p. 437*

What is a personality trait?

What are the major traits that influence personality, according to Allport and Cattell?

A personality trait is a characteristic and distinctive way in which one individual may differ from others. According to Allport, there are two types of traits: *common traits* and *personal dispositions*. The former is found in virtually everyone, and the latter is unique to some individuals. Cattell also feels that there are two types of traits: *surface traits*, which are readily observable, and *source traits*, from which surface traits develop. */p. 438*

What are the "Big Five" personality dimensions?

Recent research in personality trait theory suggests that from all of those traits that have been proposed, five emerge most regularly, although there is as yet no agreement on what to call these dimensions. One version of this theory calls them (1) Extroversion-Introversion, (2) Agreeableness or Friendliness, (3) Will or Conscientiousness, (4) Stability-Instability, and (5) Intelligence. */p. 440*

What are some of the strengths and weaknesses of each of the four approaches to personality we have discussed?

The psychoanalytic approach is the most comprehensive approach and may be credited with focusing our attention on the importance of early childhood experience, biological drives, and sexuality. Unfortunately, many of its insights and ideas are scientifically untestable. Behavioral/learning approaches profit from their strict definitions and experimental bases, but lack comprehensiveness. They put what many feel is too much emphasis on the environment as the determinant of behavior. The humanistic-phenomenological approach is positive, emphasizing personal growth and development, but many of its concepts are poorly defined and many of its predictions are difficult to test. Trait approaches provide us with possible descriptions of personality, and how to measure personality traits, but are not really theories, and as such explain very little about personality. There may be a growing consensus, but there is still no universally accepted vision of which traits are most important, how they develop, or how they are interrelated. */p. 442*

Briefly summarize the debate concerning personality versus situational influences on behavior.

One issue of interest among psychologists who study personality is the extent to which we can claim that there *are* any internal, individual traits that are consistent over time and over situations. One's personal characteristics should be discernible at least within a range of situations. The debate over the stability or consistency of personality variables begun in the late 1960s is essentially over. A point of view, called interactionism, has emerged that says that predicting how a person responds in a certain situation is determined by the interaction

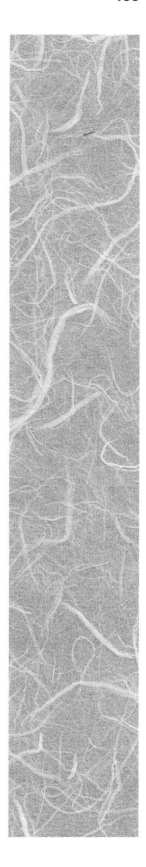

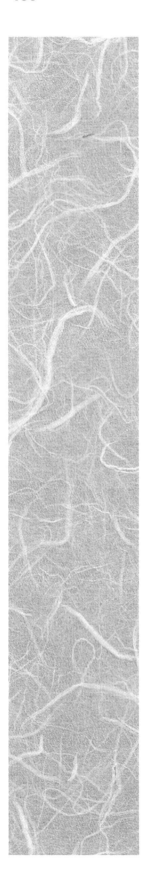

of stable personality characteristics and that person's perception of the situation. /*p. 444*

Briefly summarize what we know about gender differences in personality traits.

As much as our stereotypes would like to convince us that there are basic differences in the personalities of men and women, research continues to remind us that actual differences are few, and slight at best. The one personality trait that does seem to be more common in males than in females is aggression—at least as expressed in overt behavior, or aggressive acts. On other personality traits the data are mixed, but some possibilities include differences in communication style, body language, altruism, empathy, and self-confidence. /*p. 446*

What is a psychological test?

By what criteria do we evaluate psychological tests or assessment techniques?

A psychological test is an objective, standardized measure of a sample of behavior. The quality of a psychological test or any assessment technique is judged in terms of (1) reliability (the extent to which the measure of behavior is consistent or dependable over time), (2) validity (the extent to which the assessment actually measures what it claims to measure), and (3) the adequacy of norms (measures taken on large groups of similar subjects and that can be used as a basis of comparison). /*p. 448*

How are behavioral observations used to assess personality?

Conclusions about an individual's personality can be inferred from the observation of that individual's behaviors. Behaviors should be observed in a large number of settings. Observations should be as objective as possible and may involve the use of behavioral rating scales to check reliability. /*p. 449*

Cite an advantage and a disadvantage of the interview as a technique of personality assessment.

The major advantages of the interview are its ease and flexibility of administration, which allow the interviewer to pursue avenues of interest and abandon lines of questioning that are not informative. Unfortunately, interviews often lack demonstrated validity. /*p. 451*

What does multiphasic mean?

How was the MMPI constructed?

Multiphasic instruments attempt to measure several characteristics or traits with the same set of items. The MMPI was designed (in the early 1940s and revised, as the MMPI-2, in 1989) as an aid to psychological diagnosis. The test includes only those items that discriminate between subjects of differing diagnostic categories (including "normal"). The test also includes items to assess the extent to which the subject is doing a thorough and honest job of answering the 567 true-false questions. Paper-and-pencil tests can serve as useful screening devices to indicate which traits or patterns of traits are likely to be found within a given individual. /*p. 452*

What is the essence of a projective technique, the Rorschach and TAT in particular?

With a projective technique, the assumption is that in responding to an ambiguous stimulus (describing what is indicated in a series of inkblots with the Rorschach, or telling short stories about a set of pictures with the TAT), a subject will *project* conscious or unconscious aspects of him- or herself into his or her responses. /*p. 454*

TOPIC 9B

Provide a theoretical and an operational definition of intelligence.

In theory, we may define intelligence as David Wechsler has: the capacity of an individual to understand the world about him or her and the resourcefulness to cope with its challenges. An operational definition of intelligence would be "that which an intelligence test measures." /*p. 457*

Briefly summarize the approaches to intelligence taken by Spearman, Thurstone, Guilford, Vernon, and Sternberg.

Spearman viewed intelligence as consisting of one general factor ("g") and a number of specific abilities ("s"). Thurstone argued that intelligence reflected a combination of seven unique and primary mental abilities. Guilford argued that there are as many as 120 cognitive skills that constitute one's intelligence. Vernon suggested that intellectual skills or cognitive abilities can be arranged in a hierarchy from very general at the top to very specific at the bottom. Sternberg argues that intelligence should be conceptualized as an organized set of cognitive processes or techniques (components), not as a set of given facts or ideas. /*p. 461*

Briefly describe the Stanford-Binet Intelligence Scale.

The Stanford-Binet is the oldest of the tests of general intelligence (commonly called IQ tests). The test is individually administered. Its most recent (1986) revision yields an overall score as well as subscores for a number of abilities assumed to underlie general intelligence. The test consists of 15 subtests—each assessing a specific cognitive task—items of which are arranged in order of difficulty. Scores on the test (standard age scores) compare the performance of a subject to that of others of the same age level. /*p. 465*

What are the major features of the Wechsler intelligence scales?

The Wechsler scales are individually administered tests of general intelligence. There are three of them, each appropriate for a specific

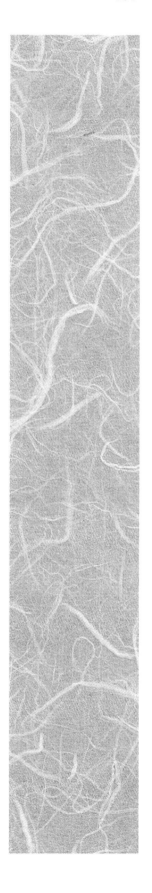

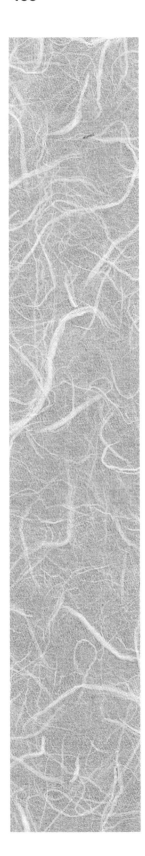

age group. Each test consists of verbal or performance subtests of varied content. Hence, three scores can be determined: an overall score, a score on the verbal subtests, and a score on the performance subtests. Scores on the Wechsler tests are standard scores that compare one's abilities to those of others of the same age. /*p. 467*

What are the advantages of group intelligence tests?

How are paper-and-pencil IQ tests and educational aptitude tests alike?

Group intelligence tests may not provide as much information or be as valid as individually administered tests, but they are much less expensive. They are best used as screening devices. Many educational aptitude tests are essentially paper-and-pencil tests of general intellectual abilities that are used to make predictions about future academic performance. /*p. 468*

If group A and group B have different IQ scores on the average, what may be true about two individuals, one from group A and the other from group B, with regard to intelligence?

Average (mean) group differences tell us little about individual differences. That is, the two individuals from groups A and B may have the same IQ score, or either may have a score higher than the other. (Review Figure 9.11.) /*p. 470*

Are there gender differences in IQ?

No and yes. There are no significant differences between men and women on virtually any test that yields a general IQ score. There are some specific skills and abilities that demonstrate sex differences, but the differences are "on the average" and quite slight. /*p. 471*

Does intelligence decline with age, increase with age, or stay the same?

Overall intelligence tends to decline slightly as one approaches the age of 50 or 60. Various skills and abilities are differentially affected by age. Fluid intelligence, for example, seems to decline with age, whereas crystallized intelligence remains constant or even increases slightly with age. Although with advanced age, one may have a more difficult time assimilating new information, there is little reason to believe that other intellectual skills will be diminished. /*p. 474*

Briefly summarize the data on racial differences in IQ scores and arguments about the causes of such differences.

There are reliable differences between the IQs of blacks and whites, most studies putting the *average* difference at about 15 points, in favor of whites, whereas Asian-American students, *on the average*, perform better on tests of academic achievement. The data on group differences tell us nothing, however, about their source. Strenuous arguments have been made favoring a genetic cause and environmental causes, including different emphases put on intellectual testing in different cultures. /*p. 476*

List six ways in which individuals can be considered gifted.

Summarize the basic findings of the Terman-Stanford study of intellectually gifted youngsters.

Giftedness can mean several things in addition to (1) overall intellectual ability as measured by IQ tests (usually taken to be an IQ over 130). Other abilities in which individuals may be gifted include (2) psychomotor skills, (3) the visual and performing arts, (4) leadership, (5) creativity, and (6) abilities in specific academic areas. The Terman-Stanford research tells us that persons who are mentally gifted experience other physical, educational, social, and economic advantages. /*p. 479*

How might we best define mental retardation?

Mental retardation is indicated by below-average intellectual functioning (usually IQ scores below 70), originating during the developmental period (within 18 years) and associated with impairment in adaptive behavior (as well as academic behaviors). /*p. 480*

List some of the possible causes of mental retardation.

In addition to genetic causes (as in Down's syndrome and Fragile X Syndrome), most known causes of mental retardation involve the health and care of the mother and fetus during pregnancy, wherein drugs, lack of oxygen, poor nutrition, and the like have been implicated in mental retardation. In other words, many causes of mental retardation appear to be preventable. /*p. 482*

chapter ten

MOTIVATION AND EMOTION

CHAPTER OUTLINE

TOPIC 10A ISSUES OF MOTIVATION
How Shall We Characterize Motivation?
    Instincts
    Needs and Drives
    Incentives
    Balance, or Equilibrium
Physiologically Based Drives
    Temperature Regulation
    Thirst and Drinking Behavior
    Hunger and Eating Behavior
Psychologically Based Motives
    Achievement Motivation
    Power Motivation
    Affiliation Motivation
TOPIC 10A SUMMARY

TOPIC 10B THE SEX DRIVE AND
HUMAN SEXUAL BEHAVIORS
The Sex Drive
The Biological Bases of Human Sexuality
    Genetic Bases
    Hormonal Bases
Homosexuality
Sexual Dysfunctions
    Sexual Dysfunctions in Males
    Sexual Dysfunctions in Females
TOPIC 10B SUMMARY

TOPIC 10C THE PSYCHOLOGY OF EMOTION
Defining and Classifying Human Emotions
    Defining Emotion
    Classifying Emotions
Physiological Aspects of Emotion
    The Role of the Autonomic Nervous System
    The Role of the Brain
Outward Expressions of Emotion
TOPIC 10C SUMMARY

CHAPTER SUMMARY

If you were like many children in kindergarten, one of the major goals in your life was to get out of kindergarten, so that you could go to elementary school with the "big kids." And, one day, off you went to grade school. Can you recall the excitement, the anticipation, the scary feeling of leaving home to go off to school? After a few years in grade school, another goal began to emerge: to get out of grade school and go to junior high. "In junior high they have different teachers, and athletic programs instead of recess." Upon entering junior high, you felt pleased with yourself: you had reached your goal. But soon, yet another goal became clear. You wanted to "get out of junior high school and go to senior high school with the big kids."

As you approached your final semester of senior high school, you may have experienced an ailment commonly called "senioritis." More than anything else, you wanted school to be over. You were motivated to get on with your life. You wanted to go to college.

Well, here you are, after all those years. You're in college taking a course in introductory psychology. If you're like many other students, a new goal may be forming: you want this term to be over. You want to get out of college so that you can get a job. The goals have changed, yet they have remained very much the same. You want to finish the task at hand so that you can move on to a new challenge.

There are two points about this scenario that will be relevant throughout this chapter. (1) The description of the events I've described here does not apply to everyone. It may not apply to you. Some people never had much of a desire to get out of junior high to get to high school. Many more have little desire or motivation to go on to college. For them, just getting out of high school was "good enough." Not all students entering college immediately start dreaming about graduation, although that goal is clear in the minds of many. The point is that different people, even in the same situation, may be motivated by different goals. This is particularly true when we consider people from varying cultures.

(2) A second point that this example makes about motivation is that it draws our attention to its *cyclical nature*. To be motivated is to be in a cycle. Soon after one goal is reached (getting out of grade school), another comes along to take its place (getting out of junior high), and then another, and another. Think of this motivational cycle in terms of something very simple, such as hunger and eating. If you are hungry, you are motivated to eat, but no matter how much you eat, you will be hungry again.

n this chapter, we'll address some important practical issues. For the first time, our focus is on questions that begin with why. "Why did she do that (as opposed to doing nothing)?" "Why did she do that (as opposed to doing something else)?" "Why does she keep doing that (as opposed to stop-ping)?" As you can see, the study of motivation gets us involved with attempts to explain the causes of one's behaviors.

We will get our discussion under way by considering some ways in which psychologists have approached the study of motivation. The theoretical approaches presented here are not always in conflict. They have much in common, and we will be able to find useful ideas within each approach. Having summarized a few approaches to motivation, the rest of Topic 10A will review two types of motivating forces: (1) those related to our survival, and rooted in our biology (physiological drives), and (2) those more clearly learned or social in nature (psychological motives).

Because sex and sexuality are so pervasive and so complex, I've chosen to deal with these matters in a separate Topic. In Topic 10B we will see how the "sex drive" in humans is different from the sex drive in nonhuman species. In this Topic we will also take time to consider sexual orientation and sexual dysfunctions. Sexually trans-mitted diseases are covered in Topic 11B.

The third Topic in this chapter deals with emotions and emotion-ality—issues very much related to motivation. Although most of us like to think of ourselves as rational, reasonable organisms, if we were totally honest with each other and with ourselves, we would admit that it is our emotions that concern us most. We enjoy reflect-ing on pleasant emotional experiences and we seek ways to minimize unpleasant ones. In Topic 10C we begin by discovering that objective-ly defining and classifying emotions has proven to be a very difficult task. We'll touch on two areas of research that have been promising: finding underlying physiological reactions that correspond to emo-tional states, and finding how emotions are reflected or expressed in behavior.

Topic 10A
ISSUES OF MOTIVATION

Motivation involves two subprocesses. First, motivation involves *arousal*—one's level of activation or excitement. Here we are using the term motivation as a force that initiates behaviors, that gets an organ-ism going, energized to *do* something and to keep doing it. The second subprocess provides *direction*, or focus, to one's behaviors. In addition to simply being aroused and active, a motivated organism's behavior is in some way goal-directed or purposeful. Thus, **motivation** is the process that arouses, directs, and maintains behavior.

motivation the process of arousing, maintaining, and directing behavior

HOW SHALL WE CHARACTERIZE MOTIVATION?

From its earliest days, psychology has tried to find some systematic theory that could summarize and organize what various motivational states have in common. Psychologists have struggled to describe one general pattern or scheme that could be used to account for *why* organisms tend to do what they do. In this section, we will review some of these theories in a somewhat chronological order. As you might anticipate, no one approach to motivation will satisfactorily answer all of our questions. Even though each of the approaches summarized below may have its drawbacks, we should focus our attention on how each contributes to our understanding of behavior and mental processes. Let me also draw your attention to Topic 15A, on industrial-organizational psychology, which also includes a section on various approaches to motivation, specifically those related to work motivation.

Instincts

In the early days of psychology, behaviors were often explained in terms of **instincts**—unlearned, complex patterns of behavior that occur in the presence of certain stimuli. They are inherited, or innate. Why do birds build nests? It's due to a nest-building instinct. When conditions are right, birds build nests. It's just part of being a bird. Why do salmon swim upstream to mate? Instinct. Swimming upstream at mating season is part of what it means to be a salmon. Yes, these behaviors can be modified by the organisms' experiences, but the force behind them is unlearned, or instinctive.

instincts unlearned, complex patterns of behavior that occur in the presence of certain stimuli

That may explain some of the behavior of birds and salmon, but what about people? William James (1890) reasoned that humans, being more complex, no doubt had many more instincts that did the

Why do salmon swim upstream at mating season? Why do birds, such as this osprey, build nests? We may "explain" these behaviors by referring to instincts, but such explanation has not proven to be useful.

"lower" animals. No one expressed the instinct explanation of human behaviors more forcefully than William McDougall (1908). He said that human behaviors were motivated by 11 basic instincts: repulsion, curiosity, flight, parenting, reproduction, gregariousness, acquisitiveness, construction, self-assertion, self-abasement, and pugnacity. Soon, McDougall extended his list to 18 instincts. As new behaviors required explanation, new instincts were devised to explain them.

As lists of human instincts got longer and longer, the basic problem with this approach became obvious. Particularly for humans, "explaining" behavior patterns by alluding to instinct only relabeled them but didn't explain anything at all. Even so, the psychologists who argued for instincts did introduce and draw attention to an idea very much with us today: we may engage in some behaviors for reasons that are basically physiological, and more inherited than learned.

Needs and Drives

One approach that provided an alternative to explaining behavior in terms of instincts was one that attempted to explain the whys of behavior in terms of needs and drives. We'll look at two theories that incorporate these concepts.

Clark Hull. Clark Hull's ideas about motivation were dominant in the 1940s and 1950s (e.g., Hull, 1943). In Hull's system, a **need** is a lack or shortage of some biological essential required for survival. A need arises from deprivation. When an organism is kept from food, it develops a need for food. A need then gives rise to a drive. A **drive** is a state of tension, arousal, or activation. If an organism is in a *drive state*, it is motivated. It is aroused and directed to engage in some behavior to satisfy the drive by reducing or eliminating the underlying need. The implication is that needs produce tensions the organism seeks to reduce; hence, this approach is referred to in terms of drive reduction.

This approach *is* less circular than a direct appeal to instincts. Instincts are tied to a specific pattern of behavior, but needs and drives are not. They are concepts that can be used to explain why we do what we do, while clearly allowing for the influence of experience and the environment. Doing without food gives rise to a need, which in turn gives rise to a drive, but expressing that drive in behavior is influenced by one's experiences and learning history.

One problem with a drive reduction approach is that it centers on the biological nature of needs. To claim that needs result only from biological deprivations seems unduly restrictive. It may be that not all of the drives that activate a person's behavior are based on biological needs. Humans often engage in behaviors to satisfy *learned* drives. Drives based on one's learning experiences are called *secondary drives,* as opposed to *primary drives,* which are based on unlearned, physiological needs. In fact, most of the drives that arouse and direct behavior have little to do with physiology.

need a lack or shortage of some biological essential resulting from deprivation

drive a state of tension resulting from a need that arouses and directs an organism's behavior

You may feel you need a new car this year. I may convince myself I need a new set of golf clubs, and we'll both work very hard to save the money to buy what we need. We may say we are "driven" to work for money, but it's difficult to imagine how your car or my golf clubs could be satisfying a biological need. A good bit of advertising is directed at trying to convince us we "need" many products and services that will have very little impact on our survival.

A related complication is that organisms continue to behave even after their biological needs are met. Think about it. Drives are states of arousal, activation, or tension. This position claims that we behave as we do in order to reduce or eliminate drives. That is, we act in order to reduce tension or arousal. Yet we know that sky divers jump out of airplanes, mountain climbers risk life and limb to scale sheer cliffs of stone, monkeys play with mechanical puzzles even when solving those puzzles leads to no other reward, and children explore the pots and pans in kitchen cabinets even when repeatedly told not to. These actions do not appear to be reducing tension, do they? We might suggest, as some psychologists have, that these organisms are trying to satisfy exploration drives, or manipulation drives, or curiosity drives. Then we run the risk of trying to explain why people behave as they do by generating longer and longer lists of drives—the same problem we have when we try to explain behavior in terms of instinct.

So, what do these complications mean? It seems that people often do behave in order to reduce drives and thereby satisfy needs. How drives are satisfied, or reduced, reflects the organism's learning history. The concept of drive reduction is a useful one and is still very

Some psychologists have argued that we all have exploration and curiosity needs—particularly in childhood.

much with us in psychology, but it cannot be accepted as a complete explanation for motivated behaviors.

Abraham Maslow. Abraham Maslow is one of the persons we associate with the humanistic movement in psychology. Humanistic psychologists emphasize the person and his or her psychological growth. Maslow combined his concern for the person with Hull's drive reduction theory and proposed that human behavior does, in fact, respond to needs. Not all of those needs are physiological. Maslow believed that the needs that motivate human action are limited in number and are arranged hierarchically. (Maslow, 1943, 1970). Figure 10.1 summarizes this hierarchy of needs.

Maslow's is basically a stage theory. It proposes that what motivates us first are *physiological needs.* At this stage are the basic needs related to survival; for example, the need for food, water, and shelter. Until these needs are met, there is little reason to suspect that an individual will be concerned with anything else. Once one's physiological needs are under control, a person is still motivated, now by *safety needs:* the need to feel secure, protected from dangers that might arise in the future. We are now motivated to see to it that the cupboard has food for later, that we won't freeze this winter, and that there's enough money saved to protect against sudden calamity. The hierarchical nature of Maslow's stages is clear already. We are not going to worry about what we'll be eating tomorrow if there's not enough to eat today; but if today's needs *are* taken care of, we can then focus on the future.

Once safety needs are met, concern shifts to *love and belongingness:* a need for someone else to care about us, to love us. If these needs are satisfied, our concern focuses on *esteem.* Our aim is to be recognized for our achievements, our efforts. In other words, once we have found that others value us for who we are, we focus on our need to be recognized for our accomplishments. These needs are not physiological, but social; they imply that our behaviors are motivated by our awareness of others and our concern for their approval. One moves higher in the hierarchy, on to higher stages, only if needs at

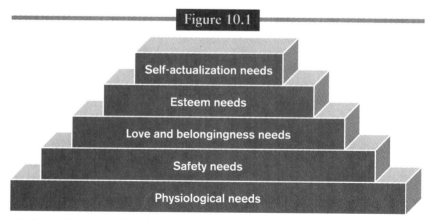

Figure 10.1

Maslow's hierarchy of needs.

lower stages are met. Ultimately, we may reach the highest stage in Maslow's hierarchy: *self-actualization needs*. We self-actualize when we become the best we can be, taking the fullest advantage of our potential as human beings. We are self-actualizing when we strive to be as creative or productive as possible.

In many ways, Maslow's arrangement of needs in a hierarchical fashion reflects many of the values of Western culture, particularly those that reflect the notion of the individual working hard to overcome obstacles and achieve. We can hardly expect people to be motivated to grow and to achieve "success" when they are concerned about their very survival on a day-to-day basis. When people's needs for safety, belonging, and esteem are reasonably fulfilled, they don't just die, unmotivated to do anything else. It should be clear to you, as it was to Maslow, that many people never make it to the self-actualization stage in the hierarchy of needs. There *are* millions of people in this world who have great difficulty dealing with the very lowest stages and who never have the time, energy, or opportunity to be concerned with such issues as self-esteem or belongingness, much less self-actualization.

As a comprehensive theory of human motivation, however, Maslow's hierarchy has some serious difficulties. Perhaps the biggest stumbling block is the idea that one can assign ranks to needs and put them in a neat order, regardless of what that order may be. It is clear that some persons are motivated in ways that violate the stage approach of this theory. Individuals will, for example, freely give up satisfying basic survival needs for the sake of "higher" principles (as in hunger strikes). For the sake of love, people may very well abandon their own needs for safety and security. The truth of the matter is, there is little empirical research support for Maslow's approach to ranking needs in a hierarchy. It remains the case, however, that because of its intuitive appeal, Maslow's approach to human motivation has found considerable favor both within and outside psychology.

Incentives

One alternative to a drive reduction approach to motivation focuses on the *end state*, or goal, of behavior, not needs or drives within the organism. According to this approach, external stimuli serve as motivating agents, or **incentives**, for behavior. Incentives are external events that act to *pull* our behavior from without, as opposed to drives, which are internal events that *push* our behavior from within.

incentives external stimuli an organism may be motivated to approach or avoid

When a mountain climber says she climbs a mountain "because it is there," the climber is indicating a type of motivation through incentive. After enjoying a large meal, we may order a piece of cherry cheesecake, not because we *need* it in any physiological sense, but because it's here on the dessert cart and *looks* so good (and because previous experience tells us that it is likely to taste very good).

Some parents want to know how to "motivate their child to clean up his or her room." We can interpret this case in terms of establishing goals or incentives. What those parents *really* want to know is how they can get their child to value, work for, and be reinforced by a clean room. What they want is a clean room, and they would like to have the child clean it. If they want the child to be motivated to clean his or her room, the child needs to learn the value or incentive of having a clean room. *How* to teach a child that a clean room is a thing to be valued is another story, probably involving other incentives the child does value. For now, let's just acknowledge that establishing a clean room as a valued goal is the major task at hand, and having a clean room is not an innate, inborn need.

If this discussion sounds like our discussion of operant conditioning (Topic 5B), you're right. Remember, the basic tenet of operant conditioning is that behaviors are controlled by their consequences. We tend to do (are motivated to do) what leads to reinforcement (positive incentives), and we tend *not* to do what leads to punishment or failure of reinforcement (negative incentives).

Before You Go On

**How have the concepts of instinct, drive,
and incentive been used to
explain motivated behaviors?**

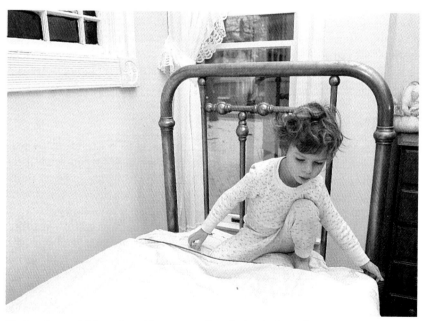

Motivating a child to clean his room and make his bed can be viewed as attempting to get the child to share some of the incentives of his parents.

Balance, or Equilibrium

A concept that has proven useful in understanding motivation is that of balance, or equilibrium. The basic idea is that we are motivated or driven to maintain a state of balance. What are we motivated to balance? Sometimes balance involves physiological processes that need to be kept at some level, or a restricted range, of activity. Sometimes equilibrium is required among our thoughts or cognitions. In this section, we'll review three of the approaches to motivation that emphasize maintaining a state of balance, equilibrium, or optimum level of functioning.

Homeostasis. One of the first references to a need to maintain a balanced state is found in the work of Walter Cannon (1932). Cannon was concerned with our internal physiological reactions, and the term he used to describe a state of balance or equilibrium within those reactions was **homeostasis**. The idea is that each of our physiological processes has a balanced, **set point** of operation. One's set point is a level of activity that can be considered "normal" or "most suitable." Whenever anything happens to upset this balance, we become motivated. We are driven to do whatever we can to return to our set point, our optimum, homeostatic level. If we drift slightly from our set point, our own physiological mechanisms act to return us to homeostasis without our intention or our awareness. If these automatic, involuntary processes are unsuccessful, we may have to take action, motivated by the drive to maintain homeostasis.

homeostasis a state of balance, or equilibrium, among internal, physiological conditions

set point a normal, optimal level (or value) of equilibrium, or balance, among physiological or psychological reactions

For example, everyone has a normal, set level of body temperature, blood pressure, basal metabolism (the rate at which energy is used by bodily functions), heart rate, and so on. When any of these are caused to deviate from their set point, homeostatic level, we become motivated to do something that will return to our state of balance. Cannon's concept of homeostasis was devised to explain physiological processes. As we shall soon see, however, the basic ideas of balance and optimum level of operation have been applied to psychological processes as well.

Arousal. **Arousal** is defined in terms of overall level of activation or excitement. A person's level of arousal may change from day to day and within the same day. After a good night's sleep and a brisk morning shower, your arousal level may be high. (It may also be high as your instructor moves through class handing out exams.) Late at night, after a busy day at school, your level of arousal may be quite low. Your arousal level is at its lowest when you are in the deepest stages of sleep.

arousal one's level of activation or excitement

Arousal theories of motivation (Berlyne, 1960, 1971; Duffy, 1962; Hebb, 1955) claim that there is an optimal level of arousal (an arousal set point) that organisms are motivated to maintain. Drive reduction approaches, remember, argue that we are motivated to reduce tension or arousal by satisfying the needs that give rise to drives. Arousal theories argue that sometimes we actually seek out arousing activities in order to maintain our optimal arousal level. If

For many of us, jumping off a high platform attached only by a bungee cord on our ankles would be overly arousing, to say the least. But for "sensation seekers," bungee jumping may provide optimum levels of arousal.

cognitive dissonance a motivating discomfort or tension caused by a lack of balance or consonance among one's cognitions

we find ourselves bored and in a rut, the idea of going to an action-adventure movie may seem like a good one. On the other hand, if we've had a very busy and hectic day, just staying at home doing nothing may sound appealing.

This approach is like Cannon's idea of homeostasis, but in more general terms than specific physiological processes. It suggests that for any situation there is a "best," or most efficient, level of arousal. To do well on an exam, for example, requires that a student have a certain level of overall arousal. If a student is tired, bored, or just doesn't care one way or the other about the exam, we can expect a poor performance. If, on the other hand, a student is *so* worried, nervous, and anxious that she or he can barely function, we'll also expect a poor exam score. The relationship between level of arousal and the efficiency of performance is depicted in Figure 10.2.

Arousal theory also takes into account the difficulty or complexity of the task or activity in which a person is engaged. For easy, simple tasks, a high level of arousal may be optimal, whereas that same high level of arousal would be disastrous for difficult, complex tasks (Brehm & Self, 1989). For example, students who were judged to be poorly, moderately, or highly motivated tried a series of difficult anagram problems (identifying a word whose letters have been scrambled). In fact, the most highly motivated subjects did significantly worse than did the moderately motivated subjects (Ford et al., 1985). The notion that optimum levels of arousal vary with the nature, or difficulty, of a task can be traced back to an article published in 1908 by Yerkes and Dodson, even though the concept of "arousal" did not appear in psychology until many decades later (Winton, 1987).

An interesting twist on the theory that we are motivated to maintain a set level of arousal is that for some unknown reason optimum levels of arousal vary widely from individual to individual. Some people seem to need and seek particularly high levels of arousal and excitement in their lives. They are what Marvin Zuckerman calls "sensation seekers" (Zuckerman et al., 1978, 1980). They enjoy sky-diving or mountain climbing and look forward to the challenge of driving in heavy city traffic.

Cognitive Dissonance. There is also a point of view that we are motivated to maintain a state of balance among our ideas or beliefs (our cognitions), as well as our physiological processes and levels of arousal. This approach claims that we are motivated to maintain what Leon Festinger (1957) calls a *state of consonance* among our cognitions.

Suppose you believe yourself to be a good student. You study very hard for an exam in biology. You think you're prepared. You judge the exam to be a fairly easy one. But when you get your exam paper back, you discover you failed the test! Now that's hard to accept. You believe you studied adequately. You believe the test wasn't difficult, but you also know you failed the test. Here are cognitions that do not fit together very well. They are not consonant; they are not balanced. You are experiencing what Festinger calls **cognitive dissonance**, a

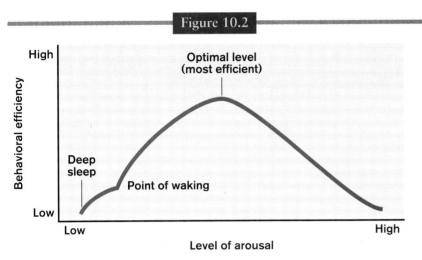

Figure 10.2

For each task we attempt, there is an optimal level of arousal. What that level is depends on several factors, including the dificulty of the task. In other words, it is possible to be too aroused (motivated), just as it is possible to be underaroused. (Hebb, 1955.)

state of tension or discomfort that exists when we hold inconsistent, dissonant cognitions. When this occurs, Festinger argues, we are motivated to bring about a change in our system of cognitions. In our example, you may come to believe you're not such a good student after all. Or you may come to believe your paper was unfairly graded. Or you may come to believe you are a poor judge of an exam's difficulty. This theory doesn't predict specifically *what* will happen, but it does predict that cognitive dissonance produces motivation to return to a balanced state of cognitive consonance.

These days, almost all smokers experience cognitive dissonance. They *know* that smoking is a very dangerous habit, and yet they continue to smoke. Some reduce their dissonance by coming to believe that although smoking is bad for one's health in general, it really isn't bad for them, at least not when compared to perceived "benefits." We'll return to Festinger and cognitive dissonance when we discuss attitude change (in Topic 14A).

Before You Go On

How can the concept of balance, or equilibrium, be used to help us understand motivated behaviors?

In what way is cognitive dissonance theory based on equilibrium?

PHYSIOLOGICALLY BASED DRIVES

Now that we have reviewed some theoretical approaches to the motives that activate and direct our behaviors, we can turn our attention to a few specific examples. As you can imagine, this discussion could be organized a number of ways. As I suggested earlier, we'll use a simple system that refers to just two major types of motivators: those that have a biological basis, which we'll call *physiologically based,* and those that are learned or social, which we'll call *psychologically based.*

There are two points for you to keep in mind as we go through this discussion. First, we will follow convention here and use the term *drive* when we're talking about those activators of behavior that have a known biological or physiological basis (e.g., hunger drive) and the term *motive* for those that do not (e.g., power motive). Second, remember that drives rooted in an organism's physiology are influenced by social and psychological factors. Also remember that we're going to treat the sex drive separately, in Topic 10B.

Temperature Regulation

Most of us seldom give our own body temperature much thought. We all have a fuzzy notion that 98.6°F is a normal, homeostatic body temperature. That one's body temperature has anything to do with motivation becomes sensible only in the context of homeostasis. Whenever anything happens to raise or lower our body temperature above or below its homeostatic, set point range, we become motivated. We become driven to return our body temperature to its normal, balanced 98.6°F. [In passing, recent research confirms the observation that body temperature normally fluctuates throughout the day, but suggests that 98.2° is a better estimate of "normal," average body temperature than is 98.6° (Mackowiak et al., 1992).]

Let's say you are outside on a bitterly cold day, and are improperly dressed for the low temperature and high wind. Soon your body temperature starts to drop, and automatically your body starts to respond to elevate your temperature back to its normal level: blood vessels in the hands and feet constrict, forcing blood back to the center of the body to conserve heat (as a result, your lips turn blue); you start to shiver (those involuntary movements of your muscles create small amounts of heat energy); and you get "goose bumps" as the skin thickens to insulate against the cold. These are exactly the sorts of automatic physiological reactions Cannon had in mind when he wrote about homeostasis.

As another example, imagine that you are fully dressed, and walking across a desert at noon on a hot day in August. Your temperature begins to rise. Automatically, blood is diverted to the body's surface, and your face becomes flushed. You perspire, and as the moisture on the surface of the skin evaporates, the skin is cooled, as is the

We are driven to maintain our body temperatures within rather strict limits.
When our autonomic nervous system cannot deal adequately with temperature
changes, we may be driven to do something that will raise or lower our body
temperatures.

blood now near the surface—all in an attempt to return your body's
temperature to its homeostatic level.

There are two centers in your brain that together act as a thermostat and start these attempts at temperature regulation. Both are
located in the **hypothalamus** deep inside the brain (Figure 10.3). One
center is particularly sensitive to elevated body temperatures, the
other to lowered temperatures. Together they act to mobilize the
internal environment when normal balance is upset.

If these automatic reactions are not successful, you may be driven
to take some voluntary action. You may have to get inside, out of the
cold or heat. You may need to turn on the furnace or the air conditioner. In fact, you may even *anticipate* the lowering or raising of your
body temperature and act accordingly—by putting on your coat
before going out on a blustery day, for example. Over and above
what your brain and body do automatically, you may have to engage
in learned behaviors in order to maintain homeostasis.

hypothalamus a small structure,
near the limbic system in the center
of the brain, associated with
temperature regulation, feeding,
drinking, and sex

Before You Go On

Given the concept of homeostasis, how might temperature
regulation be thought of as a physiologically based drive?

Thirst and Drinking Behavior

We need water for survival. If we don't drink, we die. As the need for
water increases, it gives rise to a thirst drive. The intriguing issue is
not so much that we need to drink, but how we *know* we're thirsty.
What actually causes us to seek liquid and drink it?

Figure 10.3

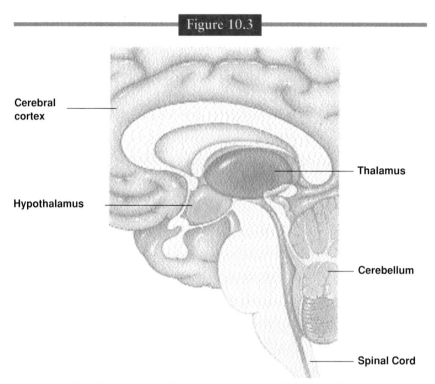

A section of the human brain, showing the location of the hypothalamus.

Internal, Physiological Cues. For a long time, we thought we drank to relieve the discomfort caused by the dryness of our mouths and throats. No doubt, the unpleasantness of a dry mouth and throat *can* cause us to drink, but there must be more to drinking behavior than this. Animals with no salivary glands, whose mouths and throats are constantly dry, drink no more than normal animals (they do drink more frequently but do not drink more in terms of quantity). Normal bodily processes (such as urination, exhaling, and perspiration) cause us to lose about 2 liters of water a day (Levinthal, 1983). That water needs to be replaced, but what motivates us to do so?

About two-thirds of the fluid in our bodies is contained *within* our body's cells (intracellular), and about one-third is held in the spaces *between* cells (extracellular). There seem to be two mechanisms sensitive to losses of fluid, one associated with each of these areas. Intracellular loss is monitored by centers in the hypothalamus. One small center acts to "turn on" the thirst drive when fluid levels are low, and another center "turns off" the thirst drive when fluid levels are adequate. Thirst that stems from extracellular loss is also monitored in the brain, through a complex chain of events, involving the kidneys, which stimulate the production of a hormone that leads to a thirst drive.

External, Psychological Cues. Our drinking behavior may be motivated by a physiological drive that arises from our physiological need for water. Sometimes, however, our drinking behavior may be influenced by external factors, or incentives. For example, the aroma of freshly brewed coffee may stimulate us to order a second (unneeded) cup. A frosty glass of iced tea may look too good to refuse. We may drink a cold beer or a soda simply because it tastes good, whether we *need* the fluid they contain or not.

Notice also that once motivated in terms of being aroused, *what* we drink will be strongly influenced by our previous learning experiences. Choices for what we drink are also shaped by availability. Even with as obvious a physiological drive as thirst, and as obvious a physiological need as our need for water, psychological factors can be very relevant.

Before You Go On

List some of the internal and external factors
that influence drinking behavior.

Hunger and Eating Behavior

Our need for food is as obvious as our need for water. If we don't eat, we die. Again, the interesting question is, what gives rise to the hunger drive? As it happens, many factors motivate a person to eat. Some are physiological. Some are more psychological and reflect learning experiences. Some involve social pressures.

Internal, Physiological Cues. People and animals with no stomachs still eat amounts of food not unlike those eaten by people with their stomachs intact. Cues from our stomachs, then, don't seem to be very important in producing a hunger drive. The two structures that seem most involved in the hunger drive are the hypothalamus (again) and the liver, which is involved in the production and breakdown of fat.

Theories of hunger that focus on the role of the hypothalamus are referred to as *dual-center* theories. This label is used because such views suggest that there are *two* regions in the hypothalamus that regulate food intake. One (the ventromedial hypothalamus) is an "eat" center that gives rise to feelings of hunger, while the other (the lateral hypothalamus) is a "no-eat" center that lets us know when we've had enough. Removing or lesioning the eat center (and leaving the no-eat center intact) in rats, for example, leads to starvation, whereas lesioning the no-eat center (leaving the eat center intact) leads to extreme overeating. Similarly, electrically stimulating the no-eat center will cause even a food-deprived rat to stop eating (Friedman & Stricker, 1976; Keesey & Powley, 1975).

Although the hypothalamus may be involved in hunger, normal eating patterns are not under the influence of electrical stimulation and brain lesioning procedures. What activates the brain's hunger-regulating centers in a normal organism? Here, we are at the level of hypothesis and conjecture, and there are several hypotheses to consider. One proposal is that the body responds to levels of blood sugar, or the amount of glucose in our blood that can be metabolized, or converted into energy, for the body's use. When glucose levels are low, which they are when we haven't eaten for a while, we are stimulated to eat. When glucose levels are adequate, we will stop eating. It may be that our *liver* most closely monitors such blood chemistry for us.

Another view holds that we respond, through a complex chain of events, not to levels of sugar but to levels of fat stored in our bodies. When fat stores are adequately filled, we feel no hunger. When fat supplies are depleted, a hunger drive arises. Once again, it is the *liver* that is involved in the cycle of storing and depleting fat supplies.

Yet another hypothesis that emphasizes the role of internal, physiological cues also relies heavily on the concept of set point, or homeostasis. The essence of this position is that a person's overall *body weight,* like blood pressure or temperature, is physiologically regulated (Nisbett, 1972). "Being so regulated, weight normally is maintained at a particular level or set-point, not only by the control of food intake, as is often assumed, but also by complementary adjustments in energy utilization and expenditure" (Keesey & Powley, 1986). An implication is that if body weight decreases significantly, through dieting or exercise, or both, the organism will be driven to return to the set point level. The result may be to abandon the diet, cut down on exercise, or both. Conversely, if one eats too much—more than is necessary to keep a homeostatic level of energy consumption and storage—one will be motivated to expend energy to return to set point levels. Still to be determined are the mechanisms involved in establishing one's set point body weight and energy utilization levels to begin with. There is evidence that these body weight set points are influenced by both genetic factors (Nisbett, 1972) and feeding behaviors during infancy (Knittle, 1975).

We are learning that there are powerful genetic forces at work that operate to determine one's body size and the distribution of fat within the body (Stunkard, 1988; Stunkard et al., 1986). One experiment (Bouchard et al., 1990) looked at the effects of overeating on 12 pairs of adult (ages 19 to 27) male identical twins. After eating normally for two weeks, the men were required to consume 1,000 excess calories of food each day for 6 days a week over a 100-day period. Weight gains between twin pairs varied considerably by the end of the study. But, significantly, there were virtually *no differences in weight gain within each pair of twins!* In addition, *where* the excess weight was stored in the body (e.g., the waist or hips) also varied between pairs, but not within twin pairs. The researchers concluded that "the most likely explanation for the intrapair similarity . . . is that genetic factors are involved" (p. 1477).

A related correlational study looked at the body weights of twins reared apart and reared together, which found that regardless of where or how the twins were reared, there was a significant relationship between genetic similarity and total body mass (Stunkard et al., 1990). Even early childhood environments had little or no effect. There is some concern that these data may be overinterpreted: "There is a risk that publishing this conclusion may lead the popular media to declare that what goes on in the home really makes no difference. That would be regrettable" (Sims, 1990). What these data suggest is that genetic factors are important in the ultimate determination of body weight and size and the distribution of fat within the body. They do not suggest that only genetic factors are involved. We probably receive many internal cues that simultaneously inform us of our physiological need for food, but as we all know, eating behavior can be influenced by factors over and above one's physiology (Friedman & Stricker, 1976).

External, Psychological Cues. We often respond to external cues that stimulate us to engage in eating behaviors. Sometimes, just the *stimulus properties* of foods—aroma, taste, and appearance—may be enough to get us to eat. You may not need or want any dessert after a large meal until the waitress shows you a piece of chocolate cake. Eating that cake has nothing to do with your internal physiological conditions. (This reminds us of the "incentive approach" to motivation described earlier.)

Sometimes people eat more from *habit* than from need (Schacter & Gross, 1968). "It's 12 o'clock. It's lunch time; so let's eat." We may fall into habits of eating at certain times, tied more to the clock than

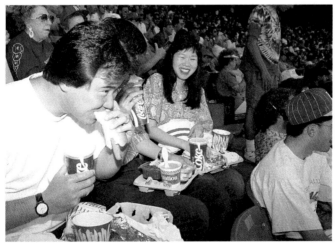

We eat for many reasons, not just simply in response to a physiological need for food. For some of us, sporting events are more enjoyable when accompanied by a hot dog and snack foods.

to internal cues from our bodies. Some people are virtually unable to watch television without poking food into their mouths, a behavioral pattern motivated more by learning than by physiology.

Occasionally, we find we eat simply because others around us are eating. Such "socially facilitated" eating has been noted in several species (e.g., Harlow, 1932; Tolman, 1969). If a caged chicken is allowed to eat its fill of grain, it eventually stops eating. When other hungry chickens are placed in the cage and begin to eat, the "full" chicken starts right in eating again. Its behaviors are not noticeably different from those of the chickens just added to the cage.

Overweight people may be less sensitive to internal hunger cues and more sensitive to external eating cues from the environment (Schacter, 1971), although there is research evidence that this logical analysis is not always true (Rodin, 1981). We also know that many people who are overweight tend to underestimate the amount of food (number of calories) they eat each day—even when they are in a controlled weight-loss program. They fail to lose weight because they really aren't dieting, even though they believe they are. They also tend to overestimate their level of exercise and physical activity (Lightman et al., 1992).

"Fully 95 percent of those starting a weight-loss program will return to their original weight within five years" (Martin et al., 1991, p. 528). For people who are overweight, it would be nice to know that there is some simple, foolproof way to lose weight. Given that there are so many factors that influence eating, such a hope is not likely to be fulfilled in the near future. No one physiological mechanism seems to have the sole control of our hunger drive (Thompson, 1980), and no one personality trait leads to obesity (Leon & Roth, 1977).

"Being hungry" and "eating" are clearly related in complex ways. Occasionally, a concern about becoming overweight can lead to seriously maladjusted behaviors, called eating disorders. It is to this issue we turn next.

Before You Go On

**List some of the internal and external factors
that influence eating.**

Eating Disorders. Eating well is something few of us do all the time. Some of us simply eat too much, and too much of the "wrong" foods—saturated fats in particular. In this section, we focus on two disorders of eating: anorexia nervosa and bulimia. Although these disorders are thought of as being independent, there are many cases in which an individual shows the symptoms of both at the same time.

Anorexia nervosa is characterized by an inability (or a refusal) to maintain one's body weight. It is essentially a condition of self-starvation, accompanied by a fear of becoming fat and a feeling that one is overweight despite the fact that the person is considerably *under-*

anorexia nervosa an eating disorder characterized by the reduction of body weight through self-starvation and/or increased activity

weight (less than 85 percent of normal weight) (APA, 1987; Yates, 1989). The person with anorexia nervosa maintains a reduced body weight by severely reducing food intake, by increasing levels of physical activity, or both. The disorder is surprisingly common, particularly among females. Nearly 1 percent of adolescent girls suffer from anorexia. The incidence of anorexia among college females is about 1 percent also (Edmands, 1993). Only about 10 to 15 percent of anorexic patients are males (Yates, 1990).

Bulimia is a disorder characterized by episodes of binge eating followed by purging—usually self-induced vomiting or the use of laxatives to rapidly rid the body of just-eaten food (APA, 1987; Yates, 1989). The binge eating episodes are often well planned, anticipated with a great deal of pleasure, and involve rapidly eating large amounts of high-calorie, sweet-tasting food. Like the anorexic patient, the person with bulimia shows great concern about weight. Unlike a person with anorexia nervosa, a bulimic patient is typically of normal to slightly below normal weight. Most bulimic patients are female, and usually from upper socioeconomic classes. Nearly 4 percent of female college freshmen suffer from the disorder, compared to only 0.4 percent of male freshmen. An estimated 15 percent of female medical students develop an eating disorder sometime in their lives (Yates, 1989).

What causes these eating disorders, and can anything be done to treat them effectively? Eating disorders have a number of interacting causes, and at present it is impossible to say which might be the most important. The high value that Western culture places on thinness is certainly one. We are constantly being bombarded with messages that communicate the same theme: "To be thin is good; to be fat is bad." Role models for many young girls include super-thin fashion models, dancers, and entertainers. More than 75 percent of adolescent girls desire to weigh less than they do (Yates, 1989). The cultural emphasis on feminine thinness likely contributes to the greater dissatisfaction among women than men with their weight and body shape (Rolls et al., 1991). In fact, one study found that women eat less when they are in the presence of a desirable male partner than when they are with a less desirable partner (Mori & Pliner, 1987).

When we look for specific behavioral or personality traits that might predict the development of an eating disorder, we find little. There is a tendency for adolescent girls with eating disorders to have rather strong needs for achievement and approval. Patients with eating disorders often show relatively high rates of depression, but such depression may be a response to an eating disorder rather than a cause (Garner et al., 1990).

Some psychologists have examined parenting and family style as contributors to eating disorders. Anorexia nervosa patients *do* tend to come from very rigid, rule-governed, overprotecting families. And bulimic patients often experienced inordinate blame and rejection in childhood (Bruch, 1980; Yates, 1990).

Obviously, researchers have considered physiological processes as causes of eating disorders. One significant line of scientific detective

bulimia an eating disorder characterized by recurrent episodes of binge eating and then purging to remove the just-eaten food

Many patients with eating disorders see themselves as overweight, even obese, when in fact their body weights are below normal.

work stems from the often-confirmed observation that bulimic patients do not "feel full" after they eat, even after they binge (Pyle et al., 1981; Walsh et al., 1989). This may be because the hormone *cholecystokinin* (CCK) is produced in very low levels in bulimic patients. This is significant because CCK is a hormone, normally produced in the small intestine, that signals that one is full and need eat no more. When drug treatment elevates CCK levels in bulimic patients, they often show fewer symptoms of the disorder.

Evidence on the treatment of eating disorders is sketchy and tentative, in part because we don't know what causes the disorders. The **prognosis**, or prediction of the course of a disorder, for anorexia nervosa is particularly poor. Nearly 50 percent of those who *are* released from treatment relapse within one year (Yates, 1990). About 5 percent of patients with anorexia actually die from excessive weight loss (Hsu, 1986). At first, treatment will be medical in response to nourishment needs. Hospitalization may be required. Virtually all forms of psychotherapy (see Topic 13B) have been tried, but with little consistent success, and no one form of therapy is significantly more effective than any other. The best predictor of the success of psychotherapy is the extent to which the family of the patient gets involved, which reinforces the notion that parental and family pressures may be part of the cause of eating disorders.

The outlook for bulimia is usually better. If nothing else, bulimic patients are seldom malnourished and do not require hospitalization for that reason. For persons with bulimia, the prognosis is better with family-oriented therapy than with individual treatment. Some success has also been reported for using a combination of behavioral and cognitive approaches to psychotherapy (e.g., Fairburn et al., 1993). With bulimic patients there has been some short-lived success with antidepressant medications (Geracioti & Liddle, 1988; Pope et al., 1985; Pope & Hudson, 1986), but when one looks at long-term success, the data are not as encouraging (Pyle et al., 1990; Walsh et al., 1991).

Anorexia nervosa and bulimia remind us how physiological processes and psychological processes can interact to produce complex patterns of behavior. Having seen how experience can impact on physiologically based drives, we can move on to consider motivators of human behavior for which there is no known physiological basis: the sources of motivation we're calling psychologically based.

prognosis the prediction of the future course of an illness or disorder

---

Before You Go On

Describe the symptoms of anorexia nervosa and bulimia.

What can we say about their causes and treatment?

PSYCHOLOGICALLY BASED MOTIVES

From time to time, you may be able to analyze your own behavior in terms of physiologically based needs and drives. That you had breakfast this morning soon after you got up might have reflected your response to a hunger drive. That you got dressed might have been your attempt to do what you could to control your body temperature, which also may have influenced your choice of clothes. Some sexual motivation (about which I'll have more to say in Topic 10B) might also have affected what you chose to wear today.

Many of our behaviors seem to be aroused and directed (motivated) by forces that are subtle and not clearly biological in origin. In this section, we'll review some of the motivators that reflect learned or social influences on our behaviors. We are going to refer to these psychologically based drives as *motives*. We'll review three that have generated considerable attention as mechanisms for "explaining" human behavior: achievement, power, and affiliation motivation.

Achievement Motivation

The hypothesis that people are motivated to varying degrees by a need to achieve was introduced to psychology in 1938 by Henry Murray. The **need to achieve (nAch)** is defined as the acquired need to meet or exceed some standard of excellence in one's behaviors. Measuring nAch and determining its sources and implications have been the major work of David McClelland and his associates (e.g., McClelland, 1985; McClelland et al., 1953).

Although there are short paper-and-pencil tests for the same purpose, nAch is usually assessed by means of the **Thematic Apperception Test (TAT)**. This is a *projective test* (see Topic 9A). People are asked to tell short stories about a series of rather ambiguous pictures depicting people in various settings (see Figure 10.4). Stories are then interpreted and scored according to a series of objective criteria that note references to attempting difficult tasks, succeeding, being rewarded for one's efforts, setting short- and long-term goals, and so on. Because there are no right or wrong responses to the TAT, judgments are made about the references to achievement a person "projects" into the picture.

One of the first things McClelland and his co-workers found was that there *were* consistent differences in measured levels of nAch. One of the most reliable findings concerning people with high needs for achievement involves the tasks they choose to attempt. When given a choice, they try to do tasks in which success is not guaranteed (otherwise, there is no challenge), but in which there still is a reasonable chance of success. Both young children (McClelland, 1958) and college students (Atkinson & Litwin, 1960) who were high in nAch were observed playing a ring-toss game, in which the object was to score points by tossing a small ring over a peg from a distance. The farther away from the peg one stood, the more points one could earn with success. High nAch subjects in both studies stood at a moderate dis-

Figure 10.4

The administration of the TAT. The subject is shown an ambiguous picture and asked such questions as, "What is going on here? What led up to this situation? What is likely to happen now?"

need to achieve (nAch) *the learned need to meet or exceed some standard of excellence in one's behaviors*

Thematic Apperception Test (TAT) *a projective personality test requiring a subject to tell a series of short stories about a set of ambiguous pictures*

tance from the peg. They didn't stand so close as to guarantee success, but they didn't choose to stand so far away that they would almost certainly fail. People with low nAch scores tended to go to either extreme—very close, earning few points for their successes, or so far away they rarely succeeded.

McClelland would argue that you are reading this text at this moment because you are motivated by a need to achieve. You want to do well on your next exam. You want to get a good grade in this course, and you have decided that to do so you need to study the assigned text material. Some students read assignments not because they are motivated by a need to achieve, but because they are motivated by a *fear of failure* (Atkinson & Feather, 1966). In such a case, the incentive is a negative one (avoid an F), which is a different matter than working toward a positive incentive (earn an A). Individuals motivated by a fear of failure tend to take very few risks. They either choose tasks they are bound to do well or tasks that are virtually impossible (if the task is impossible they don't have to blame themselves for their failures). There *are* explanations for why people choose tasks of the difficulty they do that do not rely on the notions of achievement or failure. One (e.g., Dweck, 1986) is that persons choose tasks of moderate difficulty when they are motivated to learn from their experience and improve themselves, whereas people choose easy tasks when they are motivated to "show off" and demonstrate superior performance.

In this regard, I should mention the concept of *fear of success*. This concept, introduced in 1969 by Martina Horner, was used to account for the motivation of many women who were said to back off from competition for fear of succeeding and thereby losing popularity and femininity. Although there may be some merit in the notion of a fear of success as an explanatory mechanism, it has not fared well in experimental tests (e.g., Jackaway & Teevan, 1976; Mednick, 1979). Upon close inspection, males are as likely to demonstrate a fear of success as are women.

It seems that the need to achieve is learned, usually in childhood. Children who show high levels of achievement motivation are generally those who have been encouraged in a positive way to excel ("Leslie, that grade of B is very good. You must be proud of yourself" as opposed to, "What! only a B?"). High-nAch children are generally encouraged to work things out for themselves, independently, perhaps with parental support and encouragement ("Here, Leslie, you see if you can do this" as opposed to "Here, dummy, let me do it; you'll never get it right!"). Further, McClelland is convinced that achievement motivation can be specifically taught and acquired by almost anyone, of any age, and he has developed training programs designed to increase achievement motivation levels (e.g., McClelland & Winter, 1969).

Before You Go On

What is achievement motivation, and how is it usually measured?

Power Motivation

Some people are motivated not only to excel, but to be in control, to be in charge both of the situation and of others. In such cases, we speak of a **need for power** (McClelland, 1982; Winter & Stewart, 1978). Power needs are measured the same way as achievement needs, through the interpretation of stories generated with the Thematic Apperception Test. Notice that a high need for power is, in itself, neither good nor bad. What matters is the end to which one uses one's power.

> ***need for power*** the learned need to be in control of events or persons

People with high power needs like to be admired. They prefer situations in which they can control the fate of others, usually by manipulating access to information. They present an attitude of "If you want to get this job done, you'll have to come to me to find out how to do it." People with low power needs tend to avoid situations in which others would have to depend on them, and tend to be somewhat submissive in interpersonal relationships. Even though the situation is changing slowly in Western cultures, men are more commonly to be found in positions of power than are women (Darley & Fazio, 1980; Falbo & Peplau, 1980; Mulac et al., 1985). At the same time, there are *no* reliable differences between men and women in measured *needs* for power (Winter, 1988).

Affiliation Motivation

Another psychologically based motivator that has been helpful in explaining the behaviors of some people is the **need for affiliation**. This motive involves a need to be with others, to work with others toward some end, and to form friendships and associations.

> ***need for affiliation*** the need to be with others and to form relationships

One interesting implication of having a high need for affiliation is that it is often at odds with a need for power. Logic suggests that if you are simultaneously motivated to be in control *and* to be with others in a truly supportive way, conflicts may arise. It is more difficult to exercise power over people whose friendship you value than it is to exercise power and control over people whose friendship is of little concern to you. It remains the case, however, that there *are* circumstances in which we find people who are high on both power and affiliation needs. These are often politicians who enjoy the exercise of power, but who also value being public figures and being surrounded by aides and advisors (e.g., Winter, 1987). Affiliation and achievement motives are also somewhat independent. Achievement and success can be earned either with others (high affiliation) or on one's own (low affiliation).

Although we might be quite confident that achievement and power motives are learned, and culturally determined, we are less confident about the sources of affiliation motivation. There is a reasonable argument that the need to affiliate and be with others is at

Many politicians would rate high on both a need for power and a need for affiliation.

least partly biologically based. We are social animals for whom complete social isolation is difficult, particularly when we are young (indeed, you might want to review our discussion of attachment and affiliation in Topic 8B). On the other hand, it seems clear that the extent to which we come to value affiliation relationships can be attributed to our learning experiences.

Some people are strongly influenced by a need for affiliation: to be with others, socializing, perhaps working together for common goals.

Before You Go On

Define the needs for power and affiliation.

TOPIC 10A SUMMARY

In this Topic, we have examined issues related to the psychology of motivation—attempts to explain what arouses, directs, and maintains an organism's behaviors or mental processes.

Psychologists have generated several concepts to explain why organisms do what they do: (1) *instinct* (some complex patterns of behavior are triggered in response to particular stimuli without the benefit of any learning or experience), (2) *need and drive* (an organism is aroused and directed by drives from within that are responses to biologically important (primary) needs or learned (secondary) needs, wherein a need is a real or perceived lack or shortage of something), (3) *incentives* (an organism is not pushed by internal states, but pulled by valued goals or events in the environment), (4) *homeostasis* (an organism is motivated to maintain a state of balance or equilibrium among internal, physiological conditions), (5) *arousal* (equilibrium is sought for one's overall level of activation, and there are individual differences in where that level is set; varied levels of arousal are most fitting for tasks of differing difficulty), and (6) *cognitive dissonance* (one is motivated to maintain consonance or balance among cognitive states), to name just a few. Each of these approaches has added to our understanding of motivation.

We examined in some detail temperature regulation, thirst, and hunger as examples of drives rooted in our physiology, yet still under the influence of learning and environmental pressures, taking time to explore two disorders of eating, anorexia nervosa and bulimia. Finally, we considered three psychological motives for which an underlying physiological basis is not yet identifiable. Now we move to sexuality, wherein we find an excellent example of biology and experience working together to motivate behaviors.

Topic 10B
THE SEX DRIVE AND HUMAN SEXUAL BEHAVIORS

Sex can be an important motivator for humans and nonhumans alike. What is remarkable is how sexual motivation varies, not only among individuals, but among species. Because of its importance, and because of its variability, we will consider sexuality in a separate Topic. We begin with a discussion of sex drives and then go on to consider a few aspects of human sexuality.

THE SEX DRIVE

As a physiologically based drive, the sex drive is unique in many ways. First, the survival of the individual does not depend on satisfying the sex drive. If we do not drink, we die; if we do not regulate our body temperatures, we die; if we do not eat, we die. If we don't have sex—well, we don't die. The survival of a species may require that an adequate number of its members successfully respond to a sex drive, but an individual member can get along without doing so.

Second, most physiologically based drives, including temperature regulation, thirst, and hunger, provide mechanisms that ultimately replenish or maintain the body's energy. When it is satisfied, the sex drive depletes bodily energy. In fact, the sex drive actually motivates the organism to seek tension, as opposed to most drives, which seek to reduce tension in order to return to homeostasis.

A third point about the sex drive that makes it different from other drives is that it is not present—at least in the usual sense—at birth, but requires maturation (puberty) before it is apparent. The other drives are present, and even most critical, early in life.

A fourth unique quality of the sex drive is the extent to which internal and external forces have differing degrees of impact on sexual behaviors, depending on the species involved. The importance of internal, physiological states is much greater in "lower" species than it is in humans. At the level of human sexual behaviors, sex hormones may be necessary, but they are seldom sufficient for the maintenance of sexual responding; and for the experienced human, they may not even be necessary.

For rats, matters of sex are simple and straightforward. If adequate supplies of testosterone (the male sex hormone) are present, and if there is the opportunity, a male rat will respond to its hormone-induced sex drive and will engage in sexual behaviors. If adequate supplies of estrogen and progesterone (female sex hormones) are present, and if the opportunity arises, the female rat will also engage in sexual behaviors. For rats, learning or experience have little to do with sexual behaviors—they are tied closely to physiology, to hormone level. There is little difference between the mating behaviors of sexually experienced rats, rats that have mated once or twice, and virgin rats. If the sex hormones of a female rat are removed (by removing the ovaries), there will be a total and immediate loss of sexual receptivity. If these sex hormones are replaced by injection, sexual behaviors quickly return to normal (Davidson et al., 1968). Removing the sex hormones from male rats produces a slightly different story. Sexual behaviors usually diminish and may disappear, but they take longer to do so. Injections of testosterone return the male rat to normal sexual functioning.

Removal of the sex hormones from dogs or cats ("higher" species than rats) also produces a reduction in sexual behaviors, but more gradually. An experienced male primate ("higher" still) may persist in sexual behaviors for the rest of his life, even after his sex hormones have been removed. (The same is also true of human males, but the data here are sketchy.)

So, what we find is that the sex drive in "lower" species is tied to a hormonal, physiological base. As the complexity of the organism increases, from rats to dogs, to primates, to humans, the role of internal cues becomes less certain.

No one would get far arguing that sex is not an important human motivator. However, it is easy to lose sight of the fact that it is a *physiologically* based drive. In societies such as ours, in which so much learning is involved, one could come to believe that sex drives are learned through experience and practice alone. Hormones may provide humans with an arousing force to do something, but *what* to do, *how* to do it, and *when* to do it seem to be shaped by society, religion, family, and personal experience. Sex manuals of a "how to" nature sell well, and sex therapy has become a standard practice for many psychologists trying to help people cope with pressures that external forces put on their "natural" sexual motivation.

In addition to the internal forces produced by the hormones, sex drives in humans can be aroused by a wide range of stimuli. Some people engage in sexual behaviors simply to reproduce; some do so for the physical pleasure they experience; others because they feel it demonstrates a romantic "love"; yet others want to display their sense of femininity or masculinity. Sex drives in humans are seldom satisfied with "just anybody." Social (external) constraints are often placed on one's choice of a sexual partner. Virtually any of the senses—touch, smell (particularly important in lower mammals and non-human primates), sight, and sound—can stimulate sexual arousal,

In so-called lower animals, engaging in sexual behaviors is biologically driven: There is little evidence of concern about the "quality" of one's "performance."

and there are considerable individual differences in terms of what will be effective. For example, it used to be thought that sexual arousal brought about by viewing sexual or erotic materials was much more common in men than in women (e.g., Kinsey et al., 1948, 1953). In fact, sexual arousal brought about in this way is just as common in women as in men, although women are less likely to report verbally (admit to) being sexually aroused by looking at erotic stimuli (Kelley, 1985).

Before You Go On

**In what ways is the sex drive a unique,
physiologically based drive?**

THE BIOLOGICAL BASES OF HUMAN SEXUALITY

Whether we are biologically male or female depends on the interaction of a number of factors. Among the most important are genetic and hormonal processes. For the most part, our sex is inherited, but hormones influence the expression of our genetically determined sexuality, and some of the most important hormonal influences occur well before we're born. Let's start with genetics.

Genetic Bases

When a male's sperm cell unites with a female's ovum to form a single-celled zygote, the sex of the offspring has been established. That newly formed cell holds in its nucleus 23 pairs of chromosomes. Just one of those pairs, usually counted as the twenty-third pair, will determine the sex of the person-to-be.

X and Y chromosomes the chromosomes that determine one's genetic sex; XX for females, XY for males

The chromosomes that determine one's sex are the **X** and **Y chromosomes**. Being genetically female results from receiving an X chromosome from each parent, forming an XX pair. Being male is determined by having one X chromosome and one Y chromosome, or an XY pair.

Think about that for a minute. Cells in a female's body have, in their nuclei, a pair of X chromosomes. That means that a female's sex cells (ova) must contain one X chromosome, in that a female has no Y chromosomes. Cells in a male's body, on the other hand, contain both X and Y chromosomes; so, half a male's sex cells (sperm) contain X chromosomes, and half contain Y chromosomes. Because the female always contributes an X chromosome, and because the male contributes either an X or a Y, we can say that, genetically, the sex of a child is determined by the father—or at least by the father's chromosomes. As it happens, this observation has, as yet, no practical application.

So, the first step to becoming a male is to inherit an XY chromosome pair, and the first step to becoming a female is to inherit an XX chromosome combination, but the story does not end here. Still at the level of our biological sexuality, we must next consider the role of hormones in the shaping of one's sex.

Before You Go On

How is one's sex genetically determined?

Hormonal Bases

In biological terms, human sexuality may be determined primarily by the chromosomes inherited at conception, but the expression of that sexuality requires the action of sex hormones. In fact, for about six or seven weeks after conception, there is *no differentiation* between male and female. That is, the only way to determine if the zygote is male or female is to examine the sex chromosomes, looking for the XX female pairing or the XY male pairing. At about 7 weeks, physical differentiation of the **gonads**, or sex glands, begins. Which sex glands develop is controlled by the presence of the Y chromosome. When the Y chromosome is present, the **testes**, or male sex glands, develop. When the Y chromosome is not present, the **ovaries**, or female sex glands, develop (Bernstein, 1981; Money, 1987).

Once the sex glands begin to develop, they do what they are designed to do: secrete their own variety of sex hormone. In fact, both the ovaries and the testes produce and secrete several hormones. The most important hormones produced by the testes are the **androgens**, and the most important of these is **testosterone**. The most important hormones produced by the ovaries are the **estrogens** (there are more than one) and **progesterone**. Most simply put, androgens direct the development of male reproductive organs: the penis, testes, and scrotum. Estrogens direct the development of female reproductive organs: the vagina, uterus, and ovaries. That, however, is put most simply, and the issue is far from simple.

One complication is that both male and female sex hormones are produced by both male and female sex glands. Yes, that's right; even male testes produce female estrogens, and female ovaries produce male androgens. The critical difference, of course, is the *relative amount* produced. It turns out that the development of the genitals is mostly controlled by the androgens in this way: if sufficient androgen levels are reached, the genitals will be those of a male; if there are insufficient androgen levels, the genitals will be those of a female. And remember, all of this differentiation of genitals goes on prenatally—before birth. One way to say this is to say that we are all basically female until the addition of androgens produces male development in some of us. As you might imagine, occasionally there are "errors."

gonads *the sex glands: **testes** in males, **ovaries** in females*

androgens *the male sex hormones produced by the testes*

testosterone *the most important of the male androgens, or sex hormones*

estrogens *the female sex hormones produced by the ovaries*

progesterone *one of the most important of the female estrogens, or sex hormones*

Individuals who are genetically female (XX chromosome pair) and are exposed to well-above-average amounts of male androgens may show physical signs of the external genitals of a male (perhaps a small penis and/or scrotum), as well as those of a female.

Another complication is that sex hormones are produced not only in the sex glands, but in the adrenal glands. Furthermore, the release of sex hormones is monitored and controlled by complex interactions of the pituitary gland and the hypothalamus.

Once the sex glands and their hormones have set the course of development, sex hormone production stabilizes at rather low levels through infancy and childhood. Then, in a surge of hormonal activity, the hypothalamus, adrenal glands, and gonads—all working together—bring about that developmental period we call *puberty.* We have defined puberty as the stage of development during which one becomes capable of sexual reproduction, and in Topic 8C we examined some of the psychological "fallout" of this stage of development. Puberty marks a reawakening of the hormonal basis of sexuality.

Before You Go On

Summarize the role of hormones in the determination of one's sex.

HOMOSEXUALITY

homosexuals persons who are sexually attracted to and aroused by members of their own sex

Homosexuals are individuals sexually attracted to and sexually aroused by members of their own sex, as opposed to heterosexuals, who seek outlets for their sexual drives among members of the opposite sex. Psychologists argue that homosexuality should be referred to as an orientation, *not* as a sexual preference (Committee on Lesbian and Gay Concerns, 1991). "*Sexual preference* is a moral and political term. Conceptually it implies voluntary choice. . . . The concept of voluntary choice is as much in error here as in its application to handedness or to native language. You do not choose your native language, even though you are born without it" (Money, 1987, p. 385).

Psychologists agree that homosexuality and heterosexuality are not mutually exclusive categories, but endpoints of a dimension of sexual orientations, and that many combinations are possible. Alfred Kinsey and his colleagues (1948, 1953) first brought the prevalence of homosexuality to the attention of the general public. Kinsey devised a seven-point scale (0 to 6) of sexual orientation, with those who are exclusively heterosexual at one end and persons who are exclusively homosexual at the other extreme (see Figure 10.5). Kinsey found that about half the males who responded to his surveys fell somewhere *between* these two endpoints. Even though homosexuality is now more openly discussed than it was in the 1940s and 1950s (more "out of the closet"), it is still difficult to get accurate estimates of the num-

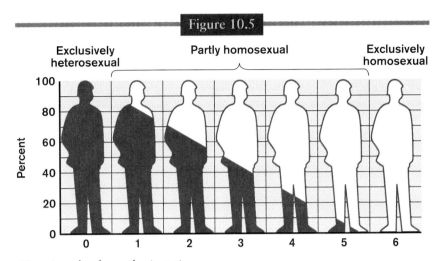

Kinsey's scale of sexual orientation.

bers of persons who are exclusively or predominantly homosexual. Conservative estimates suggest that about 1 percent of North American males are exclusively homosexual in their sexual orientation and that 8 to 10 percent have had more than an occasional homosexual encounter (e.g., Billy et al., 1993). Comparable figures indicate that lesbian sexual orientation is approximately half as prevalent as gay male sexual orientation.

In most ways, there is little difference between persons with homosexual and heterosexual orientations. Most homosexuals have experienced heterosexual sex. They simply find same-sex relationships more satisfying. In fact, homosexual couples are often more at ease and comfortable with their sexual relationship than most heterosexual couples (Masters & Johnson, 1979). Contrary to popular opinion, most gay males and lesbians are indistinguishable from persons with heterosexual orientations in their appearance and mannerisms.

As yet, we have no generally accepted theory of the causes of homosexuality. What we do know is that the matter is not simple, and probably involves an interaction of genetic, hormonal, and environmental factors (Money, 1987). For example, there is now ample evidence that homosexuality tends to "run in families" (Bailey & Pillard, 1991; Diamond & Karlen, 1980; Pool, 1993). In 1993, a team of researchers claimed they had located a segment of the X chromosome that seems certain to be the site for genes that influence the development of homosexual orientation (Hamer et al., 1993). This is only the beginning, and has not yet been confirmed. There are several hundred genes in that particular region, most of them unidentified, but "once a specific gene has been identified, we can find out where and when it is expressed and how it ultimately contributes to the development of both homosexual and heterosexual orientation" (Hamer et al., 1993, p. 326).

Although homosexuals are now able to be more open about their sexual orientation, homosexuality is still a controversial issue. This is a photo of the wedding announcement of a lesbian couple.

There is scant evidence of any significant differences in the hormone levels of heterosexuals and homosexuals at adulthood. Providing gay males and lesbians with extra amounts of sex hormones may increase overall sex drive and the incidence of sexual behaviors, but it seems to have virtually no effect on sexual orientation. One hypothesis with research support suggests that *prenatal* hormonal imbalances may affect one's sexual orientation in adulthood (Money, 1987). This hypothesis claims that embryos (genetically male or female) exposed to above-average concentrations of female hormones will develop into adults attracted to persons having masculine characteristics, and vice versa (Ellis & Ames, 1987).

In 1991, Dr. Simon LeVay of the Salk Institute in San Diego published an article on his research that became headline news (LeVay, 1991). LeVay performed a postmortem examination of the brains of 19 gay males, 16 males with heterosexual orientation, and 6 women with heterosexual orientation. He found a small area in the hypothalamus that was significantly smaller in the gay men. In gay men, this area was precisely the same size as he found in the hypothalamus of women. Here was evidence of a physical, biological correlate of homosexual orientation. Note that LeVay has not claimed he located the *cause* of homosexual orientation. His observations lead us only to an association or a correlation, from which a cause-and-effect conclusion would be unwarranted. But as one brain scientist (Dennis Landis of Case Western Reserve University) said of LeVay's work, "It would begin to suggest why male homosexuality is present in most human populations, despite cultural constraints. It suggests it's a biological phenomenon" (Barinaga, 1991).

Even as biological evidence accumulates, psychologists remain unwilling to totally abandon hypotheses that emphasize environmental influences. One thing, however, is clear: sexual orientation cannot be attributed to any one early childhood experience. Although we are not yet able to discount them totally, environmental, experiential causes of sexual orientation are mostly of theoretical interest, with little research evidence to support them. One major problem with much of our current data on the early experiences of homosexuals is that it most often comes from persons who are in therapy and are distressed with their sexual orientation. We have considerably less data about homosexuals who are comfortable with their sexuality (the majority). A reasonable position at the moment is to hypothesize that genetic and hormonal predispositions interact with environmental influences in complex ways to form one's adult sexual orientation.

Before You Go On

What is homosexuality?

What causes homosexuality?

SEXUAL DYSFUNCTIONS

Sexual drives and behaviors, which seem so natural and virtually automatic in lower species, are often the source of considerable distress for humans. **Sexual dysfunction** is the name given to any chronic (long-term) problem, disturbance, or inadequacy of sexual functioning.

Sexual dysfunctions are much more common than most people believe. As you can imagine, it is difficult to determine the number of persons who experience sexual dysfunctions. Part of the problem is the commonly held belief that everyone else's sex life is perfect, and that other couples engage in sexual activities almost constantly. People generally don't like to talk about their sex life if they think they are having problems. Physicians and therapists who ask their patients about sexual problems report many more cases than do those who wait for patients to volunteer such information (Pauly & Goldstein, 1970). Most experts agree that about 50 percent of all married couples experience some sexual dysfunction (Hyde, 1994; Masters & Johnson, 1970; McCarthy et al., 1975). That's a lot of people, and when you add in those persons with sexual problems who happen not to be married, the number is even more impressive. Once someone openly admits to having sexual problems, treatment is usually successful (Zilbergeld & Evans, 1980). Masters and Johnson (1970, 1979) claim a sex therapy failure for fewer than 20 percent of their patients. In this section, we'll review six of the most commonly reported sexual dysfunctions, three that occur in males and three that occur in females.

sexual dysfunction any of a number of chronic difficulties or problems with sexual functioning

Sexual Dysfunctions in Males

Erectile dysfunction is the inability to attain or maintain an erection long enough to experience intercourse. It is the preferred term for what many still refer to as "impotence." Impotence literally means "without power," and power is not what sex or sexual dysfunctions are all about.

This is the most commonly reported dysfunction among men seeking treatment. The dysfunction can be found in men of any age (Kaplan, 1974, 1975). By far, most cases of this dysfunction are classified as secondary, implying that there has been success at achieving an erection in the past (Masters & Johnson, 1970). Psychological reactions to erectile dysfunction can be severe. Self-esteem is often involved. Embarrassment, depression, fear of future failures, and guilt often accompany erectile dysfunction. Unfortunately, when left untreated, these reactions almost ensure that achieving an erection will be less likely in the future.

There are many possible causes of erectile dysfunction. Failure to attain or maintain an erection may be associated with short-term physical problems such as fatigue, having too much alcohol, being in a strange situation, or stress, but an occasional, isolated episode or two does not constitute a dysfunction. There *are* physical causes of erectile dysfunction, including underlying disorders or diseases such as heart disease or diabetes, injury to the spinal cord, infection in the testes or prostate, and some prescribed medications (Richardson, 1991). On the other hand, at least half of cases of erectile dysfunction seen by therapists have psychological causes, usually involving such factors as fear of failure, anxiety over the quality of one's "performance," guilt about having sex, or lack of adequate communication with one's partner.

The other two major dysfunctions of male sexual responsiveness involve the timing of ejaculation during vaginal intercourse (or coitus). *Premature ejaculation* is difficult to define. The implication, of course, is that the male ejaculates too soon. But what determines what is too soon? The most generally accepted definitions have to do with the male's voluntary control over ejaculation, rather than with time *per se* (Kaplan, 1974). In most cases, premature ejaculation is self-defined by the person (or his partner) as a condition in which ejaculation chronically occurs too early to provide satisfaction. As is the case with erectile dysfunction, premature ejaculation can result in considerable psychological distress.

A related but much less common ejaculatory problem is *retarded ejaculation*. Here the male has difficulty ejaculating at all during coitus, although he may have little difficulty doing so while masturbating or when he is with a new sex partner. When this dysfunction does occur, we tend to find frustration and anxiety on the part of the male, and a sense of rejection in his partner. As with all the sexual dysfunctions, retarded ejaculation occurs to varying degrees, with partial failure to ejaculate more common than total ejaculation failure.

Occasionally, sexual dysfunctions in men that involve the timing or adequacy of ejaculation have physical causes (such as infections or neurological problems), but almost all cases are caused by psychological factors (Hyde, 1994; Kaplan, 1974; Masters, Johnson, & Kolodny, 1992). The main issues, again, involve fear and anxiety over one's performance, and a lack of intimate communication with one's partner. Ejaculation control problems often lead to erectile dysfunctions. The male, concerned about his performance, starts to think about distracting, nonsexual issues, starts to evaluate his own performance, starts to worry about when he might ejaculate, and all in the midst of sexual intercourse. In such a case, he has taken on what Masters and Johnson call a *spectator role,* and has become more concerned about his own performance than with the needs and desires of his partner (Masters & Johnson, 1979; Masters et al., 1992).

Sexual Dysfunctions in Females

Female sexual unresponsiveness is the term that psychiatrist Helen Kaplan uses to describe what used to be referred to as "frigidity" (Kaplan, 1974, 1975). Frigidity is no longer an acceptable term for the same reason that "impotence" is no longer used: they are outdated terms that have judgmental implications. In severe forms of female sexual unresponsiveness, an actual fear or loathing of sexual activities may develop. This dysfunction is usually self-diagnosed, because what may be "acceptably responsive," or pleasurable, clearly varies from person to person. What matters is the extent to which a woman and her partner feel satisfied with the woman's ability to be sexually aroused. The causes of female sexual unresponsiveness are almost always psychological, involving feelings of shame and guilt, accompanied by a belief that sex is somehow "dirty." The dysfunction can lead to related problems, such as a lack of self-esteem and depression.

Orgasmic dysfunction is the inability to experience an orgasm. Again, this is a matter of degree; in many cases there may have been an occasional orgasm, perhaps not as forceful or timely as desired. This sexual dysfunction is the one most often mentioned by women seeking therapy for sexual problems (Wincze & Carey, 1992). Part of the problem may be the mystique that has been associated with orgasm through coitus. Many women who experience orgasm through masturbation, for example, and seldom experience orgasm through intercourse, come to believe that they are sexually inadequate, or a disappointment to their partners. Sex partners may experience guilt if orgasm is not reached. Although most women (nearly 90 percent) *can* and *do* experience orgasm, fewer than half do so with only the stimulation from vaginal intercourse (Kaplan, 1974; Masters & Johnson, 1970; Wilcox & Hager, 1980).

As with sexual dysfunctions in men, conditions such as orgasmic dysfunction in women may have a physical and/or biological basis. Orgasmic problems may be related to illness, alcohol consumption, or extreme fatigue. Most cases, however, can be traced to many of the same psychological factors that disrupt the sexual functioning of males: anxiety, fear of failure, becoming a "spectator," and—most commonly—poor communication with one's partner. Sex therapists have noted that women are even more reluctant than men to share with their partners the sorts of behaviors, touches, actions, and so on that would bring them pleasure, or orgasm, during sexual intercourse.

Vaginismus is the powerful, spasmodic, and occasionally painful contraction of the muscles surrounding the opening to the vagina. In some cases, the contractions are severe enough to prohibit the penis from entering the vagina. This is a relatively rare dysfunction, accounting for fewer than 10 percent of the cases treated by Masters and Johnson. Hypotheses about why women develop vaginismus usually refer to a reflexlike reaction of the woman against pain—either the anticipated pain of coitus not yet achieved or pain experienced in the past.

There are other difficulties associated with sexual behaviors, to be sure. This list includes only those most commonly encountered by sex therapists. Many adults will suffer the distress caused by one or more of these dysfunctions during their sexually active years. Although most sexual dysfunctions are amenable to treatment and therapy, there are steps that can be taken to help prevent these dysfunctions in the first place. Let me list a few. (1) Communicate, communicate, communicate. Try to make sure, using whatever means you can, that your partner understands those things that "turn you on," and those things you do not like, or find painful. What does your partner like and dislike? Communication also means saying "no" when that is how you feel. Trust in your partner and in yourself. (2) Don't believe everything you hear and read about the sexual exploits of others. Your aim should be to find pleasure with your sexual partner, not surpass some imagined "goal." (3) Avoid playing the "spectator." Don't spend your time and energy assessing how well you're doing, worrying about exactly what you're supposed to do next. Don't evaluate; enjoy. (4) Choose the times and situations for engaging in sex with some care. Try to avoid times when you will rushed, or when you are likely to be interrupted. (5) Be ready to seek and accept help if engaging in sexual behaviors becomes difficult, a chore, or a bore.

Before You Go On

Briefly describe some common sexual dysfunctions, and comment on their causes.

TOPIC 10B SUMMARY

In this Topic we have explored a few issues related to human sexuality. We began by noting how the sex drive in humans is significantly less physiological in its basis than is the sex drive in so-called "lower" organisms. In humans, there may be a biological-physiological basis to sexual motivation, but one's actual sexual behaviors seem greatly influenced by learning and sociocultural pressures.

To a degree, whether one is male or female depends on genetic factors (females inherit two X chromosomes, males inherit one X and one Y chromosome). The physical manifestation of one's sexuality can be determined at least in part by the subtle actions of hormones as they impact on development before birth. We saw a case of the interaction of genetic and hormonal influences when we discussed the matter of homosexual and heterosexual orientations. Evidence seems to be taking us in the direction of concluding that one's sexual orientation is more a matter of genes and hormones than any psychological experiences.

On the other hand, when we looked at sexual dysfunctions—problems or inadequacies in mature sexual functioning—we found that although physical causes are quite possible, experience, social pressures, and learning are often at the root of such problems.

T o p i c   1 0 C

THE PSYCHOLOGY OF EMOTION

Since its emergence in the late 1800s, psychology has included emotion as part of its subject matter. Psychologists have learned a great deal about emotional reactions, but answers to some critical questions have remained elusive. We wish that psychologists could tell us just what emotions are and where they come from. We want to know how to increase the pleasant emotions and decrease our experience of the unpleasant ones. Some emotional reactions *seem* quite unpleasant: fear, shame, jealousy, rage, and so on. Just the same, we would not want to give up our ability to experience emotions. To do so would be to surrender the likes of love, joy, satisfaction, and ecstasy.

We'll begin this Topic as we have begun many others—trying to generate an acceptable, working definition of "emotion." You ought to give that a try yourself before you go on. How would you define emotion?

The psychology of emotion is rich in a tradition of theories, most of which are attempts to delineate the various aspects of an emotional reaction and describe those emotional reactions that can be considered basic or primary. We'll take a brief look at a few of these attempts to describe primary human emotions. We'll end the Topic with two areas of research that have proven fruitful: the underlying physiological aspects of emotion and how inner emotional states are expressed in behavior.

DEFINING AND CLASSIFYING HUMAN EMOTIONS

In this section, we'll consider two interrelated issues: defining emotion and classifying primary emotions. The goal for this section is simple: to describe human emotions as best we can.

Defining Emotion

Try to recall the last time you experienced an emotion of some significance—perhaps the fear of going to the dentist, the joy of receiving an A on a classroom exam, the sadness at the death of a friend, or the anger at being unable to register for a class you really wanted to take. You may be able to identify as many as four components to your emotional reaction. (1) You experience a *subjective feeling*, or *affect*, which you may label fear, joy, sadness, anger, or the like. (2) You have a *cognitive* reaction; you recognize, or "know," what happened to you. (3) You have an internal, *physiological* reaction, which is largely visceral, involving glands, hormones, and internal organs. (4) You engage in an overt, observable, *behavioral* reaction. You tremble as you approach the dentist's office. You run down the hallway, a broad smile on your face, waving your exam paper over your head. You cry at the news of your friend's death. You shake your fist and yell at the registrar when you find you cannot enroll in the class of your choice.

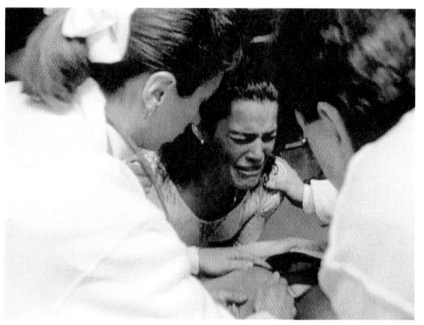

Emotions give flavor and coloring to our lives. Above, Nancy Kerrigan shows the anguish following her injury in an assault as she prepared for the 1994 winter Olympics and, at right, the joy of victory.

emotion *an experience that includes a subjective feeling, a cognitive interpretation, a physical reaction, and a behavioral expression*

Note that when we add an overt, behavioral component to emotions, we can most clearly see how emotions and motivation are related. Emotions are often viewed as motivational (Greenberg & Safran, 1989; Lang, 1985; Lazarus, 1991a, 1991b, 1993). As we saw in Topic 10A, to be motivated is to be aroused and directed to action. Emotional experiences also arouse and direct our behavior. Theorist Richard Lazarus put it this way: "Without some version of a motivational principle, emotion makes little sense, inasmuch as what is important or unimportant to us determines what we define as harmful or beneficial, hence emotional" (1991a, p. 352).

There has been considerable debate in psychology concerning how best to define emotion. As one researcher puts it, "There is no consensus about the definition of emotion; one may quarrel endlessly about the word" (Frijda, 1988). The issues have been (1) what are the basic components of an emotional reaction, and (2) in what way or ways are those components related? Answers to these questions have given rise to various classification schemes, which we'll review next. For now, we need a working definition of emotion. We will say that an **emotion** is an experience that includes a subjective feeling, a cognitive interpretation, a physiological reaction, and a behavioral expression.

Before You Go On

What are the four components that taken together define an emotional experience?

Classifying Emotions

Although cognitions, physiology, and overt behavior are involved in an emotional reaction, there seems to be little doubt that a very important aspect is the subjective-feeling component. Perhaps it would help if we had a scheme or plan that described and classified various emotional reactions or feelings in a systematic way.

In fact, there are several ways to classify emotional responses, and each has its own supporters. Wilhelm Wundt, in that first psychology laboratory in Leipzig, was concerned with emotional reactions. He believed emotions could be described in terms of three intersecting dimensions: pleasantness-unpleasantness, relaxation-tension, and calm-excitement.

Carroll Izard (1972, 1977) has proposed a classification scheme that calls for nine primary emotions. From these, he claims, all others can be constructed. Izard's nine primary emotions are fear, anger, shame, contempt, disgust, distress, interest, surprise, and joy. (Isn't it sad that six of the nine are negative emotions? Only the last three are neutral or pleasant.) Izard calls these nine emotions primary because they cannot be dissected into simpler, more basic emotions and because each is thought to have its own underlying physiological basis. Other emotions are some combination of any two or more of these nine.

Robert Plutchik (1980a) argues for eight basic emotions. What makes these emotions primary, Plutchik claims, is that each can be directly tied to some adaptive pattern of behavior; they are emotions that can be related to survival. Plutchik's eight primary emotions, and their adaptive significance, are listed in Figure 10.6. Plutchik believes that emotions in addition to these eight are variants of the primary emotions. While rage, for example, may be an extreme emotion, it is viewed as being essentially the same as anger. Anger in a weaker form is annoyance (Plutchik, 1980b).

Figure 10.7 is referred to as Plutchik's emotion solid. It shows the basic eight emotions around the top row of the solid, extreme versions of the same emotion on the top surface, and weaker versions of the same experience below them. Note also that emotions opposite each other on the solid represent opposite feelings; that is, ecstasy is taken to be the opposite of grief in this view. The smaller diameter toward the bottom of the solid is meant to represent the fact that as emotions become less intense, it is more difficult to tell them apart.

Figure 10.6

Plutchik's Eight Primary Emotions and How They Relate to Adaptive Behaviors

Emotion or feeling	Common stimulus	Typical behavior
1. Anger	Blocking of goal-directed behavior	Destruction of obstacle
2. Fear	A threat or danger	Protection
3. Sadness	Loss of something valued	Search for help and comfort
4. Disgust	Something gruesome or loathsome	Rejection; pushing away
5. Surprise	A sudden, novel stimulus	Orientation; turning toward
6. Curiosity	A new place or environment	Explore and search
7. Acceptance	A member of own group; something of value	Sharing; taking in; incorporating
8. Joy	Potential mate	Reproduction; courting; mating

Richard Lazarus (1991a, 1991b, 1993) is in the process of proposing a new theory of emotion that stresses the motivational role of emotionality. He claims that emotion is the result of specific relationships or interactions between people and their environments. Some relations are perceived as (potentially) harmful to one's well-being and yield negative emotions, such as anger, anxiety, fear, shame, or guilt. These are the emotions we are motivated to avoid. Some relations are (potentially) beneficial and give rise to positive emotions, such as joy, pride, gratitude, and love. These are emotions we are motivated to seek, or approach. Lazarus's listing of basic emotions and their relational themes is presented in Figure 10.8.

I'm sure you won't be surprised to learn that none of the approaches to classifying emotions I have listed so far has proven completely satisfactory. Psychologists continue to propose models or theories to account for the nature of an emotional reaction (e.g., Berkowitz, 1990; Buck, 1985; Ekman, 1993; Frijda, 1988; Greenberg & Safron, 1989; Oatley & Jenkins, 1992; Ortony et al., 1988; Ortony & Turner, 1990; Weiner, 1985).

Whether there are eight or nine primary emotions (or more or fewer) and how they might be combined to form other emotions will depend on one's theoretical perspective. A review by Ortony and Turner (1990) lists more than a dozen theoretical versions of basic, or primary, emotions, and *none of them is in complete agreement with any other*. The only issue on which there seems to be consensus is that emotions are *valenced* states (Ortony et al., 1988). This means that emotions can be classified as being either positive (relief, happiness, and the like) or negative (fear, anger, shame, and the like). A related problem is that there isn't even complete agreement on how to distinguish between positive and negative emotions. Fear, for example,

Figure 10.7

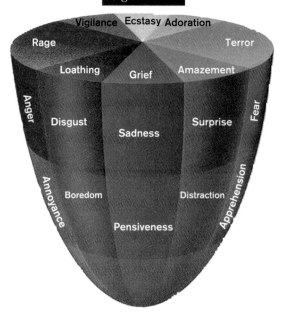

Plutchik's emotion solid.

Figure 10.8

Basic Emotions and Their Relational Themes

Emotion	Relational theme
Anger	A demeaning offense against me and mine
Anxiety	Facing an uncertain, existential threat
Fright	An immediate, concrete, and overwhelming physical danger
Guilt	Having transgressed a moral imperative
Shame	Failing to live up to an ego ideal
Sadness	Having experienced an irrevocable loss
Envy	Wanting what someone else has
Jealousy	Resenting a third party for the loss of, or a threat to, another's affection or favor
Disgust	Taking in or being too close to an indigestible (metaphorically speaking) object or idea
Happiness	Making reasonable progress toward the realization of a goal
Pride	Enhancement of one's ego-identity by taking credit for a valued object or achievement, either one's own or that of some group with which one identifies
Relief	A distressing goal-incongruent condition that has changed for the better or gone away
Hope	Fearing the worst but wanting better
Love	Desiring or participating in affection, usually but not necessarily reciprocated
Compassion	Being moved by another's suffering and wanting to help

From Lazarus, 1993. Reproduced, with permission, from the *Annual Review of Psychology*, Volume 44, © 1993 by Annual Reviews, Inc.

seems like a reasonable candidate for a list of negative emotions. Yet it is clear that fear can be *useful* and can serve to guide one's behavior in adaptive ways. On what basis shall we make our judgments of positive and negative?

So, where does this leave us? As sensible as it may sound to try to construct a system of basic, primary emotions—particularly if such a system had a physiological or evolutionary foundation—such an attempt will prove difficult at best. One problem is that there is less than total agreement on just what *basic* or *primary* means when we are talking about emotions. Ortony and Turner put it this way: "Thus, the question 'Which are the basic emotions?' is not only one that probably cannot be answered, it is a misdirected question, as though we asked, 'Which are the basic people?' and hoped to get a reply that would explain human diversity" (1990).

If there is one conclusion regarding emotion with which all theorists agree, it is that part of being emotional is a physiological, visceral response. To put it plainly, being emotional is a gut-level reaction. To be emotional involves more than our thinking, reasoning cerebral cortex. We turn next to discuss the physiological aspects of emotion.

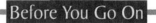

Before You Go On

Can emotions be classified?

PHYSIOLOGICAL ASPECTS OF EMOTION

Let's generate a somewhat unusual although useful example to work with. You are on a camping trip with friends. Having just eaten a large meal, you decide to take a short, solitary stroll down a nearby path through the woods. Totally relaxed, you are about 200 yards away from your friends, who are still sitting around the campfire. Just as you decide to head back, a growling black bear suddenly appears, without warning, from behind a dense thicket. It takes a look at you, bares its teeth, and roars! To say that your reaction would be an emotional one seems an understatement. You will experience affect (call it fear, if not panic). You will have a cognitive reaction (realizing you've just encountered a bear and that you'd rather you hadn't). You will engage in some overt behavior (either freezing in your tracks or racing back to the campfire). A significant part of your reaction in this situation (or one like it) will be internal, physiological, and "gut-level." Responding to a bear in the wild is not something most people would do in a purely cognitive, intellectual sort of way. When we are emotional, we respond with our insides; our viscera get involved.

Our biological reaction to emotional situations takes place at various levels. Of primary interest is the autonomic nervous system, or ANS (see Topic 2B). The brain has a role to play in emotion, but first we'll consider the autonomic response.

The Role of the Autonomic Nervous System

As you recall, the *autonomic nervous system* (*ANS*) consists of two parts, or *divisions*, that serve many of the same organs but that have quite the opposite effect on those organs. The *parasympathetic division* is actively involved in maintaining a relaxed, calm, and unemotional state. As you strolled down the path into the woods, the parasympathetic division of your ANS actively directed your digestive processes to do the best they could with the meal you'd just eaten. Blood was diverted from the extremities to the stomach and intestines. Saliva flowed freely. With your stomach full, and with blood diverted to it, you felt somewhat sleepy as your brain responded to the lower levels of blood supply. Your breathing was slow, deep, and steady, as was your heart rate. Again, all of these activities were under the control of the parasympathetic division of your autonomic nervous system.

Suddenly, there's that bear! Now the *sympathetic division* of your autonomic nervous system takes over. Automatically, many physiological changes take place—changes that are usually quite adaptive.

1. The pupils of your eyes dilate, letting in as much of what light is available, increasing your visual sensitivity.

2. Your heart rate and blood pressure are elevated (energy needs to be mobilized as fast as possible).

3. Blood is diverted away from the digestive tract toward the limbs and brain, and digestion stops; you've got a bear to deal with, so dinner can wait until later. Let's get the blood supply out there to the arms and legs where it can do some good (with what is called the fight-or-flight response).

4. Respiration increases, becoming deeper and more rapid; you'll need all the oxygen you can get.

5. Moisture is brought to the surface of the skin in the form of perspiration; as it evaporates, the body is cooled, thus conserving energy.

6. Blood sugar levels increase, making more energy readily available.

7. Blood will clot more readily than usual, for obvious but, it is hoped, unnecessary reasons.

The sympathetic system makes some of these changes directly (stopping salivation and stimulating the cardiac muscle, for example). The others are made indirectly through the release of hormones into the bloodstream, mostly epinephrine and norepinephrine from the adrenal glands of the endocrine system.

Because part of the physiological component of emotion *is* hormonal, under the control of the endocrine system, it does take a few seconds for the hormones to have their effect felt. As a result, we often sense the delayed reaction of an emotional response. If you were, in fact, confronted by a bear in the woods, you would probably not have the presence of mind to notice, but the reactions of sweaty palms, gasping breaths, and "butterflies in your stomach" take a few seconds to develop.

Is the autonomic and endocrine system reaction exactly the same for every emotion that we experience? That's a very difficult question. There may be slight differences. There appears to be a small difference in the hormones produced during rage and fear reactions. There may be differences in the biological bases of emotional reactions that prepare us for defense or retreat—fight or flight (Blanchard & Blanchard, 1988). Consistent differences in physiological reactions for the various emotional states are, at best, very slight indeed. This issue has been controversial in psychology for many years and is likely to remain so (Blanchard & Blanchard, 1988; Levinthal, 1983; Selye, 1976).

Before You Go On

Summarize the activities of the sympathetic division of the autonomic nervous system during emotional states.

The Role of the Brain

When we become emotional, our sympathetic nervous system does not spring into action on its own. Autonomic nervous system activity is closely related to, and coordinated by, central nervous system activity.

The two brain structures most intimately involved in emotionality are the *limbic system* and the *hypothalamus*, that small structure in the middle of the brain centrally involved with physiological drives. The limbic system is a "lower" center in the brain consisting of a number of small structures (the amygdala may be the most important for emotionality). These centers are "lower" in the sense of being well below the cerebral cortex, and in the sense of being present (and important) in the brains of "lower" animals, such as rats and cats.

The limbic system (you may want to refer to Fig. 2.11, page 79) is most involved in emotional responses that call for defensive or attacking responses—those emotions stimulated by threat. Electrical stimulation and/or destruction of portions of the limbic system reliably produce a variety of changes in emotional reaction.

It is to be expected that the hypothalamus would play a role in emotionality. It is involved in many motivational states. Hypothalamic stimulation can produce strong emotional reactions, including those that lead to attacking and killing any nearby prey (Flynn et al., 1970). Precisely how these lower brain centers of the limbic system and hypothalamus are coordinated in the normal experience and expression of emotion is not yet fully understood.

The role of the cerebral cortex in emotionality is also poorly understood. It seems to be largely inhibitory. That is, the limbic system and hypothalamus seem to act as the sources for extreme and rather poorly directed emotional reactions. The cortex interprets impulses from these lower centers and other information available to it and then modifies and directs the emotional reaction accordingly.

The clearest involvement of the cerebral cortex in emotionality is in the *cognitive* aspect of an emotional response. It is the cerebral cortex that is involved in the interpretation and memory of emotional events. When you get back to camp, having just been frightened by a bear, you will use your cortex to tell the emotional details of your story. There is evidence that emotional reactions tend to be processed more in the right hemisphere of the brain and that the left hemisphere is usually rather unemotional (Sperry, 1982; Tucker, 1981).

To review, along with the autonomic nervous system, the limbic system and the hypothalamus are centers of emotion. These centers are coordinated, and often controlled by, higher centers in the cerebral cortex, which, among other things, provides the cognitive interpretation of emotional responses.

Another aspect of emotion that has long intrigued psychologists is how one's inner emotional states are expressed or communicated to others. Charles Darwin was one of the first to popularize the idea that facial expressions provide a meaningful indicator of an organism's emotional state. More than a hundred years later, psychologists are discovering new evidence that suggests that Darwin was correct.

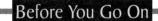

Before You Go On

What brain centers are involved in emotionality?

OUTWARD EXPRESSIONS OF EMOTION

It is very useful for one organism to let another know how it is feeling. As one wild animal approaches a second, the second had better have a good idea about the emotional state of the first. Is it angry? Does it come in peace? Is it just curious, or is it looking for dinner? Is it sad, looking for comfort, or is it sexually aroused, looking for a mating partner? An inability to make such determinations can quickly be disastrous. Animals need to know the emotional state of other animals if they are to survive for long.

Nonhuman animals have many ritualistic and instinctive patterns of behavior to communicate aggressiveness, interest in courtship, submission, and many other emotional states. Humans can also express

As animals approach each other it is important that they convey an expression of their emotional state. Is he hungry? Does he want sex? Does he come in peace?

their emotional state in a variety of ways, including verbal report. Surely, if I am happy, sad, angry, or jealous, I can try to *tell* you how I feel. In fact, the human ability to communicate with language often puts us at an advantage. Even without verbal language, there is a school of thought that suggests that the human animal, like the non-human, uses a *body language* to communicate its emotional condition (e.g., Birdwhistell, 1952; Fast, 1970). Someone sitting quietly, slumped slightly forward with head down, may be viewed as feeling sad, even from a distance. We similarly may interpret postural cues and gestures as being associated with fear, anger, happiness, and so on. But, such expressions are often the result of learning or may be modified by cultural influences.

Darwin recognized facial expression as a common cue to emotion in animals, especially mammals. Might facial expression provide the key to underlying emotions in humans, too? Are there facial expressions of emotional states that are universal among the human species, just as there appear to be among nonhumans (Andrews, 1963)? A growing body of evidence supports the hypothesis that facial expressions of one's emotional state may be an innate response, only slightly sensitive to cultural influence (Adelmann & Zajonc, 1989; Buck, 1980; Gellhorn, 1964; Oatley & Jenkins, 1992; Tomkins, 1962).

Paul Ekman and his colleagues have conducted several studies seeking a reliable relationship between emotional state and facial expression that can be found across cultures (Ekman, 1972, 1992, 1993; Ekman et al., 1987). In one large, cross-cultural study, Ekman and his associates (1973) showed college students six pictures of people's faces. In each picture, a different emotion was displayed: happiness, disgust, surprise, anger, sadness, and fear. When students from the United States, Argentina, Japan, Brazil, and Chile were asked to identify the emotion experienced by the people in the photographs, their agreement was remarkable (see Figure 10.9). One problem with this study is that all of the subjects did have many shared experiences, even though they were from basically different cultures. They were, after all, college students and had many experiences in common (perhaps they had seen the same movies, watched the same TV shows, and so on). Even though Ekman's subjects came from different countries, their agreement as raters could be explained in terms of the similarities of their experiences rather than some innate tendency to express emotions through facial expression.

An argument against this line of reasoning can be found in another project by Ekman (Ekman & Friesen, 1971; Ekman, 1972). Here, natives of a remote New Guinea tribe were asked to make faces showing various emotional reactions (for example, "A friend has come and you are happy"). No one in our culture (or any other) would have much difficulty deciding what emotion the subjects (who were videotaped) were trying to display (see Figure 10.10). These New Guinea tribesmen had little contact with persons outside New Guinea, and virtually no contact with magazines, television, or movies that could have introduced them to the facial expressions of people from other cultures. There is little doubt that distinctive, uni-

Figure 10.9

Photos Displaying Facial Expressions Like These Were Shown to Subjects from the United States, Brazil, Chile, Argentina, and Japan. (The subjects were asked to identify the emotions being displayed. The percentage of subjects who identified the photos with emotion labels is indicated.)

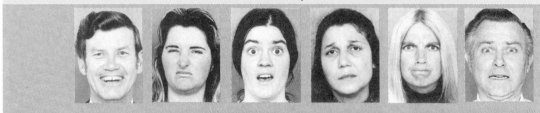

	Happiness	Disgust	Surprise	Sadness	Anger	Fear
United States (N = 99)	97%	92%	95%	84%	67%	85%
Brazil (N = 40)	95%	97%	87%	59%	90%	67%
Chile (N = 119)	95%	92%	93%	88%	94%	68%
Argentina (N = 168)	98%	92%	95%	78%	90%	54%
Japan	100%	90%	100%	62%	90%	66%

versal facial expressions have been identified for some emotions, including anger, fear, disgust, sadness, and happiness (Ekman, 1993).

Another study of facial expression (Ekman et al., 1983) has shown that simply moving one's facial muscles into the positions associated with emotional expression can cause distinctive physiological changes associated with an emotional state (see also, Adelmann & Zajonc, 1989; Laird, 1984; Matsumoto, 1987; Schiff & Lamon,

Figure 10.10

Paul Ekman and his colleagues went to New Guinea to study the relationships between facial expressions and emotional state. The man on the left was told that he was to show that he was happy because a friend was coming. The man in the second picture was told that his child had died. The man in the third picture was told that he should act angry and about to fight. The man in the last photo was told that he had just seen a dead pig that had been lying in one place for a long time. People from any culture would have no difficulty identifying these facial expressions as being correlated with happiness, grief, anger, and disgust, respectively.

1989). As bizarre as that sounds, the idea is that if you raise your eyebrows, open your eyes widely, and raise the corners of your mouth, you will produce an internal physiological change not unlike that which occurs when you are happy, and you will smile as a result!

Before You Go On

What is the relationship, if any, between facial expression and emotion?

TOPIC 10C SUMMARY

In this Topic, we summarized some of what we know about emotions. When we discuss emotion, there is little doubt our primary focus is on the subjective experience or feeling of *affect*—the *A* of our *ABC* model first introduced in Chapter 1. We began by struggling with a definition of emotion. I say "struggle" because it turns out that emotion is not a simple concept. We saw that it consists of at least four aspects: a subjective feeling, a cognitive interpretation, a visceral or physiological response, and some outward expression in overt behavior. Exactly how these components fit together, which is most important, or even if we need to consider them all seems to depend on whose theory you are dealing with. We saw that there is less than consensus on which emotional states are the most basic, or primary, ones. This reflects, among other things, one's vision of the role emotions play in our lives.

We then moved on to a couple of issues for which there is more certainty: the nature of the physiological changes that occur with emotional states, and how facial expressions are related to experienced emotion.

"I don't sing because I am happy. I am happy because I sing."

Drawing by Frascino © 1991. The New Yorker Magazine, Inc.

TOPIC 10A

How have the concepts of instinct, drive, and incentive been used to explain motivated behaviors?

In trying to explain why organisms do what they do, three concepts have proven useful. *Instincts* are complex patterns of behavior that occur in the presence of certain stimuli. Instinct approaches claim that some complex behavioral patterns are innate, or unlearned. The concept of instinct has not proven to be a satisfactory explanation of human behavior. *Needs* are shortages of some biological necessity.

CHAPTER SUMMARY

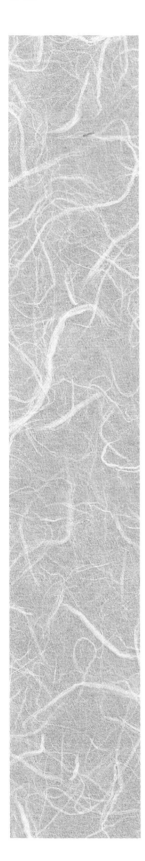

Deprivation leads to a need, which gives rise to a drive, which arouses and directs the organism's behavior. The relationship between deprivation, need, drive, and behavior is often not straightforward; many drives are more learned than biologically based. Maslow said that needs can be placed in a hierarchy, beginning with basic survival needs and ending with a need to self-actualize. Focusing on *incentives* explains behaviors in terms of goals and outcomes rather than internal driving forces. Incentives are said to "pull" behavior, whereas drives "push" behavior. In this sense, we are motivated to reach some desired end state. These approaches are not mutually exclusive. /p. 500

How can the concept of balance, or equilibrium, be used to help us understand motivated behaviors?

In what way is cognitive dissonance theory based on equilibrium?

The basic idea here is that organisms are motivated to reach and maintain a state of balance—a set point level of activity. *Homeostasis* is a general drive to maintain a state of equilibrium among internal physiological conditions such as blood pressure, metabolism, and heart rate. Others argue for a general drive to maintain a balanced state of *arousal*, with various optimal levels of arousal being best suited for various tasks or situations. Festinger claims that we are motivated to maintain consonance, or balance, among cognitive states, thereby reducing *cognitive dissonance*. /p. 503

Given the concept of homeostasis, how might temperature regulation be thought of as a physiologically based drive?

Temperature regulation can be viewed as a physiological drive because we have a need (are driven) to maintain our body temperatures within certain strict (homeostatic) levels. Doing so involves voluntary as well as involuntary, autonomic, responding. /p. 505

List some of the internal and external factors that influence drinking behavior.

We are motivated to drink for several reasons: to relieve dryness in our mouths and throats and to maintain a homeostatic level of fluid within our bodies (monitored by the hypothalamus). We also engage in drinking behavior in response to external cues (incentives), such as taste, aroma, or appearance. What we drink is often influenced by our learning experiences. /p. 507

List some of the internal and external factors that influence eating.

Several factors, both internal and external, affect eating behaviors. Internal factors include cues mediated by the hypothalamus, which may be responding to stored fat levels, blood sugar levels, or other indicators that our normal, homeostatic balance has been disrupted. Associated with this view is the position that body weight is maintained at a given set point both by food intake and by exercise levels. There is evidence that body size may be largely determined by genetic factors. The stimulus properties of foods may motivate eating, as may habit patterns and social pressures. /p. 510

Describe the symptoms of anorexia nervosa and bulimia.

What can we say about their causes and treatment?

Anorexia nervosa and bulimia are eating disorders, most commonly found in females. The anorexic patient is essentially engaged in self-starvation, significantly reducing body weight. Bulimia involves recurrent episodes of binging and purging of large amounts of sweet, high-calorie foods. We do not know what causes eating disorders, but cultural, family, and hormonal influences have been implicated. All sorts of psychotherapy have been tried as treatments for eating disorders. The prognosis for anorexia is poor. Family-oriented therapy seems most effective for bulimia, and antidepressant medication is occasionally effective in the treatment of bulimia, at least for the short term, and particularly when it is paired with psychotherapy. /p. 512

What is achievement motivation, and how is it usually measured?

Achievement motivation, based on the need to achieve (nAch), is a need to attempt and succeed at tasks so as to meet or exceed a standard of excellence. Achievement needs are usually assessed through the interpretation of short stories generated in response to the Thematic Apperception Test, or TAT, in which one looks for themes of striving and achievement. /p. 514

Define the needs for power and affiliation.

The need for power is the need to be in charge, to be in control of a situation, usually at the expense of others. Affiliation needs involve being motivated to be with others, and to form friendships and interpersonal relationships. /p. 517

TOPIC 10B

In what ways is the sex drive a unique, physiologically based drive?

There are four ways in which the sex drive is an unusual physiological drive. (1) Individual survival does not depend on its satisfaction. (2) The drive involves seeking tension rather than seeking relief from tension. (3) It is not fully present at birth, but matures later. (4) The extent to which it is influenced by learned or external influences varies from species to species. /p. 520

How is one's sex genetically determined?

At conception, a zygote receives an X chromosome from its mother's ovum and either an X or a Y chromosome from the father's sperm. If the zygote receives two X chromosomes (XX), it is genetically a

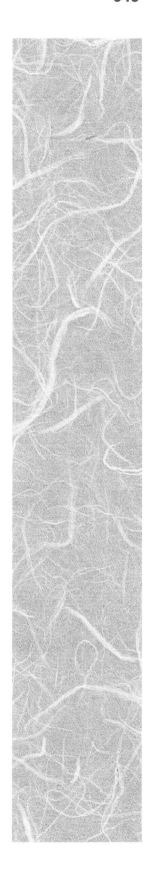

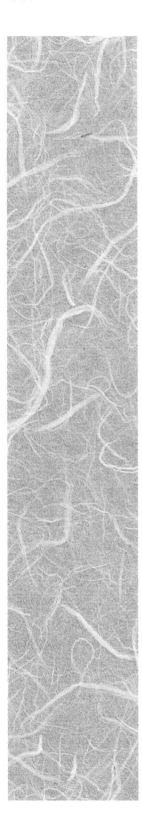

female; if it receives one X and one Y chromosome (XY), it is genetically a male. /*p. 521*

Summarize the role of hormones in the determination of one's sex.

As the sex glands develop (beginning about six weeks after conception), they begin secreting sex hormones, androgens from the male sex glands (testes) and estrogens from the female sex glands (ovaries). Androgen and estrogen levels are controlled in part by the pituitary gland and the hypothalamus. Androgens and estrogens are present in both males and females. It is the relative amounts of each that stimulate the development of the genitals and, hence, determine one's anatomical sex. /*p. 522*

What is homosexuality?

What causes homosexuality?

Homosexuals are persons who are attracted to and sexually aroused by members of their own sex. There is thought to be a continuum, or gradual dimension, that extends from exclusively homosexual on the one extreme to exclusively heterosexual on the other. Kinsey found that about half his sample of males fell somewhere between these two end points. We do not know what "causes" homosexual orientation, but strongly suspect a genetic basis or predisposition, the influence of prenatal hormone levels, and the involvement of the hypothalamus. /*p. 524*

Briefly describe some common sexual dysfunctions, and comment on their causes.

Sexual dysfunctions are chronic problems in sexual functioning. The most commonly reported by males is *erectile dysfunction*, an inability to attain or maintain an erection long enough to experience intercourse. *Premature ejaculation* and *retarded ejaculation* have to do with the timing of ejaculation during intercourse. The former problem is more common than the latter. What is "premature" or "retarded" is defined by the individual; that is, there are no "normal" time limits. *Female sexual unresponsiveness* is a condition in which a woman gains little or no satisfaction or pleasure from sexual activities. This dysfunction is usually self-diagnosed. *Orgasmic dysfunction* is the inability to experience orgasm to one's satisfaction. This is the dysfunction most commonly reported by women. *Vaginismus* is the powerful, spasmodic contraction of the muscles surrounding the opening of the vagina. It makes vaginal intercourse nearly impossible. These sexual dysfunctions, in males and females, may, in turn, create additional reactions such as loss of self-esteem, guilt, or depression. There may be a physical/biological cause (illness, fatigue, alcohol use, medication, injury) for sexual dysfunctions, but they are often caused by psychological factors. /*p. 528*

TOPIC 10C

What are the four components that taken together define an emotional experience?

There are four possible components of an emotional reaction: the experience of a subjective feeling, or *affective* component; a *cognitive* appraisal or interpretation; an internal, visceral, *physiological* reaction; and an overt *behavioral* response. /p. 531

Can emotions be classified?

There have been several attempts to categorize emotional reactions, dating back to Wundt in the late 1800s. Izard has a scheme that calls for nine primary emotions. Plutchik argues that there are eight basic emotions and many combinations and degrees of them. Other theorists have proposed as few as two or as many as dozens of primary emotions. The inconsistency among theories leads some psychologists to wonder if the attempt to classify basic emotions is misguided. /p. 534

Summarize the activities of the sympathetic division of the autonomic nervous system during emotional states.

Among the many changes that take place when we become emotional are those produced by the sympathetic division of the autonomic nervous system. Occurring to varying degrees and dependent on the situation, these reactions include dilation of the pupils, increased heart rate and blood pressure, cessation of digestive processes, deeper and more rapid breathing, increased perspiration, and elevated blood sugar levels. /p. 536

What brain centers are involved in emotionality?

The cerebral cortex is involved in the cognitive interpretation of emotional events and acts as an inhibitory mechanism, exerting some control over the activity of lower brain centers for emotionality (largely the limbic system and the hypothalamus). Basically, the brain coordinates physiological aspects of emotionality. /p. 537

What is the relationship, if any, between facial expression and emotion?

Facial expressions indicate the internal, emotional state of an individual. What leads us to believe that facial expression of emotion is unlearned (innate) is that there is such universal reliability in the interpretation of facial expressions, even across widely different cultures. Additionally, the relationship appears to be two-way because there are data indicating that one can actually change one's subjective emotional state by changing one's facial expression. /p. 541

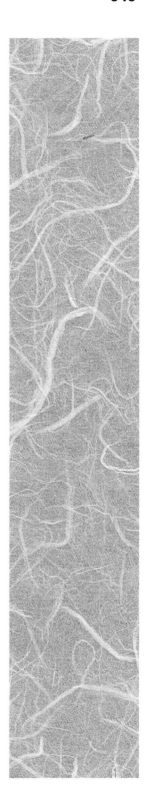

chapter eleven

PSYCHOLOGY, STRESS, AND PHYSICAL HEALTH

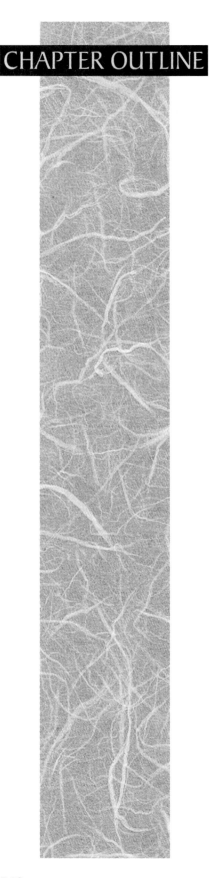

CHAPTER OUTLINE

TOPIC 11A STRESS, STRESSORS, AND HOW TO COPE
Stressors: The Causes of Stress
    Frustration-induced Stress
    Conflict-induced Stress
    Life-change-induced Stress
Reacting to the Stressors in Our Lives
    Individual Differences
    Stress as a Physiological Reaction: Selye's GAS
    Effective Strategies for Coping with Stressors
    Ineffective Strategies for Coping with Stressors
TOPIC 11A SUMMARY

TOPIC 11B HEALTH PSYCHOLOGY
Psychological Factors That Influence Physical Health
Promoting Healthy Behaviors
    Why Do People Die?
    Helping People to Stop Smoking
    Sexually Transmitted Diseases
    Helping Patients "Follow Doctors' Orders"
TOPIC 11B SUMMARY

CHAPTER SUMMARY

*I*t's Friday afternoon and you have a chance to get away for the weekend with friends. Unfortunately, you have two big exams scheduled for Monday and need the weekend to study.

—Nancy is two-thirds of the way through typing a term paper on her word processor when suddenly the power goes out. Having failed to save her work as she went along, she will have to redo it all.

—Cindy and Jerry have known each other since grade school. They dated throughout high school and college. Next week, family and friends will join in the celebration of their marriage.

—Doug wants to make the basketball team, but the coach informs him that despite his best efforts, Doug is just too short to make the team.

—Marian is excited to be in Germany in a student-exchange program, but she's also very nervous about getting along in a new country.

—After 11 years on the road as a salesman, Wayne is being promoted to district sales manager—an office job with a substantial raise in pay.

—Jake had cut back his smoking to one pack a day, and was thinking about starting an exercise program. Now he finds himself in a coronary intensive care unit, having just suffered a heart attack.

—Three-year-old Trudy keeps asking her mother for a cookie. Mother steadfastly refuses because it's almost dinner time. Trudy returns to her room and promptly pulls an arm off her favorite doll.

—You are late for class, driving down a two-lane road, when someone pulls out in front of you and drives along 10 miles an hour below the speed limit.

—For the very first time, Tom is standing on the high diving board. He wants to dive (or jump) to impress his friends, but now that he's up there, he realizes just how high that diving board really is. There's no way he'll climb back down.

Life is filled with stress, frustration, and conflict. This list provides only a very small sample of the types of stressful events people encounter on a daily basis. We'll return to each of these examples through this chapter.

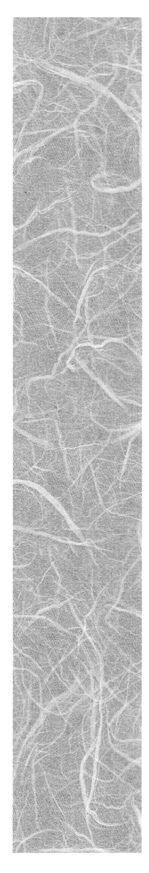

he focus of this chapter is the role of psychological factors as they affect our physical health and well-being. We have encountered this theme before: biological and psychological processes interact; body and mind are interrelated. A discussion of stress and health flows naturally from issues raised in the last chapter, which dealt with motivation and emotion. We'll see in Topic 11A that stress is like an emotion—it involves one's cognitive appraisals of a given situation, physiological reactions, and unpleasant feelings, or affects. Stress is also a motivator. People who experience stress are motivated to do something to alleviate its unpleasant aspects in their lives.

In Topic 11B we'll look at a rapidly growing subfield of psychology, called health psychology. *There are several related issues we could explore here. We'll choose two: (1) Is there a relationship between our behaviors, thoughts, and feelings and the state of our physical health? and (2) What role can psychology play in improving physical health? Let's start with the issue of stress.*

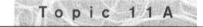

Topic 11A

STRESS, STRESSORS, AND HOW TO COPE

Our study of stress will be divided into two main sections. First, we'll see, at least in general terms, where stress comes from. What are the common stressors in our lives? Second, we'll examine the complex patterns of responses we make when we experience stress. One of the realities we'll encounter here is that often there are more unproductive, maladaptive reactions to stress than there are adaptive, mentally healthy ones. We begin by trying to see where stress comes from.

STRESSORS: THE CAUSES OF STRESS

stress *a complex set of reactions to real or perceived threats to one's well-being that motivates adaptation*

First, just what *is* stress? Although each of us is intimately familiar with stress, and how it feels, psychologists have struggled with the concept of stress for nearly sixty years, and how to define it, and the issue is far from settled (Hobfoll, 1989). We will define **stress** as a complex set of reactions made by an individual under pressure to adapt. Stress is a response one makes to real or perceived threats to one's sense of well-being. Stress is something that happens inside people. There are physiological reactions and unpleasant feelings (e.g., distress and anxiety) associated with stress.

stressors *the sources or stimuli for stress, which include frustration, conflict, and life events*

There are many circumstances or events that can produce stress. *The sources of stress are called* **stressors.** In this section, we'll consider three types of stressors: frustration, conflict, and life events. In each case, I'll provide examples, some of which you may view as being quite trivial. I've included such examples as a reminder that stress is not necessarily a response to some overwhelming, catastrophic event, such as the death of a loved one or a natural disaster. Once we've reviewed where stress comes from, we'll consider techniques people use to cope with it.

Frustration-induced Stress

As we saw in our last chapter, in Topic 10A, we can characterize motivated behaviors as being *goal-directed*. Whether by internal processes (needs and drives) or external stimuli (incentives) we are pushed or pulled toward positive goals and away from negative goals.

Now let me introduce an assumption: *Organisms don't always reach all of their goals.* Have you always gotten everything you've ever wanted? Have you always been able to avoid unpleasantness, pain, or sorrow? Do you know anyone who has?

Sometimes we are totally prohibited from ever reaching a particular goal. At other times our progress may be slower or more difficult than we would like. In either case, we are being frustrated. **Frustration** is the blocking of goal-directed behavior—blocking that may be total and permanent or partial and temporary (see Figure 11.1).

Seen in this way, stress that results from frustration is a normal, commonplace reaction. Frustration is a stressor, and the stress it produces is a fact of life. The stress that results from frustration does not imply weakness, pathology, or illness. What does matter is how individuals react to the stressors in their lives. Before we consider how one might react to frustration, let's look at some of the varieties of frustration.

To someone who feels the stress that results from frustration, the actual source of that stress may be of little consequence. However, in order to respond adaptively to frustration-induced stress, it may be helpful to recognize the source of the blocking—the particular stressor—keeping us from our goals. There are two basic types of frustration: environmental and personal.

Environmental frustration implies that the blocking or thwarting of one's goal-directed behavior is caused by something or somebody in the environment. (Note that we talk about the *source* of frustration, not *fault* or *blame*, which are evaluative terms.)

Remember Nancy, who lost most of her term paper when the power went out? This is an example of environmental frustration. Nancy wanted to get her paper typed. Her goal-directed behavior led her to use her word processor. Something in her environment—a momentary power outage—interfered with her behavior and kept her from reaching her goal. And remember Trudy? She wanted a cookie, but her mother said, "No, it's almost suppertime." Trudy is also being frustrated by her environment, but in a slightly different way. She wants a cookie, and her mother is blocking that motivated behavior. This type of environmental frustration, in which the source of the blocking is another person, is sometimes called *social frustration*.

Occasionally we are frustrated not because someone or something in our environment is blocking progress toward our goals, but because of some internal or personal reason. This is *personal frustration*. Doug fails to make the basketball team simply because he is too

Stress resulting from frustration occurs when our goal-directed behaviors are blocked or thwarted. On some days, being stuck in a traffic jam can be very frustrating.

frustration *a stressor; the blocking or thwarting of goal-directed behavior*

Figure 11.1

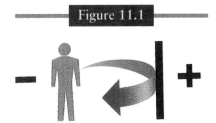

A depiction of frustration, the blocking or thwarting of goal-directed behavior.

short. Shirley, who wants to be a concert pianist, may be frustrated in her attempt to do so simply because she doesn't have sufficient talent. She may learn to be a good piano player, but she probably won't make it in the world of classical piano. Her frustration and resulting stress are certainly not her "fault" (again, fault and blame are not relevant), but if she persists in this goal-directed behavior, she will be frustrated. Some of us are learning that getting older can be stressful. I know I am often frustrated when I find I have difficulty doing things that at one time I was able to do easily. The stress we experience is frustration-induced, and this type of frustration is personal.

Before You Go On

What is meant by frustration-induced stress?

Define environmental and personal frustration, citing an example of each.

Conflict-induced Stress

conflict *a stressor in which some goals can be satisfied only at the expense of others*

Sometimes we are unable to satisfy a particular drive or motive because it is in **conflict** with other motives that are influencing us at the same time. Stress may result not from the frustration caused by the blocking of our goal-directed behaviors, but because of conflicts within our own motivational system.

With motivational conflicts, there is the implication of a decision or choice that has to be made. Sometimes the choice is relatively easy, and the resulting stress will be slight; sometimes decision making is more difficult, and the resulting stress will be greater. When discussing conflict, we talk about positive goals or incentives that one wishes to approach and negative goals or incentives one wishes to avoid. Let's look at some stress-inducing motivational conflicts.

Approach-Approach Conflicts. Conflicts are necessarily unpleasant and stress-producing situations, and will be so even when the goals involved are positive. In an *approach-approach conflict,* an organism is caught between two (or more) alternatives, and each of them is positive, or potentially reinforcing (Figure 11.2). If the person chooses alternative A, he or she will reach a desired goal. If B is chosen, a different desirable goal will be attained. What makes this a conflict is that *both* goals or alternatives are not available at the same time. It has to be one or the other. A choice has to be made.

Once an approach-approach conflict is resolved, the person *does* end up with something positive no matter which alternative is chosen. For example, if Carla enters an ice cream shop with only enough money to buy one dip of ice cream, she may experience a conflict when faced with all of the flavors from which she could choose. Typical of conflict, we will notice some vacillation in Carla's behavior, some swaying back and forth among alternatives. We can assume that

Figure 11.2

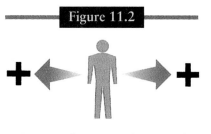

A diagram of an approach-approach conflict. In such a conflict, a person is faced with two (or more) attractive, positive goals, and must choose from among them.

this conflict will be resolved with a choice, and Carla will at least walk out of the store with an ice cream cone of some flavor she likes. Her life might have been easier (less stressful) if the store provided just one flavor in the first place and she didn't have to make such choices, but she'll contemplate that possibility with an ice cream cone.

Sometimes the choices we are called upon to make are much more serious than those involving ice cream flavors. What will be your college major? On the one hand, you'd like to go to medical school and be a surgeon (that's a positive incentive or goal). On the other hand, you'd like to cultivate your aptitude for music and study composition and conducting at a school of music (also a clear positive goal). At the moment, you cannot do both. The courses you would take as a premed student are different from those you'd take if you were to follow music as a career path. Both avenues are good, constructive, desirable alternatives; but now, at registration, you have to make a choice, one that may have long-lasting repercussions. The nature and consequences of such a conflict qualify it as a stressor.

Avoidance-Avoidance Conflicts. Perhaps the most stress-inducing and unpleasant of the motivational conflicts are the avoidance-avoidance conflicts (Figure 11.3). In this type of conflict, a person is faced with several alternatives, and each of them is negative or in some way punishing. No matter which way one turns, one is going to "get burned." To be in an avoidance-avoidance conflict is, in a way, to be boxed in so that no matter what you do, the result will be punishing or unpleasant.

This sort of conflict is not at all unusual in the workplace. Imagine you are a supervisor in charge of a reasonably large department. Your department has been doing well, making a profit, but word comes from management that you must cut your operating budget by 20 percent by next month. There *are* ways you can reduce expenses—limit travel, cut down on supplies, reduce pay, eliminate expense accounts, and so on—but each involves an action you'd rather not take. The result may be stress, and the stressor is an avoidance-avoidance conflict.

We have a number of clichés in the English language that seem to describe these conflicts: "Caught between the devil and the deep blue sea," "out of the frying pan, into the fire," and "stuck between a rock and a hard place" are three that come to mind. In each case, we are describing a situation from which a pleasant reprieve seems unlikely.

Approach-Avoidance Conflicts. With approach-avoidance conflicts, an organism is in the position of considering only one goal, one possibility (Figure 11.4). What makes this situation a conflict is that the person would very much like to reach that goal, but at the same time would very much like not to. It's a matter of "Yes, I'd love to . . . Well, as a matter of fact, I'd rather not . . . Well, maybe I would . . . No, I wouldn't . . . yes . . . no." Consider the possibility of entering into a relationship with someone you think of as special. On the one hand, such a relationship might turn out to be wonderful and rewarding. On the other hand, initiating such a relationship might put you in the position of being hurt and rejected. Typical of conflict in general, what we see in these conflicts is vacillation, swinging back and forth

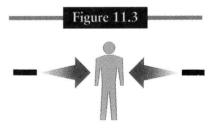

Figure 11.3

A diagram of an avoidance-avoidance conflict. In such a conflict, a person is faced with two (or more) unattractive, negative goals, and must choose from among them. This is a "no win" situation.

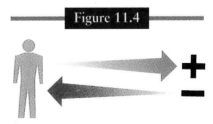

Figure 11.4

A diagram of an approach-avoidance conflict. Here, a person is faced with but one goal. What makes this a conflict is that the goal has both positive and negative aspects or features.

When at the end of a high diving board, one may find one's self in an approach-avoidance conflict, wanting to jump or dive on the one hand, but on the other hand wanting to stay safely on the board.

between alternatives—motivated to approach and, at the same time, motivated to avoid. You might find yourself in an approach-avoidance conflict if you want to interact with people who are culturally different, perhaps to show that you are unprejudiced and open-minded. At the same time, you may be reluctant to initiate such an interaction for fear that your behaviors will be inappropriate or misinterpreted.

My example of Tom on the diving board was meant to exemplify an approach-avoidance conflict. Tom really only had one option open to him—jumping off the board. On the one hand he wanted to do so, but at the same time, he was more than just a little afraid of jumping from such a height.

Multiple Approach-Avoidance Conflicts. Multiple approach-avoidance conflicts may be the most common of the conflicts experienced by adults (see Figure 11.5). This type of conflict arises when an individual is faced with a number of alternatives, each one of which is in some way positive and in some way negative.

Perhaps you and some friends are out shopping on a Saturday morning. You discover it's getting late, and you're all hungry. Where will you go to lunch? You may have a multiple approach-avoidance conflict here. "We could go to Bob's Diner, where the food is cheap and the service is fast, but the food is terrible. We could go to Cafe Olé, where the food is better, but service is a little slower, and the food is more expensive. Or we could go to The Grill, where the service is elegant and the food is superb, but the price is very high." Granted this is not an earth-shaking dilemma, but in each case there is a plus and a minus to be considered in making the choice. The more difficult the choice, the greater the induced stress.

The opening example about what to do with your upcoming weekend can be thought of as a multiple approach-avoidance conflict. If you go to the party (+), you'll probably do poorly on Monday's exams (–). But if you study for the exams and earn good scores (+), you'll miss the fun of the party (–).

Life is filled with such conflicts, and some of them can be severe and very stressful. They may encompass questions of the "What shall I do with the rest of my life?" sort. "Should I stay at home with the children (+ and –), or should I have a career (+ and –)?" "Should I get married or stay single, or is there another way (again, + and – in each case)?" "Should I work for company A (+ and –), or should I work for company B (+ and –)?" Quite clearly, lists such as this could go on and on. You might want to reflect on the conflicts you have faced during the past few weeks. You should be able to categorize each of them into one of the four types I have listed here.

Figure 11.5

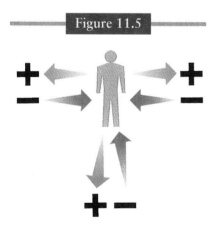

A diagram of a multiple approach-avoidance conflict. In such a conflict, a person is faced with two (or more) alternatives, each of which has both positive and negative aspects or features, and a choice must be made from among the alternatives.

Before You Go On

Name four types of motivational conflict and provide an example of each.

Life-change-induced Stress

Frustration and conflict are potent sources of stress and are often unavoidable consequences of being a motivated organism. Psychologists have also attempted to deal with sources of stress that do not fit neatly into our descriptions of either conflict or frustration. One useful approach has been to look at certain events and changes that occur in one's life as potential sources of stress.

In 1967, Thomas Holmes and Richard Rahe published the first version of their *Social Readjustment Rating Scale, or SRRS* (Holmes & Holmes, 1970). The basic idea behind this scale is that stress results whenever life situations change. The scale provides a list of life events that might be potentially stressful. The original list of such events was drawn from the reports of patients suffering from moderate to high levels of stress in their lives. Marriage was arbitrarily assigned a value of 50 stress points (*life-change units*). With "marriage = 50" as their guide, the subjects rated a number of other more or less typical life changes in terms of the amount of stress they might provide. The death of a spouse got the highest rating (100 units), followed by divorce (rated at 73 units). Pregnancy (40 units), trouble with the boss (23 units), changing to a new school (20 units), and minor violations of the law (11 units) are some other stress-inducing life-change events on the scale.

In a rather direct way, the SRRS gives us a way to measure the stress in our lives. Among other things, there is a positive correlation between scores on the SRRS and the incidence of physical illness and disease (Rahe & Arthur, 1978). People with SRRS scores between 200 and 299 have a 50-50 chance of developing noticeable symptoms of physical illness within the next two years. *Eighty* percent of those with scores above 300 develop physical symptoms within the same time period. The logic is that stress causes illness, particularly cardiovascular disorders. But we should remember what we said in Chapter 1 about correlations: They do not tell us about cause and effect. After all, some of the SRRS items themselves are related to physical illness or are in some way health related. It may not be much of a surprise, then, to find scores on this scale related to levels of physical illness. Several studies that have looked at correlations between SRRS scores and physical health problems have found the correlations to be positive (e.g., Adler et al., 1994; Brett et al., 1990; and McCrae, 1984). (We'll return to the issue of relationships between stress—and other psychological factors—and physical health in our next Topic.)

Socioeconomic status, or **SES,** is a measure that reflects one's income, educational level, and occupation. Not surprisingly, there is a correlation between socioeconomic status and experienced stress. SES is related to stress in at least two ways. (1) Persons of higher socioeconomic status are less likely than persons of low SES to encounter *negative life events* (unemployment, poor housing, less access to quality health care, and so on) in their lives (McLeod & Kessler, 1990). (2) Persons of low SES have fewer resources available to deal with stressful life events *when they do occur* (Adler et al., 1994).

socioeconomic status (SES) a measure that reflects one's income, educational, and occupational level

Richard Lazarus (1981, 1991c, 1993; Lazarus & Folkman, 1984) argues that psychologists ought to focus more attention on those causes of stress that are less dramatic than major life changes such as the death of a family member or marriage. What often matters most are life's little hassles—the traffic that goes too slowly, the toothpaste tube that splits, ants at a picnic, the cost of a pizza (compared to what it was just a few years ago), and so on. Part of Lazarus's argument is that big crises or major life-change events are often too large to have an impact on us directly. What may cause us to feel stressed are the ways in which these big events produce little, irritating changes in our lives (hassles). Being retired may mean a lack of access to friendly conversation at coffee-break time. A spouse's starting to work may make life more difficult; the other spouse may have to cook dinner for the first time. Thus, stress results not so much from the event itself, but from the hassles it creates.

As you might have predicted, Lazarus and his colleagues have constructed a scale to assess the extent to which stressorlike hassles enter peoples' lives (Kanner, Coyne, Schaefer, & Lazarus, 1981). Respondents to the *Hassles Scale,* as it is called, indicate which hassles have occurred to them and rate the severity of the experienced stress. The ten most commonly cited daily hassles for college students and for middle-aged adults are listed in Figure 11.6. Experience with the Hassle Scale indicates that it is a better predictor of problems with one's physical health and a better predictor of such psychological symptoms as anxiety and depression than is the Holmes and Rahe Social Readjustment Rating Scale (e.g., DeLongis et al., 1988).

Other scales have been designed to assess the types of stressors people encounter. One, the *Comprehensive Scale of Stress Assessment* (Sheridan & Smith, 1987), has been revised to be suitable for a population of teenagers (Sheridan & Perkins, 1992). Significant stressors for teens include such things as "having thoughts of losing your par-

---

Figure 11.6

Ten Common Stressors in the Lives of Middle-aged Adults and College Students

For middle-aged adults:	For college students:
1. Concerns about weight	1. Troubling thoughts about the future
2. Health of a family member	2. Not getting enough sleep
3. Rising prices of common goods	3. Wasting time
4. Home maintenance (interior)	4. Inconsiderate smokers
5. Too many things to do	5. Physical appearance
6. Misplacing or losing things	6. Too many things to do
7. Yard work or outside home maintenance	7. Misplacing or losing things
8. Property, investments, or taxes	8. Not enough time to do the things you need to do
9. Crime	9. Concerns about meeting high standards
10. Physical appearance	10. Being lonely

From Kanner, Coyne, Schaefer, & Lazarus, 1981.

Sometimes life events such as weddings, which are evaluated as positive events, can even be stressors.

ents or someone else dear to you," "being bombarded by questions and requests," "experiencing high-level noise at school or home," "being around angry people," and "having someone call something you have said or done 'stupid'."

A slightly different view of how life's events can produce stress claims that stressors in our lives are perceived threats to our "resources" (Hobfoll, 1988, 1989). In this model, resources are those objects, personal characteristics, conditions, or energies we value, that we work to acquire and save. The basic supposition is that most people strive to retain, protect, and build resources. When environmental events (stressors) threaten one's status, position in the community, economic stability, loved ones, home, or possessions (as examples of resources), the result is stress. An interesting aspect of this position is that we experience stress even when our *present* resources are not being threatened. Stress can also result from perceived threats to our ability to acquire more resources in the future. Retired persons, for example, are very concerned about how changes in their social security payments will impact on their lives, and some young wage earners are concerned about the extent to which they will ever be able to realize a return on the social security taxes they are paying now.

One final note about life-induced stressors: the events or changes in our lives we talk about as stressors do not have to be negative, or unpleasant events. Many events we look forward to, that we judge to be changes for the better, can bring with them many of the hassles associated with stress. I listed two examples at the beginning of the chapter. Everybody is happy about Cindy and Jerry finally getting married, no doubt a pleasant, positive life event. But at the same time—as anyone who has ever gone through the process will attest—wedding preparations are stressors. They may produce new conflicts. If Aunt Sarah is invited, does that mean that Aunt Louise must be invited as well? Cindy and Jerry are planning an outdoor reception. What if it rains?

And there's Wayne the experienced salesman, now a sales manager. Wayne may have gotten quite used to the freedom of being on the road and setting his own hours. Now that he has a promotion—"good news"—his daily routine may be drastically altered, producing new stress.

Before You Go On

In what ways might life events
produce stress?

REACTING TO THE STRESSORS IN OUR LIVES

So far we have defined stress and reviewed a number of potential stressors. Now we need to consider what someone might do when he or she experiences stress. We often hear about people trying to "cope with the stress in their lives." Consistent with the terminology we're using here, it would be more correct to speak of "coping with, or dealing with, the *stressors* in one's life." Remember, stress is a reaction to stressors (frustration, conflict, or life events). Stress may motivate us, but it motivates us to do something about the perceived threats to our well-being we are calling stressors.

Individual Differences

Before we go on, an important point needs to be made. As with so many other things, there are large individual differences in how one responds to stressors. What consitutes a stressor and what someone may do when he or she experiences stress vary considerably from person to person. Some people fall apart at weddings; others don't find them stressful at all. For some people, even simple choices are difficult to make; for others, choices are not enough, they seek challenges. The variability in stress levels we see among different people can usually be found within any one person at different times. For example, on one day, being caught in slow-moving traffic may drive you up the wall. In the very same situation a few days later, you may find you couldn't care less. So, we need to remember that reactions to stressors vary from time to time and from person to person. As it happens, the amount of stress one experiences and the means of coping with stress do *not* appear to be different for men and women (e.g., Baum & Grunberg, 1991; Lazarus, 1993). For example, in one study comparing middle-class men and women who were married and employed full-time, no gender difference was found in the degree to which work-related concerns contributed to individual levels of stress (Barnette et al., 1993).

Some people seem so generally resistant to the negative aspects of stress that they have been labeled as having *hardy personalities* (e.g., Kobasa, 1979, 1982, 1987; Maddi & Kobasa, 1984; Neubauer, 1992). Hardiness in this context is related to three things: (1) *challenge* (being able to see difficulties in one's life as an opportunity for change and growth, not threats to one's status); (2) *control* (being in charge of what is happening in one's life and believing that one is the master of one's fate); and (3) *commitment* (being engaged and involved with one's life and one's circumstances, not just watching life go by from the sidelines).

Here's another point about how we deal with stress: some responses are more effective or adaptive than others. An adaptive or effective response to stressors will ultimately reduce the experience of stress. To think that one can *avoid* stress in the first place is unrealistic. We should also acknowledge that stress, in itself, need not necessarily be a bad thing. A certain amount of stress in our lives is natural and to be expected. Stress often follows as a natural consequence of being alive, motivated in the real world. What is unfortunate is that we occasionally develop ineffective or maladaptive strategies for dealing with the stress we experience. By ineffective or maladaptive responses I mean that one's reaction will not, in the long run, be successful in reducing stress. However, before we get into the matter of effective and ineffective strategies for dealing with stress, let's look more closely at the reaction to stressors that we call stress.

Before You Go On

What does it mean to say that there are individual differences in reactions to stressors?

Stress as a Physiological Reaction: Selye's GAS

No matter how we ultimately cope with stress, stressors produce a series of physiological reactions within us. In this way, stress is much like any other reaction to emotion-producing stimuli in our environments. When we experience stress, demands are made on the physiological systems of our bodies.

The most widely accepted description of the physiological reactions one makes to stressors is described by Hans Selye's **general adaptation syndrome**, or **GAS**. According to Selye (1956, 1974), the pattern of reaction to stressors occurs in three stages: alarm, resistance, and exhaustion (see Figure 11.7).

general adaptation syndrome (GAS) Selye's description of physiological reactions made to stressors, which include the three stages of alarm, resistance, and exhaustion

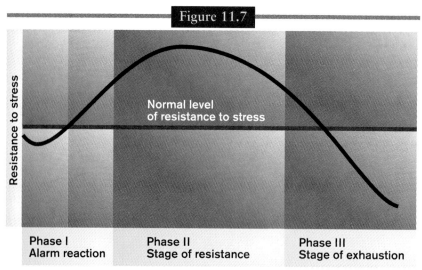

Figure 11.7

Resistance to stress

Normal level
of resistance to stress

Phase I
Alarm reaction

Phase II
Stage of resistance

Phase III
Stage of exhaustion

The general adaptation syndrome (GAS), as proposed by Hans Selye, calls for three identifiable, largely physiological, reactions to stressors. In the first stage (alarm reaction), resources are quickly mobilized as the sympathetic division of the ANS springs into action. If the stressor persists, the organism shows a defensive reaction (resistance stage) in an attempt to react to the continuing stress. Following prolonged exposure to stress, the energy necessary for adaptation may become depleted (exhaustion stage).

The first response to the perception of a stressor is *alarm*. A perceived threat produces rapid and noticeable changes in the sympathetic division of the autonomic nervous system. The sympathetic system causes an increase in blood pressure and heart rate, pupillary dilation, a cessation of digestion, and a rerouting of the blood supply to the extremities of the body. The adrenal glands secrete norepinephrine into the bloodstream and mobilize the body's resources, providing increased levels of blood sugar. These reactions are similar to those we experience in any emotional situation.

This strong, even dramatic, reaction cannot last very long. We can usually maintain high levels of sympathetic activity for no more than several minutes, a few hours at the most.

Let's start an illustrative example. Imagine Pam, a college student in the midst of a very important semester. Pam is strongly motivated to do well in all of her courses. It is just past midterm and she gets word from home that her father has had a massive heart attack. She leaves school and drives straight home, a 16-hour drive, and rushes to the hospital. Her father has never been seriously ill before; now he's in coronary intensive care. The shock and disbelief are nearly overwhelming during Pam's initial alarm-stage reaction.

In *resistance*, the second stage of the general adaptation syndrome, the stressor remains present, and Pam's body continues to fight off the challenge of the stressor. Pam's father begins to show some signs of recovery, but he will be in intensive care for at least another three days and will be hospitalized well beyond that. There's little Pam can do to help her father, but she feels she can't leave and go back to school right now. Every day she stays at home, she gets further behind in her classes.

Pam's bodily resources were mobilized in the alarm stage of the GAS. Now she has discovered that there is no means of escaping or lessening the source of her stress. The drain on her body's resources continues. If new stressors appear, Pam will be less able to deal with them effectively. She will become vulnerable to physical illness and infection to a greater degree than she would without the constant stress she is experiencing. Her internal, sympathetic responses *seem* to return to near normal, but Pam's physiological systems continue to try to mobilize to resist. High blood pressure, ulcers, skin rashes, or respiratory difficulties may develop. In the resistance stage of the GAS, a person is more susceptible to physical problems, from the common cold to cancer. Pam may appear to be in control, but the reality of her father's condition and the approach of her final exams continue to eat away at her, intruding into her awareness.

If Pam cannot discover some useful way to deal with the stress she is experiencing, her physical reaction to the still-present stressors may be *exhaustion*. In this stage, her bodily resources become nearly depleted. She is running out of energy and out of time. If effective means of coping with her father's condition and her college course work are not found, Pam may break down—psychologically or physically, or both. Although the resistance stage may last for several months, eventually one's resources become expended. In extreme cases, the exhaustion stage of the general adaptation syndrome may result in death.

For Selye, then, stress is a three-stage mobilization of the body's resources to combat real or perceived threats to our well-being. We have a limited supply of such resources. Repeated exposure to stressors tends to have cumulative effects. Dire consequences can result when a person is faced with several stressful situations in the same time frame. Selye's model focuses only on the physiological aspects of responding to stressors. It does not take into account just how a person can respond to stressors in more cognitive and behavioral ways.

The physiological reactions that Selye has noted may very well occur in the stages he described, but this model does not address ways in which we can reduce the pressure of the stressors in our lives. Let's first consider effective strategies for dealing with stress and stressors, and then look at some common ineffective strategies.

Before You Go On

Name and describe the three stages of Selye's general adaptation syndrome.

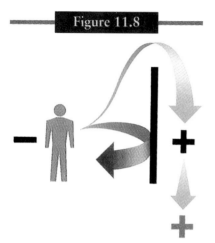

Figure 11.8

Reacting to frustration with learning is the most effective long-term reaction to stressors. That is, when one's goal-directed behaviors are continually blocked or thwarted, one should consider bringing about a relatively permanent change in those behaviors, or consider changing one's goals.

Effective Strategies for Coping with Stressors

In the long run, the most effective way to deal with stress is to make relatively permanent changes in our behaviors as a result of the experience of stress. You will recall that we defined learning as a relatively permanent change in behavior that occurs as the result of practice or experience. To respond to a stressor with learning makes particularly good sense for frustration-induced stress. Here, our pathway to a goal is being blocked or thwarted. An adaptive way to handle such a stressor is to find some new way to reach our goal or to learn to modify our goal (see Figure 11.8).

In fact, much of our everyday learning is motivated by frustration-induced stress. We've had to learn many new responses as a means of coping with frustration. Let's look at a few imaginary examples. Having been frustrated once (or twice) by locking yourself out of your house or car, you have learned to hide another set of keys somewhere where you can easily find them. Having been denied promotion because you didn't have a college degree, you are learning about general psychology on the way toward earning such a degree. Having been caught at home in a blizzard with no cookies in the house, you have learned to bake them yourself. Having discovered you're too short to make the basketball team, you have learned to play tennis. You may have learned as a child to get what you wanted from your parents by smiling sweetly and asking politely. In each of these cases, what prompted, or motivated, the learning of new responses or the establishment of new goals was the stress resulting from frustration.

Learning motivated by stress may also have taught you the value of escape and avoidance. You now know how to avoid getting into many motivational conflicts. You may have learned that the only sensible thing to do once you are in a conflict is to escape or to make major changes in what is motivating you. This is one way in which stress can be seen as a positive force in our lives. If we were never challenged, if we never set difficult goals, if we never faced stressful situations, we would miss out on many opportunities for personal growth and learning. The stress we experience might be unpleasant at the time, but it may produce positive consequences.

To say that we can, or should, respond to stressful situations by learning new, more effective behaviors is sensible enough, but are there any specific measures we can take to help alleviate the unpleasantness of stress in our lives? Indeed, there are many specific steps we can take. Here we'll review eight such strategies.

Identify the stressor. Remember that stress is a reaction to any one of several types of stressors. If you are experiencing stress in your life, perhaps the first thing you should ask is, "Where is it coming from?" Are you having difficulty resolving a motivational conflict? What positive or negative goals are involved? Is your goal-directed behavior being blocked or thwarted? If so, what is the source of your frustration? What recent changes or events in your life are particularly upsetting or problematic? Any successful strategy for coping with stress will require change—and effort—on your part. The first thing to do is to make sure your efforts are well directed.

In this regard, part of what I am talking about is directing your focus on efforts that are either *emotion-focused* or *problem-focused* (Lazarus & Folkman, 1984). The difference is rather self-evident. Strategies that are emotion focused deal with how you feel, and finding ways to feel differently. This is often one's first reaction to stressors. Real progress usually requires that you look beyond how you feel at the moment to discover the underlying situation that has caused the present feelings—a problem-focused strategy.

Remove or negate the stressor. Once a stressor has been identified, the next logical question is, "Can anything be done about it?" Do I *have* to stay in this situation, or can I bring about a change? If, for example, a particular interpersonal relationship has become a constant, nagging source of stress, might this be the time to think about breaking off the relationship? If the stress you experience at work has become overwhelming, might this be a good time to consider a different job? The issue is one of taking control, of trying to turn a challenge into an opportunity. Perhaps you recall that a tendency to take control of potentially stressful situations is one of the characteristics of people with the so-called "hardy personality" who usually manage to avoid many of the negative consequences of stress. Even people with a terminal illness fare much better if they take control, find out everything there is to know about their illness, seek second and third opinions, make the most of what time they have left, and so on (Folkman, 1984).

Reappraise the situation. We should assess whether the stressors in our lives are real or (even partially) imagined threats to our well-being. Making this determination is part of what is called a *cognitive reappraisal* of one's situation (e.g., Schultz & Decker, 1985). In the context of stress management, cognitive reappraisal means rethinking a situation to put it in the best possible light. Is that co-worker *really* trying to do you out of a promotion? Do you *really* care if you are invited to the party? *Must* you earn an A on the next test in order to pass the course? Are things *really* as bad as they seem? Lazarus (1993, p. 9) sees this as realizing that "people should try to change the noxious things that can be changed, accept those that cannot, and have the wisdom to know the difference"—a paraphrase of an ancient Hebrew prayer.

Meichenbaum (1977) argues that we can deal with a lot of stress simply by talking to ourselves, replacing negative statements (such as, "Oh boy, I'm really in trouble now. I'm sure to be called on and I'll embarrass myself in front of the whole class") with coping statements (such as, "I'll just do the best I can. I'm as prepared as anybody in here, and in a little while this will all be over"). This cognitive approach does take a bit of practice, but it can be very effective.

Inoculate against future stressors. This strategy involves accepting and internalizing much of what we have been saying about the universality of stress and stressors. It's a matter of convincing yourself that stress has occurred before, will occur again, and that this too will pass. It's a matter of anticipation and preparation—truly coming to accept the reality that "worrying about this won't make it any bet-

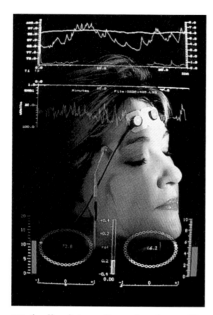

Biofeedback is an "emotion-focused" strategy for dealing with stressors. Even when effective, it won't remove the source of one's stress, but it can help one feel better.

ter," or "no matter how bad things look, I'll be able to figure out some plan to deal with it." We know, for example, that surgery patients recover faster and with fewer postsurgical complications if they are fully informed *before their surgery* of what they can expect, how they are likely to feel, and (importantly) what they can do to aid in their own recovery (MacDonald & Kuiper, 1983).

Inoculating oneself against future stressors amounts to trying to develop a sense of optimism, where optimism may be defined as the belief that good things, as opposed to bad things, will generally happen in one's life. People with this sort of optimistic outlook "routinely maintain higher levels of subjective well-being during times of stress than do people who are less optimistic" (Scheier & Carver, 1993, p. 27). Optimism also predicts such things as better adjustment in one's first year away at college, less felt depression among mothers following childbirth, and rate of recovery from heart surgery (Carver & Gaines, 1987; Scheier & Carver, 1992, 1993; Scheier et al., 1989).

Take your time with important decisions. Stress often accompanies the process of making tough decisions. You're frustrated. A goal-directed behavior is being blocked. You have to decide if you will pursue a different course of action. Which course of action? Would it be wiser to change your goal? Remember that we defined conflict in terms of making difficult decisions. Do you want to do this (+ and −) or do you want to do that (+ and −)? All I am implying with this strategy is that we make matters worse by rushing to make a decision "just to have it over with." Occasionally we are faced with deadlines by which final decisions must be made. But in many cases, we add to an already stressful situation by racing to conclusions before we have all of the facts, before we have explored all of the costs and benefits associated with the alternatives we are contemplating (e.g., Hogan, 1989). For example, if you can't make up your mind about a new car you're thinking about buying, why not rent one for a few days to see if you'd be happy with it in the long run?

So far, the strategies I've listed have made suggestions for dealing with the stressor that has caused the stress in one's life. As I've said before, being "problem focused" is the only long-term, effective way to deal with stressors. In the meantime, however, there are some things you can do to deal with the unpleasant feelings or affects that accompany stress (i.e., emotion-focused strategies). We'll look at three.

Learn techniques of relaxation. Learning effective ways to relax may not be as easy as it sounds, and may take some time and effort. The logic is simple: feeling stressed and being relaxed are incompatible responses. If you can become relaxed, the experience (feelings) of stress will be diminished (e.g., Lehrer & Woolfolk, 1984). Hypnosis may help. Meditation may help. So may relaxation training.

A variety of operant conditioning called **biofeedback** can provide relief from the tension associated with stress (Kamiya et al., 1977; Shirley, Matt, & Burish, 1992; Yates, 1980). Biofeedback is "the process of providing information to an individual about his [or her] bodily processes in some form which he [or she] might be able to use

biofeedback *a variety of operant conditioning that typically provides audio or visual information about an individual's bodily processes; the information can be used to modify these processes*

Physical exercise seldom removes stressors, but it has been found to be helpful in combatting the negative consequences of stress.

to modify those processes (Hill, 1985, p. 201). One's heart rate, let us say, is constantly monitored, and the rate is fed back to the person, perhaps in the form of an audible tone. As heart rate increases, the pitch of the tone becomes higher. As heart rate decreases, the tone gets lower. Once the learner knows (through the feedback) what his or her heart rate (or blood pressure, or muscle tension, and so on) is doing, a certain degree of control over that response is possible. The reinforcement involved here is simply the newly gained knowledge that a desired change is being made. As a result of being reinforced, the stress-fighting responses increase in their frequency (Kaplan, 1991; Kimmel, 1974; Miller, 1978; Thackwray-Emerson, 1989).

Engage in physical exercise. There is a body of evidence that claims that physical exercise can be a useful agent in the battle against stress (Brown, 1991; Crews & Landers, 1987; McCann & Holmes, 1984; Wheeler & Frank, 1988). On the other hand, there is some recent research that suggests that regular exercise and physical fitness—in themselves—are not all that important in fighting off stress, anxiety, and depression. Physical exercise may be helpful once stress is experienced. Even when it does help, it is difficult to say if exercise combats stress directly, or does so indirectly by improving physical health, stamina, self-esteem, and self-confidence. And of course, one must be careful. Deciding that tomorrow you'll start running five miles a day, rain or shine, may be a decision that in itself will create more stress than it will reduce. One needs to choose an exercise program that is enjoyable, not overly strenuous, and that helps one feel better about oneself.

Seek social support. Finally, I should mention the advantage of social support for persons who are experiencing stress. Stress is a common phenomenon. Perhaps no one else knows precisely how you feel, or has experienced exactly the same situation in which you find yourself, but all of us have known stress, and we are all aware of the types of situations that give rise to it. Social support, from friends and relatives, or from others, such as physicians, clergy, therapists, or counselors, can be very helpful (Coyne & Downey, 1991; Gottlieb, 1981; Hobfall, 1986; Janis, 1983b; Lieberman, 1983; Rook, 1987). If at all possible, one should not face stress alone.

Now that we've reviewed some of the steps one can take to help alleviate the unpleasantness of stress, let's consider some reactions stress can produce that are not as adaptive.

Before You Go On

What are some adaptive ways of dealing with stress?

Ineffective Strategies for Coping with Stressors

Simplistically speaking, if a person experiences stress and does *not* do any of the things previously listed, that person is not dealing effectively with the stressors in his or her life. More than anything else, coping effectively with stress is a matter of bringing about change. Not to change is to *fixate*, accepting the same stress from the same stressor. Fixation is seldom an adequate reaction to stress. Don't get me wrong here. "If at first you don't succeed, try, try again." Why, of course; this is sound advice. But, again, and again, and again? At some point we must be ready and able to give up a particular course of action to try something else.

In a way, procrastination is a form of fixation, isn't it? A student has a term paper due in two weeks and just can't seem to get going on it, deciding to "put if off until this weekend." This weekend may not bring any progress either, but at least the stress of dealing with the paper is momentarily postponed. The catch, of course, is that there's going to be a price to pay. Eventually, the paper will *have* to be done, and then, with very little time before the deadline, the experienced stress will probably be greater than ever before. In addition to not changing one's behavior or one's goals, or simply not doing anything at all, there are two other common reactions to stressors that are clearly maladaptive: aggression and anxiety.

It is clear that there are many sources or causes of aggression, and that one thing that motivates aggressive behavior is stress; in particular, stress that results from frustration. Remember our example of little Trudy, who was frustrated because she couldn't have a cookie, and tore the arm off her doll? At one time, it was proposed that frustration was *the* only cause of aggression, the so-called **frustration-aggression hypothesis** (Dollard et al., 1939). This point of view claimed that

frustration-aggression hypothesis the view (now discredited) that all aggression stems from frustration

Aggression that often follows frustration is an ineffective response because it does nothing to remove the stressor that caused the stress in the first place.

frustration could produce a number of reactions, including aggression, but that aggression was always caused by frustration. There *are* other sources of aggression (some view it as innate or instinctive, whereas others see it as a response learned through reinforcement or modeling that need not be stimulated by frustration). It is true, however, that frustration remains a prime candidate as the cause of aggression. It usually doesn't do much good in the long run, but a flash of aggressive behavior often follows stress (Berkowitz, 1978, 1982, 1989, 1990).

There you are in the parking lot, trying to get home from class, and your car won't start. Over and over you crank the ignition. Continuing to turn the key without success would be a good example of fixation—it's not doing you any good, but you keep at it, perhaps until you run down the battery. Still frustrated, you swing open the door, get out, kick the front left fender, throw up the hood, and glower at the engine. You're mad! Having released a bit of tension, you might feel better for a few seconds, but being angry and kicking at the car, or yelling at someone who offers to assist, won't help you solve your problem.

If stressors cannot be minimized or removed, if stressful experiences linger, the results may become debilitating. One of the consequences of stress is impaired physical health. Stress has been implicated in a number of physical disorders, mostly cardiovascular disease. We'll explore this relationship in some detail in our next Topic, on health psychology.

Another debilitating consequence of stress is *anxiety*—a general feeling of tension, apprehension, and dread that involves predictable physiological changes. Anxiety is a very difficult concept to define precisely, but everyone "knows" what you're talking about when you refer to anxiety. It is a reaction we have all experienced. Often, it is a reaction that follows or accompanies stress. In many ways we can think of anxiety as an unpleasant emotional component of the stress response. As much as anything else, we want to rid ourselves of stress in order to minimize our anxiety.

Sometimes, the amount of stress and anxiety in one's life becomes more than one can cope with effectively. Feelings of anxiety start to interfere with natural, normal adaptation to the environment and to other people. Feelings of anxiety may become the focus of one's attention. More anxiety follows, and then more distress, and more discomfort, and more pain. For many people—tens of millions of people in the United States and Canada—the anxiety that results from stress is so discomforting and so maladaptive that we say they are suffering from an anxiety-related psychological disorder. In Chapter 12 we will discuss psychological disorders, starting with the anxiety disorders. Keep in mind when you get to that discussion just how commonplace stress and anxiety are—and where most of that anxiety comes from.

Before You Go On

**What are some maladaptive reactions
to stressors?**

TOPIC 11A SUMMARY

In this Topic, we have dealt with stress, stressors, and reactions to both. I hope you now appreciate that *stress* is a strange term in common psychological usage. On the one hand, it is a response to stressors, real or perceived threats to our sense of well-being or to our resources. At the same time, stress is a motivator, stimulating us to engage in behaviors that reduce (at least) the felt negative aspects of stress.

In order to respond to (we often say "cope with") stress effectively, we need to bring about some change in the situation that caused the stress. Stressors can be either frustration (the blocking of goal-directed behaviors), conflict (motives and drives that cannot all be satisfied at the same time), or, simply, life events, particularly changes in our lives. Hans Selye saw stress as a physiological reaction to stressors involving three stages: alarm, resistance, and exhaustion. We now recognize that dealing with stress encompasses a cognitive component as well, and we can talk about effective and ineffective means of dealing with stress. Remember, stress cannot be avoided; successful reactions are aimed at the stressor that caused the stress one is experiencing.

Successful problem-oriented strategies include identifying the true stressor, removing or negating that stressor, engaging in cognitive reappraisal, inoculating oneself against future stressors, and taking one's time with important decisions. Successful emotion-oriented strategies include learning techniques of relaxation, engaging in physical exercise, and seeking social support. Ineffective strategies include fixation, aggression, and anxiety.

T o p i c   1 1 B
HEALTH PSYCHOLOGY

Health psychology is a subfield of psychology just over 25 years old, although the issues involved have been of general concern for a long time. Health psychology became a division of the American Psychological Association in 1978 (Division 38) and now has approximately 3,000 members—an increase of nearly 200 percent over 1980 membership. **Health psychology** is the study of psychological or behavioral factors affecting physical health and illness. As applied psychologists, or practitioners, health psychologists help people cope with physical diseases and illnesses, and are involved in efforts to try to prevent health problems from occurring in the first place. As research scientists, health psychologists seek to better understand the relationships between psychological functioning and physical health.

health psychology the field of applied psychology that studies psychological factors affecting physical health and illness

The involvement of psychologists in the medical realm of physical health and well-being is based on at least four assumptions:

1. Certain behaviors increase the risk of certain chronic diseases.

2. Changes in behaviors can reduce the risk of certain diseases.

3. Changing behaviors is often easier and safer than treating many diseases.

4. Behavioral interventions are comparatively cost-effective (Kaplan, 1984).

In this Topic, we'll examine two major thrusts of health psychology. We'll look at the relationships between psychological variables and physical health, an issue we anticipated in Topic 11A when we saw that stress—a psychological reaction—can have serious physical consequences. Then, we'll consider how psychologists are joining the fight against illness and disease. I'll use three extended examples: (1) attempting to get people to stop smoking, (2) dealing with the consequences of sexually transmitted diseases, AIDS in particular, and (3) helping patients follow their doctors' orders.

PSYCHOLOGICAL FACTORS THAT INFLUENCE PHYSICAL HEALTH

Is there a relationship between aspects of one's personality and one's state of physical health? Can psychological evaluations of an individual predict physical disease as well as psychological disorders? Is there such a thing as a disease-prone personality? Our response is tentative, and all of the data are not supportive, but for now we can respond, "Yes, there is a positive correlation between some personality variables and physical health."

One meta-analysis of 101 previously published research articles looked for relationships between personality measures and physical disease (including coronary heart disease, asthma, ulcers, arthritis, and headaches). The strongest associations were those that predicted coronary heart disease, although depression, anxiety, and anger or hostility were each associated to some degree with all of the physical components studied (Friedman & Booth-Kewley, 1987). On the basis of their analysis, the authors argued that there are sufficient (albeit weak) data linking some personality variables to some physical diseases to "argue for a key role for psychological research on the prevention and treatment of disease" (p. 539).

Type A behavior pattern (TABP) a collection of behaviors (competitive, achievement-oriented, impatient, easily aroused, often hostile or angry) commonly associated with coronary heart disease

When we talk about relating personality variables to physical diseases, what commonly comes to mind is the **Type A behavior pattern** (**TABP**) and coronary heart disease. As it was originally defined, TABP refers to a competitive, achievement-oriented, impatient individual who typically works at many tasks at the same time, is easily aroused, and is often hostile or angry (Friedman & Rosenman, 1959; Rosenman et al., 1964). Coronary heart disease (CHD) is a general label given to several physical symptoms, including chest pains and heart attacks, caused by a buildup of substances, such as cholesterol, that block major arteries. Some people demonstrate a *Type B behavior pattern*. These individuals show a relative lack of Type A characteristics, and are comparatively more relaxed and easygoing.

For nearly twenty years—from the early 1960s to the early 1980s—study after study found a clear, positive relationship between CHD and behaviors typical of the Type A personality (Jenkins, 1976; Rosenman et al., 1975; Wood, 1986). Persons with Type B behavior patterns were less than half as likely to experience coronary heart disease than were persons with Type A behavior patterns. A panel of the National Institutes of Health declared the Type A behavior pattern to be an independent risk factor for heart disease (National Institutes of Health, 1981). The Type A personality profile has been implicated in hypertension (chronic high blood pressure) even when no other signs of coronary heart disease are present (Irvine et al., 1991). It all seemed clear. Find people with the Type A behavior pattern, intervene to change their behaviors, and watch coronary heart disease rates decline. By now you know to be suspicious when complex problems seem to have simple solutions.

Beginning in the early 1980s, data began to surface that failed to show a clear relation between TABP and CHD (Fishman, 1987; Krantz & Glass, 1984; Matthews, 1982, 1988; Shekelle et al., 1985;

Wright, 1988). Perhaps Type A people were no more at risk for heart disease than anyone else. Perhaps studies that failed to find a relation between TABP and CHD were seriously flawed. Both of these hypotheses have evidence to support them. For one thing, the Type A behavioral pattern is complex and difficult to assess. It is likely that simple paper-and-pencil inventories—of the sort that have been used in many studies—fail to identify a large number of people with the TABP.

It also may be that the TABP, as presently defined, is too global a pattern of behaviors (Dembroski & Costa, 1987). Perhaps there is a subset of behaviors within the constellation of Type A behaviors that does predict coronary disease. This is a hypothesis now under investigation by many psychologists, including Logan Wright, a self-confessed Type A personality, who needed bypass surgery to relieve blockage of a coronary artery. As Wright put it, "... if certain so-called active ingredients, or subcomponents of the TABP are what is really responsible for coronary-prone risk, one would expect to find them to correlate more highly with CHD than does the global Type A pattern itself" (1988, p. 3).

What are Wright's candidates for the most likely active ingredients of the Type A personality?

1. *Time urgency:* concern over wasting precious, small bits of time; shifting lanes while in traffic to gain a car length

2. *Chronic activation:* the tendency to stay alert and aroused and ready all of the time; being "fired up" for everything, no matter how mundane

3. *Multiphasia:* the tendency to have several projects all going at once, having many irons in the fire; doing homework and eating while watching TV

There is research to suggest that these components, taken together, predict coronary heart disease, but the evidence is not conclusive. Other research suggests that the potent ingedients of a Type A personality are anger and hostility (Barefoot, Dahlstrom, & Williams, 1983; Dembroski et al., 1985; Houston & Vavak, 1991).

A recent meta-analysis by Scott Lyness tells us that there *is* a relationship between the Type A behavior pattern on the one hand, and heart rate and blood pressure levels on the other (Lyness, 1993). What may be most significant about these findings is that there were virtually no differences between Type A and Type B persons on *baseline* measures. Differences appeared, however, when people with these "personality types" were exposed to stressful situations. When responding to stressors, the Type A individuals showed the significant increase in blood pressure and heart rate.

Lyness found no significant gender differences in Type A and Type B patterns. This finding is consistent with data from others who have found women with Type A or Type B behavior patterns *equally* at risk for nonfatal heart attacks (e.g., Shekelle & Gale, 1985). However,

Lynda Powell and her associates have found gender differences, but in a curious way (Powell et al., 1993). These researchers found that after one has a first heart attack, women with a *Type B* behavior pattern are *more* likely than other women to have subsequent cardiovascular problems and additional heart attacks. In other words, there is a survival advantage for women with Type A behavior patterns following a heart attack (see also Eaker et al., 1988). According to Powell's research, women with Type B personality profiles, and whose aspirations to a traditional family life-style go unfulfilled, appear to be at greatest risk for subsequent cardiovascular disease.

More work needs to be done. We need research on adequately diagnosing Type A behavior patterns and on the mechanisms that underlie whatever relationships there may be between TABP and CHD. We also need research on how to bring about psychological changes in those individuals that would reduce the likelihood of their contracting any physical disease. In many ways, the ingredients of TABP are precisely the characteristics many people in our society learn to value and to imitate in their quest to "get ahead." How can psychologists intervene to help people change those behaviors that directly and indirectly impact on their state of health? It is to matters of intervention that we now turn.

Before You Go On

Briefly summarize the relationship between
the Type A behavior pattern and
coronary heart disease.

PROMOTING HEALTHY BEHAVIORS

At the very least, it is possible that some personality characteristics have an impact on one's physical health. The specific traits involved and the nature of that impact are the subject of debate and ongoing research. There is no debate and no doubt, however, that certain behaviors put people at risk for physical disease and death. One of the roles of the health psychologist is to help bring about changes in potentially dangerous behaviors (e.g., Kirscht, 1983, Levine, Toro, & Perkins, 1993; Matarazzo, 1980; Miller, 1983). This will be the focus of this section. (A concern for preventing and treating mental disorders will be the focus of Chapter 13.)

Why Do People Die?

Obviously, people die for an almost infinite number of reasons. Ultimately, death is unavoidable. On the other hand, many causes of death are "premature," and to a degree, preventable.

Let's review a few gruesome statistics. In general terms, "7 of the 10 leading causes of death in the United States are in large part behaviorally determined. We believe these unhealthy behaviors can be significantly reduced with the help of psychologists" (Heffernan & Albee, 1985, p. 202). The leading causes of death in this country are cardiovascular disorders and cancers, diseases caused and maintained by the interaction of several factors, including genetic, biological, social, environmental, and behavioral influences. Among the behavioral influences, such variables as cigarette smoking, nutrition, obesity, and stress have been identified as important risk factors (Krantz et al., 1985). What this means is that millions of people engage in what may be referred to as a deadly life-style. Consider these data from a recent review article in the *Journal of the American Medical Association.*

> In 1990 there were 2,148,000 deaths in the United States. Of these, 400,000 deaths could be traced to tobacco use; diet and activity patterns accounted for 300,000 deaths, alcohol use accounted for 100,000 deaths, microbial agents (bacteria and viruses) 90,000 deaths, toxic agents 60,000 deaths, firearms 35,000 deaths, sexual behaviors 30,000 deaths, motor vehicles 25,000 deaths, and illegal drug use 20,000 deaths. (McGinnis & Foege, 1993, p. 2207)

In many of these cases, there was probably little or nothing that could have been done to prevent or delay death. But in many cases, bringing about changes in behavior in a timely fashion might have reduced these numbers.

Notice that a deadly life-style may involve behaviors that directly lead to death; for instance, failing to wear safety belts or knowingly engaging in other unsafe behaviors at work or play. Statistics from the Department of Health and Human Services and from the Centers for Disease Control (CDC) tell us that at current rates, deaths by gunfire have surpassed deaths by traffic accidents. Nearly 50,000 children and teenagers were killed by firearms between 1979 and 1991—a number nearly equal to the American casualties in the Vietnam War.

Interventions designed to prevent health problems from arising in the first place have been applied to a range of behaviors and situations, including smoking and the misuse of alcohol. Programs have tried to impact on nutrition, physical fitness and exercise, controlling stress and high blood pressure, immunization, and unsafe sexual behaviors (Jeffery, 1989; McGinnis, 1985; Rodin & Salovey, 1989). Psychologists also use behavioral techniques in attempts to promote healthy and safe behaviors, such as the wearing of car safety belts (Geller et al., 1987). Many psychologists argue that we should be doing all we can to help promote healthy environments (such as smoke-free spaces, safe work places, opportunities for exercise at work, the installation of air bags in cars), as well as working to change individual behaviors (e.g., Aldwin & Stokals, 1988; Fielding & Phenow, 1988; Geller et al., 1982; Stokals, 1992).

For the remainder of this Topic, we will examine three areas in which health psychologists have been particularly active: helping peo-

Antismoking ads, such as this one from the American Cancer Society, are aimed at getting people to stop smoking—or not to start in the first place. Psychologists can have a powerful impact on physical health in that they can help reduce cigarette smoking.

ple to stop smoking, helping to deal with or prevent sexually transmitted diseases, and assisting patients to follow their doctors' orders.

Helping People to Stop Smoking

Although efforts to bring about attitudinal and behavioral change have been moving forward on many fronts, few have received as much attention as efforts to discourage young people from smoking. One reason for special efforts in this area is that smoking is so deadly, accounting for about one-third of all cancer deaths (Doll & Peto, 1981) and nearly 400,000 of all deaths each year (Jeffery, 1989). In 1979, the Surgeon General called cigarette smoking the single most preventable cause of death in America. Cigarettes are now viewed as one of the most addictive of substances, and among the most deadly (Fiore et al., 1989; Schelling, 1992; Surgeon General, 1988). In the 1990s, concern includes the impact of "second-hand smoke," as we see evidence that the children of parents who smoke are significantly at risk for lung cancer even if they, as adults, have never smoked. Of particular concern is the fact that an estimated 2.2 million American children ages 12 to 17 smoke cigarettes, and 9 million children under age 5 live with smokers, according to the American Heart Association. Each day an estimated 3,000 children begin smoking, claims Dr. James Moller, president of the American Heart Association.

Yet another reason for concern among health psychologists is that success rates of programs to persuade smokers to quit smoking have not been encouraging: nearly 80 percent of "quitters" relapse within a year (e.g., Cohen et al., 1989; Glasgow & Lichtenstein, 1987; Leventhal & Cleary, 1980). This statistic isn't as depressing as it may first appear when we consider that a person who finally does give up smoking permanently has quit, on the average, five times before. In fact, most smokers who quit permanently do so without any special program of intervention. And, in fact, the total number of smokers in the United States and Canada *is* decreasing, albeit at a rather slow rate (Hugick & Leonard, 1991).

Psychologists *have* been reasonably successful designing programs aimed at getting people—teenagers in particular—to refrain from smoking in the first place. Given the pressures of national advertising campaigns by the tobacco industry, the effort has not been an easy one. As more and more government and public facilities declare themselves "smoke-free environments," the more difficult it is for people to begin or continue smoking. Informational campaigns aimed at high school students *can* be effective (e.g., Evans et al., 1981). Approaches that use role models and peers to teach specific skills to be used to resist pressures to begin smoking in the first place have been successful, where the focus is on short-term benefits derived from not smoking, such as freedom from coughing and bad breath, and positive factors such as improved appearance (e.g., Murray et al., 1984).

Before You Go On

Why do psychologists care about smoking
behaviors, and what can they do about them?

Sexually Transmitted Diseases

Sexually transmitted diseases (STDs) are contagious diseases, usually
passed on through sexual contact. A review of the STDs fits into this
Topic for two reasons: (1) persons with sexually transmitted diseases
often experience as many psychological consequences as medical
ones, and (2) attempts to prevent the transmission of these diseases
involve psychological interventions to get people to change their
behaviors. Sexually transmitted diseases affect millions of individuals
each year, and for every person we know of with an STD, there may
be two to five others with the disease, but in a nonsymptomatic stage,
and, thus, not yet diagnosed. We will begin with a description of the
more common STDs, and then consider psychological interventions
aimed at controlling the spread of AIDS, the most deadly of the STDs.

   Common STDs. **Chlamydia** is one of the most common of the
STDs in North America. Chlamydia is caused by a bacterial infection.
It is usually diagnosed in sexually active persons younger than 35. Its
incidence is soaring. Approximately 4 million Americans have the disease. Symptoms include burning urination in both men and women.
Men may experience a penile discharge; women may experience a disruption in their menstrual cycle. Left untreated in women, chlamydia
can lead to pelvic inflammatory disease (PID), which can cause infertility (in about 100,000 women a year). When diagnosed, treatment
with an antibiotic, usually erythromycin, is usually effective within
one week.

   Gonorrhea also is a disease of the young and sexually active. Of
the more than 1.8 million cases that will be diagnosed this year, most
will be men between the ages of 20 and 24. It, too, is a bacterial infection that affects the moist tissue areas around the genitals. The bacteria that produce the symptoms of gonorrhea can live for only a few
seconds outside the human body, so there is little likelihood of contracting the disease from toilet seats, eating utensils, towels, or drinking fountains. One may be infected with the gonorrhea bacteria and
not even know it. This is particularly true for women, most of whom
remain relatively free of symptoms. When symptoms do develop, they
are much like those experienced with chlamydia: frequent, painful
urination, vaginal discharges, and a reddening of the genital area. In
men, there is a milky discharge from the penis and painful, frequent
urination. Treatment for this STD—penicillin, or tetracycline—is simple and usually successful, although drug-resistant strains have been
noted.

   Syphilis is caused by a bacterium called a spirochete. If left
untreated, the disease may run its course through four known stages,

*sexually transmitted diseases
(STDs) contagious diseases that are
usually transmitted through sexual
contact*

*chlamydia a common STD caused
by a bacterial infection that can lead
to PID and infertility in women if
untreated*

*gonorrhea an STD caused by a
bacterial infection of moist tissues in
the genital area*

*syphilis an STD caused by a
bacterial infection; the disease may
pass through four stages, ultimately
resulting in death*

genital herpes (herpes type II) the most common STD; a skin infection in the form of a rash or blisters in the genital area

from a relatively simple and painless sore, all the way to the infection of other, nonsexual organs, which may lead to death. Just 10 years ago it was believed that syphilis had become a disease of the past. Then, in the fall of 1990, the Centers for Disease Control (CDC) released figures indicating that since 1985, the number of syphilis cases had skyrocketed. Rates were up 60 percent (132 percent among the black population) to levels not seen since 1949. Nearly 85,000 new cases can be expected this year. It's as if, with the focus of attention on AIDS, many people have forgotten about the other STDs. A study released by the Ontario Ministry of Health in the summer of 1993 reported that females aged 15 to 19 suffered the highest rate (about 5,000 cases) of chlamydia, gonorrhea, and syphilis in 1992. Treatment for syphilis is simple once a diagnosis has been confirmed. Penicillin (or tetracycline) is used, and the prognosis is related to length of infection. As is the case for so many diseases, the sooner treatment begins, the better the prognosis.

Genital herpes (herpes type II) is a skin disease that affects the genital area, producing small sores and blisters. It is not caused by bacteria, but by a virus that was virtually unknown until the mid-1960s. Now, genital herpes is one of the most common of the STDs. Some estimates place incidence rates as high as 40 million Americans, with 500,000 new cases each year. At the moment, herpes has no cure, although medication can reduce the occasionally painful symptoms. A person with genital herpes is most infectious when the sores and blisters are active and erupting. There may be long periods during which the infected person remains symptom free, only to have the reddening and sores recur. It seems that levels of stress in one's life are related to the onset of active herpes symptoms (VanderPlate, Aral, & Magder, 1988). There are no life-threatening complications of the disease in males, but genital herpes in females increases the risk of contracting cervical cancer. Another complication arises when pregnant women contract genital herpes. The herpes virus can be passed along during childbirth, which can cause considerable damage, even death, to the newborn.

acquired immune deficiency syndrome (AIDS) a deadly disease caused by a virus (the HIV) that destroys the body's natural immune system; can be transmitted by an interchange of blood or semen

No other STD has attracted as much public attention as has **acquired immune deficiency syndrome**, or **AIDS**. AIDS was virtually unknown in the United States before 1981. Just 12 years later, over 250,000 cases and more than 160,000 deaths had been reported by the Centers for Disease Control (CDC). Of those deaths, 31,000 were in 1990 alone. In 1992, the CDC counted 47,095 new cases, up 3.5 percent over 1991 figures. Recently, AIDS has risen to be among the most common (fifth) killer of women. In 1982, 18 American women died of AIDS; in 1988, 1,430 died. By 1993, more than half of the women with AIDS were infected through heterosexual contact. Globally, estimates of the World Health Organization suggest that nearly 20 million men and women will be infected by the year 2000. After the Ninth International Conference on AIDS in June of 1993, Dr. James Curran, director of the AIDS program at CDC, said he was "more impressed with the progress of the virus than the progress of science." Also in the summer of 1993, health experts told a U.S.

Senate committee that the cost of treating Americans with AIDS could rise to $15.2 billion by 1995. Just what is AIDS?

AIDS is caused by a virus called the *human immunodeficiency virus,* or HIV. The HIV almost always enters the body through sexual contact or through the use of contaminated needles in intravenous (IV) drug use. About 1 infant in 3 born to an HIV-positive mother will also be infected. Each year, about 2,000 babies are born HIV-positive. In infected persons, concentrations of the virus are highest in the blood, semen, and vaginal fluids. An infected person may experience few symptoms other than those usually associated with the common cold. Then the person enters what is called a carrier state. He or she may pass the virus on to others, yet remain symptom free. What is not clear is just how many persons infected with the HIV will develop AIDS, or how long the process takes. Of those with a diagnosis of AIDS (not just HIV-positive), virtually all will die within four years.

The HIV directly attacks the body's immune system, which fights off infections. With a weakened or nonfunctioning immune system, someone with AIDS does not have the resources to defend against other infections that normally would not be life-threatening. In other words, patients do not die of AIDS directly, but from other diseases or opportunistic infections (e.g., pneumonia or cancer) against which the body cannot defend.

HIV cannot be transmitted by casual contact; there has to be an interchange of bodily fluids (usually blood or semen). Early in the 1980s, it was commonly believed that AIDS was restricted to homosexual males and intravenous drug users. This is clearly not the case. That in this country the disease was first noticed in the gay male population is, as much as anything else, an accident of history.

Whereas other sexually transmitted diseases can cause discomfort and pain, AIDS will be fatal. There is no vaccine to prevent it. There is no cure for AIDS, and it is unlikely that one will be discovered soon. The only reasonable way to avoid AIDS is through the monitoring of one's behaviors. Psychological interventions aimed at preventing the spread of AIDS is where we now turn.

Psychological Interventions to Decrease the Incidence of AIDS. "Behavior change remains the only means for primary prevention of HIV disease. Psychology should take a leading role in efforts to curtail the epidemic, but has not contributed to HIV prevention at a level proportionate to the urgency of the crisis" (Kelly et al., 1993, p. 1023). Attempts to prevent AIDS, or at the very least, to reduce the rate at which the disease is spreading, have met with mixed results. Successful interventions have been multifaceted, involving education, the changing of attitudes, increasing motivation to engage in safe (or safer) sexual practices, and providing people with the "negotiating skills (e.g., to say 'no' or 'please wear a condom')" to avoid high-risk situations in the first place (Brigham, 1991, p. 617).

Attempts to inform and educate have been reasonably successful. In 1987, for example, the Surgeon General's Office mailed a pamphlet describing AIDS and suggesting what could be done to avoid the HIV infection to every household in the United States. The effort was well

Knowledge and awareness of AIDS have increased in recent years, due to more educational programs, advertising regarding condoms, and movies such as Philadelphia, *starring Academy-award winner Tom Hanks.*

received and has been credited for helping increase the sales of condoms (Gerbert & Maguire, 1989; Moran et al., 1990). By and large, most Americans *are* aware of AIDS, do have a reasonable idea of what causes the disease, and are even aware of what steps need to be taken to avoid it (e.g., Levine, Toro, & Perkins, 1993; Sheridan et al., 1990).

On the assumption that many adolescents and adults will not abstain from sex altogether, many experts counsel "safe sex," but there is disagreement on just what safe sex *is*. In general, the advice seems reasonable. The fewer sexual contacts one has, the less the probability of encountering someone infected with the HIV. The more selective one is in choosing a partner, the less the risk. The use of condoms reduces, but does not eliminate, the likelihood of infection. Engaging in sexual behaviors in which there is no exchange of bodily fluids (such as mutual masturbation) also contributes to lower-risk sex (Masters, Johnson, & Kolodny, 1987). What is particularly discouraging to health officials is that even with considerable knowledge about AIDS, few people seem willing to change their sexual practices (e.g., Klepinger et al., 1993).

Young people in particular seem well aware of the AIDS epidemic, but also seem convinced that an HIV infection will happen only to someone else. For example, a report from the Centers for Disease Control released in 1991 tells us that nearly twice as many teenage girls (51.5 percent) had engaged in premarital sex by their late teens in 1988 compared to 1970 (28.6 percent), and the largest relative increase was among girls 15 years old. Many teenagers believe that they simply will not get AIDS, and most do not use condoms (Hansen, Hahn, & Wolkenstein, 1990).

Some programs that go beyond providing information and actively seek to change behaviors *have* been effective—particularly those aimed at small groups identified as members of "high risk" populations, such as gay men and IV drug users (e.g., DeJarlais & Friedman, 1988; Kelly et al., 1993; Stall et al., 1988). What seems to work particularly well are long-term, small group sessions that present information and provide social support for changing high-risk behaviors (Kelly et al., 1989; Sorensen et al., 1991). Although short-term gains (in changing attitudes and behaviors) have been noted, maintaining those gains for the long term has proven more difficult (Kelly et al., 1991). The "enormous challenge posed by HIV infection suggests that multiple approaches will be necessary to have the largest and most lasting effects" (Levine et al., 1993, p. 549).

Yes, AIDS *is* a physical disease. A biological organism, a virus, attacks the immune system, which increases the possibility of further infection, which ultimately results in death. But AIDS is a physical disease with unprecedented psychological complications. Patients who have been diagnosed with HIV but who have not yet developed AIDS tend to be more depressed and disturbed than those who have developed the full-blown and fatal symptoms of the disease (Chuang et al., 1989). At the same time, and as you might expect, people with a diagnosis of AIDS experience significant levels of stress, depression, anger, anxiety, and denial (Herek & Glunt, 1988; Kelly & St. Lawrence, 1988; Namir et al., 1987). Males with AIDS are almost 7.5 *times* more likely to commit suicide than are men in the general population (Coté et al., 1992). Because AIDS can be such a devastating disease, AIDS patients are often shunned—by loved ones and even health care professionals. In late 1987, the American Medical Association felt it had to issue a statement that it is unethical for a physician to refuse treatment to an AIDS patient. In January of 1994, the U.S. Public Health Service published a 196-page "clinical practice guideline" on how to diagnose and manage patients in the early stages of infection by HIV. The Health Service's concern was that too many primary care, general practice, physicians were unnecessarily referring suspected HIV patients to "specialists." The fear, alienation, and stress experienced by AIDS patients (and often by their friends and families) are in many ways as painful as the disease itself and require psychological treatment (e.g., Knapp & VandeCreek, 1989).

Before You Go On

Name and briefly describe five sexually transmitted diseases.

What role(s) can psychologists play in the fight against AIDS?

Helping Patients "Follow Doctors' Orders"

In addition to designing and implementing programs aimed at preventing diseases, health psychologists also intervene to help in the treatment of physical illness and disease (Meichenbaum & Turk, 1987; Rodin & Salovey, 1989). As an example of this sort of work, consider efforts to help patients comply with the orders of their physicians. Even the best of medical advice will be useless if it is not followed. I was surprised to learn that best estimates are that as many as 50 percent of patients fail to follow their doctors' orders with regard to taking prescribed medicines (Adler & Stone, 1984; DiMatteo & Friedman, 1988; Ley, 1977). This is particularly true when the illness produces no immediate discomfort or apparent risk (Rodin & Salovey, 1989). And most physicians fail to notice that their patients are not following orders (Witenberg et al., 1983).

There are many reasons why patients fail to comply with doctors' orders, including lack of communication between patient and doctor, the financial burden imposed by expensive medications, the extent of disruption of daily routine required to follow the regimen of daily medication, and the lack of clear vision of the advantage of doing so. It also may be the case that some doctors' orders are ignored because the patient (perhaps in consultation with other physicians) decides that his or her doctor's orders are "wrong," or not the best course of action.

Psychologists can assist in improving patient-physician communication with regard to medication and can assist patients in monitoring their daily medications. At the very least, it seems to help to give patients written instructions rather than oral instructions, although increased compliance does seem to be somewhat short lived (Morris & Halperin, 1979). Consistent with what we said in our last Topic, providing social support for a patient will increase compliance with doctors' orders. Consistent with what we said in our Topic on operant conditioning, providing specific reinforcers for following orders is also effective (Epstein & Cluss, 1982).

As an example, many diabetics find it difficult to maintain their daily treatment regimens. Several strategies have proven useful for this purpose, including the following:

1. *Specific assignments* that unambiguously define what is to be done

2. *Skill training* to develop new behaviors relevant to treatment

3. *Cuing* of specific behaviors with salient stimuli; that is, telling the patient precisely what is to be done under specified conditions

4. *Tailoring* of the regimen to meet the schedule and particular needs of the patient

5. *Contracts* between patient, therapist, and significant others for prescribed behavior change

6. *Shaping* of successive approximations of the desired treatment regimen

7. *Self-monitoring* of behaviors relevant to treatment

8. *Reinforcement* of new behaviors (Surwit et al., 1983, p. 260)

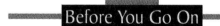

Before You Go On

How have health psychologists intervened to improve patient compliance with doctors' orders?

TOPIC 11 B SUMMARY

In this Topic, we've reviewed some of the activities that occupy today's health psychologists. The basic message is that there are many ways in which psychological factors impact on the state of one's physical health. We've seen that there are at least some personality variables, part of the "Type A behavior pattern," associated with physical disease, coronary heart disease in particular.

A major contention of health psychology is that many physical diseases or illnesses are at least partially caused by psychological or behavioral factors—that the incidence of many, often deadly, diseases could be significantly reduced if people could be helped to change some of their behaviors. We looked at three examples of interventions aimed at promoting healthy behaviors: helping people to stop smoking, helping people change their risky sexual practices in order to avoid STDs, and helping people to comply with instructions from their physicians. On each of these fronts, progress has been made; there are success stories, but there is still a long way to go.

TOPIC 11A

What is meant by frustration-induced stress?

Define environmental and personal frustration, citing an example of each.

Frustration, a stressor, is the blocking or thwarting of one's goal-directed behaviors. The type of frustration one experiences depends on the source of the blocking. If it is someone or something in one's environment thwarting goal-directed behaviors, we have *environmental frustration*. There are many examples: your car won't start; your pen runs out of ink during an exam; your dog eats your term paper. If the source of the frustration is some characteristic of the person himself or herself, we have *personal frustration*. Examples include someone who does poorly in a physics class because of a poor math background, or someone who agrees to go mountain climbing even though inexperienced and totally out of shape. /*p. 552*

Name four types of motivational conflict and provide an example of each.

Motivational conflicts are stressors. They are situations in which we find ourselves faced with difficult choices to make. In an *approach-approach conflict*, one is faced with two (or more) attractive (positive) goals and must choose among them. In an *avoidance-avoidance conflict*, a choice must be made between or among unpleasant (negative) alternatives. In an *approach-avoidance conflict*, there is but one goal under consideration; in some ways that goal is positive, in others it is negative (it attracts and repels at the same time). In a *multiple approach-avoidance conflict*, one faces a number of alternatives, each of which has its strengths and its weaknesses, and a choice must be made between or among them. /*p. 554*

In what ways might life events produce stress?

This question is not as cynical as it may sound. Many psychologists argue that life events, particularly changes in one's life situation, can act as stressors. The Social Readjustment Rating Scale (SRRS) is one

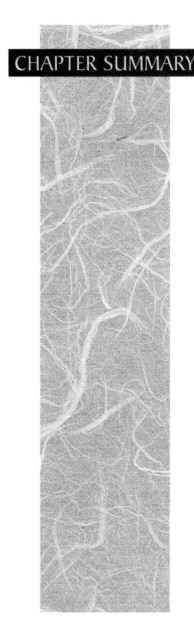

CHAPTER SUMMARY

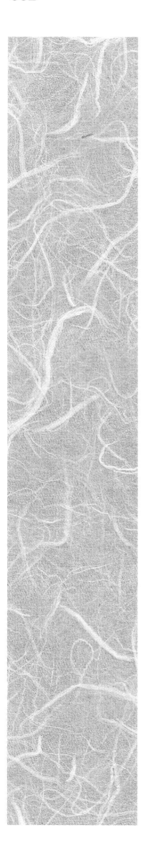

example of an instrument that attempts to measure the amount of stress in one's life by having the person indicate recent life-change events. High scores on such scales are associated with an above-average incidence of physical illness and disease. Some psychologists claim that the little "hassles" of life can be more stressful in their effects than many large-scale life events. Socioeconomic status is positively correlated with stress and health. Life-change events do not have to be evaluated as negative, unpleasant events in order to act as stressors. /p. 558

What does it mean to say that there are individual differences in reactions to stressors?

People often respond differently when presented with the same stressor. What some people find challenging, others may find overwhelmingly stressful. One's reaction to stressors also varies over time, which means that events that do not seem stressful today may seem so tomorrow. Some individuals seem particularly resistant to stressors, and have been called "hardy personalities." Such people tend to see difficulties as opportunities, have a sense of being in control of their lives, and are fully engaged and committed to life. /p. 559

Name and describe the three stages of Selye's general adaptation syndrome.

According to Hans Selye, a prolonged stress reaction progresses through three stages, collectively referred to as the general adaptation syndrome. At first there is the mobilization of the sympathetic nervous system of the ANS in the *alarm stage* as the body prepares to cope with the stressor. If the stressor is not removed, the body goes into a stage of *resistance*, in which resources continue to be mobilized but new stressors are difficultly dealt with, and in which physical illness becomes more and more likely. If the stressor remains, one may finally enter an *exhaustion stage*, in which the body's resources become depleted, adaptation breaks down, and serious illness or death may result. /p. 561

What are some adaptive ways of dealing with stress?

In general terms, the most effective means of dealing with stress is to deal with the stressors that caused it, and to do so by using the experience to bring about a relatively permanent change in one's behaviors—which is to say to learn new behaviors that will help one cope with stressors. There are two approaches to dealing with stress. One is problem focused, and includes such things as identifying the specific stressor causing one's stress, removing or minimizing the stressor, reappraising the situation, inoculating oneself against future stressors, and taking one's time in making difficult decisions. Battling the unpleasant feelings of stress, called emotion-focused approaches, include learning relaxation techniques, engaging in physical exercise, and seeking social support. /p. 566

What are some maladaptive reactions to stressors?

Maladaptive reactions to stressors are those that interfere with attempts to change one's behaviors as a result of experiencing stress. *Fixation* is the term we use to describe a pattern of behaviors in which a person tries over and over again to deal with stressors, is unsuccessful, but does not try anything new or different. *Aggression* often results from stress, particularly frustration (but not always from frustration, which is what the frustration-aggression hypothesis claims). Although aggression may yield a momentary release of tension, in itself, it usually does not remove the original stressor. *Anxiety* is yet another maladaptive response to stress. This general feeling of apprehension and dread is often the aspect of experienced stress that motivates us to do something about it. /*p. 568*

TOPIC 11B

Briefly summarize the relationship between the Type A behavior pattern and coronary heart disease.

There is a relationship between some psychological, or personality, variables and physical health; that is, some psychological traits put one at risk for disease. Beginning in the late 1950s, evidence accumulated that showed a strong, positive relationship between a Type A behavior pattern, or TABP (typified by a person who is competitive, achievement-oriented, impatient, easily aroused, often angry or hostile, and who tends to have many projects all going at once) and coronary heart disease (blockage of major arteries). The picture, it now seems, is a little less clear as psychologists seek to identify the "active ingredients" of the TABP. Some claim that time urgency, chronic activation, and multiphasia are the main culprits, whereas others have focused on the influence of anger and hostility as being best correlated with coronary disease. /*p. 572*

Why do psychologists care about smoking behaviors, and what can they do about them?

Of the leading causes of death in this country, most could be reduced by behavioral change. There are few behaviors that impact as directly on the state of one's health to any greater degree than smoking. It is a central part of what has been called a "deadly life-style." Smoking may account for as many as 400,000 deaths each year. Health psychologists continue to look for effective means of helping people to stop smoking. By and large, efforts have not met with much success. Most smokers who do quit on a "permanent" basis do so on their own. But overall, the number of smokers is decreasing, and efforts to get teens to avoid smoking in the first place have met with some success. /*p. 575*

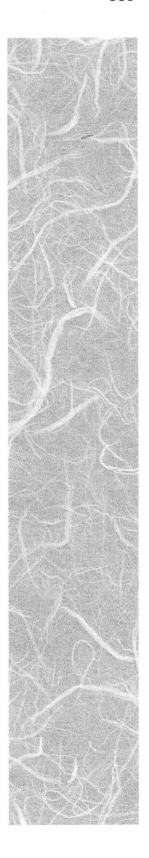

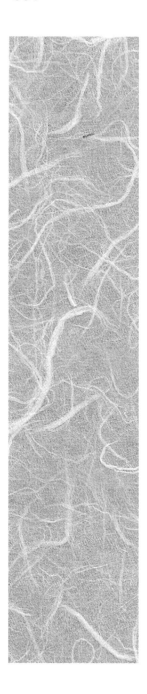

Name and briefly describe five sexually transmitted diseases.

What role(s) can psychologists play in the fight against AIDS?

Sexually transmitted diseases (STDs) are common. Among them are (1) *Chlamydia,* a bacterial infection of the genitals that results in painful urination and fluid discharge. Left untreated in women, it may lead to pelvic inflammatory disease (PID) and infertility. (2) *Gonorrhea,* a bacterial infection of the moist tissues around the genitals, is passed on only by sexual contact. If left untreated, its symptoms increase in severity. Penicillin is an effective treatment. (3) *Syphilis,* a bacterial infection, may progress through four stages as symptoms increase in severity. Left untreated, it may result in death. Again, penicillin is an effective treatment. (4) *Genital herpes,* a viral infection that affects the skin around the genitals, is a very common STD and has no known cure. (5) *Acquired immune deficiency syndrome (AIDS)* is a viral (HIV) infection transmitted through the exchange of bodily fluids, usually semen or blood. Once infected, a person may stay symptom-free (but capable of infecting others) in a "carrier state" until full-blown AIDS appears. Virtually all persons with AIDS die within four years. There is no vaccine or treatment for AIDS. For this very reason, health psychologists have been involved in helping people change their risky sexual behaviors or their behaviors in the use of intravenous drugs. Awareness of AIDS and understanding the disease has increased markedly, but many people at risk—largely sexually active, heterosexual adolescents—have made few changes in their sexual practices. Some groups of people at risk—largely gay men and IV drug users—have made changes. Health psychologists are also involved in helping AIDS sufferers (and their friends and families) deal with the deadly nature of the disease. /p. 579

How have health psychologists intervened to improve patient compliance with doctors' orders?

No medical prescription or regimen can be effective if it is not adhered to. Health psychologists have been involved in attempts to increase patient compliance with doctors' orders. Helping patients understand what their prescribed course of action should be is part of the process. Beyond that, patients need to be convinced that following orders will benefit them, that there are ways to follow orders without unduly disrupting daily routines, and so on. /p. 580

chapter twelve

THE PSYCHOLOGICAL DISORDERS

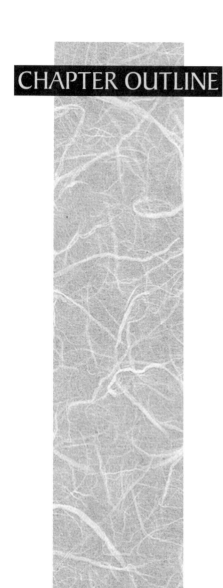

CHAPTER OUTLINE

TOPIC 12A   DEFINING AND CLASSIFYING PSYCHOLOGICAL DISORDERS
Just What *Is* "Abnormal"?
The Classification of Abnormal Reactions
    The DSM Series
    Problems with Classification and Labeling
    On "Insanity"
TOPIC 12A SUMMARY

TOPIC 12B   A SAMPLING OF PSYCHOLOGICAL DISORDERS
Anxiety Disorders
    Generalized Anxiety Disorder
    Panic Disorder
    Phobic Disorder
    Obsessive-compulsive Disorder (OCD)
    Posttraumatic Stress Disorder (PTSD)
Somatoform Disorders
    Hypochondriasis
    Conversion Disorder
Dissociative Disorders
    Dissociative Amnesia
    Dissociative Fugue
    Dissociative Identity Disorder
Personality Disorders
Disorders Usually First Diagnosed in Infancy, Childhood, or Adolescence
Delirium, Dementia, Amnestic, and Other Cognitive Disorders
Mood Disorders
    Types of Mood Disorder
    Observations on the Causes of Depression
Schizophrenia
    Incidence and Types of Schizophrenia
    Observations on the Causes of Schizophrenia
TOPIC 12B SUMMARY

CHAPTER SUMMARY

*I*ris *really* doesn't want to get out of bed this morning. She had another tough night—tossing and turning, and getting very little sleep. She's been overly tired for weeks now. Her main problem is that she feels nervous, anxious, and apprehensive, but doesn't understand why. She's been yelling at her children and nagging her husband. Iris realizes that her outbursts have not been justified, but she can't seem to stop them. She has the entire day ahead of her. Nothing *has* to get done, but she just can't decide what to do. Should she go shopping? Play tennis? Clean the house? Do the laundry? No, none of these options seems worth the effort. Once again, Iris doesn't want to do anything today. She's just too nervous.

—Steve is a 40-year-old white male who complains of chronic leg pains and headaches. He reports frequent nightmares, early morning awakenings, and a loss of interest in pleasurable activities, but he denies having thoughts of suicide. Steve spent four years in Vietnam during the war, was wounded twice, and saw heavy combat regularly. He has been married twice and is now separated. He has lost every job he has held due to his habitual outbursts of anger. He has spent the last two years living alone in a small cabin in the woods.

—David becomes absolutely petrified if he thinks he has to ride in an elevator. He has been known to walk dozens of flights of stairs to avoid taking an elevator. Recently he was in a hotel that has glass-enclosed elevators that can be seen from the lobby. Even the sight of those moving elevators created a sense of panic in David. When others try to reassure him of the inherent safety of elevators, he becomes nervous and agitated. He *knows* that elevators really are very safe.

—George announces that it's his birthday. When a friend who knows better challenges him, George responds, "Oh, yes, today I am 95. Ninety-five years old today, but not many people know that. Last year I was 94; now I'm 95. I was born in 1652 and know that Columbus sailed the ocean blue. I told him to go even though he didn't want to. He didn't think it was safe, but I knew he wouldn't fall off. . . . You gonna come to my party?"

Iris, Steve, David, and George have something in common: they each have a psychological disorder. Their symptoms are significantly different. Indeed, each would be diagnosed as having a different disorder.

*T*his chapter begins our discussion of psychological disorders, a discussion that will be continued in the next chapter, in which we consider techniques of treatment or therapy. If we can say nothing else about psychological disorders, we acknowledge that they are unpleasant, distressful, painful, and often devastating in their effects. We also can acknowledge that psychological disorders have an impact on all of us. I will spare you a lengthy recitation of the statistics on incidence and prevalence here. We will talk about these data as we discuss specific disorders. For now, we need only note that the best available estimates tell us that as you read this sentence, approximately 28 percent of U.S. adults, nearly 50 million *men and women, are suffering from some sort of psychological disorder, and fewer than one-third of those suffering from these problems are seeking help (National Institute of Mental Health, 1984, 1993; Offord et al., 1987). A recent study tells us that in their lifetimes, nearly half of all Americans will suffer from a psychological disorder (Kessler et al., 1994). In many respects, statistics such as these are both astounding and frightening; they are also impersonal. It is difficult to conceptualize what it really means to say that tens of millions of people are suffering from a psychological disorder. What we can say is that it is unlikely that any of us can be exempt from personally experiencing, or having someone close to us experience, the pain and suffering of psychological disorders.*

We begin our discussion by considering just what abnormal *means in the context of psychology, and we'll review the implications of systems for classifying the variety of psychological disorders. Having tackled these theoretical issues, I will then describe some of the common, and the more bizarre, psychological disorders. To do more than simply describe all of the known psychological disorders is well beyond the scope of our needs. The intent is to give you an idea of what psychological disorders are like.*

Topic 12A

DEFINING AND CLASSIFYING PSYCHOLOGICAL DISORDERS

We all have a basic idea of what is meant by such terms as *abnormal, mental illness,* or *psychological disorder.* The more we think about abnormality, however, the more difficult it becomes to define. In this Topic, we'll do two things: we'll generate a working definition of *abnormal* from a psychological perspective, and we'll consider the implications that follow from defining psychological disorders in terms of specific symptoms and then classifying and labeling those disorders.

JUST WHAT *IS* "ABNORMAL"?

The concept of abnormal as it is used in psychology is not a simple one. Here is the definition we'll use: **Abnormal** means maladaptive cognitions, affect, and/or behaviors that are at odds with social expectations and result in distress or discomfort. That is a lengthy definition, but to be complete, our definiton must include each of these aspects. Let's now briefly review them one at a time.

Literally, abnormal means "not of the norm" or "not average." Therefore, any behaviors or mental processes that are rare could be considered abnormal, and in a literal sense, of course, they are. The problem with this statistical approach is that it would categorize the behaviors of Robert Frost, Albert Schweitzer, Mother Theresa, and Madonna as abnormal. Statistically, they *are* abnormal; there are few others who do what these people do (or did). But, as far as we know, none of these people has (or had) a psychological disorder. Psychological disorders are not determined solely by the average or the norm in a statistical sense.

The responses of people who suffer from a psychological disorder are clearly *maladaptive*. This is a critical part of our definition. Thoughts, feelings, and behaviors are such that the individual does not function as well as he or she could without the disorder. To be different, or to be strange, does not in itself mean that someone has a psychological disorder. There must be some impairment. Psychological functioning is "abnormal *if* it is maladaptive; that is, *if* it interferes with functioning and growth, if it is self-defeating" (Carson & Butcher, 1992, p. 8).

abnormal in psychology: *maladaptive cognitions, affect, or behaviors at odds with social expectations and that result in stress or discomfort*

What is considered abnormal or deviant in one culture may be quite normal in another. Cultures vary in many respects, including styles of dress. This Arab woman's layered clothing (right) is in sharp contrast to the way these Bororo people of West Africa are dressed (above).

Another observation reflected in our definition is that abnormality may show itself in a number of ways. We have anticipated this earlier. A person with a psychological disorder may experience abnormal *affect* (moods or feelings), engage in abnormal *behaviors,* have abnormal *cognitions* (thoughts, perceptions, and beliefs), or any combination of these. Once again we see our ABCs from Chapter 1.

Any definition of psychological abnormality should acknowledge social and/or cultural expectations. What may obviously be abnormal and disordered in one culture may be viewed as quite normal or commonplace in another. In some cultures, loud crying and wailing at the funeral of a total stranger is considered strange or deviant; in others, it is common and expected. In some cultures, to claim you have been communicating with dead ancestors would be taken as a sign of mental disturbance; in others, it would be treated as a great gift. Even in your own culture, behaviors that are appropriate, or at least tolerated, in one situation, say a party, may be judged inappropriate in another context, say a religious service.

One additional issue needs to be addressed when we define psychological abnormality: psychological disorders involve *distress* or *discomfort.* People we consider abnormal are, in some way, suffering or are the source of suffering in others. Psychological disorders cause emotional distress, and individuals with such disorders are often the source of distress and discomfort to others—friends and family who care and worry about them.

So, as complex as it is, I hope you can see that there is a reason for each of the points in our definition of abnormal: behaviors or mental processes that are maladaptive, at odds with social expectations, and that result in distress or discomfort.

Before You Go On

How do we define psychological abnormality?

THE CLASSIFICATION OF ABNORMAL REACTIONS

One way of dealing with the broad concept of psychological abnormality is to consider each psychological disorder separately, in terms of how that disorder is to be diagnosed. **Diagnosis** is the process of recognizing a disorder on the basis of the presence of particular symptoms. Once we've described individual disorders, it would help if they could be organized or classified in a systematic way.

diagnosis the act of recognizing a disorder on the basis of the presence of particular symptoms

Systems of classification are common in science and are not at all new in psychology. In 1883, Emil Kraepelin published the first classification scheme for what he called "mental disturbances." His system was based on the idea that each disorder had its own collection of symptoms (a *syndrome*) and its own cause (in Kraepelin's time each disorder was thought to have a biological cause). Although we recognize that some of Kraepelin's work is no longer valid, he did demonstrate the value of classifying psychological disorders in a systematic way.

The DSM Series

In 1952, the American Psychiatric Association first published its system for classifying psychological disorders (which they called "mental disorders"). The book in which the scheme was presented was called the *Diagnostic and Statistical Manual of Mental Disorders* and became known as the *DSM*. In 1987, a revised version of the third edition, the *DSM-III-R*, was published. Even before the *DSM-III-R* was generally available, work began on its revision, the *DSM-IV*, published in 1994.

The *DSM* series is the system of classification most widely used in all mental health fields. We will follow the general outline of the *DSM-IV* in this chapter. Figure 12.1 presents a partial list of the disorders contained in the *DSM-IV*.

In fact, the *DSM-IV* is more than just an organized list of disorders in terms of symptoms. The *DSM-IV* recommends that the diagnosis of a disorder be sensitive to (1) any physical illnesses or ailments present, (2) the amount of stress the individual has recently been under, and (3) the level of adaptive functioning the individual has managed over the past three years. Except for cases for which there are known biological factors, the manual attempts to avoid any reference to the **etiology**, or causes, of disorders. It is meant to be objective, to be based on research evidence, to describe as completely as possible, and to theorize as little as possible.

etiology the cause or predisposing factors of a disorder

There are several advantages of having a single classification system for psychological disorders. The major advantage, of course, is communication. If I mean one thing when I use the term *phobia* and you mean something else, we cannot hold a very reasonable conversation about your patient's phobia. If we both agreed on the *DSM-IV*'s definition, at least we would be using the term in the same way. A related advantage is that a reliable way of classifying disorders allows one to think in terms of how to prescribe appropriate treatment or therapy most effectively. I can't leave the impression that there is only one treatment for each of the diagnostic categories of the *DSM-IV*. As we'll see in Chapter 13, on treatment and therapy, this is far from the case, but it certainly makes sense that we be able to classify disorders before we treat them. At the same time, classification can cause difficulties.

Problems with Classification and Labeling

As useful as it is to have a system for classifying psychological disorders, we must also recognize that there are problems associated with

Figure 12.1

A Sample of Psychological Disorders Listed in the *DSM-IV*

Type of disorder	Subtypes (examples)
Disorders usually first diagnosed in infancy, childhood, or adolescence	a. Mental retardation b. Learning disorders c. Autistic disorder
Delirium, dementia, amnestic and other cognitive disorders	a. Dementia of the Alzheimer's type
Substance-related disorders	a. Alcohol use disorders b. Amphetamine use disorders c. Cocaine use disorders d. Hallucinogen disorders
Schizophrenia and other psychotic disorders	a. Schizophrenia
Mood disorders	a. Depressive disorders b. Dysthymic disorder c. Bipolar disorder
Anxiety disorders	a. Panic disorder b. Specific phobia c. Obsessive-compulsive disorder d. Posttraumatic stress disorder e. Generalized anxiety disorder
Somatoform disorders	a. Conversion disorder b. Hypochondriasis
Dissociative disorders	a. Dissociative amnesia b. Dissociative fugue c. Dissociative identity disorder
Eating disorders	a. Anorexia nervosa b. Bulimia
Personality disorders	a. Paranoid personality disorder b. Schizoid personality disorder c. Antisocial personality disorder d. Histrionic personality disorder e. Narcissistic personality disorder

any such system. First, assigning labels to people may be convenient, but it can also be dehumanizing. It may be difficult to remember that Sally Jane is a complex, complicated human being with a range of feelings, thoughts, and behaviors, not just a "paranoid schizophrenic." In response to this concern, the *DSM-IV* refers only to disordered behaviors and to patterns of behaviors, not to disordered people. That is, it refers to paranoid reactions, not to individuals who are paranoid.

A second problem inherent in classification and labeling is that it is so easy to fall into the habit of believing that labels *explain*, when clearly they don't. Accurately diagnosing and labeling a pattern of behaviors does not explain those behaviors. It does not tell us why such a pattern of behaviors developed or what we can or should do about them now.

Third, labels often create unfortunate and lasting stigmas of negative attitudes about people (e.g., Piner & Kahle, 1984). To learn that someone is "psychologically disordered" may carry with it a wide range of negative reactions, and the label often sticks long after the disorder has been treated and the symptoms are gone.

One final consequence of diagnostic labeling is that the brunt of the problem tends to fall on the individual. It is the individual who has a psychological disorder in thought, affect, or behavior; seldom the group, the family, or the society of which the person is a part. Classification schemes focus on the person and not on the context in which the person lives (e.g., Gorenstein, 1984; Szasz, 1960, 1982). This issue is quite complex and has been debated within psychology for many years. An example of the difficulty is as follows: Mary Beth, a third-grader, is referred to the school psychologist because she is withdrawn, often seems to be on the verge of tears, will not talk about her home life, and is doing poorly in her academic work. Without going into the particulars of how to diagnose Mary Beth's problem, doesn't it seem misguided to focus all of our attention on Mary Beth (disregarding her family or the demands of the school) as we try to identify her problems? Is it right to diagnose and label the person without attending to the larger social networks of which that person is a part?

On "Insanity"

In common practice, the terms *psychological disorder, mental disorder,* and *behavior disorder* are often used interchangeably. There is one term, however, with which we need to exercise particular care, and that's *insanity.*

Insanity is not a psychological term. It is a legal term. It relates to problems with psychological functioning, but in a rather restricted sense. Definitions of **insanity** vary from state to state. To be judged insane usually requires evidence that a person did not know or fully understand the consequences of his or her actions at a given time (showed diminished capacity), could not discern the difference between right and wrong, and was unable to exercise control over his or her actions.

insanity a legal term for diminished capacity, inability to tell right from wrong, and inability to exercise control over one's actions

A related issue has to do with whether a person is in enough control of his or her mental and intellectual functions to understand courtroom procedures and aid in his or her own defense. If one is not, one may be ruled "not competent" to stand trial for his or her actions, whatever those actions may have been.

Having introduced the problems of defining abnormality and classifying psychological disorders, it is time to turn our attention to specific disorders. We will not cover all disorders found in the *DSM-IV.* Instead, we'll look at disorders that are among the most common or that are particularly unusual in their symptoms.

Before You Go On

What is the *DSM-IV*?

What are some of the advantages and disadvantages of classifying psychological disorders?

TOPIC 12A SUMMARY

In psychology, the concept of abnormality is a complex one, encompassing the notions of maladaptations of affects, behaviors, and/or cognitions, defined in a sociocultural context, and implying distress and discomfort. Individual psychological disorders are defined in terms of their basic symptoms, and are classified or organized in a system published as the *Diagnostic and Statistical Manual of Mental Disorders* (DSM), now in its fourth edition. The major advantage of a system of classification, such as the *DSM-IV*, is that it fosters better communication about psychological disorders. Disadvantages include the fact that naming or classifying disorders does not really explain them in any way, may put undue emphasis on the individual rather than the group of which the individual is a member, and may foster negative attitudes toward persons who are labeled as disordered. *Insanity* is a legal term, not a psychological one.

Topic 12B

A SAMPLING OF PSYCHOLOGICAL DISORDERS

For the remainder of this chapter, we will consider a variety of psychological disorders. As we do so, there are several important points you need to keep in mind.

1. Abnormal and normal are not two distinct categories. They may be thought of as endpoints on some dimension we can use to describe people, but there is a large gray area between the two in which distinctions get fuzzy.

2. Abnormal does not mean dangerous. True, some people diagnosed as having a mental disorder *may* do great violence to themselves or to others, but most people with psychological disorders are not dangerous at all.

3. Abnormal does not mean bad. People diagnosed as having a psychological disorder are not "bad people," or weak people, in any evaluative sense. They may do bad things, and bad things may have happened to them, but it is certainly not in psychology's tradition to make moral judgments about good and bad.

4. Most of our depictions of psychological disorders will be made in terms of extreme and obvious cases. Psychological disorders, like physical disorders, may occur in mild or moderate forms. As we have seen repeatedly, no two people are exactly alike; there are individual differences in psychological functioning. Such is also the case here. No two people, even with the same diagnosis of a psychological disorder, will be exactly alike in all regards.

Unless I specify otherwise, diagnostic criteria for psychological disorders are taken from the *DSM-IV*, and statistics on the prevalence of the disorders are from the National Institute of Mental Health (Freedman, 1984) or the National Comorbidity Survey (Kessler et al., 1994).

ANXIETY DISORDERS

Anxiety is a term difficult to define precisely. Even so, we can be confident claiming that everyone has experienced anxiety and recognizes it as being unpleasant. In Chapter 11, we defined **anxiety** as a feeling of general apprehension or dread accompanied by predictable physiological changes: increased muscle tension; shallow, rapid breathing; cessation of digestion; increased perspiration; and drying of the mouth. Thus, anxiety involves two levels of reaction: subjective feelings (e.g., fear or dread) and physiological responses (e.g., rapid breathing). The major symptom of *anxiety disorders* is felt anxiety, often coupled with "avoidance behavior," or attempts to resist or avoid any situation that seems to produce anxiety.

anxiety a general feeling of apprehension or dread accompanied by predictable physiological changes

Anxiety disorders are among the most common of the psychological disorders. The National Institute of Mental Health reports high rates: within a six-month period, from 7 to 15 percent of the population can be diagnosed with one or more of the several anxiety diagnoses. The National Comorbidity Survey claims that 17 percent of those surveyed had some sort of anxiety disorder in the year before the survey was taken, and 25 percent had an anxiety disorder at some time in their lives. Others have reported similar estimates (Reich, 1986; Weissman, 1988). Anxiety disorders are two to three times more likely to be diagnosed in women than in men (Kessler et al., 1994; Roth & Argyle, 1988). In any case, percentages of this sort do not convey the enormity of the problem. We're talking about real people here—people like you and me. In this section, we'll consider five types of anxiety disorders: generalized anxiety disorder, panic disorder, phobic disorder, obsessive-compulsive disorder, and posttraumatic stress disorder.

Generalized Anxiety Disorder

generalized anxiety disorder
persistent, chronic, and distressingly
high levels of unattributable and
uncontrollable anxiety or worry

The major symptom of **generalized anxiety disorder** is distressing, felt anxiety. With this disorder there is unrealistic, excessive, and persistent worry. The *DSM-IV* added the criteria that people with this disorder find it difficult to control their worry or anxiety. The anxiety may be very intense, but it is also diffuse, meaning that it does not seem to be brought on by anything specific in the person's environment; it just seems to come and go (or come and stay) without reason or warning. People with this disorder are usually in some state of uneasiness. If they are not experiencing a particularly high level of anxiety at the moment, they may be afraid that they soon will be. People with generalized anxiety disorder seldom have any clear insight or ideas about what exactly is causing the anxiety they feel. The self-reports of persons with generalized anxiety disorder show that their major concerns are with an inability to relax, tenseness, difficulty concentrating, feeling frightened, being afraid of losing control, and so on (Beck & Emery, 1985). Clearly, this is a distressing and disruptive disorder that brings with it considerable pain.

Although people with this disorder can often continue to function in social situations and on the job, they may be particularly prone to drug and alcohol abuse. This point is an important one. *Comorbidity* refers to having two or more diseases or illnesses at the same time. The 1994 National Comorbidity Survey showed us that psychological disorders are even more prevalent than previously realized. It also demonstrated that of people who experience a disorder in their lifetime, most (79 percent) will experience two or more different disorders (Kessler et al., 1994). Whereas 52 percent of the people in this survey never had any psychological disorder, 14 percent had a history of three or more disorders.

Before You Go On

Describe the symptoms of generalized
anxiety disorder.

Panic Disorder

panic disorder a disorder in which
anxiety attacks suddenly and
unpredictably; there may be periods
free from anxiety

In the generalized anxiety disorder, the experience of felt anxiety may be characterized as *chronic,* implying that the anxiety is always present, albeit sometimes more so than at other times. For a person suffering from **panic disorder**, the major symptom is more *acute*—a recurrent, unpredictable, unprovoked onset of sudden, intense anxiety, or a "panic attack." These attacks may last for a few seconds or for hours. Significantly, there is no particular stimulus to bring it on. The panic attack is unexpected. It just happens. The *DSM-IV* is quite clear on the point that panic attacks can occur in conjunction with several other disorders. They are not restricted just to panic disorder.

With panic disorder, however, it is the recurrent pattern of attacks and a building worry about future attacks that are significant.

At some time in their lives, between 1.5 and 3.5 percent of the population will experience panic disorder. (That doesn't sound very significant until we realize that that's 4 to 9 million people!) The age of onset for this disorder is usually between adolescence and the mid-twenties (Hayward et al., 1992; Markowitz et al., 1989). Initial panic attack episodes are often associated with stress, particularly from the loss of an important relationship (Ballenger, 1989). A complication of panic disorder is that it can be accompanied by feelings of depression (Noyes et al., 1990). This may be why the rate of suicide and suicide attempts is so high for persons with this diagnosis (20 percent), which is higher than for persons diagnosed with depression alone (15 percent) (Johnson et al., 1990; Weissman et al., 1989).

Before You Go On

What is a panic disorder?

Phobic Disorder

The essential feature of a **phobic disorder** (or phobia) is a persistent and excessive fear of some object, activity, or situation that consistently leads a person to avoid that object, activity, or situation. Implied in this definition is the notion that the fear is intense enough to be disruptive. The definition also implies that there is no real or significant threat involved in the stimulus that gives rise to a phobia; that is, the fear is unreasonable, exaggerated, or inappropriate.

phobic disorder an intense, irrational fear that leads a person to avoid the feared object, activity, or situation

Many things in this world are life-threatening and downright frightening. If, for example, you were driving down a rather steep hill and suddenly realized the brakes on your car were not working, you would be likely to feel an intense reaction of fear. Such a reaction would not be phobic because it is not irrational. Similarly, there are few of us who truly enjoy the company of bees. Just because we don't like bees and would rather they not be around does not qualify us as having a phobic disorder. What is missing here is *intensity* of response. People who do have a phobic reaction to bees (called mellissaphobia) may refuse to leave the house in the summer for fear of encountering a bee and may become genuinely anxious at the buzzing sound of any insect, fearing it to be a bee. People with this disorder may become uncomfortable simply reading a paragraph, such as this one, about bees. David, in our opening examples, was experiencing a phobic reaction with regard to riding in elevators.

There are many types of phobias, and the incidence of this disorder is quite high. Within one year, nearly 15 percent of the population experiences a phobic disorder. Most are named after the object or activity feared. Figure 12.2 lists a few phobic reactions. Most phobias

Figure 12.2

A Sample of Phobic Reactions

Phobia	Is a fear of
Acrophobia	High places
Agoraphobia	Open places
Algophobia	Pain
Astraphobia	Lightning and thunder
Autophobia	One's self
Claustrophobia	Small, closed places
Hematophobia	Blood
Monophobia	Being alone
Mysophobia	Dirt or contamination
Nyctophobia	The dark
Pathophobia	Illness or disease
Pyrophobia	Fire
Thanatophobia	Death and dying
Zoophobia	Animals

prognosis the prediction of the future course of an illness or disorder

agoraphobia a phobic fear of being alone, or of being in public places from which escape might be difficult

involve a fear of animals, although these phobias are not the type for which people most commonly seek treatment (Costello, 1982). In some cases, the person with a phobic disorder can successfully avoid the source of the fear and, as a result, does not seek treatment. Sometimes, avoiding the source of one's phobia is impossible. Fortunately, the **prognosis** (the prediction of the future course of a disorder) is good for phobic disorders. That is, therapy for persons with a phobia is likely to be successful. You might want to review our earlier discussion of phobias (in Topic 5A), in which we examined possible causes and treatments for simple phobias.

One of the most commonly *treated* varieties of phobia is **agoraphobia**, which literally means "fear of open places." This fear is not reserved for those occasions in which one stands in the middle of a large, open field, however. The diagnosis is for people who have an exaggerated fear of being alone or of venturing forth into the world where they may be trapped in an unpleasant or embarrassing situation. People with this disorder avoid crowds, streets, stores, and the like. They establish a safe base for themselves and may, in extreme cases, refuse to leave it altogether. It is common to find agoraphobia as an associated complication of panic disorder (comorbidity again). This is not unreasonable. After experiencing several panic attacks—brought on by no particular stimulus, remember—one finds it more and more difficult to venture out in the world, for fear of having yet another panic attack in some public place.

Before You Go On

What are the essential characteristics
of a phobic disorder?

Working as a steel worker, laboring high above the city, would be out of the question for someone suffering from acrophobia, the fear of high places. Similarly, someone with agoraphobia would find sitting in a crowd unbearably anxiety producing.

Obsessive-compulsive Disorder (OCD)

The **obsessive-compulsive disorder (OCD)** is an anxiety disorder characterized by a pattern of recurrent obsessions and compulsions. **Obsessions** are ideas or thoughts that involuntarily and constantly intrude into awareness. Generally speaking, obsessions are pointless, groundless thoughts, most commonly of violence, disease, danger, or doubt (Swedo et al., 1989a). Many of us have experienced obsessive-like thoughts. Worrying throughout the first few days of a vacation if you really did turn off the stove would be an example. Have you ever awakened to a clock radio playing some particular song? As you take your morning shower, the lyrics keep coming to mind. Even as you get dressed, you hear yourself humming the same song. There you are, driving to work, still thinking about that song. You have a feeling of "I can't get that song out of my head!" Imagine having a thought or idea constantly interrupting, coming to mind, day after day, whenever you were not consciously focusing your attention on something else. To qualify as part of OCD, obsessions must be disruptive; they must interfere with normal functioning. They are also time consuming and are the source of anxiety and distress.

Compulsions are constantly intruding, repetitive behaviors. The most commonly reported compulsions involve hand washing, grooming, and counting or checking behaviors, such as checking over and over again to be sure that the door is really locked (Swedo et al., 1989a). Again, from your own experience, have you ever found yourself walking along on a sidewalk, avoiding the cracks in the pavement? Have you ever checked an answer sheet to see that you've *real-*

obsessive-compulsive disorder (OCD) a combination of constantly intruding thoughts and constantly intruding behaviors

obsessions ideas or thoughts that involuntarily and constantly intrude into awareness

compulsions constantly intruding, repetitive, and essentially involuntary behaviors

ly answered all of the questions and then checked it again, and again, and again? To do so is a compulsive sort of response. It serves no real purpose, and it provides no sense of satisfaction, although it is done very conscientiously in an attempt to reduce anxiety or stress. The person with OCD recognizes that these behaviors serve no useful purpose, but cannot stop them. It is as if he or she engages in these behaviors in order to prevent some other (more anxiety-producing) behaviors from taking place.

In extreme cases, a particular obsession or compulsion may come to exert an enormous influence on a person's entire life. For example, consider the case of a happily married accountant, the father of three. For reasons he cannot explain, he has become obsessed with the fear of contracting AIDS. There is no reason for him to be concerned: his sexual activities are entirely monogamous; he has never used drugs; he has never had a blood transfusion. All the same, he is overwhelmed with the idea that he will contract this deadly disease. We find ritualized, compulsive behaviors associated with his obsessive thoughts: he washes his hands vigorously at every opportunity and becomes very anxious if he cannot change his clothes at least three times a day (all in his effort to avoid contact with the dreaded AIDS virus). You can imagine how distressing this must be, and you can also appreciate that OCD involves more than avoiding cracks in the sidewalk and tunes we keep humming to ourselves. Figure 12.3 lists some of the more common obsessions and ritualized compulsions found in persons with OCD.

Notice that we are using *compulsive* in an altogether different way when we refer to someone being a compulsive gambler, a compulsive eater, or a compulsive practical joker. What is different about the use of the term *compulsive* in such cases is that although the individual engages in habitual patterns of behavior, he or she gains pleasure from doing so. The compulsive gambler enjoys gambling; the compulsive eater loves to eat. Such people may not enjoy the ultimate, long-term consequences of their actions, but they feel little discomfort about the behaviors themselves. To be diagnosed as compulsive in the context of an anxiety disorder requires that behaviors be recognized as senseless and not be the source of pleasure.

Obsessive-compulsive disorder is much more common than once believed. It affects nearly 1 of every 200 teenagers (OCD is commonly diagnosed in childhood or adolescence), and a total of as many as 5 million Americans (CIBA-GEIGY, 1991; Flament et al., 1988). Unfortunately, the prognosis for OCD is not very good. One recent study, for example, found that even after as many as seven years of treatment and therapy, only 6 percent of the sample of patients with OCD in the study could be considered totally symptom-free, and 43 percent still met the diagnostic criteria for the disorder (Leonard et al., 1993).

Research suggests that obsessive-compulsive disorder has a biological basis. The most likely candidate for the source of the problem is the frontal lobes, particularly the pathways used for communication between the frontal lobes and the basal ganglia. The neurotransmitter serotonin is also directly implicated (e.g., Hollander et al.,

---

Figure 12.3

Common Obsessions and Compulsions in OCD

Common obsessions

Fear of getting dirty, contaminated, or infected by people or things in the environment
Fear of AIDS
Disgust over body wastes or secretions
Concern that a task or assignment has been done poorly or incorrectly, even when the person knows this is not the case
Extreme concern with order, symmetry, or exactness
Fear of thinking evil or sinful thoughts that go against one's religion
Fear of losing important things that will be needed later
Recurring thoughts about harming or killing others or oneself
Fear of committing a crime, such as theft
Recurring thoughts or images of a sexual nature
Extreme concern with certain sounds, images, words, or numbers
Fear of blurting out obscenities or insulting others
Fear that some disaster will occur

Common compulsive rituals

Cleaning and grooming behaviors such as washing hands, showering, and brushing teeth in particular ways
Touching certain objects in a specific way
Repeatedly cleaning items in the house
Ordering or arranging things in a certain way
Checking locks, electrical outlets, light switches, and the like repeatedly
Repeatedly putting clothes on, then taking them off
Repeating certain actions, such as going through a doorway
Counting over and over again to a certain number
Hoarding items such as old newspapers, mail, and containers
Checking to see that no one has been hurt or killed, or no other disaster has occurred because of something the person with OCD has done
Constantly seeking approval (especially children)

From CIBA-GEIGY, 1991, pp. 6–7.

1992; Swedo et al., 1989b). Partial support for the biological basis of OCD comes from the fact that drug treatment (using antidepressant medications) is often successful in eliminating the symptoms of OCD (Flament et al., 1985).

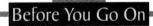

Before You Go On

What characterizes the obsessive-compulsive disorder?

Posttraumatic Stress Disorder (PTSD)

An anxiety disorder that has been the subject of much public discussion over the past decade is **posttraumatic stress disorder (PTSD)**.

posttraumatic stress disorder (PTSD) an anxiety disorder in which disruptive recollections, distressing dreams, flashbacks, and felt anxiety occur well after the experience of a traumatic event

This disorder involves distressing symptoms that arise some time *after* (usually six months) the experience of a traumatic, highly stressful event that resulted in intense fear, helplessness, or horror. The traumatic events that trigger this disorder are many, from natural disasters (e.g., Hurricane Andrew in 1992, or the floods in the Midwest in the summer of 1993), to life-threatening situations (e.g., kidnapping, rape, assault, or combat), to the loss of property (e.g., the house burns down; the car is stolen). As it happens, many associate this disorder with veterans of military conflict, the Vietnam War in particular. In fact, it is estimated that nearly 1.7 million veterans—nearly half of all who served in Southeast Asia—suffered from partial or full PTSD at some time since discharge from military service (True et al., 1993).

No psychologist will diagnose someone who had just experienced some horrendous event—such as the loss of a friend who died in the patient's arms in the midst of a furious battle—as having a disorder simply because he or she is very upset, or anxious. What makes the anxiety of PTSD qualify as a symptom of disorder is that it occurs persistently, in distressing dreams, in recurrent, disruptive recollections of the event, or in sudden feelings that the traumatic event is occurring again (in flashbacks) well *after* the event itself. Persons with this disorder try to avoid anything that would remind them of the trauma they experienced: Vietnam veterans who refuse to visit the memorial in Washington, D.C., for example. People with PTSD see themselves as special, separate, and detached from others, who cannot "share their experience." The brief case history of Steve presented in the chapter opening is typical.

Not recognized as a separate, distinct diagnostic category of anxiety disorder until 1980, posttraumatic stress disorder is certainly not rare. About 1 percent of the population can be expected to experience the disorder in their lifetime. Of those who experience a severe trauma, nearly 15 percent will experience some of the symptoms of posttraumatic stress disorder (Helzer et al., 1987).

We often find comorbidity with PTSD. It is commonly associated with alcohol and substance abuse or depression. The prognosis for posttraumatic stress disorder is related to the extent to which there are comorbid disorders (such as alcoholism) attending it, the extent to which the patient had experienced psychological problems before the traumatic event, and the extent to which social support can be made available (e.g., Jordan et al., 1992). Recent research suggests that there may be genetic factors that predispose someone to develop symptoms of the disorder (Charney et al., 1993; True et al., 1993).

Before You Go On

Describe the symptoms of posttraumatic
stress disorder.

Posttraumatic stress disorder (PTSD) may be one of the long-term effects of experiencing traumatic, life-threatening situations such as those that occur in military combat.

SOMATOFORM DISORDERS

Soma means "body." Hence, all of the **somatoform disorders** in some way involve physical, bodily symptoms or complaints. What makes these *psychological* disorders is that there is no known medical or biological cause for the symptoms. We'll consider just two somatoform disorders: one common, hypochondriasis, and the other rare but very dramatic, conversion disorder.

somatoform disorders psychological disorders reflecting physical or bodily symptoms or complaints for which there is no known physical cause

Hypochondriasis

Hypochondriasis is the appropriate diagnosis for someone preoccupied with the fear of having or developing a serious disease. Persons with this disorder are unusually aware of every ache and pain. They often read popular magazines devoted to health issues, and feel free to diagnose their own ailments. The catch is that they have no medical disorder or disease. Nonetheless, they constantly seek medical attention and will not be convinced of their good health despite the best of medical opinion and reassurance.

A man with occasional chest pains, for example, diagnoses his own condition as lung cancer. Even after many physicians reassure him that his lungs are perfectly fine and that he has no signs of lung cancer, the man's fears are not put to rest. "They are just trying to make me feel better by not telling me, but they know, as I do, that I have lung cancer and am going to die soon."

hypochondriasis a mental disorder involving the fear of developing some serious disease or medical illness

It's not too difficult to imagine why someone would develop the symptoms of hypochondriasis. If a person believes he or she (hypochondriasis is found equally in men and women) has contracted some serious disease, three problems might be solved. (1) The person now has a way to explain otherwise unexplainable anxiety: "Well, my goodness, if you had lung cancer, you'd be anxious, too." (2) The illness may be used to excuse the person from those activities he or she finds anxiety-producing: "As sick as I am, you don't possibly expect me to go to work, do you?" (3) The illness or disease may be used as a way to gain attention or sympathy: "Don't you feel sorry for me, knowing that I have such a terrible disease?"

Conversion Disorder

conversion disorder the display of a severe physical disorder for which there is no medical explanation; often accompanied by an apparent lack of concern on the part of the patient

Although **conversion disorder** is now rare (accounting for fewer than 5 percent of the anxiety-based disorders), its symptoms are striking. Here we find an individual with a loss or alteration in physical functioning that suggests a physical disorder, but which is really an expression of a psychological need or conflict. The symptoms are not intentionally produced and cannot be explained by any physical disorder. The loss in physical functioning is typically of great significance; paralysis, blindness, and deafness being classic examples. As difficult as it may be to believe, the symptoms are not fully imaginary; they are real in the sense that the person cannot feel, see, or hear.

What makes the disorder psychological is that there is no medical explanation for the symptoms. In some cases, medical explanations run contrary to the symptoms. One type of conversion disorder is called *glove anesthesia,* a condition in which the hands lose feeling and become paralyzed from the wrist down. As it happens, it is physically impossible to have such a paralysis and loss of feeling in the hands alone; normally there would be some paralysis in the forearm, upper arm, and shoulder, as well. Actual paralysis, of course, must follow neural pathways.

One of the most remarkable secondary symptoms of this disorder (occurring only in some patients) is known as *la belle indifference*—a seemingly inappropriate lack of concern over one's condition. Some persons with this disorder seem to feel comfortable with and accepting of their infirmity. Here are people who are blind, deaf, or paralyzed, and who show very little concern over their condition.

At the beginning of this section I indicated that this disorder is now quite rare. In fact, during World War I, it was the most commonly diagnosed of all psychological disorders among military personnel. It was also common during World War II (Carson & Butcher, 1992). One hypothesis about the declining incidence of this disorder is that people have become more sophisticated about medical symptoms and relationships between physical and psychological functioning. As this knowledge base grows, perhaps more people are coming to appreciate the unlikely nature of conversion disorder symptoms.

This particular disorder holds an important position in psychology's history. This was the disorder that most intrigued Sigmund Freud in his clinical practice and ultimately led him to develop a new method of therapy (see Topic 13B). The disorder was known to the Greeks, who named it hysteria, a label still used occasionally, as in "hysterical blindness." The Greeks believed the disorder was to be found only in women and reflected a disorder of the uterus, or *hysterium,* hence the name hysteria. The logic was that the disease would leave the uterus, float through the body, and settle in the eyes, hands, or whatever part of the body was affected. Of course, this notion is no longer considered valid, although the potential sexual basis for the disorder was one of the aspects that caught Freud's attention.

Before You Go On

Describe hypochondriasis and
conversion disorder.

DISSOCIATIVE DISORDERS

To *dissociate* means to become separate from or to escape. The underlying theme of disorders classified as **dissociative disorders** is that in some way a person seeks to escape from some aspect of life or personality seen as the source of stress, discomfort, or anxiety. These disorders are statistically uncommon, but they are also dramatic and are often the subject of novels, movies, and television shows. I will briefly describe three dissociative disorders: amnesia, fugue, and identity disorder.

dissociative disorder a disorder in which one escapes from aspects of one's life or personality seen as the source of discomfort

Dissociative Amnesia

Dissociative amnesia is defined as an inability to recall important personal information—an inability too extensive to be explained by ordinary forgetfulness. Before the publication of the *DSM-IV* in 1994, this disorder was known as psychogenic amnesia, where *psychogenic* means "psychological in origin," and *amnesia* refers to a loss of memory. Usually, what is forgotten is some traumatic incident and some or all of the experiences that led up to or followed the incident. As you may suspect, there is no medical explanation for the loss of memory. There can be a large range of the extent of the forgetting associated with dissociative amnesia. In some cases, a person may "lose" entire days and weeks at a time; in other cases, only specific details cannot be recalled. Not surprisingly, cases of this disorder tend to be more common in wartime, when traumatic experiences are more common.

dissociative amnesia a psychologically caused inability— too extensive to be caused by ordinary forgetfulness—to recall important personal information

Dissociative Fugue

Occasionally, amnesic forgetfulness is accompanied by a physical change of location. That is, the person finds himself or herself in a strange and different place, with no reasonable explanation for how

dissociative fugue a condition of amnesia accompanied by unexplained travel or change of location

he or she got there. When this dimension is added, we have a disorder known as **dissociative fugue**. A typical story would be of "Carol," found wandering around in the business district of a large northeastern city. She was ill-dressed for the cold winds and low temperatures. Her behaviors seemed aimless, and she was stopped by a police officer who asked if he could be of assistance. It soon became apparent that Carol did not know where she was. The officer took her to a nearby hospital. It was soon discovered that she had no memory for where she had been or what she had been doing for the last two weeks. She had no idea how she got to the city in which she was found, 350 miles from home.

Both dissociative amnesia and fugue disorder involve escape from stressful situations and, in that way, are similar to the somatoform disorders. In conversion disorders, for example, a person may escape from stress by taking on the symptoms of a major physical disorder. With amnesia and fugue, escape is more literal. People escape by forgetting, or they avoid conflict and stress by psychologically or physically running away.

Dissociative Identity Disorder

This disorder is commonly known as *multiple personality disorder*. Perhaps the most important fact to recognize about the disorder is that it is listed here as a dissociative disorder and *not* as schizophrenia. I say that because the popular press and media quite consistently give the impression that these are one in the same. They are not. Schizophrenia is a different disorder, which we will discuss shortly.

dissociative identity disorder the existence within one individual of two or more distinct personalities, each of which is dominant at a particular time

The major symptom of **dissociative identity disorder** is the existence within the same person of two or more distinct personalities or personality traits. The disorder has been very rare, although for still unknown reasons its incidence is increasing markedly (Carson & Butcher, 1992).

The very idea of this disorder—of two or more personalities inhabiting the same person—is difficult to imagine. Perhaps it would help to contrast this disorder with a pattern of behavior typical of all of us. We all change our behaviors, and in some small way, our personalities change every day, depending on the situation in which we find ourselves. We do not act, think, or feel exactly the same way at school as we do at work, at a party, or at a house of worship. We modify our behaviors to fit the circumstances in which we find ourselves. At a party, you may be carefree, happy, and uninhibited. At work, you may be a different person: reserved, quiet, serious, and concentrating on the task at hand. But, these changes do not qualify as an identity disorder. What's the difference?

The difference is one of degree and quality. For a person with a dissociative identity disorder, the change in personality is dramatic and extreme. We are not dealing with a person who slightly alters his or her behaviors; we are dealing with two or more distinct personalities, which implies a change in underlying consciousness, not just a change in behaviors. Another difference is that when we change our behaviors, we do so in response to cues in the situation in which we find ourselves. Such is not the case for a person with this dissociative disorder, whose changes in personality can take place without warning and with no particular provocation. The third major difference has to do with control. When we change our behaviors, we do so consciously or intentionally. Persons with a multiple personality disorder can seldom control or predict which of their personalities will be dominant at any one time. Persons diagnosed with multiple personality disorder have often been the victim of child abuse or sexual abuse (Putnam et al., 1986; Ross, 1989). The significantly higher incidence of multiple personality disorder in women than in men might be partially understood when we consider that girls and women are much more likely to be sexually or physically abused than are boys and men (Ross, 1989).

Before You Go On

What are the defining symptoms of
the dissociative disorders?

PERSONALITY DISORDERS

All of the psychological disorders we have reviewed so far, and those we will consider in subsequent sections, are disorders that seem to afflict people who at one time were relatively normal and undisturbed. In most cases, we can remember when the person did not show the symptoms of his or her disorder. That is more difficult to do with the personality disorders because persons with these disorders have a long-standing history of symptoms. **Personality disorders** are long-lasting patterns of perceiving, relating to, and thinking about the environment and about oneself that are maladaptive, inflexible, and that cause either impaired functioning or distress. The problems associated with personality disorders are usually identifiable by the time an individual is an adolescent.

personality disorders enduring patterns of perceiving, relating to, and thinking about the environment and oneself that are inflexible and maladaptive

The *DSM-IV* lists several personality disorders (PD), organized in three groups, or clusters. Group 1 includes disorders in which the person can be characterized as odd or eccentric in some way. People with disorders from this cluster are often difficult to get along with. Group 2 includes those disorders in which the person seems overly dramatic, emotional, or erratic, and where behaviors are quite impulsive. Group 3 includes disorders that add the dimension of anxiety or fearfulness to the standard criteria for personality disorder. Note that it is only for those varieties of personality disorder in Group 3 that we find any reports of fear, anxiety, or depression.

Rather than attempting to deal with all of the personality disorders in detail, I'll simply list and describe some of the more common PDs below. Keep in mind as you review this list that to be classified as a personality disorder, these behaviors must be relatively long-standing, generally beginning in childhood or adolescence.

1. *Cluster I:* Disorders of odd or eccentric reactions

Paranoid personality disorder: extreme sensitivity, suspiciousness, envy, and mistrust of others; the actions of other people are interpreted as deliberately demeaning or threatening. The attitude of suspicion is not justified. A person with this disorder shows a restricted range of emotional reactivity, is humorless, and rarely seeks help. Example: A person who continuously, and without justification, accuses a spouse of infidelity, and believes that every wrong number was really a call from the spouse's lover.

Schizoid personality disorder: an inability to form, and an indifference to, interpersonal relationships. A person with this disorder appears "cold and aloof," and often engages in excessive daydreaming. Example: A person who lives, as she has for years, alone in a one-room flat in a poor part of town, venturing out only to pick up a social security check and but a few necessities at the corner store.

2. *Cluster II:* Disorders of dramatic, emotional, or erratic reactions

Histrionic personality disorder: overly dramatic, reactive, and intensely expressed behaviors. A person with this disorder is very lively, tending to draw attention to himself or herself, overacting to matters of small consequence, seeking excitement while avoiding the routine. Example: A woman who spends an inordinate amount of time on her appearance, calls everyone "Darling!," seems to be constantly asking for feedback on how she looks, and describes most of her experiences as "wonderful!" and "vastly outstanding!" even when such an experience is no more than finding a detergent on sale at the grocery store.

Narcissistic personality disorder: a grandiose exaggeration of self-importance, a need for attention or admiration, and a tendency to set unrealistic goals. Someone with this disorder maintains few lasting relationships and in many ways engages in a "childish" level of behavior. Example: A person who always wants to be the topic of conversation, and shows a lack of interest in saying anything positive about anyone else. Someone who believes that no one else has ever taken a vacation as stupendous as his or hers, or understood an issue as clearly as he or she, and who will do whatever it takes to be complimented.

Antisocial personality disorder: an exceptional lack of regard for the rights and property of others; engaging in impulsive behaviors with little or no regard for the consequences of that behavior. Someone with this disorder shows early signs of lying, truancy, stealing, fighting, resisting authority, and general irresponsibility, and has difficulty maintaining a job. Example: A young man who first steals a car, then drives it down an alley, knocking over garbage cans just "for the fun of it" before abandoning the car in a deserted part of town.

3. *Cluster III:* disorders involving anxiety and fearfulness

Avoidant personality disorder: an oversensitivity to the possibility of being rejected by others and an unwillingness to enter into relationships for fear of being rejected. A person with this disorder is devastated by disapproval, but holds out a desire for social relationships. Example: A man with few close friends who almost never dates, and only talks to women who are older and less attractive than he. A man who has worked for years at the same job, never seeking a job change or promotion, who hardly ever speaks up in public, and who may attend meetings and public gatherings but does not participate.

Dependent personality disorder: allowing and seeking others to dominate and assume responsibility for one's actions; a poor self-image and lack of confidence. A person with this disorder sees himself or herself as stupid and helpless, thus deferring to others. Example: A woman whose husband commonly abuses her. Although she has from time to time reported the abuse, she refuses to take an active role in finding treatment for her husband, saying it is "her place" to do as he says, and that if she does not please him, it is her fault.

Because personality disorders are difficult to diagnose accurately, estimates of prevalence tend to be inexact. Most cases of personality disorder first come to the attention of mental health professionals on referral from the courts (or from family members), or because of related problems such as child abuse or alcoholism. What we do find is that "while the overall rate of PD [personality disorder] may be between 10% and 20%, the rates of specific disorders are very low" (Zimmerman & Coryell, 1989). About one-fourth of those with symptoms of a personality disorder fit more than one diagnostic category—another example of comorbidity (Blashfield & Breen, 1989; Zimmerman & Coryell, 1989).

The prognosis is usually poor for the personality disorders. The maladaptive patterns of behavior found in the personality disorders have often taken a lifetime to develop. Changing them is very difficult. This makes understanding the causes of these troubling disorders all the more important. What hypotheses are now under investigation? There are several. (1) There is a biologically based lack of adequate emotional arousal (Eysenck, 1960; Lykken, 1957, 1982; Raine, Venables, & Williams, 1990). (2) There is an unusually high need to seek stimulation (i.e., persons with personality disorders tend to be "sensation seekers") (Quay, 1965; Zuckerman, 1978). (3) There is some genetic basis for at least some of the personality disorders. For example, although the antisocial personality disorder is not inherited directly, it tends to "run in families" (Kendler & Gruenberg, 1982; MacMillan & Kofoed, 1984; Mednick et al., 1987). (4) There is a high incidence of parental loss. Many adults with personality disorders were abandoned in their childhood by at least one parent, usually the father (Greer, 1964; Hare, 1970). (5) There is a significantly high level of abuse in childhood (Ogata et al., 1990). (6) There was an inappropriate, or lack of, emotional "bonding" or attachment with parents in childhood (Buss, 1966).

Before You Go On

**What are the defining characteristics of
the personality disorders?**

DISORDERS USUALLY FIRST DIAGNOSED IN INFANCY, CHILDHOOD, OR ADOLESCENCE

The *Diagnostic and Statistical Manual of Mental Disorders* lists several psychological disorders that are first diagnosed in infants, children, or adolescents. As it happens, we have already discussed a couple of these: mental retardation (in Chapter 9) and eating disorders (in Chapter 10). Others include such things as disorders of language use (such as difficulties in word recognition or reading not associated with mental retardation; commonly, dyslexia), attention-deficit hyperactivity disorder (characterized by inattention, impulsiveness, and hyperactivity), and enuresis (bed-wetting). Here, we will focus on just one disorder that typically begins in infancy or childhood: autistic disorder.

The Example of Autism

autistic disorder a psychological disorder that begins in infancy or childhood and involves withdrawal from social contact, impairment in communication, a desire for sameness in the environment, and ritualistic behaviors

Autistic disorder in children was first recognized as a separate disorder in 1943 by psychiatrist Leo Kanner. Like all psychological disorders, autism occurs in a variety of extremes. There are three main symptoms. (1) A separation or withdrawal from social contact. This symptom is often referred to as an extreme "aloneness," in which the child is unresponsive to others. (2) Impairment in verbal and nonverbal communication. Consistent with withdrawal, speech is often nonexistent. When present, it is strange or stilted, often involving *echolalia*, or the simple repetition of sounds or words. When asked "How are you?" an autistic child may respond, "How are you? How are you?" (3) A desire to keep everything the same. Autistic children may seem obsessed with doing things in ritualistic, repetitive ways, and they can become very agitated whenever routines are disrupted.

Fortunately, autism is a relatively rare disorder, occurring in about 4 children in every 10,000. It is certain that autistic disorder occurs more in boys than in girls, but to what extent is unclear, with ratios ranging from 3:1 to 6:1 (Folstein & Rutter, 1988; Gordon et al., 1993; Steinhausen et al., 1986; Treffert, 1988; Wing & Gould, 1979).

One issue of special interest to psychologists has been the level of general intellectual or cognitive functioning of autistic children. For some time it was believed that, except for their symptoms, autistic children were of normal to above-normal intelligence and were likely to have parents who were above average in intelligence and education. Such beliefs turn out to be unfounded. More than two-thirds of all children with autistic disorder score in the mentally retarded range of IQ; that is, with IQs below 70 (Lockyer & Rutter, 1969; Prior & Wherry, 1986; Rutter & Schopler, 1987). An intriguing phenomenon associated with autism is that some autistic children (how many is not clear, but surely a minority) show exceptional skills in some, very specific, domain of cognitive ability. Such individuals used to be referred to by the unfortunate label of "idiot savant," where "autistic savant" is the more current and preferred term. These individuals can do

A child with autism experiences "aloneness," totally withdrawing from social contact.

remarkable things. Some seem to keep a "perpetual calendar," and can tell you the day of the week for any date that ever was or ever will be, reporting instantly, for example, that July 20, 1940, was a Saturday. Some can do arithmetic computations mentally, with an accuracy and speed that would challenge a calculator. Some demonstrate exceptional talents for music or art—all while being trapped in the disorder called autism (e.g., Treffert, 1988).

When we turn to consider the known causes and effectiveness of treatment for autistic disorder, the picture is dismal. Although parental care was once "blamed" for precipitating autistic disorder, virtually no one still believes that the behavior of parents has anything to do with the onset of this disorder (McAdoo & DeMyer, 1978). Data on genetic factors indicate a weak link at best (Folstein & Rutter, 1977; Sanua, 1987; Smalley, 1991). What we can conclude is that there is likely to be some biological basis for the autistic disorder, probably reflecting the subtle interaction of several factors, including such things as the age and general health of the mother, prenatal deficits, and imbalances in the biochemistry of the brain activity. At present, we do not know what these biological bases are.

As Hetherington and Parke (1993, p. 640) put it, "to date, autism has proven to be a discouraging disorder to treat." Only 5 to 10 percent of autistic children are able to live independently as adults, and nearly 75 percent remain either institutionalized or in need of constant care (Wing, 1989). Medical treatments of autistic disorders have not been terribly successful (Gordon et al., 1993). Although it is painstaking, behavior therapies that involve operant conditioning have been shown to have some beneficial effects (e.g., Lovaas, 1987; Lovaas & Smith, 1988). Psychologist David Holmes ends his review of the treatment of autism with this melancholy assessment: "Overall, it must be concluded that autism poses one of the most prominent and serious failures of psychology and psychiatry, and we can only hope that there will be some breakthrough in the future" (Holmes, 1991, p. 362).

Before You Go On

What characterizes the autistic disorder?

DELIRIUM, DEMENTIA, AMNESTIC, AND OTHER COGNITIVE DISORDERS

Disorders characterized as delirium, dementia, amnestic, and other cognitive disorders used to be classified as *organic mental disorders*. The implication was that what these disorders have in common is a behavioral or mental problem the cause of which involves some known organic brain dysfunction. The label "organic mental disorder" has been dropped from the *DSM-IV* because of the implication that other disorders may be independent of brain function. The new terminology tells us that the major problem with these disorders involves a disruption of cognitive functioning. The key, of course, revolves around the definition of the three terms in this category.

delirium *a clouded state of consciousness; confusion and disorientation, with difficulty in paying attention*

dementia *a marked loss of intellectual abilities in which memory is poor and deteriorates and judgment is adversely affected*

amnestic disorders *disorders in which there is impairment of memory while other intellectual functioning is intact; mostly, problems transferring information from short- to long-term memory*

1. **Delirium** is a clouded state of consciousness, involving a lessening of one's awareness and difficulty paying attention. There may be confusion and disorientation. Someone who is delirious cannot relate what is happening now to what has happened earlier.

2. **Dementia** is characterized by a marked loss of intellectual abilities. Attention may be intact, but use of memory is poor and deteriorates. Judgment and impulse control may be adversely affected.

3. **Amnestic disorders** involve an impairment of memory functioning while other intellectual skills and abilities remain intact. Most often, the problem seems to be difficulty processing information from short-term to long-term memory.

For each of the specific disorders in this category, there is the implication of a known, underlying medical condition. The most common of these disorders is dementia of the Alzheimer's type.

The Example of Alzheimer's

A slow deterioration of one's intellectual functioning is the most common symptom associated with Alzheimer's disease (Katzman, 1987). Problems of recent memory mark the early stages of the disease: "Did I take my pills this morning?" Mild personality changes—apathy, less spontaneity, withdrawal—soon follow, perhaps in an attempt to hide one's symptoms from others. The following is from a publication of the National Institute of Mental Health.

> As the disease progresses, problems in abstract thinking or in intellectual functioning take place. The individual may begin to have trouble with figures when working on bills, with understanding what is being read, or with organizing the day's work. Further disturbances in behavior, such as being agitated, irritable, quarrelsome, and less neat in appearance, may also be seen at this point. Later in the course of the disease, the afflicted may become confused or disoriented about what month or year it is and be unable to describe accurately where they live or to name correctly a place being visited. Eventually they may wander, not engage in conversation, become inattentive and erratic in mood, uncooperative, incontinent with loss of bladder and bowel control, and in extreme cases, totally incapable of caring for themselves. (Cohen, 1980)

Alzheimer's disease was first described in 1907 by Alois Alzheimer and was thought to be an inevitable process of aging (often incorrectly referred to as *senile psychosis*). The symptoms associated with dementia of the Alzheimer's type are not normal, natural, or a necessary part of growing old, but a general acceptance of this reality did not occur until the early 1970s. Among other things, Alzheimer's disease has been diagnosed in persons considerably younger than age 65. In such cases, we refer to an "early onset" form of the disease, but researchers are coming to conclude that age of onset, by itself, does not define different forms of the disease (Bondareff et al., 1993). Estimates are that 3 to 4 million Americans are afflicted with Alzheimer's disease, and over 11,000 of those afflicted die each year (Fackelman, 1992; Hostetler, 1987; Mace & Rabins, 1981; Wurtman, 1985). According to the Centers for Disease Control (CDC), the rates of death attributed to Alzheimer's disease have increased nearly *1,000 percent* since the late 1970s. This enormous increase in death rate is attributable to several factors, including an increasing awareness and willingness to diagnose the disease and an increasing number of persons living to advanced ages, when Alzheimer's is more likely to occur.

Although the major symptoms of Alzheimer's disease are psychological, it *is* a physical disease caused by abnormal changes in brain tissue. Although reliable diagnostic tests may be on the horizon, it is still the case that Alzheimer's dementia can be diagnosed only with certainty by an autopsy of the brain. At autopsy there are four signs of Alzheimer's disease. One is a mass of tangles, a "spaghetti-like jumble of abnormal protein fibers" (Butler & Emr, 1982). A second sign is the presence of plaques—waste material, degenerated nerve fibers that wrap around a core of protein. A third sign is the presence of small cavities filled with fluid and debris. The fourth sign is atrophy; some structures in the brain are reduced in size. There are two problems I need to mention here: (1) each of these signs can be found

Alzheimer's dementia involves the premature death of brain cells. Early psychological symptoms involve mild disorientation and memory loss.

in a normal brain (seldom more than one at a time, however), and (2) we don't know what causes these signs in the first place.

Scientists are beginning to understand the etiology of Alzheimer's, but we're still at the level of discussing alternative hypotheses, and some seem more promising than others. The basic issue is that nerve cells in the brains of Alzheimer's patients start to die off sooner than they should, resulting in the tangles, plaques, and other signs we see at autopsy. The crucial question is, how and why do these brain cells die (Wurtman, 1985)?

As is so often the case with psychological functioning, there is a genetic basis for Alzheimer's disease. We cannot say that the disorder is inherited in the sense that brown eyes are inherited, but there is no doubt that the disease runs in families. This is particularly true for cases for which the age of onset is younger than 60 (Marx, 1990). A breakthrough occurred in 1993 when a team of researchers at Duke University isolated a gene that might be part of the cause of Alzheimer's. How that gene may be involved is another story, yet to be understood.

Another hypothesis about the cause of Alzheimer's dementia is related to the role of a particular protein molecule. This protein is a major component of the plaques found in the brains of Alzheimer's patients. Scientists now know the specific type and structure of the protein involved. The current focus of research is to determine where this protein comes from (Marx, 1990; Selkoe, 1990).

Another model on the list of possibilities involves levels of the neurotransmitter acetylcholine. Patients with dementia of the Alzheimer's type often show a decrease in levels of acetylcholine (e.g., Coyle et al., 1983). We have already noted that acetylcholine is involved in memory; so, a belief that it is involved in memory deficit is quite understandable. Other hypotheses are also under investigation, including the possibility that Alzheimer's disease reflects the result of some low-level infection. There is the possibility that Alzheimer's is the result of a poison, or toxin (aluminum salts have been shown to produce similar symptoms). In addition, researchers are exploring the possibility that Alzheimer's dementia reflects the long-term effects of an inefficient flow of blood and oxygen to the brain. At present, there seems to be at least a shred of truth in each of these hypotheses, reminding us of a theme from Chapter 1: For many questions in psychology, there are no simple answers.

Before You Go On

What is Alzheimer's disease, and what causes it?

MOOD DISORDERS

mood disorders disorders of affect or feeling; usually depression; less frequently mania and depression occurring in cycles

The **mood disorders** (called *affective disorders* until the publication of the *DSM-III-R*) clearly demonstrate a disturbance in one's emotional reactions or feelings. We have to be a little careful here. Almost all psychological disorders have an impact on one's mood or affect. With mood disorders, however, the intensity or extremeness of mood is the major, primary symptom.

Types of Mood Disorder

Mood disorders are defined in terms of extremes of mood, depression being the more common of the two extremes. Under the label *mood disorder* are several specific disorders differentiated in terms of such criteria as length of episode and severity.

Major depression is the diagnosis for a constellation of symptoms that includes feeling sad, low, and hopeless, coupled with a loss of pleasure or interest in almost all usual activities. Associated with major depression are such factors as poor appetite, insomnia, decrease in sexual activity, loss of energy, and feelings of worthlessness. At the same time, there is no event or situation that could reasonably account for the observed depression.

major depression a mood disorder characterized by inexplicable moods of sadness and hopelessness, accompanied by a loss of pleasure or interest in usual activities

This form of mood disorder is diagnosed about two times more often in women than in men; during any 6-month period, approximately 6.6 percent of women and 3.5 percent of men will have an episode of major depression (NIMH, 1991). The ratio of about two women to every man developing major depression holds across nationalities and across ethnic groups (Cross-National Collaborative Group, 1992; McGrath et al., 1990). Worldwide, major depression is on the increase, with current rates at more than 100 million persons (Gotlib, 1992; Weissman & Klerman, 1992). Unfortunately, research also tells us that relapse and reoccurrence are common for those who have had a depressive episode (Belsher & Costello, 1988; Klerman, 1990; Lewinsohn et al., 1989). Depression as a mood disorder seldom occurs as just one episode of illness, but rather is a reasonably chronic condition (Frank et al., 1990).

Dysthymia is the name of the disorder that is essentially a mild case of major depression. The disorder is also chronic, with recurrent pessimism, low energy level, and low self-esteem. Whereas major depression tends to occur in a series of extremely debilitating episodes, dysthymia is a more continuous sense of being depressed and sad.

dysthymia a mood disorder that is basically a mild case of depression; it is chronic, with recurrent pessimism, low energy level, and low self-esteem

As in the case of major depression, there is no identifiable event that precipitates the depressed mood of dysthymia. That is, to feel even overwhelmingly depressed upon hearing of the death of a dear friend is not enough to qualify as a disorder of any sort. From time to time, we all feel periods of depression, but there is some sensible reason for that depressed mood. With these two disorders, the distressing, debilitating mood seems to be present for no good reason that anyone can determine.

In **bipolar disorder**, episodes of depression are occasionally interspersed with episodes of mania. This disorder is still often referred to as "manic depression." **Mania** is characterized as an elevated mood, with feelings of euphoria or irritability. In a manic state one shows an increase in activity, is more talkative than usual, and seems to be able to get by with less sleep than usual. Mania is a condition of mood that cannot be maintained for long. It is too tiring to stay manic for

bipolar disorder a mood disorder characterized by depression with intermittent periods of mania

mania heightened euphoria and increased activitiy, which typically occurs between episodes of depression

an extended time. As is true for depression, mania seldom occurs as an isolated episode. Follow-up studies show that recurrences of manic reactions are common. Relapse is found in approximately 40 percent of those who have been diagnosed as having a manic episode (Harrow et al., 1990; Tohen et al., 1990). People are rarely ever manic without showing interspersed periods of depression. Estimates tell us that approximately 2 million Americans presently suffer from bipolar disorder (NIMH, 1990). Having listed the symptoms of mood disorders and noting that depression is more common than mania, let's now consider *why* people develop depression.

Observations on the Causes of Depression

The answers we find to the question "What causes depression?" depend in large measure on where and how we look for such answers. It seems most likely that depression is caused by several different, but potentially interrelated, causes—both biological and psychological. In this section, I'll briefly review some of the factors that seem to influence the development of depression and the mood disorders.

Biological Factors. Bipolar mood disorder is not very common. Anyone chosen at random has less than a one-half of one percent chance of developing the symptoms of the disorder. The chances of developing the symptoms rise to 15 percent if a brother, sister, or either parent ever had the disorder. This 15-percent figure is true for fraternal twins, too. If, however, one member of a pair of identical twins has the disorder, the chances that the other twin will be diagnosed as having the disorder jump to more than 70 percent (Allen, 1976). What all this means, of course, is that there is excellent evidence for a genetic, or inherited, predisposition for the bipolar mood disorder. The data are not quite as striking for the unipolar mood disorder (depression only), for which the equivalent data is 40 percent for identical twins and 11 percent for fraternal twins. We still suspect, however, that there is some sort of genetic basis for major depression as well (Hammen et al., 1990; Kendler et al., 1993).

There was much excitement generated by published reports in 1987 that a specific gene had been localized that was the cause of bipolar mood disorder in a community of Old Order Amish living in Pennsylvania (Egeland et al., 1987). Follow-up research made it clear that the original reports were premature and overly optimistic (Baron et al., 1993). Although there may be some "linkage" between the disorder and specific sites on certain chromosomes, we realize that there are too many exceptions to claim we know the genetic basis of bipolar mood disorder (e.g., Berrettini et al., 1990).

Even if we did know the site of a specific gene, or two, or three, that provided the basis for a disorder, researchers would still be challenged to specify the biological mechanisms that then produce the symptoms of that disorder. In the case of the mood disorders, attention has been focused on neurotransmitters that appear to influence mood directly. Collectively they are referred to as *biogenic amines* and include such known neurotransmitters as serotonin, dopamine, and norepinephrine. The major breakthrough in this research came when it was discovered that a drug (reserpine) used to treat high blood pressure also produced symptoms of depression. It was then discovered that reserpine lowered the brain's normal level of norepinephrine, and the search for neurotransmitter involvement in affective disorders was on (Bennett, 1982).

One theory holds that depression is caused by a shortage of biogenic amines, and that mania is caused by an excess of these chemicals. It remains to be seen why these biochemical imbalances occur in some people and not others. Perhaps they reflect an inherited predisposition. Another argument follows from the observation that stress causes changes in the neurotransmitters in the brain—including an increase in biogenic amines (Anisman & Zacharko, 1982). If these substances are overstimulated by prolonged stress, perhaps their supply becomes depleted in the long run, leading to symptoms of depression. In cases of depression that seem to occur without any striking or unusual stressors, we may suspect that a genetic predisposition makes some people highly susceptible to the biochemical changes that accompany stress in any degree. The theory seems logical, but as yet there is insufficient evidence for us to draw any firm conclusions.

Psychological Factors. Learning theorists have attributed depression to a number of experiential phenomena, including a lack of effective reinforcers. Given a history of making responses without earning reinforcement, an individual just may stop responding and become quiet, withdrawn, passive, and depressed (Seligman, 1975). Some people, lacking in the ability to gain (or earn) reinforcers, simply respond less often to environmental cues. They enter into a long, generalized period of extinction, which ultimately leads to depression. On the other hand, some research suggests that the ineffectiveness of reinforcers in some people's lives is more a result of depression than a cause of it. *Because* they are depressed, they may find less reinforcement for their responses to the world about them (Carson & Carson, 1984).

Other theorists, most notably a psychiatrist, Aaron Beck (1967, 1976), argue that although depression is a disorder of affect, its causes are largely cognitive. Some people, the argument goes, tend to think of themselves in a poor light; they believe that they are, in many ways, ineffective people. They tend to blame themselves for a great many of their failures, whether deservedly so or not. Facing life every day with these negative attitudes about oneself tends to foster even more failures and self-doubt, and such cycles then lead to feelings of depression.

To be sure, there are other views about the causes of depression, including the psychoanalytic view that depression is a reflection of early childhood experiences that lead to anger that is directed inward. In brief, we can conclude that depression probably stems from a combination of genetic predispositions, biochemical influences, learning experiences, situational stress, and cognitive factors. Which of these is more, or most, important remains to be seen.

Before we go on, let's take a moment to consider the data on the prevalence of mood disorders that tell us that they are twice as likely to be diagnosed in women than in men. Why should this be the case?

Several hypotheses have been proposed. (1) Perhaps the genetic basis of depression is located on X-chromosomes (remember, males carry an XY pair of chromosomes, whereas women have XX pairs). Unfortunately, there is more logic than there is data to support this hypothesis. (2) Perhaps women, given their roles in our culture, are more free and open to discuss their feelings—their negative feelings in particular—than are men. This may explain why men are more likely than women to abuse alcohol: it's a male response to feelings of sadness and depression. Again, this hypothesis may sound pretty good, but there is scant data to support it. Among other things, remember that mood disorders are found to be more common in women than in men in every culture that has been studied. (3) Perhaps women are more exposed to the types of stressors (less education, poorer employment, lower pay, child-rearing responsibilities, and so on) that would lead one to become depressed. This, too, may be a valid observation, but when such factors are controlled for (when men and women are matched for such stressors), the sex difference in diagnosis remains. Even when factors such as self-esteem are controlled for, the sex difference remains.

So, once again, a common theme emerges: sex differences in depression reflect a complex interaction of genetic, biological, psychological, and cultural factors (e.g., McGrath et al., 1990).

Before You Go On

How are the mood disorders defined?

What do we know about their prevalence and their causes?

SCHIZOPHRENIA

In some ways, schizophrenia is the ultimate psychological disorder. It is "the most devastating, puzzling, and frustrating of all mental illnesses" (Bloom et al., 1985). **Schizophrenia** is the label given to what may be several different disorders, all of which have in common a distortion of reality and a retreat from others, accompanied by disturbances in affect, behavior, perception, and thinking (our ABC again).

One of the things that qualifies schizophrenia as the ultimate psychological disorder is that it impairs virtually every aspect of living. The range of symptoms is so great that it is nearly impossible to specify just which are fundamental and which are secondary.

Let's begin by summarizing some of the symptoms commonly associated with schizophrenia. First, there is usually a disturbance of thinking. In fact, schizophrenia nearly always involves delusions and hallucinations in some phase of the illness. **Delusions** are false beliefs, ideas that are firmly held regardless of what others may say.

schizophrenia a complex family of disorders characterized by impairment of cognitive functioning, delusions and hallucinations, social withdrawal, and inappropriate affect

delusions false beliefs; ideas that are firmly held regardless of evidence to the contrary

Hallucinations are false perceptions; perceiving that which is not there or failing to perceive that which is there. As reflected in their delusions, people with schizophrenia come to believe strange and unusual things that simply are not true. The delusions of someone with schizophrenia tend to be inconsistent and clearly unsupportable. Perceptions are distorted, most commonly with auditory hallucinations (hearing things, usually voices). Distortions of time are not uncommon. Sometimes a minute seems to last for hours, or hours seem to race by in seconds. A person with schizophrenia may also show unusual behaviors, typically ritualized, stereotyped, aimless, and meaningless.

One of the most obvious behavioral consequences of schizophrenia is found in language. Some schizophrenics make up words (called *neologisms*) as they talk. I once had a person with schizophrenia tell me at great length and with great animation about a "rogaritz" and what that "rogaritz" was going to do with a tree once it caught it. Others may use actual English words, but mix them up and use them inappropriately in "word salads." As an example, here is the response of a severely disturbed patient to the question, "Why are people who are born deaf usually unable to talk?" "When you swallow in your throat like a key it comes out, but not a scissors. A robin too, it means spring" (Marengo & Harrow, 1987, p. 654). You may recognize our opening example of George as fitting this diagnosis.

Persons with schizophrenia are unusually withdrawn. They seldom interact with others. Psychologists speak of "an impoverishment of interpersonal relations."

It is also common to find affect disordered. Most commonly, we find *flattened affect*, meaning that a person shows no emotional response of any kind. Occasionally there is inappropriate affect or emotion: giggling and laughing or crying and sobbing for no apparent reason.

Two things need to be made clear. First, as unsettling as these symptoms may be, the average patient with schizophrenia *does not* present the picture of the crazed, wild lunatic that is often depicted in movies and on television. Day in and day out, the average schizophrenic patient is quite colorless, socially withdrawn, and of very little danger. Although there are exceptions to this rule of thumb, it is particularly true when the patient with schizophrenia is medicated or in treatment. Their "differentness" may be frightening, but people who have schizophrenia are seldom any more dangerous than anyone else.

Second, when literally translated, schizophrenia means "splitting of the mind." This term was first used by a Swiss psychiatrist, Eugen Bleuler, in 1911. The split Bleuler was addressing was a split of the mind of the patient from the real world and the social relationships the rest of us enjoy. Never has the term been used to describe a multiple or split personality of the Dr. Jekyll and Mr. Hyde variety. Such disorders do occur, and we have seen that they are classified as dissociative identity disorders.

hallucinations false perceptions; either perceiving that which is not there or not perceiving that which is there

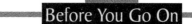

Before You Go On

What are the major symptoms
of schizophrenia?

Incidence and Types of Schizophrenia

Schizophrenia occurs around the world at the same rate: about 1 percent of the population at any point in time. This figure has been stable for many years. It is a common claim that schizophrenic patients fill more than half the hospital beds in psychiatric hospitals in the United States (Bloom et al., 1985). Once again, however, the statistics are difficult to deal with on a personal level. No matter how we state the statistics, we are talking about very large numbers of persons. Prognosis is not very encouraging. About 25 percent recover fully from their first episode of the disorder and have no recurrences; in about 50 percent of cases of schizophrenia, we have a recurrent illness with periods of remission in between, and in about 25 percent of the cases, we have no signs of recovery and a long-term deterioration in functioning. In one study, only 10 to 17 percent of patients with schizophrenia showed complete remission of symptoms in a follow-up study 5 years after initial diagnosis (Carone, Harrow, & Westermeyer, 1991). Prognosis for this disorder may be related to when intervention occurs. If treatment begins right after an initial episode, the prognosis is fairly good, with as many as 83 percent recovering (e.g., Lieberman et al., 1993). Here is a picture we also see with many physical ailments: the sooner treatment begins, the better the likelihood of recovery.

I already have indicated that schizophrenia is a label that applies to several specific disorders. In this way, the term *schizophrenia* is not unlike the term *cancer*. To say that one has cancer communicates only a general diagnosis. We then want to know what sort of cancer. Let's now consider some of the ways in which the collection of disorders called schizophrenia can be classified. Classifying varieties of schizophrenia has been motivated by an attempt to better understand what causes the disorder, and thus lead to more effective treatment. Although the subcategories that follow are common ones, the goal of demonstrating separate, distinct disorders has not been met. R. Walter Heinrichs puts it this way: "Schizophrenia is a heterogeneous illness that, paradoxically, resists subdivision" (Heinrichs, 1993, p. 221).

DSM Subtypes. The *DSM-IV* lists five subtypes of schizophrenia. These varieties share many of the same symptoms of disorganized cognition, inappropriate affect, and strange behavior, but each type has a symptom or cluster of symptoms that makes it different. (The following descriptions are from Carson & Butcher, 1992.)

The *paranoid type* diagnosis reflects a collection of sy mptoms dominated by absurd, illogical, and changeable delusions, frequently accompanied by vivid hallucinations, resulting in a severe impairment of critical judgment. Someone with paranoid schizophrenia may come to believe that others are out to do him great harm and will hear voices that tell him so.

Patients with the *disorganized type* of schizophrenia usually suffer a more severe disintegration of personality than most other patients. Emotional distortion is shown in inappropriate laughter and silliness, peculiar mannerisms, and bizarre, often obscene, behavior. Neologisms and word salad are common symptoms of this type. The *catatonic type* is characterized by alternating periods of extreme withdrawal and extreme excitement. In withdrawal, the patient may become totally motionless for hours, or even days (a condition called "catatonia"). As a stage of excitement comes on, the person may talk or shout incoherently, pace rapidly, and engage in uninhibited frenzied behavior. In this state, the individual can be dangerous.

As its name suggests, the diagnosis of *undifferentiated type* is used for those patients that show many of the symptoms of schizophrenia, but who do not meet the criteria of being paranoid, disorganized, or catatonic. In many cases, this term is used for patients in early stages of the disorder for whom a more specific diagnosis is not yet possible. The label *residual type* is reserved for persons with an indication of mild symptoms who are in the process of recovering from a clearly schizophrenic episode.

Process and Reactive. So far, we have classified psychological disorders only in terms of specific, defining symptoms. With schizophrenia, there is a distinction that is not made on the basis of the nature of symptoms, but on the basis of their *onset*. We use the term **process schizophrenia** to describe schizophrenic symptoms that have developed gradually, usually over a period of years. It is often only in retrospect, after the diagnosis of schizophrenia has been made, that we realize the patient has had a long history of symptoms that have gradually worsened to the point where intervention is required, treatment sought, and a formal diagnosis made. **Reactive schizophrenia**, on the other hand, is the term we use for the rapid, sudden onset of schizophrenic symptoms. Here we have a clinical picture of someone who was, by all accounts, quite normal and reasonably well adjusted, but who suddenly showed signs of having a psychotic episode, or "break." As we have found to be the case in other situations, we should not consider reactive and process as two separate and distinct types of schizophrenia. Rather, we should view them as extremes of a dimension that can be used to describe the nature of the onset of schizophrenic symptoms.

The significance of this distinction is that there is some reason to believe that the prognosis for schizophrenia can be, at least to a degree, based on the nature of its onset—the more toward the *process* variety, the worse the prognosis, and the more toward the *reactive* type, the better the prognosis. We need to be careful not to overinterpret what is at best a rule of thumb. Some evidence suggests that outcome, or recovery, from schizophrenia is not related to the nature of onset as clearly as once believed (e.g., Harding, 1988).

process schizophrenia
schizophrenia in which the onset of the symptoms is comparatively gradual

reactive schizophrenia
schizophrenia in which the onset of symptoms is comparatively sudden

These drawings show the varying levels of progress of a patient—an artist—with paranoid schizophrenia. The first image was chosen from a magazine for the patient to copy. The second image shows the patient's attempt at copying the picture when fully symptomatic, before therapy began, while the third image shows a picture created by the same patient after therapy.

Positive and Negative Symptoms. As early as 1919, Kraepelin claimed that schizophrenia could be divided into two types depending on the symptoms described at diagnosis. In one form of the disorder, the major symptoms are hallucinations, delusions, muscular rigidity, and/or bizarre behaviors. In the other form, the major symptoms include emotional and social withdrawal, reduced energy and motivation, apathy, and poor attention (Kay & Singh, 1989; Lenzenweger et al., 1989). Over the past decade, these two forms of the disorder have come to be known as *positive* and *negative,* respectively (Andreasen, 1982; Andreasen et al., 1990; Crow, 1980). It is a bit of an oversimplification, but it is as if in the case of positive symptoms we notice reactions of a person that have been added to his or her normal functioning, and in the case of negative symptoms we notice a lack of or the disappearance of behaviors that were once present. These two varieties are not mutually exclusive, and many patients show aspects of both forms.

Again, the usefulness of the negative-positive distinction is that there may be differences in both the causes and most effective treatment plans for the two types. In brief, we find the correlates of negative symptoms to include structural abnormalities in the brain (as seen on CAT scans, for example), a clearer genetic basis, more severe complications at birth, a lower educational level, poorer adjustment patterns before onset, and a poorer prognosis given the relative ineffectiveness of medications. Correlated with positive symptoms are an excess of the neurotransmitter dopamine, relatively normal brain configuration, severe disruptions in early family life, overactivity and aggressiveness in adolescence, and a relatively good response to treatment (Andreason et al., 1990; Breier et al., 1991; Cannon et al.,

Can you tell that this woman was diagnosed as having acute schizophrenia? There is no "typical" behavior or "look" that you can expect to find in schizophrenics.

1990; Kay & Singh, 1989; Lenzenweger et al., 1989; McGlashan & Fenton, 1992). On the other hand, we find that the distinction based on positive and negative symptoms, like the one based on nature of onset, may be of less predictive value than was once hoped (Kay, 1990; Pogue-Geile & Zubin, 1988).

Before You Go On

What characterizes the following types of schizophrenia: paranoid, disorganized, catatonic, undifferentiated, residual, process versus reactive, positive versus negative?

Observations on the Causes of Schizophrenia

Schizophrenia is a complex set of disorders. There is even disagreement on how to define schizophrenia. (In one study, a sample of patients with schizophrenia was reduced by more than half when the researchers imposed the *DSM-III* criteria rather than those from the *DSM-II* to define their subjects (Winters, Weintraub, & Neale, 1981). As you may suspect, any bottom-line conclusion on the cause of schizophrenia will be tentative and multidimensional. Although we don't know what causes the disorder, we do have a number of interesting ideas to consider.

Hereditary Factors. Schizophrenia tends to run in families (Gottesman & Bertelsen, 1989; Kessler, 1980; Rosenthal, 1970). The data are not as striking as they are for the mood disorders, but one is at a higher risk of being diagnosed as having schizophrenia if there is a history of the disorder in one's family.

Adult children of persons with schizophrenia are significantly more likely to develop the disease than are adult children of nonschizophrenic parents. If one parent has schizophrenia, his or her child is 10 to 15 times more likely to have the disorder as an adult, and when both parents have schizophrenia, their children are about 40 *times* more likely to develop this illness (Cornblatt & Erlenmeyer-Kimling, 1985; Erlenmeyer-Kimling, 1968). The risk of developing schizophrenia is 4 to 5 times greater for an identical twin than it is for a fraternal twin if the other member of the twin pair has schizophrenia. Remember that the odds of being diagnosed with this disorder, in the general population, are about 1 in 100. If adopted children develop schizophrenia, it is more likely that other cases of schizophrenia will be found among members of their biological family than their adoptive family (Bootzin & Acocella, 1984). Some of these data are presented in Figure 12.4. We need to remember that such data do not mean that schizophrenia is directly inherited. Notice, for example, that *nearly half of the identical twins of schizophrenics never do develop the disorder.* It is reasonable to say that one may inherit a predisposition to develop schizophrenia. This distinction is an important one, recalling our earlier discussions about the role of genetics in the development of psychological reactions and not drawing cause-and-effect conclusions from correlational data. And lest we get too committed to a genetic hypothesis on the causes of schizophrenia, let us consider the reality that "89 percent of diagnosed schizophrenics have no known relative who is schizophrenic (Cromwell, 1993; Plomin, 1988).

Biochemical Factors: The Dopamine Hypothesis. The neurotransmitter dopamine is found in every human brain. The role of dopamine in schizophrenia has come to light from several lines of research.

For one thing, we know that the abuse of amphetamines often leads to many of the symptoms also found in schizophrenia. We also know that amphetamines are chemically very similar to dopamine and actually may cause an increase in dopamine levels in the brain. Logic then leads us to wonder if perhaps schizophrenic symptoms (particularly those we have recognized as positive symptoms) are caused by excess amounts of dopamine.

dopamine hypothesis the view that a heightened sensitivity to the neurotransmitter dopamine may cause schizophrenic symptoms

Support for this view, or the **dopamine hypothesis,** comes from examining the action of drugs that actually reduce schizophrenic symptoms. Apparently, some drugs that alleviate schizophrenic symptoms commonly block receptor sites for dopamine in the brain (Snyder, 1980). If reducing the effectiveness of dopamine by blocking its activity at the synapse can control schizophrenic symptoms, might we assume that these symptoms are caused by dopamine in the first place (Tandon & Greden, 1989)?

The arguments for this hypothesis appear compelling, but are far from certain. For one thing, there is little evidence that persons with schizophrenia have elevated levels of dopamine in their brains (Karoum et al., 1987). Even so, there may be a heightened sensitivity in the brains of schizophrenics to whatever levels of dopamine are present (e.g., perhaps there are more receptor sites for dopamine). In other words, people with schizophrenia may not have excess levels of

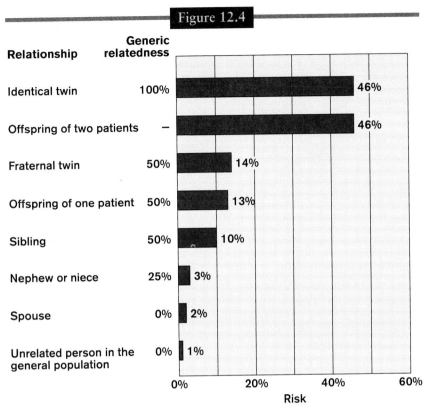

Relationship	Generic relatedness	Risk
Identical twin	100%	46%
Offspring of two patients	—	46%
Fraternal twin	50%	14%
Offspring of one patient	50%	13%
Sibling	50%	10%
Nephew or niece	25%	3%
Spouse	0%	2%
Unrelated person in the general population	0%	1%

Figure 12.4

Lifetime risks of developing schizophrenia are largely a function of how closely a person is genetically related to someone with the disease. (Data from Gottesman & Shields, 1982).

dopamine, they just may be more responsive to what they do have, thus creating schizophrenic symptoms. Again, this may sound reasonable, but there is little evidence to support such a conclusion. For another thing, not all medications used to treat schizophrenia have their effect by blocking dopamine receptor sites. It is also troublesome that when such drugs *are* effective, their effects generally take a few weeks to develop. If the effect of the drugs on receptor sites is immediate, why isn't the effect on symptoms immediate also?

Additionally, we have a "chicken and egg" problem with the dopamine hypothesis. If dopamine were shown to be related to schizophrenic symptoms, we would still have to ask if there is a direct *causal* relationship. That is, do increased levels of dopamine cause schizophrenic symptoms, or does the disorder of schizophrenia cause elevated dopamine levels? Or does some other factor—perhaps stress—cause both elevated dopamine levels and schizophrenic symptoms?

Note that we have the same chicken-and-egg problem with some interesting findings concerning brain structure and schizophrenia. The brains of many patients with schizophrenia, mostly those with positive symptoms, have abnormally large ventricles (cavities or openings that contain cerebrospinal fluid) (Andreasen et al., 1982, 1990b), and

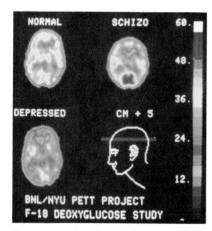

Demonstrating the involvement of the brain in psychological disorders, these PET scans show brain images of someone diagnosed with schizophrenia and of someone in a depressed state. A normal brain image is shown for comparison.

evidence suggests a lack of balance between the two hemispheres of the brain (Gur et al., 1987; Reveley et al., 1987). Even if these differences in the brain are confirmed, we still don't know if we're dealing with causes or effects. "In summary, schizophrenia may be a dopamine-related illness, but this relationship has not yet emerged as the neurological key to the disorder" (Heinrichs, 1993, p. 225).

Psychological and Social Factors. Perhaps genetic or biochemical factors, or both, predispose a person to develop the symptoms of schizophrenia. What sorts of events then turn such predispositions into reality? To this question, answers are very sketchy.

One view is that schizophrenia develops as a response to early experiences within the family unit (e.g., Lidz, 1973). The early experiences of people who later develop schizophrenic symptoms sometimes seem different from those who do not develop schizophrenia. One factor may be inefficient means of communication within the family. There may be an inability or unwillingness to share feelings and emotions or to talk openly about problems and conflicts. Early childhood experiences of adults diagnosed with schizophrenia seem filled with conflict, anxiety, doubt, and emotional tension. There also seems to be an unusually high incidence of double messages being presented to children who later develop the disorder. For example, a mother may tell her child that she becomes upset when everyone forgets about her birthday and then turn around and scold the child for spending lunch money to buy a birthday present. Parents who communicate something like, "We want you to be independent and responsible, but so long as you live in this house, you'll do things the way we say, no questions asked," are delivering a double message to their child.

There is evidence that in some people, the symptoms of schizophrenia may remain dormant, or unexpressed, until the individual is subjected to environmental stressors (e.g., Gottesman & Bertelsen, 1989; Johnson, 1989; Ventura et al., 1989). The theory here is that some people are genetically prone to develop the symptoms of schizophrenia when they are exposed to stressors. Other people faced with the same type or amount of stress might develop ulcers, might become excessively anxious, or might show no particular symptoms at all.

A word of caution. Please do not overinterpret what I have said in this section on psychosocial factors and the development of schizophrenia. Yes, it may very well be that some life experiences do bring on the symptoms of schizophrenia or tend to make those symptoms worse than they would otherwise be. The consensus is that with schizophrenia we are dealing with a complex disease of the brain, not a "disorder of living" (Johnson, 1989). "How the environment interacts with genetic risk to trigger the development of schizophrenia remains unknown" (Iacono & Grove, 1993).

Before You Go On

Describe some of the factors that have been implicated as possible causes of schizophrenic symptoms.

TOPIC 12B SUMMARY

When most people think about psychology, their first thoughts generally deal with abnormal psychology: the psychological disorders and their treatment. As we have seen in this chapter, the concept of abnormality in psychology is a very complex, multidimensional one. Even so, we have also seen that psychological disorders are much more common than any of us would like to think, afflicting tens of millions of Americans. Applying labels indicative of abnormality or disorder can have unfortunate consequences and should be done with great care. We have seen that psychologists do try to make sure that only a person's affects, behaviors, and/or cognitions—*and not the person*—are labeled as disordered.

Mostly what we have done in this Topic is briefly review, in terms of their symptoms, and where possible in terms of their etiology and prognosis, several of the more common or the more striking psychological disorders. We began with the anxiety disorders, each of which manifests high levels of anxiety in one form or another. We discussed the somatoform and dissociative disorders. We then looked at the personality disorders, characterized by lifelong patterns of inflexible and maladaptive behaviors. We saw that these disorders are difficult to diagnose and equally difficult to treat. We took a brief look at one of the disorders usually associated with infancy or childhood—autism—and found it to be a devastating disorder with poor prognosis.

We then turned our attention to psychological disorders that have symptoms of gross impairment of functioning and a loss of contact with reality. This was surely the case with our example of Alzheimer's disease. It is a distortion of affect, usually extreme depression, that marks the mood disorders. Schizophrenia is actually a set of disorders that to some degree involves impairment of all areas of functioning: affect, cognition, and behavior.

Again, the prevalence of psychological disorders is staggering. Millions of people are, at this moment, suffering from one of the disorders we've discussed in this chapter. Now it is time to consider what can be done to help and to provide relief to those who suffer the pain of the psychological disorders.

TOPIC 12A

How do we define psychological abnormality?

In the context of psychological disorders, we take abnormal to mean maladaptive behaviors, cognitions, and/or affect that are at odds with social expectations and that result in distress or discomfort. */p. 590*

What is the *DSM-IV*?

CHAPTER SUMMARY

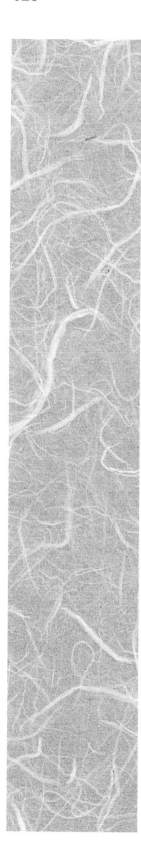

What are some of the advantages and disadvantages of classifying psychological disorders?

The *DSM-IV* is the revised fourth edition of the *Diagnostic and Statistical Manual of Mental Disorders*, the standard system of classification for the psychological disorders. The major advantage of this system is that it provides one standard label and cluster of symptoms for each disorder that all mental health practitioners can use; as such, it is a basis for improved communication. It does have its limitations, however. Such schemes of classification can be used to confuse description with explanation; classifying and labeling individuals as having psychological disorders may overlook the larger group or society of which that individual is a part. /p. 594

TOPIC 12B

Describe the symptoms of generalized anxiety disorder.

For generalized anxiety disorder, the major defining characteristic is a high level of anxiety that cannot be attributed to any particular source. With the generalized anxiety disorder, the felt anxiety is chronic, persistent, and diffuse. /p. 596

What is a panic disorder?

The defining symptom of a panic disorder is a sudden, often unpredictable, attack of intense anxiety, called a panic attack, which may last for seconds or for hours. There is no particular stimulus that prompts the attack. /p. 597

What are the essential characteristics of a phobic disorder?

By definition, a phobic disorder is typified by an intense, persistent fear of some object, activity, or situation that is in no real sense a threat to the individual's well-being; in brief, an intense, irrational fear. Phobias imply attempts to avoid the phobic object. /p. 598

What characterizes the obsessive-compulsive disorder?

Obsessions and compulsions are the main symptoms or complaints in an obsessive-compulsive disorder, or OCD. An obsession is a thought or an idea that constantly intrudes on one's awareness. A compulsion, on the other hand, is a repeated and stereotyped behavior or act that constantly intrudes on one's behavior. /p. 601

Describe the symptoms of posttraumatic stress disorder.

Posttraumatic stress disorder, or PTSD, is an anxiety disorder in which the symptoms of high levels of anxiety, recurrent and disruptive dreams, and recollections of a highly traumatic event (e.g., rape, combat, or natural disaster) occur well after the danger of the event has passed. /p. 602

Describe hypochondriasis and conversion disorder.

By definition, somatoform disorders reflect a physical or bodily symptom or complaint. In every case, however, there is no known biological cause for the complaint. In hypochondriasis, a person lives in fear and dread of contracting some serious illness or disease, when there is no medical evidence that such fears are well founded. In conversion disorder, there is an actual loss or alteration in physical functioning—often dramatic, such as blindness or deafness—not under voluntary control, suggesting a physical disorder, but without medical basis. */p. 605*

What are the defining symptoms of the dissociative disorders?

Dissociative disorders are marked by a retreat or escape from (dissociation with) some aspect of one's personality. It may be a matter of an inability to recall some life event (amnesia), sometimes accompanied by unexplained travel to a different location (fugue state). In some very rare cases, certain aspects of one's personality become so dissociated that we may say the person suffers from multiple personality disorder, where two or more personalities are found in the same individual. */p. 607*

What are the defining characteristics of the personality disorders?

Personality disorders (PDs) are enduring patterns of perceiving, relating to, and thinking about the environment and oneself that are inflexible and maladaptive. These are essentially lifelong patterns of maladjustment and may be classified as belonging to one of three groups, or clusters. Group 1 includes those PDs involving odd or eccentric reactions, such as the paranoid and schizoid personality disorder. Group 2 includes disorders of dramatic, emotional, or erratic reactions, such as the antisocial or the histrionic personality disorder. Group 3 includes disorders involving fear and anxiety, such as the avoidant or the dependent personality disorder. */p. 609*

What characterizes the autistic disorder?

Autistic disorder is usually first diagnosed in infancy or childhood (more often in boys than in girls). It includes among its symptoms a separation or withdrawal from social contact, difficulty in verbal and nonverbal communication, and an overwhelming desire or need for keeping things the same, or unchanged. Etiology is unknown and prognosis is not good. */p. 611*

What is Alzheimer's disease, and what causes it?

Alzheimer's disease is a form of degenerative dementia associated with known abnormalities in the brain—among other things, the formation of tangles and plaques. There is a strong likelihood of a genetic basis for the disease. Research is also focusing on the formation of certain brain proteins and the neurotransmitter acetylcholine. */p. 614*

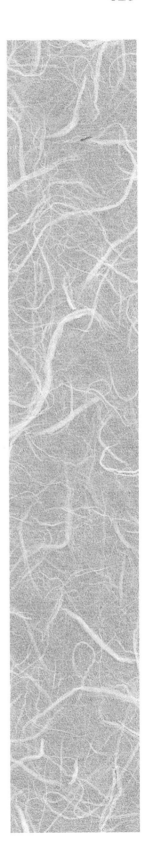

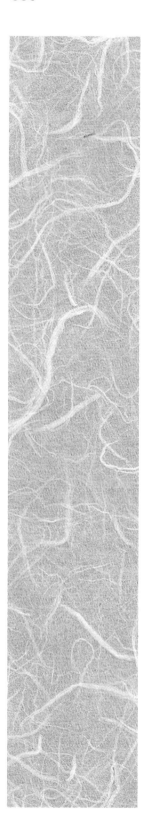

How are the mood disorders defined?

What do we know about their prevalence and their causes?

Although many psychological disorders involve disturbances of affect, in the mood disorders, a disturbance in mood or feeling is the prime, and perhaps only, major symptom. Most commonly we find the disorder to be one of depression alone; less commonly we find mania and depression occurring in cycles (bipolar mood disorder). In any case, whether the major symptom be depression or mania, there is no reason for the observed mood. Major depression is a common disorder, affecting as many as 20 percent of all women and 10 percent of all men at some time in their lives. The disorder has a strong hereditary basis. Neurotransmitters (biogenic amines) such as serotonin and dopamine have been implicated. Psychological theories of depression tend to focus on the learned ineffectiveness of reinforcers and cognitive factors, such as a poor self-image, as models for explaining the causes of depression. /p. 618

What are the major symptoms of schizophrenia?

Schizophrenia is a label applied to a number of disorders that all involve varying degrees of cognitive impairment (e.g., delusions, hallucinations, and disturbances of thought), social isolation, and disturbances of affect and behavior. /p. 620

What characterizes the following types of schizophrenia: paranoid, disorganized, catatonic, undifferentiated, residual, process versus reactive, positive versus negative?

Paranoid schizophrenia involves delusions, often of persecution, and hallucinations that support such delusions. Disorganized schizophrenia involves a severe disintegration of personality, with emotional distortions, inappropriate laughter, and bizarre behaviors. Catatonic schizophrenia is characterized by catatonia (states of physical impassivity) or extreme excitement. Undifferentiated schizophrenia involves a variety of psychotic symptoms, none of which dominates, and residual schizophrenia indicates a mild form of the disorder following a schizophrenic episode. Process schizophrenia is the term used when symptoms develop slowly; we call cases in which symptoms arise suddenly, reactive schizophrenia. The latter has a better prognosis than the former. Positive symptoms of schizophrenia include the addition of hallucinations, delusions, or bizarre behaviors to one's behaviors, whereas negative symptoms refer to losses: social withdrawal, loss of appropriate affect, apathy, or loss of attention. /p. 623

Describe some of the factors that have been implicated as possible causes of schizophrenic symptoms.

Although we do not know the causes of schizophrenia, three lines of investigation have produced hopeful leads. (1) There is a genetic predisposition for the disorder. Although schizophrenia is not inherited, it does run in families. (2) Research on biochemical correlates have localized the neurotransmitter dopamine as being involved in the production of schizophrenia-like symptoms, although dopamine's role in the disorder is now being questioned. (3) It also seems that some psychological experiences, perhaps involving parent-child interactions and communications, may predispose one toward schizophrenia. Probably the most reasonable position at the moment is that for some persons, environmental events, such as extreme stress, trigger biochemical and structural changes in the brain that result in the symptoms of schizophrenia. /p. 626

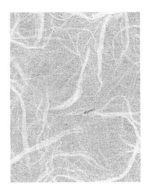

chapter thirteen

TREATMENT AND THERAPY

CHAPTER OUTLINE

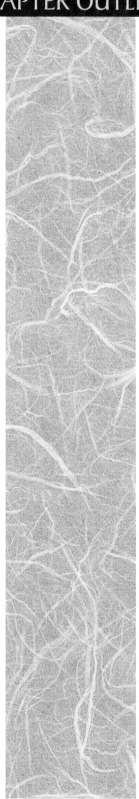

TOPIC 13A HISTORY AND BIOMEDICAL TREATMENTS
A Historical Perspective
Biomedical Treatments of Psychological Disorders
Psychosurgery
Electroconvulsive Therapy
Drug Therapy
Deinstitutionalization: Blessing or Curse?
TOPIC 13A SUMMARY

TOPIC 13B THE PSYCHOTHERAPIES
Who Provides Psychotherapy?
Psychoanalytic Techniques
Freudian Psychoanalysis
Post-Freudian Psychoanalysis
Humanistic Techniques
Behavioral Techniques
Cognitive Techniques
Rational-Emotive Therapy
Cognitive Restructuring Therapy
Group Approaches
Evaluating Psychotherapy
TOPIC 13B SUMMARY

CHAPTER SUMMARY

*B*arbara is an 18-year-old freshman at City College. Living at home with her parents and two younger brothers, she is having difficulty dealing with demands on her time. She has a job at a restaurant and is trying to manage four classes at CC. Pressures of home, school, and work are making Barbara uncharacteristically anxious and depressed. She is falling behind in her school work, doing poorly at her job, and finding life at home almost unbearable. Barbara has been seeing a counselor at the Student Services Center.

Psychotherapist: Good morning, Barbara; how do you feel today?

Barbara: [snapping back] Good lord, can't you ever say anything but "how do you feel today?" I feel fine, just fine.

P.: You sound angry.

B.: [in a sarcastically mocking tone] "You sound angry."

P.: [silence]

B.: Well, I'm not angry, so there.

P.: Um. Hmm.

B.: Yeah, so I'm angry. So big deal! So what of it? Is there something wrong with being angry?

P.: Of course not.

B.: You'd be angry too.

P.: Oh?

B.: My father threatened to throw me out of the house last night.

P.: He threatened you?

B.: He said that if I didn't get my act together and shape up, he'd send me packing. I don't know where I'd go, but if he pulls that crap on me one more time I'll show him. I will leave.

P.: Would you like to leave?

B.: Yes! No! No, I don't really want to. It's just that nobody cares about me around there. They don't know how hard it is trying to work and go to school and everything, ya' know?

P.: [nods]

B.: *They* never went to college. What do *they* know? They don't know what it's like.

P.: You feel that your parents can't appreciate your problems?

B.: Damn right! What do they know? They've never tried to work and go to college at the same time.

P.: They don't know what it's like.

B.: No, they don't. Of course, I suppose it's not all their fault. They've never been in this situation. I suppose I could try to explain it to them better.

P.: So it would be helpful to share with them how you feel, and maybe they'll understand?

B.: Yeah. Maybe that's a good idea, I'll do that. At least I'll try. I don't want to just whine and complain all the time, but maybe I can get them to understand what it's like. Boy that would help—to have somebody besides you understand and maybe be on my side once in awhile instead of on my case all the time.

This is an idealized example. Things seldom go as smoothly as depicted here, but this dialogue does reflect several of the principles of a form of psychotherapy we will be discussing in this chapter.

*I*n Chapter 13, we turn our attention to psychotherapy and to other forms of treatment designed to help people suffering from psychological disorders. To begin, we'll take a brief look at the history of treatment for psychological disorders. The premise that persons with psychological disorders should *be treated humanely is remarkably recent in our history.*

We'll then begin our discussion of treatment by considering those that typically fall outside the realm of psychology: treatments that are medical or physical in nature. We will examine psychosurgery and shock therapies, but will concentrate on the use of drugs to control and treat the symptoms of mental illness.

Most of this chapter will be devoted to types of psychotherapy—techniques "designed to influence the patient's behavior by psychological means; that is, they seek to persuade the patient to think, feel, or act differently" (Strupp, 1986, p. 128). We'll discuss five types of therapy: psychoanalytic, humanistic, behavioral, cognitive, and group techniques. Then we'll try to evaluate psychotherapy as a whole. Does it work? If so, under what circumstances?

Topic 13A
HISTORY AND BIOMEDICAL TREATMENTS

Mental illness is not a new phenomenon. Among the earliest written records from the Babylonians, Egyptians, and ancient Hebrews we find descriptions of what we now recognize as psychological disorders (Murray, 1983). How individuals with disorders were treated was consistent with the prevailing view of what caused the disorder. Let's take a brief look at some of that history.

A HISTORICAL PERSPECTIVE

The history of the treatment of psychological disorders in the Western world is not a pleasant one. By today's standards, *therapy*—in the sense of active, humane intervention to improve the condition of persons in psychological distress—does not even seem like the right term to describe the way in which most disordered persons were dealt with in the past.

The ancient Greeks and Romans believed that people who were depressed, manic, irrational, or intellectually retarded, or who had hallucinations and delusions, had in some way offended the gods. In some cases, persons were viewed as being temporarily out of favor with the gods, and it followed that their condition could be improved through prayer and religious ritual. More severely disturbed patients were seen as being physically possessed by evil spirits. These cases were more difficult, often impossible, to cure. The aim was to exorcise the evil spirits and demons inhabiting the minds and souls of the mentally deranged. Many unfortunate people died as a direct result of their treatment or were killed outright when treatment failed. Treatment was left to priests, who were, after all, thought to be skilled in the ways and means of spirit manipulation.

There were those in ancient times who had a more enlightened or reasonable view of psychological disorders. Among them was Hippocrates (460–377 B.C.), who believed that mental disorders had physical causes, not spiritual ones. He identified epilepsy as being a disorder of the brain, for example. Some of his views were wrong (e.g., that hysteria is a disorder of the uterus), but at least he tried (without success) to demystify psychological disorders. Throughout most of Western history, the impact of scientists such as Hippocrates was slight and short lived.

During the Middle Ages (1000–1500), the oppression and persecution of the mentally ill were at their peak. During this period, the prevailing view continued to be that psychologically disordered people were "bad people," under the spell of the devil and evil spirits. They had brought on their own grief, and there was no hope for them, except that they save their immortal souls and confess their evil ways.

For hundreds of years, well into the eighteenth century, the attitude toward the mentally ill continued to be that they were in league with the devil or that they were being punished by God for sinful thoughts and deeds. They were witches who could not be cured except by confession and a denunciation of their evilness. When such confessions were not forthcoming, the prescribed treatment was torture. If torture failed to evoke a confession, death was the only recourse; often death by being burned at the stake. It has been estimated that between the fourteenth and mid-seventeenth centuries, nearly 200,000 to 500,000 "witches" were put to death (Ben-Yehuda, 1980).

When the disordered were not tortured or immediately put to death, they were placed in asylums. The first insane asylum, established in 1547, was St. Mary of Bethlehem Hospital in London, to house "fools" and "lunatics." The institution became known as Bedlam (a cockney pronunciation of Bethlehem). It was a terrible place. Inmates were tortured, poorly fed, or starved to death. To remove the "bad blood" from their systems, thought to be a cause of their melancholy or delirium, patients were regularly led to bleeding chambers, where a small incision was made in a vein in the calf of their legs so that their blood would ooze into leather buckets. There was no real professional staff at Bedlam. The keepers, as they were called, could make extra money by putting their charges on view for the general public. Viewing the lunatics of Bedlam became an entertainment for the nobility. Those inmates who were able were sent into the streets to beg, wearing a sign that identified them as "fools of Bedlam." Even today we use the word *bedlam* to describe a condition of uproar and confusion.

It would be comforting to think that Bedlam was an exception, an aberration. It was not. In the eighteenth and nineteenth centuries, and in many places well into the twentieth century, similar institutions

This painting by Hieronymus Bosch depicts one of the procedures used on the psychologically disordered in the Middle Ages. Based on the belief that evil stones in the head were the cause of a patient's problems, attempts to remove them involved boring a hole in the skull—without the benefit of anesthetic.

Associating psychological disorders with witches and witchcraft was an attitude that flourished during the fifteenth and sixteenth centuries. Goay's painting, entitled The Witches Sabbath, *reflects this popular preoccupation of the times.*

were commonplace. Philippe Pinel (1745–1826) was a French physician who, in the midst of the French Revolution (on April 25, 1793), was named director of an asylum for the insane in Paris. Here, in Pinel's own words, is the scene he discovered upon taking over.

> On my entrance to the duties of that hospital, every thing presented to me the appearance of chaos and confusion. Some of my unfortunate patients labored under horrors of a most gloomy and desponding melancholy. Others were furious, and subject to the influence of a perpetual delirium. . . . Symptoms so different, and all comprehended under the general title of insanity. . . . The halls and the passages of the hospital were much confined, so arranged as to render the cold of winter and the heat of summer equally intolerable and injurious. The chambers were exceedingly small and inconvenient. Baths we had none, though I made repeated applications for them; nor had we extensive liberties for walking, gardening or other exercises. So destitute of accommodations, we found it impossible to class our patients according to the varieties and degrees of their respective maladies. (Shipley, 1961)

We know of Pinel today largely because of an act of compassion and courage. The law of the day required that inmates in an asylum be chained and confined. On September 2, 1793, Pinel ordered the chains and shackles removed from about fifty of the inmates of his "hospital." He allowed them to move freely about the institution and its grounds. This humane gesture produced surprising effects: the symptoms of the patients, in many cases, improved markedly. Pinel continued to treat those in his care with kindness and respect, which, in some cases, provided complete cures.

Unfortunately, I cannot report that Pinel's humane treatment became the norm in France and the rest of the world. It did not, but the tide did begin to turn. Pinel's unchaining of the insane and his belief in moral treatment for the mentally ill can be seen as the beginning of a gradual enlightenment concerning mental illness, even if Pinel's success did not lead to broad, sweeping reforms.

Thus, history suggests that until very recently, the prevailing understanding of the psychologically disturbed was that they were bad people, possessed by demons and devils, unable to control their behaviors and thoughts and unable to be cured. The only recourse was to separate the mentally ill from everyone else—to "put them away." Since the early 1900s, progress in providing help for the mentally ill has been both slow and unsteady. World War I and the Great Depression reduced the monies available to support state institutions for mental patients. Within the past 50 years, conditions have improved immeasurably, but there is still a long way to go. We continue to fight a prejudice against persons suffering from psychological disorders.

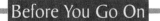
Before You Go On

Briefly trace the history of the treatment of persons with psychological disorders.

BIOMEDICAL TREATMENTS OF PSYCHOLOGICAL DISORDERS

As we have seen, biological and medical approaches to mental illness can be traced to ancient times. Psychologists today cannot use medical treatments. Currently, doing surgery, administering shock treatments, or prescribing medication requires a medical degree. Psychologists are often involved in biomedical treatments, however. Psychologists may recommend a medical treatment and refer a client to the care of a physician or psychiatrist (a person with a medical degree who specializes in mental disorders). The approaches psychologists use, the psychotherapies, will be the subject of Topic 13B.

Here we'll review three types of biomedical intervention: psychosurgery, which was common just 50 years ago, but is now rare; electroconvulsive therapy, which is far from uncommon; and drug therapy, one of the newest and most promising developments in the treatment of mental illness.

Psychosurgery

Psychosurgery is the name we give to surgical procedures, usually directed at the brain, designed to affect psychological reactions. Psychosurgical techniques in use today are largely experimental. They are aimed at making rather minimal lesions in the brain (to treat chronic pain, epilepsy, or depression, for example). Small surgical lesions in the limbic system can be effective in reducing or eliminating violent behaviors. Surgical techniques have also been used, although infrequently, to reduce extreme anxiety and the symptoms of obsessive-compulsive disorders.

psychosurgery a surgical procedure designed to affect one's psychological or behavioral reactions

Of all of the types of psychosurgery, none has ever been used as commonly as a procedure called a prefrontal lobotomy or, simply, **lobotomy** (Valenstein, 1980, 1986). This surgery severs the major neural connections between the prefrontal lobes (the area at the very front of the cerebral cortex) and lower brain centers.

lobotomy a psychosurgical technique in which the prefrontal lobes of the cerebral cortex are severed from lower brain centers

A lobotomy was first performed in 1935 by a Portuguese psychiatrist, Egas Moniz. For developing the procedure, Moniz was awarded the Nobel Prize in 1949. (The next year, in an ironic twist of fate, Moniz was shot by one of his lobotomized patients. He was rendered paraplegic and was confined to a wheelchair for the rest of his life.) The logic behind a lobotomy was that the prefrontal lobes influence the more basic emotional centers, lower in the brain (e.g., in the limbic system). Most severely disturbed patients were thought to have difficulty exercising cerebral cortex control over those lower parts of the brain. It was reasoned that if these areas of the brain were separated surgically, the more depressed, agitated, or violent patients could be brought under control.

The operation often appeared to be successful. Always used as a measure of last resort, stories of the remarkable changes it produced in chronic mental patients circulated widely. For example, *Time* magazine, in its November 30, 1942 issue, called the procedure "revolutionary," claiming that at that time, "some 300 people in the United

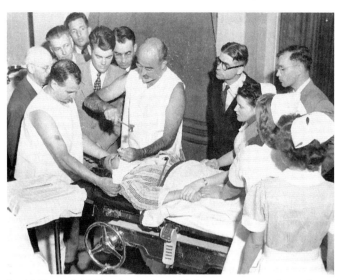

During the 1940s and 1950s, the prefontal lobotomy was performed regularly. Although psychosurgeons understood that the procedure was irreversible, it took longer to realize its destructive side effects.

States have had their psychoses surgically removed." *Life* magazine, in a very graphic photo essay titled "Psychosurgery: Operation to Cure Sick Minds Turns Surgeon's Blade into an Instrument of Mental Therapy," called the results of lobotomy procedures "spectacular," claiming that "about 30% of the lobotomized patients were able to return to everyday productive lives" (*Life*, 3/3/47, p. 93). In the 1940s and 1950s, prefrontal lobotomies were performed regularly. *Time* reported (September 15, 1952) that neurologist Walter Freeman was performing about a hundred lobotomies a week. It is difficult to estimate how many lobotomies were performed just within these two decades, but certainly they numbered in the tens of thousands.

Treating severely disturbed, depressed, and schizophrenic patients had always been difficult. Perhaps we shouldn't be surprised that this relatively simple surgical technique was accepted so widely and uncritically at first. The procedure was done under local anesthetic in the physician's office and took only 10 minutes. An instrument that looks very much like an ice pick was inserted through the eye socket, on the nasal side, and pushed up into the brain. A few movements of the instrument and the job was done—the lobes were severed from lower brain centers. Within hours, the patient would be ready to return to his or her room.

It was always appreciated that the procedure was an irreversible one. What took longer to realize was that it often carried with it terrible side effects. Between 1 and 4 percent of patients receiving prefrontal lobotomies died (Carson & Butcher, 1992, p. 610). Many who survived suffered seizures, memory loss, an inability to plan ahead, and a general listlessness and loss of affect. Many acted childishly and were difficult to manage within institutions. By the late 1950s, lobotomies had become rare. Contrary to common belief, a prefrontal lobotomy is not an illegal procedure, although the conditions under which it might even be considered are very restrictive. Prefrontal lobotomies are not done anymore for the very simple reason that they are no longer needed. There are other means, with fewer side effects, of producing similar beneficial results more safely and reliably.

Before You Go On

What is a prefrontal lobotomy?

Why was it ever used, and why is it not used today?

Electroconvulsive Therapy

As gruesome as the procedures of psychosurgery can be, many people find the very notion of **electroconvulsive therapy** (ECT), or shock treatments, even more difficult to appreciate. This technique, first introduced in 1937, involves passing an electric current of between 70 and 150 volts across a patient's head for a fraction of a second. The patient has been given a fast-acting general anesthetic and is thus unconscious when the shock is delivered. As soon as the anesthetic is administered, the patient also receives a muscle relaxant to minimize muscular contractions, which were quite common—and potentially dangerous—in the early days of ECT. The shock induces a reaction in the brain not unlike an epileptic (grand mal) seizure. The entire procedure takes about five minutes. One of the side effects of ECT is a (rather protective) memory loss for events just preceding the administration of the shock and for the shock itself.

At first, the treatment was used to help calm agitated schizophrenics, but it soon became clear that its most beneficial results were

electroconvulsive therapy (ECT) a treatment, usually for severe depression, in which an electric current passed across a patient's head causes a seizure

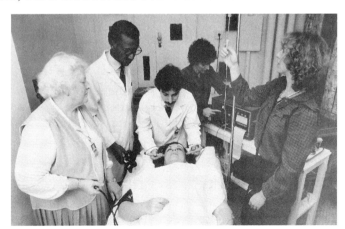

Electroconvulsive shock therapy is not pleasant to watch, and there is concern that we do not yet fully understand why the procedure often seems to be an effective treatment for extreme cases of major depression.

for those patients suffering from major depression. It often alleviates the symptoms of depression and, in some cases, has beneficial effects on other symptoms. In fact, the group of patients that seems best suited to the ECT procedure are those for whom depression is a major symptom, but for whom other symptoms (such as hallucinations or delusions) are also present (Joyce & Paykel, 1989).

Virtually all patients (97 percent) give their consent to the procedure, and negative side effects are rare. The most commonly reported side effects are memory loss and general mental confusion. In nearly all cases, these effects disappear in a few days or weeks. In one study of 99,425 treatments given to 18,627 patients, only two deaths were reported. The death rate for childbirth in the United States is nearly six times greater (Kramer, 1985). Once they have experienced the procedure, most ECT patients are far from terrorized by the notion of having an electrical shock sent through their brain. In one study, 82 percent of 166 patients surveyed rated ECT as no more upsetting than a visit to the dentist (Sackeim, 1985). The beneficial effects of ECT are reasonably long-lasting. After only 10 to 12 treatments, many patients remain free of symptoms for months.

Just why ECT produces the benefits it does is not fully understood even today. As you might guess, researchers are looking at the action of neurotransmitters in the brain for possible explanations. It seems that the effects, if not the amounts, of some neurotransmitters—GABA, serotonin, and norepinephrine, in particular—are increased by ECT.

The poor reputation ECT has among the general population, and among some psychologists and psychiatrists, did not develop without foundation. There *are* horror stories of the negative side effects that can follow abuse of the procedure. (At first, the seizures of the shock treatment were induced by drugs, not electricity, and it is largely from these drug-induced treatments we have the stories of convulsions so massive as to result in broken bones.) It is now recommended that no more than a dozen treatments be given and that they be administered over an extended period. Some patients in the past have received hundreds of ECT treatments. In such cases, there has been brain damage and permanent memory loss.

Even though we do not understand fully how ECT works, and even though it is a treatment that must be used with extreme care, ECT is very much in practice today. Although the numbers declined during the late 1970s, nearly 100,000 patients receive shock treatments each year, and numbers again are on the rise (Thompson & Blaine, 1987). For example, in 1986 payments for 88,847 ECT treatments were made by Medicare, and in 1988, 96,276 treatments were reimbursed.

The introduction of psychoactive, antidepressant medications has reduced the need for ECT. But drug treatment is not always successful, and even when it is, it often takes six to eight weeks for the drugs to produce beneficial results. Researchers have found that in many cases ECT is a more effective treatment than are antidepressant medications (Small et al., 1988). Electroconvulsive therapy is now reserved for (1) patients for whom drug therapies seem ineffective, (2) patients with acute suicidal tendencies (because drugs take so long to have their full antidepressant effects), and (3) depressed patients who also suffer from delusions (Kalat, 1984).

Administering a shock to just one side of the brain, called a *unilateral ECT,* may be a safer yet equally effective procedure with fewer side effects. More success has been found by creating seizures in the right hemisphere of the cerebral cortex (thought to be more associated with emotional reactions) than in the left hemisphere (Squire & Slater, 1978).

Before You Go On

What is ECT?

Why is it still being used?

Drug Therapy

Chemicals that have their effect on a person's cognitions, affect, or behavior are collectively referred to as *psychoactive drugs.* As we've seen, there are many of them, and most are used to produce an altered state of consciousness or awareness. Using chemicals to improve the condition of the mentally disordered is a much more recent development and has been hailed as one of the most significant scientific achievements of the latter half of the twentieth century (Snyder, 1984). In this section, we'll examine the three main types, or classes, of psychoactive drugs used as therapy: the antipsychotic, antidepressant, and antianxiety drugs.

Antipsychotic Drugs. The **antipsychotic drugs,** as their name suggests, alleviate or eliminate psychotic symptoms. **Psychotic symptoms** are those that indicate a loss of contact with reality—delusions and hallucinations, in particular—and a gross impairment of functioning. Virtually all of the symptoms of schizophrenia may be classified as psychotic. Indeed, antipsychotic medications are primarily designed and used to treat schizophenia. Nonetheless, psychotic symptoms are associated with other disorders, including extreme cases of substance abuse disorders such as alcoholism, and extreme cases of delirium and dementia.

The breakthrough in the use of antipsychotic drugs came with the introduction of *chlorpromazine.* The antipsychotic effects of chlorpromazine were first recorded in France in 1950. A neurosurgeon, Henri Laborit, was looking for a drug that would calm his patients before surgery. Before surgery, patients often feel nervous. Laborit wanted to help them relax because he knew that if they did, his patients' postsurgical recovery would be improved. A drug company supplied Laborit with chlorpromazine. It worked even better than anyone had expected, producing a state of relaxation and calm in his patients. Laborit convinced some of his colleagues to try the drug on

antipsychotic drugs *chemicals, such as chlorpromazine, effective in reducing psychotic symptoms*

psychotic symptoms *symptoms of a severe psychological disorder that indicate a loss of contact with reality and a gross impairment of functioning*

their more agitated patients, some of whom were suffering from psychological disorders. The experiments met with great success, and by the late 1950s, the drug was widely used in both North America and Europe.

The drug revolution had begun. With the success of chlorpromazine, the search for other chemicals that could improve the plight of the mentally ill began in earnest. By 1956, more than half a dozen antipsychotic medications were available in the United States. From 1976 to 1985, the use of antipsychotic medication remained stable, overall, with between 19 and 21 million prescriptions being written (Wysowski & Baum, 1989).

Chlorpromazine is just one of many drugs currently being used with success to treat psychotic symptoms. Most antipsychotic drugs are of the same general type as chlorpromazine. Although there are now many types of antipsychotic drugs, most work in essentially the same way: by influencing neurotransmitter activity in the brain. Most act by blocking receptor sites for the neurotransmitter dopamine. Antipsychotic drugs are most effective in treating the positive symptoms of schizophrenia: delusions, hallucinations, and bizarre behaviors. *Clozapine* (trade name *Clozaril*), appears to be an exception, because it is effective in reducing negative symptoms, such as social withdrawal, as well as positive ones. Unfortunately, clozapine carries with it the risk of serious side effects, some of which can be fatal. As a result, the use of this drug is very carefully monitored.

The effects of the antipsychotic drugs are remarkable and impressive, and they have revolutionized the care of psychotic patients. Nonetheless, they are not the ultimate solution for disorders such as schizophrenia. There are patients for whom the drugs either have no effect or have harmful effects. About 30 percent of patients with schizophrenia do not respond to antipsychotic medication (Kane, 1989). As you might suspect, these drugs will be most effective when they are used early on, with patients who have recently been diagnosed with schizophrenia, as opposed to those who have exhibited symptoms of the disease for some time (Lieberman et al., 1993). With high dosages or prolonged use, a variety of side effects emerge that are unpleasant at best, including dry mouth and throat, sore muscles and joints, heavy sedation, sexual impotence, and muscle tremors. Some side effects are even more negative, including seizures and cardiovascular damage. Although the most effective of the antipsychotic drugs do control or suppress symptoms, the question remains: Are they in any sense curing the disorder? In the usual sense of the word *cure*, they are not. Symptom-free patients, who are often released from institutional care to the outside world, soon stop using their medication only to find that their psychotic symptoms return.

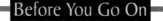

Before You Go On

What are antipsychotic drugs, and what are their effects?

Antidepressant Drugs. The **antidepressant drugs** elevate the mood of persons who are feeling depressed. The antidepressant medications used today are of two types: *MAO inhibitors* (MAO, or monoamine oxidase, is a chemical found in the brain that reduces levels of two neurotransmitters; MAO inhibitors thus increase levels of these neurotransmitters) and *tricyclics*. No one antidepressant is universally any better than any other. Each seems to be particularly effective for certain types of depressive disorders (Cole, 1988). Tricyclics are best suited for uncomplicated, major depression; the MAO inhibitors are most effective for depression accompanied by anxiety or panic symptoms (Joyce & Paykel, 1989; Tyrer & Shawcross, 1988). Some antidepressant medications may be useful in treating disorders other than depression, such as panic disorder and generalized anxiety disorder (Rickels et al., 1993). An antidepressant drug that has no effect on one person may cause severe, unpleasant side effects in another person, and have markedly beneficial effects for a third person.

These medications take 10 to 14 days to show any effect. Their full effect may take six weeks and they need to be taken on a long-term basis to prevent a recurrence of the depression (Maxman, 1991). Antidepressant drugs can elevate the mood of many truly depressed individuals, but they have virtually no effect on people who are not depressed. That is, they do not produce a euphoric high in people who are already in a good mood.

Of the two classes of antidepressants, the tricyclic types are more commonly used. As you might have guessed, the tricyclic drugs do produce unfortunate side effects in some patients, including intellectual confusion, increased perspiration, and weight gain. Some tricyclics have been implicated as a cause of heart disease. A major problem with the MAO inhibitor drugs is that they require adherence to a strict diet and carefully monitored dosages to be most effective. They, too, are associated with a range of serious side effects, such as dizziness, sexual impotence, elevated blood pressure, and liver damage, to name just a few.

A relatively new antidepressant, fluoxetine (*Prozac*) was introduced in 1987. It is the single most prescribed antidepressant; about 650,000 prescriptions are written each month. By 1996, sales of Prozac alone are projected to exceed $5 billion. It is chemically unrelated to either the tricyclics or MAO inhibitors, although it, too, affects a brain neurotransmitter (serotonin). Often an effective medication, its main advantage is that it produces fewer negative side effects. Nonetheless, these side effects (e.g., skin rashes, agitation, diarrhea, and weight loss) can be so unpleasant that patients stop using it. In test trials (before it was marketed), 15 percent of the patients receiving Prozac discontinued treatment because of adverse side effects. Because it has been on the market for a relatively short time, long-term effects of its use are as yet unknown.

This is an appropriate context in which to mention *lithium*, or lithium salts, such as lithium carbonate. Lithium salts are referred to as "mood stabilizers" (Maxman, 1991). They have been used with success in treating major depression, but are most useful in controlling the manic stage of bipolar disorders. A major benefit of lithium

antidepressant drugs chemicals, such as MAO inhibitors and tricyclics, that reduce the symptoms of depression

treatments is that they are often effective in preventing or reducing the occurrence of future episodes of mood disorder (NIMH, 1981, 1989). There are those for whom the drug has no beneficial effects, and its prolonged use can cause convulsions, kidney failure, and other serious reactions.

Unlike antipsychotic drugs, there is evidence that when antidepressant drugs *are* effective, they may actually bring about long-term cures rather than just symptom suppression. In other words, the changes in mood caused by the drugs may outlast use of the drug itself. The hope and plan, in fact, is to gradually reduce the dosage of the drug over time. For persons with mood disorders who do not respond to drugs presently available, other types are being tested. For such patients, electroconvulsive therapy may be indicated.

Before You Go On

**What are antidepressant drugs, and
what are they meant to do?**

antianxiety drugs chemicals, such as the meprobamates and benzodiazepines, that alleviate the symptoms of anxiety; also known as tranquilizers

Antianxiety Drugs. The **antianxiety drugs** (or tranquilizers) help reduce the felt aspect of anxiety. They are the most commonly prescribed of all drugs. Some antianxiety drugs, the *meprobamates* (e.g., Miltown or Equanil), are basically muscle relaxers. When muscular tension is reduced, the patient often reports feeling calm and at ease.

The other major variety of antianxiety drug is the group of chemicals called *benzodiazepines* (e.g., Librium, Valium, or Xanax). These drugs act directly on the central nervous system, and their impact is obvious and significant. They simply help anxious people feel less anxious. Initially, the only negative side effects appear to be a slight drowsiness, blurred vision, and a slight impairment of coordination.

Unfortunately, the tranquilizing effect of the drugs is not long-lasting. Patients can fall into a pattern of relying on the drugs to alleviate even the slightest of fears and worries. A dependency and addiction can develop from which withdrawal can be difficult. In fact, a danger of the antianxiety medications is the very fact that they *are* so effective. As long as one can avoid the unpleasant feelings of anxiety simply by taking a pill, there is little to motivate one to seek and deal with the actual cause of one's anxiety.

An interesting curiosity is that these drugs are significantly more likely to be prescribed for women, especially women over age 45, than they are for men (Travis, 1988). This may very well be the result of a tendency on the part of physicians to see women as more likely to be anxious in the first place (Unger & Crawford, 1992).

Before You Go On

**What are the common antianxiety drugs, and
what are the dangers inherent in their use?**

DEINSTITUTIONALIZATION: BLESSING OR CURSE?

As I have mentioned, the first institution expressly for the mentally ill was St. Mary of Bethlehem Hospital, so designated in 1547. Despite well-intentioned efforts to promote mental health (rather than just house the disordered), not much changed for nearly 400 years. By the middle of the twentieth century, large state-supported institutions were the commonplace residences of the mentally retarded and mentally ill. Lack of public support, leading to a lack of adequate funding for staff and facilities, resulted in what amounted to a national disgrace.

Mental institutions became overcrowded and unmanageable. Within the last 40 years, there has been a truly revolutionary shift in mental health care. For several seemingly sound and sensible reasons, many patients with psychological disorders have experienced **deinstitutionalization**. They have been released from the large mental institutions to return to family and community. The drop in institutional patient population has been dramatic (Figure 13.1). Compared to 1955, the number of patients in state and county mental hospitals has dropped nearly 75 percent. What has brought about this change, and has it been a change for the better or the worse?

There are several reasons for deinstitutionalization we might list. I have already alluded to some of them. Let's consider just three.

deinstitutionalization the practice, begun in the mid-1950s, of releasing patients from mental institutions and returning them to their home communities

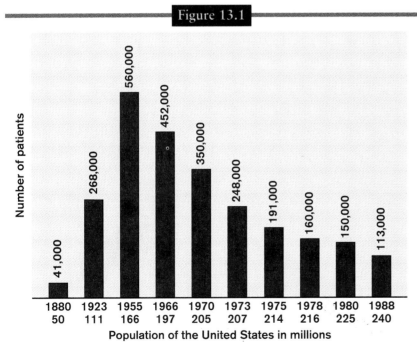

The number of patients institutionalized in county and state mental hospitals. Also indicated is the approximate U.S. population. Remember that it was in the late 1950s that antipsychotic medications became widely used. (Adapted from NIMH, 1984, and Torrey, 1988.)

1. *A concern for the rights of the patient arose.* The overcrowded and generally poor conditions that existed in many institutions became more than society was willing to bear. The courts entered the picture, ordering that either patients receive adequate and proper treatment or be released. The landmark decision was set down in 1971 in the *Wyatt* v. *Stickney* case in Alabama. Ricky Wyatt was a patient in a state hospital who felt that he (and the fellow patients who joined in his suit) was not being fairly or adequately treated. He filed suit against the Alabama mental health commissioner, Stonewall Stickney. Not only did the judge find in favor of Wyatt, but set down a list of conditions that state institutions must meet to ensure the "adequate treatment" of all patients. He further specified that if changes were not made in a timely fashion, the patients were to be released.

2. *Symptoms can be managed through chemical means.* We've already touched on this matter. In the mid-1950s, the introduction of effective drugs that at least masked or suppressed psychotic symptoms made it more reasonable that patients who no longer displayed unusual or bizarre behaviors could be released from institutional care.

3. *Community mental health centers were to be established.* Congress passed the Community Mental Health Act in 1963. This law included a provision for establishing a large number of mental health centers to be located in local communities rather than centralized in one or two state institutions. The plan was for there to be at least one easily accessible mental health center for every 50,000 people in the country. These centers would accommodate people on an outpatient basis and could provide care for those patients recently discharged from large mental hospitals. Community mental health centers were also to provide other services, including short-term inpatient care, as well as consultation, education, and prevention programs.

Has the system of deinstitutionalization worked? On this question, the house is divided. There are those who applaud the change (Braun et al., 1981), arguing that "continued optimism about community care seems warranted" (Shadish, 1984).

On the other hand, many see deinstitutionalization as trading one set of problems for a host of others. Many patients released from mental hospitals are, quite literally, "dumped" back into their home communities. There, resources for assistance are often minimal. Many require the support of the welfare system. There is seldom adequate housing for those who have been released. Patients find themselves in nursing homes, boarding houses, and other settings ill-prepared to care for their needs (Bellack & Mueser, 1986; Smith et al., 1993). Negative attitudes get involved, as in, "We don't want 'those people' living in *our* neighborhood." Many patients released from institutions become homeless "street people," particularly in large cities. The National Institute of Mental Health estimates the percentage of homeless persons with psychological disorders at 30 to 35 percent; others place the percentage at closer to 50 percent (Bellack, 1986; Levine et al., 1993; Toro et al., 1991).

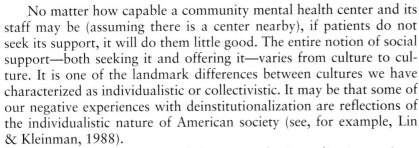

Although communities are trying to cope, many are unable to provide adequate assistance for patients released from mental hospitals. Consequently, many live on the streets, making up a significant proportion of this country's "homeless." On the positive side, many successful programs are in place and meet patients' needs after they are "deinstitutionalized."

No matter how capable a community mental health center and its staff may be (assuming there is a center nearby), if patients do not seek its support, it will do them little good. The entire notion of social support—both seeking it and offering it—varies from culture to culture. It is one of the landmark differences between cultures we have characterized as individualistic or collectivistic. It may be that some of our negative experiences with deinstitutionalization are reflections of the individualistic nature of American society (see, for example, Lin & Kleinman, 1988).

As we have noted, most of the antipsychotic medication patients require does not have lasting effects. When patients stop taking their medication (perhaps because of its expense or its side effects), symptoms return, and they will likely need to return once again to the institution. And, as many as one-half to two-thirds of released patients do stop taking their medication (e.g., McGrath et al., 1990).

It appears that the trend to reduce the population of patients in institutions is likely to continue. Effective community programs and more resources are needed to assist those released from these institutions to ensure that discharge is appropriate for them and for the community to which they return. Mental health professionals view the care and treatment of the chronically mentally disordered as a national health concern of high priority (e.g., Levine et al., 1993; Smith et al., 1993; Youngstrom, 1991).

Before You Go On

What is deinstitutionalization, why did it come about, and has it been successful?

TOPIC 13A SUMMARY

This chapter began with a synopsis of some of the history of the treatment of mental or psychological disorders. The major message here is that the basic idea of intervening on the behalf of persons with psychological disorders—particularly the most bizarre or most chronic disorders—is a relatively new direction in the history of civilization.

What treatment there was for the disordered tended to be physical, or medical. It was with biomedical treatments we began our discussion of approaches to therapy. We first considered a technique—the prefrontal lobotomy—that now is more of a historical curiosity than anything else.

We saw that there is hope that biochemical means can be found to suppress, if not eliminate, many of the symptoms associated with psychological disorders. At the moment, however, we should remain somewhat cautious. Remember that only thirty-five years ago it was widely held that lobotomies would be the ultimate treatment for persons with severe psychological disorders. Scientists do continue to learn about the delicate balance between brain and behavior. If we remain mindful of the harsh and inhumane treatment of the mentally ill that characterized our not-too-distant past, we can now be more cautiously optimistic than ever before.

Topic 13B
THE PSYCHOTHERAPIES

Because there are so many types of psychotherapy—literally hundreds—this Topic is titled The Psychothera*pies*. Here, we'll examine some of the major forms of psychotherapy.

The overriding goal of all psychotherapy is to persuade a person to think, feel, or act differently. Additionally, different types of therapy have different specific goals, or subgoals. Some attempt to help people gain insight about the true nature of their disorder and its underlying causes; some try to help people develop a sense of how they feel about themselves; some aim to alter how people think about themselves and the world in which they live; and others focus on bringing about lasting, measurable changes in overt behavior. In other words, some types of psychotherapy focus on affect or feelings, some focus on cognitions or beliefs, and some focus on overt behaviors. Once again we see that we can use our simple ABC mnemonic.

WHO PROVIDES PSYCHOTHERAPY?

Just 30 years ago, only 13 percent of the population sought psychotherapy at any time in their lives (Meredith, 1986). Now we find

Regardless of the specifics involved, all forms of psychotherapy are designed to persuade a person to think, feel, and act differently.

that 30 percent will have some experience in psychotherapy. In 1987, for example, "15 million of us [made] roughly 120 million visits to mental health professionals—nearly twice as many visits as to internists" (Hunt, 1987, p. 2). Who are these mental health professionals who provide psychotherapy?

Please keep in mind that what follows is a list of generalities; my descriptions will not hold true for everyone within a given category. Remember also that because of their experience or training, some professionals develop specialties within their fields. That is, some therapists specialize in working with the disorders of children and adolescents; some work primarily with adults; some prefer to work with families; and some devote their efforts to people with substance and alcohol abuse problems. Some have special training in dealing with clients from various cultures or ethnic groups (see Koslow & Salett, 1989; Sue & Sue, 1990). Finally, a psychotherapist can and will use several of the techniques of therapy outlined in this Topic. In other words, few therapists take one approach to treatment and no other. As many as 40 percent of therapists in the United States claim no particularly dominant approach to their psychotherapy (Norcross, 1986). The following may be considered psychotherapists:

1. The *clinical psychologist* usually has earned a Ph.D. in psychology, a program of study that provides practical, applied experience, as well as an emphasis on research. The Ph.D. clinician spends a year on an internship, usually at a mental health center or psychiatric hospital. The clinical psychologist has extensive training in psychological testing (in general, *psychodiagnostics*). Some clinical psychologists have a Psy.D. (pronounced "sigh-dee"), which is a Doctor of Psychology, rather than the Doctor of Philosophy degree.

Psy.D. programs take as long to complete as Ph.D. programs, but tend to emphasize more practical, clinical work, and place less emphasis on research.

2. Psychiatry is a specialty area in medicine. In addition to the course work required for an M.D., the *psychiatrist* spends an internship (usually one year) and a residency (usually three years) in a mental hospital, specializing in the care of psychologically disturbed patients. At the moment, the psychiatrist is the only type of psychotherapist permitted to use the biomedical treatments we reviewed in Topic 13A. (There is now a campaign under way to get some medical privileges for Ph.D. psychologists.)

3. The *counseling psychologist* usually has a Ph.D. in psychology. The focus of study (and the required one-year internship), however, is generally with patients with less severe psychological problems. For instance, rather than spending one's internship in a psychiatric hospital, a counseling psychologist would more likely spend time at a university counseling center.

4. A *licensed professional counselor* will have a degree in counselor education and will have met state requirements for a license to do psychotherapy. Counselors are found in school settings, but also work in mental health settings, specializing in family counseling and drug abuse.

5. *Psychoanalyst* is a special label given to a clinical psychologist or a psychiatrist who has also received intensive training (and certification) in the particular methods of (Freudian) psychoanalysis.

6. The terminal degree for *clinical social workers* is generally the master's degree, although Ph.D.s in social work are becoming more common. Social workers engage in a variety of psychotherapies, but their traditional role has been involvement in family and group therapy.

Some people with a master's degree in psychology provide psychotherapy (because of licensing or certification laws in many states, they cannot advertise themselves as "psychologists"). *Occupational therapists* usually have a master's degree (less frequently, a bachelor's degree) in occupational therapy, which includes many psychology classes and internship training in aiding the psychologically and physically handicapped. *Psychiatric nurses* often work in mental hospitals and clinics. In addition to their R.N. degrees, psychiatric nurses have special training in the care of mentally ill patients. *Pastoral counseling* is a specialty of those with a religious background and a master's degree in either psychology or educational counseling. The *mental health technician* usually has an associate degree in mental health technology (MHT). MHT graduates seldom provide unsupervised therapy, although they may be involved in the delivery of many mental health services.

Now that we have an idea of who may offer psychotherapy services, let's consider the types of techniques or approaches they may employ.

Before You Go On

Who may offer psychotherapy?

PSYCHOANALYTIC TECHNIQUES

Psychoanalysis began with Sigmund Freud near the end of the nineteenth century. Psychoanalysis did not really evolve from Freudian personality theory (see Topic 9A). If anything, the reverse is true. Freud was a therapist first, a personality theorist second. But his techniques of therapy and theory of personality sprang forth from the same mind, and are thus interrelated.

Psychoanalysis is based on a number of assumptions, most of them having to do with conflict and the unconscious mind. For Freud, one's life is often a struggle to resolve conflicts between naturally opposing forces. The most basic of all human conflicts are those that reflect instincts for life and instincts for death. The biological, sexual, aggressive strivings of the id are often in conflict with the superego, which is associated with guilt and overcautiousness. The strivings of the id can also be in conflict with the rational, reality-based ego, which is often called upon to mediate between the id and the superego. Anxiety-producing conflicts that go unresolved are repressed;

psychoanalysis the form of psychotherapy associated with Freud, aimed at helping the patient gain insight into unconscious conflicts

Classic, Freudian psychoanalysis required the use of a couch, where the patient would lie down, relax, and try to uncover unconscious conflicts, under the direction of the analyst.

they are forced out of awareness into the unconscious levels of the mind. Conflicts and anxiety-producing traumas of childhood can be expected to produce symptoms of psychological disturbance later on in life.

According to Freud, the best way to rid oneself of anxiety is to enter the unconscious, identify the details of the repressed, anxiety-producing conflict, bring it out into the open, and then resolve it as well as possible. The first step is to gain insight into the nature of one's problems; only then can problem solving begin. Thus, the goals of Freudian psychoanalysis are insight and resolution of repressed conflict. The entire process should be very gradual as old, repressed experiences are integrated in one's current life situation (Kaplan & Sadock, 1991).

Sigmund Freud died in 1939, but his approach to psychotherapy did not die with him. It has been modified (as Freud himself modified it over the years), but it remains true to the basic thrust of Freudian psychoanalysis. Before we consider how it has changed, let's examine Freudian analysis as Freud practiced it.

Freudian Psychoanalysis

Psychoanalysis with Sigmund Freud was a time-consuming (up to five days per week for as many as ten years), often tedious process of self-examination and introspection. The major task for the patient was to talk openly and honestly about all aspects of his or her life, from early childhood memories to the dreams of the present. The major task of the therapist, or analyst, was to interpret what was being expressed by the patient, always on the lookout for clues to possible repressed conflict. Once identified, the patient and analyst together could try to resolve the conflict(s) that brought the patient to analysis in the first place. Several procedures and processes were used in the search for repressed conflicts.

Free Association. In 1881, Freud graduated from the University of Vienna Medical School. From the start, he was interested in the treatment of what were then called nervous disorders. He went to France to study the technique of hypnosis, which many were claiming to be a worthwhile treatment for mental disorders. Freud wasn't totally convinced, but when he returned to Vienna, he and a colleague, Josef Breuer, tried hypnosis as a treatment for neurotic disorders, conversion reaction (hysteria) in particular. They both became convinced that hypnosis itself was of little benefit. What mattered more, they believed, was to have the patients talk—about anything and everything—which is what they were encouraged to do under hypnosis. In fact, Freud and Breuer's method became known as the "talking cure."

The method of **free association** became a procedure of psychoanalysis. Patients were told to say out loud whatever came into their

free association *the procedure in psychoanalysis in which the patient is to express whatever comes to mind without editing responses*

minds. Sometimes the analyst would provide a stimulus word to get a chain of freely flowing associations going. To free-associate the way Freud would have wanted you to is not an easy task. It often required many sessions for patients to learn the technique. Patients were not to edit their associations. They were to be completely honest, and say *whatever* they thought of. Many people are uncomfortable, at least initially, sharing their private, innermost thoughts and desires with anyone, much less a stranger. Here is where the Freudian couch came in. To help his patients relax, Freud would have them lie down, be comfortable, and avoid eye contact with him. The job of the analyst through all this was to try to interpret the apparently free-flowing and random verbal responses, always looking for expressions of unconscious desires and conflicts.

Resistance. During the course of psychoanalysis, particularly during periods of free association, the psychoanalyst listens very carefully to what the patient says. The analyst also carefully listens for what the patient does not say. Freud believed **resistance**, the unwillingness or inability to discuss freely some aspect of one's life, was a significant process in analysis. Resistance can show itself in many ways, from simply avoiding the mention of some topic, to joking about matters as inconsequential, to disrupting a session when a particular topic came up for discussion, to missing appointments altogether.

resistance in psychoanalysis, the inability or unwillingness to discuss freely some aspect of one's life

Let's say, for example, that over the last six months in psychoanalysis you have talked freely about a wide variety of subjects, including your early childhood memories and all the members of your family— all, that is, except your older brother. You have talked about all sorts of private experiences, some of them sexual, some of them pleasant, some unpleasant. But after six months of talking, you have not had anything to say about your older brother. Your analyst, noting this possible resistance, suggests that during your next visit, she would like to hear more about your brother. Then, for the first time since analysis began, you miss your next appointment. You do come to the following appointment, but you're 10 minutes late. Your analyst may now suspect that there is some problem with your relationship with your older brother, a problem that may have begun in childhood and has been repressed ever since. Of course, there may be *no problem* here at all, but for psychoanalysis to be successful, potential resistance needs to be broken down and investigated.

Dream Interpretation. Analyzing a patient's dreams is an important part of psychoanalysis. Freud referred to dreams as the "royal road" to the unconscious level of the mind. Freud often trained his patients to recall and record their dreams in great detail. He analyzed dreams at two levels: *manifest content,* the dream as recalled and reported, and *latent content,* the dream as a symbolic representation of the contents of the unconscious. Symbolism hidden in the latent content of dreams has been one of the most controversial aspects of Freud's theories. The idea was that true feelings, motives, and desires might be camouflaged in a dream. For example, someone who reports a dream about suffocating under a huge pile of pillows *might* be expressing negative feelings about parental overprotectiveness.

Someone who dreams about driving into an endless tunnel and becoming lost there *might* be expressing fears or concerns of a sexual nature. The job for the analyst, Freud argued, was to interpret dreams in terms of whatever insights they could provide about the true nature of the patient's unconscious mind.

Transference. Another controversial aspect of Freudian psychoanalysis is his concept of transference. **Transference** occurs when the patient unconsciously comes to view and feel about the analyst in much the same way he or she feels about some other important person in his or her life, usually a parent. As therapy continues over a long period, the relationship between analyst and patient does become a complex and often emotional one. If feelings once directed toward someone else of significance are now directed toward the analyst, they are more accessible, more easily observed by the analyst, and more readily dealt with. Therapists have to guard against doing the same thing themselves—letting their own feelings and experiences interfere with their objective interactions with their patients. Failure to do so is called *countertransference*.

transference in psychoanalysis, the situation in which the patient comes to feel about the analyst in the same way he or she once felt about some other important person

Post-Freudian Psychoanalysis

Early in the twentieth century, Freudian psychoanalysis was the only form of psychotherapy. In the 1940s and 1950s, it was *the* therapy of choice. "Psychoanalytic theory was the dominant force in psychiatry in the postwar period and was embraced by a large number of clinical psychologists. To a certain extent, and for all practical purposes, there was no rival orientation" (Garfield, 1981, p. 176). In recent years, psychoanalysis has become much less common, and strict, Freudian psychoanalysis has become rare indeed. Let's see how the Freudian notion of therapy has changed. First, however, we should note what hasn't changed: to qualify as a psychoanalytic approach, the basic aim of therapy (now called "psychoanalytic therapy") must be the uncovering of deep-seated, unconscious conflict, perhaps caused by childhood experiences, and the removal of defenses so that such conflicts can be resolved (e.g., Sandler, Dare, & Holder, 1992).

Probably the most significant change since Freud's practice is the concern for shortening the length of analysis (Strupp & Binder, 1984). Now we talk about time-limited and short-form psychoanalytic therapy (Binder, 1993; Koss & Butcher, 1986). Today's analyst will also take a more active role than did Freud. The therapist will use interviews and discussions, and is less likely to use free association. The couch as a requirement is gone; the comfort of the patient is what matters, and some patients feel more comfortable pacing or sitting than they do lying on a couch. Another shift in emphasis is that modern psychoanalysts, although not insensitive to the effects of childhood experiences, tend to spend more time exploring the present. For example, a patient may come for analysis complaining of feelings of depression and anger to the point where the analyst believes there is a real and present danger that the patient might harm himself or herself, or even commit suicide. The thrust of therapy is going to be in the here and now, dealing with the patient's current anger and depression until the analyst is convinced the patient has his or her anger under control.

Before You Go On

Describe Freudian psychoanalysis, defining some
of its major features.

How is psychoanalysis different today from
when it was practiced by Freud?

HUMANISTIC TECHNIQUES

There are many types of humanistic psychotherapy and their allied cousins, the *existential therapies*. What they all have in common is a concern for self-examination, personal growth, and development. The goal of these therapies is not to uncover deep-seated conflicts, but to foster psychological growth, to help the person take fullest advantage of life's opportunities. Based on the premise that we can take charge of ourselves and our futures, grow and change, therapy is directed at assisting us with these processes.

Client-centered therapy, also called Rogerian therapy after its founder, Carl Rogers, is the therapy that best typifies the humanistic approach. As its name suggests, the client is the center of the therapeutic interaction. Note that, given his medical training, Freud called the people he dealt with, "patients." Rogers never used the term *patient*, and before his death in 1987 began using the term *person-centered* rather than *client-centered* to describe his approach to therapy.

client-centered therapy the humanistic psychotherapy associated with Rogers, aimed at helping a person grow and self-actualize

For Rogers, therapy provides a special opportunity for a person to engage in self-discovery. Another way to express this is to say that a goal of client-centered therapy is to help the individual self-actualize. We discussed the concept of self-actualization in Chapter 9 when we covered humanistic approaches to personality (see page 440).

What are the characteristics of client-centered therapy? Again, there are many variants, but the following ideas characterize a client-centered approach. The focus is on the present, not one's past or childhood. The focus is on one's feelings or affect, not beliefs or cognitions; that is, you are more likely to hear, "How do you feel about that?" than "What do you think about that?" The therapist will attempt to reflect or mirror, not interpret, how a client is feeling (using statements such as, "You seem angry about that," or "Does that make you feel sad?"). Assessing and reflecting the true nature of a client's feelings is not necessarily easy to do. To do so requires that the therapist be an active listener and be **empathic**, or able to understand and share the essence of another's feelings.

empathic able to understand and share the essence of another's feelings, or to view from another's perspective

Throughout each session, the therapist will try to express *unconditional positive regard*. This is the expression of being accepting and noncritical. "I will not be critical. If that is the way you feel, that is the way you feel. Anything you say in here is okay, so long as you are being honest; honest with yourself. You may have done some silly things, and unfortunate things may have happened to you, but as a person, you are fine, and able to deal with these difficulties." The exchange between client and therapist presented at the beginning of the chapter is meant to reflect a client-centered approach.

A friend of mine, a Rogerian psychotherapist, was once elated about how well a session with an undergraduate student had gone. When I asked why he thought it had gone so well, he said that when the student came into his office and sat down, he asked her how she was feeling and what she'd like to talk about. She said that she didn't want to talk about anything. So my friend said, "If you don't want to talk, that's okay. If you change your mind, I'm right here, and I'm willing to listen." For the next 50 minutes, the two of them sat there, neither doing or saying anything. At the end of their hour, the therapist said, "Well, our time's up. I'll see you next week," to which the student replied, "Right, see you then." It was my friend's point of view that the value of this quiet session was that his client had learned something. She had learned that if she did not want to talk about anything, she didn't have to. That acceptance may then lead her to the realization that if she *did* want to talk about anything, no matter what, that would be okay, too.

Gestalt therapy is associated with Fritz Perls (1893–1970) and shares many of the same goals as Rogers's person-centered approach (Perls, 1967, 1971; Perls, Hefferline, & Goodman, 1951). You'll remember that we've used the term *gestalt* before (in Chapters 1 and 3), and that it means (roughly) "whole" or "totality." Thus, the goal of gestalt therapy is to assist a person to integrate his or her thoughts, feelings, and actions—to assist in increasing the person's self-awareness, self-acceptance, and growth. The therapy is aimed at helping the person become aware of his or her whole self—including conflicts and problems—and to begin working on the whole self by establishing ways to deal with conflicts and problems.

What makes Perls' therapy different from Rogers's is that it is very directive. The therapist is actively involved, challenging the client. Whereas a client-centered technique is accepting, a gestalt technique is questioning. If a patient were to say, "I never really feel very anxious," the therapist would challenge that assertion, "Oh, come on, Heather, be serious. Do you really want me to believe that you *never* feel very anxious? Being anxious from time to time is a part of being alive! Admit it. Deal with it." What we have here is "getting in touch with one's feelings," acknowledging them as valid, and moving to get on with one's life. Although the focus of gestalt therapy is the individual, sessions are often convened in small group settings. Clients may be given role-playing exercises in which they have to play several parts. They may be asked to act out how they feel in a given situation and then act out how they wish they could respond in that situation.

Before You Go On

**What are the characteristics of client-centered
and gestalt therapy?**

BEHAVIORAL TECHNIQUES

There is no one behavior therapy. **Behavior therapy** is a collection of
many specific techniques. What unites them is that they are "methods
of psychotherapeutic change founded on principles of learning established in the psychological laboratory" (Wolpe, 1981, p. 159). There
are many principles of learning and many psychological disorders to
which such methods and principles can be applied. Reflecting this
observation, we have already discussed two types of behavior therapy
in Chapter 5 (see pages 217 and 231). In this section, I will list some
of the more prominent applications that have become part of behavior therapy.

*behavior therapy techniques of
psychotherapy founded on
principles of learning established in
the psychological laboratory and
aimed at changing one's behaviors*

Systematic desensitization, applying classical conditioning in
order to alleviate feelings of anxiety, particularly those associated
with phobic disorders, is one of the first applications of learning theory to have met with success. It was formally introduced by Joseph
Wolpe in the late 1950s (Wolpe, 1958, 1982), although others had
used similar procedures earlier. You'll recall from our discussion in
Topic 5A that systematic desensitization is basically a matter of teaching a person first to relax totally and then to remain relaxed as he or
she thinks about or is exposed to stimuli that produce anxiety at ever-
increasing levels. If the person can remain calm and relaxed, that
response can be conditioned to replace the anxious or fear response
previously associated with a particular stimulus.

*systematic desensitization classical
conditioning procedures, used to
alleviate anxiety, in which anxiety-
producing stimuli are paired with a
state of relaxation*

Flooding is another behavioral procedure aimed at eliminating
anxieties or fears associated with specific stimuli. Bootzin and
Acocella describe flooding as "a cold-turkey extinction therapy"
(1984, p. 505). **Flooding** is an in vivo, or in real life, procedure in
which the client, accompanied by the therapist, is actually placed in
his or her most fear-arousing situation and is prohibited from escaping. Someone afraid of heights, for example, might be taken to the
top of a tall building or to a very high bridge. Someone afraid of
water might be taken out on a large lake. There, with the therapist
close at hand and providing encouragement and support, the individual comes face to face with his or her fear, survives the situation
(although the session may be terrifying for some), and thus comes to
learn that the fear is irrational.

*flooding a technique of behavior
therapy in which a person is
confronted (in vivo) with the object
of his or her fear while accompanied
by the therapist*

Implosive therapy is based on the same premise as flooding, but
involves the use of imagination rather than real-life situations. In
implosive therapy, you don't slowly work your way up any anxiety
hierarchy; you are forced to come to imagine your worst fear, all at
once, here and now. The therapist does not try to get the client to

*implosive therapy a behavior
therapy in which one imagines one's
worst fears, experiencing extreme
anxiety in the safe surroundings of
the therapist's office*

Behavior therapy techniques, such as systematic desensitization, are particularly useful in treating phobic disorders. A common phobia among college students is the fear of public speaking.

relax. On the contrary, the idea is to experience the full force of anxiety while in the ultimately safe surroundings of the therapist's office. Repeated trials of fear paired with the safety of the office lead to the replacement of the maladaptive fear response. Although flooding and implosive therapy do sound somewhat bizarre, and are not for everyone (some therapists have difficulty dealing with such focused anxiety), they are effective and usually require less time than does systematic desensitization.

aversion therapy *a technique of behavior therapy in which an aversive stimulus, such as a shock, is paired with an undesired behavior*

You should recognize **aversion therapy** as another example of learning applied to solving psychological problems. In aversion therapy, a stimulus that may be harmful but that produces a pleasant response is paired with an aversive, painful stimulus until the original stimulus is avoided. Every time you put a cigarette in your mouth, I deliver a painful shock to your lip. Every time you take a drink of alcohol, you get violently sick to your stomach. Every time a child molester is shown a picture of a young child, he receives a shock.

None of these situations sounds like the sort of thing anyone would agree to voluntarily. Many people do, however. They volunteer for such treatments for two reasons: (1) aversion therapy is effective at suppressing a specific behavior, at least for a while, and (2) it is seen as the lesser of two evils (shocks and nausea-producing drugs are not much fun, but people see the continuation of their inappropriate, often self-destructive, behaviors as even more dangerous in the long run).

Aversion therapy, though not a commonly used technique, is one way to help problem drinkers stop drinking. For a series of sessions, each time a person takes a drink a drug added to that drink will make him or her nauseous. Eventually, drinking becomes less desirable and the person will quit the habit—at least for a short while.

There are a couple of things we need to recognize. One is that aversion therapy, in any form, is not commonly practiced. Second, aversion therapy tends to suppress behaviors only for a relatively short time. During that time, other techniques may be used in an attempt to bring about a more lasting change in behavior. That is, the techniques of aversion therapy are seldom effective when used alone; they are used in conjunction with some other form(s) of therapy.

Contingency management and contingency contracting (introduced in Topic 5B) borrow from the learning principles of operant conditioning. The basic idea is to have a person appreciate the consequences of his or her behaviors. Appropriate behaviors lead to rewards and the opportunity to do valued things, whereas inappropriate behaviors do not lead to reinforcement and provide fewer opportunities.

In many cases, these basic procedures work very well. Their effectiveness is, as operant conditioning would predict, a function of the extent to which the therapist can effect control over the situation. If the therapist can manage the control of rewards and punishments, called **contingency management**, he or she stands a good chance of modifying the client's behavior. For example, in an institutional setting, *if* a patient (perhaps, a severely disturbed, hospitalized schizophrenic) engages in the appropriate response (leaving her room to go to dinner), *then* the patient will get something she really wants (a chance to watch TV for an extra hour). In an outpatient setting, the therapist tries to arrange the situation so that the client learns to use rewards and incentives to reinforce his or her own appropriate behaviors.

Contingency contracting amounts to establishing a contract with a client so that exhibiting certain behaviors (you prepare dinner) will

contingency management bringing about changes in one's behaviors by controlling rewards and punishments

contingency contracting establishing an agreement (contract) with one to reinforce appropriate behaviors; often involving token economies

result in certain rewards (I will wash the dishes). In many cases, contingency contracting involves establishing a token economy. What this means is that the person is first taught that some token—a checker, a poker chip, or just a check mark on a pad—can be saved. When enough tokens are accumulated, they are cashed in for something of value to the person. With contracting, the value of a token for a specific behavior is spelled out ahead of time. Because control over the environment of the person/learner is most complete in such circumstances, this technique is particularly effective in institutions and with young children. (Again, we went through examples of token economies in Topic 5B, page 231.)

modeling the acquisition of new responses through the imitation of another who responds appropriately

We have recognized that all learning cannot be explained in terms of classical or operant conditioning. It should be no surprise, then, that some types of behavior therapy use learning principles other than those from simple conditioning. **Modeling**, a term introduced by Albert Bandura, involves the acquisition of a new, appropriate response through the imitation of a model. As we saw in Topic 5C, modeling can be an effective means of learning. In a therapy situation, modeling amounts to having or letting patients watch someone else perform a certain appropriate behavior, perhaps earning a reward for it (called vicarious reinforcement). Some phobias, particularly those in children, can be overcome through modeling. A child who is afraid of dogs, for example, may profit from watching another child (which would be more effective than using an adult) playing with a dog. Modeling is also a part of what is called *assertiveness training,* which involves helping individuals stand up for their rights and come to the realization that *their* feelings and opinions matter and should be expressed. Such training actually involves many processes, including direct instruction, group discussion, role-playing, and contingency management, but often relies on modeling to help someone learn appropriate ways to express how they feel and what they think in social situations.

Before You Go On

Briefly describe some techniques used in behavior therapy, including systematic desensitization, flooding, implosive therapy, aversion therapy, contingency management and contracting, and modeling.

COGNITIVE TECHNIQUES

Psychotherapists who use cognitive techniques do not deny the importance of a person's behaviors (these therapies are often called *cognitive-behavioral*). Rather, they believe that what matters most in the therapeutic session are the client's beliefs, thoughts, perceptions, and attitudes about himself or herself and the environment. The major principle is that to change how one feels and acts, therapy should first be directed at changing how one thinks. As we have seen with other approaches to psychotherapy, there is not just one type of cognitive-behavioral therapy, there are many. A recent survey identified nearly two dozen types (Dobson, 1988). We'll examine just two: rational-emotive therapy and cognitive restructuring therapy.

Rational-Emotive Therapy

Rational-emotive therapy (RET) is associated with Albert Ellis (1970, 1973, 1991). Its basic premise is that psychological problems arise when people try to interpret (a cognitive activity) what happens in the world on the basis of irrational beliefs. Ellis put it this way: "Rational-emotive therapy (RET) hypothesizes that people largely disturb themselves by thinking in a self-defeating, illogical, and unrealistic manner—especially by escalating their natural preferences and desires into absolutistic, dogmatic musts and commands on themselves, others, and their environmental conditions" (1987, p. 364).

When compared to person-centered techniques, RET is quite directive. In fact, Ellis takes exception with techniques of psychotherapy designed to help a person *feel* better without providing useful strategies by which the person can *get* better (Ellis, 1991). In RET, the therapist takes an active role interpreting the rationality of a client's system of beliefs and encourages active change. Therapists often act as role models and make homework assignments for clients that help them bring their expectations and perceptions in line with reality.

To give a very simplified example, refer back to the dialogue between Barbara and her client-centered therapist I used to begin this chapter. A cognitive therapist might see a number of irrational beliefs operating in this scene, including two that Ellis (1970) claims are very common: (1) people should always be loved for everything they do, and (2) it's better to avoid problems than to face them. These, claims Ellis, are exactly the sort of cognitions that create psychological difficulties (others are listed in Figure 13.2). Rather than waiting for self-discovery, which might never come, a rational-emotive therapist would point out to Barbara that the fact that her parents never went to college and don't understand what it is like to work and go to school at the same time is *their* problem, not hers. Rather than agonizing over the fact that her parents don't seem to appreciate her efforts, she needs to either set them straight (pleasantly, of course, which might constitute a homework assignment for Barbara) or move out (there are several other possibilities, of course).

rational-emotive therapy (RET) a form of cognitive therapy, associated with Ellis, aimed at changing a person's irrational beliefs or maladaptive cognitions

Figure 13.2

Some Irrational Beliefs That Lead to Maladjustment and Disorder. The More Rational Alternative to These Beliefs Should Be Obvious.

1. One should be loved by everyone for everything one does.
2. Because I strongly desire to perform important tasks competently and successfully, I absolutely must perform them well at all times.
3. Because I strongly desire to be approved of by people I find significant, I absolutely must always have their approval.
4. Certain acts are wicked and people who perform them should be severely punished no matter what.
5. It is horrible when things are not the way we want them to be.
6. It is better to avoid life's problems, if possible, than to face them.
7. One needs something stronger or more powerful than oneself to rely on.
8. One must have perfect and certain self-control.
9. Because I very strongly desire people to treat me considerately and fairly, they must absolutely do so.
10. Because something once affected one's life, it will always affect it.

From Ellis, 1970, 1987.

Cognitive Restructuring Therapy

cognitive restructuring therapy a form of cognitive therapy, associated with Beck, in which an individual is led to overcome negative self-images and pessimistic views of the future

Similar to rational-emotive therapy is **cognitive restructuring therapy**, associated with Aaron Beck (1976, 1991). Although the basic goals are similar, cognitive restructuring therapy is much less confrontational and direct than RET.

Beck's assumption is that considerable psychological distress stems from a few simple, but misguided, beliefs (cognitions, again). According to Beck, people with psychological disorders (particularly those related to depression, for which cognitive restructuring was first designed) share certain characteristics. For example:

1. They tend to have very negative self-images. They do not value themselves or what they do.

2. They tend to take a very negative view of life experiences.

3. They overgeneralize. For example, having failed one test, a person comes to believe that there is no way he or she can do college work and withdraws from school and looks for work, even though he or she believes there's little chance that anyone would offer a job to someone who is such a failure and a college dropout.

4. They actually seek out experiences that reinforce their negative expectations. The student in the above example may apply for a job as a stockbroker or a law clerk. Lacking even minimal experience, he or she will not be offered either job and, thus, will confirm his or her own worthlessness.

5. They tend to hold a rather dismal outlook for the future.

6. They tend to avoid seeing the bright side of any experience.

In cognitive restructuring therapy, the patient is given opportunities to test or demonstrate his or her beliefs. The patient and therapist make up a list of hypotheses based on the patient's assumptions and beliefs and then actually go out and test these hypotheses. Obviously, the therapist tries to exercise enough control over the situation so that the experiments do not confirm the patient's beliefs about himself or herself, but will lead instead to positive outcomes. For example, given the hypothesis "Nobody cares about me," the therapist need only find one person who does care to refute it. This approach, of leading a person to the self-discovery that negative attitudes directed toward oneself are often inappropriate, has proven very successful in the treatment of depression, although it has been extended to cover a wide range of psychological disorders (Beck, 1985, 1991; Beck & Freeman, 1990; Zinbarg et al., 1992).

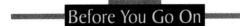

Before You Go On

Briefly summarize the logic behind rational-emotive therapy and cognitive restructuring therapy.

GROUP APPROACHES

Many patients profit from some type of *group therapy*. Group therapy is a label applied to a variety of situations in which a number of people are involved in a therapeutic setting at the same time. If nothing else, group therapy provides an economic advantage over individual psychotherapy: one therapist can interact with several people in the same time frame.

In standard forms of group therapy, clients are brought together at the same time, under the guidance of a therapist, to share their feelings and experiences. Most groups are quite informal, and no particular form of psychotherapy is dominant. In other words, meeting with people in groups is something a psychotherapist with any sort of training or background may do from time to time.

There are several possible benefits that can be derived from this procedure, including an awareness that "I'm not the only one with problems." The sense of support that one can get from someone else with problems occasionally may be even greater than that afforded by a therapist alone—a sort of "she really knows from her own experience the hell that I'm going through" logic. And there is truth in the basic notion that getting involved in helping someone else with a problem is, in itself, a therapeutic process. Yet another advantage of group therapy situations is that the person may learn new, more effective ways of "presenting" himself or herself to others.

family therapy a type of group therapy focusing on the roles, interdependence, and communication skills of family members

A group approach that has become quite popular is **family therapy,** which focuses on the roles, interdependence, and communication skills of family members. Family therapy is often begun after one member of a family enters psychotherapy. After discussing the person's problems for a while, other members of the family are invited to join in the therapy sessions. There is evidence that getting the family unit involved in therapy has benefit for patients with a wide range of disorders, from alcoholism and agoraphobia to depression and schizophrenia (Bloch & Simon, 1982; Feist, 1993; Goldfried et al., 1990).

Two related assumptions underlie a family therapy approach. One is that each family member is a part of a *system* (the family unit), and his or her feelings, thoughts, and behaviors necessarily impact on other family members (e.g., Minuchin & Fishman, 1981; Thomas, 1992). Bringing about a change (even a therapeutic one) in one member of the family system without involving the other members of the system will not last long. This is particularly true when the initial problem appears to be with a child or adolescent. I say "appears to be" because we can be confident that other family members have at least contributed to the troublesome symptoms of the child or adolescent's behavior. A therapist will have a very difficult time bringing about significant and lasting change in a child whose parents refuse to become involved in therapy.

A second assumption often relevant in family therapy sessions is that difficulties arise from improper methods of family *communication* (e.g., Satir, 1967). Quite often, individuals develop false beliefs about the feelings and/or needs of family members. The goal of therapy in such situations, then, is to meet with the family in a group setting to foster and encourage open expressions of feelings and desires. It may be very helpful for an adolescent to learn that her parents are upset and anxious about work-related stress and financial affairs. The adolescent has assumed all along that her parents yelled at her and at each other because of something *she* was doing. And the parents didn't want to share their concerns over money with the adolescent for fear that it would upset her.

Evaluating group therapy techniques is particularly difficult, and few good reviews of outcome studies are available. In general, there seems to be support for the sorts of approaches I have briefly outlined here, and there is some indication that family therapy is a better approach for some problems than is individual treatment (Gurman et al., 1986; Opalic, 1989; Yalom, 1985).

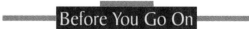

Before You Go On

What are some advantages of group therapy?

Describe two assumptions underlying
family therapy.

EVALUATING PSYCHOTHERAPY

Evaluating psychotherapy has proven to be a difficult task. Is psychotherapy effective? Compared to what? Is any type of psychotherapy better than any other? These are obviously important questions, but the best we can do, I'm afraid, is offer partial, tentative answers. Yes, psychotherapy is effective. Compared to what? Certainly when compared to doing nothing. "By about 1980 a consensus of sorts was reached that psychotherapy, as a generic treatment process, was demonstrably more effective than no treatment" (Gelso & Fassinger, 1990; Goldfried et al., 1990; VandenBos, 1986, p. 111), and more treatment appears to be better than less treatment (Howard et al., 1986) (See Figure 13.3). Research also confirms the logical assertion that the sooner one begins therapy, the better the prognosis (Kupfer, Frank, & Perel, 1989). There is also evidence that some therapists are more effective than others, regardless of what type of therapy is practiced. In other words, some people tend to be good therapists, and

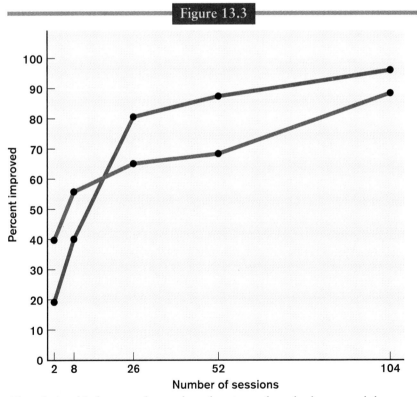

Figure 13.3

The relationship between the number of sessions of psychotherapy and the percentage of patients who showed improvement. Objective ratings made by professionals are indicated by the blue line; subjective ratings of well-being made by the patients themselves are indicated by the orange line. In other words, most improvement in psychotherapy is made early on, but improvement continues as therapy continues.

others tend to be less effective, regardless of the approach or technique they use (Beutler et al., 1986; Lafferty et al., 1989).

At this point, I need to mention a few of the problems encountered when doing research on the effectiveness of psychotherapy. First, we have little quality data on how people might have responded without treatment. In other words, we often do not have a baseline for comparison. We know that sometimes there is a spontaneous remission of symptoms. Sometimes people "get better" without the formal intervention of a therapist. To say that people get better on their own is seldom literally accurate. There are many factors that can contribute to improve one's mental health, even if one is not officially in psychotherapy (Erwin, 1980). You can imagine what such factors might be. Perhaps the source of one's stress is removed; a nagging parent moves out of state, or an aggravating boss gets transferred. Perhaps an interpersonal relationship is begun that provides needed support.

Second, we can't seem to agree on what we mean by recovery. For some, it is simply the absence of observable symptoms for a specified period. For others, however, the goal of therapy is something different: the self-report of "feeling better," personal growth, a relatively permanent change in behavior, insight into deep-seated motivational conflicts, or a restructuring of cognitions.

Finally, even when we can agree on criteria for recovery there is often concern about how to measure or assess therapy outcomes. It hardly seems realistic to expect unbiased responses from therapists *or* their patients if we were to ask them to report if therapy has been a helpful experience.

These are three of the most commonly cited general problems with designing studies to evaluate the outcome of psychotherapy. Even so, quality studies have been done. Most have focused on just one technique at a time, and generally, the results have been very positive (Erwin, 1980; Eysenck, 1952; Greenberg & Safran, 1987; Kazdin et al., 1987; Lipsey & Wilson, 1993; Marziali, 1984; Miller & Berman, 1983; Wolpe, 1981). Many studies also indicate that even when the primary treatment option is medical (say, an antidepressant drug), psychotherapy and medication together provide the best prognosis (Frank et al., 1990; Free & Oei, 1989; Klerman, 1990).

A meta-analysis by Smith, Glass, and Miller (1980) showed positive results for psychotherapy and has become a commonly cited study of its effectiveness. Smith and her colleagues found that a variety of techniques produce results that are better than what might be expected through spontaneous remission. As Figure 13.4 shows us, an average patient in psychotherapy scored better on several outcome variables than did 75 percent of control subjects who received no treatment. Remember the nature of a meta-analysis (introduced in Topic 1B). Smith, Glass, and Miller did not collect new data for their report; they carefully reviewed and statistically analyzed 475 published studies on the effectiveness of psychotherapy. A more recent meta-analysis by Mark Lipsey and David Wilson of 302 studies of psychotherapy outcomes came to the same conclusion: what psychotherapy provides is beneficial. Moreover, "the magnitude of the

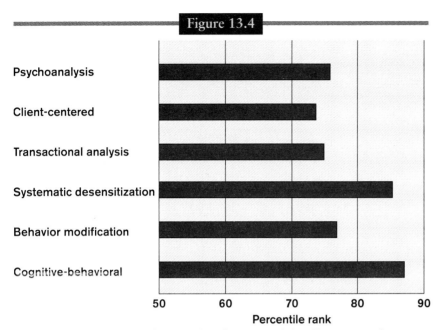

A summary of the results of 475 studies that assessed the effectiveness of psychotherapy. These data reflect the percentage of clients treated with various forms of therapy who scored higher, or more favorably, on several outcome measures than did clients who were not treated. For example, the average client in behavior modification therapy scored higher on outcome measures than did 75 percent of clients not treated.

effects for a substantial portion of those treatments is in a range of practical significance by almost any reasonable criterion" (Lipsey & Wilson, 1993).

What about comparing psychotherapy methods? Here the answer is also clear: *In general,* there are no differences. There is no evidence that any one type of therapy is universally better than any other (Stiles et al., 1986). There *is* evidence that some types of therapy may be better suited for some types of problems than for others. Each approach has its strengths and weaknesses. The psychoanalytic approaches, even in modern forms, can be time-consuming and expensive. Person-centered approaches require an introspective, non-dependent client to be most useful. Group approaches may not be effective for clients who require personal attention. Behavioral methods, such as systematic desensitization, are most useful for phobic disorders, and cognitive therapies seem to be best suited to patients with depression [although even this differentiation may be questionable (Mervis, 1986)]. None of the psychotherapeutic approaches described in this Topic will be effective, *by themselves,* for persons with psychotic disorders such as major depression or schizophrenia.

Which therapy is best suited for which particular disorder is just one of the questions to which we do not have a definitive answer, and it is one of the most active areas of research in psychotherapy today (Deffenbacher, 1988; Goldfried et al., 1990; Lipsey & Wilson, 1993).

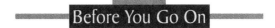

Before You Go On

Is there any evidence that psychotherapy is effective?

Is any one type of psychotherapy better than the others?

TOPIC 13B SUMMARY

In general, psychotherapy is an attempt, using psychological means, to bring about a change in the way a person thinks, feels, or acts. As Freud characterized it, it is "talking therapy," but it involves careful, interpretive listening as well. There are literally hundreds of types of such techniques, and in this Topic we have reviewed briefly only a few of the more traditional or classic approaches.

In the simplest of terms, approaches to psychotherapy can be distinguished in terms of their major goals. Psychoanalytic techniques try to uncover and resolve repressed conflicts, problems, or traumas; the humanistic approaches tend to focus on feelings, dealing with them realistically to help a person grow and flourish; behavioral approaches take their foundation from the learning laboratory and aim to change a person's overt behaviors in hopes that changes in emotion and cognitions will follow; cognitive therapies seek to help people form more realistic, rational cognitions about themselves and the world in which they live; and group therapies build on the support the interactions of several people in a therapeutic setting can provide.

Research tells us that psychotherapy—psychoanalytic, humanistic, behavioral, cognitive, or some combination—can be effective in helping people suffering from psychological distress and discomfort. We cannot say that one form of therapy is more effective than any other for any particular disorder or any particular person. "Although we know that psychotherapy works, we do not clearly understand how it works. Differently labeled therapies have demonstrably different behavioral contents, yet appear to have equivalent outcomes" (Stiles et al., 1986, p. 165).

CHAPTER SUMMARY

TOPIC 13A

Briefly trace the history of the treatment of persons with psychological disorders.

In ancient times, and throughout the Middle Ages, the prevailing view of the mentally ill was that they were possessed by evil spirits. As a result, treatment was often harsh, involving torture and placement in dungeonlike asylums for the insane, which in many ways were worse than prisons. It was not uncommon for the mentally ill, who were often viewed as witches, to be put to death for their unusual behaviors. Throughout history, there have been attempts by compassionate persons to provide humane treatment to the disordered. It wasn't until the twentieth century that what we now call the mental health movement began with an aim of treating the mentally ill in the most humane way possible. /*p. 638*

What is a prefrontal lobotomy?

Why was it ever used, and why is it not used today?

A prefrontal lobotomy is a psychosurgical technique that severs connections between the prefrontal lobes of the cerebral cortex and lower brain centers. It was first used in the mid-1930s and was a common treatment in the 1940s and 1950s. It was used because it was often successful in alleviating the worst of psychotic symptoms. It also produced many mild to severe side effects—occasionally, even death. Because of its inherent danger, and because safer, reversible treatments such as drug therapy are available today, it is no longer used. /*p. 641*

What is ECT?

Why is it still being used?

ECT stands for electroconvulsive therapy, commonly called shock therapy. In this form of treatment, a brain seizure is produced by passing an electric current across the patient's head. Upon regaining consciousness, the patient has no memory of the procedure. Although there may be negative side effects, particularly with prolonged or repeated use, the technique is demonstrably useful for most patients as a means of reducing or even eliminating severe depression and some other psychotic symptoms. /*p. 643*

What are antipsychotic drugs, and what are their effects?

Antipsychotic drugs are used to reduce or control psychotic symptoms, characterized by a loss of contact with reality and a gross impairment of functioning. Chlorpromazine was the first antipsychotic drug. Introduced in 1950, it was commonly used in the mid-1950s to suppress symptoms associated with psychosis: delusions, hallucinations, disordered thought, inappropriate affect, and the like. Antipsychotic drugs have their effect by altering the action of neurotransmitters in the brain. Although these drugs do reduce psychotic symptoms in many patients, it is not correct to say that they cure the disorder, because symptoms often return when the drugs are discontinued. /*p. 644*

What are antidepressant drugs, and what are they meant to do?

Two major types of antidepressant drugs are the MAO inhibitors and the tricyclics. They reduce episodes of depression, when they are effective. Lithium salts not only reduce depressive symptoms, but are most useful in treating bipolar disorders. Unlike the antipsychotic drugs, these may often have long-term beneficial effects (alleviating feelings of depression), even after the patient stops taking them. They

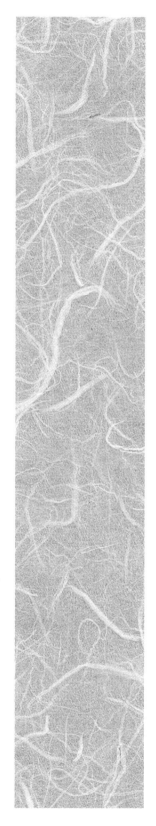

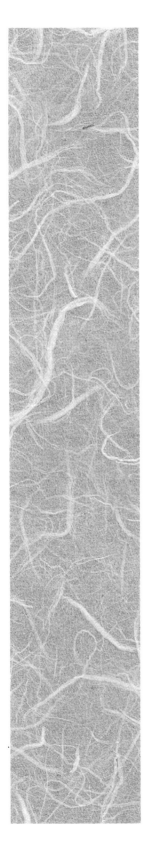

usually take weeks to produce their effects, however, and do not work for all patients. Long-term use of the drugs may produce a number of potentially harmful or unpleasant side effects. /p. 646

What are the common antianxiety drugs, and what are the dangers inherent in their use?

The most common anxiety-alleviating drugs, or tranquilizers, are the meprobamates and the benzodiazepines, including Valium and Librium, which are among the most commonly prescribed of all drugs in the world. These drugs are effective in reducing felt levels of anxiety. There is evidence that some patients who use antianxiety drugs develop addictions to them. Like many psychoactive drugs, they suppress symptoms; they do not cure the underlying anxiety, and even small overdoses can lead to severe complications. /p. 646

What is deinstitutionalization, why did it come about, and has it been successful?

Deinstitutionalization refers to the policy of taking measures to release patients from publicly supported mental institutions. As national policy, deinstitutionalization is a response to factors that became apparent in the mid-1950s: (1) conditions in mental hospitals generally were very bad, (2) antipsychotic medications significantly reduced many troublesome psychotic symptoms, and (3) community-based mental health centers were to be created to care for patients after they were released back to the community. The blessing is mixed, to be sure. Some patients are infinitely better off living at home and visiting their community mental health centers as the need arises. Others are much less fortunate. They have no nearby mental health facility and soon stop taking their medication, so psychotic symptoms return. /p. 649

TOPIC 13B

Who may offer psychotherapy?

Many different mental health professionals can provide psychotherapy. These include clinical psychologists (Ph.D.s or Psy.D.s with graduate training in psychology and a one-year internship), psychiatrists (M.D.s with an internship and residency in a mental hospital), counseling psychologists (Ph.D.s in psychology specializing in less severe disorders and with an internship in a counseling setting), licensed counselors (perhaps with degrees in education), psychoanalysts (who specialize in Freudian therapy), clinical social workers (usually with a master's degree), and others, including pastoral counselors and mental health technicians. /p. 653

Describe Freudian psychoanalysis, defining some of its major features.

How is psychoanalysis different today from when it was practiced by Freud?

Freudian psychoanalysis was aimed at uncovering repressed conflicts (usually developed in childhood) so that they can be resolved. The process involves (1) free association, in which the patient is to say anything and everything that comes to mind, without editing; (2) resistance, in which a patient seems unable or unwilling to discuss some aspect of his or her life, suggesting that the resisted experiences may be anxiety producing; (3) dream interpretation, in which one analyzes both the manifest and the latent content for insights into the nature of the patient's unconscious mind; and (4) transference, in which feelings once directed at a significant person in the patient's life become directed toward the analyst. Although basic psychoanalysis has remained unchanged since Freud's day, some changes have evolved. There is now more effort to shorten the duration of analysis; there is less emphasis on childhood experiences and more concern with the here and now. Present-day analysis is also more directive than it was in Freud's day. /p. 657

What are the characteristics of client-centered and gestalt therapy?

Client-centered, or person-centered, therapy, which we associate with Carl Rogers, is based on the belief that people can control their lives and solve their own problems if they can be helped to understand the true nature of their feelings. It promotes self-discovery and personal growth. The therapist reflects or mirrors the client's feelings, focuses on the here and now, and tries to be empathic, actively listening to and relating to the patient's feelings. Throughout therapy sessions, the therapist provides unconditional positive regard for the client. Gestalt therapy, associated with Fritz Perls, has many of the same aims, but is more directive and challenging, striving to integrate a person's thoughts, feelings, and behaviors. /p. 659

Briefly describe some techniques used in behavior therapy, including systematic desensitization, flooding, implosive therapy, aversion therapy, contingency management and contracting, and modeling.

Behavior therapies have evolved from the learning laboratory. Based on classical conditioning, systematic desensitization is a behavior therapy technique particularly well suited for the treatment of phobic reactions. A person is first taught to relax. An anxiety hierarchy is made, listing stimuli in order of their capacity to evoke fear or anxiety. Desensitization is accomplished by gradually presenting more anxiety-producing stimuli from the hierarchy while the person remains in a relaxed state in the presence of stimuli that previously elicited anxiety. Flooding and implosive therapy are two rather dramatic forms of behavior therapy useful in the treatment of phobias. In flooding, the client is confronted with the object of her or his fear in

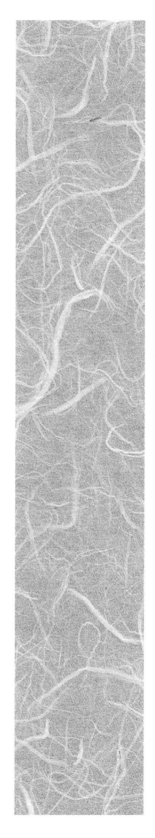

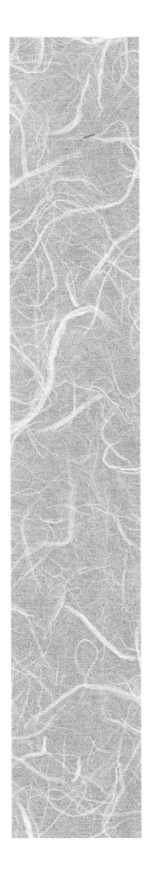

person (in vivo), accompanied by the therapist. Implosive therapy asks the client to imagine his or her fears in the most vivid way possible in an effort to increase anxiety to very high levels in the safety and security of the therapist's office. Unlike systematic desensitization, neither procedure is gradual, and neither encourages the person to remain relaxed; indeed, both require the person to become anxious in order to face and deal with that anxiety.

Aversion therapy pairs an unwanted behavior with a very negative stimulus, such as shock or a nausea-producing drug. It is an effective means of reducing unwanted behaviors, at least temporarily, but should only be thought of as therapy when someone voluntarily agrees to undergo the treatment after recognizing the long-term benefit of submitting to the aversive stimuli.

Contingency management, contingency contracting, and modeling are three specific applications of accepted learning principles used to increase the likelihood of appropriate behaviors and decrease the likelihood of inappropriate behaviors. Contingency management amounts to exercising control over the pattern of rewards a patient or subject may receive. Contracting often involves a token economy system in which a client agrees (by contract) to engage in certain behaviors in order to earn specified rewards. Modeling suggests that persons can acquire appropriate behaviors through the imitation of models, particularly when the model's behavior is reinforced. /p. 662

Briefly summarize the logic behind rational-emotive therapy and cognitive restructuring therapy.

Cognitive therapies are designed to alter the way a person perceives and thinks about himself or herself and the environment. Rational-emotive therapy (RET) works on the premise that people with problems are operating on irrational assumptions about the world and themselves. RET is directive in its attempts to change people's cognitions. Cognitive restructuring therapy is somewhat less directive, but is based on the same sort of idea as RET. The underlying premise here is that people with psychological disorders have developed negative self-images and negative views (cognitions) about the future. The therapist then provides opportunities for the patient to test those negative cognitions and discover that everything is not as bad as it may seem. /p. 665

What are some advantages of group therapy?

Describe two assumptions underlying family therapy.

There are several potential advantages to group therapy. (1) The basic problem may be an interpersonal one, and thus will be better understood and dealt with in an interpersonal situation. (2) There is value in realizing that one is not the only person in the world with a problem and that there are others who may have an even more difficult problem of the same nature. (3) There is therapeutic value in providing support for someone else. (4) The dynamics of intragroup communication can be analyzed and changed in a group setting. Family therapy is based on the assumptions that (1) family members can be seen as a part of a system in which one member (and one member's problem) affects all of the others, and that (2) many psychological problems arise because of faulty communication, and that this is particularly critical within a family. */p. 666*

Is there any evidence that psychotherapy is effective?

Is any one type of psychotherapy better than the others?

Scientifically evaluating the appropriateness and effectiveness of psychotherapy has been very difficult. Nonetheless, it is safe to conclude that, in general, psychotherapy is effective. It is significantly better than leaving disorders untreated. There are data that suggest that some therapies may be better suited to some clients and to some disorders than they are to others. There is evidence that psychotherapy provides an advantage when offered along with appropriate drug therapy. On the other hand, there is no evidence that, in general, any one type of therapy is better than any other. */p. 670*

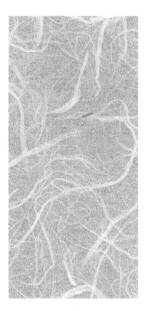

chapter fourteen

SOCIAL PSYCHOLOGY

CHAPTER OUTLINE

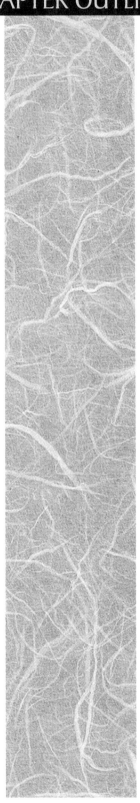

TOPIC 14A SOCIAL COGNITIONS: ATTITUDES, ATTRIBUTIONS, AND ATTRACTIONS
Attitudes
    The Components of Attitudes
    Attitude Formation
    Attitude Change and Persuasion
Attribution Theory
Interpersonal Attraction
    Theories of Interpersonal Attraction
    Factors Affecting Interpersonal Attraction
TOPIC 14A SUMMARY

TOPIC 14B SOCIAL INFLUENCE
Conformity
Obedience to Authority
    Attribution Errors and a Word of Caution
    A Reminder About Ethics in Research
Bystander Intervention
    A Cognitive Model of Bystander Intervention
    The Bystander Effect: A Conclusion
Social Loafing
Social Facilitation
Decision Making in Groups
TOPIC 14B SUMMARY

CHAPTER SUMMARY

*I*t was about thirty years ago that a New York City cocktail waitress named Kitty Genovese was brutally murdered in front of her apartment building as she returned from work about 3:30 in the morning. What made this particular murder noteworthy was that so many of Genovese's neighbors watched as she was bludgeoned and stabbed to death. Here is the account of the incident as reported in *The New York Times*.

> For more than half an hour, thirty-eight respectable law-abiding citizens in Queens watched a killer stalk and stab a woman in three separate attacks in Kew Gardens.
>
> Twice the sound of their voices and the sudden glow of their bedroom lights interrupted him and frightened him off. Each time he returned, sought her out and stabbed her again. Not one person telephoned the police during the assault; one witness called after the woman was dead. (*New York Times*, 3/27/64)

This story has become a classic example in the social psychology of bystander behaviors. I was concerned that because the incident took place so many years ago, it may have lost some of its relevance. As I pondered whether or not to tell the story of Kitty Genovese, I read this newspaper story:

> **Cheering bystanders spur on woman's killer** Oakland, Calif. (AP)–
>
> A dozen people who chanted "Kill her, kill her," as a 32-year-old woman was stabbed to death could face murder charges, authorities say.
>
> Police said Friday they were looking for members of the crowd who egged on the woman's attacker. The people could be charged with aiding and abetting a killing.
>
> "Usually, you hear of people who stand by, watch and do nothing," police Sergeant John McKenna said, "but this is the other end of things, where the people watched and participated, apparently for a thrill—to watch the kill."
>
> Police arrested Stacey Camille Grayson, 19, for investigation of murder. McKenna said Grayson told police she was angry at Dione Wells for smoking crack cocaine in the hallway of her apartment building and confronted her Wednesday night.
>
> When Wells walked away, Grayson grabbed a knife and chased her down the street. Wells tried to seek shelter in a liquor store but an employee locked the door in her path.
>
> A bystander tripped Wells as she ran by, giving Grayson a chance to stab her as the crowd urged her on, McKenna said. (The *Toronto Star*, 8/15/93)

Yes, the murder of Kitty Genovese occurred over thirty years ago. No, sadly, the story is not dated; nor is it irrelevant. There are significant differences between these two accounts, but the basic story is one that is repeated in some form or another on a nearly daily basis. "What's wrong with those people?" "How could they just stand by and watch?" "Why didn't they try to help?"

These are just some of the questions we will struggle with in this chapter on social psychology, an area of study that deals with people as they live—in a social world, influencing and being influenced by others.

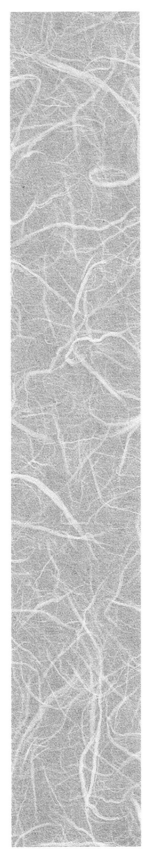

*A*s we've seen before, other areas of psychology also study reactions that are social in nature. Some developmental psychologists, for example, are interested in how styles of cooperative and competitive play change and develop through the early years of life. Personality psychologists are interested in individual characteristics that affect interpersonal behavior, such as friendliness and aggression. Learning theorists are interested in how the perception of someone else being rewarded affects behavior change. Clinical psychologists recognize that social relationships can play a pivotal role in the development of psychological disorders and their treatment.

In this chapter, we will consider two major content areas in social psychology: (1) in Topic 14A, social cognition, or the perception and evaluation of oneself and others in social situations, and (2) in Topic 14B, social influence, or how others affect the reactions of the individual.

To provide the proper context, we begin with a discussion of the perspective from which social psychologists study behavior and mental processes. Then, we'll spend the bulk of Topic 14A dealing with attitudes. We'll see how social psychologists define attitudes, how attitudes are formed, and how they may be changed. We'll look at some of the factors that determine how we process information about ourselves and others in social situations, in particular how we attribute behaviors to different causes. We'll close Topic 14A with a review of interpersonal (or social) attraction and consider some of the factors that influence how and why people are attracted to others.

The focus of Topic 14B is on social influence. We are so accustomed to the pressures of social influence that much of the time it escapes our awareness. You probably didn't consider why you happened to walk on the right side of the sidewalk the last time you were downtown, or why you took a place at the very end of the line when you bought tickets for a movie, or why you applauded at the last concert you attended. Nevertheless, each of these behaviors was shaped by social influences.

Topic 14A

SOCIAL COGNITIONS: ATTITUDES, ATTRIBUTIONS, AND ATTRACTIONS

social psychology the field of psychology concerned with how others influence the thoughts, feelings, and behaviors of the individual

Social psychology is the field of psychology concerned with how others influence the thoughts, feelings, and behaviors of the individual. Social psychologists focus their attention on the person or the individual in a group setting, and not on the group *per se* (which is more likely to be the concern of sociologists). Because we are all social organisms, we are familiar, each in our own way, with many of the concerns of social psychology.

To claim that we are familiar with the concerns of social psychology has certain implications. On the one hand, it means that social psychology tends to be perceived as interesting and relevant because it deals with everyday situations that affect us all. On the other hand, it means that we are often willing to accept common sense, our own personal experience, and even folklore as the basis for our explanations and assumptions about social behavior. Although common sense sometimes may be valid, it is not an acceptable basis for a scientific approach to understanding social behavior. Social psychology relies on experimentation and other scientific methods as sources of knowledge about social behavior, even if the results of applying these methods are contrary to intuition.

During the last 20 years, much of social psychology has taken on a cognitive flavor. That is, social psychologists are attempting to understand social behavior by examining the mental structures and processes reflected in such behavior.

A basic premise of this approach, and of this Topic, is that we do not view our social environment solely on the basis of the stimulus information it presents us (Higgins & Bargh, 1987). Instead, the argument goes, we have developed several cognitive structures and processes (attitudes, schemas, prejudices, stereotypes, and the like) that influence our interpretation of the world around us. "Discovering how people mentally organize and represent information about themselves and others has been a central task of social cognition research" (Berscheid, 1994, p. 84). Put another way, social cognition involves two related questions: What information about the social nature of the world do we have stored in memory? How does that stored information influence social judgments, choices, attractions, and behaviors (Sherman et al., 1989)? We can see these questions underlying each of the three major sections of Topic 14A. We begin with attitudes.

ATTITUDES

Since the 1920s, a central concern in social psychology has been the nature of attitudes (McGuire, 1985). We'll define **attitude** as a relatively stable disposition to evaluate an object or event. An attitude has consequences for influencing one's beliefs, feelings, and behaviors toward that object or event (Olson & Zanna, 1993).

The concept of *evaluation* in this definition refers to a dimension of attitudes that includes such notions as being for or against, pro or con, positive or negative (Eagly & Chaiken, 1992). Our definition refers to a *disposition*, or tendency, to respond to the object of an attitude (actual responding is not necessary). Note that attitudes are held in memory, which, if nothing else, makes them cognitions (e.g., Fazio, 1990). Also note that by definition attitudes have objects. We do not simply have attitudes in general; we have attitudes *about* some object or event. I recognize that the word *attitude* is occasionally used differently in common speech. We may hear that someone has a "bad atti-

attitude *a relatively stable evaluative disposition directed toward some object or event; it consists of feelings, behaviors, and beliefs*

tude" or "an attitude" in general, as in, "Boy, does he have an attitude!" In psychology, however, an attitude requires an object.

Anything can be the object of an attitude, whether it be a person, thing, or idea (Petty & Cacioppo, 1986). You may have attitudes about this course, the car you drive, your father, the president, or the corner fast-food restaurant where you eat lunch. Some of our attitudes are more important than others, of course, but the fact that we have attitudes toward so many things is precisely the reason the study of attitudes is so central in social psychology.

The Components of Attitudes

Although many definitions of attitude have been proposed over the years, most of them suggest that an attitude consists of three components (Chaiken & Stangor, 1987). When we use the term attitude in everyday conversation, we are most likely referring to the *affective component*, which consists of our feelings about the attitudinal object (Zanna & Rempel, 1988). The *behavioral component* consists of our response tendencies toward the object of our attitude. This component includes our actual behaviors and our intentions to act should the opportunity arise. The *cognitive component* includes our beliefs or thoughts about the attitudinal object. Any of these three may be primary. We may form a positive attitude toward a particular beverage because we know it is good for us (cognitive), because it is very convenient to buy (behavioral), or because we like the way it tastes (affective). By now, these three components of affect, behavior, and cognition, or ABC, ought to be familiar.

In many cases, the cognitive, affective, and behavioral components of our attitudes are consistent. We think that classical music is relaxing and like to listen to it, so we buy classical music recordings. You believe that knowledge of psychology will be an asset in your

The components of one's attitudes are not always consistent. You may feel negatively about someone and believe them to be shiftless and untrustworthy, yet when you meet that person in a social situation, you extend your hand in a pleasant greeting. This demonstrates that the behavioral component of an attitude may be inconsistent with the affective and cognitive components.

career, you are enjoying your introductory psychology class, and you plan to take more psychology classes in the future. However, there are occasions when our behaviors are not consistent with our beliefs and feelings (Ajzen & Fishbein, 1980). For example, we may have very strong, unfavorable beliefs and very negative feelings about someone, yet when we encounter that person at a social gathering, we smile, extend our hand, and say something pleasant. The situation may "overpower" the cognitive and affective components of our attitudes. This is another way of saying that the components of an attitude *may* lack consistency, and that it is the behavioral component that is most often inconsistent with the other two.

Because our actual behaviors may not reflect our feelings or our beliefs, some social psychologists (e.g., Fazio, 1989; Fishbein & Ajzen, 1975) prefer to exclude the behavioral component from their definition; they use the term *attitude* to refer only to the fundamental like or dislike for the attitudinal object. Other psychologists argue that attitude is a two-dimensional concept, involving affect *and* cognition, but not behavior (Bagozzi & Burnkrant, 1979; Zajonc & Markus, 1982).

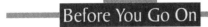

Before You Go On

What is an attitude, and what are its components?

Attitude Formation

As it happens, we have formed many attitudes about a wide range of objects and events. Let us now briefly consider where they came from. Most experts agree that attitudes are learned, and that simple conditioning processes go a long way toward explaining attitude formation.

Some attitudes are acquired through the simple associative process of *classical conditioning*. As shown in Figure 14.1, pleasant events (unconditioned stimuli) can be paired with an attitudinal object (conditioned stimulus). As a result of this association, the attitudinal object comes to elicit the same good feeling (a positive evaluation) originally produced by the unconditioned stimulus. The good feeling, originally an unconditioned response elicited by a pleasant event, now becomes a conditioned response elicited by the attitudinal object. Of course, negative attitudes can be acquired in the same way (e.g., Cacioppo et al., 1992).

Some advertising attempts to work in this way by taking an originally neutral object (the product) and trying to create positive associations for it. For instance, a soft drink advertisement may depict young, attractive people having a great time playing volleyball, dancing, or enjoying a concert while drinking a particular soft drink. The

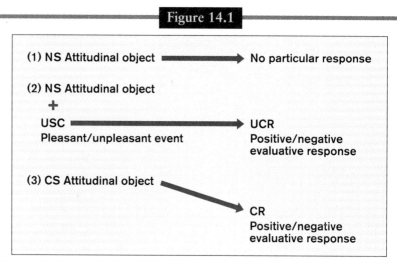

Figure 14.1

How attitudes may be classically conditioned.

obvious intent is that you and I will associate the product with good times and having fun. That sports figures often wear brand name logos or trademarks on their uniforms also suggests that manufacturers want us to learn to associate their product with the skills of the athlete we're watching. Advertisements with sexual themes operate along the same lines.

Attitudes can also be formed as a result of the reinforcement of behaviors consistent with some attitudinal position, a matter of *operant conditioning*. Several studies have shown that verbal reinforcement (saying "good" or "that's right") when subjects agree with attitudinal statements leads those subjects to develop attitudes consistent with the position expressed in those statements (Insko, 1965).

An example of classical conditioning as attitude formation. Products endorsed by celebrities become associated with those celebrities—to the benefit of the products.

Figure 14.2

Observational learning is demonstrated in advertising that uses personal testimonials of satisfied customers to promote a product or service.

As we discussed in Topic 5C, people often imitate behaviors they have seen reinforced in others (called vicarious reinforcement). To the extent we perceive that others are gaining reinforcers for having and expressing some attitude, we are likely to adopt that attitude ourselves.

Advertising that relies on the testimonials of satisfied customers is appealing to this sort of *observational learning* (Figure 14.2). The consumer is shown that someone has used a certain product with success (received reinforcement), and the advertiser hopes that this exposure will lead the observer to develop a favorable evaluation of the product. Obviously, the advertiser is going to show us only those people who are happy with their product or service. We seldom stop to think about how many people may have used the product or service and are unhappy with it.

Before You Go On

**Briefly describe three ways in which attitudes
might be acquired.**

Attitude Change and Persuasion

Much of the research on attitudes has been concerned with the very practical questions of when and how attitudes change. This research has dealt largely with conscious, planned attempts to change someone's attitude(s) by exposing them to information—a process called *persuasion* (Olson & Zanna, 1993). In this section, we will examine a few factors involved in attitude change.

Cognitive Dissonance. It seems reasonable to suggest that one's attitudes will help mold one's behaviors, and that attitude change will lead to behavior change. In 1957, Leon Festinger proposed just the reverse: that attitudes may follow behavior. Festinger's theory involves a concept he called **cognitive dissonance**. Cognitions are ideas, thoughts, beliefs, perceptions, and the like. Dissonance means discord, discomfort, or distress due to things being out of balance or inconsistent. When cognitions are dissonant, one possibility is that attitudes will change in order to reduce the unpleasantness of the dissonance. Cognitive dissonance often arises when we realize (a cognition) we have behaved in a way inconsistent (dissonant) with other cognitions. (You may recall that the concept of cognitive dissonance was introduced in Topic 10A, on motivation.)

cognitive dissonance a state of tension or distress that occurs when there is a lack of balance, or equilibrium, between or among one's cognitions

One of the best examples of how this might work is found in one of the original demonstrations of the phenomenon (Festinger & Carlsmith, 1959). Participants in the research were asked to perform an extremely boring task of rotating row after row of small wooden knobs. Following a lengthy knob-turning session, the experimenter explained that the research really had to do with the effects of motivation on such a task. The subject was told that the person in the waiting area outside the laboratory was to be the next subject in the project. This person was to be led to believe the task was interesting, fun, and educational. The experimenter then explained that his assistant, who usually told these "lies" to the waiting subject, was absent. The subject was then asked to do this "selling" job. The subject would be paid for his or her help. Subjects invariably agreed and actually worked very hard to convince the next subject the project was fun and educational. Weeks later, at the end of the semester, all subjects filled out a questionnaire that asked about their reactions to the knob-turning experiment in which they had participated.

Cognitive dissonance occurs when you find yourself test-driving and considering buying a new car that you previously have been reluctant to buy.

The only experimental manipulation was a simple one: some of the subjects were paid $20 for trying to convince the waiting person (who was really not a subject, but was in on the experiment) the obviously boring task was fun and interesting, whereas others were paid only $1. In all other respects, all subjects were treated the very same way. You must keep in mind that this was the late 1950s, and for college students living in a dormitory, $20 was a lot of money. To replicate this experiment today would require paying subjects as much as $100.

At the end of the semester, which subjects do you suppose expressed more positive attitudes about the project, the ones paid $20 or those paid $1? Doesn't it seem logical that those college students paid $20 would remember the task as being fun and enjoyable and indicate a willingness to participate in similar projects? Festinger and Carlsmith predicted just the opposite. They reasoned that students paid only $1 would feel that their behavior had not been sufficiently justified. They had told a "lie" and had been given only a trivial amount of money for doing so. These subjects would experience a great deal of tension or discomfort—cognitive dissonance would have been created. "I lied for a lousy dollar." One way to resolve this dissonance would be to modify their attitude about the project so that it fit better with their behavior—a sort of, "Well, I didn't really lie, because the experiment wasn't all that bad; in fact, it was kinda fun at that."

The subjects paid $20, on the other hand, had plenty of justification for their actions. Sure, they lied, but they had good reason to do so. These subjects would experience little cognitive dissonance and should not be expected to change their attitude about the experiment. "Yeah, I lied, but I got paid twenty bucks to do so." The results of this experiment are presented in Figure 14.3. Seldom do we find differences in an experiment as clear-cut as these.

The results of this experiment (and by now, numerous others) suggest that one way to change people's attitudes is to get them to first change their behaviors. Not only that, but there is a clear advantage in offering as little incentive as possible to bring about that change in behavior. Simply "buying one off" in order to change his or

Figure 14.3

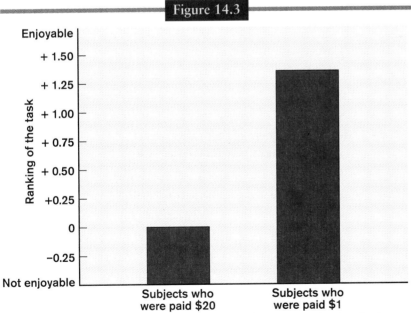

After being paid either $1 or $20 to "lie" about their paticipation in a boring task, subjects were later asked to rate that task in terms of enjoyment, interest, and educational value. As can be seen in this figure, those paid $1 (those with cognitive dissonance) gave the task much higher ratings than did subjects paid $20. (From Festinger & Carlsmith, 1959.)

her behavior may get you compliance, but it will not produce the cognitive dissonance required to bring about lasting attitude change.

You should be able to generate many other examples of cognitive dissonance influencing attitude change. A student who supports a military intervention in a Middle East conflict is invited by a friend to attend a "peace rally." Accepting that invitation may produce dissonance: "I favor military involvement, but there I was at the peace rally." These two cognitions are dissonant. What will happen next? We can't say, but we can predict that something is likely to change in order to reduce dissonance, and perhaps it will be the student's initial attitude. Consider the number of students who have changed their attitude about a course, or a discipline, just because they were required to take a course in that discipline. I know that as an undergraduate chemistry major, my (negative) attitudes about psychology and psychology classes changed because of the dissonance created when I was required to take a (very enjoyable and informative) course in introductory psychology.

More recent extensions of Festinger's cognitive dissonance approach tell us that what matters most in producing attitude change is the perception of responsibility for unfortunate or unpleasant outcomes whether those outcomes are consistent with other cognitions or not (e.g., Cooper & Scher, 1992; Scher & Cooper, 1989). In other words, when we feel our behaviors have led to some unfortunate consequence, we are more likely to end up convincing ourselves that the consequence, or outcome, really wasn't that bad after all. For example, I once bought a car I thought I really wanted to have (even though friends and relatives advised me not to). In fact, the car was a lemon, hardly ever ran properly, and spent most of its life in the shop being repaired. Nonetheless, I was continually heard to claim that "when that car is running, it's the best car I've ever had." I was responsible for an "unpleasant outcome" and I tried to resolve my dissonance by convincing myself I really had not made a mistake.

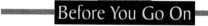

Before You Go On

What is cognitive dissonance, and how does
it operate to produce attitude change?

Cognitive Response Theory. Another theory of attitude change also cognitive in its orientation is called *cognitive response theory* (Petty et al., 1981). This theory proposes that the recipient of a persuasive communication is not at all passive, but is an active information processor who generates cognitive responses about the message as it is received. These cognitive responses can agree with and support the message, or they can be unfavorable, disagreeing and arguing with the message. This reasoning has led researchers to examine variables that affect persuasion and the cognitive responses that persuasive

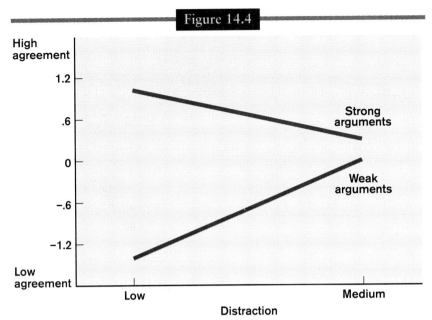

Figure 14.4

The extent to which an audience agrees with either strong arguments or weak arguments presented under conditons of low and medium distraction. Note that distraction lowered agreement when strong arguments were used, but raised agreement when weak arguments were used. (From Petty, Wells, & Brock, 1976).

messages produce. Two interesting variables that have been under study are *message quality* and *distraction.*

In one study, message quality was either high or low; that is, a persuasive speech contained either strong or weak arguments about an attitudinal object (Petty, Wells, & Brock, 1976). Subjects heard one of these two messages under conditions involving either low or moderate distraction. When the message consisted of strong arguments, agreement with the message was reduced (slightly) as distraction was increased (Figure 14.4). This occurred, the theory claims, because the distraction interfered with the listener's ability to generate cognitive responses in favor of the persuasive speech. Increasing distraction had the opposite effect when weak arguments were presented, presumably because the distraction interfered with the listener's ability to think of good arguments against the message.

Let's look at an example of how distraction influences the processing of persuasive messages. Imagine you are headed for a career in medical research and you believe strongly that research with animals is justified because of its ultimate benefit for humankind. You hear that an animal rights group is holding a rally on campus and, out of curiosity, you decide to attend. Cognitive response theory says you will generate arguments (cognitions that disagree with those being made) as you listen to the speeches at the rally. Also assume that there is some loud construction going on nearby. The noise generated by the construction may interfere with your ability to produce good counterarguments, and you will be less able to resist the persuasive speeches than you would be without all of the background noise. On the other hand, a person who went to the rally and supported the animal rights group will generate his or her own arguments that agree with the speeches being made. For this person, the construction noise may cause the speeches to be less influential than they would have been otherwise.

Cognitive response theory may be applied to advertising. Advertisers often make strong claims about their products, and they do not want potential consumers in the audience to question the validity of their claims. In that distractions interfere with the production of counterarguments, distractions leave the consumer more vulnerable to the persuasive message of the advertiser. Loud music, humor, and novelty are used as ways of creating distraction and enhancing the effectiveness of advertising.

An additional aspect of cognitive response theory is that the ultimate reaction to persuasive messages depends more on the recipient's evaluative appraisal of what was communicated than on the actual content or nature of the argument presented. What that means, of course, is that you're more likely to change your attitude if what I've said "sounds good to you," whether you fully understand all of the implications of what I've said or not (Cacioppo & Petty, 1989; DeBono & Harnish, 1988).

The Source of Persuasive Communication. A recent general theory of attitude change claims that there are two factors, or routes, involved in changing one's attitudes (Petty & Cacioppo, 1986; Tesser & Shaffer, 1990). One factor of concern is the *central route:* the nature and quality of the persuasive message itself. The other factor is the *peripheral route:* issues above and beyond the content of the message, or its source. The peripheral route will obviously be of greater concern when one has a relatively weak message to convey. What the research tells us is that in general a highly credible (believable) source will be more persuasive than will a less credible source. There are several factors involved in source credibility (e.g., such factors as vocal pleasantness and facial expressiveness) (Burgoon, Birk, & Pfau, 1990), but the two that seem especially important are *expertise* and *trustworthiness.*

Several studies (e.g., Aronson et al.,1963; Hovland & Weiss, 1951) suggest that the greater the perceived expertise of the communicator, the greater the persuasion. People convinced that they are listening to an expert are much more likely to be persuaded than they would be if they thought the speaker knew little about the subject matter—even if the messages were exactly the same. For example, I am much more likely to be persuaded by Garth Brooks if he were trying to change my mind about a guitar I was thinking about buying than I would be if he were trying to sell me a toaster oven or a spaghetti sauce. (Celebrities without any apparent expertise *are* used to promote products on the basis of the following logic: First, you will recognize them and attend to what they say. Second, their credibility and expertise in some other area, which has brought about their fame, will transfer to the product they are selling.)

Another factor that enhances a communicator's credibility is a high degree of trustworthiness (Cooper & Croyle, 1984). Studies by Walster and Festinger (1962), for example, demonstrated that more attitude change resulted when subjects overheard a persuasive communication than when they believed the communication was directed *at* them. Trustworthiness and credibility were enhanced by a perceived lack of intent to persuade ("Why should they lie; they don't even know I can hear them?").

Before You Go On

What is cognitive response theory, and how does it explain attitude change?

What communicator characteristics are known to have an impact on attitude change?

ATTRIBUTION THEORY

Another facet of the cognitive orientation we find in social psychology is called **attribution** theory. Social psychologists working with attribution theory are interested in understanding the cognitions we use when we try to explain the causes or sources of behavior. The basic question here is, "Do we tend to attribute behaviors or events we observe in the world around us to internal or to external sources—to personal dispositions or to environmental factors?" You may recognize this question as related to issues we raised in the Topic on personality when we discussed the extent to which one's behaviors are determined by personality (dispositional) factors or environmental (situational) factors (Topic 9A, page 442).

Internal attributions explain the source of a person's behavior in terms of some characteristic of the person, often a personality trait or disposition, and for this reason are sometimes called *dispositional attributions*. **External attributions** explain the sources of a person's behavior in terms of the situation or context outside the individual, and are referred to as *situational attributions*.

The evidence indicates that we tend to rely on different types of information when making judgments about the sources of behavior. Imagine, for example, that your best friend shows his temper only when he is with his girlfriend. That information is useful because of its *distinctiveness* (his bad temper shows up only when he's with his girlfriend). As a result, you may take it as a signal of a troubled relationship.

Imagine you have just received an A on a test in your history class. In this case, you could (and probably would) use information about how well everyone else did on the test before you decide about

attribution the cognitions we generate when we attempt to explain the sources of behavior

internal attribution an explanation of behavior in terms of something (a trait) within the person; a dispositional attribution

external attribution an explanation of behavior in terms of something outside the person; a situational attribution

Figure 14.5

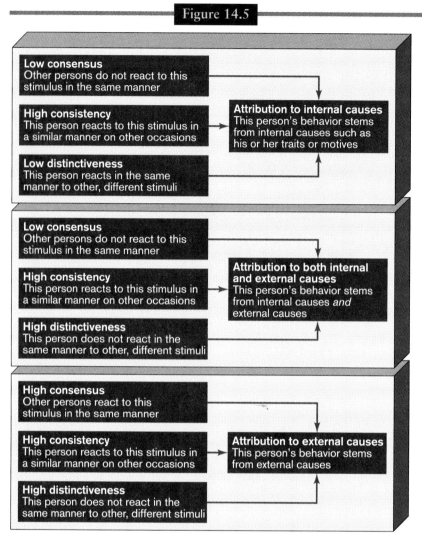

Attributing behavior: Some important considerations and possible outcomes. (From Social Psychology: Understanding Human Interaction, *Fourth, Edition, by Robert A. Baron and Donn Byrne, p. 59. Copyright © 1984, 1981, 1977, 1974 by Allyn and Bacon. Reprinted by permission.)*

your own superiority. This type of information is concerned with *consensus.* If you discover that everyone else also received an A, your explanation of your own behavior (and theirs) might be different from a situation in which you discover that yours is the only A in the class. Before you get too excited about your accomplishment, you might wait for some sign of *consistency* over time lest this one exam be just a fluke. Using information about distinctiveness, consensus, and consistency is the basis of one major theory about how attributions are made (Kelley, 1967, 1973, 1992; Kelley & Michela, 1980). Figure 14.5 shows a few of the ways in which information about distinctiveness, consensus, and consistency may lead one to attribute behavior to internal or external sources. Working through all of this information takes some time-consuming, logical reasoning on the part of the person making the attribution. Clearly, people often do not go through this reasoning procedure correctly, and attribution errors result (Allen et al., 1987).

An active area of research in social psychology deals with the errors we make in our social thinking. In general terms, we tend to make attribution errors because of preexisting cognitive biases that influence our judgments of causality. One example of such a bias is the **fundamental attribution error**—the tendency to favor internal, or personal, attributions for behaviors rather than external, situational explanations (Jones, 1979; Ross, 1977). We see a man pick up a wallet that has been dropped on the pavement and race half a block to return it to its owner. We say to ourselves, "Now there's an honest man." (And we probably would predict that that person will act honestly in a variety of situations.) The truth is, however, that the fellow returned the wallet only because he knew that we (and others) saw him pick it up. If no one else were around, the wallet may not have been returned. The fundamental attribution error is the tendency to disregard, or discount, situational factors in favor of internal, dispositional factors when we make inferences about the causes of behaviors. There is evidence that biases such as the fundamental attribution error are more common in Western cultures. People from India, for example, particularly adults, make fewer dispositional attributions than do American subjects (Miller, 1984). They are much more likely to explain behavior in terms of the situation or the environment than in terms of personality traits, abilities, or inabilities.

fundamental attribution error the tendency to overuse internal attributions when explaining behavior

As you might imagine, there are other biases that may lead us to make incorrect attributions about ourselves or others. One is called the **just world hypothesis**, in which people take on the belief that we live in a just world where good things happen only to good people and bad things happen only to bad people (Lerner, 1965, 1980). It's a sort of "everybody ultimately gets what they deserve" mentality. We see this bias (fallacy would be better) when we see people claim that victims of rape often "ask for it by the way they dress and act." In fact, even the victims of rape sometimes engage in self-blame in an attempt to explain why in the world they were singled out for a crime in which they were the victim quite by chance (Janoff-Bulman, 1979).

just world hypothesis the belief that the world is just and that people get what they deserve

Another bias that affects our attributions is the **self-serving bias**. It occurs when we attribute successes or positive outcomes to personal, internal sources and failures or negative outcomes to situational, external sources (Harvey & Weary, 1984; Miller & Ross, 1975). We tend to think that when we do well it is because we're able, talented, and work hard, whereas when we do poorly it is the fault of someone or something else. "Boy, didn't I do a great job of painting that room" versus "The room looks so shoddy because the paint was cheap and the brush was old" would be an example. (Perhaps you recall from our discussion of depression in Topic 12B that some cognitive theorists argue that some depression can be explained as a failure to apply the self-serving bias. That is, some people may get into the habit of blaming themselves for failures and negative outcomes

self-serving bias the tendency to attribute our successes to our own effort and abilities, and our failures to situational, external sources

actor-observer bias *the overuse of internal attributions to explain the behaviors of others and external attributions to explain our own behaviors*

regardless of where the real blame resides or regardless of whether there even is any blame to attribute.)

Yet another attribution error is the so-called **actor-observer bias** (Jones & Nisbett, 1971; Monson & Snyder, 1977). What we find here is a discrepancy between the way we explain our behavior (as actor) and the way we explain someone else's (as observer). What usually happens is that we use external attributions when we talk about why we do things. The basis of our explanation has to do with something about the situation. "I took that class because the instructor is entertaining." "I am dating Bill because he's so caring and considerate." "I went there because the rates were lower than anyplace else." When we explain someone else's behaviors we are more likely to use internal attributions and refer to characteristics of the person whose behaviors we have been observing. "Oh, he took that class because he's so lazy." "I know that she's dating him only because she wants to be seen with an athlete." "He went there because he wanted to show off."

That we explain our own behaviors in ways different from the ways in which we account for the behaviors of others should not be surprising. For one thing, we have much more information about ourselves and our own past experiences than we do about anyone else. In fact, the more information we have about someone else, the less likely we are to use internal attributions to explain his or her behaviors. Also, in any situation, the actor gets a different view of what is happening than does the observer. In other words, the actor and the observer both attempt to attribute the cause of behavior on the basis of different information.

Before You Go On

What are the two basic types of attribution?

Describe some ways in which attributions can be distorted or biased.

INTERPERSONAL ATTRACTION

Interpersonal attraction can be seen as an attitude toward another person—a favorable and powerful attitude at that. Interpersonal attraction reflects the extent to which a person has formed positive feelings and beliefs about another person and is prepared to act on those affects and cognitions. In this section, we'll review some of the processes that influence how these attitudes about others are formed.

Theories of Interpersonal Attraction

Social psychologists have put forth several theoretical models to explain the bases of interpersonal attraction. Let's briefly review four such theories.

Probably the simplest and most straightforward theory is one we can call the *reinforcement model* (Clore & Byrne, 1974; Lott & Lott, 1974). This model claims that we are attracted to people we associate with rewards. We are thus attracted to (have positive attitudes toward) those people we associate with rewarding experiences. It also follows that we'll tend not to be attracted to those we associate with punishment. One implication of this point of view is that you're going to like your instructor more, and seek him or her out for other classes in the future, if you get (or earn) a high grade in his or her class than you will if you get a low grade.

Another popular theory of interpersonal attraction is not as direct. It is called the *social exchange model* (Kelley & Thibault, 1978; Thibault & Kelley, 1959). According to this model, what matters most is a comparison of the costs and benefits of establishing or maintaining a relationship. For example, Leslie may judge that John is physically attractive, but that entering into an intimate relationship with him is not worth the grief she would get from friends and family, who believe John to be lazy and untrustworthy. On the other hand, if Leslie has just gone through a series of failed relationships with other men who were not physically attractive, she might take a chance on John, judging (in her frustration) that he was "worth it." This theory takes into account a series of comparative judgments that people make in social situations. Being attracted to someone else is not just a matter of "Is this a good thing?" It's more a matter of, "Is the reward I might get from this relationship worth the cost, *and* what other alternatives exist at the moment?"

A third theoretical approach to interpersonal attraction is an *equity model*, which is more an extension of social exchange theory than a departure from it (Greenberg & Cohen, 1982; Walster et al.,1978). Social exchange theory added the notion of cost to that of reward. Equity theory adds the appraisal of rewards and costs for both parties of a social relationship. That is, you may feel a relationship is worth the effort you have been putting into it, but if your partner in that relationship does not feel likewise, the relationship is in danger. What matters, then, is that both (or all) members of a relationship feel they are getting a fair deal (equity). Notice two things about this model: (1) Both members of a relationship do not have to share rewards equally. What matters is that the ratio of costs to rewards be equitable for both members. (2) If one person were to feel that he or she is getting more from a relationship than is deserved (on the basis of costs and compared to the other's rewards), the relationship would not be equitable and would be jeopardized. The best relationships are those in which all members receive an equal ratio of rewards to costs.

A more recent approach to understanding close interpersonal relationships is based more on feelings or affect than on cognitions. This model is usually referred to as *attachment theory* (Berscheid, 1994; Feeney & Noller, 1990; Hazan & Shaver, 1987). It suggests that interpersonal relationships can be classified into one of three types depending on the attitudes one has about such relationships (descriptions from Shaver, Hazan, & Bradshaw, 1988, p. 80):

Secure: "I find it relatively easy to get close to others and am comfortable depending on them and having them depend on me. I don't often worry about being abandoned or about someone getting too close to me."

Avoidant: "I am somewhat uncomfortable being close to others; I find it difficult to trust them completely, difficult to allow myself to depend on them. I get nervous when anyone gets too close, and often, partners want me to be more intimate than I feel comfortable being."

Anxious/ambivalent: "I find that others are reluctant to get as close as I would like. I often worry that my partner doesn't really love me or won't stay with me. I want to merge completely with another person, and this desire sometimes scares people away."

One of the things that makes attachment theory appealing is the evidence that suggests that one's "style" of forming attachments with others is remarkably stable throughout the life span. It may be that the types of interpersonal relationships we form as adults are influenced by the types of attachments we developed as very young children.

Finally, I should remind you of a point we first discussed in the context of mate selection (Topic 8D): few people enter into relationships having carefully considered all of the factors these models imply. That is, assessments of reinforcement, exchange, or equity value are seldom made at a conscious level; nor do we purposively seek out relationships that mirror those we had in childhood (e.g., Bargh, 1993).

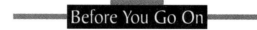

Before You Go On

Briefly summarize four theoretical models that account for interpersonal attraction.

Factors Affecting Interpersonal Attraction

Having reviewed four general models of interpersonal attraction, let's now look at some empirical evidence related to attraction. What determines who you will be attracted to? What factors tend to provide the rewards, or the positive reward/cost ratios, that serve as the basis for strong relationships? We'll consider four common determinants of interpersonal attraction.

Reciprocity, our first principle, is perhaps the most obvious. Not surprisingly, we tend to value and like people who like and value us (Backman & Secord, 1959; Curtis & Miller, 1986). We've already noted, when discussing operant conditioning (Topic 5B), that the attention of others can often be a powerful reinforcer. This is particularly true if the attention is positive, supportive, or affectionate. Research indicates that the value of someone else caring for us is particularly powerful when that someone else initially seemed to have neutral or even negative attitudes toward us (Aronson & Linder, 1965). In other words, we are most attracted to people who like us now, but who didn't originally. The logic here is related to attribution. If someone we meet for the first time expresses nothing but positive feelings and attitudes toward us, we are likely to attribute their reaction internally to the way the person is—rather shallow and the sort of person who likes everybody. But if someone at first were to express neutral, or even slightly negative, feelings toward us and then were to become more and more positive, we might have a different, more positive view of their ability to judge others.

Our second principle, *proximity*, suggests that physical closeness produces attraction. Sociologists, as well as your own experience, will tell you that people tend to establish friendships (and romances) with others with whom they have grown up, worked, or gone to school. Social-psychological studies have consistently found that residents of apartments or dormitories, for example, tend to become friends with those other residents living closest to them (Festinger et al., 1950). Being around others gives us the opportunity to discover just who can provide the interpersonal rewards we seek in friendship.

There may be a phenomenon at work here—associated with proximity—called the **mere exposure phenomenon**. Research, pioneered by Robert Zajonc (1968), has shown with a variety of stimuli that liking tends to increase with repeated exposure to stimuli. Examples of this phenomenon are abundant in everyday life. Have you ever bought a CD you had not heard previously, assuming you would like it because you have liked all the other CDs made by this performer? The first time you listen to your new CD, however, your reaction is lukewarm at best, and you are disappointed with your purchase. Not wanting to feel you've wasted your money, you play the CD a few more times over the next several days. What often happens

mere exposure phenomenon the tendency to increase our liking of people and things as a result of recurring contact

Proximity leads to liking and attraction, which is why teenagers who go to the same school and live in the same neighborhood are likely to form friendships.

is that you soon realize you like this CD. The mere exposure effect has occurred. This also commonly happens in our formation of attitudes about other people. (If this sounds like our discussion of cognitive dissonance, you're right. Why would we have repeated contacts with something or someone we don't like? That would be dissonant— and we end up liking them after all.) Apparently, familiarity is apt to breed attraction, not contempt. I have to add that although there *is* ample evidence that the mere exposure phenomenon is real, there remains considerable disagreement about *why* familiarity and repeated interactions breed attraction (e.g., Birnbaum & Mellers, 1979; Kunst-Wilson & Zajonc, 1980). I also have to add that there *are* limits. Too much exposure may lead to boredom and ultimately to devaluation (e.g., Bornstein, 1989; Bornstein, Kale, & Cornell, 1990).

The perception of *physical attractiveness* is related to interpersonal attraction. Most people are aware of the role of appearance in interpersonal relations and may spend many hours each week doing what they can to improve the way they look. The power of physical attractiveness in the context of dating has been demonstrated experimentally in a classic study directed by Elaine Walster (Walster et al., 1966). University of Minnesota freshmen completed several psychological tests as part of an orientation program. Students were then randomly matched for dates to an orientation dance, during which they took a break and evaluated their assigned partners. The researchers hoped to uncover intricate, complex, and subtle facts about interpersonal attraction, such as which personality traits might mesh in such a way as to produce attraction. As it turned out, none of these complex factors was important. The impact of physical attractiveness was so powerful it wiped out all other effects. For both men and women, the more physically attractive their date, the more they liked that date and the more they wanted to date him or her again. Numerous studies of physical attractiveness followed this one. Some of these studies gave subjects a chance to pick a date from a group of several potential partners (using descriptions and pictures). Not surprisingly, subjects almost invariably selected the most attractive person to be their date (Reis et al., 1980).

The benefits of physical attractiveness can be found in several social situations. Research suggests that attractive persons are often assumed to have other desirable characteristics (Dion et al., 1972; Hatfield & Sprecher, 1986; Vaughn & Langlois, 1983). Attractive persons—both men and women—are routinely judged to be more intelligent, to have happier marriages, to be more successful in their careers and social lives, and so on. This overgeneralization is called the *physical attractiveness stereotype,* which can have serious implications. Anderson and Nida (1978), for example, have shown that the same piece of work (in this case an essay) will be evaluated more favorably when a physically attractive person is thought to have produced it. A study by Clifford and Hatfield (1973) found fifth-grade teachers to judge attractive children to be more intelligent. Another study (Dion, 1972) found that women who were asked to recommend punishment for a child who had misbehaved were more lenient when the child was judged to be physically attractive.

It may have occurred to you that in real life we seldom have the luxury of asking for a date without the possibility of being turned down. When experiments added the possibility of rejection, an interesting effect emerged: subjects no longer chose the most attractive candidate, but selected partners whose level of physical attractiveness was more similar to their own. This behavior is called the **matching phenomenon**, which has been verified by naturalistic observation studies (Walster & Walster, 1969). Even when we consider relationships between or among friends of the same sex, we find that such friends tend to be similar when rated for physical attractiveness (Cash & Derlega, 1978).

matching phenomenon the tendency to select partners whose level of physical attractiveness matches our own

Our fourth principle is *similarity.* There is a large body of research on similarity and attraction, but the findings are consistent, and we can summarize them briefly. Much of this research has been done by Donn Byrne and his colleagues (e.g., Byrne, 1971; Smeaton et al., 1989). It indicates that there is a strong positive relationship between interpersonal attraction and the proportion of attitudes held in common. Simply put, the more similar another person is to you, the more you will tend to like that person—and the more you are likely to believe that that person likes you (Buss, 1985; Davis, 1985; Gonzales et al., 1983; Rubin, 1973). Sensibly, we also tend to be repelled, or put off, by persons we believe to be dissimilar to us (Rosenbaum, 1986).

That similarity enhances interpersonal attraction makes sense in light of the reinforcement theory of attraction previously described. Among other things, agreement with our attitudinal positions is reinforcing; it confirms that we were right all along. And, people who are similar tend to agree with us. Opposites may occasionally attract, but

The more similar another person is to you, the more you will tend to like that person. Our friends tend to be people who share our attitudes and who like to do the things we like to do.

similarity is probably the glue that over the long haul holds together romances and friendships. Obviously, it is this principle that also makes it unusual for people to form significant interpersonal relationships with persons of other cultures or other ethnic groups (e.g., Stephan, 1985).

Before You Go On

What are four determinants of interpersonal attraction?

TOPIC 14A SUMMARY

In this Topic, we've addressed a few important issues related to social cognition: perception and evaluation in a social context. We spent most of our time on attitudes, which are largely cognitive in nature, at least to the extent that they involve mental representations stored in memory, but which also involve affect and action tendencies directed toward some object or event. We have also reviewed the ways in which we develop cognitions about the sources of the behaviors we see around us. In many instances, we make erroneous attributions, based on biased expectations. We ended with a discussion of interpersonal attraction, searching for explanations (attributions again) for why some people get along so well with each other and some do not. Although the impact of group influence can be found in each of the issues we covered in this Topic, social influence and group processes will be the major focuses of Topic 14B.

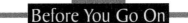

Topic 14B

SOCIAL INFLUENCE

So far, we have reviewed some of the ways in which our social nature has an impact on our cognitions—our perceptions and beliefs about ourselves and others, and how those cognitions influence us in social situations. Now it is time to consider more direct influences of the social world on our everyday behaviors. Although they have much in common, we will deal with the processes of conformity and obedience separately. We'll consider the phenomena of bystander apathy and intervention, listing some of the factors that determine how, or if, someone will intervene on behalf of someone else. We'll end our discussion by reviewing a few other situations in which social influence is a potent force in our lives. In each case, the theme will be the same: how the actions of others influence the behavior of the individual.

CONFORMITY

One of the most obvious and direct forms of social influence occurs whenever we modify our behavior, under perceived pressure to do so, so that it is consistent with the behavior of others, a process referred to as **conformity**. Although we often think of conformity in a negative way, to conform is natural and often desirable. Conformity helps make social behaviors efficient and, at least to some degree, predictable.

When he began his research on conformity, Solomon Asch believed people are not all that susceptible to social pressure when the situation in which they find themselves is clear-cut and unambiguous. Asch thought people would behave independently of group pressure when there was little doubt their own judgments were accurate, and he developed an interesting technique for testing his hypothesis (Asch, 1951, 1956).

A subject in Asch's procedure joined a group seated around a table. In his original study, the group consisted of seven people. Unknown to the real subject, six of those people in the group were confederates of the experimenter; that is, they were "in on" the experiment. A real subject was led to believe that the study dealt with the ability to make perceptual judgments. The participant had to do nothing more than decide which of three lines was the same length as a standard line (Figure 14.6). The experimenter showed each set of lines to the group and then collected responses, one by one, from each member of the group. There were 18 sets of lines to judge, and the only real subject was always the last one to respond.

conformity the changing of one's behavior, under perceived pressure, so that it is consistent with the behavior of others

---

Figure 14.6

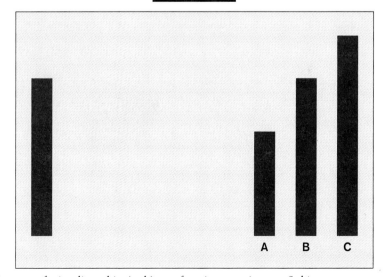

The type of stimuli used in Asch's conformity experiments. Subjects are to say which of the three lines on the right (A, B, or C) equals the line on the left. Associates of the experimenter will occasionally make incorrect choices.

Each of the judgments involved unambiguous stimuli: the correct answer was obvious. On 12 of the 18 trials, however, the confederates gave a unanimous but *incorrect* answer. What would the subjects do? How would they resolve this conflict? Their own eyes were telling them what the right answer was, but the group was saying something else. Should they trust the judgments of the others, or should they trust their own perception?

The results of his initial study surprised Asch, because they did not confirm his original hypothesis. Across all of the trials, when confederates gave "wrong" answers, conformity occurred 37 percent of the time. Subjects responded with an incorrect answer that agreed with the majority on more than one-third of the trials. Moreover, three-quarters of Asch's subjects conformed to the group pressure at least once.

In subsequent studies, Asch tried several variations of his original procedure. In one experiment, he varied the size of the unanimous, incorrect majority. As you might expect, the level of conformity increased as the size of the majority increased (leveling off at three or four people) (Asch, 1956; Knowles, 1983). Subjects gave an erroneous judgment only 4 percent of the time when just one incorrect judgment preceded their own. In another study, Asch found that subjects gave an erroneous judgment only 10 percent of the time when there was but one dissenter among the six confederates who voiced an accurate judgment before the subjects gave theirs. In other words, when the subjects had any social support for what their eyes had told them, they tended to trust their own judgment. Other researchers have demonstrated that the minority opinion (say, one dissenter) can have significant effects on conformity, especially if the minority position is held with any consistency (e.g., Moscovici et al., 1969, 1985; Nemeth, 1986).

After consistently disagreeing with other subjects in Asch's study, the lone dissenter (here, on the right) begins to doubt his judgment and looks again at the card, even though the correct answer is obvious.

Conformity involves yielding to the perceived pressure of a group. In most circumstances, it is assumed that group members are peers, or at least similar to the conformer. When one yields to the pressure of a perceived authority, the result is obedience. It is to the issue of obedience we turn next.

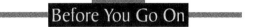

Before You Go On

Briefly describe the methodology and the basic findings of the Asch conformity studies.

OBEDIENCE TO AUTHORITY

The participants in Asch's studies no doubt took the procedure seriously, but the consequences of either conforming or maintaining independence were rather trivial. At worst, Asch's subjects might have experienced some discomfort as a result of voicing independent judgments. There were no external rewards or punishments for their behavior, and there was no one telling them how to respond. Stanley Milgram (1933–1984), a social psychologist at Yale University, went beyond Asch's procedure. Milgram's research has become among the most famous and controversial in all of psychology. His experiments pressured subjects to comply with the demand of an authority figure. The demand was both unreasonable and troubling (Milgram, 1963, 1965, 1974).

All of Milgram's studies involved the same basic procedure. Subjects arrived at the laboratory to find that they would be participating with a second person (again, a confederate of the experimenter). The experimenter explained that the research dealt with the effects of punishment on learning and that one participant would serve as "teacher," while the other would act as "learner." The two roles were assigned by a rigged drawing in which the actual subject was always assigned the role of teacher, while the confederate was always the learner. The subject watched as the learner was taken into a room and wired to electrodes to be used for delivering punishment in the form of electric shocks.

The teacher then received his instructions. First, he was to read to the learner a list of four pairs of words. The teacher was then to read the first word of one of the pairs, and the learner was to supply the second word. The teacher sat in front of a rather imposing electric "shock generator" (Figure 14.7) that had 30 switches, each with a labeled voltage. From left to right, the switches increased by increments of 15 volts, ranging from 15 volts to 450 volts. Labels were printed under the switches on the generator. These ranged from "Slight" to "Moderate" to "Extreme Intensity" to "Danger: Severe Shock." The label at the 450-volt end simply read "XXX."

As the task proceeded, the learner periodically made errors according to a prearranged schedule. The teacher had been instructed

Figure 14.7

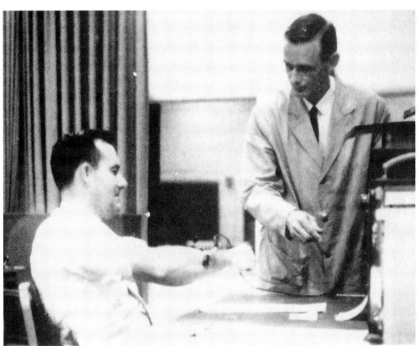

A shock generator apparatus of the sort the "teacher" would use to punish the "learner" in Stanley Milgram's research on obedience. In the bottom photo, the "learner" is given a sample shock.

to deliver an electric shock for every incorrect answer. With each error, the teacher was to move up the scale of shocks, giving the learner a more potent shock with each new mistake. (The learner, remember, was part of the act, and no one was actually receiving any shocks.)

Whenever the "teacher" hesitated or questioned whether he should continue, the experimenter was ready with a verbal prod, such as "Please continue," or "The experiment requires that you continue." If the subject protested, the experimenter would become more assertive and offer an alternative prod: "You have no choice; you must go on," he might say. The degree of obedience was determined by the level of shock at which the teacher refused to go further.

Milgram was astonished by the results of his own study, and the results still amaze us more than twenty-five years later. Twenty-six of Milgram's 40 subjects—65 percent—obeyed the demands of the experimenter and went all the way to the highest shock and closed all of the switches. In fact, no subject stopped prior to the 300-volt level, the point at which the learner pounded on the wall in protest. One later variation of this study added vocal responses from the learner, who delivered an increasingly stronger series of demands to be let out of the experiment. The level of obedience in this study was still unbelievably high, as 25 of 40 subjects (62.5 percent) continued to administer shocks to the 450-volt level.

The behavior of Milgram's subjects indicated that they *were* concerned about the learner. All subjects claimed that they experienced genuine and extreme stress in this situation. Some fidgeted, some trembled, many perspired profusely. Several subjects giggled nervously. In short, the people caught up in this situation showed obvious signs of conflict and anxiety. Nonetheless, they continued to obey the orders of the experimenter even though they had good reason to believe they might be harming the learner.

Milgram's first study was performed with male subjects ranging in age from 20 to 50. A later replication with adult women produced precisely the same results: 65 percent obeyed fully. Other variations of the basic procedure, however, uncovered several factors that could reduce the amount of obedience. Putting the learner and teacher in the same room, or having the experimenter deliver his orders over the telephone, for example, reduced obedience markedly. Another variation produced an interesting parallel to one of the Asch studies we discussed: when the shocks were delivered by a team consisting of the subject and two confederates who refused to give the shocks, full-scale obedience dropped to only 10 percent.

Attribution Errors and a Word of Caution

Upon first hearing about these distressing results, many people tend to think of Milgram's obedient subjects as cold, callous, unfeeling, unusual, or even downright cruel and sadistic people (Safer, 1980). Nothing could be further from the truth. The participants in this research were truly troubled by what was happening. If you thought Milgram's subjects must be strange or different, perhaps you were a victim of what we identified in our last Topic as an *attribution error.* You were willing to attribute the subjects' behavior to (internal) personality characteristics instead of recognizing the powerful situational forces at work.

Attributing negative personality characteristics to the "teachers" is particularly understandable in light of the unexpected nature of the results. Many psychologists in commenting on this research have suggested, in fact, that the most significant aspect of Milgram's findings is that they are so surprising. As part of his research, Milgram asked people, including a group of psychiatrists and a group of ministers, to predict what they would do under these circumstances, and asked them to predict how far others would go before refusing the authority. Respondents predicted very little obedience, expecting practically no one to proceed all the way to the final switch on the shock generator.

A Reminder About Ethics in Research

In reading about Milgram's research, it should have occurred to you that putting subjects in such a stressful situation could be considered ethically objectionable. Milgram himself was concerned with the welfare of his subjects. He took great care to debrief them fully after each session had been completed. He informed them that they had not really administered any shocks and explained why deception had been used. It is, of course, standard practice in psychological experiments to conclude the session by disclosing the true purpose of the study and alleviating any anxiety that might have arisen.

Milgram reported that after debriefing, the people in his studies were not upset over having been deceived. Their principal reaction was one of relief when they learned that no electric shock had been used. Milgram also indicated that a follow-up study performed a year later with some of the same subjects showed that no long-term adverse effects had been created by his procedure. Despite his precautions, Milgram was severely criticized for placing people in such an extremely stressful situation. One of the effects of his research was to establish in the scientific community a higher level of awareness of the need to protect the well-being of human research subjects.

Briefly describe Stanley Milgram's experimental
demonstrations of obedience.

BYSTANDER INTERVENTION

Remember the story of Kitty Genovese with which I started this chapter? Here was a young woman brutally slain in full view of (at least)

38 witnesses, none of whom came to her aid. This tragic event stimulated public concern and sparked a good deal of commentary in the media. People wondered how the witnesses could have shown such a lack of concern for another human being. *Apathy* and *alienation* were terms often used to describe what had happened. One positive outcome of this unfortunate incident was that a program of research was begun that helped establish a basic understanding of the social factors that influence people to intervene or not intervene in such a situation.

Bibb Latané and John Darley, two social psychologists who at the time were at universities in New York City, were not satisfied that terms such as bystander apathy or alienation adequately explained what happened in the Genovese case. They were not willing to attribute people's failure to help to internal, dispositional, or personality characteristics. They were convinced that situational factors make such events possible.

Latané and Darley (1970) pointed out that there are several logical reasons people should *not* be expected to offer help in an emergency. Emergencies tend to happen quickly and without advance warning. Except for medical technicians, fire fighters, and a few other select categories of individuals, people generally are not prepared to deal with emergencies when they do arise. In fact, one good predictor of who will intervene in an emergency turns out to be previous experience with similar emergency situations (Cramer et al., 1988; Huston et al., 1981).

By their nature, emergencies are not commonplace occurrences for most of us. It also goes without saying that the risk of physical injury, as was clearly present in the Genovese case and in the case of Dione Wells (from the beginning of the chapter), is an understandable deterrent to helping. Finally, people may fail to help because they want to avoid any legal consequences that might follow. They simply do not want to get involved.

A Cognitive Model of Bystander Intervention

Latané and Darley (1968) suggest that a series of cognitive events must occur before a bystander can intervene in an emergency (Figure 14.8). First, the bystander must *notice* what is going on. A person who is window shopping and thus fails to see someone collapse on the opposite side of the street cannot be expected to rush over and offer assistance. If the bystander does notice something happen, he or she still must *interpret* the situation as an emergency; perhaps the person who has collapsed is simply drunk or tired and not really having a stroke or a heart attack. The third step involves the decision that it is the bystander's (and not someone else's) *responsibility* to do something.

Even if the bystander has noticed something happening, has interpreted the situation as one calling for action, and has assumed responsibility for helping, he or she still faces the decision of what form of assistance to offer. Should he or she try to give first aid?

Figure 14.8

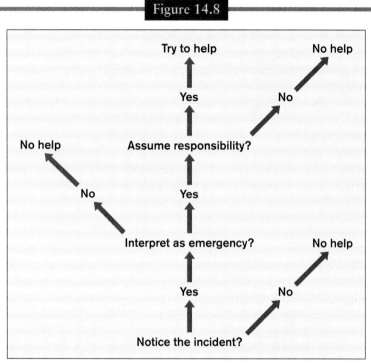

Some of the decisions and outcomes involved as a bystander considers intervening in a perceived emergency situation. (After Latané & Darley, 1968.)

Should he or she try to find the nearest telephone, or simply start shouting for help? As a final step, then, the person must decide how to *implement* his or her decision to act. What is the best first aid under these circumstances? Just where can a phone be found? Thus, we can see that intervening on behalf of someone else in a social situation involves a series of cognitive choices.

A negative outcome at any of these steps will lead to a decision to not offer assistance. When one considers the cognitive events necessary for actually helping, along with the many potential costs associated with intervention, it becomes apparent that the deck is stacked against the victim in an emergency. Ironically, it is the very presence of others that leads to this social-psychological phenomenon (Cunningham, 1984; Shotland, 1985). As Latané and Darley have suggested, perhaps we should be surprised that bystanders ever offer help. There seem to be several psychological processes that account for what is called *the social inhibition of helping,* or *bystander effect.* Let's review just three (Latané & Darley, 1970; Latané & Nida, 1981).

Audience Inhibition. **Audience inhibition** refers to our tendency to be hesitant to do things in front of others, especially when the others are strangers. We tend to be concerned about how others will evaluate us (a point we will return to later). In public, no one wants to do anything that might appear to be improper, incompetent, or

audience inhibition reluctance to intervene and offer assistance in front of others

silly. The bystander who intervenes risks embarrassment if he or she blunders. That risk increases as the number of people present increases. Those people who tend to be particularly sensitive to, or are afraid of, becoming embarrassed in public are most likely to be inhibited (Tice & Baumeister, 1985).

Pluralistic Ignorance. Emergencies tend to be ambiguous: is the man who has collapsed on the street ill or drunk? Is the commotion in a neighboring apartment an assault or a family quarrel that's just a little out of hand? When social reality is not clear, we often turn to others for clues.

While a person is in the process of getting information from others, he or she will probably try to remain calm, cool, and collected, behaving as if there is no emergency. Everyone else, of course, is doing the very same thing, showing no outward sign of concern. The result is that each person is led by the others to think that the situation is really not an emergency after all, a psychological state called **pluralistic ignorance** (Miller & McFarland, 1987). What pluralistic ignorance amounts to is the belief on the part of the individual that only she or he is confused and doesn't know what to do in an emergency, whereas everyone else is standing around doing nothing for some good reason. The group is paralyzed, in a sense, and the phenomenon can be interpreted as a type of conformity—conformity to the inaction of others.

This process was demonstrated clearly in a classic experiment by Latané and Darley (1968, 1970). Columbia University students reported to a campus building to participate in an interview. They were sent to a waiting room and were asked to fill out some preliminary forms. While they did so, smoke began to billow through a vent in the wall. After six minutes (the point at which the procedure was terminated if the "emergency" had not been reported), there was enough smoke in the room to interfere with breathing and prevent seeing across the room.

When subjects were alone in the waiting room, 75 percent of them came out to report the smoke. However, when two passive confederates were in the room with the subject, only 10 percent responded. Those people who reported the smoke did so quickly. Those from the groups who failed to do so generated all sorts of explanations for the smoke: steam, vapors from the air conditioner, smog introduced to simulate an urban environment, even "truth gas." In short, subjects who remained unresponsive had been led by the inaction of others to conclude almost anything but the obvious—that something was very wrong.

Diffusion of Responsibility. In the Kitty Genovese and Dione Wells murders, it was terribly clear that an emergency was in progress. There was very little ambiguity about what was going on. Further, the 38 witnesses in the Genovese case were not in a face-to-face group that would allow social influence processes such as pluralistic ignorance to operate. Latané and Darley suggested that a third important process is necessary to complete the explanation of bystander behavior.

pluralistic ignorance a condition in which the inaction of others leads each individual in a group to interpret a situation as a nonemergency, thus leading to general inactivity

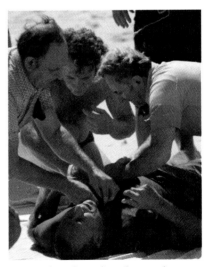

Researchers have found several reasons why people should not be expected to get involved in a perceived emergency situation. Nonetheless, some bystanders will choose to intervene, as was the case with the heart attack victim pictured here.

diffusion of responsibility the
*tendency to allow others to share in
the obligation to intervene*

A single bystander in an emergency situation must bear the full responsibility for offering assistance, but the witness who is part of a group shares that responsibility with other onlookers. The greater the number of other people present, the smaller is each individual's perceived obligation to intervene, a process referred to as **diffusion of responsibility**.

Latané and Darley devised a clever demonstration of this phenomenon. In this study, college students arrived at a laboratory to take part in a group discussion of some of the personal problems they experienced as college students at an urban campus. To reduce the embarrassment of talking about such matters in public, each group member was isolated in his or her own cubicle and could communicate with the others only through an intercom system. Actually there were no other group members, only tape-recorded voices. Thus, there was only one subject in each group, and the perceived size of the group could be manipulated to see if diffusion of responsibility would occur.

The first person to speak mentioned that he was prone to seizures when under stress, such as when studying for an exam. The others, including the actual subject, then took turns talking for about 10 minutes about their problems. A second round of discussion then began again with the seizure-prone student who, as he started talking, began to suffer one of his seizures.

It was obvious that something was wrong. As the "victim" began stammering, choking, and pleading for help, the typical subject became nervous—some trembled. The study had another feature in common with the Genovese episode: subjects could not be sure if any other bystanders (members of the group) had taken any action. (In fact, remember, there were no others.)

As expected, the likelihood of helping decreased as the perceived size of the group increased. Eighty-five percent of those in two-person groups (just subject and victim) left the cubicle to report the emergency. When the subject thought he or she was in a three-person group, 62 percent responded. Only 31 percent of the students who believed they were in a six-person group took any step to intervene. The responsibility for reporting the seizure was clearly divided (diffused) among those thought to be present.

Incidentally, diffusion of responsibility does come in forms less serious in their implications. Those of you with a few siblings can probably recall times at home when the telephone rang five or six times before anyone made a move to answer it, even though the entire family was home at the time. Some of you probably have been at parties where the doorbell went unanswered with everyone thinking that "someone else" would get it.

The Bystander Effect: A Conclusion

The situational determinants of helping behavior continued to be a popular research topic for social psychologists throughout the 1970s.

Many of these studies included a manipulation of the size of the group witnessing the event that created the need for help in the first place. Latané and Nida (1981) reviewed some 50 studies involving nearly 100 helping-not-helping situations. Although these studies involved a wide range of settings, procedures, and participants, the social inhibition of helping (the bystander effect) occurred in almost every instance. Latané and Nida combined the data from all of these studies into a single statistical analysis (a meta-analaysis of the sort introduced in Topic 1B). Their conclusion: There is little doubt that a person is more likely to help when he or she is alone rather than in a group. The bystander effect is a remarkably consistent phenomenon, perhaps as predictable as any phenomenon in social psychology.

Now let's look at a few other situations in which we can see the impact of group influence on the behavior of the individual.

Before You Go On

What effect does the presence of others have on a person's willingness to help in an emergency?

How do audience inhibition, pluralistic ignorance, and diffusion of responsibility account for the lack of bystander intervention?

SOCIAL LOAFING

Latané, Williams, and Harkins (1979) have identified a process of social influence they call **social loafing**: the tendency to work less (to decrease individual effort) as the size of the group in which one is working becomes larger. Their studies had participants shout or clap as loud as possible, either in groups or alone. If people were led to believe their performance could not be identified, they invested less and less effort in the task as group size increased. Other studies (e.g., Harkins & Petty, 1983; Petty et al., 1977; Weldon & Gargano, 1988) have used more cognitive tasks, such as evaluating poetry or brainstorming. The results tend to be consistent: when people can hide in the crowd, their effort (and hence their productivity) declines.

Although social loafing is a widespread phenomenon, it is not *always* predicted when one works in a group setting. Remember our earlier discussions of cultures that can be described in terms of the extent to which they exhibit collectivist or individualist characteristics? As you might predict, social loafing is significantly less likely in those (collectivist) cultures—such as in Japan, China, and other Asian countries—that place a high value on participation in group activities (e.g., Early, 1989; Gabrena et al., 1985). In individualist cultures, such as in the United States, and most Western countries, social loafing can be virtually eliminated if group members believe their effort is special and required for the group's success, or if group members

social loafing the tendency to decrease one's individual work effort as the size of the group in which one is working increases

believe that their performance can be identified and evaluated individually (Harkins, 1987; Harkins & Petty, 1982; Harkins & Syzmanski, 1989; Williams et al., 1981, 1989). Indeed, there are situations in which social influence actually facilitates behavior.

SOCIAL FACILITATION

Many years ago, a psychologist by the name of Norman Triplett (1898) was struck by his observation that bicycle riders competing against other cyclists outperformed those racing against a clock. He then performed what is considered the first laboratory experiment in social psychology. Triplett had children wind a fishing reel as rapidly as possible. They engaged in this task either alone or with another child alongside, doing the same thing. Just as he had noticed in his records of bicycle races, Triplett found that the children worked faster when another child was present. We now know that such an effect sometimes occurs not only with coactors (others engaged in the same task), but if a person performs before an audience. For example, joggers, both male and female, pick up their pace and run faster when running past a woman sitting on a park bench (Worringham & Messick, 1983). When the presence of others improves an individual's performance on some task, we have evidence of what is called **social facilitation**.

social facilitation improved performance due to the presence of others

Numerous studies of these phenomena were performed early in the twentieth century, but with a puzzling inconsistency in their

Because of social facilitation, we tend to perform better when we are in the presence of others—at least when we are engaged in simple or well-rehearsed behaviors. Bicycle riders, for example, ride faster when racing against other riders than when racing against the clock.

results. Sometimes social facilitation would occur, but on other occasions, just the opposite would happen. Sometimes people actually performed more poorly in the presence of others than they did alone, an effect social psychologists call **social interference**. The inconsistency in these findings was so bewildering that psychologists for the most part eventually gave up investigating social facilitation.

social interference impaired performance due to the presence of others

In 1965, Robert Zajonc resurrected the topic of social facilitation by providing a plausible interpretation for the lack of consistency in social facilitation effects. In his examination of the research, Zajonc noticed that social facilitation occurred whenever the behavior under study was simple, routine, or very well learned (e.g., bicycle riding or winding a fishing reel). Interference, on the other hand, tended to occur whenever the behavior involved was complex or not well practiced. Zajonc suggested that the presence of others creates increased arousal, which in turn energizes the dominant (most likely) response under the circumstances. When the dominant response is correct, as with a simple, well-practiced task, facilitation occurs. When the dominant response is incorrect, as with a complex task or one with which we have had little practice, the result is interference (Levine et al., 1993).

You may have experienced this effect yourself if you have ever tried to acquire a skill at a sport totally new to you. Whereas skilled athletes tend to perform better in front of audiences, the novice tends to do better when alone. (There is evidence that even skilled athletes don't always perform better in front of audiences, sometimes "choking" in front of home crowds during important games (Baumeister, 1985). You may have experienced (as a novice, that is) the frustration of finding it difficult to even make contact with a golf ball or tennis ball when there are others standing nearby, watching you.

As an overall conclusion, we may safely assume that social interference and social loafing are more common phenomena than is social facilitation. Although there are occasions in which coworkers or an audience may enhance an individual's performance, the presence of others is more likely to inhibit it—as when we are referring to people in an individualist culture.

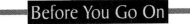
Before You Go On

What can we conclude concerning the effects of social influence on the quality of an individual's performance?

DECISION MAKING IN GROUPS

Many of the decisions we face in our daily lives are the sort made in group settings. Committees, boards, family groups, and group projects for a class are only a few examples. There is logic in the belief that group efforts to solve problems should be superior to the efforts of individuals. One might reason that problem solving ought to be more effective in a group because individuals can pool resources. Having more people available should necessarily mean having more talent and knowledge available. It also seems logical that the cohesiveness of the group might contribute to a more productive effort (and for some groups and some problems, this is exactly the case). But by now we know better than to assume that simply because a conclusion is logical it is necessarily true. In this section, we'll look briefly at two curious phenomena that can occur in the process of group decision making.

When he was an MIT graduate student in industrial management, James Stoner gave subjects in his research a series of dilemmas to grapple with (Stoner, 1961). The result of each decision was to be a statement of how much risk the fictitious character in the dilemma should take. Much to his surprise, Stoner found that the decisions rendered by groups were much riskier than those individual group members had made prior to the group decision. Stoner called this move away from conservative solutions a *risky shift*. For example, doctors, if they were asked individually, might express the opinion that a patient's problem (whatever it might be) could be handled with medication and a change in diet. If these very same doctors were to get together to discuss the patient's situation, they might very well end up concluding that what was called for here was a new and potentially dangerous (risky) surgical procedure.

group polarization the tendency for members of a group to give more extreme judgments following a discussion than they gave initially

Several hundred studies later, we now know that this effect can occur in the opposite direction (Levine & Moreland, 1990; Moscovici et al., 1985). In other words, the risky shift is simply a specific case of a more general **group polarization** effect—the implication being that group participation will make an individual's reactions more extreme, or polarized. Group discussion usually leads to an enhancement of the beliefs and attitudes of the group members that existed before the discussion began. The group process tends to push members further in the direction in which they leaned initially. One explanation for group polarization suggests that open discussion gives group members an opportunity to hear persuasive arguments they have not previously considered, leading to a strengthening of their original attitudes (Isenberg, 1986). Another possibility is that after comparing attitudinal positions with one another, some group members feel pressure to catch up with other group members who have more extreme attitudes (Hinsz & Davis, 1984).

groupthink an excessive concern for reaching a consensus in group decision making to the extent that critical evaluations of input are withheld

Irving Janis (1972, 1983a) has described a related phenomenon of social influence he calls **groupthink**, an excessive concern for reaching a consensus in group decision making to the extent that critical evaluations are withheld. Janis maintains that this style of thinking emerges when group members are so interested in maintaining harmony within the group that differences of opinion are suppressed. Groupthink is most likely to occur in cohesive groups. Alternative courses of action are not considered realistically, and often the result is a poor decision. Janis has analyzed several key historical events, including responding to the Pearl Harbor invasion, planning the Bay of Pigs invasion, and escalating the Vietnam War, in terms of the operation of groupthink. He argues that each of these situations involved a cohesive decision-making group that was relatively isolated from outside judgments, a directive leader who supplied pressure to conform to his position, and an illusion of unanimity (also, McCauley, 1989). When, for example, decisions about women or minorities are made by a group of white males, we might at least suspect that groupthink could be at work.

There *are* circumstances in which groups are more efficient than individuals working alone. As I previously implied, groups are useful when problems are complex and require skills and abilities more likely to be found in a number of different individuals working together. Group decision making can also serve to identify errors individuals might not identify.

Before You Go On

How does social influence affect decision
making in groups?

TOPIC 14B SUMMARY

We are social animals. Our behaviors as well as our feelings and cognitions are often influenced by those around us in our social environments. In this Topic, we have discussed some of the processes of group influence, and many of them seem unfavorable, leading people to

Many of the decisions we face every day are the sort that are best made in groups, whether they be committees, boards, or family groups.

avoid helping someone else in need of assistance, to actually harm someone else in obedient response to an authority figure, to exert less effort, to perform poorly, or to think inefficiently. At the same time, groups are a major part of social life, and many of our individual goals simply cannot be reached alone, without group membership. It is hoped that an awareness of the potentially negative consequences of group activity and the conditions that produce them will enable us to counter obstacles to group productivity.

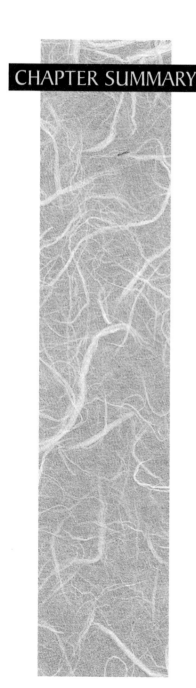

CHAPTER SUMMARY

TOPIC 14A

What is an attitude, and what are its three components?

An attitude is a relatively stable evaluative disposition (positive or negative) directed toward some object or event. An attitude consists of feelings (affects), behaviors (or action tendencies), and beliefs (cognitions). Although the affective and cognitive components of attitudes are often consistent with each other, behavior—influenced by many situational variables—may be inconsistent with the other two major components. /p. 683

Briefly describe three ways in which attitudes might be acquired.

Attitudes may be acquired through classical conditioning: after positive or negative experiences are associated with an attitudinal object, the object by itself comes to produce a positive or negative evaluation. Attitudes may develop as a result of direct reinforcement (operant conditioning), or they may be formed when they are vicariously reinforced (observational learning). /p. 685

What is cognitive dissonance, and how does it operate to produce attitude change?

Cognitive dissonance is an unpleasant state of tension between or among cognitions that may occur when we behave in a fashion inconsistent with our attitudes. Because we are motivated to reduce dissonance, we *may* do so by changing our attitudes so that they become consistent with the way we behave. /p. 688

What is cognitive response theory, and how does it explain attitude change?

What communicator characteristics are known to have an impact on attitude change?

Cognitive response theory tells us that persons receiving a persuasive message actively form cognitions in response to that message. The quality of the arguments in a persuasive communication and one's ability to form supportive or counterarguments are likely to influence the degree of persuasion the communication produces—the "central route" to attitude change. Concern with communicator characteristics and other situational variables reflects a focus on "peripheral routes" to attitude change. Those communicators perceived as being expert or trustworthy are seen as credible sources of information and are hence more persuasive. /*p. 691*

What are the two basic types of attribution?

Describe some ways in which attributions can be distorted or biased.

Attributions are cognitions we use to explain the sources of the behaviors we see in our social worlds. The two basic types of attribution are internal and external. Internal attributions identify the source of behavior as being within the person and are also called dispositional attributions. External attributions find the source of behaviors to be outside the person and are also called situational attributions. The *fundamental attribution error* leads us to overuse internal, or personal, attributions when explaining behaviors. Those persons who hold to the *just world hypothesis* are likely to believe that good things happen to good people only and that bad things happen to bad people only, who in some way deserve their misfortune. The *self-serving bias* has us tend to attribute our successes to our own efforts and actions and our failures to other, external factors. The *actor-observer* bias refers to the tendency to use external attributions to explain our own (as actor) behaviors, and internal attributions to explain the behaviors of others (as observer). /*p. 694*

Briefly summarize four theoretical models that account for interpersonal attraction.

The *reinforcement model* claims that we tend to be attracted to those persons we associate with rewards or reinforcers. The *social exchange model* adds the notion of cost to the equation, claiming that what matters in interpersonal relationships is the ratio of the benefits received to the costs invested in that relationship. The *equity model* suggests that both or all members of a relationship assess a benefit/cost ratio, and the best, most stable relationships are those in which the ratio is nearly the same (equitable) for both or all parties, no matter what the value of the benefits for any one member of the relationship. *Attachment theory* tells us that there are only a few relationship styles, and that people are consistent over their lifetime in the style they use when relating to others. /*p. 696*

What are four determinants of interpersonal attraction?

The principle of *reciprocity* states that we tend to like people who like us back. This is the most straightforward example of interpersonal attraction being based on a system of rewards. *Proximity* promotes attraction, in part, by means of the mere exposure effect: being near another person on a frequent basis gives us the opportunity to see what that other person has to offer. We also tend to be attracted to people we judge *physically attractive*. Finally, the principle of *similarity*

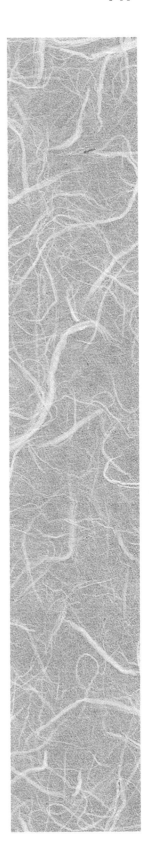

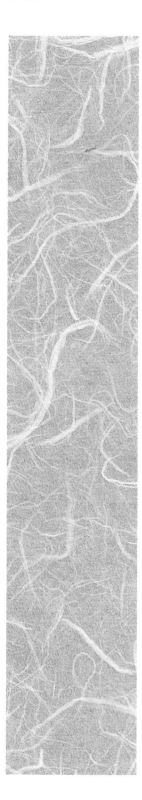

suggests that we tend to be attracted to those we believe similar to ourselves. /p. 700

TOPIC 14B

Briefly describe the methodology and the basic findings of the Asch conformity studies.

In Asch's studies, people made simple judgments about unambiguous perceptual stimuli: the length of lines. On some trials, confederates gave judgments that were clearly incorrect before the actual subject had a chance to respond. Although there were situations in which yielding to perceived group pressure could be lessened, many of Asch's subjects followed suit and conformed. /p. 703

Briefly describe Stanley Milgram's experimental demonstrations of obedience.

Subjects in Milgram's experiments were led to believe they were administering more and more potent shocks to another subject in a learning task. Whenever they hesitated to deliver shocks, an authority figure, the experimenter, prodded them to continue. All subjects obeyed to some degree, and nearly two-thirds delivered what they thought was the most intense shock, even over the protests of the learner. The individuals who obeyed in Milgram's experiments were willingly neither cruel nor inhumane. Rather, the experimenter created a powerful social situation that made it difficult to refuse the authority figure's orders. /p. 706

What effect does the presence of others have on a person's willingness to help in an emergency?

How do audience inhibition, pluralistic ignorance, and diffusion of responsibility account for the lack of bystander intervention?

The likelihood that someone will intervene on behalf of another in an emergency situation is lessened as a function of how many others (bystanders) are present at the time. Several factors have been proposed to account for this phenomenon. *Audience inhibition* is the term used to describe the hesitancy to intervene in front of others, perhaps for fear of embarrassing oneself. *Pluralistic ignorance* occurs when others lead one to think (by their inactivity) that nothing is wrong in an ambiguous emergency situation. *Diffusion of responsibility* causes a member of a group to feel less obligated to intervene (less responsible) than if he or she were alone. Each of these processes tends to discourage helping and is more likely to operate as the number of persons present increases. /p. 711

What can we conclude concerning the effects of social influence on the quality of an individual's performance?

The data suggest that as group size increases, social loafing increases. That is, one is less likely to invest full effort and energy in the task at hand as a member of a group than he or she would if working alone (at least in Western, individualist cultures). It is also the case that the quality of one's performance tends to suffer when one works in a group, a phenomenon called social interference. On the other hand, when tasks are simple or well rehearsed, performance may be enhanced, a process called social facilitation. /p. 713

How does social influence affect decision making in groups?

There are some advantages to problem solving in a group setting. With proper leadership and communication, the combined expertise present in a group may provide better solutions and provide a better check on errors than we might find if individuals worked independently. On the other hand, *group polarization*, the tendency of group discussion to solidify and enhance preexisting attitudes, and *groupthink*, the unwillingness to promote an unpopular view in front of others in a group, operate to detract from group decision making. /p. 715

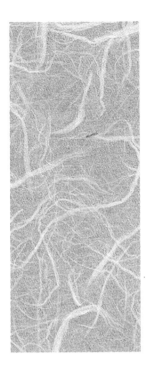

INDUSTRIAL-ORGANIZATIONAL, ENVIRONMENTAL, AND SPORT PSYCHOLOGY

CHAPTER OUTLINE

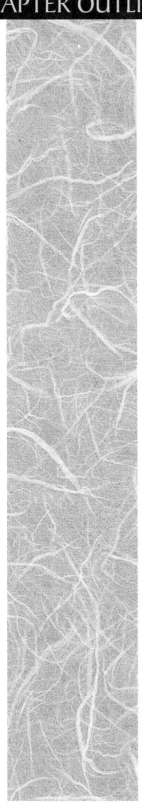

TOPIC 15A INDUSTRIAL-ORGANIZATIONAL PSYCHOLOGY
Fitting the Person to the Job
    Defining "Good Work": The Job Analysis
    Selecting People Who Can Do Good Work
    Training People to Do Good Work
    Motivating People to Do Good Work
Fitting the Job to the Person
    Job Satisfaction
    Job Satisfaction and Work Behaviors
    Worker Safety
TOPIC 15A SUMMARY

TOPIC 15B ENVIRONMENTAL AND SPORT PSYCHOLOGY
Psychology and the Environment
    Space and Territory
    Life in the City: An Example
    Noise, Temperature, and Environmental Toxins
    Changing Behaviors That Impact on the Environment
Psychology and Sport
    The Psychological Characteristics of Athletes
    Maximizing Athletic Performance
TOPIC 15B SUMMARY

CHAPTER SUMMARY

reg Farwell is plant manager for Acme Flange Fabrication, Inc., a mid-sized manufacturing company in the Midwest that is experiencing several problems. Pressures from foreign imports and a reduced demand for the high-quality flanges that AFF makes have reduced profits severely.

Greg sees the need for increased productivity as an opportunity to introduce some changes at AFF. He wants to introduce some of the new technological advances that have revolutionized flange manufacturing. He also realizes that to return Acme Flange to its once highly respected status in the industry, management will have to take a new look at techniques to motivate a group of talented but discouraged factory workers.

Installing new equipment and restructuring the organization means retraining at all levels of the company. In some cases, retraining will be directed at the acquisition of new skills; in others, it will mean fostering changes in attitudes and communication styles. To complicate matters, contract negotiations with the local union begin in two weeks. Farwell wants to be sure the changes he is proposing can be implemented while enhancing job satisfaction among AFF employees. He knows he will have to address concerns about such issues as day care, flexible time schedules, and pregnancy leaves.

Two other realities are on the mind of the plant manager. One is visits from government agencies. Inspectors will be by soon to check the plant for potential safety violations. Even more troublesome is the anticipated visit from the Environmental Protection Agency. There has been concern about waste water from the plant polluting area streams and well water.

Although Greg Farwell is the plant manager of a manufacturing firm, many of the tasks he has before him are psychological in nature. Farwell's challenges have more to do with affect, behavior, and cognition than with steel and flanges. His challenges reflect many of the concerns of industrial-organizational psychology. We will see what psychology has to say about these issues in this chapter.

e have noted repeatedly that psychology has many practical applications in everyday life. Indeed, this is one of the major themes introduced in Topic 1A. In this chapter, we continue our focus on the application of psychological principles to real-world events and issues.

Topic 15A looks at industrial-organizational, or I/O, psychology. Industrial-organizational psychologists specialize in the study of affect, behavior, and cognition in work settings. Psychologists in this field are concerned with applying psychological principles in order to improve the effectiveness and efficiency of business and industrial organizations. This does not mean that I/O psychologists are "company people," concerned only with the interests of management. The I/O psychologist cares about the workplace in general, and that includes a consideration of workers' needs, as well as management's needs.

The second Topic of this chapter will focus on two other subfields of applied psychology. First, we'll sample some of the work of psychologists concerned about interactions between the physical environment and one's psychological state of well-being. We'll examine the notions of space and territory, using life in a big city as an example. We'll review some evidence concerning the psychological reactions to environmental pollutants, such as noise, temperature, and toxins. We will see how psychologists can help people change their behaviors so as to have a positive impact on the environment. Finally, we'll look at a few ways in which psychologists apply their knowledge to the world of sports and athletics.

Topic 15A

INDUSTRIAL-ORGANIZATIONAL PSYCHOLOGY

Industrial-organizational (I/O) psychology is one of the fastest growing areas of specialization in psychology (Zedeck, 1987). We will examine two major thrusts of I/O psychology. First, we'll discuss how best to fit the right person to a given job. This will entail a brief discussion of what is meant by "doing a good job," followed by a consideration of how we can select, train, and motivate someone to do that job well. Then, we'll examine how best to fit the job to the person, which will involve examining such matters as the quality of work life, job satisfaction, and safety in the workplace. Each of the issues is relevant and meaningful to anyone who has ever entered the world of work.

FITTING THE PERSON TO THE JOB

It is to everyone's advantage to have the best available person assigned to do any particular job. Employers benefit from having workers who are well qualified and well motivated to do their work. Employees also benefit from being assigned tasks they enjoy and that are within the scope of their talents and abilities. When I was a college student, a summer job required that I fill in for another employee and drive a large truck loaded with milk from a dairy in upstate New York to various locations in New York City. That I ever got that milk delivered had more to do with good luck and youthful enthusiasm than anything else. It took me twice as long as the regular driver to make the deliveries, and, to say the least, I did not enjoy spending a summer's day being lost in New York City with a truck filled with milk. I was clearly not the best worker for the task.

What is involved in getting the best person to do a job? The relevant issues from the perspective of the I/O psychologist are personnel selection, training, and motivation. That is, one way to get a person to do good work is to *select* and hire a person who already has the ability and the motivation to do that work. On the other hand, we may choose to *train* people to do good work. We may also have to face the task of *motivating* people with ability to do good work. These are the processes we examine in this section. However, before we can select, train, or motivate someone to do a job, we need to understand the nature of the job itself.

Defining "Good Work": The Job Analysis

Assume you are an I/O psychologist hired by a company to help select a manager for one of its retail stores in a local shopping center. You could not begin to tell your employers what sort of person they were looking for until you had a complete description of the job this new manager was to do. In general terms, you would have to know the duties and responsibilities of a store manager in this company. Then, you could translate that job description into a set of measurable characteristics a successful store manager should possess. In other words, you would begin by doing a **job analysis**, "the systematic study of the tasks, duties, and responsibilities of a job and the knowledge, skills, and abilities needed to perform it" (Riggio, 1990, p. 59).

job analysis a complete and specific description of a job, including the qualities and behaviors required to do it well

Typically, writing a complete job analysis is a two-step process. The first step involves compiling a complete description of what a person in that job is expected to do. There are many sources of information one might use to generate such a description. Most companies have job descriptions for their employees, but these are usually stated in very general terms, such as "supervise workers in the store; maintain acceptable levels of sales; prepare payrolls; monitor inventory; schedule work loads," and the like. A job analysis may be written by either a person who is presently in the job in question, or a supervisor of that job position. What matters most is that the person doing the job analysis have full knowledge of the skills required (Fleishman & Mumford, 1991; Landy et al., 1994).

To be useful, a job analysis must be more specific and should describe the actual *behaviors* engaged in by someone in a given position. Does a store manager have to know how to operate the cash

One of the important roles of industrial/organizational psychologists is to help employers make the best possible personnel decisions. The first step is doing a job analysis to get a complete description of the job and of the personal qualities and behaviors required to do that job well.

register and inventory control devices? Does the manager deal with the sales staff on a one-to-one basis or in groups? Are interactions with employees informal, or are there regularly scheduled, formal meetings that need to be organized? To what extent is the store manager responsible for training and development? Will he or she be involved in labor negotiations? This list of questions can be a long one. The underlying concern at this level of analysis is, "On a daily basis, just what does a store manager do?"

Once duties and responsibilities have been specified in behavioral terms, the second step requires that these be translated into terms of measurable personal characteristics. That is, one determines the **performance criteria** required to do a job well. The goal is to generate a list of characteristics a person in a position should have in order to do that job as well as possible.

performance criteria specific behaviors or characteristics a person should have in order to do a job as well as possible

There are several areas that might be explored at this point. Smith (1976), for example, distinguishes between what she calls "hard" (or objective) criteria and "soft" (or subjective) criteria. The former come from available data—salary, number of units sold, number of days absent, and the like. Soft criteria require a degree of judgment—sense of humor, congeniality, creativity, and so on. Let's use an academic example. Suppose your psychology department wants to give an award to its "outstanding senior." Some of the criteria that determine which student has done a good job and is worthy of the award may be hard data—senior standing, a certain grade point average, and a minimum number of psychology classes. Other criteria may be subjective, or soft. The department may want to give this award to a student only if he or she is well known to many members of the faculty, has impressive communication skills, or has been active in the Psychology Club. These criteria require the judgment of those who are making the award. Most job analyses involve considering both hard (objective) and soft (subjective) criteria.

Remember that the basic task here is to find the best available person to do a job as well as possible. If we are not fully aware of the demands of a job and have not translated those demands into specific performance criteria, we will have difficulty determining if we have found the right person. In other words, we need to build in procedures early on by which our selection program can be evaluated (Dunnette & Borman, 1979). Once a job analysis has been completed—once we know what an applicant will be expected to do on the job *and* once we have translated those tasks into measurable criteria—we are ready to begin designing an assessment process.

Before You Go On

What is involved in doing a job analysis?

Selecting People Who Can Do Good Work

Personnel selection involves not only devising procedures to help one decide which of many applicants to hire, but also making decisions relating to retention, promotion, and termination (Guion & Gibson, 1988). If the job analysis has been done properly, the I/O psychologist has a complete list of those duties and characteristics in which the employer is interested. The task now is to find the individual who has those characteristics.

Some useful information can be gleaned from a well-constructed *application form*. A job application form can serve three useful functions. (1) It can be used as a rough screening device. Some applicants may be denied simply because they do not meet some basic requirement for the job, such as a minimal educational level or specified job experience. (2) It can supplement or provide cues for interviewing. Bits of data from application forms can be pursued later, during in-depth interviews. (3) It provides biographical data (called *biodata*), including educational and work history, that may be useful in making direct predictions about a candidate's potential. Some I/O psychologists list biographical information of the sort that can be uncovered on job application forms as the best source of data for predicting success on the job (Baley, 1985; Drakeley et al., 1988; Muchinsky, 1987; Mumford et al., 1992; Reilly & Chao, 1982; Rothstein et al., 1990).

An integral part of many personnel selection procedures is the *employment interview*. I have already commented (Topic 9B) on the dangers of relying too heavily on information gained through interviews. Unstructured interviews in particular are subject to error. For one thing, interviews, by their very nature, involve the interaction of two people: the interviewer and the person being interviewed. Among other things, the biases of the interviewer, conscious or unconscious, may influence the results of an interview (Cash & Kilcullen, 1985). Nonetheless, the interview remains widely used in the United States

The interview remains an integral part of the employee selection process, although research has shown that unstructured interviews may be subject to bias and misinterpretation.

(Arvey & Campion, 1982; Thayer, 1983). In addition, there are considerable individual differences in interviewer skill. That is, some interviewers consistently obtain more useful (or valid) information than do others (Thayer, 1983; Zedeck et al., 1983). Training interviewers to be sensitive to personal biases can improve the validity of the technique.

Over the last few years, the outlook for the use of the interview has become more positive and optimistic. In large measure, this is because of the increased use of the *structured interview* (Harris, 1989; Weisner & Cronshaw, 1988). As the name implies, structured interviews consist of a carefully prescribed series of questions asked of all applicants in the same order. Structured interviews take away some of the interviewer's latitude in exploring various issues, but they are much more valid than are unstructured interviews (Arvey et al., 1987; Landy et al., 1994; Schmitt & Robertson, 1990; Weisner & Cronshaw, 1988).

Beyond the job application form and the interview, personnel selection often involves the administration and interpretation of *psychological tests* (see Topic 9A). Many tests are designed to assess only one specific characteristic of the applicant (finger dexterity, for example, which a job analysis may indicate to be very relevant for an assembly line worker in an electronics plant). Others are more general, assessing a number of skills and abilities. Tests of intelligence or personality traits may be called for, particularly when evaluating candidates for managerial or supervisory positions. There are literally hundreds of published paper-and-pencil tests designed to measure a variety of characteristics, from typing skills, to mechanical aptitude, to leadership style, to motivation for sales work, to critical thinking skills. Some popular tests of general traits or abilities are being modified to focus more sharply on work-related applications (e.g., Gough, 1985). In general, the data suggest that the most useful of all psychological tests are those that assess some sort of cognitive function, such as ability or achievement tests (Guion & Gibson, 1988).

One of the most controversial questions in all of psychology (not just I/O) is whether tests of general intelligence are better predictors of job performance than are tests of specific cognitive ability or aptitude (Ackerman, 1992; Ackerman & Kanfer, 1993; Hunter, 1986; Landy et al., 1994; McClelland, 1993; Ree & Earles, 1992, 1993; Schmidt & Hunter, 1993; Sternberg & Wagner, 1993). At this point in the controversy, the best answer now seems to be "it depends." It depends on which tests of which behaviors are involved whether general measures are superior or equal to specific measures.

From time to time, it may be necessary to construct one's own test to assess some unique or special ability not measured by available instruments. A form of testing found in employment settings is called *situational testing,* in which applicants are given the opportunity to role-play the task they may be hired to do (Lin, Dobbins, & Farh, 1992; Weekley & Gier, 1987). If you were going to hire someone to work at the counter of your dry cleaning business, for instance, you might ask an applicant how he or she would respond to an irate customer whose suit was damaged in cleaning. Actually role-playing the part of an angry customer while the applicant plays the part of employee might provide very useful information.

An important consideration when using psychological tests for personnel decisions is the demonstrated validity of such tests. What is particularly crucial in employee testing is that the employer be able to demonstrate that performance on a test is actually related to performance on the job (e.g., Landy et al., 1994; Schmidt, Ones, & Hunter, 1992).

Some corporations use what is called an assessment center approach to select management personnel (both for initial hiring and promotion decisions). This approach gives evaluators opportunities to observe applicants in various social situations and under stress. The assessment center was first introduced during World War II as a device for selecting candidates for the Office of Strategic Services, now known as the CIA. The first nongovernmental application was by AT&T in the 1950s, but it wasn't until the 1960s that the approach was widely used in the private sector for selecting and promoting executives in business and industry (Bray et al., 1974).

An assessment center involves an intensive period of evaluation, typically for three or four days. Several applicants (usually 6 to 12) are brought together with executives of the company and a team of psychologists. In addition to batteries of standard paper-and-pencil tests and interviews, the applicants are given situational tests in which their behaviors in situations similar to those they might encounter on the job can be observed. One method is called the **in-basket technique**. Applicants are given a variety of tasks, memos, and assignments of the sort they might encounter in a typical day at the office (as previously determined through a job analysis). They can then be observed as they attempt to sort out and deal with the imaginary issues they find in their in-baskets.

Assessment centers are popular, and their usefulness is virtually taken for granted (Gaugler et al., 1987; Hinrichs, 1976; Saal & Knight, 1988; Schmidt et al., 1992; Schmitt, Schneider, & Cohen,

in-basket technique an assessment technique requiring applicants to respond to a variety of situations that might be encountered in a typical workday

assessment center a personnel selection procedure in which persons are tested, interviewed, and observed in a number of stressful situations by a team of evaluators

1990). Although the technique can be useful for predicting general outcomes, such as who is likely to get promoted or get larger salaries, it does not seem very useful in making specific predictions regarding specific behaviors (Hunter & Hunter, 1984; McEvoy & Beatty, 1989; Pynes & Bernardin, 1989; Zedeck & Cascio, 1984). "The research question seems not to be whether to use assessment centers but how to understand what goes on in them, how to evaluate the results, and how to make them better" (Guion & Gibson, 1988).

It may not always be practical or possible to find people who have the abilities, characteristics, and motivation for doing the type of work we have in mind. It may be that the major personnel issues facing an organization involve training and motivating existing workers to do good (or better) work. Let's first look at training.

====== Before You Go On ======

**What are some of the sources of information
that can be used in making personnel decisions?**

Training People to Do Good Work

The training of employees is one of the major concerns of business, industry, and government. The cost of such training runs into billions of dollars every year. Training or retraining present employees will become even more critical in the years ahead as the number of people entering the work force decreases (Offermann & Gowing, 1990; Tannenbaum & Yukl, 1992). Additional training needs stem from the move of many businesses to open operations overseas. Training concerning cultural issues in foreign countries is seen as essential for such businesses (e.g., Brislin, 1990, 1993; Erez & Early, 1993; Tung, 1988).

training a systematic and intentional process of altering the behaviors of employees to increase organizational effectiveness

In the context of industrial-organizational psychology, **training** means "a systematic intentional process of altering behavior of organizational members in a direction which contributes to organizational effectiveness" (Hinrichs, 1976). In other words, training is an activity intended to increase the skills or abilities of employees to do their job. Training implies a systematic intervention, as opposed to a hit-or-miss approach to instruction. Training programs have been found to be successful in many organizational settings, with various types of personnel, and as indicated by a number of productivity criteria, including quantity and quality of work, cost reduction, turnover, accident reduction, and absenteeism (Katzell & Guzzo, 1983).

Developing a successful training program is a multifaceted enterprise. Let's review some of the steps involved in designing and implementing a training program. Our discussion is based on a system proposed by Goldstein (1986, 1989) and is summarized in Figure 15.1. Assume for the moment you are an I/O psychologist in charge of training and development for Acme Flange.

Figure 15.1

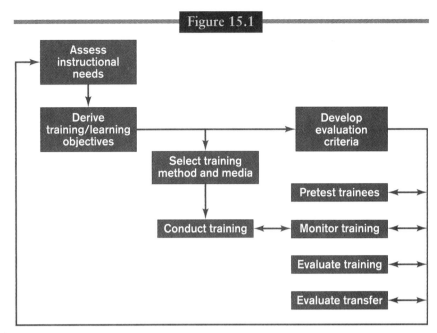

The steps involved in planning and conducting a training program. (From Goldstein, 1986.)

Assessing Training Needs. Training programs are designed to address some need within the organization. So, one of the first things you have to do is a complete assessment of instructional needs. A needs assessment in this context is very much like a job analysis in personnel selection. There are several questions that need to be raised and answered at this critical stage. What is the problem training is supposed to solve? Is production falling? Is there a new product that salespeople need to know about? Is the accident rate getting too high? Is the company reducing the number of employees? The first stage of assessing instructional needs is to state the general goals of your training program. At this point, a difficult question to face is whether a training program is the best solution for a given problem. In fact, the most crucial decision to be made about training is if it is really needed (Latham, 1988). Unfortunately, most companies do not have procedures in place to determine whether training of any sort is even needed (Saari et al., 1988).

The second stage requires translating these general goals into actual training objectives. At this stage, general statements of outcomes will no longer suffice. Now you need *specific* statements of what you expect the training program to accomplish. Just precisely what do you want trainees to know (or be able to do) at the end of the training session that they do not know (or do not do) now? Your training program will usually be evaluated in terms of these specific learning or behavioral objectives.

Training—and retraining—employees to learn new skills and procedures helps keep worker motivation high and helps companies stay abreast of new technologies.

With objectives in mind, but before you begin actual training, you will want to specify criteria by which your training can be evaluated when it is over. Clearly, your criteria for evaluating your program will be closely related to the needs and objectives of the program. For your program evaluation to be effective, it is important to list now—before training begins—how you will evaluate outcomes (Latham, 1988). There are many factors you might want to consider here. Did the trainees develop the skills and acquire the information you intended? How did the trainees feel about the program? Did the training program have an impact on the organizational needs that prompted the training in the first place? To aid in this process, you might want to consider designing a pretest procedure to assess your trainees in terms of their present skill or information level. Such pretesting may provide a means of determining the impact of your program.

Training objectives or outcomes need to be evaluated repeatedly. Evaluating training programs should be an ongoing process. What are the immediate effects of training, if any? Is the training still having the desired impact a month later? Has the training been responsible for any year-end increases in profits? In short, a training program evaluation should not be thought of as a one-shot intervention.

Training Techniques. After you have determined the criteria for assessing outcomes, you now have to decide how you will go about the actual training. Given what you know about your needs and objectives and what you know about your employees, what will be the most efficient type of training mechanism you can use to reach your specified goals?

There are many methods that might be used in a training program. In some cases, bringing workers together for classroom instruction works well. On the other hand, there are situations in which assembling large numbers of workers would be unrealistic. Automobile manufacturers, for example, can hardly be expected to have all car salespeople report to the home office for instruction on improvements in the new models of cars they will be selling. Occasionally, training has to go to the worker—in the form of printed material, audiocassettes, videotaped programs, or live presentations by a trainer—rather than having the worker go to the training.

In any case, as a designer of a training program, you will have many decisions to make about the methods you will use. Should you use "live" instructors, or should information be presented in the form of some media: print, audiotapes, videotapes, videodisks, and the like? Should training be formalized and time-limited, or can trainees be allowed to work individually, at their own pace? Will there need to be hands-on experience? Will training be in groups, or be individually oriented? Will on-the-job training be efficient or disruptive? Can the job be simulated for the purposes of training? As you can see, your options are many, and all should be considered, because some are clearly more effective than others for certain types of training. Too many trainers fall into the habit of using only one or two techniques for a range of needs and objectives. For example, televised instruction may be useful to point out a few new features of an automobile to a salesperson, but ineffective for describing the details of a new health insurance program. By and large, presenting information is less effective than demonstrating it, and involving one's audience as participants (a hands-on, or simulation, approach) is most effective. In general terms, there is no research that tells us that any particular training technique is superior to others in all circumstances. What is needed is a "fit" between present training needs and available training techniques (Campbell, 1988; Tannenbaum & Yukl, 1992; Thornton & Cleveland, 1990).

Having decided on a training technique, you are ready to begin. If you have worked through the procedures outlined so far, you'll find that actually conducting the training will be much easier than if you did not take the time to do so. You will, of course, have to monitor the effectiveness of the training program as it runs its course (review Figure 15.1). Even the best of plans sometimes need to be adjusted during actual training.

Measuring Training Effectiveness. When you have finished your training program, you are ready to consider (again) what may be the most difficult aspect of training and development. You must evaluate the success of your training. Now you need some measure of the extent to which your training transfers to the actual job in the workplace, thus meeting the organizational needs that prompted the training in the first place.

There are many difficulties involved in doing quality evaluations of training programs, and we need not review them all here. I will make only three observations:

1. Training programs can be evaluated at various levels. You may ask participants to rate *how they feel about* or evaluate the program. You may assess the extent to which the training has produced *behavioral changes*. You may measure *how much has*

been learned, perhaps with a formal testing before and after training. (Do you recognize our ABC here?) Or you may go right to the bottom line and ask about *increases in productivity or profit* (Kirkpatrick, 1976).

2. Training programs that do not include ways of evaluating both short-term and long-term effectiveness will generally be of little value. Sadly enough, very few training programs are well evaluated. Many seem to be taken simply on faith or face value because of their logical appeal (Brinkerhoff, 1989; Saari et al., 1988; Schultz & Schultz, 1990).

3. The greater the effort put into the assessment of organizational needs, job analysis, performance criteria, and the establishment of training objectives at the beginning of a training project, the easier it will be to evaluate the program when it is over.

Before You Go On

List some of the factors that need to be considered in the design, implementation, and evaluation of a training program.

People who do good work should be reinforced for their good work. Something as simple as a special parking place in the company parking lot can suffice.

Motivating People to Do Good Work

Let's review for a moment. Our major concern in this section is fitting the person to the job—finding someone to do good work. The first step in this process involves carefully delineating just what is meant by a good job. To this end, one does a job analysis and lists specific performance criteria for the job. An employer can then go through the process of selection, trying to find the best person for the job—someone who already has all of the skills to do the job well. An alternative is to train a present employee to do good (or better) work. There remains an important consideration. There may still be something missing: the motivation to do good work. Being able to do a job well and wanting to do a job well are different matters. Notice, too, that issues of training and motivation are both ongoing concerns. People change and jobs change. Seldom will one training program or one attempt to motivate employees be sufficient over the long term.

As you can imagine, I/O psychologists have long been interested in how to motivate employees to do their best work. When we talk about work motivation, we are referring to three interrelated processes: *arousing* (getting the worker to do a task), *directing* (getting the worker to do the task we want done), and *sustaining* (keeping the worker at the task). As you can also imagine, there is no one answer to questions of how to motivate workers to do a particular job and stick with it. We'll briefly review a few of the more popular approaches.

Values and Expectations. The expectancy theory of work motivation has been around for many years and has been modified by many theorists, but it is best associated with Victor Vroom (1964). Part of the appeal of this approach for I/O psychologists is that it is highly cognitive. **Expectancy theory** says that workers behave rationally and logically, making decisions based on their beliefs, judgments, and expectations.

Vroom's expression of his theory is quite complex, but what it amounts to is that we are motivated to work if (1) we expect rewards to be contingent on levels of performance, and (2) we value the rewards that are being offered. We must also believe that rewards are attainable, that we can actually do the work to a level of performance that will earn those valued rewards.

There are several implications here for employers concerned about motivating employees to do good work. For one thing, employers should see if the outcomes that follow good work are truly valued by the workers. For example, in one company, good work is rewarded by recognition with a plaque and a free trip awarded at the annual company dinner. (The company dinner is also viewed by management as a reward for a profitable year.) What if most of the work force found company dinners a huge bore, plaques an embarrassment, and free trips a nuisance (arranging for transportation, baby-sitters, and so on)? What if the employees would rather have a cash bonus or longer coffee breaks? That is, what if the employees actually believed there was little value in what the company thought were rewards?

Another implication of this theory is that workers understand the relationship between their behaviors and outcomes (e.g., Ilgen & Klein, 1989). Simply, workers need to know what to expect if they behave in a certain way. Which behaviors lead to positive outcomes, and which lead to negative outcomes? Why should an employee work very hard, put in overtime, and take work home on the weekend if he or she has little or no reason to believe that such behaviors will lead to valued rewards? In fact, fewer than one-third of workers believe their compensation is based on their work performance (Plawin & Suied, 1988). You may recognize these issues as related to our earlier discussion of basic learning principles (particularly those in Topic 5B, which covered operant conditioning).

Fair Rewards. Another approach to work motivation, called **equity theory**, is associated with J. Stacy Adams (1965). Equity theory is also cognitive, claiming that what matters most to workers is their perception of the extent to which they are being treated fairly compared to fellow workers in similar work situations.

In Adams's view, workers make a number of social comparisons (or cognitive judgments). They judge how much they are getting from the organization compared to what they are putting into it. That is, the worker judges the extent to which effort, skill, education, experience, and so on (inputs) are being rewarded by salary, praise, fringe benefits, awards, and the like (outcomes). Then, this ratio of inputs and outcomes is compared with a ratio from some other, similarly placed employee. If the relationship is perceived as being approximately the

expectancy theory the view that workers make logical choices to do what they believe will result in their attaining outcomes of highest value

equity theory the view that workers are motivated to match their inputs and outcomes with those of fellow workers in similar positions

same—or equitable—the worker will not be motivated to change. If, however, there is a perceived inequity when compared to the inputs and outcomes of a fellow worker, changes can be predicted. The worker may increase or decrease inputs (work longer or shorter hours; take fewer or more breaks) or try to effect a change in outcomes. What matters most here is not the actual value of what a worker gains for his or her efforts. What matters is the *perception* of equity—what is gained in comparison to others. A worker will be much more willing to maintain effort (input) and take a cut in pay (outcome) if he or she believes that everyone else in the company is taking a similar cut in pay (Locke, 1976; Middlemist & Peterson, 1976; Mowday, 1983).

Goal Setting. How work-related goals are set has been the centerpiece of a number of approaches to worker motivation, particularly that of Edwin Locke (1968; Locke & Latham, 1984). This approach also has a cognitive basis, assuming that workers are motivated to perform a task for which goals are clearly and specifically detailed. In order for goal setting to have a positive influence on a worker's behavior on a task, two things are necessary. First, the goal must be clear. The employee must be clearly *aware* of just what he or she is working for. Second, the employee must *accept* the goal as something worth the effort.

The mechanisms of goal setting for motivating workers have received much research interest. Here are some general conclusions. (1) Difficult but achievable goals tend to increase productivity more than easy goals. The issue here seems to hinge on the acceptance of goals as being worthwhile. Goals that are too easy may simply fail to require any change in performance. On the other hand, goals that are perceived as being *too* difficult and beyond the abilities of workers are not likely to be very useful (Erez & Zidon, 1984). (2) Specific, focused, goals are better than general ones. Simply telling workers to "do better" or "do your best" provides little information about what behaviors are expected. (3) Feedback informing workers of their progress toward established goals is important in maintaining motivated behaviors. Feedback delivered soon after an appropriate response is made is more effective than delayed feedback (e.g., Geller, Bruff, & Nimmer, 1985; Geller et al., 1987). (4) Although it may seem reasonable to predict that goals set by employers and employees working together are more effective than goals established by employers alone, the evidence suggests that this is not necessarily the case. What matters most is that the employee be aware of specific goals and accept those goals as reasonable (Locke et al., 1981). Cultural concerns are also relevant here. The more one is used to working together (as in collectivist cultures), the more important it is to be involved in goal setting. In most Western (individualistic) cultures, involvement in goal setting is less critical (e.g., Early, 1986; Erez & Early, 1987).

As you can well imagine, there are many other approaches to work motivation. Some refer directly to motivational concepts we introduced in Topic 10A, in which we discussed motivation in general. That is, some approaches stress the importance of workers' needs (as in Maslow's theory about a hierarchy from basic physiological needs to needs to self-actualize). Some stress the importance of operant conditioning procedures and attention to the consequences of behavior, reinforcers, and punishers (an approach called organizational behavior management when applied in work environments).

Here's a brief summary of our discussion. Workers will tend to be motivated to do a good job if:

1. Clear and specific goals are established and accepted.

2. The goals employers set match workers' expectations and needs.

3. Workers see clearly the relationship between their work performance and accepted outcomes.

4. Workers judge the outcomes that follow from their efforts as being in line with those earned by fellow workers making similar efforts.

5. Workers are given feedback about the nature of their work (Katzell & Thompson, 1990).

Now let's shift our emphasis slightly from a concern about finding and fitting the person to the job to the issue of fitting the job to the person. In large measure, our interest here is with what we call job satisfaction. What can be done to make jobs more satisfying? What are the consequences of doing so?

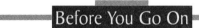

Before You Go On

Briefly summarize some of the factors that affect the motivation of workers to do a good job.

FITTING THE JOB TO THE PERSON

To this point, we have considered what an employer can do to find the best person for a given task. For the remainder of this Topic, we'll change our perspective just a bit and focus on some of the issues relevant to the person on the job in the workplace. There are two issues here. The first has to do with job satisfaction. We'll define the concept, and see if job satisfaction is correlated with job performance measures. The second issue has to do with the design of work and the workplace. How can jobs be designed to maximize such factors as employee safety and health?

Job Satisfaction

Job satisfaction refers to the attitude one holds toward one's work: "a pleasurable or positive emotional state resulting from the appraisal of one's job or job experiences" (Locke, 1976). It amounts to an employee's emotional or affective responses toward his or her job

job satisfaction an attitude; a collection of positive feelings about one's job or job experiences

(Hui, 1990). Although we may refer to job satisfaction in general terms (a "global" approach), an employee's degree of satisfaction can vary considerably for various aspects of the job itself (a "facet" approach) (Riggio, 1990). As you know from your own work experience, you might be reasonably happy with your physical working conditions, unhappy with base salary, pleased with your fringe benefits, satisfied with the level of challenge provided by the job, very dissatisfied with relationships with coworkers, and so on. In fact, there may be as many facets of job satisfaction or dissatisfaction as there are aspects to the job.

A great deal of research has looked for relationships between job satisfaction and personal characteristics of workers. Let's summarize some of that research very briefly. (1) There is a positive correlation between global job satisfaction and age. Younger workers tend to be most dissatisfied with their jobs (Rhodes, 1983), but there also is evidence that older employees develop dissatisfaction with their jobs toward the end of their careers (Kacmar & Ferris, 1989). (2) Data on gender differences in job satisfaction tend to be inconsistent. Gender differences are small (Sauser & York, 1978) and virtually nonexistent when pay, tenure, and education are controlled (Hulin & Smith, 1964). (3) Racial differences in job satisfaction have consistently been shown to be small—in the United States—with whites having more positive attitudes about their jobs than blacks (Weaver, 1980), and Mexican Americans showing more satisfaction than whites. (4) Satisfaction is positively related to the perceived level or status of one's job or occupation, wherein jobs of lowest rank tend to be filled by least satisfied workers (King et al., 1982). (5) The data are few, but there appear to be some cultural differences in job satisfaction. In one survey of ten countries, Sweden had the largest proportion of satisfied workers (63 percent), whereas Japan had the fewest (20 percent) (de Boer, 1978). The low level of job satisfaction in Japan has been reported by others (e.g., Azumi & McMillan, 1976; Lincoln & Kalleberg, 1985). Accounting for the low job satisfaction ratings in Japan, researchers cite strong commitment and motivation for success, coupled with unrealistically high expectations (Cole, 1979; de Boer, 1978). Indeed, the real challenge for I/O psychologists is to determine *why* do or do not any of these differences in job satisfaction occur.

Some I/O psychologists have become interested in a concept that is a bit broader than job satisfaction, called **quality of work life**, or **QWL**. QWL is a difficult concept to define concisely, but may be taken to include factors that influence one's attitude about one's job, such as (1) a sense of respect from supervisors; (2) security (the future of the job); (3) income adequacy and equity (present and future); (4) a sense of self-esteem, challenge, and independence; (5) opportunities for social interaction; (6) a sense of making a real contribution; (7) a relationship between life on the job and life off the job; and (8) active participation in decision making (from Davis & Cherns, 1975; Levine et al., 1984; Stein, 1983). The major concern of I/O psychology has been to develop strategies that improve the quality of work life within an organization (Beer & Walton, 1987; Lawler, 1982; Tuttle, 1983).

quality of work life (QWL) a group of factors concerning one's work that influence one's attitude toward one's job

Although it seems logical that job satisfaction be a predictor of job productivity, the relationship between satisfaction and productivity is tenuous.

It is sometimes difficult to remember that concerns about the welfare of workers and their satisfaction with any part of their job are relatively new in the history of work. Concern for the quality of work life first began to take hold only about sixty years ago (Hoppock, 1935; Mayo, 1933). Before then, workers were often viewed by those who hired them not so much as people, but as pieces of machinery—chosen, hired, and minimally trained to do a particular, often narrowly defined, task (Latham, 1988). The examples are numerous and often shameful—from assembly line work, to mining, to construction, to railroading, to textile mills, and on and on. Until recently there has been little evidence of a concern for employee safety, much less a concern for the quality of work life. Many companies now employ I/O psychologists whose main charge is to recommend changes in organizational structure that will facilitate worker satisfaction and improve the quality of work life. Is this recent emphasis on the well-being of workers motivated only by humane considerations? Is there support for the hypothesis that increased worker satisfaction leads to increased productivity and increased profitability?

Before You Go On

What are meant by job satisfaction and quality of work life?

Job Satisfaction and Work Behaviors

It may seem reasonable to assert that "a happy worker is a productive worker"—that increased job satisfaction will be reflected in increased worker productivity. For the last 50 years, many managers and executives have assumed, pretty much without question, a causal relationship between satisfaction and productivity. In many ways, satisfaction and productivity *are* related, but the relationship is not a simple one and is at best a weak one (Iaffaldano & Muchinsky, 1985). In fact, research often refutes the contention that increased performance *necessarily* results from increased satisfaction (Howell & Dipboye, 1982; Staw, 1984). Over and over, we find contradictory evidence, which, among other things, reflects the difficulties involved in agreeing on operational definitions for the quality of work life and for worker productivity (Hartman et al., 1986). The only conclusion we can draw about these two variables is that in some instances they may be correlated. Cause-and-effect statements are out of the question.

The lack of a consistent relationship between satisfaction and productivity may not be that difficult to explain. Some workers may hate their present jobs, but work hard at them so that they can be promoted to another position they believe they will prefer. Some workers may be very satisfied with their present positions simply because expectations for productivity are low; if demands for productivity increase, satisfaction may decrease. *Increasing productivity may have the effect of increasing satisfaction,* rather than vice versa. A well-motivated employee, who wants to do her best at her job, will be pleased to enter a training program to improve her on-the-job efficiency. Doing the job better leads to pride and an overall increase in satisfaction for this worker; for another, the same training program may be viewed as a ploy on the part of management to make his or her life miserable.

I should not give the impression that job satisfaction is unrelated to *all* work behaviors. There is evidence that job satisfaction measures can be used to aid the prediction of which workers are likely to be absent from work and which are likely to quit [what Saal and Knight (1988) call "withdrawal behaviors"]. As it happens, job satisfaction is not the best predictor of absenteeism [marital status, age, and size of one's work group are better (Watson, 1981)], but the positive correlations are at least consistent (Porter & Steers, 1973). The relationship between dissatisfaction with one's job and turnover seems to be even stronger, although this relationship may not be direct. That is, dissatisfaction may be an important contributing factor, but it is only one of several variables that can be used to explain why one leaves a job. (Many times people are forced to quit their jobs for reasons that have nothing to do with the job or the employer; illness and family concerns, for example.) Nonetheless, the logic that persons who are most unhappy with their work are the ones most likely to leave it does have research support (Mobley, 1977; Muchinsky & Tuttle, 1979).

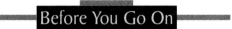
Before You Go On

**Briefly summarize the relationship between job
satisfaction and job productivity.**

Worker Safety

In this final section of Topic 15A, we review one of the oldest concerns of I/O psychologists: safety in the workplace. The statistics on industrial accidents are impressive. One compelling example is provided by Schultz and Schultz (1990, p. 445), who claim that during the peak years of the Vietnam War (1966–1970), more Americans were killed in industrial accidents than in combat. From a different perspective: accidents in the workplace cost the United States well over $100 billion a year in lost wages, insurance and medical expenses, and property loss (Riggio, 1990). The challenge is clear: increase the safety of the workplace. But how? Here are three approaches that I/O psychologists have explored (after Landy, 1989).

The Engineering Approach. This approach attempts to reduce accidents through the design and implementation of safe equipment and procedures. Of the three approaches, this one has been most successful in a wide range of applications. Examples abound. All automobiles now sold in this country are required to have a (third) stop light positioned at eye level. This requirement evolved from a safety study done with taxicabs in San Francisco in a successful attempt to reduce rear-end collisions (Voevodsky, 1974). Complex control panels are engineered with safety in mind so that the most critically important dials, meters, buttons, and switches are in clear view and easy to read and interpret (e.g., Wickens, 1992). Work areas are designed so that there is adequate illumination and sufficient space to move about, and so that scrap materials and trash can be readily removed. Heavy equipment is designed so that it can only be operated in a reasonably safe way. Computer screens have shields to protect against glare and radiation, and keyboards are now engineered to reduce physical damage to the wrist that may result from spending hours at the keyboard.

Engineering approaches to accident prevention may involve the scheduling of work time, and the design of equipment. There is ample evidence of a positive relationship between fatigue and accidents. Scheduling work time (reducing overtime work, for example) to minimize fatigue seems to improve safety (Dunham, 1979).

The Personnel Approach. This approach is based on the popular notion that some people are more "accident prone" than others, or that at least there are some personality traits consistently related to high incidences of accidents. If this were true, safety could be improved by not hiring those applicants who are prone to accidents. The problem is that the basic notion is not true. After many years of trying to identify characteristics of persons likely to behave in dangerous ways, psychologists are about to give up the search. There just don't seem to be people who are, *in general,* any more accident prone than anyone else. (Which, of course, may reflect our inability to adequately assess such a trait.) Still, there is some obvious sense to this approach that relates to a number of points we raised in the first section of this Topic. The less well qualified a person is for a job, the less well trained, or the less well motivated, the more likely that person will have an accident—particularly if the job is a dangerous one. You

Training employees to work safely involves both informing the workers about what constitutes safe work behavior and conveying the message that the employer values safe work.

wouldn't want to send an employee with poor balance and coordination to work high above the ground on scaffolding, for example.

The Industrial-Social Approach. This point of view takes the rather strange-sounding position that workers often need to be motivated to work safely. At first you might think that anyone in his or her right mind would want to work safely and avoid being in an accident. You might be right. But does the worker know *specifically* what constitutes safe behaviors? Does the worker know that the employer *values* safe work and that safe work will be rewarded? If such is not the case, workers may cut corners, working too quickly—and too dangerously—if they believe the rewards are only for amount of work and output. A long, detailed warning label, for instance, may be *so* long and *so* detailed that the worker for whom it was intended won't even bother reading it. This approach suggests that employers must make sure that workers are trained in safe ways to do their job (Levine, 1983) and that they realize that safe behaviors are valued (Zohar, 1980). What matters most, as we have seen before, is clearly establishing safety goals, providing feedback to workers, and reinforcing those behaviors that lead to attaining stated goals.

Before You Go On

What are three approaches that can be taken to improve worker safety?

TOPIC 15A SUMMARY

In this Topic, we have only scratched the surface of what industrial-organizational psychologists do in their attempt to apply principles of psychology to the world of work. We've focused on two interrelated issues. First, we considered how employers can best fit a person to a given job. This process involves several subprocesses, such as doing a complete job analysis, specifying performance criteria by which personnel can be evaluated for a given job, using a number of techniques, including application forms, interviews, and psychological tests, to select the best person for a job. We saw that even with a qualified workforce, it will be necessary from time to time to consider programs for training or motivating that workforce to do the best possible job.

Then we turned our attention to the worker in an organization, looking at such issues as job satisfaction and the quality of work life, and how these are related to productivity. We found that although enhancing workers' satisfaction with their jobs may be a noble goal, there is little evidence that improved job satisfaction will lead to increased productivity. We reviewed some of the approaches that I/O psychologists have taken to improve the safety of the workplace. In Topic 15B, we'll look at two other areas of applied psychology: environmental psychology and sport psychology.

Topic 15B

ENVIRONMENTAL AND SPORT PSYCHOLOGY

We have noted right from the start that one of the major goals of psychology is to apply what we have learned about our subject matter in the real world. Generally, we first think of applying psychology in the context of diagnosis and therapy for psychological disorders. We also think about applying principles of learning and memory to improve education and to make child rearing easier and more effective. In Topic 15A, we saw how our understanding of affect, behavior, and cognition can be applied in the workplace. In this Topic, we'll briefly examine two more areas in which psychological principles are being applied.

PSYCHOLOGY AND THE ENVIRONMENT

environmental psychology the field of applied psychology that studies how the general environment affects the behavior and mental processes of individuals and how individuals affect their environments

Environmental psychology is the study of how the general environment (as opposed to specific stimuli) affects the behavior and mental processes of those living in it, and how people, in turn, affect their environments. This field tends to be an interdisciplinary endeavor (Saegert & Winkel, 1990). Environmental psychologists work with urban planners, economists, clinical psychologists, sociologists, architects, interior decorators, landscape architects, builders, and others.

The range of specific interests within environmental psychology is large. Some psychologists are interested in such factors as how color and lighting might affect workers' productivity, students' learning, or nursing home patients' mental and physical health. Some are concerned with behavioral and psychological reactions to the poisons, or toxins, that are present in our environments. Some are interested in the design and construction of physical space that maximizes the functions for which that space is constructed. Some seek efficient means of changing behaviors in order to influence the natural environment in positive ways, through antilittering campaigns, for example. Others focus on crowding, territoriality, and adjustment to the demands of city living. Of course, many of these issues are interrelated.

Environmental psychologists recognize that what may influence behavior most is one's *perception* of the physical environment. A room with ten persons in it can appear to be terribly small and crowded if it is perceived as an office. The same room can seem quite large and uncrowded if it is perceived as a waiting area. In fact, two rooms of exactly the same area, one square and the other rectangular, can be perceived differently; the square room will appear smaller than the rectangular room (Sadalla & Oxley, 1984). Let's begin our discussion of environmental psychology by considering some of the issues involved in the perception of space and distance.

Before You Go On

Define environmental psychology, and list some of the issues environmental psychologists study.

Space and Territory

Imagine you are seated in the library, studying at a large table. There is no one else at your table. Then another student enters the room and sits right next to you. Although there are seven other chairs at your table, she chooses to sit in the one just to your left. Or imagine that you are in the process of buying a car. While you are examining a new sports car, a salesperson approaches, stands right in front of you (not more than 8 inches away), and begins to tell you about all the positive features of the car you are looking at. Or imagine that in your psychology class you always sit in the same seat. The semester is about over, and you have gotten to know some of the people who habitually sit near you. Then, the next time you go to class, you find there is someone else in "your seat." Or imagine you are a suburban homeowner. You have spent years getting your backyard to look just the way you want it to. Then, neighborhood children discover that going through your rose garden makes a great shortcut for them on their way to school.

In each of these scenarios, and in hundreds of others we can imagine, you will probably feel a sense of discomfort. Your personal space, or territory, has been invaded without invitation. The study of the effects of invading personal space and territory has been an active research area for environmental psychologists.

Personal space is mobile. It goes with you where you go. It is an imaginary "bubble" of space that surrounds you and into which others may enter comfortably by invitation only. The extent of your personal space depends on the situation, as well as on other factors, including your age (Aiello & Aiello, 1974), gender (Evans & Howard, 1973), cultural background (Pandey, 1990), and who the "intruder" happens to be. You will be more likely to allow an invasion of your personal space by someone you know well, by someone about your age, or by an attractive member of the opposite sex (Hayduk, 1983). Personal space also seems to be a bit smaller for females than for males (Heshka & Nelson, 1972). The anthropologist Edward Hall (1966) claimed that one's personal space is also determined in part by one's culture. Westerners, for example, are said to require a larger personal space than people of Arab, Japanese, or Latin cultures (Sommer, 1969). These stereotypes may be overgeneralized. The evidence that supports cultural differences in personal space is not that compelling; too many other situational factors are more powerful (Hayduk, 1983).

Hall (1966) also claimed that personal space can be subdivided into four different distances, each relevant for different types of social interaction.

personal space the mobile "bubble" of space around you reserved for intimate relationships and into which others may enter only by invitation

1. *Intimate distance* is defined as being between actual contact and about 18 inches. This space tends to be reserved for very special, intimate communications: displays of affection by lovers, offerings of comfort, and the like. This space is usually reserved only for people you know well and care about, and you will feel uncomfortable if someone else is in it.

2. *Personal distance,* according to Hall, is reserved for day-to-day interactions with acquaintances and friends. It extends from about 18 inches to approximately 4 feet, or just beyond arm's length. This space can be seen clearly in social gatherings, in which clusters of persons gather around to share in conversation. Actual physical contact in this sort of situation is unusual and unwelcomed. We typically keep our bubble of personal space adjusted to this size.

3. Hall refers to the distance of 4 to 12 feet as *social distance.* This distance is used for social interactions with persons we do not know well. It commonly includes some sort of physical barrier, such as a desk or table, between us and others around us. Within this space, communication can continue, but there is an implied message of lack of intimacy. This is the distance used for conducting routine business or for formal meetings.

4. Finally, there is *public distance,* in which personal contact is minimized, though communication remains possible. This distance is defined as being between 12 and 25 feet. Formal lectures in large classrooms, performances from a stage, and after-dinner talks presented from behind the head table are examples. Because of the distances involved, communication in these settings tends to flow in only one direction.

The point is that we will tend to feel pressured or uncomfortable whenever these distances are violated. When that perfect stranger sits right next to you in the library, she is violating your personal space. The salesperson with his or her nose almost touching yours is violating your intimate space. When a lecturer leaves the podium and begins to wander through the audience, we may feel strange because our defined public space is being invaded.

territoriality the setting off and marking of a piece of territory (a location) as one's own

Territoriality is also related to the use of space. It involves the setting off and marking of a piece of a geographical location as one's own. It is the tendency to want to declare that "this space is mine; it's my turf and someone else can enter here only at my request or with my permission."

Territoriality was first studied extensively in nonhumans (e.g., Lorenz, 1969). Many species of animals establish, mark, and defend geographical areas they use either for finding and hunting food or for mating and rearing their young. These territories are often defended vigorously—most commonly with ritualistic posturing and threats of aggression, but only occasionally with actual combat (Leger, 1992).

It seems clear that people, too, establish territories as their own, not to be entered without invitation. Reviewing the evidence for territoriality in humans, Altman (1975) noted that like personal space, our territories vary in their value to us. Some are *primary* territories, defined by us as ours and no one else's. "This is my room, and you'd better stay out of it." We often invest heavily in our primary territories. We decorate our homes, yards, dormitory rooms, or apartments to put our mark on our space. Primary territories are well marked, claimed for the long term, and defended. By controlling primary territory, we maintain a sense of privacy and a sense of identity. Evidence of such a territoriality among humans is all around us, perhaps most obvious in any teenager's room.

Altman also suggests that we are sensitive to two other types of territory: *secondary* and *public.* Secondary territories are more flexible and less well defined. They are areas we set aside for social gatherings, not so much for personal privacy. Members of the faculty may stake out a room in a college building as a faculty lounge and may be unnerved to discover students using it, even if they are using it to

Intimate distance is reserved for inter- actions with good friends, as illustrat- ed in the picture above left. Personal distance is reserved for day-to-day interactions with acquaintances (above right). Social distance is appropriate for persons we do not know well (left). Public distance minimizes per- sonal contact, although communica- tion is still possible (bottom left).

One's "territory" can take on different dimensions. We have primary territories (above right) that we think of as ours alone. We also have secondary territories (above left) that we see as primarily ours, and may mark as ours, but that are used by others. And we have a certain claim on public territories (left) that we occupy for only a short period of time and then relinquish to others.

study. Secondary territories are not "owned" by those who use them and tend not to be used for expressing personal identity. There may be a sign on the door that says Faculty Lounge, but the area *can* be used for other functions, and occasional intrusions by nonfaculty may be tolerated.

Public territories are those we tend to occupy for only a short time. They are not ours in any literal sense, and we will not feel much distress if these territories are violated. While waiting for a plane, you sit in a seat in the airport terminal and place your luggage at your feet. You get up for a minute to buy a newspaper, and when you return, you discover that someone has claimed your seat. In such a situation, you may be momentarily annoyed, but you will have less difficulty in finding another seat than in starting a major confrontation.

Personal space and territories we claim as our own serve many functions. They provide a sense of structure and continuity in what otherwise may seem to be a complex and ever-changing environment. They help us claim some sense of identity. They help us set ourselves apart from others. They regulate and reinforce needs for privacy. Although expressed differently from culture to culture, these needs appear to be universal (Lonner, 1980). When space and territory are violated, we can predict negative outcomes: anxiety, distress, and sometimes even aggressive attempts of reclamation.

Before You Go On

Define the concepts of personal space
and territoriality.

Life in the City: An Example

In 1962, John B. Calhoun published the results of his experiments on the overcrowding of rats. The data were impressive and intriguing. Calhoun raised colonies of rats in a number of environments. In some, population density was allowed, even encouraged, to increase to the point that overcrowding began to affect the behavior of the rats in the colony. Male rats became aggressive; newborn rats were often cannibalized or ignored and left to die; females became unreceptive to sexual advances from male rats; and when mating did occur, litter size decreased, apparently in response to the pressures of colony overpopulation. As you might imagine, it did not take long for some psychologists to look for parallels between Calhoun's rat studies and life in modern cities. Early investigations found correlations between population density and negative behavioral consequences, such as mental illness, crime, stress, and delinquency (Altman, 1975; Freedman, 1975; Schmitt, 1966). As psychologists began to look more closely at the lives of people in urban environments, however, it became clear that the translation of the data from Calhoun's rats to residents of our metropolitan centers was not all that straightforward.

To understand this, the first thing we need to do is distinguish between two easily confused terms (Stokols, 1972). The first is **population density**, which refers to the number of persons (or animals) per unit of area. Density is an objective, descriptive measure. **Crowding**, on the other hand, is a psychological concept. It is a *subjective feeling* of discomfort or distress produced by a perceived lack of space. Crowding may be independent of the number of persons involved. That is, you might feel very crowded and uncomfortable if you have to sit in the back seat of a small car with two other people, and not at

population density a quantitative measure of the number of persons (or animals) per unit of area

crowding the subjective feeling of discomfort caused by a sense of lack of space

all crowded when you all get to the stadium and are jammed together with 60,000 others to watch a football game (Freedman, 1975).

Crowding is a negative feeling that tends to produce a number of negative consequences. But it is not correct to conclude that living in a densely populated city *necessarily* produces negative consequences. Other potential stressors such as noise, pollution, and the threat of crime that we commonly associate with city life may be more than offset by better medical care, better sanitation, and systems for handling emergencies of all types (Creekmore, 1985). One's perception of control also matters (Rodin, 1976). When Ruback and Pandey (1988) looked at the role of perceived control for married couples in the United States and in India, they found striking similarities. In both cultures, low levels of perceived control were associated with high levels of mental distress and physical symptoms. Among other things, people who believe they can leave the city whenever they so choose will have more positive attitudes about living in that city than will people who feel "trapped" there.

Indeed, there is evidence to support the claim that living in the city *can* be healthier, in a variety of physical and psychological ways, than living in the country (Creekmore, 1985; Krupat, 1985; Milgram, 1970, 1977). Many of the advantages of city living are unavailable to residents of smaller communities. Few cities with populations of less than 50,000 can support large symphony orchestras, opera companies, museums, and art galleries (for residents who can afford them), parks and playgrounds (for those who want them), or fully staffed emergency rooms or trauma centers (for those who need them) such as those found in much larger urban areas. Nor can small communities afford stadiums and arenas for professional sports (Barker, 1968). The challenge for environmental psychologists is to help urban planners and architects design living spaces in areas of high population density that minimize the subjective experience of crowding, that maintain privacy, and that allow for expressions of individual territoriality.

Before You Go On

What is the difference between population density and crowding?

What are some of the positive and negative aspects of city living?

Noise, Temperature, and Environmental Toxins

In this section, we'll review some evidence that suggests that three aspects of the physical environment can have a profound effect on behavior. We'll consider noise, temperature, and environmental toxins (poisons) and how they affect human performance.

Noise. Noise is defined as an intrusive, unwanted, or excessive experience of sound. Almost any environment will provide some level of background noise, and sound per se need not be disruptive or stressful. In fact, the total absence of sound can induce stress. Noise becomes most stressful when it is loud, high-pitched, and unpredictable (Glass & Singer, 1972). Continued exposure to high-intensity sound can produce lasting deafness (Scharf, 1978; Taylor et al., 1965), although prolonged exposure to high levels of noise seems to produce few other serious physical problems directly (Matlin, 1983). However, there is ample evidence that prolonged exposure to noise increases levels of stress, anxiety, and aggressive behaviors (Bell et al., 1978; Smith & Stansfield, 1986).

noise an intrusive, unwanted, or excessive experience of sound

Noise levels have predictable effects on the performance of cognitive tasks, such as problem solving and school work. Sheldon Cohen and his associates (1980, 1986), for example, have shown that children who attended schools near the busy Los Angeles airport were more easily distracted from their work than children who attended schools in quieter neighborhoods. Glass and Singer (1972) suggest that absolute levels of background noise are not the major determiner of disruption. What matters more in the disruption of performance is the *predictability* of the noise and the degree of one's control over that noise. The results of one experiment demonstrating this phenomenon are presented in Figure 15.2 (Glass, Singer, & Friedman, 1969).

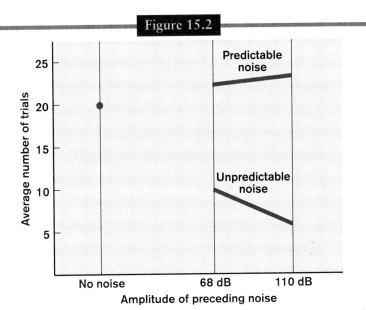

Figure 15.2

The effects of the predictability of noise as a distractor during a cognitive task. When noise occurred unpredictably, subjects spent fewer trials attempting to solve unsolvable puzzles. (From Glass, Singer, & Friedman, 1969).

Subjects were given the task of trying to solve problems that in fact had no solution. Subjects worked on these puzzles under three levels of background noise. In one condition, there was no unusual noise; in a second condition, a relatively soft (68-decibel) noise was presented; in the third condition, a loud (110-decibel) noise was introduced. In the two treatments using background noise, the predictability of the noise was also manipulated. That is, in one condition, the onset of the noise was regular and predictable; in the other, the noise was introduced on a random schedule. The introduction of predictable noise—either soft or loud—did not significantly alter the subjects' persistence in working on problems. Unpredictable noise, however, reduced the number of trials subjects were willing to invest in the problem task. Glass and Singer (1972) also reported that when subjects were able to exercise control over the occurrence of noise, their problem-solving tasks were unaffected. When noise is uncontrollable, performance levels drop, and performance often remains poor even after the stimulus noise has been removed.

Temperature. Extremes of temperature can have adverse effects on behavior. Probably any task can be accomplished most effectively within a range of moderate environmental temperatures (Baron, 1977). It is important, for example, to try to keep the temperature of a workplace within reasonable limits. If temperatures become excessively high *or* low, performance will deteriorate, although the specific effects of temperature on performance depend in large measure on the type of task being performed.

Environmental psychologists have also been concerned with the effects that extremely high temperatures have on social interactions, particularly on aggression. There is a common perception that riots and other more common displays of violent behaviors are more frequent during the long, hot days of summer. This observation is largely supported by research evidence (Anderson, 1989; Anderson & Anderson, 1984; Rotton & Frey, 1985). C. A. Anderson (1987, 1989), for example, reported on a series of studies that shows that violent crimes are more prevalent in hotter quarters of the year and in hotter years, although nonviolent crimes were less affected. Anderson also concluded that differences in crime rates between cities are better predicted by temperature than by social, demographic (age, race, education), and economic variables. Baron and Ransberger (1978) point out that riots are most likely to occur when the outside temperature is only moderately high, between about 75° and 90°. But when temperatures get much above 90°, energy (even for aggression) becomes rapidly depleted, and rioting is less likely to occur.

Environmental Toxins. As societies become more heavily invested in technological advancement, an accompanying side effect is that increased levels of toxins or pollutants find their way into the environment. Psychologists concerned with issues of the quality of life are becoming increasingly involved in issues concerning the quality of the natural environment (Daniel, 1990; Fischhoff, 1990; Kaplan, 1987; Stern, 1992; Stokols, 1990).

Of the nearly 100,000 chemicals in use in this country's industries, more than 600 have been declared dangerous in large doses by the federal government (Anderson, 1982). Many of the chemicals that pollute the natural environment are called **neurotoxins** because they have their poisonous, toxic effects on the human nervous system. Even in small doses, some can cause detectable behavioral and emotional changes in individuals.

neurotoxins chemicals (poisons) that affect psychological processes through the nervous system

Environmental psychologists are involved in research on neurotoxins at several levels. On the one hand, there is education: workers and consumers need to know about the short-term and long-term effects of contact with chemical toxins and how to deal with such materials. Because many of the effects of pollutants are psychological (e.g., disorientation, impairment of cognitive abilities, behavioral irregularities), and particularly because these chemicals may affect the behaviors of young children (and the unborn), it is becoming more common to find psychologists involved in the actual diagnosis of the effects of toxins (Fein et al., 1983). Exposure to neurotoxins may be more readily diagnosed through behavioral or psychological means than through medical diagnosis.

Before You Go On

What are some of the effects that noise, extreme temperature, and neurotoxins have on behavior?

Changing Behaviors That Impact on the Environment

In 1962, Rachel Carson published *Silent Spring*. This powerful and poignant best-seller raised public consciousness about environmental issues as no book had done before. It spoke eloquently about the fragility of the physical environment, the limits of earth's resources, and how the inhabitants of the planet impact those resources. It made clear the dangers inherent in the use of DDT and other harmful pesticides. After *Silent Spring* was published, the word *environmentalist* took on new meaning and significance. A movement had begun; a broad-based coalition of people from all walks of life became concerned with the quality of the environment and its limited resources. The environmentalist agenda is to conserve and restore: to conserve those resources that are still available and, when possible, to restore the environment to its clean and natural state. DDT use is now banned in the United States, although it is still manufactured and exported to other countries. In 1988, chemical companies began suspending the production of products that contained chlorofluorocarbons (CFCs, used in refrigeration and the manufacture of Styrofoam products). They did so because of the undeniable evidence that these chemicals, once in the atmosphere, were affecting the earth's protective ozone layer.

Environmental pollutants pose a serious threat not only to people's health but also to their entire way of life. Imagine this scene (left) as a site of illegal dumping, or an oil spill (right), and you can imagine how quality of life would be changed for persons who lived nearby.

applied behavior analysis (ABA) an approach, based on operant conditioning, that attempts to find solutions to human environment problems in the real world

Psychologists have long been active in helping to establish programs aimed at changing the behaviors of large numbers of people in such a way as to benefit the environment. In this context, finding solutions to environmental problems is one of the goals of what is called **applied behavior analysis (ABA)**. The specific techniques of applied behavior analysis derive from the work of B. F. Skinner and the procedures of operant conditioning (Topic 5B), and can be used to modify a range of behaviors. In our present context, ABA attempts to (1) operationally define some *target behavior* to be modified (e.g., the conservation of energy or water, or the reduction of roadside litter), (2) determine the antecedent environmental conditions that set the occasion for, or prompt the behavior, and (3) determine the consequences that increase, decrease, or maintain the targeted behavior (Geller, 1986; Geller & Nimmer, 1985). Programs of this sort have had a positive effect in several environmentally sensitive areas, such as energy conservation in general (Geller, 1989, 1992; Stern, 1992), conservation of natural gas (Shippee & Gregory, 1982), home-based energy conservation (Winett et al., 1985), home weatherization projects (Pavlovich & Greene, 1984), gasoline conservation (Hake & Foxx, 1978), and paper recycling (Witmer & Geller, 1976).

Let's look at one example of how this approach works: motivating waste management behavior (Geller, 1985; Geller & Lehman, 1986). First, we recognize that solid waste management *is* a problem. Millions of tons of solid waste are disposed of daily, often in ways that directly threaten environmental quality. The first step is to develop a precise, operational definition of target behaviors. Just what behavior does one want to change? Do you want to increase the use of trash receptacles? Do you want to have litter removed from roadsides? Do you want to increase the use of solid waste recycling? What waste materials do you want to emphasize?

Once you have decided which behavior is to be modified, attention shifts to antecedent strategies, or *prompting procedures*. Here, you have to let people know just what it is that you want done. This is essentially an educational component of the program. Prompts may be general ("Please dispose of properly!") or specific ("Leave your old newspapers here"). Prompts may also communicate possible consequences of one's actions ("Fine for Littering: $50" or "Bring your own container and receive a 5% discount"). Securing a behavioral commitment to a waste management program can be an effective means of prompting participation. For example, people who sign pledges or engage in a discussion of community waste management are more likely to follow through.

As we learned in our study of operant conditioning in the laboratory, behaviors will change and be maintained to the extent that those behaviors produce certain consequences. An important point for the success of programs designed to modify behavior that impacts on the environment is that consequences be tied to a person's *response*, not to some potentially *long-term outcome*. For example, scouts who pick up trash from the side of a highway should be rewarded immediately with a few cents for each bag of litter they collect rather than given an award (or reward) for providing the community with a litter-free stretch of roadway. Positive consequences for desired actions (thanking someone for picking up loose trash) typically are more effective than negative consequences (fining someone for leaving a soda can on a public beach). Intervention programs that are successful and have a positive impact should also be designed so that they can be maintained by some supporting agency or institution within the community once the program is underway.

We have come a long way since the publication of Carson's *Silent Spring*. There is still a very long way to go. Scattered and uncoordinated attempts to recycle solid waste materials, or preserve wildlife habitat, or control the pollution of industrial emissions only begin to take us in the right direction. At least there is some hope that the 1990s *can* be the decade of the environment and that significant improvements can be made.

Before You Go On

How can environmental psychologists have a positive impact on the environment?

PSYCHOLOGY AND SPORT

Sport psychology is another new and exciting area of applied psychology. Although it has had a long history in Europe, sport psychology has become an organized focus of attention in this country only within the last 20 to 25 years. **Sport psychology** is "the application of psychological principles to sport and physical activity at all levels of skill development" (Browne & Mahoney, 1984, p. 605). Although there

sport psychology the application of psychological principles to sport and physical activity at all levels of skill development

are many potential applications of psychology to sports and athletes, we'll briefly review just two: analyzing the psychological characteristics of athletes and maximizing athletic performance.

The Psychological Characteristics of Athletes

Psychology's history is filled with research on the measurement of individual differences. Wouldn't it be useful to be able to predict who might become a world-class athlete on the basis of psychological testing? It is certainly the case that there are physiological differences between athletes and nonathletes—amount of muscle, muscle type, height, weight, lung capacity, and so on. Are there any differences between athletes and nonathletes on personality measures?

Generally, research in this area has been less than satisfactory, and results often tend to confirm the obvious. Although differences tend to be small, athletes usually score higher than nonathletes on tests of assertion, dominance, aggression, and need for achievement; they score lower on anxiety level, depression, and fatigue (Browne & Mahoney, 1984; Cox, 1990; Morgan, 1980). This is particularly true when the athletes are at a high skill level. Athletes in some sports, such as hockey and football, are more tolerant of pain than are athletes in other sports, such as golf and bowling (e.g., Ryan & Kovacic, 1966). Tolerance of pain, however, may be more of an outcome (result of their activity) for some athletes than a determinant of their success. And this last point raises a problem that has plagued research on the personality of the athlete: Just how shall we define *athlete?* Given the differences among hockey players, golfers, long-distance runners, pocket billiards players, cowboys, bowlers, rock climbers, gymnasts, and so on, it is a bit surprising that research can find any significant differences between athletes and nonathletes. In fact, when general trends are sought, they often are not found (e.g., Fisher, 1977).

Maximizing Athletic Performance

Of practical importance to coaches and athletes (and psychologists) is the performance of the athlete in competition, and what can be done to maximize that performance.

One area of interest focuses on manipulating the arousal level of the athlete. The athlete in competition surely needs to be aroused and motivated to perform—"psyched up" to his or her best. Psychologists also know that too much arousal can interfere with athletic performance. They also know that optimum levels of arousal can vary as a function of the task at hand. For example, making a long putt in golf requires a relatively low level of arousal, blocking a shot in volleyball requires a slightly higher level, making a tackle in football an even higher level, and bench pressing in weight lifting requires a very high level of arousal (e.g., Cox, 1990, p. 98). (If this discussion sounds familiar, it's because we addressed these issues of arousal in general terms in the Topic on motivation, Topic 10A.) Psychologists can help athletes be sensitive to maintaining appropriate levels of arousal while maintaining concentration on the task at hand. This often involves training athletes to monitor and control arousal levels by learning to be sensitive to such indicators as their own blood pressure, respiration and heart rates, muscle tension, and the like (Harris, 1973; Landers, 1982).

Sport psychologists have tried to find evidence for a performance phenomenon that many athletes and nonathletes take for granted: the notion of developing a "hot hand," or being "in a groove," or "in the zone." The concept is not well defined, but is usually assumed to be demonstrated by a string or cluster of successful performances (e.g., made shots) than chance or past history would predict (Vallerand, Colavecchio, & Pelletier, 1988). As it happens, evidence for a "hot hand" phenomenon is virtually nonexistent. It doesn't seem to occur at all in team sports such as basketball (Adams, 1992; Gilovich et al., 1985), and occurs only minimally in individual sports such as tennis or racquetball (Iso-Ahola & Blanchard, 1986; Silva et al., 1988).

Bob Adams, of Eastern Kentucky University, may have found an exception: professional pocket billiards (Adams, 1993). Adams found that in nine-ball tournaments, there *was* evidence that a player could get on a "hot streak," make significantly more shots, and win more games than usual. Adams claims that there are two reasons why pocket billiards is different from most other sports and more susceptible to streaks or "hot hands": (1) there is not much time between opportunities to shoot (as opposed to basketball, for instance), and (2) once a player starts shooting, the opponent can do nothing to affect outcomes (as opposed to tennis, for instance).

In a similar vein, sport psychologists now claim that the so-called home field advantage (Varca, 1980) often may be exaggerated, particularly in important games (Baumeister, 1985; Baumeister & Steinhilber, 1984). The argument is that frenzied, yelling, screaming

Being "in a groove," "on a hot streak," or "in the zone" probably does not occur in any team sport. Recent evidence suggests, however, that the phenomenon may exist in very personal sports, such as pocket billiards.

hometown fans may raise arousal levels of the home team *beyond* the point of maximum efficiency. The negative effect of fans' reactions is more potent when teams are on offense than when they are playing defense, and it is clearly more potent in end-of-season playoff and championship games.

One psychologist who researches sports and athletes, Michael Mahoney, commenting on Olympic athletes, has said, "At this level of competition, the difference between two athletes is 20 percent physical and 80 percent mental" (quoted in Kiester, 1984a, pp. 20–21). To the extent that this observation is accurate, psychologists have tried to help athletes to do their best—to give what is called their *peak performance*. Mental practice, or "imagery," combined, of course, with physical practice, has proven to be beneficial (e.g., Smith, 1987). In addition to manipulating acceptable levels of arousal, mental practice is useful in the following:

1. Mentally rehearsing a particular behavioral pattern. (Think about—mentally picture—that golf swing and the flight of the ball before you step up to the tee.)

2. Reducing negative thoughts that may interfere with performance. (Forget about an earlier error and focus on positive experiences, perhaps past victories.)

3. Rehearsing one's role in a team sport. (Mentally practice what you are supposed to do and when you are supposed to do it in various game situations.)

4. Setting realistic goals. (Don't get tense worrying about a competitor in this race, simply try to better your last performance; e.g., Creekmore, 1984; Fenker & Lambiotte, 1987; Kiester, 1984a, 1984b; Ogilvie & Howe, 1984; Scott & Pelliccioni, 1982; Smith, 1987; Suinn, 1980.)

Obviously, using mental imagery is not a simple matter, nor is it the only way in which athletes can improve their performance. It's just one technique with which sports psychologists can help.

Before You Go On

What are some of the ways in which psychologists may become involved in sports and athletics?

TOPIC 15B SUMMARY

In this Topic, we've reviewed two areas in which psychological understanding can be applied to real-life situations. We've seen how the physical environment can have sweeping effects on our affects, cognitions, and behaviors, and how sports and athletics can benefit from our knowledge of human behavior.

We saw that environmental psychologists face many challenges as they try to accommodate physical space to suit the needs of those who occupy that space. We looked in some detail at issues of crowding and population density, particularly as these concepts relate to life in large cities. We also considered some of the ways in which psychologists can help bring about the sorts of changes in behavior that will be necessary to save and refurbish the natural environment.

When considering some of the things sport psychologists do, we found that attempts to find personality traits or variables that would predict athletic ability in general terms have been largely unsuccessful—as have been attempts to find data to support the notion that some athletes can get into a "groove," or develop a "hot hand" (except in professional pocket billiards). On the other hand, there is evidence that several psychological methods can be used to help athletes raise their overall levels of performance.

Psychology is a science, and it is an academic discipline. It is also a field ready and able to be a force of change in the real world.

TOPIC 15A

What is involved in doing a job analysis?

Doing a proper job analysis involves two stages: (1) constructing a complete and specific description of the activities performed by someone in a given position (i.e., a listing of the behaviors required to do the job) and (2) developing ways of evaluating the performance of a person in that job (performance criteria). Information can be accumulated from official documents, interviews, questionnaires, and the direct observation of job activities. /p. 727

What are some of the sources of information that can be used in making personnel decisions?

Once a job analysis has been completed, personnel selection involves using assessment tools to measure the relevant characteristics of applicants. There are many such tools, including application forms, interviews, psychological tests, situational tests, and assessment center approaches. Of these, casual, unstructured interviews seem to be of least value. The assessment center is one location where many applicants (or present employees) can be brought together for a period of intense evaluation. In most instances, assessment centers can simulate actual job situations and give evaluators a sense of how someone will perform on the job, in social situations, and under stress. Although assessment centers are popular, their specific role in personnel decision making has been questioned. /p. 730

List some of the factors that need to be considered in the design, implementation, and evaluation of a training program.

Several factors need to be considered in designing and implementing an employee training program. These include an assessment of the

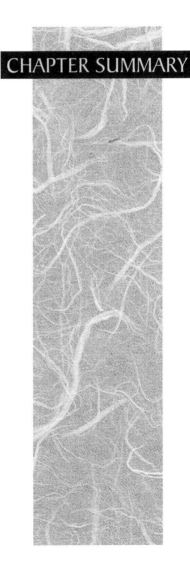

CHAPTER SUMMARY

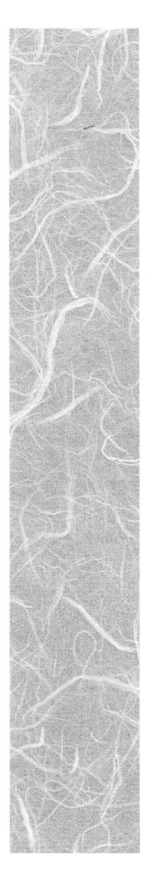

organization's instructional needs (what training, if any, is required?), the development of specific training objectives, the means by which training will be evaluated, and the selection of media and methods for the actual training. Once training has begun, it should be monitored constantly to see if objectives are being met. After training has been completed, the program itself should be evaluated in the short and long term, as should the transfer of information and skills from training to actual on-the-job performance. /*p. 734*

Briefly summarize some of the factors that affect the motivation of workers to do a good job.

Even workers with ability may not do a good job unless they are motivated to do so. There are many theories that describe what motivates workers. We looked at three approaches. Vroom's *expectancy theory* says that workers develop expectations concerning the relationship between their work behaviors and the likelihood of certain outcomes. They also assign values to outcomes. They will be most highly motivated to behave in ways that earn valued rewards. Adams's *equity theory* says that what matters most is the perception of fairness or equal reward for equal effort when one's work behaviors are compared with those of someone else at the same level. Locke's *goal-setting* approach says that what matters most is that workers be clearly aware of just what they are working for and that they accept that goal as worth the effort. /*p. 737*

What are meant by job satisfaction and the quality of work life?

Job satisfaction and quality of work life are complex concepts, usually inferred from interview and questionnaire data. In the broadest sense, job satisfaction is an attitude, a measure of an employee's evaluation of his or her position in an organization. Quality of work life (QWL) involves many factors, such as feelings about employment conditions, job security, compensation, autonomy, opportunities for social interaction, self-esteem, and participation in the decision-making process. /*p. 739*

Briefly summarize the relationship between job satisfaction and job productivity.

Although job satisfaction and productivity may be related, there is little evidence to suggest that the relationship is a strong one, and no evidence to suggest that one causes the other. Interventions designed to increase job satisfaction do sometimes have a positive impact on productivity, but interventions designed to improve productivity may also increase job satisfaction. Job satisfaction seems most closely related to employee turnover and somewhat less related to absenteeism. /*p. 740*

What are three approaches that can be taken to improve worker safety?

I/O psychologists have long been interested in making the workplace as accident-free as possible. We looked at three ways of approaching work safety. (1) *Engineering* the job and equipment to be as safe as possible has generally been an effective process. (2) Looking at *personnel* to identify accident-prone individuals or characteristics has not proven to be very worthwhile. (3) The so-called *industrial-social* approach involves motivating workers to work more safely by providing training in specific, safe behaviors and convincing them that safety is valued in the organization has been a successful approach. /p. 743

TOPIC 15B

Define environmental psychology, and list some of the issues environmental psychologists study.

Environmental psychology is the study of how the environment affects the behavior and mental processes of persons living within it, and vice versa. Environmental psychology includes such issues as crowding, interior design, territoriality, environmental pollutants, the effects of weather, and how to most effectively get people to act in ways that will improve the quality of the physical environment. /p. 744

Define the concepts of personal space and territoriality.

Personal space is the imaginary bubble of area around a person into which others enter only by invitation or in specified situations. It is mobile and goes with the person. There may be various types of personal space—acceptable distances—defined for various situations. Territoriality, on the other hand, is one's claim to certain areas in the environment. Territories may be defended against intrusion and are often used as statements of self-expression. Intrusion into one's personal space or territory without invitation may lead to tension, stress, and even aggression. /p. 749

What is the difference between population density and crowding?

What are some of the positive and negative aspects of city living?

Population density is simply a physical, quantitative measure of the number of units (e.g., people) occupying a given geographic area. Crowding, on the other hand, is a psychological reaction of distress that occurs when individuals perceive a lack of adequate space. City living increases the probability of living with crowding, noise, and other pollutants, but these stressors may be offset by the advantages of a wide range of opportunities not found outside large population centers, such as health care, police protection, and access to the arts. /p. 750

What are some of the effects that noise, extreme temperature, and neurotoxins have on behavior?

Noise, extreme temperatures, and neurotoxins may all be viewed as environmental pollutants and harmful to physical and psychological well-being. Noise per se is less stressful than is unexpected, unpredictable, or uncontrollable noise. High temperatures may lead to

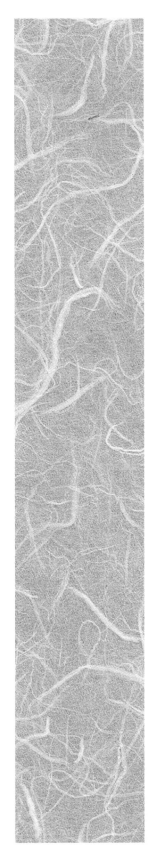

aggressive, violent reactions, but extremely high (or low) temperatures tend to decrease all levels of behavior. Many chemicals commonly found in the environment have negative consequences for behavior and mental activities; those that directly affect the nervous system are called neurotoxins. /p. 753

How can environmental psychologists help to have a positive impact on the environment?

Environmentalists work to conserve natural resources and to restore the environment to its natural and unspoiled state. Environmental psychologists can help in this effort by designing large-scale intervention programs. Programs associated with an approach called applied behavior analysis, or ABA, target specific behaviors, identify antecedent conditions that prompt these target behaviors, and attempt to control consequences of relevant behaviors to increase the rate of appropriate responses. /p. 755

What are some of the ways in which psychologists may become involved in sports and athletics?

Psychologists have become involved in sports and athletics in several ways, including trying to discover how athletes are different from nonathletes, attempting to improve an athlete's peak performance, and studying the effects of audience reactions on athletic performance. /p. 758

STATISTICAL APPENDIX

AN EXAMPLE TO WORK WITH
Organizing Data
    Frequency Distributions
    Graphic Representations
Descriptive Statistics
    Measures of Central Tendency
    Variability
Inferential Statistics
Some Normal Curve Statistics

APPENDIX SUMMARY

*D*oing research in psychology, or applying psychology, often involves the measurement of some aspect of behavior or mental processes. When we measure the affects, cognitions, or behaviors of organisms, the result of our measurement is a set of numbers. Assuming that we have adequately measured what we are interested in, we now have to deal with the numbers we have accumulated. That's where statistics come in.

It's one thing to be able to measure some psychological characteristic and something else again to make sense out of those measurements once they've been made. This is particularly true when we have a large number of measurements, either made repeatedly on the same individual or on many different individuals. After making our measurements and generating a large number of numbers, we need to be able to summarize and describe our data. We may want to make decisions based on the numbers we have collected. Statistics help us to summarize, describe, and make judgments about measurements. How they do so will be the subject of this appendix.

Before we go on, I would like to insert a word of caution. In this appendix, we are going to be dealing with numbers and a few simple formulas. Please don't let the numbers make you anxious. Some students find dealing with numbers difficult and think that statistics are not relevant for psychology students. Always keep in mind that statistics are tools, necessary tools, to help us understand our subject matter. I have long argued that (at this level at least) you don't need mathematical sophistication to appreciate statistics. What is required is a positive attitude and a few arithmetic skills, such as addition, subtraction, multiplication, and division.

AN EXAMPLE TO WORK WITH

Statistics involve numbers; when we measure something, we assign it a numerical value, and statistics help us to analyze and understand measurements once we have made them. So that we'll have some numbers to work with, let's consider the following problem.

You and your best friend are enrolled in the same introductory psychology class this semester. You have just taken your first exam, a 50-item multiple-choice test. Concerned about the possibility of cheating, your instructor provided two forms of your first exam, form A and form B. They both covered the same material, of course, but the questions were different on the two forms. By chance, you took form A of the test, and your friend took form B. You had studied together, and you thought that you both knew the material equally well. But your score on the test was eight points lower than your friend's. You suspect that perhaps the two forms of your first test were not equally difficult. You believe that your test (form A) was harder than your friend's (form B). You ask your instructor for all the grades on the test for both forms. Because of the need for confidentiality, your instructor cannot provide you with names, but does supply you with all the grades from the exam.

There are 100 students in your class who took the first exam. Fifty took form A and 50 took form B. When you get the scores from your instructor, you find that they are arranged as follows:

FORM A						FORM B				
98	86	100	60	94		82	100	90	80	60
72	80	78	66	86		72	86	82	88	80
92	62	86	96	62		82	76	84	74	84
82	86	78	88	84		86	74	78	78	78
64	86	68	76	80		78	74	84	80	80
86	96	76	72	80		90	84	68	78	86
80	82	82	64	78		80	80	80	84	80
68	74	98	98	84		76	76	80	82	82
66	64	70	90	86		86	74	70	78	76
96	92	82	68	92		82	82	80	76	80

What a mess. Just looking at all these numbers doesn't tell you much at all. Arranged as they are, it's difficult to see if either form of the exam yielded higher or lower scores. To answer your original question (was there a difference in performance on the two forms of the exam?), you're going to have to manipulate these numbers somehow. Such manipulations involve statistics. As I'll repeat throughout this appendix, statistics are tools that we use to help us make sense out of data we have collected. They will be very helpful in analyzing these data. Statistical manipulations are more useful (even necessary) when we have collected many more than 100 numbers.

ORGANIZING DATA

Let's assume that we have collected the measurements, or data, in which we are interested. Now the task before us is to make some decisions based on those data. The first thing we need to do is to assemble our data, our numbers, in some sensible way so that we can quickly and easily get some idea of what they mean. At the very least, we should put our data in the form of a frequency distribution. We might then consider some graphic representation of our data.

Frequency Distributions

Once we have collected a large set of numbers, we seek ways to organize and summarize the numbers to make them useful and meaningful. One of the easiest things to do with our numbers is to arrange

Figure A.1				
Frequency Distributions for Our Sample Data of Two Forms (A and B) of a Classroom Exam				
Scores, or Measurements, are Listed in Order in the Left Column, and the Frequency with Which Each Occurs is Indicated with Either a Hash Mark (/) or a Number				
Score	**Form A Frequency**		**Form B Frequency**	
100	/	1	/	1
98	//	2		0
96	///	3		0
94	/	1		0
92	///	3		0
90	/	1	//	2
88	/	1	/	1
86	///// //	7	////	4
84	//	2	/////	5
82	////	4	///// //	7
80	////	4	///// ///// /	11
78	///	3	///// /	6
76	//	2	/////	5
74	/	1	////	4
72	//	2	/	1
70	/	1	/	1
68	///	3	/	1
66	//	2		0
64	////	4		0
62	//	2		0
60	/	1	/	1
		N = 50		*N* = 50

frequency distribution an ordered listing of all X-values, indicating the frequency with which each occurs

them in a **frequency distribution**. As its name suggests, a frequency distribution lists, in order, all of the numbers or scores that we have collected and indicates the frequency with which each occurs.

Figure A.1 shows two types of frequency distributions for the scores earned on form A and form B of the exam we introduced in the last section as an example. One type of frequency distribution indicates the frequency of each score with a hash mark (/), while the other type simply indicates the frequency of each score with a number. In this figure, I've placed the two frequency distributions side by side. You can easily see, just by inspection of these distributions, that there is a difference between the scores earned on form A and form B of our imaginary classroom exam.

Graphic Representations

It often is helpful to go one step beyond the simple frequency distribution and draw a graph of our data. A number of different graphs have

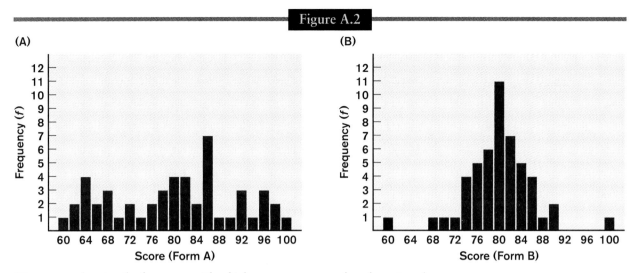

Histograms showing the frequency with which scores were earned on form A and form B of a classroom exam.

been used throughout this text. Graphs of frequencies of scores are among the most common types of graphs in psychology. For such a graph, our scores (in general referred to as *X-scores*) are plotted on the horizontal (x) axis of the graph, and frequencies (f) are plotted on the vertical (y) axis of our graph.

Figure A.2 shows one way to graph frequencies. This sort of bar graph is called a **histogram**. The frequency of each *X*-score is indicated by the height of the bar above that score. When we have few *X*-scores, and when frequencies are not too large, histograms provide clear depictions of our data. The differences between form A and form B of the classroom exam are more clearly seen in the two histograms of Figure A.2 than in a simple frequency distribution.

Figure A.3 shows the same data in a simple line graph. The advantage of this sort of graph is obvious: We can easily show both distributions of test scores on the same axes. As is the case with histograms, scores are plotted on the *x* axis and frequencies are indicated on the *y* axis. With line graphs, it is important to provide a key indicating which line represents each group of scores.

histogram a bar graph, an indication of the frequency with which X-values occur, where the height of a bar indicates the frequency of an X-value, or score

Before You Go On

What is a frequency distribution, and what is a histogram?

What are they used for?

DESCRIPTIVE STATISTICS

Let's continue working with our opening problem. We began with two sets of 50 numbers, scores earned on form A and form B of a

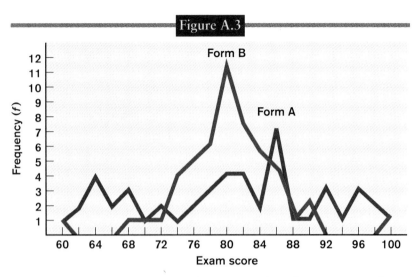

A line graph showing the frequency of scores earned on classroom exams for both form A and form B.

classroom exam. Our basic question was whether these two forms of the same test were really equally difficult. To get started, we put the scores into frequency distributions and then constructed graphs that represented our data. That helped, but there is much more we can do.

When describing collections or distributions of data, our two major concerns are usually with measures of central tendency and variability. Measures of **central tendency** are statistics that tell us where our scores tend to center. In general terms, measures of central tendency are called *averages*. If we want to know if performance on form A was better or worse *on the average* than performance on form B, we would have to compute a measure of central tendency for both distributions of scores. Measures of **variability** are statistics that tell us about the extent of dispersion, or the spread of scores within a distribution. Are scores clustered closely around the average, or are they more variable, deviating considerably from the average? First we'll deal with measures of central tendency, then with variability.

central tendency a measure of the middle, or average, score of a set of scores

variability the extent of spread or dispersion in a set or distribution of scores

Measures of Central Tendency

There are three statistics we can use to represent the central tendency of a distribution of numbers. The most commonly used is the mean. The median and mode are also measures of central tendency, but they are used less frequently.

The Mean. When we think about computing the average of a distribution of scores we are usually thinking about computing the **mean**. The mean of a set of scores is their total divided by the number of scores in the set. For example, if Max is 6 feet tall and Ruth is 4 feet tall, their mean height is 5 feet. Four inches of snow today and

mean ($\overline{X}$) the sum of all X-scores (ΣX) divided by N, the number of X-scores

2 inches yesterday yields a mean snowfall of 3 inches for the two days
(4" + 2" = 6" ÷ 2 = 3").

So, to compute the mean scores for form A of our example we
add up all the scores and divide by 50 because there are 50 scores in
the set. We'd do the very same thing for the scores earned on form
B—add them up and divide by 50. The mean of a set of numbers is
symbolized by $\overline{X}$, read *X bar*. The uppercase Greek letter sigma, Σ,
stands for "take the sum of whatever follows." We use the symbol *X*
to represent an individual score from a set of scores and *N* for the
number of scores in the set. So the formula for computing a mean
looks like this:

$$\overline{X} = \Sigma x / N$$

This is just a fancy shorthand way of expressing what you already
know: To find the mean of a set of scores ($[\overline{X}]$), add the scores (*X*)
together and then divide by the number of scores (*N*). When we do
this for form A and form B of our classroom exam example, we find
that the mean for both sets of scores is 80. That is, Σ*X* = 4000 and
N = 50 in each case, so Σ*X* ÷ *N* = 80 for both forms of the exam. In
terms of average score (as indicated by the mean), there is clearly no
difference between the two forms of the test.

The Median. Although the mean is generally the central-tendency
measure of choice, there are occasions when it may not be appropriate. These occasions occur when a distribution includes a few extreme
scores. For a simple example, the mean of the numbers, 2, 3, 3, 5, 7 is
4 (Σ*X* = 20; *N* = 5; so $\overline{X}$ = 4). Even on inspection, 4 looks right; it is a
value near the middle or center of the set. Now consider the numbers
2, 3, 3, 5, 37. What is their mean? The sum of these 5 numbers is 40,
so their mean equals 10. Here it seems by inspection that the extreme
score of 37 is adding too much weight to our measure of central tendency. For a real-life example, imagine computing the average income
of a small, working-class community that happened to include two
millionaires. The *mean* income of this community would be unduly
influenced by just two persons with unusually high incomes.

In such cases, we might prefer to use the **median** as our measure
of central tendency. The median is the value of a set of numbers that
divides it exactly in half. There are as many scores above the median
as below it. Perhaps you recognize that the median is the same as the
fiftieth percentage of a distribution—50 percent of the scores are
higher; 50 percent are lower.

Don't fall for this trick: "What is the median of these test scores:
42, 58, 37, 62, 55?" There is a tendency to want to say "37" because
it is in the middle of the list with two scores to the left and two scores
to the right. But "37" certainly isn't at the center of these scores; it's
the lowest of the five! Before you choose the median, the scores must
first be placed in order: 37, 42, 55, 58, 62. *Now* the score in the middle, 55, is the median score, the one that divides the set in half.
Whenever we have an even number of scores, there will be no one
number in the middle, will there? What is the median of these numbers: 3, 6, 8, 10, 14, 18? What we do here is calculate the mean of the

median *the score of an ordered set
above which and below which fall
half of the scores*

two numbers in the middle (here 8 and 10). So, the median of these six numbers is 9. When we have a large number of scores to deal with, the computation of the median becomes slightly more complicated. We can't always just put our scores in order and identify the median by inspection. But in such cases, the logic is the same, and we have formulas that tell us what steps to take to calculate the median. For the distributions in our example, the median for form A of the exam is 80; for form B it is 79.

mode the most frequently occurring
X-score in a set

The Mode. No doubt the easiest measure of central tendency to calculate is the **mode**. The mode is the most frequently occurring value in a set or distribution of scores. If you have already constructed a frequency distribution, finding the mode is particularly easy. Just locate the *X*-value with the greatest frequency and you've found the mode. For many psychological characteristics measured for large numbers of subjects, the mode *does* tend to fall at or near the center of the distribution of scores. For our example problem, the mode of scores earned on form A is 86, and on form B the mode is 80.

The mode is seldom used as a measure of central tendency. For one thing, computing the mode disregards all of the other values in the distribution. For another, there is no guarantee that the most frequently occurring number will be at (or even near) the middle. Notice also that it is quite possible for a collection of numbers to have two modes (be "bimodal"), or three modes, or more.

Before You Go On

Name and define three measures of central tendency.

Variability

If we know how two sets of scores, or distributions, differ "on the average," we know a lot. We know, for instance, that there is no apparent difference in central tendency for the two sets of scores we have been using as an example. There is, however, a second descriptive characteristic of distributions of numbers that may be of interest: their spread, or dispersion, or *variability.*

It is possible to have two sets of scores that have identical means but that, at the same time, are clearly different from each other. This sort of difference can be seen in Figure A.3 and is even more clearly obvious in Figure A.4. In this figure, we can see that most of the scores of distribution A are packed, or clustered, around the mean of the distribution. The scores of distribution B are much more spread out, or variable, even though the mean of this set of scores equals the mean of distribution A. Imagine for a moment that the two graphs in Figure A.4 represent grades earned by two very large classes. Further imagine that the mean grade for each class is a C. If this is the case, then these graphs tell us that almost everyone in class A received a C,

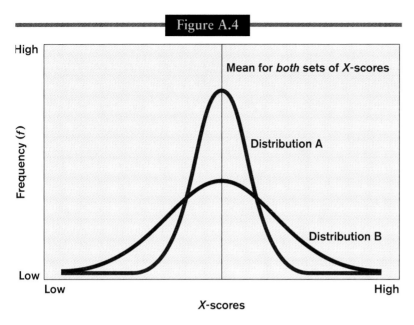

Two distributions of X-scores (A and B) that have identical means, but clearly different variabilities.

a C+, or a C−. Some may have received a B−or a D+, but most grades were near the average C. In class B, on the other hand, there were obviously many more A's, B's, D's, and F's than were earned by the other class, even though the mean grade for the two classes was a C. So knowing about a distribution's variability is to have some useful information. How shall we represent variability statistically?

One way to measure the spread of scores in a distribution is to use a statistic called the **range**. Range is one of the easiest statistics to calculate. It is found by subtracting the lowest score from the highest. Unfortunately, range simply disregards all the other scores between the highest and lowest. Even when most scores are bunched tightly around the mean, if there are just a couple of extreme scores, the range will be large. The range would be an inappropriate measure of variability for our example. Scores on both form A and form B of the classroom exam range from a high score of 100 to a low score of 60. Thus, the range for both sets of scores is 40 points. An inspection of Figure A.3, however, indicates that scores on form A are generally more variable than scores on form B.

A measure of variability that does take into account all of the scores of a distribution is **standard deviation**, usually symbolized **SD**. What it amounts to is a kind of average of the extent to which all the scores in a distribution are different from (deviate from) their mean. Let's go through the procedures that reflect this definition of standard deviation.

The first thing we need to know is the mean of our distribution ($\overline{[X]}$). Then we find the difference between each score (X, remember) and the mean ($\overline{[X]}$). This is a simple process of subtraction, yielding a

range the highest score in a distribution minus the lowest score

standard deviation (SD) a type of average of the extent to which each X-score in a distribution is different from (deviates from) the mean of that distribution

collection of $(X - [\overline{X}])$ scores. Because means are, by definition, in the middle of distributions, some X-scores will be above the mean (so $X - [\overline{X}]$ will be a positive number), and some X-scores will be below the mean (so $X - [\overline{X}]$ will be a negative number). If we then simply add up all of our deviations, $\Sigma(X - [\overline{X}])$, we will always have a sum of zero. To deal with this complication we just square each deviation score, so that we have a set of $(X - [\overline{X}])^2$ scores. Any real number, even a negative one, that is squared or multiplied by itself will yield a positive number. *Now* we add together our squared deviations, $\Sigma(X - [\overline{X}])^2$. We then find an average by dividing this total by N, the number of scores we are dealing with. In formula form, what we have so far is $\Sigma(X - [\overline{X}])^2/N$. This statistic is called *variance.*

In our calculations, we introduced a squaring operation just to get rid of negative numbers. We now reverse that operation by taking the square root of our result (variance). What we end up with then is our formula for standard deviation, and it looks like this:

$$SD = \sqrt{\frac{\Sigma(X - X)^2}{N}}$$

You may never be called on actually to compute a standard deviation using this formula. For one thing, even simple hand-held calculators often come with a button that yields a standard deviation value once you've punched in all the X-scores. For another, there are simpler computational formulas that provide the same result in fewer, easier steps. But you should appreciate what standard deviations do. They tell us the extent to which scores in a distribution deviate, or are spread from the distribution's mean. We use them often in psychology.

To reinforce our discussion, Figure A.5 depicts the computation of a standard deviation for some simple data. When the procedure is applied to our example data we find that the standard deviation for form A of the exam is 11.29; for form B, $SD = 6.18$. This result conforms to our observation that the scores on form A of the test are more variable than those earned on form B.

Before You Go On

What is the formula for standard deviation, and of what is it a measure?

INFERENTIAL STATISTICS

inferential statistics statistical tests that tell us about the significance of the results of experimental or correlational studies

We have already seen that statistics can be used to summarize and describe some of the essential characteristics of large collections of data. Statistics also can be used to guide our decision making concerning the data we have collected. That is, statistics can allow us to make inferences about our data. **Inferential statistics** tell us about the

Figure A.5		

An Example of the Computation of the Standard Deviation for a Small Distribution of X-Scores

X-scores	$X - \bar{X}$	$(X - \bar{X})^2$
12	6.5	42.25
10	4.5	20.25
7	1.5	2.25
6	.5	.25
5	−.5	.25
5	−.5	.25
4	−1.5	2.25
4	−1.5	2.25
1	−4.5	20.25
1	−4.5	20.25
		$110.50 = \Sigma(X - \bar{X})^2$

$$\Sigma X = 55$$
$$N = 10$$
$$\bar{X} = \Sigma X \div N = 5.5$$

$$SD = \sqrt{\frac{\Sigma(X - \bar{X})^2}{N}} = \sqrt{\frac{110.50}{10}} = \sqrt{11.05} = \underline{3.32}$$

significance of the results of our experimental or correlational studies. In general, they tell us the likelihood that the data we have collected might have occurred by chance. Let's use another example, again dealing with means.

For this example, let's say that our concern is with the effects of background music on studying. You want to do an experiment to determine if background music affects study skills. To keep matters simple, let's assume that you have two groups of volunteer subjects. Each group is to try to learn 50 words in a 5-minute study session. One group will practice in silence (your control group); the other will have classical music playing in the background (the experimental group). We'll call the first group, group S and the second, group C. Let's say there are 40 subjects in each group, or $N = 40$. After each group studies its word lists for 5 minutes, you test to see how many words have been learned. Then you construct a frequency distribution of your data and compute the means and standard deviations for each set of data. What you discover is that group S has a mean number of words learned equal to 26.0 and group C's mean is 28.5. Now what? There's no doubt that 28.5 is larger than 26.0, but the difference is not very large. Is the difference large enough for you to claim that the background music had an effect? We need to backtrack just a little.

Imagine that we had two groups of subjects in a similar experiment, but that both groups received exactly the same treatment. That is, both groups performed the same task under the same conditions. Some dependent variable is measured for both groups (perhaps the number of words that were learned in a 5-minute study session). Even though both groups were treated exactly the same, would we expect the mean scores for the two groups to be *exactly* equal? Wouldn't we expect *some* chance variation in scores between the two groups? If we did this same experiment again tomorrow, or next week, would we expect (again) to get exactly the same mean scores, even though experimental conditions remain the same? No. We generally anticipate that simply because of chance factors alone there will be some difference between the scores earned by two different groups of subjects—even if they are doing the same thing under the same conditions. So if mean scores for our two groups turn out to be somewhat different, we aren't surprised; we can attribute the difference to chance. But what if the groups are treated differently? What if the differences in measured responses are large? Can these differences also be attributed to chance? Or do they reflect real, significant differences between the two groups? This is where inferential statistics come in.

Inferential statistics allow us to make probability statements. They help us to determine the likelihood that observed differences in our descriptive statistics (such as means) are differences due to chance and random factors or reflect some true difference between the groups we have measured. Differences that are not likely to have occurred by chance are called **statistically significant differences**. If the difference between two calculated means is found to be statistically significant, that difference may or may not be *important* or *meaningful*, but we can claim that the difference is not likely to be due to chance.

One way to think about statistical significance is in terms of replication. If, for example, two means are found to be significantly different, it is likely that if the measurements were taken over and over again, the same difference in the same direction would show up most of the time. Inferential statistics can be used to judge the statistical significance of any statistic. They can be used to tell us about the probability with which means, or medians, or standard deviations, or proportions, or correlation coefficients are truly different or are different by chance alone.

Significance is usually stated as a proportion. We talk about means being different at the ".05 level," for instance. What this means is that the likelihood of our finding a mean difference as large as we did by chance alone is less than 5 in 100. The ".01 level of significance" is even more conservative. It implies that the difference we have observed would have occurred by chance—if in fact no real differences exist—less than 1 time in 100.

Let's return now to the example with which we are working in this section and add a small insight to this business of statistical significance. We have reported that the results of an experiment provide us with two mean scores: 26.0 for the group that studied in silence

statistically significant differences *differences between descriptive statistics not likely to have occurred by chance if those statistics were describing the same group*

and 28.5 for subjects who studied with classical music in the background. Our interest now is in determining the extent to which these means are statistically different or due to chance factors. As we have implied, there is a statistical test of significance that can be applied to our data to this very question. The statistical test is called a *t-test*.

There are *three* factors that influence a test of significance such as the one that would be applied to our data for this example. One, of course, is the size of the mean difference itself. *Everything else being equal*, the larger the measured difference, the more likely that the difference reflects a real difference and not chance factors. A second factor is the size of the sample, or the number of measurements being tested. *Everything else being equal*, differences based on large numbers of observations are more likely to be significant than the same differences based on fewer observations. The third factor that influences a measure of statistical significance is the variability of the data.

To see why variability (usually standard deviation) matters in determining the significance of difference between means, refer to Figure A.6. On the left side of Figure A.6 we see two distributions of X-scores that have different means (A and [$\bar{B}$]). The right side of the figure shows two other distributions that have the same mean difference ($\bar{C} - \bar{D}$). Because the variability (standard deviations) of distributions A and B is small, it is more likely that their means reflect significant differences than is the case for distributions C and D—even though the actual mean difference is the same in either case. In fact, the formula for the t-test of the significance of the difference between two means includes (1) the mean difference itself, (2) the size of the groups

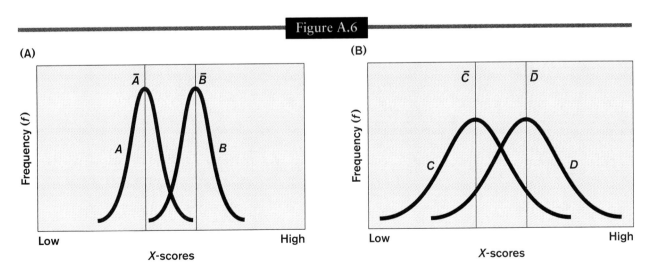

Figure A.6

(A)

Frequency (*f*)

$\bar{A}$ $\bar{B}$

A   B

Low   High

X-scores

(B)

Frequency (*f*)

$\bar{C}$ $\bar{D}$

C   D

Low   High

X-scores

The possible outcomes of two experiments. In both cases the mean differences ($\bar{B} - \bar{A}$) and ($\bar{D} - \bar{C}$) are the same, and the Ns are also the same for each distribution. Because the variabilities in the left distributions are smaller than the ones in the right, the difference between $\bar{B} - \bar{A}$ is more likely to be significant than is the difference between $\bar{D} - \bar{C}$.

involved, or N, and (3) the standard deviations of the scores from each group.

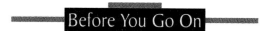

Before You Go On

What is meant by "test of statistical significance"?

What does it mean to say that two means, for example, are statistically significant at the 0.01 level?

SOME NORMAL CURVE STATISTICS

As I have suggested in our Topics on personality assessment and intelligence, many of the measurements we make in psychology tend to fall into a similar pattern. Particularly when measurements are made on large numbers of subjects, we commonly find that they fall into a distribution we call the **normal curve** (see Figure A.7). The normal curve is a frequency distribution that is symmetrical and bell shaped. As you can see, scores that are normally distributed tend to bunch

normal curve *a commonly found, symmetrical, bell-shaped frequency distribution*

Figure A.7

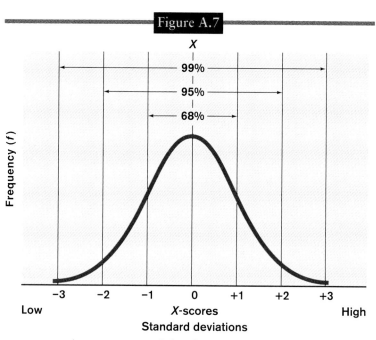

The percentage of cases in a normal distribution falling between ± 1 SD around the mean (68%), ± 2 SD (95 percent), and ± 3 SD (99 percent). The curve is symmetrical, and the mean divides it exactly in half. Also note that virtually all scores fall between 3 standard deviations below the mean and 3 standard deviations above the mean.

around the mean and become infrequent at the extreme values of *X* (whatever the *X*-scores may be). Because this normal distribution of scores does occur so often, we tend to know a lot about the nature of this curve.

The normal curve is simply a graphical representation of a collection of numbers. As such, we can compute the mean and the standard deviation of the scores that make up the distribution. Because the normal distribution is symmetrical, the mean always falls precisely in the middle of the distribution and is coincident with the median and the mode. *That is, there are just as many scores above the mean as there are below it.* We also know how many scores, or what proportion of scores, fall within standard deviation units around the mean. For example, we know that 68 percent of all scores fall between 1 standard deviation below the mean and 1 standard deviation above the mean (Figure A.7). It is also the case that 95 percent of the cases fall between ± 2 standard deviations around the mean. Almost all the cases (about 99 percent) in a normal distribution fall between −3 and +3 standard deviations around the mean. What good is this sort of information? Let's look at an example problem.

When many people are measured, IQ scores tend to fall in distributions that we may consider to be normal distributions. Figure A.8 depicts a theoretical IQ distribution where, by definition, the mean equals 100 and the standard deviation is equal to 15 IQ points. We might want to know, for instance, what percentage of the population has an IQ score above 100. Well, that's an easy one. Because the

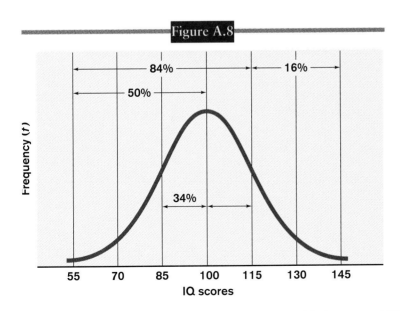

Figure A.8

A theoretical normal curve of IQ scores. Here we can see, with the mean = 100, and SD = 15, that 84 percent of the population has an IQ of 115 or less (50 percent to the mean and 34 percent from the mean to +1 SD above the mean). Thus, only 16 percent have IQs above 115.

mean equals 100, and because the mean divides the distribution exactly in half, 50 percent of the cases fall above 100 and 50 percent of the cases fall below an IQ of 100, so the answer is 50 percent.

What percentage of the population has an IQ score above 115? This takes a little more effort, and following along with Figure A.8 might help. We might work backward. If we know the percentage of cases in the shaded portion of the curve (up to IQ = 115) then the difference between that percentage and 100 will be the percentage who have IQs above 115. We can't determine the shaded percentage by inspection, but we can do so in a few easy steps. Up to the mean fall one-half, or 50 percent, of the cases (this we've already established). Now what about that segment between 100 and 115? What we do know (check Figure A.7 again) is that 68 percent of the cases fall between –1 standard deviation and +1 standard deviation. In a normal distribution, the mean divides this segment exactly in half, so that between the mean and 1 standard deviation above the mean are included 34 percent of the cases. (Note that IQ = 115 *is* 1 SD above the mean.) So now we have 50 percent to the mean of 100, and 34 percent from the mean to 115. We add the two together and determine that 84 percent of the cases fall *below* an IQ of 115, so 16 percent must fall above it. Using the same logic, we can convert any score to a percentage or proportion, if we are dealing with a normal curve. To do so for scores that do not fall precisely on standard deviation units above or below the mean involves a slight complication, but the general method is the same as we have indicated here. What percentage of the population (in accord with Figures A.7 and A.8) have earned IQ scores above 130? (The answer is 2.5 percent. Can you see where that comes from?)

Before You Go On

What is a normal curve?

In a normal curve, what percentage of the cases falls between ± 1, ± 2, and ± 3 standard deviations around the mean?

APPENDIX SUMMARY

What is a frequency distribution and what is a histogram? What are they used for?

As its name suggests, a frequency distribution is a way of organizing collected data by listing all scores (*X*-values) in order and indicating the frequency with which each occurs. A histogram is a bar graph that represents the frequency with which *X*-values occur by the height of a bar over each *X*-value. Both histograms and frequency distributions help us to summarize data so that we may make some determinations about their nature by visual inspection.

Name and define three measures of central tendency.

There are three measures of central tendency, or average: (1) the *mean* ($[\overline{X}]$), the sum of X-scores divided by the number of scores, that is, $[X] = \Sigma X/N$; (2) the *median*, the score above which and below which fall 50 percent of the scores; and (3) the *mode*, the most frequently occurring score in the distribution.

What is the formula for standard deviation, and of what is it a measure?

The standard deviation (SD) is a measure of the spread, or dispersion, of the scores in a distribution. It is the average of the extent to which each score in the distribution deviates from its mean. The formula for standard deviation is:

$$SD = \sqrt{\frac{\Sigma(X - \overline{X})^2}{N}}$$

What is meant by "test of statistical significance"?

What does it mean to say that two means, for example, are statistically significant at the 0.01 level?

A test of statistical significance tells us about the likelihood that an observed descriptive statistical difference might have occurred by chance. For example, to say that the difference between the two means is "statistically significant at the 0.01 level" means that if there were no real difference between the groups from which the means came, the likelihood of discovering a mean difference as large as the one observed is less than 1 in 100.

What is a normal curve?

In a normal curve, what percentage of the cases falls between ± 1, ± 2, and ± 3 standard deviations around the mean?

The normal curve depicts data often encountered in psychology when large numbers of measurements are made. It is a graph of frequencies of scores that is symmetrical and bell shaped. Within 1 standard deviation above the mean and 1 standard deviation below the mean fall 68 percent of all the cases measured. Between ± 2 SDs around the mean fall 95 percent of all cases, and 99 percent of all cases fall between −3 SDs and +3 SDs around the mean.

abnormal in psychology: maladaptive cognitions, affect, or behaviors at odds with social expectations and that result in stress or discomfort (p. 589)

absolute threshold the physical intensity of a stimulus that one can detect 50 percent of the time (p. 99)

accommodation in Piaget's theory, the process of changing or revising an existing schema as a result of new experiences (p. 372)

accommodation in vision, the process in which the shape of the lens is changed by the ciliary muscles to focus an image on the retina (pp. 113, 129)

acquired immune deficiency syndrome (AIDS) a deadly disease caused by a virus (the HIV) that destroys the body's natural immune system; can be transmitted by an interchange of blood or semen (p. 576)

acquisition the process in classical conditioning in which the strength of the CR increases with repeated pairings of the CS and UCS (p. 209)

acquisition the process in operant conditioning in which the rate of a reinforced response increases (p. 226)

action potential the short-lived burst caused by a change in the difference in electrical charge between the inside and outside of a neuron when it fires (p. 56)

actor-observer bias the overuse of internal attributions to explain the behaviors of others and external attributions to explain our own behaviors (p. 694)

addiction an extreme dependency, usually accompanied by symptoms of tolerance and painful withdrawal (p. 188)

adolescence the developmental period between childhood and adulthood, often begun at puberty and ending with full physical growth; generally between the ages of 12 and 20 (p. 391)

affect one's feelings or mood, or emotional state (p. 8)

agism discrimination or prejudice against someone formed solely on the basis of age (p. 410)

agoraphobia a phobic fear of being alone, or of being in public places from which escape might be difficult (p. 598)

algorithm a problem-solving strategy in which all possible solutions are generated and tested and an acceptable solution is guaranteed (p. 333)

all-or-none principle the fact that a neuron will either fire and generate a full impulse (an action potential) or not fire at all (p. 57)

alpha activity an EEG pattern associated with quiet relaxation and characterized by slow wave cycles of 8 to 12 per second (p. 173)

amnestic disorders disorders in which there is impairment of memory while other intellectual functioning is intact; mostly, problems transferring information from short- to long-term memory (p. 612)

androgens the male sex hormones produced by the testes (p. 521)

anorexia nervosa an eating disorder characterized by the reduction of body weight through self-starvation and/or increased activity (p. 510)

antianxiety drugs chemicals, such as the meprobamates and benzodiazepines, that alleviate the symptoms of anxiety; also known as tranquilizers (p. 646)

antidepressant drugs chemicals, such as MAO inhibitors and tricyclics, that reduce the symptoms of depression (p. 645)

antipsychotic drugs chemicals, such as chlorpromazine, effective in reducing psychotic symptoms (p. 643)

anxiety a general feeling of apprehension or dread accompanied by predictable physiological changes (p. 595)

applied behavior analysis (ABA) an approach, based on operant conditioning, that attempts to find solutions to human environment problems in the real world (p. 754)

aqueous humor watery fluid found in the space between the cornea and the lens that nourishes the front of the eye (p. 114)

arousal one's level of activation or excitement (p. 501)

assessment center a personnel selection procedure in which persons are tested, interviewed, and observed in a number of stressful situations by a team of evaluators (p. 729)

assimilation the process of adding new material or information to an existing schema (p. 372)

association areas the areas of the frontal, parietal, and temporal lobes in which higher mental processing occurs (p. 84)

atonia muscular immobility, associated with REM sleep, caused by the total relaxation of the muscles (p. 178)

attachment a strong two-way emotional bond, usually between a child and parent, or primary caregiver (p. 387)

attitude a relatively stable evaluative disposition directed toward some object or event; it consists of feelings, behaviors, and beliefs (p. 681)

attribution the cognitions we generate when we attempt to explain the sources of behavior (p. 691)

audience inhibition reluctance to intervene and offer assistance in front of others (p. 708)

autistic disorder a psychological disorder that begins in infancy or childhood and involves withdrawal from social contact, impairment in communication, a desire for sameness in the environment, and ritualistic behaviors (p. 610)

autokinetic effect the visual illusion of apparent motion of a stationary pinpoint of light in an otherwise dark environment (p. 135)

autonomic nervous system (ANS) neurons of the PNS that activate smooth muscles and glands (p. 63)

availability heuristic the assumption that whatever is more available in our memory is also more common or probable (p. 339)

aversion therapy a technique of behavior therapy in which an aversive stimulus, such as a shock, is paired with an undesired behavior (p. 660)

axon the long, tail-like extension of a neuron that carries an impulse away from the cell body toward a synapse (p. 53)

axon terminals the series of branching end points of an axon where one neuron communicates with the next in a series (p. 54)

babbling speech phonemes produced in rhythmic, repetitive patterns (p. 323)

basal ganglia a collection of structures in front of the limbic system that produces and depends on dopamine to control large, slow body movements (p. 80)

baseline design a method in which subjects' performance with an experimental treatment is compared with performance without that treatment (the baseline) (p. 34)

basilar membrane a structure within the cochlea that vibrates and thus stimulates the hair cells of the inner ear (p. 146)

behavior what an organism does; an action of an organism that can be observed and measured (p. 7)

behavioral observation the assessment technique of drawing conclusions about one's personality based on observations of that person's behaviors (p. 448)

behaviorism an approach to psychology emphasizing the overt, observable, measurable behavior of organisms (p. 15)

behavior therapy techniques of psychotherapy founded on principles of learning established in the psychological laboratory and aimed at changing one's behaviors (p. 659)

biofeedback a variety of operant conditioning that typically provides audio or visual information about an individual's bodily processes; the information can be used to modify these processes (p. 564)

bipolar disorder a mood disorder characterized by depression with intermittent periods of mania (p. 615)

blind spot the small region of the retina, containing no photoreceptors, where the optic nerve leaves the eye (p. 116)

brain stem the lowest part of the brain, just above the spinal cord, consisting of the medulla and the pons (p. 75)

brightness the psychological experience associated with a light's intensity, or wave amplitude (p. 109)

brightness constancy the tendency to see objects as being of constant brightness regardless of the amount or type of light available (p. 136)

British empiricists philosophers (including Locke) who claimed, among other things, that the contents of mind come from experience and observation (p. 11)

bulimia an eating disorder characterized by recurrent episodes of binge eating and then purging to remove the just-eaten food (p. 511)

case history an intensive, retrospective, and detailed study of some aspects of one (or a few) individual(s) (p. 24)

CAT scan (computerized axial tomography) a method of imaging brain structures through the computer enhancement and combining of X-ray pictures (p. 69)

cell body the largest mass of a neuron, containing the cell's nucleus (p. 53)

central nervous system (CNS) neurons and nerve fibers in the brain and spinal cord (p. 62)

cerebellum a spherical structure at the lower rear of the brain involved in the coordination of bodily movements (p. 76)

cerebral cortex (or cerebrum) the large, convoluted outer covering of the brain that is the seat of cognitive functioning and voluntary action (p. 81)

cerebral hemispheres the two halves of the cerebral cortex, separated by a deep fissure running from front to back (p. 82)

chlamydia a common STD caused by a bacterial infection that can lead to PID and infertility in women if untreated (p. 575)

chromosome literally, "colored body," found in 23 pairs in human cells; chromosomes carry genes (p. 355)

chunk a somewhat imprecise concept referring to a meaningful unit of information as represented in short-term memory (p. 264)

ciliary muscles small muscles attached to the lens that control its shape and focusing capability (p. 113)

classical conditioning learning in which an originally neutral stimulus comes to elicit a new response after having been paired with a stimulus that reflexively elicits that same response (p. 206)

client-centered therapy the humanistic psychotherapy associated with Rogers, aimed at helping a person grow and self-actualize (p. 657)

closure the Gestalt principle of organization claiming that we tend to perceive incomplete figures as whole, as complete (p. 127)

cochlea part of the inner ear where sound waves become neural impulses (p. 146)

cognitions one's perceptions, beliefs, thoughts, ideas, memories, and the like (p. 8)

cognitive dissonance a motivating discomfort or tension caused by a lack of balance or consonance among one's cognitions (pp. 502, 686)

cognitive map a mental representation of the learning situation or physical environment (p. 244)

cognitive restructuring therapy a form of cognitive therapy, associated with Beck, in which an individual is led to overcome negative self-images and pessimistic views of the future (p. 664)

collectivism in cross-cultural psychology, the tendency to set goals and make decisions based on a concern for the group or the common good (p. 381)

common fate the Gestalt principle of organization claiming that we group together, within the same figure, elements of a scene that move together in the same direction and at the same speed (p. 127)

compulsions constantly intruding, repetitive, and essentially involuntary behaviors (p. 599)

concept a mental representation of a category or class of events or objects (p. 309)

conception the moment when the father's sperm cell unites with the mother's ovum to produce a new cell (p. 355)

concrete operations stage in Piaget's theory, from age 7 years to age 12 years, when concepts can be manipulated, but not in an abstract fashion (p. 375)

conditioned response (CR) in classical conditioning, the learned response (for example, salivation) evoked by the CS after conditioning (p. 207)

conditioned stimulus (CS) in classical conditioning, an originally neutral stimulus (for example, a tone) that when paired with a UCS comes to evoke a new response (a CR) (p. 207)

cones photosensitive cells of the retina that operate best at high levels of illumination and that are responsible for color vision (p. 115)

conflict a stressor in which some goals can be satisfied only at the expense of others (p. 552)

conformity the changing of one's behavior, under perceived pressure, so that it is consistent with the behavior of others (p. 701)

consciousness the awareness or perception of the environment and of one's own mental processes (p. 166)

conservation in Piaget's theory, an appreciation that changing the physical properties of an object does not necessarily change its essence (p. 376)

contingency contracting establishing an agreement (contract) with one to reinforce appropriate behaviors; often involving token economies (p. 661)

contingency management bringing about changes in one's behaviors by controlling rewards and punishments (p. 661)

continuity the Gestalt principle of organization claiming that a stimulus or a movement will be perceived as continuing in the same smooth direction as first established (p. 126)

continuous reinforcement (CRF) schedule a reinforcement schedule in which every response is followed by a reinforcer (p. 232)

contrast the extent to which a stimulus is in some physical way different from surrounding stimuli (p. 103)

control group those participants in an experiment who do not receive any experimental treatment or manipulation (p. 33)

convergence the tendency of the eyes to move toward each other as we focus on objects close up (p. 129)

convergent thinking the reduction or focusing of many different ideas into one possible problem solution (p. 342)

conversion disorder the display of a severe physical disorder for which there is no medical explanation; often accompanied by an apparent lack of concern on the part of the patient (p. 604)

cornea the outermost structure of the eye that protects the eye and begins to focus light waves (p. 112)

corpus callosum a network of nerve fibers that connects the two hemispheres of the cerebrum (p. 85)

correlation a largely statistical technique used to determine the nature and extent of the relationship between two measured responses (p. 26)

correlation coefficient a number that indicates the nature (+ or −) and the strength (0.00 to +1.00 or −1.00) of the relationship between measured responses (p. 26)

cross laterality the process of nerve fibers crossing over at the brain stem so that the left side of the body sends impulses to, and receives impulses from, the right side of the brain, and vice versa (p. 76)

crowding the subjective feeling of discomfort caused by a sense of lack of space (p. 749)

crystallized intelligence those cognitive skills dependent on knowledge, accumulated experience, and general information (p. 473)

dark adaptation the process by which our eyes become more sensitive to light as we spend time in the dark (p. 102)

death instincts (thanatos) the inborn impulses, proposed by Freud, that compel one toward destruction; they include feelings of depression and aggression (p. 426)

debrief to inform a subject fully about the intent and/or hypotheses of one's research once data have been collected (p. 37)

decibel scale a scale of our experience of loudness in which 0 represents the absolute threshold and 120 is sensed as pain (p. 141)

defense mechanisms unconsciously applied techniques that protect the self (ego) from feelings of anxiety (p. 427)

deinstitutionalization the practice, begun in the mid-1950s, of releasing patients from mental institutions and returning them to their home communities (p. 647)

delirium a clouded state of consciousness; confusion and disorientation, with difficulty in paying attention (p. 612)

delusions false beliefs; ideas that are firmly held regardless of evidence to the contrary (p. 618)

dementia a marked loss of intellectual abilities in which memory is poor and deteriorates and judgment is adversely affected (p. 612)

dendrites extensions from a neuron's cell body where most neural impulses are received (p. 53)

denial a defense mechanism where one refuses to believe the realities of an anxiety-producing situation (p. 428)

dependence a state in which drug use is either necessary or believed to be necessary to maintain functioning at some desired level (p. 188)

dependent variables those responses measured in an experiment whose values are hypothesized to depend on manipulations of the independent variable (p. 30)

depressants drugs (such as alcohol, opiates, heroin, and barbiturates) that slow or reduce nervous system activity (p. 191)

diagnosis the act of recognizing a disorder on the basis of the presence of particular symptoms (p. 590)

difference threshold the minimal difference in a stimulus attribute that can be detected 50 percent of the time (p. 100)

diffusion of responsibility the tendency to allow others to share in the obligation to intervene (p. 710)

discrimination the phenomenon in classical conditioning in which an organism learns to make a CR in response to only one CS but not to other stimuli (p. 211)

discrimination the process of differential reinforcement wherein one stimulus is reinforced while another stimulus is not (p. 238)

displacement a defense mechanism in which one's behaviors or motives (usually aggressive) are directed at a substitute rather than the real object of those behaviors or motives (p. 429)

dissociative amnesia a psychologically caused inability—too extensive to be caused by ordinary forgetfulness—to recall important personal information (p. 605)

dissociative disorder a disorder in which one escapes from aspects of one's life or personality seen as the source of discomfort (p. 605)

dissociative fugue a condition of amnesia accompanied by unexplained travel or change of location (p. 606)

dissociative identity disorder the existence within one individual of two or more distinct personalities, each of which is dominant at a particular time (p. 606)

divergent thinking the creation of many ideas or potential problem solutions from one idea (p. 342)

dominant gene a gene that carries a trait that will be expressed regardless of the gene it is paired with (p. 355)

dopamine hypothesis the view that a heightened sensitivity to the neurotransmitter dopamine may cause schizophrenic symptoms (p. 624)

double-blind technique a protection against bias in which both subjects and data collector are kept from knowing the hypothesis of an experiment (p. 34)

Down's syndrome a condition of several symptoms, including mental retardation, caused by an extra (47th) chromosome (p. 481)

drive a state of tension resulting from a need that arouses and directs an organism's behavior (p. 496)

drug abuse a lack of control, a disruption of interpersonal relationships or difficulties at work, and a history of maladaptive use for at least one month (p. 188)

dysthymia a mood disorder that is basically a mild case of depression; it is chronic, with recurrent pessimism, low energy level, and low self-esteem (p. 615)

eardrum the outermost membrane of the ear; set in motion by the vibrations of a sound; transmits vibrations to the ossicles (p. 146)

ego the aspect of personality that encompasses the sense of "self"; it is in contact with the real world and operates on the reality principle (p. 427)

elaborative rehearsal a mechanism for processing information into LTM that involves thinking about information, organizing it, and making it meaningful (p. 271)

electroconvulsive therapy (ECT) a treatment, usually for severe depression, in which an electric current passed across a patient's head causes a seizure (p. 641)

electrode a fine wire used either to stimulate or record the electrical activity of neural tissue (p. 67)

electroencephalogram (EEG) an instrument used to measure and record the electrical activity of the brain (pp. 68, 173)

electromyogram (EMG) an instrument used to measure and record muscle tension/relaxation (p. 173)

emotion an experience that includes a subjective feeling, a cognitive interpretation, a physical reaction, and a behavioral expression (p. 530)

empathic able to understand and share the essence of another's feelings, or to view from another's perspective (p. 657)

encoding the active process of representing, or putting information into memory (p. 256)

encoding specificity principle the hypothesis that we can retrieve only what we have stored and that retrieval is enhanced to the extent that retrieval cues match encoding cues (p. 282)

endocrine system a network of glands that secrete hormones directly into the bloodstream (p. 64)

environmental psychology the field of applied psychology that studies how the general environment affects the behavior and mental processes of individuals and how individuals affect their environments (p. 744)

epigenetic model an interactionist view of development claiming that development emerges based on one's genetic programming and one's experiences (p. 356)

episodic memory a subsystem of LTM, in which personal experiences are stored (p. 273)

equity theory the view that workers are motivated to match their inputs and outcomes with those of fellow workers in similar positions (p. 735)

estrogens the female sex hormones produced by the ovaries (p. 521)

etiology the cause or predisposing factors of a disorder (p. 591)

expectancy theory the view that workers make logical choices to do what they believe will result in their attaining outcomes of highest value (p. 735)

experimental group those participants in an experiment who receive some treatment or manipulation; there may be more than one in an experiment (p. 33)

experiments operations used to investigate relationships between manipulated events (independent variables) and measured events (dependent variables) while other events (extraneous variables) are controlled or eliminated (p. 29)

external attribution an explanation of behavior in terms of something outside the person; a situational attribution (p. 691)

extinction the process in classical conditioning in which the strength of the CR decreases with repeated presentations of the CS alone (without the UCS) (p. 210)

extinction the process in operant conditioning in which the rate of a response decreases as reinforcers are withheld (p. 226)

extraneous variables those factors in an experiment that need to be minimized or eliminated so as not to affect the dependent variable (p. 30)

family therapy a type of group therapy focusing on the roles, interdependence, and communication skills of family members (p. 666)

fantasy a defense mechanism that involves the imagination or daydreaming as a reaction to stress and anxiety (p. 428)

fetal alcohol syndrome (FAS) a cluster of symptoms (e.g., low birth weight, poor muscle tone, intellectual retardation) associated with a child born to a mother who was a heavy drinker of alcohol during pregnancy (p. 362)

figure-ground relationship the Gestalt psychology principle that stimuli are selected and perceived as figures against a ground (background) (p. 124)

flashbulb memories particularly clear, vivid memories that are easily retrieved but not necessarily accurate in all detail (p. 284)

flooding a technique of behavior therapy in which a person is confronted (in vivo) with the object of his or her fear while accompanied by the therapist (p. 659)

fluid intelligence those cognitive skills dependent on speed, adaptation, flexibility, and abstract reasoning (p. 473)

formal operations stage in Piaget's theory, ages older than 12 years, when one can generate and test abstract hypotheses and manipulate symbolic concepts (p. 377)

fovea the region at the center of the retina, consisting solely of cones, where acuity is best in daylight (p. 116)

free association the procedure in psychoanalysis in which the patient is to express whatever comes to mind without editing responses (p. 654)

frontal lobes the largest of the cerebral lobes, located in front of the central fissure and above the lateral fissure (p. 82)

frustration a stressor; the blocking or thwarting of goal-directed behavior (p. 551)

frustration-aggression hypothesis the view (now discredited) that all aggression stems from frustration (p. 566)

functional fixedness a type of mental set that interferes with the discovery of a new use for an object because of the experience of using the object in some other function (p. 337)

functionalism an approach to psychology emphasizing the study of the mind and consciousness as they help an organism adapt to its environment (p. 14)

fundamental attribution error the tendency to overuse internal attributions when explaining behavior (p. 693)

"g" (g-factor) general intelligence; a global measure of intellectual ability (p. 458)

gate-control theory the theory of pain sensation that argues that there are brain centers that regulate the passage of pain messages from various parts of the body to the brain (p. 154)

gender one's maleness or femaleness; the state of being male or female (p. 384)

gender identity a basic sense or self-awareness of one's maleness or femaleness (p. 386)

gene the basic mechanism of hereditary transmission (p. 355)

general adaptation syndrome (GAS) Selye's description of physiological reactions made to stressors, which include the three stages of alarm, resistance, and exhaustion (p. 559)

generalization the phenomenon in classical conditioning in which a CR is elicited by stimuli different from, but similar to, the CS (p. 211)

generalization the phenomenon in operant conditioning in which a response that was reinforced in the presence of one stimulus appears in response to other, similar stimuli (p. 237)

generalized anxiety disorder persistent, chronic, and distressingly high levels of unattributable and uncontrollable anxiety or worry (p. 596)

genetics the science that studies the transmission of traits or characteristics from one generation to the next (p. 354)

genital herpes (herpes type II) the most common STD; a skin infection in the form of a rash or blisters in the genital area (p. 576)

gestalt whole, totality, configuration; where the whole (gestalt) is seen as more than the sum of its parts (p. 124)

Gestalt psychology the approach to psychology that emphasized perception, in particular how we select and organize information (p. 17)

gonads the sex glands: **testes** in males, **ovaries** in females (p. 521)

gonorrhea an STD caused by a bacterial infection of moist tissues in the genital area (p. 575)

group polarization the tendency for members of a group to give more extreme judgments following a discussion than they gave initially (p. 714)

groupthink an excessive concern for reaching a consensus in group decision making to the extent that critical evaluations of input are withheld (p. 714)

habituation in classical conditioning, a simple form of learning in which an organism comes to ignore a stimulus of little or no consequence (p. 207)

hair cells the receptor cells for hearing, located in the cochlea, stimulated by the vibrating basilar membrane; they send neural impulses to the temporal lobe of the brain (p. 146)

hallucinations perceptual experiences without sensory input; that is, perceiving that which is not there or not perceiving that which is there (pp. 184, 619)

hallucinogens drugs (such as LSD) whose major effect is the alteration of perceptual experience and mood (p. 193)

health psychology the field of applied psychology that studies psychological factors affecting physical health and illness (p. 569)

hertz (Hz) the standard measure of sound wave frequency that is the number of wave cycles per second (p. 142)

heuristic an informal and economical method of testing problem solutions without guarantee of success (p. 334)

holophrastic speech the use of one word to communicate a number of different meanings (p. 324)

homeostasis a state of balance, or equilibrium, among internal, physiological conditions (p. 501)

homosexuals persons who are sexually attracted to and aroused by members of their own sex (p. 522)

hormones a variety of chemical compounds, secreted by the glands of the endocrine system, many of which have effects on behavior or mental states (p. 64)

hue the psychological experience of color associated with a light's wavelength (p. 109)

humanistic psychology an approach to psychology emphasizing the person, or self, as a central matter of concern (p. 16)

hypnosis an altered state of consciousness characterized by an increase in suggestibility, attention, and imagination (p. 182)

hypochondriasis a mental disorder involving the fear of developing some serious disease or medical illness (p. 603)

hypothalamus a small structure near the limbic system in the center of the brain, associated with feeding, temperature regulation, drinking, sex and aggression (pp. 79, 505)

hypothesis a tentative explanation that can be tested and confirmed or rejected (p. 6)

id the instinctive aspect of personality that seeks immediate gratification of impulses; it operates on the pleasure principle (p. 426)

idealistic principle the force that governs the superego; opposed to the id, it seeks adherence to standards of ethics and morality (p. 427)

identity crisis the effort to define and integrate one's sense of self and what one's attitudes, beliefs, and values should be (p. 396)

illusion a perception that is at odds with (different from) what we know as physical reality (p. 135)

implosive therapy a behavior therapy in which one imagines one's worst fears, experiencing extreme anxiety in the safe surroundings of the therapist's office (p. 659)

in-basket technique an assessment technique requiring applicants to respond to a variety of situations that might be encountered in a typical workday (p. 729)

incentives external stimuli an organism may be motivated to approach or avoid (p. 499)

independent variables those events in an experiment that are manipulated by the experimenter; they are hypothesized to produce changes in responses (p. 30)

individualism in cross-cultural psychology, the tendency to set goals and make decisions based on a concern for one's self or the individual (p. 381)

inferiority complex the feeling that we are less able than others to solve life's problems and get along in the world (p. 432)

insanity a legal term for diminished capacity, inability to tell right from wrong, and inability to exercise control over one's actions (p. 593)

insomnia the inability to fall asleep and/or stay asleep (p. 180)

instinctive drift the tendency of behaviors that have been conditioned to eventually revert to more natural, instinctive behaviors (p. 241)

instincts unlearned, complex patterns of behavior that occur in the presence of certain stimuli (p. 495)

intelligence the capacity to understand the world and the resourcefulness to cope with its challenges; that which an intelligence test measures (p. 456)

interactive dualism Descartes's position that a separate body and mind influence each other and are thus knowable (p. 10)

intermittent reinforcement schedule reinforcement schedule in which responses are not reinforced every time they occur (p. 232)

internal attribution an explanation of behavior in terms of something (a trait) within the person; a dispositional attribution (p. 691)

interview the assessment technique involving a conversational interchange between an interviewer and another in order to gain information about the latter's personality (p. 450)

ion an electrically charged (either + or −) chemical particle (p. 56)

IQ (intelligence quotient) a measure of intelligence found by dividing one's mental age by one's chronological age, and multiplying the result by 100 (p. 463)

iris the colored structure of the eye that reflexively opens or closes the pupil (p. 113)

job analysis a complete and specific description of a job, including the qualities and behaviors required to do it well (p. 725)

job satisfaction an attitude; a collection of positive feelings about one's job or job experiences (p. 737)

just noticeable difference (j.n.d.) the minimal change in a stimulus attribute, such as intensity, that can be detected (p. 100)

just world hypothesis the belief that the world is just and that people get what they deserve (p. 693)

kinesthetic sense the position sense that tells us the position of various parts of our bodies and what our muscles and joints are doing (p. 153)

language a large collection of arbitrary symbols that have significance for a language-using community and that follow certain rules of combination (p. 316)

latent learning hidden learning that is not demonstrated in performance until that performance is reinforced (p. 244)

law of effect (Thorndike's) the observation that responses that lead to a "satisfying state of affairs" tend to be repeated; responses that do not lead to a satisfying state of affairs tend not to be repeated (p. 223)

learning demonstration of a relatively permanent change in behavior that occurs as the result of practice or experience (p. 204)

lens the structure behind the iris that changes shape to focus visual images in the eye (p. 113)

lesion a cut or incision that destroys specific areas of tissue (p. 67)

levels-of-processing model of memory the view that there is only one memory, but that information can be processed within that memory at distance degrees, levels, or depths (p. 257)

libido the energy that activates the sexual instincts (p. 426)

life instincts (eros) inborn impulses, proposed by Freud, that compel one toward survival; they include hunger, thirst, and sex (p. 426)

light a radiant energy that can be represented in wave form with wavelengths between 380 and 760 nanometers (p. 108)

limbic system a collection of structures, including the amygdala and septum, involved in emotionality; and the hippocampus, involved in forming long-term memories (p. 78)

linguistic intuitions judgments or decisions about the syntactic acceptability of utterances without the ability to specify why (p. 320)

lobotomy a psychosurgical technique in which the prefrontal lobes of the cerebral cortex are severed from lower brain centers (p. 639)

long-term memory (LTM) a type of memory with virtually unlimited capacity and very long, if not limitless, duration (p. 265)

loudness the psychological experience correlated with the intensity, or amplitude, of a sound wave (p. 141)

magnetic resonance imaging (MRI) a process that provides clear, detailed pictures of the brain by recording energy from cells when the brain has been placed in a magnetic field (p. 69)

maintenance rehearsal a process of rote repetition (reattending) to keep information in short-term memory (p. 262)

major depression a mood disorder characterized by inexplicable moods of sadness and hopelessness, accompanied by a loss of pleasure or interest in usual activities (p. 615)

malleus, incus, and stapes (collectively, *ossicles*) three small bones that intensify sound vibrations and transmit them from the eardrum to the oval window (p. 146)

mania heightened euphoria and increased activity, which typically occurs between episodes of depression (p. 615)

matching phenomenon the tendency to select partners whose level of physical attractiveness matches our own (p. 699)

meaningfulness the extent to which new information evokes associations with information already in memory (p. 286)

meditation a self-induced state of altered consciousness characterized by a focusing of attention and relaxation (p. 185)

medulla an area of the brain stem that monitors breathing and heart rate, and where most cross laterality occurs (p. 76)

memory the cognitive capacity to encode, store, and retrieve information (p. 256)

menarche a female's first menstrual period, a sure sign of the beginning of adolescence (p. 394)

mental processes internal activities of consciousness, including cognitions and affect (p. 8)

mental retardation a condition indicated by an IQ below 70 that begins during the developmental period and is associated with impairment in adaptive functioning (p. 479)

mental set a predisposed (set) way to perceive or respond to something; an expectation (pp. 106, 336)

mere exposure phenomenon the tendency to increase our liking of people and things as a result of recurring contact (p. 697)

meta-analysis a statistical procedure of combining the results of many studies to see more clearly any relationships among observations that may be present (p. 35)

method of loci the mnemonic device that mentally places information to be retrieved at a series of familiar locations (loci) (p. 289)

microsleep a very brief episode of sleep discernible only by examination of an EEG record (p. 179)

MMPI a paper-and-pencil personality test designed to indicate the presence of a psychological disorder (p. 451)

mnemonic devices strategies for improving retrieval that take advantage of existing memories in order to make new material more meaningful (p. 287)

modeling the acquisition of new responses through the imitation of another who responds appropriately (p. 662)

monochromatic literally *one-colored*; a pure light consisting of light waves all of the same wavelength (p. 111)

mood disorders disorders of affect or feeling; usually depression; less frequently mania and depression occurring in cycles (p. 614)

morpheme the smallest unit of meaning in a language (p. 319)

motivation the process of arousing, maintaining, and directing behavior (p. 494)

motor areas the strips at the back of the frontal lobes that control voluntary movement (p. 84)

multistore models of memory descriptions of memory that propose a number of distinct types (or stores) of memory, each with its own manner of processing information (p. 257)

myelin a white, fatty covering found on some axons that serves to insulate and protect them, while increasing the speed of impulses (p. 53)

nanometer (nm) one millionth of a millimeter; the unit of measurement for the wavelength of light (p. 109)

narcolepsy a disorder that involves unintentional sleeping, muscle paralysis, and immediate REM sleep; is resistant to treatment (p. 180)

narrative chaining the mnemonic device of relating words in a story, thus organizing them in a meaningful way (p. 287)

naturalistic observation the method of observing and noting behaviors as they occur, without the involvement of the observer (p. 21)

need a lack or shortage of some biological essential resulting from deprivation (p. 496)

need for affiliation the need to be with others and to form relationships (p. 515)

need for power the learned need to be in control of events or persons (p. 515)

need to achieve (nAch) the learned need to meet or exceed some standard of excellence in one's behaviors (p. 513)

negative reinforcer a stimulus that increases the rate of a response when that stimulus is removed after the response is made (p. 229)

neo-Freudians theorists (including Adler, Jung, and Horney) who supported the basics of psychoanalytic theory, but differed from Freud (p. 431)

neonate the newborn, from birth through the first 2 weeks (p. 365)

neural impulse a sudden and reversible change in the electrical charges within and outside a neuron, which travels from the dendrite to the axon terminal of a neuron (p. 55)

neural threshold the minimum stimulation required to produce an impulse within a neuron (p. 58)

neuron a nerve cell that transmits neural impulses; the basic building block of the nervous system (p. 52)

neurotoxins chemicals (poisons) that affect psychological processes through the nervous system (p. 753)

neurotransmitters chemical molecules released at a synapse that will, in general, either excite or inhibit neural impulse transmission (p. 58)

noise an intrusive, unwanted, or excessive experience of sound (p. 751)

norms in testing, results of a test taken by a large sample of persons whose scores can be used to make comparisons, or give meaning to new scores (p. 448)

nuclei small collections or bundles of neural cell bodies (p. 76)

object permanence the appreciation that an object no longer in view can still exist and reappear later (p. 373)

observer bias when one's own motives, expectations, and past experiences interfere with the objectivity of one's observations (p. 22)

obsessions ideas or thoughts that involuntarily and constantly intrude into awareness (p. 599)

obsessive-compulsive disorder (OCD) a combination of constantly intruding thoughts and constantly intruding behaviors (p. 599)

occipital lobes the cerebral lobes at the very back of the brain (p. 82)

operant behavior(s) used by an organism to operate on its environment (p. 223)

operant conditioning a procedure that changes the rate of a response on the basis of the consequences that result from that response (p. 223)

operational definition a definition of a concept given in terms of the methods (or operations) used to measure or create that concept (p. 8)

optic chiasma the location in the brain where impulses from light in the left visual field cross to the right side of the brain, and impulses from light in the right visual field cross to the left side of the brain (p. 119)

optic nerve the fiber, consisting of many neurons, that leaves the eye and carries impulses to the occipital lobe of the brain (p. 116)

orienting reflex the simple, unlearned response of orienting toward, or attending to, a new or unusual stimulus (p. 207)

overlearning the practice or rehearsal of material over and above what is needed to learn it (p. 293)

overregularization the excessive application of an acquired language rule (e.g., for plurals or past tense) in a situation where it is not appropriate (p. 326)

panic disorder a disorder in which anxiety attacks suddenly and unpredictably; there may be periods free from anxiety (p. 596)

parasympathetic division neurons (of the ANS) involved in the maintenance of states of calm and relaxation (p. 64)

parietal lobes the lobes of the cerebrum found behind the frontal lobes, in front of the occipital lobes, and above the temporal lobes (p. 82)

Parkinson's disease a disorder of movement caused by damage to tissues in the basal ganglia (p. 80)

perception the cognitive process of selecting, organizing, and interpreting stimuli (p. 97)

performance criteria specific behaviors or characteristics a person should have in order to do a job as well as possible (p. 726)

peripheral nervous system (PNS) neurons not found in the brain or spinal cord, but in the periphery of the body (p. 62)

personality those affects, behaviors, and cognitions that characterize a person in a variety of situations. (p. 424)

personality disorders enduring patterns of perceiving, relating to, and thinking about the environment and oneself that are inflexible and maladaptive (p. 607)

personal space the mobile "bubble" of space around you reserved for intimate relationships and into which others may enter only by invitation (p. 745)

PET scan (positron emission tomography) a picture of brain functioning provided by an image of radioactive chemicals in a living, intact brain (p. 69)

phenomenology the study of events as they are experienced by the individual, not as they actually occur (p. 40)

phenylketonuria (PKU) a genetically caused disorder that produces mental retardation and that is now detectable and, thus, preventable (p. 482)

pheromones chemicals that produce an odor used as a method of communication between organisms (p. 150)

phi phenomenon the visual illusion of the apparent motion of stationary lights flashing on and off alternately (p. 135)

phobic disorder an intense, irrational fear that leads a person to avoid the feared object, activity, or situation (pp. 216, 597)

phoneme the smallest unit of sound in the spoken form of a language (p. 318)

photoreceptors light-sensitive cells (cones and rods) of the retina that convert light energy into neural energy (p. 115)

pinna the outer ear, which collects and funnels sound waves into the auditory canal toward the eardrum (p. 146)

pitch the psychological experience that corresponds to sound wave frequency and gives rise to high (treble) or low (bass) sounds (p. 142)

placebo an inactive substance that has its effect because a person believes it will be effective (p. 156)

plasticity a capacity to be molded and shaped by experiences with the environment (p. 357)

pleasure principle the impulse of the id to seek immediate gratification to reduce tensions (p. 427)

pluralistic ignorance a condition in which the inaction of others leads each individual in a group to interpret a situation as a nonemergency, thus leading to general inactivity (p. 709)

pons a brain stem structure, forming a bridge between the brain and the spinal cord, that monitors the sleep-wake cycle (p. 76)

population density a quantitative measure of the number of persons (or animals) per unit of area (p. 749)

positive reinforcer a stimulus that increases the rate of a response it follows (p. 229)

positive test strategy the heuristic of sticking with an acceptable decision or solution, even if a better one might exist (p. 340)

posttraumatic stress disorder (PTSD) an anxiety disorder in which disruptive recollections, distressing dreams, flashbacks, and felt anxiety occur well after the experience of a traumatic event (p. 601)

pragmatics the study of how social context affects the meaning of linguistic events (p. 321)

prenatal period the period of development from conception to birth (p. 358)

preoperational stage in Piaget's theory, from age 2 to 6 years, characterized by egocentrism and the beginning of symbol development (p. 375)

primary hues red, green, and blue; those colors of light from which all others can be produced (p. 121)

primary mental abilities in Thurstone's model, the seven distinct abilities that constitute intelligence (p. 458)

primary reinforcers stimuli (usually biologically or physiologically based) that increase the rate of a response with no previous experience required (p. 230)

proactive interference the inhibition of retrieval of recently learned material caused by material learned earlier (p. 298)

problem a situation in which there is a discrepancy between one's current state and one's desired, or goal, state, with no clear way of getting from one to the other (p. 328)

procedural memory a subsystem of LTM, in which stimulus-response associations and skilled patterns of responses are stored (p. 272)

process schizophrenia schizophrenia in which the onset of the symptoms is comparatively gradual (p. 621)

progesterone one of the most important of the female estrogens, or sex hormones (p. 521)

prognosis the prediction of the future course of an illness or disorder (pp. 512, 598)

projection a defense mechanism that involves seeing in others traits or motives that would make one anxious if seen in oneself (p. 428)

projective technique an assessment technique requiring a person to respond to ambiguous stimuli in hopes that the person will reveal aspects of his or her personality (p. 452)

prototype the member of a category that best typifies or represents that category (p. 310)

proximity the Gestalt principle of organization claiming that stimuli will be perceived as belonging together if they occur together in space or time (p. 125)

psychiatry the subfield of medicine that studies, diagnoses, and treats mental disorders (p. 168)

psychoactive drug a chemical that affects psychological processes and consciousness (p. 188)

psychoanalysis the form of psychotherapy associated with Freud, aimed at helping the patient gain insight into unconscious conflicts (p. 653)

psychoanalytic the approach to personality associated with Freud and his followers that relies on instincts and the unconscious as explanatory concepts (p. 425)

psychoanalytic psychology the approach to psychology associated with Freud that emphasizes instincts and unconscious mental processes (p. 16)

psycholinguistics the science that studies the cognitive processes involved in the use and acquisition of language (p. 316)

psychological test an objective, standardized measure of a sample of behavior (p. 446)

psychology the science of behavior and mental processes (p. 4)

psychophysics the study of the relationship between the physical attributes of stimuli and the psychological experiences they produce (p. 97)

psychosurgery a surgical procedure designed to affect one's psychological or behavioral reactions (p. 639)

psychotic symptoms symptoms of a severe psychological disorder that indicate a loss of contact with reality and a gross impairment of functioning (p. 643)

puberty the stage of physical development at which one becomes capable of sexual reproduction (p. 394)

publicly verifiable the agreement (verifiability) of observers (public) that a behavior or an event did or did not take place (p. 7)

punishment the administration of a punisher, which is a stimulus that decreases the rate, or probability, of a response that precedes it (p. 235)

pupil the opening of the iris, which changes size in relation to the amount of light available and to emotional factors (p. 113)

quality of work life (QWL) a group of factors concerning one's work that influence one's attitude toward one's job (p. 738)

random assignment the selection of members of a population in such a way that each has an equal chance of being assigned to any one group (p. 33)

rational-emotive therapy (RET) a form of cognitive therapy, associated with Ellis, aimed at changing a person's irrational beliefs or maladaptive cognitions (p. 663)

rationalization a defense mechanism that excuses one's behaviors rather than facing the anxiety-producing reasons for them (p. 428)

reactive schizophrenia schizophrenia in which the onset of symptoms is comparatively sudden (p. 621)

reality principle the force that governs the ego, arbitrating between the demands of the id, the superego, and the real world (p. 427)

recall a measure of retrieval in which an individual is given the fewest possible cues to aid retrieval and must produce information to which he or she has been previously exposed (p. 278)

recessive gene a gene that carries a trait that will be expressed only if it is paired with another similar recessive gene (p. 355)

recognition a measure of retrieval in which an individual is required to identify material previously learned (p. 278)

reflex an unlearned, automatic response that occurs in the presence of a specific stimulus (p. 206)

regression a defense mechanism that involves returning to earlier, more primitive levels of behavior that were once effective (p. 429)

reinforcement a process that increases the rate, or probability, of the response it follows (p. 228)

reinforcers stimuli that increase the rate, or probability, of the responses they follow (p. 228)

relearning a technique of noting the improvement in performance when learning material a second time (p. 280)

reliability consistency or dependability; in testing, the consistency of test scores (p. 447)

REM sleep rapid-eye-movement sleep, during which vivid dreaming occurs, as do heightened levels of physiological functioning (p. 176)

representativeness heuristic the assumption that judgments made about a prototypic member of a category will hold for all members of the category (p. 339)

repression a defense mechanism referring to motivated forgetting of an anxiety-producing event or desire (p. 428)

resistance in psychoanalysis, the inability or unwillingness to discuss freely some aspect of one's life (p. 655)

resting potential the difference in electrical charge between the inside of a neuron and the outside when it is at rest (p. 56)

reticular activating system (RAS) a network of nerve fibers, extending from the brain stem to the cerebrum, involved in maintaining levels of arousal (p. 78)

retina layers of cells at the back of the eye that contain the photosensitive rod and cone cells (p. 115)

retinal disparity the phenomenon in which each retina receives a different (disparate) view of the same three-dimensional object (p. 129)

retrieval the process of locating, removing, and using information stored in memory (p. 257)

retroactive interference the inhibition of retrieval of previously learned material caused by material learned later (p. 297)

rods photosensitive cells of the retina that are most active in low levels of illumination and do not respond differentially to various wavelengths of light (p. 115)

Rorschach inkblot test a projective technique in which a person is asked to say what he or she sees in a series of inkblots (p. 453)

sample the subset or portion of a larger population chosen for study (p. 24)

saturation the psychological experience associated with the purity of a light wave; the most saturated lights are monochromatic and the least saturated are white light (p. 111)

schema a system of organized, general knowledge, stored in long-term memory, that guides the encoding and retrieval of information (p. 290)

schemas organized mental representations of the world that are adaptive and formed by experience (p. 372)

schizophrenia a complex family of disorders characterized by impairment of cognitive functioning, delusions and hallucinations, social withdrawal, and inappropriate affect (p. 618)

science an organized body of knowledge gained through application of scientific methods (p. 5)

scientific methods a series of procedures that involve observation, description, control, and replication used to explain phenomena (p. 5)

secondary reinforcers stimuli that increase the rate of a response because of their having been associated with other reinforcers; also called *conditioned, or learned, reinforcers* (p. 231)

self-serving bias the tendency to attribute our successes to our own effort and abilities, and our failures to situational, external sources (p. 693)

semantic memory a subsystem of LTM, in which vocabulary, facts, simple concepts, and rules are stored (p. 272)

semantics the study of the meaning of words and sentences (p. 319)

sensation the process of receiving information from the environment and changing that input into nervous system activity (p. 96)

sensorimotor stage in Piaget's theory, from birth to age 2 years, when a child learns by sensing and doing (p. 373)

sensory adaptation the process in which our sensory experience tends to decrease or diminish with continued exposure to a stimulus (p. 101)

sensory areas those areas of the cerebral cortex that receive impulses from sense receptors (p. 83)

sensory memory a type of memory that stores large amounts of information for very brief periods (a few seconds or less) (p. 258)

set point a normal, optimal level (or value) of equilibrium, or balance, among physiological or psychological reactions (p. 501)

sexual dysfunction any of a number of chronic difficulties or problems with sexual functioning (p. 525)

sexually transmitted diseases (STDs) contagious diseases that are usually transmitted through sexual contact (p. 575)

s-factors specific cognitive, intellectual skills or abilities; for Spearman, what makes up intelligence, when combined with a g-factor (p. 458)

shape constancy the tendency to see objects as being of constant shape regardless of the shape of the retinal image (p. 136)

shaping a procedure of reinforcing successive approximations of a desired response until that desired response is made (p. 226)

short-term memory (STM) a type of memory with limited capacity and limited duration; also called working memory (p. 259)

signal detection theory the view that signal detection is a matter of decision making, of separating a signal from ground (background) noise (p. 101)

similarity the Gestalt principle of organization claiming that stimuli will be perceived together if they share some common characteristics (p. 126)

single-blind technique a protection against bias in which subjects are kept from knowing the purpose, or hypothesis, of an experiment (p. 34)

size constancy the tendency to see objects as being of constant size regardless of the size of the retinal image (p. 136)

sleep apnea involves patterns of sleep during which breathing stops entirely (p. 181)

social facilitation improved performance due to the presence of others (p. 712)

social interference impaired performance due to the presence of others (p. 713)

social learning theory the theory that learning takes place through observation and imitation of models (p. 246)

social loafing the tendency to decrease one's individual work effort as the size of the group in which one is working increases (p. 711)

social psychology the field of psychology concerned with how others influence the thoughts, feelings, and behaviors of the individual (p. 680)

socioeconomic status (SES) a measure that reflects one's income, educational, and occupational level (p. 555)

somatic nervous system sensory and motor neurons outside the CNS that serve sense receptors and skeletal muscles (p. 63)

somatoform disorders psychological disorders reflecting physical or bodily symptoms or complaints for which there is no known physical cause (p. 603)

spinal cord a mass of interconnected neurons within the spine that conveys impulses to and from the brain and is involved in some reflex behaviors (p. 72)

spinal reflex an automatic, involuntary response to a stimulus that involves sensory neurons, interneurons, and motor neurons (p. 73)

split-brain procedure a surgical technique of severing the corpus callosum, allowing the two hemispheres to operate independently (p. 85)

spontaneous recovery the phenomenon in classical conditioning in which a previously extinguished CR returns after a rest interval (p. 210)

spontaneous recovery the phenomenon in operant conditioning in which a previously extinguished response returns after a rest interval (p. 227)

sport psychology the application of psychological principles to sport and physical activity at all levels of skill development (p. 755)

stage of the embryo developmental period from 2 to 8 weeks (p. 359)

stage of the fetus developmental period from week 8 until birth (p. 359)

stage of the zygote developmental period from conception to the age of 2 weeks (p. 358)

state-dependent memory the hypothesis that retrieval can be enhanced by the extent to which one's state of mind at retrieval matches one's state of mind at encoding (p. 284)

stimulants drugs (such as caffeine, cocaine, and amphetamines) that increase nervous system activities (p. 189)

storage the process of holding encoded information in memory (p. 256)

strategy in problem solving, a systematic plan for generating possible solutions that can be tested to see if they are correct (p. 332)

stress a complex set of reactions to real or perceived threats to one's well-being that motivates adaptation (p. 550)

stressors the sources or stimuli for stress, which include frustration, conflict, and life events (p. 550)

structuralism the approach to psychology associated with Wundt that concerned itself with the structure and operations of the human mind and consciousness (p. 13)

subjective contours the perception of a contour (a line or plane) that is not there, but is suggested by other aspects of a scene (p. 127)

subliminal perception the process of perceiving and responding to stimuli presented at levels below one's absolute threshold (p. 171)

superego the aspect of personality that refers to ethical or moral considerations; it operates on the idealistic principle (p. 427)

survey a means of collecting observations from a large number of subjects, usually by interview or questionnaire (p. 23)

sympathetic division neurons (of the ANS) involved in states of emotionality (p. 64)

synapse the location at which an impulse is relayed from one neuron to another by means of neurotransmitters (p. 58)

synaptic cleft the space between the membrane of an axon terminal and the membrane of the next neuron in a sequence (p. 58)

syntax the rules that govern how the morphemes of a language may be combined to form meaningful utterances (p. 320)

syphilis an STD caused by a bacterial infection; the disease may pass through four stages, ultimately resulting in death (p. 575)

systematic desensitization the application of classical conditioning procedures to alleviate anxiety; each item in a hierarchy of anxiety-producing stimuli is paired with a state of relaxation (pp. 217, 659)

taste buds the receptors for taste located on the tongue (p. 148)

telegraphic speech utterances characterized by the use of nouns, verbs, and adjectives and generally few "function words" (p. 324)

temporal lobes the lobes of the cerebrum, located at the temples (p. 82)

territoriality the setting off and marking of a piece of territory (a location) as one's own (p. 746)

testosterone the most important of the male androgens, or sex hormones (p. 521)

thalamus the last sensory relay station; it sends impulses to the appropriate area of the cerebral cortex (p. 81)

Thematic Apperception Test (TAT) a projective personality test requiring a subject to tell a series of short stories about a set of ambiguous pictures (pp. 454, 513)

theory an organized collection of ultimately testable ideas used to explain a particular subject matter (p. 424)

timbre the psychological experience of wave purity by which we differentiate the qualities of tones (p. 143)

tolerance in using a drug, a state in which more and more of the drug is required to produce the same desired effect (p. 188)

training a systematic and intentional process of altering the behaviors of employees to increase organizational effectiveness (p. 730)

trait a distinguishable, relatively enduring way in which individuals may be described and in which they may differ (p. 437)

transducer a mechanism that converts energy from one form to another—a basic process common to all of our senses (p. 97)

transference in psychoanalysis, the situation in which the patient comes to feel about the analyst in the same way he or she once felt about some other important person (p. 656)

tremors involuntary, trembling, jerky movements (p. 77)

Type A behavior pattern (TABP) a collection of behaviors (competitive, achievement-oriented, impatient, easily aroused, often hostile or angry) commonly associated with coronary heart disease (p. 570)

unconditioned response (UCR) in classical conditioning, a response (for example, salivation) reliably and reflexively evoked by a stimulus (p. 207)

unconditioned stimulus (UCS) in classical conditioning, a stimulus (for example, food powder) that reflexively and reliably evokes a response (p. 207)

validity in testing, the extent to which a test measures what it claims to measure (p. 447)

vesicles the small containers, concentrated in axon terminals, that hold neurotransmitter molecules (p. 58)

vestibular sense the position sense that tells us about balance, where we are in relation to gravity, and acceleration or deceleration (p. 153)

viability the ability to survive without interference or intervention (p. 360)

vicarious reinforcement (or punishment) increasing the rate (with reinforcement) or decreasing the rate (with punishment) of responses due to observing the consequences of someone else's behaviors (p. 247)

vitreous humor the thick fluid behind the lens of the eye that helps keep the eyeball spherical (p. 115)

wave amplitude a characteristic of a wave form (the height of a wave) that determines the brightness of light (p. 109)

wavelength the distance between any point on a wave and the corresponding point on the next cycle of the wave (p. 109)

white light a light of the lowest possible saturation, containing a mixture of all visible wavelengths (p. 111)

white noise a sound consisting of a random assortment of all wave frequencies from the audible spectrum (p. 145)

withdrawal a negative reaction that may occur when one stops taking a drug (p. 188)

X and Y chromosomes the chromosomes that determine one's genetic sex; XX for females, XY for males (p. 520)

zygote the one-cell product of the union of sperm and ovum at conception (p. 357)

Abel, E. L. (1981). Behavioral teratology. *Psychological Bulletin, 90,* 564–581.

Ackerman, P. L. (1992). Predicting individual differences in complex skill acquisition: Dynamics of ability determinants. *Journal of Applied Psychology, 77,* 598–614.

Ackerman, P. L., & Kanfer, R. (1993). Integrating laboratory and field study for improving selection: Development of a battery for predicting air traffic controller success. *Journal of Applied Psychology, 78,* 413–432.

Adams, G. R. (1977). Physical attractiveness, personality, and social reactions to peer pressure. *Journal of Psychology, 96,* 287–296.

Adams, G. R., & Gullotta, T. (1983). *Adolescent life experiences.* Monterey, CA: Brooks/Cole.

Adams, J. L. (1974). *Conceptual blockbusting.* Stanford, CA: Stanford Alumni Association. Cited in A. L. Glass, K. J. Holyoak, & J. L. Santa (1979). *Cognition.* Reading, MA: Addison-Wesley.

Adams, J. S. (1965). Inequity in social exchange. In L. Berkowitz (Ed.), *Advances in experimental social psychology.* New York: Academic Press.

Adams, R. M. (1992). The "hot hand" revisited: Successful basketball shooting as a function of intershot interval. *Perceptual and Motor Skills, 74,* 934.

Adams, R. M. (1993). Momentum in the performance of professional tournament pocket billiards players. *International Journal of Sport Psychology,* in press.

Adelmann, P. K., & Zajonc, R. B. (1989). Facial efference and the experience of emotion. *Annual Review of Psychology, 40,* 249–280.

Adler, N. E., Boyce, T., Chesney, M. A., Cohen, S., Folkman, S., Kahn, R. L., & Syme, S. L. (1994). Socioeconomic status and health: The challenge of the gradient. *American Psychologist, 49,* 15–24.

Adler, N. E., & Stone, G. (1984). Psychology in the health system. In J. Ruffini (Ed.). *Advances in medical social science.* New York: Gordon & Breach.

Adler, R., & Cohen, N. (1993). Psychoneuroimmunology: Conditioning and stress. *Annual Review of Psychology, 44,* 23–51.

Adler, T. (1989). Cocaine babies face behavior deficits. *APA Monitor, 20,* 14.

Adler, T. (1990). Does the "new" MMPI beat the "classic"? *APA Monitor, 21,* 18–19.

Agnew, H. W., Webb, W. W., & Williams, R. L. (1964). The effects of stage 4 sleep deprivation. *Electroencephalography and Clinical Neurophysiology, 17,* 68–70.

Aiello, J. R., & Aiello, T. D. (1974). The development of personal space: Proxemic behavior of children 6 through 16. *Human Ecology, 2,* 177–189.

Aiken, L. R. (1984). *Psychological testing and assessment* (4th ed.). Boston: Allyn & Bacon.

Ainsworth, M. D. S. (1979). Infant–mother attachment. *American Psychologist, 34,* 932–937.

Ainsworth, M. D. S. (1989). Attachments beyond infancy. *American Psychologist, 44,* 709–716.

Ajzen, I., & Fishbein, M. (1980). *Understanding attitudes and predicting social behavior.* Englewood Cliffs, NJ: Prentice-Hall.

Alba, J. W., & Hasher, L. (1983). Is memory schematic? *Psychological Bulletin, 93,* 201–231.

Aldwin, C., & Stokals, D. (1988). The effects of environmental change on individuals and groups: Some neglected issues in stress research. *Journal of Environmental Psychology, 8,* 57–75.

Allen, J. L., Walker, L. D., Schroeder, D. A., & Johnson, D. E. (1987). Attributions and attribution-behavior relations: The effect of level of cognitive development. *Journal of Personality and Social Psychology, 52,* 1099–1109.

Allen, M. G. (1976). Twin studies of affective illness. *Archives of General Psychiatry, 33,* 1476–1478.

Allport, G. W. (1961). *Pattern and growth in personality.* New York: Holt, Rinehart & Winston.

Altman, I. (1975). *The environment and social behavior.* Monterey, CA: Brooks/Cole.

Amabile, T. M. (1985). Motivation and creativity. *Journal of Personality and Social Psychology, 48,* 393–399.

American Association of Retired Persons. (1993). Census Bureau ups 65+ population estimates. *AARP Bulletin, 34,* 2.

American Psychiatric Association. (1987). *Diagnostic and statistical manual of mental disorders* (3rd rev. ed.). Washington, DC: American Psychiatric Association.

American Psychiatric Association. (1994). *Diagnostic and statistical manual of mental disorders* (4th ed.). Washington, DC: American Psychiatric Association.

American Psychological Association. (1992). Ethical principles of psychologists and code of conduct. *American Psychologist, 47,* 1597–1611.

Amoore, J. E. (1970). *Molecular basis of odor.* Springfield, IL: Thomas.

Anastasi, A. (1988). *Psychological testing* (6th ed.). New York: Macmillan.

Anderson, C. A. (1987). Temperature and aggression: Effects on quarterly, yearly, and city rates of violent and nonviolent crime. *Journal of Personality and Social Psychology, 52,* 1161–1173.

Anderson, C. A. (1989). Temperature and aggression: Ubiquitous effects of heat on occurrence of human violence. *Psychological Bulletin, 106,* 74–96.

Anderson, C. A., & Anderson, D. C. (1984). Ambient temperature and violent crime: Tests of the linear and curvilinear hypotheses. *Journal of Personality and Social Psychology, 46,* 91–97.

Anderson, J. R. (1976). *Language, memory, and thought.* Hillsdale, NJ: Erlbaum.

Anderson, J. R. (1983a). *The architecture of cognition.* Cambridge, MA: Harvard University Press.

Anderson, J. R. (1983b). A spreading activation theory of memory. *Journal of Verbal Learning and Verbal Behavior, 22,* 261–295.

Anderson, J. R. (1986). Knowledge compilation: The general learning mechanism. In R. Michalski, J. Carbonnell, & T. Mitchell (Eds.), *Machine learning II.* Palo Alto, CA: Tioga Press.

Anderson, J. R. (1987). Skill acquisition: Compilation of weak-method problem solutions. *Psychological Review, 94,* 192–210.

Anderson, R., & Nida, S. A. (1978). Effect of physical attractiveness on opposite- and same-sex evaluations. *Journal of Personality, 46,* 401–413.

Anderson, R. C., & Pichert, J. W. (1978). Recall of previously unrecallable information following a shift in perspective. *Journal of Verbal Learning and Verbal Behavior, 17,* 1–12.

Andreasen, N. C. (1982). Negative versus positive schizophrenia: Definition and validation. *Archives of General Psychiatry, 39,* 789–794.

Andreasen, N. C., Ehrhardt, J. C., Swayze, V. W., Alliger, R. J., Yuh, W. T. C., Cohen, G., & Ziebell, S. (1990a). Magnetic resonance imaging of the brain in schizophrenia. *Archives of General Psychiatry, 47,* 35–44.

Andreasen, N. C., Flaum, M., Swayze, V. W., Tyrrell, G., & Arndt, S. (1990). Positive and negative symptoms in schizophrenia. *Archives of General Psychiatry, 47,* 615–621.

Andreasen, N. C., Olsen, S. A., Dennert, J. W., & Smith, M. R. (1982). Ventricular enlargement in schizophrenia: Definition and prevalence. *American Journal of Psychiatry, 139,* 292–296.

Andrews, R. J. (1963). Evolution of facial expression. *Science, 142,* 1034–1041.

Angoff, W. H. (1988). The nature-nurture debate, aptitudes, and group differences. *American Psychologist, 43,* 713–720.

Anisfeld, M. (1984). *Language development from birth to three.* Hillsdale, NJ: Erlbaum.

Anisman, H., & Zacharko, R. M. (1982). Depression: The predisposing influence of stress. *The Behavioral and Brain Sciences, 5,* 89–137.

Aronson, E., & Linder, D. (1965). Gain and loss of esteem as determinants of interpersonal attractiveness. *Journal of Personality and Social Psychology, 1,* 156–171.

Aronson, E., Turner, J. A., & Carlsmith, J. M. (1963). Communicator credibility and communication discrepancy as a determinant of opinion change. *Journal of Abnormal and Social Psychology, 67,* 31–36.

Arvey, R. D., & Campion, J. E. (1982). The employee interview: A summary and review of recent research. *Personnel Psychology, 35,* 281–322.

Arvey, R. D., Miller, H. E., Gould, R., & Burch, P. (1987). Interview validity for selecting sales clerks. *Personnel Psychology, 40,* 1–12.

Asch, S. E. (1951). The effects of group pressure upon the modification and distortion of judgment. In H. Guetzkow (Ed.), *Groups, leadership, and men.* Pittsburgh: Carnegie Press.

Asch, S. E. (1956). Studies of independence and conformity: I. A minority of one against a unanimous majority. *Psychological Monographs: General and Applied, 70* (Whole No. 416), 1–70.

Aserinsky, E., & Kleitman, N. (1953). Regularly occurring periods of eye mobility and concomitant phenomena during sleep. *Science, 118,* 273–274.

Aslin, R. N., & Smith, L. B. (1988). Perceptual development. *Annual Review of Psychology, 39,* 435–473.

Atkinson, J. W., & Feather, N. T. (1966). *A theory of achievement motivation.* New York: Wiley.

Atkinson, J. W., & Litwin, G. H. (1960). Achievement motive and test anxiety conceived as motive to approach success and motive to avoid failure. *Journal of Abnormal and Social Psychology, 60,* 27–36.

Atkinson, R. C. (1975). Mnemotechnics in second-language learning. *American Psychologist, 30,* 821–828.

Atkinson, R. C., & Shiffrin, R. M. (1968). Human memory: A proposed system and its control processes. In K. W. Spence & J. T. Spence (Eds.), *The psychology of learning and motivation: Advances in research and theory.* New York: Academic Press.

Atwood, M. E., & Polson, P. G. (1976). A process model for water jug problems. *Cognitive Psychology, 8,* 191–216.

Auletta, K. (1984). Children of children. *Parade Magazine, 17,* 4–7.

Axelrod, S., & Apsche, J. (1983). *The effects of punishment on human behavior.* New York: Academic Press.

Azrin, N. H., & Holz, W. C. (1966). Punishment. In W. K. Honig (Ed.), *Operant behavior: Areas of research and application.* Englewood Cliffs, NJ: Prentice-Hall.

Azumi, K., & McMillan, C. J., (1976). Worker sentiment in the Japanese factory: Its organizational determinants. In L. Austin (Ed.), *Japan: The paradox of progress.* New Haven, CT: Yale University Press.

Babor, T. F., Berglas, S., Mendelson, J. H., Ellinboe, J., &

Miller, K. (1983). Alcohol, effect and the disinhibition of behavior. *Psychopharmacology, 80,* 53–60.

Backman, C. W., & Secord, P. F. (1959). The effect of perceived liking on interpersonal attraction. *Human Relations, 12,* 379–384.

Baddeley, A. (1990). *Human memory: Theory and practice.* Boston: Allyn & Bacon.

Baddeley, A. (1992). Working memory. *Science, 225,* 556–559.

Baddeley, A. D. (1982). Domains of recollection. *Psychological Review, 89,* 708–729.

Bagozzi, R. P., & Burnkrant, R. E. (1979). Attitude organization and the attitude-behavior relationship. *Journal of Personality and Social Psychology, 37,* 913–929.

Bahrick, H. P. (1984). Semantic memory content in permastore. *Journal of Experimental Psychology: General, 113,* 1–29.

Bailey, J. M., & Pillard, R. C. (1991). A genetic study of male sexual orientation. *Archives of General Psychiatry, 48,* 1089–1096.

Balay, J., & Shevrin, H. (1988). The subliminal psychodynamic activation method: A critical review. *American Psychologist, 43,* 161–174.

Baley, S. (1985). The legalities of hiring in the 80s. *Personnel Journal, 64,* 112–115.

Ballenger, J. C. (1989). Toward an integrated model of panic disorder. *American Journal of Orthopsychiatry, 59,* 284–293.

Bandura, A. (1965). Influence of models' reinforcement contingencies on the acquisition of imitative responses. *Journal of Personality and Social Psychology, 1,* 589–595.

Bandura, A. (1974). Behavior theory and the models of man. *American Psychologist, 29,* 859–869.

Bandura, A. (1976). Modeling theory: Some traditions, trends and disputes. In W. S. Sahakian (Ed.), *Learning: Systems, models, and theories.* Skokie, IL: Rand McNally.

Bandura, A. (1977). *Social learning theory.* Englewood Cliffs, NJ: Prentice-Hall.

Bandura, A. (1978). The self-system in reciprocal determinism. *American Psychologist, 33,* 344–358.

Bandura, A. (1982). Self-efficacy mechanism in human agency. *American Psychologist, 37,* 122–147.

Bandura, A., Ross, D., & Ross, S. A. (1963). Imitation of film-mediated aggressive models. *Journal of Abnormal and Social Psychology, 66,* 3–11.

Barber, T. F. X. (1972). Suggested (hypnotic) behavior: The trace paradigm vs. an alternative paradigm. In E. Fromm & R. E. Shorr (Eds.), *Hypnosis: Research developments and perspectives.* Chicago: Aldine-Atherton.

Barefoot, J. C., Dahlstrom, W. D., & Williams, R. B. (1983). Hostility, CHD incidence, and total mortality: A 25-year follow-up study of 255 physicians. *Psychosomatic Medicine, 45,* 59–63.

Bargh, J. A. (1993). The four horsemen of automaticity: Awareness, intention, efficiency and control in social cog-

nition. In R. S. Wyer & T. K. Srull (Eds.), *Handbook of social cognition.* Hillsdale, NJ: Erlbaum.

Barinaga, M. (1991). Is homosexuality biological? *Science, 253,* 956–957.

Barker, R. (1968). *Ecological psychology.* Stanford, CA: Stanford University Press.

Barnette, R. C., Marshall, N. L., Raudenbush, S. W., & Brennan, R. T. (1993). Gender and the relationship between job experiences and psychological distress: A study of dual-earner couples. *Journal of Personality and Social Psychology, 64,* 794–806.

Baron, M., Freimer, N. F., Risch, N., Lerer, B., Alexander, J. R., et al. (1993). Diminished support for linkage between manic depressive illness and X-chromosome markers in three Israeli pedigrees. *Natural Genetics, 3,* 49–55.

Baron, R. A. (1977). *Human aggression.* New York: Plenum.

Baron, R. A., & Ransberger, V. M. (1978). Ambient temperature and the occurrence of collective violence: The "long hot summer" revisited. *Journal of Personality and Social Psychology, 36,* 351–360.

Barr, H. M., Streissguth, A. P., Darby, B. L., & Sampson, P. D. (1990). Prenatal exposure to alcohol, caffeine, tobacco, and aspirin: Effects on fine and gross motor performance in 4-year-old children. *Developmental Psychology, 26,* 339–348.

Barrett, G. V., & Depinet, R. L. (1991). A reconsideration of testing for competence rather than for intelligence. *American Psychologist, 46,* 1012–1024.

Barron, F., & Harrington, D. M. (1981). Creativity, intelligence, and personality. *Annual Review of Psychology, 32,* 439–476.

Barsalou, L. W. (1983). Ad hoc categories. *Memory and Cognition, 11,* 211–227.

Barsalou, L. W. (1989). Intra-concept similarity and its implications for inter-concept similarity. In S. Vosniadou & A. Ortony (Eds.), *Similarity and analogical reasoning.* New York: Cambridge University Press.

Bartlett, F. C. (1932). *Remembering.* Cambridge: Cambridge University Press.

Bartus, R. T., Dean, R. L., Beer, B., & Lippa, A. S. (1982). The cholinergic hypothesis of geriatric memory dysfunction. *Science, 217,* 408–417.

Basso, K. (1970). To give up words: Silence in Western Apache culture. *Southwestern Journal of Anthropology, 26,* 213–230.

Baum, A., & Grunberg, N. E. (1991). Gender, stress, and health. *Health Psychology, 10,* 80–85.

Baumeister, A. A. (1987). Mental retardation: Some conceptions and dilemmas. *American Psychologist, 42,* 796–800.

Baumeister, R. F. (1985). The championship choke. *Psychology Today, 19,* 48–52.

Baumeister, R. F. (1987). How the self became a problem: A psychological review of historical research. *Journal of Personality and Social Psychology, 52,* 163–176.

Baumeister, R. F., & Steinhilber, A. (1984). Paradoxical effects of supportive audiences on performance under pressure: The home field disadvantage in sports championships. *Journal of Personality and Social Psychology, 47,* 85–93.

Beauvais, F., Oetting, E. R., Wolf, W., & Edwards, R. W. (1989). American Indian youth and drugs: 1975–1987, a continuing problem. *American Journal of Public Health, 79,* 634–636.

Beck, A. T. (1967). *Depression: Clinical, experimental, and theoretical aspects.* New York: HarperCollins.

Beck, A. T. (1976). *Cognitive therapy and the emotional disorders.* New York: International University Press.

Beck, A. T. (1985). Theoretical perspectives in clinical anxiety. In A. H. Tuma & J. D. Master (Eds.), *Anxiety and the anxiety disorders.* Hillsdale, NJ: Erlbaum.

Beck, A. T. (1991). Cognitive therapy: A 30-year retrospective. *American Psychologist, 46,* 368–375.

Beck, A. T., & Emery, G. (1985). *Anxiety disorders and phobias: A cognitive perspective.* New York: Basic Books.

Beck, A. T., & Freeman, A. (1990). *Cognitive therapy of personality disorders.* New York: Guilford.

Beckman, L. J., & Houser, B. B. (1982). The consequences of childlessness on the social-psychological well-being of older women. *Journal of Gerontology, 37,* 243–250.

Bee, H. (1995). *The developing child* (7th ed.). New York: HarperCollins.

Beecroft, R. (1966). *Classical conditioning.* Goleta, CA: Psychonomic Press.

Beer, M., & Walton, A. E. (1987). Organization change and development. *Annual Review of Psychology, 38,* 339–367.

Begg, I., & Paivio, A. (1969). Concreteness and imagery in sentence meaning. *Journal of Verbal Learning and Verbal Behavior, 8,* 821–817.

Bekerian, D. A. (1993). In search of the typical eyewitness. *American Psychologist, 48,* 574–576.

Bell, P. A., Fisher, J. D., & Loomis, R. J. (1978). *Environmental psychology.* Philadelphia: Saunders.

Bellack, A. S. (1986). Schizophrenia: Behavior therapy's forgotten child. *Behavior Therapy, 17,* 199–214.

Bellack, A. S., & Mueser, K. T. (1986). A comprehensive treatment program for schizophrenia and chronic mental illness. *Community Mental Health Journal, 22,* 175–189.

Belsher, G., & Costello, C. G. (1988). Relapse after recovery from unipolar depression: A critical review. *Psychological Bulletin, 104,* 84–96.

Belsky, J. (1990). The "effects" of infant day care reconsidered. In N. Fox & G. G. Fein (Eds.), *Infant day care: The current debate.* Norwood, NJ: Ablex.

Belsky, J., & Rovine, M. (1988). Nonmaternal care in the first year of life and the security of infant–parent attachment. *Child Development, 59,* 157–167.

Bem, S. (1981). Gender schema theory: A cognitive account of sex typing. *Psychological Review, 88,* 354–364.

Benbow, C. P. (1987). Possible biological correlates of precocious mathematical reasoning ability. *Trends in Neuroscience, 10,* 17–20.

Benbow, C. P. (1990). Gender differences: Searching for facts. *American Psychologist, 45,* 988.

Benedict, H. (1979). Early lexical development: Comprehension and production. *Journal of Child Language, 6,* 183–200.

Bennett, T. L. (1982). *Introduction to physiological psychology.* Monterey, CA: Brooks/Cole.

Bennett, W. (1980). The cigarette century. *Science, 80,* 36–43.

Ben-Porath, Y. S., & Butcher, J. N. (1989). The comparability of MMPI and MMPI-2 scales and profiles. *Psychological Assessment, 1,* 345–347.

Benson, H. (1975). *The relaxation response.* New York: Morrow.

Ben-Yehuda, N. (1980). The European witch craze. *American Journal of Sociology, 86,* 1–31.

Berkowitz, L. (1978). What ever happened to the frustration-aggression hypothesis? *American Behavioral Scientist, 21,* 691–708.

Berkowitz, L. (1982). Aversive conditions as stimuli to aggression. *Advances in Experimental Social Psychology, 15,* 249–288.

Berkowitz, L. (1989). Frustration-aggression hypothesis: Examination and reformulation. *Psychological Bulletin, 106,* 59–73.

Berkowitz, L. (1990). On the formation and regulation of anger and aggression. *American Psychologist, 45,* 494–503.

Berlyne, D. E. (1960). *Conflict, arousal, and curiosity.* New York: McGraw-Hill.

Berlyne, D. E. (1971). *Aesthetics and psychobiology.* Englewood Cliffs, NJ: Prentice-Hall.

Bernstein, I. (1978). Learned taste aversion in children receiving chemotherapy. *Science, 200,* 1302–1303.

Bernstein, R. (1981). The Y chromosome and primary sexual differentiation. *Journal of the American Medical Association, 245,* 1953–1956.

Berrettini, W. H., Golden, L. R., Gelernter, J., Gejman, P. V., Gershon, E. S., & Datera-Wadleigh, S. (1990). X-chromosome markers and manic-depressive illness. *Archives of General Psychiatry, 47,* 366–374.

Berscheid, E. (1994). Interpersonal relationships. *Annual Review of Psychology, 45,* 79–129.

Bertenthal, B. I., & Campos, J. J. (1989). A systems approach to the organizing effects of self-produced locomotion during infancy. In C. Rovee-Collier & L. P. Lipsett (Eds.), *Advances in infancy research.* Norwood, NJ: Ablex.

Beutler, L. E., Crago, M., & Arizmendi, T. G. (1986). Therapist variables in psychotherapy process and outcome. In S. L. Garfield & A. E. Bergin (Eds.), *Handbook of psychotherapy and behavior change* (3rd ed.), New York: Wiley.

Bhawuk, D. P. S., & Brislin, R. (1992). The measurement of

intercultural sensitivity using the concepts of individualism and collectivism. *International Journal of Intercultural Relations, 16,* 413–436.

Billy, J. O. G., Tanfer, K., Grady, W. R., & Klepinger, D. H. (1993). The sexual behavior of men in the United States. *Family Planning Perspectives, 25,* 52–60.

Binder, J. L. (1993). Research findings on short-term psychodynamic therapy techniques. *Directions in Clinical Psychology, 3,* 10.3–10.13.

Birch, E. E., Gwiazda, J., & Held, R. (1983). The development of vergence does not account for the onset of stereopsis. *Perception, 12,* 331–336.

Birdwhistell, R. L. (1952). *Introduction to kinesics.* Louisville, KY: University of Louisville Press.

Birnbaum, M. H., & Mellers, B. A. (1979). Stimulus recognition may mediate exposure effects. *Journal of Personality and Social Psychology, 37,* 391–394.

Bjorklund, A., Dunnett, S. B., & Stenevi, U. (1980). Reinnervation of the denervated striatum by substantia nigra transplants: Functional consequences as revealed by pharmacological and sensorimotor testing. *Brain Research, 199,* 307–333.

Blanchard, D. C., & Blanchard, R. J. (1988). Ethoexperimental approaches to the biology of emotion. *Annual Review of Psychology, 39,* 43–68.

Blaney, P. H. (1986). Affect and memory: A review. *Psychological Bulletin, 99,* 229–246.

Blashfield, R. K., & Breen, M. J. (1989). Face validity of the DSM-III-R personality disorders. *American Journal of Psychiatry, 146,* 1575–1579.

Blass, E. M., Ganchow, J. R., & Steiner, J. E. (1984). Classical conditioning in newborn human infants 2–48 hours of age. *Infant Behavior and Development, 7,* 223–235.

Bleier, R., Houston, L., & Byne, W. (1987). Can the corpus callosum predict gender, age, handedness, or cognitive differences? *Trends in Neuroscience, 9,* 391–394.

Bloch, D., & Simon, R. (Eds.). (1982). *The strength of family therapy: Selected papers of Nathan Ackerman.* New York: Brunner/Mazel.

Block, J. (1965). *The challenge of response sets.* Englewood Cliffs, NJ: Prentice-Hall.

Bloodworth, R. C. (1987). Major problems associated with marijuana abuse. *Psychiatric Medicine, 3,* 173–184.

Bloom, F. E., Lazerson, A., & Hotstadter, L. (1985). *Brain, mind, and behavior.* San Francisco: Freeman.

Blum, J. E., Jarvik, L. F., & Clark, E. T. (1970). Rate of change on selective tests of intelligence: A twenty-year longitudinal study. *Journal of Gerontology, 25,* 171–176.

Bolles, R. C. (1970). Species-specific defense reactions and avoidance learning. *Psychological Review, 71,* 32–48.

Bolles, R. C. (1972). Reinforcement, expectancy, and learning. *Psychological Review, 79,* 394–409.

Bolles, R. C. (1975). Learning, motivation, and cognition. In W. K. Estes (Ed.), *Handbook of learning and cognitive processes* (Vol. 1). Hillsdale, NJ: Erlbaum.

Bondareff, W., Mountjoy, C. Q., Wischik, C. M., Hauser, D. L., LaBree, L. D., & Roth, M. (1993). Evidence of subtypes of Alzheimer's Disease and implications for etiology. *Archives of General Psychiatry, 50,* 350–356.

Bootzin, R. R., & Acocella, J. R. (1984). *Abnormal psychology: Current perspectives* (4th ed.). New York: Random House.

Borbely, A. (1986). *Secrets of sleep.* New York: Basic Books.

Bordens, K. S., & Abbott, B. B. (1991). *Research design and methods: A process approach.* Mountain View, CA: Mayfield.

Bornstein, R. F. (1989). Exposure and affect: Overview and meta-analysis of research 1968–1987. *Psychological Bulletin, 106,* 265–289.

Bornstein, R. F., Kale, A. R., & Cornell, K. R. (1990). Boredom as a limiting condition of the mere exposure effect. *Journal of Personality and Social Psychology, 58,* 791–800.

Bouchard, C., Tremblay, A., Després, J., et al. (1990). The response to long-term overfeeding in identical twins. *The New England Journal of Medicine, 322,* 1477–1482.

Bourne, L. E. (1992). Cognitive psychology: A brief overview. *Psychology Science Agenda, 5(5),* 5, 20.

Bourne, L. E., Dominowski, R. L., & Loftus, E. F. (1983). *Cognitive process.* Englewood Cliffs, NJ: Prentice-Hall.

Bousfield, W. A. (1953). The occurrence of clustering in the free recall of randomly arranged associates. *Journal of General Psychology, 49,* 229–240.

Bower, G. H. (1970). Imagery as a relational organizer in associative learning. *Journal of Verbal Learning and Verbal Behavior, 9,* 529–533.

Bower, G. H. (1972). Mental imagery and associative learning. In L. W. Gregg (Ed.), *Cognition in learning and memory.* New York: Wiley.

Bower, G. H. (1981). Mood and memory. *American Psychologist, 36,* 129–148.

Bower, G. H., & Clark, M. C. (1969). Narrative stories as mediators for serial learning. *Psychonomic Science, 14,* 181–182.

Bower, G. H., Monteiro, K. P., & Gilligan, S. G. (1978). Emotional mood as a context for learning and recall. *Journal of Verbal Learning and Verbal Behavior, 17,* 573–587.

Bower, G. H., & Springston, F. (1970). Pauses as recoding points in letter series. *Journal of Experimental Psychology, 83,* 421–430.

Bower, T. G. R., Broughton, J. M., & Moore, M. K. (1971). Infant responses to approaching objects: An indicator of response to distal variables. *Perception and Psychophysics, 9,* 193–196.

Bowers, J. S., & Schacter, D. L. (1990). Implicit memory and test awareness. *Journal of Experimental Psychology: Learning, Memory, and Cognition, 16,* 404–416.

Bowlby, J. (1982). *Attachment and loss: Vol. 1. Attachment* (2nd ed.). New York: Basic Books.

Bradbard, M. R., & Endsley, R. C. (1983). The effects of sex-typed labelling on preschool children's information seeking and retention. *Sex Roles, 9,* 247–260.

Bradley, D. R., & Dumais, S. T. (1975). Ambiguous cognitive contours. *Nature, 257,* 582–584.

Bradshaw, J. L., & Nettleton, N. C. (1983). *Human cerebral asymmetry.* Englewood Cliffs, NJ: Prentice-Hall.

Braine, M. D. S. (1976). Children's first word combinations. *Monographs for the Society for Research in Child Development, 41* (Serial No. 164).

Bransford, J. D., & Johnson, M. K. (1972). Contextual prerequisites for understanding: Some investigations of comprehension and recall. *Journal of Verbal Learning and Verbal Behavior, 11,* 717–720.

Bratic, E. B. (1982). Healthy mothers, healthy babies coalition. *Prevention, 97,* 503–509.

Braun, P., Kochansky, G., Shapiro, R., Greenberg, S., Gudeman, J. E., Johnson, S., & Shore, M. (1981). Overview: Deinstitutionalization of psychiatric patients, a critical review of outcome studies. *American Journal of Psychiatry, 138,* 736–749.

Bray, D. W., Campbell, R. J., & Grant, D. L. (1974). *Formative years in business: A long-term AT&T study of managerial lives.* New York: Wiley.

Bregman, J., Dykens, E., Watson, M., & Leckman, J. (1987). Fragile X syndrome: Variability in phenotype expression. *Journal of the American Academy of Child and Adolescent Psychiatry, 26,* 463–471.

Brehm, J. W., & Self, E. A. (1989). The intensity of motivation. *Annual Review of Psychology, 40,* 109–131.

Breier, A., Schreiber, J. L., Dyer, J., & Pickar, D. (1991). National Institute of Mental Health longitudinal study of chronic schizophrenia: Prognosis and predictors of outcome. *Archives of General Psychiatry, 48,* 239–246.

Breland, K., & Breland, M. (1961). This misbehavior of organisms. *American Psychologist, 16,* 681–684.

Brett, J. F., Brief, A. P., Burke, M. J., George, J. M., & Webster, J. (1990). Negative affectivity and the reporting of stressful events. *Health Psychology, 9,* 57–68.

Brewer, W. F., & Nakamura, G. V. (1984). The nature and function of schemas. In R. S. Wyler & T. K. Sroll (Eds.), *Handbook of social cognition.* Hillsdale, NJ: Erlbaum.

Briggs, G. G., Freeman, R. K., & Yaffe, S. J. (1986). *Drugs in pregnancy and lactation* (2nd ed.). Baltimore: Williams & Wilkins.

Brigham, J. C. (1991). *Social psychology* (2nd ed.). New York: HarperCollins.

Brinkerhoff, R. O. (1989). *Evaluating training programs in business and industry.* San Francisco: Jossey-Bass.

Brislin, R. W. (1990). *Applied cross-cultural psychology.* Newbury Park, Ca: Sage.

Brislin, R. W. (1993). *Understanding culture's influence on behavior.* Fort Worth, TX: Harcourt Brace.

Brody, E. M. (1981). Women in the middle and family help to older people. *Gerontologist, 21,* 471–480.

Brody, E. M. (1985). Parent care as a normative family stress. *Gerontologist, 25,* 19–29.

Brown, J. (1958). Some tests of the decay theory of immediate memory. *Quarterly Journal of Experimental Psychology, 10,* 12–21.

Brown, J. (1976). An analysis of recognition and recall and of problems in their comparison. In J. Brown (Ed.), *Recall and recognition.* New York: Wiley.

Brown, J. D. (1991). Staying fit and staying well. *Journal of Personality and Social Psychology, 60,* 555–561.

Brown, J. I. (1973). *The Nelson-Denny reading test.* Boston: Houghton Mifflin.

Brown, N. A. (1985). Are offspring at risk from their father's exposure to toxins? *Nature, 316,* 110.

Brown, R. (1973). *A first language: The early stages.* Cambridge, MA: Harvard University Press.

Brown, R., Cazden, C. B., & Bellugi, U. (1969). The child's grammar from 1 to 3. *Symposia on child language* (Vol. 2). Minneapolis: University of Minnesota Press.

Brown, R., & Kulik, J. (1977). Flashbulb memories. *Cognition, 5,* 73–99.

Browne, M. A., & Mahoney, M. J. (1984). Sport psychology. *Annual Review of Psychology, 35,* 605–626.

Bruch, H. (1980). Preconditions for the development of anorexia nervosa. *American Journal of Psychoanalysis, 40,* 169–172.

Bruner, J. S., Goodnow, J. J., & Austin, G. A. (1956). *A study of thinking.* New York: Wiley.

Buck, R. (1980). Nonverbal behavior and the theory of emotion: The facial feedback hypothesis. *Journal of Personality and Social Psychology, 38,* 811–824.

Buck, R. (1985). Prime theory: An integrated view of motivation and emotion. *Psychological Review, 92,* 389–413.

Buckhout, R. (1975). Nearly 2000 witnesses can be wrong. *Social Action and the Law, 2,* 7.

Burgoon, J. K., Birk, T., & Pfau, M. (1990). Non-verbal behaviors, persuasion, and credibility. *Human Communication Research, 17,* 140–169.

Bushnell, I. W. R., Sai, F., & Mullin, J. T. (1989). Neonatal recognition of the mother's face. *British Journal of Developmental Psychology, 7,* 3–15.

Buss, A. H. (1966). *Psychopathology.* New York: Wiley.

Buss, D. M. (1984). Evolutionary biology and personality psychology. *American Psychologist, 39,* 1135–1147.

Buss, D. M. (1985). Human mate selection. *American Scientist, 73,* 47–51.

Buss, D. M. (1989). Personality as traits. *American Psychologist, 44,* 1378–1388.

Buss, D. M., Abbott, M., Angleitner, A., Asherian, A., Biaggio, A., Blanco-Villasenor, A., et al. (1990). International preferences in mate selection: A study of 37 cultures. *Journal of Cross-Cultural Psychology, 21,* 5–47.

Buss, D. M., & Barnes, M. (1986). Preferences in human mate selection. *Journal of Personality and Social Psychology, 50,* 559–570.

Butler, R., & Emr, M. (1982). SDAT research: Current trends. *Generations, 7,* 14–18.

Butler, R., & Lewis, M. (1981). *Aging and mental health.* St. Louis: Mosby.

Byrne, D. (1971). *The attraction paradigm.* New York: Academic Press.

Cacioppo, J. T., Marshall-Goodell, B. S., Tassinary, L. G., & Petty, R. E. (1992). Rudimentary determinants of attitudes: Classical conditioning is more effective when prior knowledge about the attitude stimulus is low than high. *Journal of Experimental Social Psychology, 28,* 207–233.

Cacioppo, J. T., & Petty, R. E. (1989). Effects of message repetition on argument processing, recall, and persuasion. *Basic Applied Social Psychology, 10,* 3–12.

Calhoun, J. B. (1962). Population density and social pathology. *Scientific American, 206,* 139–148.

Campbell, J. P. (1988). Training design for performance improvement. In J. P. Campbell & R. J. Campbell (Eds.), *Productivity in organizations.* San Francisco: Jossey-Bass.

Campos, J. J. (1976). Heart rates: A sensitive tool for the study of emotional development. In L. Lipsett (Ed.), *Developmental psychobiology: The significance of infancy.* Hillsdale, NJ: Erlbaum.

Campos, J. J., Hiatt, S., Ramsey, D., Henderson, C., & Svejda, M. (1978). The emergence of fear on the visual cliff. In M. Lewis & L. A. Rosenbaum (Eds.), *The development of affect.* New York: Plenum.

Cannon, T. D., Mednick, S. A., & Parnas, J. (1990). Antecedents of predominantly negative- and predominantly positive-symptom schizophrenia in a high-risk population. *Archives of General Psychiatry, 47,* 622–632.

Cannon, W. B. (1932). *The wisdom of the body.* New York: Norton.

Caplan, N. (1989). *The boat people and achievement in America: A study of family life, hard work, and cultural values.* Ann Arbor: University of Michigan Press.

Carey, S. (1978). The child as word learner. In M. Halle, J. Bresnan, & G. A. Miller (Eds.), *Linguistic theory and psychological reality.* Cambridge, MA: MIT Press.

Carlson, N. R. (1991). *Physiology of behavior* (4th ed.). Boston: Allyn & Bacon.

Carone, B. J., Harrow, M., & Westermeyer, J. F. (1991). Posthospital course and outcome in schizophrenia. *Archives of General Psychiatry, 48,* 247–253.

Carson, R. C. (1989). Personality. *Annual review of psychology, 40,* 227–248.

Carson, R. C., & Butcher, J. N. (1992). *Abnormal psychology and modern life* (9th ed.). New York: HarperCollins.

Carson, R. L. (1962). *Silent spring.* Boston: Houghton Mifflin.

Carson, T. P., & Carson, R. C. (1984). The affective disorders. In H. E. Adams & P. B. Sutker (Eds.), *Comprehensive handbook of psychopathology.* New York: Plenum.

Carver, C. S., & Gaines, J. G. (1987). Optimism, pessimism, and postpartum depression. *Cognitive Therapy and Research, 11,* 449–462.

Cash, T. F., & Derlega, V. J. (1978). The matching hypothesis: Physical attractiveness among same-sexed friends. *Personality and Social Psychology Bulletin, 4,* 240–243.

Cash, T. F., & Kilcullen, R. N. (1985). The eye of the beholder: Susceptibility to sexism and beautyism in the evaluation of managerial applicants. *Journal of Applied Social Psychology, 15,* 591–605.

Cattell, R. B. (1973). *Personality and mood by questionnaire.* San Francisco: Jossey-Bass.

Cattell, R. B. (1979). *The structure of personality in its environment.* New York: Springer.

Cavanaugh, J. C., & Park, D. C. (1993). Vitality for life: Psychological research for productive aging. *APS Observer,* Special Issue: December.

Cermak, L. S., & Craik, F. I. M. (Eds.). (1979). *Levels of processing in human memory.* Hillsdale, NJ: Erlbaum.

Chagnon, N. A. (1983). *Yanomamö: The fierce people* (3rd ed.). New York: Holt, Rinehart & Winston.

Chaiken, S., & Stangor, C. (1987). Attitudes and attitude change. *Annual Review of Psychology, 38,* 575–630.

Charney, D. S., Deutch, A. Y., Krystal, J. H., Southwick, S. M., & Davis, M. (1993). Psychobiological mechanisms of posttraumatic stress disorder. *Archives of General Psychiatry, 50,* 294–305.

Chase, M. H., & Morales, F. R. (1990). The atonia and myoclonia of active (REM) sleep. *Annual Review of Psychology, 41,* 557–584.

Chase, W. G., & Simon, H. A. (1973). The mind's eye in chess. In W. G. Chase (Ed.), *Visual information processing.* New York: Academic Press.

Chasnoff, I. J., Griffith, D. R., MacGregor, S., Dirkes, K., & Burns, K. (1989). Temporal patterns of cocaine use in pregnancy. *Journal of the American Medical Association, 261,* 1741–1744.

Cheesman, J., & Merikle, P. M. (1984). Priming with and without awareness. *Perception and Psychophysics, 36,* 387–395.

Chi, M. T. H., & Glaser, R. (1985). Problem solving ability. In R. J. Sternberg (Ed.), *Advances in the psychology of human intelligence.* San Francisco: Freeman.

Chilman, C. S. (1980). Parent satisfactions, concerns, and goals for their children. *Family Relations, 29,* 339–346.

Chilman, C. S. (1983). *Adolescent sexuality in a changing American society: Social and psychological perspectives for the human services profession* (2nd ed.). New York: Wiley.

Chomsky, N. (1957). *Syntactic structures.* The Hague: Mouton.

Chomsky, N. (1965). *Aspects of a theory of syntax.* Cambridge, MA: Harvard University Press.

Chomsky, N. (1975). *Reflections on language.* New York: Pantheon Books.

Chomsky, N. (1986). *Knowledge of language: Its nature, origin, and use.* New York: Praeger.

Chuang, H. T., Devins, G. M., Hunsley, J., & Gill, M. J. (1989). Psychosocial distress and well-being among gay and bisexual men with immunodeficiency virus infection. *American Journal of Psychiatry, 146,* 876–880.

CIBA-GEIGY. (1991). *OCD: When a habit isn't just a habit.* Pine Brook, NJ: CIBA-GEIGY Corporation.

Clarkson-Smith, L., & Hartley, A. A. (1989). Relationships between physical exercise and cognitive abilities in older adults. *Psychology and Aging, 4,* 183–189.

Clifford, B. R., & Lloyd-Bostock, S. (Eds.). (1983). *Evaluating witness evidence: Recent psychological research and new perspectives.* Norwood, NJ: Ablex.

Clifford, M. M., & Hatfield, E. (1973). The effect of physical attractiveness on teacher expectation. *Sociology of Education, 46,* 248–258.

Clore, G. L., & Byrne, D. (1974). A reinforcement-affect model of attraction. In T. L. Huston (Ed.), *Foundations of interpersonal attraction.* New York: Academic Press.

Cohen, G. D. (1980). *Fact sheet: Senile dementia (Alzheimer's disease).* [No. ADM 80-929]. Washington, DC: Center for Studies of the Mental Health of the Aging.

Cohen, L. R., DeLoach, J., & Strauss, M. (1978). Infant visual perception. In J. Osofky (Ed.), *The handbook of infant development.* New York: Wiley.

Cohen, S., Evans, G. W., Krantz, D. S., Stokols, D., & Kelly, S. (1980). Aircraft noise and children: Longitudinal and cross-sectional evidence on the adaptation to noise and the effectiveness of noise abatement. *Journal of Personality and Social Psychology, 40,* 331–345.

Cohen, S., Evans, G. W., Stokols, D., & Krantz, D. S. (1986). *Behavior, health, and environmental stress.* New York: Plenum.

Cohen, S., Lichtenstein, E., Prochaska, J. O., Rossi, J. S., Gritz, E. R., Carr, C. R., et al. (1989). Debunking myths about self-quitting: Evidence from 10 prospective studies of persons who attempt to quit smoking by themselves. *American Psychologist, 44,* 1355–1365.

Colby, A., & Kohlberg, L. (1984). Invariant sequence and internal consistency in moral judgment stages. In W. M. Kurtines & J. L. Gewitz (Eds.), *Morality, moral behavior, and moral development.* New York: Wiley.

Cole, J. O. (1988). Where are those new antidepressants we were promised? *Archives of General Psychiatry, 45,* 193–194.

Cole, R. E. (1979). *Work, mobility, and participation.* Berkeley: University of California Press.

Coles, R., & Stokes, G. (1985). *Sex and the American teenager.* New York: HarperCollins.

College Board. (1989). *College-bound seniors: 1989 SAT profile.* New York: College Entrance Examination Board.

Collins, A. M., & Loftus, E. F. (1975). A spreading activation theory of semantic processing. *Psychological Review, 82,* 407–428.

Collins, A. M., & Quillian, M. R. (1969). Retrieval time from semantic memory. *Journal of Verbal Learning and Verbal Behavior, 8,* 240–247.

Collins, W. A., & Gunnar, M. R. (1990). Social and personality development. *Annual Review of Psychology, 41,* 387–416.

Committee on an Aging Society. (1986). *America's aging: Productive roles in an older society.* Washington, DC: National Academy Press.

Committee on Lesbian and Gay Concerns. (1991). Avoiding heterosexual bias in language. *American Psychologist, 46,* 973–974.

Conger, J. J. (1991). *Adolescence and youth* (4th ed.). New York: HarperCollins.

Conger, J. J., & Peterson, A. C. (1984). *Adolescence and youth: Psychological development in a changing world.* New York: HarperCollins.

Conrad, R. (1963). Acoustic confusions and memory span for words. *Nature, 197,* 1029–1030.

Conrad, R. (1964). Acoustic confusions in immediate memory. *British Journal of Psychology, 55,* 75–84.

Cooper, J., & Croyle, R. T. (1984). Attitudes and attitude change. *Annual Review of Psychology, 35,* 395–426.

Cooper, J., & Scher, S. J. (1992). Actions and attitudes: The role of responsibility and aversive consequences in persuasion. In T. Brock & S. Shavitt (Eds.), *The psychology of persuasion.* San Fransisco: Freeman.

Cooper, L. A., & Shepard, R. N. (1973). Chronometric studies of the rotation of mental images. In W. G. Chase (Ed.), *Visual information processing.* New York: Academic Press.

Cordua, G. D., McGraw, K. O., & Drabman, R. S. (1979). Doctor or nurse: Children's perception of sex typed occupations. *Child Development, 50,* 590–593.

Coren, S. (1972). Subjective contours and apparent depth. *Psychological Review, 79,* 359–367.

Coren, S., & Girgus, J. S. (1978). *Seeing is deceiving: The psychology of visual illusions.* Hillsdale, NJ: Erlbaum.

Corkin, S. (1984). Lasting consequences of bilateral medial temporal lobectomy: Clinical course and experimental findings in H. M. *Seminars in Neurology, 4,* 249–259.

Cornblatt, B. A., & Erlenmeyer-Kimling, L. (1985). Global attention deviance as a marker of risk for schizophrenia: Specificity and predictive validity. *Journal of Abnormal Psychology, 94,* 470–486.

Costa, P. T., & McCrae, R. R. (1980). Still stable after all these years: Personality as a key to some issues in adulthood and old age. In P. B. Baltes & O. G. Brim, Jr. (Eds.), *Life-span development and behavior.* New York: Academic Press.

Costello, C. G. (1982). Fears and phobias in women: A community study. *Journal of Abnormal Psychology, 91,* 280–286.

Coté, T. R., Biggar, R. J., & Dannenberg, A. L. (1992). Risk of suicide among persons with AIDS: A national assessment. *Journal of the American Medical Association, 268,* 2066–2068.

Coulter, W. A., & Morrow, H. W. (Eds.). (1978). *Adaptive behavior: Concepts and measurements.* New York: Grune & Stratton.

Council, J. R. (1993). Context effects in personality research. *Current Directions in Psychological Science, 2,* 31–34.

Cowan, N. (1984). On short and long auditory stores. *Psychological Bulletin, 96,* 341–370.

Cowan, W. M. (1979). The development of the brain. In *The brain* (pp. 56–69). San Francisco: Freeman.

Cox, R. H. (1990). *Sport psychology: Concepts and applications.* Dubuque, IA: Brown.

Coyle, J. T., Price, D. L., & DeLong, M. H. (1983). Alzheimer's disease: A disorder of central cholinergic innervation. *Science, 219,* 1184–1189.

Coyne, J. C., & Downey, G. (1991). Social factors and psychopathology: Stress, social support, and coping processes. *Annual Review of Psychology, 42,* 401–425.

Cozby, P. C. (1973). Self-disclosure: A literature review. *Psychological Bulletin, 79,* 73–91.

Craik, F. I. M. (1970). The fate of primary memory items in free recall. *Journal of Verbal Learning and Verbal Behavior, 9,* 143–148.

Craik, F. I. M., & Lockhart, R. S. (1972). Levels of processing: A framework for memory research. *Journal of Verbal Learning and Verbal Behavior, 11,* 671–684.

Craik, F. I. M., & Tulving, E. (1975). Depth of processing and the retention of words in episodic memory. *Journal of Experimental Psychology: General, 104,* 268–294.

Cramer, R. E., McMaster, M. R., Bartell, P. A., & Dragna, M. (1988). Subject competence and minimization of the bystander effect. *Journal of Applied Social Psychology, 18,* 1133–1148.

Creekmore, C. R. (1984). Games athletes play. *Psychology Today, 19,* 40–44.

Creekmore, C. R. (1985). Cities won't drive you crazy. *Psychology Today, 19,* 46–53.

Crews, D. J., & Landers, D. M. (1987). A meta-analytic review of aerobic fitness and reactivity to psychosocial stressors. *Medicine and Science in Sport and Exercise, 19,* 114–120.

Crockett, L. J., & Peterson, A. C. (1987). Pubertal status and psychosocial development: Findings from the Early Adolescence Study. In R. M. Lerner & T. T. Foch (Eds.), *Biological-psychosocial interactions in early adolescence: A life-span approach.* Hillsdale, NJ: Erlbaum.

Cromwell, R. L. (1993). Searching for the origins of schizophrenia. *Psychological Science, 4,* 276–279.

Cross-National Collaborative Group. (1992). The changing rate of major depression: Cross-national comparisons. *Journal of the American Medical Association, 268,* 3098–3105.

Crow, T. J. (1980). Molecular pathology of schizophrenia: More than one disease process? *The British Medical Journal, 280,* 66–68.

Cunningham, S. (1984). Genovese: 20 years later, few heed stranger's cries. *APA Monitor, 15,* 30.

Curtis, R. C., & Miller, K. (1986). Believing another likes or dislikes you: Behaviors making the beliefs come true. *Journal of Personality and Social Psychology, 51,* 284–290.

Cushner, K. (1990). Cross-cultural psychology and the formal classroom. In R. W. Brislin (Ed.), *Applied cross-cultural psychology.* Newbury Park, CA: Sage.

Cutler, W. B., Preti, G., Krieger, A., Huggins, G. R., Ramon Garcia, C., & Lawley, H. J. (1986). Human axillary secretions influence women's menstrual cycles: The role of donor extract from men. *Hormones and Behavior, 20,* 463–473.

Dahlstrom, W. G. (1993). Tests: Small samples, large consequences. *American Psychologist, 48,* 393–399.

Daniel, T. C. (1990). Measuring the quality of the natural environment: A psychophysical approach. *American Psychologist, 45,* 633–637.

Darley, J. M., & Fazio, R. H. (1980). Expectancy confirmation processes arising in the interaction sequence. *American Psychologist, 35,* 861–866.

Darley, J. M., & Schultz, T. R. (1990). Moral rules: Their content and acquisition. *Annual Review of Psychology, 41,* 525–556.

Darling, C. A., & Davidson, J. K. (1986). Coitally active university students: Sexual behaviors, concerns, and challenges. *Adolescence, 21,* 403–419.

Darwin, C. T., Turvey, M. T., & Crowder, R. G. (1972). An auditory analogue of the Sperling partial report procedure: Evidence for brief auditory storage. *Cognitive Psychology, 3,* 255–267.

Dasen, P., & Heron, A. (1981). Cross-cultural tests of Piaget's theory. In H. C. Triandis & A. Heron (Eds.), *Handbook of cross-cultural psychology; Vol. 4: Developmental Psychology.* Boston: Allyn & Bacon.

Dasen, P. R., & de Ribaupierre, A. (1987). Neo-Piagetian theories: Cross-cultural and differential perspectives. *International Journal of Psychology, 22,* 793–832.

Datan, N., Rodeheaver, D., & Hughes, F. (1987). Adult development and aging. *Annual Review of Psychology, 38,* 153–180.

Davidoff, J. B. (1975). *Differences in visual perception: The individual eye.* New York: Academic Press.

Davidson, J. M., Smith, E. R., Rodgers, C. H., & Bloch, G. J. (1968). Relative thresholds of behavioral and somatic responses to estrogen. *Physiology and Behavior, 3,* 227–229.

Davis, K. (1985). Near and dear: Friendship and love compared. *Psychology Today, 19,* 22–30.

Davis, L. E., & Cherns, A. B. (1975). *The quality of working life: Vol. I. Problems, prospects and the state of the art.* New York: Free Press.

DeAngelis, T. (1989). Behavior is included in report on smoking. *APA Monitor, 20,* 3–4.

de Boer, C. (1978). The polls: Attitudes toward work. *Public Opinion Quarterly, 42,* 414–423.

DeBono, K. G., & Harnish, R. J. (1988). Source expertise, source attractiveness, and the processing of persuasive information: A functional approach. *Journal of Personality and Social Psychology, 55,* 541–546.

DeCasper, A. J., & Fifer, W. P. (1980). Of human bonding: Newborns prefer their mother's voice. *Science, 208,* 1174–1176.

DeCasper, A. J., & Sigafoos, A. D. (1983). The interuterine heartbeat: A potent reinforcer for newborns. *Infant Behavior and Development, 6,* 19–25.

de Cuevas, J. (1990, September/October). "No, she held them loosely." *Harvard Magazine,* pp. 60–67.

Deffenbacher, J. L. (1988). Some recommendations and directions. *Counseling Psychology, 35,* 234–236.

DeGroot, A. D. (1965). *Thought and chance in chess.* The Hague: Mouton.

DeGroot, A. D. (1966). Perception and memory versus thought: Some old ideas and recent findings. In B. Kleinmuntz (Ed.), *Problem solving.* New York: Wiley.

DeJarlais, D. C., & Friedman, S. R. (1988). The psychology of preventing AIDS among intravenous drug users: A social learning conceptualization. *American Psychologist, 43,* 865–870.

DeLongis, A., Folkman, S., & Lazarus, R. S. (1988). The impact of daily stress on health and mood: Psychological and social resources as mediators. *Journal of Personality and Social Psychology, 54,* 486–495.

Dembroski, T. M., & Costa, P. T., Jr. (1987). Coronary prone behavior: Components of the Type A pattern and hostility. *Journal of Personality, 55,* 211–235.

Dembroski, T. M., MacDougall, J. M., Williams, R. B., Haney, T. I., & Blumenthal, J. A. (1985). Components of Type A, hostility, and anger in relationship to angiographic findings. *Psychosomatic Medicine, 47,* 219–233.

Dement, W. C. (1974). *Some must watch while some must sleep.* San Francisco: Freeman.

Deregowski, J. B. (1972). Pictorial perception and culture. *Scientific American, 83.*

Deregowski, J. B. (1973). Illusion and culture. In R. L. Gregory & G. H. Gombrich (Eds.), *Illusion in nature and art.* New York: Scribner's (pp. 161–192).

Deutsch, J. A. (1973). The cholinergic synapse and the site of memory. In J. A. Deutsch (Ed.), *The physiological basis of memory.* New York: Academic Press.

deVilliers, J. G., & deVilliers, P. A. (1978). *Language acquisition.* Cambridge, MA: Harvard University Press.

Diamond, M., & Karlen, A. (1980). *Sexual decisions.* Boston: Little, Brown.

Digman, J. M. (1990). Personality structure: Emergence of the five-factor model. *Annual Review of Psychology, 41,* 417–440.

DiMatteo, M. R., & Friedman, H. S. (1988). *Social Psychology and medicine.* Cambridge, MA: Oeleschlager, Gunn & Hain.

Dion, K. K. (1972). Physical attractiveness and evaluation of children's transgressions. *Journal of Personality and Social Psychology, 24,* 207–213.

Dion, K. K., Berscheid, E., & Walster (Hatfield), E. (1972). What is beautiful is good. *Journal of Personality and Social Psychology, 24,* 285–290.

Dirkes, M. A. (1978). The role of divergent production in the learning process. *American Psychologist, 33,* 815–820.

Dixon, N. F. (1971). *Subliminal perception: The nature of a controversy.* New York: McGraw-Hill.

Dixon, N. F. (1981). *Preconscious processing.* New York: Wiley.

Dobson, K. S. (1988). *Handbook of cognitive-behavioral therapies.* New York: Guilford.

Doll, R., & Peto, R. (1981). *The causes of cancer.* New York: Oxford University Press.

Dollard, J., Doob, L., Miller, N., Mowrer, O. H., & Sears, R. R. (1939). *Frustration and aggression.* New Haven, CT: Yale University Press.

Domjan, M. (1987). Animal learning comes of age. *American Psychologist, 42,* 556–564.

Donnenberg, G. R., & Hoffman, L. W. (1988). Gender differences in moral development. *Sex Roles, 18,* 701–717.

Doty, R. Y. (1986). Gender and endocrine-related influences on human olfactory perception. In H. Meiselman & R. S. Rivlin (Eds.), *Clinical measurement of taste and smell.* New York: Macmillan.

Doweiko, H. E. (1993). *Concepts of chemical dependency* (2nd ed.). Pacific Grove, CA: Brooks/Cole.

Drakeley, R. J., Herriot, P., & Jones, A. (1988). Biographical data, training success and turnover. *Journal of Occupational Psychology, 61,* 145–152.

Duffy, E. (1962). *Activation and behavior.* New York: Wiley.

Duncan, J. (1985). Two techniques for investigating perception without awareness. *Perception and Psychophysics, 38,* 296–298.

Dunham, R. B. (1979). Job design and redesign. In S. Kerr (Ed.), *Organizational behavior.* Columbus, OH: Grid.

Dunker, K. (1945). On problem solving. *Psychological Monographs, 58* (Whole No. 270).

Dunnette, M. D., & Borman, W. C. (1979). Personnel selection and classification systems. *Annual Review of Psychology, 30,* 477–525.

Dywan, J., & Bowers, K. (1983). The use of hypnosis to enhance recall. *Science, 222,* 184–185.

Dweck, C. S. (1986). Motivational processes affecting learning. *American Psychologist, 41,* 1040–1048.

Eagly, A. H., & Chaiken, S. (1992). *The psychology of attitudes.* San Diego: Harcourt Brace Jovanovich.

Eagly, A. H., & Steffen, V. J. (1986). Gender and aggressive behavior: A meta-analytic review of the social psychological literature. *Psychological Bulletin, 100,* 309–330.

Eaker, E. D., Packard, B., Wenger, N. K., et al. (1988). Coronary heart disease in women. *American Journal of Cardiology, 61,* 641–644.

Early, C. (1989). Social loafing and collectivism: A comparison of the United States and the People's Republic of China. *Administrative Science Quarterly, 34,* 555–581.

Early, P. C. (1986). Supervisors and shop stewards as sources of contextual information in goal-setting: A comparison of the U.S. with England. *Journal of Applied Psychology, 71,* 111–118.

Eaton, W. O., & Enns, L. R. (1986). Sex differences in human motor activity level. *Psychological Bulletin, 100,* 19–28.

Ebbinghaus, H. E. (1885/1964). *Memory: A contribution to experimental psychology.* New York: Dover.

Eccles, J., Wigfield, A., Harold, R. D., & Blumenfeld, P. (1993). Age and gender differences in children's self- and task perceptions during elementary school. *Child Development, 64,* 830–847.

Edelman, G. (1992). *Bright air, brilliant fire: On the matter of mind.* New York: Basic Books.

Edmands, M. S. (1993). Caring for students with eating disorders on college and university campuses. *Advances in Medical Psychotherapy, 6,* 59–75.

Edwards, C. P. (1977). The comparative study of the development of moral judgment and reasoning. In R. L. Munroe, R. Munroe, & B. B. Whiting (Eds.), *Handbook of cross-cultural human development.* New York: Garland.

Edwards, C. P. (1981). The development of moral reasoning in cross-cultural perspective. In R. H. Munroe, R. L. Munroe, & B. B. Whiting (Eds.), *Handbook of cross-cultural human development.* New York: Garland.

Edwards, L. K., & Edwards, A. L. (1991). A principal components analysis of the Minnesota Multiphasic Personality Inventory Factor Scales. *Journal of Personality and Social Psychology, 60,* 766–772.

Egeland, J. A., Gerhard, D. S., Pauls, D. L., Suddex, J. N., Kidd, K. K., Allen, C. R., Hostetter, A. M., & Housman, D. E. (1987). Bipolar affective disorders linked to DNA markers on chromosome 11. *Nature, 325,* 783–787.

Egeth, H. E. (1993). What do we *not* know about eyewitness identification? *American Psychologist, 48,* 577–580.

Eich, J. E., Weingartner, H., Stillman, R. C., & Gillan, J. C. (1975). State-dependent accessibility of retrieval cues in the retention of a categorized list. *Journal of Verbal Learning and Verbal Behavior, 14,* 408–417.

Ekman, P. (1972). Universals and cultural differences in facial expression of emotion. In J. K. Cole (Ed.), *Nebraska symposium on motivation.* Lincoln: University of Nebraska Press.

Ekman, P. (1973). Cross-cultural studies in facial expression. In P. Ekman (Ed.), *Darwin and facial expressions: A century of research in review.* New York: Academic Press.

Ekman, P. (1992). Facial expression and emotion: New findings, new questions. *Psychological Science, 3,* 34–38.

Ekman, P. (1993). Facial expression and emotion. *American Psychologist, 48,* 384–392.

Ekman, P., & Friesen, W. V. (1971). Constants across cultures in the face and emotion. *Journal of Personality and Social Psychology, 17,* 124–129.

Ekman, P., Friesen, W. V., O'Sullivan, M., Diacoyanni-Tarlatzis, I., Krause, R., et al. (1987). Universals and cultural differences in the judgment of facial expressions of emotion. *Journal of Personality and Social Psychology, 53,* 712–717.

Ekman, P., Levenson, R. W, & Friesen, W. V. (1983). Autonomic nervous system activity distinguishes among emotions. *Science, 221,* 1208–1210.

Ellis, A. (1970). *Reason and emotion in psychotherapy.* Secaucus, NJ: Stuart.

Ellis, A. (1973). *Humanistic psychotherapy: The rational-emotive approach.* New York: McGraw-Hill.

Ellis, A. (1987). The impossibility of achieving consistently good mental health. *American Psychologist, 42,* 364–375.

Ellis, A. (1991). How can psychological treatment aim to be briefer and better? The rational-emotive approach to brief therapy. In K. N. Anchor (Ed.), *Handbook of medical psychotherapy.* Toronto: Hogrefe & Huber.

Ellis, L., & Ames, M. A. (1987). Neurohormonal functioning and sexual orientation: A theory of homosexuality-heterosexuality. *Psychological Bulletin, 101,* 233–258.

Epstein, L. H., & Cluss, P. A. (1982). A behavioral medicine perspective on adherence to long-term medical regimes. *Journal of Consulting and Clinical Psychology, 50,* 950–971.

Epstein, S. (1979). The stability of behavior: On predicting most of the people much of the time. *Journal of Personality and Social Psychology, 37,* 1097–1126.

Erdelyi, M. H. (1985). *Psychoanalysis: Freud's cognitive psychology.* New York: Freeman.

Erdelyi, M. H. (1992). Psychodynamics and the unconscious. *American Psychologist, 47,* 784–787.

Erdelyi, M. H., & Goldberg, B. (1979). Let's not sweep repression under the rug: Toward a cognitive psychology of repression. In J. F. Kihlstrom & F. J. Evans (Eds.), *Functional disorders of memory.* Hillsdale, NJ: Erlbaum.

Erez, M., & Early, P. C. (1987). Comparative analysis of goal-setting strategies across cultures. *Journal of Applied Psychology, 72,* 658–665.

Erez, M., & Early, P. C. (1993). *Culture, self-identity, and work.* New York: Oxford University Press.

Erez, M., & Zidon, I. (1984). Effect of goal acceptance on the relationship of goal difficulty to performance. *Journal of Applied Psychology, 69,* 69–78.

Ericsson, K. A., & Chase, W. G. (1982). Exceptional memory. *American Scientist, 70,* 607–615.

Erikson, E. H. (1963). *Childhood and society.* New York: Norton.

Erikson, E. H. (1965). *The challenge of youth.* Garden City, NY: Doubleday (Anchor Books).

Erikson, E. H. (1968). *Identity: Youth and crisis.* New York: Norton.

Erlenmeyer-Kimling, L. (1968). Studies on the offspring of two schizophrenic parents. In D. Rosenthal & S. S. Kety (Eds.), *The transmission of schizophrenia*. Elmsford, NY: Pergamon Press.

Erwin, E. (1980). Psychoanalytic therapy: The Eysenck argument. *American Psychologist, 35,* 435–443.

Etaugh, C. (1980). Effects of nonmaternal care on children. *American Psychologist, 35,* 309–316.

Evans, G. W., & Howard, R. B. (1973). Personal space. *Psychological Bulletin, 80,* 334–344.

Evans, R. I., Rozelle, R. M., Maxwell, S. E., Raines, B. E., et al. (1981). Social modeling films to deter smoking in adolescents: Results of a three-year field investigation. *Journal of Applied Psychology, 66,* 399–414.

Eveleth, P., & Tanner, J. (1978). *Worldwide variations in human growth.* New York: Cambridge University Press.

Eysenck, H. J. (1952). The effects of psychotherapy: An evaluation. *Journal of Consulting Psychology, 16,* 319–324.

Eysenck, H. J. (1960). *Behavior therapy and neurosis.* London: Pergamon.

Fackelman, K. A. (1992). Anatomy of Alzheimer's: Do immune proteins help destroy brain cells? *Science News, 142,* 394–396.

Fagan, J. F., & Singer, L. T. (1979). The role of single feature differences in infant recognition of faces. *Infant Behavior and Development, 2,* 39–45.

Fahn, S. (1992). Fetal-tissue transplants in Parkinson's disease. *The New England Journal of Medicine, 327,* 1589–1590.

Fairburn, C. G., Jones, R., Peveler, R. C., Hope, R. A., & O'Conner, M. (1993). Psychotherapy and bulimia nervosa. *Archives of General Psychiatry, 50,* 419–428.

Falbo, T., & Peplau, L. A. (1980). Power strategies in intimate relationships. *Journal of Personality and Social Psychology, 38,* 618–628.

Fantz, R. L. (1961). The origin of form perception. *Scientific American, 204,* 66–72.

Fantz, R. L. (1963). Pattern vision in newborn infants. *Science, 140,* 296–297.

Farrell, M. P., & Rosenberg, S. D. (1981). *Men at midlife.* Boston: Auburn House.

Fast, J. (1970). *Body language.* New York: M. Evans.

Fazio, R. H. (1989). On the power and functionality of attitudes: The role of attitude accessibility. In A. R. Pratkanis, S. J. Breckler, & A. G. Greenwald (Eds.), *Attitude structure and function.* Hillsdale, NJ: Erlbaum.

Fazio, R. H. (1990). Multiple processes by which attitudes guide behavior: The MODE model as an integrative framework. *Advances in Experimental Social Psychology, 23,* 75–109.

Feeney, J. A., & Noller, P. (1990). Attachment style as a predictor of adult romantic relationships. *Journal of Personality and Social Psychology, 58,* 281–291.

Fein, G. G., Schwartz, P. M., Jacobson, S. W., & Jacobson, J. L. (1983). Environmental toxins and behavior development. *American Psychologist, 38,* 1188–1197.

Feist, S. C. (1993). Marriage and family therapy: Theories and applications. *Directions in Clinical Psychology, 3,* 4.3–4.24.

Fenker, R. M., & Lambiotte, J. G. (1987). A performance enhancement program for a college football team: One incredible season. *The Sport Psychologist, 1,* 224–236.

Festinger, L. (1957). *A theory of cognitive dissonance.* Stanford, CA: Stanford University Press.

Festinger, L, & Carlsmith, J. M. (1959). Cognitive consequences of forced compliance. *Journal of Abnormal and Social Psychology, 58,* 203–210.

Festinger, L., Schachter, S., & Back, K. (1950). *Social processes in informal groups: A study of human factors in housing.* New York: HarperCollins.

Fielding, J. E., & Phenow, K. J. (1988). Health effects of involuntary smoking. *The New England Journal of Medicine, 319,* 1452–1460.

Finnegan, L. P. (1982). Outcome of children born to women dependent upon narcotics. In B. Stimmel (Ed.), *The effects of maternal alcohol and drug abuse on the newborn.* New York: Haworth.

Fiore, M. C., Novotny, T. E., Pierce, J. P., Hatzlandreu, E. J., Patel, K. M., & Davis, R. M. (1989). Trends in cigarette smoking in the United States: The changing influence of gender and race. *Journal of the American Medical Association, 261,* 49–55.

Fischhoff, B. (1990). Psychology and public policy: Tool or toolmaker? *American Psychologist, 45,* 647–653.

Fishbein, M., & Ajzen, I. (1975). *Belief, attitude, intention, and behavior: An introduction to theory and research.* Reading, MA: Addison-Wesley.

Fisher, A. C. (1977). Sport personality assessment: Facts, fallacies, and perspectives. *Motor Skills: Theory into Practice, 1,* 87–97.

Fishman, J. (1987). Type A on trial. *Psychology Today, 21,* 42–50.

Fitzgerald, L. (1993). Sexual harassment: Violence against women in the workplace. *American Psychologist, 48,* 1070–1076.

Flament, M. F., Rapoport, J. L., Berg, C. J., Sceery, W., Kilts, C., Mellstrom, B., & Linnoila, M. (1985). Clomipramine treatment of childhood obsessive-compulsive disorder: A double-blind study. *Archives of General Psychiatry, 42,* 977–983.

Flament, M. F., Whitaker, A., Rapoport, J. L., Davies, M., Berg, C. Z., Kalikow, K., Sceery, W., & Shaffer, D. (1988). Obsessive-compulsive disorder in adolescence: An epidemiologic study. *Journal of the American Academy of Child and Adolescent Psychiatry, 27,* 289–296.

Flavell, J. H. (1982). On cognitive development. *Child Development, 53,* 1–10.

Fleishman, E. A., & Mumford, M. D. (1991). Evaluating classifications of job behavior: A construct of the ability requirement scales. *Personnel Psychology, 44,* 523–575.

Flexser, A. J., & Tulving, E. (1982). Priming and recognition failure. *Journal of Verbal Learning and Verbal Behavior, 21,* 237–248.

Flynn, J. P., Vanegas, H., Foote, W., & Edwards, S. (1970). Neural mechanisms involved in a cat's attack on a rat. In R. E. Whalen, R. F. Thompson, M. Verzeano, & N. M. Weinberger (Eds.), *The neural control of behavior.* New York: Academic Press.

Folkman, S. (1984). Personal control and stress and coping processes: A theoretical analysis. *Journal of Personality and Social Psychology, 46,* 839–852.

Folstein, S. E., & Rutter, M. L. (1977). Genetic influences and infantile autism. *Nature, 265,* 726–728.

Folstein, S. E., & Rutter, M. L. (1988). Autism: Familial aggregation and genetic implications. *Journal of Autism and Developmental Disorders, 18,* 3–30.

Ford, C. E., Wright, R. A., & Haythornwaite, J. (1985). Task performance and magnitude of goal valence. *Journal of Research in Personality, 19,* 253–260.

Ford, M. R., & Lowery, C. R. (1986). Gender differences in moral reasoning: A comparison of justice and care orientations. *Journal of Personality and Social Psychology, 4,* 777–783.

Fowler, C. A., Wolford, G., Slade, R., & Tassinary, L. (1981). Lexical access with and without awareness. *Journal of Experimental Psychology: General, 110,* 341–362.

Fowler, R. D. (1992). Report of the Chief Executive Officer: A year of building for the future. *American Psychologist, 47,* 876–883.

Fowles, D. G. (1990). *A profile of older Americans: 1989.* Washington, DC: American Association of Retired Persons.

Fox, R., Aslin, R. N., Shea, S. L., & Dumais, S. T. (1980). Stereopsis in human infants. *Science, 207,* 323–324.

Frank, E., Kupfer, D. J., Perel, J. M., Cornes, C., Jarrett, D. B., et al. (1990). Three-year outcomes for maintenance therapies in recurrent depression. *Archives of General Psychiatry, 47,* 1093–1099.

Frankenburg, W. K., & Dodds, J. B. (1967). The Denver Developmental Screening Test. *Journal of Pediatrics, 71,* 181–191.

Frazier, T. M., David, G. H., Goldstein, H., & Goldberg, I. D. (1961). Cigarette smoking and prematurity. *American Journal of Obstetrics and Gynecology, 81,* 988–996.

Frederickson, P. A. (1987). The relevance of sleep disorders medicine to psychiatric practice. *Psychiatric Annals, 17,* 91–100.

Free, M. L., & Oei, T. P. S. (1989). Biological and psychological processes in the treatment and maintenance of depression. *Clinical Psychology Review, 9,* 653–688.

Freed, C. R., Breeze, R. E., Rosenberg, N. L., et al. (1992). Survival of implanted fetal dopamine cells and neurologic improvement 12 to 46 months after transplantation for Parkinson's disease. *The New England Journal of Medicine, 327,* 1549–1555.

Freedman, D. X. (1984). Psychiatric epidemiology counts. *Archives of General Psychiatry, 41,* 931–934.

Freedman, J. L. (1975). *Crowding and behavior.* New York: Viking Press.

Freud, A. (1958). *Adolescence: Psychoanalytic study of the child.* New York: Academic Press.

Freud, S. (1900). *The interpretation of dreams.* In J. Strachey (Ed.), *The complete psychological works of Sigmund Freud.* London: Hogarth Press.

Fribourg, S. (1982). Cigarette smoking and sudden infant death syndrome. *Journal of Obstetrics and Gynecology, 142,* 934–941.

Fried, P. A. (1993). Prenatal exposure to tobacco and marijuana: Effects during pregnancy, infancy, and early childhood. *Clinical Obstetrics and Gynecology, 36,* 319–337.

Friedman, H. S., & Booth-Kewley, S. (1987). The "disease-prone personality": A meta-analytic review of the construct. *American Psychologist, 42,* 539–555.

Friedman, M., & Rosenman, R. (1959). Association of specific overt behavior patterns with blood and cardiovascular findings. *Journal of the American Medical Association, 169,* 1286.

Friedman, M. I., & Stricker, E. M. (1976). The physiological psychology of hunger: A physiological perspective. *Psychological Review, 83,* 409–431.

Friedman, S. (1972). Habituation and recovery of visual response in the alert human newborn. *Journal of Experimental Child Psychology, 13,* 339–349.

Frijda, N. H. (1988). The laws of emotion. *American Psychologist, 43,* 349–358.

Furstenberg, F. F., Brooks-Gunn, J., & Chase-Lansdale, L. (1989). Teenaged pregnancy and childbearing. *American Psychologist, 44,* 313–320.

Furumoto, L., & Scarborough, E. (1986). Placing women in the history of psychology: The first American women psychologists. *American Psychologist, 41,* 35–42.

Gabrena, W., Wang, Y., Latané, B. (1985). Social loafing on an optimizing task: Cross-cultural differences among Chinese and Americans. *Journal of Cross-cultural Psychology, 16,* 223–242.

Gagné, R. M. (1984). Learning outcomes and their effects: Useful categories of human performance. *American Psychologist, 39,* 377–385.

Galanter, E. (1962). Contemporary psychophysics. In R. Brown et al. (Eds.), *New directions in psychology.* New York: Holt, Rinehart & Winston.

Gallagher, J. J., & Ramey, C. T. (1987). *The malleability of children.* Baltimore: Paul H. Brooks.

Galton, F. (1879). *Hereditary genius: An inquiry into its laws and consequences.* Englewood Cliffs, NJ: Prentice-Hall.

Gans, J. E., & Blyth, D. A. (1990). *American adolescents: How healthy are they?* AMA Profiles of Adolescent Health series. Chicago: American Medical Association.

Garbarino, J. (1985). *Adolescent development: An ecological perspective.* Columbus, OH: Merrill.

Garcia, J., Ervin, F. R., & Koelling, R. A. (1966). Learning with prolonged delay of reinforcement. *Psychonomic Science, 5,* 121–122.

Garfield, S. L. (1981). Psychotherapy: A 40-year appraisal. *American Psychologist, 36,* 174–183.

Garner, D. M., Olmsted, M. P., Davis, R., Rockert, W., Goldbloom, D., & Eagle, M. (1990). The association between bulimic symptoms and reported psychopathology. *International Journal of Eating Disorders, 9,* 1–15.

Gaugler, B. B., Rosenthal, D. B., Thornton, G. C., & Bentson, C. (1987). Meta-analysis of assessment center validity. *Journal of Applied Psychology, 72,* 493–511.

Gazzaniga, M. S., & LeDoux, J. E. (1978). *The integrated mind.* New York: Plenum.

Geller, E. S. (1985). The behavior change approach to litter management. *Journal of Resource Management, 14,* 117–122.

Geller, E. S. (1986). Prevention of environmental problems. In B. A. Edelstein & L. Michelson (Eds.), *Handbook of prevention.* New York: Plenum.

Geller, E. S. (1989). Applied behavioral analysis and social marketing: An integration to preserve the environment. *Journal of Social Issues, 45,* 17–36.

Geller, E. S. (1992). It takes more than information to save energy. *American Psychologist, 47,* 814–815.

Geller, E. S., Bruff, C. D., & Nimmer, J. G. (1985). "Flash for life": Community-based prompting for safety belt promotion. *Journal of Applied Behavioral Analysis, 18,* 309–314.

Geller, E. S., & Lehman, G. R. (1986). Motivating desirable waste management behavior: Applications of behavioral analysis. *Journal of Resource Management, 15,* 58–68.

Geller, E. S., & Nimmer, J. G. (1985). *Social marketing and applied behavior analysis: An integration for quality of life intervention.* Blacksburg: Virginia Polytechnic Institute and State University.

Geller, E. S., Rudd, J. R., Kalsher, M. J., Sreff, F. M., & Lehman, G. R. (1987). Employer-based programs to motivate safety belt use: A review of short-term and long-term effects. *Journal of Safety Research, 18,* 1–17.

Geller, E. S., Winett, R. A., & Everett, P. B. (1982). *Preserving the environment: New strategies for behavior change.* New York: Pergamon Press.

Gellhorn, E. (1964). Motion and emotion: The role of proprioception in the physiology and pathology of the emotions. *Psychological Review, 71,* 457–472.

Gelman, D., Doherty, S., Joseph, N., & Carroll, G. (1987, Spring). How infants learn to talk. *Newsweek: On Health.*

Gelman, R. (1978). Cognitive development. *Annual Review of Psychology, 29,* 297–332.

Gelso, C. J., & Fassinger, R. E. (1990). Counseling psychology: Theory and research on interventions. *Annual Review of Psychology, 41,* 355–386.

Gemberling, G. A., & Domjan, M. (1982). Selective associations in one-day-old rats: Taste toxicosis and texture-shock aversion learning. *Journal of Comparative and Physiological Psychology, 96,* 105–113.

Geracioti, T. D., & Liddle, R. A. (1988). Impaired cholecystokinin secretion in bulimia nervosa. *New England Journal of Medicine, 319,* 683–688.

Gerbert, B., & Maguire, B. (1989). Public acceptance of the Surgeon General's brochure on AIDS. *Public Health Report, 104,* 130–133.

Gerow, J. R., & Murphy, D. P. (1980). The validity of the Nelson-Denny Reading Test as a predictor of performance in introductory psychology. *Educational and Psychological Measurement, 40,* 553–556.

Gibson, E. J. (1987). Introductory essay: What does infant perception tell us about theories of perception? *Journal of Experimental Psychology: Perception and Performance, 13,* 515–523.

Gibson, E. J. (1988). Exploratory behavior in the development of perceiving, acting, and the acquiring of knowledge. *Annual Review of Psychology, 39,* 1–41.

Gibson, E. J., & Walk, R. D. (1960). The visual cliff. *Scientific American, 202,* 64–71.

Gillam, B. (1980). Geometrical illusions. *Scientific American, 242,* 102–111.

Gilligan, C. (1982). *In a different voice.* Cambridge, MA: Harvard University Press.

Gilovich, T., Vallone, R., & Tversky, A. (1985). The hot hand in basketball: On the misperception of random sequences. *Cognitive Psychology, 17,* 295–314.

Glaser, R. (1984). Education and thinking. *American Psychologist, 39,* 93–104.

Glasgow, R. E., & Lichtenstein, E. (1987). Long-term effects of behavioral smoking cessation interventions. *Behavior Therapy, 18,* 297–324.

Glass, A. L., Holyoak, K. J., & Santa, J. L. (1979). *Cognition.* Reading, MA: Addison-Wesley.

Glass, D. C., & Singer, J. E. (1972). *Urban stress.* Hillsdale, NJ: Erlbaum.

Glass, D. C., Singer, J. E., & Friedman, L. N. (1969). Psychic cost of adaptation to an environmental stressor. *Journal of Personality and Social Psychology, 12,* 200–210.

Glenn, N. D., & Weaver, C. N. (1981). The contribution of marital happiness to global happiness. *Journal of Marriage and the Family, 43,* 161–168.

Glucksberg, S., & Danks, J. H. (1968). Effects of discriminative labels and of nonsense labels upon the availability of novel function. *Journal of Verbal Learning and Verbal Behavior, 7,* 72–76.

Golbus, M. S. (1980). Teratology for the obstetrician: Current status. *American Journal of Obstetrics and Gynecology, 55,* 269.

Gold, P. E. (1987). Sweet memories. *American Scientist, 75,* 151–155.

Goldberg, L. R. (1993). The structure of phenotypic personality traits. *American Psychologist, 48,* 26–34.

Goldfried, M. R., Greenberg, L. S., & Marmar, C. (1990). Individual psychotherapy: Process and outcome. *Annual Review of Psychology, 41,* 659–688.

Goldstein, I. L. (1986). *Training in organizations.* Monterey, CA: Brooks/Cole.

Goldstein, I. L. (1989). *Training and development in organizations.* San Francisco: Jossey-Bass.

Goleman, O. (1980). 1,528 little geniuses and how they grew. *Psychology Today, 14,* 28–53.

Gonzales, M. H., Davis, J. M., Loney, G. L., Lukens, C. K., & Junghans, C. M. (1983). Interactional approach to interpersonal attraction. *Journal of Personality and Social Psychology, 44,* 1192–1197.

Gooden, D., & Baddeley, A. D. (1975). Context-dependent memory in two natural environments: On land and under water. *British Journal of Psychology, 66,* 325–331.

Goodwin, D. W., Powell, B., Bremer, D., Hoine, H., & Stein, J. (1969). Alcohol and recall: State-dependent effects in man. *Science, 163,* 1358–1360.

Gordon, C. T., State, R. C., Nelson, J. E., Hamburger, S. D., & Rapoport, J. L. (1993). A double-blind comparison of clomipramine, desipramine, and placebo in the treatment of autistic disorder. *Archives of General Psychiatry, 50,* 441–447.

Gorenstein, E. E. (1984). Debating mental illness. *American Psychologist, 39,* 50–56.

Gormezano, I. (1972). Investigations of defense and reward conditioning in the rabbit. In A. H. Black & W. F. Prokasy (Eds.), *Classical conditioning II: Current theory and research.* Englewood Cliffs, NJ: Prentice-Hall.

Gotlib, I. H. (1992). Interpersonal and cognitive aspects of depression. *Current Directions in Psychological Science, 1,* 149–156.

Gottesman, I. I., & Bertelsen, A. (1989). Confirming unexpressed genotypes for schizophrenia. *Archives of General Psychiatry, 46,* 867–872.

Gottesman, I. I., & Shields, J. (1982). *Schizophrenia: The epigenetic puzzle.* Cambridge, UK: Cambridge University Press.

Gottlieb, B. H. (1981). *Social networks and social support.* Beverly Hills, CA: Sage.

Gottlieb, G. (1970). Conceptions of prenatal development. In L. R. Aronson, E. Tobach, D. S. Lehrman, & J. S. Rosenblatt (Eds.), *Development and evolution of behavior.* San Francisco: Freeman.

Gough, H. G. (1985). A work orientation scale for the California Psychological Inventory. *Journal of Applied Psychology, 70,* 505–513.

Govoni, L. E., & Hayes, J. E. (1988). *Drugs and nursing implications* (6th ed.). Norwalk, CT: Appleton & Lange.

Gracely, R. H., Lynch, S., & Bennett, G. J. (1991). The central process responsible for A_LTM-mediated allodynia in some patients with RSD is sensitive to perfusion of the microenvironment of nociceptor terminals. Paper presented at the 21st Annual Meeting of the Society for Neuroscience. New Orleans.

Graf, P., & Mandler, G. (1984). Activation makes words more accessible, but not necessarily more retrievable. *Journal of Verbal Learning and Verbal Behavior, 23,* 553–568.

Graf, P., & Schacter, D. A. (1985). Implicit and explicit memory for new associations in normal and amnesic subjects. *Journal of Experimental Psychology: Learning, Memory, and Cognition, 11,* 501–518.

Graziano, A. M., & Raulin, M. L. (1993). *Research methods: A process of inquiry.* New York: HarperCollins.

Green, D. M., & Swets, J. A. (1966). *Signal detection theory and psychophysics.* New York: Wiley.

Greenberg, J., & Cohen, R. L. (1982). *Equity and justice in social behavior.* New York: Academic Press.

Greenberg, L. S., & Safran, J. D. (1987). *Emotion in psychotherapy.* New York: Guilford.

Greenberg, L. S., & Safran, J. D. (1989). Emotion in psychotherapy. *American Psychologist, 44,* 19–29.

Greeno, J. G. (1978). Natures of problem-solving abilities. In W. K. Estes (Ed.), *Handbook of learning and cognitive processes* (Vol. 5). Hillsdale, NJ: Erlbaum.

Greeno, J. G. (1989). A perspective on thinking. *American Psychologist, 44,* 134–141.

Greenough, W. T. (1984). Structural correlates of information storage in mammalian brain. *Trends in Neurosciences, 7,* 229–233.

Greenwald, A. G. (1992) New look 3: Unconsciousness reclaimed. *American Psychologist, 47,* 776–779.

Greenwald, A. G., Spangenberg, E. R., Pratkais, A. R., & Eskenazi, J. (1991). Double-blind tests of subliminal self-help audio tapes. *Psychological Science, 2,* 119–122.

Greer, S. (1964). Study of parental loss in neurotics and sociopaths. *Archives of General Psychiatry, 11,* 177–180.

Gregory, R. L. (1977). *Eye and brain: The psychology of seeing* (3rd ed.). New York: New World Library.

Grice, G. R. (1948). The relation of secondary reinforcement to delayed reward in visual discrimination learning. *Journal of Experimental Psychology, 38,* 1–16.

Grinspoon, L. (1977). *Marihuana reconsidered* (2nd ed.). Cambridge, MA: Harvard University Press.

Grob, C., & Dobkin de Rois, M. (1992). Adolescent drug use in cross-cultural perspective. *Journal of Drug* 121–138.

Gross, R. T., & Duke, P. M. (1980). The effect of early and late maturation on adolescent behavior. *Pediatric Clinics of North America, 27,* 71–77.

Grossman, H. J. (Ed.). (1973). *Manual on terminology and classification in mental retardation.* Washington, DC: American Association on Mental Deficiency.

Groves, P. M., & Rebec, G. V. (Introduction to biological psychology (4th ed.). Brown.

Guilford, J. P. (1959a). *Personality.* New York: McGraw-Hill.

Guilford, J. P. (1959b). Traits of creativity. In H. H. Anderson (Ed.), *Creativity and its cultivation.* New York: HarperCollins.

Guilford, J. P. (1967). *The nature of human intelligence.* New York: McGraw-Hill.

Guilford, J. P. (1988). Some changes in the structure-of-intellect model. *Educational and Psychological Measurement, 48,* 1–4.

Guion, R. M., & Gibson, W. M. (1988). Personnel selection and placement. *Annual Review of Psychology, 39,* 349–374.

Gur, R. E., Resnick, S. M., Alavi, A., Gur, R. C., Caroff, S., Dann, R., et al. (1987). Regional brain function in schizophrenia. *Archives of General Psychiatry, 44,* 119–125.

Gurman, A. S., Kniskern, D. P., & Pinsof, W. M. (1986). Research on the process and outcome of marital and family therapy. In S. L. Garfield & A. E. Bergin (Eds.), *Handbook of psychotherapy and behavior change* (3rd ed.). New York: Wiley.

Haist, F., Shimamura, A. P., & Squire, L. R. (1992). On the relationship between recall and recognition memory. *Journal of Experimental Psychology: Learning, Memory and Cognition, 18,* 691–702.

Hake, D. F., & Foxx, R. M. (1978). Promoting gasoline conservation: The effects of reinforcement schedules, a leader, and self-recording. *Behavior Modification, 2,* 339–369.

Halberstadt, A. G., & Saitta, M. B. (1987). Gender, nonverbal behavior, and perceived dominance: A test of the theory. *Journal of Personality and Social Psychology, 53,* 257–272.

Hall, E. T. (1966). *The hidden dimension.* Garden City, NY: Doubleday.

Hall, G. S. (1904). *Adolescence.* Englewood Cliffs, NJ: Prentice-Hall.

Hall, J. A. (1978). Gender effects in decoding nonverbal cues. *Psychological Bulletin, 85,* 845–857.

Hall, J. F. (1976). *Classical conditioning and instrumental conditioning: A contemporary approach.* Philadelphia: Lippincott.

Hall, W. G., & Oppenheim, R. W. (1987). Developmental psychology. *Annual Review of Psychology, 38,* 91–128.

Halpern, D. F. (1986). *Sex differences in cognitive abilities.* Hillsdale, NJ: Erlbaum.

Hamburg, D. A., & Takanishi, R. (1989). Preparing for life: The critical transition of adolescence. *American Psychologist, 44,* 825–827.

Hamer, D. H., Hu, S., Magnuson, V. L., Hu, N., & Pattatucci, A. M. (1993). A linkage between DNA markers on the X chromosome and male sexual orientation. *Science, 261,*

Hammen, C., Burge, D., Burney, E., & Adrian, C. (1990). Longitudinal study of diagnoses in children of women with unipolar and bipolar affective disorder. *Archives of General Psychiatry,* 112–1117.

Hansen, W. B., Hahn, G. L., & Wolkenstein, J. (1990). Perceived personal immunity: Beliefs about susceptibility to AIDS. *Journal of Sex Research, 27,* 622–628.

Harding, C. M. (1988). Course types in schizophrenia: An analysis of European and American studies. *Schizophrenia Bulletin, 14,* 633–642.

Hare, R. D. (1970). *Psychopathology: Theory and research.* New York: Wiley.

Harkins, S. (1987). Social loafing and social facilitation. *Journal of Experimental Socialpsychology, 23,* 1–18.

Harkins, S. G., & Petty, R. E. (1982). Effects of task difficulty and task uniqueness on social loafing. *Journal of Personality and Social Psychology, 43,* 1214–1229.

Harkins, S. G., & Petty, R. E. (1983). Social context effects in persuasion: The effects of multiple sources and multiple targets. In P. B. Paulus (Ed.), *Basic group processes.* New York: Springer-Verlag.

Harkins, S. G., & Szymanski, K. (1989). Social loafing and group evaluation. *Journal of Personality and Social Psychology, 56,* 934–941.

Harlow, H. F. (1932). Social facilitation of feeding in the albino rat. *Journal of Genetic Psychology, 41,* 211–221.

Harlow, H. F. (1959). Love in infant monkeys. *Scientific American, 200,* 68–74.

Harlow, H. F., Harlow, M. K., & Suomi, S. J. (1971). From thought to therapy: Lessons from a private library. *American Scientist, 59,* 536–549.

Harris, B. (1979). What ever happened to Little Albert? *American Psychologist, 34,* 151–160.

Harris, D. V. (1973). *Involvement in sport: A somatopsychic rationale for physical activity.* Philadelphia: Lea & Febiger.

Harris, L., & Associates. (1975, 1981, 1983). *The myth and reality of aging in America.* Washington, DC: The National Council on Aging.

Harris, M. M. (1989). Reconsidering the employment interview: A review of recent literature and suggestions for future research. *Personnel Psychology, 42,* 691–726.

Harris, P. L. (1983). Infant cognition. In P. H. Mussen (Ed.), *Handbook of child psychology* (Vol. 2). New York: Wiley.

Harrow, M., Goldberg, J. F., Grossman, L. S., & Meltzer, H. Y. (1990). Outcome in manic disorders. *Archives of General Psychiatry, 47,* 665–671.

Hartman, S., Grigsby, D. W., Crino, M. D., & Chhokar, J. (1986). The measurement of job satisfaction by action tendencies. *Educational and Psychological Measurement, 46,* 317–329.

Hartup, W. W. (1989). Social relationships and their developmental significance. *American Psychologist, 44,* 120–126.

Haruki, T., Shigehisa, T., Nedate, K., Wajima, M., & Ogawa, R. (1984). Effects of alien-reinforcement and its combined type of learning behavior and efficacy in relation to personality. *International Journal of Psychology, 19,* 527–545.

Harvey, J. H., & Weary, G. (1984). Current issues in attribution theory. *Annual Review of Psychology, 35,* 427–459.

Hastie, R., & Park, B. (1986). The relationship between memory and judgment depends on whether the judgement task is memory-based or on-line. *Psychological Review, 93,* 258–268.

Hastorf, A. H., & Cantril, H. (1954). They saw a game: A case study. *Journal of Abnormal and Social Psychology, 49,* 129–134.

Hatfield, E., & Sprecher, S. (1986). *Mirror, mirror . . . The importance of looks in everyday life.* Albany: State University of New York Press.

Havighurst, R. J. (1972). *Developmental tasks and education* (3rd ed.). New York: McKay.

Hayduk, L. A. (1983). Personal space: Where we now stand. *Psychological Bulletin, 94,* 293–335.

Hayes, C. D. (Ed.). (1987). *Risking the future* (Vol. 1). Washington, DC: National Academy Press.

Hayman, C. A. G., & Tulving, E. (1989). Contingent dissociation between recognition and fragment completion: The method of triangulation. *Journal of Experimental Psychology: Learning, Memory, and Cognition, 15,* 220–224.

Haynes, S. G., McMichael, A. J., & Tyroler, H. A. (1978). Survival after early and normal retirement. *Journal of Gerontology, 33,* 872–883.

Hayward, C., Killan, J. D., Hammer, L. D., Litt, I. F., Wilson, D. M., Simmonds, B., & Taylor, C. B. (1992). Pubertal stage and panic attack history in sixth- and seventh-grade girls. *American Journal of Psychiatry, 149,* 1239–1243.

Hazan, C., & Shaver, P. (1987). Romantic love conceptualized as an attachment process. *Journal of Personality and Social Psychology, 52,* 511–524.

Hebb, D. O. (1955). Drives and the C.N.S. (conceptual nervous system). *Psychological Review, 62,* 243–254.

Heffernan, J. A., & Albee, G. W. (1985). Prevention perspectives. *American Psychologist, 40,* 202–204.

Heidbreder, E. (1946). The attainment of concepts. *Journal of General Psychology, 24,* 93–108.

Heinrichs, R. W. (1993). Schizophrenia and the brain: Conditions for a neuropsychology of madness. *American Psychologist, 48,* 221–233.

Hellige, J. B. (1990). Hemispheric asymmetry. *Annual Review of Psychology, 41,* 55–80.

Hellige, J. B. (Ed.). (1983). *Cerebral hemisphere asymmetry: Method, theory, and application.* New York: Praeger.

Helms, J. E. (1992). Why is there no study of cultural equivalence in standardized cognitive ability testing? *American Psychologist, 47,* 1083–1101.

Helzer, J. E., Robins, L. N., & McEnvoy, L. (1987). Post-traumatic stress disorder in the general population. *New England Journal of Medicine, 317,* 1630–1634.

Henley, T. B., Johnson, M. G., Jones, E. M., & Herzog, H. A. (1989). Definitions of psychology. *The Psychological Record, 39,* 143–152.

Hennessy, J., & Melhuish, E. C. (1991). Early day care and the development of school-age children. *Journal of Reproduction and Infant Psychology, 9,* 117–136.

Herek, G. M., & Glunt, E. K. (1988). An epidemic of stigma: Public reactions to AIDS. *American Psychologist, 43,* 886–891.

Heshka, S., & Nelson, Y. (1972). Interpersonal speaking distance as a function of age, sex, and relationship. *Sociometry, 35,* 491–498.

Hetherington, E. M., & Parke, R. D. (1993). *Child psychology: A contemporary viewpoint.* New York: McGraw-Hill.

Higgins, E. T., & Bargh, J. A. (1987). Social cognition and social perception. *Annual Review of Psychology, 38,* 369–426.

Hilgard, E. R. (1975). Hypnosis. *Annual Review of Psychology, 26,* 19–44.

Hilgard, E. R. (1978, January). Hypnosis and consciousness. *Human Nature,* pp. 42–49.

Hilgard, E. R. (1992). Divided consciousness and dissociation. *Consciousness and Cognition, 1,* 16–31.

Hilgard, E. R., & Hilgard, J. R. (1975). *Hypnosis in the relief of pain.* Los Altos, CA: W. Kaufman.

Hilgard, J. R. (1970). *Personality and hypnosis: A study of imaginative involvement.* Chicago: University of Chicago Press.

Hill, W. F. (1985). *Learning: A survey of psychological interpretations* (4th ed.). New York: HarperCollins.

Hinrichs, J. R. (1976). Personnel training. In M. Dunnette (Ed.), *Handbook of industrial and organizational psychology.* Skokie, IL: Rand McNally.

Hinsz, V. B., & Davis, J. H. (1984). Persuasive arguments theory, group polarization, and choice shifts. *Personality and Social Psychology Bulletin, 10,* 260–268.

Hobfoll, S. E. (1986). *Stress, social support, and women.* Washington, DC: Hemisphere.

Hobfoll, S. E. (1988). *The ecology of stress.* Washington, DC: Hemisphere.

Hobfoll, S. E. (1989). Conservation of resources: A new attempt at conceptualizing stress. *American Psychologist, 44,* 513–524.

Hobson, J. A. (1977). The reciprocal interaction model of sleep cycle control: Implications for PGO wave generation and dream amnesia. In R. R. Drucker-Colin & J. L. McGaugh (Eds.), *Neurobiology of sleep and memory.* New York: Academic Press.

Hobson, J. A. (1988). *The dreaming brain.* New York: Basic Books.

Hobson, J. A., & McCarley, R. W. (1977). The brain as a dream state generator: An activation-synthesis hypothesis of the dream process. *American Journal of Psychiatry, 134,* 1335–1348.

Hofferth, S. L., & Hayes, C. D. (Eds.). (1987). *Risking the future: Adolescent sexuality, pregnancy, and childbearing.* Washington, DC: National Academy Press.

Hoffman, D. D. (1983). The interpretation of visual illusions. *Scientific American, 245,* 154–162.

Hogan, J. (1989). Personality correlates of physical fitness. *Journal of Personality and Social Psychology, 56,* 284–288.

Hogan, R., & Nicholson, R. A. (1988). The meaning of personality test scores. *American Psychologist, 43,* 621–626.

Holden, C. (1980). A new visibility for gifted children. *Science, 210,* 879–882.

Hollander, E., DeCaria, C. M., Nitescu, A., Gully, R., Suckow, R. F., et al. (1992). Serotonergic function in obsessive-compulsive disorder. *Archives of General Psychiatry, 49,* 21–28.

Holman, B. L., & Tumeh, S. S. (1990). Single-photon emission computed tomography (SPECT): Applications and potential. *Journal of the American Medical Association, 263,* 561–564.

Holmes, D. (1994). *Abnormal psychology* (2nd ed.). New York: HarperCollins.

Holmes, D. S. (1984). Meditation and somatic arousal reduction: A review of the experimental evidence. *American Psychologist, 39,* 1–10.

Holmes, D. S. (1985). To meditate or simply rest, that is the question: A response to the comments of Shapiro. *American Psychologist, 40,* 722–725.

Holmes, D. S. (1987). The influence of meditation versus rest on physiological arousal: A second examination. In M. West (Ed.), *The psychology of meditation.* Oxford: Oxford University Press.

Holmes, T. S., & Holmes, T. H. (1970). Short-term intrusions into the life-style routine. *Journal of Psychosomatic Research, 14,* 121–132.

Holyoak, K. J., & Spellman, B. A. (1993). Thinking. *Annual Review of Psychology, 44,* 265–315.

Hood, R. D. (1990). Paternally mediated effects. In R. D. Hood (Ed.), *Developmental toxicology: Risk assessment and the future.* New York: Van Nostrand Reinhold.

Hoppock, R. (1935). *Job satisfaction.* New York: HarperCollins.

Hörmann, H. (1986). *Meaning and context.* New York: Plenum.

Horn, J. L. (1976). Human abilities: A review of research and theories in the early 1970s. *Annual Review of Psychology, 27,* 437–485.

Horn, J. L., & Cattell, R. B. (1966). Refinement and test of the theory of fluid and crystallized intelligence. *Journal of Educational Psychology, 57,* 253–276.

Horne, J. A. (1988). *Why we sleep: The function of sleep in humans and other mammals.* Oxford: Oxford University Press.

Horner, M. S. (1969). Women's will to fail. *Psychology Today, 3,* 36.

Horowitz, F. D., & O'Brien, M. (Eds.). (1985). *The gifted and talented: Developmental perspectives.* Washington, DC: American Psychological Association.

Hoshmand, T. L., & Polkinghorne, D. E. (1992). Redefining the science-practice relationship and professional training. *American Psychologist, 47,* 55–66.

Hostetler, A. J. (1987). Alzheimer's trials hinge on early diagnosis. *APA Monitor, 18,* 14–15.

Houston, B. K., & Vavak, C. R. (1991). Cynical hostility: Developmental factors, psycho-social correlates, and health behaviors. *Health Psychology, 10,* 9–17.

Houston, J. P. (1986). *Fundamentals of learning and memory* (3rd ed.). New York: Harcourt Brace Jovanovich.

Hovland, C. I., & Weiss, W. (1951). The influence of source credibility on communication effectiveness. *Public Opinion Quarterly, 15,* 635–650.

Howard, D. V. (1983). *Cognitive psychology.* New York: Macmillan.

Howard, K. I., Kopata, S. M., Krause, M. S., & Orlinsky, D. E. (1986). The dose-effect relationship in psychotherapy. *American Psychologist, 41,* 159–164.

Howell, W. C., & Dipboye, R. L. (1982). *Essentials of industrial and organizational psychology.* Homewood, IL: Dorsey Press.

Howes, C. (1990). Can the age of entry into child care and the quality of child care predict adjustment in kindergarten? *Developmental Psychology, 26,* 292–303.

Hsia, J. (1988). Limits on affirmative action: Asian American access to higher education. *Educational Policy, 2,* 117–136.

Hsu, L. K. G. (1986). The treatment of anorexia nervosa. *American Journal of Psychiatry, 143,* 573–581.

Hubel, D. H. (1979). The brain. *Scientific American, 241,* 45–53.

Hubel, D. H., & Wiesel, T. N. (1979). Brain mechanisms of vision. *Scientific American, 241,* 150–162.

Hudson, W. (1960). Pictorial depth perception in subcultural groups in Africa. *Journal of Social Psychology, 52,* 183–208.

Hughes, F. P., & Noppe, L. D. (1985). *Human development.* St. Paul, MN: West.

Hughes, J., Smith, T. W., Kosterlitz, H. W., Fothergill, L. A., Morgan, G. A., & Morris, H. R. (1975). Identification of two related peptides from the brain with potent opiate agonist activity. *Nature, 258,* 577–579.

Hughes, J. R., Gust, S. W., & Pechacek, T. F. (1987). Prevalence of tobacco dependence and withdrawal. *American Journal of Psychiatry, 144,* 205–208.

Hugick, L., & Leonard, J. (1991). Despite increasing hostility, one in four Americans still smokes. *Gallup Poll Monthly, 315,* 2–10.

Hui, C. H. (1990). Work attitudes, leadership styles, and managerial behaviors in different cultures. In R. W. Brislin (Ed.), *Applied cross-cultural psychology.* Newbury Park, CA: Sage.

Hulin, C. L., & Smith, P. C. (1964). Sex differences in job satisfaction. *Journal of Applied Psychology, 48,* 88–92.

Hull, C. L. (1943). *Principles of behavior.* Englewood Cliffs, NJ: Prentice-Hall.

Hunt, M. (1987, August 30). Navigating the therapy maze. *The New York Times Magazine,* pp. 28–31, 37, 44, 46, 49.

Hunter, J. E. (1986). Cognitive ability, cognitive aptitudes, job knowledge, and job performance. *Journal of Vocational Behavior, 29,* 340–362.

Hunter, J. E., & Hunter, R. F. (1984). Validity and utility of alternative predictors of job performance. *Psychological Bulletin, 96,* 72–98.

Hunter, S., & Sundel, M. (Eds.). (1989). *Midlife myths.* Newbury Park, CA: Sage.

Huston, A. C. (1985). The development of sex-typing: Themes from recent research. *Developmental Review, 5,* 1–17.

Huston, T. L., Ruggiero, M., Conner, R., & Geis, G. (1981). Bystander intervention into crime: A study based on naturally occurring episodes. *Social Psychology Quarterly, 44,* 14–23.

Hyde, J. S. (1984). How large are gender differences in aggression? A developmental meta-analysis. *Developmental Psychology, 20,* 697–706.

Hyde, J. S. (1986). *Understanding human sexuality* (3rd ed.). New York: McGraw-Hill.

Hyde, J. S. (1994). *Understanding human sexuality,* (5th ed.). New York: McGraw-Hill.

Hyde, J. S., Fennema, E., & Lamon, S. J. (1990). Gender differences in mathematics performance: A meta-analysis. *Psychological Bulletin, 107,* 139–155.

Iacono, W. G., & Grove, W. M. (1993). Schizophrenia reviewed: Toward an integrative genetic model. *Psychological Science, 4,* 273–276.

Iaffaldano, M. T., & Muchinsky, P. M. (1985). Job satisfaction and job performance: A meta-analysis. *Psychological Bulletin, 97,* 251–273.

Ilgen, D. R., & Klein, H. J. (1989). Organizational behavior. *Annual Review of Psychology, 40,* 327–351.

Insko, C. A. (1965). Verbal reinforcement of attitude. *Journal of Personality and Social Psychology, 2,* 621–623.

Irvine, J., Garner, D. M., Craig, H. M., & Logan, A. G. (1991). Prevalence of Type A behavior in untreated hypertensive individuals. *Hypertension, 18,* 72–78.

Isenberg, D. J. (1986). Group polarization: A critical review and meta-analysis. *Journal of Personality and Social Psychology, 50,* 1141–1151.

Iso-Ahola, S. E., & Blanchard, W. J. (1986). Psychological momentum and competitive sport performance: A field study. *Perceptual and Motor Skills, 62,* 763–768.

Istvan, J. (1986). Stress, anxiety, and birth outcomes: A critical review of the evidence. *Psychological Bulletin, 100,* 331–348.

Izard, C. E. (1972). *Patterns of emotion: A new analysis of anxiety and aggression.* New York: Academic Press.

Izard, C. E. (1977). *Human emotions.* New York: Plenum.

Jackaway, R., & Teevan, R. (1976). Fear of failure and fear of success: Two dimensions of the same motive. *Sex Roles, 2,* 283–294.

Jacklin, C. N. (1989). Female and male: Issues of gender. *American Psychologist, 44,* 127–133.

Jacklin, C. N., & Maccoby, E. E. (1978). Social behavior at 33 months in same-sex and mixed-sex dyads. *Child Development, 49,* 557–569.

Jacobs, B. L. (1987). How hallucinogenic drugs work. *American Scientist, 75,* 386–392.

Jacobs, B. L., & Trulson, M. E. (1979). Mechanisms of action of LSD. *American Scientist, 67,* 396–404.

Jacobson, D. S. (1984). Neonatal correlates of prenatal exposure to smoking, caffeine, and alcohol. *Infant Behavior and Development, 7,* 253–265.

Jacoby, L. L., & Dallas, M. (1981). On the relationship between autobiographical memory and perceptual learning. *Journal of Experimental Psychology: General, 3,* 306–340.

James, W. (1890). *Principles of psychology.* New York: Holt, Rinehart & Winston.

James, W. (1892). *Psychology: Briefer course.* New York: Holt, Rinehart & Winston.

James, W. (1904). Does consciousness exist? *Journal of Philosophy, 1,* 477–491.

Janis, I. L. (1972). *Victims of groupthink.* Boston: Houghton Mifflin.

Janis, I. L. (1983a). *Groupthink: Psychological studies of policy decisions and fiascos* (2nd ed.). Boston: Houghton Mifflin.

Janis, I. L. (1983b). The role of social support in adherence to stressful decisions. *American Psychologist, 38,* 143–160.

Janoff-Bulman, R. (1979). Characterological versus behavioral self-blame: Inquiries into depression and rape. *Journal of Personality and Social Psychology, 37,* 1798–1809.

Jeffery, R. W. (1989). Risk behaviors and health: Contrasting individual and population perspectives. *American Psychologist, 44,* 1194–1202.

Jenkins, C. D. (1976). Recent evidence supporting psychological and social risk factors for coronary disease. *New England Journal of Medicine, 294,* 1033–1038.

Jenkins, J. G., & Dallenbach, K. M. (1924). Oblivescence during sleep and waking. *American Journal of Psychology, 35,* 605–12.

Jensen, A. R. (1969). How much can we boost IQ and scholastic achievement? *Harvard Educational Review, 39,* 1–123.

Jensen, A. R. (1980). *Bias in mental testing.* New York: Free Press.

Jensen, A. R. (1981). *Straight talk about mental tests.* London: Methuen.

Jessor, R. (1993). Successful adolescent development among youth in high-risk settings. *American Psychologist, 48,* 117–126.

Johnson, D. L. (1989). Schizophrenia as a brain disease. *American Psychologist, 44,* 553–555.

Johnson, E. H. (1978). Validation of concept-learning strategies. *Journal of Experimental Psychology, 107,* 237–265.

Johnson, J., Weissman, M. M., & Klerman, G. L. (1990). Panic disorder, comorbidity, and suicide attempts. *Archives of General Psychiatry, 47,* 805–808.

Johnson, M. K., & Hasher, L. (1987). Human learning and memory. *Annual Review of Psychology, 38,* 631–668.

Jones, E. E. (1979). The rocky road from acts to dispositions. *American Psychologist, 34,* 107–117.

Jones, E. E., & Nisbett, R. E. (1971). *The actor and the observer: Divergent perceptions of behavior.* Morristown, NJ: General Learning Press.

Jones, K. L., Smith, D. W., Ulleland, C. N., & Streissgoth, A. P. (1973). Patterns of malformation in offspring of chronic alcoholic mothers. *Lancet, 3,* 1267–1271.

Jones, M. C. (1957). The careers of boys who were early or late maturing. *Child Development, 28,* 113–128.

Jordan, B. K., Marmar, C. R., Fairbank, J. A., Schlenger, W. E., Kulka, R. A., Hough, R. L., & Weiss, D. S. (1992). Problems in families of male Vietnam veterans with post-traumatic stress disorder. *Journal of Consulting and Clinical Psychology, 60,* 916–926.

Joyce, P. R., & Paykel, E. S. (1989). Predictors of drug response in depression. *Archives of General Psychiatry, 46,* 89–99.

Julien, R. M. (1985). *A primer of drug action* (4th ed.). San Francisco: Freeman.

Julien, R. M. (1988). *A primer of drug addiction* (5th ed.). New York: Freeman.

Kacmar, K. M., & Ferris, G. R. (1989). Theoretical and methodological considerations in the age-job satisfaction relationship. *Journal of Applied Psychology, 74,* 201–207.

Kagan, J. (1988). The meanings of personality predicates. *American Psychologist, 43,* 614–620.

Kahn, S., Zimmerman, G., Csikzentmihalyi, M., & Getzels, J. W. (1985). Relations between identity in young adulthood and intimacy at midlife. *Journal of Personality and Social Psychology, 49,* 1316–1322.

Kahneman, D., & Tversky, A. (1973). On the psychology of prediction. *Psychological Review, 80,* 237–251.

Kahneman, D., & Tversky, A. (1979). On the interpretation of intuitive probability: A reply to Jonathan Cohen. *Cognition, 7,* 409–411.

Kahneman, D., & Tversky, A. (1984). Choices, values, and frames. *American Psychologist, 39,* 341–350.

Kalat, J. W. (1984). *Biological psychology* (2nd ed.). Belmont, CA: Wadsworth.

Kales, A., Scharf, M. B., Kales, J. D., & Soldatos, C. R. (1979). Rebound insomnia: A potential hazard following withdrawal of certain benzodiazepines. *Journal of the American Medical Association, 241,* 1692–1695.

Kalish, R. A. (1976). Death and dying in a social context. In R. H. Binstock & E. Shanas (Eds.), *Handbook of aging and the social sciences.* New York: Van Nostrand Reinhold.

Kalish, R. A. (1982). *Late adulthood: Perspectives on human development.* Monterey, CA: Brooks/Cole.

Kamin, L. (1968). Attention-like processes in classical conditioning. In M. Jones (Ed.), *Miami symposium on the prediction of behavior: Aversive stimulation.* Miami: University of Miami Press.

Kamin, L. (1969). Predictability, surprise, attention, and conditioning. In R. Church & B. Campbell (Eds.), *Punishment and aversive behaviors.* Englewood Cliffs, NJ: Prentice-Hall.

Kamiya, J., Barber, T. X., Miller, N. E., Shapiro, D., & Stoyva, J. (1977). *Biofeedback and self-control.* Chicago: Aldine.

Kandel, E. R., & Schwartz, J. H. (1982). Molecular biology of learning: Modulation of transmitter release. *Science, 218,* 433–443.

Kane, J. (1989). The current status of neuroleptics. *Journal of Clinical Psychiatry, 50,* 322–328.

Kanizsa, G. (1976). Subjective contours. *Scientific American, 234,* 48–52.

Kanner, A. D., Coyne, J. C., Schaefer, C., & Lazarus, R. S. (1981). Comparison of two modes of stress measurement: Daily hassles and uplifts versus major life events. *Journal of Behavioral Medicine, 4,* 1–39.

Kanner, L. (1943). Autistic disturbances of affective contact. *Nervous Child, 2,* 217–250.

Kaplan, G. M. (1991). The use of biofeedback in the treatment of chronic facial tics: A case study. *Medical Psychotherapy, 4,* 71–84.

Kaplan, H. S. (1974). *The new sex therapy: Active treatment of sexual dysfunction.* New York: Quadrangle.

Kaplan, H. S. (1975). *The illustrated manual of sex therapy.* New York: Quadrangle.

Kaplan, H. S., & Sadock, B. J. (1991). *Synopsis of psychiatry.* Baltimore: Williams & Wilkins.

Kaplan, R. M. (1984). The connection between clinical health promotion and health status. *American Psychologist, 39,* 755–765.

Kaplan, R. M., & Saccuzzo, D. P. (1989). *Psychological testing* (2nd ed.). Monterey, CA: Brooks/Cole.

Kaplan, S. (1987). Aesthetics, affect and cognition: Environmental preference from an evolutionary perspective. *Environment and Behavior, 19,* 3–32.

Karoum, F., Karson, C. N., Bigelow, L. B., Lawson, W. B., & Wyatt, R. J. (1987). Preliminary evidence of reduced combined output of dopamine and its metabolites in chronic schizophrenia. *Archives of General Psychiatry, 44,* 604–607.

Kassin, S. M., Ellsworth, P. C., & Smith, V. L. (1989). The "general acceptance" of psychological research on eyewitness testimony: A survey of experts. *American Psychologist, 44,* 1089–1098.

Kastenbaum, R., & Costa, P. (1977). Psychological perspectives on death. *Annual Review of Psychology, 28,* 225–249.

Katzell, R. A., & Guzzo, R. A. (1983). Psychological approaches to productivity improvement. *American Psychologist, 38,* 468–472.

Katzell, R. A., & Thompson, D. E. (1990). Work motivation: Theory and practice. *American Psychologist, 45,* 144–153.

Katzman, R. (1987). Alzheimer's disease. *New England Journal of Medicine, 314,* 964–973.

Kay, S. R. (1990). Significance of the positive-negative distinction in schizophrenia. *Schizophrenia Bulletin, 16,* 635–652.

Kay, S. R., & Singh, M. M. (1989). The positive-negative distinction in drug-free schizophrenic patients. *Archives of General Psychiatry, 46,* 711–717.

Kazdin, A. E., Esveldt-Dawson, K., French, N. H., & Unis, A. S. (1987). Problem-solving skills training and relationship therapy in the treatment of antisocial child behavior. *Journal of Consulting and Clinical Psychology, 55,* 76–85.

Keating, D. P. (1980). Thinking processes in adolescents. In J. Adelson (Ed.), *Handbook of adolescent psychology.* New York: Wiley.

Keesey, R. E., & Powley, T. L. (1975). Hypothalamic regulation of body weight. *American Scientist, 63,* 558–565.

Keesey, R. E., & Powley, T. L. (1986). The regulation of body weight. *Annual Review of Psychology, 37,* 109–133.

Keith, P. M. (1983). A comparison of the resources of parents and childless men and women in very old age. *Family Relations, 32,* 403–409.

Kelley, H. H. (1967). Attribution theory in social psychology. In D. Levine (Ed.), *Nebraska symposium on motivation.* Lincoln: University of Nebraska Press.

Kelley, H. H. (1973). The process of causal attribution. *American Psychologist, 28,* 107–128.

Kelley, H. H. (1992). Common-sense psychology and scientific psychology. *Annual Review of Psychology, 43,* 1–24.

Kelley, H. H., & Michela, J. L. (1980). Attribution theory and research. *Annual Review of Psychology, 31,* 457–501.

Kelley, H. H., & Thibault, J. W. (1978). *Interpersonal relations: A theory of interdependence.* New York: Wiley.

Kelley, K. (1985). Sex, sex guilt, and authoritarianism: Differences in responses to explicit heterosexual and masturbatory slides. *The Journal of Sex Research, 21,* 68–85.

Kelly, J. A., Kalichman, S. C., Kauth, M. R., Kilgore, H. G., Hood, H. V., et al. (1991). Situational factors associated with AIDS risk behavior lapses and coping strategies used by gay men who successfully avoid lapses. *American Journal of Public Health, 81,* 1335–1338.

Kelly, J. A., Murphy, D. A., Sikkema, K. J., & Kalichman, S. C. (1993). Psychological interventions to prevent HIV infection are urgently needed. *American Psychologist, 48,* 1023–1034.

Kelly, J. A., & St. Lawrence, J. S. (1988). *The AIDS health crisis.* New York: Plenum.

Kelly, J. A., St. Lawrence, J. S., Hood, H. V., & Brasfield, T. L. (1989). Behavior intervention to reduce AIDS risk activities. *Journal of Consulting and Clinical Psychology, 57,* 60–67.

Kempler, D., & Van Lanker, D. (1987). The right turn of phrase. *Psychology Today, 21,* 20–22.

Kendler, K. S., & Gruenberg, A. M. (1982). Genetic relationship between paranoid personality disorder and the "schizophrenic" spectrum disorders. *American Journal of Psychiatry, 139,* 1185–1186.

Kendler, K. S., Neale, M. C., Kessler, R. C., Heath, A. C., & Eaves, L. J. (1993). A longitudinal twin study of 1-year prevalence of major depression in women. *Archives of General Psychiatry, 50,* 843–852.

Kendrick, D. T., & Funder, D. C. (1988). Profiting from controversy: Lessons from the person-situation debate. *American Psychologist, 43,* 23–34.

Kermis, M. D. (1984). *The psychology of human aging.* Boston: Allyn & Bacon.

Kershner, J. R., & Ledger, G. (1985). Effect of sex, intelligence, and style of thinking on creativity: A comparison of gifted and average IQ children. *Journal of Personality and Social Psychology, 48,* 1033–1040.

Kessler, R. C., McGonagle, K. A., Zhao, S., Nelson, C. P., et al. (1994). Lifetime and 12-month prevalence of DSM-III-R psychiatric disorders in the United States: Results from the National Comorbidity Survey. *Archives of General Psychiatry, 51,* 88–19.

Kessler, S. (1980). The genetics of schizophrenia: A review. In S. J. Keith & L. R. Mosher (Eds.), *Special report: Schizophrenia.* Washington, DC: U.S. Government Printing Office.

Kett, J. F. (1977). *Rites of passage: Adolescence in America from 1790 to the present.* New York: Basic Books.

Key, M. R. (1975). *Male/female language.* Metuchen, NJ: Scarecrow Press.

Kientzle, M. J. (1946). Properties of learning curves under varied distributions of practice. *Journal of Experimental Psychology, 36,* 187–211.

Kiester, E. (1984a). The playing fields of the mind. *Psychology Today, 18,* 18–24.

Kiester, E. (1984b). The uses of anger. *Psychology Today, 18,* 26.

Kiester, E., Jr. (1980). Images of the night: The physiological roots of dreaming. *Science 80, 1,* 36–43.

Kihlstrom, J. F. (1985). Hypnosis. *Annual Review of Psychology, 26,* 557–591.

Kihlstrom, J. F. (1987). The cognitive unconscious. *Science, 327,* 1445–1452.

Kimball, M. M. (1989). A new perspective on women's math achievement. *Psychological Bulletin, 105,* 198–214.

Kimble, G. A. (1981). Biological and cognitive constraints on learning. In L. Benjamin (Ed.), *The G. Stanley Hall Lecture*

Series (Vol. 1). Washington, DC: American Psychological Association.

Kimble, G. A. (1989). Psychologist from the standpoint of a generalist. *American Psychologist, 44,* 491–499.

Kimmel, D. C. (1988). Ageism, psychology, and public policy. *American Psychologist, 43,* 175–178.

Kimmel, H. D. (1974). Instrumental conditioning of autonomically-mediated responses in human beings. *American Psychologist, 29,* 325–335.

King, M., Murray, M. A., & Atkinson, T. (1982). Background, personality, job characteristics, and satisfaction with work in a national sample. *Human Relations, 35,* 119–133.

King, M. J., Zir, L. M., Kaltman, A. J., & Fox, A. C. (1973). Variant angina associated with angiographically demonstrated coronary artery system spasm and REM sleep. *American Journal of Medical Science, 265,* 419–422.

Kinsbourne, M. (1982). Hemispheric specialization and the growth of human understanding. *American Psychologist, 37,* 411–420.

Kinsey, A. C., Pomeroy, W. B., & Martin, C. E. (1948). *Sexual behavior in the human male.* Philadelphia: Saunders.

Kinsey, A. C., Pomeroy, W. B., Martin, C. E., & Gebhard, P. H. (1953). *Sexual behavior in the human female.* Philadelphia: Saunders.

Kirby, D. A., & Verrier, R. L. (1989). Differential effects of sleep stage on coronary hemodynamic function during stenosis. *Physiology and Behavior, 45,* 1017–1020.

Kirkpatrick, D. L. (1976). Evaluation of training. In R. L. Craig (Ed.), *Training and development handbook* (2nd ed.) New York: McGraw-Hill.

Kirscht, J. P. (1983). Preventive health behavior: A review of research and issues. *Health Psychology, 2,* 277–301.

Klayman, J., & Ha, Y-W. (1987). Confirmation, disconfirmation, and information in hypothesis testing. *Psychological Review, 94,* 211–228.

Kleitman, N. (1963a). Patterns of dreaming. *Scientific American, 203,* 82–88.

Kleitman, N. (1963b). *Sleep and wakefulness.* Chicago: University of Chicago Press.

Klepinger, D. H., Billy, J. O. G., Tanfer, K., & Grady, W. R. (1993). Perceptions of AIDS risk and severity and their association with risk-related behavior among U.S. men. *Family Planning Perspectives, 25,* 74–82.

Klerman, G. L. (1990). Treatment of recurrent unipolar major depressive disorder. *Archives of General Psychiatry, 47,* 1158–1162.

Knapp, S., & VandeCreek, L. (1989). What psychologists need to know about AIDS. *The Journal of Training and Practice in Professional Psychology, 3,* 3–16.

Knittle, J. L. (1975). Early influences on development of adipose tissue. In G. A. Bray (Ed.), *Obesity in perspective.* Washington, DC: U.S. Government Printing Office.

Knowles, E. S. (1983). Social physics and the effects of others: Tests of the effects of audience size and distance on social

judgments and behavior. *Journal of Personality and Social Psychology, 45,* 1263–1279.

Kobasa, S. C. (1979). Stressful life events, personality, and health: An inquiry into hardiness. *Journal of Personality and Social Psychology, 37,* 1–11.

Kobasa, S. C. (1982). The hardy personality: Toward a social psychology of stress and health. In G. S. Sanders & J. Suls (Eds.), *Social psychology of health and illness.* Hillsdale, NJ: Erlbaum.

Kobasa, S. C. (1987). Stress responses and personality. In R. C. Barnette, L. Beiner, & G. K. Baruch (Eds.), *Gender and stress.* New York: Free Press.

Kocel, K. M. (1977). Cognitive abilities: Handedness, familial sinistrality, and sex. *Annal of the New York Academy of Sciences, 299,* 233–243.

Koestler, A. (1964). *The act of creation.* New York: Macmillan.

Kohlberg, L. (1963). Moral development and identification. In H. W. Stevenson (Ed.), *Child psychology.* Chicago: University of Chicago Press.

Kohlberg, L. (1969). *Stages in the development of moral thought and action.* New York: Holt, Rinehart & Winston.

Kohlberg, L. (1981). *Philosophy of moral development.* New York: HarperCollins.

Kohlberg, L. (1985). *The psychology of moral development.* New York: HarperCollins.

Köhler, W. (1969). *The task of Gestalt psychology.* Princeton, NJ: Princeton University Press.

Kolata, G. (1987). What babies know, and noises parents make. *Science, 237,* 726.

Kolb, B. (1989). Brain development, plasticity, and behavior. *American Psychologist, 44,* 1203–1212.

Korchin, S. J., & Scheldberg, D. (1981). The future of clinical assessment. *American Psychologist, 36,* 1147–1158.

Koslow, D. R., & Salett, E. P. (1989). *Crossing cultures in mental health.* Washington, DC: SIETAR International.

Koss, M. P., & Butcher, J. N. (1986). Research on brief psychotherapy. In S. L. Garfield & A. E. Bergin (Eds.), *Handbook of psychotherapy and behavior change* (3rd ed.). New York: Wiley.

Kosslyn, S. M. (1987). Seeing and imagining in the cerebral hemispheres: A computational approach. *Psychological Review, 94,* 148–175.

Kraepelin, E. (1883). *Compendium der psychiatrie.* Leipzig: Abel.

Kramer, B. A. (1985). The use of ECT in California, 1977–1983. *The American Journal of Psychiatry, 142,* 1190–1192.

Krantz, D. S., & Glass, D. C. (1984). Personality, behavior patterns, and physical illness: Conceptual and methodological issues. In W. D. Gentry (Ed.), *Handbook of behavioral medicine.* New York: Guilford.

Krantz, D. S., Grunberg, N. E., & Braum, A. (1985). Health psychology. *Annual Review of Psychology, 36,* 349–383.

Kripke, D. F., & Gillin, J. C. (1985). Sleep disorders. In J. O. Cavenar (Ed.), *Psychiatry.* Philadelphia: Lippincott.

Krueger, J. M., & Obal, F. (1993). A neuronal group theory of sleep function. *Journal of Sleep Research, 2,* 63–69.

Krueger, W. C. F. (1929). The effect of overlearning on retention. *Journal of Experimental Psychology, 12*, 71–78.

Krupat, E. (1985). *People in cities: The urban environment and its effects.* New York: Cambridge University Press.

Kübler-Ross, E. (1969). *On death and dying.* New York: Macmillan.

Kübler-Ross, E. (1981). *Living with death and dying.* New York: Macmillan.

Kunst-Wilson, W. R., & Zajonc, R. B. (1980). Affective discrimination that cannot be recognized. *Science, 207*, 557–558.

Kupfer, D. J., Frank, E., & Perel, J. M. (1989). The advantage of early treatment intervention in recurrent depression. *Archives of General Psychiatry, 46*, 771–775.

Labov, W. (1973). The boundaries of words and their meaning. In C. J. N. Bailey & R. W. Shuy (Eds.), *New ways of analyzing variations in English.* Washington, DC: Georgetown University Press.

Lafferty, P., Beutler, L. E., & Crago, M. (1989). Differences between more and less effective psychotherapists: A study of select therapist variables. *Journal of Consulting and Clinical Psychology, 57*, 76–80.

Laird, J. (1984). The real role of facial response in the experience of emotion: A reply to Tourangeau and Ellsworth, and others. *Journal of Personality and Social Psychology, 47*, 909–917.

Laird, J. M. A., & Bennett, G. J. (1991). *Dorsal horn neurons in rats with an experimental peripheral mononeuropathy.* Paper presented at the 21st Annual Meeting of the Society for Neuroscience, New Orleans.

Lakoff, R. (1975). *Language and women's place.* New York: HarperCollins.

Lamb, M. E. (1977). Father-infant and mother-infant interaction in the first year of life. *Child Development, 48*, 167–181.

Lamb, M. E. (1979). Paternal influences and the father's role: A personal perspective. *American Psychologist, 34*, 938-943.

Lamb, M. E., Hwang, C. P., Frodi, A. M., & Frodi, M. (1982). Security of mother and father infant attachment and its relation to sociability with strangers in traditional and non-traditional Swedish families. *Infant Behavior and Development, 5*, 355–368.

Lamb, M. E., & Sternberg, K. J. (1990). Do we really know how day care affects children? *Journal of Applied Developmental Psychology, 11*, 499.

Landers, D. M. (1982). Arousal, attention, and skilled performance: Further considerations. *Quest, 33*, 271–283.

Landers, S. (1987). Panel urges teen contraception. *APA Monitor, 18*, 6.

Landesman, S., & Butterfield, E. C. (1987). Normalization and deinstitutionalization of mentally retarded individuals. *American Psychologist, 42*, 809–816.

Landesman, S., & Ramey, C. (1989). Developmental psychology and mental retardation: Integrating scientific principles with treatment practices. *American Psychologist, 44*, 409–415.

Landy, F. J. (1989). *Psychology of work behavior* (2nd ed.). Homewood, IL: Dorsey Press.

Landy, F. J., Shankster, L. J., & Köhler, S. S. (1994). Personnel selection and placement. *Annual Review of Psychology, 45*, 261–296.

Lanetto, R. (1980). *Children's conceptions of death.* New York: Springer.

Lang, P. J. (1985). The cognitive psychophysiology of emotion: Fear and anxiety. In A. H. Tuma & J. D. Maser (Eds.), *Anxiety and the anxiety disorders.* Hillsdale, NJ: Erlbaum.

Langer, S. K. (1951). *Philosophy in a new key.* New York: New American Library.

Larson, R., & Ham, M. (1993). Stress and "storm and stress" in early adolescence: The relationship of negative events with dysphoric affect. *Developmental Psychology, 29*, 130–140.

Larson, R., & Lampman-Petraitis, R. (1989). Daily emotional states as reported by children and adolescents. *Child Development, 60*, 1250–1260.

Lasky, R. E., & Kallio, K. D. (1978). Transformation rules in concept learning. *Memory and Cognition, 6*, 491–495.

Latané, B., & Darley, J. M. (1968). Group inhibition of bystander intervention in emergencies. *Journal of Personality and Social Psychology, 10*, 215–221.

Latané, B., & Darley, J. M. (1970). *The unresponsive bystander: Why doesn't he help?* Englewood Cliffs, NJ: Prentice-Hall.

Latané, B., & Nida, S. (1981). Ten years of research on group size and helping. *Psychological Bulletin, 89*, 308–324.

Latané, B., Williams, K., & Harkins, S. (1979). Many hands make light work: The causes and consequences of social loafing. *Journal of Personality and Social Psychology, 37*, 822–832.

Latham, G. P. (1988). Human resource training and development. *Annual Review of Psychology, 39*, 545–582.

Lattal, K. A. (1992). B. F. Skinner and psychology: Introduction to the special issue. *American Psychologist, 47*, 1269–1272.

Lauer, J., & Lauer, R. (1985). Marriages made to last. *Psychology Today, 19*, 22–26.

Lavond, D. G., Kim, J. J., & Thompson, R. F. (1993). Mammalian brain substrates of aversive classical conditioning. *Annual Review of Psychology, 44*, 317–342.

Lawler, E. E. (1982). Strategies for improving the quality of work life. *American Psychologist, 37*, 486–493.

Lazarus, R. S. (1981). Little hassles can be hazardous to your health. *Psychology Today, 15*, 58–62.

Lazarus, R. S. (1991a). Cognition and motivation in emotion. *American Psychologist, 46*, 352–367.

Lazarus, R. S. (1991b). Progress on a cognitive-motivational-relational theory of emotion. *American Psychologist, 46*, 819–834.

Lazarus, R. S. (1991c). *Emotion and adaptation.* New York: Oxford University Press.

Lazarus, R. S. (1993). From psychological stress to the emotions: A history of changing outlooks. *Annual Review of Psychology, 44,* 1–21.

Lazarus, R. S., & Folkman, S. (1984). *Stress, appraisal, and coping.* New York: Springer.

Leahey, T. H., & Harris, R. J. (1989). *Human learning* (2nd ed.). Englewood Cliffs, NJ: Prentice-Hall.

Leger, D. W. (1992). *Biological foundations of behavior: An integrative approach.* New York: HarperCollins.

Lehrer, P. M., & Woolfolk, R. L. (1984). Are stress reduction techniques interchangeable, or do they have specific effects? A review of the comparative empirical literature. In L. Woolfolk & P. M. Lehrer (Eds.), *Principles and practice of stress management.* New York: Guilford.

Lempers, J. D., Flavell, E. R., & Flavell, J. H. (1977). The development in very young children of tactile knowledge concerning visual perception. *Genetic Psychology Monographs, 95,* 3–53.

Lenneberg, E. H. (1967). *Biological foundations of language.* New York: Wiley.

Lenneberg, E. H., Rebelsky, F. G., & Nichols, I. A. (1965). The vocalizations of infants born to deaf and hearing parents. *Human Development, 8,* 23–27.

Lenzenweger, M. F., Dworkin, R. H., & Wethington, E. (1989). Models of positive and negative symptoms in schizophrenia: An empirical evaluation of latent structures. *Journal of Abnormal Psychology, 98,* 62–70.

Leon G. R., & Roth, L. (1977). Obesity: Psychological causes, correlations and speculations. *Psychological Bulletin, 84,* 117–139.

Leonard, H. L., Swedo, S. E., Lenane, M. C., Rettew, D. C., Hamburger, S. D., et al. (1993). A 2- to 7-year follow-up study of 54 obsessive-compulsive children and adolescents. *Archives of General Psychiatry, 50,* 429–439.

Lerner, M. J. (1965). The effect of responsibility and choice on a partner's attractiveness following failure. *Journal of Personality, 33,* 178–187.

Lerner, M. J. (1980). *The belief in a just world.* New York: Plenum.

Lerner, R. M. (1978). Nature, nurture, and dynamic interactionism. *Human Development, 21,* 1–20.

LeVay, S. (1991). A difference in hypothalamic structure between heterosexual and homosexual men. *Science, 253,* 1034–1037.

Leventhal, H., & Cleary, P. D. (1980). The smoking problem: A review of the research and theory in behavioral risk modification. *Psychological Bulletin, 88,* 370–405.

Levine, H. Z. (1983). Safety and health programs. *Personnel, 3,* 4–9.

Levine, J. D., Gordon, N. C., & Fields, H. L. (1979). Naloxone dose dependently produces analgesia and hyperalgesia in post-operative pain. *Nature, 278,* 740–741.

Levine, J. M., & Moreland, R. L. (1990). Progress in small group research. *Annual Review of Psychology, 41,* 585–634.

Levine, J. M., Resnick, L. B., & Higgins, E. T. (1993). Social foundations of cognition. *Annual Review of Psychology, 44,* 585–612.

Levine, M., Toro, P. A., & Perkins, D. V. (1993). Social and community interventions. *Annual Review of Psychology, 44,* 525–558.

Levine, M. F., Taylor, J. C., & Davis, L. E. (1984). Defining quality of work life. *Human Relations, 37,* 81–104.

Levine, M. W., & Shefner, J. M. (1991). *Fundamentals of sensation and perception* (2nd ed.). Pacific Grove, CA: Brooks/Cole.

Levinson, D. J. (1978). *The seasons of a man's life.* New York: Ballantine Books.

Levinson, D. J. (1986). A conception of adult development. *American Psychologist, 41,* 3–13.

Levinson, D. J., Darrow, C. M., Klein, E. B., Levinson, M. H., & McKee, B. (1974). *The seasons of a man's life.* New York: Knopf.

Levinthal, C. F. (1983). *Introduction to physiological psychology* (2nd ed.). Englewood Cliffs, NJ: Prentice-Hall.

Lewinsohn, P. M., Zeiss, A. M., & Duncan, E. M. (1989). Probability of relapse after recovery from an episode of depression. *Journal of Abnormal Psychology, 98,* 107–116.

Ley, B. W. (1985). Alcohol problems in special populations. In J. H. Mendelson & N. K. Mello (Eds.), *The diagnosis and treatment of alcoholism* (2nd ed.). New York: McGraw-Hill.

Ley, P. (1977). Psychological studies of doctor-patient communication. In S. Rachman (Ed.), *Contributions to medical psychology* (Vol. 1). Elmsford, NY: Pergamon Press.

Lidz, T. (1973). *The origin and treatment of schizophrenic disorders.* New York: Basic Books.

Lieberman, J., Jody, D., Geisler, S., Alvir, J., Loebel, A., et al. (1993). Time course and biological correlates of treatment response in first-episode schizophrenia. *Archives of General Psychiatry, 50,* 369–376.

Lieberman, M. A. (1983). The effects of social support on response to stress. In L. Goldbert & D. S. Breznitz (Eds.), *Handbook of stress management.* New York: Free Press.

Lightman, S. W., Pisarska, K., Berman, E. R., Pestone, M., et al. (1992). Discrepancy between self-reported and actual caloric intake in obese subjects. *The New England Journal of Medicine, 327,* 1893–1898.

Lin, E., & Kleinman, A. (1988). Psychopathology and clinical course of schizophrenia: A cross-cultural perspective. *Schizophrenia Bulletin, 14,* 555–567.

Lin, T. R., Dobbins, G. H., & Farh, J. L. (1992). A field study of race and similarity effects on interview ratings in conventional and situational interviews. *Journal of Applied Psychology, 77,* 363–371.

Lincoln, J. R., & Kalleberg, A. L. (1985). Work organization and workforce commitment: A study of plants and employees in the U.S. and Japan. *American Sociological Review, 50,* 738–760.

Lindsley, D. B., Bowden, J., & Magoun, H. W. (1949). Effect upon EEG of acute injury to the brain stem activating system. *Electroencephalography and Clinical Neurophysiology, 1,* 475–486.

Linn, M. C., & Peterson, A. C. (1985). Emergence and characterization of sex differences in spatial ability: A meta-analysis. *Child Development, 56,* 1479–1498.

Lipsey, M. W., & Wilson, D. B. (1993). The efficacy of psychological, educational, and behavioral treatment: Confirmation from meta-analysis. *American Psychologist, 48,* 1181–1209.

Litt, M. D. (1988). Self-efficacy and perceived control: Cognitive mediators of pain tolerance. *Journal of Personality and Social Psychology, 54,* 149–160.

Locke, E. A. (1968). Toward a theory of task motivation and incentives. *Organizational Behavior and Human Performance, 3,* 157–189.

Locke, E. A. (1976). The nature and causes of job satisfaction. In M. D. Dunnette (Ed.), *Handbook of industrial and organizational psychology.* Skokie, IL: Rand McNally.

Locke, E. A., & Latham, G. P. (1984). *Goal setting: A motivational technique that works.* Englewood Cliffs, NJ: Prentice-Hall.

Locke, E. A., Shaw, K. N., Saari, L. M., & Latham, G. (1981). Goal-setting and task performance: 1969–1980. *Psychological Bulletin, 90,* 124–152.

Lockhard, J. S., & Paulus, D. L. (Eds.). (1988). *Self-deception: An adaptive mechanism?* Englewood Cliffs, NJ: Prentice-Hall.

Lockyer, L., & Rutter, M. L. (1969). A five- to fifteen-year follow-up study of infantile psychosis. *British Journal of Psychiatry, 115,* 865–882.

Loftus, E. F. (1984). The eyewitness on trial. In B. D. Sales & A. Alwork (Eds.), *With liberty and justice for all.* Englewood Cliffs, NJ: Prentice-Hall.

Loftus, E. F. (1991). The glitter of everyday memory . . . and the gold. *American Psychologist, 46,* 16–18.

Loftus, E. F. (1993a). The reality of repressed memories. *American Psychologist, 48,* 518–537.

Loftus, E. F. (1993b). *Therapeutic memories of early childhood abuse: Fact or fiction.* Paper presented at the Annual Meeting of the American Psychological Association, Toronto.

Loftus, E. F., & Klinger, M. R. (1992). Is the unconscious smart or dumb? *American Psychologist, 47,* 761–765.

Loftus, E. F., & Loftus, G. R. (1980). On the permanence of stored information in the human brain. *American Psychologist, 35,* 409–420.

Loftus, E. F., Miller, D. G. & Burns, H. J. (1978). Semantic integration of verbal information into a visual memory. *Journal of Experimental Psychology: Human Learning and Memory, 4,* 19–31.

Loftus, E. F., & Zanni, G. (1975). Eyewitness testimony: The influence of wording on a question. *Bulletin of the Psychonomic Society, 5,* 86–88.

Londerville, S., & Main, M. (1981). Security of attachment and compliance in maternal training methods in the second year of life. *Developmental Psychology, 17,* 289–299.

Long, P. (1986). Medical mesmerism. *Psychology Today, 20*(1), 28–29.

Lonner, W. J. (1980). The search for psychological universals. In H. C. Triandis & W. W. Lambert (Eds.), *Handbook of cross-cultural psychology* (Vol. I). Boston: Allyn & Bacon.

Lord, C. G. (1980). Schemas and images as memory aids. *Journal of Personality and Social Psychology, 38,* 257–269.

Lorenz, K. (1969). *On aggression.* New York: Bantam Books.

Lott, A. J., & Lott, B. E. (1974). The role of reward in the formation of positive interpersonal attitudes. In T. L. Huston (Ed.), *Foundations of interpersonal attraction.* New York: Academic Press.

Lovaas, O. I. (1987). Behavioral treatment and normal educational and intellectual functioning in young autistic children. *Journal of Consulting and Clinical Psychology, 55,* 3–9.

Lovaas, O. I., & Smith, P. (1988). Intensive behavioral treatment for young autistic children. In B. Lahey & A. Kazdin (Eds.), *Advances in clinical child psychology* (Vol. 2). New York: Plenum.

Lozoff, B. (1989). Nutrition and behavior. *American Psychologist, 44,* 231–236.

Lubin, B., Larsen, R. M., & Matarazzo, J. D. (1984). Patterns of psychological test usage in the United States: 1935–1982. *American Psychologist, 39,* 451–454.

Lucas, E. A., Foutz, A. S., Dement, W. C., & Mittler, M. M. (1979). Sleep cycle organization in narcoleptic and normal dogs. *Physiology and Behavior, 23,* 325–331.

Lugaresi, E., Medori, R., Montagna, P., Baruzzi, A., Cortelli, P., Lugaresi, A., Tinuper, P., Zucconi, M., & Gambetti, P. (1986). Fatal familial insomnia and dyautonomia with selective degeneration of the thalamic nuclei. *New England Journal of Medicine, 315,* 997–1003.

Luh, C. W. (1922). The conditions of retention. *Psychological Monographs* (Whole No. 142).

Lykken, D. T. (1957). A study of anxiety in sociopathic personality. *Journal of Abnormal and Social Psychology, 55,* 6–10.

Lykken, D. T. (1982). Fearlessness: Its carefree charm and deadly risk. *Psychology Today, 16,* 20–28.

Lykken, D. T., McGue, M., Tellegen, A., & Bouchard, T. J., Jr. (1992). Emergenesis: Genetic traits that may not run in families. *American Psychologist, 47,* 1565–1577.

Lynch, G., & Baudry, M. (1984). The biochemistry of memory: A new and specific hypothesis. *Science, 224,* 1057–1063.

Lyness, S. A. (1993). Predictors of differences between Type A and B individuals in heart rate and blood pressure reactivity. *Psychological Bulletin, 114,* 266–295.

Lynn, D. (1974). *The father: His role in child development.* Monterey, CA: Brooks/Cole.

Lynn, R. (1977). The intelligence of the Japanese. *Bulletin of the British Psychological Society, 30,* 69–72.

Lynn, R. (1982). IQ in Japan and the United States shows a greater disparity. *Nature, 297,* 222–223.

Lynn, R. (1987). The intelligence of the Mongoloids: A psychometric, evolutionary, and neurological theory. *Personality and Individual Differences, 8,* 813–844.

Lynn, R. (1991). Educational achievements of Asian Americans. *American Psychologist, 46,* 875–876.

Lynn, S. J., & Rhue, J. W. (1986). The fantasy-prone person: Hypnosis, imagination, and creativity. *Journal of Personality and Social Psychology, 51,* 404–408.

Lynn, S. J., Rhue, J. W., & Weekes, J. R. (1990). Hypnotic involuntariness: A social cognitive analysis. *Psychological Review, 97,* 69–184.

Lytton, H., & Romney, D. M. (1991). Parents' differential socialization of boys and girls: A meta-analysis. *Psychological Bulletin, 109,* 267–296.

Maccoby, E. E. (1988). Gender as a social category. *Developmental Psychology, 24,* 755–765.

Maccoby, E. E. (1990). Gender and relationships: A developmental account. *American Psychologist, 45,* 513–520.

Maccoby, E. E., & Jacklin, C. N. (1974). *The psychology of sex differences.* Stanford, CA: Stanford University Press.

Maccoby, E. E., & Jacklin, C. N. (1980). Sex differences in aggression: A rejoinder and reprise. *Child Development, 51,* 964–980.

Maccoby, E. E., & Jacklin, C. N. (1987). Gender segregation in childhood. In E. H. Reese (Ed.), *Advances in child development and behavior* (Vol. 23). New York: Academic Press.

MacDonald, M. R., & Kuiper, N. A. (1983). Cognitive-behavioral preparations for surgery: Some theoretical and methodological concerns. *Clinical Psychology Review, 3,* 27–39.

Mace, N. L., & Rabins, P. V. (1981). *The 36-hour day.* Baltimore: Johns Hopkins University Press.

Mackenzie, B. (1984). Explaining race differences in IQ: The logic, the methodology, and the evidence. *American Psychologist, 39,* 1214–1233.

Mackintosh, N. J. (1975). A theory of attention: Variations in the associability of stimuli with reinforcement. *Psychological Review, 82,* 276–298.

Mackintosh, N. J. (1986). The biology of intelligence? *British Journal of Psychology, 77,* 1–18.

Mackowiak, P. A., Wasserman, S. S., & Levine, M. M. (1992). A critical appraisal of 98.6F, the upper limit of the normal body temperature, and other legacies of Carl Reinhold August Wunderlich. *Journal of the American Medical Association, 268,* 1578–1580.

MacLeod, M. D., & Ellis, H. D. (1986). Modes of presentation in eyewitness testimony research. *Human Learning Journal of Practical Research and Applications, 5,* 39–44.

MacMillan, J., & Kofoed, L. (1984). Sociobiology and antisocial personality: An alternative perspective. *Journal of Mental Disorders, 172,* 701–706.

Maddi, S. R., & Kobasa, S. C. (1984). *The hardy executive: Health and stress.* Homewood, IL: Dorsey Press.

Madigan, S., & O'Hara, R. (1992). Short-term memory at the turn of the century: Mary Whiton Calkin's memory research. *American Psychologist, 47,* 170–174.

Magnusson, D., & Edler, N. S. (Eds.). (1977). *Personality at the crossroads: An international perspective.* Hillsdale, NJ: Erlbaum.

Magsud, M. (1979). Resolution of moral dilemmas by Nigerian secondary school pupils. *Journal of Moral Education, 7,* 40–49.

Maguire, J. (1990). *Care and feeding of the brain.* New York: Doubleday.

Maharishi, Mahesh Yogi. (1963). *The science of living and art of being.* London: Unwin.

Mahowald, M. W., & Schenck, C. H. (1989). REM sleep behavior disorder. In M. H. Krygr, T. Roth, & W. C. Dement (Eds.), *Principles and practice of sleep medicine.* Philadelphia: Saunders.

Maier, N. R. F. (1931). Reasoning in humans II: The solution of a problem and its appearance in consciousness. *Journal of Experimental Psychology, 105,* 181–194.

Malatesta, C. A., & Isard, C. E. (1984). The ontogenesis of human social signals: From biological imperative to symbol utilization. In N. A. Fox & R. J. Davidson (Eds.), *The psychobiology of affective development.* Hillsdale, NJ: Erlbaum.

Mandler, G. (1980). Recognizing: The judgment of previous occurrence. *Psychological Review, 87,* 252–271.

Manning, M. L. (1983). Three myths concerning adolescence. *Adolescence, 18,* 823–829.

Marengo, J. T., & Harrow, M. (1987). Schizophrenic thought disorder at follow-up. *Archives of General Psychiatry, 44,* 651–659.

Markowitz, J. S., Weissman, M. M., Ouellete, R., Lish, J. D., & Klerman, G. L. (1989). Quality of life in panic disorder. *Archives of General Psychiatry, 46,* 984–992.

Marks, I. M. (1986). Epidemiology of anxiety. *Social Psychiatry, 21,* 167–171.

Marschark, M., Richmond, C. L., Yuille, J. C., & Hunt, R. R. (1987). The role of imagery in memory: On shared and distinctive information. *Psychological Bulletin, 102,* 28–41.

Martin, B. J. (1986). Sleep deprivation and exercise. In K. B. Pandolf (Ed.), *Exercise and sport sciences review* (pp. 213–229). New York: Macmillan.

Martin, C. L. (1991). The role of cognition in understanding gender effects. In H. W. Reese (Ed.), *Advances in child development and behavior* (Vol. 23). New York: Academic Press.

Martin, G. B., & Clark, R. D. (1982). Distress crying in neonates: Species and peer specificity. *Developmental Psychology, 18,* 3–9.

Martin, R. J., White, B. D., & Hulsey, M. G. (1991). The regulation of body weight. *American Scientist, 79,* 528–541.

Martindale, C. (1981). *Cognition and consciousness.* Homewood, IL: Dorsey Press.

Marx, J. (1990). Alzheimer's pathology explored. *Science, 249,* 984–986.

Marziali, E. (1984). Prediction of outcome of brief psychotherapy from therapist interpretive interactions. *Archives of General Psychiatry, 41,* 301–304.

Maslow, A. H. (1943). A theory of human motivation. *Psychological Review, 50,* 370–396.

Maslow, A. H. (1954). *Motivation and personality.* New York: Harper.

Maslow, A. H. (1970). *Motivation and personality* (2nd ed.). New York: HarperCollins.

Massaro, D. W. (1975). *Experimental psychology and information processing.* Skokie, IL: Rand McNally.

Masters, W., & Johnson, V. (1970). *Human sexual inadequacy.* Boston: Little, Brown.

Masters, W., & Johnson, V. (1979). *Homosexuality in perspective.* Boston: Little, Brown.

Masters, W., Johnson, V., & Kolodny, R. C. (1987). *Human sexuality* (3rd ed.). Glenview, IL: Scott, Foresman/Little, Brown.

Masters, W. H., Johnson, V. E., & Kolodny, R. C. (1992). *Human sexuality* (4th ed.). New York: HarperCollins.

Matarazzo, J. D. (1980). Behavioral health and behavioral medicine: Frontiers for a new health psychology. *American Psychologist, 35,* 807–817.

Matarazzo, J. D. (1990). Psychological assessment versus psychological testing: Validation from Binet to the school, clinic, and courtroom. *American Psychologist, 45,* 999–1017.

Matlin, M. W. (1983). *Perception.* Boston: Allyn & Bacon.

Matsumoto, D. (1987). The role of facial response in the experience of emotion: More methodological problems and a meta-analysis. *Journal of Personality and Social Psychology, 52,* 769–774.

Matthews, K. A. (1982). Psychological perspectives on the Type A behavior pattern. *Psychological Bulletin, 91,* 293–323.

Matthews, K. A. (1988). Coronary heart disease and Type A behavior: Update on an alternative to the Booth-Kewley and Friedman (1987) quantitative review. *Psychological Bulletin, 104,* 373–380.

Matthies, H. (1989). Neurobiological aspects of learning and memory. *Annual Review of Psychology, 40,* 381–404.

Mattson, S. N., Barron, S., & Riley, E. P. (1988). The behavioral effects of prenatal alcohol exposure. In K. Kuriyama, A. Takada, & H. Ishii (Eds.), *Biomedical and social aspects of alcohol and alcoholism.* Tokyo: Elsevier.

Maxman, J. S. (1991). *Psychotropic drugs: Fast facts.* New York: Norton.

Mayer, R. E. (1983). *Thinking, problem solving, cognition.* San Francisco: Freeman.

Mayo, E. (1933). *The human problems of an industrial civilization.* Cambridge, MA: Harvard University Press.

McAdoo, W. G., & DeMyer, M. K. (1978). Personality characteristics of parents. In M. Rutter & E. Schopler (Eds.), *Autism: A reappraisal of concepts and treatment.* New York: Plenum.

McCann, I. L., & Holmes, D. S. (1984). Influence of aerobic exercise on depression. *Journal of Personality and Social Psychology, 46,* 1142–1147.

McCarthy, B. W., Ryan, M., & Johnson, F. (1975). *Sexual awareness.* San Francisco: Boyd & Fraser.

McCauley, C. (1989). The nature of social influence in groupthink: Compliance and internalization. *Journal of Personality and Social Psychology, 57,* 250–260.

McClelland, D. C. (1958). Risk-taking in children with high and low need for achievement. In J. W. Atkinson (Ed.), *Motives in fantasy, action, and society.* New York: Van Nostrand Reinhold.

McClelland, D. C. (1973). Testing for competence rather than for "intelligence." *American Psychologist, 28,* 1–14.

McClelland, D. C. (1982). The need for power, sympathetic activation, and illness. *Motivation and Emotion, 6,* 31–41.

McClelland, D. C. (1985). *Human motivation.* Glenview, IL: Scott, Foresman.

McClelland, D. C. (1993). Intelligence is not the best predictor of job performance. *Current Directions in Psychological Science, 2,* 5–6.

McClelland, D. C., Atkinson, J. W., Clark, R. A., & Lowell, E. L. (1953). *The achievement motive.* Englewood Cliffs, NJ: Prentice-Hall.

McClelland, D. C., & Winter, D. G. (1969). *Motivating economic development.* New York: Free Press.

McClintock, M. K. (1971). Menstrual synchrony and suppression. *Nature, 229,* 244–245.

McClintock, M. K. (1979). Estrous synchrony and its mediation by airborne chemical communication. *Hormones and Behavior, 10,* 264.

McCloskey, M., & Egeth, H. (1983). Eyewitness identification: What can a psychologist tell a jury? *American Psychologist, 38,* 550–563.

McCloskey, M., Wible, C., & Cohen, N. J. (1988). Is there a special flashbulb-memory mechanism? *Journal of Experimental Psychology: General, 117,* 171–181.

McCloskey, M., & Zaragoza, M. (1985). Misleading postevent information and memory for events: Arguments and evidence against memory impairment hypotheses. *Journal of Experimental Psychology: General, 114,* 1–16.

McCrae, R. (1984). Situational determinants of coping responses: Loss, threat, and challenge. *Journal of Personality and Social Psychology, 46,* 919–928.

McCrae, R. R., & Costa, P. T. (1984). *Emerging lives, enduring dispositions: Personality in adulthood.* Boston: Little, Brown.

McCrae, R. R., & Costa, P. T. (1986). Clinical assessment can benefit from recent advances in personality psychology. *American Psychologist, 41,* 1001–1002.

McCrae, R. R., & Costa, P. T. (1987). Validation of the five-factor model of personality across instruments and observers. *Journal of Personality and Social Psychology, 52,* 81–90.

McCrae, R. R., & John, O. P. (1992). An introduction to the five-factor model and its applications. *Journal of Personality, 60,* 175–215.

McDougall, W. (1908). *An introduction to social psychology.* London: Methuen.

McEvoy, G. M., & Beatty, R. W. (1989). Assessment centers and subordinate appraisals of managers: A seven-year examination of predictive validity. *Personnel Psychology, 42,* 37–52.

McGaugh, J. L. (1983). Hormonal influences on memory. *Annual Review of Psychology, 34,* 297–323.

McGee, M. G. (1979). Human spatial abilities: Psychometric studies and environmental, genetic, hormonal, and neurological influences. *Psychological Bulletin, 86,* 889–918.

McGeoch, J. A., & McDonald, W. T. (1931). Meaningful relation and retroactive inhibition. *American Journal of Psychology, 43,* 579–588.

McGinnis, J. M. (1985). Recent history of federal initiatives in prevention policy. *American Psychologist, 40,* 205–212.

McGinnis, J. M., & Foege, W. H. (1993). Actual causes of death in the United States. *Journal of the American Medical Association, 270,* 2207–2212.

McGlashen, T. H., & Fenton, W. S. (1992). The positive-negative distinction in schizophrenia: Review of natural history indicators. *Archives of General Psychiatry, 49,* 63–72.

McGlone, J. (1977). Sex differences in the cerebral organization of verbal functions in patients with unilateral lesions. *Brain, 100,* 775–793.

McGlone, J. (1978). Sex differences in functional brain asymmetry. *Cortex, 14,* 122–128.

McGlone, J. (1980). Sex differences in human brain asymmetry: A critical survey. *The Behavioral and Brain Sciences, 3,* 215–227.

McGrath, E., Keita, G. P., Strickland, B., & Russo, N. F. (Eds.). (1990). *Women and depression: Risk factors and treatment issues.* Washington, DC: American Psychological Association.

McGraw, K. O. (1987). *Developmental psychology.* San Diego: Harcourt Brace Jovanovich.

McGue, M., & Lykken, D. T. (1992). Genetic influence on risk of divorce. *Psychological Science, 3,* 368–373.

McGuire, W. J. (1985). Attitudes and attitude change. In G. Lindzey & E. Aronson (Eds.), *Handbook of social psychology.* New York: Random House.

McKim, W. A. (1986). *Drugs and behavior.* Englewood Cliffs, NJ: Prentice-Hall.

McLoed, J. D., & Kessler, R. C. (1990). Socioeconomic status and differences in vulnerability to undesirable life events. *Journal of Health and Social Behavior, 31,* 162–172.

McNaughton, B. L., & Morris, R. G. M. (1987). Hippocampal synaptic enhancement and information storage within a distributed memory system. *Trends in Neuroscience, 10,* 408–415.

McNeil, D. (1970). *The acquisition of language: The study of developmental psycholinguistics.* New York: HarperCollins.

Medin, D. L. (1989). Concepts and concept structure. *American Psychologist, 44,* 1469–1481.

Mednick, M. T. (1989). On the politics of psychological constructs: Stop the bandwagon, I want to get off. *American Psychologist, 44,* 1118–1123.

Mednick, M. T. S. (1979). The new psychology of women: A feminist analysis. In J. E. Gullahorn (Ed.), *Psychology and women: In transition.* New York: Wiley.

Mednick, S. A., Moffitt, T. E., & Stack, S. (1987). *The causes of crime: New biological approaches.* New York: Cambridge University Press.

Meer, J. (1986). The reason of age. *Psychology Today, 20,* 60–64.

Meichenbaum, D. (1977). *Cognitive-behavior modification: An integrative approach.* New York: Plenum.

Meichenbaum, D., & Turk, D. C. (1987). *Facilitating treatment adherence.* New York: Plenum.

Meltzoff, A. N., & Moore, M. K. (1977). Imitation of facial and manual gestures by human neonates. *Science, 198,* 75–78.

Meltzoff, A. N., & Moore, M. K. (1989). Imitation in newborn infants: Exploring the range of gestures imitated and the underlying mechanism. *Developmental Psychology, 25,* 954–962.

Melzack, R. (1973). *The puzzle of pain.* Baltimore: Penguin Books.

Melzack, R., & Wall, P. D. (1965). Pain mechanisms: A new theory. *Science, 150,* 971–979.

Meredith, N. (1986). Testing the talking cure. *Science 86, 7*(5), 30–37.

Mervis, J. (1986). NIMH data points the way to effective treatment. *APA Monitor, 17,* 1, 13.

Metcalfe, J., & Wiebe, D. (1987). Intuition and insight and noninsight problem solving. *Memory and Cognition, 15,* 238–246.

Michael, J. L. (1985). Behavior analysis: A radical perspective. In B. L. Hammonds (Ed.), *Psychology and learning.* Washington, DC: American Psychological Association.

Middlemist, R. D., & Peterson, R. B. (1976). Test of equity theory by controlling for comparison of workers' efforts. *Organizational Behavior and Human Performance, 15,* 335–354.

Milgram, S. (1963). Behavioral studies of obedience. *Journal of Abnormal and Social Psychology, 67,* 371–378.

Milgram, S. (1965). Some conditions of obedience and disobedience to authority. *Human Relations, 18,* 57–76.

Milgram, S. (1970). The experience of living in cities. *Science, 167,* 1461–1468.

Milgram, S. (1974). *Obedience to authority.* New York: HarperCollins.

Milgram, S. (1977). *The individual in a social world.* Reading, MA: Addison-Wesley.

Miller, D. T., & McFarland, C. (1987). Pluralistic ignorance: When similarity is interpreted as dissimilarity. *Journal of Personality and Social Psychology, 53,* 298–305.

Miller, D. T., & Ross, M. (1975). Self-serving biases in the attribution of causality: Fact or Fiction? *Psychological Bulletin, 82,* 213–225.

Miller, J. G. (1984). Culture and the development of everyday social explanation. *Journal of Personality and Social Psychology, 46,* 961–978.

Miller, N. E. (1944). Experimental studies of conflict. In J. M. Hunt (Ed.), *Personality and the behavior disorders.* New York: Ronald Press.

Miller, N. E. (1978). Biofeedback and visceral learning. *Annual Review of Psychology, 29,* 373–404.

Miller, N. E. (1983). Behavioral medicine: Symbiosis between laboratory and clinic. *Annual Review of Psychology, 34,* 1–31.

Miller, R. C., & Berman, J. S. (1983). The efficacy of cognitive behavior therapies: A quantitative review of the research evidence. *Psychological Bulletin, 94,* 39–53.

Miller, R. R., & Spear, N. E. (Eds.). (1985). *Information processing in animals: Conditioned inhibition.* Hillsdale, NJ: Erlbaum.

Miller, W. R. (1992) Client/treatment matching in addictive behaviors. *The Behavior Therapist, 15,* 7–8.

Millstein, S. G. (1989). Adolescent health: Challenges for behavioral scientists. *American Psychologist, 44,* 837–842.

Milner, B. (1959). The memory deficit in bilateral hippocampal lesions. *Psychiatric Research Reports, 11,* 43–52.

Milner, B. (1965). Memory disturbances after bilateral hippocampal lesions. In B. Milner & S. Glickman (Eds.), *Cognitive processes and the brain.* New York: Van Nostrand Reinhold.

Milner, B., Corkin, S., & Teuber, H. L. (1968). Further analysis of the hippocampal amnesic syndrome: 14-year follow-up study of H. M. *Neuropsychologica, 6,* 215–234.

Minami, H., & Dallenbach, K. M. (1946). The effect of activity upon learning and retention in the cockroach. *American Journal of Psychology, 59,* 682–697.

Minuchin, S., & Fishman, H. C. (1981). *Family therapy techniques.* Cambridge, MA: Harvard University Press.

Mirin, S. M., Weiss, R. D., & Greenfield, S. F. (1991). Psychoactive substance abuse disorders. In A. J. Galenberg, E. L. Bassuk, & S. C. Schoonover (Eds.), *The practitioner's guide to psychoactive drugs.* New York: Plenum.

Mischel, W. (1968). *Personality and assessment.* New York: Wiley.

Mischel, W. (1979). On the interface of cognition and personality. *American Psychologist, 34,* 740–754.

Mischel, W. (1981). *Introduction to personality* (3rd ed.). New York: Holt, Rinehart & Winston.

Mischel, W., & Peake, P. K. (1982). Beyond déja vu in the search for cross-situational consistency. *Psychological Review, 89,* 730–755.

Mobley, W. H. (1977). Intermediate linkages in the relationship between job satisfaction and employee turnover. *Journal of Applied Psychology, 62,* 237–240.

Moncher, M. S., Holden, G. W., & Trimble, J. E. (1990). Substance abuse among Native American youth. *Journal of Consulting and Clinical Psychology, 58,* 408–415.

Money, J. (1972). *Man woman/boy girl.* Baltimore: Johns Hopkins University Press.

Money, J. (1987). Sin, sickness, or status? Homosexual gender identity and psychoneuroendocrinology. *American Psychologist, 42,* 384–399.

Monson, T. C., & Snyder, M. (1977). Actors, observers, and the attribution process. *Journal of Experimental Social Psychology, 13,* 89–111.

Moon, C., & Fifer, W. P. (1990). Syllables as signals for 2-day old infants. *Infant Behavior and Development, 13,* 377–390.

Moore, K. (1992). *Facts at a glance.* Washington, DC: Childtrends.

Moore, K. L. (1982). *The developing human* (3rd ed.). Philadelphia: Saunders.

Moorecroft, W. H. (1987). An overview of sleep. In J. Gackenback (Ed.), *Sleep and dreams.* New York: Garland.

Moorecroft, W. H. (1989). *Sleep, dreaming, and sleep disorders.* Latham, MD: University Press of America.

Moran, J. S., Janes, H. R., Peterman, T. A., & Stone, K. M. (1990). Increase in condom sales following AIDS education and publicity, United States. *American Journal of Public Health, 80,* 607–608.

Morgan, W. P. (1980). The trait psychology controversy. *Research Quarterly for Exercise and Sport, 51,* 50–76.

Mori, D., & Pliner, P. L. (1987). "Eating lightly" and the self-presentation of femininity. *Journal of Social and Personality Psychology, 53,* 693–702.

Morris, C. W. (1946). *Signs, language, and behavior.* Englewood Cliffs, NJ: Prentice-Hall.

Morris, L. A., & Halperin, J. (1979). Effects of written drug information on patient knowledge and compliance: A literature review. *American Journal of Public Health, 69,* 47–52.

Morrison, D. M. (1985). Adolescent contraceptive behavior: A review. *Psychological Bulletin, 98,* 538–568.

Moruzzi, G. (1975). The sleep-wake cycle. *Reviews of Psychology, 64,* 1–165.

Moruzzi, G., & Magoun, H. W. (1949). Brain stem reticular formation and activation of the EEG. *Electroencephalography and Clinical Neurophysiology, 1,* 455–473.

Moscovici, S., Lage, E., & Naffrechoux, M. (1969). Influences of a consistent minority on the response of a majority in a color perception task. *Sociometry, 32,* 365–380.

Moscovici, S., Mugny, G., & Van Avermaet, E. (1985). *Perspectives on minority influence.* New York: Cambridge University Press.

Mowday, R. T. (1983). Equity theory prediction of behavior in organizations. In R. M. Steers & L. W. Porter (Eds.), *Motivation and work behavior* (3rd ed.). New York: McGraw-Hill.

Mshelia, A. Y., & Lapidus, L. B. (1990). Depth picture perception in relation to cognitive style and training in non-Western children. *Journal of Cross-Cultural Psychology, 21,* 414–433.

Muchinsky, P. M. (1987). *Psychology applied to work* (2nd ed.). Homewood, IL: Dorsey Press.

Muchinsky, P. M., & Tuttle, M. L. (1979). Employee turnover: An empirical and methodological assessment. *Journal of Vocational Behavior, 14,* 43–77.

Mulac, A., Incontro, C. R., & James, M. R. (1985). Comparison of gender-linked language effect and sex role stereotypes. *Journal of Personality and Social Psychology, 49,* 1098–1109.

Mumford, M. D., Uhlman, C. E., & Kilcullen, R. N. (1992). The structure of life history: Implications for the construct validity of background data scales. *Human Performance, 5,* 109–137.

Munn, N. L. (1956). *Introduction to psychology.* Boston: Houghton Mifflin.

Murdock, B. B. (1974). *Human memory: Theory and data.* New York: Wiley.

Murray, D. J. (1983). *A history of Western psychology.* Englewood Cliffs, NJ: Prentice-Hall.

Murray, D. M., Johnson, C. A., Leupker, R. F., & Mittlemark, M. B. (1984). The prevention of cigarette smoking in children: A comparison of four strategies. *Journal of Applied Social Psychology, 14,* 274–288.

Murray, H. A. (1938). *Explorations in personality.* New York: Oxford University Press.

Nakazima, S. (1962). A comparative study of the speech developments of Japanese and American English in children. *Studies in Phonology, 2,* 27–39.

Namir, S., Wolcott, D. L., Fawzy, F. I., & Alumbaugh, M. J. (1987). Coping with AIDS: Psychological and health implications. *Journal of Applied Social Psychology, 17,* 309–328.

Nash, M. (1987). What, if anything, is regressed about hypnotic age regression? *Psychological Bulletin, 102,* 42–52.

National Commission on Sleep Disorders Research (NCSDR). (1993). *Wake up America: A national sleep alert.* Washington, DC: Department of Health and Human Services.

National Institute on Drug Abuse. (1987). *National household survey on drug abuse: Population estimates 1985.* Rockville, MD.

National Institute of Mental Health (NIMH). (1981). Depressive disorders: Causes and treatment (DHEW Publication No. ADM 81–108). Washington, DC: U.S. Government Printing Office.

National Institute of Mental Health. (1984). The NIMH epidemiologic catchment area program. *Archives of General Psychiatry, 41,* 931–1011.

National Institute of Mental Health. (1989). *Information on lithium.* Rockville, MD: U.S. Department of Health and Human Services.

National Institute of Mental Health. (1990). *Bipolar disorder: Manic-depressive illness.* Washington, DC: U.S. Government Printing Office.

National Institute of Mental Health. (1991). *Information about D/Art and depression.* Rockville, MD: U.S. Department of Health and Human Services.

National Institute of Mental Health. (1993). The NIMH epidemiologic catchment area program. *Archives of General Psychiatry, 50.*

National Institutes of Health, Review Panel on Coronary Prone Behavior and Coronary Heart Disease. (1981). Coronary-prone behavior and coronary heart disease: A critical review. *Circulation, 63,* 1199-1215.

Neisser, U. (1982). *Memory observed.* San Francisco: Freeman.

Neisser, U. (1991). A case of misplaced nostalgia. *American Psychologist, 46,* 34–36.

Nelson, K. (1993). The psychological and social origins of autobiographical memory. *Psychological Science, 4,* 7–14.

Nemeth, C. (1986). Differential contributions of majority and minority influence. *Psychological Review, 93,* 23–32.

Neubauer, P. J. (1992). The impact of stress, hardiness, home and work environment on job satisfaction, illness, and absenteeism in critical care nurses. *Medical Psychotherapy, 5,* 109–122.

Neugarten, B. L., & Neugarten, D. A. (1986). Changing meanings of age in the aging society. In A. Piter & L. Bronte (Eds.), *Our aging society: Paradox and promise.* New York: Norton.

Neugarten, B. L., & Neugarten, D. A. (1989). Policy issues in an aging society. In M. Storandt & G. R. VandenBos (Eds.), *The adult years: Continuity and change.* Washington, DC: American Psychological Association.

Newby, R. W. (1987). Contextual areas in item recognition following verbal discrimination learning. *Journal of General Psychology, 114,* 281–287.

Newcomb, M. D., & Bentler, P. M. (1989). Substance abuse among children and teenagers. *American Psychologist, 44,* 242–248.

Newcomb, N., & Dubas, J. S. (1987). Individual differences in cognitive ability: Are they related to timing of puberty? In R. M. Lerner & T. T. Foch (Eds.), *Biological-psychosocial interactions in early adolescence: A life-span approach.* Hillsdale, NJ: Erlbaum.

Newell, A., Shaw, J. C., & Simon, H. A. (1962). The process of creative thinking. In H. E. Gruber, G. Terrell, & M. Wertheimer (Eds.), *Contemporary approaches to creative thinking.* New York: Atherton Press.

Newell, A., & Simon, H. A. (1972). *Human problem solving.* Englewood Cliffs, NJ: Prentice-Hall.

Newman, B. M., & Newman, P. R. (1984). *Development through life: A psychosocial approach.* Homewood, IL: Dorsey Press.

Nickerson, R. S., & Adams, M. J. (1979). Long-term memory for a common object. *Cognitive Psychology, 11,* 287–307.

Nisan, M., & Kohlberg, L. (1982). Universality and variation in moral judgement: A longitudinal and cross-sectional study in Turkey. *Child Development, 53,* 865–876.

Nisbett, R. E. (1972). Hunger, obesity, and the ventromedial hypothalamus. *Psychological Review, 79,* 433–453.

Norcross, J. C. (1986). *Handbook of eclectic psychotherapy.* New York: Brunner/Mazel.

Norman, G. R., Brooks, L. R., & Allen, S. W. (1989). Recall by expert medical practitioners and novices as a record of processing attention. *Journal of Experimental Psychology: Learning, Memory, and Cognition, 15,* 1166–1174.

Noyes, R., Reich, J., Christiansen, J., Suelzer, M., Pfohl, B., & Coryell, W. A. (1990). Outcome of panic disorder. *Archives of General Psychiatry, 47,* 809–818.

Oatley, K., & Jenkins, J. M. (1992). Human emotions: Function and dysfunction. *Annual Review of Psychology, 43,* 55–85.

Oden, G. C. (1987). Concept, knowledge, and thought. *Annual Review of Psychology, 38,* 203–227.

Oden, M. H. (1968). The fulfillment of promise: 40-year follow-up of the Terman gifted group. *Genetic Psychology Monographs, 77*(1), 3–93.

Oetting, E. R., & Beauvais, F. (1987). Peer cluster theory, socialization characteristics and adolescent drug use: A path analysis. *Journal of Counseling Psychology, 34,* 205–213.

Oetting, E. R., & Beauvais, F. (1990). Adolescent drug use: Findings of national and local surveys. *Journal of Consulting and Clinical Psychology, 58,* 385–394.

Offer, D., & Offer, J. (1975). *From teenage to young manhood: A psychological study.* New York: Basic Books.

Offermann, L. R., & Gowing, M. K. (1990). Organizations of the future: Changes and challenges. *American Psychologist, 45,* 95–108.

Offord, D. R., Boyle, M. H., Szatmari, P., Rae-Grant, N. I., Links, P. S., et al. (1987). Ontario child health study. *Archives of General Psychiatry, 44,* 832–836.

Ogata, S. N., Silk, K. R., Goodrich, S., Lohr, N. E., & Hill, E. M. (1990). Childhood sexual and physical abuse in patients with borderline personality. *American Journal of Psychiatry, 147,* 1008–1013.

Ogilvie, B. C., & Howe, M. A. (1984). Beating slumps at their game. *Psychology Today, 18,* 28–32.

Oller, D. K. (1981). Infant vocalization. In R. E. Stark (Ed.), *Language behavior in infancy and early childhood.* New York: Elsevier.

Olson, J. M., & Zanna, M. P. (1993). Attitudes and attitude change. *Annual Review of Psychology, 44,* 117–154.

Olton, D. S. (1978). Characteristics of spatial memory. In S. H. Hule, H. F. Fowler, & W. K. Honig (Eds.), *Cognitive processes in animal behavior.* Hillsdale, NJ: Erlbaum.

Olton, D. S. (1979). Mazes, maps, and memory. *American Psychologist, 34,* 583-596.

Opalic, P. (1989). Existential and psychopathological evaluation of group psychotherapy of neurotic and psychotic patients. *International Journal of Group Psychotherapy, 39,* 389–422.

Orne, M. (1969). Demand characteristics and the concept of quasi-controls. In R. Rosenthal & R. Rosnow (Eds.), *Artifact in behavioral research.* New York: Academic Press.

Ortony, A., Clore, G. L., & Collins, A. (1988). *The cognitive structure of emotions.* New York: Cambridge University Press.

Ortony, A., & Turner, T. J. (1990). What's basic about basic emotions? *Psychological Review, 97,* 315–331.

Paivio, A. (1971). *Imagery and verbal processes.* New York: Holt, Rinehart & Winston.

Palfai, T., & Jankiewicz, H. (1991). *Drugs and human behavior.* Dubuque, IA: Brown.

Paludi, M. A., & Gullo, D. F. (1986). The effect of sex labels on adults' knowledge of infant development. *Sex Roles, 16,* 19–30.

Pandey, J. (1990). The environment, culture, and behavior. In R. W. Brislin (Ed.), *Applied cross-cultural psychology.* Newbury Park, CA: Sage.

Parke, R. D. (1981). *Fathers.* Cambridge, MA: Harvard University Press.

Parke, R. D., & Tinsley, B. J. (1987). Family interaction in infancy. In J. D. Osofsky (Ed.), *Handbook of infant development* (2nd ed.). New York: Wiley.

Parker, E. S., Birnbaum, I. M., & Noble, E. P. (1976). Alcohol and memory: Storage and state dependency. *Journal of Verbal Learning and Verbal Behavior, 15,* 691–702.

Pauly, I. B., & Goldstein, S. G. (1970, November). Prevalence of significant sexual problems in medical practice. *Medical Aspects of Human Sexuality,* pp. 48–63.

Paunonen, S. P., Jackson, D. N., Trzebinski, J., & Fosterling, F. (1992). Personality structures across cultures: A multimethod evaluation. *Journal of Personality and Social Psychology, 62,* 447–456.

Pavlov, I. (1927). *Conditioned reflexes.* New York: Oxford University Press.

Pavlov, I. (1928). *Lectures on conditioned reflexes: The higher nervous activity of animals* (Vol. I) (H. Gantt, Trans.). London: Lawrence and Wishart.

Pavlovich, M., & Greene, B. F. (1984). A self-instructional manual for installing low-cost/no-cost weatherization material: Experimental validation with scouts. *Journal of Applied Behavior Analysis, 17,* 105–109.

Payne, J. W., Bettman, J. R., & Johnson, E. J. (1992). Behavioral decision research: A constructive processing perspective. *Annual Review of Psychology, 43,* 87–131.

Peabody, D., & Goldberg, L. R. (1989). Some determinants of factor structures from personality trait descriptors. *Journal of Personality and Social Psychology, 57,* 552–567.

Pearce, J. M., & Hall, G. (1980). A model for Pavlovian conditioning: Variations in the effectiveness of conditioned but not of unconditioned stimuli. *Psychological Review, 87,* 532–552.

Pearson, J. C., Turner, L. H., & Todd-Mancillas, W. (1991). *Gender and communication* (2nd ed.), Dubuque, IA: Brown.

Pederson, D. R., Morgan, G., Sitko, C., Campbell, K., Ghesquire, K., & Acton, H. (1990). Maternal sensitivity and the security of infant-mother attachment: A Q-sort study. *Child Development, 61,* 1974–1983.

Peele, S., Brodsky, A., & Arnold, M. (1991). *The truth about addiction and recovery.* New York: Simon & Schuster.

Penfield, W. (1975). *The mystery of the mind.* Princeton, NJ: Princeton University Press.

Penfield, W., & Rasmussen, T. (1950). *The cerebral cortex of man.* New York: Macmillan.

Perls, F. S. (1967). Group vs. individual psychotherapy. *ECT: A Review of General Semantics, 34,* 306–312.

Perls, F. S. (1971). *Gestalt therapy verbatim.* New York: Bantam Books.

Perls, F. S., Hefferline, R. F., & Goodman, P. (1951). *Gestalt therapy.* New York: Julien Press.

Peterson, A. C. (1988). Adolescent development. *Annual Review of Psychology, 39,* 583–607.

Peterson, A. C., & Ebata, A. T. (1987). Developmental transitions and adolescent problem behavior: Implications for prevention and intervention. In K. Hurrelmann (Ed.), *Social prevention and intervention,* New York: de Gruyter.

Peterson, L. R., & Peterson, M. J. (1959). Short-term retention of individual verbal items. *Journal of Experimental Psychology, 58,* 193–198.

Petty, R. E., & Cacioppo, J. T. (1986). The elaboration likelihood model of persuasion. *Advances in Experimental Social Psychology, 19,* 123–205.

Petty, R. E., Harkins, S. G., Williams, K. D., & Latané, B. (1977). The effects of group size on cognitive effort and evaluation. *Personality and Social Psychology Bulletin, 3,* 579–582.

Petty, R. E., Ostrow, T. M., & Brock, T. C. (1981). *Cognitive responses in persuasive communications: A text in attitude change.* Hillsdale, NJ: Erlbaum.

Petty, R. E., Wells, G. L., & Brock, T. C. (1976). Distraction can enhance or reduce yielding to propaganda: Thought disruption versus effort justification. *Journal of Personality and Social Psychology, 34,* 874–884.

Phares, V., & Compas, B. E. (1993). Fathers and developmental psychopathology. *Current Directions in Psychological Science, 2,* 162–165.

Phillips, D., McCartney, K., & Scarr, S. (1987). Child-care quality and children's social development. *Developmental Psychology, 23,* 537–543.

Piaget, J. (1932/1948). *The moral judgment of the child.* New York: Free Press.

Piaget, J. (1954). *The construction of reality in the child.* New York: Basic Books.

Piaget, J. (1967). *Six psychological studies.* New York: Random House.

Pillemer, D. B., & White, S. H. (1989). Childhood events recalled by children and adults. In H. W. Reese (Ed.), *Advances in child development and behavior* (Vol. 21). New York: Academic Press.

Piner, K. E., & Kahle, L. R. (1984). Adapting to the stigmatizing label of mental illness: Foregone but not forgotten. *Journal of Personality and Social Psychology, 47,* 805–811.

Plawin, P., & Suied, M. (1988, December). Can't get no satisfaction. *Changing Times,* p. 106.

Plomin, R. (1988). The nature and nurture of cognitive abilities. In J. Sternberg (Ed.), *Advances in the psychology of human intelligence* (Vol. 4). Hillsdale, NJ: Erlbaum.

Plomin, R. (1989). Environment and genes: Determinants of behavior. *American Psychologist, 44,* 105–111.

Plomin, R., DeFries, J. C., & Fulker, D. W. (1988). *Nature and nurture during infancy and early childhood.* New York: Cambridge University Press.

Plutchik, R. (1980a). *Emotion: A psychoevolutionary synthesis.* New York: HarperCollins.

Plutchik, R. (1980b, February). A language for the emotions. *Psychology Today,* pp. 68–78.

Pogue-Geile, M. F., & Zubin, J. (1988). Negative symptomatology and schizophrenia: A conceptual and empirical review. *International Journal of Mental Health, 16,* 3–45.

Pola, J., & Martin, L. (1977). Eye movements following autokinesis. *Bulletin of the Psychonomic Society, 10,* 397–398.

Pool, R. (1993). Evidence for homosexuality gene. *Science, 261,* 291–292.

Pope, H. G., & Hudson, J. I. (1986). Antidepressant therapy for bulimia: Current status. *Journal of Clinical Psychiatry, 47,* 339–345.

Pope, H. G., Hudson, J. I., Jonas, J. M., & Yurgelun-Todd, D. (1985). Antidepressant treatment of bulimia: A two-year follow-up study. *Journal of Clinical Psychopharmacology, 5,* 320–327.

Porter, L. W., & Steers, R. M. (1973). Organizational, work, and personal factors in employee turnover and absenteeism. *Psychological Bulletin, 80,* 151–176.

Posner, M. I. (1973). *Cognition: An introduction.* Glenview, IL: Scott, Foresman.

Posner, M. I., & Keele, S. W. (1968). On the genesis of abstract ideas. *Journal of Experimental Psychology, 77,* 353–363.

Posner, M. I., & Keele, S. W. (1970). Retention of abstract ideas. *Journal of Experimental Psychology, 83,* 304–308.

Post, R. B., & Leibowitz, H. W. (1985). A revised analysis of the role of efference in motion perception. *Perception, 14,* 631–643.

Powell, L. H., Shaker, L. A., Jones, B. A., Vaccarino, L. V., et al. (1993). Psychosocial predictors of mortality in 83 women with premature acute myocardial infarction. *Psychosomatic Medicine, 55,* 221–225.

Powers, S. I., Hauser, S. T., & Kilner, L. A. (1989). Adolescent mental health. *American Psychologist, 44,* 200–208.

Pressley, M., Levin, J. R., & Delaney, H. D. (1982). The mnemonic keyword method. *Review of Educational Research, 52,* 61–91.

Price-Williams, D. R., Gordon, W., & Ramirez, M. (1969). Skill and conservation. *Developmental Psychology, 1,* 769.

Prior, M., & Wherry, J. S. (1986). Autism, schizophrenia, and allied disorders. In H. C. Quay & J. S. Wherry (Eds.), *Psychopathological disorders of childhood* (3rd ed.). New York: Wiley.

Putnam, F. W., Guroff, J. J., Silberman, E. K., Barban, L., & Post, R. M. (1986). The clinical phenomenology of multiple personality disorder: Review of 100 recent cases. *Journal of Clinical Psychology, 47,* 285–293.

Pyle, R. L., Mitchell, J. E., & Eckert, E. D. (1981). Bulimia: Report of 34 cases. *Journal of Clinical Psychiatry, 42,* 60–64.

Pyle, R. L., Mitchell, J. E., Eckert, E. D., Hatsukami, D. K., Pomeroy, C., & Zimmerman, R. (1990). Maintenance treatment and 6-month outcome for bulimic patients who respond to initial treatment. *American Journal of Psychiatry, 147,* 871–875.

Pynes, J., & Bernardin, H. J. (1989). Predictive validity of an entry-level police officer assessment center. *Journal of Applied Psychology, 74,* 831–833.

Quadrel, M. J., Fishhoff, B., & Davis, W. (1993). Adolescent (in)vulnerability. *American Psychologist, 48,* 102–116.

Quay, H. C. (1965). Psychopathic personality as pathological sensation seeking. *American Journal of Psychiatry, 122,* 180–183.

Quina, K., Wingard, J. A., & Bates, H. G. (1987). Language style and gender stereotypes in person perception. *Psychology of Women Quarterly, 11,* 111–222.

Radford, A. (1990). *Syntactic theory and the acquisition of English syntax: The nature of early child grammars of English.* Oxford: Blackwell.

Rahe, R. H., & Arthur, R. J. (1978). Life changes and illness reports. In K. E. Gunderson & R. H. Rahe (Eds.), *Life stress and illness.* Springfield, IL: Thomas.

Raine, A., Venables, P. H., & Williams, M. (1990). Relationship between central and autonomic measures of arousal at age 15 years and criminality at age 24 years. *Archives of General Psychiatry, 46,* 1003–1007.

Ray, O. S., & Ksir, C. (1987). *Drugs, society, and human behavior.* St. Louis: Mosby.

Ree, M. J., & Earles, J. A. (1992). Intelligence is the best predictor of job performance. *Current Directions in Psychological Science, 1,* 86–89.

Ree, M. J., & Earles, J. A. (1993). g is to psychology what carbon is to chemistry: A reply to Sternberg and Wagner, McClelland, and Calfee. *Current Directions in Psychological Science, 2,* 11–12.

Reich, J. (1986). The epidemiology of anxiety. *The Journal of Nervous and Mental Disease, 174,* 129–136.

Reilly, R. R., & Chao, G. T. (1982). Validity and fairness of some alternative employee selection procedures. *Personnel Psychology, 35,* 1–62.

Reinisch, J. M., & Sanders, S. A. (1992). Effects of prenatal exposure to diethylstilbestrol (DES) on hemispheric laterality and spatial ability in human males. *Hormones and Behavior, 26,* 62–75.

Reinke, B. J., Ellicott, A. M., Harris, R. L., & Hancock, E. (1985). Timing of psychological changes in women's lives. *Human Development, 28,* 259–280.

Reis, H. T., Nezlek, J., & Wheeler, L. (1980). Physical attractiveness in social interaction. *Journal of Personality and Social Psychology, 38,* 604–617.

Reis, S. M. (1989). Reflections on policy affecting the education of gifted and talented students: Past and future perspectives. *American Psychologist, 44,* 399–408.

Rescorla, R. A. (1968). Probability of shock in the presence and absence of CS in fear conditioning. *Journal of Comparative and Physiological Psychology, 66,* 1–5.

Rescorla, R. A. (1987). A Pavlovian analysis of goal-directed behavior. *American Psychologist, 42,* 119–129.

Rescorla, R. A. (1988). Pavlovian conditioning: It's not what you think it is. *American Psychologist, 43,* 151–160.

Rescorla, R. A., & Wagner, A. R. (1972). A theory of Pavlovian conditioning: Variations in the effectiveness of reinforcement and nonreinforcement. In A. H. Black & W. F. Prokasy (Eds.), *Classical conditioning II: Current research and theory.* Englewood Cliffs, NJ: Prentice-Hall.

Resnick, L. B. (1987). *Education and learning to think.* Washington, DC: National Academy Press.

Rest, J. R. (1983). Morality. In J. Flavell & E. Markman (Eds.), *Handbook of child development: Cognitive development.* New York: Wiley.

Reveley, M. A., Reveley, A. M., & Baldy, R. (1987). Left cerebral hemisphere hypodensity in discordant schizophrenic twins. *Archives of General Psychiatry, 44,* 624–632.

Revelle, W. (1987). Personality and motivation: Sources of inefficiency in cognitive performance. *Journal of Research in Personality, 21,* 436–452.

Revulsky, S. H. (1985). The general process approach to animal learning. In T. D. Johnston & A. T. Petrewicz (Eds.), *Issues in the ecological study of learning.* Hillsdale, NJ: Erlbaum.

Revulsky, S. H., & Garcia, J. (1970). Learned associations over long delays. In G. H. Bower & J. T. Spence (Eds.), *The psychology of learning and motivation* (Vol. 4). New York: Academic Press.

Reynolds, A. G., & Flagg, P. W. (1983). *Cognitive psychology.* Boston: Little, Brown.

Reynolds, B. A., & Weiss, S. (1992). Generation of neurons and astrocytes from isolated cells of the adult mammalian nervous system. *Science, 225,* 1707–1710.

Rhodes, S. R. (1983). Age-related differences in work attitudes and behaviors: A review and conceptual analysis. *Psychological Bulletin, 93,* 328–367.

Rhyne, D. (1981). Bases of marital satisfaction among men and women. *Journal of Marriage and the Family, 43,* 941–954.

Rice, M. L. (1989). Children's language acquisition. *American Psychologist, 44,* 149–156.

Richardson, J. D. (1991). Medical causes of male sexual dysfunction. *Medical Journal of Australia, 155,* 29–33.

Richardson-Klavehn, A., & Bjork, R. A. (1988). Measures of memory. *Annual Review of Psychology, 39,* 475–543.

Rickels, K., Downing, R., Schweizer, E., & Hassman, H. (1993). Antidepressants for the treatment of generalized anxiety disorder. *Archives of General Psychiatry, 50,* 884–895.

Riggio, R. E. (1990). *Introduction to industrial/organizational psychology.* Glenview, IL: Scott, Foresman.

Robins, L. N., Helzer, J. E., Weissman, M. M., Orvaschel, H., Guenberg, E., Burke, J. D., & Regier, D. A. (1984). Lifetime prevalence of specific psychiatric disorders in three sites. *Archives of General Psychiatry, 41,* 949–958.

Roche, A. F., & Davila, G. H. (1972). Late adolescent growth in stature. *Pediatrics, 50,* 874–880.

Rock, I. (1986). The description and analysis of object and event perception. In K. R. Boff, L. Kaufman, & J. P. Thomas (Eds.), *Handbook of perception and human performance: Vol. 2. Cognitive processes and performance.* New York: Wiley.

Rodin, J. (1976). Crowding, perceived choice and response to controllable and uncontrollable outcomes. *Journal of Experimental Social Psychology, 12,* 564–578.

Rodin, J. (1981). Current status of the internal-external hypothesis of obesity: What went wrong? *American Psychologist, 36,* 361–372.

Rodin, J., & Salovey, P. (1989). Health psychology. *Annual Review of Psychology, 40,* 533–579.

Roediger, H. L. (1990). Implicit memory: Retention without remembering. *American Psychologist, 45,* 1043–1056.

Rolls, B. J., Federoff, I. C., & Guthrie, J. F. (1991). Gender differences in eating behavior and body weight regulation. *Health Psychology, 10,* 133–142.

Rook, K. S. (1987). Social support versus companionship: Effects of life stress, loneliness, and evaluation by others. *Journal of Personality and Social Psychology, 52,* 1132–1147.

Rorschach, H. (1921). *Psychodiagnostics.* Bern: Huber.

Rosch, E. (1973). Natural categories. *Cognitive Psychology, 4,* 328–350.

Rosch, E. (1975). Cognitive representations of semantic categories. *Journal of Experimental Psychology: General, 104,* 192–253.

Rosch, E. (1978). Principles of categorization. In E. Rosch & B. B. Lloyd (Eds.), *Cognition and categorization.* Hillsdale, NJ: Erlbaum.

Rose, A. S., & Blank, M. (1974). The potency of context in children's cognition: An illustration through conservation. *Child Development, 45,* 499–502.

Rosenbaum, M. E. (1986). The repulsion hypothesis: On the nondevelopment of relationships. *Journal of Personality and Social Psychology, 51,* 1156–1166.

Rosenman, R. H., Brand, R. J., Jenkins., C. D., Friedman, M., Strauss. R., & Wurm, M. (1975). Coronary heart disease in the Western Collaborative Group Study: Final follow-up experience of $8\frac{1}{2}$ years. *Journal of the American Medical Association, 233,* 872–877.

Rosenman, R. H., Friedman, M., Strauss, R., Wurm, M., Kositcheck, R., Hahn, W., & Werthessen, N. T. (1964). A predictive study of coronary heart disease. *Journal of the American Medical Association, 189,* 15–22.

Rosenthal, D. (1970). *Genetics of psychopathology.* New York: McGraw-Hill.

Rosenzweig, M. R. (1992). Psychological science around the world. *American Psychologist, 47,* 718–722.

Rosenzweig, M. R., Bennett, E. L., & Diamond, M. C. (1972). Brain changes in response to experiences. *Scientific American, 226,* 22–29.

Ross, C. A. (1989). *Multiple personality disorder: Diagnosis, clinical features, and treatment.* New York: Wiley.

Ross, G., Kagan, J., Zelazo, P., & Kotelchuck, M. (1975). Separation protest in infants in home and laboratory. *Developmental Psychology, 11,* 256–257.

Ross, L. D. (1977). The intuitive psychologist and his shortcomings: Distortions in the attributional process. In L. Berkowitz (Ed.), *Advances in experimental social psychology* (Vol. 10). New York: Academic Press.

Rossi, A. S. (1980). Aging and parenthood in the middle years. In P. B. Baltes & O. G. Brim, Jr. (Eds.), *Lifespan development and behavior* (Vol. III). New York: Academic Press.

Roth, E. M., & Shoben, E. J. (1983). The effect of context on the structure of categories. *Cognitive Psychology, 15,* 346–378.

Roth M., & Argyle, N. (1988). Anxiety, panic and phobic disorders: An overview, *Journal of Psychiatric Research, 22* (Suppl. 1), 33–54.

Rothstein, H. R., Schmidt, F. L., Erwin, F. W., Owens, W. A., & Sparks, C. P. (1990). Biographical data in employment selection: Can validities be made generalizable? *Journal of Applied Psychology, 75,* 175–184.

Rotton, J., & Frey, J. (1985). Air pollution, weather, and violent crimes: Concomitant analysis of archival data. *Journal of Personality and Social Psychology, 49,* 1207–1220.

Rowe, D. C. (1981). Environmental and genetic influences on dimensions of perceived parenting: A twin study. *Developmental Psychology, 17,* 203–208.

Rowe, D. C. (1987). Resolving the person-situation debate. *American Psychologist, 42,* 218–227.

Rowe, J. W., & Kahn, R. L. (1987). Human aging: Usual and successful. *Science, 237,* 143–149.

Ruback, R. B., & Pandey, J. (1988). Crowding and perceived control in India. Unpublished manuscript, cited in J. Pandet (1990).

Rubin, D. C., & Kontis, T. C. (1983). A schema for common cents. *Memory and Cognition, 11,* 335–341.

Rubin, Z. (1973). *Liking and loving: An invitation to social psychology.* New York: Holt, Rinehart & Winston.

Rushton, J. P. (1988). Race differences in behavior: A review and evolutionary analysis. *Personality and Individual Differences, 9,* 1009–1024.

Rushton, J. P., Fulker, D. W., Neale, M. C., Nias, D. K. B., & Eysenck, H. J. (1986). Altruism and aggression: The heritability of individual differences. *Journal of Personality and Social Psychology, 50,* 1192–1198.

Rutter, M., Graham, P., Chadwick, O., & Yule, W. (1976). Adolescent turmoil: Fact or fiction? *Journal of Child Psychology and Psychiatry, 17,* 35–56.

Rutter, M., & Schopler, E. (1987). Autism and pervasive developmental disorders: Concepts and diagnostic uses. *Journal of Autism and Developmental Disorders, 17,* 159–186.

Ryan, E. D., & Kovacic, C. R. (1966). Pain tolerance and athletic participation. *Journal of Personality and Social Psychology, 22,* 383–390.

Saal, F. E., & Knight, P. A. (1988). *Industrial/organizational psychology.* Monterey, CA: Brooks/Cole.

Saari, L. M., Johnson, T. R., McLaughlin, S. D., & Zimerle, D. M. (1988). A survey of management training and education practices in U.S. companies. *Personnel Psychology, 41,* 731–743.

Sackeim, H. A. (1985). The case for ECT. *Psychology Today, 19,* 36–40.

Sadalla, E. K., & Oxley, D. (1984). The perception of room size: The rectangularity illusion. *Environment and Behavior, 16,* 394–405.

Saegert, S., & Winkel, G. H. (1990). Environmental psychology. *Annual Review of Psychology, 41,* 441–477.

Safer, M. (1980). Attributing evil to the subject, not the situation: Student reactions to Milgram's film on obedience. *Personality and Social Psychology Bulletin, 6,* 205–209.

Sakai, K. (1985). Neurons responsible for paradoxical sleep. In A. Wauquier (Ed.), *Sleep: Neurotransmitters and neuromodulators.* New York: Raven Press.

Salthouse, T. A. (1989). Age-related changes in basic cognitive processes. In M. Storandt & G. R. VandenBos (Eds.), *The adult years: Continuity and change.* Washington, DC: American Psychological Association.

Sameroff, A. J., & Cavanaugh, P. J. (1979). Learning in infancy: A developmental perspective. In J. D. Osofsky (Ed.), *Handbook of infant development.* New York: Wiley.

Samuelson, F. J. B. (1980). Watson's Little Albert, Cyril Burt's twins, and the need for a critical science. *American Psychologist, 35,* 619–625.

Sandler, J., Dare, C., & Holder, A. (1992). *The patient and the analyst: The basis of the psychoanalytic process* (2nd ed.). Madison, CT: International University Press.

Sands, L. P., Terry, H., & Meredith, W. (1989). Change and stability in adult intellectual functioning assessed by Wechsler item responses. *Psychology and Aging, 4,* 79–87.

Sanua, V. D. (1987). Standing against an established ideology: Infantile autism, a case in point. *Clinical Psychology, 4,* 96–110.

Satir, V. (1967). *Conjoint family therapy.* Palo Alto, CA: Science and Behavior Books.

Saunders, N. A., & Sullivan, C. E. (Eds.). (1994). *Sleep and breathing* (2nd ed.). New York: Marcel Dekker.

Sauser, W. J., & York, C. M. (1978). Sex differences in job satisfaction: A reexamination. *Personnel Psychology, 31,* 537-547.

Scarborough, E., & Furumoto, L. (1987). *Untold lives: The first generation of American women psychologists.* New York: Columbia University Press.

Scarr, S., & Eisenberg, M. (1993). Child care research: Issues, perspectives, and results. *Annual Review of Psychology, 44,* 613–644.

Schacter, D. L. (1987). Implicit memory: History and current status. *Journal of Experimental Psychology: Learning, Memory, and Cognition. 13,* 501–518.

Schacter, D. L. (1992). Understanding implicit memory: A cognitive neuroscience approach. *American Psychologist, 47,* 559–569.

Schacter, S. (1971). Some extraordinary facts about obese humans and rats. *American Psychologist, 26,* 129–144.

Schacter, S., & Gross, L. P. (1968). Manipulated time and eating behavior. *Journal of Personality and Social Psychology, 10,* 98–106.

Schaie, K. W. (1974). Translations in gerontology—from lab to life: Intellectual functioning. *American Psychologist, 29,* 802–807.

Schaie, K. W. (1983). The Seattle Longitudinal Study: A 21-year exploration of psychometric intelligence in adulthood. In K. W. Schaie (Ed.), *Longitudinal studies of adult psychological development.* New York: Guilford.

Schaie, K. W. (1993). The Seattle Longitudinal Studies of

Adult Intelligence. *Current Directions in Psychological Science, 2,* 171–175.

Schaie, K. W., & Strother, C. R. (1968) A cross-sequential study of age changes in cognitive behavior. *Psychological Bulletin, 70,* 671–680.

Schaie, K. W., & Willis, S. L. (1986). *Adult development and aging* (2nd ed.). Boston: Little, Brown.

Scharf, B. (1978). Loudness. In E. C. Carterette & M. P. Friedman (Eds.), *Handbook of perception.* New York: Academic Press.

Schau, C. G., Kahn, L., Diepold, J. H., Cherry, F. (1980). The relationships of parental expectations and preschool children's verbal sex typing to their sex-typed toy play behavior. *Child Development, 51,* 266–270.

Scheerer, M. (1963). Problem solving. *Scientific American, 208,* 118–128.

Scheier, M. F., & Carver, C. S. (1992). Effects of optimism on psychological and physical well-being: Theoretical overview and empirical update. *Cognitive Therapy and Research, 16,* 201–228.

Scheier, M. F., & Carver, C. S. (1993). On the power of positive thinking: The benefits of being optimistic. *Current Directions in Psychological Science, 2,* 26–30.

Scheier, M. F., Matthews, K. A., Owens, J. F., Magovern, G. J., Lefebvre, R., Abbott, R. C., & Carver, C. S. (1989). Dispositional optimism and recovery from coronary artery bypass surgery: The beneficial effects of optimism on physical and psychological well-being. *Journal of Personality and Social Psychology, 57,* 1024–1040.

Schelling, T. C. (1992). Addictive drugs: The cigarette experience. *Science, 255,* 430–433.

Scher, S. J., & Cooper, J. (1989). Motivational basis of dissonance: The singular role of behavioral consequences. *Journal of Personality and Social Psychology, 56,* 899–906.

Schiff, B. B., & Lamon, M. (1989). Inducing emotion by unilateral contraction of facial muscles: A new look at hemispheric specialization and the experience of emotion. *Neuropsychologia, 27,* 923–925.

Schmidt, F. L. (1992). What do data really mean? Research findings, meta-analysis, and cumulative knowledge in psychology. *American Psychologist, 47,* 1173–1181.

Schmidt, F. L., & Hunter, J. E. (1993). Tacit knowledge, practical intelligence, general mental ability, and job knowledge. *Current Directions in Psychological Science, 2,* 8–9.

Schmidt, F. L., Ones, D. S., & Hunter, J. E. (1992). Personnel selection. *Annual Review of Psychology, 43,* 627–670.

Schmitt, H. N., Schneider, J. R., & Cohen, S. A. (1990). Factors affecting validity of a regionally administered assessment center. *Personnel Psychology, 43,* 1–12.

Schmitt, N., & Robertson, I. (1990). Personnel selection. *Annual Review of Psychology, 41,* 289–319.

Schmitt, R. C. (1966). Density, health, and social disorganization. *American Institute of Planners Journal, 32,* 38–40.

Schroeder, S. R., Schroeder, C. S., & Landesman, S. (1987). Psychological services in educational settings to persons with mental retardation. *American Psychologist, 42,* 805–808.

Schuckit, M. A. (1989). *Drug and alcohol abuse: A clinical guide to diagnosis and treatment* (3rd ed.). New York: Plenum.

Schultz, D. P., & Schultz, S. E. (1990). *Psychology and industry today.* New York: Macmillan.

Schultz, R., & Alderman, D. (1974). Clinical research on the "stages of dying." *Omega, 5,* 137–144.

Schultz, R., & Decker, S. (1985). Long-term adjustment to physical disability: The role of social support, perceived control and self-blame. *Journal of Personality and Social Psychology, 48,* 1162–1172.

Schwartz, P. (1983). Length of day-care attendance and attachment behavior in eighteen-month-old infants. *Child Development, 54,* 1073–1078.

Scott, K. G., & Carran, D. T. (1987). The epidemiology and prevention of mental retardation. *American Psychologist, 42,* 801–804.

Scott, M. D., & Pelliccioni, L., Jr. (1982). *Don't choke: How athletes become winners.* Englewood Cliffs, NJ: Prentice-Hall.

Sears, P. S., & Barbee, A. H. (1977). Career and life satisfaction among Terman's gifted women. In J. Stanley et al. (Eds.), *The gifted and the creative: Fifty year perspective.* Baltimore: Johns Hopkins University Press.

Segall, M., Dasen, P., Berry, J., & Poortinga, Y. (1990). *Human behavior in global perspective.* Elmsford, NY: Pergamon.

Segall, M. H., Campbell, D. T., & Herskovits, M. J. (1966). *The influence of culture on visual perception.* Indianapolis: Bobbs-Merrill.

Seligman, M. E. P. (1975). *Helplessness: On depression development and death.* San Francisco: Freeman.

Selkoe, D. J. (1990). Deciphering Alzheimer's disease: The amyloid precursor protein yields new clues. *Science, 248,* 1058.

Selye, H. (1974). *Stress without distress.* Philadelphia: Lippincott.

Selye, H. (1976). *The stress of life.* New York: McGraw-Hill.

Sennecker, P., & Hendrick, C. (1983). Androgyny and helping behavior. *Journal of Personality and Social Psychology, 45,* 916–925.

Serbin, L. A., Sprafkin, C., Elman, M., & Doyle, A. B. (1984). The early development of sex differentiated patterns of social influence. *Canadian Journal of Social Science, 14,* 350–363.

Serpell, R., & Deregowski, J. B. (1980). The skill of pictorial perception: An interpretation of cross-cultural evidence. *International Journal of Psychology, 15,* 145–180.

Shadish, W. R. (1984). Policy research: Lessons from the implementation of deinstitutionalization. *American Psychologist, 39,* 725–738.

Shaffer, M. (1982). *Life after stress*. New York: Knopf.

Shapiro, D. H., Jr. (1985). Clinical use of meditation as a self-regulation strategy: Comment on Holmes's conclusions and implications. *American Psychologist, 40,* 719–722.

Shaver, P., Hazan, C., & Bradshaw, D. (1988). Love as attachment: The integration of three behavioral systems. In R. J. Sternberg & M. L. Barnes (Eds.), *The psychology of love*. New Haven, CT: Yale University Press.

Shedler, J., & Block, J. (1990). Adolescent drug use and psychological health: A longitudinal study. *American Psychologist, 45,* 612–630.

Sheer, D. E. (Ed.). (1961). *Electrical stimulation of the brain*. Austin: University of Texas Press.

Shekelle, B., Hulley, S. B., Neaton, J. D., Billings, J. H., Borhani, N. O., et al. (1985). The MRFIT behavior pattern study II: Type A behavior and the incidence of coronary heart disease. *American Journal of Epidemiology, 122,* 559–570.

Shekelle, R. B., Gale, M. E., & Norvis, M. (1985). Type A scores (Jenkins Activity Survey) and risk of recurrent coronary heart disease in the Aspirin Myocardial Infarction Study. *American Journal of Cardiology, 56,* 221–225.

Sheridan, C. L., & Perkins, A. (1992). Cross-validation of an inventory of stressors for teenagers. *Medical Psychotherapy, 5,* 103–108.

Sheridan, C. L., & Smith, L. K. (1987). Toward a comprehensive scale of stress assessment: Norms, reliability, and validity. *International Journal of Psychometrics, 34,* 48–54.

Sheridan, K., Humfleet, G., Phair, J., & Lyons, J. (1990). The effects of AIDS education on the knowledge and attitudes of community leaders. *Journal of Community Psychology, 18,* 354–360.

Sherman, S. J., Judd, C. M., & Park, B. (1989). Social cognition. *Annual Review of Psychology, 40,* 281–326.

Shertzer, B. (1985). *Career planning* (3rd ed.). Boston: Houghton Mifflin.

Shiffman, L. B., Fischer, L. B., Zettler-Segal, M., & Benowitz, N. L. (1990). Nicotine exposure among nondependent smokers. *Archives of General Psychiatry, 47,* 333–340.

Shiffman, S. (1992). Relapse process and relapse prevention in addictive behaviors. *The Behavior Therapist, 15,* 99–111.

Shimamura, A. P. (1986). Priming effects in amnesia: Evidence for a dissociable memory function. *Quarterly Journal of Experimental Psychology, 38A,* 619–644.

Shipley, T. (1961). *Classics in psychology*. New York: Philosophical Library.

Shippee, G., & Gregory, W. L. (1982). Public commitment and energy conservation. *American Journal of Community Psychology, 10,* 81–93.

Shirley, M. C., Matt, D. A., & Burish, T. G. (1992). Comparison of frontalis, multiple muscle site, and reactive muscle site feedback in reducing arousal under stressful and nonstressful conditions. *Medical Psychotherapy, 5,* 133–148.

Shotland, R. L. (1985). When bystanders just stand by. *Psychology Today, 19,* 50–55.

Shulman, H. G. (1971). Similarity effects in short-term memory. *Psychological Bulletin, 75,* 399–415.

Shulman, H. G. (1972). Semantic confusion errors in short-term memory. *Journal of Verbal Learning and Verbal Behavior, 11,* 221–227.

Shweder, R. A., & Sullivan, M. A. (1993). Cultural psychology: Who needs it? *Annual Review of Psychology, 44,* 497–523.

Sibai, B. M., Caritis, S. N., Thom, E., Klebanoff, M., McNellis, D., et al. (1993). Prevention of preeclampsia with low-dose aspirin in healthy, nulliparous pregnant women. *The New England Journal of Medicine, 329,* 1213–1218.

Siegler, R. S. (1983). Five generalizations about cognitive development. *American Psychologist, 38,* 263–277.

Siegler, R. S. (1989). Mechanisms of cognitive development. *Annual Review of Psychology, 40,* 353–379.

Silva, J. M., Hardy, C. J., & Crace, R. K. (1988). Analysis of momentum in intercollegiate tennis. *Journal of Sport and Exercise Psychology, 10,* 346–354.

Simkins-Bullock, J. A., & Wildman, B. G. (1991). An investigation into the relationships between gender and language. *Sex Roles, 24,* 149–160.

Simon, H. A. (1990). Invariants of human behavior. *Annual Review of Psychology, 41,* 1–19.

Sims, E. A. H. (1990). Destiny rides again as twins overeat. *New England Journal of Medicine, 322,* 1522–1523.

Skinner, B. F. (1938). *The behavior of organisms: A behavioral analysis*. Englewood Cliffs, NJ: Prentice-Hall.

Skinner, B. F. (1956). A case history in the scientific method. *American Psychologist, 11,* 221–233.

Skinner, B. F. (1957). *Verbal behavior*. Englewood Cliffs, NJ: Prentice-Hall.

Skinner, B. F. (1983). Intellectual self-management in old age. *American Psychologist, 38,* 239–244.

Skinner, B. F. (1984). *A matter of consequence*. New York: Knopf.

Skinner, B. F. (1987). What ever happened to psychology as the science of behavior? *American Psychologist, 42,* 780–786.

Skinner, B. F. (1989). The origins of cognitive thought. *American Psychologist, 44,* 13–18.

Skinner, B. F. (1990). Can psychology be a science of mind? *American Psychologist, 45,* 1206–1210.

Skolnick, A. (1979). *The intimate environment* (2nd ed.). Boston: Little, Brown.

Slobin, D. I. (1979). *Psycholinguistics*. Glenview, IL: Scott, Foresman.

Small, J. G., Klapper, M. H., Kellams, J. J., Miller, M. J., Milstein, V., Sharpley, P. H., & Small, I. F. (1988). Electroconvulsive treatment compared with lithium in the management of manic states. *Archives of General Psychiatry, 45,* 727–732.

Smalley, S. L. (1991). Genetic influences in autism. *Psychiatric Clinics of North America, 14,* 125–139.

Smeaton, G., Byrne, D., & Murnen, S. (1989). The repulsion hypothesis revisited: Similarity irrelevance or dissimilarity bias? *Journal of Personality and Social Psychology, 56,* 54–59.

Smith, A., & Stansfield, S. (1986). Aircraft noise exposure, noise sensitivity, and everyday errors. *Environment and Behavior, 18,* 214–226.

Smith, D. (1987). Conditions that facilitate the development of sport imagery training. *The Sport Psychologist, 1,* 237–247.

Smith, G. B., Schwebel, A. I., Dunn, R. L., & McIver, S. D. (1993). The role of psychologists in the treatment, management, and prevention of chronic mental illness. *American Psychologist, 48,* 966–971.

Smith, M. L., Glass, G. V., & Miller, T. I. (1980). *The benefits of psychotherapy.* Baltimore: Johns Hopkins University Press.

Smith, P. C. (1976). Behavior, results, and organizational effectiveness: The problem of criteria. In M. D. Dunnette (Ed.), *Handbook of industrial and organizational psychology.* Skokie, IL: Rand McNally.

Smith, S. (1979). Remembering in and out of context. *Journal of Experimental Psychology: Human Learning and Memory, 5,* 460–471.

Snarey, J. (1987). A question of morality. *Psychology Today, 21,* 6–8.

Snarey, J. R., Reimer, J., & Kohlberg, L. (1985). Development of social-moral reasoning among kibbutz adolescents: A longitudinal cross-sectional study. *Developmental Psychology, 21,* 3–17.

Snow, M. E., Jacklin, C. N., & Maccoby, E. E. (1983). Sex-of-child differences in father-child interaction at one year of age. *Child Development, 54,* 227–232.

Snyder, S. H. (1984, November). Medicated minds. *Science 84,* pp. 141–142.

Snyderman, M., & Rothman, S. (1987). Survey of expert opinion on intelligence and aptitude testing. *American Psychologist, 42,* 137–144.

Somers, V. K., Dyken, M. E., Mark, A. L., & Abboud, F. M. (1993). Sympathetic-nerve activity during sleep in normal subjects. *The New England Journal of Medicine, 328,* 303–307.

Sommer, R. (1969). *Personal space: The behavioral basis of designs.* Englewood Cliffs, NJ: Prentice-Hall.

Sorensen, J. L., Wermuth, L. A., Gibson, D. R., Choi, K., et al. (1991). *Preventing AIDS in drug users and their sexual partners.* New York: Guilford.

Soyka, L. F., & Joffee, J. M. (1980). Male mediated drug effects on offspring. In R. H. Schwarz & S. J. Yaffe (Eds.), *Drug and chemical risks to the fetus and newborn.* New York: Alan R. Liss.

Spanos, N. P., & Barber, T. F. X. (1974). Toward convergence in hypnosis research. *American Psychologist, 29,* 500–511.

Spanos, N. P., Menary, E., Gabora, N. J., DuBreuil, S. C., & Dewhirst, B. (1991). Secondary identity enactments during past-life regression: A sociocognitive perspective. *Journal of Personality and Social Psychology, 61,* 308–320.

Spear, N. E., Miller, J. S., & Jagielo, J. A. (1990). Animal learning and memory. *Annual Review of Psychology, 41,* 169–211.

Spearman, C. (1904). "General intelligence" objectively determined and measured. *American Journal of Psychology, 15,* 201–293.

Spence, J. T. (1985). Gender identity and its implications for concepts of masculinity and femininity. In T. Sondregger (Ed.), *Nebraska symposium on motivation.* Lincoln: University of Nebraska Press.

Spencer, D. D., Robbins, R. J., Naftolin, F., et al. (1992). Unilateral transplantation of human fetal mesencephalic tissue into the caudate nucleus of patients with Parkinson's disease. *The New England Journal of Medicine, 327,* 1541–1548.

Sperling, G. (1960). The information available in brief visual presentation. *Psychological Monographs, 74* (Whole No. 498).

Sperling, G. (1963). A model for visual memory tasks. *Human Factors, 5,* 19–31.

Sperry, R. (1968). Hemispheric disconnection and unity in conscious awareness. *American Psychologist, 23,* 723–733.

Sperry, R. (1982). Some effects of disconnecting the cerebral hemispheres. *Science, 217,* 1223–1226.

Spitz, H. (1986). *The raising of intelligence: A selected history of attempts to raise retarded intelligence.* Hillsdale, NJ: Erlbaum.

Springer, J. P., & Deutsch, G. (1981). *Left brain, right brain.* San Francisco: Freeman.

Squire, L. R., Knowlton, B., & Mussen, G. (1993). The structure and organization of memory. *Annual Review of Psychology, 44,* 453–495.

Squire, L. R., & Slater, P. C. (1978). Bilateral and unilateral ECT: Effects on verbal and nonverbal memory. *American Journal of Psychiatry, 135,* 1316–1320.

Stall, R. D., Coates, T. J., & Huff, C. (1988). Behavioral risk reduction for HIV infection among gay and bisexual men: A review of results from the United States. *American Psychologist, 43,* 878–885.

Standing, L. (1973). Learning 10,000 pictures. *Quarterly Journal of Experimental Psychology, 25,* 207–222.

Standing, L., Canezio, J., & Haber, R. N. (1970). Perception and memory for pictures: Single-trial learning 2500 visual stimuli. *Psychonomic Science, 19,* 73–74.

Staw, B. M. (1984). Organized behavior: A review and reformation of the field's outcome variables. *Annual Review of Psychology, 35,* 627–666.

Stechler, G., & Halton, A. (1982). Prenatal influences on human development. In B. B. Woolman (Ed.), *Handbook of developmental psychology.* Englewood Cliffs, NJ: Prentice-Hall.

Stein, B. A. (1983). *Quality of work life in action: Managing for effectiveness.* New York: American Management Association.

Stein, J. A., Newcomb, M. D., & Bentler, P. M. (1990). The relative influence of vocational behavior and family involvement on self-esteem: Longitudinal analyses of young adult women and men. *Journal of Vocational Behavior, 36,* 320–328.

Steinhausen, H. C., Göbel, D., Breinlinger, M., & Wolleben, B. (1986). A community survey of infantile autism. *Journal of the American Academy of Child Psychiatry, 25,* 186–189.

Stenchever, M. A., Williamson, R. A., Leonard, J., Karp, L. E., Ley, B., Shy, K., & Smith, D. (1981). Possible relationship between in utero diethylstibestrol exposure and male infertility. *American Journal of Obstetrics and Gynecology, 140,* 186–193.

Stephan, W. (1985). Intergroup relations. In G. Lindsey & E. Aronson (Eds.), *Handbook of social psychology* (3rd ed.). New York: Random House.

Stern, D. (1977). *The first relationship.* Cambridge, MA: Harvard University Press.

Stern, L. (1985). *The structures and strategies of human memory.* Homewood, IL: Dorsey Press.

Stern, P. C. (1992). Psychological dimensions of global environmental change. *Annual Review of Psychology, 43,* 269–302.

Sternberg, R. J. (1979). The nature of mental abilities. *American Psychologist, 34,* 214–230.

Sternberg, R. J. (1981). Testing and cognitive psychology. *American Psychologist, 36,* 1181–1189.

Sternberg, R. J. (1985). *Beyond IQ.* New York: Cambridge University Press.

Sternberg, R. J. (1988). *The triarchic mind.* New York: Viking Press.

Sternberg, R. J., & Wagner, R. K. (1993). The g-centric view of intelligence and job performance is wrong. *Current Directions in Psychological Science, 2,* 1–5.

Stevenson, H. W., Lee, S. Y., & Stigler, J. W. (1986). Mathematics achievement of Chinese, Japanese, and American children. *Science, 231,* 693–696.

Stiles, W. B., Shapiro, D. A., & Elliot, R. (1986). "Are all psychotherapies equivalent?" *American Psychologist, 41,* 165–180.

Stinnett, N., Walters, J., & Kaye, E. (1984). *Relationships in marriage and family* (2nd ed.). New York: Macmillan.

Stokols, D. (1992). Establishing and maintaining healthy environments. *American Psychologist, 47,* 6–22.

Stokols, D. (1972). On the distinction between density and crowding: Some implications for future research. *Psychological Review, 79,* 275–277.

Stokols, D. (1990). Instrumental and spiritual views of people–environment relations. *American Psychologist, 45,* 641–646.

Stoner, J. A. F. (1961). *A comparison of individual and group decisions involving risk.* Unpublished master's thesis, Massachusetts Institute of Technology, Cambridge.

Storandt, M. (1983). Psychology's response to the graying of America. *American Psychologist, 38,* 323–326.

Streissguth, A. P., Aase, J. M., Clarren, S. K., Randels, S. P., La Due, R. A., & Smith, D. F. (1991). Fetal alcohol syndrome in adolescents and adults. *Journal of the American Medical Association, 265,* 1961–1967.

Strupp, H. H. (1986). Psychotherapy: Research, practice, and public policy (How to avoid dead ends). *American Psychologist, 41,* 120–130.

Strupp, H. H., & Binder, J. L. (1984). *Psychotherapy in a new key.* New York: Guilford.

Stunkard, A. J. (1988). Some perspectives on human obesity: Its causes. *Bulletin of the New York Academy of Medicine, 64,* 902–923.

Stunkard, A. J., Harris, J. R., Pederson, N. L., & McClearn, G. E. (1900). The body-mass index of twins who have been reared apart. *New England Journal of Medicine, 322,* 1483–1487.

Stunkard, A. J., Sørensen, T. I. A., Hanis, C., et al. (1986). An adoption study of human obesity. *New England Journal of Medicine, 314,* 193–198.

Sue, D. W., & Sue, D. (1990). *Counseling the culturally different: Theory and practice* (2nd ed.). New York: Wiley.

Sue, S., & Okasaki, S. (1990). Asian-American educational achievements: A phenomenon in search of an explanation. *American Psychologist, 45,* 913–920.

Suinn, R. M. (1980). *Psychology in sports: Methods and applications.* Minneapolis: Burgess.

Suler, J. R. (1985). Meditation and somatic arousal: A comment on Holmes's review. *American Psychologist, 40,* 717.

Surgeon General. (1988). *The health consequences of smoking: Nicotine addiction.* Rockville, MD: U.S. Department of Health and Human Services.

Surwit, R. S., Feinglos, M. N., & Scovern, A. W. (1983). Diabetes and behavior. *American Psychologist, 38,* 255–262.

Swaim, R. C., Oetting, E. R., Thurman, P. J., Beauvais, F., & Edwards, R. W. (1993). American Indian adolescent drug use and socialization characteristics: A cross-cultural comparison. *Journal of Cross-Cultural Psychology, 24,* 53–70.

Swedo, S. E., Rapoport, J. L., Leonard, H., Lenane, M., & Cheslow, D. (1989a). Obsessive-compulsive disorder in children and adolescents. *Archives of General Psychiatry, 46,* 335–341.

Swedo, S. E., Schapiro, M. B., Grady, C. L., Cheslow, D. L., et al. (1989b). Cerebral glucose metabolism in childhood-onset obsessive-compulsive disorder. *Archives of General Psychiatry, 46,* 518–523.

Szasz, T. S. (1960). *The myth of mental illness.* New York: HarperCollins.

Szasz, T. S. (1982). The psychiatric will: A new mechanism for protecting persons against "psychosis" *and* psychiatry. *American Psychologist 37,* 762–770.

Takanishi, R. (1993). The opportunities of adolescence—research, interventions, and policy. *American Psychologist, 48,* 85–87.

Tandon, R., & Greden, J. F. (1989). Cholinergic hyperactivity and negative schizophrenic symptoms. *Archives of General Psychiatry 46*, 745–753.

Tannenbaum, S. I., & Yukl, G. (1992). Training and development in work organizations. *Annual Review of Psychology, 43*, 399–441.

Tanner, J. M. (1973). Growing up. *Scientific American, 179*, 34–43.

Tanner, J. M. (1981). Growth and maturation during adolescence. *Nutrition Review, 39*, 43–55.

Taylor, W., Pearson, J., Mair, A., & Burns, W. (1965). Study of noise and hearing in jute weaving. *Journal of the Acoustical Society of America, 4*, 144–152.

Tenopyr, M. L. (1981). The realities of employment testing. *American Psychologist, 36*, 1120–1127.

Terenius, L. (1982). Endorphins and modulation of pain. *Advances in Neurology, 33*, 59–64.

Termine, N., Hrynick, T., Kestenbaum, R., Gleitman, H., & Spelke, E. S. (1987). Perceptual completion of surfaces in infancy. *Journal of Experimental Psychology: Perception and Performance, 13*, 524–532.

Tesser, A., & Shaffer, D. R. (1990). Attitudes and attitude change. *Annual Review of Psychology, 41*, 479–523.

Thackwray-Emerson, D. (1989). The effect of self-motivation on headache reduction through biofeedback training. *Medical Psychotherapy, 2, 125*–130.

Thayer, W. P. (1983). Industrial/organizational psychology: Science and application. In C. J. Scheirer & A. M. Rogers (Eds.), *The G. Stanley Hall lecture series* (Vol. 3). Washington, DC: American Psychological Association.

Thibault, J. W., & Kelley, H. H. (1959). *The social psychology of groups.* New York: Wiley.

Thomas, A., & Chess, S. (1977). *Temperament and development.* New York: Brunner/Mazel.

Thomas, M. B. (1992). *An introduction to marital and family therapy.* New York: Macmillan.

Thompson, C. I. (1980). *Controls of eating.* Jamaica, NY: Spectrum.

Thompson, C. P. (1982). Memory for unique personal events: The roommate study. *Memory and Cognition, 10*, 324–332.

Thompson, J. W., & Blaine, J. D. (1987). Use of ECT in the United States in 1975 and 1980. *American Journal of Psychiatry, 144*, 557–562.

Thorndike, A. L., Hagen, E. P., & Sattler, J. M. (1986). *The Stanford-Binet intelligence scale, Fourth edition: Technical manual.* Chicago: Riverside.

Thorndike, E. L. (1911). *Animal intelligence.* New York: Macmillan.

Thornton, G. C., III, & Cleveland, J. N. (1990). Developing managerial talent through simulation. *American Psychologist, 45*, 190–199.

Thurstone, L. L. (1938). Primary mental abilities. *Psychometric Monographs* (No. 1).

Tice, D. M., & Baumeister, R. F. (1985). Masculinity inhibits helping in emergencies: Personality does predict the bystander effect. *Journal of Personality and Social Psychology, 49*, 420–428.

Tilley, A. J., & Empson, J. A. C. (1978). REM sleep and memory consolidation. *Biological Psychology, 6*, 293–300.

Tobin-Richards, M., Boxer, A., & Peterson, A. C. (1984). The psychological impact of pubertal change: Sex differences in perceptions of self during early adolescence. In J. Brooks-Gunn & A. C. Peterson (Eds.), *Girls at puberty: Biological, psychological, and social perspectives.* New York: Plenum.

Tohen, M., Waternaux, C. M., & Tsuang, M. T. (1990). Outcome in mania. *Archives of General Psychiatry, 47*, 1106–1111.

Tolman, C. W. (1969) Social feeding in domestic chicks: Effects of food deprivation of non-feeding companions. *Psychonomic Science, 15*, 234.

Tolman, E. C. (1932). *Purposive behaviorism in animals and men.* Englewood Cliffs, NJ: Prentice-Hall.

Tolman, E. C., & Honzik, C. H. (1930). Introduction and removal of reward and maze performance in rats. *University of California Publication in Psychology, 4*, 257–275.

Tomkins, S. S. (1962). *Affect, imagery, consciousness: Vol. I. The positive affects.* New York: Springer.

Toro, P. A., Trickett, E. J., Wall, D. D., & Salem, D. A. (1991). Homelessness in the United States: An ecological perspective. *American Psychologist, 46*, 1208–1218.

Torrey, E. F. (1988). *Surviving schizophrenia: A family manual.* New York: HarperCollins.

Torrey, T. W., & Feduccia, A. (1979). *Morphogenesis of the vertebrates.* New York: Wiley.

Travis, C. B. (1988). *Women and health psychology: Mental health issues.* Hillsdale, NJ: Erlbaum.

Treffert, D. A. (1988). The idiot savant: A review of the syndrome. *American Journal of Psychiatry, 145*, 563–572.

Triandis, H. C. (1990). Theoretical concepts that are applicable to the analysis of ethnocentrism. In R. W. Brislin (Ed.), *Applied cross-cultural psychology.* Newbury Park, CA: Sage.

Triandis, H. C. (1993). Collectivism and individualism as cultural syndromes. *Cross-Cultural Research, 27*, 155–180.

Triandis, H. C., Brislin, R., & Hui, C. H. (1988). Cross-cultural training across the individualism-collectivism divide. *International Journal of Intercultural Relations, 12*, 269–289.

Triplett, N. (1898). The dynamogenic factors in pacemaking and competition. *American Journal of Psychology, 9*, 507–533.

True, W. R., Rice, J., Eisen, S. A., Heath, A. C., Goldberg, J., Lyons, M. J., & Nowak, J. (1993). A twin study of genetic and environmental contributions to liability for posttraumatic stress symptoms. *Archives of General Psychiatry, 50*, 257–264.

Tucker, D. M. (1981). Lateral brain function, emotion, and conceptualization. *Psychological Bulletin, 89*, 19–46.

Tulving, E. (1962). Subjective organization in free recall of "unrelated" words. *Psychological Review, 69,* 344–354.

Tulving, E. (1972). Episodic and semantic memory. In E. Tulving & W. Donaldson (Eds.), *Organization of memory.* New York: Academic Press.

Tulving, E. (1983). *Elements of episodic memory.* New York: Oxford University Press.

Tulving, E. (1985). How many memory systems are there? *American Psychologist, 40,* 385–398.

Tulving, E. (1986). What kind of a hypothesis is the distinction between episodic and semantic memory? *Journal of Experimental Psychology: Learning, Memory, and Cognition, 12,* 307–311.

Tulving, E., & Schacter, D. L. (1990). Priming and human memory systems. *Science, 247,* 301–306.

Tulving, E., & Thompson, D. M. (1973). Encoding specificity and retrieval processes in episodic memory. *Journal of Experimental Psychology: Learning, Memory, and Cognition, 8,* 336–342.

Tung, R. (1988). *The new expatriates: Managing human resources abroad.* New York: HarperCollins.

Turnbull, C. (1961). Some observations regarding the experiences and behaviors of the Bambuti pygmies. *American Journal of Psychology, 74,* 304–308.

Turner, J. S., & Helms, D. B. (1987). *Contemporary adulthood.* New York: Holt, Rinehart & Winston.

Tuttle, T. C. (1983). Organizational productivity: A challenge for psychologists. *American Psychologist, 38,* 479–486.

Tversky, A., & Kahneman, D. (1974). Judgment under uncertainty: Heuristics and biases. *Science, 125,* 1124–1131.

Tyrer, P., & Shawcross, C. (1988). Monoamine oxidase inhibitors in anxiety disorders. *Journal of Psychiatric Research, 22* (Suppl. 1), 87–98.

Ulrich, R. E., Stachnick, T. J., & Stainton, N. R. (1963). Student acceptance of Generalized Personality Inventory. *Psychological Reports, 13,* 831–834.

Underwood, B. J. (1957). Interference and forgetting. *Psychological Review, 64,* 49–60.

Unger, R., & Crawford, M. (1992). *Women and gender: A feminist psychology.* New York: McGraw-Hill.

U.S. Bureau of the Census. (1991). *Statistical Abstract of the United States* (111th ed.). Washington, DC: U.S. Government Printing Office.

U.S. General Accounting Office. (1992). *Elderly Americans: Health, housing, and nutritional gaps between the poor and the nonpoor.* Washington, DC: United States General Accounting Office.

Valenstein, E. S. (1980). *The psychosurgery debate: Scientific, legal, and ethical perspectives.* San Francisco: Freeman.

Valenstein, E. S. (1986). *Great and desperate cures.* New York: Basic Books.

Vallerand, R. J., Colavecchio, P. G., & Pelletier, L. G. (1988).

Psychological momentum and performance inferences: A preliminary test of the antecedents-consequences psychological momentum model. *Journal of Sport and Exercise Psychology, 10,* 92–108.

Valliant, G. E. (1983). *The natural history of alcoholism: Causes, patterns and paths to recovery.* Cambridge, MA: Harvard University Press.

Valliant, G. E., & Valliant, C. O. (1990). Natural history of male psychological health, XII: A 45-year study of predictors of successful aging at age 65. *American Journal of Psychiatry, 147,* 31–37.

VandenBos, G. R. (1986). Psychotherapy research: A special issue. *American Psychologist, 41,* 111–112.

VanderPlate, C., Aral, S. O., & Magder, L. (1988). The relationship among genital herpes simplex virus, stress, and social support. *Health Psychology, 7,* 159–168.

Vander Wall, S. B. (1982). An experimental analysis of cache recovery in the Clark's nutcracker. *Animal Behavior, 30,* 84–94.

van Ijzendoorn, M. H., & Kroonenberg, P. M. (1988). Cross-cultural patterns of attachment: A meta-analysis. *Child Development, 59,* 147–156.

Varca, P. E. (1980). An analysis of home and away game performance of male college basketball teams. *Journal of Sport Psychology, 2,* 245–257.

Vaughn, B. E., & Langlois, J. H. (1983). Physical attractiveness as a correlate of peer status and social competence in preschool children. *Developmental Psychology, 19,* 561–567.

Ventura, J., Nuechterlein, K. H., Lukoff, D., & Hardesty, J. P. (1989). A prospective study of stressful life events and schizophrenic relapse. *Journal of Abnormal Psychology, 98,* 407–411.

Verillo, R. T. (1975). Cutaneous sensation. In B. Scharf (Ed.), *Experimental sensory psychology.* Glenview, IL: Scott, Foresman.

Vernon, P. E. (1960). *The structure of human abilities* (rev. ed.). London: Methuen.

Vernon, P. E. (1979). *Intelligence: Heredity and environment.* San Francisco: Freeman.

Vinacke, W. E. (1974). *The psychology of thinking* (2nd ed.). New York: McGraw-Hill.

Vitz, P. C. (1990). The use of stories in moral development. *American Psychologist, 45,* 709–720.

Voevodsky, J. (1974). Evaluations of a deceleration warning light for reducing rear-end automobile collisions. *Journal of Applied Psychology, 59,* 270–273.

Vokey, J. R., & Read, J. D. (1985). Subliminal messages: Between the devil and the media. *American Psychologist, 40,* 1231–1239.

Vorhees, C. F., & Mollnow, E. (1987). Behavioral teratogenesis: Long-term influences on behavior from early exposure to environmental agents. In J. O. Osofsky (Ed.), *Handbook of infant development* (2nd ed.). New York: Wiley.

Vroom, V. (1964). *Work and motivation.* New York: Wiley.

Walker, L. J. (1989). A longitudinal study of moral reasoning. *Child Development, 60,* 157–166.

Wallace, P. (1977). Individual discrimination of humans by odor. *Physiology and Behavior, 19,* 577–579.

Wallace, R. K., & Benson, H. (1972). The physiology of meditation. *Scientific American, 226,* 85–90.

Wallach, H. (1987). Perceiving a stable environment when one moves. *Annual Review of Psychology, 38,* 1–28.

Wallas, G. (1926). *The art of thought.* New York: Harcourt Brace Jovanovich.

Walsh, B. T., Hadigan, C. M., Devlin, M. J., Gladis, M., & Roose, S. P. (1991). Long-term outcome of antidepressant treatment for bulimia nervosa. *American Journal of Psychiatry, 148,* 1206–1212.

Walsh, B. T., Kissileff, H. R., Cassidy, S. M., & Dantzic, S. (1989). Eating behavior of women with bulimia. *Archives of General Psychiatry, 46,* 54–58.

Walster, E., Aronson, V., Abrahams, D., & Rottman, L. (1966). Importance of physical attractiveness in dating behavior. *Journal of Personality and Social Psychology, 4,* 508–516.

Walster, E., & Festinger, L. (1962). The effectiveness of "overheard" and persuasive communications. *Journal of Abnormal and Social Psychology, 65,* 395–402.

Walster, E., Walster, G. W., & Berschied, E. (1978). *Equity: Theory and research.* Boston: Allyn & Bacon.

Walters, G. C., & Grusec, J. E. (1977). *Punishment.* San Francisco: Freeman.

Walton, G. E., Bower, N. J. A., & Bower, T. G. R. (1992). Recognition of familiar faces by newborns. *Infant Behavior and Development, 15,* 265–269.

Walton, G. E., & Bower, T. G. R. (1993). Newborns form "prototypes" in less than 1 minute. *Psychological Science, 4,* 203–205.

Wamboldt, F. S., & Reiss, D. (1989). Defining a family heritage and a new relationship identity: Two central tasks in the making of a marriage. *Family Process, 28,* 317–335.

Warrington, E. K., & Weiskrantz, L. (1968). New method of testing long-term retention with special reference to amnesic patients. *Nature, 217,* 972–974.

Warrington, E. K., & Weiskrantz, L. (1970). Amnesic syndrome: Consolidation or retrieval? *Nature, 228,* 629–630.

Watkins, M. J. (1990). Mediationism and the obfuscation of memory. *American Psychologist, 45,* 328–335.

Watson, C. J. (1981). An evaluation of some aspects of the Steers and Rhodes model of employee attendance. *Journal of Applied Psychology, 66,* 385–389.

Watson, J. B. (1919). *Psychology from the standpoint of a behaviorist.* Philadelphia: Lippincott.

Watson, J. B. (1925). *Behaviorism.* New York: Norton.

Watson, J. B. (1926). What is behaviorism? *Harper's Monthly Magazine, 152,* 723–729.

Watson, M. W., & Amgott-Kwan, T. (1984). Development of family-role concepts in school-age children. *Developmental Psychology, 20,* 953–959.

Waugh, N. C., & Norman, D. A. (1965). Primary memory. *Psychological Review, 72,* 89–104.

Weaver, C. N. (1980). Job satisfaction in the United States in the 1970s. *Journal of Applied Psychology, 65,* 364–367.

Webb, W. B. (1975). *Sleep, the gentle tyrant.* Englewood Cliffs, NJ: Prentice-Hall.

Webb, W. B. (1981). The return of consciousness. In L. T. Benjamin (Ed.), *The G. Stanley Hall lecture series* (Vol. I). Washington, DC: American Psychological Association.

Webb, W. B., & Cartwright, R. D. (1978). Sleep and dreams. *Annual Review of Psychology, 29,* 223–252.

Wechsler, D. (1958). *The measurement and appraisal of adult intelligence* (4th ed.). Baltimore: Williams & Wilkins.

Wechsler, D. (1975). Intelligence defined and undefined: A relativistic reappraisal. *American Psychologist, 30,* 135–139.

Wechsler, D. (1981). *Manual for the Wechsler Adult Intelligence Scale—Revised.* New York: The Psychological Corporation.

Weekley, J. A., & Gier, J. A. (1987). Reliability and validity of the situational interview for a sales position. *Journal of Applied Psychology, 72,* 484–487.

Weil, A. T., Zinberg, N., & Nelson, J. M. (1968). Clinical and psychological effects of marijuana in man. *Science, 162,* 1234–1242.

Weisberg, R. W. (1986). *Creativity: Genius and other myths.* San Francisco: Freeman.

Weisner, W. H., & Cronshaw, S. F. (1988). A meta-analytic investigation of the impact of interview format and degree of structure on the validity of the employment interview. *Journal of Occupational Psychology, 61,* 275–290.

Weissman, M. M. (1988). The epidemiology of anxiety disorders: Rates, risks and familial patterns. *Journal of Psychiatric Research, 22,* (Suppl. 1), 99–114.

Weissman, M. M., & Klerman, G. L. (1992). The changing rate of major depression. *Journal of the American Medical Association, 268,* 3098.

Weissman, M. M., Klerman, G. L., Markowitz, J. S., & Ouellette, R. (1989). Suicidal ideation and suicide attempts in panic disorders and attacks. *The New England Journal of Medicine, 321,* 1209–1214.

Welch, W. W., Anderson, R. E., & Harris, L. J. (1982). The effects of schooling on mathematics achievement. *American Educational Research Journal, 19,* 145–153.

Weldon, E., & Gargano, G. M. (1988). Cognitive loading: The effects of accountability and shared responsibility on cognitive effort. *Personality and Social Psychology Bulletin, 14,* 159–171.

Wellman, H. M., & Gellman, S. A. (1992). Cognitive development: Fundamental theories of core domains. *Annual Review of Psychology, 43,* 337–375.

Wells, G. L. (1993). What do we know about eyewitness identification? *American Psychologist, 48,* 553–571.

Wertheimer, M. (1961). Psychomotor coordination of auditory and visual space at birth. *Science, 134,* 1692.

West, M. A. (1985). Meditation and somatic arousal reduction. *American Psychologist, 40,* 717–719.

Wheeler, R. J., & Frank, M. A. (1988). Identification of stress buffers. *Behavioral Medicine, 14,* 78–89.

Whitehurst, G. (1982). Language development. In B. Wolman (Ed.), *Handbook of developmental psychology.* Englewood Cliffs, NJ: Prentice-Hall.

Whiting, B., & Edwards, C. P. (1973). A cross-cultural analysis of sex differences in the behavior of children ages three through eleven. *Journal of Social Psychology, 91,* 177–188.

Whyte, L. L. (1960). *The unconscious before Freud.* New York: Basic Books.

Wickens, C. D. (1992). *Engineering psychology and human performance* (2nd ed.). New York: HarperCollins.

Wickens, D. D. (1973). Some characteristics of word encoding. *Memory and Cognition, 1,* 485–490.

Widner, H., Tetrud, J., Rehncrona, S., et al. (1992). Bilateral fetal mesencephalic grafting in two patients with Parkinsonism induced by 1-methyl-4-phenyl-1,2,3,6 tetrahydropridine (MPTP). *The New England Journal of Medicine, 327,* 1556–1563.

Wiggins, J. S., & Pincus, A. L. (1992). Personality: Structure and assessment. *Annual Review of Psychology, 43,* 473–504.

Wilcox, D., & Hager, R. (1980). Toward realistic expectations for orgasmic response in women. *Journal of Sex Research, 16,* 162–179.

Wilkes, J. (1986). Conversation with Ernest R. Hilgard: A study in hypnosis. *Psychology Today, 20*(1), 23–27.

Williams, J. E., & Best, D. L. (1990). *Measuring sex stereotypes: A multination study.* Newbury Park, CA: Sage.

Williams, K., Harkins, S., & Latané, B. (1981). Identifiability as a deterrent to social loafing: Two cheering experiments. *Journal of Personality and Social Psychology, 40,* 303–311.

Williams, K., Nida, S. A., Baca, L. D., & Latané, B. (1989). Social loafing and swimming: Effects of identifiability of individual and relay performance of intercollegiate swimmers. *Basic and Applied Social Psychology, 10,* 73–82.

Wilson, G. T. (1982). Adult disorders. In G. T. Wilson & C. M. Franks (Eds.), *Contemporary behavior therapy: Conceptual and empirical foundations.* New York: Guilford.

Wincze, J. P., & Carey, M. P. (1992). *Sexual dysfunctions: A guide for assessment and treatment.* New York: Guilford.

Wing, L. (1989). *Diagnosis and treatment of autism.* New York: Plenum.

Wing, L., & Gould, J. (1979). Severe impairment of social interaction and associated abnormalities in children: Epidemiology and classification. *Journal of Autism and Developmental Disorders, 9,* 11–29.

Winter, D. G. (1987). Leader appeal, leader performance, and the motive profiles of leaders and followers: A study of American presidents and elections. *Journal of Personality and Social Psychology, 52,* 196–202.

Winter, D. G. (1988). The power motive in women—and men. *Journal of Personality and Social Psychology, 54,* 510–519.

Winter, D. G., & Stewart, A. J. (1978). The power motive. In H. London & J. E. Exner (Eds.), *Dimensions of personality.* New York: Wiley.

Winters, K. C., Weintraub, S., & Neale, J. M. (1981). Validity of MMPI code types in identifying DSM-III schizophrenics. *Journal of Consulting and Clinical Psychology, 49,* 486–487.

Winton, W. M. (1987). Do introductory textbooks present the Yerkes-Dodson Law correctly? *American Psychologist, 42,* 202–203.

Witenberg, S. H., Blanchard, E. B., McCoy, G., Suls, J., & McGoldrick, M. D. (1983). Evaluation of compliance in home and center hemodialysis patients. *Health Psychology, 2,* 227–238.

Witmer, J. F., & Geller, E. S. (1976). Facilitating paper recycling: Effects of prompts, raffles, and contests. *Journal of Applied Behavior Analysis, 9,* 315–322.

Wollen, K. A., Weber, A., & Lowry, D. H. (1972). Bizarreness versus interaction of mental images as determinants of learning. *Cognitive Psychology, 3,* 518–523.

Wolpe, J. (1958). *Psychotherapy by reciprocal inhibition.* Stanford, CA: Stanford University Press.

Wolpe, J. (1969). Basic principles and practices of behavior therapy of neuroses. *American Journal of Psychiatry, 125,* 1242–1247.

Wolpe, J. (1981). Behavior therapy versus psychoanalysis. *American Psychologist, 36,* 159–164.

Wolpe, J. (1982). *The practice of behavior therapy* (3rd ed.). New York: Pergamon Press.

Wood, C. (1986). The hostile heart. *Psychology Today, 20,* 10–12.

Worringham, C. J., & Messick, D. M. (1983). Social facilitation of running: An unobtrusive study. *Journal of Social Psychology, 121,* 23–29.

Wright, L. (1988). The Type A behavior pattern and coronary artery disease. *American Psychologist, 43,* 2–14.

Wurtman, R. J. (1985). Alzheimer's disease. *Scientific American, 247,* 62–74.

Wysowski, D. K., & Baum, C. (1989). Antipsychotic drug use in the United States, 1976–1985. *Archives of General Psychiatry, 46,* 929–932.

Yalom, I. D. (1985). *The theory and practice of group psychotherapy.* New York: Basic Books.

Yaniv, I., & Meyer, D. E. (1987). Activation and metacognition of inaccessible stored information: Potential basis for incubation effects in problem solving. *Journal of Experimental Psychology: Learning, Memory, and Cognition, 13,* 187–205.

Yates, A. (1989). Current perspectives on the eating disorders: I History, psychological and biological aspects. *Journal of the American Academy of Child and Adolescent Psychiatry, 28,* 813–828.

Yates, A. (1990). Current perspectives on eating disorders: II Treatment, outcome, and research directions. *Journal of the American Academy of Child and Adolescent Psychiatry, 29,* 1–9.

Yates, A. J. (1980). *Biofeedback and the modification of behavior.* New York: Plenum.

Yates, F. A. (1966). *The art of memory.* Chicago: University of Chicago Press.

Youngstrom, N. (1991, May). Serious mental illness issues need leadership. *APA Monitor,* p. 27.

Yuille, J. C. (1993). We must study forensic eyewitnesses to know about them. *American Psychologist, 48,* 572–573.

Zadeh, L. (1965). Fuzzy sets. *Information and Control, 8,* 338–353.

Zajonc, R. B. (1968). Attitudinal effects of mere exposure. *Journal of Personality and Social Psychology* (Monograph Suppl.), *9,* 1–27.

Zajonc, R. B., & Markus, H. (1982). Affective and cognitive factors in preferences. *Journal of Consumer Research, 9,* 123–131.

Zanna, M. P., & Rempel, J. K. (1988). Attitudes: A new look at an old concept. In D. Bartal & A. W. Kruglanski (Eds.), *The social psychology of knowledge.* New York: Cambridge University Press.

Zedeck, S. (1987). *The science and practice of industrial and organizational psychology.* College Park, MD: Society for Industrial and Organizational Psychology.

Zedeck, S., & Cascio, W. F. (1984). Psychological issues in personnel decisions. *Annual Review of Psychology, 35,* 461–518.

Zedeck, S., Tziner, A., & Middlestadt, S. E. (1983). Interviewer validity and reliability: An individual analysis approach. *Personnel Psychology, 36,* 230–237.

Zelnik, M., & Kantner, J. F. (1980). Sexual activity, contraceptive use, and pregnancy among metropolitan-area teenagers: 1971–1979. *Family Planning Perspectives, 12,* 230–237.

Zigler, E., & Hodapp, R. M. (1991). Behavioral functioning in individuals with mental retardation. *Annual Review of Psychology, 42,* 29–50.

Zilbergeld, B., & Evans, M. (1980). The inadequacy of Masters and Johnson. *Psychology Today, 14,* 28–43.

Zimmerman, M., & Coryell, W. (1989). *DSM-III* personality disorder diagnoses in a nonpatient sample. *Archives of General Psychiatry, 46,* 682–689.

Zinbarg, R. E., Barlow, D. H., Brown, T. A., & Hertz, R. M. (1992). Cognitive-behavioral approaches to the nature and treatment of anxiety disorders. *Annual Review of Psychology, 43,* 235–267.

Zohar, D. (1980). Safety climate in industrial organizations: Theoretical and applied implications. *Journal of Applied Psychology, 65,* 96–102.

Zuckerman, B., & Bresnahan, K. (1991). Developmental and behavioral consequences of prenatal drug and alcohol exposure. *Pediatrics Clinics of North America, 38,* 1387–1406.

Zuckerman, M. (1978). Sensation seeking and psychopathology. In R. D. Hare & D. Shalling (Eds.), *Psychopathic behavior.* New York: Wiley.

Zuckerman, M., Buchsbaum, M. S., & Murphy, D. L. (1980). Sensation seeking and its biological correlates. *Psychological Bulletin, 88,* 187–214.

Zuckerman, M., Eysenck, S., & Eysenck, H. J. (1978). Sensation seeking in England and America: Cross-cultural, age, and sex comparisons. *Journal of Consulting and Clinical Psychology, 46,* 139–149.

CREDITS

PHOTO CREDITS

Unless otherwise acknowledged, all photographs are the property of Scott, Foresman. Page abbreviations are as follows: (L) left, (R) right, (T) top, (B) bottom.

Cover and **iii** David Madison/Tony Stone Images; **ix** (T) G&J Images/The Image Bank; **ix** (B) Elisabeth Wettand/Photo Researchers; **x** Marc Romanelli/The Image Bank; **xi** (T) Zefa-Norman/The Stock Market; **xi** (B) Eric Kamp/Phototake; **xii** Richard Gross/The Stock Market; **xiii** (T) Jean Miele/ The Stock Market; **xiii** (B) Michael Hart/FPG; **xiv** N. Markus/Photo Researchers; **xv** Terence Turner/FPG; **xvi** (T) David Ball/The Picture Cube; **xvi** (B) Phil Schofield; **xvii**(T) Comstock Inc.; **xvii** (B) Bob Daemmrich/Uniphoto; **xviii** Frank Cezus/Tony Stone Images.

Chapter 1: 1 G&J Images/ The Image Bank; **4** Martin Rogers/Tony Stone Images; **8** Will and Deni McIntyre/Photo Researchers; **13** Archives of the History of American Psychology, University of Akron; **15** Joe McNally; **16** Bettmann Archive; **17** Historical Pictures/Stock Montage, Inc.; **18** (all) Nathan Benn/ Woodfin Camp & Associates; **22** Merlin D. Tuttle/National Audubon Society Collection/Photo Researchers; **24** Rhoda Sidney/Photo Edit; **28** Focus On Sports; **38** UPI/Bettmann; **41** (R) *Ascending and Descending*, Escher, 1960—M. C./Cordon Art—Baarn—Holland; **42** Uniphoto.

Chapter 2: 49 Elisabeth Wettand/Photo Researchers; **54** Secch-Lecaque/Roussel–UCLAF/SPL/Photo Researchers; **66** Warren Anatomical Museum, Harvard Medical School; **70** (TL) Shambroom/Photo Researchers; **70** (TR and B) Dan McCoy/Rainbow; **77** Bruce Curtis/Peter Arnold, Inc.; **87** (R) David Young-Wolff/Photo Edit.

Chapter 3: 93 Marc Romanelli/The Image Bank; **100** J. P. Ferrero/Explorer/Photo Researchers; **103** Nancy Gerow; **117** (**both**) Pat Field; **118** E. R. Degginger; **130** (B) J. Sohm/The Image Works; **130** (T) Nancy Gerow; **131** Dennis Kucharzak; **132** (T) DeRichemond/ The Image Works; **132** (B) Murray & Associates, Inc.; **145** Larry Mulvehill/Photo Researchers; **152** Tony Freeman/Photo Edit; **154** Bob Daemmrich/The Image Works.

Chapter 4: 163 Zefa-Norman/The Stock Market; **174** Will and Deni McIntyre/Photo Researchers; **176** Alan Hobson/Photo Researchers; **179** (**all**) Patrick Ward/Discover Syndication/Walt Disney Publications; **183** Bart Bartholomew/Black Star; **186** Dan McCoy/Rainbow; **190** Richard Hutchings/Photo Researchers; **191** (L) Rick Friedman/The Picture Cube; **191** (R) Robert E. Daemmrich/Tony Stone Images; **194** Claudia Andujar/Photo Researchers.

Chapter 5: 201 Eric Kamp/Phototake; **208** Tass/SOVFOTO; **214** (T) Vloo/Stockphotos; **214** (B) Courtesy of the Archives: The Coca-Cola Company; **217** Scott Pauly/Black Star; **221** Michael Newman/Photo Edit; **225** Richard Wood/The Picture Cube; **227** Susan Van Etten/Photo Edit; **228** The *Hartford Courant*/The Image Works; **237** David Young-Wolff/Photo Edit; **238** Hank Morgan/Discover Syndication/Walt Disney Publications; **240** Animal Behavior Enterprises; **246** (all) From A. Bandura and R. Walters/Photos courtesy of Dr. Albert Bandura (1963), *Social Learning and Personality*; **247** Nancy S. Gerow.

Chapter 6: 253 Richard Gross/The Stock Market; **261** Michael Dwyer/Stock Boston; **263** D. and I. MacDonald/ The Picture Cube; **266** PhotoFest; **269** Bettmann; **274** (TL) John Coletti/ The Picture Cube; **274** (TR) Myrleen Ferguson Cate/Photo Edit; **274** Doug Menuez/Stock Boston; **283** (L) Cleo/Photo Edit; **283** (R) Hangarter/ The Picture Cube: **285** (**both**) AP Wide World; **293** SuperStock, Inc.

Chapter 7: 305 Jean Miele/The Stock Market; **308** ESTO; **309** G. Bassignac-Sirpa/Gamma-Liaison; **311** SuperStock, Inc. **314** Bruce Kliewe/The Picture Cube; **317** Four by Five Inc./Superstock; **318** Burk Uzzle/Magnum Photos; **323** Hiroji Kubota/Magnum Photos; **328** Dennis MacDonald/Photo Edit; **333** Roger Ball/Picturesque; **341** Rube Goldberg/Reprinted with special permission of King Features Syndicate; **344** Beringer/Dratch/The Image Works.

Chapter 8: 351 Michael Hart/FPG; **359** Petit Format/Nestlé/SS/Photo Researchers; **362** Courtesy, American Cancer Society; **365** Peter Vandermark/Stock Boston; **369** Enrique Ferorelli Enterprises, Inc.; **372** Bill Anderson/Monkmeyer Press Photo Service; **374** (all) George Zimbel/Monkmeyer Press Photo Service; **376** Laura Dwight/Peter Arnold, Inc.; **385** (**both**) The Huntington Library and Art Gallery, San Marino, CA; **386** Elizabeth Zuckerman/Photo Edit; **387** Martin Rogers/Stock Boston; **389** Jeffrey W. Myers/The Stock Market; **394** Robert W. Ginn/The Picture Cube; **397** Susan Oristaglio/The Stock Market; **398** Ken Kaminsky/The Picture Cube; **400** Bob Daemmrich/Stock Boston; **406** Myrleen Ferguson/Photo Edit; **407** Sidney Harris; **409** SuperStock, Inc.; **411** Ellis Herwig/The Picture Cube; **413** Michael L. Osborne.

Chapter 9: 421 N. Markus/Photo Researchers; **431** Mugshots/Gabe Palmer/The Stock Market; **434** Bob Daemmrich/Stock Boston; **443** Bob Daemmrich/The Image Works; **449** Blair Seitz/Photo Researchers; **450** Peter Steiner/The Stock Market; **457** Mark Antman/The Image Works; **471** Loren Santow/Tony Stone Images; **477** (I) Roger Ball/Picturesque; **477** (BL) Frank Siteman/The Picture Cube; **477** (BR) L. Kolvoord/The Image Works; **481** Dan McCoy/Rainbow.

Abbott, B. B., 6
Abbott, M., 405
Abbott, R. C., 564
Abboud, F. M., 178
Abel, E. L., 362
Abrahams, D., 698
Ackerman, P. L., 729
Acocella, J. R., 624, 659
Acton, H., 388
Adams, G. R., 393
Adams, J. L., 307, 344
Adams, J. S., 735
Adams, M. J., 282
Adams, R. M., 757, 760
Adelmann, P. K., 539, 540
Adler, A., 431, 432, 484
Adler, N. E., 555
Adler, R., 218
Adler, T., 69, 362, 451
Adrian, C., 616
Agnew, H. W., 179
Aiello, J. R., 745
Aiello, T. D., 745
Aiken, L. R., 450, 470
Ainsworth, M. D. S.,
    387–389
Ajzen, I., 683
Alavi, A., 626
Alba, J. W., 291
Albee, G. W., 43, 573
Alderman, D., 413
Aldwin, C., 573
Alexander, J. R., 616
Allen, C. R., 616
Allen, J. L., 693
Allen, M. G., 616
Allen, S. W., 292
Allport, G., 437–439, 485
Altman, I., 746, 749
Alvir, J., 620, 644
Alzheimer, A., 612–614
Amabile, T. M., 478
Ames, M. A., 524
Amgott-Kwan, T., 315
Amoore, J. E., 151
Anastasi, A., 446
Anderson, C. A., 752, 753
Anderson, D. C., 752
Anderson, J. R., 263, 272,
    273
Anderson, R., 698
Anderson, R. C., 292
Anderson, R. E., 471

Andreasen, N. C., 622, 625
Andrews, R. J., 539
Angleitner, A., 405
Anisfeld, M., 326
Anisman, H., 617
Apsche, J., 236
Aral, S. O., 400, 576
Argyle, N., 595
Aristotle, 11
Arizmendi, T. G., 668
Arndt, S., 625
Arnold, M., 189
Aronson, E., 690, 697
Aronson, V., 698
Arthur, R. J., 555
Arvey, R. D., 728
Asch, S., 701–704, 718
Aserinsky, E., 176
Asherian, A., 405
Aslin, R. N., 368, 369
Atkinson, J. W., 513, 514
Atkinson, R. C., 257, 288
Atkinson, T., 738
Atwood, M. E., 335
Auletta, K., 401
Austin, G. A., 314
Axelrod, S., 236
Azrin, N. H., 236
Azumi, K., 738

Babor, T. F., 192
Baca, L. D., 712
Back, K., 697
Backman, C. W., 696
Baddeley, A. D., 255, 257,
    259, 268, 274, 284
Bagozzi, R. P., 683
Bahrick, H. P., 278
Bailey, J. M., 523
Balay, J., 171
Baldy, R., 626
Baley, S., 727
Ballenger, J. C., 597
Bandura, A., 242, 245–248,
    434, 441, 444, 484, 662
Barban, L., 607
Barbee, A. H., 478, 479
Barber, T. F. X., 184, 564
Barefoot, J. C., 571
Bargh, J. A., 681, 696
Barinaga, M., 524
Barker, R., 750
Barlow, D. H., 665

Barnes, M., 404
Barnette, R. C., 559
Baron, M., 616
Baron, R. A., 692, 752
Barr, H. M., 362
Barrett, G. V., 458
Barron, F., 341
Barron, S., 362
Barsalou, L. W., 309, 315
Bartell, P. A., 707
Bartlett, F., 290, 291
Bartus, R. T., 275
Baruzzi, A., 81
Basso, K., 322
Bates, H. G., 322
Baudry, M., 276
Baum, A., 558
Baum, C., 644
Baumeister, A. A., 479
Baumeister, R. F., 425, 472,
    709, 713, 757
Beatty, R. W., 730
Beauvais, F., 192, 398
Beck, A. T., 596, 617, 664,
    665
Beckman, L. J., 406
Bee, H., 388, 389
Beecroft, R., 221
Beer, B., 275
Beer, M., 738
Begg, I., 287
Bekerian, D. A., 270, 271
Bellack, A. S., 648
Bellugi, U., 327
Belsher, G., 615
Belsky, J., 389
Bem, S., 386
Benbow, C. P., 471
Benedict, H., 324
Bennett, E. L., 275
Bennett, G. J., 156
Bennett, T. L., 196, 617
Bennett, W., 190
Benowitz, N. L., 189
Ben-Porath, Y. S., 451
Benson, H., 186
Bentler, P. M., 398, 406
Bentson, C., 729
Ben-Yehuda, N., 637
Berg, C. J., 601
Berg, C. Z., 600
Berger, H., 68
Berglas, S., 192

Berkowitz, L., 532, 567
Berlyne, D. E., 501
Berman, E. R., 510
Berman, J. S., 668
Bernardin, H. J., 730
Bernstein, I., 221
Bernstein, R., 521
Berrettini, W. H., 616
Berry, J., 378
Berscheid, E., 681, 695, 698
Bertelsen, A., 623, 626
Bertenthal, B. I., 369
Best, D. L., 386
Bettman, J. R., 339
Beutler, L. E., 668
Bhawuk, D. P. S., 381
Biaggio, A., 405
Bigelow, L. B., 624
Billy, J. O. G., 523, 578
Binder, J. L., 656
Binet, A., 462, 465, 467, 478
Birch, E. E., 369
Birdwhistell, R. L., 539
Birk, T., 690
Birnbaum, I. M., 284
Birnbaum, M. H., 698
Bjork, R. A., 280
Bjorklund, A., 80
Blaine, J. W., 642
Blanchard, D. C., 536
Blanchard, R. J., 536
Blanchard, W. J., 757
Blanco-Villasenor, A., 405
Blaney, P. H., 284
Blank, M., 379
Blashfield, R. K., 609
Blass, E. M., 370
Bleier, R., 88
Bleuler, E., 619
Bloch, D., 666
Bloch, G. J., 518
Block, J., 101, 398
Bloodworth, R. C., 196
Bloom, F. E., 618, 620
Blum, J. E., 473
Blumenfeld, P., 385
Blyth, D. A., 398
Bolles, R. C., 242
Bondareff, W., 613
Booth-Kewley, S., 570
Bootzin, R. R., 624, 659
Borbely, A., 174
Bordens, K. S., 6

Borman, W. C., 727
Bornstein, R. F., 698
Bouchard, C., 508
Bouchard, T. J., Jr., 39
Bourne, L. E., 8, 309, 332
Bousfield, W. A., 273
Bowden, J., 78
Bower, G. H., 30, 264, 284, 287–289
Bower, T. G. R., 369
Bowers, J. S., 281
Bowers, K., 185
Bowlby, J., 387, 389
Boxer, A., 396
Boyce, T., 555
Boyle, M. H., 588
Bradbard, M. R., 387
Bradley, D. R., 127
Bradshaw, D., 695
Bradshaw, J. L., 87
Braine, M. D. S., 324
Brand, R. J., 570
Bransford, J. D., 291, 300
Brasfield, T. L., 578
Bratic, E. B., 361
Braum, A., 573
Braun, P., 648
Bray, D. W., 729
Breen, M. J., 609
Breeze, R. E., 80
Bregman, J., 481
Brehm, J. W., 502
Breier, A., 622
Breinlinger, M., 610
Breland, K., 240, 241
Breland, M., 240, 241
Bremer, D., 284
Brennan, R. T., 559
Bresnahan, K., 362
Brett, J. F., 555
Breuer, J., 654
Brewer, W. F., 292
Brief, A. P., 555
Briggs, G. G., 363
Brigham, J. C., 577
Brinkerhoff, R. O., 734
Brislin, R. W., 229, 322, 378, 381, 730
Broca, P.-P., 65, 84
Brock, T. C., 688, 689
Brodsky, A., 189
Brody, E. M., 409
Brogan, J., 85
Brooks, L. R., 292
Brooks-Gunn, J., 400
Brown, J., 260, 278
Brown, J. D., 565
Brown, J. I., 26
Brown, N. A., 362
Brown, R., 284, 324, 327
Brown, T. A., 665
Browne, M. A., 755, 756
Bruch, H., 511
Bruff, C. D., 736
Bruner, J. S., 314

Buchsbaum, M. S., 502
Buck, R., 532, 539
Buckhout, R., 268
Burch, P., 728
Burge, D., 616
Burgoon, J. K., 690
Burish, T. G., 564
Burke, J. D., 217
Burke, M. J., 555
Burney, E., 616
Burnkrant, R. E., 683
Burns, H. J., 269
Burns, K., 362
Burns, W., 751
Buss, A., 437
Buss, A. H., 609
Buss, D. M., 404, 425, 699
Butcher, J. N., 451, 589, 604, 606, 620, 640, 656
Butler, R., 413, 613
Butterfield, E. C., 480
Byne, W., 88
Byrne, D., 692, 695, 699

Cacioppo, J. T., 682, 683, 690
Calhoun, J. B., 749
Calkins, M., 14
Campbell, D. T., 139
Campbell, J. P., 733
Campbell, K., 388
Campbell, R. J., 729
Campion, J. E., 728
Campos, J. J., 369
Cannon, T. D., 622
Cannon, W., 501, 502, 504
Cantril, H., 106
Caplan, N., 476
Carey, M. P., 527
Carey, S., 324
Caritis, S. N., 363
Carlsmith, J. M., 686, 687, 690
Carlson, N. R., 78
Caroff, S., 626
Carone, B. J., 620
Carr, C., 574
Carran, D. T., 482
Carroll, G., 23
Carson, R., 753, 755
Carson, R. C., 439, 443, 589, 604, 606, 617, 620, 640
Carson, T. P., 617
Cartwright, R. D., 179
Carver, C. S., 564
Cascio, W. F., 730
Cash, T. F., 699, 727
Cassidy, S. M., 512
Cattell, R. B., 438, 452, 473, 485
Cavanaugh, P. J., 370
Cavenaugh, J. C., 410
Cazden, C. B., 327
Cermak, L. S., 257, 272

Chadwick, O., 392
Chagnon, N. A., 194
Chaiken, S., 681, 682
Chao, G. T., 727
Charney, D. S., 602
Chase, M. H., 178
Chase, W. G., 264, 292
Chase-Lansdale, L., 400
Chasnoff, I. J., 362
Cheesman, J., 171
Cherns, A. B., 738
Cherry, F., 384
Cheslow, D. L., 599, 601
Chesney, M. A., 555
Chess, S., 384
Chhokar, J., 740
Chi, M. T. H., 345
Chilman, C. S., 400, 405
Choi, K., 578
Chomsky, N., 320, 326
Christiansen, J., 597
Chuang, H. T., 578
Clark, E. T., 473
Clark, M. C., 30, 287, 288, 289
Clark, R. A., 513
Clark, R. D., 369
Clarkson-Smith, L., 412
Cleary, P. D., 574
Cleveland, J. N., 733
Clifford, B. R., 268
Clifford, M. M., 698
Clore, G. L., 532, 695
Cluss, P. A., 580
Coates, T. J., 578
Cohen, G. D., 612
Cohen, L. R., 368
Cohen, N., 218
Cohen, N. J., 284
Cohen, R. L., 695
Cohen, S., 555, 573
Cohen, S., 751
Cohen, S. A., 729
Colavecchio, P. G., 757
Colby, A., 381
Cole, J. O., 645
Cole, R. E., 738
Coles, R., 400
Collins, A., 532
Collins, A. M., 273
Collins, W. A., 387
Compas, Bruce, 364
Conezio, J., 266
Conger, J. J., 392, 395
Conner, R., 707
Conrad, R., 265
Cooper, J., 688, 691
Cooper, L. A., 265
Cordua, G. D., 387
Coren, S., 127, 138
Cornblatt, B. A., 624
Cornell, K. R., 698
Cornes, C., 615, 668
Cortelli, P., 81
Coryell, W. A., 597, 609

Costa, P. T., 402, 408, 413, 439
Costa, P. T., Jr., 571
Costello, C. G., 598, 615
Coté, T. R., 579
Coulter, W. A., 480
Council, J. R., 443
Cowan, N., 258
Cowan, W. M., 55
Cox, R. H., 756
Coyle, J. T., 614
Coyne, J. C., 556, 566
Cozby, P. C., 322, 445
Crace, R. K., 757
Crago, M., 668
Craig, H. M., 570
Craik, F. I. M., 257, 271, 272, 285
Cramer, R. E., 707
Crawford, M., 88, 646
Creekmore, C. R., 750, 758
Crews, D. J., 564
Crino, M. D., 740
Crockett, L. J., 395
Cromwell, R. L., 624
Cronshaw, S. F., 728
Crotle, R. T., 691
Crow, T. J., 622
Crowder, R. G., 258
Csikzentmihalyi, M., 403
Cunningham, S., 708
Curran, J., 576
Curtis, R. C., 696
Cushner, K., 229
Cutler, W. B., 151

Dahlstrom, W. D., 571
Dahlstrom, W. G., 446
Dallas, M., 172
Dallenbach, K. M., 297, 298
Daniel, T. C., 752
Danks, J. H., 337
Dann, R., 626
Dantzic, S., 512
Darby, B. L., 362
Dare, C., 656
Darley, J. M., 379, 382, 515, 707–710
Darling, C. A., 400
Darrow, C. M., 408
Darwin, C., 11, 13, 14, 44, 537, 538
Darwin, C. T., 258
Dasen, P. R., 378
Datan, N., 402
Datera-Wadleigh, S., 616
David, G. G., 362
Davidoff, J. B., 138
Davidson, J. K., 400
Davies, M., 600
Davila, G. H., 392
Davis, J. H., 714
Davis, J. M., 699
Davis, K., 699
Davis, L. E., 738

Davis, M., 602
Davis, R., 511
Davis, R. M., 574
Davis, W., 392
Dean, R. L., 275
DeAngelis, T., 189
De Boer, C., 738
DeBono, K. G., 690
DeCaria, C. M., 600
DeCasper, A. J., 369, 370
Decker, S., 563
de Cuevas, J., 323
Deffenbacher, J. L., 669
DeGroot, A. D., 291
DeJarlais, D. C., 578
Delaney, H. D., 289
DeLoach, J., 368
DeLong, M. H., 614
DeLongis, A., 556
Dembroski, T. M., 571
Dement, W. C., 173, 179, 180
DeMyer, M. K., 611
Depinet, R. L., 458
Deregowski, J. B., 133
de Ribaupierre, A., 378
Derlaga, V. J., 699
Descartes, R., 10, 44
Després, J., 508
Deutch, A. Y., 602
Deutsch, G., 85
Deutsch, J. A., 275
de Villers, J. G., 325
de Villers, P. A., 325
Devins, G. M., 578
Devlin, M. J., 512
Dewhirst, B., 185
Diacoyanni-Tarlatzis, I., 539
Diamond, M., 523
Diamond, M. C., 275
Diepold, J. H., 384
Digman, J. M., 439, 440, 443
DiMatteo, M. R., 579
Dion, K. K., 698
Dipboye, R. L., 740
Dirkes, K., 362
Dirkes, M. A., 342
Dixon, N. F., 171, 172
Dobbins, G. H., 729
Dobkin de Rois, M., 194
Dobson, K. S., 663
Dodds, J. B., 368
Doherty, S., 23
Doll, R., 574
Dollard, J., 434, 441, 484, 566
Dominowski, R. L., 309, 332
Domjan, M., 218, 221, 247
Donneberg, G. R., 382
Doob, L., 566
Doty, R. Y., 151
Doweiko, H. E., 189, 190, 193, 196
Downey, G., 566

Downing, R., 645
Doyle, A. B., 386
Drabman, R. S., 387
Dragna, M., 707
Drakeley, R. J., 727
Dubas, J. S., 395
DuBreuil, S. C., 185
Duffy, E., 501
Duke, P. M., 395
Dumais, S. T., 127, 369
Duncan, E. M., 615
Duncan, J., 171
Duncker, K., 307, 337, 339
Dunham, R. B., 741
Dunn, R. L., 648, 649
Dunnett, S. B., 80
Dunnette, M. D., 727
Dweck, C. S., 514
Dworkin, R. H., 622
Dyer, J., 622
Dyken, M. E., 178
Dykens, E., 481
Dywan, J., 185

Eagle, M., 511
Eagly, A. H., 445, 681
Eaker, E. D., 572
Earles, J. A., 458, 729
Early, C., 711
Early, P. C., 381, 730, 736
Eaton, W. O., 384
Eaves, L. J., 616
Ebata, A. T., 391, 392
Ebbinghaus, H. E., 280, 294
Eccles, J., 385
Eckert, E. D., 512
Edelman, G., 53
Edler, N. S., 444
Edwards, A. L., 451
Edwards, C. P., 381, 445
Edwards, L. K., 451
Edwards, R. W., 192
Edwards, S., 537
Egeland, J. A., 616
Egeth, H. E., 269, 271
Eich, J. E., 284
Eisen, S. A., 602
Eisenberg, M., 389
Ekman, P., 532, 539, 540
Ellicott, A. M., 402
Ellinboe, J., 192
Elliot, R., 669
Ellis, A., 663, 664
Ellis, H. D., 269
Ellis, L., 524
Ellsworth, P. C., 270
Elman, M., 386
Emery, G., 596
Empson, J. A. C., 177
Emr, M., 613
Endsley, R. C., 387
Enns, L. R., 384
Epstein, L. H., 580
Epstein, S., 443
Erdelyi, M. H., 170, 268

Erez, M., 381, 730, 736
Ericsson, K. A., 264
Erikson, E. H., 370, 382–384, 396, 397, 402, 403, 405, 409, 418–420
Erlenmeyer-Kimling, L., 624
Ervin, F. R., 221
Erwin, E., 668
Erwin, F. W., 727
Eskenazi, J., 171
Esveldt-Dawson, K., 668
Etaugh, C., 389
Evans, G. W., 745
Evans, M., 525
Evans, R. I., 574
Eveleth, P., 394
Everett, P. B., 573
Eysenck, H. J., 445, 502, 609, 668
Eysenck, S., 502

Fackelman, K. A., 613
Fagan, J. F., 386
Fahn, S., 80
Fairbank, J. A., 602
Fairburn, C. G., 512
Falbo, T., 515
Farh, J. L., 729
Farrell, M. P., 408
Fassinger, R. E., 667
Fast, J., 539
Fazio, R. H., 515, 681, 683
Feather, N. T., 514
Fechner, G., 11–12, 44
Federoff, I. C., 511
Feeney, J. A., 695
Fein, G. G., 753
Feinglos, M. N., 580
Feist, S. C., 666
Fenker, R. M., 758
Fennema, E., 35, 470, 471
Fenton, W. S., 623
Ferris, G. R., 738
Festinger, L., 502, 503, 542, 686, 687, 691, 697
Fielding, J. E., 573
Fields, H. L., 156
Fifer, W. P., 369, 370
Finnegan, L. P., 362
Fiore, M. C., 574
Fischer, L. B., 189
Fischhoff, B., 752
Fishbein, M., 683
Fisher, A. C., 756
Fishhoff, B., 392
Fishman, H. C., 666
Fishman, J., 570
Fitzgerald, L., 22
Flagg, P. W., 333
Flament, M. F., 600, 601
Flaum, M., 625
Flavell, E. R., 378
Flavell, J. H., 378
Fleishman, E. A., 725

Flexser, A. J., 282
Flynn, J. P., 537
Foege, W. H., 573
Folkman, S., 555, 556, 563
Folstein, S. E., 610, 611
Foote, W., 537
Ford, C. E., 502
Ford, M. R., 381
Fosterling, F., 440
Fothergill, L. A., 155
Foutz, A. S., 180
Fowler, C. A., 172
Fowler, R. D., 17
Fowles, D. G., 410
Fox, A. C., 178
Fox, R., 369
Foxx, R. M., 754
Frank, E., 615, 667, 668
Frank, M. A., 565
Frankenburg, W. K., 368
Frazier, T. M., 362
Fredrickson, P. A., 180
Free, M. L., 668
Freed, C. R., 80
Freedman, D. X., 595
Freedman, J. L., 749, 750
Freeman, A., 665
Freeman, R. K., 363
Freeman, W., 640
Freimer, N. F., 616
French, N. H., 668
Freud, A., 382, 392
Freud, S., 16, 45, 168–170, 177, 197, 382, 425–427, 429–433, 435, 441, 454, 483, 484, 604—605, 653–657, 673
Frey, J., 752
Fribourg, S., 362
Fried, P. A., 362
Friedman, H. S., 570, 579
Friedman, L. N., 751
Friedman, M., 570
Friedman, M. I., 508, 509
Friedman, S. R., 578
Friesen, W. V., 539, 540
Frijda, N. H., 530, 532
Frodi, A. M., 388
Frodi, M., 388
Fulker, D. W., 445
Funder, D. C., 443
Furstenberg, F. F., 400
Furumoto, L., 14

Gabora, N. J., 185
Gabrena, W., 711
Gage, P., 66
Gagné, R. M., 332
Gaines, J. G., 564
Galanter, E., 99
Gale, M. E., 570
Gallagher, J. J., 357
Galton, F., 452
Gambetti, P., 81
Ganchow, J. R., 370

Gans, J. E., 398
Garbarino, J., 392
Garber, D. M., 511
Garcia, J., 221
Gardner, R., 179
Garfield, S. L., 656
Gargano, G. M., 711
Garner, D. M., 570
Gaugler, B. B., 729
Gazzaniga, M. S., 86
Gebhard, P. H., 520, 522
Geis, G., 707
Geisler, S., 620, 644
Gejman, P. V., 616
Gelernter, J., 616
Geller, E. S., 573, 736, 754
Gellhorn, E., 539
Gelman, D., 23
Gelman, R., 378
Gelman, S. A., 372, 378
Gelso, C. J., 667
Gemberling, G. A., 221
Genovese, K., 679, 706–707, 709
George, J. M., 555
Geracioti, T. D., 512
Gerbert, B., 578
Gerhard, D. S., 616
Gerow, J. R., 27
Gershon, E. S., 616
Ghesquire, K., 388
Gibson, D. R., 578
Gibson, E. J., 368, 369
Gibson, W. M., 727, 728, 730
Gier, J. A., 729
Gill, M. J., 578
Gillam, B., 137, 138
Gilligan, C., 381, 384
Gilligan, S. G., 284
Gillin, J. C., 180
Gilovich, T., 757
Girgus, J. S., 138
Gladis, M., 512
Glaser, R., 343–345
Glasgow, R. E., 574
Glass, A. L., 343
Glass, D. C., 570, 751, 752
Glass, G. V., 668
Gleitman, H., 368
Glenn, N. D., 403
Glucksberg, S., 337
Glunt, E. K., 579
Gobel, D., 610
Golbus, M. S., 362
Gold, P. E., 284
Goldberg, B., 268
Goldberg, I. D., 362
Goldberg, J., 602
Goldberg, J. F., 616
Goldberg, L. R., 439
Goldbloom, D., 511
Golden, L. R., 616
Goldfried, M. R., 666–668
Goldstein, H., 362

Goldstein, I. L., 730, 731
Goldstein, S. G., 525
Goleman, O., 478
Gonzales, M. H., 699
Gooden, D., 284
Goodman, P., 658
Goodnow, J. J., 314
Goodrich, S., 609
Goodwin, D. W., 284
Gordon, C. T., 610, 611
Gordon, N. C., 156
Gordon, W., 378
Gorenstein, E. E., 593
Gormezano, I., 221
Gotlib, I. H., 615
Gottesman, I. I., 623, 625, 626
Gottlieb, B. H., 566
Gottlieb, G., 356
Gough, H. G., 728
Gould, J., 610
Gould, R., 728
Govoni, L. E., 363
Gowing, M. K., 730
Gracely, R. H., 156
Grady, C. L., 601
Grady, W. R., 523, 578
Graf, P., 280, 281
Graham, P., 392
Grant, D. L., 729
Grayson, S., 679
Graziano, A. M., 6
Greden, J. F., 624
Green, D. M., 101
Greenberg, J., 695
Greenberg, L. S., 530, 532, 666–668
Greenberg, S., 648
Greene, B. F., 754
Greenfield, S. F., 195
Greeno, J. G., 3444
Greenough, W. T., 275
Greenwald, A. G., 168, 170, 171
Greer, S., 609
Gregory, R. L., 134, 138, 139
Gregory, W. L., 754
Grice, G. R., 235
Grigsby, D. W., 740
Grinspoon, L., 196
Gritz, E. R., 574
Grob, C., 194
Gross, L. P., 509
Gross, R. J., 395
Grossman, H. J., 479
Grossman, L. S., 616
Grove, W. M., 626
Groves, P. M., 61
Gruenberg, A. M., 609
Grunberg, N. E., 558, 573
Grusec, J. E., 236
Gudeman, J. E., 648
Guenberg, E., 217
Guilford, J. P., 342, 437,

459, 460, 487
Guion, R. M., 727, 728, 730
Gullo, D. F., 384, 386
Gullotta, T., 393
Gully, R., 600
Gunnar, M. R., 387
Gur, R. C., 626
Gur, R. E., 626
Gurman, A. S., 666
Guroff, J. J., 607
Gust, S. M., 189
Guthrie, J. F., 511
Guzzo, R. A., 730
Gwiazda, J., 369

Ha, Y-W., 340
Haber, R. N., 266
Hadigan, C. M., 512
Hagen, E. P., 462, 463
Hager, R., 527
Hahn, G. L., 578
Hahn, W., 570
Haist, F., 279
Hake, D. F., 754
Halberstadt, A. G., 445
Hall, E., 745–746
Hall, G., 220
Hall, G. S., 392
Hall, J. A., 445
Hall, J. F., 235
Hall, W. G., 357, 368
Halperin, J., 580
Halpern, D. F., 470
Halton, A., 363
Ham, M., 392
Hamburg, D. A., 394
Hamburger, S. D., 600, 610, 611
Hamer, D. H., 523
Hammen, C., 616
Hammer, L. D., 597
Hancock, E., 402
Hanis, C., 508
Hansen, W. B., 578
Hardesty, J. P., 626
Harding, C. M., 621
Hardy, C. J., 757
Hare, R. D., 609
Harkins, S., 711, 712
Harlow, H. F., 387, 389, 510
Harnish, R. J., 690
Harold, R. D., 385
Harrington, D. M., 341
Harris, B., 215, 216
Harris, D. V., 757
Harris, J. R., 509
Harris, L., 411
Harris, L. J., 471
Harris, M. M., 728
Harris, P. L., 378, 409
Harris, R. J., 284
Harris, R. L., 402
Harrow, M., 616, 619, 620
Hartley, A. A., 412
Hartman, S., 740

Hartup, W. W., 387
Haruki, T., 248
Harvey, J. H., 693
Hasher, L., 272, 291
Hassman, H., 645
Hastie, R., 339
Hastorf, A. H., 106
Hatfield, E., 698
Hatsukami, D. K., 512
Hatzlandreu, E. J., 574
Hauser, D. L., 613
Hauser, S. T., 392
Havighurst, R. J., 408
Hayduk, L. A., 745
Hayes, C. D., 344, 401
Hayes, J. E., 363
Hayman, C. A. G., 279
Haynes, S. G., 411
Haythornwaite, J., 502
Hayward, C., 597
Hazan, C., 695
Heath, A. C., 602, 616
Hebb, D. O., 501, 503
Hefferline, R. F., 658
Heffernan, J. A., 43, 573
Heidbreder, E., 312–315
Heinrichs, R. W., 620, 626
Held, R., 369
Hellige, J. B., 86
Helmholz, H. von, 12, 44, 121, 122, 159
Helms, D., 406
Helms, J. E., 458, 474
Helzer, J. E., 217, 602
Henderson, C., 369
Hendrick, C., 445
Henley, M. G., 4
Hennessy, J., 389
Herek, G. M., 579
Hering, E., 122, 159
Heron, A., 378
Herriot, P., 727
Herskovits, M. J., 139
Hertz, R. M., 665
Herzog, H. A., 4
Heshka, S., 745
Hetherington, E. M., 611
Hiatt, J. J., 369
Higgins, E. T., 681, 713
Hilgard, E. R., 168, 182–184
Hilgard, J. R., 182–184
Hill, E. M., 609
Hill, W. F., 565
Hinrichs, J. R., 729, 730
Hinsz, V., 714
Hippocrates, 637
Hobfoll, S. E., 550, 557, 566
Hobson, J. A., 176, 177
Hodapp, R. M., 481, 482
Hofferth, S. L., 401
Hoffman, D. D., 138
Hoffman, L. W., 382
Hogan, J., 564
Hogan, R., 437
Hoine, H., 284

Holden, C., 479
Holden, G. W., 192
Holder, A., 656
Hollander, E., 600
Holman, B. L., 70
Holmes, D. S., 186–187, 403, 565, 611
Holmes, T. H., 555
Holmes, T. S., 555, 556
Holyoak, K. J., 170, 343
Holz, W. C., 236
Honzik, C. H., 242, 243
Hood, H. V., 578
Hood, R. D., 364
Hope, R. A., 512
Hoppock, R., 739
Hörmann, H., 310
Horn, J. L., 341, 473, 478
Horne, J. A., 179
Horner, M., 514
Horney, K., 432–433, 484
Horowitz, F. D., 478
Hoshmand, T. L., 7
Hostetler, A. J., 613
Hostetter, A. M., 616
Hotstadter, L., 618, 620
Hough, R. L., 602
Houser, B. B., 406
Housman, D. E., 616
Houston, B. K., 571
Houston, J., 279
Houston, L., 88
Hovland, C. I., 690
Howard, D. V., 320
Howard, K. I., 667
Howard, R. B., 745
Howe, M. A., 758
Howell, W. C., 740
Howes, C., 389
Hrynick, T., 368
Hsia, J., 474
Hsu, L. K. G., 512
Hu, N., 523
Hu, S., 523
Hubel, D. H., 52, 68
Hudson, J. I., 512
Hudson, W., 133
Huff, C., 578
Huggins, G. R., 151
Hughes, F., 402
Hughes, F. P., 362
Hughes, J., 155
Hughes, J. R., 189
Hugick, L., 574
Hui, C. H., 381
Hui, C. P., 738
Hulin, C. L., 738
Hull, C., 496, 499
Hulsey, M. G., 510
Humfleet, G., 578
Hunsley, J., 578
Hunt, M., 651
Hunter, J. E., 729, 730
Hunter, R. F., 730
Hunter, S., 408

Huston, A. C., 445
Huston, T. L., 707
Hwang, C. P., 388
Hyde, J. S., 35, 384, 445, 470, 471, 525, 526

Iacono, W. G., 626
Iaffaldano, M. T., 740
Ilgen, D. R., 735
Incontro, C. R., 515
Insko, C. A., 684
Irvine, J., 570
Isenberg, D. J., 714
Iso-Ahola, S. E., 757
Istvan, J., 363
Izard, C., 531

Jackaway, R., 514
Jacklin, C., 385, 386, 445, 470, 471
Jackson, D. N., 440
Jacobs, B. L., 194
Jacobson, D. S., 362
Jacobson, J. L., 753
Jacobson, S. W., 753
Jacoby, L. L., 172
Jagielo, J. A., 218, 219, 283
James, M. R., 515
James, W., 13–14, 17, 44, 166, 167, 197, 495
Janes, H. R., 578
Janis, I. L., 566, 714
Jankiewicz, H., 60, 180
Janoff-Bulman, R., 693
Jarrett, D. B., 615, 668
Jarvik, L. F., 473
Jefferson, T., 436
Jeffery, R. W., 573
Jenkins, C. D., 570
Jenkins, J. G., 297
Jenkins, J. M., 532, 539
Jensen, A. R., 474, 475
Jessor, R., 392
Jody, D., 620
Jody, J., 644
Joffee, J. M., 364
John, O. P., 439
Johnson, C. A., 574
Johnson, D. E., 693
Johnson, D. L., 626
Johnson, E. H., 314
Johnson, E. J., 339
Johnson, F., 525
Johnson, J., 597
Johnson, L., 398
Johnson, M. G., 4
Johnson, M. K., 272, 291, 300
Johnson, S., 648
Johnson, T. R., 731, 734
Johnson, V., 523, 525–527, 578
Jonas, J. M., 512
Jones, A., 727
Jones, B. A., 572

Jones, E. E., 693, 694
Jones, E. M., 4
Jones, K. L., 362
Jones, M. C., 395
Jones, R., 512
Jordan, B. K., 602
Joseph, N., 23
Joyce, P. R., 642, 645
Judd, C. M., 681
Julien, R. M., 189, 190, 196
Jung, C., 432, 484
Junghans, C. M., 699

Kacmar, K. M., 738
Kagan, J., 389, 437
Kahle, L. R., 593
Kahn, L., 384
Kahn, R. L., 412, 555
Kahn, S., 403
Kahneman, D., 339
Kalat, J. W., 643
Kale, A. R., 698
Kales, A., 180
Kales, J. D., 180
Kalikow, K., 600
Kalish, R. A., 411, 413
Kalleberg, A. L., 738
Kallio, K. D., 310
Kalsher, M. J., 573, 736
Kaltman, A. J., 178
Kamin, L., 219, 220, 242
Kamiya, J., 564
Kandel, E. R., 275
Kanfer, R., 729
Kanizsa, G., 127
Kanner, A. D., 556
Kanner, L., 610
Kantner, J. F., 401
Kaplan, G. M., 565
Kaplan, H. S., 525–527, 654
Kaplan, R. M., 447, 569
Kaplan, S., 752
Karlen, A., 523
Karoum, F., 624
Karp, L. E., 363
Karson, C. N., 624
Kassin, S. M., 270
Kastenbaum, R., 413
Katzell, R. A., 730, 737
Katzman, R., 612
Kauth, M. R., 578
Kay, S. R., 622, 623
Kazdin, A. E., 668
Keating, D. P., 396
Keele, S. W., 315
Keesey, R. E., 508
Keita, G. P., 615, 618, 649
Keith, P. M., 406
Kellams, J. J., 642
Kelley, H. H., 692, 695
Kelley, K., 520
Kelly, J. A., 577, 578, 579
Kempler, D., 86
Kendler, K. S., 609, 616

Kendrick, D. T., 443
Kermis, M. D., 410
Kershner, J. R., 341, 478
Kessler, R. C., 555, 588, 595, 596, 616
Kessler, S., 623
Kestenbaum, R., 368
Kett, J. F., 391
Key, M. R., 322, 445
Kidd, K. K., 616
Kientzle, M. J., 295
Kiester, E., 758
Kiester, E., Jr., 176
Kihlstrom, J. F., 168, 185
Kilcullen, R. C., 727
Kilgore, H. G., 578
Killian, J. D., 597
Kilner, L. A., 392
Kilys, C., 601
Kim, J. J., 218, 275
Kimball, M. M., 471
Kimble, G. A., 8, 36–37, 39, 229
Kimmel, D. C., 410
Kimmel, H. D., 565
King, M., 738
King, M. J., 178
Kinsbourne, M., 85
Kinsey, A. C., 520, 522
Kirby, V. A., 178
Kirkpatrick, D. L., 734
Kirscht, J. P., 572
Kissileff, H. R., 512
Klapper, M. H., 642
Klayman, J., 340
Klebanoff, M., 363
Klein, E. B., 408
Klein, H. J., 735
Kleinman, A., 649
Kleitman, N., 176
Klepinger, D. H., 523, 578
Klerman, G. L., 597, 615, 668
Klinger, M. R., 170, 172
Knapp, S., 579
Knight, P. A., 729, 740
Kniskern, D. P., 666
Knittle, J. L., 508
Knowles, E. S., 702
Knowlton, B., 257, 265, 279
Kobasa, S. C., 559
Kocel, K. M., 88
Kochansky, G., 648
Koelling, R. A., 221
Koestler, A., 343
Kofoed, L., 609
Kohlberg, L., 370, 379–381, 384, 417
Köhler, S. S., 725, 728, 729
Köhler, W., 307, 330
Kolata, G., 369
Kolb, B., 52, 54, 357
Kolodny, R. C., 526, 578
Kontis, T. C., 282

Koonenberg, P. M., 388
Koop, C. E., 189
Kopata, S. M., 667
Korchin, S. J., 452
Kositcheck, R., 570
Koslow, D. R., 651
Koss, M. P., 656
Kosslyn, S. M., 87
Kosterlitz, H. W., 155
Kotelchuck, M., 389
Kovacic, C. R., 756
Kraepelin, E., 590, 591, 622
Krantz, D. S., 570, 573
Krause, M. S., 667
Krause, R., 539
Krieger, A., 151
Kripke, D. F., 180
Krueger, J. M., 178
Krueger, W. C. F., 294
Krupat, E., 750
Krystal, J. H., 602
Kübler-Ross, E., 412, 413
Kuiper, N. A., 564
Kulik, J., 284
Kulka, R. A., 602
Kunst-Wilson, W. R., 698
Kupfer, D. J., 615, 667, 668

Laborit, Henri, 643
Labov, W., 309
LaBree, L. D., 613
Ladd-Franklin, C., 14
Lafferty, P., 668
Laird, J., 540
Laird, J. M. A., 156
Lakoff, R., 322
Lamb, M. E., 388, 389
Lambiotte, J. C., 758
Lamon, M., 540
Lamon, S. J., 35, 470, 471
Lampman-Petraitis, R., 392
Landers, D. M., 565, 757
Landers, S., 401
Landesman, S., 479, 480, 482
Landis, D., 524
Landy, F. J., 725, 728, 741
Lang, P. J., 530
Langer, S., 316
Langlois, J. H., 698
Lapidus, L. B., 134
Larsen, R. M., 451, 465
Larson, R., 392
Lasky, R. E., 310
Latané, B., 707–712
Latham, G. P., 731, 732, 736, 739
Lattal. K. A., 15
Lauer, J., 405
Lauer, R., 405
Lavond, D. G., 218, 275
Lawler, E. E., 738
Lawley, H. J., 151
Lawson, W. B., 624
Lazarus, R. S., 530, 532,

533, 556, 558, 563
Lazerson, A., 618, 620
Leahy, T. H., 284
Leckman, J., 481
Ledger, G., 341, 478
LeDoux, J. E., 86
Lee, S. Y., 474, 476
Lefebvre, R., 564
Leger, D. W., 746
Lehman, G. R., 573, 736, 754
Lehrer, P. M., 564
Leibowitz, H. W., 135
Lempers, J. D., 378
Lenane, M., 599, 600
Lenneberg, E. H., 323, 326
Lenzenweger, M. F., 622, 623
Leon, G. R., 510
Leonard, H. L., 599, 600
Leonard, J., 363, 574
Lerer, B., 616
Lerner, M. J., 693
Lerner, R. M., 356
Leupker, R. F., 574
LeVay, S., 524
Levenson, R. W., 540
Leventhal, H., 574
Levin, J. R., 289
Levine, H. Z., 742
Levine, J. D., 156
Levine, J. M., 713, 714
Levine, M., 572, 578, 648, 649
Levine, M. F., 738
Levine, M. M., 504
Levine, M. W., 97
Levinson, D. J., 402, 403, 406, 408
Levinson, M. H., 408
Levinthal, C. F., 506, 536
Lewinsohn, P. M., 615
Lewis, M., 413
Ley, B., 363
Ley, B. W., 192
Lichtenstein, E., 574
Liddle, R. A., 512
Lidz, T., 626
Lieberman, J., 620
Lieberman, M. A., 566
Lightman, S. W., 510
Lin, E., 649
Lin, T. R., 729
Lincoln, J. R., 738
Linder, D., 697
Lindsley, D. B., 78
Links, P. S., 588
Linn, M. C., 471
Linnoila, M., 601
Lippa, A. S., 275
Lipsey, M. W., 668, 669
Lish, R., 597
Litt, I. F., 597
Litt, M. D., 156
Litwin, G. H., 513

Lloyd-Bostock, S., 268
Locke, E., 736, 737, 760
Locke, J., 10, 11, 40, 44, 311
Lockhard, J. S., 170
Lockhart, R. S., 257, 271
Lockyer, M. L., 610
Loebel, A., 620, 644
Loftus, E. F., 170, 172, 257, 267, 268, 269, 273, 309, 332
Loftus, G., 267
Logan, A. G., 570
Lohr, N. E., 609
Londerville, S., 388
Loney, G. L., 699
Lonner, W. J., 749
Lord, C. G., 291
Lorenz, K., 746
Lott, A. J., 695
Lott, B. E., 695
Lovaas, O. I., 611
Lowell, E. L., 513
Lowery, C. R., 381
Lowry, D. H., 289, 290
Lozoff, B., 361
Lubin, B., 451, 465
Lucas, E. A., 180
Lugaresi, A., 81
Lugaresi, E., 81
Luh, C. W., 279
Lukens, C. K., 699
Lukoff, D., 626
Luons, J., 578
Lykken, D. T., 39, 609
Lynch, G., 276
Lynch, S., 156
Lyness, S., 571
Lynn, D., 388
Lynn, R., 474, 476
Lynn, S. J., 182, 183
Lyons, M. J., 602
Lytton, H., 384

McAdoo, W. G., 611
McCann, I. L., 403, 565
McCarley, R. W., 177
McCarthy, B. W., 525
McCartney, K., 389
McCauley, C., 471
McClearn, G. E., 509
McClelland, D. C., 458, 513–515, 729
McClintock, M. K., 151
McCloskey, M., 267, 269, 284
Maccoby, Eleanor, 385, 386, 445, 470
McCrae, R. R., 402, 408, 439, 555
MacDonald, M. R., 564
McDonald, W. T., 299
McDougall, W., 496
Mace, N. L., 613
McEnvoy, L., 602

McEvoy, G. M., 730
McFarland, C., 709
McGee, M. G., 471
McGeoch, J. A., 299
McGinnis, J. M., 573
McGlashan, T. H., 623
McGlone, J., 88
McGonagle, K. A., 588, 595, 596
McGrath, E., 615, 618, 649
McGraw, K. O., 357, 387
MacGregor, S., 362
McGue, M., 39
McGuire, W. J., 681
McIver, S. D., 648, 649
McKee, B., 408
Mackenzie, B., 475
McKim, W. A., 189, 191, 196
Mackintosh, N. J., 221, 470, 475
Mackowiak, P. A., 504
McLaughlin, S. D., 731, 734
McLeod, J. D., 555
MacLeod, M. D., 269
McMaster, M. R., 707
McMichael, A. J., 411
McMillan, C. J., 738
MacMillan, J., 609
McNaughton, B. L., 275
McNeil, D., 326
McNellis, D., 363
Maddi, S. R., 559
Madigan, S., 14
Magder, L., 570
Magnuson, V. L., 523
Magnusson, D., 444
Magoun, H. W., 78
Magovern, G. J., 564
Magsud, M., 381
Maguire, B., 578
Maguire, J., 192
Maharishi Yogi, 185
Mahoney, M. J., 755, 756, 758
Mahowald, M. W., 178
Maier, N. R. F., 337, 338
Main, M., 388
Mair, A., 751
Mandler, G., 279, 281
Manning, M. L., 392
Marengo, J. T., 619
Mark, A. L., 178
Markowitz, J. S., 597
Marks, I. M., 217
Markus, H., 683
Marmar, C., 666–668
Marmar, C. R., 602
Marschark, M., 288
Marshall, N. L., 559
Marshall-Goodell, B. S., 683
Martin, B. J., 179
Martin, C. E., 520, 522

Martin, C. L., 387
Martin, G. B., 369
Martin, L., 135
Martin, R. J., 510
Martindale, C., 265
Marx, J., 614
Marziali, E., 668
Maslow, A., 16–17, 45, 436, 484, 498, 499, 542, 737
Massaro, D. W., 258
Masters, W., 523, 525–527, 578
Matarazzo, J. D., 43, 451, 464, 465, 572
Matlin, M. W., 751
Matsumoto, D., 540
Matt, D. A., 564
Matthews, K. A., 564, 570
Matthies, H., 275
Maxman, J. S., 645
Maxwell, S. E., 574
Mayer, D. J., 61
Mayer, R. A., 290
Mayo, E., 739
Medin, D. L., 309, 315
Mednick, M. T. S., 382, 514
Mednick, S. A., 609, 622
Medori, R., 81
Meer, J., 410
Meichenbaum, D., 563, 579
Melhuish, E. C., 389
Mellers, B. A., 698
Mellstrom, B., 601
Meltzer, H. Y., 616
Melzack, R., 154, 156
Menary, E., 185
Mendel, G., 355
Mendelson, J. H., 192
Meredith, N., 650
Meredith, W., 473
Merikle, P. M., 172
Mervis, J., 669
Messick, D. M., 712
Metcalfe, J., 343
Meyer, D. E., 343
Michael, J. A., 229
Michela, J. L., 692
Middlemist, R. D., 736
Middlestadt, S. E., 728
Milgram, S., 703–706, 718, 750
Miller, D. G., 269
Miller, D. T., 693, 709
Miller, G., 263
Miller, H. E., 728
Miller, J. G., 442, 693
Miller, J. S., 218, 219, 283
Miller, K., 192, 696
Miller, M. J., 642
Miller, N. E., 43, 434, 441, 484, 564–566, 572
Miller, R. C., 668
Miller, R. R., 220
Miller, T. I., 668
Miller, W. R., 188

Millstein, S. G., 398, 401
Milstein, V., 642
Minami, H., 298
Minuchin, S., 666
Mirin, S. M., 195
Mischel, W., 443, 444
Mitchell, J. E., 512
Mittlemark, M. B., 574
Mittler, M. M., 180
Mobley, W. H., 740
Moffitt, T. E., 609
Moller, J., 574
Mollnow, E., 362
Moncher, M. S., 192
Money, J., 386, 521–524
Moniz, E., 639
Monson, T. C., 694
Montagna, P., 81
Monteiro, K. P., 284
Moon, C., 370
Moore, K. L., 357, 360, 361, 401
Moorecroft, W. H., 179
Morales, F. R., 178
Moran, J. S., 578
Moreland, R. L., 714
Morgan, G., 388
Morgan, G. A., 155
Morgan, W. P., 756
Mori, D., 511
Morris, C. W., 316
Morris, H. R., 155
Morris, L. A., 580
Morris, R. G. M., 275
Morrison, D. M., 401
Morrow, H. W., 480
Moruzzi, G., 78, 81
Moscovici, S., 702, 714
Mountjoy, C. Q., 613
Mowday, R. T., 736
Mowrer, O. H., 566
Mshelia, A. Y., 134
Muchinsky, P. M., 727, 740
Mueser, K. T., 648
Mugny, G., 702, 714
Mulac, A., 515
Mumford, M. D., 725, 727
Munn, N. L., 423
Murdock, B. B., 257
Murnen, S., 699
Murphy, D. A., 577, 578
Murphy, D. L., 502
Murphy, D. P., 27
Murray, D. J., 636
Murray, D. M., 574
Murray, H., 454, 513
Murray, M. A., 738
Mussen, G., 257, 265, 279

Naftolin, F., 80
Nakamura, G. V., 292
Nakazima, S., 323
Nash, M., 185
Neale, J. M., 623
Neale, M. C., 445, 616

Nedate, K., 248
Neisser, U., 284
Nelson, C. P., 588, 595, 596
Nelson, J. E., 610, 611
Nelson, J. M., 196
Nelson, K., 275
Nelson, Y., 745
Nemeth, C., 702
Nettleton, N. C., 87
Neubauer, P. J., 559
Neugarten, B. L., 409, 411, 412
Neugarten, D. A., 409, 411, 412
Newby, R. W., 282
Newcomb, M. B., 398
Newcomb, M. D., 406
Newcomb, N., 395
Newell, A., 334, 341, 344
Newman, B. M., 403
Newman, P. R., 403
Nezler, J., 698
Nias, D. K. B., 445
Nichols, I. A., 323
Nicholson, R. A., 437
Nickerson, R. S., 282
Nida, S. A., 698, 708, 711
Nimmer, J. G., 736, 754
Nisan, M., 381
Nisbett, R. E., 508, 694
Nitescu, A., 600
Noble, E. P., 284
Noller, P., 695
Noppe, L. D., 362
Norcross, J. C., 651
Norman, D. A., 257
Norman, G. R., 292
Norvis, M., 570
Novotny, T. E., 574
Nowak, J., 602
Noyes, R., 597
Nuechterlein, K. H., 626

Oatley, K., 532, 539
Obal, F., 178
O'Brien, M., 478
O'Conner, M., 512
Oden, M. H., 309, 310, 478
Oei, T. P. S., 668
Oetting, E. R., 192, 398
Offer, D., 392
Offer, J., 392
Offermann, L. R., 730
Offord, D. R., 588
Ogata, S. N., 609
Ogawa, R., 248
Ogilvie, B. C., 758
O'Hara, R., 14
Okasaki, S., 474, 476
Oller, D. K., 323
Olmsted, M. P., 511
Olson, J. M., 681, 686
Olton, D., 242, 244, 248
Ones, D. S., 729
Opalic, P., 666

Oppenheim, R. W., 357, 368
Orlinsky, D. E., 667
Orne, M., 184
Ortony, A., 532, 534
Orvaschel, H., 217
Ostrow, T. M., 688
O'Sullivan, M., 539
Ouellete, R., 597
Owens, J. F., 564
Owens, W. A., 727
Oxley, D., 744

Packard, B., 572
Paivio, A., 288
Palfai, T., 60, 180
Paludi, M. A., 384, 386
Pandey, J., 745
Park, B., 339, 681
Park, D. C., 410
Parke, R. D., 389, 611
Parker, E. S., 284
Parnas, J., 622
Patel, K. M., 574
Pattatucci, A. M. L., 523
Pauls, D. L., 616
Paulus, D. L., 170
Pauly, I. B., 525
Paunonen, S. P., 440
Pavlov, I., 206–209, 219, 220, 250
Pavlovich, M., 754
Paykel, E. S., 642, 645
Payne, J. W., 339
Peabody, D., 439
Peake, P. K., 443
Pearce, J. M., 220
Pearson, J., 751
Pearson, J. C., 322
Pechacek, T. F., 189
Pederson, D. R., 388
Pederson, N. L., 509
Peele, S., 189
Pelletier, L. G., 757
Pelliccioni, L., Jr., 758
Penfield, W., 67
Peplau, L. A., 515
Perel, J. M., 615, 667, 668
Perkins, A., 556
Perkins, D. V., 572, 578, 648, 649
Perls, F., 658, 673
Pestone, M., 510
Peterman, T. A., 578
Peterson, A. C., 391, 392, 395, 396, 471
Peterson, L. R., 261, 262
Peterson, M. J., 261, 262
Peterson, R. B., 736
Peto, R., 574
Petty, R. E., 682, 683, 688–690, 711, 712
Peveler, R. C., 512
Pfau, M., 690
Pfohl, B., 597
Phair, J., 578

Phares, V., 364
Phenow, K. J., 573
Phillips, D., 389
Piaget, J., 370, 372, 373, 375–379, 382, 384, 396, 416, 417
Pichert, J. W., 292
Pickar, D., 622
Pierce, J. P., 574
Pillard, R. C., 523
Pillemer, D. B., 275
Pincus, A. L., 439, 440, 443
Pinel, P., 638
Piner, K. E., 593
Pinker, S., 325
Pinsof, W. M., 666
Pisarska, K., 510
Plawin, P., 735
Pliner, P. L., 511
Plomin, R., 356, 357, 624
Plutchik, R., 530, 531, 533, 545
Pogue-Geile, M. F., 623
Pola, J., 135
Polkinghorne, D. E., 7
Polson, P. G., 335
Pomeroy, C., 512
Pomeroy, W. B., 520, 522
Pool, R., 523
Poortinga, Y., 378
Pope, H. G., 512
Porter, L. W., 740
Posner, M. I., 315, 331
Post, J. M., 607
Post, R. B., 135
Powell, B., 284
Powell, L., 572
Powers, S. I., 392
Powley, T. L., 508
Pratkais, A. R., 171
Pressley, M., 289
Preti, G., 151
Price, D. L., 614
Price-Williams, D. R., 378
Prior, M., 610
Prochaska, J. O., 574
Putnam, F. W., 607
Pyle, R. L., 512
Pynes, J., 730

Quadrel, M. J., 392
Quay, H. C., 609
Quillian, M. R., 273
Quina, K., 322

Rabins, P. V., 613
Radford, A., 324
Rae-Grant, N. I., 588
Rahe, Richard, 555, 556
Raine, A., 609
Raines, B. E., 574
Ramey, C. T., 357, 479, 482
Ramirez, M., 378
Ramon Garcia, C., 151
Ramsey, D., 369

Ransberger, V. M., 752
Rapoport, J. L., 599, 601, 610, 611
Rasmussen, T., 67
Raudenbush, S. W., 559
Raulin, M. L., 6
Rayner, R., 214–216, 220, 249
Read, J. D., 171
Rebec, G. V., 61
Rebelsky, F. G., 323
Ree, M. J., 458, 729
Regier, D. A., 217
Rehncrona, S., 80
Reich, J., 595, 597
Reilly, R. R., 727
Reimer, J., 381
Reinisch, J. M., 363
Reinke, B. J., 402
Reis, H. T., 698
Reis, S. M., 478
Reiss, D., 405
Rempel, J. K., 682
Rescorla, R. A., 218–220, 242
Resnick, L. B., 344, 713
Resnick, S. M., 626
Rest, J. R., 380
Rettew, D. C., 600
Reveley, A. M., 626
Reveley, M. A., 626
Revelle, W., 440
Revulsky, S. H., 221
Reynolds, A. G., 333
Reynolds, B. A., 55
Rhodes, S. R., 406, 738
Rhue, J. W., 182, 183
Rhyne, D., 405
Rice, J., 602
Rice, M., 327
Richardson, J. D., 526
Richardson-Klavehn, A., 280
Rickels, K., 645
Riggio, R. E., 725, 738, 741
Riley, E. P., 362
Risch, N., 616
Robbins, R. J., 80
Robertson, I., 728
Robins, L. N., 217, 602
Roche, A. F., 392
Rockert, W., 511
Rodeheaver, D., 402
Rodgers, C. H., 518
Rodin, J., 510, 573, 579, 750
Roediger, H. L., 257, 280
Rogers, C., 16–17, 45, 435, 484, 657, 658, 673
Rolls, B. J., 511
Romney, D. M., 384
Rook, K. S., 566
Roose, S. P., 512
Roosevelt, E., 436
Rorschach, H., 453
Rosch, E., 310, 311
Rose, A. S., 379

Rosenbaum, M. E., 699
Rosenberg, N. L., 80
Rosenberg, S. D., 408
Rosenman, R. H., 570
Rosenthal, D., 623
Rosenthal, D. B., 729
Rosenzweig, M. R., 17, 275
Ross, C. A., 607
Ross, D., 246
Ross, G., 389
Ross, L. D., 693
Ross, M., 693
Ross, S. A., 246
Rossi, A. S., 408
Rossi, J. S., 574
Roth, E. M., 311
Roth, L., 510
Roth, M., 595, 613
Rothman, S., 467
Rothstein, H. R., 727
Rottman, L., 698
Rotton, J., 752
Rovine, M., 389
Rowe, D. C., 356, 443
Rowe, J. W., 412
Rozelle, R. M., 574
Rubin, D. C., 282
Rubin, Z., 699
Rudd, J. R., 573, 736
Ruggiero, M., 707
Rushton, J. P., 445, 474
Russo, N. F., 615, 618, 649
Rutter, M., 392
Rutter, M. L., 610, 611
Ryan, E. D., 756
Ryan, M., 525

Saal, F. E., 729, 740
Saari, L. M., 731, 734
Saccuzzo, D. P., 447
Sackeim, H. A., 642
Sadalla, E. K., 744
Sadock, B. J., 654
Saegert, S., 744
Safer, M., 705
Safran, J. D., 530, 532, 668
St. Lawrence, J. S., 578, 579
Saitta, M. B., 445
Sakai, K., 76
Salem, D. A., 648
Salett, E. P., 651
Salovey, P., 573, 579
Salthouse, T. A., 410, 474
Sameroff, A. J., 370
Sampson, P. D., 362
Samuelson, F. J. B., 214
Sanau, V. D., 611
Sanders, S. A., 363
Sandler, J., 656
Sands, L. P., 473
Santa, J. L., 343
Satir, V., 666
Sattler, J. M., 462, 463
Saunders, N. A., 178
Sauser, W. J., 738

Scarborough, E., 14
Scarr, S., 389
Sceery, W., 600
Schachter, S., 697
Schacter, D. A., 280
Schacter, D. L., 257, 278, 280, 281
Schacter, S., 509, 510
Schaefer, C., 556
Schaie, K. W., 406, 412, 473
Schapiro, M. B., 601
Scharf, B., 751
Scharf, M. B., 180
Schau, C. G., 384
Scheerer, M., 307, 337
Scheier, M. F., 564
Scheldberg, D., 452
Schelling, T. C., 574
Schenck, C. H., 178
Scher, S. J., 688
Schiff, B. B., 540
Schlenger, W. E., 602
Schmidt, F. L., 35, 727, 729
Schmitt, H. N., 729
Schmitt, N., 728
Schmitt, R. C., 749
Schneider, J. R., 729
Schopler, E., 610
Schreiber, J. L., 622
Schroeder, C. S., 480
Schroeder, D. A., 693
Schroeder, S. R., 480
Schuckit, M. A., 188, 191
Schultz, D. P., 734, 741
Schultz, R., 413, 563
Schultz, S. E., 734, 741
Schultz, T. R., 379, 382
Schwartz, J. H., 275
Schwartz, P., 389
Schwartz, P. M., 753
Schwebel, A. I., 648, 649
Schweizer, E., 645
Scott, K. G., 482
Scovern, A. W., 580
Sears, P. S., 478, 479
Sears, R. R., 566
Secord, P. F., 696
Segall, M., 378
Segall, M. H., 139
Self, E. A., 502
Seligman, M. E. P., 617
Selkoe, D. J., 614
Selye, H., 536, 559–561, 582
Sennecker, P., 445
Serbin, L. A., 386
Serpell, R., 133
Shadish, W. R., 648
Shaffer, D., 600
Shaffer, D. R., 690
Shaffer, M., 403
Shaker, L. A., 572
Shankster, L. J., 725, 728, 729
Shapiro, D., 564
Shapiro, D. A., 669

Shapiro, D. H., Jr., 187
Shapiro, R., 648
Sharpley, P. H., 642
Shaver, P., 695
Shaw, J. C., 341
Shaw, K. N., 736
Shawcross, C., 645
Shea, S. L., 369
Shedler, J., 398
Sheer, D. E., 67
Shefner, J. M., 97
Shekelle, B., 570, 571
Shepard, R. N., 265
Sheridan, C. L., 556
Sheridan, K., 578
Sherman, S. J., 681
Shertzer, B., 406
Shevrin, H., 171
Shields, J., 625
Shiffman, L. B., 189
Shiffman, S., 189
Shiffrin, R. M., 257
Shigehisa, T., 248
Shimamura, A. P., 279, 281
Shipley, T., 638
Shippee, G., 754
Shirley, M. C., 564
Shoben, E. J., 311
Shore, M., 648
Shotland, R. L., 708
Shulman, H. G., 265
Shweder, R. A., 20, 442
Shy, K., 363
Sibai, B. M., 363
Siegler, R. S., 371
Sigafoos, A. D., 370
Sikkema, K. J., 577, 578
Silberman, E. K., 607
Silk, K. R., 609
Silva, J. M., 757
Simkins-Bullock, J. A., 322
Simmonds, B., 597
Simon, H. A., 6, 292, 334,
    341, 344
Simon, R., 666
Simon, T., 462
Simonides, 289
Sims, E. A. H., 509
Singer, J. E., 751, 752
Singer, L. T., 386
Singh, M. M., 622, 623
Sitko, C., 388
Skinner, B. F., 15, 45, 222,
    223, 225, 228, 231, 232,
    240, 325, 343, 410, 434,
    441, 754
Skolnick, A., 406
Slade, R., 172
Slater, P. C., 643
Slobin, D. I., 316, 317, 320,
    327
Small, I. F., 642
Small, J. G., 642
Smalley, S. L., 611
Smeaton, G., 699

Smith, A., 751
Smith, D., 363, 758
Smith, D. W., 362
Smith, E. R., 518
Smith, G. B., 648, 649
Smith, L. B., 368
Smith, L. K., 556
Smith, M. L., 668
Smith, P., 611
Smith, P. C., 726, 738
Smith, S., 283
Smith, T. W., 155
Smith, V. L., 270
Snarey, J. R., 381
Snow, M. E., 385
Snyder, M., 694
Snyder, S. H., 624, 643
Snyderman, M., 467
Soldatos, C. R., 180
Somers, V. K., 178
Sommer, R., 745
Sorensen, J. L., 578
Southwick, S. M., 602
Soyka, L. F., 364
Spagenberg, E. R., 171
Spanos, N. P., 184, 185
Sparks, C. P., 727
Spear, N. E., 218–220, 283
Spearman, C., 457–459, 460,
    462, 487
Spelke, E. S., 368
Spellman, B. A., 170
Spence, J. T., 386
Spencer, D. D., 80
Sperling, G., 258
Sperry, R., 85, 537
Spitz, H., 482
Sprafkin, C., 386
Sprecher, S., 698
Springer, J. P., 85
Springston, F., 264
Squire, L. R., 257, 265, 279,
    643
Sreff, F. M., 573, 736
Stachnick, T. J., 423
Stacvk, S., 609
Stainton, N. R., 423
Stall, R. D., 578
Standing, L., 266
Stangor, C., 682
Stansfield, S., 751
State, R. C., 610, 611
Staw, B. M., 740
Stechler, G., 363
Steers, R. M., 740
Steffen, V. J., 445
Stein, B. A., 738
Stein, J., 284
Stein, J. A., 406
Steiner, J. E., 370
Steinhausen, H. C., 610
Steinhilber, A., 757
Stenchever, M. A., 363
Stenevi, U., 80
Stephan, W., 700

Stern, D., 388
Stern, L. W., 315
Stern, P. C., 752, 754
Sternberg, K. J., 389
Sternberg, R. J., 458, 460,
    487, 729
Stevenson, H. W., 474, 476
Stewart, A. J., 515
Stickney, S., 648
Stigler, J. W., 474, 476
Stiles, W. B., 669
Stinnett, N., 403
Stokals, D., 573
Stokes, G., 400
Stokols, D., 749, 752
Stone, K. M., 578
Stoner, James, 714
Storandt, M., 410
Stoyva, J., 564
Strauss, M., 368
Strauss, R., 570
Streissguth, A. P., 362
Stricker, E. M., 508, 509
Strickland, B., 615, 618, 649
Strother, C. R., 473
Strupp, H. H., 636, 656
Stunkard, A. J., 508, 509
Suckow, R. F., 600
Suddes, J. N., 616
Sue, D., 651
Sue, D. W., 651
Sue, S., 474, 476
Suelzer, M., 597
Suied, M., 735
Suinn, R. M., 758
Suler, J. R., 187
Sullivan, C. E., 178
Sullivan, M. A., 20, 442
Sundel, M., 408
Surwit, R. S., 580
Suzuki, S., 323
Svejda, M., 369
Swaim, R. C., 192
Swayze, V. W., 625
Swedo, S. E., 599, 601
Swets, J. A., 101
Symanski, K., 712
Syme, S. L., 555
Szasz, T. S., 593
Szatmari, P., 588

Takanishi, R., 392, 394
Tandon, R., 624
Tanfer, K., 523, 578
Tannenbaum, S. I., 730, 733
Tanner, J. M., 392–395
Tassinary, L. G., 172, 683
Taylor, C. B., 597
Taylor, J. C., 738
Taylor, W., 751
Teevan, R., 514
Tellegen, A., 39
Tenopyr, M. L., 450
Terenius, L., 155
Terman, L. M., 462, 478,

479
Termine, N., 368
Terry, H., 473
Tesser, A., 690
Tetrud, J., 80
Thackwray-Emerson, D.,
    565
Thayer, W. P., 728
Thibault, J. W., 695
Thom, E., 363
Thomas, A., 384
Thomas, M. B., 666
Thompson, C. I., 510
Thompson, C. P., 284
Thompson, D. E., 737
Thompson, D. M., 282, 283
Thompson, J. D., 642
Thompson, R. F., 218, 275
Thorndike, A. L., 462, 463
Thorndike, E. L., 223–225,
    228
Thornton, G. C., 729, 733
Thurman, P. J., 192
Thurstone, L. L., 458–460
Tice, D. M., 709
Tilley, A. J., 177
Tinsley, B. J., 389
Tinuper, P., 81
Tobin-Richards, M., 396
Todd-Mancillas, W., 322
Tohen, M., 616
Tolman, C. W., 510
Tolman, E., 242–245, 248,
    252
Tomkins, S. S., 539
Toro, P. A., 572, 578, 648,
    649
Torrey, E. F., 647
Torrey, T. W., 357
Travis, C. B., 646
Treffert, D. A., 610, 611
Tremblay, A., 508
Triandis, H. C., 229, 381
Trickett, E. J., 648
Trimble, J. E., 192
Triplett, N., 712
True, W. R., 602
Trulson, M. E., 194
Trzebinski, J., 440
Tsuang, M. T., 616
Tucker, D. M., 537
Tulving, E., 172, 257, 272,
    273, 279, 282, 283, 285
Tumeh, S. S., 70
Tung, R., 730
Turk, D. C., 579
Turnbull, C., 133
Turner, J., 406
Turner, J. A., 690
Turner, L. H., 322
Turner, T. J., 532, 534
Turvey, M. T., 258
Tuttle, T. C., 738, 740
Tversky, Amos, 339, 757
Tyrer, P., 645

Tyroler, H. A., 411
Tyrrell, G., 625
Tziner, A., 728

Uhlman, C. E., 727
Ulleland, C. N., 362
Ulrich, R. E., 423
Underwood, B. J., 279, 299
Unger, R., 88, 646
Unis, A. S., 668

Vaccarino, L. V., 572
Valenstein, E. S., 639
Vallerand, R. J., 757
Valliant, C. O., 412
Valliant, G. E., 192, 412
Vallone, R., 757
Van Avermaet, E., 702, 714
VandeCreek, L., 579
VandenBos, G. R., 667
VanderPlate, C., 576
Vander Wall, S. B., 245
Vanegas, H., 537
Van Ijzendorn, M. H., 388
Van Lanker, D., 86
Varca, P. E., 757
Vaughn, B. E., 698
Vavak, C. R., 571
Venables, P. H., 609
Ventura, J., 626
Verillo, R. T., 154
Vernon, P. E., 460, 461, 473, 487
Verrier, R. L., 178
Vinacke, W. E., 341
Vitz, P. C., 379
Voevodsky, J., 741
Vokey, J. R., 171
Vorhees, C. F., 362
Vroom, V., 735, 760

Wagner, A. R., 220
Wagner, R. K., 458, 729
Wajima, M., 248
Walk, R., 369
Walker, L. D., 693
Walker, L. J., 382
Wall, D. D., 648
Wall, P. D., 154
Wallace, P., 151
Wallace, R. K., 186
Wallach, H., 134
Wallas, G., 342, 343
Walsh, B. T., 512
Walster, E., 691, 695, 698, 699
Walster, G. W., 695, 699
Walters, G. C., 236
Walton, A. E., 738
Wamboldt, F. S., 405
Wang, Y., 711
Warrington, E. K., 281
Washburn, M. F., 14, 44

Wasserman, S. S., 504
Waternaux, C. M., 616
Watkins, L. R., 61
Watkins, M. J., 257, 267
Watson, C. J., 740
Watson, J. B., 14–17, 45, 166, 214–216, 249, 433–434, 441, 484
Watson, M., 481
Watson, M. W., 315
Waugh, N. C., 257
Wearing, C., 255
Weary, G., 693
Weaver, C. N., 403, 738
Webb, M., 166
Webb, W. B., 179, 187
Webb, W. W., 179
Weber, A., 289, 290
Webster, J., 555
Wechsler, D., 456, 465–467, 473, 487
Weekes, J. R., 182
Weekley, J. A., 729
Weil, A. T., 196
Weintraub, S., 623
Weisberg, R. W., 478
Weiskrantz, L., 281
Weisner, W. H., 728
Weiss, D. S., 602
Weiss, R. D., 195
Weiss, S., 55
Weiss, W., 690
Weissman, M. M., 217, 595, 597, 615
Welch, W. W., 471
Wellman, H. M., 372, 378
Wells, D., 679, 707, 709
Wells, G. L., 689
Wells, Gary, 270
Welson, E., 711
Wenger, N. K., 572
Wermuth, L. A., 578
Wertheimer, M., 17, 369
Werthessen, N. T., 570
West, M. A., 187
Westermeyer, J. F., 620
Weston, M., 179
Wethington, E., 622
Wheeler, L., 698
Wheeler, R. J., 565
Wherry, J. S., 610
Whitaker, A., 600
White, B. D., 510
White, S. H., 275
Whitehurst, G., 325
Whiting, B., 445
Whyte, L. L., 168
Wible, C., 284
Wickens, C. D., 741
Wickens, D. D., 265
Widner, H., 80
Wiebe, D., 343
Wiesel, T., 68

Wigfield, A., 385
Wiggins, J. S., 439, 440, 443
Wilcox, D., 527
Wildman, B. G., 322
Wilkes, J., 183
Williams, J. E., 386
Williams, K., 711, 712
Williams, M., 609
Williams, R. B., 571
Williams, R. L., 179
Williamson, R. A., 363
Willis, S. L., 406
Wilson, D. B., 668, 669
Wilson, D. M., 597
Wilson, G. T., 218
Wincze, J. P., 527
Winett, R. A., 573, 754
Wing, L., 610, 611
Wingard, J. A., 322
Winkel, G. H., 744
Winter, D. G., 514, 515
Winters, K. C., 623
Winton, W. M., 502
Wischik, C. M., 613
Witenberg, S. H., 579
Witmer, J. F., 754
Wolf, W., 192
Wolford, G., 172
Wolkenstein, J., 578
Wolleben, B., 610
Wollen, K. A., 289, 290
Wolpe, J., 217, 659, 668
Wood, C., 570
Woolfolk, R. L., 564
Worrington, C. J., 712
Wright, L., 571
Wright, R. A., 502
Wundt, W., 12–13, 17, 44, 97, 166, 531, 545
Wurm, M., 570
Wurtman, R. J., 613, 614
Wyatt, R., 648
Wyatt, R. J., 624
Wysowski, D. K., 644

Yaffe, S. J., 363
Yalom, I. D., 666
Yaniv, I., 343
Yates, A. J., 564
Yates, F. A., 289
Yerkes, R. M., 502
York, C. M., 738
Young, T., 121, 122, 159
Youngstrom, N., 649
Yuille, J. C., 270, 271
Yukl, G., 730, 733
Yule, W., 392
Yurgelun-Todd, D., 512

Zacharko, R. M., 617
Zadeh, L., 309
Zajonc, R. B., 539, 540, 683, 697, 698, 713

Zanna, M. P., 681, 682, 686
Zanni, G., 269
Zaragoza, M., 267
Zedeck, S., 724, 728, 730
Zeiss, A. M., 615
Zelazo, P., 389
Zelnick, M., 401
Zettler-Segal, M., 189
Zhao, S., 588, 595, 596
Zidon, I., 736
Zigler, E., 481, 482
Zilbergeld, B., 525
Zimerle, D. M., 731, 734
Zimmerman, G., 403
Zimmerman, M., 609
Zimmerman, R., 512
Zinbarg, R. E., 665
Zinberg, N., 196
Zir, L. M., 178
Zohar, D., 742
Zubin, J., 623
Zucconi, M., 81
Zuckerman, B., 362
Zuckerman, M., 502, 609

Abnormal psychology. *See* Psychological disorders
Abortion, 401
Absolute thresholds, 97–99, 101
Acceptance, of dying, 413
Accommodation, 113, 129, 160, 372–373
Acetylcholine (ACh), 60, 90, 276, 614, 629
Achievement motivation, 513–514, 543
Acquired immune deficiency syndrome (AIDS), 576–579, 584
Acquisition, in conditioning, 209, 226, 227, 249, 251
Acrophobia, 598, 599
ACT (American College Testing Program), 468
Action potential, 56
Actor-observer bias, 694, 717
Acupuncture, 156
Adaptation, 11
Addiction, drug, 188, 190, 199
Adolescence
  characterizations of, 391–392
  defined, 391, 418–419
  drug use in, 397–399, 419
  eating disorders, 510–512, 543
  identity formation in, 396–397, 419
  physical changes during, 392–396, 419
  puberty, 394–396, 399–401, 419, 430, 522
  sexuality in, 399–401, 419
Adrenal glands, 522
Adulthood, development in
  early, 402–407, 420
  late, 410, 420
  middle, 408–409, 420
Advertising, 213–214, 683–685, 690
Affective component of attitude, 682, 716
Affective disorders. *See* Mood disorders
Affects, defined, 8
Affiliation motivation, 515–516, 543
Aggression, 388, 566–567, 583
  gender and, 445, 486

social learning theory and, 246–247
Agism, 410
Agoraphobia, 598, 599
Agreeableness/friendliness, 439–440, 485
AIDS. *See* Acquired immune deficiency syndrome (AIDS)
Alarm stage, 559–561, 582
Alcohol, 191–192, 199, 362, 398, 415
Algophobia, 598
Algorithms, 333–334, 349
All-or-none principle, 57, 58, 89
Alpha activity, 173, 174, 186, 198
Altruism, gender and, 445, 486
Alzheimer's disease, 60, 612–614, 629
Ambiguity, in language, 321
American Association of Mental Deficiency (AAMD), 479, 480
American Psychological Association (APA), 17, 36
Amnesia, 281
  psychogenic, 605
Amnestic disorders, 611, 612
Amphetamines, 189–191, 199, 624
Amplitude of sound, 141, 143, 160
Amygdala, 78–79, 91
Analgesics, 192
Anal stage, 430, 484
Androgens, 394, 521, 544
Anger, at dying, 412
Animal Mind, The (Washburn), 14
Anorexia nervosa, 510–512, 543
Antianxiety drugs, 646, 672
Antidepressant drugs, 642–643, 645–646, 671–672
Antipsychotic drugs, 643–644, 671
Antisocial personality disorder, 608, 609, 629
Anxiety, 567–568, 595
Anxiety disorders, 595–603, 628
Apparent motion, 134–135
Applied behavior analysis (ABA), 754, 762
Applied psychology
  environmental, 744–755, 761

health, 19, 45, 569–580
industrial/organizational. *See* Industrial-organizational (I/O) psychology
  sports, 755–758
Approach-approach conflicts, 552–553, 581
Approach-avoidance conflicts, 553–554, 581
Aptitude tests, 467–468
Aqueous humor, 114–115, 158
Archetypes, 432
Armed Forces Qualification Test (AFQT), 467
Army Alpha Test, 467
Army Beta Test, 467
Arousal, 68
  athletes and, 756–757
  motivation and, 501–502, 542
  sexual, 518–520
Assertiveness training, 662
Assessment centers, 729–730
Assimilation, 372
Association areas, 82, 84, 91
Astraphobia, 598
Asylums, 637–638
Athletes, 755–758
Atonia, 178, 198
Attachment, 387–389, 418, 695–696, 717
Attention span, 388
Attitudes
  changing, 503, 686–691, 716
  components of, 682–683, 716
  defined, 681, 716
  formation of, 683–685, 716
Attractiveness, 698–699, 717
Attribution theory, 691–694, 717
Audience inhibition, 708–709, 718
Audition. *See* Hearing
Auditory canal, 146, 147, 160
Authority, obedience to, 703–706, 718
Autism, 610–611, 629
Autobiographical memory, 274–275, 302
Autokinetic effect, 135, 160
Autonomic nervous system (ANS), 63–64, 90, 534–536, 545
Autonomy versus self-doubt crisis, 383, 418

Autophobia, 598
Availability heuristic, 339, 349
Aversion therapy, 660–661, 674
Avoidance-avoidance conflicts, 553, 581
Avoidant personality disorder, 608–609, 629
Axons, 53–55
Axon terminals, 54, 55, 58–60

Babbling, 323, 348
Babinski reflex, 366
Balance (equilibrium) in motivation, 501–503, 542
Bambuti people, 133
Barbiturates, 193, 199
Bargaining, 412–413
Basal ganglia, 75, 80–81, 84, 91, 600
Baseline design, 34, 47
Basic anxiety, 432
Basic hostility, 432
Basilar membrane, 146, 147, 161
Behavior, defined, 7
Behavioral component of attitude, 682, 716
Behavioral/learning approach to personality, 433–434, 441, 484, 485
Behavioral observation, 448–449, 486
Behavior disorders. *See* Psychological disorders
Behaviorism, 15–16, 45
Behavior of Organisms, The (Skinner), 240
Behavior therapy, 659–662, 673–674
Benzodiazepines, 646, 672
Bias, 34–35
  in attribution theory, 693–694, 717
  cultural, 466
  observer, 22
Binocular cues, 129
Biofeedback, 564–565
Biogenic amines, 616–617, 630
Bipolar cells, 116
Bipolar disorder, 615, 616, 630, 645
Birth defects, 360–362, 364
Blind spot, 116

Blocking, 219
Blood alcohol level (BAL), 192
Body language, 539
  gender and, 445, 486
Body weight, 508–510
Bottom-up processing, 107, 125
Bound morphemes, 326, 327
Brain. *See also* Cental nervous
    system (CNS)
  Alzheimer's disease and,
    613–614
  cerebral cortex, 75, 81–88,
    91, 154, 537, 545
  damage to, 65–67, 77–78
  electrical stimulation of,
    67–69
  electroconvulsive therapy
    (ECT), 641–643, 671
  emotions and, 536–537, 545
  hemispheres of, 82, 85–87,
    92
  homosexuality and, 524
  hypothalamus, 75, 79–80, 91,
    505, 506, 508, 522, 536,
    537, 544, 545
  lobes and localization of,
    82–85, 91
  lower centers of, 75–81
  male and female, 87–88, 92
  memory and, 275–276
  observation of, 69–70
  pain and, 154–156, 161
  schizophrenia and, 624–626
  surgery and, 67, 639–641,
    671
  transplantation issues, 80–81
  vision and, 116, 119–121,
    159
Brain stem, 75–76, 90–91
Brightness, 109–110, 112, 146
Brightness constancy, 136, 160
British empiricists, 11
Broca's area, 83
Bulimia, 510–512, 542
Bystander intervention, 679,
    700, 706–711, 718

Caffeine, 189, 199
California Personality Inventory
    (CPI), 452
Cannabis plant, 195–196
Cardinal traits, 438
Career choice, 406–407, 420
Case histories, 24–25, 46
Catatonic schizophrenia, 621,
    630
CAT scan (computerized axial
    tomography), 69
Cell body, 53
Central nervous system (CNS),
    62–64, 90
  cerebral cortex, 75, 81–88,
    91, 154, 537, 545
  lower brain centers, 75–81
  spinal cord, 71–74
  study of, 65–70

Central traits, 438
Cephalocaudal sequencing, 367,
    416
Cerebellum, 75–77, 80, 91
Cerebral cortex, 75, 81–88, 91,
    154, 537, 545
Cerebral hemispheres, 82
Chastity, 405
Chemical senses. *See* Smell;
    Taste
Child abuse, 268
Child development, 353
  cognitive, 370–379, 416–417
  gender identity, 384–387,
    418
  moral, 379–382, 417
  motor, 365–368, 415–416
  psychosocial, 382–384, 418
  sensory and perceptual,
    367–370, 416
  social attachments, 387–389,
    418
Chlamydia, 575, 584
Chlorpromazine, 643–644, 671
Chlorofluorocarbons (CFCs),
    753
Cholecystokinin (CCK), 512
Chromosomes, 355, 357, 415,
    481
Chronic activation, 571
Chronological age (CA),
    463–464
Chunking, 264, 301–302
Ciliary muscles, 113
Classical conditioning,
    206–222, 249, 326, 370,
    416, 683–684, 716
Claustrophobia, 598
Client-centered therapy,
    657–658, 673
Clinical psychologists, 651–652,
    672
Clinical psychology, 19, 45
Clinical social workers, 652,
    672
Closure, 125, 127, 135, 159
Clozapine, 644
Cocaine, 61, 189, 190, 199,
    362
Cochlea, 146, 147, 161
Codeine, 192, 199
Coding (Morse code), 318
Cognitions, defined, 8
Cognitive approaches to learn-
    ing, 241–248
Cognitive component of atti-
    tude, 682, 716
Cognitive development
  of neonates, 370–372, 416
  Piaget's theory of, 372–379,
    416–417
Cognitive disorders, 611–614,
    629
Cognitive dissonance, 502–503,
    542, 686–688, 698, 716
Cognitive map, 244–245, 252

Cognitive psychology, 19, 45
Cognitive reappraisal, 563
Cognitive response theory,
    688–691, 716
Cognitive restructuring therapy,
    664–665, 674
Cognitive therapy, 662–665,
    674
Collective monologues, 375
Collective unconscious, 432,
    484
Collectivism, 381
College Entrance Examination
    Board, 468
Common fate, 125, 127, 159
Common traits, 437–438, 485
Communication
  gender and, 445, 486
  patient-physician, 578–580,
    584
  persuasion, 686–691,
    716–717
Community Mental Health Act
    (1963), 648
Comorbidity, 596, 602
Competence versus inferiority
    crisis, 383, 384, 418
Comprehensive Scale of Stress
    Assessment, 556
Compulsions, 599
Conception, 355, 358
Concepts
  defined, 308–311, 346
  forming, 311–315, 346
Concrete operations stage of
    child development,
    375–377, 417
Conditioned emotional repons-
    es, 212–214, 249
Conditioned response (CR),
    207–211, 213, 215, 249
Conditioned stimulus (CS),
    207–211, 213, 215,
    219–221, 249, 250
Conditioning
  classical, 206–222, 249, 326,
    370, 416, 683–684, 716
  operant, 222–241, 250–251,
    326, 370, 416, 500, 684,
    716, 754, 755
Cones, 115–119, 158–159
Confidentiality, 37
Conflict-induced stress,
    552–554, 581
Conformity, 701–703, 718
Conscientiousness, 440, 485
Consciousness. *See also* Sleep;
    Unconscious
  basic characteristics of,
    166–167, 197
  defined, 166, 197
  drugs and, 188–196, 199
  hypnosis and, 182–185,
    199
  levels of, 167–170, 197,
    425–426, 483

  meditation and, 185–187,
    199
Conservation, in Piaget's theory,
    376, 378–379
Constancy of perception,
    135–140, 160
Contact comfort, 388, 418
Context, effects of, 282–285
Contiguity, 125–126
Contingency contracting, 231,
    661–662, 674
Contingency management, 661,
    674
Continuity, 125–127, 159
Continuous reinforcement
    (CRF) schedule, 232, 233,
    251
Contraception, 401
Contrast, stimulus factor of,
    103, 104
Control group, 33
Conventional morality, 380, 417
Convergence, 129, 160
Convergent thinking, 342, 349
Conversion disorder, 604–605,
    629
Cornea, 112, 113, 115, 158
Coronary heart disease (CHD),
    570–572, 583
Corpus callosum, 75, 79, 85, 86,
    88
Correlation, defined, 26
Correlational methods, 25–29
Correlation coefficient, 26–28,
    46
Cortex. *See* Cerebral cortex
Counseling psychologists, 652,
    672
Counseling psychology, 19, 45
Counterirritation, 156
Crack cocaine, 190, 362
Creative problem solving,
    340–343, 349–350
Criterion-referenced test, 451
Cross laterality, 76, 84, 91, 120
Cross-sectional method, 473
Crowding, 749–750, 761
Crystallized intelligence, 462,
    463, 473
Cultural bias, 466
Cultural psychology, 20, 45

Dark adaptation, 102, 118–119
Day care, 389, 418
Death and dying, 412–413
Death instincts (thanatos), 426
Debriefing, 37
Decibel scale, 141, 144
Decision making, group,
    713–715, 719
Defense mechanisms, 427–428,
    483–484
Deinstitutionalization, 647–649,
    672
Delirium, 611, 612, 643
Delta waves, 174–175, 198

Delusions, 618, 630, 643, 671
Dementia, 611, 612, 643
Dendrites, 53, 55
Denial, 428, 483
  of dying, 412
Dependence, drug, 188, 190, 199
Dependent personality disorder, 609, 629
Dependent variables, 30–32, 46
Depressants, 191–193, 199
Depression, 413, 615–618, 630, 642
Depth perception, 128–134, 159–160
DES (diethylstilbestrol), 363
Developmentally delayed, 480
Developmental psychology. *See* Adolescence; Adulthood, development in; Child development; Prenatal development
Diagnosis, 590
Diagnostic and Statistical Manual of Mental Disorders series, 591, 592, 595, 596, 605, 607, 611, 614, 620, 628
Dichromatism, 123
Difference thresholds, 100, 157–158
Differential reinforcement, 238, 252
Diffusion of responsibility, 710, 718
Discrimination, in conditioning, 211, 238–239, 249, 252
Disorganized schizophrenia, 621, 630
Displacement, 429, 484
Dissociative amnesia, 605, 629
Dissociative fugue, 605–606, 629
Dissociative identity disorder, 606–607, 619, 629
Distance perception, 128–134, 159–160
Distributed practice, 295–296, 304
Divergent thinking, 342, 349
Dominant gene, 355
Dopamine, 61, 80, 190, 199, 616, 624–625, 631
Dorsal roots, 72
Double-blind technique, 34, 47
Down's syndrome, 364, 481, 489
Dreaming, REM and NREM sleep and, 176–178, 198
Dream interpretation, 655–656, 673
Drinking behavior, 505–507, 542
Drives, 496–499, 541–542
Drugs

  adolescent use of, 398–399, 419
  antianxiety, 646, 672
  antidepressant, 642–643, 645–646, 671–672
  antipsychotic, 67, 643–644
  depressants, 191–193, 199
  hallucinogens, 193–195, 199–200
  marijuana, 195–196, 200
  pregnancy and, 362–363, 415
  stimulants, 189–191, 199
Dysthymia, 615

Ear, structures of, 145–147, 160–161
Eardrum, 146, 147, 160
Early adulthood, development in, 402–407, 420
Eating behavior, 507–510, 542–543
Eating disorders, 510–512, 543
Ebene, 194
Echolalia, 610
Educational/instructional psychology, 19, 45
Ego, 426, 427, 430, 434, 483
Egocentrism, 375, 378
Elaborative rehearsal, 271, 286, 302
Elderly, 410–413, 420, 472–474, 488
Electra complex, 430
Electroconvulsive therapy (ECT), 641–643, 671
Electrodes, 67–68
Electroencephalogram (EEG), 68, 173–175, 186, 198
Electromagnetic energy, 110
Electromyogram (EMG), 173, 175, 198
Embryo, 359, 415
Emotions
  classifying, 531–534, 545
  defined, 529–530, 545
  memory and, 284, 285, 303
  outward expressions of, 537–541, 545
  physiological aspects of, 534–537, 545
Empathy, 388, 657, 673
  gender and, 445–446, 486
Employment interview, 727–728, 759
Encapsulated nerve endings, 151
Encoding, 256, 301. *See also* Memory
  retrieval and, 281–296, 303
Encoding specificity principle, 282–283
Endocrine system, 64
Endorphins, 61, 155–156
Engineering approach to worker safety, 741, 761
Environmental frustration, 551, 581

Environmentalist movement, 753, 762
Environmental psychology, 744–755, 761
Environmental toxins, 752–753, 762
Epigenetic model of development, 356–357, 415
Epilepsy, 637
Epinephrine, 535
Episodic memory, 273–274, 302
Equity model of interpersonal attraction, 695, 717
Equity theory of work motivation, 735–736, 760
Erectile dysfunction, 525–526, 544
Esteem needs, 498
Estrogens, 394, 518, 521, 544
Ethical Principles of Psychologists (American Psychological Association), 36
Ethics, 36–38, 47, 706
Ethnic differences, in intelligence, 474–476, 488–489
Exhaustion stage, 559–561, 582
Existential therapies, 657
Expectancy theory of work motivation, 735, 760
Experimental group, 33
Experimental methods, 29–36, 46–47
External attribution, 691, 717
Extinction, in conditioning, 210, 226–227, 249, 251
Extraneous variables, 30–33, 46
Extroversion/introversion, 439, 485
Eye
  neural impulses, 119–121
  structures of, 112–119, 158
Eyewitness testimony, 268–271

Facial expressions, 539–541, 545
Factor analysis, 438
Failure, fear of, 514
Family therapy, 666, 674–675
Fantasy, 428, 483
Farsightedness, 114
Fear. *See* Phobic disorders
Feelings. *See* Emotions
Female sexual unresponsiveness, 526–527, 544
Fetal alcohol syndrome (FAS), 362
Fetus, 359–361, 415
Figure–ground relationship, 124–125
Fixation, 566, 567, 583
Fixed-interval (FI) reinforcement schedule, 233, 251
Fixed-ratio (FR) reinforcement schedule, 232, 251
Flashbulb memories, 284, 285

Flattened affect, 619
Flooding, 659, 673
Fluoxetine (Prozac), 645
Fluid-analytic abilities, 462, 463
Fluid intelligence, 473
Formal operations stage of child development, 377, 417
Fovea, 116–118, 159
Fragile X syndrome, 481, 489
Free association, 654–656, 673
Free nerve endings, 151
Free recall, 278
Frontal lobes, 82, 83, 600
Frustration-aggression hypothesis, 566–567, 583
Frustration-induced stress, 551–552, 562, 581
Functional fixedness, 337–338, 342, 349
Functionalism, 14, 44
Fundamental attribution error, 693, 717

GABA, 642
Ganglion cells, 116
Gate-control theory of pain, 154–156, 161
Gender
  brain and, 87–88, 92
  intelligence and, 470–471, 488
  mood disorders and, 617–618
  personality and, 444–446, 486
  stress and, 558–559
Gender identity, 384–387, 418
General adaptation syndrome (GAS), 559–561, 582
Generalization, in conditioning, 211, 215, 237–238, 249, 252
Generalized anxiety disorder, 596, 628
Generalized Personality Test (GPT), 423
Generate-test strategy, 333
Generativity, process of, 405
Generativity versus stagnation crisis, 383, 409
Genes, 355, 415
Genetics, 354–357, 415, 443
Genital herpes (herpes type II), 576, 584
Genital stage, 430, 484
Geometric illusions, 137–139, 160
Gestalt psychology, 17, 45, 124–127
Gestalt therapy, 658, 673
g-factor, 458, 462, 463, 487
Giftedness, 476–479, 489
Glaucoma, 115
Glove anesthesia, 604
Goals. *See* Motivation
Goal-setting approach to work motivation, 736, 760

Gonads, 521, 522
Gonorrhea, 575, 584
Grasping reflex, 366, 416
Group decision making, 713–715, 719
Group intelligence tests, 467–468, 488
Group polarization effect, 714, 719
Group therapy, 665–666, 674–675
Groupthink, 714–715, 719
Gustation. *See* Taste

Habituation, 207, 371
Hair cells, 146, 161
Hallucinations, 184, 619, 630, 643, 671
Hallucinogens, 193–195, 199–200
Hashish, 195–196
Hassles Scale, 556
Health psychology, 19, 45, 569–580
Hearing
    of neonates, 369, 416
    receptor for, 145–146, 160–161
    stimulus for, 141–145, 160
Hematophobia, 598
Hemispheres of brain, 82, 85–87, 92
Heroin, 193, 199, 362
Hertz (Hz), 142
Heterosexuality, 522
Heuristics, 334–333, 349
    biased, 338–340, 349
Hierarchical model of intelligence, 460, 461, 487
Hierarchy of needs, 436, 498–499, 542
Hill climbing strategy, 334–336
Hippocampus, 79
Histrionic personality disorder, 608, 629
HIV. *See* Human immunodeficiency virus (HIV)
Holophrastic speech, 324, 348
Homelessness, 648, 649
Homeostasis, 501, 502, 504, 505, 518, 542
Homosexuality, 522–524, 544
Hormones, 64
    emotions and, 535–536
    in puberty, 394
    sex, 521–522, 544
Hue, 109, 112, 146
Human immunodeficiency virus (HIV), 577–579, 584
Humanistic/phenomenological approach to personality, 435–436, 441, 484, 485
Humanistic psychology, 16–17, 45, 498, 657–658, 673
Hunger, 507–510
Hypnosis, 182–185, 199, 654

Hypochondriasis, 603–604, 629
Hypothalamus, 75, 79–80, 91, 505, 506, 508, 522, 536, 537, 544, 545
Hypothesis
    defined, 6, 29
    testing, 314–315, 346
Hysteria, 605, 637, 654

Id, 426, 427, 430, 434, 483
Idealistic principle, 427, 482
Identity formation in adolescence, 396–397, 419
Illusion, 135
Implosive therapy, 659–660, 674
In-basket technique, 729
Incentives, 499–500, 542
Incus, 146, 147, 160
Independent variables, 30, 32, 33, 46
Individualism, 381
Industrial-organizational (I/O) psychology, 6, 20, 45, 495
    job analysis in, 725–727, 759
    job satisfaction and, 737–740, 760
    motivation in, 734–737, 760
    personnel selection in, 727–730, 759
    training in, 730–734, 759–760
    worker safety and, 741–742, 760–761
Industrial-social approach to worker safety, 742, 761
Inferiority complex, 432
Inhibitory synapse, 59–60
Initiative versus guilt crisis, 383–384, 418
Insanity, defined, 593
Insomnia, 180, 198
Instinctive drift, 241, 252
Instincts, 495–496, 541
Intellect, structure of, 459–460, 487
Intelligence, 440, 455, 485
    age differences in, 472–474, 488
    defined, 9, 456, 487
    extremes of, 476–482, 489
    gender differences in, 470–471, 488
    group differences in, 468–470, 488
    psychological tests of, 461–468, 487–488
    racial-ethnic differences in, 474–476, 488–489
    theoretical models of, 457–461, 487
Interactionism, 444, 485
Interactive dualism, 10
Interference, 296–299
Intermittent (partial) reinforcement schedules, 232

Internal attribution, 691, 717
Interpersonal attraction, 405, 694–700, 717–718
Interposition, 130, 133, 160
Interviews
    employment, 727–728, 759
    personality assessment, 450, 486
Intimacy versus isolation crisis, 383, 403, 420
Intimate distance, 745, 747
Ions, 56
IQ (intelligence quotient), 463–464
Iris, 113, 158

Job analysis, 725–727, 759
Job application form, 727
Job productivity, 740, 760
Job satisfaction, 737–740, 760
Job training, 730–734, 759–760
Just noticible difference (j.n.d.), 100, 158
Just world hypothesis, 693, 717

Key word method of study, 289, 290, 304
Kinesthetic sense, 153–154, 161

Language
    acquisition of, 322–327, 348
    defined, 316–318, 346–347
    pragmatics, 321–322, 347
    structure of, 318–321
Language acquisition device (LAD), 326
Late adulthood, development in, 410, 420
Latency stage, 430, 484
Latent content of dreams, 655, 673
Latent learning, 244, 245, 252
Law of effect, 223–225
L-dopa, 80
Learned drives, 496
Learning
    classical conditioning and, 206–222, 249
    cognitive approaches to, 241–248
    defined, 204–206, 249
    language acquisition and, 325–327, 348
    latent, 244, 245, 252
    operant conditioning and, 222–241, 250–251
    personality theory and, 433–434, 441, 484, 485
    social learning theory, 245–248, 252
Lens of eye, 113
Lesion, 67
Levels-of-processing model of memory, 257
Libido, 426, 432
Librium, 646, 672

Licensed professional counselors, 652, 672
Life-change-induced stress, 555–558, 581–582
Life instincts (Eros), 426
Light, 108–109, 158
Limbic system, 78–79, 91, 536, 537, 545
Linear perspective, 130, 160
Linguistic intuitions, 320–321, 347
Lithium, 645–646, 671
Little Albert demonstration, 214–216, 249, 433
Lobes, of brain, 82–85, 91
Lobotomy, 639–641, 671
Longitudinal method, 473
Long-term memory, 260, 265–275, 302
Loudness, 141, 146, 160
Love and belongingness needs, 498
LSD (lysergic acid diethylamide), 194–195, 199–200

Magnetic resonance imaging (MRI), 69, 70
Magnetoencephalogram (MEG), 68
Maintenance rehearsal, 262, 271, 302
Major depression, 615, 630
Malleus, 146, 147, 160
Mania, 615–617
Manifest content of dreams, 655, 673
MAO (monoamine oxidase) inhibitors, 645, 671
Marijuana, 195–196, 200, 398
Marriage, 403–405, 420, 555, 557–558
Massed practice, 295–296, 304
Masturbation, 527, 578
Matching phenomenon, 699
Maternal stress, 363, 415
Meaningfulness, 286–288, 303
Means-ends analysis, 334–335
Meditation, 185–187, 199
Medulla, 76, 81, 90–91
Memory, 255–304. *See also* Retrieval
    autobiographical, 274–275, 302
    episodic, 273–274, 302
    flashbulb, 284, 285
    levels-of-processing model of, 257
    long-term, 260, 265–275, 302
    multistore models of, 257
    in neonates, 371, 416
    procedural, 272, 274, 280–281
    repressed, 268
    semantic, 272–274, 302
    sensory, 258–258, 260, 301

short-term, 259–265, 301–302
state-dependent, 284
Menarche, 394
Mental age (MA), 463–464
Mental disorders. *See* Psychological disorders
Mental health technicians, 652, 672
Mental images, 287, 288
Mentally gifted, 478
Mental processes, defined, 7–8
Mental retardation, 362, 363, 479–482, 489
Mental set, 106, 128, 159, 336–338, 342, 349
Meprobamates, 646, 672
Mere exposure phenomenon, 697–698, 717
Mescaline, 194
Meta-analysis, 35, 47
Methadone, 193
Method of loci, 289–290, 304
Microsleep, 179
Middle adulthood, development in, 408–409, 420
Midlife crisis, 408
Minnesota Multiphasic Personality Inventory (MMPI), 451–452, 486
Mnemonic devices, 287–290, 303–304
Modeling, 246–248, 252, 662, 674
Monochromatic light, 111
Monocular cues, 129
Monophobia, 598
Mood disorders, 614–618, 630, 646
Moral development, 379–382, 417
Moro reflex, 366, 416
Morphemes, 319, 323, 325, 326, 347
Morphine, 192, 199
Motion
perception of, 134–135, 160
stimulus factor of, 104
Motion parallax, 132–133, 160
Motion sickness, 153
Motivated forgetting, 428
Motivation, 17, 106, 107, 128, 134, 159
balance (equilibrium) in, 501–503, 542
cyclical nature of, 493
defined, 494
incentives in, 499–500, 542
instincts and, 495–496, 541
needs and drives in, 496–499, 541–542
physiologically based, 504–512, 542–543
psychologically based, 513–516, 543
sex drive, 518–520, 543

work, 495, 734–737, 760
Motor areas, 83, 84, 91
Motor development
of children, 367, 368, 416
of neonates, 365–366, 415–416
Müller-Lyer illusion, 137–139
Multiphasia, 571
Multiple approach-avoidance conflicts, 554, 581
Multiple personality disorder, 606–607, 629
Multistore models of memory, 257
Myelin, 53–55, 89
Mysophobia, 598

Nanometer, 109
Narcissistic personality disorder, 608
Narcolepsy, 165, 180–181, 198
Narrative chaining, 287, 289, 303–304
National Commission on Sleep Disorder Research (NCSDR), 165
Naturalistic observation, 21–23, 45–46
Nearsightedness, 114
Needs, 496–499
achievement, 513–514, 543
affiliation, 515–516, 543
defined, 496
Maslow's hierarchy of, 436, 498–499, 542
power, 515, 516, 543
Negative afterimages, 123
Negative reinforcers, 229–230, 251
Neo-Freudians, 431–433, 440, 441, 484
Neologisms, 619, 621
Neonates
motor development of, 365–366
reflexes of, 365–366, 415–416
sensory and perceptual development, 367–370, 416
Nervous systems
autonomic, 63–64, 90, 534–536, 545
central. *See* Central nervous system (CNS)
peripheral, 62–63, 90
somatic, 63
Neural impulse, 55, 58–61, 89
Neural threshold, 58, 60, 89
Neurons
defined, 52, 89
functions of, 55–58
structure of, 52–55
synapses, 58–61
Neurotoxins, 753
Neurotransmitters, 58–61, 89, 90, 190, 276, 302,

616–617, 642, 645
Neutral stimulus, 207
Nicotine, 60, 189–190, 199
Nocturnal animals, 118
Noise, 751–752, 761
Norepinephrine, 60–61, 190, 199, 535, 616, 617, 642
Norms in testing, adequacy of, 447–448, 486
Novelty-familiarity, stimulus factor of, 104
NREM (nonrapid eye movement) sleep, 176, 179, 198
Nuclei, 76, 79, 81
Nutrition, in pregnancy, 361–362, 415
Nyctophobia, 598

Obedience to authority, 703–706, 718
Objectivity in testing, 447
Object permanence, 373
Observational learning, 685, 716
Observational methods
case histories, 24–25, 46
naturalistic, 21–23, 45–46
surveys, 23–24, 46
Observer bias, 22
Obsessions, 599
Obsessive-compulsive disorder (OCD), 599–601, 628
Occipital lobes, 82, 83
Occupational therapists, 652
Ocular cues, 129, 159–160
Oedipus complex, 430
Old-old, 411, 420
Olfaction. *See* Smell
On Death and Dying (Kübler-Ross), 412
Operant conditioning, 222–241, 250–251, 326, 370, 416, 500, 684, 716, 754, 755
Operational definitions, 8–9, 44, 456, 487
Opiates, 192–193, 199
Opponent-process theory of color vision, 122–124, 159
Optic chiasma, 119–120, 159
Optic nerve, 116
Oral stage, 430, 484
Organic mental disorders, 611
Orgasmic dysfunction, 527, 544
Orienting reflex, 207
Origin of the Species, The (Darwin), 11
Oval window, 146, 147, 160
Ovaries, 521
Overlearning, 293–294, 304
Overregularization, 326

Pain, 154–157, 161
analgesics and, 192
hypnosis and, 184
Pain threshold, 61

Panic disorder, 596–597, 628
Paper-and-pencil tests, 451–452, 467, 486–488
Paralysis, 73, 90
Paranoid personality disorder, 608, 629
Paranoid schizophrenia, 620–621, 630
Parasympathetic division, 64, 535
Parenthood, 405–406
Parietal lobes, 82, 83
Parkinson's disease, 80
Past experience, 106, 128, 159
Pastoral counseling, 652, 672
Pathophobia, 598
Patient–physician communication, 578–580, 584
Patterns of shading, 131–132, 160
Pavlovian conditioning, 206–222, 249
Peak performance, 758, 762
Pelvic inflammatory disease (PID), 575
Perception, 94–95. *See also* Sensation
constancy of, 135–140, 160
defined, 97, 157
of depth and distance, 128–134, 159–160
of motion, 134–135, 160
organization of, 124–128, 159
personal factors in selection of, 105–107, 158
stimulus factors in selection of, 103–105, 158
subliminal, 171
Performance criteria, 726, 759
Peripheral nervous system (PNS), 62–63, 90
Personal dispositions, 437–438, 485
Personal distance, 745, 747
Personal factors, and perception, 105–107, 128, 158, 159
Personal frustration, 551–552, 581
Personality. *See also* Intelligence
assessment, 446–454, 486–487
behavioral/learning approach to, 433–434, 441, 484, 485
consistency of, 442–444, 485–486
defined, 424–425
gender and, 444–446, 486
humanistic/phenomenological approach to, 435–436, 441, 484, 485
interactionism and, 444, 485
psychoanalytic approach to, 425–433, 440–441, 483–485

Personality *(Continued)*
    trait approach to, 437–442, 485
Personality disorders, 607–609, 629
Personality psychology, 19–20, 45
Personal space, 744–749, 761
Personal unconscious, 432
Personnel approach to worker safety, 741–742, 761
Personnel selection, 727–730, 759
Persuasion, 686–691, 716–717
Pesticides, 753
PET scan (positron emission tomography), 69–70
Phallic stage, 430, 484
Phantom-limb pain, 156
Phenomenology, 40
Phenylketonuria (PKU), 482
Pheromones, 150–151
Philosophy, psychology and, 10–12
Phi phenomenon, 135, 160
Phobic disorders, 216–218, 250, 597–598, 628
Phonemes, 318–319, 323, 347
Photoreceptors, 115–119, 158
Physical attractiveness, 698–699, 717
Physical cues, 129, 130–133, 160
Physical exercise, stress and, 565
Physiological/biological psychology, 18, 45
Physiological needs, 498
Pictorial cues, 130–133
Pinna, 146, 147, 160
Pitch, 142, 143, 146, 160
Placebos, 156
Plasticity, 357, 415
Pleasure principle, 427, 483
Pluralistic ignorance, 709, 718
Pons, 75, 76, 81, 91
Population density, 749, 761
Position senses, 153–154, 161
Positive reinforcers, 229, 251
Positive test strategy, 340
Postconventional morality, 380, 417
Posttraumatic stress disorder (PTSD), 601–603, 628
Power motivation, 515, 516, 543
Pragmatics, 321–322, 347
Preconscious mind, 169, 197, 425, 483
Preconventional morality, 379–380, 417
Prefrontal lobotomy, 639–641, 671
Premature ejaculation, 526, 544
Prematurity, 481
Prenatal development
    drugs and, 362–363, 415
    environmental influences on, 361–365, 415

genetics and, 354–357, 415
    stages of, 357–361, 415
Prenatal period, 358
Preoperational stage of child development, 375, 417
Primary drives, 496
Primary hues, 121
Primary mental abilities, 458–459, 487
Primary reinforcers, 230
Principles of Psychology (James), 13
Proactive interference, 298–299, 304
Problems
    components of, 329, 348
    defined, 328–329
    well-defined and ill-defined, 329, 348
Problem solving, 388
    barriers to effective, 336–343, 349
    creative, 340–343, 349–350
    representation in, 330–332, 348–349
    strategies in, 332–336, 349
    teaching, 343–345, 350
Procedural memory, 272, 274, 280–281
Process schizophrenia, 621, 630
Procrastination, 566
Progesterone, 518, 521
Prognosis, 512, 598
Projection, 428, 483
Projective techniques, 452–454, 487
Projective tests, 513
Prompting procedures, 754–755
Prototypes, 310–311, 346
Proximity, 125–126, 159
    interpersonal attraction and, 697–698, 717
Proximodistal sequencing, 367, 416
Pseudoinsomnia, 180
Psychiatric nurses, 652
Psychiatrists, 652, 672
Psychiatry, defined, 168
Psychoactive drugs, 188–196, 199
Psychoanalysis, 168
    Freudian, 16, 45, 653–656, 673
    neo-Freudian, 431–433, 484
    personality theory and, 425–431, 440–441, 483–485
Psychoanalysts, 652, 672
Psychodiagnostics, 651
Psychogenic amnesia, 605
Psycholinguistics, 19, 316, 318
Psychological disorders, 568
    anxiety, 595–603, 628
    autism, 610–611, 629
    classification of, 590–594, 628

cognitive, 611–614, 629
    defined, 589–590, 627
    dissociative, 605–607, 629
    humanistic techniques, 657–658, 673
    incidence of, 588
    mood, 614–618, 630
    personality, 607–609, 629
    schizophrenia, 618–626, 630–631
    somatoform, 603–605, 629
    treatment for. *See* Treatments
Psychological tests
    characteristics of good, 446–448, 486
    defined, 446
    for employment, 728–729, 759
    of intelligence, 461–468, 487–488
Psychology
    contemporary approaches to, 17–20
    correlational methods in, 25–29, 46
    defined, 3–7, 13, 20
    early history of, 12–14
    ethical considerations in, 36–38, 47
    experimental methods in, 29–36, 46–47
    goals of, 5–7, 20, 44
    key themes and general principles in, 38–43, 47
    observational methods in, 21–25, 45–46
    origins of, 10–12, 20–21
    subject matter of, 7–9
Psychometrics, 19, 45
Psychophysics, 97, 157
Psychosexual stages of personality development, 429–430, 484
Psychotherapy, 17
    behavioral techniques, 659–662, 673–674
    cognitive techniques, 662–665, 674
    eating disorders and, 512
    evaluating, 667–669, 675
    Freudian psychoanalysis, 16, 45, 653–656, 673
    group therapy, 665–666, 674–675
    post-Freudian psychoanalysis, 656, 673
    providers of, 650–653, 672
Psychotic symptoms, 643
Puberty, 394–396, 399–401, 419, 430, 522
Public distance, 746, 747
Public territory, 746, 748–749
Public verifiability, 7
Punishment, 235–237, 252, 500
Pupil, 113, 158
Purity of sound, 141, 160

Quality of work life (QWL), 738, 739, 760

Racial differences, in intelligence, 474–476, 488–489
Random assignment, 33, 46
Rating scales, 449
Rational-emotive therapy, 663–664, 674
Rationalization, 428, 483
Reactive schizophrenia, 621, 630
Reality principle, 427, 483
Real motion, 134
Recall, 278–279, 303
Recessive gene, 355
Reciprocity, interpersonal attraction and, 696–697, 717
Recognition, 278–279, 303
Reflex, 206
Regression, 429, 484
Reinforcement, 500
    defined, 228, 251
    differential, 238, 252
    model of interpersonal attraction, 695, 717
    positive and negative, 228–230, 251
    primary and secondary, 230–232, 251
    scheduling, 232–235, 251–252
Relative size, 131, 133, 160
Relaxation, 564–565
Relearning, 280, 303
Reliability in testing, 447, 486
REM (rapid eye movement)
    rebound effect, 179
    sleep, 176–178, 198
    sleep disorder, 178
Repetition, stimulus factor of, 104–105
Representativeness heuristic, 339–340, 349
Repressed memory, 268
Repression, 428, 483
Research methods
    correlational, 25–29
    ethical considerations in, 36–38
    experimental, 29–36
    observational, 21–25
Reserpine, 617
Residual schizophrenia, 621, 630
Resistance, 559–561, 582, 655, 673
Responsibility, diffusion of, 710, 718
Resting potential, 56, 57
Retarded ejaculation, 526, 544
Reticular activating system (RAS), 75, 78–79, 91
Retina, 115–119, 158
Retinal disparity, 129, 159–160
Retraining, 732

Retrieval, 257, 301
  encoding and, 281–296, 303
  interference and, 296–299
  measuring, 277–281, 303
  practicing, 300–301
Retroactive interference, 297–298, 304
Rods, 115–119, 158, 159
Rogerian therapy, 657–658, 673
Role confusion, 397
Role-playing, 449
Rooting reflex, 366, 415
Rorschach inkblot test, 453–454, 487
Rotter Incomplete Sentences Blank, 453
Rubella (German measles), 361

Safety, worker, 741–742, 760–761
Safety needs, 498
Sample, 24
Sandwich generation, 409
SAT (Scholastic Aptitude Test), 468, 471
Saturation, 111, 112, 146
Schemas, 290–293, 304, 372–373
Schizoid personality disorder, 608, 629
Schizophrenia, 618–619, 630–631, 644
  causes of, 40–41, 623–626
  types of, 620–623, 630
Science
  defined, 5
  psychology as, 5–7, 44
  roots of psychology in, 11–12
Scientific methods, 5–6
Scientist-practitioners, 6
Secondary drives, 496
Secondary reinforcers, 230
Secondary territory, 746, 748
Secondary traits, 438
Self-actualization needs, 436, 498, 499, 542, 657
Self-confidence, gender and, 445–446, 487
Self-esteem, 388, 395
Self-serving bias, 693–694, 717
Semantic memory, 272–274, 302
Semantics, 319–320, 347
Senile psychosis, 612
Sensation, 94–95. *See also* Perception
  absolute thresholds and, 97–99, 101
  defined, 96, 157
  difference thresholds and, 100, 157–158
  hearing. *See* Hearing
  pain, 154–157, 161
  position senses, 153–154, 161
  sensory adaptation, 101–103, 158
  sight. *See* Vision

signal detection theory and, 101, 158
  skin senses, 151–153, 161
  smell, 147, 148–151, 161
  taste, 147–149, 161
Sensorimotor stage of child development, 373–374, 416
Sensory adaptation, 101–103, 158
Sensory areas, 83, 91
Sensory memory, 258–258, 260, 301
Sentence completion test, 453
Sentences, 320–321, 347
Septum, 78–79, 91
Serial recall, 278
Serotonin, 194–195, 600, 616, 642, 645
Set point, 501
Sex drive, 518–520, 543
Sexual dysfunctions, 525–528, 544
Sexuality
  genetic bases of, 520–521, 543–544
  homosexuality, 522–524, 544
  hormonal bases of, 521–522, 544
  sexual dysfunctions, 525–528, 544
Sexually transmitted diseases (STDs), 575–579, 584
Sexual preference, 522
s-factors, 458, 487
Shading, patterns of, 131–132, 160
Shape constancy, 136, 160
Shaping, in conditioning, 225–226, 251
Shock treatments, 641–643, 671
Short-term memory, 259–265, 301–302, 462, 463
Sibling relationships, 388
Signal detection theory, 101, 158
Signing (American Sign Language), 318
Silent Spring (Carson), 753
Similarity, 125, 126, 159
  interpersonal attraction and, 699–700, 717–718
Single-blind technique, 34, 47
Situational testing, 729
16 PF Questionnaire, 452
Size, stimulus factor of, 104
Size constancy, 136, 160
Skin (cutaneous) senses, 151–153, 161
Skinner box, 225
Sleep, 68, 81
  deprivation, 178–179, 198
  disorders, 180–181, 198
  REM and NREM, 176–178, 198
  stages of, 173–176, 198
Sleep apnea, 181, 198
Sleep debt, 179

Sleeping pills, 180
Sleep spindles, 174, 198
Smell, 147, 148–151, 161, 369, 416
Smoking, 60, 189–190, 362, 398, 415, 503, 573, 574, 583
Social attachments, 387–389, 418
Social cognitions
  attitudes in, 681–691, 716
  attribution theory in, 691–694, 717
  interpersonal attraction in, 694–700, 717–718
Social distance, 746, 747
Social exchange model of interpersonal attraction, 695, 717
Social facilitation, 712–713, 719
Social frustration, 551
Social influence
  bystander intervention, 679, 700, 706–711, 718
  conformity, 701–703, 718
  group decision making, 713–716, 719
  obedience to authority, 703–706, 718
  social facilitation, 712–713, 719
  social loafing, 711–712, 719
Social interference, 713, 719
Social learning theory, 245–248, 252
Social loafing, 711–712, 719
Social psychology. *See* Social cognitions; Social influence
Social Readjustment Rating Scale (SRRS), 555–556, 581–582
Sociocultural factors, drug use and abuse and, 192, 199
Somatic nervous system, 63
Somatoform disorders, 603–605, 629
Sound, 141–146, 160–161
Source traits, 438–439, 485
Spanking, 236, 237
SPECT scan (single-photon-emission computed tomography), 70
Speech, 318–319, 347
  holophrastic, 324, 348
  telegraphic, 324–325
Speed, 189–191, 199
Sperm, 364
Spinal cord, 71–74, 90
Spinal reflexes, 73–74
Split-brain procedure, 85–86, 91–92
Spontaneous recovery, in conditioning, 210, 227, 249, 251
Sport psychology, 755–758

Stability/instability, 440, 485
Stanford-Binet Intelligence Scale, 462–465, 473–474, 487
Stapes, 146, 147, 160
State-dependent memory, 284
Stereochemical theory, 151
Stimulants, 189–191, 199
Stimulus factors, and perception, 103–105, 125–127, 158, 159
Storage, 256, 301. *See also* Memory
Stress, 549
  conflict-induced, 552–554, 581
  coping with, 562–568, 582–583
  defined, 550
  frustration-induced, 551–552, 562, 581
  life-change-induced, 555–558, 581–582
  maternal, 363, 415
  reactions to, 558–561, 582
Stressors, defined, 550
Structuralism, 13, 44
Subjective contours, 127
Subliminal perception, 171
Success, fear of, 514
Sucking reflex, 366, 416
Sudden Infant Death Syndrome (SIDS), 181
Suicide, 597
Superego, 426–428, 430, 434, 483
Superior colliculus, 120
Surface traits, 438, 485
Surveys, 23–24, 46
Symbols of language, 316–317
Sympathetic division, 64, 535–536, 545
Synapses, 58–61, 89, 275
Synaptic cleft, 58, 59
Synesthesia, 195, 199–200
Syntax, 320–321, 323, 324, 327, 347
Syphilis, 575–576, 584
Systematic desensitization, 217–218, 250, 659, 660, 673

Tabula rasa, 11
Taste, 147–149, 161, 369, 416
Taste aversion, 221, 250
Taste buds, 148, 149
Taylor Manifest Anxiety Scale, 452
Teenage pregnancy, 400–401, 419
Telegraphic speech, 324–325
Temperature extremes, 752, 761–762
Temperature regulation, 504–505, 542
Temporal lobes, 82, 83

Terman-Stanford study, 478–479
Territoriality, 746, 761
Testosterone, 518, 521
Texture gradient, 131, 132, 160
Thalamus, 75, 79, 81, 91
Thalidomide, 363
Thanatophobia, 598
THC (tetrahydrocannabinol), 195, 200
Thematic Apperception Test (TAT), 454, 487, 513
Theory, defined, 424
Therapy. *See* Psychotherapy
Theta waves, 174, 198
Thirst, 505–507, 542
Three-dimensionality, 128, 129, 132, 159
Timbre, 143–144, 146, 160
Time urgency, 571
Token economy, 231
Tolerance, drug, 188, 193
Tonic neck reflex, 366
Top-down processing, 107, 125
Touch, 416
Training programs, 730–734, 759–760
Trait approach to personality, 437–442, 485
Tranquilizers, 646, 672
Transcendental meditation (TM), 185–186
Transducer, 97
Transference in psychoanalysis, 656, 673

Treatments
  deinstitutionalization, 647–649, 672
  drug therapy, 643–646, 671
  electroconvulsive therapy (ECT), 641–643, 671
  historical perspective on, 636–638, 670–671
  psychosurgery, 639–641, 671
Tremors, 77–78
Triarchic model of intelligence, 460, 487
Trichromatic theory of color vision, 121, 124, 159
Tricyclics, 645, 671
Trust versus mistrust crisis, 382, 383, 418
Two-dimensionality, 129, 159–160
Two-string problem, 337, 338
Type A behavior pattern (TABP), 570–572, 583

Unconditional positive regard, 658, 673
Unconditioned response (UCR), 207–209, 213, 215, 249
Unconditioned stimulus (UCS), 207–210, 213, 215, 219–221, 249, 250
Unconscious, 16, 426, 432, 483
  contemporary investigations of, 170–172
  Freud on, 168, 169, 197
Undifferentiated schizophrenia, 621, 630

Unilateral ECT, 643
Urban environment, 749–750, 761

Vaginismus, 527, 544
Validity in testing, 447, 486
Valium, 646, 672
Variable-interval (VI) reinforcement schedule, 234–235, 251
Variable-ratio (VR) reinforcement schedule, 234, 251
Ventral roots, 72
Vertical-horizontal illusion, 137
Vesicles, 58, 59
Vestibular sense, 153, 161
Viability of fetus, 360–361
Vicarious punishment, 247, 252
Vicarious reinforcement, 247, 252
Vision, 67, 68
  color vision and color blindness, 121–124, 159
  dark adaptation, 118–118
  of neonates, 368–369, 416
  receptor for, 112–121, 158
  stimulus for, 108–112
Visual cliff, 369
Visual field, 119, 159
Visual imagery, 287, 288, 304, 758
Vitreous humor, 115
Volunteers, 37

Walking reflex, 366, 416
Waste management, 754–755

Wave amplitude, 108–112, 158
Wave frequency, 141–143, 160
Wavelength, 108–112, 158
Wave purity, 108, 111, 112, 158
Wechsler intelligence scales, 465–467, 487–488
White light, 111–112
White noise, 145
Will, 440, 485
Witches, 637, 670
Withdrawal, drugs and, 188
Word association technique, 452–453
Worker safety, 741–742, 760–761
Working backward strategy, 334–336
Working memory. *See* Short-term memory
Wyatt v. *Stickney* (1971), 648

Xanax, 646
X chromosome, 520–521, 523
X-ray technology, 69

Yanomamö Indians, 194
Y chromosome, 520–521
Young-old, 411, 420

Zoophobia, 598
Zulu people, 139
Zygote, 357–359, 415, 520, 543